Books by William L. Shirer

BERLIN DIARY (1941)

END OF A BERLIN DIARY (1947)

THE TRAITOR (1950)

MIDCENTURY JOURNEY (1952)

STRANGER, COME HOME (1954)

THE CHALLENGE OF SCANDINAVIA (1955)

THE CONSUL'S WIFE (1956)

THE RISE AND FALL OF ADOLF HITLER (1961)

THE SINKING OF THE *BISMARCK* (1962)

THE COLLAPSE OF THE THIRD REPUBLIC (1969)

20TH CENTURY JOURNEY: THE START:
1904–1930 (1976)

GANDHI — A MEMOIR (1980)

20TH CENTURY JOURNEY: THE NIGHTMARE YEARS:
1930–1940 (1984)

20TH CENTURY JOURNEY: A NATIVE'S RETURN:
1945–1988 (1990)

LOVE AND HATRED: THE TROUBLED MARRIAGE OF
LEO AND SONYA TOLSTOY (1994)

THE
RISE AND FALL
OF THE
THIRD REICH

✦✦✦

A History of Nazi Germany

William L. Shirer

With a New Introduction by
Ron Rosenbaum

SIMON & SCHUSTER
New York   London   Toronto   Sydney   New Delhi

Simon & Schuster
1230 Avenue of the Americas
New York, NY 10020

First Simon & Schuster hardcover edition 1960

SIMON & SCHUSTER and colophon are registered trademarks
of Simon & Schuster, Inc.

For information about special discounts for bulk purchases,
please contact Simon & Schuster Special Sales at
1-866-506-1949 or business@simonandschuster.com.

The Simon & Schuster Speakers Bureau can bring authors
to your live event. For more information or to book an event,
contact the Simon & Schuster Speakers Bureau at
1-866-248-3049 or visit our website at www.simonspeakers.com.

Manufactured in the United States of America

10   9

ISBN 978-1-4516-4259-9
ISBN 978-1-4516-5168-3 (pbk)

CONTENTS

Book Four: WAR: EARLY VICTORIES AND THE TURNING POINT

Book Five: BEGINNING OF THE END

Book Six: THE FALL OF THE THIRD REICH

I have often felt a bitter sorrow at the thought of the German people, which is so estimable in the individual and so wretched in the generality . . . —GOETHE

Hitler was the fate of Germany and this fate could not be stayed.
—FIELD MARSHAL WALTHER VON BRAUCHITSCH, Commander in Chief of the German Army, 1938–41

A thousand years will pass and the guilt of Germany will not be erased.
—HANS FRANK, Governor General of Poland, before he was hanged at Nuremberg

Those who do not remember the past are condemned to relive it.
—SANTAYANA

A NEW INTRODUCTION

Ron Rosenbaum

Nineteen Sixty: Only fifteen years had passed since the Second World War ended. But already one could read an essay describing a "wave of amnesia that has overtaken the West"* with regard to the events of 1933 to 1945.

At the time, there was no Spielberg-produced HBO *Band of Brothers,* no "Greatest Generation" celebration, there was no Holocaust Museum on the Washington Mall. There was, instead, the beginning of a kind of willed forgetfulness of the horror of those years.

No wonder. It was not merely the Second World War, it was war to the second power, exponentially more horrific. Not merely in degree and quantity—in death toll and geographic reach—but also in consequences, if one considered the new modes of mass murder witnessed at Auschwitz and Hiroshima.

But in 1960, there were two notable developments, two captures: In May, Adolf Eichmann was apprehended by Israeli agents in Argentina and flown to Jerusalem for trial. And in October, William L. Shirer captured something else, both massive and elusive, in the four corners of a book: *The Rise and Fall of the Third Reich.* He captured it in a way that made amnesia no longer an option.

The arrest of Eichmann, chief operating officer of the Final Solution, reawakened the question *Why?* Why had Germany, long one of the most ostensibly civilized, highly educated societies on earth, a repository of learning and decorum, transformed itself into an instrument of savage mass murder that turned a continent into a charnel house? Why had Germany delivered itself over to the raving exterminationist dictates of

---

*Quoted in Gavriel D. Rosenfeld, "The Reception of William L. Shirer's *The Rise and Fall of the Third Reich* in the United States and West Germany 1960–62," *Journal of Contemporary History,* Vol. 29, p. 124.

one man, the man Shirer refers to disdainfully as the "vagabond." Why
did the world allow a "street tramp," a Chaplinesque figure whose 1923
"beerhall putsch" was a comic fiasco, transform himself into a genocidal
Führer whose rule spanned a continent and threatened to last a thousand
years?

Why? William Shirer offered a 1250-page answer.

It wasn't a final answer, a final solution to the final solution. After tens,
perhaps hundreds of thousands of pages of further attempts at answers by
others—Ian Kershaw, Saul Friedlander, Richard Evans, Andrew Roberts,
to name but a few—the answer to "why" is still a matter of contention.
Perhaps Shirer's contribution is better described as an attempt to remind
the world of "what." What happened to civilization and humanity in those
years. But that in itself was a major contribution to a post-war generation
that came of age in the '60s, many of whom read Shirer as their parents'
Book of the Month Club selection and have told me the unforgettable
impact it had on them.

Shirer had been known previously as a journalist who spent six years
(1934–1940) stationed in Berlin and Vienna, reporting on the rise of the
Reich for Hearst's newspapers and Edward R. Murrow's radio broadcast.
A witness to history rather than a professional historian, he was only
twenty-one when he arrived in Paris from the Midwest. Initially, he
planned to make the Hemingway-like transition from newsman to
novelist, but events overtook him.

One of his first big assignments, covering the Lindbergh landing, was
his introduction to the mass hysteria of hero worship, and he soon found
himself covering an even more profoundly charismatic figure: Mahatma
Gandhi. But nothing prepared him for the demonic spellbinding spectacle
he witnessed when he took up residence in Berlin and began to chronicle
the Rise of the Third Reich under the rule of Adolf Hitler.

If journalism is "the first rough draft of history," Shirer gave us his
first rough draft of the *The Rise and Fall* in his bestselling *Berlin Diary,*
published shortly after he was forced to leave Nazi-conquered Europe in
December 1940. In it we get some of the private reflections and reactions
Shirer kept to himself while he was filing copy under threat of censorship
and expulsion, which prevented him from detailing the worst excesses,
including the murder of Hitler's opponents, the beginnings of the Final
Solution, and the explicit preparations for upcoming war. (A valuable
account of Shirer and his fellow journalists' struggles with this situation
can be found in *The Long Night,* a recent portrait of Shirer in those years,
by Steve Wick.)

After war broke out he covered the savagery of the German invasion of Poland and drove into Paris in the wake of the Wehrmacht, before he was finally forced to leave in December 1940. And so *The Rise and Fall* was a kind of leap from eyewitness war correspondent to archival historian. He was present at the rise, distant from the fall. In his 1250-page magnum opus, he sought, though he did not always find, a longer focal distance, the perspective not of a journalist but of a historian. His model, consciously or unconsciously, was the kind of historian, who, like Thucydides, had first-hand experience of war and then sought to adopt the analytic distance of the historian. His talent, which bridged journalism and history, was for narrative, for weaving together individuals and ideas, the personal and the impersonal factors of history into the tapestry of a vast, multifaceted story. The Greek and Roman historians we reread are the ones who survive as storytellers.

Unlike Thucydides, Shirer had the advantage of access to the kind of treasure previous historians always sought but mostly failed to find. After the German defeat, the Allies made available warehouses full of captured German military and diplomatic documents—the Pentagon Papers/Wikileaks of their time—that enabled Shirer to see the war from the other side. He also had access to the remarkably candid interviews with the German generals conducted after the surrender by B. H. Liddell-Hart, the British strategic thinker who invented the concept of lightning offensive warfare that the Germans adopted and called "blitzkreig." All of which gave a documentary substructure to his account of the fall.

And by 1960, Shirer also had those fifteen more years of distance, an interval that, while not enough for some purposes, gave him a balance between personal experience and the perspective of time. Fifteen more years to think about what he'd seen, fifteen years to distance himself and then to return from that distance. Fifteen years that often served to sharpen rather than diminish his horror at what he'd seen.

He doesn't pretend to have *all* the answers, indeed one of the most admirable attributes of this work is his willingness to admit to mystery and inexplicability when he finds it. Later historians had access—as Shirer did not—to knowledge of the Enigma machine, the British code-breaking apparatus that gave the Allies the incalculable advantage of anticipating the movements of enemy forces mid-battle, an advantage that changed the course of the war. Details of Enigma only began to become public in 1974, and as more and more top secret documents are declassified, we are learning more and more about the crucial role the Enigma code breakers at Bletchley Park, north of London, played in the fall of the Reich.

But Shirer could draw on first-hand clues to a different *kind* of enigma:

he had first hand, up-close-and-personal experience of the enigma that was Adolf Hitler and the enigma of his relationship to the German people. He had lived in Hitler's Germany, lived amidst Hitler's mass cult following during the rise. He emerged from that experience and from observing the fall that finally followed with the desire to decode that enigma for the world. It is remarkable how much difference it makes in their accounts: the difference between those historians who were able to witness personally whatever mesmeric hysteria Hitler was able to stir up in person, and those, like most of us, who only *read* about the effect of his presence and wonder how it came to be, what it was like to be an ordinary inhabitant of hell. It is the difference between witnessing a murder and reading trial testimony about it. The ones who saw it found they were witness to something virtually incommunicable.

There have been other books that sought to chronicle the war or to explain Hitler, but Shirer made it his mission to take on the entire might and scope of *the Reich*, the fusion of people and state Hitler forged. It was an extraordinary act of daring, one might almost say an act of literary-historical generalship. To conquer a veritable continent of information.

It will remain an awe-inspiring achievement that he could capture that terrain of horror in *merely* 1250 pages. Re-reading the book one sees how subtle he is in shifting between telescope and microscope— even, one might say, stethoscope. He gives us Tolstoyan vistas of battle, interwoven with intimate close-ups of the key players, the minds and hearts behind the mayhem. He is particularly skilled at showing the drama both internal and external of war-changing decision-making moments— Munich, Dunkirk, Stalingrad—disentangling the strategic shifts the Enigma machine could record but not necessarily explain.

And one can't help but admire Shirer's ability to single out the way, amidst all the pre-war geopolitical maneuvering, a single cunning Hitler lie was as effective as a blitzkrieg in disarming the West.

For instance, in August 1939 on the verge of unleashing the fury of his battalions on Poland, Hitler is quoted by Shirer as reassuring the British ambassador in Berlin that he had no such plans. Indeed, as the panzers massed, he told the ambassador that he wanted nothing more than a peaceful resolution, friendship with England, and most of all sought to "end his life as an artist not a warmonger."

One of Shirer's most difficult and successful tasks was returning readers to the mind-set of the pre-war years—that fatal wishful thinking that allowed the world to swallow such lies. The world that saw Hitler as just another statesman—perhaps a bit overwrought—pursuing realistic national goals rather than hysterical delusions that justified any crime including genocide. (Shirer had no patience for the post war "normalizing" vision that the Oxford historian A.J.P. Taylor sought to resurrect: Hitler as just another "foreign policy realist" of his time, pursuing rational national interests. This point of view continues to be taken seriously, by some).

It becomes clear all too late, Shirer shows us, that the diplomats and statesmen of the day were not aware that they were dealing with a different kind of animal for whom the lie was a chief weapon of war, and mass murder was "realism."

Of course Shirer's "capture" didn't succeed in undoing what Hitler and Eichmann and the Reich had done, but it did its part to ensure that what had been done — the full depths of horror — would never be lost in oblivion. And, in a way, the values Shirer displayed — of thoughtfulness, coherence, rationality, discernment, and empathy for the suffering of the victims — were a vindication of the values the Allies fought for.

But in addition to the grand sweep of his gaze, which reached from the Irish Sea to the steppes beyond the Urals, Shirer had a remarkable eye for the singular detail that was key to a close reading of character.

As an illustration, return for a moment to Hitler and Eichmann, and the prescience of the one Eichmann quote Shirer included in the book — a remarkable quote from Eichmann about his "conscience," in which he reveals his true feelings about the Holocaust. It's a quote that impresses the student of this vast subject because Shirer chose to single it out from the astonishing welter of details available to him. It can be found in a bottom-of-the-page footnote that was written before Eichmann's apprehension in Argentina made headlines and drew the attention of the world to this previously little-known figure, the chief executioner of the Final Solution. It's a remark that goes to the heart of the subsequent debate about the phenomenon of Eichmann — the why — and offers a persuasive answer.

We know Shirer wrote this footnote before Eichmann's capture because of a last minute footnote *to* that footnote. It's an un-numbered but capitalized "NOTE" Shirer appends to his original Eichmann footnote (thus probably the very last words he wrote in the book). In it Shirer tells us: "As this book went on press the government of Israel announced that it had apprehended Eichmann."

And so his decision to give us the initial footnote, with its devastating characterization of Eichmann, was not some hasty, news-flash, add-on but grew out of a kind of a depth and breadth of knowledge and understanding of the Nazi mind and its exterminationist intentionality which some subsequent Eichmann commenters such as Hannah Arendt in her famous "banality of evil" analysis were blind to.

The Eichmann remark can be found on p. 978 in chapter 27, The New Order, a section whose title Shirer intended as an ironic echo of Hitler's original grandiose phrase: "The New Order" had collapsed, and Shirer was summoning up the death tolls, horrors, and depredations Hitler's regime had perpetrated in its name.

It's a section devoted to the Final Solution, the Nazi euphemism for what was not then widely called "The Holocaust." In it Shirer takes up the question of the actual number of Jews murdered and tells us, "According to two S.S. witnesses at Nuremberg the total was put at between five and six millions by one of the great Nazi experts on the subject, Karl Eichmann, chief of the Jewish office of the Gestapo, who carried out the final solution . . ." (Note that he uses Eichmann's first name not the middle name that would soon become inseparable from him: Adolf.)

Here is the damning quote Shirer spots and footnotes from Eichmann:

> Eichmann, according to one of his henchmen, said just before the German collapse, that "he would leap laughing into the grave because the feeling that he had five million people on his conscience would be for him a source of extraordinary satisfaction."

What's important is that Shirer has at his fingertips the damning evidence of Eichmann's true *attitude* toward the mass murder he was administering and a sense that this question would become important, although he could not have imagined the world-wide controversy Arendt made it become. For Shirer, Eichmann was no bloodless paper-pusher, no middle-manager just following orders as Eichmann and his defense lawyer—and later Hannah Arendt and others—sought to convince the world. He was not an emblem, an embodiment of "the banality of evil" as Arendt tried to portray him. Shirer will not countenance the exculpation of individual moral responsibility in the "just following orders" defense.

This is Shirer at his best: he has read through a vast portion of the warehouses full of captured German diplomatic and military documents and interrogation transcripts but is able, in his conspectus, to select with precision the most telling remark, the proverbial hypodermic in the haystack: "leap laughing into the grave."

Clearly this footnote was intended not merely to subtantiate the 5 million number but to illustrate a mindset. It is unlikely Shirer could have imagined someone would seek to construe Eichmann's self-evident bloodthirstiness as somehow bloodless and banal. But just in case there are any still taken in by Arendt, the world's worst court reporter, parroting the Eichmann line of defense, this laughing admission of that ghoulish "joyfulness," that mockery of conscience, that exulting in having engineered one of the greatest crimes in history, puts the lie to all foolish imputations of "banality." Q.E.D.

It is difficult to speak of Shirer's distinctive and singular eye without mentioning a curious detail: Shirer did his reporting and writing on the Third Reich with only one eye. He arrived in Berlin in 1934 ready to report on the gathering darkness but without the eye whose vision he had lost in a skiing accident the year before. He never mentions it in *The Rise and Fall* or in his bestselling *Berlin Diary*. (I only came across the detail in a posthumous afterword to an edition of *Berlin Diary* by his colleague Gordon Craig.) One is tempted to use this excruciatingly painful accident—it was the result of swerving to avoid crashing into a fallen fellow skier on an icy chute of a trail—as a metaphor for the magnitude and acuity of Shirer's achievement: With his one eye he saw more than most who had two.

In any case, he saw reflected in Eichmann's joyfulness something of the other Adolf's horrific enthusiasm for the task. But despite his understanding of the genocidal mentality, this is not a history of Hitler and that other parallel war, "The War Against the Jews," as the historian Lucy Dawidowicz called it.

Shirer's was an even more encompassing objective. His intention was to show that the obscene criminality was a communal atrocity, not a case of one person's racial hatred, but of the hatred that drove an entire nation, the Reich itself. A central theme of his book was to show that Hitler and his exterminationist drive was as much a creation, a distillation of the Reich, a quintessence brewed from the darkest elements of German history, an entire culture. His intention was announced in the title: it was not *The Rise and Fall of Adolf Hitler* (although he did a Young Adult version of this book with that exact title). But *The Rise and Fall of the Third Reich*.

It was a challenging decision: he wanted to challenge the "Hitler-centric" point of view of previous treatments of the war. The most well known of these was Alan Bullock's *Hitler: A Study in Tyranny* and the influential H. R. Trevor-Roper's *The Last Days of Hitler,* an enterprise with more scope than the title suggests, which used that final Götterdämmerung in the bunker as a way of looking back upon what brought Hitler and history to that bitter end.

No, Shirer's book declared itself to be not about a man or an ideology (it was not *The Rise and Fall of Nazism* either) but about a *regime,* albeit he comes close to arguing the regime was itself a distillation of a specifically German history. A Reich.

"Third Reich" was not a term of Hitler's invention; it was concocted in a 1922 book by a German nationalist crank named Arthur Moeller van den Bruck who believed in the divine destiny of a German history, a history that could be divided into three momentous acts: Charlemagne's first Reich. The second Reich, resurrected by Bismark with his Prussian "blood and iron," whose glory was purportedly betrayed by the so-called "stab in the back"—the Jews and socialists on the homefront whose supposed treachery brought the noble German army defeat just as it was on the verge of victory in November 1918. And thus all Germany was awaiting the savior who would arise to restore, with a Third Reich, the destiny that was theirs.

Hitler heard the call, or at least liked the slogan. He'd already heard the call, some say as far back as his youth in Vienna or as late as his confinement in a sanitarium at the tail end of the First World War, where he had some kind of vision that cured his hysterical blindness aka nervous breakdown by endowing him with a sense he must regain his sight to fulfill a mission of historical destiny on Germany's behalf.

The German Problem

In emphasizing the Germanness of the Hitler Reich, Shirer opened himself to charges of exchanging Hitler-centrism for German-centrism. That was the theme of the initial debate over Shirer's book.* Not that there was much debate in America. There was no arguing its immense popular success. Some 10 million copies sold by century's end, 12 million copies of the *Reader's Digest* digestion. A year on the best seller list. After the wave of amnesia, a hunger for an answer broke out, a "why" arose, and Shirer was there to offer a *because.*

More surprising was the almost unanimous praise from professional, academic historians for a work by a journalist. Trevor-Roper himself, then at Oxford and known for his scathing demolitions of fellow academic historians, hailed Shirer's work on the front page of *The New York Times Book Review* in an October 16, 1960, front page essay entitled LIGHT ON OUR CENTURY'S DARKEST NIGHT.

Trevor-Roper offered special praise for Shirer's discoveries in the vast storehouses of captured Third Reich documents: "In a nauseating story, few

---

*Rosenfeld, op. cit.

things are more nauseating than the documents printed by Mr. Shirer which show German businessmen unctuously competing for contracts to supply poison gas, gas chambers, and crematoria for Nazi extermination camps . . ."

However, the reception of Shirer's work in Germany was—certainly at first—quite different, particularly in West Germany, which was struggling to fulfill its Cold War role as bulwark of Western democratic values against barbarous communism next door. Reminders of Germany's recent past were not welcome, especially if they emphasized some kind of malevolent Germanness. In addition to carping from the German press and academic historians, Germany's august Chancellor Konrad Adenauer actually personally requested of Gardner Cowles, the publisher of the *Saturday Evening Post,* that he cancel planned serialization of Shirer's work. (Cowles refused.)*

But German attitudes toward Shirer's position changed over the years as dramatically evidenced by the reception received in Germany by Daniel Goldhagen's 1996 book *Hitler's Willing Executioners.* Goldhagen's book can almost be seen as a direct reproof to the original West German critique of Shirer. Goldhagen castigates historians for playing down the Germanness of the Holocaust, the enthusiastic "willingness" of the German people's participation, which Goldhagen traces to nineteenth-century German "scientific racism" and its characterization of Jews as a "racial bacillus," the medical rhetoric taken up by Hitler and the Nazis.

Goldhagen goes much further than Shirer in "Germanizing" the crimes. But while there was a initial wave of resistance in the German press, something remarkable happened by the time Goldhagen arrived in Germany to publicize the German translation of his book. The German people hailed him and his work—and the way it singled out German ideology for guilt. There was a veritable tidal wave of approbation, which made Goldhagen's German book tour a kind of excuse for Germans of the new generation to express—and go on record with—their remorse, expiate the shame of their forebears, and define their own Germanness against the Germanness of the Reich.

These were Germans two generations removed from the war, Germans who almost reveled in an occasion to distance themselves from the perpetrators, at last finding an opportunity to say, "We too despise what they did. It's time to end the amnesia, the denial, and the blame-shifting here."

Did Shirer have a "German problem"? The opportunistic German embrace of Goldhagen did not necessarily vindicate Shirer's German-centric theory. In a sense, Goldhagen's focus on the Germanism of

---

*Rosenfeld, op. cit.

European anti-Semitism downplayed two millennia of Christian anti-Semitism, and tended to excuse individual Third Reich Germans from moral responsibility by portraying them as helplessly driven by an ineradicable ideology. And it tends to ignore both Eastern European ethnic hatred of the Jews and Western European apathetic complicity of the Vichy France variety.

In Shirer one can see an evolution: in *Berlin Diary* the emphasis on the Germanic character is more visceral than ideological. It's impossible to overestimate the effect six years of living in Hitler's Gemany, seeing the viciousness and brutality of its Nazi-intoxicated inhabitants, had on Shirer.

He was forced to witness daily cruelty through gritted teeth if he wanted to remain in Germany to report on it. For a journalist, he had an invaluable eyewitness standpoint, but it inevitably affected his feelings toward the culture that acceded to Hitler and Naziism so readily.

Here's an early instance of his visceral response to personal experience as chronicled in *Berlin Diary,* published in 1941, before we were at war. It began with his arrival in Berlin in 1934, shortly after the Night of Long Knives, in which Hitler slit the throats of his closest comrades in the SA (the uniformed "stormtrooper" street-thug army) to seal in blood his bond with the official German Army and win their approval for his assumption of the role of President, Chancellor, and Führer. Shirer's first personal experience of Hitler was as the godlike icon buoyed up by tens of thousands of cultists at Nuremberg in 1934.

Witnessing a Hitler harangue in person for the first time, he wrote in *Berlin Diary*:

> "We are strong and will get stronger," Hitler shouted at them through the microphone, his words echoing across the hushed field from the loudspeakers. And there in the floodlit night, massed together like sardines in one mass formation, the little men of Germany who have made Naziism possible achieved the highest state of being the Germanic man knows: the shedding of the individual souls and minds—with the personal responsibilities and doubts and problems—until under the mystic lights at the sound of the magic words of the Austrian they were merged completely in the Germanic herd.

Shirer's contempt here is palpable, physical, immediate, and personal. Contempt not for Hitler, so much as for the "little men of Germany." The use of the word "herd" casts them as subhuman. Hitler, like Circe, transformed men into swine, only these went willingly. In the *The Rise and Fall* Shirer searches for a deeper "why": Was it a unique one-time phenomenon, or do humans possess some ever-present receptivity to the appeal of primal herd-like hatred?

One can see this search for a deeper "why" in Shirer's attempt to view the entire phenomenon from more abstract philosophic, historic, and cultural perspectives without displacing personal responsibility. Hitler may have been a quintessential distillation of centuries of German culture and philosophy, but Shirer was careful in not letting him or this heritage become an *excuse* for his accomplices.

There *were* Germans, Christian and Jewish, who resisted, however few and ineffectual. I was surprised, indeed pleasantly shocked, when researching *Explaining Hitler,* to discover a Munich archive of the anti-Hitler Munich newspaper the *Münchener Post.* Until it was sacked by storm trooper mobs in the wake of the Hitler takeover, its reporters and editors jeopardized life and limb to uncover Nazi Party scandals, desperately seeking to warn the world that there was more to Hitler than merely fanatic nationalism. It was the *Post* that discovered and published on December 9, 1931, a secret Nazi Party post-takeover plan for the Jews in which can be found the first known use of the Nazi party euphemism for genocide— "Endlossung," Final Solution.

The *Post* was published by the much maligned German Social Democratic party, a party attacked by both Hitler's Nazis and Stalin's Communists (as "social fascists"). They failed to stop Hitler but succeeded to an extent they're rarely credited with in saving the German character from collective obloquy. There were other German reporters as well, notably Konrad Heiden and Rudolf Olden, who tried to tell the world the truth.

It doesn't strike me as if Shirer is attributing the malevolent aspect of the "Germanic" to an ethnic, or racial trait, the mirror image of how Hitler saw the Jews. Rather he sought scrupulously to trace these traits not to genetics but to a shared intellectual tradition, or perhaps delusion might be a better word. Malignant nurture not nature. And so, twenty years later, *The Rise and Fall*'s appraisal is less visceral than *Berlin Diary*'s, as he tries to trace what you might call the intellectual DNA of the Third Reich as opposed to its ethnic chromosomal code.

In these pages, one can sense as well a desire to put Hitler in perspective, in historical context. Some might call it a desire on Shirer's part to put himself at a distance from Hitler—after all, the world makes more sense and human nature seems less potentially demonic if a way can be found to explain Hitler rationally by means of a philosophic tradition of Prussian national chauvinism than if one is to face the implications of a potential for the eruption of unfathomable evil in individual human nature.

And so Shirer gives, for instance, as much attention to the lasting impact of Johann Gottlieb Fichte's 1804 speeches after the German defeat at Jena as he does to *The Protocols of the Elders of Zion* in shaping the Third Reich and Hitler's mind. He forces fanatical pro-Germanism to take its place beside fanatical anti-Semitism in that chamber of horrors.

Few outside the academy are aware of Fichte's 1804 speeches. In his section on "The Intellectual Roots of the Third Reich," Shirer speaks of the way that—following the humiliating German defeat by Napoleon at Jena—the philosopher Fichte delivered a lecture cum harangue at the University of Berlin whose incitements to rise from the ashes, Shirer tells us, "stirred and rallied a divided and defeated people and their resounding echoes could still be heard in the Third Reich."

(It's probably worth noting another testament to Shirer's ear and eye that, in one of the best twenty-first century meditations on Hitler, *Hitler's Private Library,* historian Timothy Ryback discovers, in an interview with Leni Riefenstahl, that she gave Hitler a very special, very personal gift, a gift of a white leather-bound edition of the collected works of Johann Gottlieb Fichte. Also worth noting: the ideology of "Germanism" is itself largely traceable to the Roman historian Tacitus's largely fictional portrait of Teutonic forest tribes.* History: so often the history of lie upon lie.)

Shirer's emphasis on the power of this hortatory-verging-on-hysterical aspect of German nationalism, that it recurrently needed to be revised and reconstructed by charismatic, even operatic philosophers, such as Nietsche and Wagner, helps explain Hitler's initial excited reception of it at an impressionable age. Hitler was still a youth when he came under the spell of one of his history teachers at Linz, Dr. Leopold Poetsch. Shirer brings forth from the shadows of amnesia this nearly forgotten figure, an acolyte of the Pan-German League, who may have been the most decisive in shaping—distorting—the pliant young mind of Adolf Hitler with his "dazzling eloquence" which "carr[ied] us away with him," as Hitler describes Poetsch's effect in *Mein Kampf*. It was undoubtedly Poetsch, the miserable little schoolteacher, who foisted Fichte on Hitler.

Shirer does not condemn Germans as Germans. He's faithful to the idea that all men are created equal, but he won't countenance the relativistic notion that all *ideas* are equal as well, and in bringing Fichte and Poetsch

---

*Christopher B. Krebs, *The Most Dangerous Book: Tacitus' *Germania *from the Roman Empire to the Third Reich*. New York: W. W. Norton, 2011.

to the fore, he shows that stupid and evil ideas played as crucial a role in Hitler's development as stupid and evil people.

Shirer and Postwar Controversies

There are so many what-if's in the history of the Third Reich. What if Hitler had another teacher, if he had not been given this lens of a German hysteria through which to focus all else in the world . . . who knows? Was his flight from "Jew infested" Vienna to Germany in 1913, his enlistment in the German army in 1914, his later belief that the brave and noble German army lost the war because of an illusory "stab in the back" by Jews and socialists . . . was it all fated?

Shirer doesn't address the question of "inevitability"; it's hard to say if he'd dispute or endorse the scholar-polemicist Milton Himmelfarb's contention in a well-known 1983 essay entitled "No Hitler, No Holocaust." Himmelfarb maintained there might have been another world war, an anti-Semitic regime in Germany, even pogroms, but that without Hitler, without his singleminded exterminationist drive, there would be no *Einsatzgruppen* killing squads, no Auschwitz, no Final Solution. Whether this is true may be an unanswerable question of the sort Shirer is too shrewd to digress upon. But throughout his narrative, particularly of "the Rise" he seems to be asking that contentious "inevitability" question.

One has to respect Shirer's reluctance to take sides on certain wartime controversies that still beset Third Reich historians today and may forever remain inexplicable, irresolvable. Why did Hitler hold his panzers back at Dunkirk for a crucial 48 hours and forgo a clear opportunity to destroy what was left of the British army, instead permitting the evacuation of some 380,000 British troops who would come storming back across the channel to defeat him? Shirer examines all explanations and finds them insufficient.

He does take a stand on what has become a controversial question: Chamberlain and appeasement. In the first decade of the twenty-first century there arose a number of revisionist analyses of the 1938 crisis over Czechoslovakia, which could have led to war that year. Hitler demanded the Czechs eviscerate their nation by giving Germany the Sudetenland, (the northern more Germanic province of the artificial nation created by Versailles). The Czechs asked British Prime Minister Chamberlain for a "guarantee" of Czech territorial integrity. Hitler threatened war. Suddenly, dramatically, Chamberlain flew to Munich for a summit with Hitler, Mussolini, and Daladier of France.

When Chamberlain returned boasting he had achieved "peace in our time," he had effectively handed half of Czechoslovakia to Hitler in return for a guarantee that the rest of Czechoslovakia would remain independent, a guarantee which Hitler treated like toilet paper.

But revisionists have argued that Chamberlain's appeasement was canniness, that he knew the British rearmament was not sufficient to stop Hitler if he chose war for Czechoslovakia in 1938 but might be ready by 1939.

Shirer had accompanied Hitler on his mission to Munich to meet with Chamberlain and knew Hitler saw it as a victory. It also served to cut the ground out from under those in the German military who thought they could use the opportunity of a foolhardy Hitler-provoked Czech crisis as an excuse for a coup against the Führer, an idea that they abandoned in Hitler's moment of triumph. However, it must also be said that the German military opponents of Hitler were almost always able to find an excuse not to act.

The argument over appeasement—and whether or not it was tactically valuable—was settled as much as these things ever are in Shirer's (and Churchill's) favor in 2010 when Niall Ferguson published (in *The War of the World*) a crushing rebuttal to the "military balance" aspect of the pro-appeasement revisionists. It concluded that the British-French alliance was measurably superior in ordnance in 1938—much more so than a year later—and would have enjoyed a strategic advantage had battle broken out at the Czech border.

Chamberlain's failure of nerve at Munich led to the feckless "guarantee" of the defense of Poland in 1939; full scale war soon destroyed Poland and conquered France after Hitler's treaty with Stalin had eliminated the threat from the East.

There is one battle, one turning point in which Shirer's analysis of Hitler's decision-making process seems to mirror the analysis of the evolution of Hitler's mind engaged in by the two giants of British World War II history, Trevor-Roper and Bullock. I'm speaking here of Stalingrad, where many believe Hitler's suicidal "stand or die" (in effect, "stand and die") order to his encircled Sixth Army, his refusal to allow them a tactical retreat from Stalingrad, insured the capture and loss of an entire 200,000-man army and a decisive reversal of fortune on the Russian front that was the beginning of the end of the war itself.

The mindset that produced this disastrous stance was the result of an evolution—a dialectic—Bullock introduced me to when I spoke to him in his study at Oxford's St. Catherine's College. In his first book *Hitler: A Study in Tyranny,* he said he had focused on Hitler the petty criminal, thief, scoundrel, con man, blackmailer, someone who rose to power with the ratlike cunning of the criminal underworld. His favorite term for Hitler was "mountebank"—con man—as applied to an international diplomacy ripe for the taking.

Initially he thought Hitler was an adventurer, a cynic, an *actor,* Bullock said disdainfully. He didn't even believe in his anti-Semitism, or so Bullock first thought; it was just an opportunistic way of swaying the German masses readily disposed to search for a World War I scapegoat. He was, as Bullock construed him, a depraved recrudescence of Louis Napoleon, the mountebank adventurer who seized the French throne in the mid-nineteenth century and whose claims for a Napoleonic dynasty brought France to ruin. (Curiously enough, *The Protocols of the Elders of Zion,* the ur-Jewish conspiracy theory work, Hitler's shaping text on Jews, and which informs *Mein Kampf,* was based originally on a satiric attack on Louis Napoleon.)

But in any case, Bullock told me, he'd found himself attacked for this vision of Hitler by his great rival on the subject, Trevor-Roper. Trevor-Roper thought that whatever his disreputable origins were, Hitler had developed a demonic, mesmeric, almost occult power over his audiences, one that depended on a belief in his own chosenness for a divine mission—a kind of possession that may have been self-deluded but was not cynical or calculated. The Führer *believed* in the Führer myth. (Some said Trevor-Roper himself had half-succumbed to its power if not its ideology in describing it in mystical, hyperbolic terms).

When I spoke to Trevor-Roper, he told me, "Hitler was convinced of his own rectitude"; Hitler was a true believer in the grandiosity of his own fatedness and his duty to humanity to exterminate the "racial bacillus" that had infected the Aryan race. His anti-Semitism, according to Trevor-Roper, was all too utterly sincere.

Bullock later told me something remarkable: Trevor-Roper had forced him to rethink his own vision of Hitler. Now, Bullock said, he tried to incorporate them both into a synthesis, a dynamic. Hitler was an actor at first, but he became "an actor who became convinced by his own act."

"And that," Bullock said, "was when he began to lose the war. That was the meaning of Stalingrad." Hitler had come to believe, because of a previous astonishing series of victories, in his own divine invincibility, he lost the ratlike craftiness that would have allowed him to make a tactical retreat from Stalingrad. But perhaps because of the symbolic name of the city, he felt the occult destiny that had brought him so far would not falter, that his shattered legions would prevail.

He might have lost anyway, but he was no longer calculating troop strength; he was gambling on will and divine favor alone.

It is a tribute to Shirer as a reporter and to Bullock as a historian that they both came to see how the shift in balance between actor and believer came to a head in that climactic battle.

In *The Rise and Fall,* Shirer captures a remarkable exchange (at the end of November 1941) between Hitler and von Rundstedt, the senior officer in the German army on the Stalingrad front, who was about to lose a good portion of it if he didn't execute a tactical retreat:

> Suddenly an order came to me from the Führer: "Remain where you are, and retreat no further." I immediately wired back: "It is madness to attempt to hold. . . . I repeat that this order be rescinded or that you find someone else." That same night the Führer's reply arrived: "I am acceding to your request. Please give up your command."

"This mania for ordering distant troops to stand fast no matter what their peril," Shirer writes, " . . . was to lead to Stalingrad and other disasters and to help seal Hitler's fate."

Indeed if one were seeking the foremost object lesson from rereading Shirer's remarkable work fifty years on, it might be Shirer's look at this glorification of suicidal martyrdom, its inseparability from delusion and defeat, because of the way it blinds its adherents to anything but murderous faith—and leads to little more than the slaughter.

And, yes, perhaps one corollary of Shirer's account that almost need not be spelled out: the danger of giving up our sense of selfhood for the illusory unity of a frenzied mass movement, of devolving from human to herd for some homicidal abstraction. It is a problem we can never be reminded of enough and for this we will always owe William Shirer a debt of gratitude.

Ron Rosenbaum is the author of *Explaining Hitler: The Search for the Origins of His Evil.*

FOREWORD

THOUGH I LIVED and worked in the Third Reich during the first half of its brief life, watching at first hand Adolf Hitler consolidate his power as dictator of this great but baffling nation and then lead it off to war and conquest, this personal experience would not have led me to attempt to write this book had there not occurred at the end of World War II an event unique in history.

This was the capture of most of the confidential archives of the German government and all its branches, including those of the Foreign Office, the Army and Navy, the National Socialist Party and Heinrich Himmler's secret police. Never before, I believe, has such a vast treasure fallen into the hands of contemporary historians. Hitherto the archives of a great state, even when it was defeated in war and its government overthrown by revolution, as happened to Germany and Russia in 1918, were preserved by it, and only those documents which served the interests of the subsequent ruling regime were ultimately published.

The swift collapse of the Third Reich in the spring of 1945 resulted in the surrender not only of a vast bulk of its secret papers but of other priceless material such as private diaries, highly secret speeches, conference reports and correspondence, and even transcripts of telephone conversations of the Nazi leaders tapped by a special office set up by Hermann Goering in the Air Ministry.

General Franz Halder, for instance, kept a voluminous diary, jotted down in Gabelsberger shorthand not only from day to day but from hour to hour during the day. It is a unique source of concise information for the period between August 14, 1939, and September 24, 1942, when he was Chief of the Army General Staff and in daily contact with Hitler and the other leaders of Nazi Germany. It is the most revealing of the German diaries, but there are others of great value, including those of Dr. Joseph Goebbels, the Minister of Propaganda and close party associate of Hitler, and of General Alfred Jodl, Chief of Operations of the High Command of the Armed Forces (OKW). There are diaries of the OKW itself and of the Naval High Command. Indeed the sixty thousand files of the German Naval Archives, which were captured at Schloss Tambach near Coburg, contain practically all the signals, ships' logs, diaries, memoranda, etc., of the German Navy from April 1945, when they were found, back to 1868, when the modern German Navy was founded.

The 485 tons of records of the German Foreign Office, captured by the U.S. First Army in various castles and mines in the Harz Mountains just as they were about to be burned on orders from Berlin, cover not only the period of the Third Reich but go back through the Weimar Republic to the beginning of the Second Reich of Bismarck. For many years after the war tons of Nazi documents lay sealed in a large U.S. Army warehouse in Alexandria, Virginia, our government showing no interest in even opening the packing cases to see what of historical interest might lie within them. Finally in 1955, ten years after their capture, thanks to the initiative of the American Historical Association and the generosity of a couple of private foundations, the Alexandria papers were opened and a pitifully small group of scholars, with an inadequate staff and equipment, went to work to sift through them and photograph them before the government, which was in a great hurry in the matter, returned them to Germany. They proved a rich find.

So did such documents as the partial stenographic record of fifty-one "Fuehrer Conferences" on the daily military situation as seen and discussed at Hitler's headquarters, and the fuller text of the Nazi warlord's table talk with his old party cronies and secretaries during the war; the first of these was rescued from the charred remains of some of Hitler's papers at Berchtesgaden by an intelligence officer of the U.S. 101st Airborne Division, and the second was found among Martin Bormann's papers.

Hundreds of thousands of captured Nazi documents were hurriedly assembled at Nuremberg as evidence in the trial of the major Nazi war criminals. While covering the first part of that trial I collected stacks of mimeographed copies and later the forty-two published volumes of testimony and documents, supplemented by ten volumes of English translations of many important papers. The text of other documents published in a fifteen-volume series on the twelve subsequent Nuremberg trials was also of value, though many papers and much testimony were omitted.

Finally, in addition to this unprecedented store of documents, there are the records of the exhaustive interrogation of German military officers and party and government officials and their subsequent testimony under oath at the various postwar trials, which provide material the like of which was never available, I believe, from such sources after previous wars.

I have not read, of course, all of this staggering amount of documentation—it would be far beyond the power of a single individual. But I have worked my way through a considerable part of it, slowed down, as all toilers in this rich vineyard must be, by the lack of any suitable indexes.

It is quite remarkable how little those of us who were stationed in Germany during the Nazi time, journalists and diplomats, really knew of what was going on behind the façade of the Third Reich. A totalitarian dictatorship, by its very nature, works in great secrecy and knows how to preserve that secrecy from the prying eyes of outsiders. It was easy enough to record and describe the bare, exciting and often revolting events in the Third Reich: Hitler's accession to power, the Reichstag fire, the Roehm Blood Purge, the Anschluss with Austria, the surrender of Chamberlain at Munich, the occupation of Czechoslovakia, the attacks on Poland, Scandinavia, the West, the Balkans and Russia, the horrors of the Nazi occupation and of the concentration camps and the liquidation of the Jews. But the fateful decisions secretly made, the intrigues, the treachery, the motives and the aberrations which led up to them, the parts played by the principal actors behind the scenes, the extent of the terror they exercised and their technique of organizing it—all this and much more remained largely hidden from us until the secret German papers turned up.

Some may think that it is much too early to try to write a history of the Third Reich, that such a task should be left to a later generation of writers to whom time has given perspective. I found this view especially prevalent in France when I went to do some research there. Nothing more recent than the Napoleonic era, I was told, should be tackled by writers of history.

There is much merit in this view. Most historians have waited fifty years or a hundred, or more, before attempting to write an account of a country, an empire, an era. But was this not principally because it took that long for the pertinent documents to come to light and furnish them with the authentic material they needed? And though perspective was gained, was not something lost because the authors necessarily lacked a personal acquaintance with the life and the atmosphere of the times and with the historical figures about which they wrote?

In the case of the Third Reich, and it is a unique case, almost all of the documentary material became available at its fall, and it has been enriched by the testimony of all the surviving leaders, military and civilian, in some instances before their death by execution. With such incomparable sources so soon available and with the memory of life in Nazi Germany and of the appearance and behavior and nature of the men who ruled it, Adolf Hitler above all, still fresh in my mind and bones, I decided, at any rate, to make an attempt to set down the history of the rise and fall of the Third Reich.

"I lived through the whole war," Thucydides remarks in his *History of the Peloponnesian War,* one of the greatest works of history ever written, "being of an age to comprehend events and giving my attention to them in order to know the exact truth about them."

I found it extremely difficult and not always possible to learn the exact truth about Hitler's Germany. The avalanche of documentary material helped one further along the road to truth than would have seemed possible twenty years ago, but its very vastness could often be confusing. And in all human records and testimony there are bound to be baffling contradictions.

No doubt my own prejudices, which inevitably spring from my experience and make-up, creep through the pages of this book from time to time. I detest totalitarian dictatorships in principle and came to loathe this one the more I lived through it and watched its ugly assault upon the human spirit. Nevertheless, in this book I have tried to be severely objective, letting the facts speak for themselves and noting the source for each. No incidents, scenes or quotations stem from the imagination; all are based on documents, the testimony of eyewitnesses or my own personal observation. In the half-dozen or so occasions in which there is some speculation, where the facts are missing, this is plainly labeled as such.

My interpretations, I have no doubt, will be disputed by many. That is inevitable, since no man's opinions are infallible. Those that I have ventured here in order to add clarity and depth to this narrative are merely the best I could come by from the evidence and from what knowledge and experience I have had.

Adolf Hitler is probably the last of the great adventurer-conquerors in the tradition of Alexander, Caesar and Napoleon, and the Third Reich the last of the empires which set out on the path taken earlier by France, Rome and Macedonia. The curtain was rung down on that phase of history, at least, by the sudden invention of the hydrogen bomb, of the ballistic missile and of rockets that can be aimed to hit the moon.

In our new age of terrifying, lethal gadgets, which supplanted so swiftly the old one, the first great aggressive war, if it should come, will be launched by suicidal little madmen pressing an electronic button. Such a war will not last long and none will ever follow it. There will be no conquerors and no conquests, but only the charred bones of the dead on an uninhabited planet.

Book One

✛ ✛ ✛

THE RISE
OF
ADOLF HITLER

1

BIRTH OF THE THIRD REICH

ON THE VERY EVE of the birth of the Third Reich a feverish tension gripped Berlin. The Weimar Republic, it seemed obvious to almost everyone, was about to expire. For more than a year it had been fast crumbling. General Kurt von Schleicher, who like his immediate predecessor, Franz von Papen, cared little for the Republic and less for its democracy, and who, also like him, had ruled as Chancellor by presidential decree without recourse to Parliament, had come to the end of his rope after fifty-seven days in office.

On Saturday, January 28, 1933, he had been abruptly dismissed by the aging President of the Republic, Field Marshal von Hindenburg. Adolf Hitler, leader of the National Socialists, the largest political party in Germany, was demanding for himself the chancellorship of the democratic Republic he had sworn to destroy.

The wildest rumors of what might happen were rife in the capital that fateful winter weekend, and the most alarming of them, as it happened, were not without some foundation. There were reports that Schleicher, in collusion with General Kurt von Hammerstein, the Commander in Chief of the Army, was preparing a putsch with the support of the Potsdam garrison for the purpose of arresting the President and establishing a military dictatorship. There was talk of a Nazi putsch. The Berlin storm troopers, aided by Nazi sympathizers in the police, were to seize the Wilhelmstrasse, where the President's Palace and most of the government ministries were located. There was talk also of a general strike. On Sunday, January 29, a hundred thousand workers crowded into the Lustgarten in the center of Berlin to demonstrate their opposition to making Hitler Chancellor. One of their leaders attempted to get in touch with General von Hammerstein to propose joint action by the Army and organized labor should Hitler be named to head a new government.[1] Once before, at the time of the Kapp putsch in 1920, a general strike had saved the Republic after the government had fled the capital.

Throughout most of the night from Sunday to Monday Hitler paced

3

up and down his room in the Kaiserhof hotel on the Reichskanzlerplatz, just down the street from the Chancellery.[2] Despite his nervousness he was supremely confident that his hour had struck. For nearly a month he had been secretly negotiating with Papen and the other leaders of the conservative Right. He had had to compromise. He could not have a purely Nazi government. But he could be Chancellor of a coalition government whose members, eight out of eleven of whom were not Nazis, agreed with him on the abolition of the democratic Weimar regime. Only the aged, dour President had seemed to stand in his way. As recently as January 26, two days before the advent of this crucial weekend, the grizzly old Field Marshal had told General von Hammerstein that he had "no intention whatsoever of making that Austrian corporal either Minister of Defense or Chancellor of the Reich."[3]

Yet under the influence of his son, Major Oskar von Hindenburg, of Otto von Meissner, the State Secretary to the President, of Papen and other members of the palace camarilla, the President was finally weakening. He was eighty-six and fading into senility. On the afternoon of Sunday, January 29, while Hitler was having coffee and cakes with Goebbels and other aides, Hermann Goering, President of the Reichstag and second to Hitler in the Nazi Party, burst in and informed them categorically that on the morrow Hitler would be named Chancellor.[4]

Shortly before noon on Monday, January 30, 1933, Hitler drove over to the Chancellery for an interview with Hindenburg that was to prove fateful for himself, for Germany and for the rest of the world. From a window in the Kaiserhof, Goebbels, Roehm and other Nazi chiefs kept an anxious watch on the door of the Chancellery, where the Fuehrer would shortly be coming out. "We would see from his face whether he had succeeded or not," Goebbels noted. For even then they were not quite sure. "Our hearts are torn back and forth between doubt, hope, joy and discouragement," Goebbels jotted down in his diary. "We have been disappointed too often for us to believe wholeheartedly in the great miracle."[5]

A few moments later they witnessed the miracle. The man with the Charlie Chaplin mustache, who had been a down-and-out tramp in Vienna in his youth, an unknown soldier of World War I, a derelict in Munich in the first grim postwar days, the somewhat comical leader of the Beer Hall Putsch, this spellbinder who was not even German but Austrian, and who was only forty-three years old, had just been administered the oath as Chancellor of the German Reich.

He drove the hundred yards to the Kaiserhof and was soon with his old cronies, Goebbels, Goering, Roehm and the other Brownshirts who had helped him along the rocky, brawling path to power. "He says nothing, and all of us say nothing," Goebbels recorded, "but his eyes are full of tears."[6]

That evening from dusk until far past midnight the delirious Nazi storm troopers marched in a massive torchlight parade to celebrate the victory. By the tens of thousands, they emerged in disciplined columns from the depths of the Tiergarten, passed under the triumphal arch of the Brandenburg Gate and down the Wilhelmstrasse, their bands blaring the old martial airs to the thunderous beating of the drums, their voices bawling the new Horst Wessel song and other tunes that were as old as Germany, their jack boots beating a mighty rhythm on the pavement, their torches held high ánd forming a ribbon of flame that illuminated the night and kindled the hurrahs of the onlookers massed on the sidewalks. From a window in the palace Hindenburg looked down upon the marching throng, beating time to the military marches with his cane, apparently pleased that at last he had picked a Chancellor who could arouse the people in a traditionally German way. Whether the old man, in his dotage, had any inkling of what he had unleashed that day is doubtful. A story, probably apocryphal, soon spread over Berlin that in the midst of the parade he had turned to an old general and said, "I didn't know we had taken so many Russian prisoners."

A stone's throw down the Wilhelmstrasse Adolf Hitler stood at an open window of the Chancellery, beside himself with excitement and joy, dancing up and down, jerking his arm up continually in the Nazi salute, smiling and laughing until his eyes were again full of tears.

One foreign observer watched the proceedings that evening with different feelings. "The river of fire flowed past the French Embassy," André François-Poncet, the ambassador, wrote, "whence, with heavy heart and filled with foreboding, I watched its luminous wake."[7]

Tired but happy, Goebbels arrived home that night at 3 A.M. Scribbling in his diary before retiring, he wrote: "It is almost like a dream . . . a fairy tale . . . The new Reich has been born. Fourteen years of work have been crowned with victory. The German revolution has begun!"[8]

The Third Reich which was born on January 30, 1933, Hitler boasted, would endure for a thousand years,[9] and in Nazi parlance it was often referred to as the "Thousand-Year Reich." It lasted twelve years and four months, but in that flicker of time, as history goes, it caused an eruption on this earth more violent and shattering than any previously experienced, raising the German people to heights of power they had not known in more than a millennium, making them at one time the masters of Europe from the Atlantic to the Volga, from the North Cape to the Mediterranean, and then plunging them to the depths of destruction and desolation at the end of a world war which their nation had cold-bloodedly provoked and during which it instituted a reign of terror over the conquered peoples which, in its calculated butchery of human life and the human spirit, outdid all the savage oppressions of the previous ages.

The man who founded the Third Reich, who ruled it ruthlessly and often with uncommon shrewdness, who led it to such dizzy heights and to such a sorry end, was a person of undoubted, if evil, genius. It is true that he found in the German people, as a mysterious Providence and centuries of experience had molded them up to that time, a natural instrument which he was able to shape to his own sinister ends. But without

Adolf Hitler, who was possessed of a demonic personality, a granite will, uncanny instincts, a cold ruthlessness, a remarkable intellect, a soaring imagination and—until toward the end, when, drunk with power and success, he overreached himself—an amazing capacity to size up people and situations, there almost certainly would never have been a Third Reich.

"It is one of the great examples," as Friedrich Meinecke, the eminent German historian, said, "of the singular and incalculable power of personality in historical life."[10]

To some Germans and, no doubt, to most foreigners it appeared that a charlatan had come to power in Berlin. To the majority of Germans Hitler had—or would shortly assume—the aura of a truly charismatic leader. They were to follow him blindly, as if he possessed a divine judgment, for the next twelve tempestuous years.

THE ADVENT OF ADOLF HITLER

Considering his origins and his early life, it would be difficult to imagine a more unlikely figure to succeed to the mantle of Bismarck, the Hohenzollern emperors and President Hindenburg than this singular Austrian of peasant stock who was born at half past six on the evening of April 20, 1889, in the Gasthof zum Pommer, a modest inn in the town of Braunau am Inn, across the border from Bavaria.

The place of birth on the Austro–German frontier was to prove significant, for early in his life, as a mere youth, Hitler became obsessed with the idea that there should be no border between these two German-speaking peoples and that they both belonged in the same Reich. So strong and enduring were his feelings that at thirty-five, when he sat in a German prison dictating the book that would become the blueprint for the Third Reich, his very first lines were concerned with the symbolic significance of his birthplace. *Mein Kampf* begins with these words:

Today it seems to me providential that fate should have chosen Braunau am Inn as my birthplace. For this little town lies on the boundary between two German states which we of the younger generation at least have made it our life-work to reunite by every means at our disposal. . . . This little city on the border seems to me the symbol of a great mission.[11]

Adolf Hitler was the third son of the third marriage of a minor Austrian customs official who had been born an illegitimate child and who for the first thirty-nine years of his life bore his mother's name, Schicklgruber. The name Hitler appears in the maternal as well as the paternal line. Both Hitler's grandmother on his mother's side and his grandfather on his father's side were named Hitler, or rather variants of it, for the family name was variously written as Hiedler, Huetler, Huettler and Hitler.

Adolf's mother was his father's second cousin, and an episcopal dispensation had to be obtained for the marriage.

The forebears of the future German Fuehrer, on both sides, dwelt for generations in the Waldviertel, a district in Lower Austria between the Danube and the borders of Bohemia and Moravia. In my own Vienna days I sometimes passed through it on my way to Prague or to Germany. It is a hilly, wooded country of peasant villages and small farms, and though only some fifty miles from Vienna it has a somewhat remote and impoverished air, as if the main currents of Austrian life had passed it by. The inhabitants tend to be dour, like the Czech peasants just to the north of them. Intermarriage is common, as in the case of Hitler's parents, and illegitimacy is frequent.

On the mother's side there was a certain stability. For four generations Klara Poelzl's family remained on peasant holding Number 37 in the village of Spital.[12] The story of Hitler's paternal ancestors is quite different. The spelling of the family name, as we have seen, changes; the place of residence also. There is a spirit of restlessness among the Hitlers, an urge to move from one village to the next, from one job to another, to avoid firm human ties and to follow a certain bohemian life in relations with women.

Johann Georg Hiedler, Adolf's grandfather, was a wandering miller, plying his trade in one village after another in Lower Austria. Five months after his first marriage, in 1824, a son was born, but the child and the mother did not survive. Eighteen years later, while working in Duerenthal, he married a forty-seven-year-old peasant woman from the village of Strones, Maria Anna Schicklgruber. Five years before the marriage, on June 7, 1837, Maria had had an illegitimate son whom she named Alois and who became Adolf Hitler's father. It is most probable that the father of Alois was Johann Hiedler, though conclusive evidence is lacking. At any rate Johann eventually married the woman, but contrary to the usual custom in such cases he did not trouble himself with legitimizing the son after the marriage. The child grew up as Alois Schicklgruber.

Anna died in 1847, whereupon Johann Hiedler vanished for thirty years, only to reappear at the age of eighty-four in the town of Weitra in the Waldviertel, the spelling of his name now changed to Hitler, to testify before a notary in the presence of three witnesses that he was the father of Alois Schicklgruber. Why the old man waited so long to take this step, or why he finally took it, is not known from the available records. According to Heiden, Alois later confided to a friend that it was done to help him obtain a share of an inheritance from an uncle, a brother of the miller, who had raised the youth in his own household.[13] At any rate, this tardy recognition was made on June 6, 1876, and on November 23 the parish priest at Doellersheim, to whose office the notarized statement had been forwarded, scratched out the name of Alois Schicklgruber in the baptismal registry and wrote in its place that of Alois Hitler.

From that time on Adolf's father was legally known as Alois Hitler, and the name passed on naturally to his son. It was only during the

1930s that enterprising journalists in Vienna, delving into the parish archives, discovered the facts about Hitler's ancestry and, disregarding old Johann Georg Hiedler's belated attempt to do right by a bastard son, tried to fasten on the Nazi leader the name of Adolf Schicklgruber.

There are many weird twists of fate in the strange life of Adolf Hitler, but none more odd than this one which took place thirteen years before his birth. Had the eighty-four-year-old wandering miller not made his un-expected reappearance to recognize the paternity of his thirty-nine-year-old son nearly thirty years after the death of the mother, Adolf Hitler would have been born Adolf Schicklgruber. There may not be much or anything in a name, but I have heard Germans speculate whether Hitler could have become the master of Germany had he been known to the world as Schicklgruber. It has a slightly comic sound as it rolls off the tongue of a South German. Can one imagine the frenzied German masses acclaiming a Schicklgruber with their thunderous "Heils"? "Heil Schickl-gruber!"? Not only was "Heil Hitler!" used as a Wagnerian, paganlike chant by the multitude in the mystic pageantry of the massive Nazi rallies, but it became the obligatory form of greeting between Germans during the Third Reich, even on the telephone, where it replaced the conventional "Hello." "Heil Schicklgruber!"? It is a little difficult to imagine.*

Since the parents of Alois apparently never lived together, even after they were married, the future father of Adolf Hitler grew up with his uncle, who though a brother of Johann Georg Hiedler spelled his name dif-ferently, being known as Johann von Nepomuk Huetler. In view of the undying hatred which the Nazi Fuehrer would develop from youth on for the Czechs, whose nation he ultimately destroyed, the Christian name is worthy of passing mention. Johann von Nepomuk was the national saint of the Czech people and some historians have seen in a Hitler's being given this name an indication of Czech blood in the family.

Alois Schicklgruber first learned the trade of shoemaker in the village of Spital, but being restless, like his father, he soon set out to make his fortune in Vienna. At eighteen he joined the border police in the Austrian customs service near Salzburg, and on being promoted to the customs service itself nine years later he married Anna Glasl-Hoerer, the adopted daughter of a customs official. She brought him a small dowry and in-creased social status, as such things went in the old Austro-Hungarian petty bureaucracy. But the marriage was not a happy one. She was four-teen years older than he, of failing health, and she remained childless. After sixteen years they were separated and three years later, in 1883, she died.

Before the separation Alois, now legally known as Hitler, had taken up

---

* Hitler himself seems to have recognized this. In his youth he confided to the only boyhood friend he had that nothing had ever pleased him as much as his father's change of names. He told August Kubizek that the name Schicklgruber "seemed to him so uncouth, so boorish, apart from being so clumsy and unpractical. He found 'Hiedler' . . . too soft; but 'Hitler' sounded nice and was easy to remember." (August Kubizek, *The Young Hitler I Knew*, p. 40.)

with a young hotel cook, Franziska Matzelsberger, who bore him a son, named Alois, in 1882. One month after the death of his wife he married the cook and three months later she gave birth to a daughter, Angela. The second marriage did not last long. Within a year Franziska was dead of tuberculosis. Six months later Alois Hitler married for the third and last time.

The new bride, Klara Poelzl, who would shortly become the mother of Adolf Hitler, was twenty-five, her husband forty-eight, and they had long known each other. Klara came from Spital, the ancestral village of the Hitlers. Her grandfather had been Johann von Nepomuk Huetler, with whom his nephew, Alois Schicklgruber-Hitler, had grown up. Thus Alois and Klara were second cousins and they found it necessary, as we have seen, to apply for episcopal dispensation to permit the marriage.

It was a union which the customs official had first contemplated years before when he had taken Klara into his childless home as a foster daughter during his first marriage. The child had lived for years with the Schicklgrubers in Braunau, and as the first wife ailed Alois seems to have given thought to marrying Klara as soon as his wife died. His legitimation and his coming into an inheritance from the uncle who was Klara's grandfather occurred when the young girl was sixteen, just old enough to legally marry. But, as we have seen, the wife lingered on after the separation, and, perhaps because Alois in the meantime took up with the cook Franziska Matzelsberger, Klara, at the age of twenty, left the household and went to Vienna, where she obtained employment as a household servant.

She returned four years later to keep house for her cousin; Franziska too, in the last months of her life, had moved out of her husband's home. Alois Hitler and Klara Poelzl were married on January 7, 1885, and some four months and ten days later their first child, Gustav, was born. He died in infancy, as did the second child, Ida, born in 1886. Adolf was the third child of this third marriage. A younger brother, Edmund, born in 1894, lived only six years. The fifth and last child, Paula, born in 1896, lived to survive her famous brother.

Adolf's half-brother, Alois, and his half-sister, Angela, the children of Franziska Matzelsberger, also lived to grow up. Angela, a handsome young woman, married a revenue official named Raubal and after his death worked in Vienna as a housekeeper and for a time, if Heiden's information is correct, as a cook in a Jewish charity kitchen.[14] In 1928 Hitler brought her to Berchtesgaden as his housekeeper, and thereafter one heard a great deal in Nazi circles of the wondrous Viennese pastries and desserts she baked for him and for which he had such a ravenous appetite. She left him in 1936 to marry a professor of architecture in Dresden, and Hitler, by then Chancellor and dictator, was resentful of her departure and declined to send a wedding present. She was the only person in the family with whom, in his later years, he seems to have been close—with one exception. Angela had a daughter, Geli Raubal, an attractive young blond woman with whom, as we shall see, Hitler had the only truly deep love affair of his life.

Adolf Hitler never liked to hear mention of his half-brother. Alois Matzelsberger, later legitimized as Alois Hitler, became a waiter, and for many years his life was full of difficulties with the law. Heiden records that at eighteen the young man was sentenced to five months in jail for theft and at twenty served another sentence of eight months on the same charge. He eventually moved to Germany, only to become embroiled in further troubles. In 1924, while Adolf Hitler was languishing in prison for having staged a political revolt in Munich, Alois Hitler was sentenced to six months in prison by a Hamburg court for bigamy. Thereafter, Heiden recounts, he moved on to England, where he quickly established a family and then deserted it.[15]

The coming to power of the National Socialists brought better times to Alois Hitler. He opened a *Bierstube*—a small beerhouse—in a suburb of Berlin, moving it shortly before the war to the Wittenbergplatz in the capital's fashionable West End. It was much frequented by Nazi officials and during the early part of the war when food was scarce it inevitably had a plentiful supply. I used to drop in occasionally at that time. Alois was then nearing sixty, a portly, simple, good-natured man with little physical resemblance to his famous half-brother and in fact indistinguishable from dozens of other little pub keepers one had seen in Germany and Austria. Business was good and, whatever his past, he was now obviously enjoying the prosperous life. He had only one fear: that his half-brother, in a moment of disgust or rage, might revoke his license. Sometimes there was talk in the little beerhouse that the Chancellor and Fuehrer of the Reich regretted this reminder of the humble nature of the Hitler family. Alois himself, I remember, refused to be drawn into any talk whatsoever about his half-brother—a wise precaution but frustrating to those of us who were trying to learn all we could about the background of the man who by that time had already set out to conquer Europe.

Except in *Mein Kampf,* where the sparse biographical material is often misleading and the omissions monumental, Hitler rarely discussed—or permitted discussion of in his presence—his family background and early life. We have seen what the family background was. What was the early life?

THE EARLY LIFE OF ADOLF HITLER

The year his father retired from the customs service at the age of fifty-eight, the six-year-old Adolf entered the public school in the village of Fischlham, a short distance southwest of Linz. This was in 1895. For the next four or five years the restless old pensioner moved from one village to another in the vicinity of Linz. By the time the son was fifteen he could remember seven changes of address and five different schools. For two years he attended classes at the Benedictine monastery at Lambach, near which his father had purchased a farm. There he sang in the choir, took singing lessons and, according to his own account,[16] dreamed of one day taking holy orders. Finally the retired customs official settled down for good in the village of Leonding, on the southern outskirts of Linz, where the family occupied a modest house and garden.

At the age of eleven, Adolf was sent to the high school at Linz. This represented a financial sacrifice for the father and indicated an ambition that the son should follow in his father's footsteps and become a civil servant. That, however, was the last thing the youth would dream of.

"Then barely eleven years old," Hitler later recounted,[17] "I was forced into opposition (to my father) for the first time. . . . I did not want to become a civil servant."

The story of the bitter, unrelenting struggle of the boy, not yet in his teens, against a hardened and, as he said, domineering father is one of the few biographical items which Hitler sets down in great detail and with apparent sincerity and truth in *Mein Kampf*. The conflict aroused the first manifestation of that fierce, unbending will which later would carry him so far despite seemingly insuperable obstacles and handicaps and which, confounding all those who stood in his way, was to put an indelible stamp on Germany and Europe.

I did not want to become a civil servant, no, and again no. All attempts on my father's part to inspire me with love or pleasure in this profession by stories from his own life accomplished the exact opposite. I . . . grew sick to my stomach at the thought of sitting in an office, deprived of my liberty; ceasing to be master of my own time and being compelled to force the content of my whole life into paper forms that had to be filled out. . . .

One day it became clear to me that I would become a painter, an artist . . . My father was struck speechless.

"Painter? Artist?"

He doubted my sanity, or perhaps he thought he had heard wrong or mis-understood me. But when he was clear on the subject, and particularly after he felt the seriousness of my intention, he opposed it with all the determination of his nature. . . .

"Artist! No! Never as long as I live!" . . . My father would never depart from his "Never!" And I intensified my "Nevertheless!"[18]

One consequence of this encounter, Hitler later explained, was that he stopped studying in school. "I thought that once my father saw how little progress I was making at high school he would let me devote myself to my dream, whether he liked it or not."[19]

This, written thirty-four years later, may be partly an excuse for his failure at school. His marks in grade school had been uniformly good. But at the Linz high school they were so poor that in the end, without obtaining the customary certificate, he was forced to transfer to the state high school at Steyr, some distance from Linz. He remained there but a short time and left before graduating.

Hitler's scholastic failure rankled in him in later life, when he heaped ridicule on the academic "gentry," their degrees and diplomas and their pedagogical airs. Even in the last three or four years of his life, at Supreme Army Headquarters, where he allowed himself to be overwhelmed with details of military strategy, tactics and command, he would take an evening off to reminisce with his old party cronies on the stupidity of the teachers he had had in his youth. Some of these meanderings of this mad genius, now the Supreme Warlord personally directing his vast armies from the Volga to the English Channel, have been preserved.

When I think of the men who were my teachers, I realize that most of them were slightly mad. The men who could be regarded as good teachers were exceptional. It's tragic to think that such people have the power to bar a young man's way.—*March 3, 1942.*[20]

I have the most unpleasant recollections of the teachers who taught me. Their external appearance exuded uncleanliness; their collars were unkempt . . . They were the product of a proletariat denuded of all personal independence of thought, distinguished by unparalleled ignorance and most admirably fitted to become the pillars of an effete system of government which, thank God, is now a thing of the past.—*April 12, 1942.*[21]

When I recall my teachers at school, I realize that half of them were abnormal. . . . We pupils of old Austria were brought up to respect old people and women. But on our professors we had no mercy; they were our natural enemies. The majority of them were somewhat mentally deranged, and quite a few ended their days as honest-to-God lunatics! . . . I was in particular bad odor with the teachers. I showed not the slightest aptitude for foreign languages—though I might have, had not the teacher been a congenital idiot. I could not bear the sight of him.—*August 29, 1942.*[22]

Our teachers were absolute tyrants. They had no sympathy with youth; their one object was to stuff our brains and turn us into erudite apes like themselves. If any pupil showed the slightest trace of originality, they persecuted him relentlessly, and the only model pupils whom I have ever got to know have all been failures in after-life.—*September 7, 1942.*[23]

To his dying day, it is obvious, Hitler never forgave his teachers for the poor marks they had given him—nor could he forget. But he could distort to a point of grotesqueness.

The impression he made on his teachers, recollected after he had become a world figure, has been briefly recorded. One of the few instructors Hitler seems to have liked was Professor Theodor Gissinger, who strove to teach him science. Gissinger later recalled, "As far as I was concerned, Hitler left neither a favorable nor an unfavorable impression in Linz. He was by no means a leader of the class. He was slender and erect, his face pallid and very thin, almost like that of a consumptive, his gaze unusually open, his eyes brilliant."[24]

Professor Eduard Huemer, apparently the "congenital idiot" mentioned by Hitler above—for he taught French—came to Munich in 1923 to testify for his former pupil, who was then being tried for treason as the result of the Beer Hall Putsch. Though he lauded Hitler's aims and said that he wished from the bottom of his heart to see him fulfill his ideals, he gave the following thumbnail portrait of the young high-school student:

Hitler was certainly gifted, although only for particular subjects, but he lacked self-control and, to say the least, he was considered argumentive, autocratic, self-opinionated and bad-tempered, and unable to submit to school discipline. Nor was he industrious; otherwise he would have achieved much better results, gifted as he was.[25]

There was one teacher at the Linz high school who exercised a strong and, as it turned out, a fateful influence on the young Adolf Hitler. This was a history teacher, Dr. Leopold Poetsch, who came from the southern German-language border region where it meets that of the South Slavs and whose experience with the racial struggle there had made him a fanatical German nationalist. Before coming to Linz he had taught at Marburg, which later, when the area was transferred to Yugoslavia after the First World War, became Maribor.

Though Dr. Poetsch had given his pupil marks of only "fair" in history, he was the only one of Hitler's teachers to receive a warm tribute in *Mein Kampf*. Hitler readily admitted his debt to this man.

It was perhaps decisive for my whole later life that good fortune gave me a history teacher who understood, as few others did, this principle . . . —of retaining the essential and forgetting the nonessential . . . In my teacher, Dr. Leopold Poetsch of the high school in Linz, this requirement was fulfilled in a truly ideal manner. An old gentleman, kind but at the same time firm, he was able not only to hold our attention by his dazzling eloquence but to carry us away with him. Even today I think back with genuine emotion on this gray-haired man who, by the fire of his words, sometimes made us forget the present; who, as if by magic, transported us into times past and, out of the millennium mists of time, transformed dry historical facts into vivid reality. There we sat, often aflame with enthusiasm, sometimes even moved to tears . . . He used our budding national fanaticism as a means of educating us, frequently appealing to our sense of national honor.

This teacher made history my favorite subject.

And indeed, though he had no such intention, it was then that I became a young revolutionary.[26]

Some thirty-five years later, in 1938, while touring Austria in triumph after he had forced its annexation to the Third Reich, Chancellor Hitler stopped off at Klagenfurt to see his old teacher, then in retirement. He was delighted to find that the old gentleman had been a member of the underground Nazi S.S., which had been outlawed during Austria's independence. He conversed with him alone for an hour and later confided to members of his party, "You cannot imagine how much I owe to that old man."[27]

Alois Hitler died of a lung hemorrhage on January 3, 1903, at the age of sixty-five. He was stricken while taking a morning walk and died a few moments later in a nearby inn in the arms of a neighbor. When his thirteen-year-old son saw the body of his father he broke down and wept.[28]

His mother, who was then forty-two, moved to a modest apartment in Urfahr, a suburb of Linz, where she tried to keep herself and her two surviving children, Adolf and Paula, on the meager savings and pension left her. She felt obligated, as Hitler remarks in *Mein Kampf,* to continue his education in accordance with his father's wishes—"in other words," as he puts it, "to have me study for the civil servant's career." But though the young widow was indulgent to her son, and he seems to have loved her dearly, he was "more than ever determined absolutely," he says, "not to undertake this career." And so, despite a tender love between mother and son, there was friction and Adolf continued to neglect his studies.

"Then suddenly an illness came to my help and in a few weeks decided my future and the eternal domestic quarrel."[29]

The lung ailment which Hitler suffered as he was nearing sixteen necessitated his dropping out of school for at least a year. He was sent for a time to the family village of Spital, where he recuperated at the home of his mother's sister, Theresa Schmidt, a peasant woman. On his recovery he returned briefly to the state high school at Steyr. His last report, dated September 16, 1905, shows marks of "adequate" in German, chemistry, physics, geometry and geometrical drawing. In geography and history he was "satisfactory"; in free-hand drawing, "excellent." He felt so excited at the prospect of leaving school for good that for the first and last time in his life he got drunk. As he remembered it in later years he was picked up at dawn, lying on a country road outside of Steyr, by a milkmaid and helped back to town, swearing he would never do it again.* In this matter, at least, he was as good as his word, for he became a teetotaler, a nonsmoker and a vegetarian to boot, at first out of necessity as a penniless vagabond in Vienna and Munich, and later out of conviction.

The next two or three years Hitler often described as the happiest days of his life.† While his mother suggested—and other relatives urged—that he go to work and learn a trade he contented himself with dreaming of

---

* He told this story on himself in one of his reminiscing moods on the evening of January 8–9, 1942, at Supreme Headquarters. (*Hitler's Secret Conversations,* p. 160.)

† "These were the happiest days of my life and seemed to me almost a dream . . ." (*Mein Kampf,* p. 18.) In a letter dated August 4, 1933, six months after he became Chancellor, Hitler wrote his boyhood friend, August Kubizek: "I should be very glad . . . to revive once more with you those memories of the best years of my life." (Kubizek, *The Young Hitler I Knew,* p. 273.)

his future as an artist and with idling away the pleasant days along the Danube. He never forgot the "downy softness" of those years from sixteen to nineteen when as a "mother's darling" he enjoyed the "hollowness of a comfortable life."[30] Though the ailing widow found it difficult to make ends meet on her meager income, young Adolf declined to help out by getting a job. The idea of earning even his own living by any kind of regular employment was repulsive to him and was to remain so throughout his life.

What apparently made those last years of approaching manhood so happy for Hitler was the freedom from having to work, which gave him the freedom to brood, to dream, to spend his days roaming the city streets or the countryside declaiming to his companion what was wrong with the world and how to right it, and his evenings curled up with a book or standing in the rear of the opera house in Linz or Vienna listening enraptured to the mystic, pagan works of Richard Wagner.

A boyhood friend later remembered him as a pale, sickly, lanky youth who, though usually shy and reticent, was capable of sudden bursts of hysterical anger against those who disagreed with him. For four years he fancied himself deeply in love with a handsome blond maiden named Stefanie, and though he often gazed at her longingly as she strolled up and down the Landstrasse in Linz with her mother he never made the slightest effort to meet her, preferring to keep her, like so many other objects, in the shadowy world of his soaring fantasies. Indeed, in the countless love poems which he wrote to her but never sent (one of them was entitled "Hymn to the Beloved") and which he insisted on reading to his patient young friend, August Kubizek,* she became a damsel out of *Die Walkuerie,* clad in a dark-blue flowing velvet gown, riding a white steed over the flowering meadows.[31]

Although Hitler was determined to become an artist, preferably a painter or at least an architect, he was already obsessed with politics at the age of sixteen. By then he had developed a violent hatred for the Hapsburg monarchy and all the non-German races in the multinational Austro–Hungarian Empire over which it ruled, and an equally violent love for everything German. At sixteen he had become what he was to remain till his dying breath: a fanatical German nationalist.

He appears to have had little of the carefree spirit of youth despite all the loafing. The world's problems weighed down on him. Kubizek later recalled, "He saw everywhere only obstacles and hostility . . . He was

---

* Kubizek, who appears to have been the only friend Hitler ever had in his youth, has given in his book, *The Young Hitler I Knew,* an interesting picture of his companion in the last four years before, at the age of nineteen, he skidded down to the life of a vagabond in Vienna—a portrait, incidentally, that not only fills a biographical gap in the life of the German Fuehrer but corrects somewhat the hitherto prevalent impressions of his early character. Kubizek was as unlike Hitler as can be imagined. He had a happy home in Linz, learned his father's trade as an upholsterer, worked diligently at it while studying music, was graduated with honors from the Vienna Conservatory of Music and began a promising professional career as a conductor and composer which was shattered by the First World War.

always up against something and at odds with the world . . . I never saw him take anything lightly . . ."[32]

It was at this period that the young man who could not stand school became a voracious reader, subscribing to the Library of Adult Education in Linz and joining the Museum Society, whose books he borrowed in large numbers. His young friend remembered him as always surrounded by books, of which his favorites were works on German history and German mythology.[33]

Since Linz was a provincial town, it was not long before Vienna, the glittering baroque capital of the empire, began to beckon a youth of such ambition and imagination. In 1906, just after his seventeenth birthday, Hitler set out with funds provided by his mother and other relations to spend two months in the great metropolis. Though it was later to become the scene of his bitterest years when, at times, he literally lived in the gutter, Vienna on this first visit enthralled him. He roamed the streets for days, filled with excitement at the sight of the imposing buildings along the Ring and in a continual state of ecstasy at what he saw in the museums, the opera house, the theaters.

He also inquired about entering the Vienna Academy of Fine Arts, and a year later, in October 1907, he was back in the capital to take the entrance examination as the first practical step in fulfilling his dream of becoming a painter. He was eighteen and full of high hopes, but they were dashed. An entry in the academy's classification list tells the story.

The following took the test with insufficient results, or were not admitted . . . Adolf Hitler, Braunau a. Inn, April 20, 1889, German, Catholic. Father civil servant. 4 classes in High School. Few Heads. Test drawing unsatisfactory.[34]

Hitler tried again the following year and this time his drawings were so poor that he was not admitted to the test. For the ambitious young man this was, as he later wrote, a bolt from the blue. He had been absolutely convinced that he would be successful. According to his own account in *Mein Kampf*, Hitler requested an explanation from the rector of the academy.

That gentleman assured me that the drawings I had submitted incontrovertibly showed my unfitness for painting, and that my ability obviously lay in the field of architecture; for me, he said, the Academy's School of Painting was out of the question, the place for me was at the School of Architecture.[35]

The young Adolf was inclined to agree but quickly realized to his sorrow that his failure to graduate from high school might well block his entry into the architectural school.

In the meantime his mother was dying of cancer of the breast and he returned to Linz. Since Adolf's departure from school Klara Hitler and her relatives had supported the young man for three years, and they could see nothing to show for it. On December 21, 1908, as the town began to assume its festive Christmas garb, Adolf Hitler's mother died, and two days later she was buried at Leonding beside her husband. To the nineteen-year-old youth

it was a dreadful blow . . . I had honored my father, but my mother I had loved . . . [Her] death put a sudden end to all my highflown plans . . . Poverty and hard reality compelled me to take a quick decision . . . I was faced with the problem of somehow making my own living.[36]

Somehow! He had no trade. He had always disdained manual labor. He had never tried to earn a cent. But he was undaunted. Bidding his relatives farewell, he declared that he would never return until he had made good.

With a suitcase full of clothes and underwear in my hand and an indomitable will in my heart, I set out for Vienna. I too hoped to wrest from fate what my father had accomplished fifty years before; I too hoped to become "something"—but in no case a civil servant.[37]

"THE SADDEST PERIOD OF MY LIFE"

The next four years, between 1909 and 1913, turned out to be a time of utter misery and destitution for the conquering young man from Linz. In these last fleeting years before the fall of the Hapsburgs and the end of the city as the capital of an empire of fifty-two million people in the heart of Europe, Vienna had a gaiety and charm that were unique among the capitals of the world. Not only in its architecture, its sculpture, its music, but in the lighthearted, pleasure-loving, cultivated spirit of its people, it breathed an atmosphere of the baroque and the rococo that no other city of the West knew.

Set along the blue Danube beneath the wooded hills of the Wienerwald, which were studded with yellow-green vineyards, it was a place of natural beauty that captivated the visitor and made the Viennese believe that Providence had been especially kind to them. Music filled the air, the towering music of gifted native sons, the greatest Europe had known, Haydn, Mozart, Beethoven and Schubert, and, in the last Indian-summer years, the gay, haunting waltzes of Vienna's own beloved Johann Strauss. To a people so blessed and so imprinted with the baroque style of living, life itself was something of a dream and the good folk of the city passed the pleasant days and nights of their lives waltzing and wining, in light talk in the congenial coffeehouses, listening to music and viewing the make-believe of theater and opera and operetta, in flirting and making love, abandoning a large part of their lives to pleasure and to dreams.

To be sure, an empire had to be governed, an army and navy manned, communications maintained, business transacted and labor done. But few in Vienna worked overtime—or even full time—at such things.

There was a seamy side, of course. This city, like all others, had its poor: ill-fed, ill-clothed and living in hovels. But as the greatest industrial center in Central Europe as well as the capital of the empire, Vienna was prosperous, and this prosperity spread among the people and sifted down. The great mass of the lower middle class controlled the city politically; labor was organizing not only trade unions but a powerful political party of its own, the Social Democrats. There was a ferment in the life of the city, now grown to a population of two million. Democracy was forcing out the ancient autocracy of the Hapsburgs, education and culture were opening up to the masses so that by the time Hitler came to Vienna in 1909 there was opportunity for a penniless young man either to get a higher education or to earn a fairly decent living and, as one of a million wage earners, to live under the civilizing spell which the capital cast over its inhabitants. Was not his only friend, Kubizek, as poor and as obscure as himself, already making a name for himself in the Academy of Music?

But the young Adolf did not pursue his ambition to enter the School of Architecture. It was still open for him despite his lack of a high-school diploma—young men who showed "special talent" were admitted without such a certificate—but so far as is known he made no application. Nor was he interested in learning a trade or in taking any kind of regular employment. Instead he preferred to putter about at odd jobs: shoveling snow, beating carpets, carrying bags outside the West Railroad Station, occasionally for a few days working as a building laborer. In November 1909, less than a year after he arrived in Vienna to "forestall fate," he was forced to abandon a furnished room in the Simon Denk Gasse, and for the next four years he lived in flophouses or in the almost equally miserable quarters of the men's hostel at 27 Meldemannstrasse in the Twentieth District of Vienna, near the Danube, staving off hunger by frequenting the charity soup kitchens of the city.

No wonder that nearly two decades later he could write:

To me Vienna, the city which to so many is the epitome of innocent pleasure, a festive playground for merrymakers, represents, I am sorry to say, merely the living memory of the saddest period of my life.

Even today this city can arouse in me nothing but dismal thoughts. For me the name of this Phaeacial city represents five years of hardship and misery. Five years in which I was forced to earn a living, first as a day laborer, then as a small painter; a truly meager living which never sufficed to appease even my daily hunger.[38]

Always, he says of these times, there was hunger.

Hunger was then my faithful bodyguard; he never left me for a moment and partook of all I had . . . My life was a continual struggle with this pitiless friend.[39]

It never, however, drove him to the extremity of trying to find a regular job. As he makes clear in *Mein Kampf,* he had the petty bourgeoisie's gnawing fear of sliding back into the ranks of the proletariat, of the manual laborers—a fear he was later to exploit in building up the National Socialist Party on the broad foundation of the hitherto leaderless, ill-paid, neglected white-collar class, whose millions nourished the illusion that they were at least socially better off than the "workers."

Although Hitler says he eked out at least part of a living as "a small painter," he gives no details of this work in his autobiography except to remark that in the years 1909 and 1910 he had so far improved his position that he no longer had to work as a common laborer.

"By this time," he says, "I was working independently as a small draftsman and painter of water colors."[40]

This is somewhat misleading, as is so much else of a biographical nature in *Mein Kampf*. Though the evidence of those who knew him at the time appears to be scarcely more trustworthy, enough of it has been pieced together to give a picture that is probably more accurate and certainly more complete.*

That Adolf Hitler was never a house painter, as his political opponents taunted him with having been, is fairly certain. At least there is no evidence that he ever followed such a trade. What he did was draw or paint crude little pictures of Vienna, usually of some well-known landmark such as St. Stephen's Cathedral, the opera house, the Burgtheater, the Palace of Schoenbrunn or the Roman ruins in Schoenbrunn Park. According to his acquaintances he copied them from older works; apparently he could not draw from nature. They are rather stilted and lifeless, like a beginning architect's rough and careless sketches, and the human figures he sometimes added are so bad as to remind one of a comic strip. I find a note of my own made once after going through a portfolio of Hitler's original sketches: "Few faces. Crude. One almost ghoulish face." To Heiden, "they stand like tiny stuffed sacks outside the high, solemn palaces."[41]

Probably hundreds of these pitiful pieces were sold by Hitler to the petty traders to ornament a wall, to dealers who used them to fill empty picture frames on display and to furniture makers who sometimes tacked them to the backs of cheap sofas and chairs after a fashion in Vienna in those days. Hitler could also be more commercial. He often drew posters for shopkeepers advertising such products as Teddy's Perspiration Powder, and there was one, perhaps turned out to make a little money at Christmas time, depicting Santa Claus selling brightly colored candles, and another showing St. Stephen's Gothic spire, which Hitler never tired of copying, rising out of a mountain of soap cakes.

---

* See *Das Ende des Hitler-Mythos*, by Josef Greiner, who was personally acquainted with Hitler during part of his Vienna days. See also *Hitler the Pawn*, by Rudolf Olden; Olden's book includes statements from Reinhold Hanisch, a Sudeten tramp who for a time was a roommate of Hitler's in the men's hostel and who hawked some of his paintings. Konrad Heiden, in *Der Fuehrer*, also quotes material from Hanisch, including the court records of a lawsuit which Hitler brought against the tramp for cheating him out of a share of a painting which Hanisch allegedly sold for him.

This was the extent of Hitler's "artistic" achievement, yet to the end of his life he considered himself an "artist."

Bohemian he certainly looked in those vagabond years in Vienna. Those who knew him then remembered later his long black shabby overcoat, which hung down to his ankles and resembled a caftan and which had been given him by a Hungarian Jewish old-clothes dealer, a fellow inmate of the dreary men's hostel who had befriended him. They remembered his greasy black derby, which he wore the year round; his matted hair, brushed down over his forehead as in later years and, in the back, hanging disheveled over his soiled collar, for he rarely appeared to have had a haircut or a shave and the sides of his face and his chin were usually covered with the black stubble of an incipient beard. If one can believe Hanisch, who later became something of an artist, Hitler resembled "an apparition such as rarely occurs among Christians."[42]

Unlike some of the shipwrecked young men with whom he lived, he had none of the vices of youth. He neither smoked nor drank. He had nothing to do with women—not, so far as can be learned, because of any abnormality but simply because of an ingrained shyness.

"I believe," Hitler remarked afterward in *Mein Kampf,* in one of his rare flashes of humor, "that those who knew me in those days took me for an eccentric."[43]

They remembered, as had his teachers, the strong, staring eyes that dominated the face and expressed something embedded in the personality that did not jibe with the miserable existence of the unwashed tramp. And they recalled that the young man, for all his laziness when it came to physical labor, was a voracious reader, spending much of his days and evenings devouring books.

At that time I read enormously and thoroughly. All the free time my work left me was employed in my studies. In this way I forged in a few years' time the foundations of a knowledge from which I still draw nourishment today.[44]

In *Mein Kampf* Hitler discourses at length on the art of reading.

By "reading," to be sure, I mean perhaps something different than the average member of our so-called "intelligentsia."

I know people who "read" enormously . . . yet whom I would not describe as "well-read." True, they possess a mass of "knowledge," but their brain is unable to organize and register the material they have taken in . . . On the other hand, a man who possesses the art of correct reading will . . . instinctively and immediately perceive everything which in his opinion is worth permanently remembering, either because it is suited to his purpose or generally worth knowing . . . The art of reading, as of learning, is this: . . . *to retain the essential, to forget the nonessential.** . . . Only this kind of reading has meaning and purpose . . . Viewed in this light, my Vienna period was especially fertile and valuable.[45]

---

* The italics are Hitler's.

Valuable for what? Hitler's answer is that from his reading and from his life among the poor and disinherited of Vienna he learned all that he needed to know in later life.

Vienna was and remained for me the hardest, though most thorough, school of my life. I had set foot in this town while still half a boy and I left it a man, grown quiet and grave.

In this period there took shape within me a world picture and a philosophy which became the granite foundation of all my acts. In addition to what I then created, I have had to learn little; and I have had to alter nothing.[46]

What, then, had he learned in the school of those hard knocks which Vienna had so generously provided? What were the ideas which he acquired there from his reading and his experience and which, as he says, would remain essentially unaltered to the end? That they were mostly shallow and shabby, often grotesque and preposterous, and poisoned by outlandish prejudices will become obvious on the most cursory examination. That they are important to this history, as they were to the world, is equally obvious, for they were to form part of the foundation for the Third Reich which this bookish vagrant was soon to build.

THE BUDDING IDEAS OF ADOLF HITLER

They were, with one exception, not original but picked up, raw, from the churning maelstrom of Austrian politics and life in the first years of the twentieth century. The Danube monarchy was dying of indigestion. For centuries a minority of German–Austrians had ruled over the polyglot empire of a dozen nationalities and stamped their language and their culture on it. But since 1848 their hold had been weakening. The minorities could not be digested. Austria was not a melting pot. In the 1860s the Italians had broken away and in 1867 the Hungarians had won equality with the Germans under a so-called Dual Monarchy. Now, as the twentieth century began, the various Slav peoples—the Czechs, the Slovaks, the Serbs, the Croats and the others—were demanding equality and at least national autonomy. Austrian politics had become dominated by the bitter quarrel of the nationalities.

But this was not all. There was social revolt too and this often transcended the racial struggle. The disenfranchised lower classes were demanding the ballot, and the workers were insisting on the right to organize trade unions and to strike—not only for higher wages and better working conditions but to gain their democratic political ends. Indeed a general strike had finally brought universal manhood suffrage and with this the end of political dominance by the Austrian Germans, who numbered but a third of the population of the Austrian half of the empire.

To these developments Hitler, the fanatical young German-Austrian nationalist from Linz, was bitterly opposed. To him the empire was sinking into a "foul morass." It could be saved only if the master race, the Germans, reasserted their old absolute authority. The non-German races, especially the Slavs and above all the Czechs, were an inferior people. It was up to the Germans to rule them with an iron hand. The Parliament must be abolished and an end put to all the democratic "nonsense."

Though he took no part in politics, Hitler followed avidly the activities of the three major political parties of old Austria: the Social Democrats, the Christian Socialists and the Pan-German Nationalists. And there now began to sprout in the mind of this unkempt frequenter of the soup kitchens a political shrewdness which enabled him to see with amazing clarity the strengths and weaknesses of contemporary political movements and which, as it matured, would make him the master politician of Germany.

At first contact he developed a furious hatred for the party of the Social Democrats. "What most repelled me," he says, "was its hostile attitude toward the struggle for the preservation of Germanism [and] its disgraceful courting of the Slavic 'comrade' . . . In a few months I obtained what might have otherwise required decades: an understanding of a pestilential whore,* cloaking herself as social virtue and brotherly love."[47]

And yet he was already intelligent enough to quench his feelings of rage against this party of the working class in order to examine carefully the reasons for its popular success. He concluded that there were several reasons, and years later he was to remember them and utilize them in building up the National Socialist Party of Germany.

One day, he recounts in *Mein Kampf,* he witnessed a mass demonstration of Viennese workers. "For nearly two hours I stood there watching with bated breath the gigantic human dragon slowly winding by. In oppressed anxiety I finally left the place and sauntered homeward."[48]

At home he began to read the Social Democratic press, examine the speeches of its leaders, study its organization, reflect on its psychology and political techniques and ponder the results. He came to three conclusions which explained to him the success of the Social Democrats: They knew how to create a mass movement, without which any political party was useless; they had learned the art of propaganda among the masses; and, finally, they knew the value of using what he calls "spiritual and physical terror."

This third lesson, though it was surely based on faulty observation and compounded of his own immense prejudices, intrigued the young Hitler. Within ten years he would put it to good use for his own ends.

I understood the infamous spiritual terror which this movement exerts, particularly on the bourgeoisie, which is neither morally nor mentally equal to such attacks; at a given sign it unleashes a veritable barrage of lies and slanders against whatever adversary seems most dangerous, until the nerves of the attacked persons break down . . . This is a tactic based on precise calculation

---

* The word was cut out in the second and all subsequent editions of *Mein Kampf,* and the noun "pestilence" substituted.

of all human weaknesses, and its result will lead to success with almost mathematical certainty . . .

I achieved an equal understanding of the importance of physical terror toward the individual and the masses . . . For while in the ranks of their supporters the victory achieved seems a triumph of the justice of their own cause, the defeated adversary in most cases despairs of the success of any further resistance.[49]

No more precise analysis of Nazi tactics, as Hitler was eventually to develop them, was ever written.

There were two political parties which strongly attracted the fledgling Hitler in Vienna, and to both of them he applied his growing power of shrewd, cold analysis. His first allegiance, he says, was to the Pan-German Nationalist Party founded by Georg Ritter von Schoenerer, who came from the same region near Spital in Lower Austria as had Hitler's family. The Pan-Germans at that time were engaged in a last-ditch struggle for German supremacy in the multinational empire. And though Hitler thought that Schoenerer was a "profound thinker" and enthusiastically embraced his basic program of violent nationalism, anti-Semitism, anti-socialism, union with Germany and opposition to the Hapsburgs and the Holy See, he quickly sized up the causes for the party's failure:

"This movement's inadequate appreciation of the importance of the social problem cost it the truly militant mass of the people; its entry into Parliament took away its mighty impetus and burdened it with all the weaknesses peculiar to this institution; the struggle against the Catholic Church . . . robbed it of countless of the best elements that the nation can call its own."[50]

Though Hitler was to forget it when he came to power in Germany, one of the lessons of his Vienna years which he stresses at great length in *Mein Kampf* is the futility of a political party's trying to oppose the churches. "Regardless of how much room for criticism there was in any religious denomination," he says, in explaining why Schoenerer's Los-von-Rom (Away from Rome) movement was a tactical error, "a political party must never for a moment lose sight of the fact that in all previous historical experience a purely political party has never succeeded in producing a religious reformation."[51]

But it was the failure of the Pan-Germans to arouse the masses, their inability to even understand the psychology of the common people, that to Hitler constituted their biggest mistake. It is obvious from his recapitulation of the ideas that began to form in his mind when he was not much past the age of twenty-one that to him this was the cardinal error. He was not to repeat it when he founded his own political movement.

There was another mistake of the Pan-Germans which Hitler was not to make. That was the failure to win over the support of at least some of the powerful, established institutions of the nation—if not the Church, then the Army, say, or the cabinet or the head of state. Unless a political movement gained such backing, the young man saw, it would be difficult if not impossible for it to assume power. This support was precisely what Hitler had the shrewdness to arrange for in the crucial January days of 1933 in Berlin and what alone made it possible for him and his National Socialist Party to take over the rule of a great nation.

There was one political leader in Vienna in Hitler's time who understood this, as well as the necessity of building a party on the foundation of the masses. This was Dr. Karl Lueger, the burgomaster of Vienna and leader of the Christian Social Party, who more than any other became Hitler's political mentor, though the two never met. Hitler always regarded him as "the greatest German mayor of all times . . . a statesman greater than all the so-called 'diplomats' of the time . . . If Dr. Karl Lueger had lived in Germany he would have been ranked among the great minds of our people."[52]

There was, to be sure, little resemblance between Hitler as he later became and this big, bluff, genial idol of the Viennese lower middle classes. It is true that Lueger became the most powerful politician in Austria as the head of a party which was drawn from the disgruntled petty bourgeoisie and which made political capital, as Hitler later did, out of a raucous anti-Semitism. But Lueger, who had risen from modest circumstances and worked his way through the university, was a man of considerable intellectual attainments, and his opponents, including the Jews, readily conceded that he was at heart a decent, chivalrous, generous and tolerant man. Stefan Zweig, the eminent Austrian Jewish writer, who was growing up in Vienna at this time, has testified that Lueger never allowed his official anti-Semitism to stop him from being helpful and friendly to the Jews. "His city administration," Zweig recounted, "was perfectly just and even typically democratic . . . The Jews who had trembled at this triumph of the anti-Semitic party continued to live with the same rights and esteem as always."[53]

This the young Hitler did not like. He thought Lueger was far too tolerant and did not appreciate the racial problem of the Jews. He resented the mayor's failure to embrace Pan-Germanism and was skeptical of his Roman Catholic clericalism and his loyalty to the Hapsburgs. Had not the old Emperor Franz-Josef twice refused to sanction Lueger's election as burgomaster?

But in the end Hitler was forced to acknowledge the genius of this man who knew how to win the support of the masses, who understood modern social problems and the importance of propaganda and oratory in swaying the multitude. Hitler could not help but admire the way Lueger dealt with the powerful Church—"his policy was fashioned with infinite shrewdness." And, finally, Lueger "was quick to make use of all available means for winning the support of long-established institutions, so as to be able to derive the greatest possible advantage for his movement from those old sources of power."[54]

Here in a nutshell were the ideas and techniques which Hitler was later to use in constructing his own political party and in leading it to power in Germany. His originality lay in his being the only politician of the Right to apply them to the German scene after the First World War. It was then that the Nazi movement, alone among the nationalist and conservative parties, gained a great mass following and, having achieved this, won over the support of the Army, the President of the Republic and the associations of big business—three "long-established institutions" of great power, which led to the chancellorship of Germany. The lessons learned in Vienna proved useful indeed.

Dr. Karl Lueger had been a brilliant orator, but the Pan-German Party had lacked effective public speakers. Hitler took notice of this and in *Mein Kampf* makes much of the importance of oratory in politics.

The power which has always started the greatest religious and political avalanches in history rolling has from time immemorial been the magic power of the spoken word, and that alone.

The broad masses of the people can be moved only by the power of speech. All great movements are popular movements, volcanic eruptions of human passions and emotional sentiments, stirred either by the cruel Goddess of Distress or by the firebrand of the word hurled among the masses; they are not the lemonade-like outpourings of the literary aesthetes and drawing-room heroes.[55]

Though refraining from actual participation in Austrian party politics, young Hitler already was beginning to practice his oratory on the audiences which he found in Vienna's flophouses, soup kitchens and on its street corners. It was to develop into a talent (as this author, who later was to listen to scores of his most important speeches, can testify) more formidable than any other in the Germany between the wars, and it was to contribute in a large measure to his astounding success.

And finally in Hitler's Vienna experience there were the Jews. In Linz, he says, there had been few Jews. "At home I do not remember having heard the word during my father's lifetime." At high school there was a Jewish boy—"but we didn't give the matter any thought . . . I even took them [the Jews] for Germans."[56]

According to Hitler's boyhood friend, this is not the truth. "When I first met Adolf Hitler," says August Kubizek, recalling their days together in Linz, "his anti-Semitism was already pronounced . . . Hitler was already a confirmed anti-Semite when he went to Vienna. And although his experiences in Vienna might have deepened this feeling, they certainly did not give birth to it."[57]

"Then," says Hitler, "I came to Vienna."

Preoccupied by the abundance of my impressions . . . oppressed by the hardship of my own lot, I gained at first no insight into the inner stratification of the people in this gigantic city. Notwithstanding that Vienna in those days counted nearly two hundred thousand Jews among its two million inhabitants,

I did not see them . . . The Jew was still characterized for me by nothing but his religion, and therefore on grounds of human tolerance I maintained my rejection of religious attacks in this case as in others. Consequently the tone of the Viennese anti-Semitic press seemed to me unworthy of the cultural tradition of a great nation.[58]

One day, Hitler recounts, he went strolling through the Inner City. "I suddenly encountered an apparition in a black caftan and black sidelocks. Is this a Jew? was my first thought. For, to be sure, they had not looked like that in Linz. I observed the man furtively and cautiously, but the longer I stared at this foreign face, scrutinizing feature for feature, the more my first question assumed a new form: Is this a German?"[59]

Hitler's answer may be readily guessed. He claims, though, that before answering he decided "to try to relieve my doubts by books." He buried himself in anti-Semitic literature, which had a large sale in Vienna at the time. Then he took to the streets to observe the "phenomenon" more closely. "Wherever I went," he says, "I began to see Jews, and the more I saw, the more sharply they became distinguished in my eyes from the rest of humanity . . . Later I often grew sick to the stomach from the smell of these caftan-wearers."[60]

Next, he says, he discovered the "moral stain on this 'chosen people' . . . Was there any form of filth or profligacy, particularly in cultural life, without at least one Jew involved in it? If you cut even cautiously into such an abscess, you found, like a maggot in a rotting body, often dazzled by the sudden light—a kike!" The Jews were largely responsible, he says he found, for prostitution and the white-slave traffic. "When for the first time," he relates, "I recognized the Jew as the cold-hearted, shameless and calculating director of this revolting vice traffic in the scum of the big city, a cold shudder ran down my back."[61]

There is a great deal of morbid sexuality in Hitler's ravings about the Jews. This was characteristic of Vienna's anti-Semitic press of the time, as it later was to be of the obscene Nuremberg weekly *Der Stuermer*, published by one of Hitler's favorite cronies, Julius Streicher, Nazi boss of Franconia, a noted pervert and one of the most unsavory characters in the Third Reich. *Mein Kampf* is sprinkled with lurid allusions to uncouth Jews seducing innocent Christian girls and thus adulterating their blood. Hitler can write of the "nightmare vision of the seduction of hundreds of thousands of girls by repulsive, crooked-legged Jew bastards." As Rudolf Olden has pointed out, one of the roots of Hitler's anti-Semitism may have been his tortured sexual envy. Though he was in his early twenties, so far as is known he had no relations of any kind with women during his sojourn in Vienna.

"Gradually," Hitler relates, "I began to hate them . . . For me this was the time of the greatest spiritual upheaval I have ever had to go through. I had ceased to be a weak-kneed cosmopolitan and become an anti-Semite."[62]

He was to remain a blind and fanatical one to the bitter end; his last testament, written a few hours before his death, would contain a final blast against the Jews as responsible for the war which he had started and which was now finishing him and the Third Reich. This burning hatred, which was to infect so many Germans in that empire, would lead ultimately to a massacre so horrible and on such a scale as to leave an ugly scar on civilization that will surely last as long as man on earth.

In the spring of 1913, Hitler left Vienna for good and went to live in Germany, where his heart, he says, had always been. He was twenty-four and to everyone except himself he must have seemed a total failure. He had not become a painter, nor an architect. He had become nothing, so far as anyone could see, but a vagabond—an eccentric, bookish one, to be sure. He had no friends, no family, no job, no home. He had, however, one thing: an unquenchable confidence in himself and a deep, burning sense of mission.

Probably he left Austria to escape military service.* This was not because he was a coward but because he loathed the idea of serving in the ranks with Jews, Slavs and other minority races of the empire. In *Mein Kampf* Hitler states that he went to Munich in the spring of 1912, but this is an error. A police register lists him as living in Vienna until May 1913.

His own stated reasons for leaving Austria are quite grandiose.

My inner revulsion toward the Hapsburg State steadily grew . . . I was repelled by the conglomeration of races which the capital showed me, repelled by this whole mixture of Czechs, Poles, Hungarians, Ruthenians, Serbs, and Croats, and everywhere the eternal mushroom of humanity—Jews, and more Jews. To me the giant city seemed the embodiment of racial desecration . . . The longer I lived in this city the more my hatred grew for the foreign mixture of peoples which had begun to corrode this old site of German culture . . . For all these reasons a longing rose stronger and stronger in me to go at last whither since my childhood secret desires and secret love had drawn me.[63]

---

* Since 1910, when he was twenty-one, he had been subject to military service. According to Heiden the Austrian authorities could not put their finger on him while he was in Vienna. They finally located him in Munich and ordered him to report for examination in Linz. Josef Greiner, in his *Das Ende des Hitler-Mythos,* publishes some of the correspondence between Hitler and the Austrian military authorities in which Hitler denies that he went to Germany to avoid Austrian military service. On the ground that he lacked funds, he requested to be allowed to take his examination in Salzburg because of its nearness to Munich. He was examined there on February 5, 1914, and found unfit for military or even auxiliary service on account of poor health—apparently he still had a lung ailment. His failure to report for military service until the authorities finally located him at the age of twenty-four must have bothered Hitler when his star rose in Germany. Greiner confirms a story that was current in anti-Nazi circles when I was in Berlin that when the German troops occupied Austria in 1938 Hitler ordered the Gestapo to find the official papers relating to his military service. The records in Linz were searched in vain—to Hitler's mounting fury. They had been removed by a member of the local government, who, after the war, showed them to Greiner.

His destiny in that land he loved so dearly was to be such as not even he, in his wildest dreams, could have then imagined. He was, and would remain until shortly before he became Chancellor, technically a foreigner, an Austrian, in the German Reich. It is only as an Austrian who came of age in the last decade before the collapse of the Hapsburg Empire, who failed to take root in its civilized capital, who embraced all the preposterous prejudices and hates then rife among its German-speaking extremists and who failed to grasp what was decent and honest and honorable in the vast majority of his fellow citizens, were they Czechs or Jews or Germans, poor or well off, artists or artisans, that Hitler can be understood. It is doubtful if any German from the north, from the Rhineland in the west, from East Prussia or even from Bavaria in the south could have had in his blood and mind out of any possible experience exactly the mixture of ingredients which propelled Adolf Hitler to the heights he eventually reached. To be sure, there was added a liberal touch of unpredictable genius.

But in the spring of 1913 his genius had not yet shown. In Munich, as in Vienna, he remained penniless, friendless and without a regular job. And then in the summer of 1914 the war came, snatching him, like millions of others, into its grim clutches. On August 3 he petitioned King Ludwig III of Bavaria for permission to volunteer in a Bavarian regiment and it was granted.

This was the heaven-sent opportunity. Now the young vagabond could satisfy not only his passion to serve his beloved adopted country in what he says he believed was a fight for its existence—"to be or not to be"— but he could escape from all the failures and frustrations of his personal life.

"To me," he wrote in *Mein Kampf,* "those hours came as a deliverance from the distress that had weighed upon me during the days of my youth. I am not ashamed to say that, carried away by the enthusiasm of the moment, I sank down on my knees and thanked Heaven out of the fullness of my heart for granting me the good fortune of being permitted to live in such a time . . . For me, as for every German, there now began the most memorable period of my life. Compared to the events of this gigantic struggle all the past fell away into oblivion."[64]

For Hitler the past, with all its shabbiness, loneliness and disappointments, was to remain in the shadows, though it shaped his mind and character forever afterward. The war, which now would bring death to so many millions, brought for him, at twenty-five, a new start in life.

2

BIRTH OF THE NAZI PARTY

O<small>N THE DARK AUTUMN</small> Sunday of November 10, 1918, Adolf Hitler experienced what out of the depths of his hatred and frustration he called the greatest villainy of the century.* A pastor had come bearing unbelievable news for the wounded soldiers in the military hospital at Pasewalk, a small Pomeranian town northeast of Berlin, where Hitler was recovering from temporary blindness suffered in a British gas attack a month before near Ypres.

That Sunday morning, the pastor informed them, the Kaiser had abdicated and fled to Holland. The day before a republic had been proclaimed in Berlin. On the morrow, November 11, an armistice would be signed at Compiègne in France. The war had been lost. Germany was at the mercy of the victorious Allies. The pastor began to sob.

"I could stand it no longer," Hitler says in recounting the scene. "Everything went black again before my eyes; I tottered and groped my way back to the ward, threw myself on my bunk, and dug my burning head into my blanket and pillow . . . So it had all been in vain. In vain all the sacrifices and privations; . . . in vain the hours in which, with mortal fear clutching at our hearts, we nevertheless did our duty; in vain the death of two millions who died . . . Had they died for this? . . . Did all this happen only so that a gang of wretched criminals could lay hands on the Fatherland?"[1]

For the first time since he had stood at his mother's grave, he says, he broke down and wept. "I could not help it." Like millions of his fellow countrymen then and forever after, he could not accept the blunt and shattering fact that Germany had been defeated on the battlefield and had lost the war.

Like millions of other Germans, too, Hitler had been a brave and courageous soldier. Later he would be accused by some political oppo-

---

* The expression appeared in the first German edition of *Mein Kampf*, but was changed to "revolution" in all subsequent editions.

29

nents of having been a coward in combat, but it must be said, in fairness, that there is no shred of evidence in his record for such a charge. As a dispatch runner in the First Company of the 16th Bavarian Reserve Infantry Regiment, he arrived at the front toward the end of October 1914 after scarcely three months of training, and his unit was decimated in four days of hard fighting at the first Battle of Ypres, where the British halted the German drive to the Channel. According to a letter Hitler wrote his Munich landlord, a tailor named Popp, his regiment was reduced in four days of combat from 3,500 to 600 men; only thirty officers survived, and four companies had to be dissolved.

During the war he was wounded twice, the first time on October 7, 1916, in the Battle of the Somme, when he was hit in the leg. After hospitalization in Germany he returned to the List Regiment—it was named after its original commander—in March 1917 and, now promoted to corporal, fought in the Battle of Arras and the third Battle of Ypres during that summer. His regiment was in the thick of the fighting during the last all-out German offensive in the spring and summer of 1918. On the night of October 13 he was caught in a heavy British gas attack on a hill south of Werwick during the last Battle of Ypres. "I stumbled back with burning eyes," he relates, "taking with me my last report of the war. A few hours later, my eyes had turned into glowing coals; it had grown dark around me."[2]

He was twice decorated for bravery. In December 1914 he was awarded the Iron Cross, Second Class, and in August 1918 he received the Iron Cross, First Class, which was rarely given to a common soldier in the old Imperial Army. One comrade in his unit testified that he won the coveted decoration for having captured fifteen Englishmen single-handed; another said it was Frenchmen. The official history of the List Regiment contains no word of any such exploit; it is silent about the individual feats of many members who received decorations. Whatever the reason, there is no doubt that Corporal Hitler earned the Iron Cross, First Class. He wore it proudly to the end of his life.

And yet, as soldiers go, he was a peculiar fellow, as more than one of his comrades remarked. No letters or presents from home came to him, as they did to the others. He never asked for leave; he had not even a combat soldier's interest in women. He never grumbled, as did the bravest of men, about the filth, the lice, the mud, the stench, of the front line. He was the impassioned warrior, deadly serious at all times about the war's aims and Germany's manifest destiny.

"We all cursed him and found him intolerable," one of the men in his company later recalled. "There was this white crow among us that didn't go along with us when we damned the war to hell."[3] Another man described him as sitting "in the corner of our mess holding his head between his hands, in deep contemplation. Suddenly he would leap up and, running about excitedly, say that in spite of our big guns victory would be denied us, for the invisible foes of the German people were a greater danger than the biggest cannon of the enemy."[4] Whereupon he would launch into a vitriolic attack on these "invisible foes"—the Jews and the Marxists. Had he not learned in Vienna that they were the source of all evil?

And indeed had he not seen this for himself in the German homeland while convalescing from his leg wound in the middle of the war? After his discharge from the hospital at Beelitz, near Berlin, he had visited the capital and then gone on to Munich. Everywhere he found "scoundrels" cursing the war and wishing for its quick end. Slackers abounded, and who were they but Jews? "The offices," he found, "were filled with Jews. Nearly every clerk was a Jew and nearly every Jew was a clerk . . . In the year 1916–17 nearly the whole production was under control of Jewish finance . . . The Jew robbed the whole nation and pressed it beneath his domination . . . I saw with horror a catastrophe approaching . . ."[5] Hitler could not bear what he saw and was glad, he says, to return to the front.

He could bear even less the disaster which befell his beloved Fatherland in November 1918. To him, as to almost all Germans, it was "monstrous" and undeserved. The German Army had not been defeated in the field. It had been stabbed in the back by the traitors at home.

Thus emerged for Hitler, as for so many Germans, a fanatical belief in the legend of the "stab in the back" which, more than anything else, was to undermine the Weimar Republic and pave the way for Hitler's ultimate triumph. The legend was fraudulent. General Ludendorff, the actual leader of the High Command, had insisted on September 28, 1918, on an armistice "at once," and his nominal superior, Field Marshal von Hindenburg, had supported him. At a meeting of the Crown Council in Berlin on October 2 presided over by Kaiser Wilhelm II, Hindenburg had reiterated the High Command's demand for an immediate truce. "The Army," he said, "cannot wait forty-eight hours." In a letter written on the same day Hindenburg flatly stated that the *military* situation made it imperative "to stop the fighting." No mention was made of any "stab in the back." Only later did Germany's great war hero subscribe to the myth. In a hearing before the Committee of Inquiry of the National Assembly on November 18, 1919, a year after the war's end, Hindenburg declared, "As an English general has very truly said, the German Army was 'stabbed in the back.' "*

---

* The attribution of the myth to an English general was hardly factual. Wheeler-Bennett, in *Wooden Titan: Hindenburg,* has explained that, ironically, two British generals did have something to do—inadvertently—with the perpetration of the false legend. "The first was Maj.-Gen. Sir Frederick Maurice, whose book *The Last Four Months,* published in 1919, was grossly misrepresented by reviewers in the German press as proving that the German Army had been betrayed by the Socialists on the Home Front and not been defeated in the field." The General denied this interpretation in the German press, but to no avail. Ludendorff made use of the reviews to convince Hindenburg. "The other officer," says Wheeler-Bennett, "was Maj.-Gen. Malcolm, head of the British Military Mission in Berlin. Ludendorff was dining with the General one evening, and with his usual turgid eloquence was expatiating on how the High Command had always suffered lack of support from the Civilian Govern-

In point of fact, the civilian government headed by Prince Max of Baden, which had not been told of the worsening military situation by the High Command until the end of September, held out for several weeks against Ludendorff's demand for an armistice.

One had to live in Germany between the wars to realize how widespread was the acceptance of this incredible legend by the German people. The facts which exposed its deceit lay all around. The Germans of the Right would not face them. The culprits, they never ceased to bellow, were the "November criminals"—an expression which Hitler hammered into the consciousness of the people. It mattered not at all that the German Army, shrewdly and cowardly, had maneuvered the republican government into signing the armistice which the military leaders had insisted upon, and that it thereafter had advised the government to accept the Peace Treaty of Versailles. Nor did it seem to count that the Social Democratic Party had accepted power in 1918 only reluctantly and only to preserve the nation from utter chaos which threatened to lead to Bolshevism. It was not responsible for the German collapse. The blame for that rested on the old order, which had held the power.* But millions of Germans refused to concede this. They had to find scapegoats for the defeat and for their humiliation and misery. They easily convinced themselves that they had found them in the "November criminals" who had signed the surrender and established democratic government in the place of the old autocracy. The gullibility of the Germans is a subject which Hitler often harps on in *Mein Kampf*. He was shortly to take full advantage of it.

When the pastor had left the hospital in Pasewalk that evening of November 10, 1918, "there followed terrible days and even worse nights" for Adolf Hitler. "I knew," he says, "that all was lost. Only fools, liars and criminals could hope for mercy from the enemy. In these nights hatred grew in me, hatred for those responsible for this deed . . . Miserable and degenerate criminals! The more I tried to achieve clarity on the monstrous event in this hour, the more the shame of indignation and disgrace burned my brow. What was all the pain in my eyes compared to this misery?"

And then: "My own fate became known to me. I decided to go into politics."[6]

As it turned out, this was a fateful decision for Hitler and for the world.

---

ment and how the Revolution had betrayed the Army. In an effort to crystallize the meaning of Ludendorff's verbosity into a single sentence, General Malcolm asked him: 'Do you mean, General, that you were stabbed in the back?' Ludendorff's eyes lit up and he leapt upon the phrase like a dog on a bone. 'Stabbed in the back?' he repeated. 'Yes, that's it exactly. We were stabbed in the back.' "

* A few generals were courageous enough to say so. On August 23, 1924, the *Frankfurter Zeitung* published an article by General Freiherr von Schoenaich analyzing the reasons for Germany's defeat. He came to "the irresistible conclusion that we owe our ruin to the supremacy of our military authorities over civilian authorities . . . In fact, German militarism simply committed suicide." (Quoted by Telford Taylor in *Sword and Swastika*, p. 16.)

THE BEGINNING OF THE NAZI PARTY

The prospects for a political career in Germany for this thirty-year-old Austrian without friends or funds, without a job, with no trade or profession or any previous record of regular employment, with no experience whatsoever in politics, were less than promising, and at first, for a brief moment, Hitler realized it. "For days," he says, "I wondered what could be done, but the end of every meditation was the sober realization that I, nameless as I was, did not possess the least basis for any useful action."[7]

He had returned to Munich at the end of November 1918, to find his adopted city scarcely recognizable. Revolution had broken out here too. The Wittelsbach King had also abdicated. Bavaria was in the hands of the Social Democrats, who had set up a Bavarian "People's State" under Kurt Eisner, a popular Jewish writer who had been born in Berlin. On November 7, Eisner, a familiar figure in Munich with his great gray beard, his pince-nez, his enormous black hat and his diminutive size, had traipsed through the streets at the head of a few hundred men and, without a shot being fired, had occupied the seat of parliament and government and proclaimed a republic. Three months later he was assassinated by a young right-wing officer, Count Anton Arco-Valley. The workers thereupon set up a soviet republic, but this was short-lived. On May 1, 1919, Regular Army troops dispatched from Berlin and Bavarian "free corps" (*Freikorps*) volunteers entered Munich and overthrew the Communist regime, massacring several hundred persons, including many non-Communists, in revenge for the shooting of a dozen hostages by the soviet. Though a moderate Social Democratic government under Johannes Hoffmann was nominally restored for the time being, the real power in Bavarian politics passed to the Right.

What was the Right in Bavaria at this chaotic time? It was the Regular Army, the Reichswehr; it was the monarchists, who wished the Wittelbachs back. It was a mass of conservatives who despised the democratic Republic established in Berlin; and as time went on it was above all the great mob of demobilized soldiers for whom the bottom had fallen out of the world in 1918, uprooted men who could not find jobs or their way back to the peaceful society they had left in 1914, men grown tough and violent through war who could not shake themselves from ingrained habit and who, as Hitler, who for a while was one of them, would later say, "became revolutionaries who favored revolution for its own sake and desired to see revolution established as a permanent condition."

Armed free-corps bands sprang up all over Germany and were secretly equipped by the Reichswehr. At first they were mainly used to fight the Poles and the Balts on the disputed eastern frontiers, but soon they were backing plots for the overthrow of the republican regime. In March 1920, one of them, the notorious Ehrhardt Brigade, led by a freebooter, Captain Ehrhardt, occupied Berlin and enabled Dr. Wolfgang Kapp,* a mediocre

---

* Kapp was born in New York on July 24, 1868.

politician of the extreme Right, to proclaim himself Chancellor. The Regular Army, under General von Seeckt, had stood by while the President of the Republic and the government fled in disarray to western Germany. Only a general strike by the trade unions restored the republican government.

In Munich at the same time a different kind of military *coup d'état* was more successful. On March 14, 1920, the Reichswehr overthrew the Hoffmann Socialist government and installed a right-wing regime under Gustav von Kahr. And now the Bavarian capital became a magnet for all those forces in Germany which were determined to overthrow the Republic, set up an authoritarian regime and repudiate the *Diktat* of Versailles. Here the *condottieri* of the free corps, including the members of the Ehrhardt Brigade, found a refuge and a welcome. Here General Ludendorff settled, along with a host of other disgruntled, discharged Army officers.* Here were plotted the political murders, among them that of Matthias Erzberger, the moderate Catholic politician who had had the courage to sign the armistice when the generals backed out; and of Walther Rathenau, the brilliant, cultured Foreign Minister, whom the extremists hated for being a Jew and for carrying out the national government's policy of trying to fulfill at least some of the provisions of the Versailles Treaty.

It was in this fertile field in Munich that Adolf Hitler got his start.

When he had come back to Munich at the end of November 1918, he had found that his battalion was in the hands of the "Soldiers' Councils." This was so repellent to him, he says, that he decided "at once to leave as soon as possible." He spent the winter doing guard duty at a prisoner-of-war camp at Traunstein, near the Austrian border. He was back in Munich in the spring. In *Mein Kampf* he relates that he incurred the "disapproval" of the left-wing government and claims that he avoided arrest only by the feat of aiming his carbine at three "scoundrels" who had come to fetch him. Immediately after the Communist regime was overthrown Hitler began what he terms his "first more or less political activity." This consisted of giving information to the commission of inquiry set up by the 2nd Infantry Regiment to investigate those who shared responsibility for the brief soviet regime in Munich.

Apparently Hitler's service on this occasion was considered valuable enough to lead the Army to give him further employment. He was assigned to a job in the Press and News Bureau of the Political Department

---

* At the war's end Ludendorff fled to Sweden disguised in false whiskers and blue spectacles. He returned to Germany in February 1919, writing his wife: "It would be the greatest stupidity for the revolutionaries to allow us all to remain alive. Why, if ever I come to power again there will be no pardon. Then with an easy conscience, I would have Ebert, Scheidemann and Co. hanged, and watch them dangle." (Margaritte Ludendorff, *Als ich Ludendorffs Frau war,* p. 229.) Ebert was the first President and Scheidemann the first Chancellor of the Weimar Republic. Ludendorff, though second-in-command to Hindenburg, had been the virtual dictator of Germany for the last two years of the war.

of the Army's district command. The German Army, contrary to its traditions, was now deep in politics, especially in Bavaria, where at last it had established a government to its liking. To further its conservative views it gave the soldiers courses of "political instruction," in one of which Adolf Hitler was an attentive pupil. One day, according to his own story, he intervenéd during a lecture in which someone had said a good word for the Jews. His anti-Semitic harangue apparently so pleased his superior officers that he was soon posted to a Munich regiment as an educational officer, a *Bildungsoffizier,* whose main task was to combat dangerous ideas—pacifism, socialism, democracy; such was the Army's conception of its role in the democratic Republic it had sworn to serve.

This was an important break for Hitler, the first recognition he had won in the field of politics he was now trying to enter. Above all, it gave him a chance to try out his oratorical abilities—the first prerequisite, as he had always maintained, of a successful politician. "All at once," he says, "I was offered an opportunity of speaking before a larger audience; and the thing that I had always presumed from pure feeling without knowing it was now corroborated: I could 'speak.' " The discovery pleased him greatly even if it came as no great surprise. He had been afraid that his voice might have been permanently weakened by the gassing he had suffered at the front. Now he found it had recovered sufficiently to enable him to make himself heard "at least in every corner of the small squad rooms."[8] This was the beginning of a talent that was to make him easily the most effective orator in Germany, with a magic power, after he took to radio, to sway millions by his voice.

One day in September 1919, Hitler received orders from the Army's Political Department to have a look at a tiny political group in Munich which called itself the German Workers' Party. The military were suspicious of workers' parties, since they were predominantly Socialist or Communist, but this one, it was believed, might be different. Hitler says it was "entirely unknown" to him. And yet he knew one of the men who was scheduled to speak at the party's meeting which he had been assigned to investigate.

A few weeks before, in one of his Army educational courses, he had heard a lecture by Gottfried Feder, a construction engineer and a crank in the field of economics, who had become obsessed with the idea that "speculative" capital, as opposed to "creative" and "productive" capital, was the root of much of Germany's economic trouble. He was for abolishing the first kind and in 1917 had formed an organization to achieve this purpose: the German Fighting League for the Breaking of Interest Slavery. Hitler, ignorant of economics, was much impressed by Feder's lecture. He saw in Feder's appeal for the "breaking of interest slavery." one of the "essential premises for the foundation of a new party." In Feder's lecture, he says, "I sensed a powerful slogan for this coming struggle."[9]

But at first he did not sense any importance in the German Workers' Party. He went to its meeting because he was ordered to, and, after sitting through what he thought was a dull session of some twenty-five persons gathered in a murky room in the Sterneckerbräu beer cellar, he was not impressed. It was "a new organization like so many others. This was a time," he says, "in which anyone who was not satisfied with developments . . . felt called upon to found a new party. Everywhere these organizations sprang out of the ground, only to vanish silently after a time. I judged the German Workers' Party no differently."[10] After Feder had finished speaking Hitler was about to leave, when a "professor" sprang up, questioned the soundness of Feder's arguments and then proposed that Bavaria should break away from Prussia and found a South German nation with Austria. This was a popular notion in Munich at the time, but its expression aroused Hitler to a fury and he rose to give "the learned gentleman," as he later recounted, a piece of his mind. This apparently was so violent that, according to Hitler, the "professor" left the hall "like a wet poodle," while the rest of the audience looked at the unknown young speaker "with astonished faces." One man—Hitler says he did not catch his name—came leaping after him and pressed a little booklet into his hands.

This man was Anton Drexler, a locksmith by trade, who may be said to have been the actual founder of National Socialism. A sickly, bespectacled man, lacking a formal education, with an independent but narrow and confused mind, a poor writer and a worse speaker, Drexler was then employed in the Munich railroad shops. On March 7, 1918, he had set up a "Committee of Independent Workmen" to combat the Marxism of the free trade unions and to agitate for a "just" peace for Germany. Actually, it was a branch of a larger movement established in North Germany as the Association for the Promotion of Peace on Working-Class Lines (the country was then and would continue to be until 1933 full of countless pressure groups with highfalutin titles).

Drexler never recruited more than forty members, and in January 1919 he merged his committee with a similar group, the Political Workers' Circle, led by a newspaper reporter, one Karl Harrer. The new organization, which numbered less than a hundred, was called the German Workers' Party and Harrer was its first chairman. Hitler, who has little to say in *Mein Kampf* of some of his early comrades whose names are now forgotten, pays Harrer the tribute of being "honest" and "certainly widely educated" but regrets that he lacked the "oratorical gift." Perhaps Harrer's chief claim to fleeting fame is that he stubbornly maintained that Hitler was a poor speaker, a judgment which riled the Nazi leader ever after, as he makes plain in his autobiography. At any rate, Drexler seems to have been the chief driving force in this small, unknown German Workers' Party.

The next morning Hitler turned to a perusal of the booklet which Drexler had thrust into his hands. He describes the scene at length in *Mein Kampf*. It was 5 A.M. Hitler had awakened and, as he says was his custom, was reclining on his cot in the barracks of the 2nd Infantry Regiment watching the mice nibble at the bread crumbs which he invariably scattered on the floor the night before. "I had known so much poverty in my life," he muses, "that I was well able to imagine the hunger and hence also the pleasure of the little creatures." He remembered the little pamphlet and began to read it. It was entitled "My Political Awakening." To Hitler's surprise, it reflected a good many ideas which he himself had acquired over the years. Drexler's principal aim was to build a political party which would be based on the masses of the working class but which, unlike the Social Democrats, would be strongly nationalist. Drexler had been a member of the patriotic Fatherland Front but had soon become disillusioned with its middle-class spirit which seemed to have no contact at all with the masses. In Vienna, as we have seen, Hitler had learned to scorn the bourgeoisie for the same reason—its utter lack of concern with the working-class families and their social problems. Drexler's ideas, then, definitely interested him.

Later that day Hitler was astonished to receive a postcard saying that he had been accepted in the German Workers' Party. "I didn't know whether to be angry or to laugh," he remembered later. "I had no intention of joining a ready-made party, but wanted to found one of my own. What they asked of me was presumptuous and out of the question."[11] He was about to say so in a letter when "curiosity won out" and he decided to go to a committee meeting to which he had been invited and explain in person his reasons for not joining "this absurd little organization."

The tavern in which the meeting was to take place was the Alte Rosenbad in the Herrenstrasse, a very run-down place . . . I went through the ill-lit dining room in which not a soul was sitting, opened the door to the back room, and there I was face to face with the Committee. In the dim light of a grimy gas lamp four young people sat at a table, among them the author of the little pamphlet, who at once greeted me most joyfully and bade me welcome as a new member of the German Workers' Party.

Really, I was somewhat taken aback. The minutes of the last meeting were read and the secretary given a vote of confidence. Next came the treasury report—all in all the association possessed seven marks and fifty pfennigs—for which the treasurer received a vote of confidence. This too was entered in the minutes. Then the first chairman read the answers to a letter from Kiel, one from Duesseldorf, and one from Berlin and everyone expressed approval. Next a report was given on the incoming mail . . .

Terrible, terrible! This was club life of the worst manner and sort. Was I to join this organization?[12]

Yet there was something about these shabby men in the ill-lit back room that attracted him: "the longing for a new movement which should be more than a party in the previous sense of the word." That evening he returned to the barracks to "face the hardest question of my life: should I join?" Reason, he admits, told him to decline. And yet . . . The very unimportance of the organization would give a young man of energy and ideas an opportunity "for real personal activity." Hitler thought over what he could "bring to this task."

That I was poor and without means seemed to me the most bearable part of it, but it was harder that I was numbered among the nameless, that I was one of the millions whom chance permits to live or summons out of existence without even their closest neighbors condescending to take any notice of it. In addition, there was the difficulty which inevitably arose from my lack of schooling.

After two days of agonized pondering and reflection, I finally came to the conviction that I had to take this step.

It was the most decisive resolve of my life. From here there was and could be no turning back.[13]

Adolf Hitler was then and there enrolled as the seventh member of the committee of the German Workers' Party.

There were two members of this insignificant party who deserve mention at this point; both were to prove important in the rise of Hitler. Captain Ernst Roehm, on the staff of the Army's District Command VII in Munich, had joined the party before Hitler. He was a stocky, bull-necked, piggish-eyed, scar-faced professional soldier—the upper part of his nose had been shot away in 1914—with a flair for politics and a natural ability as an organizer. Like Hitler he was possessed of a burning hatred for the democratic Republic and the "November criminals" he held responsible for it. His aim was to re-create a strong nationalist Germany and he believed with Hitler that this could be done only by a party based on the lower classes, from which he himself, unlike most Regular Army officers, had come. A tough, ruthless, driving man—albeit, like so many of the early Nazis, a homosexual—he helped to organize the first Nazi strongarm squads which grew into the S.A., the army of storm troopers which he commanded until his execution by Hitler in 1934. Roehm not only brought into the budding party large numbers of ex-servicemen and freecorps volunteers, who formed the backbone of the organization in its early years, but, as an officer of the Army, which controlled Bavaria, he obtained for Hitler and his movement the protection and sometimes the support of the authorities. Without this help, Hitler probably could never have got a real start in his campaign to incite the people to overthrow the Republic. Certainly he could not have got away with his methods of terror and intimidation without the tolerance of the Bavarian government and police.

Dietrich Eckart, twenty-one years older than Hitler, was often called the spiritual founder of National Socialism. A witty journalist, a mediocre poet and dramatist, he had translated Ibsen's *Peer Gynt* and written a number of unproduced plays. In Berlin for a time he had led, like Hitler in Vienna, the bohemian vagrant's life, become a drunkard, taken to morphine and, according to Heiden, been confined to a mental institution, where he was finally able to stage his dramas, using the inmates as actors. He had returned to his native Bavaria at the war's end and held forth before a circle of admirers at the Brennessel wine cellar in Schwabling, the artists' quarter in Munich, preaching Aryan superiority and calling for the elimination of the Jews and the downfall of the "swine" in Berlin.

"We need a fellow at the head," Heiden, who was a working newspaperman in Munich at the time, quotes Eckart as declaiming to the habitues of the Brennessel wine cellar in 1919, "who can stand the sound of a machine gun. The rabble need to get fear into their pants. We can't use an officer, because the people don't respect them any more. The best would be a worker who knows how to talk . . . He doesn't need much brains . . . He must be a bachelor, then we'll get the women."[14]

What more natural than that the hard-drinking poet* should find in Adolf Hitler the very man he was looking for? He became a close adviser to the rising young man in the German Workers' Party, lending him books, helping to improve his German—both written and spoken—and introducing him to his wide circle of friends, which included not only certain wealthy persons who were induced to contribute to the party's funds and Hitler's living but such future aides as Rudolf Hess and Alfred Rosenberg. Hitler's admiration for Eckart never flagged, and the last sentence of *Mein Kampf* is an expression of gratitude to this erratic mentor: He was, says Hitler in concluding his book, "one of the best, who devoted his life to the awakening of our people, in his writings and his thoughts and finally in his deeds."[15]

Such was the weird assortment of misfits who founded National Socialism, who unknowingly began to shape a movement which in thirteen years would sweep the country, the strongest in Europe, and bring to Germany its Third Reich. The confused locksmith Drexler provided the kernel, the drunken poet Eckart some of the "spiritual" foundation, the economic crank Feder what passed as an ideology, the homosexual Roehm the support of the Army and the war veterans, but it was now the former tramp, Adolf Hitler, not quite thirty-one and utterly unknown, who took the lead in building up what had been no more than a back-room debating society into what would soon become a formidable political party.

All the ideas which had been bubbling in his mind since the lonesome days of hunger in Vienna now found an outlet, and an inner energy which had not been observable in his make-up burst forth. He prodded his timid committee into organizing bigger meetings. He personally typed out and distributed invitations. Later he recalled how once, after he had distributed eighty of these, "we sat waiting for the masses who were expected to appear. An hour late, the 'chairman' had to open the 'meeting.' We were again seven, the old seven."[16] But he was not to be discouraged. He increased the number of invitations by having them mimeographed. He collected a few marks to insert a notice of a meeting in a local newspaper. "The success," he says, "was positively amazing. One hundred and eleven people were present." Hitler was to make his first "public"

---

* Eckart died of overdrinking in December 1923.

speech, following the main address by a "Munich professor." Harrer, nominal head of the party, objected. "This gentleman, who was certainly otherwise honest," Hitler relates, "just happened to be convinced that I might be capable of doing certain things, but not of speaking. I spoke for thirty minutes, and what before I had simply felt within me, without in any way knowing it, was now proved by reality: I could speak!"[17] Hitler claims the audience was "electrified" by his oratory and its enthusiasm proved by donations of three hundred marks, which temporarily relieved the party of its financial worries.

At the start of 1920, Hitler took over the party's propaganda, an activity to which he had given much thought since he had observed its importance in the Socialist and Christian Social parties in Vienna. He began immediately to organize by far the biggest meeting ever dreamt of by the pitifully small party. It was to be held on February 24, 1920, in the Festsaal of the famous Hofbräuhaus, with a seating capacity of nearly two thousand. Hitler's fellow committeemen thought he was crazy. Harrer resigned in protest and was replaced by Drexler, who remained skeptical.* Hitler emphasizes that he personally conducted the preparations. Indeed the event loomed so large for him that he concludes the first volume of *Mein Kampf* with a description of it, because, he explains, it was the occasion when "the party burst the narrow bonds of a small club and for the first time exerted a determining influence on the mightiest factor of our time: public opinion."

Hitler was not even scheduled as the main speaker. This role was reserved for a certain Dr. Johannes Dingfelder, a homeopathic physician, a crackpot who contributed articles on economics to the newspapers under the pseudonym of "Germanus Agricola," and who was soon to be forgotten. His speech was greeted with silence; then Hitler began to speak. As he describes the scene:

> There was a hail of shouts, there were violent clashes in the hall, a handful of the most faithful war comrades and other supporters battled with the disturbers . . . Communists and Socialists . . . and only little by little were able to restore order. I was able to go on speaking. After half an hour the applause slowly began to drown out the screaming and shouting . . . When after nearly four hours the hall began to empty I knew that now the principles of the movement which could no longer be forgotten were moving out among the German people.[18]

In the course of his speech Hitler had enunciated for the first time the twenty-five points of the program of the German Workers' Party. They had been hastily drawn up by Drexler, Feder and Hitler. Most of the heckling at Hitler had really been directed against parts of the program which he read out, but he nevertheless considered all the points as having

---

* Harrer also was opposed to Hitler's violent anti-Semitism and believed that Hitler was alienating the working-class masses. These were the real reasons why he resigned.

been adopted and they became the official program of the Nazi Party when its name was altered on April 1, 1920, to the National Socialist German Workers' Party. Indeed, for tactical reasons Hitler in 1926 declared them "unalterable."

They are certainly a hodgepodge, a catchall for the workers, the lower middle class and the peasants, and most of them were forgotten by the time the party came to power. A good many writers on Germany have ridiculed them, and the Nazi leader himself was later to be embarrassed when reminded of some of them. Yet, as in the case of the main principles laid down in *Mein Kampf,* the most important of them were carried out by the Third Reich, with consequences disastrous to millions of people, inside and outside of Germany.

The very first point in the program demanded the union of all Germans in a Greater Germany. Was this not exactly what Chancellor Hitler would insist on and get when he annexed Austria and its six million Germans, when he took the Sudetenland with its three million Germans? And was it not his demand for the return of German Danzig and the other areas in Poland inhabited predominantly by Germans which led to the German attack on Poland and brought on World War II? And cannot it be added that it was one of the world's misfortunes that so many in the interwar years either ignored or laughed off the Nazi aims which Hitler had taken the pains to put down in writing? Surely the anti-Semitic points of the program promulgated in the Munich beer hall on the evening of February 24, 1920, constituted a dire warning. The Jews were to be denied office and even citizenship in Germany and excluded from the press. All who had entered the Reich after August 2, 1914, were to be expelled.

A good many paragraphs of the party program were obviously merely a demagogic appeal to the mood of the lower classes at a time when they were in bad straits and were sympathetic to radical and even socialist slogans. Point 11, for example, demanded abolition of incomes unearned by work; Point 12, the nationalization of trusts; Point 13, the sharing with the state of profits from large industry; Point 14, the abolishing of land rents and speculation in land. Point 18 demanded the death penalty for traitors, usurers and profiteers, and Point 16, calling for the maintenance of "a sound middle class," insisted on the communalization of department stores and their lease at cheap rates to small traders. These demands had been put in at the insistence of Drexler and Feder, who apparently really believed in the "socialism" of National Socialism. They were the ideas which Hitler was to find embarrassing when the big industrialists and landlords began to pour money into the party coffers, and of course nothing was ever done about them.

There were, finally, two points of the program which Hitler would carry out as soon as he became Chancellor. Point 2 demanded the abrogation of the treaties of Versailles and St. Germain. The last point, number 25, insisted on "the creation of a strong central power of the State." This, like Points 1 and 2 demanding the union of all Germans in the Reich and the abolition of the peace treaties, was put into the program at Hitler's insistence and it showed how even then, when his party was hardly known outside Munich, he was casting his eyes on further horizons even at the risk of losing popular support in his own bailiwick.

Separatism was very strong in Bavaria at the time and the Bavarians, constantly at odds with the central government in Berlin, were demanding less, not more, centralization, so that Bavaria could rule itself. In fact, this was what it was doing at the moment; Berlin's writ had very little authority in the states. Hitler was looking ahead for power not only in Bavaria but eventually in the Reich, and to hold and exercise that power a dictatorial regime such as he already envisaged needed to constitute itself as a strong centralized authority, doing away with the semiautonomous states which under the Weimar Republic, as under the Hohenzollern Empire, enjoyed their own parliaments and governments. One of his first acts after January 30, 1933, was to swiftly carry out this final point in the party's program which so few had noticed or taken seriously. No one could say he had not given ample warning, in writing, from the very beginning.

Inflammatory oratory and a radical, catchall program, important as they were for a fledgling party out to attract attention and recruit mass support, were not enough, and Hitler now turned his attention to providing more—much more. The first signs of his peculiar genius began to appear and make themselves felt. What the masses needed, he thought, were not only ideas—a few simple ideas, that is, that he could ceaselessly hammer through their skulls—but symbols that would win their faith, pageantry and color that would arouse them, and acts of violence and terror, which if successful, would attract adherents (were not most Germans drawn to the strong?) and give them a sense of power over the weak.

In Vienna, as we have seen, he was intrigued by what he called the "infamous spiritual and physical terror" which he thought was employed by the Social Democrats against their political opponents.* Now he turned it to good purpose in his own anti-Socialist party. At first ex-servicemen were assigned to the meetings to silence hecklers and, if necessary, toss them out. In the summer of 1920, soon after the party had added "National Socialist" to the name of the "German Workers' Party" and became the National Socialist German Workers' Party, or N.S.D.A.P., as it was now to be familiarly known, Hitler organized a bunch of roughneck war veterans into "strong-arm" squads, *Ordnertruppe,* under the command of Emil Maurice, an ex-convict and watchmaker. On October 5, 1921, after camouflaging themselves for a short time as the "Gymnastic and Sports Division" of the party to escape suppression by the Berlin government, they were officially named the Sturmabteilung, from which the name S.A. came. The storm troopers, outfitted in brown uniforms, were recruited largely from the freebooters of the free corps and placed under the command of Johann Ulrich Klintzich, an aide of the notorious

---

* See above, pp. 22–23.

Captain Ehrhardt, who had recently been released from imprisonment in connection with the murder of Erzberger.

These uniformed rowdies, not content to keep order at Nazi meetings, soon took to breaking up those of the other parties. Once in 1921 Hitler personally led his storm troopers in an attack on a meeting which was to be addressed by a Bavarian federalist by the name of Ballerstedt, who received a beating. For this Hitler was sentenced to three months in jail, one of which he served. This was his first experience in jail and he emerged from it somewhat of a martyr and more popular than ever. "It's all right," Hitler boasted to the police. "We got what we wanted. Ballerstedt did not speak." As Hitler had told an audience some months before, "The National Socialist Movement will in the future ruthlessly prevent—if necessary by force—all meetings or lectures that are likely to distract the minds of our fellow countrymen."[19]

In the summer of 1920 Hitler, the frustrated artist but now becoming the master propagandist, came up with an inspiration which can only be described as a stroke of genius. What the party lacked, he saw, was an emblem, a flag, a symbol, which would express what the new organization stood for and appeal to the imagination of the masses, who, as Hitler reasoned, must have some striking banner to follow and to fight under. After much thought and innumerable attempts at various designs he hit upon a flag with a red background and in the middle a white disk on which was imprinted a black swastika. The hooked cross—the hakenkreuz—of the swastika, borrowed though it was from more ancient times, was to become a mighty and frightening symbol of the Nazi Party and ultimately of Nazi Germany. Whence Hitler got the idea of using it for both the flag and the insignia of the party he does not say in a lengthy dissertation on the subject in *Mein Kampf*.

The hakenkreuz is as old, almost, as man on the planet. It has been found in the ruins of Troy and of Egypt and China. I myself have seen it in ancient Hindu and Buddhist relics in India. In more recent times it showed up as an official emblem in such Baltic states as Estonia and Finland, where the men of the German free corps saw it during the fighting of 1918–19. The Ehrhardt Brigade had it painted on their steel helmets when they entered Berlin during the Kapp putsch in 1920. Hitler had undoubtedly seen it in Austria in the emblems of one or the other anti-Semitic parties and perhaps he was struck by it when the Ehrhardt Brigade came to Munich. He says that numerous designs suggested to him by party members invariably included a swastika and that a "dentist from Sternberg" actually delivered a design for a flag that "was not bad at all and quite close to my own."

For the colors Hitler had of course rejected the black, red and gold of the hated Weimar Republic. He declined to adopt the old imperial flag of red, white and black, but he liked its colors not only because, he says, they form "the most brilliant harmony in existence," but because they were the colors of a Germany for which he had fought. But they had to be given a new form, and so a swastika was added.

Hitler reveled in his unique creation. "*A symbol it really is!*" he exclaims in *Mein Kampf*. "In *red* we see the social idea of the movement, in *white* the nationalist idea, in the *swastika* the mission of the struggle for the victory of the Aryan man."[20]

Soon the swastika armband was devised for the uniforms of the storm troopers and the party members, and two years later Hitler designed the Nazi standards which would be carried in the massive parades and would adorn the stages of the mass meetings. Taken from old Roman designs, they consisted of a black metal swastika on top with a silver wreath surmounted by an eagle, and, below, the initials NSDAP on a metal rectangle from which hung cords with fringe and tassels, a square swastika flag with "*Deutschland Erwache!* (Germany Awake!)" emblazoned on it.

This may not have been "art," but it was propaganda of the highest order. The Nazis now had a symbol which no other party could match. The hooked cross seemed to possess some mystic power of its own, to beckon to action in a new direction the insecure lower middle classes which had been floundering in the uncertainty of the first chaotic postwar years. They began to flock under its banner.

ADVENT OF THE "FUEHRER"

In the summer of 1921 the rising young agitator who had shown such surprising talents not only as an orator but as an organizer and a propagandist took over the undisputed leadership of the party. In doing so, he gave his fellow workers a first taste of the ruthlessness and tactical shrewdness with which he was to gain so much success in more important crises later on.

Early in the summer Hitler had gone to Berlin to get in touch with North German nationalist elements and to speak at the National Club, which was their spiritual headquarters. He wanted to assess the possibilities of carrying his own movement beyond the Bavarian borders into the rest of Germany. Perhaps he could make some useful alliances for that purpose. While he was away the other members of the committee of the Nazi Party decided the moment was opportune to challenge his leadership. He had become too dictatorial for them. They proposed some alliances themselves with similarly minded groups in South Germany, especially with the "German Socialist Party" which a notorious Jew-baiter, Julius Streicher, a bitter enemy and a rival of Hitler, was building up in Nuremberg. The committee members were sure that if these groups, with their ambitious leaders, could be merged with the Nazis, Hitler would be reduced in size.

Sensing the threat to his position, Hitler hurried back to Munich to quell the intrigues of these "foolish lunatics," as he called them in *Mein Kampf*. He offered to resign from the party. This was more than the party could afford, as the other members of the committee quickly realized. Hitler was not only their most powerful speaker but their best organizer and propagandist. Moreover, it was he who was now bringing in most of the organization's funds—from collections at the mass meetings at which he spoke and from other sources as well, including the Army. If he left, the budding Nazi Party would surely go to pieces. The committee refused to accept his resignation. Hitler, reassured of the strength of his position, now forced a complete capitulation on the other leaders. He demanded dictatorial powers for himself as the party's sole leader, the abolition of the committee itself and an end to intrigues with other groups such as Streicher's.

This was too much for the other committee members. Led by the party's founder, Anton Drexler, they drew up an indictment of the would-be dictator and circulated it as a pamphlet. It was the most drastic accusation Hitler was ever confronted with from the ranks of his own party—from those, that is, who had firsthand knowledge of his character and how he operated.

A lust for power and personal ambition have caused Herr Adolf Hitler to return to his post after his six weeks' stay in Berlin, of which the purpose has not yet been disclosed. He regards the time as ripe for bringing disunion and schism into our ranks by means of shadowy people behind him, and thus to further the interests of the Jews and their friends. It grows more and more clear that his purpose is simply to use the National Socialist party as a springboard for his own immoral purposes, and to seize the leadership in order to force the Party onto a different track at the psychological moment. This is most clearly shown by an ultimatum which he sent to the Party leaders a few days ago, in which he demands, among other things, that he shall have a sole and absolute dictatorship of the Party, and that the Committee, including the locksmith Anton Drexler, the founder and leader of the Party, should retire. . . .

And how does he carry on his campaign? Like a Jew. He twists every fact . . . National Socialists! Make up your minds about such characters! Make no mistake. Hitler is a demagogue . . . He believes himself capable . . . of filling you up with all kinds of tales that are anything but the truth.[21]

Although weakened by a silly anti-Semitism (Hitler acting like a Jew!), the charges were substantially true, but publicizing them did not get the rebels as far as might be supposed. Hitler promptly brought a libel suit against the authors of the pamphlet, and Drexler himself, at a public meeting, was forced to repudiate it. In two special meetings of the party Hitler dictated his peace terms. The statutes were changed to abolish the committee and give him dictatorial powers as president. The humiliated Drexler was booted upstairs as honorary president, and he soon passed out of the picture.* As Heiden says, it was the victory of the Cavaliers over the Roundheads of the party. But it was more than that. Then and

---

* He left the party in 1923 but served as Vice-President of the Bavarian Diet from 1924 to 1928. In 1930 he became reconciled with Hitler, but he never returned to active politics. The fate of all discoverers, as Heiden observed, overtook Drexler.

there, in Júly 1921, was established the "leadership principle" which was to be the law first of the Nazi Party and then of the Third Reich. The "Fuehrer" had arrived on the German scene.

The "leader" now set to work to reorganize the party. The gloomy taproom in the back of the Sterneckerbräu, which to Hitler was more of "a funeral vault than an office," was given up and new offices in another tavern in the Corneliusstrasse occupied. These were lighter and roomier. An old Adler typewriter was purchased on the installment plan, and a safe, filing cabinets, furniture, a telephone and a full-time paid secretary were gradually acquired.

Money was beginning to come in. Nearly a year before, in December of 1920, the party had acquired a run-down newspaper badly in debt, the *Voelkischer Beobachter,* an anti-Semitic gossip sheet which appeared twice a week. Exactly where the sixty thousand marks for its purchase came from was a secret which Hitler kept well, but it is known that Eckart and Roehm persuaded Major General Ritter von Epp, Roehm's commanding officer in the Reichswehr and himself a member of the party, to raise the sum. Most likely it came from Army secret funds. At the beginning of 1923 the *Voelkischer Beobachter* became a daily, thus giving Hitler the prerequisite of all German political parties, a daily newspaper in which to preach the party's gospels. Running a daily political journal required additional money, and this now came from what must have seemed to some of the more proletarian roughnecks of the party like strange sources. Frau Helene Bechstein, wife of the wealthy piano manufacturer, was one. From their first meeting she took a liking to the young firebrand, inviting him to stay at the Bechstein home when he was in Berlin, arranging parties in which he could meet the affluent, and donating sizable sums to the movement. Part of the money to finance the new daily came from a Frau Gertrud von Seidlitz, a Balt, who owned stock in some prosperous Finnish paper mills.

In March 1923, a Harvard graduate, Ernst (Putzi) Hanfstaengl, whose mother was American and whose cultivated and wealthy family owned an art-publishing business in Munich, loaned the party one thousand dollars against a mortgage on the *Voelkischer Beobachter.** This was a fabulous

---

* In his memoirs, *Unheard Witness,* Hanfstaengl says that he was first steered to Hitler by an American. This was Captain Truman Smith, then an assistant military attaché at the American Embassy in Berlin. In November 1922 Smith was sent by the embassy to Munich to check on an obscure political agitator by the name of Adolf Hitler and his newly founded National Socialist Labor Party. For a young professional American Army officer, Captain Smith had a remarkable bent for political analysis. In one week in Munich, November 15–22, he managed to see Ludendorff, Crown Prince Rupprecht and a dozen political leaders in Bavaria, most of whom told him that Hitler was a rising star and his movement a rapidly growing political force. Smith lost no time in attending an outdoor Nazi rally at which Hitler spoke. "Never saw such a sight in my life!" he scribbled in his diary immediately afterward. "Met Hitler," he wrote, "and he promises to talk to me Monday and explain his aims." On the Monday, Smith made his way to Hitler's residence—"a little bare bedroom on the second floor of a run-down house," as he described it—and had a long talk with the future dictator, who was scarcely known

sum in marks in those inflationary days and was of immense help to the party and its newspaper. But the friendship of the Hanfstaengls extended beyond monetary help. It was one of the first respectable families of means in Munich to open its doors to the brawling young politician. Putzi became a good friend of Hitler, who eventually made him chief of the Foreign Press Department of the party. An eccentric, gangling man, whose sardonic wit somewhat compensated for his shallow mind, Hanfstaengl was a virtuoso at the piano and on many an evening, even after his friend came to power in Berlin, he would excuse himself from the company of those of us who might be with him to answer a hasty summons from the Fuehrer. It was said that his piano-playing—he pounded the instrument furiously—and his clowning soothed Hitler and even cheered him up after a tiring day. Later this strange but genial Harvard man, like some other early cronies of Hitler, would have to flee the country for his life.*

Most of the men who were to become Hitler's closest subordinates were now in the party or would shortly enter it. Rudolf Hess joined in 1920. Son of a German wholesale merchant domiciled in Egypt, Hess had spent the first fourteen years of his life in that country and had then come to the Rhineland for his education. During the war he served for a time in the List Regiment with Hitler—though they did not become acquainted

---

outside Munich. "A marvelous demagogue!" the assistant U.S. military attaché began his diary that evening. "Have rarely listened to such a logical and fanatical man." The date was November 22, 1922.

Just before leaving for Berlin that evening Smith saw Hanfstaengl, told him of his meeting with Hitler and advised him to take a look at the man. The Nazi leader was to address a rally that evening and Captain Smith turned over his press ticket to Hanfstaengl. The latter, like so many others, was overwhelmed by Hitler's oratory, sought him out after the meeting and quickly became a convert to Nazism.

Back in Berlin, which at that time took little notice of Hitler, Captain Smith wrote a lengthy report which the embassy dispatched to Washington on November 25, 1922. Considering when it was written, it is a remarkable document.

The most active political force in Bavaria at the present time [Smith wrote] is the National Socialist Labor Party. Less a political party than a popular movement, it must be considered as the Bavarian counterpart to the Italian fascisti . . . It has recently acquired a political influence quite disproportionate to its actual numerical strength. . . .

Adolf Hitler from the very first has been the dominating force in the movement, and the personality of this man has undoubtedly been one of the most important factors contributing to its success . . . His ability to influence a popular assembly is uncanny. In private conversation he disclosed himself as a forceful and logical speaker, which, when tempered with a fanatical earnestness, made a very deep impression on a neutral listener.

Colonel Smith, who later served as American military attaché in Berlin during the early years of the Nazi regime, kindly placed his diary and notes of his trip to Munich at the disposal of this writer. They have been invaluable in the preparation of this chapter.

* Hanfstaengl spent part of World War II in Washington, ostensibly as an interned enemy alien but actually as an "adviser" to the United States government on Nazi Germany. This final role of his life, which seemed so ludicrous to Americans who knew him and Nazi Germany, must have amused him.

then—and after being twice wounded became a flyer. He enrolled in the University of Munich after the war as a student of economics but seems to have spent much of his time distributing anti-Semitic pamphlets and fighting with the various armed bands then at loose in Bavaria. He was in the thick of the firing when the soviet regime in Munich was overthrown on May 1, 1919, and was wounded in the leg. One evening a year later he went to hear Hitler speak, was carried away by his eloquence and joined the party, and soon he became a close friend, a devoted follower and secretary of the leader. It was he who introduced Hitler to the geopolitical ideas of General Karl Haushofer, then a professor of geopolitics at the university.

Hess had stirred Hitler with a prize-winning essay which he wrote for a thesis, entitled "How Must the Man Be Constituted Who Will Lead Germany Back to Her Old Heights?"

Where all authority has vanished, only a man of the people can establish authority . . . The deeper the dictator was originally rooted in the broad masses, the better he understands how to treat them psychologically, the less the workers will distrust him, the more supporters he will win among these most energetic ranks of the people. He himself has nothing in common with the mass; like every great man he is all personality . . . When necessity commands, he does not shrink before bloodshed. Great questions are always decided by blood and iron . . . In order to reach his goal, he is prepared to trample on his closest friends . . . The lawgiver proceeds with terrible hardness . . . As the need arises, he can trample them [the people] with the boots of a grenadier . . .[22]

No wonder Hitler took to the young man. This was a portrait perhaps not of the leader as he was at the moment but of the leader he wanted to become—and did. For all his solemnity and studiousness, Hess remained a man of limited intelligence, always receptive to crackpot ideas, which he could adopt with great fanaticism. Until nearly the end, he would be one of Hitler's most loyal and trusted followers and one of the few who was not bitten by consuming personal ambition.

Alfred Rosenberg, although he was often hailed as the "intellectual leader" of the Nazi Party and indeed its "philosopher," was also a man of mediocre intelligence. Rosenberg may with some truth be put down as a Russian. Like a good many Russian "intellectuals," he was of Baltic German stock. The son of a shoemaker, he was born January 12, 1893, at Reval (now Tallinn) in Estonia, which had been a part of the Czarist Empire since 1721. He chose to study not in Germany but in Russia and received a diploma in architecture from the University of Moscow in 1917. He lived in Moscow through the days of the Bolshevik revolution and it may be that, as some of his enemies in the Nazi Party later said, he flirted with the idea of becoming a young Bolshevik revolutionary. In February 1918, however, he returned to Reval, volunteered for service in the German Army when it reached the city, was turned down as a "Russian" and finally, at the end of 1918, made his way to Munich, where he first became active in White Russian émigré circles.

Rosenberg then met Dietrich Eckart and through him Hitler, and joined the party at the end of 1919. It was inevitable that a man who had actually received a diploma in architecture would impress the man who had failed even to get into a school of architecture. Hitler was also impressed by Rosenberg's "learning," and he liked the young Balt's hatred of the Jews and the Bolsheviks. Shortly before Eckart died, toward the end of 1923, Hitler made Rosenberg editor of the *Voelkischer Beobachter,* and for many years he continued to prop up this utterly muddled man, this confused and shallow "philosopher," as the intellectual mentor of the Nazi movement and as one of its chief authorities on foreign policy.

Like Rudolf Hess, Hermann Goering had also come to Munich some time after the war ostensibly to study economics at the university, and he too had come under the personal spell of Adolf Hitler. One of the nation's great war heroes, the last commander of the famed Richthofen Fighter Squadron, holder of the Pour le Mérite, the highest war decoration in Germany, he found it even more difficult than most war veterans to return to the humdrum existence of peacetime civilian life. He became a transport pilot in Denmark for a time and later in Sweden. One day he flew Count Eric von Rosen to the latter's estate some distance from Stockholm and while stopping over as a guest fell in love with Countess Rosen's sister, Carin von Kantzow, née Baroness Fock, one of Sweden's beauties. Some difficulties arose. Carin von Kantzow was epileptic and was married and the mother of an eight-year-old son. But she was able to have the marriage dissolved and marry the gallant young flyer. Possessed of considerable means, she went with her new husband to Munich, where they lived in some splendor and he dabbled in studies at the university.

But not for long. He met Hitler in 1921, joined the party, contributed generously to its treasury (and to Hitler personally), threw his restless energy into helping Roehm organize the storm troopers and a year later, in 1922, was made commander of the S.A.

A swarm of lesser-known and, for the most part, more unsavory individuals joined the circle around the party dictator. Max Amann, Hitler's first sergeant in the List Regiment, a tough, uncouth character but an able organizer, was named business manager of the party and the *Voelkischer Beobachter* and quickly brought order into the finances of both. As his personal bodyguard Hitler chose Ulrich Graf, an amateur wrestler, a butcher's apprentice and a renowned brawler. As his "court photographer," the only man who for years was permitted to photograph him, Hitler had the lame Heinrich Hoffmann, whose loyalty was doglike and profitable, making him in the end a millionaire. Another favorite brawler was Christian Weber, a horse dealer, a former bouncer in a Munich dive and a lusty beer drinker. Close to Hitler in these days was Hermann Esser, whose oratory rivaled the leader's and whose Jew-baiting articles in the *Voelkischer Beobachter* were a leading feature of the party newspaper. He made no secret that for a time he lived well off the generosity of some of his mistresses. A notorious blackmailer, resorting to threats to "expose" even his own party comrades who crossed him, Esser became so repulsive to some of the older and more decent men in the movement that they demanded his expulsion. "I know Esser is a scoundrel," Hitler retorted in public, "but I shall hold on to him as long as he can be of use to me."[23] This was to be his attitude toward almost all of his close collaborators, no matter how murky their past—or indeed their present. Murderers, pimps, homosexual perverts, drug addicts or just plain rowdies were all the same to him if they served his purposes.

He stood Julius Streicher, for example, almost to the end. This depraved sadist, who started life as an elementary-school teacher, was one of the most disreputable men around Hitler from 1922 until 1939, when his star finally faded. A famous fornicator, as he boasted, who blackmailed even the husbands of women who were his mistresses, he made his fame and fortune as a blindly fanatical anti-Semite. His notorious weekly, *Der Stuermer,* thrived on lurid tales of Jewish sexual crimes and Jewish "ritual murders"; its obscenity was nauseating, even to many Nazis. Streicher was also a noted pornographist. He became known as the "uncrowned King of Franconia" with the center of his power in Nuremberg, where his word was law and where no one who crossed him or displeased him was safe from prison and torture. Until I faced him slumped in the dock at Nuremberg, on trial for his life as a war criminal, I never saw him without a whip in his hand or in his belt, and he laughingly boasted of the countless lashings he had meted out.

Such were the men whom Hitler gathered around him in the early years for his drive to become dictator of a nation which had given the world a Luther, a Kant, a Goethe and a Schiller, a Bach, a Beethoven and a Brahms.

On April 1, 1920, the day the German Workers' Party became the National Socialist German Workers' Party—from which the abbreviated name "Nazi" emerged—Hitler left the Army for good. Henceforth he would devote all of his time to the Nazi Party, from which neither then nor later did he accept any salary.

How, then, it might be asked, did Hitler live? His fellow party workers themselves sometimes wondered. In the indictment which the rebel members of the party committee drew up in July 1921, the question was bluntly posed: "If any member asks him how he lives and what was his former profession, he always becomes angry and excited. Up to now no answer has been supplied to these questions. So his conscience cannot be clean, especially as his excessive intercourse with ladies, to whom he often describes himself as 'King of Munich,' costs a great deal of money."

Hitler answered the question during the subsequent libel action which he brought against the authors of the pamphlet. To the question of the court as to exactly how he lived, he replied, "If I speak for the National Socialist Party I take no money for myself. But I also speak for other organizations . . . . and then of course I accept a fee. I also have my midday meal with various party comrades in turn. I am further assisted to a modest extent by a few party comrades."[24]

Probably this was very close to the truth. Such well-heeled friends as Dietrich Eckart, Goering and Hanfstaengl undoubtedly "lent" him money to pay his rent, purchase clothes and buy a meal. His wants were certainly modest. Until 1929 he occupied a two-room flat in a lower-middle-class district in the Thierschstrasse near the River Isar. In the winter he wore an old trench coat—it later became familiar to everyone in Germany from numerous photographs. In the summer he often appeared in shorts, the *Lederhosen* which most Bavarians donned in seasonable weather. In 1923 Eckart and Esser stumbled upon the Platterhof, an inn near Berchtesgaden, as a summer retreat for Hitler and his friends. Hitler fell in love with the lovely mountain country; it was here that he later built the spacious villa, Berghof, which would be his home and where he would spend much of his time until the war years.

There was, however, little time for rest and recreation in the stormy years between 1921 and 1923. There was a party to build and to keep control of in the face of jealous rivals as unscrupulous as himself. The N.S.D.A.P. was but one of several right-wing movements in Bavaria struggling for public attention and support, and beyond, in the rest of Germany, there were many others.

There was a dizzy succession of events and of constantly changing situations for a politician to watch, to evaluate and to take advantage of. In April 1921 the Allies had presented Germany the bill for reparations, a whopping 132 billion gold marks—33 billion dollars—which the Germans howled they could not possibly pay. The mark, normally valued at four to the dollar, had begun to fall; by the summer of 1921 it had dropped to seventy-five, a year later to four hundred, to the dollar Erzberger had been murdered in August 1921. In June 1922, there was an attempt to assassinate Philipp Scheidemann, the Socialist who had proclaimed the Republic. The same month, June 24, Foreign Minister Rathenau was shot dead in the street. In all three cases the assassins had been men of the extreme Right. The shaky national government in Berlin finally answered the challenge with a special Law for the Protection of the Republic, which imposed severe penalties for political terrorism. Berlin demanded the dissolution of the innumerable armed leagues and the end of political gangsterism. The Bavarian government, even under the moderate Count Lerchenfeld, who had replaced the extremist Kahr in 1921, was finding it difficult to go along with the national regime in Berlin. When it attempted to enforce the law against terrorism, the Bavarian Rightists, of whom Hitler was now one of the acknowledged young leaders, organized a conspiracy to overthrow Lerchenfeld and march on Berlin to bring down the Republic.

The fledgling democratic Weimar Republic was in deep trouble, its very existence constantly threatened not only from the extreme Right but from the extreme Left.

3

VERSAILLES, WEIMAR

AND THE BEER HALL PUTSCH

To MOST MEN in the victorious Allied lands of the West, the proclamation of the Republic in Berlin on November 9, 1918, had
appeared to mark the dawn of a new day for the German people and their
nation. Woodrow Wilson, in the exchange of notes which led to the
armistice, had pressed for the abolition of the Hohenzollern militarist
autocracy, and the Germans had seemingly obliged him, although reluctantly. The Kaiser had been forced to abdicate and to flee; the monarchy
was dissolved, all the dynasties in Germany were quickly done away with,
and republican government was proclaimed.

But proclaimed by accident! On the afternoon of November 9, the
so-called Majority Social Democrats under the leadership of Friedrich
Ebert and Philipp Scheidemann met in the Reichstag in Berlin following
the resignation of the Chancellor, Prince Max of Baden. They were
sorely puzzled as to what to do. Prince Max had just announced the
abdication of the Kaiser. Ebert, a saddler by trade, thought that one of
Wilhelm's sons—anyone except the dissolute Crown Prince—might succeed him, for he favored a constitutional monarchy on the British pattern.
Ebert, though he led the Socialists, abhorred social revolution. "I hate it
like sin," he had once declared.

But revolution was in the air in Berlin. The capital was paralyzed by a
general strike. Down the broad Unter den Linden, a few blocks from the
Reichstag, the Spartacists, led by the Left Socialists Rosa Luxemburg and
Karl Liebknecht, were preparing from their citadel in the Kaiser's palace
to proclaim a soviet republic. When word of this reached the Socialists
in the Reichstag they were consternated. Something had to be done at
once to forestall the Spartacists. Scheidemann thought of something.
Without consulting his comrades he dashed to the window overlooking the
Koenigsplatz, where a great throng had gathered, stuck his head out and
on his own, as if the idea had just popped into his head, proclaimed the
Republic! The saddle maker Ebert was furious. He had hoped, somehow,
to save the Hohenzollern monarchy.

Thus was the German Republic born, as if by a fluke. If the Socialists themselves were not staunch republicans it could hardly be expected that the conservatives would be. But the latter had abdicated their responsibility. They and the Army leaders, Ludendorff and Hindenburg, had pushed political power into the hands of the reluctant Social Democrats. In doing so they managed also to place on the shoulders of these democratic working-class leaders apparent responsibility for signing the surrender and ultimately the peace treaty, thus laying on them the blame for Germany's defeat and for whatever suffering a lost war and a dictated peace might bring upon the German people. This was a shabby trick, one which the merest child would be expected to see through, but in Germany it worked. It doomed the Republic from the start.

Perhaps it need not have. In November 1918 the Social Democrats, holding absolute power, might have quickly laid the foundation for a lasting democratic Republic. But to have done so they would have had to suppress permanently, or at least curb permanently, the forces which had propped up the Hohenzollern Empire and which would not loyally accept a democratic Germany: the feudal Junker landlords and other upper castes, the magnates who ruled over the great industrial cartels, the roving *condottieri* of the free corps, the ranking officials of the imperial civil service and, above all, the military caste and the members of the General Staff. They would have had to break up many of the great estates, which were wasteful and uneconomic, and the industrial monopolies and cartels, and clean out the bureaucracy, the judiciary, the police, the universities and the Army of all who would not loyally and honestly serve the new democratic regime.

This the Social Democrats, who were mostly well-meaning trade-unionists with the same habit of bowing to old, established authority which was ingrained in Germans of other classes, could not bring themselves to do. Instead they began by abdicating their authority to the force which had always been dominant in modern Germany, the Army. For though it had been defeated on the battlefield the Army still had hopes of maintaining itself at home and of defeating the revolution. To achieve these ends it moved swiftly and boldly.

On the night of November 9, 1918, a few hours after the Republic had been "proclaimed," a telephone rang in the study of Ebert in the Reich Chancellery in Berlin. It was a very special telephone, for it was linked with Supreme Headquarters at Spa by a private and secret line. Ebert was alone. He picked up the telephone. "Groener speaking," a voice said. The former saddle maker, still bewildered by the day's events which had suddenly thrust into his unwilling hands whatever political power remained in a crumbling Germany, was impressed. General Wilhelm Groener was the successor of Ludendorff as First Quartermaster General. Earlier on that very day at Spa it was he who, when Field Marshal von Hindenburg faltered, had bluntly informed the Kaiser that he no longer commanded the loyalty of his troops and must go—a brave act for which the military caste never forgave him. Ebert and Groener had developed a bond of mutual respect since 1916, when the General, then in charge of war production, had worked closely with the Socialist leader. Early in November —a few days before—they had conferred in Berlin on how to save the monarchy and the Fatherland.

Now at the Fatherland's lowest moment a secret telephone line brought them together. Then and there the Socialist leader and the second-in-command of the German Army made a pact which, though it would not be publicly known for many years, was to determine the nation's fate. Ebert agreed to put down anarchy and Bolshevism and maintain the Army in all its tradition. Groener thereupon pledged the support of the Army in helping the new government establish itself and carry out its aims.

"Will the Field Marshal (Hindenburg) retain the command?" Ebert asked.

General Groener replied that he would.

"Convey to the Field Marshal the thanks of the government," Ebert replied.[1]

The German Army was saved, but the Republic, on the very day of its birth, was lost. The generals, with the honorable exception of Groener himself and but few others, would never serve it loyally. In the end, led by Hindenburg, they betrayed it to the Nazis.

At the moment, to be sure, the specter of what had just happened in Russia haunted the minds of Ebert and his fellow Socialists. They did not want to become the German Kerenskys. They did not want to be supplanted by the Bolshevists. Everywhere in Germany the Soldiers' and Workers' Councils were springing up and assuming power, as they had done in Russia. It was these groups which on November 10 elected a Council of People's Representatives, with Ebert at its head, to govern Germany for the time being. In December the first Soviet Congress of Germany met in Berlin. Composed of delegates from the Soldiers' and Workers' Councils throughout the country, it demanded the dismissal of Hindenburg, the abolition of the Regular Army and the substitution of a civil guard whose officers would be elected by the men and which would be under the supreme authority of the Council.

This was too much for Hindenburg and Groener. They declined to recognize the authority of the Soviet Congress. Ebert himself did nothing to carry out its demands. But the Army, fighting for its life, demanded more positive action from the government it had agreed to support. Two days before Christmas the People's Marine Division, now under the control of the Communist Spartacists, occupied the Wilhelmstrasse, broke into the Chancellery and cut its telephone wires. The secret line to Army headquarters, however, continued to function and over it Ebert appealed for help. The Army promised liberation by the Potsdam garrison, but before it could arrive the mutinous sailors retired to their quarters in the stables of the imperial palace, which the Spartacists still held.

The Spartacists, with Karl Liebknecht and Rosa Luxemburg, the two most effective agitators in Germany, at their head, continued to push for a soviet republic. Their armed power in Berlin was mounting. On Christmas Eve the Marine Division had easily repulsed an attempt by regular troops from Potsdam to dislodge it from the imperial stables. Hindenburg and Groener pressed Ebert to honor the pact between them and suppress the Bolshevists. This the Socialist leader was only too glad to do. Two days after Christmas he appointed Gustav Noske as Minister of National Defense, and from this appointment events proceeded with a logic which all who knew the new Minister might have expected.

Noske was a master butcher by trade who had worked his way up in the trade-union movement and the Social Democratic Party, becoming a member of the Reichstag in 1906, where he became recognized as the party's expert on military affairs. He also became recognized as a strong nationalist and as a strong man. Prince Max of Baden had picked him to put down the naval mutiny at Kiel in the first days of November and he had put it down. A stocky, square-jawed man of great physical strength and energy, though of abbreviated intelligence—typical, his enemies said, of his trade—Noske announced on his appointment as Defense Minister that "someone must be the bloodhound."

Early in January 1919 he struck. Between January 10 and 17— "Bloody Week," as it was called in Berlin for a time—regular and free-corps troops under the direction of Noske and the command of General von Luettwitz* crushed the Spartacists. Rosa Luxemburg and Karl Liebknecht were captured and murdered by officers of the Guard Cavalry Division.

As soon as the fighting in Berlin was over, elections were held throughout Germany for the National Assembly, which was to draw up the new constitution. The voting, which took place on January 19, 1919, revealed that the middle and upper classes had regained some of their courage in the little more than two months which had elapsed since the "revolution." The Social Democrats (the Majority and Independent Socialists), who had governed alone because no other group would share the burden, received 13,800,000 votes out of 30,000,000 cast and won 185 out of 421 seats in the Assembly, but this was considerably less than a majority. Obviously the new Germany was not going to be built by the working class alone. Two middle-class parties, the Center, representing the political movement of the Roman Catholic Church, and the Democratic Party, born of a fusion in December of the old Progressive Party and the left

---

* A year later General Freiherr Walther von Luettwitz, a reactionary officer of the old school, would show how loyal he was to the Republic in general and to Noske in particular when he led free-corps troops in the capture of Berlin in support of the Kapp putsch. Ebert, Noske and the other members of the government were forced to flee at five in the morning of March 13, 1920. General von Seeckt, Chief of Staff of the Army and nominally subordinate to Noske, the Minister of Defense, had refused to allow the Army to defend the Republic against Luettwitz and Kapp. "This night has shown the bankruptcy of all my policy," Noske cried out. "My faith in the Officer Corps is shattered. You have all deserted me." (Quoted by Wheeler-Bennett in *The Nemesis of Power*, p. 77.)

wing of the National Liberals, polled 11,500,000 votes between them and obtained 166 seats in the Assembly. Both parties professed support for a moderate, democratic Republic, though there was considerable sentiment for an eventual restoration of the monarchy.

The Conservatives, some of whose leaders had gone into hiding in November and others who, like Count von Westarp, had appealed to Ebert for protection, showed that though reduced in numbers they were far from extinguished. Rechristened the German National People's Party, they polled over three million votes and elected 44 deputies; their right-wing allies, the National Liberals, who had changed their name to the German People's Party, received nearly a million and a half votes and won 19 seats. Though decidedly in the minority, the two conservative parties had won enough seats in the Assembly to be vocal. Indeed, no sooner had the Assembly met in Weimar on February 6, 1919, than the leaders of these two groups sprang up to defend the name of Kaiser Wilhelm II and the way he and his generals had conducted the war. Gustav Stresemann, the head of the People's Party, had not yet experienced what later seemed to many to be a change of heart and mind. In 1919 he was still known as the man who had been the Supreme Command's mouthpiece in the Reichstag—"Ludendorff's young man," as he was called—a violent supporter of the policy of annexation, a fanatic for unrestricted submarine warfare.

The constitution which emerged from the Assembly after six months of debate—it was passed on July 31, 1919, and ratified by the President on August 31—was, on paper, the most liberal and democratic document of its kind the twentieth century had seen, mechanically well-nigh perfect, full of ingenious and admirable devices which seemed to guarantee the working of an almost flawless democracy. The idea of cabinet government was borrowed from England and France, of a strong popular President from the United States, of the referendum from Switzerland. An elaborate and complicated system of proportional representation and voting by lists was established in order to prevent the wasting of votes and give small minorities a right to be represented in Parliament.*

---

* There were flaws, to be sure, and in the end some of them proved disastrous. The system of proportional representation and voting by list may have prevented the wasting of votes, but it also resulted in the multiplication of small splinter parties which eventually made a stable majority in the Reichstag impossible and led to frequent changes in government. In the national elections of 1930 some twenty-eight parties were listed.

The Republic might have been given greater stability had some of the ideas of Professor Hugo Preuss, the principal drafter of the constitution, not been rejected. He proposed at Weimar that Germany be made into a centralized state and that Prussia and the other single states be dissolved and transformed into provinces. But the Assembly turned his proposals down.

Finally, Article 48 of the constitution conferred upon the President dictatorial powers during an emergency. The use made of this clause by Chancellors Bruening, von Papen and von Schleicher under President Hindenburg enabled them to govern without approval of the Reichstag and thus, even before the advent of Hitler, brought an end to democratic parliamentary government in Germany.

The wording of the Weimar Constitution was sweet and eloquent to the ear of any democratically minded man. The people were declared sovereign: "Political power emanates from the people." Men and women were given the vote at the age of twenty. "All Germans are equal before the law . . . Personal liberty is inviolable . . . Every German has a right . . . to express his opinion freely . . . All Germans have the right to form associations or societies . . . All inhabitants of the Reich enjoy complete liberty of belief and conscience . . ." No man in the world would be more free than a German, no government more democratic and liberal than his. On paper, at least.

THE SHADOW OF VERSAILLES

Before the drafting of the Weimar Constitution was finished an inevitable event occurred which cast a spell of doom over it and the Republic which it was to establish. This was the drawing up of the Treaty of Versailles. During the first chaotic and riotous days of the peace and even after the deliberations of the National Assembly got under way in Weimar the German people seemed to give little thought to the consequences of their defeat. Or if they did, they appeared to be smugly confident that having, as the Allies urged, got rid of the Hohenzollerns, squelched the Bolshevists and set about forming a democratic, republican government, they were entitled to a just peace based not on their having lost the war but on President Wilson's celebrated Fourteen Points.

German memories did not appear to stretch back as far as one year, to March 3, 1918, when the then victorious German Supreme Command had imposed on a defeated Russia at Brest Litovsk a peace treaty which to a British historian, writing two decades after the passions of war had cooled, was a "humiliation without precedent or equal in modern history."[2] It deprived Russia of a territory nearly as large as Austria-Hungary and Turkey combined, with 56,000,000 inhabitants, or 32 per cent of her whole population; a third of her railway mileage, 73 per cent of her total iron ore, 89 per cent of her total coal production; and more than 5,000 factories and industrial plants. Moreover, Russia was obliged to pay Germany an indemnity of six billion marks.

The day of reckoning arrived for the Germans in the late spring of 1919. The terms of the Versailles Treaty, laid down by the Allies without negotiation with Germany, were published in Berlin on May 7. They came as a staggering blow to a people who had insisted on deluding themselves to the last moment. Angry mass meetings were organized throughout the country to protest against the treaty and to demand that Germany refuse to sign it. Scheidemann, who had become Chancellor during the Weimar Assembly, cried, "May the hand wither that signs this treaty!" On May 8 Ebert, who had become Provisional President, and the government publicly branded the terms as "unrealizable and unbearable." The next day the German delegation at Versailles wrote the unbending Clemenceau that such a treaty was "intolerable for any nation."

What was so intolerable about it? It restored Alsace-Lorraine to France, a parcel of territory to Belgium, a similar parcel in Schleswig to Denmark—after a plebiscite—which Bismarck had taken from the Danes in the previous century after defeating them in war. It gave back to the Poles the lands, some of them only after a plebiscite, which the Germans had taken during the partition of Poland. This was one of the stipulations which infuriated the Germans the most, not only because they resented separating East Prussia from the Fatherland by a corridor which gave Poland access to the sea, but because they despised the Poles, whom they considered an inferior race. Scarcely less infuriating to the Germans was that the treaty forced them to accept responsibility for starting the war and demanded that they turn over to the Allies Kaiser Wilhelm II and some eight hundred other "war criminals."

Reparations were to be fixed later, but a first payment of five billion dollars in gold marks was to be paid between 1919 and 1921, and certain deliveries in kind—coal, ships, lumber, cattle, etc.—were to be made in lieu of cash reparations.

But what hurt most was that Versailles virtually disarmed Germany* and thus, for the time being anyway, barred the way to German hegemony in Europe. And yet the hated Treaty of Versailles, unlike that which Germany had imposed on Russia, left the Reich geographically and economically largely intact and preserved her political unity and her potential strength as a great nation.

The provisional government at Weimar, with the exception of Erzberger, who urged acceptance of the treaty on the grounds that its terms could be easily evaded, was strongly against accepting the Versailles *Diktat*, as it was now being called. Behind the government stood the overwhelming majority of citizens, from right to left.

And the Army? If the treaty were rejected, could the Army resist an inevitable Allied attack from the west? Ebert put it up to the Supreme Command, which had now moved its headquarters to Kolberg in Pomerania. On June 17 Field Marshal von Hindenburg, prodded by General Groener, who saw that German military resistance would be futile, replied:

In the event of a resumption of hostilities we can reconquer the province of Posen [in Poland] and defend our frontiers in the east. In the west, however, we can scarcely count upon being able to withstand a serious offensive on the part of the enemy in view of the numerical superiority of the Entente and their ability to outflank us on both wings.

The success of the operation as a whole is therefore very doubtful, but as a soldier I cannot help feeling that it were better to perish honorably than accept a disgraceful peace.

---

* It restricted the Army to 100,000 long-term volunteers and prohibited it from having planes or tanks. The General Staff was also outlawed. The Navy was reduced to little more than a token force and forbidden to build submarines or vessels over 10,000 tons.

The concluding words of the revered Commander in Chief were in the best German military tradition but their sincerity may be judged by knowledge of the fact which the German people were unaware of—that Hindenburg had agreed with Groener that to try to resist the Allies now would not only be hopeless but might result in the destruction of the cherished officer corps of the Army and indeed of Germany itself.

The Allies were now demanding a definite answer from Germany. On June 16, the day previous to Hindenburg's written answer to Ebert, they had given the Germans an ultimatum: Either the treaty must be accepted by June 24 or the armistice agreement would be terminated and the Allied powers would "take such steps as they think necessary to enforce their terms."

Once again Ebert appealed to Groener. If the Supreme Command thought there was the slightest possibility of successful military resistance to the Allies, Ebert promised to try to secure the rejection of the treaty by the Assembly. But he must have an answer immediately. The last day of the ultimatum, June 24, had arrived. The cabinet was meeting at 4:30 P.M. to make its final decision. Once more Hindenburg and Groener conferred. "You know as well as I do that armed resistance is impossible," the aging, worn Field Marshal said. But once again, as at Spa on November 9, 1918, when he could not bring himself to tell the Kaiser the final truth and left the unpleasant duty to Groener, he declined to tell the truth to the Provisional President of the Republic. "You can give the answer to the President as well as I can," he said to Groener.[3] And again the courageous General took the final responsibility which belonged to the Field Marshal, though he must have known that it would eventually make doubly sure his being made a scapegoat for the officer corps. He telephoned the Supreme Command's view to the President.

Relieved at having the Army's leaders take the responsibility—a fact that was soon forgotten in Germany—the National Assembly approved the signing of the peace treaty by a large majority and its decision was communicated to Clemenceau a bare nineteen minutes before the Allied ultimatum ran out. Four days later, on June 28, 1919, the treaty of peace was signed in the Hall of Mirrors in the Palace of Versailles.

A HOUSE DIVIDED

From that day on Germany became a house divided.

The conservatives would accept neither the treaty of peace nor the Republic which had ratified it. Nor, in the long run, would the Army—General Groener excepted—though it had sworn to support the new democratic regime and had itself made the final decision to sign at Versailles. Despite the November "revolution," the conservatives still held the economic power. They owned the industries, the large estates and most of the country's capital. Their wealth could be used, and was, to subsidize

political parties and a political press that would strive from now on to
undermine the Republic.

The Army began to circumvent the military restrictions of the peace
treaty before the ink on it was scarcely dry. And thanks to the timidity
and shortsightedness of the Socialist leaders, the officer corps managed not
only to maintain the Army in its old Prussian traditions, as we have seen,
but to become the real center of political power in the new Germany. The
Army did not, until the last days of the short-lived Republic, stake its
fortunes on any one political movement. But under General Hans von
Seeckt, the brilliant creator of the 100,000-man Reichswehr, the Army,
small as it was in numbers, became a state within a state, exerting an increasing influence on the nation's foreign and domestic policies until a
point was reached where the Republic's continued existence depended on
the will of the officer corps.

As a state within a state it maintained its independence of the national
government. Under the Weimar Constitution the Army could have been
subordinated to the cabinet and Parliament, as the military establishments
of the other Western democracies were. But it was not. Nor was the
officer corps purged of its monarchist, antirepublican frame of mind. A
few Socialist leaders such as Scheidemann and Grzesinski urged "democ-
ratizing" the armed forces. They saw the danger of handing the Army
back to the officers of the old authoritarian, imperialist tradition. But they
were successfully opposed not only by the generals but by their fellow
Socialists, led by the Minister of Defense, Noske. This proletarian minister
of the Republic openly boasted that he wanted to revive "the proud soldier
memories of the World War." The failure of the duly elected government
to build a new Army that would be faithful to its own democratic spirit
and subordinate to the cabinet and the Reichstag was a fatal mistake for
the Republic, as time would tell.

The failure to clean out the judiciary was another. The administrators
of the law became one of the centers of the counterrevolution, perverting
justice for reactionary political ends. "It is impossible to escape the conclusion," the historian Franz L. Neumann declared, "that political justice
is the blackest page in the life of the German Republic."[4] After the
Kapp putsch in 1920 the government charged 705 persons with high
treason; only one, the police president of Berlin, received a sentence—five
years of "honorary confinement." When the state of Prussia withdrew
his pension the Supreme Court ordered it restored. A German court in
December 1926 awarded General von Luettwitz, the military leader of
the Kapp putsch, back payment of his pension to cover the period when
he was a rebel against the government and also the five years that he was
a fugitive from justice in Hungary.

Yet hundreds of German liberals were sentenced to long prison terms on
charges of treason because they revealed or denounced in the press or by
speech the Army's constant violations of the Versailles Treaty. The
treason laws were ruthlessly applied to the supporters of the Republic;
those on the Right who tried to overthrow it, as Adolf Hitler was soon to

learn, got off either free or with the lightest of sentences. Even the assassins, if they were of the Right and their victims democrats, were leniently treated by the courts or, as often happened, helped to escape from the custody of the courts by Army officers and right-wing extremists.

And so the mild Socialists, aided by the democrats and the Catholic Centrists, were left to carry on the Republic, which tottered from its birth. They bore the hatred, the abuse and sometimes the bullets of their opponents, who grew in number and in resolve. "In the heart of the people," cried Oswald Spengler, who had skyrocketed to fame with his book *The Decline of the West,* "the Weimar Constitution is already doomed." Down in Bavaria the young firebrand Adolf Hitler grasped the strength of the new nationalist, antidemocratic, antirepublican tide. He began to ride it.

He was greatly aided by the course of events, two in particular: the fall of the mark and the French occupation of the Ruhr. The mark, as we have seen, had begun to slide in 1921, when it dropped to 75 to the dollar; the next year it fell to 400 and by the beginning of 1923 to 7,000. Already in the fall of 1922 the German government had asked the Allies to grant a moratorium on reparation payments. This the French government of Poincaré had bluntly refused. When Germany defaulted in deliveries of timber, the hardheaded French Premier, who had been the wartime President of France, ordered French troops to occupy the Ruhr. The industrial heart of Germany, which, after the loss of Upper Silesia to Poland, furnished the Reich with four fifths of its coal and steel production, was cut off from the rest of the country.

This paralyzing blow to Germany's economy united the people momentarily as they had not been united since 1914. The workers of the Ruhr declared a general strike and received financial support from the government in Berlin, which called for a campaign of passive resistance. With the help of the Army, sabotage and guerrilla warfare were organized. The French countered with arrests, deportations and even death sentences. But not a wheel in the Ruhr turned.

The strangulation of Germany's economy hastened the final plunge of the mark. On the occupation of the Ruhr in January 1923, it fell to 18,000 to the dollar; by July 1 it had dropped to 160,000; by August 1 to a million. By November, when Hitler thought his hour had struck, it took four billion marks to buy a dollar, and thereafter the figures became trillions. German currency had become utterly worthless. Purchasing power of salaries and wages was reduced to zero. The life savings of the middle classes and the working classes were wiped out. But something even more important was destroyed: the faith of the people in the economic structure of German society. What good were the standards and practices of such a society, which encouraged savings and investment and solemnly promised a safe return from them and then defaulted? Was this not a fraud upon the people?

And was not the democratic Republic, which had surrendered to the enemy and accepted the burden of reparations, to blame for the disaster? Unfortunately for its survival, the Republic did bear a responsibility. The inflation could have been halted by merely balancing the budget—a difficult but not impossible feat. Adequate taxation might have achieved this, but the new government did not dare to tax adequately. After all, the cost of the war—164 billion marks—had been met not even in part by direct taxation but 93 billions of it by war loans, 29 billions out of Treasury bills and the rest by increasing the issue of paper money. Instead of drastically raising taxes on those who could pay, the republican government actually reduced them in 1921.

From then on, goaded by the big industrialists and landlords, who stood to gain though the masses of the people were financially ruined, the government deliberately let the mark tumble in order to free the State of its public debts, to escape from paying reparations and to sabotage the French in the Ruhr. Moreover, the destruction of the currency enabled German heavy industry to wipe out its indebtedness by refunding its obligations in worthless marks. The General Staff, disguised as the "Truppenamt" (Office of Troops) to evade the peace treaty which supposedly had outlawed it, took notice that the fall of the mark wiped out the war debts and thus left Germany financially unencumbered for a new war.

The masses of the people, however, did not realize how much the industrial tycoons, the Army and the State were benefiting from the ruin of the currency. All they knew was that a large bank account could not buy a straggly bunch of carrots, a half peck of potatoes, a few ounces of sugar, a pound of flour. They knew that as individuals they were bankrupt. And they knew hunger when it gnawed at them, as it did daily. In their misery and hopelessness they made the Republic the scapegoat for all that had happened.

Such times were heaven-sent for Adolf Hitler.

REVOLT IN BAVARIA

"The government calmly goes on printing these scraps of paper because, if it stopped, that would be the end of the government," he cried. "Because once the printing presses stopped—and that is the prerequisite for the stabilization of the mark—the swindle would at once be brought to light . . . Believe me, our misery will increase. The scoundrel will get by. The reason: because the State itself has become the biggest swindler and crook. A robbers' state! . . . If the horrified people notice that they can starve on billions, they must arrive at this conclusion: we will no longer submit to a State which is built on the swindling idea of the majority. We want a dictatorship . . ."[5]

No doubt the hardships and uncertainties of the wanton inflation were driving millions of Germans toward that conclusion and Hitler was ready to lead them on. In fact, he had begun to believe that the chaotic conditions of 1923 had created an opportunity to overthrow the Republic which might not recur. But certain difficulties lay in his way if he were himself to lead the counterrevolution, and he was not much interested in it unless he was.

In the first place, the Nazi Party, though it was growing daily in numbers, was far from being even the most important political movement in Bavaria, and outside that state it was unknown. How could such a small party overthrow the Republic? Hitler, who was not easily discouraged by odds against him, thought he saw a way. He might unite under his leadership all the antirepublican, nationalist forces in Bavaria. Then with the support of the Bavarian government, the armed leagues and the Reichswehr stationed in Bavaria, he might lead a march on Berlin —as Mussolini had marched on Rome the year before—and bring the Weimar Republic down. Obviously Mussolini's easy success had given him food for thought.

The French occupation of the Ruhr, though it brought a renewal of German hatred for the traditional enemy and thus revived the spirit of nationalism, complicated Hitler's task. It began to unify the German people behind the republican government in Berlin which had chosen to defy France. This was the last thing Hitler wanted. His aim was to do away with the Republic. France could be taken care of after Germany had had its nationalist revolution and established a dictatorship. Against a strong current of public opinion Hitler dared to take an unpopular line: "No—not down with France, but down with the traitors of the Fatherland, down with the November criminals! That must be our slogan."[6]

All through the first months of 1923 Hitler dedicated himself to making the slogan effective. In February, due largely to the organizational talents of Roehm, four of the armed "patriotic leagues" of Bavaria joined with the Nazis to form the so-called Arbeitsgemeinschaft der Vaterlaendischen Kampfverbaende (Working Union of the Fatherland Fighting Leagues) under the political leadership of Hitler. In September an even stronger group was established under the name of the Deutscher Kampfbund (German Fighting Union), with Hitler one of a triumvirate of leaders. This organization sprang from a great mass meeting held at Nuremberg on September 2 to celebrate the anniversary of the German defeat of France at Sedan in 1870. Most of the fascist-minded groups in southern Germany were represented and Hitler received something of an ovation after a violent speech against the national government. The objectives of the new Kampfbund were openly stated: overthrow of the Republic and the tearing up of the Treaty of Versailles.

At the Nuremberg meeting Hitler had stood in the reviewing stand next to General Ludendorff during a parade of the demonstrators. This was not by accident. For some time the young Nazi chief had been cultivating the war hero, who had lent his famous name to the makers of the Kapp putsch in Berlin and who, since he continued to encourage counterrevolution from the Right, might be tempted to back an action which was beginning to germinate in Hitler's mind. The old General had no political sense; living now outside Munich, he did not disguise his contempt for Bavarians, for Crown Prince Rupprecht, the Bavarian pretender, and for the Catholic Church in this most Catholic of all states in Germany. All this Hitler knew, but it suited his purposes. He did not want Ludendorff as the political leader of the nationalist counterrevolution, a role which it was known the war hero was ambitious to assume. Hitler insisted on that role for himself. But Ludendorff's name, his renown in the officer corps and among the conservatives throughout Germany would be an asset to a provincial politician still largely unknown outside Bavaria. Hitler began to include Ludendorff in his plans.

In the fall of 1923 the German Republic and the state of Bavaria reached a point of crisis. On September 26, Gustav Stresemann, the Chancellor, announced the end of passive resistance in the Ruhr and the resumption of German reparation payments. This former mouthpiece of Hindenburg and Ludendorff, a staunch conservative and, at heart, a monarchist, had come to the conclusion that if Germany were to be saved, united and made strong again it must, at least for the time being, accept the Republic, come to terms with the Allies and obtain a period of tranquillity in which to regain its economic strength. To drift any further would only end in civil war and perhaps in the final destruction of the nation.

The abandonment of resistance to the French in the Ruhr and the resumption of the burden of reparations touched off an outburst of anger and hysteria among the German nationalists, and the Communists, who also had been growing in strength, joined them in bitter denunciation of the Republic. Stresemann was faced with serious revolt from both extreme Right and extreme Left. He had anticipated it by having President Ebert declare a state of emergency on the very day he announced the change of policy on the Ruhr and reparations. From September 26, 1923, until February 1924, executive power in Germany under the Emergency Act was placed in the hands of the Minister of Defense, Otto Gessler, and of the Commander of the Army, General von Seeckt. In reality this made the General and his Army virtual dictators of the Reich.

Bavaria was in no mood to accept such a solution. The Bavarian cabinet of Eugen von Knilling proclaimed its own state of emergency on September 26 and named the right-wing monarchist and former premier Gustav von Kahr as State Commissioner with dictatorial powers. In Berlin it was feared that Bavaria might secede from the Reich, restore the Wittelsbach monarchy and perhaps form a South German union with Austria. A meeting of the cabinet was hastily summoned by President Ebert, and General von Seeckt was invited to attend. Ebert wanted to know where the Army stood. Seeckt bluntly told him. "The Army, Mr. President, stands behind me."[7]

The icy words pronounced by the monocled, poker-faced Prussian Commander in Chief did not, as might have been expected, dismay the German President or his Chancellor. They had already recognized the Army's position as a state within the State and subject only to itself. Three years before, as we have seen, when the Kapp forces had occupied

Berlin and a similar appeal had been made to Seeckt, the Army had stood not behind the Republic but behind the General. The only question now, in 1923, was where Seeckt stood.

Fortunately for the Republic he now chose to stand behind it, not because he believed in republican, democratic principles but because he saw that for the moment the support of the existing regime was necessary for the preservation of the Army, itself threatened by revolt in Bavaria and in the north, and for saving Germany from a disastrous civil war. Seeckt knew that some of the leading officers of the Army division in Munich were siding with the Bavarian separatists. He knew of a conspiracy of the "Black Reichswehr" under Major Buchrucker, a former General Staff officer, to occupy Berlin and turn the republican government out. He now moved with cool precision and absolute determination, to set the Army right and end the threat of civil war.

On the night of September 30, 1923, "Black Reichswehr" troops under the command of Major Buchrucker seized three forts to the east of Berlin. Seeckt ordered regular forces to besiege them, and after two days Buchrucker surrendered. He was tried for high treason and actually sentenced to ten years of fortress detention. The "Black Reichswehr," which had been set up by Seeckt himself under the cover name of Arbeitskommandos (Labor Commandos) to provide secret reinforcements for the 100,000-man Reichswehr, was dissolved.*

Seeckt next turned his attention to the threats of Communist uprisings in Saxony, Thuringia, Hamburg and the Ruhr. In suppressing the Left the loyalty of the Army could be taken for granted. In Saxony the Socialist–Communist government was arrested by the local Reichswehr commander and a Reich Commissioner appointed to rule. In Hamburg and in the other areas the Communists were quickly and severely squelched. It now seemed to Berlin that the relatively easy suppression of the Bolshevists had robbed the conspirators in Bavaria of the pretext that they were really acting to save the Republic from Communism, and that they would now recognize the authority of the national government. But it did not turn out that way.

Bavaria remained defiant of Berlin. It was now under the dictatorial control of a triumvirate: Kahr, the State Commissioner, General Otto von Lossow, commander of the Reichswehr in Bavaria, and Colonel Hans von Seisser, the head of the state police. Kahr refused to recognize that President Ebert's proclamation of a state of emergency in Germany had

---

* The "Black Reichswehr" troops, numbering roughly twenty thousand, were stationed on the eastern frontier to help guard it against the Poles in the turbulent days of 1920–23. The illicit organization became notorious for its revival of the horrors of the medieval *Femegerichte*—secret courts—which dealt arbitrary death sentences against Germans who revealed the activities of the "Black Reichswehr" to the Allied Control Commission. Several of these brutal murders reached the courts. At one trial the German Defense Minister, Otto Gessler, who had succeeded Noske, denied any knowledge of the organization and insisted that it did not exist. But when one of his questioners protested against such innocence Gessler cried, "He who speaks of the 'Black Reichswehr' commits an act of high treason!"

any application in Bavaria. He declined to carry out any orders from Berlin. When the national government demanded the suppression of Hitler's newspaper, the *Voelkischer Beobachter,* because of its vitriolic attacks on the Republic in general and on Seeckt, Stresemann and Gessler in particular, Kahr contemptuously refused.

A second order from Berlin to arrest three notorious leaders of some of the armed bands in Bavaria, Captain Heiss, Captain Ehrhardt (the "hero" of the Kapp putsch) and Lieutenant Rossbach (a friend of Roehm), was also ignored by Kahr. Seeckt, his patience strained, ordered General von Lossow to suppress the Nazi newspaper and arrest the three free-corps men. The General, himself a Bavarian and a confused and weak officer who had been taken in by Hitler's eloquence and Kahr's persuasiveness, hesitated to obey. On October 24 Seeckt sacked him and appointed General Kress von Kressenstein in his place. Kahr, however, would not take this kind of dictation from Berlin. He declared that Lossow would retain the command of the Reichswehr in Bavaria and defying not only Seeckt but the constitution, forced the officers and the men of the Army to take a special oath of allegiance to the Bavarian government.

This, to Berlin, was not only political but military rebellion, and General von Seeckt was now determined to put down both.[8]

He issued a plain warning to the Bavarian triumvirate and to Hitler and the armed leagues that any rebellion on their part would be opposed by force. But for the Nazi leader it was too late to draw back. His rabid followers were demanding action. Lieutenant Wilhelm Brueckner, one of his S.A. commanders, urged him to strike at once. "The day is coming," he warned, "when I won't be able to hold the men back. If nothing happens now, they'll run away from us."

Hitler realized too that if Stresemann gained much more time and began to succeed in his endeavor to restore tranquillity in the country, his own opportunity would be lost. He pleaded with Kahr and Lossow to march on Berlin before Berlin marched on Munich. And his suspicion grew that either the triumvirate was losing heart or that it was planning a separatist coup without him for the purpose of detaching Bavaria from the Reich. To this, Hitler, with his fanatical ideas for a strong, nationalist, unified Reich, was unalterably opposed.

Kahr, Lossow and Seisser were beginning to lose heart after Seeckt's warning. They were not interested in a futile gesture that might destroy them. On November 6 they informed the Kampfbund, of which Hitler was the leading political figure, that they would not be hurried into precipitate action and that they alone would decide when and how to act. This was a signal to Hitler that he must seize the initiative himself. He did not possess the backing to carry out a putsch a'one. He would have to have the support of the Bavarian state, the Army and the police—this was a lesson he had learned in his beggarly Vienna days. Somehow he would have to put Kahr, Lossow and Seisser in a position where they would have to act with him and from which there would be no turning back. Boldness, even recklessness, was called for, and that Hitler now proved he had. He decided to kidnap the triumvirate and force them to use their power at his bidding.

The idea had first been proposed to Hitler by two refugees from Russia, Rosenberg and Scheubner-Richter. The latter, who had ennobled himself with his wife's name and called himself Max Erwin von Scheubner-Richter, was a dubious character who, like Rosenberg, had spent most of his life in the Russian Baltic provinces and after the war made his way with other refugees from the Soviet Union to Munich, where he joined the Nazi Party and became one of Hitler's close confidants.

On November 4, Germany's Memorial Day (*Totengedenktag*) would be observed by a military parade in the heart of Munich, and it had been announced in the press that not only the popular Crown Prince Rupprecht but Kahr, Lossow and Seisser would take the salute of the troops from a stand in a narrow street leading from the Feldherrnhalle. Scheubner-Richter and Rosenberg proposed to Hitler that a few hundred storm troopers, transported by trucks, should converge on the little street before the parading troops arrived and seal it off with machine guns. Hitler would then mount the tribune, proclaim the revolution and at pistol point prevail upon the notables to join it and help him lead it. The plan appealed to Hitler and he enthusiastically endorsed it. But, on the appointed day, when Rosenberg arrived early on the scene for purposes of reconnaissance he discovered to his dismay that the narrow street was fully protected by a large body of well-armed police. The plot, indeed the "revolution," had to be abandoned.

Actually it was merely postponed. A second plan was concocted, one that could not be balked by the presence of a band of strategically located police. On the night of November 10–11, the S.A. and the other armed bands of the Kampfbund would be concentrated on the Froettmaninger Heath, just north of Munich, and on the morning of the eleventh, the anniversary of the hated, shameful armistice, would march into the city, seize strategic points, proclaim the national revolution and present the hesitant Kahr, Lossow and Seisser with a *fait accompli*.

At this point a not very important public announcement induced Hitler to drop that plan and improvise a new one. A brief notice appeared in the press that, at the request of some business organizations in Munich, Kahr would address a meeting at the Buergerbräukeller, a large beer hall on the southeastern outskirts of the city. The date was November 8, in the evening. The subject of the Commissioner's speech, the notice said, would be the program of the Bavarian government. General von Lossow, Colonel von Seisser and other notables would be present.

Two considerations led Hitler to a rash decision. The first was that he suspected Kahr might use the meeting to announce the proclamation of Bavarian independence and the restoration of the Wittelsbachs to the Bavarian throne. All day long on November 8 Hitler tried in vain to see Kahr, who put him off until the ninth. This only increased the Nazi leader's suspicions. He must forestall Kahr. Also, and this was the second consideration, the Buergerbräukeller meeting provided the opportunity which had been missed on November 4: the chance to rope in all three members of the triumvirate and at the point of a pistol force them to join the Nazis in carrying out the revolution. Hitler decided to act at once. Plans for the November 10 mobilization were called off; the storm troops were hastily alerted for duty at the big beer hall.

THE BEER HALL PUTSCH

About a quarter to nine on the evening of November 8, 1923, after Kahr had been speaking for half an hour to some three thousand thirsty burghers, seated at roughhewn tables and quaffing their beer out of stone mugs in the Bavarian fashion, S.A. troops surrounded the Buergerbräukeller and Hitler pushed forward into the hall. While some of his men were mounting a machine gun in the entrance, Hitler jumped up on a table and to attract attention fired a revolver shot toward the ceiling. Kahr paused in his discourse. The audience turned around to see what was the cause of the disturbance. Hitler, with the help of Hess and of Ulrich Graf, the former butcher, amateur wrestler and brawler and now the leader's bodyguard, made his way to the platform. A police major tried to stop him, but Hitler pointed his pistol at him and pushed on. Kahr, according to one eyewitness, had now become "pale and confused." He stepped back from the rostrum and Hitler took his place.

"The National Revolution has begun!" Hitler shouted. "This building is occupied by six hundred heavily armed men. No one may leave the hall. Unless there is immediate quiet I shall have a machine gun posted in the gallery. The Bavarian and Reich governments have been removed and a provisional national government formed. The barracks of the Reichswehr and police are occupied. The Army and the police are marching on the city under the swastika banner."

This last was false; it was pure bluff. But in the confusion no one knew for sure. Hitler's revolver was real. It had gone off. The storm troopers with their rifles and machine guns were real. Hitler now ordered Kahr, Lossow and Seisser to follow him to a nearby private room off stage. Prodded by storm troopers, the three highest officials of Bavaria did Hitler's bidding while the crowd looked on in amazement.

But with growing resentment too. Many businessmen still regarded Hitler as something of an upstart. One of them shouted to the police, "Don't be cowards as in 1918. Shoot!" But the police, with their own chiefs so docile and the S.A. taking over the hall, did not budge. Hitler had arranged for a Nazi spy at police headquarters, Wilhelm Frick, to telephone the police on duty at the beer hall not to interfere but merely to report. The crowd began to grow so sullen that Goering felt it necessary to step to the rostrum and quiet them. "There is nothing to fear," he cried. "We have the friendliest intentions. For that matter, you've no cause to grumble, you've got your beer!" And he informed them that in the next room a new government was being formed.

It was, at the point of Adolf Hitler's revolver. Once he had herded his prisoners into the adjoining room, Hitler told them, "No one leaves this room alive without my permission." He then informed them they would all have key jobs either in the Bavarian government or in the Reich government which he was forming with Ludendorff. With Ludendorff? Earlier in the evening Hitler had dispatched Scheubner-Richter to Ludwigshoehe to fetch the renowned General, who knew nothing of the Nazi conspiracy, to the beerhouse at once.

The three prisoners at first refused even to speak to Hitler. He continued to harangue them. Each of them must join him in proclaiming the revolution and the new governments; each must take the post he, Hitler, assigned them, or "he has no right to exist." Kahr was to be the Regent of Bavaria; Lossow, Minister of the National Army; Seisser, Minister of the Reich Police. None of the three was impressed at the prospect of such high office. They did not answer.

Their continued silence unnerved Hitler. Finally he waved his gun at them. "I have four shots in my pistol! Three for my collaborators, if they abandon me. The last bullet for myself!" Pointing the weapon to his forehead, he cried, "If I am not victorious by tomorrow afternoon, I shall be a dead man!"

Kahr was not a very bright individual but he had physical courage. "Herr Hitler," he answered, "you can have me shot or shoot me yourself. Whether I die or not is no matter."

Seisser also spoke up. He reproached Hitler for breaking his word of honor not to make a putsch against the police.

"Yes, I did," Hitler replied. "Forgive me, but I had to for the sake of the Fatherland."

General von Lossow disdainfully maintained silence. But when Kahr started to whisper to him, Hitler snapped, "Halt! No talking without my permission!"

He was getting nowhere with his own talk. Not one of the three men who held the power of the Bavarian state in their hands had agreed to join him, even at pistol point. The putsch wasn't going according to plan. Then Hitler acted on a sudden impulse. Without a further word, he dashed back into the hall, mounted the tribune, faced the sullen crowd and announced that the members of the triumvirate in the next room had joined him in forming a new national government.

"The Bavarian Ministry," he shouted, "is removed. . . . The government of the November criminals and the Reich President are declared to be removed. A new national government will be named this very day here in Munich. A German National Army will be formed immediately . . . I propose that, until accounts have been finally settled with the November criminals, the direction of policy in the National Government be taken over by me. Ludendorff will take over the leadership of the German National Army . . . The task of the provisional German

National Government is to organize the march on that sinful Babel, Berlin, and save the German people . . . Tomorrow will find either a National Government in Germany or us dead!"

Not for the first time and certainly not for the last, Hitler had told a masterful lie, and it worked. When the gathering heard that Kahr, General von Lossow and Police Chief von Seisser had joined Hitler its mood abruptly changed. There were loud cheers, and the sound of them impressed the three men still locked up in the little side room.

Scheubner-Richter now produced General Ludendorff, as if out of a hat. The war hero was furious with Hitler for pulling such a complete surprise on him, and when, once closeted in the side room, he learned that the former corporal and not he was to be the dictator of Germany his resentment was compounded. He spoke scarcely a word to the brash young man. But Hitler did not mind so long as Ludendorff lent his famous name to the desperate undertaking and won over the three re-calcitrant Bavarian leaders who thus far had failed to respond to his own exhortations and threats. This Ludendorff proceeded to do. It was now a question of a great national cause, he said, and he advised the gentlemen to co-operate. Awed by the attention of the generalissimo, the trio appeared to give in, though later Lossow denied that he had agreed to place himself under Ludendorff's command. For a few minutes Kahr fussed over the question of restoring the Wittelsbach monarchy, which was so dear to him. Finally he said he would co-operate as the "King's deputy."

Ludendorff's timely arrival had saved Hitler. Overjoyed at this lucky break, he led the others back to the platform, where each made a brief speech and swore loyalty to each other and to the new regime. The crowd leaped on chairs and tables in a delirium of enthusiasm. Hitler beamed with joy. "He had a childlike, frank expression of happiness that I shall never forget," an eminent historian who was present later declared.[9]

Again mounting the rostrum, Hitler spoke his final word to the gathering:

I want now to fulfill the vow which I made to myself five years ago when I was a blind cripple in the military hospital: to know neither rest nor peace until the November criminals had been overthrown, until on the ruins of the wretched Germany of today there should have arisen once more a Germany of power and greatness, of freedom and splendor.

This meeting began to break up. At the exits Hess, aided by storm troopers, detained a number of Bavarian cabinet members and other notables who were trying to slip out with the throng. Hitler kept his eye on Kahr, Lossow and Seisser. Then news came of a clash between storm troopers of one of the fighting leagues, the Bund Oberland, and regular troops at the Army Engineers' barracks. Hitler decided to drive to the scene and settle the matter personally, leaving the beer hall in charge of Ludendorff.

This turned out to be a fatal error. Lossow was the first to slip away.

He informed Ludendorff he must hurry to his office at Army headquarters to give the necessary orders. When Scheubner-Richter objected, Ludendorff rejoined stiffly, "I forbid you to doubt the word of a German officer." Kahr and Seisser vanished too.

Hitler, in high spirits, returned to the Buergerbräu to find that the birds had flown the coop. This was the first blow of the evening and it stunned him. He had confidently expected to find his "ministers" busy at their new tasks while Ludendorff and Lossow worked out plans for the march on Berlin. But almost nothing was being done. Not even Munich was being occupied by the revolutionary forces. Roehm, at the head of a detachment of storm troopers from another fighting league, the Reichskriegsflagge, had seized Army headquarters at the War Ministry in the Schoenfeldstrasse but no other strategic centers were occupied, not even the telegraph office, over whose wires news of the coup went out to Berlin and orders came back, from General von Seeckt to the Army in Bavaria, to suppress the putsch.

Though there were some defections among the junior officers and some of the troops, whose sympathies were with Hitler and Roehm, the higher officers, led by General von Danner, commander of the Munich garrison, not only were prepared to carry out Seeckt's command but were bitterly resentful of the treatment meted out to General von Lossow. In the Army's code a civilian who pointed a revolver at a general deserved to be smitten by an officer's side arms. From headquarters at the 19th Infantry barracks, where Lossow had joined Danner, messages went out to outlying garrisons to rush reinforcements to the city. By dawn Regular Army troops had drawn a cordon around Roehm's forces in the War Ministry.

Before this action Hitler and Ludendorff joined Roehm at the ministry for a time, to take stock of the situation. Roehm was shocked to find that no one besides himself had taken military action and occupied the key centers. Hitler tried desperately to re-establish contact with Lossow, Kahr and Seisser. Messengers were dispatched to the 19th Infantry barracks in the name of Ludendorff but they did not return. Poehner, the former Munich police chief and now one of Hitler's supporters, was sent with Major Huehnlein and a band of the S.A. troopers to occupy police headquarters. They were promptly arrested there.

And what of Gustav von Kahr, the head of the Bavarian government? After leaving the Buergerbräukeller he had quickly recovered his senses and his courage. Not wishing to take any more chances on being made a prisoner of Hitler and his rowdies, Kahr moved the government to Regensburg. But not before he had ordered placards posted throughout Munich carrying the following proclamation:

The deception and perfidy of ambitious comrades have converted a demonstration in the interests of national reawakening into a scene of disgusting violence. The declarations extorted from myself, General von Lossow and

Colonel Seisser at the point of the revolver are null and void. The National
Socialist German Workers' Party, as well as the fighting leagues Oberland and
Reichskriegsflagge, are dissolved.

VON KAHR
General State Commissioner

The triumph which earlier in the evening had seemed to Hitler so
near and so easily won was rapidly fading with the night. The basis for a
successful political revolution on which he had always insisted—the
support of existing institutions such as the Army, the police, the political
group in power—was now crumbling. Not even Ludendorff's magic name,
it was now clear, had won over the armed forces of the state. Hitler suggested that perhaps the situation could be retrieved if he and the General
withdrew to the countryside near Rosenheim and rallied the peasants
behind the armed bands for an assault on Munich, but Ludendorff
promptly rejected the idea.

Or perhaps there was another way out which at least would avert
disaster. On first hearing of the putsch, Crown Prince Rupprecht, a
bitter personal enemy of Ludendorff, had issued a brief statement calling
for its prompt suppression. Now Hitler decided to appeal to the Prince
to intercede with Lossow and Kahr and obtain an honorable, peaceful
settlement. A Lieutenant Neunzert, a friend of Hitler and of Rupprecht,
was hurried off at dawn to the Wittelsbach castle near Berchtesgaden
on the delicate mission. Unable to find an automobile, he had to wait for
a train and did not arrive at his destination until noon, at which hour
events were taking a turn not foreseen by Hitler nor dreamt of as possible
by Ludendorff.

Hitler had planned a putsch, not a civil war. Despite his feverish state
of excitement he was in sufficient control of himself to realize that he
lacked the strength to overcome the police and the Army. He had wanted
to make a revolution *with* the armed forces, not *against* them. Bloodthirsty though he had been in his recent speeches and during the hours he
held the Bavarian triumvirs at gunpoint, he shrank from the idea of men
united in their hatred of the Republic shedding the blood of each other.

So did Ludendorff. He would, as he had told his wife, string up President Ebert "and Co." and gladly watch them dangle from the gallows.
But he did not wish to kill policemen and soldiers who, in Munich at least,
believed with him in the national counterrevolution.

To the wavering young Nazi leader Ludendorff now proposed a plan
of his own that might still bring them victory and yet avoid bloodshed.
German soldiers, even German police—who were mostly ex-soldiers—
would never dare, he was sure, to fire on the legendary commander who
had led them to great victories on both the Eastern and the Western fronts.
He and Hitler would march with their followers to the center of the
city and take it over. Not only would the police and the Army not dare
to oppose him, he was certain; they would join him and fight under his
orders. Though somewhat skeptical, Hitler agreed. There seemed no

other way out. The Crown Prince, he noted, had not replied to his plea for mediation.

Toward eleven o'clock on the morning of November 9, the anniversary of the proclamation of the German Republic, Hitler and Ludendorff led a column of some three thousand storm troopers out of the gardens of the Buergerbräukeller and headed for the center of Munich. Beside them in the front rank marched Goering, commander of the S.A., Scheubner-Richter, Rosenberg, Ulrich Graf, Hitler's bodyguard, and half a dozen other Nazi officials and leaders of the Kampfbund. A swastika flag and a banner of the Bund Oberland were unfurled at the head of the column. Not far behind the first ranks a truck chugged along, loaded with machine guns and machine gunners. The storm troopers carried carbines, slung over their shoulders, some with fixed bayonets. Hitler brandished his revolver. Not a very formidable armed force, but Ludendorff, who had commanded millions of Germany's finest troops, apparently thought it sufficient for his purposes.

A few hundred yards north of the beer cellar the rebels met their first obstacle. On the Ludwig Bridge, which leads over the River Isar toward the center of the city, stood a detachment of armed police barring the route. Goering sprang forward and, addressing the police commander, threatened to shoot a number of hostages he said he had in the rear of his column if the police fired on his men. During the night Hess and others had rounded up a number of hostages, including two cabinet members, for just such a contingency. Whether Goering was bluffing or not, the police commander apparently believed he was not and let the column file over the bridge unmolested.

At the Marienplatz the Nazi column encountered a large crowd which was listening to an exhortation of Julius Streicher, the Jew-baiter from Nuremberg, who had rushed to Munich at the first news of the putsch. Not wishing to be left out of the revolution, he cut short his speech and joined the rebels, jumping into step immediately behind Hitler.

Shortly after noon the marchers neared their objective, the War Ministry, where Roehm and his storm troopers were surrounded by soldiers of the Reichswehr. Neither besiegers nor besieged had yet fired a shot. Roehm and his men were all ex-soldiers and they had many wartime comrades on the other side of the barbed wire. Neither side had any heart for killing.

To reach the War Ministry and free Roehm, Hitler and Ludendorff now led their column through the narrow Residenzstrasse, which, just beyond the Feldherrnhalle, opens out into the spacious Odeonsplatz. At the end of the gullylike street a detachment of police about one hundred strong, armed with carbines, blocked the way. They were in a strategic spot and this time they did not give way.

But once again the Nazis tried to talk their way through. One of them, the faithful bodyguard Ulrich Graf, stepped forward and cried out to the police officer in charge, "Don't shoot! His Excellency Ludendorff is coming!" Even at this crucial, perilous moment, a German revolutionary, even an old amateur wrestler and professional bouncer, remembered to give a gentleman his proper title. Hitler added another cry. "Surrender! Surrender!" he called out. But the unknown police officer did not surrender. Apparently Ludendorff's name had no magic sound for him; this was the police, not the Army.

Which side fired first was never established. Each put the blame on the other. One onlooker later testified that Hitler fired the first shot with his revolver. Another thought that Streicher did, and more than one Nazi later told this author that it was this deed which, more than any other, endeared him so long to Hitler.*

At any rate a shot was fired and in the next instant a volley of shots rang out from both sides, spelling in that instant the doom of Hitler's hopes. Scheubner-Richter fell, mortally wounded. Goering went down with a serious wound in his thigh. Within sixty seconds the firing stopped, but the street was already littered with fallen bodies—sixteen Nazis and three police dead or dying, many more wounded and the rest, including Hitler, clutching the pavement to save their lives.

There was one exception, and had his example been followed, the day might have had a different ending. Ludendorff did not fling himself to the ground. Standing erect and proud in the best soldierly tradition, with his adjutant, Major Streck, at his side, he marched calmly on between the muzzles of the police rifles until he reached the Odeonsplatz. He must have seemed a lonely and bizarre figure. Not one Nazi followed him. Not even the supreme leader, Adolf Hitler.

The future Chancellor of the Third Reich was the first to scamper to safety. He had locked his left arm with the right arm of Scheubner-Richter (a curious but perhaps revealing gesture) as the column approached the police cordon, and when the latter fell he pulled Hitler down to the pavement with him. Perhaps Hitler thought he had been wounded; he suffered sharp pains which, it was found later, came from a dislocated shoulder. But the fact remains that according to the testimony of one of his own Nazi followers in the column, the physician Dr. Walther Schulz, which was supported by several other witnesses, Hitler "was the first to get up and turn back," leaving his dead and wounded comrades lying in the street. He was hustled into a waiting motorcar and spirited off to the country home of the Hanfstaengls at Uffing, where Putzi's wife and sister nursed him and where, two days later, he was arrested.

Ludendorff was arrested on the spot. He was contemptuous of the rebels who had not had the courage to march on with him, and so bitter against the Army for not coming over to his side that he declared hence-

---

* Some years later, in approving Streicher's appointment as Nazi leader for Franconia over the opposition of many party comrades, Hitler declared, "Perhaps there are one or two who don't like the shape of Comrade Streicher's nose. But when he lay beside me that day on the pavement by the Feldherrnhalle, I vowed to myself never to forsake him so long as he did not forsake me." (Heiden, *Hitler: A Biography,* p. 157.)

forth he would not recognize a German officer nor ever again wear an officer's uniform. The wounded Goering was given first aid by the Jewish proprietor of a nearby bank into which he had been carried and then smuggled across the frontier into Austria by his wife and taken to a hospital in Innsbruck. Hess also fled to Austria. Roehm surrendered at the War Ministry two hours after the collapse before the Feldherrnhalle. Within a few days all the rebel leaders except Goering and Hess were rounded up and jailed. The Nazi putsch had ended in a fiasco. The party was dissolved. National Socialism, to all appearances, was dead. Its dictatorial leader, who had run away at the first hail of bullets, seemed utterly discredited, his meteoric political career at an end.

TRIAL FOR TREASON

As things turned out, that career was merely interrupted, and not for long. Hitler was shrewd enough to see that his trial, far from finishing him, would provide a new platform from which he could not only discredit the compromised authorities who had arrested him but—and this was more important—for the first time make his name known far beyond the confines of Bavaria and indeed of Germany itself. He was well aware that correspondents of the world press as well as of the leading German newspapers were flocking to Munich to cover the trial, which began on February 26, 1924, before a special court sitting in the old Infantry School in the Blutenburgstrasse. By the time it had ended twenty-four days later Hitler had transformed defeat into triumph, made Kahr, Lossow and Seisser share his guilt in the public mind to their ruin, impressed the German people with his eloquence and the fervor of his nationalism, and emblazoned his name on the front pages of the world.

Although Ludendorff was easily the most famous of the ten prisoners in the dock, Hitler at once grabbed the limelight for himself. From beginning to end he dominated the courtroom. Franz Guertner, the Bavarian Minister of Justice and an old friend and protector of the Nazi leader, had seen to it that the judiciary would be complacent and lenient. Hitler was allowed to interrupt as often as he pleased, cross-examine witnesses at will and speak on his own behalf at any time and at any length—his opening statement consumed four hours, but it was only the first of many long harangues.

He did not intend to make the mistake of those who, when tried for complicity in the Kapp putsch, had pleaded, as he later said, that "they knew nothing, had intended nothing, wished nothing. That was what destroyed the bourgeois world—that they had not the courage to stand by their act . . . to step before the judge and say, 'Yes, that was what we *wanted* to do; we wanted to destroy the State.' "

Now before the judges and the representatives of the world press in Munich, Hitler proclaimed proudly, "I alone bear the responsibility. But I am not a criminal because of that. If today I stand here as a revolutionary, it is as a revolutionary against the revolution. There is no such thing as high treason against the traitors of 1918."

If there were, then the three men who headed the government, the Army and the police in Bavaria and who had conspired with him against the national government were equally guilty and should be in the dock beside him instead of in the witness stand as his chief accusers. Shrewdly he turned the tables on the uneasy, guilt-ridden triumvirs:

One thing was certain, Lossow, Kahr and Seisser had the same goal that we had—to get rid of the Reich government . . . If our enterprise was actually high treason, then during the whole period Lossow, Kahr and Seisser must have been committing high treason along with us, for during all these weeks we talked of nothing but the aims of which we now stand accused.

The three men could scarcely deny this, for it was true. Kahr and Seisser were no match for Hitler's barbs. Only General von Lossow defended himself defiantly. "I was no unemployed *komitadji*," he reminded the court. "I occupied a high position in the State." And the General poured all the scorn of an old Army officer on his former corporal, this unemployed upstart, whose overpowering ambition had led him to try to dictate to the Army and the State. How far this unscrupulous demagogue had come, he exclaimed, from the days, not so far distant, when he had been willing to be merely "the drummer" in a patriotic movement!

A drummer merely? Hitler knew how to answer that:

How petty are the thoughts of small men! Believe me, I do not regard the acquisition of a minister's portfolio as a thing worth striving for. I do not hold it worthy of a great man to endeavor to go down in history just by becoming a minister. One might be in danger of being buried beside other ministers. My aim from the first was a thousand times higher than becoming a minister. I wanted to become the destroyer of Marxism. I am going to achieve this task, and if I do, the title of Minister will be an absurdity so far as I am concerned.

He invoked the example of Wagner.

When I stood for the first time at the grave of Richard Wagner my heart overflowed with pride in a man who had forbidden any such inscription as "Here lies Privy Councilor, Music Director, His Excellency Baron Richard von Wagner." I was proud that this man and so many others in German history were content to give their names to history without titles. It was not from modesty that I wanted to be a drummer in those days. That was the highest aspiration—the rest is nothing.

He had been accused of wanting to jump from drummer to dictator. He would not deny it. Fate had decreed it.

The man who is born to be a dictator is not compelled. He wills it. He is not driven forward, but drives himself. There is nothing immodest about this. Is it immodest for a worker to drive himself toward heavy labor? Is it presumptuous of a man with the high forehead of a thinker to ponder through the nights till he gives the world an invention? The man who feels called upon to govern a people has no right to say, "If you want me or summon me, I will co-operate." No! It is his duty to step forward.

Though he might be in the dock facing a long prison sentence for high treason against his country, his confidence in himself, in the call to "govern a people," was undiminished. While in prison awaiting trial, he had already analyzed the reasons for the failure of the putsch and had vowed that he would not commit the same mistakes in the future. Recalling his thoughts thirteen years later after he had achieved his goal, he told his old followers, assembled at the Buergerbräukeller to celebrate the anniversary of the putsch, "I can calmly say that it was the rashest decision of my life. When I think back on it today, I grow dizzy . . . If today you saw one of our squads from the year 1923 marching by, you would ask, 'What workhouse have they escaped from?' . . . But fate meant well with us. It did not permit an action to succeed which, if it had succeeded, would in the end have inevitably crashed as a result of the movement's inner immaturity in those days and its deficient organizational and intellectual foundation . . . We recognized that it is not enough to overthrow the old State, but that the new State must previously have been built up and be ready to one's hand . . . In 1933 it was no longer a question of overthrowing a State by an act of violence; meanwhile the new State had been built up and all that remained to do was to destroy the last remnants of the old State—and that took but a few hours."

How to build the new Nazi State was already in his mind as he fenced with the judges and his prosecutors during the trial. For one thing, he would have to have the German Army *with* him, not *against* him, the next time. In his closing address he played on the idea of reconciliation with the armed forces. There was no word of reproach for the Army.

I believe that the hour will come when the masses, who today stand in the street with our swastika banner, will unite with those who fired upon them . . . When I learned that it was the Green police which fired, I was happy that it was not the Reichswehr which had stained the record; the Reichswehr stands as untarnished as before. One day the hour will come when the Reichswehr will stand at our side, officers and men.

It was an accurate prediction, but here the presiding judge intervened. "Herr Hitler, you say that the Green police was stained. That I cannot permit."

The accused paid not the slightest attention to the admonition. In a peroration that held the audience in the courtroom spellbound Hitler spoke his final words:

The army we have formed is growing from day to day . . . I nourish the proud hope that one day the hour will come when these rough companies will grow to battalions, the battalions to regiments, the regiments to divisions, that the old cockade will be taken from the mud, that the old flags will wave again, that there will be a reconciliation at the last great divine judgment which we are prepared to face.

He turned his burning eyes directly on the judges.

For it is not you, gentlemen, who pass judgment on us. That judgment is spoken by the eternal court of history. What judgment you will hand down I know. But that court will not ask us, "Did you commit high treason or did you not?" That court will judge us, the Quartermaster General of the old Army [Ludendorff], his officers and soldiers, as Germans who wanted only the good of their own people and Fatherland, who wanted to fight and die. You may pronounce us guilty a thousand times over, but the goddess of the eternal court of history will smile and tear to tatters the brief of the state prosecutor and the sentence of this court. For she acquits us.[10]

The sentences, if not the verdicts, of the actual judges were, as Konrad Heiden wrote, not so far from the judgment of history. Ludendorff was acquitted. Hitler and the other accused were found guilty. But in the face of the law—Article 81 of the German Penal Code—which declared that "whosoever attempts to alter by force the Constitution of the German Reich or of any German state shall be punished by lifelong imprisonment," Hitler was sentenced to five years' imprisonment in the old fortress of Landsberg. Even then the lay judges protested the severity of the sentence, but they were assured by the presiding judge that the prisoner would be eligible for parole after he had served six months. Efforts of the police to get Hitler deported as a foreigner—he still held Austrian citizenship—came to nothing. The sentences were imposed on April 1, 1924. A little less than nine months later, on December 20, Hitler was released from prison, free to resume his fight to overthrow the democratic state. The consequences of committing high treason, if you were a man of the extreme Right, were not unduly heavy, despite the law, and a good many antirepublicans took notice of it.

The putsch, even though it was a fiasco, made Hitler a national figure and, in the eyes of many, a patriot and a hero. Nazi propaganda soon transformed it into one of the great legends of the movement. Each year, even after he came to power, even after World War II broke out, Hitler returned on the evening of November 8 to the beer hall in Munich to address his Old Guard comrades—the *alte Kaempfer,* as they were called —who had followed the leader to what seemed then such a grotesque disaster. In 1935 Hitler, the Chancellor, had the bodies of the sixteen Nazis who had fallen in the brief encounter dug up and placed in vaults in the Feldherrnhalle, which became a national shrine. Of them Hitler said, in dedicating the memorial, "They now pass into German immortality. Here they stand for Germany and keep guard over our people. Here they lie as true witnesses to our movement." He did not add, and no German seemed to recall, that they were also the men whom Hitler had abandoned to their dying when he had picked himself up from the pavement and ran away.

That summer of 1924 in the old fortress at Landsberg, high above the River Lech, Adolf Hitler, who was treated as an honored guest, with a room of his own and a splendid view, cleared out the visitors who flocked to pay him homage and bring him gifts, summoned the faithful Rudolf Hess, who had finally returned to Munich and received a sentence, and began to dictate to him chapter after chapter of a book.*

---

* Before the arrival of Hess, Emil Maurice, an ex-convict, a watchmaker and the first commander of the Nazi "strong-arm" squads, took some preliminary dictation.

4

THE MIND OF HITLER

AND THE ROOTS

OF THE THIRD REICH

Hitler wanted to call his book "Four and a Half Years of Struggle against Lies, Stupidity and Cowardice," but Max Amann, the hard-headed manager of the Nazi publishing business, who was to bring it out, rebelled against such a ponderous—and unsalable—title and shortened it to *My Struggle* (*Mein Kampf*). Amann was sorely disappointed in the contents. He had hoped, first, for a racy personal story in which Hitler would recount his rise from an unknown "worker" in Vienna to world renown. As we have seen, there was little autobiography in the book. The Nazi business manager had also counted on an inside story of the Beer Hall Putsch, the drama and double-dealing of which, he was sure, would make good reading. But Hitler was too shrewd at this point, when the party fortunes were at their lowest ebb, to rake over old coals.* There is scarcely a word of the unsuccessful putsch in *Mein Kampf*.

The first volume was published in the autumn of 1925. A work of some four hundred pages, it was priced at twelve marks (three dollars), about twice the price of most books brought out in Germany at that time. It did not by any means become an immediate best seller. Amann boasted that it sold 23,000 copies the first year and that sales continued upward—a claim that was received with skepticism in anti-Nazi circles.

Thanks to the Allied seizure in 1945 of the royalty statements of the Eher Verlag, the Nazi publishing firm, the facts about the actual sale of *Mein Kampf* can now be disclosed. In 1925 the book sold 9,473 copies, and thereafter for three years the sales decreased annually. They slumped

---

* "It is useless," he wrote at the end of the second volume, "to reopen wounds that seem scarcely healed; . . . useless to speak of guilt regarding men who in the bottom of their hearts, perhaps, were all devoted to their nation with equal love, and who only missed or failed to understand the common road." For a man so vindictive as Hitler, this showed unexpected tolerance of those who had crushed his rebellion and jailed him; or, in view of what happened later to Kahr and others who crossed him, it was perhaps more a display of will power—an ability to restrain himself momentarily for tactical reasons. At any rate, he refrained from recrimination.

to 6,913 in 1926, to 5,607 in 1927 and to a mere 3,015 in 1928, counting both volumes. They were up a little—to 7,664—in 1929, rose with the fortunes of the Nazi Party in 1930, when an inexpensive one-volume edition at eight marks appeared, to 54,086, dropped slightly to 50,808 the following year and jumped to 90,351 in 1932.

Hitler's royalties—his chief source of income from 1925 on—were considerable when averaged over those first seven years. But they were nothing compared to those received in 1933, the year he became Chancellor. In his first year of office *Mein Kampf* sold a million copies, and Hitler's income from the royalties, which had been increased from 10 to 15 per cent after January 1, 1933, was over one million marks (some $300,-000), making him the most prosperous author in Germany and for the first time a millionaire.* Except for the Bible, no other book sold as well during the Nazi regime, when few family households felt secure without a copy on the table. It was almost obligatory—and certainly politic—to present a copy to a bride and groom at their wedding, and nearly every school child received one on graduation from whatever school. By 1940, the year after World War II broke out, six million copies of the Nazi bible had been sold in Germany.[1]

Not every German who bought a copy of *Mein Kampf* necessarily read it. I have heard many a Nazi stalwart complain that it was hard going and not a few admit—in private—that they were never able to get through to the end of its 782 turgid pages. But it might be argued that had more non-Nazi Germans read it before 1933 and had the foreign statesmen of the world perused it carefully while there still was time, both Germany and the world might have been saved from catastrophe. For whatever other accusations can be made against Adolf Hitler, no one can accuse him of not putting down in writing exactly the kind of Germany he intended to make if he ever came to power and the kind of world he meant to create by armed German conquest. The blueprint of the Third Reich and, what is more, of the barbaric New Order which Hitler inflicted on conquered Europe in the triumphant years between 1939 and 1945 is set down in all its appalling crudity at great length and in detail between the covers of this revealing book.

As we have seen, Hitler's basic ideas were formed in his early twenties in Vienna, and we have his own word for it that he learned little afterward and altered nothing in his thinking.† When he left Austria for Germany in 1913 at the age of twenty-four, he was full of a burning passion for German nationalism, a hatred for democracy, Marxism and the Jews and a certainty that Providence had chosen the Aryans, especially the Germans, to be the master race.

---

* Like most writers, Hitler had his difficulties with the income tax collector—at least, as we shall see, until he became the dictator of Germany.
† See above, p. 21.

In *Mein Kampf* he expanded his views and applied them specifically to the problem of not only restoring a defeated and chaotic Germany to a place in the sun greater than it had ever had before but making a new kind of state, one which would be based on race and would include all Germans then living outside the Reich's frontiers, and in which would be established the absolute dictatorship of the Leader—himself—with an array of smaller leaders taking orders from above and giving them to those below. Thus the book contains, first, an outline of the future German state and of the means by which it can one day become "lord of the earth," as the author puts it on the very last page; and, second, a point of view, a conception of life, or, to use Hitler's favorite German word, a *Weltanschauung*. That this view of life would strike a normal mind of the twentieth century as a grotesque hodgepodge concocted by a half-baked, uneducated neurotic goes without saying. What makes it important is that it was embraced so fanatically by so many millions of Germans and that if it led, as it did, to their ultimate ruin it also led to the ruin of so many millions of innocent, decent human beings inside and especially outside Germany.

Now, how was the new Reich to regain her position as a world power and then go on to world mastery? Hitler pondered the question in the first volume, written mostly when he was in prison in 1924, returning to it at greater length in Volume Two, which was finished in 1926.

In the first place, there must be a reckoning with France, "the inexorable mortal enemy of the German people." The French aim, he said, would always be to achieve a "dismembered and shattered Germany . . . a hodgepodge of little states." This was so self-evident, Hitler added, that ". . . if I were a Frenchman . . . I could not and would not act any differently from Clemenceau." Therefore, there must be "a final active reckoning with France . . . a last decisive struggle . . . only then will we be able to end the eternal and essentially so fruitless struggle between ourselves and France; presupposing, of course, that Germany actually regards the destruction of France as only a means which will afterward enable her finally to give our people the expansion made possible elsewhere."[2]

Expansion elsewhere? Where? In this manner Hitler leads to the core of his ideas on German foreign policy which he was to attempt so faithfully to carry out when he became ruler of the Reich. *Germany, he said bluntly, must expand in the East—largely at the expense of Russia.*

In the first volume of *Mein Kampf* Hitler discoursed at length on this problem of *Lebensraum*—living space—a subject which obsessed him to his dying breath. The Hohenzollern Empire, he declared, had been mistaken in seeking colonies in Africa. "Territorial policy cannot be fulfilled in the Cameroons but today almost exclusively in Europe." But the soil of Europe was already occupied. True, Hitler recognized, "but nature has not reserved this soil for the future possession of any particular nation or race; on the contrary, this soil exists for the people which possesses the force to take it." What if the present possessors object? "Then the law of self-preservation goes into effect; and what is refused to amicable methods, it is up to the fist to take."[3]

Acquisition of new soil, Hitler continued, in explaining the blindness of German prewar foreign policy, "was possible only in the East . . . If land was desired in Europe, it could be obtained by and large only at the expense of Russia, and this meant that the new Reich must again set itself on the march along the road of the Teutonic Knights of old, to obtain by the German sword sod for the German plow and daily bread for the nation."[4]

As if he had not made himself entirely clear in the initial volume, Hitler returned to the subject in the second one.

Only an adequate large space on this earth assures a nation of freedom of existence . . . Without consideration of "traditions" and prejudices [the National Socialist movement] must find the courage to gather our people and their strength for an advance along the road that will lead this people from its present restricted living space to new land and soil . . . The National Socialist movement must strive to eliminate the disproportion between our population and our area—viewing this latter as a source of food as well as a basis for power politics . . . We must hold unflinchingly to our aim . . . to secure for the German people the land and soil to which they are entitled . . .[5]

How much land are the German people entitled to? The bourgeoisie, says Hitler scornfully, "which does not possess a single creative political idea for the future," had been clamoring for the restoration of the 1914 German frontiers.

The demand for restoration of the frontiers of 1914 is a political absurdity of such proportions and consequences as to make it seem a crime. Quite aside from the fact that the Reich's frontiers in 1914 were anything but logical. For in reality they were neither complete in the sense of embracing the people of German nationality nor sensible with regard to geomilitary expediency. They were not the result of a considered political action, but momentary frontiers in a political struggle that was by no means concluded . . . With equal right and in many cases with more right, some other sample year of German history could be picked out, and the restoration of the conditions at that time declared to be the aim in foreign affairs.[6]

Hitler's "sample year" would go back some six centuries, to when the Germans were driving the Slavs back in the East. The push eastward must be resumed. "Today we count eighty million Germans in Europe! This foreign policy will be acknowledged as correct only if, after scarcely a hundred years, there are two hundred and fifty million Germans on this continent."[7] And all of them within the borders of the new and expanded Reich.

Some other peoples, obviously, will have to make way for so many Germans. What other peoples?

And so we National Socialists . . . take up where we broke off six hundred years ago. We stop the endless German movement to the south and west, and turn our gaze toward the land in the East.

If we speak of soil in Europe today, we can primarily have in mind only Russia and her vassal border states.[*8]

Fate, Hitler remarks, was kind to Germany in this respect. It had handed over Russia to Bolshevism, which, he says, really meant handing over Russia to the Jews. "The giant empire in the East," he exults, "is ripe for collapse. And the end of Jewish rule in Russia will also be the end of Russia as a state." So the great steppes to the East, Hitler implies, could be taken over easily on Russia's collapse without much cost in blood to the Germans.

Can anyone contend that the blueprint here is not clear and precise? France will be destroyed, but that is secondary to the German drive eastward. First the immediate lands to the East inhabited predominantly by Germans will be taken. And what are these? Obviously Austria, the Sudetenland in Czechoslovakia and the western part of Poland, including Danzig. After that, Russia herself. Why was the world so surprised, then, when Chancellor Hitler, a bare few years later, set out to achieve these very ends?

On the nature of the future Nazi State, Hitler's ideas in *Mein Kampf* are less concise. He made it clear enough that there would be no "democratic nonsense" and that the Third Reich would be ruled by the *Fuehrerprinzip,* the leadership principle—that is, that it would be a dictatorship. There is almost nothing about economics in the book. The subject bored Hitler and he never bothered to try to learn something about it beyond toying with the crackpot ideas of Gottfried Feder, the crank who was against "interest slavery."

What interested Hitler was political power; economics could somehow take care of itself.

The state has nothing at all to do with any definite economic conception or development . . . The state is a racial organism and not an economic organization . . . The inner strength of a state coincides only in the rarest cases with so-called economic prosperity; the latter, in innumerable cases, seems to indicate the state's approaching decline . . . Prussia demonstrates with marvelous sharpness that not material qualities but ideal virtues alone make possible the formation of a state. Only under their protection can economic life flourish. Always when in Germany there was an upsurge of political power

---

The italics are mine.

the economic conditions began to improve; but always when economics became the sole content of our people's life, stifling the ideal virtues, the state collapsed and in a short time drew economic life with it . . . Never yet has a state been founded by peaceful economic means . . .[9]

Therefore, as Hitler said in a speech in Munich in 1923, "no economic policy is possible without a sword, no industrialization without power." Beyond that vague, crude philosophy and a passing reference in *Mein Kampf* to "economic chambers," "chambers of estates" and a "central economic parliament" which "would keep the national economy functioning," Hitler refrains from any expression of opinion on the economic foundation of the Third Reich.

And though the very name of the Nazi Party proclaimed it as "socialist," Hitler was even more vague on the kind of "socialism" he envisaged for the new Germany. This is not surprising in view of a definition of a "socialist" which he gave in a speech on July 28, 1922:

Whoever is prepared to make the national cause his own to such an extent that he knows no higher ideal than the welfare of his nation; whoever has understood our great national anthem, "Deutschland ueber Alles," to mean that nothing in the wide world surpasses in his eyes this Germany, people and land—that man is a Socialist.[10]

Considerable editorial advice and even pruning on the part of at least three helpers could not prevent Hitler from meandering from one subject to another in *Mein Kampf*. Rudolf Hess, who took most of the dictation first at Landsberg prison and later at Haus Wachenfeld near Berchtesgaden, did his best to tidy up the manuscript, but he was no man to stand up to the Leader. More successful in this respect was Father Bernhard Stempfle, a former member of the Hieronymite order and an anti-Semitic journalist of some notoriety in Bavaria. This strange priest, of whom more will be heard in this history, corrected some of Hitler's bad grammar, straightened out what prose he could and crossed out a few passages which he convinced the author were politically objectionable. The third adviser was Josef Czerny, of Czech origin, who worked on the Nazi newspaper, *Voelkischer Beobachter,* and whose anti-Jewish poetry endeared him to Hitler. Czerny was instrumental in revising the first volume of *Mein Kampf* for its second printing, in which certain embarrassing words and sentences were eliminated or changed; and he went over carefully the proofs of Volume Two.

Nevertheless, most of the meanderings remained. Hitler insisted on airing his thoughts at random on almost every conceivable subject, including culture, education, the theater, the movies, the comics, art, literature, history, sex, marriage, prostitution and syphilis. Indeed, on the subject of syphilis, Hitler devotes ten turgid pages, declaring it is "*the* task of the nation—not just *one more* task,"* to eradicate it. To combat this dread disease Hitler demands that all the propaganda resources of the nation be mobilized. "Everything," he says, "depends on the solution of this question." The problem of syphilis and prostitution must also be attacked, he states, by facilitating earlier marriages, and he gives a foretaste of the eugenics of the Third Reich by insisting that "marriage cannot be an end in itself, but must serve the one higher goal: the increase and preservation of the species and the race. This alone is its meaning and its task."[11]

And so with this mention of the preservation of the species and of the race in *Mein Kampf* we come to the second principal consideration: Hitler's *Weltanschauung,* his view of life, which some historians, especially in England, have seen as a crude form of Darwinism but which in reality, as we shall see, has its roots deep in German history and thought. Like Darwin but also like a whole array of German philosophers, historians, kings, generals and statesmen, Hitler saw all life as an eternal struggle and the world as a jungle where the fittest survived and the strongest ruled—a "world where one creature feeds on the other and where the death of the weaker implies the life of the stronger."

Mein Kampf is studded with such pronouncements: "In the end only the urge for self-preservation can conquer . . . Mankind has grown great in eternal struggle, and only in eternal peace does it perish. . . . Nature . . . puts living creatures on this globe and watches the free play of forces. She then confers the master's right on her favorite child, the strongest in courage and industry . . . The stronger must dominate and not blend with the weaker, thus sacrificing his own greatness. Only the born weakling can view this as cruel . . ." For Hitler the preservation of culture "is bound up with the rigid law of necessity and the right to victory of the best and strongest in the world. Those who want to live, let them fight, and those who do not want to fight, in this world of eternal struggle, do not deserve to live. Even if this were hard—that is how it is!"[12]

And who is "nature's favorite child, the strongest in courage and industry" on whom Providence has conferred "the master's right"? The Aryan. Here in *Mein Kampf* we come to the kernel of the Nazi idea of race superiority, of the conception of the master race, on which the Third Reich and Hitler's New Order in Europe were based.

All the human culture, all the results of art, science and technology that we see before us today, are almost exclusively the creative product of the Aryan. This very fact admits of the not unfounded inference that he alone was the founder of all higher humanity, therefore representing the prototype of all that we understand by the word "man." He is the Prometheus of mankind from whose shining brow the divine spark of genius has sprung at all times,

---

* The italics are Hitler's.

forever kindling anew that fire of knowledge which illumined the night of silent mysteries and thus caused man to climb the path to mastery over the other beings of this earth . . . It was he who laid the foundations and erected the walls of every great structure in human culture.[13]

And how did the Aryan accomplish so much and become so supreme? Hitler's answer is: By trampling over others. Like so many German thinkers of the nineteenth century, Hitler fairly revels in a sadism (and its opposite, masochism) which foreign students of the German spirit have always found so difficult to comprehend.

Thus, for the formation of higher cultures the existence of lower human types was one of the most essential preconditions . . . It is certain that the first culture of humanity was based less on the tamed animal than on the use of lower human beings. Only after the enslavement of subject races did the same fate strike beasts. For first the conquered warrior drew the plow—and only after him the horse. Hence it is no accident that the first cultures arose in places where the Aryan, in his encounters with lower peoples, subjugated them and bent them to his will . . . As long as he ruthlessly upheld the master attitude, not only did he remain master, but also the preserver and increaser of culture.[14]

Then something happened which Hitler took as a warning to the Germans.

As soon as the subjected people began to raise themselves up and approach the level of their conqueror, a phase of which probably was the use of his language, the barriers between master and servant broke down.

But even worse than sharing the master's language was something else.

The Aryan gave up the purity of his blood and, therefore, lost his sojourn in the paradise which he had made for himself. He became submerged in a racial mixture and gradually lost his cultural creativeness.

To the young Nazi leader this was the cardinal error.

Blood mixture and the resultant drop in the racial level is the sole cause of the dying out of old cultures; for men do not perish as a result of lost wars, but by the loss of that force of resistance which is continued only in pure blood. All who are not of good race in this world are chaff.[15]

Chaff were the Jews and the Slavs, and in time, when he became dictator and conqueror, Hitler would forbid the marriage of a German with any member of these races, though a fourth-grade schoolmarm could have told him that there was a great deal of Slavic blood in the Germans, especially in those who dwelt in the eastern provinces. In carrying out his racial ideas, it must again be admitted, Hitler was as good as his word. In the New Order which he began to impose on the Slavs in the East during the war, the Czechs, the Poles, the Russians were—and were to remain, if the grotesque New Order had endured—the hewers of wood and the drawers of water for their German masters.

It was an easy step for a man as ignorant of history and anthropology as Hitler to make of the Germans the modern Aryans—and thus the master race. To Hitler the Germans are "the highest species of humanity on this earth" and will remain so if they "occupy themselves not merely with the breeding of dogs, horses and cats but also with care for the purity of their own blood."[16]

Hitler's obsession with race leads to his advocacy of the "folkish" state. Exactly what kind of state that was—or was intended to be—I never clearly understood despite many rereadings of *Mein Kampf* and listening to dozens of addresses on the subject by the Fuehrer himself, though more than once I heard the dictator declare that it was the central point of his whole thinking. The German word *Volk* cannot be translated accurately into English. Usually it is rendered as "nation" or "people," but in German there is a deeper and somewhat different meaning that connotes a primitive, tribal community based on blood and soil. In *Mein Kampf* Hitler has a difficult time trying to define the folkish state, announcing, for example, on page 379 that he will clarify "the 'folkish' concept" only to shy away from any clarification and wander off on other subjects for several pages. Finally he has a go at it:

In opposition to [the bourgeois and the Marxist-Jewish worlds], the folkish philosophy finds the importance of mankind in its basic racial elements. In the state it sees only a means to an end and construes its end as the preservation of the racial existence of man. Thus, it by no means believes in an equality of races, but along with their difference it recognizes their higher or lesser value and feels itself obligated to promote the victory of the better and stronger, and demand the subordination of the inferior and weaker in accordance with the eternal will that dominates this universe. Thus, in principle, it serves the basic aristocratic idea of nature and believes in the validity of this law down to the last individual. It sees not only the different value of the races, but also the different value of individuals. From the mass it extracts the importance of the individual personality and thus . . . it has an organizing effect. It believes in the necessity of an idealization of humanity, in which alone it sees the premise for the existence of humanity. But it cannot grant the right to existence even to an ethical idea if this idea represents a danger for the racial life of the bearers of a higher ethics; for in a bastardized and niggerized world all the concepts of the humanly beautiful and sublime, as well as all ideas of an idealized future of our humanity, would be lost forever . . .

And so the folkish philosophy of life corresponds to the innermost will of nature, since it restores that free play of forces which must lead to a continuous mutual higher breeding, until at last the best of humanity, having achieved possession of this earth, will have a free path for activity in domains which will lie partly above it and partly outside it.

We all sense that in the distant future humanity must be faced by problems which only a highest race, become master people and supported by the means and possibilities of an entire globe, will be equipped to overcome.[17]

"Thus," Hitler declares a little farther on, "the highest purpose of a folkish state is concern for the preservation of those original racial elements which bestow culture and create the beauty and dignity of a higher mankind."[18] This again leads him to a matter of eugenics:

The folkish state . . . must set race in the center of all life. It must take care to keep it pure . . . It must see to it that only the healthy beget children; that there is only one disgrace: despite one's own sickness and deficiencies, to bring children into the world; and one highest honor: to renounce doing so. And conversely it must be considered reprehensible to withhold healthy children from the nation. Here the [folkish] state must act as guardian of a millennial future in the face of which the wishes and the selfishness of the individual must appear as nothing and submit . . . A folkish state must therefore begin by raising marriage from the level of a continuous defilement of the race and give it the consecration of an institution which is called upon to produce images of the Lord and not monstrosities halfway between man and ape.[19]

Hitler's fantastic conception of the folkish state leads to a good many other wordy considerations which, if heeded, he says, will bring the Germans the mastery of the earth—German domination has become an obsession with him. At one point he argues that the failure to keep the Germanic race simon-pure "has robbed us of world domination. If the German people had possessed that herd unity which other peoples enjoyed, the German Reich today would doubtless be mistress of the globe."[20] Since a folkish state must be based on race, "the German Reich must embrace all Germans"—this is a key point in his argument, and one he did not forget nor fail to act upon when he came to power.

Since the folkish state is to be based "on the aristocratic idea of nature" it follows that democracy is out of the question and must be replaced by the *Fuehrerprinzip*. The authoritarianism of the Prussian Army is to be adopted by the Third Reich: "authority of every leader downward and responsibility upward."

There must be no majority decisions, but only responsible persons . . . Surely every man will have advisers by his side, but *the decision will be made by one man.** . . . only he alone may possess the authority and the right to command . . . It will not be possible to dispense with Parliament. But their councilors will then actually give counsel . . . In no chamber does a

---

* The italics are Hitler's.

vote ever take place. They are working institutions and not voting machines. This principle—absolute responsibility unconditionally combined with absolute authority—will gradually breed an elite of leaders such as today, in this era of irresponsible parliamentarianism, is utterly inconceivable.[21]

Such were the ideas of Adolf Hitler, set down in all their appalling crudeness as he sat in Landsberg prison gazing out at a flowering orchard above the River Lech,* or later, in 1925–26, as he reclined on the balcony of a comfortable inn at Berchtesgaden and looked out across the towering Alps toward his native Austria, dictating a torrent of words to his faithful Rudolf Hess and dreaming of the Third Reich which he would build on the shoddy foundations we have seen, and which he would rule with an iron hand. That one day he would build it and rule it he had no doubts whatsoever, for he was possessed of that burning sense of mission peculiar to so many geniuses who have sprouted, seemingly, from nowhere and from nothing throughout the ages. He would unify a chosen people who had never before been politically one. He would purify their race. He would make them strong. He would make them lords of the earth.

A crude Darwinism? A sadistic fancy? An irresponsible egoism? A megalomania? It was all of these in part. But it was something more. For the mind and the passion of Hitler—all the aberrations that possessed his feverish brain—had roots that lay deep in German experience and thought. Nazism and the Third Reich, in fact, were but a logical continuation of German history.

THE HISTORICAL ROOTS OF THE THIRD REICH

In the delirious days of the annual rallies of the Nazi Party at Nuremberg at the beginning of September, I used to be accosted by a swarm of hawkers selling a picture postcard on which were shown the portraits of Frederick the Great, Bismarck, Hindenburg and Hitler. The inscription read: "What the King conquered, the Prince formed, the Field Marshal defended, the Soldier saved and unified." Thus Hitler, the soldier, was portrayed not only as the savior and unifier of Germany but as the successor of these celebrated figures who had made the country great. The implication of the continuity of German history, culminating in Hitler's rule, was not lost upon the multitude. The very expression "the Third Reich" also served to strengthen this concept. The First Reich had been

---

* "Without my imprisonment," Hitler remarked long afterward, "*Mein Kampf* would never have been written. That period gave me the chance of deepening various notions for which I then had only an instinctive feeling . . . It's from this time, too, that my conviction dates—a thing that many of my supporters never understood—that we could no longer win power by force. The state had had time to consolidate itself, and it had the weapons." (*Hitler's Secret Conversations*, p. 235.) The remark was made to some of his cronies at headquarters on the Russian front on the night of February 3–4, 1942.

the medieval Holy Roman Empire; the Second Reich had been that which was formed by Bismarck in 1871 after Prussia's defeat of France. Both had added glory to the German name. The Weimar Republic, as Nazi propaganda had it, had dragged that fair name in the mud. The Third Reich restored it, just as Hitler had promised. Hitler's Germany, then, was depicted as a logical development from all that had gone before— or at least of all that had been glorious.

But the onetime Vienna vagabond, however littered his mind, knew enough history to realize that there had been German failures in the past, failures that must be set against the successes of France and Britain. He never forgot that by the end of the Middle Ages, which had seen Britain and France emerge as unified nations, Germany remained a crazy patchwork of some three hundred individual states. It was this lack of national development which largely determined the course of German history from the end of the Middle Ages to midway in the nineteenth century and made it so different from that of the other great nations of Western Europe.

To the lack of political and dynastic unity was added, in the sixteenth and seventeenth centuries, the disaster of religious differences which followed the Reformation. There is not space in this book to recount adequately the immense influence that Martin Luther, the Saxon peasant who became an Augustinian monk and launched the German Reformation, had on the Germans and their subsequent history. But it may be said, in passing, that this towering but erratic genius, this savage anti-Semite and hater of Rome, who combined in his tempestuous character so many of the best and the worst qualities of the German—the coarseness, the boisterousness, the fanaticism, the intolerance, the violence, but also the honesty, the simplicity, the self-scrutiny, the passion for learning and for music and for poetry and for righteousness in the eyes of God— left a mark on the life of the Germans, for both good and bad, more indelible, more fateful, than was wrought by any other single individual before or since. Through his sermons and his magnificent translation of the Bible, Luther created the modern German language, aroused in the people not only a new Protestant vision of Christianity but a fervent German nationalism and taught them, at least in religion, the supremacy of the individual conscience. But tragically for them, Luther's siding with the princes in the peasant risings, which he had largely inspired, and his passion for political autocracy ensured a mindless and provincial political absolutism which reduced the vast majority of the German people to poverty, to a horrible torpor and a demeaning subservience. Even worse perhaps, it helped to perpetuate and indeed to sharpen the hopeless divisions not only between classes but also between the various dynastic and political groupings of the German people. It doomed for centuries the possibility of the unification of Germany.

The Thirty Years' War and the Peace of Westphalia of 1648, which ended it, brought the final catastrophe to Germany, a blow so devastating that the country has never fully recovered from it. This was the last of Europe's great religious wars, but before it was over it had degenerated from a Protestant–Catholic conflict into a confused dynastic struggle between the Catholic Austrian Hapsburgs on the one side and the Catholic French Bourbons and the Swedish Protestant monarchy on the other. In the savage fighting, Germany itself was laid waste, the towns and countryside were devastated and ravished, the people decimated. It has been estimated that one third of the German people perished in this barbarous war.

The Peace of Westphalia was almost as disastrous to the future of Germany as the war had been. The German princes, who had sided with France and Sweden, were confirmed as absolute rulers of their little domains, some 350 of them, the Emperor remaining merely as a figurehead so far as the German lands were concerned. The surge of reform and enlightenment which had swept Germany at the end of the fifteenth and the beginning of the sixteenth centuries was smothered. In that period the great free cities had enjoyed virtual independence; feudalism was gone in them, the arts and commerce thrived. Even in the countryside the German peasant had secured liberties far greater than those enjoyed in England and France. Indeed, at the beginning of the sixteenth century Germany could be said to be one of the fountains of European civilization.

Now, after the Peace of Westphalia, it was reduced to the barbarism of Muscovy. Serfdom was reimposed, even introduced in areas where it had been unknown. The towns lost their self-government. The peasants, the laborers, even the middle-class burghers, were exploited to the limit by the princes, who held them down in a degrading state of servitude. The pursuit of learning and the arts all but ceased. The greedy rulers had no feeling for German nationalism and patriotism and stamped out any manifestations of them in their subjects. Civilization came to a standstill in Germany. The Reich, as one historian has put it, "was artificially stabilized at a medieval level of confusion and weakness."[22]

Germany never recovered from this setback. Acceptance of autocracy, of blind obedience to the petty tyrants who ruled as princes, became ingrained in the German mind. The idea of democracy, of rule by parliament, which made such rapid headway in England in the seventeenth and eighteenth centuries, and which exploded in France in 1789, did not sprout in Germany. This political backwardness of the Germans, divided as they were into so many petty states and isolated in them from the surging currents of European thought and development, set Germany apart from and behind the other countries of the West. There was no natural growth of a nation. This has to be borne in mind if one is to comprehend the disastrous road this people subsequently took and the warped state of mind which settled over it. In the end the German nation was forged by naked force and held together by naked aggression

Beyond the Elbe to the east lay Prussia. As the nineteenth century waned, this century which had seen the sorry failure of the confused and timid liberals at Frankfurt in 1848–49 to create a somewhat democratic, unified Germany, Prussia took over the German destiny. For centuries this Germanic state had lain outside the main stream of German historical development and culture. It seemed almost as if it were a freak of history. Prussia had begun as the remote frontier state of Brandenburg on the sandy wastes east of the Elbe which, beginning with the eleventh century, had been slowly conquered from the Slavs. Under Brandenburg's ruling princes, the Hohenzollerns, who were little more than military adventurers, the Slavs, mostly Poles, were gradually pushed back along the Baltic. Those who resisted were either exterminated or made landless serfs. The imperial law of the German Empire forbade the princes from assuming royal titles, but in 1701 the Emperor acquiesced in the Elector Frederick III's being crowned King *in* Prussia at Koenigsberg.

By this time Prussia had pulled itself up by its own bootstraps to be one of the ranking military powers of Europe. It had none of the resources of the others. Its land was barren and bereft of minerals. The population was small. There were no large towns, no industry and little culture. Even the nobility was poor, and the landless peasants lived like cattle. Yet by a supreme act of will and a genius for organization the Hohenzollerns managed to create a Spartan military state whose well-drilled Army won one victory after another and whose Machiavellian diplomacy of temporary alliances with whatever power seemed the strongest brought constant additions to its territory.

There thus arose quite artificially a state born of no popular force nor even of an idea except that of conquest, and held together by the absolute power of the ruler, by a narrow-minded bureaucracy which did his bidding and by a ruthlessly disciplined army. Two thirds and sometimes as much as five sixths of the annual state revenue was expended on the Army, which became, under the King, the state itself. "Prussia," remarked Mirabeau, "is not a state with an army, but an army with a state." And the state, which was run with the efficiency and soullessness of a factory, became all; the people were little more than cogs in the machinery. Individuals were taught not only by the kings and the drill sergeants but by the philosophers that their role in life was one of obedience, work, sacrifice and duty. Even Kant preached that duty demands the suppression of human feeling, and the Prussian poet Willibald Alexis gloried in the enslavement of the people under the Hohenzollerns. To Lessing, who did not like it, "Prussia was the most slavish country of Europe."

The Junkers, who were to play such a vital role in modern Germany, were also a unique product of Prussia. They were, as they said, a master race. It was they who occupied the land conquered from the Slavs and who farmed it on large estates worked by these Slavs, who became landless serfs quite different from those in the West. There was an essential difference between the agrarian system in Prussia and that of western Germany and Western Europe. In the latter, the nobles, who owned most of the land, received rents or feudal dues from the peasants, who though often kept in a state of serfdom had certain rights and privileges and could, and did, gradually acquire their own land and civic freedom. In the West, the peasants formed a solid part of the community; the landlords, for all their drawbacks, developed in their leisure a cultivation which led to, among other things, a civilized quality of life that could be seen in the refinement of manners, of thought and of the arts.

The Prussian Junker was not a man of leisure. He worked hard at managing his large estate, much as a factory manager does today. His landless laborers were treated as virtual slaves. On his large properties he was the absolute lord. There were no large towns nor any substantial middle class, as there were in the West, whose civilizing influence might rub against him. In contrast to the cultivated *grand seigneur* in the West, the Junker developed into a rude, domineering, arrogant type of man, without cultivation or culture, aggressive, conceited, ruthless, narrow-minded and given to a petty profit-seeking that some German historians noted in the private life of Otto von Bismarck, the most successful of the Junkers.

It was this political genius, this apostle of "blood and iron," who between 1866 and 1871 brought an end to a divided Germany which had existed for nearly a thousand years and, by force, replaced it with Greater Prussia, or what might be called Prussian Germany. Bismarck's unique creation is the Germany we have known in our time, a problem child of Europe and the world for nearly a century, a nation of gifted, vigorous people in which first this remarkable man and then Kaiser Wilhelm II and finally Hitler, aided by a military caste and by many a strange intellectual, succeeded in inculcating a lust for power and domination, a passion for unbridled militarism, a contempt for democracy and individual freedom and a longing for authority, for authoritarianism. Under such a spell, this nation rose to great heights, fell and rose again, until it was seemingly destroyed with the end of Hitler in the spring of 1945—it is perhaps too early to speak of that with any certainty.

"The great questions of the day," Bismarck declared on becoming Prime Minister of Prussia in 1862, "will not be settled by resolutions and majority votes—that was the mistake of the men of 1848 and 1849—but by blood and iron." That was exactly the way he proceeded to settle them, though it must be said that he added a touch of diplomatic finesse, often of the most deceitful kind. Bismarck's aim was to destroy liberalism, bolster the power of conservatism—that is, of the Junkers, the Army and the crown—and make Prussia, as against Austria, the dominant power not only among the Germans but, if possible, in Europe as well. "Germany looks not to Prussia's liberalism," he told the deputies in the Prussian parliament, "but to her force."

Bismarck first built up the Prussian Army and when the parliament re-fused to vote the additional credits he merely raised them on his own and finally dissolved the chamber. With a strengthened Army he then struck in three successive wars. The first, against Denmark in 1864, brought the duchies of Schleswig and Holstein under German rule. The second, against Austria in 1866, had far-reaching consequences. Austria, which for centuries had been first among the German states, was finally excluded from German affairs. It was not allowed to join the North German Confederation which Bismarck now proceeded to establish.

"In 1866," the eminent German political scientist Wilhelm Roepke once wrote, "Germany ceased to exist." Prussia annexed outright all the German states north of the Main which had fought against her, except Saxony; these included Hanover, Hesse, Nassau, Frankfurt and the Elbe duchies. All the other states north of the Main were forced into the North German Confederation. Prussia, which now stretched from the Rhine to Koenigsberg, completely dominated it, and within five years, with the defeat of Napoleon III's France, the southern German states, with the considerable kingdom of Bavaria in the lead, would be drawn into Prussian Germany.[23]

Bismarck's crowning achievement, the creation of the Second Reich, came on January 18, 1871, when King Wilhelm I of Prussia was proclaimed Emperor of Germany in the Hall of Mirrors at Versailles. Germany had been unified by Prussian armed force. It was now the greatest power on the Continent; its only rival in Europe was England.

Yet there was a fatal flaw. The German Empire, as Treitschke said, was in reality but an extension of Prussia. "Prussia," he emphasized, "is the dominant factor . . . The will of the Empire can be nothing but the will of the Prussian state." This was true, and it was to have disastrous consequences for the Germans themselves. From 1871 to 1933 and indeed to Hitler's end in 1945, the course of German history as a consequence was to run, with the exception of the interim of the Weimar Republic, in a straight line and with utter logic.

Despite the democratic façade put up by the establishment of the Reichstag, whose members were elected by universal manhood suffrage, the German Empire was in reality a militarist autocracy ruled by the King of Prussia, who was also Emperor. The Reichstag possessed few powers; it was little more than a debating society where the representatives of the people let off steam or bargained for shoddy benefits for the classes they represented. The throne had the power—by divine right. As late as 1910 Wilhelm II could proclaim that the royal crown had been "granted by God's Grace alone and not by parliaments, popular assemblies and popular decision . . . Considering myself an instrument of the Lord," he added, "I go my way."

He was not impeded by Parliament. The Chancellor he appointed was responsible to him, not to the Reichstag. The assembly could not overthrow a Chancellor nor keep him in office. That was the prerogative of the monarch. Thus, in contrast to the development in other countries in the West, the idea of democracy, of the people sovereign, of the supremacy of parliament, never got a foothold in Germany, even after the twentieth century began. To be sure, the Social Democrats, after years of persecution by Bismarck and the Emperor, had become the largest single political party in the Reichstag by 1912. They loudly demanded the establishment of a parliamentary democracy. But they were ineffective. And, though the largest party, they were still a minority. The middle classes, grown prosperous by the belated but staggering development of the industrial revolution and dazzled by the success of Bismarck's policy of force and war, had traded for material gain any aspirations for political freedom they may have had.* They accepted the Hohenzollern autocracy. They gladly knuckled under to the Junker bureaucracy and they fervently embraced Prussian militarism. Germany's star had risen and they—almost all the people—were eager to do what their masters asked to keep it high.

At the very end, Hitler, the Austrian, was one of them. To him Bismarck's Second Reich, despite its mistakes and its "terrifying forces of decay" was a work of splendor in which the Germans at last had come into their own.

Was not Germany above all other countries a marvelous example of an empire which had risen from foundations of a policy purely of power? Prussia, the germ cell of the Empire, came into being through resplendent heroism and not through financial operations or commercial deals, and the Reich itself in turn was only the glorious reward of aggressive political leadership and the death-defying courage of its soldiers . . .

The very founding of the [Second] Reich seemed gilded by the magic of an event which uplifted the entire nation. After a series of incomparable victories, a Reich was born for the sons and grandsons—a reward for immortal heroism . . . This Reich, which did not owe its existence to the trickery of parliamentary fractions, towered above the measure of other states by the very exalted manner of its founding; for not in the cackling of a parliamentary battle of words but in the thunder and rumbling of the front surrounding Paris was the solemn act performed: a proclamation of our will, declaring that the Germans, princes and people, were resolved in the future to constitute a Reich and once again to raise the imperial crown to symbolic heights . . . No deserters and slackers were the founders of the Bismarckian state, but the regiments at the front.

This unique birth and baptism of fire in themselves surrounded the Reich with a halo of historic glory such as only the oldest states—and they but seldom—could boast.

And what an ascent now began!

Freedom on the outside provided daily bread within. The nation became rich in numbers and earthly goods. The honor of the state, and with it that

---

* In a sense the German working class made a similar trade. To combat socialism Bismarck put through between 1883 and 1889 a program for social security far beyond anything known in other countries. It included compulsory insurance for workers against old age, sickness, accident and incapacity, and though organized by the State it was financed by employers and employees. It cannot be said that it stopped the rise of the Social Democrats or the trade unions, but it did have a profound influence on the working class in that it gradually made them value security over political freedom and caused them to see in the State, however conservative, a benefactor and a protector. Hitler, as we shall see, took full advantage of this state of mind. In this, as in other matters, he learned much from Bismarck. "I studied Bismarck's socialist legislation," Hitler remarks in *Mein Kampf* (p. 155), "in its intention, struggle and success."

of the whole people, was protected and shielded by an army which could point most visibly to the difference from the former German Union.[24]

That was the Germany which Hitler resolved to restore. In *Mein Kampf* he discourses at great length on what he believes are the reasons for its fall: its tolerance of Jews and Marxists, the crass materialism and selfishness of the middle class, the nefarious influence of the "cringers and lickspittles" around the Hohenzollern throne, the "catastrophic German alliance policy" which linked Germany to the degenerate Hapsburgs and the untrustworthy Italians instead of with England, and the lack of a fundamental "social" and racial policy. These were failures which, he promised, National Socialism would correct.

THE INTELLECTUAL ROOTS OF THE THIRD REICH

But aside from history, where did Hitler get his ideas? Though his opponents inside and outside Germany were too busy, or too stupid, to take much notice of it until it was too late, he had somehow absorbed, as had so many Germans, a weird mixture of the irresponsible, megalomaniacal ideas which erupted from German thinkers during the nineteenth century. Hitler, who often got them at second hand through such a muddled pseudo philosopher as Alfred Rosenberg or through his drunken poet friend Dietrich Eckart, embraced them with all the feverish enthusiasm of a neophyte. What was worse, he resolved to put them into practice if the opportunity should ever arise.

We have seen what they were as they thrashed about in Hitler's mind: the glorification of war and conquest and the absolute power of the authoritarian state; the belief in the Aryans, or Germans, as the master race, and the hatred of Jews and Slavs; the contempt for democracy and humanism. They are not original with Hitler—though the means of applying them later proved to be. They emanate from that odd assortment of erudite but unbalanced philosophers, historians and teachers who captured the German mind during the century before Hitler with consequences so disastrous, as it turned out, not only for the Germans but for a large portion of mankind.

There had been among the Germans, to be sure, some of the most elevated minds and spirits of the Western world—Leibnitz, Kant, Herder, Humboldt, Lessing, Goethe, Schiller, Bach and Beethoven—and they had made unique contributions to the civilization of the West. But the German culture which became dominant in the nineteenth century and which coincided with the rise of Prussian Germany, continuing from Bismarck through Hitler, rests primarily on Fichte and Hegel, to begin with, and then on Treitschke, Nietzsche, Richard Wagner, and a host of lesser lights not the least of whom, strangely enough, were a bizarre Frenchman and an eccentric Englishman. They succeeded in establishing a spiritual break with the West; the breach has not been healed to this day.

In 1807, following Prussia's humiliating defeat by Napoleon at Jena, Johann Gottlieb Fichte began his famous "Addresses to the German Nation" from the podium of the University of Berlin, where he held the chair of philosophy. They stirred and rallied a divided, defeated people and their resounding echoes could still be heard in the Third Reich. Fichte's teaching was heady wine for a frustrated folk. To him the Latins, especially the French, and the Jews are the decadent races. Only the Germans possess the possibility of regeneration. Their language is the purest, the most original. Under them a new era in history would blossom. It would reflect the order of the cosmos. It would be led by a small elite which would be free of any moral restraints of a "private" nature. These are some of the ideas we have seen Hitler putting down in *Mein Kampf*.

On Fichte's death in 1814, he was succeeded by Georg Wilhelm Friedrich Hegel at the University of Berlin. This is the subtle and penetrating mind whose dialectics inspired Marx and Lenin and thus contributed to the founding of Communism and whose ringing glorification of the State as supreme in human life paved the way for the Second and Third Reichs of Bismarck and Hitler. To Hegel the State is all, or almost all. Among other things, he says, it is the highest revelation of the "world spirit"; it is the "moral universe"; it is "the actuality of the ethical idea . . . ethical mind . . . knowing and thinking itself"; the State "has the supreme right against the individual, whose supreme duty is to be a member of the State . . . for the right of the world spirit is above all special privileges . . ."

And the happiness of the individual on earth? Hegel replies that "world history is no empire of happiness. The periods of happiness," he declares, "are the empty pages of history because they are the periods of agreement, without conflict." War is the great purifier. In Hegel's view, it makes for "the ethical health of peoples corrupted by a long peace, as the blowing of the winds preserves the sea from the foulness which would be the result of a prolonged calm."

No traditional conception of morals and ethics must disturb either the supreme State or the "heroes" who lead it. "World history occupies a higher ground . . . Moral claims which are irrelevant must not be brought into collision with world-historical deeds and their accomplishments. The litany of private virtues—modesty, humility, philanthropy and forbearance—must not be raised against them . . . So mighty a form [the State] must trample down many an innocent flower—crush to pieces many an object in its path."

Hegel foresees such a State for Germany when she has recovered her God-given genius. He predicts that "Germany's hour" will come and that its mission will be to regenerate the world. As one reads Hegel one realizes how much inspiration Hitler, like Marx, drew from him, even if it was at second hand. Above all else, Hegel in his theory of "heroes," those great agents who are fated by a mysterious Providence to carry out "the will of the world spirit," seems to have inspired Hitler, as we shall see at the end of this chapter, with his own overpowering sense of mission.

Heinrich von Treitschke came later to the University of Berlin. From 1874 until his death in 1896 he was a professor of history there and a popular one, his lectures being attended by large and enthusiastic gatherings which included not only students but General Staff officers and officials of the Junker bureaucracy. His influence on German thought in the last quarter of the century was enormous and it continued through Wilhelm II's day and indeed Hitler's. Though he was a Saxon, he became the great Prussianizer; he was more Prussian than the Prussians. Like Hegel he glorifies the State and conceives of it as supreme, but his attitude is more brutish: the people, the subjects, are to be little more than slaves in the nation. "It does not matter what you think," he exclaims, "so long as you obey."

And Treitschke outdoes Hegel in proclaiming war as the highest expression of man. To him "martial glory is the basis of all the political virtues; in the rich treasure of Germany's glories the Prussian military glory is a jewel as precious as the masterpieces of our poets and thinkers." He holds that "to play blindly with peace . . . has become the shame of the thought and morality of our age."

War is not only a practical necessity, it is also a theoretical necessity, an exigency of logic. The concept of the State implies the concept of war, for the essence of the State is power . . . That war should ever be banished from the world is a hope not only absurd, but profoundly immoral. It would involve the atrophy of many of the essential and sublime forces of the human soul . . . A people which become attached to the chimerical hope of perpetual peace finishes irremediably by decaying in its proud isolation . . ."

Nietzsche, like Goethe, held no high opinion of the German people,* and in other ways, too, the outpourings of this megalomaniacal genius differ from those of the chauvinistic German thinkers of the nineteenth century. Indeed, he regarded most German philosophers, including Fichte and Hegel, as "unconscious swindlers." He poked fun at the "Tartuffery of old Kant." The Germans, he wrote in *Ecce Homo,* "have no conception how vile they are," and he came to the conclusion that "wheresoever Germany penetrated, she ruins culture." He thought that Christians, as much as Jews, were responsible for the "slave morality" prevalent in the world; he was never an anti-Semite. He was sometimes fearful of Prussia's future, and in his last years, before insanity closed down his mind, he even toyed with the idea of European union and world government.

---

* "I have often felt," Goethe once said, "a bitter sorrow at the thought of the German people, which is so estimable in the individual and so wretched in the generality. A comparison of the German people with other peoples arouses a painful feeling, which I try to overcome in every possible way." (Conversation with H. Luden on December 13, 1813, in *Goethes Gespraeche,* Auswahl Biedermann; quoted by Wilhelm Roepke in *The Solution of the German Problem,* p. 131.)

Yet I think no one who lived in the Third Reich could have failed to be impressed by Nietzsche's influence on it. His books might be full, as Santayana said, of "genial imbecility" and "boyish blasphemies." Yet Nazi scribblers never tired of extolling him. Hitler often visited the Nietzsche museum in Weimar and publicized his veneration for the philosopher by posing for photographs of himself staring in rapture at the bust of the great man.

There was some ground for this appropriation of Nietzsche as one of the originators of the Nazi *Weltanschauung*. Had not the philosopher thundered against democracy and parliaments, preached the will to power, praised war and proclaimed the coming of the master race and the superman—and in the most telling aphorisms? A Nazi could proudly quote him on almost every conceivable subject, and did. On Christianity: "the one great curse, the one enormous and innermost perversion . . . I call it the one immortal blemish of mankind . . . This Christianity is no more than the typical teaching of the Socialists." On the State, power and the jungle world of man: "Society has never regarded virtue as anything else than as a means to strength, power and order. The State [is] unmorality organized . . . the will to war, to conquest and revenge . . . Society is not entitled to exist for its own sake but only as a substructure and scaffolding, by means of which a select race of beings may elevate themselves to their higher duties . . . There is no such thing as the right to live, the right to work, or the right to be happy: in this respect man is no different from the meanest worm."* And he exalted the superman as the beast of prey, "the magnificent blond brute, avidly rampant for spoil and victory."

And war? Here Nietzsche took the view of most of the other nineteenth-century German thinkers. In the thundering Old Testament language in which *Thus Spake Zarathustra* is written, the philosopher cries out: "Ye shall love peace as a means to new war, and the short peace more than the long. You I advise not to work, but to fight. You I advise not to peace but to victory . . . Ye say it is the good cause which halloweth even war? I say unto you: it is the good war which halloweth every cause. War and courage have done more great things than charity."

Finally there was Nietzsche's prophecy of the coming elite who would rule the world and from whom the superman would spring. In *The Will to Power* he exclaims: "A daring and ruler race is building itself up . . . The aim should be to prepare a transvaluation of values for a particularly

---

* Women, whom Nietzsche never had, he consigned to a distinctly inferior status, as did the Nazis, who decreed that their place was in the kitchen and their chief role in life to beget children for German warriors. Nietzsche put the idea this way: "Man shall be trained for war and woman for the procreation of the warrior. All else is folly." He went further. In *Thus Spake Zarathustra* he exclaims: "Thou goest to woman? Do not forget thy whip!"—which prompted Bertrand Russell to quip, "Nine women out of ten would have got the whip away from him, and he knew it, so he kept away from women . . ."

strong kind of man, most highly gifted in intellect and will. This man and the elite around him will become the "lords of the earth."

Such rantings from one of Germany's most original minds must have struck a responsive chord in Hitler's littered mind. At any rate he appropriated them for his own—not only the thoughts but the philosopher's penchant for grotesque exaggeration, and often his very words. "Lords of the Earth" is a familiar expression in *Mein Kampf*. That in the end Hitler considered himself the superman of Nietzsche's prophecy can not be doubted.

"Whoever wants to understand National Socialist Germany must know Wagner," Hitler used to say.* This may have been based on a partial misconception of the great composer, for though Richard Wagner harbored a fanatical hatred, as Hitler did, for the Jews, who he was convinced were out to dominate the world with their money, and though he scorned parliaments and democracy and the materialism and mediocrity of the bourgeoisie, he also fervently hoped that the Germans, "with their special gifts," would "become not rulers, but ennoblers of the world."

It was not his political writings, however, but his towering operas, recalling so vividly the world of German antiquity with its heroic myths, its fighting pagan gods and heroes, its demons and dragons, its blood feuds and primitive tribal codes, its sense of destiny, of the splendor of love and life and the nobility of death, which inspired the myths of modern Germany and gave it a Germanic *Weltanschauung* which Hitler and the Nazis, with some justification, took over as their own.

From his earliest days Hitler worshiped Wagner, and even as his life neared a close, in the damp and dreary bunker at Army headquarters on the Russian front, with his world and his dreams beginning to crack and crumble, he loved to reminisce about all the times he had heard the great Wagnerian works, of what they had meant to him and of the inspiration he had derived from the Bayreuth Festival and from his countless visits to Haus Wahnfried, the composer's home, where Siegfried Wagner, the composer's son, still lived with his English-born wife, Winifred, who for a while was one of his revered friends.

"What joy each of Wagner's works has given me!" Hitler exclaims on the evening of January 24–25, 1942, soon after the first disastrous German defeats in Russia, as he discourses to his generals and party cronies, Himmler among them, in the depths of the underground shelter of Wolfsschanze at Rastenburg in East Prussia. Outside there is snow and an arctic cold, the elements which he so hated and feared and which had contributed to the first German military setback of the war. But in the warmth of the bunker his thoughts on this night, at least, are on one of the great inspirations of his life. "I remember," he says, "my emotion the first time I entered Wahnfried. To say I was moved is an understate-

---

* My own recollection is confirmed by Otto Tolischus in his *They Wanted War*, p. 11.

ment! At my worst moments, they never ceased to sustain me, even Siegfried Wagner. I was on Christian-name terms with them. I loved them all, and I also love Wahnfried . . . The ten days of the Bayreuth season were always one of the blessed seasons of my existence. And I rejoice at the idea that one day I shall be able to resume the pilgrimage! . . . On the day following the end of the Bayreuth Festival . . . I'm gripped by a great sadness—as when one strips the Christmas tree of its ornaments."[25]

Though Hitler reiterated in his monologue that winter evening that to him *Tristan und Isolde* was "Wagner's masterpiece," it is the stupendous *Nibelungen Ring,* a series of four operas which was inspired by the great German epic myth, *Nibelungenlied,* and on which the composer worked for the better part of twenty-five years, that gave Germany and especially the Third Reich so much of its primitive Germanic *mythos.* Often a people's myths are the highest and truest expression of its spirit and culture, and nowhere is this more true than in Germany. Schelling even argued that "a nation comes into existence with its mythology . . . The unity of its thinking, which means a collective philosophy, [is] presented in its mythology; therefore its mythology contains the fate of the nation." And Max Mell, a contemporary poet, who wrote a modern version of the *Song of the Nibelungs,* declared, "Today only little has remained of the Greek gods that humanism wanted to implant so deeply into our culture . . . But Siegfried and Kriemhild were always in the people's soul!"

Siegfried and Kriemhild, Brunhild and Hagen—these are the ancient heroes and heroines with whom so many modern Germans liked to identify themselves. With them, and with the world of the barbaric, pagan Nibelungs—an irrational, heroic, mystic world, beset by treachery, overwhelmed by violence, drowned in blood, and culminating in the *Goetterdaemmerung,* the twilight of the gods, as Valhalla, set on fire by Wotan after all his vicissitudes, goes up in flames in an orgy of self-willed annihilation which has always fascinated the German mind and answered some terrible longing in the German soul. These heroes, this primitive, demonic world, were always, in Mell's words, "in the people's soul." In that German soul could be felt the struggle between the spirit of civilization and the spirit of the Nibelungs, and in the time with which this history is concerned the latter seemed to gain the upper hand. It is not at all surprising that Hitler tried to emulate Wotan when in 1945 he willed the destruction of Germany so that it might go down in flames with him.

Wagner, a man of staggering genius, an artist of incredible magnitude, stood for much more than has been set down here. The conflict in the Ring operas often revolves around the theme of greed for gold, which the composer equated with the "tragedy of modern capitalism," and which he saw, with horror, wiping out the old virtues which had come down from an earlier day. Despite all his pagan heroes he did not entirely despair of Christianity, as Nietzsche did. And he had great compassion for the erring, warring human race. But Hitler was not entirely wrong in saying that to understand Nazism one must first know Wagner.

Wagner had known, and been influenced by, first Schopenhauer and then Nietzsche, though the latter quarreled with him because he thought his operas, especially *Parsifal,* showed too much Christian renunciation. In the course of his long and stormy life, Wagner came into contact with two other men, one a Frenchman, the other an Englishman, who are important to this history not so much for the impression they made on him, though in one case it was considerable, as for their effect on the German mind, which they helped to direct toward the coming of the Third Reich.

These individuals were Count Joseph Arthur de Gobineau, a French diplomat and man of letters, and Houston Stewart Chamberlain, one of the strangest Englishmen who ever lived.

Neither man, be it said at once, was a mountebank. Both were men of immense erudition, deep culture and wide experience of travel. Yet both concocted racial doctrines so spurious that no people, not even their own, took them seriously with the single exception of the Germans. To the Nazis their questionable theories became gospel. It is probably no exaggeration to say, as I have heard more than one follower of Hitler say, that Chamberlain was the spiritual founder of the Third Reich. This singular Englishman, who came to see in the Germans the master race, the hope of the future, worshiped Richard Wagner, one of whose daughters he eventually married; he venerated first Wilhelm II and finally Hitler and was the mentor of both. At the end of a fantastic life he could hail the Austrian corporal—and this long before Hitler came to power or had any prospect of it—as a being sent by God to lead the German people out of the wilderness. Hitler, not unnaturally, regarded Chamberlain as a prophet, as indeed he turned out to be.

What was it in the teaching of these two men that inoculated the Germans with a madness on the question of race and German destiny?

Gobineau's chief contribution was a four-volume work which was published in Paris between 1853 and 1855, entitled *Essai sur l'Inégalité des Races Humaines* (Essay on the Inequality of the Human Races). Ironically enough, this French aristocrat, after serving as an officer in the Royal Guard, had started his public career as *chef de cabinet* to Alexis de Tocqueville when the distinguished author of *Democracy in America* served a brief term of office in 1848. He had then gone to Hanover and Frankfurt as a diplomat and it was from his contact with the Germans, rather than with De Tocqueville, that he derived his theories on racial inequalities, though he once confessed that he wrote the volumes partly to prove the superiority of his own aristocratic ancestry.

To Gobineau, as he stated in his dedication of the work to the King of Hanover, the key to history and civilization was race. "The racial question dominates all the other problems of history . . . the inequality of races suffices to explain the whole unfolding of the destiny of peoples." There were three principal races, white, yellow and black, and the white was the superior. "History," he contended, "shows that all civilization flows from the white race, that no civilization can exist without the co-operation of this race." The jewel of the white race was the Aryan, "this illustrious human family, the noblest among the white race," whose origins he traced back to Central Asia. Unfortunately, Gobineau says, the contemporary Aryan suffered from intermixture with inferior races, as one could see in the southern Europe of his time. However, in the northwest, above a line running roughly along the Seine and east to Switzerland, the Aryans, though far from simon-pure, still survived as a superior race. This took in some of the French, all of the English and the Irish, the people of the Low Countries and the Rhine and Hanover, and the Scandinavians. Gobineau seemingly excluded the bulk of the Germans, who lived to the east and southeast of his line—a fact which the Nazis glossed over when they embraced his teachings.

Still, to Gobineau's mind the Germans, or at least the West Germans, were probably the best of all the Aryans, and this discovery the Nazis did *not* gloss over. Wherever they went, the Germans, he found, brought improvement. This was true even in the Roman Empire. The so-called barbaric German tribes who conquered the Romans and broke up their empire did a distinct service to civilization, for the Romans, by the time of the fourth century, were little better than degenerate mongrels, while the Germans were relatively pure Aryans. "The Aryan German," he declared, "is a powerful creature . . . Everything he thinks, says and does is thus of major importance."

Gobineau's ideas were quickly taken up in Germany. Wagner, whom the Frenchman met in 1876 toward the close of his life (he died in 1882) espoused them with enthusiasm, and soon Gobineau societies sprang up all over Germany.*

THE STRANGE LIFE AND WORKS OF
H. S. CHAMBERLAIN

Among the zealous members of the Gobineau Society in Germany was Houston Stewart Chamberlain, whose life and works constitute one of the most fascinating ironies in the inexorable course of history which led to the rise and fall of the Third Reich.

This son of an English admiral, nephew of a British field marshal, Sir Neville Chamberlain, and of two British generals, and eventually son-in-law of Richard Wagner, was born at Portsmouth in 1855. He was destined for the British Army or Navy, but his delicate health made such a calling out of the question and he was educated in France and Geneva, where French became his first language. Between the ages of fifteen and nineteen fate brought him into touch with two Germans and thereafter he was drawn irresistibly toward Germany, of which he ultimately became a citizen and one of the foremost thinkers and in whose language he wrote all of his many books, several of which had an almost blinding influence on Wilhelm II, Adolf Hitler and countless lesser Germans.

---

* Though not in France.

In 1870, when he was fifteen, Chamberlain landed in the hands of a remarkable tutor, Otto Kuntze, a Prussian of the Prussians, who for four years imprinted on his receptive mind and sensitive soul the glories of militant, conquering Prussia and also—apparently unmindful of the contrasts—of such artists and poets as Beethoven, Goethe, Schiller and Wagner. At nineteen Chamberlain fell madly in love with Anna Horst, also a Prussian, ten years his senior and, like him, highly neurotic. In 1882, at the age of twenty-seven, he journeyed from Geneva, where he had been immersed for three years in studies of philosophy, natural history, physics, chemistry and medicine, to Bayreuth. There he met Wagner who, as he says, became the sun of his life, and Cosima, the composer's wife, to whom he would remain passionately and slavishly devoted all the rest of his days. From 1885, when he went with Anna Horst, who had become his wife, to live for four years in Dresden, he became a German in thought and in language, moving on to Vienna in 1889 for a decade and finally in 1909 to Bayreuth, where he dwelt until his death in 1927. He divorced his idolized Prussian wife in 1905, when she was sixty and even more mentally and physically ill than he (the separation was so painful that he said it almost drove him mad) and three years later he married Eva Wagner and settled down near Wahnfried, where he could be near his wife's mother, the revered, strong-willed Cosima.

Hypersensitive and neurotic and subject to frequent nervous breakdowns, Chamberlain was given to seeing demons who, by his own account, drove him on relentlessly to seek new fields of study and get on with his prodigious writings. One vision after another forced him to change from biology to botany to the fine arts, to music, to philosophy, to biography to history. Once, in 1896, when he was returning from Italy, the presence of a demon became so forceful that he got off the train at Gardone, shut himself up in a hotel room for eight days and, abandoning some work on music that he had contemplated, wrote feverishly on a biological thesis until he had the germ of the theme that would dominate all of his later works: race and history.

Whatever its blemishes, his mind had a vast sweep ranging over the fields of literature, music, biology, botany, religion, history and politics. There was, as Jean Réal[26] has pointed out, a profound unity of inspiration in all his published works and they had a remarkable coherence. Since he felt himself goaded on by demons, his books (on Wagner, Goethe, Kant, Christianity and race) were written in the grip of a terrible fever, a veritable trance, a state of self-induced intoxication, so that, as he says in his autobiography, *Lebenswege,* he was often unable to recognize them as his own work, because they surpassed his expectations. Minds more balanced than his have subsequently demolished his theories of race and much of his history, and to such a French scholar of Germanism as Edmond Vermeil Chamberlain's ideas were essentially "shoddy." Yet to the anti-Nazi German biographer of Hitler, Konrad Heiden, who deplored the influence of his racial teachings, Chamberlain "was one of the most astonishing talents in the history of the German mind, a mine of knowledge and profound ideas."

The book which most profoundly influenced that mind, which sent Wilhelm II into ecstasies and provided the Nazis with their racial aberrations, was *Foundations of the Nineteenth Century* (*Grundlagen des Neunzehnten Jahrhunderts*) a work of some twelve hundred pages which Chamberlain, again possessed of one of his "demons," wrote in nineteen months between April 1, 1897, and October 31, 1898, in Vienna, and which was published in 1899.

As with Gobineau, whom he admired, Chamberlain found the key to history, indeed the basis of civilization, to be race. To explain the nineteenth century, that is, the contemporary world, one had to consider first what it had been bequeathed from ancient times. Three things, said Chamberlain: Greek philosophy and art, Roman law and the personality of Christ. There were also three legatees: the Jews and the Germans, the "two pure races," and the half-breed Latins of the Mediterranean—"a chaos of peoples," he called them. The Germans alone deserved such a splendid heritage. They had, it is true, come into history late, not until the thirteenth century. But even before that, in destroying the Roman Empire, they had proved their worth. "It is not true," he says, "that the Teutonic barbarian conjured up the so-called 'Night of the Middle Ages'; this night followed rather upon the intellectual and moral bankruptcy of the raceless chaos of humanity which the dying Roman Empire had nurtured; but for the Teuton, everlasting night would have settled upon the world." At the time he was writing he saw in the Teuton the only hope of the world.

Chamberlain included among the "Teutons" the Celts and the Slavs, though the Teutons were the most important element. However, he is quite woolly in his definitions and at one point declares that "whoever behaves as a Teuton is a Teuton whatever his racial origin." Perhaps here he was thinking of his own non-German origin. Whatever he was, the Teuton, according to Chamberlain, was "the soul of our culture. The importance of each nation as a living power today is dependent upon the proportion of genuinely Teutonic blood in its population . . . True history begins at the moment when the Teuton, with his masterful hand, lays his grip upon the legacy of antiquity."

And the Jews? The longest chapter in *Foundations* is devoted to them. As we have seen, Chamberlain claimed that the Jews and the Teutons were the only pure races left in the West. And in this chapter he condemns "stupid and revolting anti-Semitism." The Jews, he says, are not "inferior" to the Teuton, merely "different." They have their own grandeur; they realize the "sacred duty" of man to guard the purity of race. And yet as he proceeds to analyze the Jews, Chamberlain slips into the very vulgar anti-Semitism which he condemns in others and which leads, in the end, to the obscenities of Julius Streicher's caricatures of the Jews in *Der Stuermer* in Hitler's time. Indeed a good deal of the "philosophical" basis of Nazi anti-Semitism stems from this chapter.

The preposterousness of Chamberlain's views is quickly evident. He has declared that the personality of Christ is one of the three great bequests of antiquity to modern civilization. He then sets out to "prove" that Jesus was not a Jew. His Galilean origins, his inability to utter correctly the Aramaic gutturals, are to Chamberlain "clear signs" that Jesus had "a large proportion of non-Semitic blood." He then makes a typically flat statement: "Whoever claimed that Jesus was a Jew was either being stupid or telling a lie. . . . Jesus was not a Jew."

What was he then? Chamberlain answers: Probably an Aryan! If not entirely by blood, then unmistakably by reason of his moral and religious teaching, so opposed to the "materialism and abstract formalism" of the Jewish religion. It was natural then—or at least it was to Chamberlain—that Christ should become "the God of the young Indo-European peoples overflowing with life," and above all the God of the Teuton, because "no other people was so well equipped as the Teutonic to hear this divine voice."

There follows what purports to be a detailed history of the Jewish race from the time of the mixture of the Semite or Bedouin of the desert with the roundheaded Hittite, who had a "Jewish nose," and finally with the Amorites, who were Aryans. Unfortunately the Aryan mixture—the Amorites, he says, were tall, blond, magnificent—came too late to really improve the "corrupt" Hebrew strain. From then on the Englishman, contradicting his whole theory of the purity of the Jewish race, finds the Jews becoming a "negative" race, "a bastardy," so that the Aryans were justified in "denying" Israel. In fact, he condemns the Aryans for giving the Jews "a halo of false glory." He then finds the Jews "lamentably lacking in true religion."

Finally, for Chamberlain the way of salvation lies in the Teutons and their culture, and of the Teutons the Germans are the highest-endowed, for they have inherited the best qualities of the Greeks and the Indo-Aryans. This gives them the right to be masters of the world. "God builds today upon the Germans alone," he wrote in another place. "This is the knowledge, the certain truth, that has filled my soul for years."

Publication of *Foundations of the Nineteenth Century* created something of a sensation and brought this strange Englishman sudden fame in Germany. Despite its frequent eloquence and its distinguished style—for Chamberlain was a dedicated artist—the book was not easy reading. But it was soon taken up by the upper classes, who seem to have found in it just what they wanted to believe. Within ten years it had gone through eight editions and sold 60,000 copies and by the time of the outbreak of the First World War in 1914 it had reached a sale of 100,000. It flourished again in the Nazi time and I remember an announcement of its twenty-fourth edition in 1938, by which time it had sold more than a quarter of a million copies.

Among its first and most enthusiastic readers was Kaiser Wilhelm II. He invited Chamberlain to his palace at Potsdam and on their very first meeting a friendship was formed that lasted to the end of the author's life in 1927. An extensive correspondence between the two followed. Some of the forty-three letters which Chamberlain addressed to the Emperor (Wilhelm answered twenty-three of them) were lengthy essays which the ruler used in several of his bombastic speeches and statements. "It was God who sent your book to the German people, and you personally to me," the Kaiser wrote in one of his first letters. Chamberlain's obsequiousness, his exaggerated flattery, in these letters can be nauseating. "Your Majesty and your subjects," he wrote, "have been born in a holy shrine," and he informed Wilhelm that he had placed his portrait in his study opposite one of Christ by Leonardo so that while he worked he often paced up and down between the countenance of his Savior and his sovereign.

His servility did not prevent Chamberlain from continually proffering advice to the headstrong, flamboyant monarch. In 1908 the popular opposition to Wilhelm had reached such a climax that the Reichstag censored him for his disastrous intervention in foreign affairs. But Chamberlain advised the Emperor that public opinion was made by idiots and traitors and not to mind it, whereupon Wilhelm replied that the two of them would stand together—"You wield your pen; I my tongue (and) my broad sword."

And always the Englishman reminded the Emperor of Germany's mission and its destiny. "Once Germany has achieved the power," he wrote after the outbreak of the First World War, "—and we may confidently expect her to achieve it—she must immediately begin to carry out a scientific policy of genius. Augustus undertook a systematic transformation of the world, and Germany must do the same . . . Equipped with offensive and defensive weapons, organized as firmly and flawlessly as the Army, superior to all in art, science, technology, industry, commerce, finance, in every field, in short; teacher, helmsman, and pioneer of the world, every man at his post, every man giving his utmost for the holy cause—thus Germany . . . will conquer the world by inner superiority."

For preaching such a glorious mission for his adopted country (he became a naturalized German citizen in 1916, halfway through the war) Chamberlain received from the Kaiser the Iron Cross.

But it was on the Third Reich, which did not arrive until six years after his death but whose coming he foresaw, that this Englishman's influence was the greatest. His racial theories and his burning sense of the destiny of the Germans and Germany were taken over by the Nazis, who acclaimed him as one of their prophets. During the Hitler regime books, pamphlets and articles poured from the presses extolling the "spiritual founder" of National Socialist Germany. Rosenberg, as one of Hitler's mentors, often tried to impart his enthusiasm for the English philosopher to the Fuehrer. It is likely that Hitler first learned of Chamberlain's writings before he left Vienna, for they were popular among the Pan-German and anti-Semitic groups whose literature he devoured so avidly in those early days. Probably too he read some of Chamberlain's chauvinistic articles during the war. In *Mein Kampf* he expresses the regret that Chamberlain's observations were not more heeded during the Second Reich.

Chamberlain was one of the first intellectuals in Germany to see a great future for Hitler—and new opportunities for the Germans if they followed him. Hitler had met him in Bayreuth in 1923, and though ill, half paralyzed, and disillusioned by Germany's defeat and the fall of the Hohenzollern Empire—the collapse of all his hopes and prophecies!—Chamberlain was swept off his feet by the eloquent young Austrian. "You have mighty things to do," he wrote Hitler on the following day, ". . . My faith in Germanism had not wavered an instant, though my hope—I confess—was at a low ebb. With one stroke you have transformed the state of my soul. That in the hour of her deepest need Germany gives birth to a Hitler proves her vitality; as do the influences that emanate from him; for these two things—personality and influence—belong together . . . May God protect you!"

This was at a time when Adolf Hitler, with his Charlie Chaplin mustache, his rowdy manners and his violent, outlandish extremism, was still considered a joke by most Germans. He had few followers then. But the hypnotic magnetism of his personality worked like a charm on the aging, ill philosopher and renewed his faith in the people he had chosen to join and exalt. Chamberlain became a member of the budding Nazi Party and so far as his health would permit began to write for its obscure publications. One of his articles, published in 1924, hailed Hitler, who was then in jail, as destined by God to lead the German people. Destiny had beckoned Wilhelm II, but he had failed; now there was Adolf Hitler. This remarkable Englishman's seventieth birthday, on September 5, 1925, was celebrated with five columns of encomiums in the Nazi *Voelkischer Beobachter,* which hailed his *Foundations* as the "gospel of the Nazi movement," and he went to his grave sixteen months later—on January 11, 1927—with high hope that all he had preached and prophesied would yet come true under the divine guidance of this new German Messiah.

Aside from a prince representing Wilhelm II, who could not return to German soil, Hitler was the only public figure at Chamberlain's funeral. In reporting the death of the Englishman the *Voelkischer Beobachter* said that the German people had lost "one of the great armorers whose weapons have not yet found in our day their fullest use." Not the half-paralyzed old man, dying, not even Hitler, nor anyone else in Germany, could have foreseen in that bleak January month of 1927, when the fortunes of the Nazi Party were at their lowest ebb, how soon, how very soon, those weapons which the transplanted Englishman had forged would be put to their fullest use, and with what fearful consequences.[27]

Yet Adolf Hitler had a mystical sense of his personal mission on earth in those days, and even before. "From millions of men . . . *one* man must step forward," he wrote in *Mein Kampf* (the italics are his), "who with apodictic force will form granite principles from the wavering idea-world of the broad masses and take up the struggle for their sole correct-ness, until from the shifting waves of a free thought-world there will arise a brazen cliff of solid unity in faith and will."[28]

He left no doubt in the minds of readers that he already considered himself that *one* man. *Mein Kampf* is sprinkled with little essays on the role of the genius who is picked by Providence to lead a great people, even though they may not at first understand him or recognize his worth, out of their troubles to further greatness. The reader is aware that Hitler is re-ferring to himself and his present situation. He is not yet recognized by the world for what he is sure he is, but that has always been the fate of geniuses—in the beginning. "It 'nearly always takes some stimulus to bring the genius on the scene," he remarks. "The world then resists and does not want to believe that the type, which apparently is identical with it, is suddenly a very different being; a process which is repeated with every eminent son of man . . . The spark of a genius," he declares, "exists in the brain of the truly creative man from the hour of his birth. True genius is always inborn and never cultivated, let alone learned."[29]

Specifically, he thought, the great men who shaped history were a blend of the practical politician and the thinker. "At long intervals in human history it may occasionally happen that the politician is wedded to the theoretician. The more profound this fusion, the greater are the obstacles opposing the work of the politician. He no longer works for necessities which will be understood by the first good shopkeeper, but for aims which only the fewest comprehend. Therefore his life is torn between love and hate. The protest of the present, which does not understand him, struggles with the recognition of posterity—for which he also works. For the greater a man's works are for the future, the less the present can com-prehend them; the harder his fight . . ."[30]

These lines were written in 1924, when few understood what this man, then in prison and discredited by the failure of his comic-opera putsch, had in mind to do. But Hitler had no doubts himself. Whether he actually read Hegel or not is a matter of dispute. But it is clear from his writings and speeches that he had some acquaintance with the philosopher's ideas, if only through discussions with his early mentors Rosenberg, Eckart and Hess. One way or another Hegel's famous lectures at the University of Berlin must have caught his attention, as did numerous dictums of Nietzsche. We have seen briefly* that Hegel developed a theory of "heroes" which had great appeal to the German mind. In one of the Berlin lectures he discussed how the "will of the world spirit" is carried out by "world-historical individuals."

They may be called Heroes, inasmuch as they have derived their purposes and their vocation, not from the calm regular course of things, sanctioned by the existing order; but from a concealed fount, from that inner Spirit, still

---

* See above, p. 98.

hidden beneath the surface, which impinges on the outer world as on a shell and bursts it into pieces. Such were Alexander, Caesar, Napoleon. They were practical, political men. But at the same time they were thinking men, who had an insight into the requirements of the time—what was ripe for development. This was the very Truth for their age, for their world . . . It was theirs to know this nascent principle, the necessary, directly sequent step in progress, which their world was to take; to make this their aim, and to expend their energy in promoting it. World-historical men—the Heroes of an epoch—must therefore be recognized as its clear-sighted ones; *their* deeds, *their* words are the best of their time.[31]

Note the similarities between this and the above quotation from *Mein Kampf*. The fusion of the politician and the thinker—that is what produces a hero, a "world-historical figure," an Alexander, a Caesar, a Napoleon. If there was in him, as Hitler had now come to believe, the same fusion, might he not aspire to their ranks?

In Hitler's utterances there runs the theme that the supreme leader is above the morals of ordinary man. Hegel and Nietzsche thought so too. We have seen Hegel's argument that "the private virtues" and "irrelevant moral claims" must not stand in the way of the great rulers, nor must one be squeamish if the heroes, in fulfilling their destiny, trample or "crush to pieces" many an innocent flower. Nietzsche, with his grotesque exaggeration, goes much further.

The strong men, the masters, regain the pure conscience of a beast of prey; monsters filled with joy, they can return from a fearful succession of murder, arson, rape and torture with the same joy in their hearts, the same contentment in their souls as if they had indulged in some student's rag . . . When a man is capable of commanding, when he is by nature a "Master," when he is violent in act and gesture, of what importance are treaties to him? . . . To judge morality properly, it must be replaced by two concepts borrowed from zoology: the *taming* of a beast and the *breeding* of a specific species.[32]

Such teachings, carried to their extremity by Nietzsche and applauded by a host of lesser Germans, seem to have exerted a strong appeal on Hitler.* A genius with a mission was above the law; he could not be bound by "bourgeois" morals. Thus, when his time for action came, Hitler could justify the most ruthless and cold-blooded deeds, the suppression of personal freedom, the brutal practice of slave labor, the depravities of the concentration camp, the massacre of his own followers in June 1934, the killing of war prisoners and the mass slaughter of the Jews.

When Hitler emerged from Landsberg prison five days before Christmas, 1924, he found a situation which would have led almost any other man to retire from public life. The Nazi Party and its press were banned;

---

* See above, pp. 86–87, for quotations from *Mein Kampf*.

the former leaders were feuding and falling away. He himself was forbidden to speak in public. What was worse, he faced deportation to his native Austria; the Bavarian state police had strongly recommended it in a report to the Ministry of the Interior. Even many of his old comrades agreed with the general opinion that Hitler was finished, that now he would fade away into oblivion as had so many other provincial politicians who had enjoyed a brief moment of notoriety during the strife-ridden years when it seemed that the Republic would totter.*

But the Republic had weathered the storms. It was beginning to thrive. While Hitler was in prison a financial wizard by the name of Dr. Hjalmar Horace Greeley Schacht had been called in to stabilize the currency, and he had succeeded. The ruinous inflation was over. The burden of reparations was eased by the Dawes Plan. Capital began to flow in from America. The economy was rapidly recovering. Stresemann was succeeding in his policy of reconciliation with the Allies. The French were getting out of the Ruhr. A security pact was being discussed which would pave the way for a general European settlement (Locarno) and bring Germany into the League of Nations. For the first time since the defeat, after six years of tension, turmoil and depression, the German people were beginning to have a normal life. Two weeks before Hitler was released from Landsberg, the Social Democrats—the "November criminals," as he called them—had increased their vote by 30 per cent (to nearly eight million) in a general election in which they had championed the Republic. The Nazis, in league with northern racial groups under the name of the National Socialist German Freedom movement, had seen their vote fall from nearly two million in May 1924 to less than a million in December. Nazism appeared to be a dying cause. It had mushroomed on the country's misfortunes; now that the nation's outlook was suddenly bright it was rapidly withering away. Or so most Germans and foreign observers believed.

But not Adolf Hitler. He was not easily discouraged. And he knew how to wait. As he picked up the threads of his life in the little two-room apartment on the top floor of 41 Thierschstrasse in Munich during the winter months of 1925 and then, when summer came, in various inns on the Obersalzberg above Berchtesgaden, the contemplation of the misfortunes of the immediate past and the eclipse of the present, served only to strengthen his resolve. Behind the prison gates he had had time to range over in his mind not only his own past and its triumphs and mistakes, but the tumultuous past of his German people and *its* triumphs and errors. He saw both more clearly now. And there was born in him anew a burning sense of mission—for himself and for Germany—from

---

* As late as 1929, Professor M. A. Gerothwohl, the editor of Lord D'Abernon's diaries, wrote a footnote to the ambassador's account of the Beer Hall Putsch in which, after mention of Hitler's being sentenced to prison, he added: "He was finally released after six months and bound over for the rest of his sentence, thereafter fading into oblivion." Lord D'Abernon was the British ambassador in Berlin from 1920 to 1926 and worked with great skill to strengthen the Weimar Republic.

which all doubts were excluded. In this exalted spirit he finished dictating the torrent of words that would go into Volume One of *Mein Kampf* and went on immediately to Volume Two. The blueprint of what the Almighty had called upon him to do in this cataclysmic world and the philosophy, the *Weltanschauung*, that would sustain it were set down in cold print for all to ponder. That philosophy, however demented, had roots, as we have seen, deep in German life. The blueprint may have seemed preposterous to most twentieth-century minds, even in Germany. But it too possessed a certain logic. It held forth a vision. It offered, though few saw this at the time, a continuation of German history. It pointed the way toward a glorious German destiny.

Book Two

✠ ✠ ✠

TRIUMPH
AND
CONSOLIDATION

5

THE ROAD TO POWER: 1925–31

THE YEARS FROM 1925 until the coming of the depression in 1929 were lean years for Adolf Hitler and the Nazi movement, but it is a measure of the man that he persevered and never lost hope or confidence. Despite the excitability of his nature, which often led to outbursts of hysteria, he had the patience to wait and the shrewdness to realize that the climate of material prosperity and of a feeling of relaxation which settled over Germany in those years was not propitious for his purposes.

He was confident that the good times would not last. So far as Germany was concerned, he said, they depended not on her own strength but on that of others—of America above all, from whose swollen coffers loans were pouring in to make and keep Germany prosperous. Between 1924 and 1930 German borrowing amounted to some seven billion dollars and most of it came from American investors, who gave little thought to how the Germans might make eventual repayment. The Germans gave even less thought to it.

The Republic borrowed to pay its reparations and to increase its vast social services, which were the model of the world. The states, cities and municipalities borrowed to finance not only needed improvements but building of airfields, theaters, sport stadiums and fancy swimming pools. Industry, which had wiped out its debts in the inflation, borrowed billions to retool and to rationalize its productive processes. Its output, which in 1923 had dropped to 55 per cent of that in 1913, rose to 122 per cent by 1927. For the first time since the war unemployment fell below a million—to 650,000—in 1928. That year retail sales were up 20 per cent over 1925 and the next year real wages reached a figure 10 per cent higher than four years before. The lower middle classes, all the millions of shopkeepers and small-salaried folk on whom Hitler had to draw for his mass support, shared in the general prosperity.

My own acquaintance with Germany began in those days. I was stationed in Paris and occasionally in London at that time, and fascinating though those capitals were to a young American happy to have escaped from the incredible smugness and emptiness of the Calvin Coolidge era, they paled a little when one came to Berlin and Munich. A wonderful ferment was working in Germany. Life seemed more free, more modern, more exciting than in any place I had ever seen. Nowhere else did the arts or the intellectual life seem so lively. In contemporary writing, painting, architecture, in music and drama, there were new currents and fine talents. And everywhere there was an accent on youth. One sat up with the young people all night in the sidewalk cafés, the plush bars, the summer camps, on a Rhineland steamer or in a smoke-filled artist's studio and talked endlessly about life. They were a healthy, carefree, sun-worshiping lot, and they were filled with an enormous zest for living to the full and in complete freedom. The old oppressive Prussian spirit seemed to be dead and buried. Most Germans one met—politicians, writers, editors, artists, professors, students, businessmen, labor leaders—struck you as being democratic, liberal, even pacifist.

One scarcely heard of Hitler or the Nazis except as butts of jokes— usually in connection with the Beer Hall Putsch, as it came to be known. In the elections of May 20, 1928, the Nazi Party polled only 810,000 votes out of a total of thirty-one million cast and had but a dozen of the Reichstag's 491 members. The conservative Nationalists also lost heavily, their vote falling from six million in 1924 to four million, and their seats in Parliament diminished from 103 to 73. In contrast, the Social Democrats gained a million and a quarter votes in the 1928 elections, and their total poll of more than nine million, with 153 seats in the Reichstag, made them easily the largest political party in Germany. Ten years after the end of the war the German Republic seemed at last to have found its feet.

The membership of the National Socialist Party in that anniversary year—1928—was 108,000. Small as the figure was, it was slowly growing. A fortnight after leaving prison at the end of 1924, Hitler had hurried to see Dr. Heinrich Held, the Prime Minister of Bavaria and the head of the Catholic Bavarian People's Party. On the strength of his promise of good behavior (Hitler was still on parole) Held had lifted the ban on the Nazi Party and its newspaper. "The wild beast is checked," Held told his Minister of Justice, Guertner. "We can afford to loosen the chain." The Bavarian Premier was one of the first, but by no means the last, of Germany's politicians to fall into this fatal error of judgment.

The *Voelkischer Beobachter* reappeared on February 26, 1925, with a long editorial written by Hitler, entitled "A New Beginning." The next day he spoke at the first mass meeting of the resurrected Nazi Party in the Buergerbraükeller, which he and his faithful followers had last seen on the morning of November 9, a year and a half before, when they set out on their ill-fated march. Many of the faithful were absent. Eckart and Scheubner-Richter were dead. Goering was in exile. Ludendorff and Roehm had broken with the leader. Rosenberg, feuding with Streicher and Esser, was sulking and stayed away. So did Gregor Strasser, who with Ludendorff had led the National Socialist German Freedom movement while Hitler was behind bars and the Nazi Party itself banned. When

Hitler asked Anton Drexler to preside at the meeting the old locksmith and founder of the party told him to go to the devil. Nevertheless some four thousand followers gathered in the beer hall to hear Hitler once again and he did not disappoint them. His eloquence was as moving as ever. At the end of a two-hour harangue, the crowd roared with applause. Despite the many desertions and the bleak prospects, Hitler made it clear that he still considered himself the dictatorial leader of the party. "I alone lead the movement, and no one can impose conditions on me so long as I personally bear the responsibility," he declared, and added, "Once more I bear the whole responsibility for everything that occurs in the movement."

Hitler had gone to the meeting with his mind made up on two objectives which he intended henceforth to pursue. One was to concentrate all power in his own hands. The other was to re-establish the Nazi Party as a political organization which would seek power exclusively through constitutional means. He had explained the new tactics to one of his henchmen, Karl Ludecke, while still in prison: "When I resume active work it will be necessary to pursue a new policy. Instead of working to achieve power by armed coup, we shall have to hold our noses and enter the Reichstag against the Catholic and Marxist deputies. If outvoting them takes longer than outshooting them, at least the result will be guaranteed by their own constitution. Any lawful process is slow . . . Sooner or later we shall have a majority—and after that, Germany."[1] On his release from Landsberg, he had assured the Bavarian Premier that the Nazi Party would henceforth act within the framework of the constitution.

But he allowed himself to be carried away by the enthusiasm of the crowd in his reappearance at the Buergerbraükeller on February 27. His threats against the State were scarcely veiled. The republican regime, as well as the Marxists and the Jews, was "the enemy." And in his peroration he had shouted, "To this struggle of ours there are only two possible issues: either the enemy passes over our bodies or we pass over theirs!"

The "wild beast," in this, his first public appearance after his imprisonment, did not seem "checked" at all. He was again threatening the State with violence, despite his promise of good behavior. The government of Bavaria promptly forbade him to speak again in public—a ban that was to last two years. The other states followed suit. This was a heavy blow to a man whose oratory had brought him so far. A silenced Hitler was a defeated Hitler, as ineffective as a handcuffed pugilist in a ring. Or so most people thought.

But again they were wrong. They forgot that Hitler was an organizer as well as a spellbinder. Curbing his ire at being forbidden to speak in public, he set to work with furious intent to rebuild the National Socialist German Workers' Party and to make of it an organization such as Germany had never seen before. He meant to make it like the Army—a state within a state. The first job was to attract dues-paying members. By the end of 1925 they numbered just 27,000. The going was slow, but each year some progress was made: 49,000 members in 1926; 72,000 in 1927; 108,000 in 1928; 178,000 in 1929.

More important was the building up of an intricate party structure which corresponded to the organization of the German government and indeed of German society. The country was divided into districts, or *Gaue,* which corresponded roughly with the thirty-four Reichstag electoral districts and at the head of which was a gauleiter appointed by Hitler. There were an additional seven *Gaue* for Austria, Danzig, the Saar and the Sudetenland in Czechoslovakia. A *Gau* was divided into *Kreise*—circles —and presided over by a *Kreisleiter.* The next smallest party unit was an *Ortsgruppe*—a local group—and in the cities these were further subdivided into street cells and blocks.

The political organization of the Nazi Party was divided into two groups: P.O. I, as it was known, designed to attack and undermine the government, and P.O. II to establish a state within a state. Thus the second group had departments of agriculture, justice, national economy, interior and labor—and, with an eye to the future, of race and culture, and of engineering. P.O. I had departments of foreign affairs and of labor unions and a Reich Press Office. The Propaganda Division was a separate and elaborate office.

Though some of the party roughnecks, veterans of street fighting and beerhouse brawls, opposed bringing women and children into the Nazi Party, Hitler soon provided organizations for them too. The Hitler Youth took in youngsters from fifteen to eighteen who had their own departments of culture, schools, press, propaganda, "defense sports," etc., and those from ten to fifteen were enrolled in the Deutsches Jungvolk. For the girls there was the Bund Deutscher Maedel and for the women the N. S. Frauenschaften. Students, teachers, civil servants, doctors, lawyers, jurists—all had their separate organizations, and there was a Nazi Kulturbund to attract the intellectuals and artists.

After considerable difficulties the S.A. was reorganized into an armed band of several hundred thousand men to protect Nazi meetings, to break up the meetings of others and to generally terrorize those who opposed Hitler. Some of its leaders also hoped to see the S.A. supplant the Regular Army when Hitler came to power. To prepare for this a special office under General Franz Ritter von Epp was set up, called the Wehrpolitische Amt. Its five divisions concerned themselves with such problems as external and internal defense policy, defense forces, popular defense potential, and so on. But the brown-shirted S.A. never became much more than a motley mob of brawlers. Many of its top leaders, beginning with its chief, Roehm, were notorious homosexual perverts. Lieutenant Edmund Heines, who led the Munich S.A., was not only a homosexual but a convicted murderer. These two and dozens of others quarreled and feuded as only men of unnatural sexual inclinations, with their peculiar jealousies, can.

To have at hand a more dependable band Hitler created the S.S.— Schutzstaffel—put their members in black uniforms similar to those worn by the Italian Fascisti and made them swear a special oath of loyalty to him personally. At first the S.S. was little more than a bodyguard for the Fuehrer. Its first leader was a newspaperman named Berchtold. As he preferred the relative quiet of the newsroom of the *Voelkischer Beobachter* to playing at cop and soldier, he was replaced by one Erhard Heiden, a former police stool pigeon of unsavory reputation. It was not until 1929 that Hitler found the man he was looking for as the ideal leader of the S.S., in the person of a chicken farmer in the village of Waldtrudering, near Munich, a mild-mannered fellow whom people mistook (as did this author when he first met him) for a small-town schoolmaster and whose name was Heinrich Himmler. When Himmler took over the S.S. it numbered some two hundred men. By the time he finished his job with it, the S.S. dominated Germany and was a name that struck terror throughout occupied Europe.

At the top of the pyramid of the intricate party organization stood Adolf Hitler with the highfalutin title of Partei-und-Oberster-S.A.-Fuehrer, Vorsitzender der N.S.D.A.V.—which may be translated as "Supreme Leader of the Party and the S.A., Chairman of the National Socialist German Labor Organization." Directly attached to his office was the Reich Directorate (Reichsleitung) which was made up of the top bosses of the party and such useful officials as the "Reich Treasurer" and the "Reich Business Manager." Visiting the palatial Brown House in Munich, the national headquarters of the party, during the last years of the Republic, one got the impression that here indeed were the offices of a state within a state. That, no doubt, was the impression Hitler wished to convey, for it helped to undermine confidence, both domestic and foreign, in the actual German State, which he was trying to overthrow.

But Hitler was intent on something more important than making an impression. Three years after he came to power, in a speech to the "old fighters" at the Buergerbräu on the anniversary evening of November 9, 1936, he explained one of the objectives he had had in building the party up into such a formidable and all-embracing organization. "We recognized," he said, in recalling the days when the party was being re-formed after the putsch, "that it is not enough to overthrow the old State, but that the new State must previously have been built up and be practically ready to one's hand. . . . In 1933 it was no longer a question of overthrowing a state by an act of violence; meanwhile the new State had been built up and all that there remained to do was to destroy the last remnants of the old State—and that took but a few hours."[2]

An organization, however streamlined and efficient, is made up of erring human beings, and in those years when Hitler was shaping his party to take over Germany's destiny he had his fill of troubles with his chief lieutenants, who constantly quarreled not only among themselves but with him. He, who was so monumentally intolerant by his very nature, was strangely tolerant of one human condition—a man's morals. No other party in Germany came near to attracting so many shady characters. As we have seen, a conglomeration of pimps, murderers, homosexuals, alcoholics and blackmailers flocked to the party as if to a natural haven. Hitler did not care, as long as they were useful to him. When he emerged from prison he found not only that they were at each other's throats but that there was a demand from the more prim and respectable leaders such as Rosenberg and Ludendorff that the criminals and especially the perverts be expelled from the movement. This Hitler frankly refused to do. "I do not consider it to be the task of a political leader," he wrote in his editorial, "A New Beginning," in the *Voelkischer Beobachter* of February 26, 1925, "to attempt to improve upon, or even to fuse together, the human material lying ready to his hand."

By 1926, however, the charges and countercharges hurled by the Nazi chieftains at one another became so embarrassing that Hitler set up a party court to settle them and to prevent his comrades from washing their dirty linen in public. This was known as the USCHLA, from Untersuchung-und-Schlichtungs-Ausschuss—Committee for Investigation and Settlement. Its first head was a former general, Heinemann, but he was unable to grasp the real purpose of the court, which was not to pronounce judgment on those accused of common crimes but to hush them up and see that they did not disturb party discipline or the authority of the Leader. So the General was replaced by a more understanding ex-officer, Major Walther Buch, who was given two assistants. One was Ulrich Graf, the former butcher who had been Hitler's bodyguard; the other was Hans Frank, a young Nazi lawyer, of whom more will be heard later when it comes time to recount his bloodthirstiness as Governor General of occupied Poland, for which he paid on the gallows at Nuremberg. This fine judicial triumvirate performed to the complete satisfaction of the Fuehrer. A party leader might be accused of the most nefarious crime. Buch's answer invariably was, "Well, what of it?" What he wanted to know was whether it hurt party discipline or offended the Fuehrer.

It took more than this party court, effective though it was in thousands of instances, to keep the ambitious, throat-cutting, big Nazi fry in line. Often Hitler had to intervene personally not only to keep a semblance of harmony but to prevent his own throat from being cut.

While he had languished at Landsberg, a young man by the name of Gregor Strasser had suddenly risen in the Nazi movement. A druggist by profession and a Bavarian by birth, he was three years younger than Hitler; like him, he had won the Iron Cross, First Class, and during the war he had risen from the ranks to be a lieutenant. He had become a Nazi in 1920 and soon became the district leader in Lower Bavaria. A big, stocky man, somewhat of a *bon vivant,* bursting with energy, he developed into an effective public speaker more by the force of his personality than by the oratorical gifts with which Hitler was endowed. Moreover, he was a born organizer. Fiercely independent in spirit and mind, Strasser refused to kowtow to Hitler or to take very seriously the Austrian's claims to be absolute dictator of the Nazi movement. This was to prove, in the long run, a fatal handicap, as was his sincere enthusiasm for the "socialism" in National Socialism.

Over the opposition of the imprisoned Hitler, Strasser joined Ludendorff and Rosenberg in organizing a Nazi *Voelkisch* movement to contest the state and national elections in the spring of 1924. In Bavaria the bloc polled enough votes to make it the second largest party; in Germany, as we have seen, under the name of the National Socialist German Freedom movement it won two million votes and obtained thirty-two seats in the Reichstag, one of which went to Strasser. Hitler took a dark view of the young man's activities and an even darker one of his successes. Strasser, for his part, was not disposed to accept Hitler as the Lord, and he pointedly stayed away from the big rally in Munieh on February 27, 1925, which relaunched the Nazi Party.

If the movement was to become truly national, Hitler realized, it must get a footing in the north, in Prussia, and above all in the citadel of the enemy, Berlin. In the election of 1924 Strasser had campaigned in the north and made alliances with ultranational groups there led by Albrecht von Graefe and Count Ernst zu Reventlow. He thus had personal contacts and a certain following in this area and he was the only Nazi leader who had. Two weeks after the February 27 meeting, Hitler swallowed his personal pique, sent for Strasser, induced him to come back to the fold and proposed that he organize the Nazi Party in the north. Strasser accepted. Here was an opportunity to exercise his talents without the jealous, arrogant Leader being in a position to breathe down his neck.

Within a few months he had founded a newspaper in the capital, the *Berliner Arbeiterzeitung,* edited by his brother, Otto Strasser, and a fortnightly newsletter, the *N. S. Briefe,* which kept the party officials informed of the party line. And he had laid the foundations for a political organization that stretched through Prussia, Saxony, Hanover and the industrial Rhineland. A veritable dynamo, Strasser traveled all over the north, addressing meetings, appointing district leaders and setting up a party apparatus. Being a Reichstag deputy gave him two immediate advantages over Hitler: he had a free pass on the railroads, so travel was no expense to him or the party; and he enjoyed parliamentary immunity. No authority could ban him from public speaking; no court could try him for slandering anyone or anything he wanted to. As Heiden wrote sardonically, "Free travel and free slander—Strasser had a big head start over his Fuehrer."

As his secretary and editor of the *N. S. Briefe* Gregor Strasser took on a twenty-eight-year-old Rhinelander named Paul Joseph Goebbels.

THE EMERGENCE OF PAUL JOSEPH GOEBBELS

This swarthy, dwarfish young man, with a crippled foot, a nimble mind and a complicated and neurotic personality, was not a stranger to the Nazi movement. He had discovered it in 1922 when he first heard Hitler speak in Munich, was converted, and became a member of the party. But the movement did not really discover him until three years later, when Gregor Strasser, hearing him speak, decided that he could use a young man of such obvious talents. Goebbels at twenty-eight was already an impassioned orator, a fanatical nationalist and, as Strasser knew, possessed of a vituperative pen and, rare for Nazi leaders, a sound university education. Heinrich Himmler had just resigned as Strasser's secretary to devote more of his time to raising chickens. Strasser appointed Goebbels in his place. It was to prove a fateful choice.

Paul Joseph Goebbels was born on October 29, 1897, in Rheydt, a textile center of some thirty thousand people in the Rhineland. His father, Fritz Goebbels, was a foreman in a local textile plant. His mother, Maria Katharina Odenhausen, was the daughter of a blacksmith. Both parents were pious Catholics.

Through the Catholics, Joseph Goebbels received most of his education. He attended a Catholic parochial grade school and then the *Gymnasium* in Rheydt. A scholarship from the Catholic Albert Magnus Society enabled him to go on to the university—in fact, to eight universities. Before he received his Ph.D. from Heidelberg in 1921 at the age of twenty-four, he had studied at the universities of Bonn, Freiburg, Wuerzburg, Cologne, Frankfurt, Munich and Berlin. In these illustrious institutions—the flower of German higher learning—Goebbels had concentrated on the study of philosophy, history, literature and art and had continued his work in Latin and Greek.

He intended to become a writer. The year he received his doctorate he wrote an autobiographical novel, *Michael,* which no publisher would take at the time, and in the next couple of years he finished two plays, *The Wanderer* (about Jesus Christ) and *The Lonesome Guest,* both in verse, which no producer would stage.* He had no better luck in journalism. The great liberal daily, *Berliner Tageblatt,* turned down the dozens of articles he submitted and his application for a reporter's job.

His personal life also was full of frustrations in the early days. Because he was a cripple he could not serve in the war and thus was cheated of the experience which seemed, at least in the beginning, so glorious for the young men of his generation and which was a requisite for leadership in the Nazi Party. Goebbels was not, as most people believed, born with a club foot. At the age of seven he had suffered an attack of osteomyelitis, an inflammation of the bone marrow. An operation on his left thigh was not successful and the left leg remained shorter than the right and somewhat withered. This handicap, which forced him to walk with a noticeable limp, riled him all the days of his life and was one of the causes of his early embitterment. In desperation, during his university days and during

---

* *Michael* was finally published in 1929, after Goebbels had become nationally known as a Nazi leader. *The Wanderer* reached the stage after Goebbels became Propaganda Minister and the boss of the German theater. It had a short run.

the brief period when he was an agitator against the French in the Ruhr, he often passed himself off as a wounded war veteran.

Nor was he lucky in love, though all his life he mistook his philanderings, which became notorious in his years of power, for great amours. His diaries for 1925–26, when he was twenty-eight and twenty-nine and just being launched into Nazi politics by Strasser, are full of moonings over loved ones—of whom he had several at a time.* Thus:

August 14, 1925: Alma wrote me a postcard from Bad Harzburg. The first sign of her since that night. This teasing, charming Alma!

Received first letter from Else in Switzerland. Only Else dear can write like that . . . Soon I am going to the Rhine for a week to be quite alone. Then Else will come . . . How happy I am in anticipation!

August 15: In these days I must think so often of Anke . . . How wonderful it was to travel with her. This wonderful wench!

I am yearning for Else. When shall I have her in my arms again?

Else dear, when shall I see you again?

Alma, you dear featherweight!

Anke, never can I forget you!

August 27: Three days on the Rhine . . . Not a word from Else . . . Is she angry with me? How I pine for her! I am living in the same room as I did with her last Whitsuntide. What thoughts! What feeling! Why doesn't she come?

September 3: Else is here! On Tuesday she returned from Switzerland— fat, buxom, healthy, gay, only slightly tanned. She is very happy and in the best of spirits. She is good to me, and gives me much joy.

October 14: Why did Anke have to leave me? . . . I just mustn't think of these things.

December 21: There is a curse on me and the women. Woe to those who love me!

December 29: To Krefeld last night with Hess. Christmas celebration. A delightful, beautiful girl from Franconia. She's my type. Home with her through rain and storm. Au revoir!

Else arrived.

February 6, 1926: I yearn for a sweet woman! Oh, torturing pain!

Goebbels never forgot "Anke"—Anke Helhorn, his first love, whom he had met during his second semester at Freiburg. His diary is full of

---

* These early diaries, unearthed by Allied intelligence agents after the war, are a rich source of information for this period of Goebbel's life.

ravings about her dark-blond beauty and his subsequent disillusionment when she left him. Later, when he became Propaganda Minister, he revealed to friends, with typical vanity and cynicism, why she had left him. "She betrayed me because the other guy had more money and could afford to take her out to dinner and to shows. How foolish of her! . . . Today she might be the wife of the Minister of Propaganda! How frustrated she must feel!" Anke married and divorced "the other guy" and in 1934 came to Berlin, where Goebbels got her a job on a magazine.[3]

It was Strasser's radicalism, his belief in the "socialism" of National Socialism, which attracted the young Goebbels. Both wanted to build the party on the proletariat. The diary of Goebbels is full of expressions of sympathy for Communism at this time. "In the final analysis," he wrote on October 23, 1925, "it would be better for us to end our existence under Bolshevism than to endure slavery under capitalism." On January 31, 1926, he told himself in his diary: "I think it is terrible that we [the Nazis] and the Communists are bashing in each other's heads . . . Where can we get together sometime with the leading Communists?" It was at this time that he published an open letter to a Communist leader assuring him that Nazism and Communism were really the same thing. "You and I," he declared, "are fighting one another, but we are not really enemies."

To Adolf Hitler this was rank heresy, and he watched with increasing uneasiness the success of the Strasser brothers and Goebbels in building up a vigorous, radical, proletarian wing of the party in the north. If left to themselves these men might capture the party, and for objectives which Hitler violently opposed. The inevitable showdown came in the fall of 1925 and in February of the following year.

It was forced by Gregor Strasser and Goebbels over an issue which aroused a good deal of feeling in Germany at that time. This was the proposal of the Social Democrats and the Communists that the extensive estates and fortunes of the deposed royal and princely families be expropriated and taken over by the Republic. The question was to be settled by a plebiscite of the people, in accordance with the Weimar Constitution. Strasser and Goebbels proposed that the Nazi Party jump into the fray with the Communists and the Socialists and support the campaign to expropriate the nobles.

Hitler was furious. Several of these former rulers had kicked in with contributions to the party. Moreover, a number of big industrialists were beginning to become financially interested in Hitler's reborn movement precisely because it promised to be effective in combating the Communists, the Socialists and the trade unions. If Strasser and Goebbels got away with their plans, Hitler's sources of income would immediately dry up.

Before the Fuehrer could act, however, Strasser called a meeting of the northern district party leaders in Hanover on November 22, 1925. Its purpose was not only to put the northern branch of the Nazi Party behind the expropriation drive but to launch a new economic program which would do away with the "reactionary" twenty-five points that had been adopted back in 1920. The Strassers and Goebbels wanted to nationalize the big industries and the big estates and substitute a chamber of corporations on fascist lines for the Reichstag. Hitler declined to attend the meeting, but sent his faithful Gottfried Feder to represent him and to squelch the rebels. Goebbels demanded that Feder be thrown out— "We don't want any stool pigeons!" he cried. Several leaders who would later make their mark in the Third Reich were present—Bernhard Rust, Erich Koch, Hans Kerrl and Robert Ley—but only Ley, the alcoholic chemist who was leader of the Cologne district, supported Hitler. When Dr. Ley and Feder argued that the meeting was out of order, that nothing could be done without Hitler, the Supreme Leader, Goebbels shouted (according to Otto Strasser, who was present), "I demand that the petty bourgeois Adolf Hitler be expelled from the Nazi Party!"

The vituperative young Goebbels had come a long way since he had first fallen under Hitler's spell three years before—or so it must have seemed to Gregor Strasser.

"At that moment I was reborn!" Goebbels exclaimed in recording his impressions of the first time he heard Hitler speak, in the Circus Krone in Munich in June 1922. "Now I knew which road to take . . . This was a command!" He was even more ecstatic over Hitler's behavior during the trial of the Munich putschists. After the verdicts were in, Goebbels wrote the Fuehrer:

Like a rising star you appeared before our wondering eyes, you performed miracles to clear our minds and, in a world of skepticism and desperation, gave us faith. You towered above the masses, full of faith and certain of the future, and possessed by the will to free those masses with your unlimited love for all those who believe in the new Reich. For the first time we saw with shining eyes a man who tore off the mask from the faces distorted by greed, the faces of mediocre parliamentary busybodies . . .

In the Munich court you grew before us to the greatness of the Fuehrer. What you said are the greatest words spoken in Germany since Bismarck. You expressed more than your own pain . . . You named the need of a whole generation, searching in confused longing for men and task. What you said is the catechism of the new political belief, born out of the despair of a collapsing, Godless world . . . We thank you. One day, Germany will thank you . . .

But now, a year and a half later, Goebbels' idol had fallen. He had become a "petty bourgeois" who deserved being booted out of the party. With only Ley and Feder dissenting, the Hanover meeting adopted Strasser's new party program and approved the decision to join the Marxists in the plebiscite campaign to deprive the former kings and princes of their possessions.

Hitler bided his time and then on February 14, 1926, struck back. He called a meeting at Bamberg, in southern Germany, shrewdly picking a weekday, when it was difficult for the northern leaders to get away from their jobs. In fact, only Gregor Strasser and Goebbels were able to attend. They were greatly outnumbered by Hitler's hand-picked leaders in the south. And at the Fuehrer's insistence they were forced to capitulate and abandon their program. Such German historians of Nazism as Heiden and Olden, and the non-German writers who have been guided by them, have recounted that at the Bamberg meeting Goebbels openly deserted Strasser and went over to Hitler. But the Goebbels diaries, discovered after Heiden and Olden wrote their books, reveal that he did not betray Strasser quite so abruptly. They show that Goebbels, though he joined Strasser in surrendering to Hitler, thought the Fuehrer was utterly wrong, and that, for the moment at least, he had no intention whatever of going over to him. On February 15, the day after the Bamberg meeting, he confided to his diary:

Hitler talks for two hours. I feel as though someone had beaten me. What sort of Hitler is this? A reactionary? Extremely awkward and unsteady. Completely wrong on the Russian question. Italy and England are our natural allies! Horrible! . . . We must annihilate Russia! . . . The question of the private property of the nobility must not even be touched upon. Terrible! . . . I cannot utter a word. I feel as though I've been hit over the head . . .

Certainly one of the great disappointments of my life. I no longer have complete faith in Hitler. That is the terrible thing: my props have been taken from under me.

To show where his loyalties stood, Goebbels went to the station with Strasser and tried to console him. A week later, on February 23, he records: "Long conference with Strasser. Result: we must not begrudge the Munich crowd their Pyrrhic victory. We must begin again our fight for socialism."

But Hitler had sized up the flamboyant young Rhinelander better than Strasser. On March 29 Goebbels noted: "This morning a letter from Hitler. I shall make a speech on April 8 at Munich." He arrived there on April 7. "Hitler's car is waiting," he recorded. "What a royal reception! I will speak at the historic Buergerbräu." The next day he did, from the same platform as the Leader. He wrote it all down in his diary entry of April 8:

Hitler phones . . . His kindness in spite of Bamberg makes us feel ashamed . . . At 2 o'clock we drive to the Buergerbräu. Hitler is already there. My heart is beating so wildly it is about to burst. I enter the hall. Roaring welcome . . . And then I speak for two and a half hours . . . People roar and shout. At the end Hitler embraces me. I feel happy . . . Hitler is always at my side.

A few days later Goebbels surrendered completely. "*April 13:* Hitler spoke for three hours. Brilliantly. He can make you doubt your own views. Italy and England our allies. Russia wants to devour us . . . I love him . . . He has thought everything through. His ideal: a just collectivism and individualism. As to soil—everything belongs to the people. Production to be creative and individualistic. Trusts, transport, etc., to be socialized . . . I am now at ease about him . . . I bow to the greater man, to the political genius."

When Goebbels left Munich on April 17 he was Hitler's man and was to remain his most loyal follower to his dying breath. On April 20 he wrote the Fuehrer a birthday note: "Dear and revered Adolf Hitler! I have learned so much from you . . . You have finally made me see the light . . ." And that night in his diary: "He is thirty-seven years old. Adolf Hitler, I love you because you are both great and simple. These are the characteristics of the genius."

Goebbels spent a good part of the summer with Hitler at Berchtesgaden, and his diary is full of further encomiums to the Leader. In August he publicly broke with Strasser in an article in the *Voelkischer Beobachter.*

Only now do I recognize you for what you are: revolutionaries in speech but not in deed [he told the Strassers and their followers] . . . Don't talk so much about ideals and don't fool yourselves into believing that you are the inventors and protectors of these ideals . . . We are not doing penance by standing solidly behind the Fuehrer. We . . . bow to him . . . with the manly, unbroken pride of the ancient Norsemen who stand upright before their Germanic feudal lord. We feel that he is greater than all of us, greater than you and I. He is the instrument of the Divine Will that shapes history with fresh, creative passion.

Late in October 1926 Hitler made Goebbels Gauleiter of Berlin. He instructed him to clean out the quarreling Brownshirt rowdies who had been hampering the growth of the movement there and conquer the capital of Germany for National Socialism. Berlin was "red." The majority of its voters were Socialists and Communists. Undaunted, Goebbels, who had just turned twenty-nine, and who in a little more than a year's time had risen from nothing to be one of the leading lights of the Nazi Party, set out to fulfill his assignment in the great Babylonian city.

AN INTERLUDE OF REST AND ROMANCE
FOR ADOLF HITLER

The politically lean years for Adolf Hitler were, as he later said, the best years of his personal life. Forbidden to speak in public until 1927, intent on finishing *Mein Kampf* and plotting in his mind the future of the Nazi Party and of himself, he spent most of his time on the Obersalzberg above the market village of Berchtesgaden in the Bavarian Alps. It was a haven for rest and relaxation.

Hitler's monologues at his headquarters at the front during the war, when late at night he would relax with the old party comrades and his faithful women secretaries and reminisce about past times, are full of nostalgic talk about what this mountain retreat, where he established the only home he ever owned, meant to him. "Yes," he exclaimed during one of these sessions on the night of January 16–17, 1942, "there are so many links between Obersalzberg and me. So many things were born there . . . I spent there the finest hours of my life . . . It is there that all my great projects were conceived and ripened. I had hours of leisure in those days, and how many charming friends!"

During the first three years after his release from prison Hitler lived in various inns on the Obersalzberg and in that winter reminiscence in 1942 he talked for an hour about them. He finally settled down in the Deutsche Haus, where he spent the best part of two years and in which he finished dictating *Mein Kampf*. He and his party cronies, he says, were "very fond of visiting the Dreimaederlhaus, where there were always pretty girls. This," he adds, "was a great treat for me. There was one of them, especially, who was a real beauty."

That evening in the headquarters bunker on the Russian front, Hitler made a remark to his listeners that recalls two preoccupations he had during the pleasant years at Berchtesgaden.

At this period [on the Obersalzberg] I knew a lot of women. Several of them became attached to me. Why, then, didn't I marry? To leave a wife behind me? At the slightest imprudence, I ran the risk of going back to prison for six years. So there could be no question of marriage for me. I therefore had to renounce certain opportunities that offered themselves.[4]

Hitler's fear in the mid-Twenties of being sent back to prison or of being deported was not without some foundation. He was still on parole. Had he openly evaded the ban against his speaking in public the Bavarian government might well have clapped him behind the bars again or sent him back over the border to his native Austria. One reason that he had chosen the Obersalzberg as a refuge was its proximity to the Austrian frontier; on a moment's notice he could have slipped over the line and evaded arrest by the German police. But to have returned to Austria, voluntarily or by force, would have ruined his prospects. To lessen the risk of deportation, Hitler formally renounced his Austrian citizenship on April 7, 1925—a step that was promptly accepted by the Austrian government. This, however, left him *staatenlos,* a man without a country. He gave up his Austrian citizenship but he did not become a citizen of Germany. This was a considerable handicap for a politician in the Reich. For one thing, he could not be elected to office. He had publicly declared that he would never beg the republican government for a citizenship which he felt should have been his because of his services to Imperial Germany in the war. But all through the last half of the 1920s, he secretly sought to have the Bavarian government make him a German national. His efforts failed.

As to women and marriage, there was also some truth in what Hitler related that evening of 1942. Contrary to the general opinion, he liked the company of women, especially if they were beautiful. He returns to the subject time and again in his table talk at Supreme Headquarters during the war. "What lovely women there are in the world!" he exclaims to his cronies on the night of January 25–26, 1942, and he gives several examples in his personal experience. adding the boast, "In my youth in Vienna, I knew a lot of lovely women!" Heiden has recounted some of his romantic yearnings of the early days: for a Jenny Haug, whose brother was Hitler's chauffeur and who passed as his sweetheart in 1923; for the tall and stately Erna Hanfstaengl, sister of Putzi; for Winifred Wagner, daughter-in-law of Richard Wagner. But it was with his niece that Adolf Hitler had, so far as is known, the only deep love affair of his life.

In the summer of 1928 Hitler rented the villa Wachenfeld on the Obersalzberg above Berchtesgaden for a hundred marks a month ($25) from the widow of a Hamburg industrialist and induced his widowed half-sister, Angela Raubal, to come from Vienna to keep house for him in the first home which he could call his own.* Frau Raubal brought along her two daughters, Geli and Friedl. Geli was twenty, with flowing blond hair, handsome features, a pleasant voice and a sunny disposition which made her attractive to men.[5]

Hitler soon fell in love with her. He took her everywhere, to meetings and conferences, on long walks in the mountains and to the cafés and theaters in Munich. When in 1929 he rented a luxurious nine-room apartment in the Prinzregentenstrasse, one of the most fashionable thoroughfares in Munich, Geli was given her own room in it. Gossip about the party leader and his beautiful blond niece was inevitable in Munich and throughout Nazi circles in southern Germany. Some of the more prim—or envious—leaders suggested that Hitler cease showing off his youthful sweetheart in public, or that he marry her. Hitler was furious at such talk and in one quarrel over the matter he fired the Gauleiter of Wuerttemberg.

It is probable that Hitler intended to marry his niece. Early party comrades who were close to him at that time subsequently told this author that a marriage seemed inevitable. That Hitler was deeply in love with her they had no doubt. Her own feelings are a matter of conjecture. That she was flattered by the attentions of a man now becoming famous, and indeed enjoyed them, is obvious. Whether she reciprocated her uncle's love is not known; probably not, and in the end certainly not. Some deep rift whose origins and nature have never been fully ascertained grew between them. There has been much speculation but little evidence. Each was apparently jealous of the other. She resented his attentions to other

* Later he bought it and, after becoming Chancellor, rebuilt it on a vast and lavish scale, changing the name from Haus Wachenfeld to Berghof.

women—to Winifred Wagner, among others. He suspected that she had had a clandestine affair with Emil Maurice, the ex-convict who had been his bodyguard. She objected too to her uncle's tyranny over her. He did not want her to be seen in the company of any man but himself. He forbade her to go to Vienna to continue her singing lessons, squelching her ambition for a career on the operatic stage. He wanted her for himself alone.

There are dark hints too that she was repelled by the masochistic inclinations of her lover, that this brutal tyrant in politics yearned to be enslaved by the woman he loved—a not uncommon urge in such men, according to the sexologists. Heiden tells of a letter which Hitler wrote to his niece in 1929 confessing his deepest feelings in this regard. It fell into the hands of his landlady's son—with consequences which were tragic to more than one life.[6]

Whatever it was that darkened the love between the uncle and his niece, their quarrels became more violent and at the end of the summer of 1931 Geli announced that she was returning to Vienna to resume her voice studies. Hitler forbade her to go. There was a scene between the two, witnessed by neighbors, when Hitler left his Munich apartment to go to Hamburg on September 17, 1931. The young girl was heard to cry to him from the window as her uncle was getting into his car, "Then you won't let me go to Vienna?" and he was heard to respond, "No!"

The next morning Geli Raubal was found shot dead in her room. The state's attorney, after a thorough investigation, found that it was a suicide. The coroner reported that a bullet had gone through her chest below the left shoulder and penetrated the heart; it seemed beyond doubt that the shot was self-inflicted.

Yet for years afterward in Munich there was murky gossip that Geli Raubal had been murdered—by Hitler in a rage, by Himmler to eliminate a situation that had become embarrassing to the party. But no credible evidence ever turned up to substantiate such rumors.

Hitler himself was struck down by grief. Gregor Strasser later recounted that he had had to remain for the following two days and nights at Hitler's side to prevent him from taking his own life. A week after Geli's burial in Vienna, Hitler obtained special permission from the Austrian government to go there; he spent an evening weeping at the grave. For months he was inconsolable.

Three weeks after the death of Geli, Hitler had his first interview with Hindenburg. It was his first bid for the big stakes, for the chancellorship of the Reich. His distraction on this momentous occasion—some of his friends said he did not seem to be in full possession of his faculties during the conversation, which went badly for the Nazi leader—was put down by those who knew him as due to the shock of the loss of his beloved niece.

From this personal blow stemmed, I believe, an act of renunciation, his decision to abstain from meat; at least, some of his closest henchmen seemed to think so. To them he declared forever afterward that Geli Raubal was the only woman he ever loved, and he always spoke of her with the deepest reverence—and often in tears. Servants said that her room in the villa at Obersalzberg, even after it was rebuilt and enlarged in the days of Hitler's chancellorship, remained as she had left it. In his own room there, and in the Chancellery in Berlin, portraits* of the young woman always hung and when the anniversaries of her birth and death came around each year flowers were placed around them.

For a brutal, cynical man who always seemed to be incapable of love of any other human being, this passion of Hitler's for the youthful Geli Raubal stands out as one of the mysteries of his strange life. As with all mysteries, it cannot be rationally explained, merely recounted. Thereafter, it is almost certain, Adolf Hitler never seriously contemplated marriage until the day before he took his own life fourteen years later.

The compromising letter from Hitler to his niece was retrieved from the landlord's son through the efforts of Father Bernhard Stempfle, the Hieronymite Catholic priest and anti-Semitic journalist who had helped the Nazi leader in tidying up *Mein Kampf* for publication. The money for its purchase, according to Heiden, was supplied by Franz Xavier Schwarz, the party treasurer. Thus Father Stempfle was one of the few persons who knew something of the secrets of Hitler's love for Geli Raubal. Apparently he did not keep his knowledge of the affair entirely to himself. He was to pay for this lapse with his life when the author of *Mein Kampf* became dictator of Germany and one day settled accounts with some of his old friends.

The source of Hitler's income during those personally comfortable years when he acquired a villa at Obersalzberg and a luxurious apartment in Munich and drove about in a flashy, chauffeured automobile, for which he paid 20,000 marks ($5,000), has never been established. But his income tax files, which turned up after the war, shed some light on the subject.[7] Until he became Chancellor and had himself declared exempt from taxation, he was in continual conflict with the tax authorities, and a considerable file accumulated in the Munich Finance Office between 1925 and 1933.

That office notified him on May 1, 1925, that he had failed to file a return for 1924 or for the first quarter of 1925. Hitler replied, "I had no income in 1924 [when he was in prison], or in the first quarter of 1925. I have covered my living expenses by raising a bank loan." What about that $5,000 automobile? the tax collector shot back. Hitler answered that he had raised a bank loan for that too. In all his tax returns, Hitler listed his profession as "writer" and, as such, attempted to justify a high proportion of his income as deductible expenses—he doubtless was aware of the practice of writers everywhere. His first income tax declaration, for the third quarter of 1925, listed a gross income of 11,231 R.M., deductible

---

* Painted after her death by Adolf Ziegler, Hitler's favorite painter.

professional expenses of 6,540 R.M. and interest payments on loans of 2,245 R.M., which left a net taxable income of 2,446 R.M.

In a three-page typewritten explanation Hitler defended his large deductions for professional expenses, arguing that though a large part of them appeared to be due to his political activities, such work provided him with the material he needed as a political writer and also helped increase the sales of his book.

Without my political activity my name would be unknown, and I would be lacking materials for the publication of a political work . . . Accordingly in my case as a political writer, the expenses of my political activity, which is the necessary condition of my professional writing as well as its assurance of financial success, cannot be regarded as subject to taxation. . . .

The Finance Office can see that out of the income from my book, for this period, only a very small fraction was expended for myself; *nowhere do I possess property or other capital assets that I can call my own.** I restrict of necessity my personal wants so far that I am a complete abstainer from alcohol and tobacco, take my meals in most modest restaurants, and aside from my minimal apartment rent make no expenditures that are not chargeable to my expenses as a political writer . . . *Also the automobile is for me but a means to an end. It alone makes it possible for me to accomplish my daily work.*[8]

The Finance Office allowed but one half of the deductions, and when Hitler appealed to the Review Board it upheld the original assessment. Thereafter only one half of his expense deductions were allowed by the tax authorities. He protested but paid.

The Nazi leader's reported gross income in his tax returns correspond pretty accurately to his royalties from *Mein Kampf:* 19,843 R.M. in 1925, 15,903 R.M. in 1926, 11,494 R.M. in 1927, 11,818 R.M. in 1928 and 15,448 R.M. in 1929. Since publishers' books were subject to inspection by the tax office, Hitler could not safely report an income less than his royalties. But what about other sources of income? These were never reported. It was known that he demanded, and received, a high fee for the many articles which he wrote in those days for the impoverished Nazi press. There was much grumbling in party circles over the high cost of Hitler. These items are absent from his tax declarations. As the Twenties neared their end, money started to flow into the Nazi Party from a few of the big Bavarian and Rhineland industrialists who were attracted by Hitler's opposition to the Marxists and the trade unions. Fritz Thyssen, head of the German steel trust, the Vereinigte Stahlwerke (United Steel Works), and Emil Kirdorf, the Ruhr coal king, contributed sizable sums. Often the money was handed over directly to Hitler. How much he kept for himself will probably never be known. But his scale of living in the last few years before he became Chancellor indicates that not all of the money he received from his backers was turned over to the party treasury.

---

* The italics in this declaration are Hitler's.

To be sure, from 1925 to 1928 he complained of difficulty in meeting his income tax payments; he was constantly in arrears and invariably asking for further postponements. In September of 1926 he wrote the Finance Office: "At the moment I am not in a position to pay the taxes; to cover my living expenses I have had to raise a loan." Later he claimed of that period that "for years I lived on Tyrolean apples. It's unbelievable what economies we had to make. Every mark saved was for the party." And between 1925 and 1928 he contended, to the tax collector, that he was going ever deeper in debt. In 1926 he reported expenditures of 31,-209 R.M. against an income of 15,903 R.M. and stated the deficit had been made up by further "bank loans."

Then, miraculously, in 1929, though his declared income was considerably less than in 1925, the item of interest on or repayment of loans disappears from his tax declaration—and never reappears. As Professor Hale, on whose studies the foregoing is based, remarked, "a financial miracle had been wrought and he had liquidated his indebtedness."[9]

Hitler, it must be said in fairness, never seemed to care much about money—if he had enough to live on comfortably and if he did not have to toil for it in wages or a salary. At any rate, beginning with 1930, when his book royalties suddenly tripled from the previous year to some $12,-000 and money started pouring in from big business, any personal financial worries he may have had were over for good. He could now devote his fierce energies and all his talents to the task of fulfilling his destiny. The time for his final drive for power, for the dictatorship of a great nation, had arrived.

THE OPPORTUNITIES OF THE DEPRESSION

The depression which spread over the world like a great conflagration toward the end of 1929 gave Adolf Hitler his opportunity, and he made the most of it. Like most great revolutionaries he could thrive only in evil times, at first when the masses were unemployed, hungry and desperate, and later when they were intoxicated by war. Yet in one respect he was unique among history's revolutionaries: He intended to make his revolution *after* achieving political power. There was to be no revolution to gain control of the State. That goal was to be reached by mandate of the voters or by the consent of the rulers of the nation—in short, by constitutional means. To get the votes Hitler had only to take advantage of the times, which once more, as the Thirties began, saw the German people plunged into despair; to obtain the support of those in power he had to convince them that only he could rescue Germany from its disastrous predicament. In the turbulent years from 1930 to 1933 the shrewd and daring Nazi leader set out with renewed energy to obtain these twin objectives. In retrospect it can be seen that events themselves and the weakness and confusion of the handful of men who were bound by their oath to loyally defend the democratic Republic which they governed played into Hitler's hands. But this was by no means foreseeable at the beginning of 1930.

Gustav Stresemann died on October 3, 1929. He had exhausted himself by his strenuous labors, as Foreign Minister over the preceding six years, to restore defeated Germany to the ranks of the big powers and to guide the German people toward political and economic stability. His successes had been prodigious. He had brought Germany into the League of Nations, negotiated the Dawes Plan and the Young Plan which reduced reparations to a level which Germany could easily pay, and in 1925 had been one of the chief architects of the Pact of Locarno which brought Western Europe the first tranquillity its war-weary, strife-ridden people had known in a generation.

Three weeks after Stresemann's death, on October 24, the stock market in Wall Street crashed. The results in Germany were soon felt—and disastrously. The cornerstone of German prosperity had been loans from abroad, principally from America, and world trade. When the flow of loans dried up and repayment on the old ones became due the German financial structure was unable to stand the strain. When world trade sagged following the general slump Germany was unable to export enough to pay for essential imports of the raw materials and food which she needed. Without exports, German industry could not keep its plants going, and its production fell by almost half from 1929 to 1932. Millions were thrown out of work. Thousands of small business enterprises went under. In May of 1931 Austria's biggest bank, the Kreditanstalt, collapsed, and this was followed on July 13 by the failure of one of Germany's principal banks, the Darmstaedter und Nationalbank, which forced the government in Berlin to close down all banks temporarily. Not even President Hoover's initiative in establishing a moratorium on all war debts, including German reparations, which became effective on July 6, could stem the tide. The whole Western world was stricken by forces which its leaders did not understand and which they felt were beyond man's control. How was it possible that suddenly there could be so much poverty, so much human suffering, in the midst of so much plenty?

Hitler had predicted the catastrophe, but no more than any other politician did he understand what had brought it about; perhaps he had less understanding than most, since he was both ignorant of and uninterested in economics. But he was not uninterested in or ignorant of the opportunities which the depression suddenly gave him. The misery of the German people, their lives still scarred by disastrous experience of the collapse of the mark less than ten years before, did not arouse his compassion. On the contrary, in the darkest days of that period, when the factories were silent, when the registered unemployed numbered over six million and bread lines stretched for blocks in every city in the land, he could write in the Nazi press: "Never in my life have I been so well disposed and inwardly contented as in these days. For hard reality has opened the eyes of millions of Germans to the unprecedented swindles, lies and betrayals of the Marxist deceivers of the people."[10] The suffering of his fellow

Germans was not something to waste time sympathizing with, but rather to transform, cold-bloodedly and immediately, into political support for his own ambitions. This he proceeded to do in the late summer of 1930.

Hermann Mueller, the last Social Democrat Chancellor of Germany and the head of the last government based on a coalition of the democratic parties which had sustained the Weimar Republic, had resigned in March 1930 because of a dispute among the parties over the unemployment insurance fund. He had been replaced by Heinrich Bruening, the parliamentary leader of the Catholic Center Party, who had won the Iron Cross as a captain of a machine gun company during the war and whose sober, conservative views in the Reichstag had attracted the favorable attention of the Army and in particular of a general by the name of Kurt von Schleicher, who was then quite unknown to the German public. Schleicher, a vain, able, ambitious "desk officer," already acknowledged in military circles as a talented and unscrupulous intriguer, had suggested Bruening's name to President von Hindenburg. The new Chancellor, though he may not have realized it fully, was the Army's candidate. A man of sterling personal character, unselfish, modest, honest, dedicated, somewhat austere in nature, Bruening hoped to restore stable parliamentary government in Germany and rescue the country from the growing slump and political chaos. It was the tragedy of this well-meaning and democratically minded patriot that, in trying to do so, he unwittingly dug the grave for German democracy and thus, unintentionally, paved the way for the coming of Adolf Hitler.

Bruening was unable to induce a majority of the Reichstag to approve certain measures in his financial program. He thereupon asked Hindenburg to invoke Article 48 of the constitution and under its emergency powers approve his financial bill by presidential decree. The chamber responded by voting a demand for the withdrawal of the decree. Parliamentary government was breaking down at a moment when the economic crisis made strong government imperative. In an effort to find a way out of the impasse, Bruening requested the President in July 1930 to dissolve the Reichstag. New elections were called for September 14. How Bruening expected to get a stable parliamentary majority in a new election is a question that was never answered. But Hitler realized that his own opportunity had come sooner than he expected.

The hard-pressed people were demanding a way out of their sorry predicament. The millions of unemployed wanted jobs. The shopkeepers wanted help. Some four million youths who had come of voting age since the last election wanted some prospect of a future that would at least give them a living. To all the millions of discontented Hitler in a whirlwind campaign offered what seemed to them, in their misery, some measure of hope. He would make Germany strong again, refuse to pay reparations, repudiate the Versailles Treaty, stamp out corruption, bring the money barons to heel (especially if they were Jews) and see to it that every

German had a job and bread. To hopeless, hungry men seeking not only relief but new faith and new gods, the appeal was not without effect.

Though his hopes were high, Hitler was surprised on the night of September 14, 1930, when the election returns came in. Two years before, his party had polled 810,000 votes and elected 12 members to the Reichstag. This time he had counted on quadrupling the Nazi vote and securing perhaps 50 seats in Parliament. But on this day the vote of the N.S.D.A.P. rose to 6,409,600, entitling the party to 107 seats in the Reichstag and propelling it from the ninth and smallest party in Parliament to the second largest.

At the other extreme, the Communists had also gained, from 3,265,000 votes in 1928 to 4,592,000, with their representation in the Reichstag increased from 54 to 77. The moderate middle-class parties, with the exception of the Catholic Center, lost over a million votes, as did the Social Democrats, despite the addition of four million new voters at the polls. The vote of the right-wing Nationalists of Hugenberg dropped from four to two million. It was clear that the Nazis had captured millions of adherents from the other middle-class parties. It was also clear that henceforth it would be more difficult than ever for Bruening—or for anyone else—to command a stable majority in the Reichstag. Without such a majority how could the Republic survive?

This was a question which on the morrow of the 1930 elections became of increased interest to two pillars of the nation whose leaders had never really accepted the Republic except as a passing misfortune in German history: the Army and the world of the big industrialists and financiers. Flushed by his success at the polls, Hitler now turned his attention toward winning over these two powerful groups. Long ago in Vienna, as we have seen, he had learned from the tactics of Mayor Karl Lueger the importance of bringing "powerful existing institutions" over to one's side.

A year before, on March 15, 1929, Hitler had made a speech in Munich in which he appealed to the Army to reconsider its enmity toward National Socialism and its support of the Republic.

The future does not lie with the parties of destruction, but rather with the parties who carry in themselves the strength of the people, who are prepared and who wish to bind themselves to this Army in order to aid the Army someday in defending the interests of the people. In contrast we still see the officers of our Army belatedly tormenting themselves with the question as to how far one can go along with Social Democracy. But, my dear sirs, do you really believe that you have anything in common with an ideology which stipulates the dissolution of all that which is the basis of the existence of an army?

This was a skillful bid for the support of the officers of the Army which, as most of them believed and as Hitler now repeated for the hundredth time, had been stabbed in the back and betrayed by the very Republic which they were now supporting and which, moreover, had no love for the military caste and all that it stood for. And then in words which were prophetic of what he himself one day would do, he warned the officers of what would happen to them if the Marxists triumphed over the Nazis. Should that happen, he said,

> You may write over the German Army: "The end of the German Army." For then, gentlemen, you must definitely become political. . . . You may then become hangmen of the regime and political commissars, and if you do not behave your wife and child will be put behind locked doors. And if you still do not behave, you will be thrown out and perhaps stood up against a wall . . .[11]

Relatively few persons heard the speech, but in order to propagate it in Army circles the *Voelkischer Beobachter* published it verbatim in a special Army edition and it was discussed at length in the columns of a Nazi monthly magazine, *Deutscher Wehrgeist,* a periodical devoted to military affairs which had recently appeared.

In 1927 the Army had forbidden the recruitment of Nazis in the 100,000-man Reichswehr and even banned their employment as civilians in the arsenals and supply depots. But by the beginning of 1930 it became obvious that Nazi propaganda was making headway in the Army, especially among the younger officers, many of whom were attracted not only by Hitler's fanatical nationalism but by the prospects he held out for an Army restored to its old glory and size in which there would be opportunities, now denied them in such a small military force, to advance to higher rank.

The Nazi infiltration into the armed services became serious enough to compel General Groener, now the Minister of Defense, to issue an order of the day on January 22, 1930, which recalled a similar warning to the Army by General von Seeckt on the eve of the Beer Hall Putsch seven years before. The Nazis, he declared, were greedy for power. "They therefore woo the Wehrmacht. In order to use it for the political aims of their party, they attempt to dazzle us [into believing] that the National Socialists alone represent the truly national power." He requested the soldiers to refrain from politics and to "serve the state" aloof from all party strife.

That some of the young Reichswehr officers were not refraining from politics, or at least not from Nazi politics, came to light shortly afterward and aroused a furor in Germany, dissension in the highest echelons of the officer corps, and delight in the Nazi camp. In the spring of 1930 three young lieutenants, Ludin, Scheringer and Wendt, of the garrison at Ulm were arrested for spreading Nazi doctrines in the Army and for trying to induce their fellow officers to agree that in the case of an armed Nazi revolt they would not fire on the rebels. This last was high treason, but General Groener, not wishing to publicize the fact that treason existed in the Army, attempted to hush up the affair by arranging for the accused to be tried before a court-martial for a simple breach of discipline. The defiance of Lieutenant Scheringer, who smuggled out an inflammatory article for the *Voelkischer Beobachter,* made this impossible. A week after the Nazi successes in the September elections of 1930, the three subalterns were arraigned before the Supreme Court at Leipzig on charges of high treason. Among their defenders were two rising Nazi lawyers, Hans Frank and Dr. Carl Sack.*

But it was neither the lawyers nor the accused who occupied the limelight at the trial, but Adolf Hitler. He was called by Frank as a witness. His appearance represented a calculated risk. It would be embarrassing to disown the three lieutenants, whose activities were proof of the growth of Nazi sentiment in the Army, which he did not want to discourage. It was embarrassing that Nazi efforts to subvert the Army had been uncovered. And it was not helpful to his present tactics that the prosecution had charged the Nazi Party with being a revolutionary organization intent on overthrowing the government by force. To deny that last charge, Hitler arranged with Frank to testify for the defense. But in reality the Fuehrer had a much more important objective. That was, as leader of a movement which had just scored a stunning popular triumph at the polls, to assure the Army and especially its leading officers that National Socialism, far from posing a threat to the Reichswehr, as the case of the Nazi subalterns implied, was really its salvation and the salvation of Germany.

From this national forum which the witness box afforded, Hitler made good use of all his forensic talents and his subtle sense of political strategy, and if his masterly display was full of deceit, as it was, few in Germany, even among the generals, seemed to be aware of it. Blandly Hitler assured the court (and the Army officers) that neither the S.A. nor the party was fighting the Army. "I have always held the view," he declared, "that any attempt to replace the Army was madness. None of us have any interest in replacing the Army . . . We will see to it, when we have come to power, that out of the present Reichswehr a great Army of the German people shall arise."

And he reiterated to the court (and the generals) that the Nazi Party was seeking to capture power only by constitutional means and that the young officers were mistaken if they anticipated an armed revolt.

Our movement has no need of force. The time will come when the German nation will get to know of our ideas; then thirty-five million Germans will stand behind me . . . When we do possess constitutional rights, then we will form the State in the manner which we consider to be the right one.

THE PRESIDENT OF THE COURT: This, too, by constitutional means?

HITLER: Yes.

---

* Both of whom would end their lives on the gallows, Sack for his part in the conspiracy against Hitler on July 20, 1944, and Frank for what he did on behalf of Hitler in Poland.

But Hitler, though he was addressing mainly the Army and the other conservative elements in Germany, had to consider the revolutionary fervor of his own party followers. He could not let them down, as he had the three accused. He therefore seized on the opportunity presented when the president of the court recalled a statement of his in 1923, a month before his unsuccessful putsch, that "heads will roll in the sand." Did the Nazi leader repudiate that utterance today?

> I can assure you [Hitler replied] that when the National Socialist movement is victorious in this struggle, then there will be a National Socialist Court of Justice too. Then the November 1918 revolution will be avenged and heads will roll![12]

No one can say that Hitler did not give warning of what he would do if he came to power, but the audience in the courtroom apparently welcomed it, for they applauded the threat loudly and long, and though the presiding judge took exception to the interruption neither he nor the public prosecutor made objection to the remark. It made a sensational headline in newspapers throughout Germany and in many outside. Lost in the excitement of Hitler's utterances was the actual case in hand. The three young officers, their zeal for National Socialism disavowed by the Supreme Leader of National Socialism himself, were found guilty of conspiracy to commit high treason and given the mild sentence of eighteen months of fortress detention—in republican Germany the severe sentences on this charge were reserved for those who supported the Republic.*

The month of September 1930 marked a turning point in the road that was leading the Germans inexorably toward the Third Reich. The surprising success of the Nazi Party in the national elections convinced not only millions of ordinary people but many leaders in business and in the Army that perhaps here was an upsurge that could not be stopped. They might not like the party's demagoguery and its vulgarity, but on the other hand it was arousing the old feelings of German patriotism and nationalism which had been so muted during the first ten years of the Republic. It promised to lead the German people away from communism, socialism, trade-unionism and the futilities of democracy. Above all, it had caught fire throughout the Reich. It was a success.

Because of this and of Hitler's public assurances to the Army at the Leipzig trial, some of the generals began to ponder whether National Socialism might not be just what was needed to unify the people, restore the old Germany, make the Army big and great once more and enable

---

* Lieutenant Scheringer, embittered by what he considered Hitler's betrayal, renounced the Nazi Party while in prison and became a fanatical Communist. He was marked—as were so many who crossed Hitler—for liquidation in the June 30, 1934, purge, but somehow escaped and lived to see the end of Hitler. Lieutenant Ludin remained an enthusiastic Nazi, was elected to the Reichstag in 1932, became a high officer in the S.A. and the S.S., and served as German minister to the puppet state of Slovakia, where he was arrested at the time of the liberation and executed by the Czechoslovaks.

the nation to shake off the shackles of the humiliating Treaty of Versailles. They had been pleased with Hitler's retort to the presiding judge of the Supreme Court, who had asked him what he meant when he kept talking about the "German National Revolution."

"This means," Hitler had said, "exclusively the rescue of the enslaved German nation we have today. Germany is bound hand and foot by the peace treaties . . . The National Socialists do not regard these treaties as law, but as something imposed upon Germany by constraint. We do not admit that future generations, who are completely innocent, should be burdened by them. If we protest against them with every means in our power, then we find ourselves on the path of revolution."

That was the view of the officer corps too. Some of its leading members had bitterly criticized General Groener, the Minister of Defense, for allowing the three subalterns to be tried by the Supreme Court. General Hans von Seeckt, the recently deposed Commander in Chief and generally acknowledged as the postwar genius of the German Army, the worthy successor of Scharnhorst and Gneisenau, complained to Groener that it had weakened the spirit of solidarity within the officer corps. Colonel Ludwig Beck, who was soon to become Chief of Staff and later an even more important figure in this history but who in 1930 was the commander of the 5th Artillery Regiment at Ulm from which the three lieutenants had come, not only protested vehemently to his superiors against their arrest but testified in their defense at Leipzig.

Now that the trial was over and Hitler had spoken, the generals felt better disposed toward a movement which they had previously regarded as a threat to the Army. General Alfred Jodl, Chief of Operations of the Armed Forces High Command during World War II, told the military tribunal at Nuremberg just what the Nazi leader's statement at Leipzig had meant to the officer corps. Until that time, he said, the senior officers had believed Hitler was trying to undermine the Army; now they were reassured. General von Seeckt himself, after his election to the Reichstag in 1930, openly allied himself with Hitler for a while and in 1932 urged his sister to vote for Hitler—instead of for his old chief, Hindenburg— in the presidential elections.

The political blindness of the German Army officers, which was to prove so fatal to them in the end, had begun to grow and to show.

The political ineptitude of the magnates of industry and finance was no less than that of the generals and led to the mistaken belief that if they coughed up large enough sums for Hitler he would be beholden to them and, if he ever came to power, do their bidding. That the Austrian upstart, as many of them had regarded him in the Twenties, might well take over the control of Germany began to dawn on the business leaders after the sensational Nazi gains in the September elections of 1930.

By 1931, Walther Funk testified at Nuremberg, "my industrial friends and I were convinced that the Nazi Party would come to power in the not too distant future."

In the summer of that year Funk, a greasy, shifty-eyed, paunchy little man whose face always reminded this writer of a frog, gave up a lucrative job as editor of a leading German financial newspaper, the *Berliner Boersenzeitung,* joined the Nazi Party and became a contact man between the party and a number of important business leaders. He explained at Nuremberg that several of his industrialist friends, especially those prominent in the big Rhineland mining concerns, had urged him to join the Nazi movement "in order to persuade the party to follow the course of private enterprise."

At that time the leadership of the party held completely contradictory and confused views on economic policy. I tried to accomplish my mission by personally impressing on the Fuehrer and the party that private initiative, self-reliance of the businessman, the creative powers of free enterprise, et cetera, be recognized as the basic economic policy of the party. The Fuehrer personally stressed time and again during talks with me and industrial leaders to whom I had introduced him, that he was an enemy of state economy and of so-called "planned economy" and that he considered free enterprise and competition as absolutely necessary in order to gain the highest possible production.[13]

Hitler, then, as his future Reichsbank president and Minister of Economics says, was beginning to see the men in Germany who had the money, and he was telling them more or less what they wanted to hear. The party needed large sums to finance election campaigns, pay the bill for its widespread and intensified propaganda, meet the payroll of hundreds of full-time officials and maintain the private armies of the S.A. and the S.S., which by the end of 1930 numbered more than 100,000 men —a larger force than the Reichswehr. The businessmen and the bankers were not the only financial sources—the party raised sizable sums from dues, assessments, collections and the sale of party newspapers, books and periodicals—but they were the largest. And the more money they gave the Nazis, the less they would have for the other conservative parties which they had been supporting hitherto.

"In the summer of 1931," Otto Dietrich, Hitler's press chief first for the party and later for the Reich, relates, "the Fuehrer suddenly decided to concentrate systematically on cultivating the influential industrial magnates."[14]

What magnates were they?

Their identity was a secret which was kept from all but the inner circle around the Leader. The party had to play both sides of the tracks. It had to allow Strasser, Goebbels and the crank Feder to beguile the masses with the cry that the National Socialists were truly "socialists" and against the money barons. On the other hand, money to keep the party going had to be wheedled out of those who had an ample supply of it. Throughout the latter half of 1931, says Dietrich, Hitler "traversed Germany from end to end, holding private interviews with prominent [business] personalities." So hush-hush were some of these meetings that they had to be held "in some lonely forest glade. Privacy," explains Dietrich, "was absolutely imperative; the press must have no chance of doing mischief. Success was the consequence."

So was an almost comical zigzag in Nazi politics. Once in the fall of 1930 Strasser, Feder and Frick introduced a bill in the Reichstag on behalf of the Nazi Party calling for a ceiling of 4 per cent on all interest rates, the expropriation of the holdings of "the bank and stock exchange magnates" and of all "Eastern Jews" without compensation, and the nationalization of the big banks. Hitler was horrified; this was not only Bolshevism, it was financial suicide for the party. He peremptorily ordered the party to withdraw the measure. Thereupon the Communists reintroduced it, word for word. Hitler bade his party vote against it.

We know from the interrogations of Funk in the Nuremberg jail after the war who some, at least, of the "influential industrial magnates" whom Hitler sought out were. Emil Kirdorf, the union-hating coal baron who presided over a political slush fund known as the "Ruhr Treasury" which was raised by the West German mining interests, had been seduced by Hitler at the party congress in 1929. Fritz Thyssen, the head of the steel trust, who lived to regret his folly and to write about it in a book called *I Paid Hitler,* was an even earlier contributor. He had met the Nazi leader in Munich in 1923, been carried away by his eloquence and forthwith made, through Ludendorff, an initial gift of 100,000 gold marks ($25,-000) to the then obscure Nazi Party. Joining Thyssen was Albert Voegler, also a power in the United Steel Works. In fact the coal and steel interests were the principal sources of the funds that came from the industrialists to help Hitler over his last hurdles to power in the period between 1930 and 1933.

But Funk named other industries and concerns whose directors did not want to be left out in the cold should Hitler make it in the end. The list is a long one, though far from complete, for Funk had a wretched memory by the time he arrived for trial at Nuremberg. It included Georg von Schnitzler, a leading director of I. G. Farben, the giant chemical cartel; August Rosterg and August Diehn of the potash industry (Funk speaks of this industry's "positive attitude toward the Fuehrer"); Cuno of the Hamburg-Amerika line; the brown-coal industry of central Germany; the Conti rubber interests; Otto Wolf, the powerful Cologne industrialist; Baron Kurt von Schroeder, the Cologne banker, who was to play a pivotal role in the final maneuver which hoisted Hitler to power; several leading banks, among which were the Deutsche Bank, the Commerz und Privat Bank, the Dresdener Bank, the Deutsche Kredit Gesellschaft; and Germany's largest insurance concern, the Allianz.

Wilhelm Keppler, one of Hitler's economic advisers, brought in a number of South German industrialists and also formed a peculiar society of businessmen devoted to the S.S. chief, Himmler, called the Circle of Friends of the Economy (Freundeskreis der Wirtschaft), which later became known as the Circle of Friends of the Reichsfuehrer S.S., who was

Himmler, and which raised millions of marks for this particular gangster to pursue his "researches" into Aryan origins. From the very beginning of his political career Hitler had been helped financially—and socially— by Hugo Bruckman, the wealthy Munich publisher, and by Carl Bechstein, the piano manufacturer, both of whose wives developed a touching fondness for the rising young Nazi leader. It was in the Bechstein mansion in Berlin that Hitler first met many of the business and Army leaders and it was there that some of the decisive secret meetings took place which led him finally to the chancellorship.

Not all German businessmen jumped on the Hitler bandwagon after the Nazi election showing in 1930. Funk mentions that the big electric corporations Siemens and A.E.G. stood aloof, as did the king of the munition makers, Krupp von Bohlen und Halbach. Fritz Thyssen in his confessions declares that Krupp was a "violent opponent" of Hitler and that as late as the day before Hindenburg appointed him Chancellor Krupp urgently warned the old Field Marshal against such a folly. However, Krupp soon saw the light and quickly became, in the words of the repentant Thyssen, "a super Nazi."[15]

It is obvious, then, that in his final drive for power Hitler had considerable financial backing from a fairly large chunk of the German business world. How much the bankers and businessmen actually contributed to the Nazi Party in those last three years before January 1933 has never been established. Funk says it probably amounted to no more than "a couple of million marks." Thyssen estimates it at two millions a year; he says he himself personally gave one million marks. But judged by the large sums which the party had at its disposal in those days, though Goebbels complained it was never enough, the total gifts from business were certainly larger than these estimates by many times. What good they eventually did these politically childish men of the business world will be seen later in this narrative. One of the most enthusiastic of them at this time—as he was one of the most bitterly disillusioned of them afterward—was Dr. Schacht, who resigned his presidency of the Reichsbank in 1930 because of his opposition to the Young Plan, met Goering in that year and Hitler in 1931 and for the next two years devoted all of his considerable abilities to bringing the Fuehrer closer to his banker and industrialist friends and ever closer to the great goal of the Chancellor's seat. By 1932 this economic wizard, whose responsibility for the coming of the Third Reich and for its early successes proved to be so immeasurably great, was writing Hitler: "I have no doubt that the present development of things can only lead to your becoming Chancellor . . . Your movement is carried internally by so strong a truth and necessity that victory cannot elude you long . . . No matter where my work may take me in the near future, even if someday you should see me imprisoned in a fortress, you can always count on me as your loyal supporter." One of the two letters from which these words are taken was signed: "With a vigorous 'Heil.' "[16]

One "so strong a truth" of the Nazi movement, which Hitler had never made any secret of, was that if the party ever took over Germany it would stamp out a German's personal freedom, including that of Dr. Schacht and his business friends. It would be some time before the genial Reichsbank president, as he would again become under Hitler, and his associates in industry and finance would wake up to this. And since this history, like all history, is full of sublime irony, it would not be too long a time before Dr. Schacht proved himself to be a good prophet not only about Hitler's chancellorship but about the Fuehrer's seeing him imprisoned, if not in a fortress then in a concentration camp, which was worse, and not as Hitler's "loyal supporter"—here he was wrong—but in an opposite capacity.

Hitler had now, by the start of 1931, gathered around him in the party the little band of fanatical, ruthless men who would help him in his final drive to power and who, with one exception, would be at his side to help him sustain that power during the years of the Third Reich, though another of them, who was closest of all to him and perhaps the ablest and most brutish of the lot, would not survive, even with his life, the second year of Nazi government. There were five who stood above the other followers at this time. These were Gregor Strasser, Roehm, Goering, Goebbels and Frick.

Goering had returned to Germany at the end of 1927, following a general political amnesty which the Communists had helped the parties of the Right put through the Reichstag. In Sweden, where he had spent most of his exile since the 1923 putsch, he had been cured of addiction to narcotics at the Langbro Asylum and when he was well had earned his living with a Swedish aircraft company. The dashing, handsome World War ace had now grown corpulent but had lost none of his energy or his zest for life. He settled down in a small but luxurious bachelor's flat in the Badischestrasse in Berlin (his epileptic wife, whom he deeply loved, had contracted tuberculosis and remained, an invalid, in Sweden), earned his living as adviser to aircraft companies and the German airline, Lufthansa, and cultivated his social contacts. These contacts were considerable and ranged from the former Crown Prince and Prince Philip of Hesse, who had married Princess Mafalda, the daughter of the King of Italy, to Fritz Thyssen and other barons of the business world, as well as to a number of prominent officers of the Army.

These were the very connections which Hitler lacked but needed, and Goering soon became active in introducing the Nazi leader to his friends and in counteracting in upper-class circles the bad odor which some of the Brownshirt ruffians exuded. In 1928 Hitler chose Goering as one of the twelve Nazi deputies to represent the party in the Reichstag, of which he became President when the Nazis became the largest party in 1932. It was in the official residence of the Reichstag President that many of the meetings were held and intrigues hatched which led to the party's ultimate triumph, and it was here—to jump ahead in time a little—that a plan was connived that helped Hitler to stay in power after he became Chancellor: to set the Reichstag on fire.

Ernst Roehm had broken with Hitler in 1925 and not long afterward gone off to join the Bolivian Army as a lieutenant colonel. Toward the end of 1930 Hitler appealed to him to return and take over again the leadership of the S.A., which was getting out of hand. Its members, even its leaders, apparently believed in a coming Nazi revolution by violence, and with increasing frequency they were taking to the streets to molest and murder their political opponents. No election, national, provincial or municipal, took place without savage battles in the gutters.

Passing notice must here be taken of one of these encounters, for it provided National Socialism with its greatest martyr. One of the neighborhood leaders of the S.A. in Berlin was Horst Wessel, son of a Protestant chaplain, who had forsaken his family and his studies and gone to live in a slum with a former prostitute and devote his life to fighting for Nazism. Many anti-Nazis always held that the youth earned his living as a pimp, though this charge may have been exaggerated. Certainly he consorted with pimps and prostitutes. He was murdered by some Communists in February 1930 and would have passed into oblivion along with hundreds of other victims of both sides in the street wars had it not been for the fact that he left behind a song whose words and tune he had composed. This was the Horst Wessel song, which soon became the official song of the Nazi party and later the second official anthem—after "Deutschland ueber Alles"—of the Third Reich. Horst Wessel himself, thanks to Dr. Goebbels' skillful propaganda, became one of the great hero legends of the movement, hailed as a pure idealist who had given his life for the cause.

At the time Roehm took over the S.A., Gregor Strasser was undoubtedly the Number Two man in the Nazi Party. A forceful speaker and a brilliant organizer, he was the head of the party's most important office, the Political Organization, a post which gave him great influence among the provincial and local leaders whose labors he supervised. With his genial Bavarian nature, he was the most popular leader in the party next to Hitler, and, unlike the Fuehrer he enjoyed the personal trust and even liking of most of his political opponents. There were a good many at that time, within and without the party, who believed that Strasser might well supplant the moody, incalculable Austrian leader. This view was especially strong in the Reichswehr and in the President's Palace.

Otto, Gregor Strasser's brother, had fallen by the wayside. Unfortunately for him, he had taken seriously not only the word "socialist" but the word "workers" in the party's official name of National Socialist German Workers' Party. He had supported certain strikes of the socialist trade unions and demanded that the party come out for nationalization of industry. This of course was heresy to Hitler, who accused Otto Strasser of professing the cardinal sins of "democracy and liberalism." On May 21 and 22, 1930, the Fuehrer had a showdown with his rebellious subordinate and demanded complete submission. When Otto refused, he was booted out of the party. He tried to form a truly national "socialist" movement, the Union of Revolutionary National Socialists, which became known only as the Black Front, but in the September elections it failed completely to win any sizable number of Nazi votes away from Hitler.

Goebbels, the fourth member of the Big Five around Hitler, had remained an enemy and rival of Gregor Strasser ever since their break in 1926. Two years after that he had succeeded Strasser as propaganda chief of the party when the latter was moved up to head the Political Organization. He had remained as Gauleiter of Berlin, and his achievements in reorganizing the party there as well as his talents for propaganda had favorably impressed the Fuehrer. His glib but biting tongue and his nimble mind had not endeared him to Hitler's other chief lieutenants, who distrusted him. But the Nazi leader was quite content to see strife among his principal subordinates, if only because it was a safeguard against their conspiring together against his leadership. He never fully trusted Strasser, but in the loyalty of Goebbels he had complete confidence; moreover, the lame little fanatic was bubbling with ideas which were useful to him. Finally, Goebbels' talents as a rowdy journalist—he now had a Berlin newspaper of his own, *Der Angriff,* to spout off in—and as a rabble-rousing orator were invaluable to the party.

Wilhelm Frick, the fifth and last member of the group, was the only colorless personality in it. He was a typical German civil servant. As a young police officer in Munich before 1923 he had served as one of Hitler's spies at police headquarters, and the Fuehrer always felt grateful to him. Often he had taken on the thankless tasks. On Hitler's instigation he had become the first Nazi to hold provincial office—in Thuringia—and later he became the leader of the Nazi Party in the Reichstag. He was doggedly loyal, efficient and, because of the façade of his retiring nature and suave manners, useful in contacts with wavering officials in the republican government.

Some of the lesser men in the party in the early Thirties would subsequently gain notoriety and frightening personal power in the Third Reich. Heinrich Himmler, the poultry farmer, who, with his pince-nez, might be mistaken for a mild, mediocre schoolmaster—he had a degree in agronomy from the Munich Technische Hochschule—was gradually building up Hitler's praetorian guard, the black-coated S.S. But he worked under the shadow of Roehm, who was commander of both the S.A. and the S.S., and he was little known, even in party circles, outside his native Bavaria. There was Dr. Robert Ley, a chemist by profession and a habitual drunkard, who was the Gauleiter of Cologne, and Hans Frank, the bright young lawyer and leader of the party's legal division. There was Walther Darré, born in 1895 in the Argentine, an able agronomist who was won over to National Socialism by Hess and whose book *The Peasantry as the Life Source of the Nordic Race* brought him to Hitler's attention and to a job as head of the Agricultural Department of the party. Rudolf Hess himself, personally unambitious and doggedly loyal to the Leader, held only the title of private secretary to the Fuehrer. The second private secretary was one Martin Bormann, a molelike man who preferred to burrow in the dark recesses of party life to further his intrigues and who once had served a year in prison for complicity in a political murder. The Reich Youth Leader was Baldur von Schirach, a romantically minded young man and an energetic organizer, whose mother was an American and whose great-grandfather, a Union officer, had lost a leg at Bull Run; he told his American jailers at Nuremberg that he had become an anti-Semite at the age of seventeen after reading a book called *Eternal Jew,* by Henry Ford.

There was also Alfred Rosenberg, the ponderous, dim-witted Baltic pseudo philosopher who, as we have seen, was one of Hitler's earliest mentors and who since the putsch of 1923 had poured out a stream of books and pamphlets of the most muddled content and style, culminating in a 700-page work entitled *The Myth of the Twentieth Century.* This was a ludicrous concoction of his half-baked ideas on Nordic supremacy palmed off as the fruit of what passed for erudition in Nazi circles—a book which Hitler often said jokingly he had tried unsuccessfully to read and which prompted Schirach, who fancied himself as a writer, to remark once that Rosenberg was "a man who sold more copies of a book no one ever read than any other author," for in the first ten years after its publication in 1930 it sold more than half a million copies. From the beginning to the end Hitler always had a warm spot in his heart for this dull, stupid, fumbling man, rewarding him with various party jobs such as editor of the *Voelkischer Beobachter* and other Nazi publications and naming him as one of the party's deputies in the Reichstag in 1930, where he represented the movement in the Foreign Affairs Committee.

Such was the conglomeration of men around the leader of the National Socialists. In a normal society they surely would have stood out as a grotesque assortment of misfits. But in the last chaotic days of the Republic they began to appear to millions of befuddled Germans as saviors. And they had two advantages over their opponents: They were led by a man who knew exactly what he wanted and they were ruthless enough, and opportunist enough, to go to any lengths to help him get it.

As the year of 1931 ran its uneasy course, with five million wage earners out of work, the middle classes facing ruin, the farmers unable to meet their mortgage payments, the Parliament paralyzed, the government floundering, the eighty-four-year-old President fast sinking into the befuddlement of senility, a confidence mounted in the breasts of the Nazi chieftains that they would not have long to wait. As Gregor Strasser publicly boasted, "All that serves to precipitate the catastrophe . . . is good, very good for us and our German revolution."

6

THE LAST DAYS

OF THE REPUBLIC:

1931–33

O UT OF THE TURMOIL and chaos of German life there now emerged a curious and devious figure who, more than any other single individual, was destined to dig the grave of the Republic—one who would serve briefly as its last Chancellor and, ironically, in one of the final twists of his astonishing career desperately try to save it, when it was too late. This was Kurt von Schleicher, whose name in German means "intriguer" or "sneak."

In 1931 he was a lieutenant general in the Army.* Born in 1882, he had entered military service at eighteen as a subaltern in Hindenburg's old regiment, the 3rd Foot Guards, where he became a close friend of Oskar von Hindenburg, the son of the Field Marshal and President. His second friendship proved almost as valuable. This was with General Groener, who was impressed by his brilliance as a student at the War Academy, and who, when he replaced Ludendorff at Supreme Headquarters in 1918, brought along the young officer as his adjutant. Primarily a "desk officer"—he had seen but a short period of service on the Russian front—Schleicher remained thereafter close to the sources of power in the Army and in the Weimar Republic, where his nimble mind, affable manners and flair for politics impressed both the generals and the politicians. Under General von Seeckt he played an increasingly important role in helping to organize the illegal free corps and the equally illegal and highly secret "Black Reichswehr," and he was a key figure in the confidential negotiations with Moscow which led to the camouflaged training of German tank and air officers in Soviet Russia and in the establishment of German-run arms factories there. A gifted manipulator, with a passion for intrigue, Schleicher worked best under cover in the dark. Until the beginning of the Thirties his name was unknown to the general public, but for some time previously it had been attracting increasing notice in the Bendlerstrasse, where the War Ministry was, and in the Wilhelmstrasse, where the government ministries were situated.

---

* Equivalent to a major general in the U.S. Army.

In January 1928 he had used his growing influence with President Hindenburg, with whom he had become close through his friendship with Oskar, to have his old chief, General Groener, appointed as Minister of Defense, the first military man to hold that post during the Republic. Groener made Schleicher his right-hand man in the ministry, putting him in charge of a new office, the Ministry Bureau (Ministeramt), where he handled the political and press affairs of the Army and Navy. "My cardinal in politics," Groener called his assistant and entrusted him with the Army's relations with the other ministries and the political leaders. In this position Schleicher not only was a power in the officer corps but began to be a power in politics. In the Army he could make and break the higher officers and began to do so, getting rid of General von Blomberg, the second-in-command of the Army, in 1930 by a piece of trickery and replacing him with an old friend from the 3rd Foot Guards, General von Hammerstein. In the spring of the same year, as we have seen, he made his first effort to select the Chancellor himself and, with the backing of the Army, talked Hindenburg into appointing Heinrich Bruening to that post.

In achieving this political triumph Schleicher carried out what he thought would be the first step in a grandiose scheme to make over the Republic, an idea which had been forming for some time in his agile mind. He saw clearly enough—as who didn't?—the causes of the weakness of the Weimar regime. There were too many political parties (in 1930 ten of them each polled over a million votes) and they were too much at cross-purposes, too absorbed in looking after the special economic and social interests they represented to be able to bury their differences and form an enduring majority in the Reichstag that could back a stable government capable of coping with the major crisis which confronted the country at the beginning of the Thirties. Parliamentary government had become a matter of what the Germans called *Kuhhandel* —cattle trading—with the parties bargaining for special advantages for the groups which elected them, and the national interests be damned. No wonder that when Bruening took over as Chancellor on March 28, 1930, it had become impossible to achieve a majority in the Reichstag for any policy—of the Left, the Center or the Right—and that merely to carry on the business of government and do something about the economic paralysis he had to resort to Article 48 of the constitution, which permitted him in an emergency, if the President approved, to govern by decree.

This was exactly the way Schleicher wished the Chancellor to govern. It made for strong government under the forceful hand of the President, who, after all (Schleicher argued), through his popular election represented the will of the people and was backed by the Army. If the democratically elected Reichstag couldn't provide stable government, then the democratically elected President must. What the majority of Germans wanted, Schleicher was sure, was a government that would take a firm stand and lead them out of their hopeless plight. Actually, as the elections which Bruening called in September showed, that was not what the majority of Germans wanted. Or at least they did not want to be led out of the wilderness by the kind of government which Schleicher and his friends in the Army and in the Presidential Palace had chosen.

In truth, Schleicher had committed two disastrous mistakes. By putting up Bruening as Chancellor and encouraging him to rule by presidential decree, he had cracked the foundation of the Army's strength in the nation—its position *above* politics, the abandonment of which would lead to its own and Germany's ruin. And he had made a bad miscalculation about the voters. When six and a half million of them, against 810,000 two years before, voted for the Nazi Party on September 14, 1930, the political General realized that he must take a new tack. By the end of the year he was in touch with Roehm, who had just returned from Bolivia, and with Gregor Strasser. This was the first serious contact between the Nazis and those who held the political power in the Republic. In just two years its development was to lead Adolf Hitler to his goal and General von Schleicher to his fall and ultimate murder.

On October 10, 1931, three weeks after the suicide of his niece and sweetheart, Geli Raubal, Hitler was received by President Hindenburg for the first time. Schleicher, busy weaving a new web of intrigue, had made the appointment. Earlier that autumn he had conferred with Hitler and arranged for him to see both the Chancellor and the President. In the back of his mind, as well as that of Bruening, was the question of what to do when Hindenburg's seven-year term of office came to an end in the spring of 1932. The Field Marshal would be eighty-five then, and the periods when his mind was lucid were diminishing. Still, as everyone realized, if he were not a candidate to succeed himself, Hitler, though he was not legally a German citizen, might contrive to become one, run for the office, win the election and become President.

During the summer the scholarly Chancellor had pondered long hours over the desperate plight of Germany. He quite realized that his government had become the most unpopular one the Republic had ever had. To cope with the depression he had decreed lower wages and salaries as well as lower prices and had clamped down severe restrictions on business, finance and the social services. The "Hunger Chancellor" he had been called by both the Nazis and the Communists. Yet he thought he saw a way out that in the end would re-establish a stable, free, prosperous Germany. He would try to negotiate with the Allies a cancellation of reparations, whose payment had been temporarily stopped by the Hoover moratorium. In the disarmament conference scheduled to begin the following year he would try either to get the Allies to honor their pledge in the Versailles Treaty to disarm to the level of Germany or to allow Germany to embark openly on a modest program of rearmament, which in fact, with his connivance, and in secret, it had already started to do.

Thus the last shackle of the peace treaty would be thrown off and Germany would emerge as an equal among the big powers. This would be not only a boon to the Republic but might launch, Bruening thought, a new era of confidence in the Western world that would put an end to the economic depression which had brought the German people such misery. And it would take the wind out of the Nazi sails.

Bruening planned to move boldly on the home front too and to bring about by agreement of all the major parties save the Communists a fundamental change in the German constitution. He meant to restore the Hohenzollern monarchy. Even if Hindenburg could be persuaded to run again, he could not be expected at his age to live out another full term of seven years. Should he die in another year or two, the way would still be open to Hitler to be elected President. To forestall that, to assure permanency and stability in the office of head of state, Bruening broached the following plan: The 1932 presidential elections would be called off and Hindenburg's term of office simply extended, as it could be, by a two-thirds vote in the two houses of Parliament, the Reichstag and the Reichsrat. As soon as that was achieved, he would propose that Parliament proclaim a monarchy with the President as regent. On his death one of the sons of the Crown Prince would be put on the Hohenzollern throne. This act too would take the wind out of the Nazis; in fact Bruening was confident that it would mean their end as a political force.

But the aged President was not interested. He, whose duty it had been as Commander of the Imperial Army to tell the Kaiser on that dark fall day of November 1918 at Spa that he must go, that the monarchy was at an end, would not consider any Hohenzollern's resuming the throne except the Emperor himself, who still lived in exile at Doorn, in Holland. When Bruening explained to him that the Social Democrats and the trade unions, which with the greatest reluctance had given some encouragement to his plan if only because it might afford the last desperate chance of stopping Hitler, would not stand for the return of either Wilhelm II or his eldest son and that moreover if the monarchy were restored it must be a constitutional and democratic one on the lines of the British model, the grizzly old Field Marshal was so outraged he summarily dismissed his Chancellor from his presence. A week later he recalled him to inform him that he would not stand for re-election.

In the meantime first Bruening and then Hindenburg had had their first meeting with Adolf Hitler. Both talks went badly for the Nazi leader. He had not yet recovered from the blow of Geli Raubal's suicide; his mind wandered and he was unsure of himself. To Bruening's request for Nazi support for the continuance in office of Hindenburg Hitler answered with a long tirade against the Republic which left little doubt that he would not go along with the Chancellor's plans. With Hindenburg, Hitler was ill at ease. He tried to impress the old gentleman with a long harangue but it fell flat. The President, at this first meeting, was not impressed by the "Bohemian corporal," as he called him, and told Schleicher that such a man might become Minister of Posts but never Chancellor—words which the Field Marshal would later have to eat.

Hitler, in a huff, hastened off to Bad Harzburg, where on the next day, October 11, he joined a massive demonstration of the "National Opposition" against the governments of Germany and Prussia. This was an assembly not so much of the radical Right, represented by the National Socialists, as of the older, conservative forces of reaction: Hugenberg's German National Party, the right-wing veterans' private army, the Stahlhelm, the so-called Bismarck Youth, the Junkers' Agrarian League, and an odd assortment of old generals. But the Nazi leader did not have his heart in the meeting. He despised the frock-coated, top-hatted, bemedaled relics of the old regime, with whom, he saw, it might be dangerous to associate a "revolutionary" movement like his own too closely. He raced through his speech in a perfunctory manner and left the field before the parade of the Stahlhelm, which, to his annoyance, had shown up in larger numbers than the S.A. The Harzburg Front which was formed that day and which represented an effort of the old-line conservatives to bring the Nazis into a united front to begin a final assault on the Republic (it demanded the immediate resignation of Bruening) was thus stillborn. Hitler had no intention of playing second fiddle to these gentlemen whose minds, he thought, were buried in the past to which he knew there was no return. He might use them for the moment if they helped to undermine the Weimar regime and made available to him, as they did, new financial sources. But he would not, in turn, be used by them. Within a few days the Harzburg Front was facing collapse; the various elements of it were once more at each other's throats.

Except on one issue. Both Hugenberg and Hitler refused to agree to Bruening's proposal that Hindenburg's term of office be prolonged. At the beginning of 1932 the Chancellor renewed his effort to get them to change their minds. With great difficulty he had prevailed on the President to agree to serving further if Parliament prolonged his term and thus made it unnecessary for him to have to shoulder the burden of a bitter election campaign. Now Bruening invited Hitler to come to Berlin for fresh discussions. The telegram arrived while the Fuehrer was conferring with Hess and Rosenberg in the editorial offices of the *Voelkischer Beobachter* in Munich. Thrusting the paper into their faces, Hitler cried, "Now I have them in my pocket! They have recognized me as a partner in their negotiations."[1]

On January 7 Hitler conferred with Bruening and Schleicher, and there was a further meeting on January 10. Bruening repeated his proposal that the Nazi Party agree to prolonging Hindenburg's term. If this were done, and as soon as he had settled the problem of cancellation of reparations and equality of armaments, he himself would retire. According to some sources—it is a disputed point—Bruening held out a further bait: he offered to suggest Hitler's name to the President as his successor.[2]

Hitler did not immediately give a definite reply. He adjourned to the Kaiserhof hotel and took counsel with his advisers. Gregor Strasser was in favor of accepting Bruening's plan, arguing that if the Nazis forced an election Hindenburg would win it. Goebbels and Roehm were for an outright rejection. In his diary for January 7, Goebbels wrote: "The Presidency is not the issue. Bruening merely wants to strengthen his own position indefinitely . . . The chess game for power begins. . . . The chief thing is that we remain strong and make no compromises." The night before, he had written: "There is a man in the organization that no one trusts . . . This is Gregor Strasser."[3]

Hitler himself saw no reason to strengthen Bruening's hand and thus give the Republic a further lease on life. But unlike the thickheaded Hugenberg, who rejected the plan outright on January 12, Hitler was more subtle. He replied not to the Chancellor but over his head to the President, declaring that he regarded Bruening's proposal as unconstitutional but that he would support Hindenburg's re-election if the Field Marshal would reject Bruening's plan. To Otto von Meissner, the nimble Secretary of State at the Presidential Chancellery, who had zealously served in that capacity first the Socialist Ebert and then the conservative Hindenburg and who was beginning to think of a third term in office for himself with whoever the President might be—perhaps even Hitler?—the Nazi leader, in a secret conversation at the Kaiserhof, offered to support Hindenburg in the elections if he would first get rid of Bruening, name a "National" government and decree new elections for the Reichstag and the Prussian Diet.

To this Hindenburg would not agree. Nettled by the refusal of the Nazis and the Nationalists, the latter his friends and supposed supporters, to agree to spare him the strain of an election battle, Hindenburg agreed to run again. But to his resentment against the nationalist parties was added a curious spleen against Bruening, who he felt had handled the whole matter badly and who was now forcing him into bitter conflict with the very nationalist forces which had elected him President in 1925 against the liberal–Marxist candidates. Now he could win only with the support of the Socialists and the trade unions, for whom he had always had an undisguised contempt. A marked coolness sprang up in his dealings with his Chancellor—"the best," he had said not so long ago, "since Bismarck."

A coolness toward Bruening also came over the General who had propelled him into the chancellorship. To Schleicher the austere Catholic leader had been a disappointment after all. He had become the most unpopular Chancellor the Republic had ever had. He had been unable to obtain a majority in the country; he had failed to curb the Nazis or to win them over; he had bungled the problem of keeping Hindenburg on. Therefore he must go—and perhaps with him General Groener, Schleicher's revered chief, who did not seem to grasp the ideas for the future which he, Schleicher, had in mind. The scheming General was not exactly in a hurry. Bruening and Groener, the two strong men of the government, must remain in power until Hindenburg was re-elected; without their support the old Field Marshal might not make it. After the elections their usefulness would be over.

HITLER AGAINST HINDENBURG

There were a number of occasions in the career of Adolf Hitler when, faced with a difficult decision, he seemed unable to make up his mind, and this was one of them. The question he faced in January 1932 was: to run or not to run for President? Hindenburg seemed unbeatable. The legendary hero would be supported not only by many elements of the Right but by the democratic parties which had been against him in the election of 1925 but which now saw him as the savior of the Republic. To run against the Field Marshal and be beaten, as he almost certainly would be—was that not to risk the reputation for invincibility which the Nazis had been building up in one provincial election after another since their spectacular triumph in the national poll in 1930? And yet, not to run—was that not a confession of weakness, a demonstration of a lack of confidence that National Socialism was on the threshold of power? There was another consideration. Hitler was at the moment not even eligible to run. He was not a German citizen.

Joseph Goebbels urged him to announce his candidacy. On January 19 they journeyed to Munich together and that evening Goebbels recorded in his diary: "Discussed the question of the presidency with the Fuehrer. No decision has yet been reached. I pleaded strongly for his own candidacy." For the next month the diary of Goebbels reflected the ups and downs in Hitler's mind. On January 31: "The Fuehrer's decision will be made on Wednesday. It can no longer be in doubt." On February 2 it seemed that he had made it. Goebbels noted: "He decides to be a candidate himself." But Goebbels adds that the decision will not be made public until it is seen what the Social Democrats do. Next day the party leaders assemble in Munich to hear Hitler's decision. "They wait in vain," Goebbels grumbles. "Everyone," he adds, "is nervous and strained." That evening the little propaganda chief seeks relief; he steals away to see Greta Garbo in a movie and is "moved and shaken" by this "greatest living actress." Later that night "a number of old party comrades come to me. They are depressed at the lack of a decision. They fear that the Fuehrer is waiting too long."

He may be waiting too long, but Hitler's confidence in his ultimate triumph does not weaken. One night in Munich, the diary records, the Fuehrer has a long discussion with Goebbels on which post the latter will have in the Third Reich. The Leader has in mind for him, Goebbels says, a "Ministry of Popular Education which will deal with films, radio, art, culture and propaganda." On another evening Hitler has a long discussion with his architect, Professor Troost, over plans for a "grandiose alteration of the national capital." And Goebbels adds: "The Fuehrer has his plans all finished. He speaks, acts and feels as if we were already in power."

But he does not speak yet as if he were anxious to run against Hindenburg. On February 9, Goebbels records, "the Fuehrer is back in Berlin. More debates at the Kaiserhof over the presidential election. Everything is left in suspense." Three days later Goebbels goes over his calculations of votes with the Fuehrer. "It's a risk," he says, "but it must be taken." Hitler goes off to Munich to think it over still further.

In the end his mind is made up for him by Hindenburg. On February 15 the aged President formally announces his candidacy. Goebbels is happy. "Now we have a free hand. Now we need no longer hide our decision." But Hitler does hide it until February 22. At a meeting that day in the Kaiserhof "the Fuehrer gives me permission," Goebbels rejoices, "to announce his candidacy at the Sport Palace tonight."

It was a bitter and confusing campaign. In the Reichstag Goebbels branded Hindenburg as "the candidate of the party of the deserters" and was expelled from the chamber for insulting the President. In Berlin the nationalist *Deutsche Zeitung,* which had backed Hindenburg's election in 1925, now turned on him vehemently. "The present issue," it declared, "is whether the internationalist traitors and pacifist swine, with the approval of Hindenburg, are to bring about the final ruin of Germany."

All the traditional loyalties of classes and parties were upset in the confusion and heat of the electoral battle. To Hindenburg, a Protestant, a Prussian, a conservative and a monarchist, went the support of the Socialists, the trade unions, the Catholics of Bruening's Center Party and the remnants of the liberal, democratic middle-class parties. To Hitler, a Catholic, an Austrian, a former tramp, a "national socialist," a leader of the lower-middle-class masses, was rallied, in addition to his own followers, the support of the upper-class Protestants of the north, the conservative Junker agrarians and a number of monarchists, including, at the last minute, the former Crown Prince himself. The confusion was further compounded by the entrance of two other candidates, neither of whom could hope to win but both of whom might poll enough votes to prevent either of the leading contestants from obtaining the absolute majority needed for election. The Nationalists put up Theodor Duesterberg, second-in-command of the Stahlhelm (of which Hindenburg was the honorary commander), a colorless former lieutenant colonel whom the Nazis, to their glee, soon discovered to be the great-grandson of a Jew. The Communists, shouting that the Social Democrats were "betraying the workers" by supporting Hindenburg, ran their own candidate, Ernst Thaelmann, the party's leader. It was not the first time, nor the last, that the Communists, on orders from Moscow, risked playing into Nazi hands.

Before the campaign was scarcely under way Hitler solved the problem of his citizenship. On February 25 it was announced that the Nazi Minister of the Interior of the state of Brunswick had named Herr Hitler an attaché of the legation of Brunswick in Berlin. Through this comic-opera maneuver the Nazi leader became automatically a citizen of Brunswick and hence of Germany and was therefore eligible to run for President of the German Reich. Having leaped over this little hurdle with ease, Hitler threw himself into the campaign with furious energy, crisscrossing the country, addressing large crowds at scores of mass meetings and whipping them up into a state of frenzy. Goebbels and Strasser, the other two spellbinders of the party, followed a similar schedule. But this was not all.

They directed a propaganda campaign such as Germany had never seen. They plastered the walls of the cities and towns with a million screeching colored posters, distributed eight million pamphlets and twelve million extra copies of their party newspapers, staged three thousand meetings a day and, for the first time in a German election, made good use of films and gramophone records, the latter spouting forth from loudspeakers on trucks.

Bruening also worked tirelessly to win the election for the aged President. For once this fair-minded man was ruthless enough to reserve all radio time on the government-controlled networks for his own side—a tactic which infuriated Hitler. Hindenburg spoke only once, in a recorded broadcast on March 10, on the eve of the polling. It was a dignified utterance, one of the few made during the campaign, and it was effective.

Election of a party man, representing one-sided extremist views, who would consequently have the majority of the people against him, would expose the Fatherland to serious disturbances whose outcome would be incalculable. Duty commanded me to prevent this . . . If I am defeated, I shall at least not have incurred the reproach that of my own accord I deserted my post in an hour of crisis . . . I ask for no votes from those who do not wish to vote for me.

Those who voted for him fell .4 per cent short of the needed absolute majority. When the polls closed on March 13, 1932, the results were:

Hindenburg	18,651,497	49.6%
Hitler	11,339,446	30.1%
Thaelmann	4,983,341	13.2%
Duesterberg	2,557,729	6.8%

The figures were a disappointment to both sides. The old President had led the Nazi demagogue by over seven million votes but had just failed to win the required absolute majority; this necessitated a second election, in which the candidate receiving the most votes would be elected. Hitler had increased the Nazi vote over 1930 by nearly five million—some 86 per cent—but he had been left far behind Hindenburg. Late on the evening of the polling there was deep despair at the Goebbels home in Berlin, where many of the party leaders had gathered to listen to the results over the radio. "We're beaten; terrible outlook," Goebbels wrote in his diary that night. "Party circles badly depressed and dejected . . . We can save ourselves only by a clever stroke."

But in the *Voelkischer Beobachter* the next morning Hitler announced: "The first election campaign is over. The second has begun today. I shall lead it." Indeed, he campaigned as vigorously as before. Chartering a Junkers passenger plane, he flew from one end of Germany to the other— a novelty in electioneering at that time—addressing three or four big rallies a day in as many cities. Shrewdly, he altered his tactics to attract more votes. In the first campaign he had harped on the misery of the people, the impotence of the Republic. Now he depicted a happy future for all Germans if he were elected: jobs for the workers, higher prices for the farmers, more business for the businessmen, a big Army for the militarists, and once in a speech at the Lustgarten in Berlin he promised, "In the Third Reich every German girl will find a husband!"

The Nationalists withdrew Duesterberg from the race and appealed to their followers to vote for Hitler. Again even the dissolute former Crown Prince, Friedrich Wilhelm, fell into line. "I shall vote for Hitler," he announced.

April 10, 1932, the day of the second election, was dark and rainy, and a million fewer citizens cast their votes. The results announced late that night were:

Hindenburg	19,359,983	53%
Hitler	13,418,547	36.8%
Thaelmann	3,706,759	10.2%

Though Hitler had increased his total vote by two million and Hindenburg had gained only one million, the President was in by a clear, absolute majority. More than half the German people had thus given expression to their belief in the democratic Republic; they had decisively rejected the extremists of both Right and Left. Or so they thought.

Hitler himself had much to ponder. He had made an impressive showing. He had doubled the Nazi vote in two years. And yet a majority still eluded him—and with it the political power he sought. Had he reached the end of this particular road? In the party discussions that followed the April 10 poll, Strasser frankly argued that this was indeed Hitler's position. Strasser urged a deal with those in power: with the President, with the government of Bruening and General Groener, with the Army. Hitler distrusted his chief lieutenant but he did not dismiss his idea. He had not forgotten one of the lessons of his Vienna days, that to attain power one must win the support of some of the existing "powerful institutions."

Before he could make up his mind as to the next step, one of these "powerful institutions," the government of the Republic, struck him a blow.

For more than a year the Reich government and various state governments had been coming into possession of documents which showed that a number of high Nazi leaders, especially in the S.A., were preparing to take over Germany by force and institute a reign of terror. On the eve of the first presidential elections the S.A., now 400,000 strong, had been fully mobilized and had thrown a cordon around Berlin. Though Captain Roehm, the S.A. chief, assured General von Schleicher that the measure was merely "precautionary," the Prussian police had seized documents at Nazi headquarters in Berlin which made it pretty clear that the S.A. meant to carry out a *coup d'état* on the following evening should Hitler be elected President—such was Roehm's hurry. Goebbels in a diary notation on the night of March 11 had confirmed that something was afoot. "Talked over instructions with the S.A. and S.S. commanders. Deep uneasiness is rife everywhere. The word Putsch haunts the air."

Both the national and the state governments were alarmed. On April 5 representatives of several of the states, led by Prussia and Bavaria, the two largest, had demanded that the central government suppress the S.A. or else they would do it themselves in their respective territories. Chancellor Bruening was away from Berlin electioneering, but Groener, who received the delegates in his capacity of Minister of the Interior and of Defense, promised action as soon as Bruening returned, which was on April 10, the day of the second election. Bruening and Groener thought they had good reasons for stamping out the S.A. It would end the threat of civil war and might be a prelude to the end of Hitler as a major factor in German politics. Certain of Hindenburg's re-election by an absolute majority, they felt that the voters were giving them a mandate to protect the Republic against the threats of the Nazis to forcibly overthrow it. The time had come to use force against force. Also, unless they acted vigorously, the government would lose the support of the Social Democrats and the trade unions, which were providing most of the votes for Hindenburg and the chief backing for the continuance of Bruening's government.

The cabinet met on April 10, in the midst of the polling, and decided to immediately suppress Hitler's private armies. There was some difficulty in getting Hindenburg to sign the decree—Schleicher, who had first approved it, began to whisper objections in the President's ear—but he finally did so on April 13 and it was promulgated on April 14.

This was a stunning blow to the Nazis. Roehm and some of the hotheads in the party urged resistance to the order. But Hitler, shrewder than his lieutenants, ruled that it must be obeyed. This was no moment for armed rebellion. Besides, there was interesting news about Schleicher. Goebbels noted it in his diary on that very day, April 14: "We are informed that Schleicher does not approve Groener's action . . ." And later that day: ". . . a telephone call from a well-known lady who is a close friend of General Schleicher. She says the General wants to resign."[4]

Goebbels was interested but skeptical. "Perhaps," he added, "it is only a maneuver." Neither he nor Hitler nor anyone else, certainly not Bruening and most certainly not Groener, to whom Schleicher owed his rapid rise in the Army and in the councils of government, had as yet surmised the infinite capacity for treachery of the scheming political General. But they were soon to learn.

Even before the ban on the S.A. was promulgated, Schleicher, who had won over the weak-minded commander of the Reichswehr, General von Hammerstein, confidentially informed the commanders of the seven military districts that the Army opposed the move. Next he persuaded Hindenburg to write a cantankerous letter to Groener, on April 16, asking why the Reichsbanner, the paramilitary organization of the Social Democrats, had not been suppressed along with the S.A. Schleicher took a further step to undermine his chief's position. He inspired a malicious smear campaign against General Groener, spreading tales that he was too ill to remain in office, that he had become a convert to Marxism and even to pacifism and proclaiming that the Defense Minister had disgraced the Army by having a child born five months after his recent marriage—the baby, he told Hindenburg, had been nicknamed "Nurmi" in Army circles, after the fleet Finnish runner of Olympic fame.

In the meantime, Schleicher renewed his contacts with the S.A. He held talks with both Roehm, the S.A. chief, and Count von Helldorf, the S.A. leader of Berlin. On April 26, Goebbels noted that Schleicher had informed Helldorff he "wanted to change his course." Two days later Schleicher saw Hitler, and Goebbels reported that "the talk went off well."

Even at this stage of the game it is evident that with regard to one question Roehm and Schleicher were conspiring behind Hitler's back. Both men wanted the S.A. incorporated into the Army as a militia, a step to which the Fuehrer was unalterably opposed. This was a matter over which Hitler had often quarreled with his S.A. chief of staff, who saw the storm troopers as a potential military force to strengthen the country, whereas Hitler regarded them as purely a *political* force, a band to strike terror in the streets against his political opponents and to keep up political enthusiasm in the Nazi ranks. But in his conversations with the Nazi leaders, Schleicher had another objective in mind. He wanted the S.A. attached to the Army, where he could control it; but he also wanted Hitler, the only conservative nationalist with any mass following, in the government—where he could control *him*. The *Verbot* of the S.A. hindered progress toward both objectives.

By the end of the first week of May 1932, Schleicher's intrigues reached one of their climaxes. Goebbels notes on May 4 that "Hitler's mines are beginning to go off. First Groener and then Bruening must go." On May 8, Goebbels reported in his diary, Hitler had a "decisive conference with General Schleicher and with some gentlemen close to the President. Everything goes well. Bruening will fall in a few days. The President will withdraw his confidence in him." He then outlines the plan which Schleicher and the President's camarilla had hatched with Hitler: The Reichstag will be dissolved, a presidential cabinet will be installed and all prohibitions against the S.A. and the Nazi Party lifted. To avoid arousing Bruening's suspicion of what is up, Goebbels adds, Hitler will keep away from Berlin. Late that evening he spirits his chief away to Mecklenburg and into virtual hiding.

For the Nazis, the presidential cabinet is regarded, Goebbels notes the next day, as merely an "interim" affair. Such a "colorless" transitional government, he says, "will clear the way for us. The weaker it is the easier we can do away with it." This, of course, is not the view of Schleicher, who already is dreaming of a new government which will dispense with Parliament until the constitution can be changed and which he will dominate. Already, it is clear, he and Hitler believe they can each get the best of the other. But for the moment he has an ace to play. He can assure the tired old President that he can offer what Bruening could not: a government supported by Hitler and yet without the inconvenience of having the fanatical demagogue in it.

So all was ready, and on May 10, two days after his meeting with Hitler and the men around Hindenburg, Schleicher struck. The blow was delivered at the Reichstag. General Groener rose to defend the banning of the S.A. and was violently attacked by Goering. Ill with diabetes and sick at heart at the treachery already wrought by Schleicher, the Defense Minister tried to defend himself as best he could but he was overwhelmed by a torrent of abuse from the Nazi benches. Exhausted and humiliated, he started to leave the chamber, only to run into General von Schleicher, who informed him coldly that he "no longer enjoyed the confidence of the Army and must resign." Groener appealed to Hindenburg, for whom he had loyally fronted—and taken the blame—when the crucial moment had come, first, in 1918, to tell the Kaiser to go, and then, in 1919, to advise the republican government to sign the Versailles Treaty. But the old Field Marshal, who had never ceased resenting his obligation to the younger officer, replied that he "regretted" he could do nothing in the matter. On May 13, bitter and disillusioned,* Groener resigned. That evening Goebbels recorded in his diary: "We have news from General Schleicher. Everything is going according to plan."

The plan called for Bruening's head next, and it was not long before the conniving General was able to slip it on the block. Groener's fall had been a grave setback for the tottering Republic; almost alone among the military men he had served it ably and devotedly, and there was no one else in the Army of his stature and loyalty to replace him. But the stubborn, hard-working Bruening was still a power. He had secured the backing of the majority of Germans for Hindenburg's re-election and, as he believed, for the continuance of the Republic. He seemed to be on the eve of sensational successes in foreign policy with regard to both the cancellation of reparations and equality of armament for the Reich. But the aging President, as we have seen, had rewarded with a remarkable coolness the Chancellor's superhuman efforts in winning him a further term of office. His attitude became more frigid when Bruening proposed that the State take over a number of bankrupt Junker estates in East Prussia, after generous compensation, and give them to the landless peasants. When Hindenburg went off for the Easter holidays at the middle of May to Neudeck, the East Prussian estate which the Junkers, with the financial help of the industrialists, had given him as a present on his eightieth birthday, he got an earful from his aristocratic neighbors, who clamored for the dismissal of a Chancellor whom they now called "an agrarian Bolshevist."

The Nazis, undoubtedly through Schleicher, learned before Bruening that the Chancellor was on his way out. On May 18 Goebbels returned

---

* "Scorn and rage boil within me," Groener wrote Schleicher a few months later (November 29), "because I have been deceived in you, my old friend, disciple, adopted son." (See Gordon A. Craig, "Reichswehr and National Socialism: The Policy of Wilhelm Groener," *Political Science Quarterly*, June 1948.)

from Munich to Berlin and, noting that the "Easter spirit" was still lingering, wrote in his diary: "For Bruening alone winter seems to have set in. The funny thing is he doesn't realize it. He can't find men for his cabinet. The rats are leaving the sinking ship." It might have been more accurate to say that the leading rat, far from leaving the sinking ship of state, was merely making ready to put in a new captain. The next day Goebbels recorded: "General Schleicher has refused to take over the Ministry of Defense." This was true but also not quite accurate. Bruening had indeed made the request of Schleicher after upbraiding him for undermining Groener. "I will," Schleicher had replied, "but not in your government."[5]

On May 19 Goebbels' diary recorded: "Message from Schleicher. The list of ministers is ready. For the transition period it is not so important." Thus at least a week in advance of Bruening the Nazis knew his goose was cooked. On Sunday, May 29, Hindenburg summoned Bruening to his presence and abruptly asked for his resignation, and on the following day it was given him.

Schleicher had triumphed. But not only Bruening had fallen; the democratic Republic went down with him, though its death agonies would continue for another eight months before the final *coup de grâce* was administered. Bruening's responsibility for its demise was not small. Though democratic at heart, he had allowed himself to be maneuvered into a position where he had perforce to rule much of the time by presidential decree without the consent of Parliament. The provocation to take such a step admittedly had been great; the politicians in their blindness had made it all but inevitable. As recently as May 12, though, he had been able to win a vote of confidence in the Reichstag for his finance bill. But where Parliament could not agree he had relied on the authority of the President to govern. Now that authority had been withdrawn. From now on, from June 1932 to January 1933, it would be granted to two lesser men who, though not Nazis, felt no urge to uphold a democratic Republic, at least as it was presently constituted.

The political power in Germany no longer resided, as it had since the birth of the Republic, in the people and in the body which expressed the people's will, the Reichstag. It was now concentrated in the hands of a senile, eighty-five-year-old President and in those of a few shallow ambitious men around him who shaped his weary, wandering mind. Hitler saw this very clearly, and it suited his purposes. It seemed most unlikely that he would ever win a majority in Parliament. Hindenburg's new course offered him the only opportunity that was left of coming to power. Not at the moment, to be sure, but soon.

He hurried back to Berlin from Oldenburg, where on May 29 the Nazis had won an absolute majority in the election for the local diet. The next day he was received by Hindenburg, who confirmed the points of the deal which the Nazi leader had secretly worked out with Schleicher on May 8: the lifting of the ban on the S.A., a presidential cabinet of Hindenburg's own choosing, dissolution of the Reichstag. Would Hitler support the new government? Hindenburg asked. Hitler replied that he would. That evening of May 30, the Goebbels' diary was brought up to date: "Hitler's talk with the President went well . . . V. Papen is spoken of as Chancellor. But that interests us little. The important thing is that the Reichstag is dissolved. Elections! Elections! Direct to the people! We are all very happy."[6]

FIASCO OF FRANZ VON PAPEN

There now appeared briefly on the center of the stage an unexpected and ludicrous figure. The man whom General von Schleicher foisted upon the octogenarian President and who on June 1, 1932, was named Chancellor of Germany was the fifty-three-year-old Franz von Papen, scion of an impoverished family of the Westphalian nobility, a former General Staff officer, a crack gentleman rider, an unsuccessful and amateurish Catholic Centrist politician, a wealthy industrialist by marriage and little known to the public except as a former military attaché in Washington who had been expelled during the war for complicity in the planning of such sabotage as blowing up bridges and railroad lines while the United States was neutral.

"The President's choice met with incredulity," wrote the French ambassador in Berlin. "No one but smiled or tittered or laughed because Papen enjoyed the peculiarity of being taken seriously by neither his friends nor his enemies . . . He was reputed to be superficial, blundering, untrue, ambitious, vain, crafty and an intriguer."[7] To such a man— and M. François-Poncet was not exaggerating—Hindenburg, at Schleicher's prompting, had entrusted the fate of the floundering Republic.

Papen had no political backing whatsoever. He was not even a member of the Reichstag. The furthest he had got in politics was a seat in the Prussian Landtag. On his appointment as Chancellor his own Center Party, indignant at the treachery of Papen toward its leader, Bruening, unanimously expelled him from the party. But the President had told him to form a government above parties, and this he was able to do at once because Schleicher already had a list of ministers at hand. It comprised what became known as the "barons' cabinet." Five members were of the nobility, two were corporation directors, and one, Franz Guertner, named Minister of Justice, had been Hitler's protector in the Bavarian government during the troubled days before and after the Beer Hall Putsch. General von Schleicher was smoked out by Hindenburg from his preferred position behind the scenes and made Minister of Defense. The "barons' cabinet" was received by much of the country as a joke, though the stamina of a number of its members, Baron von Neurath, Baron von Eltz-Rubenach, Count Schwerin von Krosigk and Dr. Guertner, was such that they lingered on at their posts far into the era of the Third Reich.

Papen's first act was to honor Schleicher's pact with Hitler. On June 4 he dissolved the Reichstag and convoked new elections for July 31, and after some prodding from the suspicious Nazis, he lifted the ban on the S.A. on June 15. A wave of political violence and murder such as even Germany had not previously seen immediately followed. The storm troopers swarmed the streets seeking battle and blood and their challenge was often met, especially by the Communists. In Prussia alone between June 1 and 20 there were 461 pitched battles in the streets which cost eighty-two lives and seriously wounded four hundred men. In July, thirty-eight Nazis and thirty Communists were listed among the eighty-six persons killed in riots. On Sunday, July 10, eighteen persons were done to death in the streets, and on the following Sunday, when the Nazis, under police escort, staged a march through Altona, a working-class suburb of Hamburg, nineteen persons were shot dead and 285 wounded. The civil war which the barons' cabinet had been called in to halt was growing steadily worse. All the parties save the Nazis and the Communists demanded that the government take action to restore order.

Papen responded by doing two things. He banned all political parades for the fortnight prior to the July 31 elections. And he took a step which was aimed not only at placating the Nazis but at destroying one of the few remaining pillars of the democratic Republic. On July 20 he deposed the Prussian government and appointed himself Reich Commissioner for Prussia. This was a daring move toward the kind of authoritarian government he was seeking for the whole of Germany. Papen's excuse was that the Altona riots had shown the Prussian government could not maintain law and order. He also charged, on "evidence" hastily produced by Schleicher, that the Prussian authorities were in cahoots with the Communists. When the Socialist ministers refused to be deposed except by force, Papen obligingly supplied it.

Martial law was proclaimed in Berlin and General von Rundstedt, the local Reichswehr commander, sent a lieutenant and a dozen men to make the necessary arrests. This was a development which was not lost on the men of the Right who had taken over the federal power, nor did it escape Hitler's notice. There was no need to worry any longer that the forces of the Left or even of the democratic center would put up serious resistance to the overthrow of the democratic system. In 1920 a general strike had saved the Republic from being overthrown. Such a measure was debated now among the trade-union leaders and the Socialists and rejected as too dangerous. Thus by deposing the constitutional Prussian government Papen had driven another nail into the coffin of the Weimar Republic. It had taken, as he boasted, only a squad of soldiers to do it.

For their part, Hitler and his lieutenants were determined to bring down not only the Republic but Papen and his barons too. Goebbels expressed the aim in his diary on June 5: "We must disassociate ourselves at the earliest possible moment from this transitional bourgeois cabinet." When Papen saw Hitler for the first time on June 9, the Nazi leader told him, "I regard your cabinet only as a temporary solution and will continue my efforts to make my party the strongest in the country. The chancellorship will then devolve on me."[8]

The Reichstag elections of July 31 were the third national elections held in Germany within five months, but, far from being weary from so much electioneering, the Nazis threw themselves into the campaign with more fanaticism and force than ever before. Despite Hitler's promise to Hindenburg that the Nazis would support the Papen government, Goebbels unleashed bitter attacks on the Minister of the Interior and as early as July 9 Hitler went to Schleicher and complained bitterly of the government's policies. From the size of the crowds that turned out to see Hitler it was evident that the Nazis were gaining ground. In one day, July 27, he spoke to 60,000 persons in Brandenburg, to nearly as many in Potsdam, and that evening to 120,000 massed in the giant Grunewald Stadium in Berlin while outside an additional 100,000 heard his voice by loudspeaker.

The polling on July 31 brought a resounding victory for the National Socialist Party. With 13,745,000 votes, the Nazis won 230 seats in the Reichstag, making them easily the largest party in Parliament though still far short of a majority in a house of 608 members. The Social Democrats, no doubt because of the timidity shown by their leaders in Prussia, lost ten seats and were reduced to 133. The working class was swinging over to the Communists, who gained 12 seats and became the third largest party, with 89 members in the Reichstag. The Catholic Center increased its strength somewhat, from 68 to 73 seats, but the other middle-class parties and even Hugenberg's German National Party, the only one which had supported Papen in the election, were overwhelmed. Except for the Catholics, the middle and upper classes, it was evident, had gone over to the Nazis.

On August 2 Hitler took stock of his triumph at Tegernsee, near Munich, where he conferred with his party leaders. Since the last Reichstag elections two years before, the National Socialists had gained over seven million votes and increased their representation in Parliament from 107 to 230. In the four years since the 1928 elections, the Nazis had won some thirteen million new votes. Yet the majority which would sweep the party into power still eluded Hitler. He had won only 37 per cent of the total vote. The majority of Germans was still against him.

Far into the night he deliberated with his lieutenants. Goebbels recorded the results in his diary entry of August 2: "The Fuehrer faces difficult decisions. Legal? With the Center?" With the Center the Nazis could form a majority in the Reichstag. But to Goebbels this is "unthinkable." Still, he notes, "the Fuehrer comes to no final decision. The situation will take a little time to ripen."

But not much. Hitler, flushed with his victory, though it was less than decisive, was impatient. On August 4 he hurried to Berlin to see not Chancellor von Papan, but General von Schleicher, and, as Goebbels noted, "to present his demands. They will not be too moderate," he added. On August 5, at the Fuerstenberg barracks near Berlin, Hitler outlined his terms to General von Schleicher: the chancellorship for himself; and for his party, the premiership of Prussia, the Reich and Prussian Ministries of Interior, the Reich Ministries of Justice, Economy, and Aviation, and a new ministry for Goebbels, that of Popular Enlightenment and Propaganda. As a sop to Schleicher, Hitler promised him the Defense Ministry. Furthermore, Hitler said he would demand an enabling act from the Reichstag authorizing him to rule by decree for a specified period; if it were refused, the Reichstag would be "sent home."

Hitler left the meeting convinced that he had won over Schleicher to his program and hurried south in good spirits to his mountain retreat on the Obersalzberg. Goebbels, always cynical in regard to the opposition and always distrustful of the political General, was not so sure. "It is well to be skeptical about further developments," he confided to his diary on August 6 after he had listened to the Leader's optimistic report of his meeting with Schleicher. Goebbels was sure of one thing, though: "Once we have the power we will never give it up. They will have to carry our dead bodies out of the ministries."

All was not as well as Hitler seemed to think. On August 8 Goebbels wrote: "Telephone call from Berlin. It is full of rumors. The whole party is ready to take over power. The S.A. men are leaving their places of work in order to make themselves ready. The party leaders are preparing for the great hour. If all goes well, fine. If things go badly there will be a terrible setback." The next day Strasser, Frick and Funk arrived at Obersalzberg with news that was not exactly encouraging. Schleicher was turning again, like a worm. He was now insisting that if Hitler got the chancellorship he must rule with the consent of the Reichstag. Funk reported that his business friends were worried about the prospects of a Nazi government. He had a message from Schacht confirming it. Finally, the Wilhelmstrasse, the trio told Hitler, was worried about a Nazi putsch.

This worry was not without foundation. Next day, August 10, Goebbels learned that in Berlin the S.A. was "in a state of armed readiness . . . The S.A. is throwing an ever stronger ring around Berlin . . . The Wilhelmstrasse is very nervous about it. But that is the point of our mobilization." On the following day the Fuehrer could stand the waiting no longer. He set out by motorcar for Berlin. He would make himself "scarce" there, Goebbels says, but on the other hand he would be ready when he was called. When the call did not come he himself requested to see the President. But first he had to see Schleicher and Papen.

This interview took place at noon on August 13. It was a stormy one. Schleicher had slid away from his position of a week before. He supported Papen in insisting that the most Hitler could hope for was the vice-chancellorship. Hitler was outraged. He must be Chancellor or nothing. Papen terminated the interview by saying he would leave the "final decision" up to Hindenburg.*

---

* Papen, in his memoirs, does not mention Schleicher's presence at this meeting, but it is clear from other sources that he was there. It is an important point, in view of subsequent events.

Hitler retired in a huff to the nearby Kaiserhof. There at 3 P.M. a phone call came from the President's office. Someone—probably Goebbels, judging from his diary—asked, "Has a decision already been made? If so, there is no point in Hitler's coming over." The President, the Nazis were told, "wishes first to speak to Hitler."

The aging Field Marshal received the Nazi leader standing up and leaning on his cane in his study, thus setting the icy tone for the interview. For a man in his eighty-fifth year who only ten months before had suffered a complete mental relapse lasting more than a week, Hindenburg was in a surprisingly lucid frame of mind. He listened patiently while Hitler reiterated his demand for the chancellorship and full power. Otto von Meissner, chief of the Presidential Chancellery, and Goering, who had accompanied Hitler, were the only witnesses to the conversation, and though Meissner is not a completely dependable source, his affidavit at Nuremberg is the only firsthand testimony in existence of what followed. It has a ring of truth.

Hindenburg replied that because of the tense situation he could not in good conscience risk transferring the power of government to a new party such as the National Socialists, which did not command a majority and which was intolerant, noisy and undisciplined.

At this point, Hindenburg, with a certain show of excitement, referred to several recent occurrences—clashes between the Nazis and the police, acts of violence committed by Hitler's followers against those who were of a different opinion, excesses against Jews and other illegal acts. All these incidents had strengthened him in his conviction that there were numerous wild elements in the Party beyond control . . . After extended discussion Hindenburg proposed to Hitler that he should declare himself ready to co-operate with the other parties, in particular with the Right and Center, and that he should give up the one-sided idea that he must have complete power. In co-operating with other parties, Hindenburg declared, he would be able to show what he could achieve and improve upon. If he could show positive results, he would acquire increasing and even dominating influence even in a coalition government. Hindenburg stated that this also would be the best way to eliminate the widespread fear that a National Socialist government would make ill use of its power and would suppress all other viewpoints and gradually eliminate them. Hindenburg stated that he was ready to accept Hitler and the representatives of his movement in a coalition government, the precise combination to be a matter of negotiation, but that he could not take the responsibility of giving exclusive power to Hitler alone . . . Hitler was adamant, however, in refusing to put himself in the position of bargaining with the leaders of the other parties and in such manner to form a coalition government.[9]

The discussion, then, ended without agreement, but not before the old President, still standing, had delivered a stern lecture to the Nazi leader. In the words of the official communiqué issued immediately afterward, Hindenburg "regretted that Herr Hitler did not see himself in a position to support a national government appointed with the confidence of the Reich President, as he had agreed to do before the Reichstag elections." In the view of the venerable President, Hitler had broken his word, but let him beware of the future. "The President," the communiqué stated further, "gravely exhorted Herr Hitler to conduct the opposition on the part of the N.S. Party in a chivalrous manner, and to bear in mind his responsibility to the Fatherland and to the German people."

The communiqué giving Hindenburg's version of the meeting and insisting that Hitler had demanded "complete control of the State" was published in such a hurry that it caught Goebbels' propaganda machine napping and did much harm to Hitler's cause, not only among the general public but among the Nazis themselves. In vain did Hitler respond that he had not asked for "complete power" but only for the chancellorship and a few ministries. Hindenburg's word was generally accepted.

In the meantime, the mobilized storm troopers were chafing at the bit. Hitler called in their leaders and spoke to them that same evening. "It's a difficult task," Goebbels noted. "Who knows if their formations can be held together? Nothing is more difficult than to tell victory-flushed troops that victory has been snatched out of their hand." Late that night the little Doktor sought consolation in the reading of the letters of Frederick the Great. Next day he raced off for a vacation on the beaches of the Baltic. "Great hopelessness reigns among the party comrades," he wrote. He declined to leave his room even to speak with them. "I don't want to hear about politics for at least a week. I want only sun, light, air and peace."

Hitler retired to the Obersalzberg to imbibe the same elements and ponder the immediate future. As Goebbels said, "the first big chance has been missed." Hermann Rauschning, the then Nazi leader in Danzig, found the Fuehrer brooding sullenly on his mountaintop. "We must be ruthless," Hitler told him, and launched into a tirade against Papen. But he had not lost hope. At times he spoke as if he were already Chancellor. "My task is more difficult than Bismarck's," he said. "I must first create the nation before even beginning to tackle the national tasks before us." But supposing the Nazis were suppressed by a military dictatorship under Papen and Schleicher? Hitler abruptly asked Rauschning whether Danzig, an independent city-state then under the protection of the League of Nations, had an extradition agreement with Germany. Rauschning did not at first understand the question, but it later became evident that Hitler was looking for a place that might serve as an asylum.[10] In his diary Goebbels noted "rumors that the Fuehrer is to be arrested." Yet even now, after his rebuff by the Reich President and the government of Papen and Schleicher, and despite his fears that his party might be outlawed, he was determined to stick to his path of "legality." He squelched all talk of a putsch by the S.A. Except for occasional spells of depression he remained confident that he would achieve his goal—not by force and scarcely by winning a parliamentary majority, but by the means which had carried

Schleicher and Papen to the top: by backstairs intrigue, a game that two could play.

It was not long before he gave an example. On August 25 Goebbels conferred with Hitler at Berchtesgaden and noted: "We have got into touch with the Center Party, if only to bring pressure on our opponents." Next day Goebbels was back in Berlin, where he found that Schleicher had already found out "about our feelers to the Center." On the following day he went to see the General just to make sure. He thought Schleicher appeared worried at the prospect of Hitler and the Catholic Center getting together, for between them they commanded an absolute majority in the Reichstag. As to Schleicher, Goebbels wrote: "I don't know what is genuine or false in him."

The contacts with the Center Party, though never intended, as Goebbels said, to be much more than a means of applying pressure on the Papen government, paid off in a farcical event which now occurred in the Reichstag and which marked the beginning of the end for the cavalryman Chancellor. When the chamber convened on August 30 the Centrists joined the Nazis in electing Goering President of the Reichstag. For the first time, then, a National Socialist was in the chair when the Reichstag reconvened on September 12 to begin its working session. Goering made the most of his opportunity. Chancellor von Papen had obtained in advance from the President a decree for the dissolution of the chamber— the first time that the death warrant of the Reichstag had been signed before it met to transact business. But for this first working session he neglected to bring it along. He had with him instead a speech outlining the program of his government, having been assured that one of the Nationalist deputies, in agreement with most of the other parties, would object to a vote on the expected Communist motion for censure of the government. In this case a single objection from any one of the 600-odd members was enough to postpone a vote.

When Ernst Torgler, the Communist leader, introduced his motion as an amendment to the order of the day, however, neither a Nationalist deputy nor any other rose to object. Finally Frick asked for a half hour's adjournment on behalf of the Nazis.

"The situation was now serious," Papen says in his memoirs, "and I had been caught unawares." He sent a messenger posthaste to the Chancellery to fetch the dissolution order.

In the meantime Hitler conferred with his parliamentary party group in the Reichstag President's Palace across the street. The Nazis were in a dilemma, and they were embarrassed. The Nationalists, they felt, had double-crossed them by not moving to postpone the vote. Now Hitler's party, in order to bring down the Papen government, would have to vote with the Communists on a Communist motion. Hitler decided to swallow the pill of such an unsavory association. He ordered his deputies to vote for the Communist amendment and overthrow Papen before the Chancellor could dissolve the Reichstag. To accomplish this, of course, Goering, as presiding officer, would have to pull some fast and neat tricks of parliamentary procedure. The former air ace, a man of daring and of many abilities, as he was to prove on a larger stage later, was equal to the occasion.

When the session reconvened Papen appeared with the familiar red dispatch case which, by tradition, carried the dissolution order he had so hastily retrieved. But when he requested the floor to read it, the President of the Reichstag managed not to see him, though Papen, by now red-faced, was on his feet brandishing the paper for all in the assembly to see. All but Goering. His smiling face was turned the other way. He called for an immediate vote. By now Papen's countenance, according to eyewitnesses, had turned from red to white with anger. He strode up to the President's rostrum and plunked the dissolution order on his desk. Goering took no notice of it and ordered the vote to proceed. Papen, followed by his ministers, none of whom were members of the chamber, stalked out. The deputies voted: 513 to 32 against the government. Only then did Goering notice the piece of paper which had been thrust so angrily on his desk. He read it to the assembly and ruled that since it had been countersigned by a Chancellor who already had been voted out of office by a constitutional majority it had no validity.

Which elements in Germany gained and which lost by this farcical incident, and how much, was not immediately clear. That the dandy, Papen, had been made a joke of there was no doubt; but then he had always been somewhat of a joke, even, as Ambassador François-Poncet said, to his friends. That the Reichstag had shown that the overwhelming majority of Germans opposed Hindenburg's hand-picked presidential government was clear enough. But in the process had it not further sapped public confidence in the parliamentary system? As for the Nazis, had they not again shown themselves to be not only irresponsible but ready to connive even with the Communists to achieve their ends? Moreover, were the citizens not weary of elections and did the Nazis not face losing votes in the inevitable new election, the fourth within the year? Gregor Strasser and even Frick thought that they did, and that such a loss might be disastrous to the party.

Hitler, however, Goebbels reported that same evening, "was beside himself with joy. Again he has made a clear, unmistakable decision."

The Reichstag quickly recognized its dissolution, and new elections were set for November 6. For the Nazis they presented certain difficulties. For one thing, as Goebbels noted, the people were tired of political speeches and propaganda. Even the party workers, as he admitted in his diary of October 15, had "become very nervous as the result of these everlasting elections. They are overworked . . ." Also there were financial difficulties. Big business and big finance were swinging behind Papen, who had given them certain concessions. They were becoming increasingly distrustful, as Funk had warned, of Hitler's refusal to co-operate with Hindenburg and with what seemed to them his growing radicalism and his tendency to work even with the Communists, as the

Reichstag episode had shown. Goebbels took notice of this in his diary of October 15: "Money is extraordinarily hard to obtain. All the gentlemen of 'Property and Education' are standing by the government."

A few days before the election the Nazis had joined the Communists in staging a strike of the transport workers in Berlin, a strike disavowed by the trade unions and the Socialists. This brought a further drying up of financial sources among the businessmen just when the Nazi Party needed funds most to make a whirlwind finish in the campaign. Goebbels noted lugubriously on November 1: "Scarcity of money has become a chronic illness with us. We lack enough to really carry out a big campaign. Many bourgeois circles have been frightened off by our participation in the strike. Even many of our party comrades are beginning to have their doubts." On November 5, the eve of the elections: "Last attack. Desperate drive of the party against defeat. We succeed in getting 10,000 marks at the last minute. This will be thrown into the campaign Saturday afternoon. We have done everything that could be done. Now let fate decide."

Fate, and the German electorate, decided on November 6 a number of things, none of them conclusive for the future of the crumbling Republic. The Nazis lost two million votes and 34 seats in the Reichstag, reducing them to 196 deputies. The Communists gained three quarters of a million votes and the Social Democrats lost the same number, with the result that the Communist seats rose from 89 to 100 and the Socialist seats dropped from 133 to 121. The German National Party, the sole one which had backed the government, won nearly a million additional votes—obviously from the Nazis—and now had 52 seats instead of 37. Though the National Socialists were still the largest party in the country, the loss of two million votes was a severe setback. For the first time the great Nazi tide was ebbing, and from a point far short of a majority. The legend of invincibility had been shattered. Hitler was in a weaker position to bargain for power than he had been since July.

Realizing this, Papen put aside what he calls his "personal distaste" for Hitler and wrote him a letter on November 13 inviting him to "discuss the situation." But Hitler made so many conditions in his reply that Papen abandoned all hope of obtaining an understanding with him. The Nazi leader's intransigence did not surprise the breezy, incompetent Chancellor, but a new course which his friend and mentor, Schleicher, now proposed did surprise him. For the slippery kingmaker had come to the conclusion that Papen's usefulness, like that of Bruening before him, had come to an end. New plans were sprouting in his fertile mind. His good friend Papen must go. The President must be left completely free to deal with the political parties, especially with the largest. He urged Papen's resignation, and on November 17 Papen and his cabinet resigned. Hindenburg sent immediately for Hitler.

Their meeting on November 19 was less frigid than that of August 13. This time the President offered chairs and allowed his caller to remain for over an hour. Hindenburg presented Hitler with two choices: the chancellorship if he could secure a workable majority in the Reichstag for a definite program, or the vice-chancellorship under Papen in another presidential cabinet that would rule by emergency decrees. Hitler saw the President again on the twenty-first and he also exchanged several letters with Meissner. But there was no agreement. Hitler could not get a workable majority in Parliament. Though the Center Party agreed to support him on condition that he would not aspire to dictatorship, Hugenberg withheld the co-operation of the Nationalists. Hitler therefore resumed his demand for the chancellorship of a presidential government, but this the President would not give him. If there was to be a cabinet governing by decree Hindenburg preferred his friend Papen to head it. Hitler, he said in a letter on his behalf dispatched by Meissner, could not be given such a post "because such a cabinet is bound to develop into a party dictatorship. . . . I cannot take the responsibility for this before my oath and my conscience."[11]

The old Field Marshal was more prophetic on the first point than on the second. As for Hitler, once more he had knocked on the door of the Chancellery, had seen it open a crack only to be slammed shut in his face.

This was just what Papen had expected, and when he and Schleicher went to see Hindenburg on the evening of December 1 he was sure that he would be reappointed Chancellor. Little did he suspect what the scheming General had been up to. Schleicher had been in touch with Strasser and had suggested that if the Nazis would not come into a Papen government perhaps they would join a cabinet in which he himself were Chancellor. Hitler was asked to come to Berlin for consultations with the General, and according to one version widely publicized in the German press and later accepted by most historians, the Fuehrer actually took the night train to Berlin from Munich but was hauled off in the dead of the night by Goering at Jena and spirited away to Weimar for a meeting of the top Nazi leaders. Actually the Nazi version of this incident is, surprisingly, probably the more accurate. Goebbels' diary for November 30 recounts that a telegram came for Hitler asking him to hurry to Berlin, but that he decided to let Schleicher wait while he conferred with his comrades at Weimar, where he was scheduled to open the campaign for the Thuringian elections. At this conference, attended by the Big Five leaders, Goering, Goebbels, Strasser, Frick and Hitler, on December 1, there was considerable disagreement. Strasser, supported by Frick, urged at least Nazi toleration of a Schleicher government, though he himself preferred joining it. Goering and Goebbels argued strenuously against such a course and Hitler sided with them. Next day Hitler advised a certain Major Ott, whom Schleicher had sent to him, to counsel the General not to take the chancellorship, but it was too late.

Papen had been blandly unaware of the intrigue which Schleicher was weaving behind his back. At the beginning of the meeting with the President on December 1 he had confidently outlined his plans for the future. He should continue as Chancellor, rule by decree and let the Reichstag go hang for a while until he could "amend the constitution." In effect,

Papen wanted "amendments" which would take the country back to the days of the empire and re-establish the rule of the conservative classes. At his Nuremberg trial and in his memoirs he admitted, as indeed he did to the Field Marshal, that his proposals involved "a breach of the present constitution by the President," but he assured Hindenburg that "he might be justified in placing the welfare of the nation above his oath to the constitution," as, he added, Bismarck once had done "for the sake of the country."[13]

To Papen's great surprise, Schleicher broke in to object. He played upon the aged President's obvious reluctance to violate his oath to uphold the constitution, if it could be avoided—and the General thought it could. He believed a government which could command a majority in the Reichstag was possible if he himself headed it. He was sure he could detach Strasser and at least sixty Nazi deputies from Hitler. To this Nazi fraction he could add the middle-class parties and the Social Democrats. He even thought the trade unions would support him.

Hindenburg was shocked at such an idea and, turning to Papen, asked him then and there to go ahead with the forming of a new government. "Schleicher," says Papen, "appeared dumfounded." They had a long argument after they had left the President but could reach no agreement. As they parted, Schleicher, in the famous words addressed to Luther as he set out for the fateful Diet of Worms, said to Papen, "Little Monk, you have chosen a difficult path."

How difficult it was Papen learned the next morning at nine o'clock at a cabinet meeting which he had called.

> Schleicher rose [Papen says] and declared that there was no possibility of carrying out the directive that the President had given me. Any attempt to do so would reduce the country to chaos. The police and the armed services could not guarantee to maintain transport and supply services in the event of a general strike, nor would they be able to ensure law and order in the event of a civil war. The General Staff had made a study in this respect and he had arranged for Major Ott [its author] to place himself at the Cabinet's disposal and present a report.[13]

Whereupon the General produced the major. If Schleicher's remarks had shaken Papen, the conveniently timed report of Major Eugen Ott (who would later be Hitler's ambassador to Tokyo) demolished him. Ott simply stated that "the defense of the frontiers and the maintenance of order against both Nazis and Communists was beyond the strength of the forces at the disposal of the federal and state governments. It is therefore recommended that the Reich government should abstain from declaring a state of emergency."[14]

To Papen's pained surprise, the German Army which had once sent the Kaiser packing and which more recently, at Schleicher's instigation, had eliminated General Groener and Chancellor Bruening, was now cashiering him. He went immediately to Hindenburg with the news, hoping that the President would fire Schleicher as Minister of Defense and retain Chancellor Papen—and indeed proposing that he do so.

"My dear Papen," the stout old President replied, "you will not think much of me if I change my mind. But I am too old and have been through too much to accept the responsibility for a civil war. Our only hope is to let Schleicher try his luck."

"Two great tears," Papen swears, rolled down Hindenburg's cheeks. A few hours later, as the deposed Chancellor was clearing his desk, a photograph of the President arrived for him with the inscription, "*Ich hatt' einen Kameraden!*" The next day the President wrote him in his own handwriting of the "heavy heart" he felt in relieving him of his post and reiterating that his confidence in him "remains unshaken." That was true and would shortly be proved.

On December 2 Kurt von Schleicher became Chancellor, the first general to occupy that post since General Count Georg Leo von Caprivi de Caprara de Montecuccoli, who had succeeded Bismarck in 1890. Schleicher's tortuous intrigues had at last brought him to the highest office at a moment when the depression, which he little understood, was at its height; when the Weimar Republic, which he had done so much to undermine, was already crumbling; when no one any longer trusted him, not even the President, whom he had manipulated so long. His days on the heights, it seemed obvious to almost everyone but himself, were strictly numbered. The Nazis were sure of it. Goebbels' diary for December 2 included this entry: "Schleicher is named Chancellor. He won't last long."

Papen thought so too. He was smarting from wounded vanity and thirsting for revenge against his "friend and successor," as he calls him in his memoirs. To get Papen out of the way Schleicher offered him the Paris embassy, but he declined. The President, Papen says, wanted him to remain in Berlin "within reach." That was the most strategic place to weave his own web of intrigues against the archintriguer. Busy and agile as a spider, Papen set to work. As the strife-ridden year of 1932 approached its end, Berlin was full of cabals, and of cabals within cabals. Besides those of Papen and Schleicher, there was one at the President's Palace, where Hindenburg's son, Oskar, and his State Secretary, Meissner, held sway behind the throne. There was one at the Kaiserhof hotel, where Hitler and the men around him were plotting not only for power but against each other. Soon the webs of intrigue became so enmeshed that by New Year's, 1933, none of the cabalists was sure who was double-crossing whom. But it would not take long for them to find out.

SCHLEICHER: THE LAST CHANCELLOR OF THE REPUBLIC

"I stayed in power only fifty-seven days," Schleicher remarked once in the hearing of the attentive French ambassador, "and on each and every one of them I was betrayed fifty-seven times. Don't ever speak to me of

'German loyalty'!"[15] His own career and doings had certainly made him an authority on the subject.

He began his chancellorship by making Gregor Strasser an offer to become Vice-Chancellor of Germany and Premier of Prussia. Having failed to get Hitler to join his government, Schleicher now tried to split the Nazis by this bait to Strasser. There was some reason to believe he might succeed. Strasser was the Number Two man in the party, and among the left-wing element, which really believed in a national socialism, he was more popular than Hitler. As leader of the Party Organization he was in direct touch with all the provincial and local leaders and seemingly had earned their loyalty. He was now convinced that Hitler had brought the movement to a dead end. The more radical followers were going over to the Communists. The party itself was financially bankrupt. In November Fritz Thyssen had warned that he could make no further contributions to the movement. There were simply no funds to meet the payroll of thousands of party functionaries or to maintain the S.A., which alone cost two and a half million marks a week. The printers of the extensive Nazi press were threatening to stop the presses unless they received payment on overdue bills. Goebbels had touched on this in his diary on November 11: "The financial situation of the Berlin organization is hopeless. Nothing but debts and obligations." And in December he was regretting that party salaries would have to be cut. Finally, the provincial elections in Thuringia on December 3, the day Schleicher called in Strasser, revealed a loss of 40 per cent in the Nazi vote. It had become obvious, at least to Strasser, that the Nazis would never obtain office through the ballot.

He therefore urged Hitler to abandon his "all or nothing" policy and take what power he could by joining in a coalition with Schleicher. Otherwise, he feared, the party would fall to pieces. He had been pressing this line for some months, and Goebbels' diary from midsummer to December is full of bitter references to Strasser's "disloyalty" to Hitler.

The showdown came on December 5 at a meeting of the party leaders at the Kaiserhof in Berlin. Strasser demanded that the Nazis at least "tolerate" the Schleicher government, and he was backed by Frick, who headed the Nazi bloc in the Reichstag, many of whose members feared losing their seats and their deputy's salary if Hitler provoked any more elections. Goering and Goebbels strenuously opposed Strasser and won Hitler to their side. Hitler would not "tolerate" the Schleicher regime, but, it developed, he was still ready to "negotiate" with it. For this task, however, he appointed Goering—he had already heard, Goebbels reveals, of Strasser's private talk with the Chancellor two days before. On the seventh, Hitler and Strasser had a conversation at the Kaiserhof that degenerated into a bitter quarrel. Hitler accused his chief lieutenant of trying to stab him in the back, oust him from his leadership of the party and break up the Nazi movement. Strasser heatedly denied this, swore that he had been loyal but accused Hitler of leading the party to destruction. Apparently he left unsaid a number of things that had been swelling within him since 1925. Back at his room in the Excelsior Hotel he put them all in writing in a letter to Hitler which ended with his resignation of all his offices in the party.

The letter, which reached Hitler on the eighth, fell, as Goebbels' diary says, "like a bombshell." The atmosphere in the Kaiserhof was that of a graveyard. "We are all dejected and depressed," Goebbels noted. It was the greatest blow Hitler had suffered since he rebuilt the party in 1925. Now, on the threshold of power, his principal follower had deserted him and threatened to smash all he had built up in seven years.

> In the evening [Goebbels wrote], the Fuehrer comes to our home. It is difficult to be cheerful. We are all depressed, above all because of the danger of the whole party falling apart, and all our work having been in vain . . . Telephone call from Dr. Ley. The situation in the party worsens from hour to hour. The Fuehrer must return immediately to the Kaiserhof.

Goebbels was called to join him there at two o'clock in the morning. Strasser had given his story to the morning newspapers, which were just then appearing on the streets. Hitler's reaction was described by Goebbels:

> Treason! Treason! Treason!
> For hours the Fuehrer paces up and down in the hotel room. He is embittered and deeply wounded by this treachery. Finally he stops and says: If the party once falls to pieces I'll put an end to it all in three minutes with a pistol shot.

The party did not fall apart and Hitler did not shoot himself. Strasser might have achieved both these ends, which would have radically altered the course of history, but at the crucial moment he himself gave up. Frick, with Hitler's permission, had been searching all Berlin for him, it having been agreed that the quarrel must somehow be patched over to rescue the party from disaster. But Strasser, fed up with it all, had taken a train south for a vacation in sunny Italy. Hitler, always at his best when he detected weakness in an opponent, struck swiftly and hard. The Political Organization which Strasser had built up was taken over by the Fuehrer himself, with Dr. Ley, the Gauleiter from Cologne, as his staff chief. Strasser's friends were purged and all party leaders convoked to Berlin to sign a new declaration of loyalty to Adolf Hitler, which they did.

The wily Austrian had once more extricated himself from a tight fix that might easily have proved disastrous. Gregor Strasser, whom so many had thought to be a greater man than Hitler, was quickly destroyed. "A dead man," Goebbels called him in his diary notation of December 9. This was to become literally true within two years when Hitler decided to settle accounts.

On December 10, a week after he had been tripped by General von Schleicher, Franz von Papen began to spin his own web of intrigues. Following a speech that evening to the exclusive Herrenklub, from whose aristocratic and wealthy members he had recruited his short-lived cabinet, he had a private talk with Baron Kurt von Schroeder, the Cologne banker who had contributed funds to the National Socialist Party. He suggested that the financier arrange for him to see Hitler on the sly. In his memoirs Papen claims that it was Schroeder who made the suggestion but admits that he agreed. By a strange coincidence, Wilhelm Keppler, Hitler's economic adviser and one of his contact men with business circles, made the same suggestion on behalf of the Nazi leader.

The two men, who had been at such odds only a few weeks before, met in what they hoped was the greatest of secrecy at the home of Schroeder in Cologne on the morning of January 4. Papen was surprised when a photographer snapped him at the entrance, but gave it little thought until the next day. Hitler was accompanied by Hess, Himmler and Keppler, but he left his aides in the parlor and retired to Schroeder's study, where he was closeted for two hours with Papen and their host. Though the conversation started badly, with Hitler complaining bitterly of the way Papen had treated the Nazis while Chancellor, it soon developed to a point that was to prove fateful for both men and their country. This was a crucial moment for the Nazi chief. By a superhuman effort he had kept the party intact after Strasser's defection. He had traveled up and down the country addressing three and four meetings a day, exhorting the party leaders to keep together behind him. But Nazi spirits remained at a low ebb, and the party was financially bankrupt. Many were saying it was finished. Goebbels had reflected the general feeling in his diary the last week of the year: "1932 has brought us eternal bad luck . . . The past was difficult and the future looks dark and gloomy; all prospects and hopes have quite disappeared."

Hitler therefore was not nearly in so favorable a position to bargain for power as he had been during the previous summer and autumn. But neither was Papen; he was out of office. In their adversity, their minds met.

The terms on which they met are a matter of dispute. In his trial at Nuremberg and in his memoirs Papen blandly maintained that, ever loyal to Schleicher, he merely suggested to Hitler that he join the General's government. In view, however, of Papen's long record of deceit, of his quite natural desire to present himself in the most favorable light at Nuremberg and in his book, and of subsequent events, it seems certain that Schroeder's quite different account, which was given at Nuremberg, is the more truthful one. The banker maintained that what Papen suggested was the replacement of the Schleicher government by a Hitler–Papen government in which the two of them would be coequal. But:

Hitler . . . said if he were made Chancellor it would be necessary for him to be the head of the government but that supporters of Papen could go into his government as ministers when they were willing to go along with him in his policy of changing many things. These changes included elimination of Social

Democrats, Communists and Jews from leading positions in Germany and the restoration of order in public life. Von Papen and Hitler reached agreement in principle . . . They agreed that further details would have to be worked out and that this could be done in Berlin or some other convenient place.[16]

And in the greatest secrecy, of course. But, to the consternation of Papen and Hitler, the newspapers in Berlin came out with flaming headlines on the morning of January 5 over accounts of the Cologne meeting, accompanied by editorial blasts against Papen for his disloyalty to Schleicher. The wily General had placed his spies with his usual acumen; one of them, Papen later learned, had been that photographer who had snapped his picture as he entered Schroeder's home.

Besides his deal with Papen, Hitler got two other things out of the Cologne meeting which were of great value to him. He learned from the ex-Chancellor that Hindenburg had not given Schleicher power to dissolve the Reichstag. This meant that the Nazis, with the help of the Communists, could overthrow the General any time they wished. Secondly, out of the meeting came an understanding that West German business interests would take over the debts of the Nazi Party. Two days after the Cologne talks Goebbels noted "pleasing progress in political developments" but still complained of the "bad financial situation." Ten days later, on January 16, he reported that the financial position of the party had "fundamentally improved overnight."

In the meantime Chancellor Schleicher went about—with an optimism that was myopic, to say the least—trying to establish a stable government. On December 15 he made a fireside broadcast to the nation begging his listeners to forget that he was a general and assuring them that he was a supporter "neither of capitalism nor of socialism" and that to him "concepts such as private economy or planned economy have lost their terrors." His principal task, he said, was to provide work for the unemployed and get the country back on its economic feet. There would be no tax increase, no more wage cuts. In fact, he was canceling the last cut in wages and relief which Papen had made. Furthermore, he was ending the agricultural quotas which Papen had established for the benefit of the large landowners and instead was launching a scheme to take 800,000 acres from the bankrupt Junker estates in the East and give them to 25,000 peasant families. Also prices of such essentials as coal and meat would be kept down by rigid control.

This was a bid for the support of the very masses which he had hitherto opposed or disregarded, and Schleicher followed it up with conversations with the trade unions, to whose leaders he gave the impression that he envisaged a future in which organized labor and the Army would be twin pillars of the nation. But labor was not to be taken in by a man whom it profoundly mistrusted, and it declined its co-operation.

The industrialists and the big landowners, on the other hand, rose up in arms against the new Chancellor's program, which they clamored was nothing less than Bolshevism. The businessmen were aghast at Schleicher's sudden friendliness to the unions. The owners of large estates were infuriated at his reduction of agricultural protection and livid at the prospect of his breaking up the bankrupt estates in the East. On January 12 the Landbund, the association of the larger farmers, bitterly attacked the government, and its leaders, two of whom were Nazis, called on the President with their protests. Hindenburg, now a Junker landowner himself, called his Chancellor to account. Schleicher's answer was to threaten to publish a secret Reichstag report on the Osthilfe (Eastern Relief) loans— a scandal which, as everyone knew, implicated hundreds of the oldest Junker families, who had waxed fat on unredeemed government "loans," and which indirectly involved even the President himself, since the East Prussian estate which had been presented to him had been illegally deeded to his son to escape inheritance taxes.

Despite the uproar among the industrialists and landowners and the coolness of the trade unions, Schleicher remained unaccountably confident that all was going well. On New Year's Day, 1933, he and his cabinet called on the aged President, who proceeded to express his gratitude that "the gravest hardships are overcome and the upward path is now open to us." On January 4, the day Papen and Hitler were conferring in Cologne, the Chancellor arranged for Strasser, who had returned from his holiday in the Italian sun, to see Hindenburg. The former Number Two Nazi, when he saw the President a few days later, expressed willingness to join the Schleicher cabinet. This move threw consternation into the Nazi camp, which at the moment was pitched in the tiny state of Lippe, where Hitler and all his principal aides were fighting furiously to score a local election success in order to improve the Fuehrer's bargaining position with Papen. Goebbels recounts the arrival of Goering at midnight of January 13 with the bad news of Strasser and of how the party chiefs had sat up all night discussing it, agreeing that if he took office it would be a grave setback to the party.

Schleicher thought so too, and on January 15 when Kurt von Schuschnigg, then the Austrian Minister of Justice, visited him he assured him that "Herr Hitler was no longer a problem, his movement had ceased to be a political danger, and the whole problem had been solved, it was a thing of the past."[17]

But Strasser did not come into the cabinet, nor did the leader of the Nationalist Party, Hugenberg, who on the day before, the fourteenth, had assured Hindenburg that he would. Both men soon turned to Hitler, Strasser to be turned down cold and Hugenberg with more success. On January 15, at the very moment when Schleicher was gloating to Schuschnigg about the end of Hitler, the Nazis scored a local success in the elections of little Lippe. It was not much of an achievement. The total vote was only 90,000, of which the Nazis obtained 38,000, or 39 per cent, an increase of some 17 per cent over their previous poll. But, led by Goebbels, the Nazi leaders beat the drums over their "victory," and strangely enough it seems to have impressed a number of conservatives, including the men behind Hindenburg, of whom the principal ones were State Secretary Meissner and the President's son, Oskar.

On the evening of January 22, these two gentlemen stole out of the presidential quarters, grabbed a taxi, as Meissner says, to avoid being noticed and drove to the suburban home of a hitherto unknown Nazi by the name of Joachim von Ribbentrop, who was a friend of Papen—they had served together on the Turkish front during the war. There they met Papen, Hitler, Goering and Frick. According to Meissner, Oskar von Hindenburg had been opposed to any truck with the Nazis up to this fateful evening. Hitler may have known this; at any rate he insisted on having a talk with him "under four eyes," and to Meissner's astonishment young Hindenburg assented and withdrew with Hitler to another room, where they were closeted together for an hour. What Hitler said to the President's son, who was not noted for a brilliant mind or a strong character, has never been revealed. It was generally believed in Nazi circles that Hitler made both offers and threats, the latter consisting of hints to disclose to the public Oskar's involvement in the Osthilfe scandal and the tax evasion on the Hindenburg estate. One can only judge the offers by the fact that a few months later five thousand tax-free acres were added to the Hindenburg family property at Neudeck and that in August 1934 Oskar was jumped from colonel to major general in the Army.

At any rate there is no doubt that Hitler made a strong impression on the President's son. "In the taxi on the way back," Meissner later recounted in his affidavit at Nuremberg, "Oskar von Hindenburg was extremely silent, and the only remark which he made was that it could not be helped—the Nazis had to be taken into the government. My impression was that Hitler had succeeded in getting him under his spell."

It only remained for Hitler to cast the spell over the father. This admittedly was more difficult, for whatever the old Field Marshal's deficiencies of mind, age had not softened his granite character. More difficult, but not impossible. Papen, busy as a beaver, was working daily on the old man. And it was easy to see that, for all his cunning, Schleicher was fast stumbling to a fall. He had failed to win over the Nazis or to split them. He could get no backing from the Nationalists, the Center or the Social Democrats.

On January 23, therefore, Schleicher went to see Hindenburg, admitted that he could not find a majority in the Reichstag and demanded its dissolution and emergency powers to rule by decree under Article 48 of the constitution. According to Meissner, the General also asked for the "temporary elimination" of the Reichstag and frankly acknowledged that he would have to transform his government into "a military dictatorship."[18] Despite all his devious plotting, Schleicher was back where Papen had been early in December, but their roles were now reversed. Then Papen had demanded emergency powers and Schleicher had opposed him and proposed that he himself form a majority government with the backing of the Nazis. Now the General was insisting on dictatorial rule, and the sly fox Papen was assuring the Field Marshal that he himself could corral Hitler for a government that would have a majority in the Reichstag. Such are the ups and downs of rogues and intriguers!

Hindenburg, reminding Schleicher of the reasons he had given on December 2 for upsetting Papen, informed him that they still held good. He bade him return to his task of finding a Reichstag majority. Schleicher was finished, and he knew it. So did everyone else who was in on the secret. Goebbels, one of the few in on it, commented the next day: "Schleicher will fall any moment, he who brought down so many others."

His end came finally and officially on January 28, when he called on the President and tendered the resignation of his government. "I have already one foot in the grave, and I am not sure that I shall not regret this action in heaven later on," Hindenburg told the disillusioned General. "After this breach of trust, sir, I am not sure that you will go to heaven," Schleicher replied, and quickly faded out of German history.[19]

At noon of the same day Papen was entrusted by the President to explore the possibilities of forming a government under Hitler "within the terms of the constitution." For a week this sly, ambitious man had been flirting with the idea of double-crossing Hitler after all and becoming Chancellor again of a presidential government backed by Hugenberg. On January 27 Goebbels noted: "There is still the possibility that Papen will again be made Chancellor." The day before, Schleicher had sent the Commander in Chief of the Army, General von Hammerstein, to the President to warn him against selecting Papen. In the maze of intrigues with which Berlin was filled, Schleicher was at the last minute plumping for Hitler to replace him. Hindenburg assured the Army commander he had no intention of appointing "that Austrian corporal."

The next day, Sunday, January 29, was a crucial one, with the conspirators playing their last desperate hands and filling the capital with the most alarming and conflicting rumors, not all of them groundless by any means. Once more Schleicher dispatched the faithful Hammerstein to stir up the brew. The Army chief sought out Hitler to warn him once again that Papen might leave him out in the cold and that it might be wise for the Nazi leader to ally himself with the fallen Chancellor and the Army. Hitler was not much interested. He returned to the Kaiserhof to have cakes and coffee with his aides and it was at this repast that Goering appeared with the tidings that the Fuehrer would be named Chancellor on the morrow.

That night the Nazi chieftains were celebrating the momentous news at Goebbels' home on the Reichskanzlerplatz when another emissary from Schleicher arrived with startling news. This was Werner von Alvensleben, a man so given to conspiracy that when one did not exist he invented one. He informed the jubilant party that Schleicher and Hammerstein had put the Potsdam garrison on an alarm footing and were preparing to bundle the old President off to Neudeck and establish a military dictatorship. This was a gross exaggeration. It is possible that the two generals were playing with the idea but most certain that they had not taken any action. The Nazis, however, became hysterical with alarm. Goering hastened as fast as his bulk allowed across the square to alert the President and Papen. What Hitler did he later described himself.

My immediate counteraction to this planned [military] putsch was to send for the Commander of the Berlin S.A., Count von Helldorf, and through him to alert the whole S.A. of Berlin. At the same time I instructed Major Wecke of the Police, whom I knew I could trust, to prepare for a sudden seizure of the Wilhelmstrasse by six police battalions . . . Finally I instructed General von Blomberg (who had been selected as Reichswehr Minister-elect) to proceed at once, on arrival in Berlin at 8 A.M. on January 30, direct to the Old Gentleman to be sworn in, and thus to be in a position, as Commander in Chief of the Reichswehr, to suppress any possible attempts at a *coup d'état*.[20]

Behind the backs of Schleicher and the Commander in Chief of the Army—everything in this frenzied period was being done behind someone's back—General Werner von Blomberg had been summoned, not by Hitler, who was not yet in power, but by Hindenburg and Papen from Geneva, where he was representing Germany at the Disarmament Conference, to become the new Minister of Defense in the Hitler–Papen cabinet. He was a man who, as Hitler later said, already enjoyed his confidence and who had come under the spell of his chief of staff in East Prussia, Colonel Walter von Reichenau, an outspoken Nazi sympathizer. When Blomberg arrived in Berlin, early on the morning of January 30, he was met at the station by two Army officers with conflicting orders for him. A Major von Kuntzen, Hammerstein's adjutant, commanded him to report to the Commander in Chief of the Army. Colonel Oskar von Hindenburg, adjutant to his father, ordered the bewildered Blomberg to report to the President of the Republic. Blomberg went to the President, was immediately sworn in as Defense Minister, and thus was given the authority not only to put down any attempted coup by the Army but to see that the military supported the new government, which a few hours later would be named. Hitler was always grateful to the Army for accepting him at that crucial moment. Not long afterward he told a party rally, "If in the days of our revolution the Army had not stood on our side, then we would not be standing here today." It was a responsibility which would weigh heavily on the officer corps in the days to come and which, in the end, they would more than regret.

On this wintry morning of January 30, 1933, the tragedy of the Weimar Republic, of the bungling attempt for fourteen frustrating years of the Germans to make democracy work, had come to an end—but not before, at the very last moment, as the final curtain fell, a minor farce took place among the motley group of conspirators gathered to bury the republican regime. Papen later described it.

At about half-past ten the members of the proposed Cabinet met in my house and walked across the garden to the Presidential palace, where we waited in Meissner's office. Hitler immediately renewed his complaints about not being appointed Commissioner for Prussia. He felt that this severely restricted his power. I told him . . . the Prussian appointment could be left until later. To this, Hitler replied that if his powers were to be thus limited, he must insist on new Reichstag elections.

This produced a completely new situation and the debate became heated. Hugenberg, in particular, objected to the idea, and Hitler tried to pacify him by stating that he would make no changes in the Cabinet, whatever the result might be . . . By this time it was long past eleven o'clock, the time that had been appointed for our interview with the President, and Meissner asked me to end our discussion, as Hindenburg was not prepared to wait any longer.

We had had such a sudden clash of opinions that I was afraid our new coalition would break up before it was born . . . At last we were shown in to the President and I made the necessary formal introductions. Hindenburg made a short speech about the necessity of full co-operation in the interests of the nation, and we were then sworn in. The Hitler cabinet had been formed.[21]

In this way, by way of the back door, by means of a shabby political deal with the old-school reactionaries he privately detested, the former tramp from Vienna, the derelict of the First World War, the violent revolutionary, became Chancellor of the great nation.

To be sure, the National Socialists were in a decided minority in the government; they had only three of the eleven posts in the cabinet and except for the chancellorship these were not key positions. Frick was Minister of the Interior but he did not control the police as this minister did in most European countries—the police in Germany were in the hands of the individual states. The third Nazi cabinet member was Goering, but no specific office could be found for him; he was named Minister without Portfolio, with the understanding that he would become Minister of Aviation as soon as Germany had an air force. Little noticed was the naming of Goering to be also Minister of the Interior of Prussia, an office that controlled the Prussian police; for the moment public attention was focused on the Reich cabinet. Goebbels' name, to the surprise of many, did not appear in it; momentarily he was left out in the cold.

The important ministries went to the conservatives, who were sure they had lassoed the Nazis for their own ends: Neurath continued as Minister of Foreign Affairs; Blomberg was Minister of Defense; Hugenberg took over the combined Ministries of Economy and Agriculture; Seldte, the Stahlhelm leader, was made Minister of Labor; the other ministries were left in the hands of nonparty "experts" whom Papen had appointed eight months before. Papen himself was Vice-Chancellor of the Reich and Premier of Prussia, and Hindenburg had promised him that he would not receive the Chancellor except in the company of the Vice-Chancellor. This unique position, he was sure, would enable him to put a brake on the radical Nazi leader. But even more: This government was Papen's conception, his creation, and he was confident that with the help of the staunch old President, who was his friend, admirer and protector, and with the knowing support of his conservative colleagues, who outnumbered the obstreperous Nazis eight to three, he would dominate it.

But this frivolous, conniving politician did not know Hitler—no one really knew Hitler—nor did he comprehend the strength of the forces which had spewed him up. Nor did Papen, or anyone else except Hitler, quite realize the inexplicable weakness, that now bordered on paralysis, of existing institutions—the Army, the churches, the trade unions, the political parties—or of the vast non-Nazi middle class and the highly organized proletariat all of which, as Papen mournfully observed much later, would "give up without a fight."

No class or group or party in Germany could escape its share of responsibility for the abandonment of the democratic Republic and the advent of Adolf Hitler. The cardinal error of the Germans who opposed Nazism was their failure to unite against it. At the crest of their popular strength, in July 1932, the National Socialists had attained but 37 per cent of the vote. But the 63 per cent of the German people who expressed their opposition to Hitler were much too divided and shortsighted to combine against a common danger which they must have known would overwhelm them unless they united, however temporarily, to stamp it out. The Communists, at the behest of Moscow, were committed to the last to the silly idea of first destroying the Social Democrats, the Socialist trade unions and what middle-class democratic forces there were, on the dubious theory that although this would lead to a Nazi regime it would be only temporary and would bring inevitably the collapse of capitalism, after which the Communists would take over and establish the dictatorship of the proletariat. Fascism, in the Bolshevik Marxist view, represented the last stage of a dying capitalism; after that, the Communist deluge!

Fourteen years of sharing political power in the Republic, of making all the compromises that were necessary to maintain coalition governments, had sapped the strength and the zeal of the Social Democrats until their party had become little more than an opportunist pressure organization, determined to bargain for concessions for the trade unions on which their strength largely rested. It might be true, as some Socialists said, that fortune had not smiled on them: the Communists, unscrupulous and undemocratic, had split the working class; the depression had further hurt the Social Democrats, weakening the trade unions and losing the party the support of millions of unemployed, who in their desperation turned either to the Communists or the Nazis. But the tragedy of the Social Democrats could not be explained fully by bad luck. They had had their chance to take over Germany in November 1918 and to found a state based on what they had always preached: social democracy. But they lacked the decisiveness to do so. Now at the dawn of the third decade they were a tired, defeatist party, dominated by old, well-meaning but mostly mediocre men. Loyal to the Republic they were to the last, but in the end too confused, too timid to take the great risks which alone could have preserved it, as they had shown by their failure to act when Papen turned out a squad of soldiers to destroy constitutional government in Prussia.

Between the Left and the Right, Germany lacked a politically powerful middle class, which in other countries—in France, in England, in the United States—had proved to be the backbone of democracy. In the first year of the Republic the middle-class parties, the Democrats, the People's Party, the Center, had polled a total of twelve million votes, only two million less than the two Socialist groups. But thereafter their strength had waned as their supporters gravitated toward Hitler and the Nationalists. In 1919, the Democrats had elected 74 members to the Reichstag; by 1932 they held just 2 seats. The strength of the People's Party fell from 62 seats in 1920 to 11 seats in 1932. Only the Catholic Center retained its voting strength to the end. In the first republican elections in 1919 the Center had 71 deputies in the Reichstag; in 1932 it had 70. But even more than the Social Democrats, the Center Party since Bismarck's time had been largely opportunist, supporting whatever government made concessions to its special interests. And though it seemed to be loyal to the Republic and to subscribe to its democracy, its leaders, as we have seen, were negotiating with the Nazis to give Hitler the chancellorship before they were outbid by Papen and the Nationalists.

If the German Republic was bereft of a middle-of-the-road political class, it also lacked that stability provided in many other countries by a truly conservative party. The German Nationalists at their peak in 1924 had polled six million votes and sent 103 deputies to the Reichstag, in which they formed the second largest party. But then, as at almost all times during the Weimar regime, they refused to take a responsible position either in the government or in opposition, the only exception being their participation in two short-lived cabinets in the Twenties. What the German Right, whose vote went largely to the Nationalists, wanted was an end to the Republic and a return to an imperialist Germany in which all of their old privileges would be restored. Actually the Republic had treated the Right both as individuals and as classes with the utmost generosity and, considering their aim, with exceptional tolerance. It had, as we have seen, allowed the Army to maintain a state within a state, the businessmen and bankers to make large profits, the Junkers to keep their uneconomic estates by means of government loans that were never repaid and seldom used to improve their land. Yet this generosity had won neither their gratitude nor their loyalty to the Republic. With a narrowness, a prejudice, a blindness which in retrospect seem inconceivable to this chronicler, they hammered away at the foundations of the Republic until, in alliance with Hitler, they brought it down.

In the former Austrian vagabond the conservative classes thought they had found a man who, while remaining their prisoner, would help them attain their goals. The destruction of the Republic was only the first step. What they then wanted was an authoritarian Germany which at home would put an end to democratic "nonsense" and the power of the trade unions and in foreign affairs undo the verdict of 1918, tear off the shackles of Versailles, rebuild a great Army and with its military power restore the country to its place in the sun. These were Hitler's aims too. And though he brought what the conservatives had lacked, a mass following, the Right was sure that he would remain in its pocket—was he not outnumbered eight to three in the Reich cabinet? Such a commanding position also would allow the conservatives, or so they thought, to achieve their ends without the barbarism of unadulterated Nazism. Admittedly they were decent, God-fearing men, according to their lights.

The Hohenzollern Empire had been built on the armed triumphs of Prussia, the German Republic on the defeat by the Allies after a great war. But the Third Reich owed nothing to the fortunes of war or to foreign influence. It was inaugurated in peacetime, and peacefully, by the Germans themselves, out of both their weaknesses and their strengths. The Germans imposed the Nazi tyranny on themselves. Many of them, perhaps a majority, did not quite realize it at that noon hour of January 30, 1933, when President Hindenburg, acting in a perfectly constitutional manner, entrusted the chancellorship to Adolf Hitler.

But they were soon to learn.

7

THE NAZIFICATION OF GERMANY:

1933–34

THE THEORY WHICH HITLER had evolved in his vagabond days in Vienna and never forgotten—that the way to power for a revolutionary movement was to ally itself with some of the powerful institutions in the State—had now worked out in practice pretty much as he had calculated. The President, backed by the Army and the conservatives, had made him Chancellor. His political power, though great, was, however, not complete. It was shared with these three sources of authority, which had put him into òffice and which were outside and, to some extent, distrustful of the National Socialist movement.

Hitler's immediate task, therefore, was to quickly eliminate them from the driver's seat, make his party the exclusive master of the State and then with the power of an authoritarian government and its police carry out the Nazi revolution. He had been in office scarcely twenty-four hours when he made his first decisive move, springing a trap on his gullible conservative "captors" and setting in motion a chain of events which he either originated or controlled and which at the end of six months would bring the complete Nazification of Germany and his own elevation to dictator of the Reich, unified and defederalized for the first time in German history.

Five hours after being sworn in, at 5 P.M. on January 30, 1933, Hitler held his first cabinet meeting. The minutes of the session, which turned up at Nuremberg among the hundreds of tons of captured secret documents, reveal how quickly and adroitly Hitler, aided by the crafty Goering, began to take his conservative colleagues for a ride.*[1] Hindenburg had named

---

* This cabinet meeting, of course, was private, and, like most of the other conferences, many of them taking place in the strictest secrecy, held by Hitler and his political and military aides during the Third Reich, its proceèdings and decisions were not accessible to the public until the captured German documents were first perused during the Nuremberg trial.

A great many of these highly confidential discussions and the decisions emanating from them—all regarded as state secrets—will henceforth be chronicled in this book, which, from here to the end, largely rests on the documents which recorded them at the time. At the risk of somewhat cluttering the pages with numbers indicat-

Hitler to head not a presidential cabinet but one based on a majority in the Reichstag. However, the Nazis and the Nationalists, the only two parties represented in the government, had only 247 seats out of 583 in Parliament and thus lacked a majority. To attain it they needed the backing of the Center Party with its 70 seats. In the very first hours of the new government Hitler had dispatched Goering to talk with the Centrist leaders, and now he reported to the cabinet that the Center was demanding "certain concessions." Goering therefore proposed that the Reichstag be dissolved and new elections held, and Hitler agreed. Hugenberg, a man of wooden mind for all his success in business, objected to taking the Center into the government but on the other hand opposed new elections, well knowing that the Nazis, with the resources of the State behind them, might win an absolute majority at the polls and thus be in a position to dispense with his own services and those of his conservative friends. He proposed simply suppressing the Communist Party; with its 100 seats eliminated, the Nazis and the Nationalists would have a majority. But Hitler would not go so far at the moment, and it was finally agreed that the Chancellor himself would confer with the Center Party leaders on the following morning and that if the talks were fruitless the cabinet would then ask for new elections.

Hitler easily made them fruitless. At his request the Center leader, Monsignor Kaas, submitted as a basis for discussion a list of questions which added up to a demand that Hitler promise to govern constitutionally. But Hitler, tricking both Kaas and his cabinet members, reported to the latter that the Center had made impossible demands and that there was no chance of agreement. He therefore proposed that the President be asked to dissolve the Reichstag and call new elections. Hugenberg and Papen were trapped, but after a solemn assurance from the Nazi leader that the cabinet would remain unchanged however the elections turned out, they agreed to go along with him. New elections were set for March 5.

For the first time—in the last relatively free election Germany was to have—the Nazi Party now could employ all the vast resources of the government to win votes. Goebbels was jubilant. "Now it will be easy," he wrote in his diary on February 3, "to carry on the fight, for we can call on all the resources of the State. Radio and press are at our disposal. We shall stage a masterpiece of propaganda. And this time, naturally, there is no lack of money."[2]

The big businessmen, pleased with the new government that was going to put the organized workers in their place and leave management to run its businesses as it wished, were asked to cough up. This they agreed to do at a meeting on February 20 at Goering's Reichstag President's Palace, at which Dr. Schacht acted as host and Goering and Hitler laid down the line to a couple of dozen of Germany's leading magnates, including Krupp

ing notes, these sources will be indicated. No other history of a nation over a specific epoch has been so fully documented, I believe, as that of the Third Reich, and to have left out reference to the documents, it seemed to the author, would have greatly weakened whatever value this book may have as an authentic historical record.

von Bohlen, who had become an enthusiastic Nazi overnight, Bosch and Schnitzler of I. G. Farben, and Voegler, head of the United Steel Works. The record of this secret meeting has been preserved.

Hitler began a long speech with a sop to the industrialists. "Private enterprise," he said, "cannot be maintained in the age of democracy; it is conceivable only if the people have a sound idea of authority and personality . . . All the worldly goods we possess we owe to the struggle of the chosen . . . We must not forget that all the benefits of culture must be introduced more or less with an iron fist." He promised the businessmen that he would "eliminate" the Marxists and restore the Wehrmacht (the latter was of special interest to such industries as Krupp, United Steel and I. G. Farben, which stood to gain the most from rearmament). "Now we stand before the last election," Hitler concluded, and he promised his listeners that "regardless of the outcome, there will be no retreat." If he did not win, he would stay in power "by other means . . . with other weapons." Goering, talking more to the immediate point, stressed the necessity of "financial sacrifices" which "surely would be much easier for industry to bear if it realized that the election of March fifth will surely be the last one for the next ten years, probably even for the next hundred years."

All this was made clear enough to the assembled industrialists and they responded with enthusiasm to the promise of the end of the infernal elections, of democracy and disarmament. Krupp, the munitions king, who, according to Thyssen, had urged Hindenburg on January 29 not to appoint Hitler, jumped up and expressed to the Chancellor the "gratitude" of the businessmen "for having given us such a clear picture." Dr. Schacht then passed the hat. "I collected three million marks," he recalled at Nuremberg.[3]

On January 31, 1933, the day after Hitler was named Chancellor, Goebbels wrote in his diary: "In a conference with the Fuehrer we lay down the line for the fight against the Red terror. For the moment we shall abstain from direct countermeasures. The Bolshevik attempt at revolution must first burst into flame. At the proper moment we shall strike."

Despite increasing provocation by the Nazi authorities there was no sign of a revolution, Communist or Socialist, bursting into flames as the electoral campaign got under way. By the beginning of February the Hitler government had banned all Communist meetings and shut down the Communist press. Social Democrat rallies were either forbidden or broken up by the S.A. rowdies, and the leading Socialist newspapers were continually suspended. Even the Catholic Center Party did not escape the Nazi terror. Stegerwald, the leader of the Catholic Trade Unions, was beaten by Brownshirts when he attempted to address a meeting, and Bruening was obliged to seek police protection at another rally after S.A. troopers had wounded a number of his followers. Altogether fifty-one anti-Nazis were listed as murdered during the electoral campaign, and the

Nazis claimed that eighteen of their own number had been done to death.

Goering's key position as Minister of the Interior of Prussia now began to be noticed. Ignoring the restraining hand of Papen, who as Premier of Prussia was supposedly above him, Goering removed hundreds of republican officials and replaced them with Nazis, mostly S.A. and S.S. officers. He ordered the police to avoid "at all costs" hostility to the S.A., the S.S. and the Stahlhelm but on the other hand to show no mercy to those who were "hostile to the State." He urged the police "to make use of firearms" and warned that those who didn't would be punished. This was an outright call for the shooting down of all who opposed Hitler by the police of a state (Prussia) which controlled two thirds of Germany. Just to make sure that the job would be ruthlessly done, Goering on February 22 established an auxiliary police force of 50,000 men, of whom 40,000 were drawn from the ranks of the S.A. and the S.S. and the rest from the Stahlhelm. Police power in Prussia was thus largely carried out by Nazi thugs. It was a rash German who appealed to such a "police" for protection against the Nazi terrorists.

And yet despite all the terror the "Bolshevik revolution" which Goebbels, Hitler and Goering were looking for failed to "burst into flames." If it could not be provoked, might it not have to be invented?

On February 24, Goering's police raided the Karl Liebknecht Haus, the Communist headquarters in Berlin. It had been abandoned some weeks before by the Communist leaders, a number of whom had already gone underground or quietly slipped off to Russia. But piles of propaganda pamphlets had been left in the cellar and these were enough to enable Goering to announce in an official communiqué that the seized "documents" proved that the Communists were about to launch the revolution. The reaction of the public and even of some of the conservatives in the government was one of skepticism. It was obvious that something more sensational must be found to stampede the public before the election took place on March 5.

THE REICHSTAG FIRE

On the evening of February 27, four of the most powerful men in Germany were gathered at two separate dinners in Berlin. In the exclusive Herrenklub in the Vosstrasse, Vice-Chancellor von Papen was entertaining President von Hindenburg. Out at Goebbels' home, Chancellor Hitler had arrived to dine *en famille*. According to Goebbels, they were relaxing, playing music on the gramophone and telling stories. "Suddenly," he recounted later in his diary, "a telephone call from Dr. Hanfstaengl: 'The Reichstag is on fire!' I am sure he is telling a tall tale and decline even to mention it to the Fuehrer."[4]

But the diners at the Herrenklub were just around the corner from the Reichstag.

Suddenly [Papen later wrote] we noticed a red glow through the windows and heard sounds of shouting in the street. One of the servants came hurrying up to me and whispered: "The Reichstag is on fire!" which I repeated to the President. He got up and from the window we could see the dome of the Reichstag looking as though it were illuminated by searchlights. Every now and again a burst of flame and a swirl of smoke blurred the outline.[5]

The Vice-Chancellor packed the aged President home in his own car and hurried off to the burning building. In the meantime Goebbels, according to his account, had had second thoughts about Putzi Hanfstaengl's "tall tale," had made some telephone calls and learned that the Reichstag was in flames. Within a few seconds he and his Fuehrer were racing "at sixty miles an hour down the Charlottenburger Chaussee toward the scene of the crime."

That it was a crime, a Communist crime, they proclaimed at once on arrival at the fire. Goering, sweating and puffing and quite beside himself with excitement, was already there ahead of them declaiming to heaven, as Papen later recalled, that "this is a Communist crime against the new government." To the new Gestapo chief, Rudolf Diels, Goering shouted, "This is the beginning of the Communist revolution! We must not wait a minute. We will show no mercy. Every Communist official must be shot, where he is found. Every Communist deputy must this very night be strung up."[6]

The whole truth about the Reichstag fire will probably never be known. Nearly all those who knew it are now dead, most of them slain by Hitler in the months that followed. Even at Nuremberg the mystery could not be entirely unraveled, though there is enough evidence to establish beyond a reasonable doubt that it was the Nazis who planned the arson and carried it out for their own political ends.

From Goering's Reichstag President's Palace an underground passage, built to carry the central heating system, ran to the Reichstag building. Through this tunnel Karl Ernst, a former hotel bellhop who had become the Berlin S.A. leader, led a small detachment of storm troopers on the night of February 27 to the Reichstag, where they scattered gasoline and self-igniting chemicals and then made their way quickly back to the palace the way they had come. At the same time a half-witted Dutch Communist with a passion for arson, Marinus van der Lubbe, had made his way into the huge, darkened and to him unfamiliar building and set some small fires of his own. This feeble-minded pyromaniac was a godsend to the Nazis. He had been picked up by the S.A. a few days before after having been overheard in a bar boasting that he had attempted to set fire to several public buildings and that he was going to try the Reichstag next.

The coincidence that the Nazis had found a demented Communist arsonist who was out to do exactly what they themselves had determined to do seems incredible but is nevertheless supported by the evidence. The idea for the fire almost certainly originated with Goebbels and Goering. Hans Gisevius, an official in the Prussian Ministry of the Interior at the time, testified at Nuremberg that "it was Goebbels who first thought of setting the Reichstag on fire," and Rudolf Diels, the Gestapo chief, added in an affidavit that "Goering knew exactly how the fire was to be started" and had ordered him "to prepare, prior to the fire, a list of people who were to be arrested immediately after it." General Franz Halder, Chief of the German General Staff during the early part of World War II, recalled at Nuremberg how on one occasion Goering had boasted of his deed.

At a luncheon on the birthday of the Fuehrer in 1942 the conversation turned to the topic of the Reichstag building and its artistic value. I heard with my own ears when Goering interrupted the conversation and shouted: "The only one who really knows about the Reichstag is I, because I set it on fire!" With that he slapped his thigh with the flat of his hand.*

Van der Lubbe, it seems clear, was a dupe of the Nazis. He was encouraged to try to set the Reichstag on fire. But the main job was to be done—without his knowledge, of course—by the storm troopers. Indeed, it was established at the subsequent trial at Leipzig that the Dutch half-wit did not possess the means to set so vast a building on fire so quickly. Two and a half minutes after he entered, the great central hall was fiercely burning. He had only his shirt for tinder. The main fires, according to the testimony of experts at the trial, had been set with considerable quantities of chemicals and gasoline. It was obvious that one man could not have carried them into the building, nor would it have been possible for him to start so many fires in so many scattered places in so short a time.

Van der Lubbe was arrested on the spot and Goering, as he afterward told the court, wanted to hang him at once. The next day Ernst Torgler, parliamentary leader of the Communists, gave himself up to the police when he heard that Goering had implicated him, and a few days later Georgi Dimitroff, a Bulgarian Communist who later became Prime Minister of Bulgaria, and two other Bulgarian Communists, Popov and Tanev, were apprehended by the police. Their subsequent trial before the Supreme Court at Leipzig turned into something of a fiasco for the Nazis and especially for Goering, whom Dimitroff, acting as his own lawyer, easily provoked into making a fool of himself in a series of stinging cross-examinations. At one point, according to the court record, Goering screamed at the Bulgarian, "Out with you, you scoundrel!"

JUDGE [to the police officer]: Take him away.

DIMITROFF [being led away by the police]: Are you afraid of my questions, Herr Ministerpraesident?

GOERING: You wait until we get you outside this court, you scoundrel!

Torgler and the three Bulgarians were acquitted, though the German Communist leader was immediately taken into "protective custody,"

---

* Both in his interrogations and at his trial at Nuremberg, Goering denied to the last that he had had any part in setting fire to the Reichstag.

where he remained until his death during the second war. Van der Lubbe was found guilty and decapitated.[7]

The trial, despite the subserviency of the court to the Nazi authorities, cast a great deal of suspicion on Goering and the Nazis, but it came too late to have any practical effect. For Hitler had lost no time in exploiting the Reichstag fire to the limit.

On the day following the fire, February 28, he prevailed on President Hindenburg to sign a decree "for the Protection of the People and the State" suspending the seven sections of the constitution which guaranteed individual and civil liberties. Described as a "defensive measure against Communist acts of violence endangering the state," the decree laid down that:

Restrictions on personal liberty, on the right of free expression of opinion, including freedom of the press; on the rights of assembly and association; and violations of the privacy of postal, telegraphic and telephonic communications; and warrants for house searchers, orders for confiscations as well as restrictions on property, are also permissible beyond the legal limits otherwise prescribed.

In addition, the decree authorized the Reich government to take over complete power in the federal states when necessary and imposed the death sentence for a number of crimes, including "serious disturbances of the peace" by armed persons.[8]

Thus with one stroke Hitler was able not only to legally gag his opponents and arrest them at his will but, by making the trumped-up Communist threat "official," as it were, to throw millions of the middle class and the peasantry into a frenzy of fear that unless they voted for National Socialism at the elections a week hence, the Bolsheviks might take over. Some four thousand Communist officials and a great many Social Democrat and liberal leaders were arrested, including members of the Reichstag, who, according to the law, were immune from arrest. This was the first experience Germans had had with Nazi terror backed up by the government. Truckloads of storm troopers roared through the streets all over Germany, breaking into homes, rounding up victims and carting them off to S.A. barracks, where they were tortured and beaten. The Communist press and political meetings were suppressed; the Social Democrat newspapers and many liberal journals were suspended and the meetings of the democratic parties either banned or broken up. Only the Nazis and their Nationalist allies were permitted to campaign unmolested.

With all the resources of the national and Prussian governments at their disposal and with plenty of money from big business in their coffers, the Nazis carried on an election propaganda such as Germany had never seen before. For the first time the State-run radio carried the voices of Hitler, Goering and Goebbels to every corner of the land. The streets, bedecked with swastika flags, echoed to the tramp of the storm troopers. There were mass rallies, torchlight parades, the din of loudspeakers in the squares. The billboards were plastered with flamboyant Nazi posters and at night bonfires lit up the hills. The electorate was in turn cajoled with promises of a German paradise, intimidated by the brown terror in the streets and frightened by "revelations" about the Communist "revolution." The day after the Reichstag fire the Prussian government issued a long statement declaring that it had found Communist "documents" proving:

Government buildings, museums, mansions and essential plants were to be burned down . . . Women and children were to be sent in front of terrorist groups . . . The burning of the Reichstag was to be the signal for a bloody insurrection and civil war . . . It has been ascertained that today was to have seen throughout Germany terrorist acts against individual persons, against private property, and against the life and limb of the peaceful population, and also the beginning of general civil war.

Publication of the "documents proving the Communist conspiracy" was promised, but never made. The fact, however, that the Prussian government itself vouched for their authenticity impressed many Germans.

The waverers were also impressed perhaps by Goering's threats. At Frankfurt on March 3, on the eve of the elections, he shouted:

Fellow Germans, my measures will not be crippled by any judicial thinking . . . I don't have to worry about justice; my mission is only to destroy and exterminate, nothing more! . . . Certainly, I shall use the power of the State and the police to the utmost, my dear Communists, so don't draw any false conclusions; but the struggle to the death, in which my fist will grasp your necks, I shall lead with those down there—the Brownshirts.[9]

Almost unheard was the voice of former Chancellor Bruening, who also spoke out that day, proclaiming that his Center Party would resist any overthrow of the constitution, demanding an investigation of the suspicious Reichstag fire and calling on President Hindenburg "to protect the oppressed against their oppressors." Vain appeal! The aged President kept his silence. It was now time for the people, in their convulsion, to speak.

On March 5, 1933, the day of the last democratic elections they were to know during Hitler's life, they spoke with their ballots. Despite all the terror and intimidation, the majority of them rejected Hitler. The Nazis led the polling with 17,277,180 votes—an increase of some five and a half million, but it comprised only 44 per cent of the total vote. A clear majority still eluded Hitler. All the persecution and suppression of the previous weeks did not prevent the Center Party from actually increasing its vote from 4,230,600 to 4,424,900; with its ally, the Catholic Bavarian People's Party, it obtained a total of five and a half million votes. Even the Social Democrats held their position as the second largest party, polling 7,181,629 votes, a drop of only 70,000. The Communists lost a million supporters but still polled 4,848,058 votes. The Nationalists, led by Papen and Hugenberg, were bitterly disappointed with their own showing, a vote of 3,136,760, a mere 8 per cent of the votes cast and a gain of less than 200,000.

Still, the Nationalists' 52 seats, added to the 288 of the Nazis, gave the government a majority of 16 in the Reichstag. This was enough, perhaps, to carry on the day-to-day business of government but it was far short of the two-thirds majority which Hitler needed to carry out a new, bold plan to establish his dictatorship by consent of Parliament.

GLEICHSCHALTUNG: THE "CO-ORDINATION"
OF THE REICH

The plan was deceptively simple and had the advantage of cloaking the seizure of absolute power in legality. The Reichstag would be asked to pass an "enabling act" conferring on Hitler's cabinet exclusive legislative powers for four years. Put even more simply, the German Parliament would be requested to turn over its constitutional functions to Hitler and take a long vacation. But since this necessitated a change in the constitution, a two-thirds majority was needed to approve it.

How to obtain that majority was the main order of business at a cabinet meeting on March 15, 1933, the minutes of which were produced at Nuremberg.[10] Part of the problem would be solved by the "absence" of the eighty-one Communist members of the Reichstag. Goering felt sure that the rest of the problem could be easily disposed of "by refusing admittance to a few Social Democrats." Hitler was in a breezy, confident mood. After all, by the decree of February 28, which he had induced Hindenburg to sign the day after the Reichstag fire, he could arrest as many opposition deputies as was necessary to assure his two-thirds majority. There was some question about the Catholic Center, which was demanding guarantees, but the Chancellor was certain that this party would go along with him. Hugenberg, the Nationalist leader, who had no desire to put all the power in Hitler's hands, demanded that the President be authorized to participate in preparing laws decreed by the cabinet under the enabling act. Dr. Meissner, the State Secretary in the Presidential Chancellery, who had already committed his future to the Nazis, replied that "the collaboration of the Reich President would not be necessary." He was quick to realize that Hitler had no wish to be tied down by the stubborn old President, as the republican chancellors had been.

But Hitler wished, at this stage, to make a grandiose gesture to the aged Field Marshal and to the Army and the nationalist conservatives as well, and in so doing link his rowdy, revolutionary regime with Hindenburg's venerable name and with all the past military glories of Prussia. To accomplish this he and Goebbels, who on March 13 became Minister of Propaganda, conceived a master stroke. Hitler would open the new Reichstag, which he was about to destroy, in the Garrison Church at Potsdam, the great shrine of Prussianism, which aroused in so many Germans memories of imperial glories and grandeur, for here lay buried the bones of Frederick the Great, here the Hohenzollern kings had worshiped, here Hindenburg had first come in 1866 on a pilgrimage when he returned as a young Guards officer from the Austro–Prussian War, a war which had given Germany its first unification.

The date chosen for the ceremonial opening of the first Reichstag of the Third Reich, March 21, was significant too, for it fell on the anniversary of the day on which Bismarck had opened the first Reichstag of the Second Reich in 1871. As the old field marshals, generals and admirals from imperial times gathered in their resplendent uniforms in the Garrison Church, led by the former Crown Prince and Field Marshal von Mackensen in the imposing dress and headgear of the Death's-Head Hussars, the shades of Frederick the Great and the Iron Chancellor hovered over the assembly.

Hindenburg was visibly moved, and at one point in the ceremony Goebbels, who was staging the performance and directing the broadcasting of it to the nation, observed—and noted in his diary—that the old Field Marshal had tears in his eyes. Flanked by Hitler, who appeared ill at ease in his formal cutaway morning coat, the President, attired in field-gray uniform with the grand cordon of the Black Eagle, and carrying a spiked helmet in one hand and his marshal's baton in the other, had marched slowly down the aisle, paused to salute the empty seat of Kaiser Wilhelm II in the imperial gallery, and then in front of the altar had read a brief speech giving his blessings to the new Hitler government.

May the old spirit of this celebrated shrine permeate the generation of today, may it liberate us from selfishness and party strife and bring us together in national self-consciousness to bless a proud and free Germany, united in herself.

Hitler's reply was shrewdly designed to play on the sympathies and enlist the confidence of the Old Order so glitteringly represented.

Neither the Kaiser nor the government nor the nation wanted the war. It was only the collapse of the nation which compelled a weakened race to take upon itself, against its most sacred convictions, the guilt for this war.

And then, turning to Hindenburg, who sat stiffly in his chair a few feet in front of him:

By a unique unheaval in the last few weeks our national honor has been restored and, thanks to your understanding, Herr Generalfeldmarschall, the union between the symbols of the old greatness and the new strength has been celebrated. We pay you homage. A protective Providence places you over the new forces of our nation.[11]

Hitler, with a show of deep humility toward the President he intended to rob of his political power before the week was up, stepped down, bowed low to Hindenburg and gripped his hand. There in the flashing lights of camera bulbs and amid the clicking of movie cameras, which Goebbels had placed along with microphones at strategic spots, was recorded for the nation and the world to see, and to hear described, the solemn hand-clasp of the German Field Marshal and the Austrian corporal uniting the new Germany with the old.

"After the dazzling pledge made by Hitler at Potsdam," the French ambassador, who was present at the scene, later wrote, "how could such men—Hindenburg and his friends, the Junkers and monarchist barons, Hugenberg and his German Nationalists, the officers of the Reichswehr— how could they fail to dismiss the apprehension with which they had begun to view the excesses and abuses of his party? Could they now hesitate to grant him their entire confidence, to meet all his requests, to concede the full powers he claimed?"[12]

The answer was given two days later, on March 23, in the Kroll Opera House in Berlin, where the Reichstag convened. Before the house was the so-called Enabling Act—the "Law for Removing the Distress of People and Reich (*Gesetz zur Behebung der Not von Volk und Reich*)," as it was officially called. Its five brief paragraphs took the power of legislation, including control of the Reich budget, approval of treaties with foreign states and the initiating of constitutional amendments, away from Parliament and handed it over to the Reich cabinet for a period of four years. Moreover, the act stipulated that the laws enacted by the cabinet were to be drafted by the Chancellor and "might deviate from the constitution." No laws were to "affect the position of the Reichstag"—surely the cruelest joke of all—and the powers of the President remained "undisturbed."[13]

Hitler reiterated these last two points in a speech of unexpected restraint to the deputies assembled in the ornate opera house, which had long specialized in the lighter operatic works and whose aisles were now lined with brown-shirted storm troopers, whose scarred bully faces indicated that no nonsense would be tolerated from the representatives of the people.

The government [Hitler promised] will make use of these powers only inso-far as they are essential for carrying out vitally necessary measures. Neither the existence of the Reichstag nor that of the Reichsrat is menaced. The posi-tion and rights of the President remain unaltered . . . The separate existence of the federal states will not be done away with. The rights of the churches will not be diminished and their relationship to the State will not be modified. The number of cases in which an internal necessity exists for having recourse to such a law is in itself a limited one.

The fiery Nazi leader sounded quite moderate and almost modest; it was too early in the life of the Third Reich for even the opposition members to know full well the value of Hitler's promises. Yet one of them, Otto Wells, leader of the Social Democrats, a dozen of whose deputies had been "detained" by the police, rose—amid the roar of the storm troopers outside yelling, "Full powers, or else!"—to defy the would-be dictator. Speaking quietly and with great dignity, Wells declared that the government might strip the Socialists of their power but it could never strip them of their honor.

> We German Social Democrats pledge ourselves solemnly in this historic hour to the principles of humanity and justice, of freedom and socialism. No enabling act can give you the power to destroy ideas which are eternal and indestructible.

Furious, Hitler jumped to his feet, and now the assembly received a real taste of the man.

> You come late, but yet you come! [he shouted] . . . You are no longer needed . . . The star of Germany will rise and yours will sink. Your death knell has sounded. . . . I do not want your votes. Germany will be free, but not through you! [Stormy applause.]

The Social Democrats, who bore a heavy responsibility for the weakening of the Republic, would at least stick to their principles and go down—this one time—defiantly. But not the Center Party, which once had successfully defied the Iron Chancellor in the Kulturkampf. Monsignor Kaas, the party leader, had demanded a written promise from Hitler that he would respect the President's power of veto. But though promised before the voting, it was never given. Nevertheless the Center leader rose to announce that his party would vote for the bill. Bruening remained silent. The vote was soon taken: 441 for, and 84 (all Social Democrats) against. The Nazi deputies sprang to their feet shouting and stamping deliriously and then, joined by the storm troopers, burst into the Horst Wessel song, which soon would take its place alongside "Deutschland ueber Alles" as one of the two national anthems:

> Raise high the flags! Stand rank on rank together.
> Storm troopers march with steady, quiet tread. . . .

Thus was parliamentary democracy finally interred in Germany. Except for the arrests of the Communists and some of the Social Democratic deputies, it was all done quite legally, though accompanied by terror. Parliament had turned over its constitutional authority to Hitler and thereby committed suicide, though its body lingered on in an embalmed state to the very end of the Third Reich, serving infrequently as a sounding board for some of Hitler's thunderous pronunciamentos, its members henceforth hand-picked by the Nazi Party, for there were to be no more real elections. It was this Enabling Act alone which formed the legal basis for Hitler's dictatorship. From March 23, 1933, on, Hitler was the dictator of the Reich, freed of any restraint by Parliament or, for all practical purposes, by the weary old President. To be sure, much remained to be done to bring the entire nation and all its institutions completely under the Nazi heel, though, as we shall see, this also was accomplished with breathless speed and with crudeness, trickery and brutality.

"The street gangs," in the words of Alan Bullock, "had seized control of the resources of a great modern State, the gutter had come to power." But—as Hitler never ceased to boast—"legally," by an overwhelming vote of Parliament. The Germans had no one to blame but themselves.

One by one, Germany's most powerful institutions now began to surrender to Hitler and to pass quietly, unprotestingly out of existence.

The states, which had stubbornly maintained their separate powers throughout German history, were the first to fall. On the evening of March 9, two weeks before the passage of the Enabling Act, General von Epp, on orders from Hitler and Frick and with the help of a few storm troopers, turned out the government of Bavaria and set up a Nazi regime. Within a week Reich Commissars were appointed to take over in the other states, with the exception of Prussia, where Goering was already firmly in the saddle. On March 31, Hitler and Frick, using the Enabling Act for the first time, promulgated a law dissolving the diets of all states except Prussia and ordering them reconstituted on the basis of the votes cast in the last Reichstag election. Communist seats were not to be filled. But this solution lasted only a week. The Chancellor, working at feverish haste, issued a new law on April 7, appointing Reich Governors (*Reichsstaathaelter*) in all the states and empowering them to appoint and remove local governments, dissolve the diets, and appoint and dismiss state officials and judges. Each of the new governors was a Nazi and they were "required" to carry out "the general policy laid down by the Reich Chancellor."

Thus, within a fortnight of receiving full powers from the Reichstag, Hitler had achieved what Bismarck, Wilhelm II and the Weimar Republic had never dared to attempt: he had abolished the separate powers of the historic states and made them subject to the central authority of the Reich, which was in his hands. He had, for the first time in German history, really unified the Reich by destroying its age-old federal character. On January 30, 1934, the first anniversary of his becoming Chancellor, Hitler would formally complete the task by means of a Law for the Reconstruction of the Reich. "Popular assemblies" of the states were abolished, the sovereign powers of the states were transferred to the Reich, all state governments were placed under the Reich government and the state governors put under the administration of the Reich Minister of the Interior.[14] As this Minister, Frick, explained it, "The state governments from now on are merely administrative bodies of the Reich."

The preamble to the law of January 30, 1934, proclaimed that it was "promulgated with the unanimous vote of the Reichstag." This was true, for by this time all the political parties of Germany except the Nazis had been quickly eliminated.

It cannot be said that they went down fighting. On May 19, 1933, the Social Democrats—those who were not in jail or in exile—voted in the Reichstag without a dissenting voice to approve Hitler's foreign policy. Nine days before, Goering's police had seized the party's buildings and newspapers and confiscated its property. Nevertheless, the Socialists still tried to appease Hitler. They denounced their comrades abroad who were attacking the Fuehrer. On June 19 they elected a new party committee, but three days later Frick put an end to their attempts to compromise by dissolving the Social Democratic Party as "subversive and inimical to the State." Paul Lobe, the surviving leader, and several of his party members in the Reichstag were arrested. The Communists, of course, had already been suppressed.

This left the middle-class parties, but not for long. The Catholic Bavarian People's Party, whose government had been kicked out of office by the Nazi coup on March 9, announced its own dissolution on July 4, and its ally, the Center Party, which had defied Bismarck so strenuously and been a bulwark of the Republic, followed suit the next day, leaving Germany for the first time in the modern era without a Catholic political party—a fact which did not discourage the Vatican from signing a concordat with Hitler's government a fortnight later. Stresemann's old party, the People's Party, committed hara-kiri on the Fourth of July; the Democrats (*Staatspartei*) had already done so a week before.

And what of Hitler's partner in government, the German National Party, without whose support the former Austrian corporal could never have come legally to power? Despite its closeness to Hindenburg, the Army, the Junkers and big business and the debt owed to it by Hitler, it went the way of all other parties and with the same meekness. On June 21 the police and the storm troopers took over its offices throughout the country, and on June 29 Hugenberg, the bristling party leader, who had helped boost Hitler into the Chancellery but six months before, resigned from the government and his aides "voluntarily" dissolved the party.

The Nazi Party alone remained, and on July 14 a law decreed:

The National Socialist German Workers' Party constitutes the only political party in Germany.

Whoever undertakes to maintain the organizational structure of another political party or to form a new political party will be punished with penal servitude up to three years or with imprisonment of from six months to three years, if the deed is not subject to a greater penalty according to other regulations.[15]

The one-party totalitarian State had been achieved with scarcely a ripple of opposition or defiance, and within four months after the Reichstag had abdicated its democratic responsibilities.

The free trade unions, which, as we have seen, once had crushed the fascist Kapp putsch by the simple means of declaring a general strike, were disposed of as easily as the political parties and the states—though not until an elaborate piece of trickery had been practiced on them. For half a century May Day had been the traditional day of celebration for the German—and European—worker. To lull the workers and their leaders before it struck, the Nazi government proclaimed May Day, 1933, as a national holiday, officially named it the "Day of National Labor" and prepared to celebrate it as it had never been celebrated before. The trade-union leaders were taken in by this surprising display of friendliness toward the working class by the Nazis and enthusiastically co-operated with the government and the party in making the day a success. Labor leaders were flown to Berlin from all parts of Germany, thousands of banners were unfurled acclaiming the Nazi regime's solidarity with the worker, and out at Tempelhof Field Goebbels prepared to stage the greatest mass demonstration Germany had ever seen. Before the massive rally, Hitler himself received the workers' delegates, declaring, "You will see how untrue and unjust is the statement that the revolution is directed against the German workers. On the contrary." Later in his speech to more than 100,000 workers at the airfield Hitler pronounced the motto, "Honor work and respect the worker!" and promised that May Day would be celebrated in honor of German labor "throughout the centuries."

Late that night Goebbels, after describing in his most purple prose the tremendous enthusiasm of the workers for this May Day celebration which he had so brilliantly staged, added a curious sentence in his diary: "Tomorrow we shall occupy the trade-union buildings. There will be little resistance."*[16]

That is what happened. On May 2 the trade-union headquarters throughout the country were occupied, union funds confiscated, the unions dissolved and the leaders arrested. Many were beaten and lodged in concentration camps. Theodor Leipart and Peter Grassmann, the chairmen of the Trade Union Confederation, had openly pledged themselves to co-operate with the Nazi regime. No matter, they were arrested. "The Leiparts and Grassmanns," said Dr. Robert Ley, the alcoholic Cologne party boss who was assigned by Hitler to take over the unions and establish the German Labor Front, "may hypocritically declare their devotion to the Fuehrer as much as they like—but it is better that they should be in prison." And that is where they were put.

At first, though, both Hitler and Ley tried to assure the workers that their rights would be protected. Said Ley in his first proclamation: "Workers! Your institutions are sacred to us National Socialists. I my-

---

* A document which came to light at Nuremberg shows that the Nazis had been planning for some time to destroy the trade unions. A secret order dated April 21 and signed by Dr. Ley contained detailed instructions for "co-ordinating" the unions on May 2. S.A. and S.S. troops were to carry out the "occupation of trade-union properties" and to "take into protective custody" all union leaders. Union funds were to be seized.[17] The Christian (Catholic) Trade Unions were not molested on May 2. Their end came on June 24.

self am a poor peasant's son and understand poverty . . . I know the exploitation of anonymous capitalism. Workers! I swear to you, we will not only keep everything that exists, we will build up the protection and the rights of the workers still further."

Within three weeks the hollowness of another Nazi promise was exposed when Hitler decreed a law bringing an end to collective bargaining and providing that henceforth "labor trustees," appointed by him, would "regulate labor contracts" and maintain "labor peace."[18] Since the decisions of the trustees were to be legally binding, the law, in effect, outlawed strikes. Ley promised "to restore absolute leadership to the natural leader of a factory—that is, the employer . . . Only the employer can decide. Many employers have for years had to call for the 'master in the house.' Now they are once again to be the 'master in the house.' "

For the time being, business management was pleased. The generous contributions which so many employers had made to the National Socialist German Workers' Party were paying off. Yet for business to prosper a certain stability of society is necessary, and all through the spring and early summer law and order were crumbling in Germany as the frenzied brown-shirted gangs roamed the streets, arresting and beating up and sometimes murdering whomever they pleased while the police looked on without lifting a nightstick. The terror in the streets was not the result of the breakdown of the State's authority, as it had been in the French Revolution, but on the contrary was carried out with the encouragement and often on the orders of the State, whose authority in Germany had never been greater or more concentrated. Judges were intimidated; they were afraid for their lives if they convicted and sentenced a storm trooper even for cold-blooded murder. Hitler was now the law, as Goering said, and as late as May and June 1933 the Fuehrer was declaiming that "the National Socialist Revolution has not yet run its course" and that "it will be victoriously completed only if a new German people is educated." In Nazi parlance, "educated" meant "intimidated"—to a point where all would accept docilely the Nazi dictatorship and its barbarism. To Hitler, as he had publicly declared a thousand times, the Jews were not Germans, and though he did not exterminate them at once (only a relative few—a few thousand, that is—were robbed, beaten or murdered during the first months), he issued laws excluding them from public service, the universities and the professions. And on April 1, 1933, he proclaimed a national boycott of Jewish shops.

The businessmen, who had been so enthusiastic over the smashing of the troublesome labor unions, now found that left-wing Nazis, who really believed in the party's socialism, were trying to take over the employers' associations, destroy the big department stores and nationalize industry. Thousands of ragged Nazi Party officials descended on the business houses of those who had not supported Hitler, threatening to seize them in some cases, and in others demanding well-paying jobs in the management. Dr. Gottfried Feder, the economic crank, now insisted that the party program be carried out—nationalization of big business, profit sharing and the abolition of unearned incomes and "interest slavery." As if this were not enough to frighten the businessmen, Walther Darré, who had just been named Minister of Agriculture, threw the bankers into jitters by promising a big reduction in the capital debts of the farmers and a cut in the interest rate on what remained to 2 per cent.

Why not? Hitler was, by midsummer of 1933, the master of Germany. He could now carry out his program. Papen, for all his cunning, had been left high and dry, and all his calculations that he and Hugenberg and the other defenders of the Old Order, with their 8-to-3 majority in the cabinet against the Nazis, could control Hitler and indeed use him for their own conservative ends, had exploded in his face. He himself had been booted out of his post as Prime Minister of Prussia and replaced by Goering. Papen remained Vice-Chancellor in the Reich cabinet but, as he ruefully admitted later, "this position turned out to be anomalous." Hugenberg, the apostle of business and finance, was gone, his party dissolved. Goebbels, the third most important man in the Nazi Party, had been brought into the cabinet on March 13 as Minister of Popular Enlightenment and Propaganda. Darré, regarded as a "radical," as was Goebbels, was Minister of Agriculture.

Dr. Hans Luther, the conservative president of the Reichsbank, the key post in the German economic system, was fired by Hitler and packed off to Washington as ambassador. Into his place, on March 17, 1933, stepped the jaunty Dr. Schacht, the former head of the Reichsbank and devoted follower of Hitler, who had seen the "truth and necessity" of Nazism. No single man in all of Germany would be more helpful to Hitler in building up the economic strength of the Third Reich and in furthering its rearmament for the Second World War than Schacht, who later became also Minister of Economics and Plenipotentiary-General for War Economy. It is true that shortly before the second war began he turned against his idol, eventually relinquished or was fired from all his offices and even joined those who were conspiring to assassinate Hitler. But by then it was too late to stay the course of the Nazi leader to whom he had for so long given his loyalty and lent his prestige and his manifest talents.

"NO SECOND REVOLUTION!"

Hitler had conquered Germany with the greatest of ease, but a number of problems remained to be faced as summer came in 1933. There were at least five major ones: preventing a second revolution; settling the uneasy relations between the S.A. and the Army; getting the country out of its economic morass and finding jobs for the six million unemployed; achieving equality of armaments for Germany at the Disarmament Conference in Geneva and accelerating the Reich's secret rearming, which had begun during the last years of the Republic; and deciding who should succeed the ailing Hindenburg when he died.

It was Roehm, chief of the S.A., who coined the phrase "the second revolution," and who insisted that it be carried through. He was joined by Goebbels, who in his diary of April 18, 1933, wrote: "Everyone among the people is talking of a second revolution which must come. That means that the first revolution is not at an end. Now we shall settle with the *Reaktion*. The revolution must nowhere come to a halt."[19]

The Nazis had destroyed the Left, but the Right remained: big business and finance, the aristocracy, the Junker landlords and the Prussian generals, who kept tight rein over the Army. Roehm, Goebbels and the other "radicals" in the movement wanted to liquidate them too. Roehm, whose storm troopers now numbered some two million—twenty times as many as the troops in the Army—sounded the warning in June:

One victory on the road of German revolution has been won . . . The S.A. and S.S., who bear the great responsibility of having set the German revolution rolling, will not allow it to be betrayed at the halfway mark . . . If the Philistines believe that the national revolution has lasted too long . . . it is indeed high time that the national revolution should end and become a National Socialist one . . . We shall continue our fight—with them or without them. And, if necessary, against them . . . We are the incorruptible guarantors of the fulfillment of the German revolution.[20]

And in August he added, in a speech, "There are still men in official positions today who have not the least idea of the spirit of the revolution. We shall ruthlessly get rid of them if they dare to put their reactionary ideas into practice."

But Hitler had contrary thoughts. For him the Nazi socialist slogans had been merely propaganda, means of winning over the masses on his way to power. Now that he had the power he was uninterested in them. He needed time to consolidate his position and that of the country. For the moment at least the Right—business, the Army, the President—must be appeased. He did not intend to bankrupt Germany and thus risk the very existence of his regime. There must be no second revolution.

This he made plain to the S.A. and S.S. leaders themselves in a speech to them on July 1. What was needed now in Germany, he said, was order. "I will suppress every attempt to disturb the existing order as ruthlessly as I will deal with the so-called second revolution, which would lead only to chaos." He repeated the warning to the Nazi state governors gathered in the Chancellery on July 6:

The revolution is not a permanent state of affairs, and it must not be allowed to develop into such a state. The stream of revolution released must be guided into the safe channel of evolution . . . We must therefore not dismiss a businessman if he is a good businessman, even if he is not yet a National Socialist, and especially not if the National Socialist who is to take his place knows nothing about business. In business, ability must be the only standard . . .

History will not judge us according to whether we have removed and imprisoned the largest number of economists, but according to whether we have succeeded in providing work . . . The ideas of the program do not oblige us to act like fools and upset everything, but to realize our trains of thought wisely and carefully. In the long run our political power will be all the more secure, the more we succeed in underpinning it economically. The state governors must therefore see to it that no party organizations assume the functions of government, dismiss individuals and make appointments to offices, to do which the Reich government—and in regard to business, the Reich Minister of Economics—is competent.[21]

No more authoritative statement was ever made that the Nazi revolution was political, not economic. To back up his words, Hitler dismissed a number of Nazi "radicals" who had tried to seize control of the employers' associations. He restored Krupp von Bohlen and Fritz Thyssen to their positions of leadership in them, dissolved the Combat League of Middle-Class Tradespeople, which had annoyed the big department stores, and in place of Hugenberg named Dr. Karl Schmitt as Minister of Economics. Schmitt was the most orthodox of businessmen, director general of Allianz, Germany's largest insurance company, and he lost no time in putting an end to the schemes of the National Socialists who had been naïve enough to take their party program seriously.

The disillusion among the rank-and-file Nazis, especially among the S.A. storm troopers, who formed the large core of Hitler's mass movement, was great. Most of them had belonged to the ragged army of the dispossessed and the unsatisfied. They were anticapitalist through experience and they believed that the revolution which they had fought by brawling in the streets would bring them loot and good jobs, either in business or in the government. Now their hopes, after the heady excesses of the spring, were dashed. The old gang, whether they were party members or not, were to keep the jobs and to keep control of jobs. But this development was not the only reason for unrest in the S.A.

The old quarrel between Hitler and Roehm about the position and purpose of the S.A. cropped up again. From the earliest days of the Nazi movement Hitler had insisted that the storm troopers were to be a political and not a military force; they were to furnish the physical violence, the terror, by which the party could bludgeon its way to political power. To Roehm, the S.A. had been not only the backbone of the Nazi revolution but the nucleus of the future revolutionary army which would be for Hitler what the French conscript armies were to Napoleon after the French Revolution. It was time to sweep away the reactionary Prussian generals— those "old clods," as he contemptuously called them—and form a revolutionary fighting force, a people's army, led by himself and his tough aides who had conquered the streets of Germany.

Nothing could be further from Hitler's thoughts. He realized more clearly than Roehm or any other Nazi that he could not have come to power without the support or at least the toleration of the Army generals and that, for the time being at least, his very survival at the helm depended in part on their continued backing, since they still retained the physical power to remove him if they were so minded. Also Hitler foresaw that the Army's loyalty to him personally would be needed at that crucial moment, which could not be far off, when the eighty-six-year-old Hindenburg, the Commander in Chief, would pass on. Furthermore, the Nazi leader was certain that only the officer corps, with all its martial traditions and abilities, could achieve his goal of building up in a short space of time a strong, disciplined armed force. The S.A. was but a mob—good enough for street fighting but of little worth as a modern army. Moreover, its purpose had now been served and from now on it must be eased tactfully out of the picture. The views of Hitler and Roehm were irreconcilable, and from the summer of 1933 to June 30 of the following year a struggle literally to the death was to be fought between these two veterans of the Nazi movement who were also close friends (Ernst Roehm was the only man whom Hitler addressed by the familiar personal pronoun *du*).

Roehm expressed the deep sense of frustration in the ranks of the storm troopers in a speech to fifteen thousand S.A. officers in the Sportpalast in Berlin on November 5, 1933. "One often hears . . . that the S.A. had lost any reason for existence," he said, warning that it had not. But Hitler was adamant. "The relation of the S.A. to the Army," he had warned at Bad Godesberg on August 19, "must be the same as that of the political leadership." And on September 23 at Nuremberg he spoke out even more clearly:

On this day we should particularly remember the part played by our Army, for we all know well that if, in the days of our revolution, the Army had not stood on our side, then we should not be standing here today. We can assure the Army that we shall never forget this, that we see in them the bearers of the tradition of our glorious old Army, and that with all our heart and all our powers we will support the spirit of this Army.

Some time before this, Hitler had secretly given the armed forces assurances which had brought many of the higher officers to his side. On February 2, 1933, three days after assuming office, he had made a two-hour address to the top generals and admirals at the home of General von Hammerstein, the Army Commander in Chief. Admiral Erich Raeder revealed at Nuremberg the tenor of this first meeting of the Nazi Chancellor with the officer corps.[22] Hitler, he said, freed the military elite from its fears that the armed services might be called upon to take part in a civil war and promised that the Army and Navy could now devote themselves unhindered to the main task of quickly rearming the new Germany. Admiral Raeder admitted that he was highly pleased at the prospect of a new Navy, and General von Blomberg, whose hasty assumption of the office of Minister of Defense on January 30, 1933, had stamped out any temptation on the part of the Army to revolt against Hitler's becoming Chancellor, declared later in his unpublished memoirs that the Fuehrer opened up "a field of activities holding great possibilities for the future."

Further to augment the enthusiasm of the military leaders Hitler created, as early as April 4, the Reich Defense Council to spur a new and secret rearmament program. Three months later, on July 20, the Chancellor promulgated a new Army Law, abolishing the jurisdiction of the civil courts over the military and doing away with the elected representation of the rank and file, thus restoring to the officer corps its ancient military prerogatives. A good many generals and admirals began to see the Nazi revolution in a different and more favorable light.

As a sop to Roehm, Hitler named him—along with Rudolf Hess, the deputy leader of the party—a member of the cabinet on December 1 and on New Year's Day, 1934, addressed to the S.A. chief a warm and friendly letter. While reiterating that "the Army has to guarantee the protection of the nation against the world beyond our frontiers," he acknowledged that "the task of the S.A. is to secure the victory of the National Socialist Revolution and the existence of the National Socialist State" and that the success of the S.A. had been "primarily due" to Roehm. The letter concluded:

At the close of the year of the National Socialist Revolution, therefore, I feel compelled to thank you, my dear Ernst Roehm, for the imperishable services which you have rendered to the National Socialist movement and the German people, and to assure you how very grateful I am to fate that I am able to call such men as you my friends and fellow combatants.

In true friendship and grateful regard,
Your ADOLF HITLER[23]

The letter, employing the familiar *du,* was published in the chief Nazi daily paper, the *Voelkischer Beobachter,* on January 2, 1934, and did much to ease for the moment the feelings of resentment in the S.A. In the atmosphere of good feeling that prevailed over the Christmas and New Year holidays, the rivalry between the S.A. and the Army and the clamor of the radical Nazis for the "second revolution" was temporarily stilled.

THE BEGINNINGS OF NAZI FOREIGN POLICY

"It is no victory, for the enemies were lacking," observed Oswald Spengler in commenting on how easily Hitler had conquered and Nazified Germany in 1933. "This seizure of power—" the author of *The Decline of the West* wrote early in the year, "it is with misgiving that I see it celebrated each day with so much noise. It would be better to save that for a day of real and definitive successes, that is, in the foreign field. There are no others."[24]

The philosopher-historian, who for a brief moment was an idol of the Nazis until a mutual disenchantment set in, was unduly impatient. Hitler had to conquer Germany before he could set out to conquer the world. But once his German opponents were liquidated—or had liquidated themselves—he lost no time in turning to what had always interested him the most: foreign affairs.

Germany's position in the world in the spring of 1933 could hardly have been worse. The Third Reich was diplomatically isolated and militarily impotent. The whole world had been revolted by Nazi excesses, especially the persecution of the Jews. Germany's neighbors, in particular France and Poland, were hostile and suspicious, and as early as March 1933, following a Polish military demonstration in Danzig, Marshal Pilsudski suggested to the French the desirability of a joint preventive war against Germany. Even Mussolini, for all his outward pose of welcoming the advent of a second fascist power, had not in fact been enthusiastic about Hitler's coming to power. The Fuehrer of a country potentially so much stronger than Italy might soon put the Duce in the shade. A rabidly Pan-German Reich would have designs on Austria and the Balkans, where the Italian dictator had already staked out his claims. The hostility toward Nazi Germany of the Soviet Union, which had been republican Germany's one friend in the years since 1921, was obvious. The Third Reich was indeed friendless in a hostile world. And it was disarmed, or relatively so in comparison with its highly armed neighbors.

The immediate strategy and tactics of Hitler's foreign policy therefore were dictated by the hard realities of Germany's weak and isolated position. But, ironically, this situation also provided natural goals which corresponded to his own deepest desires and those of the vast majority of the German people: to get rid of the shackles of Versailles without provoking sanctions, to rearm without risking war. Only when he had achieved these dual short-term goals would he have the freedom and the military power to pursue the long-term diplomacy whose aims and methods he had set down so frankly and in such detail in *Mein Kampf*.

The first thing to do, obviously, was to confound Germany's adversaries in Europe by preaching disarmament and peace and to keep a sharp eye for a weakness in their collective armor. On May 17, 1933, before the Reichstag, Hitler delivered his "Peace Speech," one of the greatest of his career, a masterpiece of deceptive propaganda that deeply moved the German people and unified them behind him and which made a profound and favorable impression on the outside world. The day before, President Roosevelt had sent a ringing message to the chiefs of state of forty-four nations outlining the plans and hopes of the United States for disarmament and peace and calling for the abolition of all offensive weapons—bombers, tanks and mobile heavy artillery. Hitler was quick to take up the President's challenge and to make the most of it.

The proposal made by President Roosevelt, of which I learned last night, has earned the warmest thanks of the German government. It is prepared to agree to this method of overcoming the international crisis . . . The President's proposal is a ray of comfort for all who wish to co-operate in the maintenance of peace . . . Germany is entirely ready to renounce all offensive weapons if the armed nations, on their side, will destroy their offensive weapons . . . Germany would also be perfectly ready to disband her entire military establishment and destroy the small amount of arms remaining to her, if the neighboring countries will do the same . . . Germany is prepared to agree to any solemn pact of nonaggression, because she does not think of attacking but only of acquiring security.

There was much else in the speech, whose moderateness and profession of love for peace pleasantly surprised an uneasy world. Germany did not want war. War was "unlimited madness." It would "cause the collapse of the present social and political order." Nazi Germany had no wish to "Germanize" other peoples. "The mentality of the last century, which led people to think that they would make Germans out of Poles and Frenchmen, is alien to us . . . Frenchmen, Poles and others are our neighbors, and we know that no event that is historically conceivable can change this reality."

There was one warning. Germany demanded equality of treatment with all other nations, especially in armaments. If this was not to be obtained, Germany would prefer to withdraw from both the Disarmament Conference and the League of Nations.

The warning was forgotten amid the general rejoicing throughout the Western world at Hitler's unexpected reasonableness. The *Times* of London agreed that Hitler's claim for equality was "irrefutable." The *Daily Herald* of London, official organ of the Labor Party, demanded that Hitler be taken at his word. The conservative weekly *Spectator* of London concluded that Hitler had grasped the hand of Roosevelt and that this gesture provided new hope for a tormented world. In Washington the President's secretary was quoted by the official German news bureau as saying, "The President was enthusiastic at Hitler's acceptance of his proposals."

From the Nazi firebrand dictator had come not brutal threats, as so many had expected, but sweetness and light. The world was enchanted. And in the Reichstag even the Socialists' deputies, those who were not in jail or in exile, voted without dissent to make the assembly's approval of Hitler's foreign policy declaration unanimous.

But Hitler's warning was not an empty one, and when it became clear early in October that the Allies would insist on an interval of eight years to bring their armaments down to Germany's level, he abruptly announced on October 14 that, denied equality of rights by the other powers at Geneva, Germany was immediately withdrawing from the Disarmament Conference and from the League of Nations. At the same time he took three other steps: He dissolved the Reichstag, announced that he would submit his decision to leave Geneva to a national plebiscite and ordered General von Blomberg, the Minister of Defense, to issue secret directives to the armed forces to resist an armed attack should the League resort to sanctions.[25]

This precipitate action revealed the hollowness of the Hitler conciliatory speech in the spring. It was Hitler's first open gamble in foreign affairs. It meant that from now on Nazi Germany intended to rearm itself in defiance of any disarmament agreement and of Versailles. This was a calculated risk—also the first of many—and Blomberg's secret directive to the Army and Navy, which came to light at Nuremberg, reveals not only that Hitler gambled with the possibility of sanctions but that Germany's position would have been hopeless had they been applied.* In the West against France and in the East against Poland and Czechoslovakia, the directive laid down definite defense lines which the German forces were ordered "to hold as long as possible." It is obvious from Blomberg's orders that the German generals, at least, had no illusions that the defenses of the Reich could be held for any time at all.

This, then, was the first of many crises over a period that would extend for three years—until after the Germans reoccupied the demilitarized left bank of the Rhine in 1936—when the Allies could have applied sanctions, not for Hitler's leaving the Disarmament Conference and the League but for violations of the disarmament provisions of Versailles which had been going on in Germany for at least two years, even before Hitler. That the Allies at this time could easily have overwhelmed Germany is as certain as it is that such an action would have brought the end of the Third Reich in the very year of its birth. But part of the genius of this one-time Austrian waif was that for a long time he knew the mettle of his foreign adversaries as expertly and as uncannily as he had sized up that of his opponents at home. In this crisis, as in those greater ones which were to follow in rapid succession up to 1939, the victorious Allied nations took no action, being too divided, too torpid, too blind to grasp the nature or the direction of what was building up beyond the Rhine. On this, Hitler's calculations were eminently sound, as they had been and were to be in regard to his own people. He knew well what the German people would say in the plebiscite, which he fixed—along with new elections of a single-party Nazi slate to the Reichstag—for November 12, 1933, the day after the anniversary of the 1918 armistice, a black day that still rankled in German memories.

"See to it that this day," he told an election rally at Breslau on November 4, "shall later be recorded in the history of our people as a day of salvation—that the record shall run: On an eleventh of November the German people formally lost its honor; fifteen years later came a twelfth of November and then the German people restored its honor to itself." On the eve of the polling, November 11, the venerable Hindenburg added his support in a broadcast to the nation: "Show tomorrow your firm national unity and your solidarity with the government. Support with me and the

---

* Some months previously, on May 11, Lord Hailsham, the British Secretary of State for War, had publicly warned that any attempt of Germany to rearm would be a breach of the peace treaty and would be answered by sanctions, in accordance with the treaty. In Germany it was thought that sanctions would mean armed invasion.

Reich Chancellor the principle of equal rights and of peace with honor, and show the world that we have recovered, and with the help of God will maintain, German unity!"

The response of the German people, after fifteen years of frustration and of resentment against the consequences of a lost war, was almost unanimous. Some 96 per cent of the registered voters cast their ballots and 95 per cent of these approved Germany's withdrawal from Geneva. The vote for the single Nazi list for the Reichstag (which included Hugenberg and a half-dozen other non-Nazis) was 92 per cent. Even at the Dachau concentration camp 2,154 out of 2,242 inmates voted for the government which had incarcerated them! It is true that in many communities threats were made against those who failed to vote or who voted the wrong way; and in some cases there was fear that anyone who cast his vote against the regime might be detected and punished. Yet even with these reservations the election, whose count at least was honest, was a staggering victory for Adolf Hitler. There was no doubt that in defying the outside world as he had done, he had the overwhelming support of the German people.

Three days after the plebiscite and election, Hitler sent for the new Polish ambassador, Josef Lipski. At the end of their talk a joint communiqué was issued which amazed not only the German public but the outside world. The Polish and German governments agreed "to deal with the questions touching both countries by means of direct negotiations and to renounce all application of force in their relations with each other for the consolidation of European peace."

Even more than France, Poland was the hated and despised enemy in the minds of the Germans. To them the most heinous crime of the Versailles peacemakers had been to separate East Prussia from the Reich by the Polish Corridor, to detach Danzig and to give to the Poles the province of Posen and part of Silesia, which, though predominantly Polish in population, had been German territory since the days of the partition of Poland. No German statesmen during the Republic had been willing to regard the Polish acquisitions as permanent. Stresemann had refused even to consider an Eastern Locarno pact with Poland to supplement the Locarno agreement for the West. And General von Seeckt, father of the Reichswehr and arbiter of foreign policy during the first years of the Republic, had advised the government as early as 1922, "Poland's existence is intolerable, incompatible with the essential conditions of Germany's life. Poland," he insisted, "must go and will go." Its obliteration, he added, "must be one of the fundamental drives of German policy . . . With the disappearance of Poland will fall one of the strongest pillars of the Versailles Peace, the hegemony of France."[26]

Before Poland could be obliterated, Hitler saw, it must be separated from its alliance with France. The course he now embarked on offered several immediate advantages besides the ultimate one. By renouncing the use of force against Poland he could strengthen his propaganda for peace and allay the suspicions aroused in both Western and Eastern Europe by his hasty exit from Geneva. By inducing the Poles to conduct direct negotiations he could bypass the League of Nations and then weaken its authority. And he could not only deal a blow to the League's conception of "collective security" but undermine the French alliances in Eastern Europe, of which Poland was the bastion. The German people, with their traditional hatred of the Poles, might not understand, but to Hitler one of the advantages of a dictatorship over democracy was that unpopular policies which promised significant results ultimately could be pursued temporarily without internal rumpus.

On January 26, 1934, four days before Hitler was to meet the Reichstag on the first anniversary of his accession to power, announcement was made of the signing of a ten-year nonaggression pact between Germany and Poland. From that day on, Poland, which under the dictatorship of Marshal Pilsudski was itself just eliminating the last vestiges of parliamentary democracy, began gradually to detach itself from France, its protector since its rebirth in 1919, and to grow ever closer to Nazi Germany. It was a path that was to lead to its destruction long before the treaty of "friendship and nonaggression" ran out.

When Hitler addressed the Reichstag on January 30, 1934, he could look back on a year of achievement without parallel in German history. Within twelve months he had overthrown the Weimar Republic, substituted his personal dictatorship for its democracy, destroyed all the political parties but his own, smashed the state governments and their parliaments and unified and defederalized the Reich, wiped out the labor unions, stamped out democratic associations of any kind, driven the Jews out of public and professional life, abolished freedom of speech and of the press, stifled the independence of the courts and "co-ordinated" under Nazi rule the political, economic, cultural and social life of an ancient and cultivated people. For all these accomplishments and for his resolute action in foreign affairs, which took Germany out of the concert of nations at Geneva, and proclaimed German insistence on being treated as an equal among the great powers, he was backed, as the autumn plebiscite and election had shown, by the overwhelming majority of the German people.

Yet as the second year of his dictatorship got under way clouds gathered on the Nazi horizon.

THE BLOOD PURGE OF JUNE 30, 1934

The darkening of the sky was due to three unresolved problems, and they were interrelated: the continued clamor of radical party and S.A. leaders for the "second revolution"; the rivalry of the S.A. and the Army; and the question of the succession to President Hindenburg, the sands of whose life at last began to run out with the coming of spring.

Roehm, the chief of staff of the S.A., now swollen to two and a half million storm troopers, had not been put off by Hitler's gesture of appointing him to the cabinet nor by the Fuehrer's friendly personal letter on New Year's Day. In February he presented to the cabinet a lengthy memorandum proposing that the S.A. should be made the foundation of a new People's Army and that the armed forces, the S.A. and S.S. and all veterans' groups should be placed under a single Ministry of Defense, over which—the implication was clear—he should preside. No more revolting idea could be imagined by the officer corps, and its senior members not only unanimously rejected the proposal but appealed to Hindenburg to support them. The whole tradition of the military caste would be destroyed if the roughneck Roehm and his brawling Brownshirts should get control of the Army. Moreover, the generals were shocked by the tales, now beginning to receive wide circulation, of the corruption and debauchery of the homosexual clique around the S.A. chief. As General von Brauchitsch would later testify, "rearmament was too serious and difficult a business to permit the participation of peculators, drunkards and homosexuals."

For the moment Hitler could not afford to offend the Army, and he gave no support to Roehm's proposal. Indeed, on February 21 he secretly told Anthony Eden, who had come to Berlin to discuss the disarmament impasse, that he was prepared to reduce the S.A. by two thirds and to agree to a system of inspection to make sure that the remainder received neither military training nor arms—an offer which, when it leaked out, further inflamed the bitterness of Roehm and the S.A. As the summer of 1934 approached, the relations between the S.A. chief of staff and the Army High Command continued to deteriorate. There were stormy scenes in the cabinet between Roehm and General von Blomberg, and in March the Minister of Defense protested to Hitler that the S.A. was secretly arming a large force of special staff guards with heavy machine guns—which was not only a threat against the Army but, General von Blomberg added, an act done so publicly that it threatened Germany's clandestine rearmament under the auspices of the Reichswehr.

It is plain that at this juncture Hitler, unlike the headstrong Roehm and his cronies, was thinking ahead to the day when the ailing Hindenburg would breathe his last. He knew that the aged President as well as the Army and other conservative forces in Germany were in favor of a restoration of the Hohenzollern monarchy as soon as the Field Marshal had passed away. He himself had other plans, and when early in April the news was secretly but authoritatively conveyed to him and Blomberg from Neudeck that the President's days were numbered, he realized that a bold stroke must soon be made. To ensure its success he would need the backing of the officer corps; to obtain that support he was prepared to go to almost any length.

The occasion for confidential parleys with the Army soon presented itself. On April 11 the Chancellor, accompanied by General von Blomberg and the commanders in chief of the Army and the Navy, General Freiherr von Fritsch and Admiral Raeder, set out on the cruiser *Deutschland* from Kiel for Koenigsberg to attend the spring maneuvers in East Prussia. The Army and Navy commanders were told of Hindenburg's worsening condition and Hitler, backed by the compliant Blomberg, bluntly proposed that he himself, with the Reichswehr's blessing, be the President's successor. In return for the support of the military, Hitler offered to suppress Roehm's ambitions, drastically reduce the S.A. and guarantee the Army and Navy that they would continue to be the sole bearers of arms in the Third Reich. It is believed that Hitler also held out to Fritsch and Raeder the prospect of an immense expansion of the Army and Navy, if they were prepared to go along with him. With the fawning Raeder there was no question but that he would, but Fritsch, a tougher man, had first to consult his senior generals.

This consultation took place at Bad Nauheim on May 16, and after the "Pact of the *Deutschland*" had been explained to them, the highest officers of the German Army unanimously endorsed Hitler as the successor to President Hindenburg.[27] For the Army this *political* decision was to prove of historic significance. By voluntarily offering to put itself in the unrestrained hands of a megalomaniacal dictator it was sealing its own fate. As for Hitler, the deal would make his dictatorship supreme. With the stubborn Field Marshal out of the way, with the prospect of the restoration of the Hohenzollerns snuffed out, with himself as head of state as well as of government, he could go his way alone and unhindered. The price he paid for this elevation to supreme power was paltry: the sacrifice of the S.A. He did not need it, now that he had all the authority. It was a raucous rabble that only embarrassed him. Hitler's contempt for the narrow minds of the generals must have risen sharply that spring. They could be had, he must have thought, for surprisingly little. It was a judgment that he held, unaltered, except for one bad moment in June, to the end—his end and theirs.

Yet, as summer came, Hitler's troubles were far from over. An ominous tension began to grip Berlin. Cries for the "second revolution" multiplied, and not only Roehm and the storm troop leaders but Goebbels himself, in speeches and in the press which he controlled, gave vent to them. From the conservative Right, from the Junkers and big industrialists around Papen and Hindenburg, came demands that a halt be called to the revolution, that the arbitrary arrests, the persecution of the Jews, the attacks against the churches, the arrogant behavior of the storm troopers be curbed, and that the general terror organized by the Nazis come to an end.

Within the Nazi Party itself there was a new and ruthless struggle for power. Roehm's two most powerful enemies, Goering and Himmler, were uniting against him. On April 1 Himmler, chief of the black-coated S.S., which was still an arm of the S.A. and under Roehm's command, was named by Goering to be chief of the Prussian Gestapo, and he immediately began to build up a secret-police empire of his own. Goering, who had been made a *General der Infanterie* by Hindenburg the previous August (though he was Minister of Aviation), gladly shed his shabby brown

S.A. uniform for the more showy one of his new office, and the change was symbolic: as a general and a member of a family from the military caste, he quickly sided with the Army in its fight against Roehm and the S.A. To protect himself in the jungle warfare which was now going on, Goering also recruited his own personal police force, the Landespolizeigruppe General Goering, several thousand men strong, which he concentrated in the former Cadet School at Lichterfelde, where he had first entered the Army and which was strategically located on the outskirts of Berlin.

Rumors of plots and counterplots added to the tension in the capital. General von Schleicher, unable to bear a decent obscurity or to remember that he no longer enjoyed the confidence of Hindenburg, the generals or the conservatives and was therefore powerless, had begun to mix again in politics. He was in touch with Roehm and Gregor Strasser and there were reports, some of which reached Hitler, that he was busy trying to make a deal whereby he would become Vice-Chancellor in place of his old enemy, Papen, Roehm would become Minister of Defense and the S.A. would be amalgamated with the Army. Cabinet "lists" circulated by the dozen in Berlin; in some of them Bruening was to be made Foreign Minister and Strasser Minister of Economics. These reports had little foundation but they were grist to the mill of Goering and Himmler, who, desirous each for his own reasons to destroy Roehm and the S.A., and at the same time to settle accounts with Schleicher and the disgruntled conservatives, embroidered them and brought them to Hitler, who at any time needed little prodding to have his suspicions aroused. What Goering and his Gestapo chief had in mind was not only to purge the S.A. but to liquidate other opponents on the Left and Right, including some who had opposed Hitler in the past and were no longer politically active. At the end of May Bruening and Schleicher were warned that they were marked for murder. The former slipped quietly out of the country in disguise, the latter went off on a vacation to Bavaria but returned to Berlin toward the end of June.

At the beginning of June, Hitler had a showdown with Roehm which, according to his own account given to the Reichstag later, lasted for nearly five hours and which "dragged on until midnight." It was, Hitler said, his "last attempt" to come to an understanding with his closest friend in the movement.

I informed him that I had the impression from countless rumors and numerous declarations of faithful old party members and S.A. leaders that conscienceless elements were preparing a national Bolshevist action that could bring nothing but untold misfortune to Germany . . . I implored him for the last time to voluntarily abandon this madness and instead to lend his authority to prevent a development that, in any event, could only end in disaster.

According to Hitler, Roehm left him with the "assurance that he would do everything possible to put things right." Actually, Hitler later claimed, Roehm began "preparations to eliminate me personally."

This was almost certainly untrue. Though the whole story of the purge, like that of the Reichstag fire, will probably never be known, all the evidence that has come to light indicates that the S.A. chief never plotted to put Hitler out of the way. Unfortunately the captured archives shed no more light on the purge than they do on the Reichstag fire; in both cases it is likely that all the incriminating documents were destroyed on the orders of Goering.

Whatever was the real nature of the long conversation between the two Nazi veterans, a day or two after it took place Hitler bade the S.A. go on leave for the entire month of July, during which the storm troopers were prohibited from wearing uniforms or engaging in parades or exercises. On June 7, Roehm announced that he himself was going on sick leave but at the same time he issued a defiant warning: "If the enemies of S.A. hope that the S.A. will not be recalled, or will be recalled only in part after its leave, we may permit them to enjoy this brief hope. They will receive their answer at such time and in such form as appears necessary. The S.A. is and remains the destiny of Germany."

Before he left Berlin Roehm invited Hitler to confer with the S.A. leaders at the resort town of Wiessee, near Munich, on June 30. Hitler readily agreed and indeed kept the appointment, though not in a manner which Roehm could possibly have imagined. Perhaps not in a way, either, that Hitler himself at this moment could foresee. For, as he later admitted to the Reichstag, he hesitated "again and again before taking a final decision . . . I still cherished the secret hope that I might be able to spare the movement and my S.A. the shame of such a disagreement and that it might be possible to remove the mischief without severe conflicts."

"It must be confessed," he added, "that the last days of May continuously brought to light more and more disquieting facts." But did they? Later Hitler claimed that Roehm and his conspirators had made preparations to seize Berlin and take him into custody. But if this were so why did all the S.A. leaders depart from Berlin early in June, and—even more important—why did Hitler leave Germany at this moment and thus provide an opportunity for the S.A. chiefs to grab control of the State in his absence?

For on June 14 the Fuehrer flew to Venice to hold the first of many conversations with his fellow fascist dictator, Mussolini. The meeting, incidentally, did not go off well for the German leader, who, in his soiled raincoat and battered soft hat, seemed ill at ease in the presence of the more experienced Duce, resplendent in his glittering, bemedaled black Fascisti uniform and inclined to be condescending to his visitor. Hitler returned to Germany in a state of considerable irritation and called a meeting of his party leaders in the little town of Gera in Thuringia for Sunday, June 17, to report on his talks with Mussolini and to assess the worsening situation at home. As fate would have it, another meeting took place on that Sunday in the old university town of Marburg which attracted much more attention in Germany and indeed in the world, and which helped bring the critical situation to a climax.

The dilettante Papen, who had been rudely shoved to the sidelines by Hitler and Goering but who was still nominally Vice-Chancellor and still enjoyed the confidence of Hindenburg, summoned enough courage to speak out publicly against the excesses of the regime which he had done so much to foist on Germany. In May he had seen the ailing President off to Neudeck—it was the last time he was to see his protector alive— and the grizzly but enfeebled old Field Marshal had said to him: "Things are going badly, Papen. See what you can do to put them right."

Thus encouraged, Papen had accepted an invitation to make an address at the University of Marburg on June 17. The speech was largely written by one of his personal advisers, Edgar Jung, a brilliant Munich lawyer and writer and a Protestant, though certain ideas were furnished by one of the Vice-Chancellor's secretaries, Herbert von Bose, and by Erich Klausener, the leader of Catholic Action—a collaboration that soon cost all three of them their lives. It was a courageous utterance and, thanks to Jung, eloquent in style and dignified in tone. It called for an end of the revolution, for a termination of the Nazi terror, for the restoration of normal decencies and the return of some measure of freedom, especially of freedom of the press. Addressing Dr. Goebbels, the Propaganda Minister, Papen said:

> Open manly discussions would be of more service to the German people than, for instance, the present state of the German press. The government [must be] mindful of the old maxim, "Only weaklings suffer no criticism" . . . Great men are not created by propaganda . . . If one desires close contact and unity with the people, one must not underestimate their understanding. One must not everlastingly keep them on leading strings . . . No organization, no propaganda, however excellent, can alone maintain confidence in the long run. It is not by incitement . . . and not by threats against the helpless part of the nation but only by talking things over with people that confidence and devotion can be maintained. People treated as morons, however, have no confidence to give away . . . It is time to join together in fraternal friendship and respect for all our fellow countrymen, to avoid disturbing the labors of serious men and to silence fanatics.[28]

The speech, when it became known, was widely heralded in Germany, but it fell like a bombshell on the little group of Nazi leaders gathered at Gera, and Goebbels moved quickly to see that it became known as little as possible. He forbade the broadcast of a recording of the speech scheduled for the same evening as well as any reference to it in the press, and ordered the police to seize copies of the *Frankfurter Zeitung* which were on the streets with a partial text. But not even the absolute powers of the Propaganda Minister were sufficient to keep the German people and the outside world from learning the contents of the defiant address. The wily Papen had provided the foreign correspondents and diplomats in Berlin with advance texts, and several thousand copies were hastily run off on the presses of Papen's newspaper, *Germania,* and secretly distributed.

On learning of the Marburg speech, Hitler was stung to fury. In a speech the same afternoon at Gera he denounced the "pygmy who imagines he can stop, with a few phrases, the gigantic renewal of a people's life." Papen was furious too, at the suppression of his speech. He rushed to Hitler on June 20 and told him he could not tolerate such a ban "by a junior minister," insisted that he had spoken "as a trustee for the President," and then and there submitted his resignation, adding a warning that he "would advise Hindenburg of this immediately."[29]

This was a threat that obviously worried Hitler, for he was aware of reports that the President was so displeased with the situation that he was considering declaring martial law and handing over power to the Army. In order to size up the seriousness of this danger to the very continuance of the Nazi regime, he flew to Neudeck on the following day, June 21, to see Hindenburg. His reception could only have increased his fears. He was met by General von Blomberg and quickly saw that his Defense Minister's usual lackeylike attitude toward him had suddenly disappeared. Blomberg instead was now the stern Prussian general and he brusquely informed Hitler that he was authorized by the Field Marshal to tell him that unless the present state of tension in Germany was brought quickly to an end the President would declare martial law and turn over the control of the State to the Army. When Hitler was permitted to see Hindenburg for a few minutes in the presence of Blomberg, the old President confirmed the ultimatum.

This was a disastrous turn of affairs for the Nazi Chancellor. Not only was his plan to succeed the President in jeopardy; if the Army took over, that would be the end of him and of Nazi government. Flying back to Berlin the same day he must have reflected that he had only one choice to make if he were to survive. He must honor his pact with the Army, suppress the S.A. and halt the continuance of the revolution for which the storm troop leaders were pressing. The Army, backed by the venerable President, it was obvious, would accept no less.

And yet, in that last crucial week of June, Hitler hesitated—as least as to how drastic to be with the S.A. chiefs to whom he owed so much. But now Goering and Himmler helped him to make up his mind. They had already drawn up the scores they wanted to settle, long lists of present and past enemies they wished to liquidate. All they had to do was convince the Fuehrer of the enormity of the "plot" against him and of the necessity for swift and ruthless action. According to the testimony at Nuremberg of Wilhelm Frick, the Minister of the Interior and one of Hitler's most faithful followers, it was Himmler who finally succeeded in convincing Hitler that "Roehm wanted to start a putsch. The Fuehrer," Frick added, "ordered Himmler to suppress the putsch." Himmler, he explained, was instructed to put it down in Bavaria, and Goering in Berlin.[30]

The Army prodded Hitler too and thereby incurred a responsibility for the barbarity which was soon to take place. On June 25 General von Fritsch, the Commander in Chief, put the Army in a state of alert, canceling all leaves and confining the troops to barracks. On June 28 Roehm was expelled from the German Officers' League—a plain warning that the S.A. chief of staff was in for trouble. And just to make sure that no one, Roehm above all, should have any illusions about where the Army stood, Blomberg took the unprecedented step of publishing a signed article on June 29 in the *Voelkischer Beobachter,* affirming that "the Army . . . stands behind Adolf Hitler . . . who remains one of ours."

The Army, then, was pressing for the purge, but it did not want to soil its own hands. That must be done by Hitler, Goering and Himmler, with their black-coated S.S. and Goering's special police.

Hitler left Berlin on Thursday, June 28, for Essen to attend the wedding of a local Nazi gauleiter, Josef Terboven. The trip and its purpose hardly suggest that he felt a grave crisis to be imminent. On the same day Goering and Himmler ordered special detachments of the S.S. and the "Goering Police" to hold themselves in readiness. With Hitler out of town, they evidently felt free to act on their own. The next day, the twenty-ninth, the Fuehrer made a tour of Labor Service camps in Westphalia, returning in the afternoon to Godesberg on the Rhine, where he put up at a hotel on the riverbank run by an old war comrade, Dreesen. That evening Goebbels, who seems to have hesitated as to which camp to join—he had been secretly in touch with Roehm—arrived in Godesberg, his mind made up, and reported what Hitler later described as "threatening intelligence" from Berlin. Karl Ernst, a former hotel bellhop and ex-bouncer in a café frequented by homosexuals, whom Roehm had made leader of the Berlin S.A., had alerted the storm troopers. Ernst, a handsome but not a bright young man, believed then and for the remaining twenty-four hours or so of his life that he was faced by a putsch from the Right, and he would die shouting proudly, "Heil Hitler!"

Hitler later claimed that up to this moment, June 29, he had decided merely to "deprive the chief of staff [Roehm] of his office and for the time being keep him in custody and arrest a number of S.A. leaders whose crimes were unquestioned . . . and in an earnest appeal to the others, I would recall them to their duty."

However, [he told the Reichstag on July 13] . . . at one o'clock in the night I received from Berlin and Munich two urgent messages concerning alarm summonses: first, in Berlin an alarm muster had been ordered for four P.M. . . . and at five P.M. action was to begin with a surprise attack; the government buildings were to be occupied . . . Second, in Munich the alarm summons had already been given to the S.A.; they had been ordered to assemble at nine o'clock in the evening . . . That was mutiny! . . . In these circumstances I could make but one decision . . . Only a ruthless and bloody intervention might still perhaps stifle the spread of the revolt . . .

At two o'clock in the morning I flew to Munich.

Hitler never revealed from whom the "urgent messages" came but the implication is that they were sent by Goering and Himmler. What is certain is that they were highly exaggerated. In Berlin, S.A. Leader Ernst thought of nothing more drastic than to drive to Bremen that Saturday with his bride to take ship for a honeymoon at Madeira. And in the south, where the S.A. "conspirators" were concentrated?

At the moment of 2 A.M. on June 30 when Hitler, with Goebbels at his side, was taking off from Hangelar Airfield near Bonn, Captain Roehm and his S.A. lieutenants were peacefully slumbering in their beds at the Hanslbauer Hotel at Wiessee on the shores of the Tegernsee. Edmund Heines, the S.A. Obergruppenfuehrer of Silesia, a convicted murderer, a notorious homosexual with a girlish face on the brawny body of a piano mover, was in bed with a young man. So far did the S.A. chiefs seem from staging a revolt that Roehm had left his staff guards in Munich. There appeared to be plenty of carousing among the S.A. leaders but no plotting.

Hitler and his small party (Otto Dietrich, his press chief, and Viktor Lutze, the colorless but loyal S.A. leader of Hanover, had joined it) landed in Munich at 4 A.M. on Saturday, June 30, and found that some action already had been taken. Major Walther Buch, head of USCHLA, the party court, and Adolf Wagner, Bavarian Minister of the Interior, aided by such early cronies of Hitler as Emil Maurice, the ex-convict and rival for Geli Raubal's love, and Christian Weber, the horse dealer and former cabaret bouncer, had arrested the Munich S.A. leaders, including Obergruppenfuehrer Schneidhuber, who was also chief of police in Munich. Hitler, who was now working himself up to a fine state of hysteria, found the prisoners in the Ministry of the Interior. Striding up to Schneidhuber, a former Army colonel, he tore off his Nazi insignia and cursed him for his "treason."

Shortly after dawn Hitler and his party sped out of Munich toward Wiessee in a long column of cars. They found Roehm and his friends still fast asleep in the Hanslbauer Hotel. The awakening was rude. Heines and his young male companion were dragged out of bed, taken outside the hotel and summarily shot on the orders of Hitler. The Fuehrer, according to Otto Dietrich's account, entered Roehm's room alone, gave him a dressing down and ordered him to be brought back to Munich and lodged in Stadelheim prison, where the S.A. chief had served time after his participation with Hitler in the Beer Hall Putsch in 1923. After fourteen stormy years the two friends, who more than any others were responsible for the launching of the Third Reich, for its terror and its degradation, who though they had often disagreed had stood together in the moments of crisis and defeats and disappointments, had come to a parting of the ways, and the scar-faced, brawling battler for Hitler and Nazism had come to the end of his violent life.

Hitler, in a final act of what he apparently thought was grace, gave orders that a pistol be left on the table of his old comrade. Roehm refused to make use of it. "If I am to be killed, let Adolf do it himself," he is reported to have said. Thereupon two S.A. officers, according to the testimony of an eyewitness, a police lieutenant, given twenty-three years later in a postwar trial at Munich in May 1957, entered the cell and fired their revolvers at Roehm point-blank. "Roehm wanted to say something," said this witness, "but the S.S. officer motioned him to shut up. Then Roehm stood at attention—he was stripped to the waist—with his face full of contempt."* And so he died, violently as he had lived, contemptuous of the friend he had helped propel to the heights no other German had ever reached, and almost certainly, like hundreds of others who were slaughtered that day—like Schneidhuber, who was reported to have cried, "Gentlemen, I don't know what this is all about, but shoot straight"—without any clear idea of what was happening, or why, other than that it was an act of treachery which he, who had lived so long with treachery and committed it so often himself, had not expected from Adolf Hitler.

In Berlin, in the meantime, Goering and Himmler had been busy. Some 150 S.A. leaders were rounded up and stood against a wall of the Cadet School at Lichterfelde and shot by firing squads of Himmler's S.S. and Goering's special police.

Among them was Karl Ernst, whose honeymoon trip was interrupted by S.S. gunmen as his car neared Bremen. His bride and his chauffeur were wounded; he himself was knocked unconscious and flown back to Berlin for his execution.

The S.A. men were not the only ones to fall on that bloody summer weekend. On the morning of June 30, a squad of S.S. men in mufti rang the doorbell at General von Schleicher's villa on the outskirts of Berlin. When the General opened the door he was shot dead in his tracks, and when his wife, whom he had married but eighteen months before—he had been a bachelor until then—stepped forward, she too was slain on the spot. General Kurt von Bredow, a close friend of Schleicher, met a similar fate the same evening. Gregor Strasser was seized at his home in Berlin at noon on Saturday and dispatched a few hours later in his cell in the Prinz Albrechtstrasse Gestapo jail on the personal orders of Goering.

Papen was luckier. He escaped with his life. But his office was ransacked by an S.S. squad, his principal secretary, Bose, shot down at his desk, his confidential collaborator, Edgar Jung, who had been arrested a few days earlier by the Gestapo, murdered in prison, another collabora-

---

* The Munich trial in May 1957 was the first occasion on which actual eyewitnesses and participants in the June 30, 1934, purge talked in public. During the Third Reich it would not have been possible. Sepp Dietrich, whom this author recalls personally as one of the most brutal men of the Third Reich, commanded Hitler's S.S. Bodyguard in 1934 and directed the executions in Stadelheim prison. Later a colonel general in the Waffen S.S. during the war, he was sentenced to twenty-five years in prison for complicity in the murder of American prisoners of war during the Battle of the Bulge in 1944. Released after ten years, he was brought to Munich in 1957 and sentenced on May 14 to eighteen months in prison for his part in the June 30, 1934, executions. His sentence and that of Michael Lippert, who was convicted as being one of the two S.S. officers who actually killed Roehm, was the first punishment given to the Nazi executioners who took part in the purge.

tor, Erich Klausener, leader of Catholic Action, slain in his office in the Ministry of Communications, and the rest of his staff, including his private secretary, Baroness Stotzingen, carted off to concentration camp. When Papen went to protest to Goering, the latter, who at that moment had no time for idle talk, "more or less," he later recalled, threw him out, placing him under house arrest at his villa, which was surrounded by heavily armed S.S. men and where his telephone was cut and he was forbidden to have any contact with the outside world—an added humiliation which the Vice-Chancellor of Germany swallowed remarkably well. For within less than a month he defiled himself by accepting from the Nazi murderers of his friends a new assignment as German minister to Vienna, where the Nazis had just slain Chancellor Dollfuss.

How many were slain in the purge was never definitely established. In his Reichstag speech of July 13, Hitler announced that sixty-one persons were shot, including nineteen "higher S.A. leaders," that thirteen more died "resisting arrest" and that three "committed suicide"—a total of seventy-seven. *The White Book of the Purge,* published by émigrés in Paris, stated that 401 had been slain, but it identified only 116 of them. At the Munich trial in 1957, the figure of "more than 1,000" was given.

Many were killed out of pure vengeance for having opposed Hitler in the past, others were murdered apparently because they knew too much, and at least one because of mistaken identity. The body of Gustav von Kahr, whose suppression of the Beer Hall Putsch in 1923 we have already recounted, and who had long since retired from politics, was found in a swamp near Dachau hacked to death, apparently by pickaxes. Hitler had neither forgotten nor forgiven him. The body of Father Bernhard Stempfle of the Hieronymite Order, who, it will be remembered from earlier pages, helped edit *Mein Kampf* and later talked too much, perhaps, about his knowledge of why Hitler's love, Geli Raubal, committed suicide, was found in the forest of Harlaching near Munich, his neck broken and three shots in the heart. Heiden says the murder gang that killed him was led by Emil Maurice, the ex-convict who had also made love to Geli Raubal. Others who "knew too much" included three S.A. men who were believed to have been accomplices of Ernst in setting the Reichstag on fire. They were dispatched with Ernst.

One other murder deserves mention. At seven-twenty on the evening of June 30, Dr. Willi Schmid, the eminent music critic of the *Muenchener Neueste Nachrichten,* a leading Munich daily newspaper, was playing the cello in his study while his wife prepared supper and their three children, aged nine, eight and two, played in the living room of their apartment in the Schackstrasse in Munich. The doorbell rang, four S.S. men appeared and without explanation took Dr. Schmid away. Four days later his body was returned in a coffin with orders from the Gestapo not to open it in any circumstances. Dr. Willi Schmid, who had never participated in politics, had been mistaken by the S.S. thugs for Willi Schmidt, a local S.A. leader, who in the meantime had been arrested by another S.S. detachment and shot.*

Was there a plot against Hitler at all? There is only his word for it, contained in the official communiqués and in his Reichstag speech of July 13. He never presented a shred of evidence. Roehm had made no secret of his ambition to see the S.A. become the nucleus of the new Army and to head it himself. He had certainly been in touch with Schleicher about the scheme, which they had first discussed when the General was Chancellor. Probably, as Hitler stated, Gregor Strasser "was brought in." But such talks certainly did not constitute treason. Hitler himself was in contact with Strasser and early in June, according to Otto Strasser, offered him the post of Minister of Economics.

At first Hitler accused Roehm and Schleicher of having sought the backing of a "foreign power"—obviously France—and charged that General von Bredow was the intermediary in "foreign policy." This was part of the indictment of them as "traitors." And though Hitler repeated the charges in his Reichstag speech and spoke sarcastically of "a foreign diplomat [who could have been no other than François-Poncet, the French ambassador] explaining that the meeting with Schleicher and Roehm was of an entirely harmless character," he was unable to substantiate his accusations. It was crime enough, he said lamely, for any responsible German in the Third Reich even to see foreign diplomats without his knowledge.

When three traitors in Germany arrange . . . a meeting with a foreign statesman . . . and give orders that no word of this meeting shall reach me, then I shall have such men shot dead even when it should prove true that at such a consultation which was thus kept secret from me they talked of nothing more than the weather, old coins and like topics.

When François-Poncet protested vigorously against the insinuation that he had participated in the Roehm "plot" the German Foreign Office officially informed the French government that the accusations were wholly without foundation and that the Reich government hoped the ambassador would remain in his post. Indeed, as this writer can testify, François-Poncet continued to remain on better personal terms with Hitler than any other envoy from a democratic state.

In the first communiqués, especially in a blood-curdling eyewitness account given the public by Otto Dietrich, the Fuehrer's press chief, and even in Hitler's Reichstag speech, much was made of the depraved morals

---

* Kate Eva Hoerlin, former wife of Willi Schmid, told the story of her husband's murder in an affidavit sworn on July 7, 1945, at Binghamton, N.Y. She became an American citizen in 1944. To hush up the atrocity Rudolf Hess himself visited the widow, apologized for the "mistake" and secured for her a pension from the German government. The affidavit is given in Nuremberg Document L-135, NCA, VII, pp. 883–90.

of Roehm and the other S.A. leaders who were shot. Dietrich asserted that the scene of the arrest of Heines, who was caught in bed at Wiessee with a young man, "defied description," and Hitler in addressing the surviving storm troop leaders in Munich at noon on June 30, just after the first executions, declared that for their corrupt morals alone these men deserved to die.

And yet Hitler had known all along, from the earliest days of the party, that a large number of his closest and most important followers were sexual perverts and convicted murderers. It was common talk, for instance, that Heines used to send S.A. men scouring all over Germany to find him suitable male lovers. These things Hitler had not only tolerated but defended; more than once he had warned his party comrades against being too squeamish about a man's personal morals if he were a fanatical fighter for the movement. Now, on June 30, 1934, he professed to be shocked by the moral degeneration of some of his oldest lieutenants.

Most of the killing was over by Sunday afternoon, July 1, when Hitler, who had flown back to Berlin from Munich the night before, was host at a tea party in the gardens of the Chancellery. On Monday President Hindenburg thanked Hitler for his "determined action and gallant personal intervention which have nipped treason in the bud and rescued the German people from great danger." He also congratulated Goering for his "energetic and successful action" in suppressing "high treason." On Tuesday General von Blomberg expressed to the Chancellor the congratulations of the cabinet, which proceeded to "legalize" the slaughter as a necessary measure "for the defense of the State." Blomberg also issued an order of the day to the Army expressing the High Command's satisfaction with the turn of events and promising to establish "cordial relations with the new S.A."

It was natural, no doubt, that the Army should be pleased with the elimination of its rival, the S.A., but what about the sense of honor, let alone of decency, of an officer corps which not only condoned but openly praised a government for carrying out a massacre without precedent in German history, during which two of its leading officers, Generals von Schleicher and von Bredow, having been branded as traitors, were coldbloodedly murdered? Only the voices of the eighty-five-year-old Field Marshal von Mackensen and of General von Hammerstein, the former Commander in Chief of the Army, were raised in protest against the murder of their two fellow officers and the charges of treason which had been the excuse for it.* This behavior of the corps was a black stain on the

---

* The two senior officers continued their efforts to clear the names of Schleicher and Bredow, and succeeded in getting Hitler, at a secret meeting of party and military leaders in Berlin on January 3, 1935, to admit that the killing of the two generals had been "in error" and to announce that their names would be restored to the honor rolls of their regiments. This "rehabilitation" was never published in Germany, but the officer corps accepted it as such. (See Wheeler-Bennett, *The Nemesis of Power*, p. 337.)

honor of the Army; it was also a mark of its unbelievable shortsightedness.

In making common cause with the lawlessness, indeed the gangsterism, of Hitler on June 30, 1934, the generals were putting themselves in a position in which they could never oppose future acts of Nazi terrorism not only at home but even when they were aimed across the frontiers, even when they were committed against their own members. For the Army was backing Hitler's claim that he had become the law, or, as he put it in his Reichstag speech of July 13, "If anyone reproaches me and asks why I did not resort to the regular courts of justice, then all I can say is this: In this hour I was responsible for the fate of the German people, and thereby I became the supreme judge [*oberster Gerichtsherr*] of the German people." And Hitler added, for good measure, "Everyone must know for all future time that if he raises his hand to strike the State, then certain death is his lot." This was a warning that was to catch up with the generals in ten years almost to a day when at last the more desperate of them dared to raise their hand to strike down their "supreme judge."

Moreover, the officer corps only deluded itself in thinking that on June 30 it got rid forever of the threat of the Nazi movement against its traditional prerogatives and power. For in the place of the S.A. came the S.S. On July 26 the S.S., as a reward for carrying out the executions, was made independent of the S.A., with Himmler—as its Reichsfuehrer—responsible only to Hitler. Soon this much-better-disciplined and loyal force would become much more powerful than the S.A. had ever been and as a rival to the Army would succeed where Roehm's ragged Brownshirts had failed.

For the moment, however, the generals were smugly confident. As Hitler reiterated in his Reichstag address on July 13, the Army was to remain "the sole bearer of arms." At the High Command's bidding, the Chancellor had got rid of the S.A., which had dared to dispute that dictum. The time now came when the Army had to carry out its part of the "Pact of the *Deutschland*."

THE DEATH OF HINDENBURG

All through the summer the seemingly indestructible Hindenburg had been sinking and on August 2, at nine in the morning, he died in his eighty-seventh year. At noon, three hours later, it was announced that according to a law enacted by the cabinet on the *preceding* day the offices of Chancellor and President had been combined and that Adolf Hitler had taken over the powers of the head of state and Commander in Chief of the Armed Forces. The title of President was abolished; Hitler would be known as Fuehrer and Reich Chancellor. His dictatorship had become complete. To leave no loopholes Hitler exacted from all officers and men of the armed forces an oath of allegiance—not to Germany, not to the constitution, which he had violated by not calling for the election of Hindenburg's successor, but to himself. It read:

I swear by God this sacred oath, that I will render unconditional obedience to Adolf Hitler, the Fuehrer of the German Reich and people, Supreme Commander of the Armed Forces, and will be ready as a brave soldier to risk my life at any time for this oath.

From August 1934 on, the generals, who up to that time could have overthrown the Nazi regime with ease had they so desired, thus tied themselves to the person of Adolf Hitler, recognizing him as the highest legitimate authority in the land and binding themselves to him by an oath of fealty which they felt honor-bound to obey in all circumstances no matter how degrading to them and the Fatherland. It was an oath which was to trouble the conscience of quite a few high officers when their acknowledged leader set off on a path which they felt could only lead to the nation's destruction and which they opposed. It was also a pledge which enabled an even greater number of officers to excuse themselves from any personal responsibility for the unspeakable crimes which they carried out on the orders of a Supreme Commander whose true nature they had seen for themselves in the butchery of June 30. One of the appalling aberrations of the German officer corps from this point on rose out of this conflict of "honor"—a word which, as this author can testify by personal experience, was often on their lips and of which they had such a curious concept. Later and often, by honoring their oath they dishonored themselves as human beings and trod in the mud the moral code of their corps.

When Hindenburg died, Dr. Goebbels, the Minister of Propaganda, officially announced that no last will and testament of the Field Marshal had been found and that it must be presumed there was none. But on August 15, four days before the plebiscite in which the German people were asked to approve Hitler's taking over the President's office, Hindenburg's political testament turned up, delivered to Hitler by none other than Papen. Its words of praise for Hitler provided strong ammunition to Goebbels in the final days of the plebiscite campaign, and it was reinforced on the eve of the voting by a broadcast of Colonel Oskar von Hindenburg:

My father had himself seen in Adolf Hitler his own direct successor as head of the German State, and I am acting according to my father's intention when I call on all German men and women to vote for the handing over of my father's office to the Fuehrer and Reich Chancellor.*

Almost certainly this was not true. For Hindenburg, on the best evidence available, had recommended as his last wish a restoration of the monarchy after his death. This part of the testament Adolf Hitler suppressed.

---

* It is interesting and perhaps revealing that Hitler now promoted Oskar from colonel to major general. See above, p. 181.

Some, if not all, of the mystery which cloaked the truth about the aged President's testament was cleared up after the war by Papen's interrogation at Nuremberg and later in his memoirs. And while Papen is not an unimpeachable witness and may not have told all he knew, his testimony cannot be ignored. He himself wrote the initial draft of Hindenburg's last will, and, according to him, at the Field Marshal's request.

My draft [he says in his memoirs] recommended that after his death a constitutional monarchy should be adopted, and I made a point of the inadvisability of combining the offices of President and Chancellor. In order to avoid giving any offense to Hitler, there were also certain approving references to some of the positive accomplishments of the Nazi regime.

Papen delivered his draft to Hindenburg in April 1934, he says.

A few days later he asked me to call on him again, and told me that he had decided not to approve the document in the form I had suggested. He felt . . . that the nation as a whole should make up its mind as to the form of State it desired. He therefore intended to regard the account of his service as a testament, and his recommendations concerning the return of the monarchy would be expressed, as his last wish, in a private letter to Hitler. This meant, of course, that the whole point of my original suggestion had been lost, as the recommendation concerning the monarchy was no longer addressed to the nation; a fact of which Hitler later took full advantage.

No German was as well placed as Papen to observe how Hitler took the advantage.

When I returned to Berlin after Hindenburg's funeral at Tannenberg, Hitler rang me up. He asked me if a political testament by Hindenburg existed, and if I knew where it was. I said that I would ask Oskar von Hindenburg. "I should be obliged," said Hitler, "if you would ensure that this document comes into my possession as soon as possible." I therefore told Kageneck, my private secretary, to go to Neudeck and ask Hindenburg's son if the testament still existed, and whether I could have it to pass it on to Hitler. As I had not seen Hindenburg after he left Berlin at the end of May, I had no idea whether he had destroyed the testament or not.

Oskar, who had not been able to find the important document immediately after his father's death, suddenly found it. That this could not have been a very difficult feat was attested to by Count von der Schulenburg, Hindenburg's adjutant, in his testimony at Papen's denazification trial. He revealed that the President on May 11 signed two documents, his testament and his last wishes. The first was addressed to "the German People" and the second to the "Reich Chancellor." When Hindenburg left Berlin on his last journey to Neudeck Schulenburg took the papers with him. Papen says he did not know this at the time. But in due course his secretary returned from Neudeck bringing two sealed envelopes turned over to him by Oskar von Hindenburg.

On August 15 Papen delivered them to Hitler at Berchtesgaden.

Hitler read both documents with great care and discussed the contents with us. It was obvious that Hindenburg's recommendations in the document expressing his last wishes were contrary to Hitler's intentions. He therefore took advantage of the fact that the envelope bore the address "Reich Chancellor Adolf Hitler." "These recommendations of the late President," he said, "are given to me personally. Later I shall decide if and when I shall permit their publication." In vain I begged him to publish both documents. The only one handed to his press chief for publication was Hindenburg's account of his service, in which he included praise of Hitler.[31]

What happened to the second document recommending that not Hitler but a Hohenzollern become head of state Papen does not say and perhaps does not know. Since it has never turned up among the hundreds of tons of captured secret Nazi documents it is likely that Hitler lost no time in destroying it.

Perhaps it would have made little difference if Hitler had been courageous and honest enough to publish it. Even before Hindenburg's death, he had made the cabinet promulgate a law giving him the President's powers. This was on August 1, the day before the Field Marshal died. That the "law" was illegal also made little difference in a Germany where the former Austrian corporal had now become the law itself. That it was illegal was obvious. On December 17, 1932, during the Schleicher government, the Reichstag had passed by the necessary two-thirds majority an amendment to the constitution providing that the president of the High Court of Justice, instead of the Chancellor, should act as President until a new election could be held. And while the Enabling Act, which was the "legal" basis of Hitler's dictatorship, gave the Chancellor the right to make laws which deviated from the constitution, it specifically forbade him to tamper with the institution of the Presidency.

But what mattered the law now? It mattered not to Papen, who cheerfully went off to serve Hitler as minister in Vienna and smooth over the mess caused by the murder of Chancellor Dollfuss by the Nazis. It mattered not to the generals, who went eagerly to work to build up Hitler's Army. It mattered not to the industrialists, who turned enthusiastically to the profitable business of rearmament. Conservatives of the old school, "decent" Germans like Baron von Neurath in the Foreign Office and Dr. Schacht in the Reichsbank, did not resign. No one resigned. In fact, Dr. Schacht took on the added duties of Minister of Economics on August 2, the day Hitler seized the powers of the expiring President.

And the German people? On August 19, some 95 per cent of those who had registered went to the polls, and 90 per cent, more than thirty-eight million of them, voted approval of Hitler's usurpation of complete power. Only four and a quarter million Germans had the courage—or the desire—to vote "No."

No wonder that Hitler was in a confident mood when the Nazi Party Congress assembled in Nuremberg on September 4. I watched him on the morning of the next day stride like a conquering emperor down the center aisle of the great flag-bedecked Luitpold Hall while the band blared forth "The Badenweiler March" and thirty thousand hands were raised in the Nazi salute. A few moments later he sat proudly in the center of the vast stage with folded arms and shining eyes as Gauleiter Adolf Wagner of Bavaria read the Fuehrer's proclamation.

The German form of life is definitely determined for the next thousand years. The Age of Nerves of the nineteenth century has found its close with us. There will be no other revolution in Germany for the next one thousand years!

Being mortal, he would not live a thousand years, but as long as he lived he would rule this great people as the most powerful and ruthless autocrat they had ever had. The venerable Hindenburg was no longer there to dispute his authority, the Army was in his hands, bound to obedience by an oath no German soldier would lightly break. Indeed, all Germany and all the Germans were in his bloodstained hands now that the last recalcitrants had been done away with or had disappeared for good.

"It is wonderful!" he exulted at Nuremberg to the foreign correspondents at the end of the exhausting week of parades, speeches, pagan pageantry and the most frenzied adulation for a public figure this writer had ever seen. Adolf Hitler had come a long way from the gutters of Vienna. He was only forty-five, and this was just the beginning. Even one returning to Germany for the first time since the death of the Republic could see that, whatever his crimes against humanity, Hitler had unleashed a dynamic force of incalculable proportions which had long been pent up in the German people. To what purpose, he had already made clear in the pages of *Mein Kampf* and in a hundred speeches which had gone unnoticed or unheeded or been ridiculed by so many—by almost everyone—within and especially without the Third Reich.

8

LIFE IN THE THIRD REICH:

1933–37

I T WAS AT THIS TIME, in the late summer of 1934, that I came to live and work in the Third Reich. There was much that impressed, puzzled and troubled a foreign observer about the new Germany. The overwhelming majority of Germans did not seem to mind that their personal freedom had been taken away, that so much of their culture had been destroyed and replaced with a mindless barbarism, or that their life and work had become regimented to a degree never before experienced even by a people accustomed for generations to a great deal of regimentation.

In the background, to be sure, there lurked the terror of the Gestapo and the fear of the concentration camp for those who got out of line or who had been Communists or Socialists or too liberal or too pacifist, or who were Jews. The Blood Purge of June 30, 1934, was a warning of how ruthless the new leaders could be. Yet the Nazi terror in the early years affected the lives of relatively few Germans and a newly arrived observer was somewhat surprised to see that the people of this country did not seem to feel that they were being cowed and held down by an unscrupulous and brutal dictatorship. On the contrary, they supported it with genuine enthusiasm. Somehow it imbued them with a new hope and a new confidence and an astonishing faith in the future of their country.

Hitler was liquidating the past, with all its frustrations and disappointments. Step by step, and rapidly (as we shall see in detail later), he was freeing Germany from the shackles of Versailles, confounding the victorious Allies and making Germany militarily strong again. This was what most Germans wanted and they were willing to make the sacrifices which the Leader demanded of them to get it: the loss of personal freedom, a Spartan diet ("Guns before Butter") and hard work. By the autumn of 1936 the problem of unemployment had been largely licked, almost everyone had a job again* and one heard workers who had been deprived of their trade-union rights joking, over their full dinner pails,

---

* From February 1933 to the spring of 1937, the number of registered unemployed fell from six million to less than one million.

that at least under Hitler there was no more freedom to starve. *"Gemein-nutz vor Eigennutz!"* (The Common Interest before Self!) was a popular Nazi slogan in those days, and though many a party leader, Goering above all, was secretly enriching himself and the profits of business were mounting, there was no doubt that the masses were taken in by the new "national socialism" which ostensibly put the welfare of the community above one's personal gain.

The racial laws which excluded the Jews from the German community seemed to a foreign observer to be a shocking throwback to primitive times, but since the Nazi racial theories exalted the Germans as the salt of the earth and the master race they were far from being unpopular. A few Germans one met—former Socialists or liberals or devout Christians from the old conservative classes—were disgusted or even revolted by the persecution of the Jews, but though they helped to alleviate hardship in a number of individual cases they did nothing to help stem the tide. What could they do? They would often put the question to you, and it was not an easy one to answer.

The Germans heard vaguely in their censored press and broadcasts of the revulsion abroad but they noticed that it did not prevent foreigners from flocking to the Third Reich and seemingly enjoying its hospitality. For Nazi Germany, much more than Soviet Russia, was open for all the world to see.* The tourist business thrived and brought in vast sums of badly needed foreign currency. Apparently the Nazi leaders had nothing to hide. A foreigner, no matter how anti-Nazi, could come to Germany and see and study what he liked—with the exception of the concentration camps and, as in all countries, the military installations. And many did. And many returned who if they were not converted were at least rendered tolerant of the "new Germany" and believed that they had seen, as they said, "positive achievements." Even a man as perspicacious as Lloyd George, who had led England to victory over Germany in 1918, and who in that year had campaigned with an election slogan of "Hang the Kaiser" could visit Hitler at Obersalzberg in 1936 and go away enchanted with the Fuehrer and praise him publicly as "a great man" who had the vision and the will to solve a modern nation's social problems—above all, unemployment, a sore which still festered in England and in regard to which the great wartime Liberal leader with his program We Can Conquer Unemployment had found so little interest at home.

The Olympic games held in Berlin in August 1936 afforded the Nazis a golden opportunity to impress the world with the achievements of the Third Reich, and they made the most of it. The signs *"Juden uner-*

---

* Also, in contrast to the Soviet Union, Nazi Germany permitted all but a few thousand of its citizens who were in the black book of the secret police to travel abroad, though this was severely curtailed by currency restrictions because of the country's lack of foreign exchange. However, the currency restrictions were no more stringent than those for British citizens after 1945. The point is that the Nazi rulers did not seem to be worried that the average German would be contaminated by anti-Nazism if he visited the democratic countries.

wuenscht" (Jews Not Welcome) were quietly hauled down from the shops, hotels, beer gardens and places of public entertainment, the persecution of the Jews and of the two Christian churches temporarily halted, and the country put on its best behavior. No previous games had seen such a spectacular organization nor such a lavish display of entertainment. Goering, Ribbentrop and Goebbels gave dazzling parties for the foreign visitors—the Propaganda Minister's "Italian Night" on the Pfaueninsel near Wannsee gathered more than a thousand guests at dinner in a scene that resembled the Arabian Nights. The visitors, especially those from England and America, were greatly impressed by what they saw: apparently a happy, healthy, friendly people united under Hitler—a far different picture, they said, than they had got from reading the newspaper dispatches from Berlin.

And yet underneath the surface, hidden from the tourists during those splendid late-summer Olympic days in Berlin and indeed overlooked by most Germans or accepted by them with a startling passivity, there seemed to be—to a foreigner at least—a degrading transformation of German life.

There was nothing hidden, of course, about the laws which Hitler decreed against the Jews or about the government-sponsored persecution of these hapless people. The so-called Nuremberg Laws of September 15, 1935, deprived the Jews of German citizenship, confining them to the status of "subjects." It also forbade marriage between Jews and Aryans as well as extramarital relations between them, and it prohibited Jews from employing female Aryan servants under thirty-five years of age. In the next few years some thirteen decrees supplementing the Nuremberg Laws would outlaw the Jew completely. But already by the summer of 1936, when the Germany which was host to the Olympic games was enchanting the visitors from the West, the Jews had been excluded either by law or by Nazi terror—the latter often preceded the former—from public and private employment to such an extent that at least one half of them were without means of livelihood. In the first year of the Third Reich, 1933, they had been excluded from public office, the civil service, journalism, radio, farming, teaching, the theater, the films; in 1934 they were kicked out of the stock exchanges, and though the ban on their practicing the professions of law and medicine or engaging in business did not come legally until 1938 they were in practice removed from these fields by the time the first four-year period of Nazi rule had come to an end.

Moreover, they were denied not only most of the amenities of life but often even the necessities. In many a town the Jew found it difficult if not impossible to purchase food. Over the doors of the grocery and butcher shops, the bakeries and the dairies, were signs, "Jews Not Admitted." In many communities Jews could not procure milk even for their young children. Pharmacies would not sell them drugs or medicine. Hotels would not give them a night's lodging. And always, wherever they went, were the taunting signs "Jews Strictly Forbidden in This Town" or "Jews Enter This Place at Their Own Risk." At a sharp bend in the road near

Ludwigshafen was a sign, "Drive Carefully! Sharp Curve! Jews 75 Miles an Hour!"*

Such was the plight of the Jews at about the time the Festival of the Olympics was held in Germany. It was but the beginning of a road that would soon lead to their extinction by massacre.

THE PERSECUTION OF THE CHRISTIAN CHURCHES

The Nazi war on the Christian churches began more moderately. Though Hitler, nominally a Catholic, had inveighed against political Catholicism in *Mein Kampf* and attacked both of the Christian churches for their failure to recognize the racial problem, he had, as we have seen, warned in his book that "a political party must never . . . lose sight of the fact that in all previous historical experience a purely political party has never succeeded in producing a religious reformation." Article 24 of the party program had demanded "liberty for all religious denominations in the State so far as they are not a danger to . . . the moral feelings of the German race. The party stands for positive Christianity." In his speech of March 23, 1933, to the Reichstag when the legislative body of Germany abandoned its functions to the dictator, Hitler paid tribute to the Christian faiths as "essential elements for safeguarding the soul of the German people," promised to respect their rights, declared that his government's "ambition is a peaceful accord between Church and State" and added—with an eye to the votes of the Catholic Center Party, which he received—that "we hope to improve our friendly relations with the Holy See."

Scarcely four months later, on July 20, the Nazi government concluded a concordat with the Vatican in which it guaranteed the freedom of the Catholic religion and the right of the Church "to regulate her own affairs." The agreement, signed on behalf of Germany by Papen and of the Holy See by the then Papal Secretary of State, Monsignor Pacelli, later Pope Pius XII, was hardly put to paper before it was being broken by the Nazi government. But coming as it did at a moment when the first excesses of the new regime in Germany had provoked world-wide revulsion, the concordat undoubtedly lent the Hitler government much badly needed prestige.†

On July 25, five days after the ratification of the concordat, the German government promulgated a sterilization law, which particularly offended

---

* The author was violently attacked in the German press and on the radio, and threatened with expulsion, for having written a dispatch saying that some of these anti-Semitic signs were being removed for the duration of the Olympic games.

† In an allocution to the Sacred College on June 2, 1945, Pope Pius XII defended the concordat which he had signed, but described National Socialism, as he later came to know it, as "the arrogant apostasy from Jesus Christ, the denial of His doctrine and of His work of redemption, the cult of violence, the idolatry of race and blood, the overthrow of human liberty and dignity."

the Catholic Church. Five days later the first steps were taken to dissolve the Catholic Youth League. During the next years thousands of Catholic priests, nuns and lay leaders were arrested, many of them on trumped-up charges of "immorality" or of "smuggling foreign currency." Erich Klausener, leader of Catholic Action, was, as we have seen, murdered in the June 30, 1934, purge. Scores of Catholic publications were suppressed, and even the sanctity of the confessional was violated by Gestapo agents. By the spring of 1937 the Catholic hierarchy in Germany, which, like most of the Protestant clergy, had at first tried to co-operate with the new regime, was thoroughly disillusioned. On March 14, 1937, Pope Pius XI issued an encyclical, "Mit Brennender Sorge" (With Burning Sorrow), charging the Nazi government with "evasion" and "violation" of the concordat and accusing it of sowing "the tares of suspicion, discord, hatred, calumny, of secret and open fundamental hostility to Christ and His Church." On "the horizon of Germany" the Pope saw "the threatening storm clouds of destructive religious wars . . . which have no other aim than . . . of extermination."

The Reverend Martin Niemoeller had personally welcomed the coming to power of the Nazis in 1933. In that year his autobiography, *From U-Boat to Pulpit,* had been published. The story of how this submarine commander in the First World War had become a prominent Protestant pastor was singled out for special praise in the Nazi press and became a best seller. To Pastor Niemoeller, as to many a Protestant clergyman, the fourteen years of the Republic had been, as he said, "years of darkness"[1] and at the close of his autobiography he added a note of satisfaction that the Nazi revolution had finally triumphed and that it had brought about the "national revival" for which he himself had fought so long— for a time in the free corps, from which so many Nazi leaders had come.

He was soon to experience a terrible disillusionment.

The Protestants in Germany, as in the United States, were a divided faith. Only a very few—some 150,000 out of forty-five million of them— belonged to the various Free Churches such as the Baptists and Methodists. The rest belonged to twenty-eight Lutheran and Reformed Churches of which the largest was the Church of the Old Prussian Union, with eighteen million members. With the rise of National Socialism there came further divisions among the Protestants. The more fanatical Nazis among them organized in 1932 "The German Christians' Faith Movement" of which the most vehement leader was a certain Ludwig Mueller, army chaplain of the East Prussian Military District, a devoted follower of Hitler who had first brought the Fuehrer together with General von Blomberg when the latter commanded the district. The "German Christians" ardently supported the Nazi doctrines of race and the leadership principle and wanted them applied to a Reich Church which would bring all Protestants into one all-embracing body. In 1933 the "German Christians" had some three thousand out of a total of seventeen thousand pastors, though their lay followers probably represented a larger percentage of churchgoers.

Opposed to the "German Christians" was another minority group which called itself the "Confessional Church." It had about the same number of pastors and was eventually led by Niemoeller. It opposed the Nazification of the Protestant churches, rejected the Nazi racial theories and denounced the anti-Christian doctrines of Rosenberg and other Nazi leaders. In between lay the majority of Protestants, who seemed too timid to join either of the two warring groups, who sat on the fence and eventually, for the most part, landed in the arms of Hitler, accepting his authority to intervene in church affairs and obeying his commands without open protest.

It is difficult to understand the behavior of most German Protestants in the first Nazi years unless one is aware of two things: their history and the influence of Martin Luther.* The great founder of Protestantism was both a passionate anti-Semite and a ferocious believer in absolute obedience to political authority. He wanted Germany rid of the Jews and when they were sent away he advised that they be deprived of "all their cash and jewels and silver and gold" and, furthermore, "that their synagogues or schools be set on fire, that their houses be broken up and destroyed . . . and they be put under a roof or stable, like the gypsies . . . in misery and captivity as they incessantly lament and complain to God about us" —advice that was literally followed four centuries later by Hitler, Goering and Himmler.[2]

In what was perhaps the only popular revolt in German history, the peasant uprising of 1525, Luther advised the princes to adopt the most ruthless measures against the "mad dogs," as he called the desperate, downtrodden peasants. Here, as in his utterances about the Jews, Luther employed a coarseness and brutality of language unequaled in German history until the Nazi time. The influence of this towering figure extended down the generations in Germany, especially among the Protestants. Among other results was the ease with which German Protestantism became the instrument of royal and princely absolutism from the sixteenth century until the kings and princes were overthrown in 1918. The hereditary monarchs and petty rulers became the supreme bishops of the Protestant Church in their lands. Thus in Prussia the Hohenzollern King was the head of the Church. In no country with the exception of Czarist Russia did the clergy become by tradition so completely servile to the political authority of the State. Its members, with few exceptions, stood solidly behind the King, the Junkers and the Army, and during the nineteenth century they dutifully opposed the rising liberal and democratic movements. Even the Weimar Republic was anathema to most Protestant pastors, not only because it had deposed the kings and princes but because it drew its

---

* To avoid any misunderstanding, it might be well to point out here that the author is a Protestant.

main support from the Catholics and the Socialists. During the Reichstag elections one could not help but notice that the Protestant clergy—Niemoeller was typical—quite openly supported the Nationalist and even the Nazi enemies of the Republic. Like Niemoeller, most of the pastors welcomed the advent of Adolf Hitler to the chancellorship in 1933.

They were soon to become acquainted with the very strong-arm Nazi tactics which had swept Hitler to political power. In July 1933 representatives of the Protestant churches had written a constitution for a new "Reich Church," and it was formally recognized by the Reichstag on July 14. Immediately there broke out a heated struggle over the election of the first Reich Bishop. Hitler insisted that his friend, Chaplain Mueller, whom he had appointed his adviser on Protestant church affairs, be given this highest office. The leaders of the Church Federation proposed an eminent divine, Pastor Friedrich von Bodelschwingh. But they were naïve. The Nazi government intervened, dissolved a number of provincial church organizations, suspended from office several leading dignitaries of the Protestant churches, loosed the S.A. and the Gestapo on recalcitrant clergymen—in fact, terrorized all who supported Bodelschwingh. On the eve of the elections of delegates to the synod which would elect the Reich Bishop, Hitler personally took to the radio to "urge" the election of "German Christians" whose candidate Mueller was. The intimidation was highly successful. Bodelschwingh in the meantime had been forced to withdraw his candidacy, and the "elections" returned a majority of "German Christians," who in September at the synod in Wittenberg, where Luther had first defied Rome, elected Mueller Reich Bishop.

But the new head of the Church, a heavy-handed man, was not able to establish a unified Church or to completely Nazify the Protestant congregations. On November 13, 1933, the day after the German people had overwhelmingly backed Hitler in a national plebiscite, the "German Christians" staged a massive rally in the Sportpalast in Berlin. A Dr. Reinhardt Krause, the Berlin district leader of the sect, proposed the abandonment of the Old Testament, "with its tales of cattle merchants and pimps" and the revision of the New Testament with the teaching of Jesus "corresponding entirely with the demands of National Socialism." Resolutions were drawn up demanding "One People, One Reich, One Faith," requiring all pastors to take an oath of allegiance to Hitler and insisting that all churches institute the Aryan paragraph and exclude converted Jews. This was too much even for the timid Protestants who had declined to take any part in the church war, and Bishop Mueller was forced to suspend Dr. Krause and disavow him.

In reality the struggle between the Nazi government and the churches was the age-old one of what to render unto Caesar and what to God. So far as the Protestants were concerned, Hitler was insistent that if the Nazi "German Christians" could not bring the evangelical churches into line under Reich Bishop Mueller then the government itself would have to take over the direction of the churches. He had always had a certain contempt for the Protestants, who, though a tiny minority in his native Catholic Austria, comprised two thirds of the citizens of Germany. "You can do anything you want with them," he once confided to his aides. "They will submit . . . they are insignificant little people, submissive as dogs, and they sweat with embarrassment when you talk to them."[3] He was well aware that the resistance to the Nazification of the Protestant churches came from a minority of pastors and an even smaller minority of worshipers.

By the beginning of 1934, the disillusioned Pastor Niemoeller had become the guiding spirit of the minority resistance in both the "Confessional Church" and the Pastors' Emergency League. At the General Synod in Barmen in May 1934, and at a special meeting in Niemoeller's Church of Jesus Christ at Dahlem, a suburb of Berlin, in November, the "Confessional Church" declared itself to be the legitimate Protestant Church of Germany and set up a provisional church government. Thus there were now two groups—Reich Bishop Mueller's and Niemoeller's— claiming to legally constitute the Church.

It was obvious that the former army chaplain, despite his closeness to Hitler, had failed to integrate the Protestant churches, and at the end of 1935, after the Gestapo had arrested seven hundred "Confessional Church" pastors, he resigned his office and faded out of the picture. Already, in July 1935, Hitler had appointed a Nazi lawyer friend, Dr. Hans Kerrl, to be Minister for Church Affairs, with instructions to make a second attempt to co-ordinate the Protestants. One of the milder Nazis and a somewhat cautious man, Kerrl at first had considerable success. He succeeded not only in winning over the conservative clergy, which constituted the majority, but in setting up a Church Committee headed by the venerable Dr. Zoellner, who was respected by all factions, to work out a general settlement. Though Niemoeller's group co-operated with the committee, it still maintained that it was the only legitimate Church. When, in May 1936, it addressed a courteous but firm memorandum to Hitler protesting against the anti-Christian tendencies of the regime, denouncing the government's anti-Semitism and demanding an end to State interference in the churches, Frick, the Nazi Minister of the Interior, responded with ruthless action. Hundreds of "Confessional Church" pastors were arrested, one of the signers of the memorandum, Dr. Weissler, was murdered in the Sachsenhausen concentration camp, the funds of the "Confessional Church" were confiscated and it was forbidden to make collections.

On February 12, 1937, Dr. Zoellner resigned from the Church Committee—he had been restrained by the Gestapo from visiting Luebeck, where nine Protestant pastors had been arrested—complaining that his work had been sabotaged by the Church Minister. Dr. Kerrl replied the next day in a speech to a group of submissive churchmen. He accused the venerable Zoellner of failing to appreciate the Nazi doctrine of Race, Blood and Soil, and clearly revealed the government's hostility to both Protestant and Catholic churches.

The party [Kerrl said] stands on the basis of Positive Christianity, and Positive Christianity *is* National Socialism . . . National Socialism is the doing of God's will . . . God's will reveals itself in German blood . . . Dr. Zoellner and Count Galen [the Catholic bishop of Muenster] have tried to make clear to me that Christianity consists in faith in Christ as the Son of God. That makes me laugh . . . No, Christianity is not dependent upon the Apostle's Creed . . . True Christianity is represented by the party, and the German people are now called by the party and especially by the Fuehrer to a real Christianity . . . The Fuehrer is the herald of a new revelation.[4]

On the first of July, 1937, Dr. Niemoeller was arrested and confined to Moabit prison in Berlin. On June 27 he had preached to the congregation, which always overflowed his church at Dahlem, what was to be his last sermon in the Third Reich. As if he had a foreboding of what was to come he said, "We have no more thought of using our own powers to escape the arm of the authorities than had the Apostles of old. No more are we ready to keep silent at man's behest when God commands us to speak. For it is, and must remain, the case that we must obey God rather than man."

After eight months in prison he was tried on March 2, 1938, before a *Sondergericht,* one of the "Special Courts" set up by the Nazis to try offenders against the State, and though acquitted of the main charge of "underhand attacks against the State" was fined two thousand marks and sentenced to seven months' imprisonment for "abuse of the pulpit" and holding collections in his church. Since he had served more than this time, the court ordered his release, but he was seized by the Gestapo as he was leaving the courtroom, placed in "protective custody" and confined in concentration camps, first at Sachsenhausen and then at Dachau, where he remained for seven years until liberated by Allied troops.

Some 807 other pastors and leading laymen of the "Confessional Church" were arrested in 1937, and hundreds more in the next couple of years. If the resistance of the Niemoeller wing of the church was not completely broken, it was certainly bent. As for the majority of Protestant pastors, they, like almost everyone else in Germany, submitted in the face of Nazi terror. By the end of 1937 the highly respected Bishop Marahrens of Hanover was induced by Dr. Kerrl to make a public declaration that must have seemed especially humiliating to tougher men of God such as Niemoeller: "The National Socialist conception of life is the national and political teaching which determines and characterizes German manhood. As such, it is obligatory upon German Christians also." In the spring of 1938 Bishop Marahrens took the final step of ordering all pastors in his diocese to swear a personal oath of allegiance to the Fuehrer. In a short time the vast majority of Protestant clergymen took the oath, thus binding themselves legally and morally to obey the commands of the dictator.

It would be misleading to give the impression that the persecution of

Protestants and Catholics by the Nazi State tore the German people asunder or even greatly aroused the vast majority of them. It did not. A people who had so lightly given up their political and cultural and economic freedoms were not, except for a relatively few, going to die or even risk imprisonment to preserve freedom of worship. What really aroused the Germans in the Thirties were the glittering successes of Hitler in providing jobs, creating prosperity, restoring Germany's military might, and moving from one triumph to another in his foreign policy. Not many Germans lost much sleep over the arrests of a few thousand pastors and priests or over the quarreling of the various Protestant sects. And even fewer paused to reflect that under the leadership of Rosenberg, Bormann and Himmler, who were backed by Hitler, the Nazi regime intended eventually to destroy Christianity in Germany, if it could, and substitute the old paganism of the early tribal Germanic gods and the new paganism of the Nazi extremists. As Bormann, one of the men closest to Hitler, said publicly in 1941, "National Socialism and Christianity are irreconcilable."

What the Hitler government envisioned for Germany was clearly set out in a thirty-point program for the "National Reich Church" drawn up during the war by Rosenberg, an outspoken pagan, who among his other offices held that of "the Fuehrer's Delegate for the Entire Intellectual and Philosophical Education and Instruction for the National Socialist Party." A few of its thirty articles convey the essentials:

1. The National Reich Church of Germany categorically claims the exclusive right and the exclusive power to control all churches within the borders of the Reich: it declares these to be national churches of the German Reich.

5. The National Church is determined to exterminate irrevocably . . . the strange and foreign Christian faiths imported into Germany in the ill-omened year 800.

7. The National Church has no scribes, pastors, chaplains or priests, but National Reich orators are to speak in them.

13. The National Church demands immediate cessation of the publishing and dissemination of the Bible in Germany . . .

14. The National Church declares that to it, and therefore to the German nation, it has been decided that the Fuehrer's Mein Kampf is the greatest of all documents. It . . . not only contains the greatest but it embodies the purest and truest ethics for the present and future life of our nation.

18. The National Church will clear away from its altars all crucifixes, Bibles and pictures of saints.

19. On the altars there must be nothing but Mein Kampf (to the German nation and therefore to God the most sacred book) and to the left of the altar a sword.

30. On the day of its foundation, the Christian Cross must be removed from all churches, cathedrals and chapels . . . and it must be superseded by the only unconquerable symbol, the swastika.[5]

THE NAZIFICATION OF CULTURE

On the evening of May 10, 1933, some four and a half months after Hitler became Chancellor, there occurred in Berlin a scene which had not been witnessed in the Western world since the late Middle Ages. At about midnight a torchlight parade of thousands of students ended at a square on Unter den Linden opposite the University of Berlin. Torches were put to a huge pile of books that had been gathered there, and as the flames enveloped them more books were thrown on the fire until some twenty thousand had been consumed. Similar scenes took place in several other cities. The book burning had begun.

Many of the books tossed into the flames in Berlin that night by the joyous students under the approving eye of Dr. Goebbels had been written by authors of world reputation. They included, among German writers, Thomas and Heinrich Mann, Lion Feuchtwanger, Jakob Wassermann, Arnold and Stefan Zweig, Erich Maria Remarque, Walther Rathenau, Albert Einstein, Alfred Kerr and Hugo Preuss, the last named being the scholar who had drafted the Weimar Constitution. But not only the works of dozens of German writers were burned. A good many foreign authors were also included: Jack London, Upton Sinclair, Helen Keller, Margaret Sanger, H. G. Wells, Havelock Ellis, Arthur Schnitzler, Freud, Gide, Zola, Proust. In the words of a student proclamation, any book was condemned to the flames "which acts subversively on our future or strikes at the root of German thought, the German home and the driving forces of our people."

Dr. Goebbels, the new Propaganda Minister, who from now on was to put German culture into a Nazi strait jacket, addressed the students as the burning books turned to ashes. "The soul of the German people can again express itself. These flames not only illuminate the final end of an old era; they also light up the new."

The new Nazi era of German culture was illuminated not only by the bonfires of books and the more effective, if less symbolic, measures of proscribing the sale or library circulation of hundreds of volumes and the publishing of many new ones, but by the regimentation of culture on a scale which no modern Western nation had ever experienced. As early as September 22, 1933, the Reich Chamber of Culture had been set up by law under the direction of Dr. Goebbels. Its purpose was defined, in the words of the law, as follows: "In order to pursue a policy of German culture, it is necessary to gather together the creative artists in all spheres into a unified organization under the leadership of the Reich. The Reich must not only determine the lines of progress, mental and spiritual, but also lead and organize the professions."

Seven subchambers were established to guide and control every sphere of cultural life: the Reich chambers of fine arts, music, the theater, literature, the press, radio and the films. All persons engaged in these fields were obligated to join their respective chambers, whose decisions and directives had the validity of law. Among other powers, the chambers could expel—or refuse to accept—members for "political unreliability," which meant that those who were even lukewarm about National Socialism could be, and usually were, excluded from practicing their profession or art and thus deprived of a livelihood.

No one who lived in Germany in the Thirties, and who cared about such matters, can ever forget the sickening decline of the cultural standards of a people who had had such high ones for so long a time. This was inevitable, of course, the moment the Nazi leaders decided that the arts, literature, the press, radio and the films must serve exclusively the propaganda purposes of the new regime and its outlandish philosophy. Not a single living German writer of any importance, with the exception of Ernst Juenger and Ernst Wiechert in the earlier years, was published in Germany during the Nazi time. Almost all of them, led by Thomas Mann, emigrated; the few who remained were silent or were silenced. Every manuscript of a book or a play had to be submitted to the Propaganda Ministry before it could be approved for publication or production.

Music fared best, if only because it was the least political of the arts and because the Germans had such a rich store of it from Bach through Beethoven and Mozart to Brahms. But the playing of Mendelssohn was banned because he was a Jew (the works of all Jewish composers were *verboten*) as was the music of Germany's leading modern composer, Paul Hindemith. Jews were quickly weeded out of the great symphony orchestras and the opera. Unlike the writers, most of the great figures of the German music world chose to remain in Nazi Germany and indeed lent their names and their talent to the New Order. Wilhelm Furtwaengler, one of the finest conductors of the century, remained. He was out of favor for a year in 1934 because of his defense of Hindemith, but returned to activity for the remaining years of Hitler's rule. Richard Strauss, perhaps the world's leading living composer, remained and indeed for a time became president of the Reich Music Chamber, lending his great name to Goebbels' prostituting of culture. Walter Gieseking, the eminent pianist, spent much of his time making tours in foreign countries which were organized or approved by the Propaganda Minister to promote German "culture" abroad. But because the musicians did not emigrate and because of Germany's great treasure of classical music, one could hear during the days of the Third Reich symphony music and opera performed magnificently. In this the Berlin Philharmonic Orchestra and the Berlin State Opera were pre-eminent. The excellent music fare did much to make people forget the degradation of the other arts and of so much of life under the Nazis.

The theater, it must be said, retained much of its excellence as long as it stuck to classical plays. Max Reinhardt, of course, was gone, along with all other Jewish producers, directors and actors. The Nazi playwrights were so ludicrously bad that the public stayed away from their offerings, which invariably had short runs. The president of the Reich Theater Chamber was one Hans Johst, an unsuccessful playwright who once had publicly boasted that whenever someone mentioned the word "culture" to him he wanted to reach for his revolver. But even Johst and Goebbels, who determined what was played on the stage and who played and directed it, were unable to prevent the German theater from giving commendable and often moving performances of Goethe, Schiller and Shakespeare.

Strangely enough, some of Shaw's plays were permitted to be performed in Nazi Germany—perhaps because he poked fun at Englishmen and lampooned democracy and perhaps too because his wit and left-wing political views escaped the Nazi mind.

Strangest of all was the case of Germany's great playwright, Gerhart Hauptmann. Because he had been an ardent Socialist his plays had been banned from the imperial theaters during Kaiser Wilhelm II's time. During the Republic he had been the most popular playwright in Germany, and indeed he retained that position in the Third Reich. His plays continued to be produced. I shall never forget the scene at the close of the first night of his last play, *The Daughter of the Cathedral,* when Hauptmann, a venerable figure with his flowing white hair tumbling down over his black cape, strode out of the theater arm in arm with Dr. Goebbels and Johst. He, like so many other eminent Germans, had made his peace with Hitler, and Goebbels, a shrewd man, had made much effective propaganda out of it, tirelessly reminding the German people and the outside world that Germany's greatest living playwright, a former Socialist and the champion of the common man, had not only remained in the Third Reich but had continued to write and have his plays produced.

How sincere or opportunistic or merely changeable this aging playwright was may be gathered from what happened after the war. The American authorities, believing that Hauptmann had served the Nazis too well, banned his plays from the theaters in their sector in West Berlin. Whereupon the Russians invited him to Berlin, welcomed him as a hero and staged a gala cycle of his plays in East Berlin. And on October 6, 1945, Hauptmann sent a message to the Communist-dominated "Kulturbund for the Democratic Revival of Germany" wishing it well and expressing the hope that it would succeed in bringing about a "spiritual rebirth" of the German people.

The Germany which had given the world a Duerer and a Cranach had not been pre-eminent in the fine arts in modern times, though German expressionism in painting and the Munich Bauhaus architecture were interesting and original movements and German artists had participated in all the twentieth-century evolutions and eruptions represented by impressionism, cubism and Dadaism.

To Hitler, who considered himself a genuine artist despite his early failures as one in Vienna, all modern art was degenerate and senseless. In *Mein Kampf* he had delivered a long tirade on the subject, and one of his first acts after coming to power was to "cleanse" Germany of its "decadent" art and to attempt to substitute a new "Germanic" art. Some 6,500 modern paintings—not only the works of Germans such as Kokoschka and Grosz but those of Cézanne, Van Gogh, Gauguin, Matisse, Picasso and many others—were removed from German museums.

What was to replace them was shown in the summer of 1937 when Hitler formally opened the "House of German Art" in Munich in a drab, pseudoclassic building which he had helped design and which he described as "unparalleled and inimitable" in its architecture. In this first exhibition of Nazi art were crammed some nine hundred works, selected from fifteen thousand submitted, of the worst junk this writer has ever seen in any country. Hitler himself made the final selection and, according to some of the party comrades who were with him at the time, had become so incensed at some of the paintings accepted by the Nazi jury presided over by Adolf Ziegler, a mediocre painter who was president of the Reich Chamber of Art,* that he had not only ordered them thrown out but had kicked holes with his jack boot through several of them. "I was always determined," he said in a long speech inaugurating the exhibition, "if fate ever gave us power, not to discuss these matters [of artistic judgment] but to make decisions." And he had made them.

In his speech—it was delivered on July 18, 1937—he laid down the Nazi line for "German art":

Works of art that cannot be understood but need a swollen set of instructions to prove their right to exist and find their way to neurotics who are receptive to such stupid or insolent nonsense will no longer openly reach the German nation. Let no one have illusions! National Socialism has set out to purge the German Reich and our people of all those influences threatening its existence and character . . . With the opening of this exhibition has come the end of artistic lunacy and with it the artistic pollution of our people . . .

And yet some Germans at least, especially in the art center of Germany which Munich was, preferred to be artistically polluted. In another part of the city in a ramshackle gallery that had to be reached through a narrow stairway was an exhibition of "degenerate art" which Dr. Goebbels had organized to show the people what Hitler was rescuing them from. It contained a splendid selection of modern paintings—Kokoschka, Chagall and expressionist and impressionist works. The day I visited it, after panting through the sprawling House of German Art, it was crammed, with a long line forming down the creaking stairs and out into the street. In fact, the crowds besieging it became so great that Dr. Goebbels, incensed and embarrassed, soon closed it.

THE CONTROL OF PRESS, RADIO, FILMS

Every morning the editors of the Berlin daily newspapers and the correspondents of those published elsewhere in the Reich gathered at the

---

* Ziegler owed his position to the happy circumstance that he had painted the portrait of Geli Raubal.

Propaganda Ministry to be told by Dr. Goebbels or by one of his aides what news to print and suppress, how to write the news and headline it, what campaigns to call off or institute and what editorials were desired for the day. In case of any misunderstanding a daily written directive was furnished along with the oral instructions. For the smaller out-of-town papers and the periodicals the directives were dispatched by telegram or by mail.

To be an editor in the Third Reich one had to be, in the first place, politically and racially "clean." The Reich Press Law of October 4, 1933, which made journalism a "public vocation," regulated by law, stipulated that all editors must possess German citizenship, be of Aryan descent and not married to a Jew. Section 14 of the Press Law ordered editors "to keep out of the newspapers anything which in any manner is misleading to the public, mixes selfish aims with community aims, tends to weaken the strength of the German Reich, outwardly or inwardly, the common will of the German people, the defense of Germany, its culture and economy . . . or offends the honor and dignity of Germany"—an edict which, if it had been in effect before 1933, would have led to the suppression of every Nazi editor and publication in the country. It now led to the ousting of those journals and journalists who were not Nazi or who declined to become so.

One of the first to be forced out of business was the *Vossische Zeitung*. Founded in 1704 and numbering among its contributors in the past such names as Frederick the Great, Lessing and Rathenau, it had become the leading newspaper of Germany, comparable to the *Times* of London and the New York *Times*. But it was liberal and it was owned by the House of Ullstein, a Jewish firm. It went out of business on April 1, 1934, after 230 years of continuous publication. The *Berliner Tageblatt,* another world-renowned liberal newspaper, lingered on a little longer, until 1937, though its owner, Hans Lackmann-Mosse, a Jew, was forced to surrender his interest in the newspaper in the spring of 1933. Germany's third great liberal newspaper, the *Frankfurter Zeitung,* also continued to publish after divesting itself of its Jewish proprietor and editors. Rudolf Kircher, its London correspondent, an Anglophile and a liberal, became the editor and, like Karl Silex, editor of the conservative *Deutsche Allgemeine Zeitung* of Berlin, who had also been a London correspondent, a Rhodes scholar, a passionate admirer of the British and a liberal, served the Nazis well, often becoming, as Otto Dietrich, the Reich press chief, once said of the former "opposition papers," "more papal than the Pope." That the last three newspapers survived was due partly to the influence of the German Foreign Office, which wanted these internationally known journals as a kind of showpiece to impress the outside world. They gave a respectability to Nazi Germany and at the same time peddled its propaganda.

With all newspapers in Germany being told what to publish and how to write the news and editorials, it was inevitable that a deadly conformity would come over the nation's press. Even a people so regimented and so given to accepting authority became bored by the daily newspapers. Circulation declined even for the leading Nazi daily newspapers such as the morning *Voelkischer Beobachter* and the evening *Der Angriff*. And the total circulation of all journals fell off steeply as one paper after another went under or was taken over by Nazi publishers. In the first four years of the Third Reich the number of daily newspapers declined from 3,607 to 2,671.

But the country's loss of a free and varied press was the party's gain—at least financially. Max Amann, Hitler's top sergeant during the First World War and head of the Eher Verlag, the party's publishing firm, became the financial dictator of the German press. As Reich Leader for the Press and president of the Press Chamber, he had the legal right to suppress any publication he pleased and the consequent power to buy it up for a song. In a short time the Eher Verlag became a gigantic publishing empire, probably the largest and most lucrative in the world.* Despite the drop in sales of many Nazi publications, the daily newspapers owned or controlled by the party or individual Nazis had two thirds of the total daily circulation of twenty-five million by the time of the outbreak of the second war. In an affidavit made at Nuremberg, Amann described how he operated:

After the party came to power in 1933 . . . many of these concerns, such as the Ullstein House, which were owned or controlled by Jewish interests, or by political or religious interests hostile to the Nazi Party, found it expedient to sell their newspapers or assets to the Eher concern. There was no free market for the sale of such properties and the Eher Verlag was generally the only bidder. In this matter the Eher Verlag, together with publishing concerns owned or controlled by it, expanded into a monopoly of the newspaper publishing business in Germany . . . The party investment in these publishing enterprises became financially very successful. It is a true statement to say that the basic purpose of the Nazi press program was to eliminate all the press which was in opposition to the party.[6]

At one period in 1934 both Amann and Goebbels appealed to the obsequious editors to make their papers less monotonous. Amann said he deplored "the present far-reaching uniformity of the press, which is not a product of government measures and does not conform to the will of the government." One rash editor, Ehm Welke of the weekly *Gruene Post*, made the mistake of taking Amann and Goebbels seriously. He chided the Propaganda Ministry for its red tape and for the heavy hand with which it held down the press and made it so dull. His publication was promptly suspended for three months and he himself dismissed by Goebbels and carted off to a concentration camp.

---

* Amann's own income skyrocketed from 108,000 marks in 1934 to 3,800,000 marks in 1942. (Letter to the author from Professor Oron J. Hale, who has made a study of the surviving records of the Nazi publishing firm.)

The radio and the motion pictures were also quickly harnessed to serve the propaganda of the Nazi State. Goebbels had always seen in radio (television had not yet come in) the chief instrument of propaganda in modern society and through the Radio Department of his ministry and the Chamber of Radio he gained complete control of broadcasting and shaped it to his own ends. His task was made easier because in Germany, as in the other countries of Europe, broadcasting was a monopoly owned and operated by the State. In 1933 the Nazi government automatically found itself in possession of the Reich Broadcasting Corporation.

The films remained in the hands of private firms but the Propaganda Ministry and the Chamber of Films controlled every aspect of the industry, their task being—in the words of an official commentary—"to lift the film industry out of the sphere of liberal economic thoughts . . . and thus enable it to receive those tasks which it has to fulfill in the National Socialist State."

The result in both cases was to afflict the German people with radio programs and motion pictures as inane and boring as were the contents of their daily newspapers and periodicals. Even a public which usually submitted without protest to being told what was good for it revolted. The customers stayed away in droves from the Nazi films and jammed the houses which showed the few foreign pictures (mostly B-grade Hollywood) which Goebbels permitted to be exhibited on German screens. At one period in the mid-Thirties the hissing of German films became so common that Wilhelm Frick, the Minister of the Interior, issued a stern warning against "treasonable behavior on the part of cinema audiences." Likewise the radio programs were so roundly criticized that the president of the Radio Chamber, one Horst Dressler-Andress, declared that such carping was "an insult to German culture" and would not be tolerated. In those days, in the Thirties, a German listener could still turn his dial to a score of foreign radio stations without, as happened later when the war began, risking having his head chopped off. And perhaps quite a few did, though it was this observer's impression that as the years went by, Dr. Goebbels proved himself right, in that the radio became by far the regime's most effective means of propaganda, doing more than any other single instrument of communication to shape the German people to Hitler's ends.

I myself was to experience how easily one is taken in by a lying and censored press and radio in a totalitarian state. Though unlike most Germans I had daily access to foreign newspapers, especially those of London, Paris and Zurich, which arrived the day after publication, and though I listened regularly to the BBC and other foreign broadcasts, my job necessitated the spending of many hours a day in combing the German press, checking the German radio, conferring with Nazi officials and going to party meetings. It was surprising and sometimes consternating to find that notwithstanding the opportunities I had to learn the facts and despite one's inherent distrust of what one learned from Nazi sources, a steady diet over the years of falsifications and distortions made a certain impression on one's mind and often misled it. No one who has not lived for years in a totalitarian land can possibly conceive how difficult it is to escape the dread consequences of a regime's calculated and incessant propaganda. Often in a German home or office or sometimes in a casual conversation with a stranger in a restaurant, a beer hall, a café, I would meet with the most outlandish assertions from seemingly educated and intelligent persons. It was obvious that they were parroting some piece of nonsense they had heard on the radio or read in the newspapers. Sometimes one was tempted to say as much, but on such occasions one was met with such a stare of incredulity, such a shock of silence, as if one had blasphemed the Almighty, that one realized how useless it was even to try to make contact with a mind which had become warped and for whom the facts of life had become what Hitler and Goebbels, with their cynical disregard for truth, said they were.

EDUCATION IN THE THIRD REICH

On April 30, 1934, Bernhard Rust, an *Obergruppenfuehrer* in the S.A., onetime Gauleiter of Hanover, a Nazi Party member and friend of Hitler since the early Twenties, was named Reich Minister of Science, Education and Popular Culture. In the bizarre, topsy-turvy world of National Socialism, Rust was eminently fitted for his task. Since 1930 he had been an unemployed provincial schoolmaster, having been dismissed in that year by the local republican authorities at Hanover for certain manifestations of instability of mind, though his fanatical Nazism may have been partly responsible for his ouster. For Dr. Rust preached the Nazi gospel with the zeal of a Goebbels and the fuzziness of a Rosenberg. Named Prussian Minister of Science, Art and Education in February 1933, he boasted that he had succeeded overnight in "liquidating the school as an institution of intellectual acrobatics."

To such a mindless man was now entrusted dictatorial control over German science, the public schools, the institutions of higher learning and the youth organizations. For education in the Third Reich, as Hitler envisaged it, was not to be confined to stuffy classrooms but to be furthered by a Spartan, political and martial training in the successive youth groups and to reach its climax not so much in the universities and engineering colleges, which absorbed but a small minority, but first, at the age of eighteen, in compulsory labor service and then in service, as conscripts, in the armed forces.

Hitler's contempt for "professors" and the intellectual academic life had peppered the pages of *Mein Kampf,* in which he had set down some of his ideas on education. "The whole education by a national state," he had written, "must aim primarily not at the stuffing with mere knowledge but at building bodies which are physically healthy to the core." But, even more important, he had stressed in his book the importance of winning over and then training the youth in the service "of a new national state" —a subject he returned to often after he became the German dictator. "When an opponent declares, 'I will not come over to your side,' " he said in a speech on November 6, 1933, "I calmly say, 'Your child belongs to us already . . . What are you? You will pass on. Your descendants, however, now stand in the new camp. In a short time they will know nothing else but this new community.' " And on May 1, 1937, he declared, "This new Reich will give its youth to no one, but will itself take youth and give to youth its own education and its own upbringing." It was not an idle boast; that was precisely what was happening.

The German schools, from first grade through the universities, were quickly Nazified. Textbooks were hastily rewritten, curricula were changed, *Mein Kampf* was made—in the words of *Der Deutsche Erzieher,* official organ of the educators—"our infallible pedagogical guiding star" and teachers who failed to see the new light were cast out. Most instructors had been more or less Nazi in sentiment when not outright party members. To strengthen their ideology they were dispatched to special schools for intensive training in National Socialist principles, emphasis being put on Hitler's racial doctrines.

Every person in the teaching profession, from kindergarten through the universities, was compelled to join the National Socialist Teachers' League which, by law, was held "responsible for the execution of the ideological and political co-ordination of all teachers in accordance with the National Socialist doctrine." The Civil Service Act of 1937 required teachers to be "the executors of the will of the party-supported State" and to be ready "at any time to defend without reservation the National Socialist State." An earlier decree had classified them as civil servants and thus subject to the racial laws. Jews, of course, were forbidden to teach. All teachers took an oath to "be loyal and obedient to Adolf Hitler." Later, no man could teach who had not first served in the S.A., the Labor Service or the Hitler Youth. Candidates for instructorships in the universities had to attend for six weeks an observation camp where their views and character were studied by Nazi experts and reported to the Ministry of Education, which issued licenses to teach based on the candidates' political "reliability."

Prior to 1933, the German public schools had been under the jurisdiction of the local authorities and the universities under that of the individual states. Now all were brought under the iron rule of the Reich Minister of Education. It was he who also appointed the rectors and the deans of the universities, who formerly had been elected by the full professors of the faculty. He also appointed the leaders of the university students' union, to which all students had to belong, and of the lecturers ûnion, comprising all instructors. The N.S. Association of University Lecturers, under the tight leadership of old Nazi hands, was given a decisive role in selecting who was to teach and to see that what they taught was in accordance with Nazi theories.

The result of so much Nazification was catastrophic for German education and for German learning. History was so falsified in the new text-books and by the teachers in their lectures that it became ludicrous. The teaching of the "racial sciences," exalting the Germans as the master race and the Jews as breeders of almost all the evil there was in the world, was even more so. In the University of Berlin alone, where so many great scholars had taught in the past, the new rector, a storm trooper and by profession a veterinarian, instituted twenty-five new courses in *Rassenkunde*—racial science—and by the time he had really taken the university apart he had eighty-six courses connected with his own profession.

The teaching of the natural sciences, in which Germany had been so pre-eminent for generations, deteriorated rapidly. Great teachers such as Einstein and Franck in physics, Haber, Willstaetter and Warburg in chemistry, were fired or retired. Those who remained, many of them, were bitten by the Nazi aberrations and attempted to apply them to pure science. They began to teach what they called *German* physics, *German* chemistry, *German* mathematics. Indeed, in 1937 there appeared a journal called *Deutsche Mathematik,* and its first editorial solemnly proclaimed that any idea that mathematics could be judged nonracially carried "within itself the germs of destruction of German science."

The hallucinations of these Nazi scientists became unbelievable, even to a layman. "German Physics?" asked Professor Philipp Lenard of Heidelberg University, who was one of the more learned and internationally respected scientists of the Third Reich. " 'But,' it will be replied, 'science is and remains international.' It is false. In reality, science, like every other human product, is racial and conditioned by blood." Professor Rudolphe Tomaschek, director of the Institute of Physics at Dresden, went further. "Modern Physics," he wrote, "is an instrument of [world] Jewry for the destruction of Nordic science . . . True physics is the creation of the German spirit . . . In fact, all European science is the fruit of Aryan, or, better, German thought." Professor Johannes Stark, head of the German National Institute of Physical Science, thought so too. It would be found, he said, that the "founders of research in physics, and the great discoverers from Galileo to Newton to the physical pioneers of our time, were almost exclusively Aryan, predominantly of the Nordic race."

There was also Professor Wilhelm Mueller, of the Technical College of Aachen, who in a book entitled *Jewry and Science* saw a world-wide Jewish plot to pollute science and thereby destroy civilization. To him Einstein, with his theory of relativity, was the archvillain. The Einstein theory, on which so much of modern physics is based, was to this singular Nazi professor "directed from beginning to end toward the goal of transforming the living—that is, the non-Jewish—world of living essence, born from a mother earth and bound up with blood, and bewitching it into spectral abstraction in which all individual differences of peoples and nations, and all inner limits of the races, are lost in unreality, and in which only an unsubstantial diversity of geometric dimensions survives which produces all events out of the compulsion of its godless subjection to laws." The world-wide acclaim given to Einstein on the publication of his theory of relativity, Professor Mueller proclaimed, was really only a rejoicing over "the approach of Jewish world rule which was to force down German manhood irrevocably and eternally to the level of the lifeless slave."

To Professor Ludwig Bieberback, of the University of Berlin, Einstein was "an alien mountebank." Even to Professor Lenard, "the Jew conspicuously lacks understanding for the truth . . . being in this respect in contrast to the Aryan research scientist with his careful and serious will to truth . . . Jewish physics is thus a phantom and a phenomenon of degeneration of fundamental German Physics."[7]

And yet from 1905 to 1931 ten German Jews had been awarded Nobel Prizes for their contributions to science.

During the Second Reich, the university professors, like the Protestant clergy, had given blind support to the conservative government and its expansionist aims, and the lecture halls had been breeding grounds of virulent nationalism and anti-Semitism. The Weimar Republic had insisted on complete academic freedom, and one result had been that the vast majority of university teachers, antiliberal, antidemocratic, anti-Semitic as they were, had helped to undermine the democratic regime. Most professors were fanatical nationalists who wished the return of a conservative, monarchical Germany. And though to many of them, before 1933, the Nazis were too rowdy and violent to attract their allegiance, their preachments helped prepare the ground for the coming of Nazism. By 1932 the majority of students appeared to be enthusiastic for Hitler.

It was surprising to some how many members of the university faculties knuckled under to the Nazification of higher learning after 1933. Though official figures put the number of professors and instructors dismissed during the first five years of the regime at 2,800—about one fourth of the total number—the proportion of those who lost their posts through defying National Socialism was, as Professor Wilhelm Roepke, himself dismissed from the University of Marburg in 1933, said, "exceedingly small." Though small, there were names famous in the German academic world: Karl Jaspers, E. I. Gumbel, Theodor Litt, Karl Barth, Julius Ebbinghaus and dozen of others. Most of them emigrated, first to Switzerland, Holland and England and eventually to America. One of them, Professor Theodor Lessing, who had fled to Czechoslovakia, was tracked down by Nazi thugs and murdered in Marienbad on August 31, 1933.

A large majority of professors, however, remained at their posts, and as early as the autumn of 1933 some 960 of them, led by such luminaries as Professor Sauerbruch, the surgeon, Heidegger, the existentialist philosopher, and Pinder, the art historian, took a public vow to support Hitler and the National Socialist regime.

"It was a scene of prostitution," Professor Roepke later wrote, "that has stained the honorable history of German learning."[8] And as Professor Julius Ebbinghaus, looking back over the shambles in 1945, said, "The

German universities failed, while there was still time, to oppose publicly with all their power the destruction of knowledge and of the democratic state. They failed to keep the beacon of freedom and right burning during the night of tyranny."[9]

The cost of such failure was great. After six years of Nazification the number of university students dropped by more than one half—from 127,920 to 58,325. The decline in enrollment at the institutes of technology, from which Germany got its scientists and engineers, was even greater—from 20,474 to 9,554. Academic standards fell dizzily. By 1937 there was not only a shortage of young men in the sciences and engineering but a decline in their qualifications. Long before the outbreak of the war the chemical industry, busily helping to further Nazi rearmament, was complaining through its organ, *Die Chemische Industrie,* that Germany was losing its leadership in chemistry. Not only the national economy but national defense itself was being jeopardized, it complained, and it blamed the shortage of young scientists and their mediocre caliber on the poor quality of the technical colleges.

Nazi Germany's loss, as it turned out, was the free world's gain, especially in the race to be the first with the atom bomb. The story of the successful efforts of Nazi leaders, led by Himmler, to hamstring the atomic-energy program is too long and involved to be recounted here. It was one of the ironies of fate that the development of the bomb in the United States owed so much to two men who had been exiled because of race from the Nazi and Fascist dictatorships: Einstein from Germany and Fermi from Italy.

To Adolf Hitler it was not so much the public schools, from which he himself had dropped out so early in life, but the organizations of the Hitler Youth on which he counted to educate the youth of Germany for the ends he had in mind. In the years of the Nazi Party's struggle for power the Hitler Youth movement had not amounted to much. In 1932, the last year of the Republic, its total enrollment was only 107,956, compared to some ten million youths who belonged to the various organizations united in the Reich Committee of German Youth Associations. In no country in the world had there been a youth movement of such vitality and numbers as in republican Germany. Hitler, realizing this, was determined to take it over and Nazify it.

His chief lieutenant for this task was a handsome young man of banal mind but of great driving force, Baldur von Schirach, who, falling under Hitler's spell, had joined the party in 1925 at the age of eighteen and in 1931 had been named Youth Leader of the Nazi Party. Among the scarfaced, brawling Brownshirts, he had the curious look of an American college student, fresh and immature, and this perhaps was due to his having had, as we have seen, American forebears (including two signers of the Declaration of Independence).[10]

Schirach was named "Youth Leader of the German Reich" in June 1933. Aping the tactics of his elder party leaders, his first action was to send an armed band of fifty husky Hitler Youth men to occupy the national offices of the Reich Committee of German Youth Associations, where an old Prussian Army officer, General Vogt, head of the committee, was put to rout. Schirach next took on one of the most celebrated of German naval heroes, Admiral von Trotha, who had been Chief of Staff of the High Seas Fleet in the First World War and who was now president of the Youth Associations. The venerable admiral too was put to flight and his position and organization were dissolved. Millions of dollars' worth of property, chiefly in hundreds of youth hostels scattered throughout Germany, was seized.

The concordat of July 20, 1933, had specifically provided for the unhindered continuance of the Catholic Youth Association. On December 1, 1936, Hitler decreed a law outlawing it and all other non-Nazi organizations for young people.

> . . . All of the German youth in the Reich is organized within the Hitler Youth.
>
> The German youth, besides being reared within the family and schools, shall be educated physically, intellectually and morally in the spirit of National Socialism . . . through the Hitler Youth.[11]

Schirach, whose office had formerly been subordinate to the Ministry of Education, was made responsible directly to Hitler.

This half-baked young man of twenty-nine, who wrote maudlin verse in praise of Hitler ("this genius grazing the stars") and followed Rosenberg in his weird paganism and Streicher in his virulent anti-Semitism, had become the dictator of youth in the Third Reich.

From the age of six to eighteen, when conscription for the Labor Service and the Army began, girls as well as boys were organized in the various cadres of the Hitler Youth. Parents found guilty of trying to keep their children from joining the organization were subject to heavy prison sentences even though, as in some cases, they merely objected to having their daughters enter some of the services where cases of pregnancy had reached scandalous proportions.

From the age of six to ten, a boy served a sort of apprenticeship for the Hitler Youth as a *Pimpf*. Each youngster was given a performance book in which would be recorded his progress through the entire Nazi youth movement, including his ideological growth. At ten, after passing suitable tests in athletics, camping and Nazified history, he graduated into the Jungvolk ("Young Folk"), where he took the following oath:

> In the presence of this blood banner, which represents our Fuehrer, I swear to devote all my energies and my strength to the savior of our country, Adolf Hitler. I am willing and ready to give up my life for him, so help me God.

At fourteen the boy entered the Hitler Youth proper and remained there until he was eighteen, when he passed into the Labor Service and the Army. It was a vast organization organized on paramilitary lines similar to the S.A. and in which the youngsters approaching manhood received systematic training not only in camping, sports and Nazi ideology but in soldiering. On many a weekend in the environs of Berlin this writer would be interrupted in his picnicking by Hitler Youths scrambling through the woods or over the heath, rifles at the ready and heavy army packs on their backs.

Sometimes the young ladies would be playing at soldiering, too, for the Hitler Youth movement did not neglect the maidens. From ten to fourteen, German girls were enrolled as *Jungmaedel*—literally, "young maidens"—and they too had a uniform, made up of a white blouse, full blue skirt, socks and heavy—and most unfeminine—marching shoes. Their training was much like that of the boys of the same age and included long marches on weekends with heavy packs and the usual indoctrination in the Nazi philosophy. But emphasis was put on the role of women in the Third Reich—to be, above all, healthy mothers of healthy children. This was stressed even more when the girls became, at fourteen, members of the B.D.M.—Bund Deutscher Maedel (League of German Maidens).

At eighteen, several thousand of the girls in the B.D.M. (they remained in it until 21) did a year's service on the farms—their so-called *Land Jahr,* which was equivalent to the Labor Service of the young men. Their task was to help both in the house and in the fields. The girls lived sometimes in the farmhouses and often in small camps in rural districts from which they were taken by truck early each morning to the farms. Moral problems soon arose. The presence of a pretty young city girl sometimes disrupted a peasant's household, and angry complaints from parents about their daughters' having been made pregnant on the farms began to be heard. But that wasn't the only problem. Usually a girls' camp was located near a Labor Service camp for young men. This juxtaposition seems to have made for many pregnancies too. One couplet—a take-off on the "Strength through Joy" movement of the Labor Front, but it applied especially to the *Land Jahr* of the young maidens—went the rounds of Germany:

> In the fields and on the heath
> I lose Strength through Joy.

Similar moral problems also arose during the Household Year for Girls, in which some half a million Hitler Youth maidens spent a year at domestic service in a city household. Actually, the more sincere Nazis did not consider them moral problems at all. On more than one occasion I listened to women leaders of the B.D.M.—they were invariably of the plainer type and usually unmarried—lecture their young charges on the moral and patriotic duty of bearing children for Hitler's Reich—within wedlock if possible, but without it if necessary.

By the end of 1938 the Hitler Youth numbered 7,728,259. Large as this number was, obviously some four million youth had managed to stay out of the organization, and in March 1939 the government issued a law conscripting all youth into the Hitler Youth on the same basis as they were drafted into the Army. Recalcitrant parents were warned that their children would be taken away from them and put into orphanages or other homes unless they enrolled.

The final twist to education in the Third Reich came in the establishment of three types of schools for the training of the elite: the Adolf Hitler Schools, under the direction of the Hitler Youth, the National Political Institutes of Education and the Order Castles—the last two under the aegis of the party. The Adolf Hitler Schools took the most promising youngsters from the Jungvolk at the age of twelve and gave them six years of intensive training for leadership in the party and in the public services. The pupils lived at the school under Spartan discipline and on graduation were eligible for the university. There were ten such schools founded after 1937, the principal one being the *Akademie* at Brunswick.

The purpose of the Political Institutes of Education was to restore the type of education formerly given in the old Prussian military academies. This, according to one official commentary, cultivated "the soldierly spirit, with its attributes of courage, sense of duty and simplicity." To this was added special training in Nazi principles. The schools were under the supervision of the S.S., which furnished the headmasters and most of the teachers. Three such schools were established in 1933 and grew to thirty-one before the outbreak of the war, three of them for women.

At the very top of the pyramid were the so-called Order Castles, the Ordensburgen. In these, with their atmosphere of the castles of the Order of Teutonic Knights of the fourteenth and fifteenth centuries, were trained the elite of the Nazi elite. The knightly order had been based on the principle of absolute obedience to the Master, the *Ordensmeister,* and devoted to the German conquest of the Slavic lands in the East and the enslavement of the natives. The Nazi Order Castles had similar discipline and purposes. Only the most fanatical young National Socialists were chosen, usually from the top ranks of the graduates of the Adolf Hitler Schools and the Political Institutes. There were four Castles, and a student attended successively all of them. The first of six years was spent in one which specialized in the "racial sciences" and other aspects of Nazi ideology. The emphasis was on mental training and discipline, with physical training subordinated to it. This was reversed the second year at a Castle where athletics and sports, including mountain climbing and parachute jumping, came first. The third Castle, where the students spent the next year and a half, offered political and military instruction. Finally, in the fourth and last stage of his education, the student was sent for a year and a half to the Ordensburg in Marienburg in East Prussia, near the Polish frontier. There, within the walls of the very Order Castle which had been a stronghold of the Teutonic Knights five centuries before, his political and military training was concentrated on the Eastern question and

Germany's need (and right!) of expanding into the Slavic lands in its eternal search for *Lebensraum*—an excellent preparation, as it turned out and no doubt was meant to turn out, for the events of 1939 and thereafter.

In such a manner were the youth trained for life and work and death in the Third Reich. Though their minds were deliberately poisoned, their regular schooling interrupted, their homes largely replaced so far as their rearing went, the boys and the girls, the young men and women, seemed immensely happy, filled with a zest for the life of a Hitler Youth. And there was no doubt that the practice of bringing the children of all classes and walks of life together, where those who had come from poverty or riches, from a laborer's home or a peasant's or a businessman's, or an aristocrat's, shared common tasks, was good and healthy in itself. In most cases it did no harm to a city boy and girl to spend six months in the compulsory Labor Service, where they lived outdoors and learned the value of manual labor and of getting along with those of different backgrounds. No one who traveled up and down Germany in those days and talked with the young in their camps and watched them work and play and sing could fail to see that, however sinister the teaching, here was an incredibly dynamic youth movement.

The young in the Third Reich were growing up to have strong and healthy bodies, faith in the future of their country and in themselves and a sense of fellowship and camaraderie that shattered all class and economic and social barriers. I thought of that later, in the May days of 1940, when along the road between Aachen and Brussels one saw the contrast between the German soldiers, bronzed and clean-cut from a youth spent in the sunshine on an adequate diet, and the first British war prisoners, with their hollow chests, round shoulders, pasty complexions and bad teeth— tragic examples of the youth that England had neglected so irresponsibly in the years between the wars.

THE FARMER IN THE THIRD REICH

When Hitler came to power in 1933 the farmer, as in most countries, was in desperate straits. According to a writer in the *Frankfurter Zeitung*, his situation was worse than at any time since the disastrous Peasants' War of 1524–25 devastated the German land. Agricultural income in 1932–33 had fallen to a new low, more than a billion marks below the worst postwar year, 1924–25. The farmers were in debt to the amount of twelve billions, almost all of it incurred in the last eight years. Interest on these debts took some 14 per cent of all farm income, and to this was added a comparable burden in taxes and contributions to social services.

"My party comrades, make yourselves clear about one thing: There is only one last, one final last chance for the German peasantry," Hitler warned at the outset of his chancellorship, and in October 1933 he declared that "the ruin of the German peasant will be the ruin of the German people."

For years the Nazi Party had cultivated the backing of the farmers. Point 17 of the "inalterable" party program promised them "land reform . . . a law for confiscation without compensation of land for common purposes; abolition of interest on farm loans, and prevention of all speculation in land." Like most of the other points of the program, the promises to the farmers were not kept—with the exception of the last provision against land speculation. In 1938, after five years of Nazi rule, land distribution remained more lopsided than in any other country in the West. Figures published that year in the official *Statistical Year Book* showed that the smallest two and a half million farms had less land than the top .1 per cent. The Nazi dictatorship, like the Socialist-bourgeois governments of the Republic, did not dare to break up the immense feudal estates of the Junkers, which lay to the east of the Elbe.

Nevertheless, the Nazi regime did inaugurate a sweeping new farm program accompanied by much sentimental propaganda about *"Blut und Boden"* (Blood and Soil) and the peasant's being the salt of the earth and the chief hope of the Third Reich. To carry it out Hitler appointed Walther Darré, one of the few party leaders who, though he subscribed to most of the Nazi myths, knew his field professionally and well. An outstanding agricultural specialist with suitable academic training, he had served in the Agriculture Ministries of Prussia and the Reich. Forced to leave them because of conflicts with his superiors, he retired to his home in the Rhineland in 1929 and wrote a book entitled *The Peasantry as the Life Source of the Nordic Race*. Such a title was bound to attract the attention of the Nazis. Rudolf Hess brought Darré to Hitler, who was so impressed with him that he commissioned him to draw up a suitable farm program for the party.

With Hugenberg's dismissal in June 1933, Darré became Minister of Food and Agriculture. By September he was ready with his plans to make over German agriculture. Two basic laws promulgated in that month reorganized the entire structure of production and marketing, with a view to ensuring higher prices for farmers, and at the same time put the German peasant on a new footing—accomplishing this, paradoxically, by putting him back on a very old footing in which farms were entailed, as in feudal days, and the farmer and successive inheritors compulsorily attached to their particular plot of soil (provided they were Aryan Germans) to the end of time.

The Hereditary Farm Law of September 29, 1933, was a remarkable mixture of pushing back the peasants to medieval days and of protecting them against the abuses of the modern monetary age. All farms up to 308 acres (125 hectares) which were capable of providing a decent living for a family were declared to be hereditary estates subject to the ancient laws of entailment. They could not be sold, divided, mortgaged or foreclosed for debts. Upon the death of the owner they had to be passed on to the oldest or youngest son, in accordance with local customs, or to the nearest male relative, who was obliged to provide a living and an education for his brothers and sisters until they were of age. Only an Aryan German citizen who could prove the purity of his blood back to 1800 could own such a farm. And only such a man, the law stipulated, could bear the "honored title" *Bauer,* or Peasant, which he forfeited if he broke the "peasant honor code" or ceased, because of incapacity or otherwise, to actively farm. Thus the heavily indebted German farmer, at the beginning of the Third Reich, was protected from losing his property by foreclosures or from seeing it shrink in size (there being no necessity to sell a piece of it to repay a debt), but at the same time he was bound to the soil as irrevocably as the serfs of feudal times.

And every aspect of his life and work was strictly regulated by the Reich Food Estate, which Darré established by a law of September 13, 1933, a vast organization with authority over every conceivable branch of agricultural production, marketing and processing, and which he himself headed in his capacity of Reich Peasant Leader. Its chief objectives were two: to obtain stable and profitable prices for the farmer and to make Germany self-sufficient in food.

How well did it succeed? In the beginning, certainly, the farmer, who for so long had felt himself neglected in a State which seemed to be preoccupied with the interests of business and labor, was flattered to be singled out for so much attention and proclaimed a national hero and an honored citizen. He was more pleased at the rise in prices which Darré obtained for him by simply arbitrarily fixing them at a profitable level. In the first two years of Nazi rule wholesale agricultural prices increased by 20 per cent (in vegetables, dairy products and cattle the rise was a little more) but this advantage was partially offset by a similar rise in the things which the farmer had to buy—above all in machinery and fertilizer.

As for self-sufficiency in food, which was deemed necessary by the Nazi leaders, who already, as we shall see, were plotting war, the goal was never achieved, nor—given the quality and quantity of German soil in relation to its population—could it ever be. The best the country could do, despite all Nazi efforts in the much-advertised "Battle of Production," was to reach 83 per cent of self-sufficiency and it was only by the conquest of foreign lands that the Germans obtained enough food to enable them to hold out during the second war as long as they did.

THE ECONOMY OF THE THIRD REICH

The foundation of Hitler's success in the first years rested not only on his triumphs in foreign affairs, which brought so many bloodless conquests, but on Germany's economic recovery, which in party circles and even among some economists abroad was hailed as a miracle. And indeed it might have seemed so to a good many people. Unemployment, the curse of the Twenties and early Thirties, was reduced, as we have seen, from six million in 1932 to less than a million four years later. National production rose 102 per cent from 1932 to 1937 and the national income was doubled. To an observer, Germany in the mid-Thirties seemed like one vast beehive. The wheels of industry were humming and everyone was as busy as a bee.

For the first year Nazi economic policies, which were largely determined by Dr. Schacht—for Hitler was bored with economics, of which he had an almost total ignorance—were devoted largely to putting the unemployed back to work by means of greatly expanded public works and the stimulation of private enterprise. Government credit was furnished by the creation of special unemployment bills, and tax relief was generously given to firms which raised their capital expenditures and increased employment.

But the real basis of Germany's recovery was rearmament, to which the Nazi regime directed the energies of business and labor—as well as of the generals—from 1934 on. The whole German economy came to be known in Nazi parlance as *Wehrwirtschaft,* or war economy, and it was deliberately designed to function not only in time of war but during the peace that led to war. General Ludendorff, in his book *Total War (Der Totale Krieg)* whose title was mistranslated into English as *The Nation at War,* published in Germany in 1935, had stressed the necessity of mobilizing the economy of the nation on the same totalitarian basis as everything else in order to properly prepare for total war. It was not exactly a new idea among the Germans, for in Prussia during the eighteenth and nineteenth centuries some five sevenths of the government's revenue, as we have seen, was spent on the Army and that nation's whole economy was always regarded as primarily an instrument not of the people's welfare but of military policy.

It was left to the Nazi regime to adapt *Wehrwirtschaft* to the third decade of the twentieth century. The results were truthfully summed up by Major General Georg Thomas, chief of the Military Economic Staff: "History will know only a few examples of cases where a country has directed, even in peacetime, all its economic forces deliberately and systematically toward the requirements of war, as Germany was compelled to do in the period between the two World Wars."[12]

Germany, of course, was not "compelled" to prepare on such a scale for war—that was a deliberate decision taken by Hitler. In the secret Defense Law of May 21, 1935, he appointed Schacht Plenipotentiary-General for War Economy, ordering him to "begin his work already in peacetime" and giving him the authority to "direct the economic preparations for war." The inimitable Dr. Schacht had not waited until the spring of 1935 to start building up the German economy for war. On September 30, 1934, less than two months after he had become Minister of Economics, he submitted a report to the Fuehrer entitled "Report on the State of Work for War-Economic Mobilization as of September 30, 1934," in which he proudly stressed that his ministry "has been charged with the economic preparation for war." On May 3, 1935, four weeks before he was made Plenipotentiary for War Economy, Schacht submitted a personal memorandum to Hitler which began with the statement that "the accomplishment of the armament program with speed and in quantity is *the* [italics his] problem of German politics; everything else therefore should be subordinate to this purpose . . ." Schacht explained to Hitler that since "armament had to be camouflaged completely until March 16, 1935 [when Hitler announced conscription for an army of thirty-six divisions], it was necessary to use the printing press" to finance the first stages. He also pointed out with some glee that the funds confiscated from the enemies of the State (mostly Jews) and others taken from blocked foreign accounts had helped pay for Hitler's guns. "Thus," he cracked, "our armaments are partially financed with the credits of our political enemies."[13]

Though at his trial at Nuremberg he protested in all innocence against the accusations that he had participated in the Nazi conspiracy to make aggressive war—he had done just the contrary, he proclaimed—the fact remains that no single person was as responsible as Schacht for Germany's *economic* preparation for the war which Hitler provoked in 1939. This was freely acknowledged by the Army. On the occasion of Schacht's sixtieth birthday the Army publication *Militaer-Wochenblatt* in its issue of January 22, 1937, hailed him as "the man who made the reconstruction of the Wehrmacht economically possible." And it added: "The Defense Force owes it to Schacht's skill and great ability that, in defiance of all currency difficulties, it has been able to grow up to its present strength from an army of 100,000 men."

All of Schacht's admitted wizardry in finance was put to work to pay for getting the Third Reich ready for war. Printing banknotes was merely one of his devices. He manipulated the currency with such legerdemain that at one time it was estimated by foreign economists to have 237 different values. He negotiated amazingly profitable (for Germany) barter deals with dozens of countries and to the astonishment of orthodox economists successfully demonstrated that the more you owed a country the more business you did with it. His creation of credit in a country that had little liquid capital and almost no financial reserves was the work of genius, or—as some said—of a master manipulator. His invention of the so-called "Mefo" bills was a good example. These were simply bills created by the Reichsbank and guaranteed by the State and used to pay armament manufacturers. The bills were accepted by all German banks and ultimately discounted by the Reichsbank. Since they appeared neither in the published statements of the national bank nor in the government's budget they helped maintain secrecy as to the extent of Germany's rearmament. From 1935 to 1938 they were used exclusively to finance rearmament and amounted to a total of twelve billion marks. In explaining them once to Hitler, Count Schwerin von Krosigk, the harassed Minister of Finance, remarked that they were merely a way of "printing money."[14]

In September 1936, with the inauguration of the Four-Year Plan under the iron control of Goering, who replaced Schacht as economic dictator though he was almost as ignorant of business as was Hitler, Germany went over to a total war economy. The purpose of the plan was to make Germany self-sufficient in four years, so that a wartime blockade would not stifle it. Imports were reduced to a bare minimum, severe price and wage controls were introduced, dividends restricted to 6 per cent, great factories set up to make synthetic rubber, textiles, fuel and other products from Germany's own sources of raw materials, and a giant Hermann Goering Works established to make steel out of the local low-grade ore. In short, the German economy was mobilized for war, and businessmen, though their profits soared, became mere cogs in a war machine, their work circumscribed by so many restrictions, by so many forms to fill out, that Dr. Funk, who succeeded Schacht in 1937 as Minister of Economics and in 1939 as president of the Reichsbank, was forced to admit ruefully that "official communications now make up more than one half of a German manufacturer's entire correspondence" and that "Germany's export trade involves 40,000 separate transactions daily; yet for a single transaction as many as forty different forms must be filled out."

Buried under mountains of red tape, directed by the State as to what they could produce, how much and at what price, burdened by increasing taxation and milked by steep and never ending "special contributions" to the party, the businessmen, who had welcomed Hitler's regime so enthusiastically because they expected it to destroy organized labor and allow an entrepreneur to practice untrammeled free enterprise, became greatly disillusioned. One of them was Fritz Thyssen, one of the earliest and biggest contributors to the party. Fleeing Germany at the outbreak of the war, he recognized that the "Nazi regime has ruined German industry." And to all he met abroad he proclaimed, "What a fool [*Dummkopf*] I was!"[15]

In the beginning, however, the businessmen fooled themselves into believing that Nazi rule was the answer to all their prayers. To be sure, the "inalterable" party program had sounded ominous to them with its promises of nationalization of trusts, profit sharing in the wholesale trade, "communalization of department stores and their lease at a cheap rate to small traders" (as Point 16 read), land reform and the abolition of interest on mortgages. But the men of industry and finance soon learned that Hitler had not the slightest intention of honoring a single economic plank in the party program—the radical promises had been thrown in merely to attract votes. For the first few months in 1933, a few party radicals tried to get control of the business associations, take over the department stores and institute a corporate state on lines which Mussolini was attempting to establish. But they were quickly thrown out by Hitler and replaced by conservative businessmen. Gottfried Feder, Hitler's early mentor in economics, the crank who wanted to abolish "interest slavery," was given a post as undersecretary in the Ministry of Economics, but his superior, Dr. Karl Schmitt, the insurance magnate, who had spent his life lending money and collecting interest, gave him nothing to do, and when Schacht took over the ministry he dispensed with Feder's services.

The little businessmen, who had been one of the party's chief supports and who expected great things from Chancellor Hitler, soon found themselves, many of them, being exterminated and forced back into the ranks of wage earners. Laws decreed in October 1937 simply dissolved all corporations with a capital under $40,000 and forbade the establishment of new ones with a capital less than $200,000. This quickly disposed of one fifth of all small business firms. On the other hand the great cartels, which even the Republic had favored, were further strengthened by the Nazis. In fact, under a law of July 15, 1933, they were made compulsory. The Ministry of Economics was empowered to organize new compulsory cartels or order firms to join existing ones.

The system of myriad business and trade associations organized during the Republic was maintained by the Nazis, though under the basic law of February 27, 1934, they were reorganized on the streamlined leadership principle and put under the control of the State. All businesses were forced to become members. At the head of an incredibly complex structure was the Reich Economic Chamber, whose leader was appointed by the State, and which controlled seven national economic groups, twenty-three economic chambers, one hundred chambers of industry and commerce and the seventy chambers of handicrafts. Amidst this labyrinthine organization and all the multitude of offices and agencies of the Ministry of Economics and the Four-Year Plan and the Niagara of thousands of special decrees and laws even the most astute businessman was often lost, and special lawyers had to be employed to enable a firm to function. The graft involved in finding one's way to key officials who could make decisions on which orders depended or in circumventing the endless rules and regulations of the government and the trade associations became in the late Thirties astronomical. "An economic necessity," one businessman termed it to this writer.

Despite his harassed life, however, the businessman made good profits. The heavy industries, chief beneficiaries of rearmament, increased theirs from 2 per cent in the boom year of 1926 to 6½ per cent in 1938, the last full year of peace. Even the law limiting dividends to 6 per cent worked no hardship on the companies themselves. Just the opposite. In theory, according to the law, any amount above that had to be invested in government bonds—there was no thought of confiscation. Actually most firms reinvested in their own businesses the undistributed profits, which rose from 175 million marks in 1932 to five billion marks in 1938, a year in which the total savings in the savings banks amounted to only two billions, or less than half the undistributed profits, and in which the distributed profits in form of dividends totaled only 1,200,000,000 marks. Besides his pleasant profits, the businessman was also cheered by the way the workers had been put in their place under Hitler. There were no more unreasonable wage demands. Actually, wages were reduced a little despite a 25 per cent rise in the cost of living. And above all, there were no costly strikes. In fact, there were no strikes at all. Such manifestations of unruliness were *verboten* in the Third Reich.

THE SERFDOM OF LABOR

Deprived of his trade unions, collective bargaining and the right to strike, the German worker in the Third Reich became an industrial serf, bound to his master, the employer, much as medieval peasants had been bound to the lord of the manor. The so-called Labor Front, which in theory replaced the old trade unions, did not represent the worker. According to the law of October 24, 1934, which created it, it was "the organization of creative Germans of brain and fist." It took in not only wage and salary earners but also the employers and members of the professions. It was in reality a vast propaganda organization and, as some workers said, a gigantic fraud. Its aim, as stated in the law, was not to protect the worker but "to create a true social and productive community of all Germans. Its task is to see that every single individual should be able . . . to perform the maximum of work." The Labor Front was not an independent administrative organization but, like almost every other group in Nazi Germany except the Army, an integral part of the N.S.D.A.P., or, as its leader, Dr. Ley—the "stammering drunkard," to use Thyssen's phrase—said, "an instrument of the party." Indeed, the October 24 law stipulated that its officials should come from the ranks of the party, the former Nazi unions, the S.A. and the S.S.—and they did.

Earlier, the Law Regulating National Labor of January 20, 1934, known as the "Charter of Labor," had put the worker in his place and raised the employer to his old position of absolute master—subject, of course, to interference by the all-powerful State. The employer became the "leader of the enterprise," the employees the "following," or *Gefolgschaft*. Paragraph Two of the law set down that "the leader of the enterprise makes the decisions for the employees and laborers in all matters concerning the enterprise." And just as in ancient times the lord was supposed to be responsible for the welfare of his subjects so, under the Nazi law, was the employer made "responsible for the well-being of the employees and laborers." In return, the law said, "the employees and laborers owe him faithfulness"—that is, they were to work hard and long, and no back talk or grumbling, even about wages.

Wages were set by so-called labor trustees, appointed by the Labor Front. In practice, they set the rates according to the wishes of the employer—there was no provision for the workers even to be consulted in such matters—though after 1936, when help became scarce in the armament industries and some employers attempted to raise wages in order to attract men, wage scales were held down by orders of the State. Hitler was quite frank about keeping wages low. "It has been the iron principle of the National Socialist leadership," he declared early in the regime, "not to permit any rise in the hourly wage rates but to raise income solely by an increase in performance."[16] In a country where most wages were based at least partly on piecework, this meant that a worker could hope to earn more only by a speed-up and by longer hours.

Compared to the United States, and after allowances were made for the difference in the cost of living and in social services, wages in Germany had always been low. Under the Nazis they were slightly lower than before. According to the Reich Statistical Office, they declined for skilled workers from 20.4 cents an hour in 1932, at the height of the depression, to 19.5 cents during the middle of 1936. Wage scales for unskilled labor fell from 16.1 cents to 13 cents an hour. At the party congress in Nuremberg in 1936 Dr. Ley stated that the average earnings of full-time workers in the Labor Front amounted to $6.95 a week. The Reich Statistical Office put the figure for all German workers at $6.29.

Although millions more had jobs, the share of all German workers in the national income fell from 56.9 per cent in the depression year of 1932 to 53.6 per cent in the boom year of 1938. At the same time income from capital and business rose from 17.4 per cent of the national income to 26.6 per cent. It is true that because of much greater employment the total income from wages and salaries grew from twenty-five billion marks to forty-two billions, an increase of 66 per cent. But income from capital and business rose much more steeply—by 146 per cent. All the propagandists in the Third Reich from Hitler on down were accustomed to rant in their public speeches against the bourgeois and the capitalist and proclaim their solidarity with the worker. But a sober study of the official statistics, which perhaps few Germans bothered to make, revealed that the much maligned capitalists, not the workers, benefited most from Nazi policies.

Finally, the take-home pay of the German worker shrank. Besides stiff income taxes, compulsory contributions to sickness, unemployment and disability insurance, and Labor Front dues, the manual worker—like everyone else in Nazi Germany—was constantly pressured to make increasingly large gifts to an assortment of Nazi charities, the chief of which was Winterhilfe (Winter Relief). Many a workman lost his job because he failed to contribute to Winterhilfe or because his contribution was deemed too small. Such failure was termed by one labor court, which upheld the dismissal of an employee without notice, "conduct hostile to the community of the people . . . to be most strongly condemned." In the mid-Thirties it was estimated that taxes and contributions took from 15 to 35 per cent of a worker's gross wage. Such a cut out of $6.95 a week did not leave a great deal for rent and food and clothing and recreation.

As with the medieval serfs, the workers in Hitler's Germany found themselves being more and more bound to their place of labor, though here it was not the employer who bound them but the State. We have seen how the peasant in the Third Reich was bound to his land by the Hereditary Farm Law. Likewise the agricultural laborer, by law, was attached to the land and forbidden to leave it for work in the city. In practice, it must be said, this was one Nazi law which was not obeyed; between 1933 and 1939 more than a million (1,300,000) farm workers migrated to jobs in industry and trade. But for industrial laborers the law was enforced. Various government decrees beginning with the law of May 15, 1934, severely restricted a worker's freedom of movement from one job to another. After June 1935 the state employment offices were given exclusive control of employment; they determined who could be hired for what and where.

The "workbook" was introduced in February 1935, and eventually no worker could be hired unless he possessed one. In it was kept a record of his skills and employment. The workbook not only provided the State and the employer with up-to-date data on every single employee in the nation but was used to tie a worker to his bench. If he desired to leave for other employment his employer could retain his workbook, which meant that he could not legally be employed elsewhere. Finally, on June 22, 1938, a special decree issued by the Office of the Four-Year Plan instituted labor conscription. It obliged every German to work where the State assigned him. Workers who absented themselves from their jobs without a very good excuse were subject to fine and imprisonment. There was, it is obvious, another side to this coin. A worker thus conscripted could not be fired by his employer without the consent of the government employment office. He had job security, something he had rarely known during the Republic.

Tied down by so many controls at wages little above the subsistence level, the German workers, like the Roman proletariat, were provided with circuses by their rulers to divert attention from their miserable state. "We had to divert the attention of the masses from material to moral values," Dr. Ley once explained. "It is more important to feed the souls of men than their stomachs."

So he came up with an organization called Kraft durch Freude ("Strength through Joy"). This provided what can only be called regimented leisure. In a twentieth-century totalitarian dictatorship, as perhaps with older ones, it is deemed necessary to control not only the working hours but the leisure hours of the individual. This was what "Strength through Joy" did. In pre-Nazi days Germany had tens of thousands of clubs devoted to everything from chess and soccer to bird watching. Under the Nazis no organized social, sport or recreational group was allowed to function except under the control and direction of Kraft durch Freude.

To the ordinary German in the Third Reich this official all-embracing recreational organization no doubt was better than nothing at all, if one could not be trusted to be left to one's own devices. It provided members of the Labor Front, for instance, with dirt-cheap vacation trips on land and sea. Dr. Ley built two 25,000-ton ships, one of which he named after himself, and chartered ten others to handle ocean cruises for Kraft durch Freude. This writer once participated in such a cruise; though life aboard was organized by Nazi leaders to a point of excruciation (for him), the German workers seemed to have a good time. And at bargain rates! A cruise to Madeira, for instance, cost only $25, including rail fare to and from the German port, and other jaunts were equally inexpensive. Beaches on the sea and on lakes were taken over for thousands of summer vacationers—one at Ruegen on the Baltic, which was not completed by the time the war came, called for hotel accommodations for twenty thousand persons—and in winter special skiing excursions to the Bavarian Alps were organized at a cost of $11 a week, including carfare, room and board, rental of skis and lessons from a ski instructor.

Sports, every branch of which was controlled by the "Strength through Joy," were organized on a massive scale, more than seven million persons, according to the official figures, participating in them annually. The organization also made available at bargain rates tickets to the theater, the opera and concerts, thus making available more high-brow entertainment to the laboring man, as Nazi officials often boasted. Kraft durch Freude also had its own ninety-piece symphony orchestra which continually toured the country, often playing in the smaller places where good music was not usually available. Finally, the organization took over the 200-odd adult education institutions which had flourished during the Republic —a movement which had originated in Scandinavia—and continued them, though adding a strong mixture of Nazi ideology to the instruction.

In the end, of course, the workers paid for their circuses. The annual income from dues to the Labor Front came to $160,000,000 in 1937 and passed the $200,000,000 point by the time the war started, according to Dr. Ley—the accounting was exceedingly vague, being handled not by the State but by the Finance Office of the party, which never published its accounts. From the dues, 10 per cent was earmarked for Kraft durch Freude. But the fees paid by individuals for vacation trips and entertainment, cheap as they were, amounted in the year before the war to $1,250,-000,000. There was another heavy cost to the wage earner. As the largest single party organization in the country, with twenty-five million members, the Labor Front became a swollen bureaucracy, with tens of thousands of full-time employees. In fact, it was estimated that from 20 to 25 per cent of its income was absorbed by administration expense.

One particular swindle perpetrated by Hitler on the German workers deserves passing mention. This had to do with the Volkswagen (the "People's Car")—a brainstorm of the Fuehrer himself. Every German, or at least every German workman, he said, should own an automobile, just as in the United States. Heretofore in this country where there was only one motorcar for every fifty persons (compared to one for every five in America) the workman had used a bicycle or public transportation to get about. Now Hitler decreed that a car should be built for him to sell for only 990 marks—$396 at the official rate of exchange. He himself, it was said, took a hand in the actual designing of the car, which was done under the supervision of the Austrian automobile engineer Dr. Ferdinand Porsche.

Since private industry could not turn out an automobile for $396, Hitler ordered the State to build it and placed the Labor Front in charge of the project. Dr. Ley's organization promptly set out in 1938 to build at Fallersleben, near Braunschweig, "the biggest automobile factory in the world," with a capacity for turning out a million and a half cars a year—"more than Ford," the Nazi propagandists said. The Labor Front advanced fifty million marks in capital. But that was not the main financing. Dr. Ley's ingenious plan was that the workers themselves should furnish the capital by means of what became known as a "pay-before-you-get-it" installment plan—five marks a week, or if a worker thought he could afford it, ten or fifteen marks a week. When 750 marks had been paid in, the buyer received an order number entitling him to a car as soon as it could be turned out. Alas for the worker, not a single car was ever turned out for any customer during the Third Reich. Tens of millions of marks were paid in by the German wage earners, not a pfennig of which was ever to be refunded. By the time the war started the Volkswagen factory turned to the manufacture of goods more useful to the Army.

Swindled though he was in this instance and in many others, reduced, as we have seen, to a sort of industrial serfdom on subsistence wages, and less prone than any other segment of German society to subscribe to Nazism or to be taken in by its ceaseless propaganda, the German worker, it is only fair to say, did not appear to resent very bitterly his inferior status in the Third Reich. The great German war machine that hurtled over the Polish border at dawn on September 1, 1939, could never have been fashioned without the very considerable contribution that the German workman made to it. Regimented he was and sometimes terrorized, but so was everyone else—and centuries of regimentation had accustomed him, as it had all other Germans, to being told what to do. Though it is perhaps unwise to attempt to generalize about such things, this writer's own impression of the workingman in Berlin and in the Ruhr was that while he was somewhat cynical about the promises of the regime he had no more hankering for revolt than anyone else in the Third Reich. Unorganized as he was and lacking leadership, what could he do? A workman often put that question to you.

But the greatest cause of his acceptance of his role in Nazi Germany was, without any doubt at all, that he had a job again and the assurance that he would keep it. An observer who had known something about his precarious predicament during the Republic could understand why he did not seem to be desperately concerned with the loss of political freedom and even of his trade unions as long as he was employed full-time. In the past, for so many, for as many as six million men and their families, such rights of free men in Germany had been overshadowed, as he said, by the freedom to starve. In taking away that last freedom, Hitler assured himself of the support of the working class, probably the most skillful and industrious and disciplined in the Western world. It was a backing given not to his half-baked ideology or to his evil intentions, as such, but to what counted most: the production of goods for war.

JUSTICE IN THE THIRD REICH

From the very first weeks of 1933, when the massive and arbitrary arrests, beatings and murders by those in power began, Germany under National Socialism ceased to be a society based on law. "Hitler is the law!" the legal lights of Nazi Germany proudly proclaimed, and Goering emphasized it when he told the Prussian prosecutors on July 12, 1934, that "the law and the will of the Fuehrer are one." It was true. The law was what the dictator said it was and in moments of crisis, as during the Blood Purge, he himself, as we have seen in his speech to the Reichstag immediately after that bloody event, proclaimed that he was the "supreme judge" of the German people, with power to do to death whomever he pleased.

In the days of the Republic, most judges, like the majority of the Protestant clergy and the university professors, had cordially disliked the Weimar regime and in their decisions, as many thought, had written the blackest page in the life of the German Republic, thus contributing to its fall. But at least under the Weimar Constitution judges were independent, subject only to the law, protected from arbitrary removal and bound at least in theory by Article 109 to safeguard equality before the law. Most of them had been sympathetic to National Socialism, but they were hardly prepared for the treatment they soon received under its actual rule. The Civil Service law of April 7, 1933, was made applicable to all magistrates and quickly rid the judiciary not only of Jews but of those whose Nazism was deemed questionable, or, as the law stipulated, "who indicated that he was no longer prepared to intercede at all times for the National Socialist State." To be sure, not many judges were eliminated by this law, but they were warned where their duty lay. Just to make sure that they understood, Dr. Hans Frank, Commissioner of Justice and Reich Law Leader, told the jurists in 1936, "The National Socialist ideology is the foundation of all basic laws, especially as explained in the party program and in the speeches of the Fuehrer." Dr. Frank went on to explain what he meant:

There is no independence of law against National Socialism. Say to yourselves at every decision which you make: "How would the Fuehrer decide in my place?" In every decision ask yourselves: "Is this decision compatible with the National Socialist conscience of the German people?" Then you will have a firm iron foundation which, allied with the unity of the National Socialist People's State and with your recognition of the eternal nature of the will of Adolf Hitler, will endow your own sphere of decision with the authority of the Third Reich, and this for all time.[17]

That seemed plain enough, as did a new Civil Service law of the following year (January 26, 1937), which called for the dismissal of all officials, including judges, for "political unreliability." Furthermore, all jurists were forced to join the League of National Socialist German Jurists, in which they were often lectured on the lines of Frank's talk.

Some judges, however antirepublican they may have been, did not respond avidly enough to the party line. In fact, a few of them, at least, attempted to base their judgments on the law. One of the worst examples of this, from the Nazi point of view, was the decision of the Reichsgericht, Germany's Supreme Court, to acquit on the basis of evidence three of the four Communist defendants in the Reichstag fire trial in March 1934. (Only Van der Lubbe, the half-witted Dutchman, who confessed, was found guilty.) This so incensed Hitler and Goering that within a month, on April 24, 1934, the right to try cases of treason, which heretofore had been under the exclusive jurisdiction of the Supreme Court, was taken away from that august body and transferred to a new court, the Volksgerichtshof, the People's Court, which soon became the most dreaded tribunal in the land. It consisted of two professional judges and five others chosen from among party officials, the S.S. and the armed forces, thus giving the latter a majority vote. There was no appeal from its decisions or sentences and usually its sessions were held in camera. Occasionally, however, for propaganda purposes when relatively light sentences were to be given, the foreign correspondents were invited to attend.

Thus this writer once observed a case before the People's Court in 1935. It struck him more as a drumhead court-martial than a civil-court trial. The proceedings were finished in a day, there was practically no opportunity to present defense witnesses (if any had dared to appear in defense of one accused of "treason") and the arguments of the defense lawyers, who were "qualified" Nazis, seemed weak to the point of ludicrousness. One got the impression from reading the newspapers, which merely announced the verdicts, that most of the unfortunate defendants (though not on the day I attended) received a death sentence. No figures were ever published, though in December 1940 Roland Freisler, the much-feared president of the People's Court (who was killed during the war when an American bomb demolished his courtroom during a trial) claimed that "only four per cent of the accused were put to death."

Established even earlier than the sinister People's Court was the Sondergericht, the Special Court, which took over from the ordinary courts cases of political crime or, as the Law of March 21, 1933, which established the new tribunal, put it, cases of "insidious attacks against the government." The Special Courts consisted of three judges, who invariably had to be trusted party members, without a jury. A Nazi prosecutor had the choice of bringing action in such cases before either an ordinary court or the Special Court, and invariably he chose the latter, for obvious reasons. Defense lawyers before this court, as before the Volksgerichtshof, had to be approved by Nazi officials. Sometimes even if they were approved they fared badly. Thus the lawyers who attempted to represent the widow of Dr. Klausener, the Catholic Action leader murdered in the Blood Purge, in her suit for damages against the State were whisked off to Sachsenhausen concentration camp, where they were kept until they formally withdrew the action.

Hitler, and for some time Goering, had the right to quash criminal proceedings. In the Nuremberg documents[18] a case came to light in which the Minister of Justice strongly recommended the prosecution of a high Gestapo official and a group of S.A. men whom the evidence, he thought, plainly proved guilty of the most shocking torture of inmates of a concentration camp. He sent the evidence to Hitler. The Fuehrer ordered the prosecution dropped. Goering too, in the beginning, had such power. Once in April 1934 he halted criminal proceedings against a well-known businessman. It soon became known that the defendant paid Goering some three million marks. As Gerhard F. Kramer, a prominent lawyer in Berlin at the time, later commented, "It was impossible to establish whether Goering blackmailed the industrialist or whether the industrialist bribed the Prussian Prime Minister."[19] What *was* established was that Goering quashed the case.

On the other hand, Rudolf Hess, deputy of the Fuehrer, was empowered to take "merciless action" against defendants who in his opinion got off with too light sentences. A record of all court sentences of those found guilty of attacking the party, the Fuehrer or the State were forwarded to Hess, who if he thought the punishment too mild could take the "merciless" action. This usually consisted of hauling the victims off to a concentration camp or having him bumped off.

Sometimes, it must be said, the judges of the *Sondergericht* did display some spirit of independence and even devotion to the law. In such cases either Hess or the Gestapo stepped in. Thus, as we have seen, when Pastor Niemoeller was acquitted by the Special Court of the main charges against him and sentenced only to a short term, which he had already served while awaiting trial, the Gestapo snatched him as he was leaving the courtroom and carted him off to a concentration camp.

For the Gestapo, like Hitler, was also the law. It originally was established for Prussia by Goering on April 26, 1933, to replace Department IA of the old Prussian political police. He had at first intended to designate it merely as the Secret Police Office (Geheimes Polizei Amt) but the German initials GPA sounded too much like the Russian GPU. An obscure post office employee who had been asked to furnish a franking stamp for the new bureau suggested that it be called the Geheime Staatspolizei, simply the "Secret State Police"—GESTAPO for short— and thus unwittingly created a name the very mention of which was to inspire terror first within Germany and then without.

In the beginning the Gestapo was little more than a personal instrument of terror employed by Goering to arrest and murder opponents of the regime. It was only in April 1934, when Goering appointed Himmler deputy chief of the Prussian Secret Police, that the Gestapo began to expand as an arm of the S.S. and, under the guiding genius of its new chief, the mild-mannered but sadistic former chicken farmer, and of Reinhard Heydrich, a young man of diabolical cast[20] who was head of the S.S. Security Service, or S.D. (Sicherheitsdienst), become such a scourge, with the power of life and death over every German.

As early as 1935 the Prussian Supreme Court of Administration, under Nazi pressure, had ruled that the orders and actions of the Gestapo were not subject to judicial review. The basic Gestapo law promulgated by the government on February 10, 1936, put the secret police organization above the law. The courts were not allowed to interfere with its activities in any way. As Dr. Werner Best, one of Himmler's right-hand men in the Gestapo, explained, "As long as the police carries out the will of the leadership, it is acting legally."[21]

A cloak of "legality" was given to the arbitrary arrests and the incarceration of victims in concentration camps. The term was *Schutzhaft,* or "protective custody," and its exercise was based on the Law of February 28, 1933, which, as we have seen, suspended the clauses of the constitution which guaranteed civil liberties. But protective custody did not protect a man from possible harm, as it did in more civilized countries. It punished him by putting him behind barbed wire.

The first concentration camps sprang up like mushrooms during Hitler's first year of power. By the end of 1933 there were some fifty of them, mainly set up by the S.A. to give its victims a good beating and then ransom them to their relatives or friends for as much as the traffic would bear. It was largely a crude form of blackmail. Sometimes, however, the prisoners were murdered, usually out of pure sadism and brutality. At the Nuremberg trial four such cases came to light that took place in the spring of 1933 at the S.S. concentration camp at Dachau, near Munich. In each instance a prisoner was cold-bloodedly murdered, one by whipping, another by strangulation. Even the public prosecutor in Munich protested.

Since after the Blood Purge of June 1934 there was no more resistance to the Nazi regime, many Germans thought that the mass "protective custody" arrests and the confinement of thousands in the concentration camps would cease. On Christmas Eve, 1933, Hitler had announced an amnesty for twenty-seven thousand inmates of the camps, but Goering and Himmler got around his orders and only a few were actually released. Then Frick, the rubber-stamp bureaucrat who was Minister of the Interior, had tried in April 1934 to reduce the abuses of the Nazi thugs by issuing secret decrees placing restrictions on the wholesale use of *Schutzhaft* arrests and reducing commitments to concentration camps, but Himmler had persuaded him to drop the matter. The S.S. Fuehrer saw more clearly than the Minister that the purpose of the concentration camps was not only to punish enemies of the regime but by their very existence to terrorize the people and deter them from even contemplating any resistance to Nazi rule.

Shortly after the Roehm purge, Hitler turned the concentration camps over to the control of the S.S., which proceeded to organize them with the efficiency and ruthlessness expected of this elite corps. Guard duty was given exclusively to the Death's-Head units (*Totenkopfverbaende*) whose members were recruited from the toughest Nazi elements, served an enlistment of twelve years and wore the familiar skull-and-bones insignia on their black tunics. The commander of the first Death's-Head detachment and the first commander of the Dachau camp, Theodor Eicke, was put in charge of all the concentration camps. The fly-by-night ones were closed down and larger ones constructed, the chief of which (until the war came, when they were expanded into occupied territory) were Dachau near Munich, Buchenwald near Weimar, Sachsenhausen, which replaced the Oranienburg camp of initial fame near Berlin, Ravensbrueck in Mecklenburg (for women) and, after the occupation of Austria in 1938, Mauthausen near Linz—names which, with Auschwitz, Belsec and Treblinka, which were later established in Poland, were to become all too familiar to most of the world.

In them, before the end mercifully came, millions of hapless persons were done to death and millions of others subjected to debasement and torture more revolting than all but a few minds could imagine. But at the beginning—in the Thirties—the population of the Nazi concentration camps in Germany probably never numbered more than from twenty to thirty thousand at any one time, and many of the horrors later invented and perpetrated by Himmler's men were as yet unknown. The extermination camps, the slave labor camps, the camps where the inmates were used as guinea pigs for Nazi "medical research," had to wait for the war.

But the early camps were not exactly humane. I have before me a copy of the regulations drawn up for Dachau on November 1, 1933, by its first commander, Theodor Eicke, who when he became head of all the camps applied them throughout.

Article 11. The following offenders, considered as agitators, will be hanged: Anyone who . . . politicizes, holds inciting speeches and meetings, forms cliques, loiters around with others; who for the purpose of supplying the propaganda of the opposition with atrocity stories, collects true or false information about the concentration camp; receives such information, buries it, talks about it to others, smuggles it out of the camp into the hands of foreign visitors, etc.

Article 12. The following offenders, considered as mutineers, will be shot on the spot or later hanged. Anyone attacking physically a guard or S.S. man, refusing to obey or to work while on detail. . . or bawling, shouting, inciting or holding speeches while marching or at work.

Milder sentences of two weeks' solitary confinement and twenty-five lashings were given "anyone making depreciatory remarks in a letter or other documents about National Socialist leaders, the State and Government . . . [or] glorifying Marxist or Liberal leaders of the old democratic parties."

Allied with the Gestapo was the Security Service, the Sicherheitsdienst, or S.D., which formed another set of initials that struck fear in the bosoms of all Germans—and later of the occupied peoples. Originally formed by Himmler in 1932 as the intelligence branch of the S.S., and placed by him under the direction of Reinhard Heydrich, later internationally renowned as "Hangman Heydrich," its initial function had been to watch over members of the party and report any suspicious activity. In 1934 it became also the intelligence unit for the secret police, and by 1938 a new law gave it this function for the entire Reich.

Under the expert hand of Heydrich, a former intelligence officer in the Navy who had been cashiered by Admiral Raeder in 1931 at the age of twenty-six for refusing to marry the daughter of a shipbuilder whom he had compromised, the S.D. soon spread its net over the country, employing some 100,000 part-time informers who were directed to snoop on every citizen in the land and report the slightest remark or activity which was deemed inimical to Nazi rule. No one—if he were not foolish—said or did anything that might be interpreted as "anti-Nazi" without first taking precautions that it was not being recorded by hidden S.D. microphones or overheard by an S.D. agent. Your son or your father or your wife or your cousin or your best friend or your boss or your secretary might be an informer for Heydrich's organization; you never knew, and if you were wise nothing was ever taken for granted.

The full-time sleuths of the S.D. probably never numbered more than three thousand during the Thirties and most of them were recruited from the ranks of the displaced young intellectuals—university graduates who had been unable to find suitable jobs or any secure place in normal society. Thus among these professional spies there was always the bizarre atmosphere of pedantry. They had a grotesque interest in such side lines as the study of Teutonic archeology, the skulls of the inferior races and the eugenics of a master race., A foreign observer, however, found difficulty in making contacts with these odd men, though Heydrich himself, an arrogant, icy and ruthless character, might occasionally be seen at a Berlin night club surrounded by some of his blond young thugs. They not only kept out of the spotlight because of the nature of their work but, in 1934 and 1935 at least, because a number of them who had spied on Roehm and his confederates in the S.A. were bumped off by a secret band that called itself "Roehm's Avengers" and took care to pin that label on the bodies.

One of the interesting, if subordinate, tasks of the S.D. was to ascertain who voted "No" in Hitler's plebiscites. Among the numerous Nuremberg documents is a secret report of the S.D. in Kochem on the plebiscite of April 10, 1938:

Copy is attached enumerating the persons who cast "No" votes or invalid votes at Kappel. The control was affected in the following way: some members of the election committee marked all the ballots with numbers. During the balloting a voters' list was made up. The ballots were handed out in numerical order, therefore it was possible afterward . . . to find out the persons who cast "No" votes or invalid votes. The marking was done on the back of the ballot with skimmed milk.

The ballot cast by the Protestant parson Alfred Wolfers is also enclosed.[22]

On June 16, 1936, for the first time in German history, a unified police was established for the whole of the Reich—previously the police had been organized separately by each of the states—and Himmler was put in charge as Chief of the German Police. This was tantamount to putting the police in the hands of the S.S., which since its suppression of the Roehm "revolt" in 1934 had been rapidly increasing its power. It had become not only the praetorian guard, not only the single armed branch of the party, not only the elite from whose ranks the future leaders of the new Germany were being chosen, but it now possessed the police power. The Third Reich, as is inevitable in the development of all totalitarian dictatorships, had become a police state.

GOVERNMENT IN THE THIRD REICH

Though the Weimar Republic was destroyed, the Weimar Constitution was never formally abrogated by Hitler. Indeed—and ironically—Hitler based the "legality" of his rule on the despised republican constitution. Thus thousands of decreed laws—there were no others in the Third Reich —were explicitly based on the emergency presidential decree of February 28, 1933, for the Protection of the People and the State, which Hindenburg, under Article 48 of the constitution, had signed. It will be remembered that the aged President was bamboozled into signing the decree the day after the Reichstag fire when Hitler assured him that there was grave danger of a Communist revolution. The decree, which suspended all civil rights, remained in force throughout the time of the Third Reich, enabling the Fuehrer to rule by a sort of continual martial law.

The Enabling Act too, which the Reichstag had voted on March 24, 1933, and by which it handed over its legislative functions to the Nazi government, was the second pillar in the "constitutionality" of Hitler's rule. Each four years thereafter it was dutifully prolonged for another four-year period by a rubber-stamp Reichstag, for it never occurred to the dictator to abolish this once democratic institution but only to make it nondemocratic. It met only a dozen times up to the war, "enacted" only four laws,* held no debates or votes and never heard any speeches except those made by Hitler.

After the first few months of 1933 serious discussions ceased in the cabinet, its meetings became more and more infrequent after the death of Hindenburg in August 1934, and after February 1938 the cabinet was

---

* The Reconstruction Law of January 30, 1934, and the three anti-Semitic Nuremberg Laws of September 15, 1935.

never convened. However, individual cabinet members held the considerable power of being authorized to promulgate decrees which, with the Fuehrer's approval, automatically became laws. The Secret Cabinet Council (Geheimer Kabinettsrat), set up with great fanfare in 1938, perhaps to impress Prime Minister Chamberlain, existed only on paper. It never met once. The Reich Defense Council (Reichsverteidigungsrat), established early in the regime as a war-planning agency under the chairmanship of Hitler, met formally only twice, though some of its working committees were exceedingly active.

Many cabinet functions were delegated to special agencies such as the Office of the Deputy of the Fuehrer (Hess and later Martin Bormann), of the Plenipotentiaries for War Economy (Schacht) and Administration (Frick), and of the Delegate for the Four-Year Plan (Goering). In addition there were what was known as the "supreme government agencies" and "national administrative agencies," many of them holdovers from the Republic. In all, there were some 42 executive agencies of the national government under the direct jurisdiction of the Fuehrer.

The diets and governments of the separate states of Germany were, as we have seen, abolished in the first year of the Nazi regime when the country was unified, and governors for the states, which were reduced to provinces, were appointed by Hitler. Local self-government, the only field in which the Germans had seemed to be making genuine progress toward democracy, was also wiped out. A series of laws decreed between 1933 and 1935 deprived the municipalities of their local autonomy and brought them under the direct control of the Reich Minister of the Interior, who appointed their mayors—if they had a population of over 100,000—and reorganized them on the leadership principle. In towns under 100,000, the mayors were named by the provincial governors. For Berlin, Hamburg and Vienna (after 1938, when Austria was occupied) Hitler reserved the right to appoint the burgomasters.

The offices through which Hitler exercised his dictatorial powers consisted of four chancelleries: those of the President (though the title had ceased to exist after 1934), the Chancellor (the title was abandoned in 1939) and the party, and a fourth known as the Chancellery of the Fuehrer which looked after his personal affairs and carried out special tasks.

In truth, Hitler was bored by the details of day-to-day governing and after he had consolidated his position following the death of Hindenburg he left them largely to his aides. Old party comrades such as Goering, Goebbels, Himmler, Ley and Schirach were given free rein to carve out their own empires of power—and usually profit. Schacht was given a free hand at first to raise the money for expanding government expenditures by whatever sleight of hand he could think up. Whenever these men clashed over the division of power or spoils, Hitler intervened. He did not mind these quarrels. Indeed, he often encouraged them, because they added status to his position as supreme arbiter and prevented any closing of the ranks against him. Thus he seemed to take delight at the spectacle of three men competing with each other in foreign affairs: Neurath, the Foreign Minister, Rosenberg, the head of the party's Foreign Affairs Department, and Ribbentrop, who had his own "Ribbentrop Bureau" which dabbled in foreign policy. All three men were at loggerheads with each other and Hitler kept them so by maintaining their rival offices until in the end he chose the dull-witted Ribbentrop to become his Foreign Minister and carry out his orders in foreign affairs.

Such was the government of the Third Reich, administered from top to bottom on the so-called leadership principle by a vast and sprawling bureaucracy, having little of the efficiency usually credited to the Germans, poisoned by graft, beset by constant confusion and cutthroat rivalries augmented by the muddling interference of party potentates and often rendered impotent by the terror of the S.S.-Gestapo.

At the top of the swarming heap stood the onetime Austrian vagabond, now become, with the exception of Stalin, the most powerful dictator on earth. As Dr. Hans Frank reminded a convention of lawyers in the spring of 1936, "There is in Germany today only one authority, and that is the authority of the Fuehrer."[23]

With that authority Hitler had quickly destroyed those who opposed him, unified and Nazified the State, regimented the country's institutions and culture, suppressed individual freedom, abolished unemployment and set the wheels of industry and commerce humming—no small achievement after only three or four years in office. Now he turned—in fact, he already had turned—to the two chief passions of his life: the shaping of Germany's foreign policy toward war and conquest and the creation of a mighty military machine which would enable him to achieve his goal.

It is time now to turn to the story, more fully documented than that of any other in modern history, of how this extraordinary man, at the head of so great and powerful a nation, set out to attain his ends.

Book Three

✚ ✚ ✚

THE ROAD TO WAR

9

THE FIRST STEPS: 1934–37

To talk peace, to prepare secretly for war and to proceed with enough caution in foreign policy and clandestine rearmament to avoid any preventive military action against Germany by the Versailles powers—such were Hitler's tactics during the first two years.

He stumbled badly with the Nazi murder of the Austrian Chancellor Dollfuss in Vienna on July 25, 1934. At noon on that day 154 members of the S.S. Standarte 89, dressed in Austrian Army uniforms, broke into the Federal Chancellery and shot Dollfuss in the throat at a range of two feet. A few blocks away other Nazis seized the radio station and broadcast the news that Dollfuss had resigned. Hitler received the tidings while listening to a performance of *Das Rheingold* at the annual Wagner Festival at Bayreuth. They greatly excited him. Friedelind Wagner, granddaughter of the great composer, who sat in the family box nearby, was a witness. Two adjutants, Schaub and Brueckner, she later told, kept receiving the news from Vienna on a telephone in the anteroom of her box and then whispering it to Hitler.

After the performance the Fuehrer was most excited. This excitement mounted as he told us the horrible news . . . Although he could scarcely wipe the delight from his face Hitler carefully ordered dinner in the restaurant as usual.

"I must go across for an hour and show myself," he said, "or people will think I had something to do with this."[1]

They would not have been far from right. In the first paragraph of *Mein Kampf*, it will be remembered, Hitler had written that the reunion of Austria and Germany was a "task to be furthered with every means our lives long." Soon after becoming Chancellor he had appointed a Reichstag deputy, Theodor Habicht, as inspector of the Austrian Nazi Party, and a little later he had set up Alfred Frauenfeld, the self-exiled Austrian party leader, in Munich, whence he broadcast nightly, inciting his com-

279

rades in Vienna to murder Dollfuss. For months prior to July 1934 the Austrian Nazis, with weapons and dynamite furnished by Germany, had instituted a reign of terror, blowing up railways, power stations and government buildings and murdering supporters of the Dollfuss clerical-fascist regime. Finally, Hitler had approved the formation of an Austrian Legion, several thousand strong, which camped along the Austrian border in Bavaria, ready to cross over and occupy the country at an opportune moment.

Dollfuss died of his wounds at about 6 P.M., but the Nazi putsch, due largely to the bungling of the conspirators who had seized the Chancellery, failed. Government forces, led by Dr. Kurt von Schuschnigg, quickly regained control, and the rebels, though promised safe-conduct to Germany through the intervention of the German minister, were arrested and thirteen of them later hanged. In the meantime Mussolini, to whom Hitler only a month before at their meeting in Venice had promised to leave Austria alone, caused uneasiness in Berlin by hastily mobilizing four divisions on the Brenner Pass.

Hitler quickly backed down. The news story prepared for the press by the official German news agency, D.N.B., rejoicing at the fall of Dollfuss and proclaiming the Greater Germany that must inevitably follow, was hastily withdrawn at midnight and a new version substituted expressing regret at the "cruel murder" and declaring that it was a purely Austrian affair. Habicht was removed, the German minister in Vienna recalled and dismissed and Papen, who had narrowly escaped Dollfuss' fate just a month before during the Roehm purge, was packed off to Vienna posthaste to restore, as Hitler directed him, "normal and friendly relations."

Hitler's first joyous excitement had given way to fear. "We are faced with a new Sarajevo!" Papen says he shouted at him when the two conferred about how to overcome the crisis.[2] But the Fuehrer had learned a lesson. The Nazi putsch in Vienna, like the Beer Hall Putsch in Munich in 1923, had been premature. Germany was not yet militarily strong enough to back up such a venture by force. It was too isolated diplomatically. Even Fascist Italy had joined Britain and France in insisting on Austria's continued independence. Moreover, the Soviet Union was showing interest for the first time in joining the West in an Eastern Locarno which would discourage any moves of Germany in the East. In the autumn it joined the League of Nations. The prospects for dividing the Great Powers seemed dimmer than ever throughout the crucial year of 1934. All that Hitler could do was to preach peace, get along with his secret rearmament and wait and watch for opportunities.

Besides the Reichstag, Hitler had another means of communicating his peace propaganda to the outside world: the foreign press, whose correspondents, editors and publishers were constantly seeking interviews with him. There was Ward Price, the monocled Englishman, and his newspaper, the London *Daily Mail,* who were always ready at the drop of a hint to accommodate the German dictator. So in August 1934, in another one of the series of interviews which would continue up to the eve of the war, Hitler told Price—and his readers—that "war will not come again," that Germany had "a more profound impression than any other of the evil that war causes," that "Germany's problems cannot be settled by war."[3] In the fall he repeated these glowing sentiments to Jean Goy, a French war veterans' leader and a member of the Chamber of Deputies, who passed them on in an article in the Paris daily *Le Matin*.[4]

THE BREACHING OF VERSAILLES

In the meantime Hitler pursued with unflagging energy his program of building up the armed services and procuring arms for them. The Army was ordered to treble its numerical strength—from 100,000 to 300,000 by October 1, 1934—and in April of that year General Ludwig Beck, Chief of the General Staff, was given to understand that by April 1 of the following year the Fuehrer would openly decree conscription and publicly repudiate the military restrictions of the Versailles Treaty.[5] Until then the utmost secrecy must be observed. Goebbels was admonished never to allow the words "General Staff" to appear in the press, since Versailles forbade the very existence of this organization. The annual official rank list of the German Army ceased to be published after 1932 so that its swollen lists of officers would not give the game away to foreign intelligence. General Keitel, chairman of the Working Committee of the Reich Defense Council, admonished his aides as early as May 22, 1933, "No document must be lost, since otherwise enemy propaganda will make use of it. Matters communicated orally cannot be proven; they can be denied."[6]

The Navy too was warned to keep its mouth shut. In June 1934 Raeder had a long conversation with Hitler and noted down:

Fuehrer's instructions: No mention must be made of a displacement of 25–26,000 tons, but only of improved 10,000-ton ships . . . The Fuehrer demands complete secrecy on the construction of the U-boats.[7]

For the Navy had commenced the construction of two battle cruisers of 26,000 tons (16,000 tons above the Versailles limit) which would eventually be known as the *Scharnhorst* and the *Gneisenau*. Submarines, the building of which Versailles had prohibited, had been secretly constructed in Finland, Holland and Spain during the German Republic, and recently Raeder had stored the frames and parts of a dozen of them at Kiel. When he saw Hitler in November 1934 he asked permission to assemble six of them by "the time of the critical situation in the first quarter of 1935" (obviously he too knew what Hitler planned to do at that time) but the Fuehrer merely replied that "he would tell me when the situation demanded that the assembly should commence."[8]

At this meeting Raeder also pointed out that the new shipbuilding program (not to mention the tripling of naval personnel) would take more money than he had available, but Hitler told him not to worry. "In case of need, he will get Dr. Ley to put 120–150 million from the Labor Front at the disposal of the Navy, as the money would still benefit the workers."[9] Thus the dues of the German workers were to finance the naval program.

Goering too was busy those first two years, establishing the Air Force. As Minister of Aviation—supposedly *civil* aviation—he put the manufacturers to work designing warplanes. Training of military pilots began immediately under the convenient camouflage of the League for Air Sports.

A visitor to the Ruhr and Rhineland industrial areas in those days might have been struck by the intense activity of the armament works, especially those of Krupp, chief German gunmakers for three quarters of a century, and I. G. Farben, the great chemical trust. Although Krupp had been forbidden by the Allies to continue in the armament business after 1919, the company had really not been idle. As Krupp would boast in 1942, when the German armies occupied most of Europe, "the basic principle of armament and turret design for tanks had already been worked out in 1926 . . . Of the guns being used in 1939–41, the most important ones were already fully complete in 1933." Farben scientists had saved Germany from early disaster in the First World War by the invention of a process to make synthetic nitrates from air after the country's normal supply of nitrates from Chile was cut off by the British blockade. Now under Hitler the trust set out to make Germany self-sufficient in two materials without which modern war could not be fought: gasoline and rubber, both of which had had to be imported. The problem of making synthetic gasoline from coal had actually been solved by the company's scientists in the mid-Twenties. After 1933, the Nazi government gave I. G. Farben the go-ahead with orders to raise its synthetic oil production to 300,000 tons a year by 1937. By that time the company had also discovered how to make synthetic rubber from coal and other products of which Germany had a sufficiency, and the first of four plants was set up at Schkopau for large-scale production of *buna,* as the artificial rubber became known. By the beginning of 1934, plans were approved by the Working Committee of the Reich Defense Council for the mobilization of some 240,000 plants for war orders. By the end of that year rearmament, in all its phases, had become so massive it was obvious that it could no longer be concealed from the suspicious and uneasy powers of Versailles.

These powers, led by Great Britain, had been flirting with the idea of recognizing a *fait accompli,* that is, German rearmament, which was not nearly so secret as Hitler supposed. They would concede Hitler complete arms equality in return for Germany's joining in a general European settlement which would include an Eastern Locarno and thus provide the Eastern countries, especially Russia, Poland and Czechoslovakia, with the same security which the Western nations enjoyed under the Locarno Treaty—and, of course, furnish Germany with the same guarantees of security. In May of 1934 Sir John Simon, the British Foreign Secretary, who was to be a good forerunner of Neville Chamberlain in his inability to comprehend the mind of Adolf Hitler, actually proposed equality of armaments to Germany. The French sharply rejected such an idea.

But the proposals for a general settlement, including equality of armaments and an Eastern Locarno, were renewed jointly by the British and French governments early in February 1935. The month before, on January 13, the inhabitants of the Saar had voted overwhelmingly— 477,000 to 48,000—to return their little coal-rich territory to the Reich and Hitler had taken the occasion to publicly proclaim that Germany had no further territorial claims on France, which meant the abandoning of German claims on Alsace and Lorraine. In the atmosphere of optimism and good will which the peaceful return of the Saar and Hitler's remarks engendered, the Anglo–French proposals were formally presented to Hitler at the beginning of February 1935.

Hitler's reply of February 14 was somewhat vague—and, from his viewpoint, understandably so. He welcomed a plan which would leave Germany free to rearm in the open. But he was evasive on Germany's willingness to sign an Eastern Locarno. That would be tying his hands in the main area where, as he had always preached, Germany's *Lebensraum* lay. Might not Britain be detached in this matter from France, which with its mutual-assistance pacts with Poland, Czechoslovakia and Rumania, was more interested in Eastern security? Hitler must have thought so, for in his cautious reply he suggested that bilateral discussions precede general talks and invited the British to come to Berlin for preliminary discussions. Sir John Simon readily agreed, and a meeting was arranged for March 6 in Berlin. Two days before that date the publication of a British White Paper caused a great deal of simulated anger in the Wilhelmstrasse. Actually the White Paper struck most foreign observers in Berlin as a sober observation on Germany's clandestine rearmament, the acceleration of which had moved Britain to a modest increase of her own. But Hitler was reported furious with it. Neurath informed Simon on the very eve of his departure for Berlin that the Fuehrer had a "cold" and the talks would have to be postponed.

Whether he had a cold or not, Hitler certainly had a brain storm. It would be embarrassing to have Simon and Eden around if he transformed it into a bold act. He thought he had found a pretext for dealing the Versailles *Diktat* a mortal blow. The French government had just introduced a bill extending military service from eighteen months to two years because of the shortage of youth born during the First World War. On March 10, Hitler sent up a trial balloon to test the mettle of the Allies. The accommodating Ward Price was called in and given an interview with Goering, who told him officially what all the world knew, that Germany had a military Air Force. Hitler confidently awaited the reaction in London to this unilateral abrogation of Versailles. It was just what he expected. Sir John Simon told the Commons that he still counted on going to Berlin.

A SATURDAY SURPRISE

On Saturday, March 16—most of Hitler's surprises were reserved for Saturdays—the Chancellor decreed a law establishing universal military service and providing for a peacetime army of twelve corps and thirty-six divisions—roughly half a million men. That was the end of the military restrictions of Versailles—unless France and Britain took action. As Hitler had expected, they protested but they did not act. Indeed, the British government hastened to ask whether Hitler would still receive its Foreign Secretary—a query which the dictator graciously answered in the affirmative.

Sunday, March 17, was a day of rejoicing and celebration in Germany. The shackles of Versailles, symbol of Germany's defeat and humiliation, had been torn off. No matter how much a German might dislike Hitler and his gangster rule, he had to admit that the Fuehrer had accomplished what no republican government had ever dared attempt. To most Germans the nation's honor had been restored. That Sunday was also Heroes' Memorial Day (*Heldengedenktag*). I went to the ceremony at noon at the State Opera House and there witnessed a scene which Germany had not seen since 1914. The entire lower floor was a sea of military uniforms, the faded gray uniforms and spiked helmets of the old Imperial Army mingling with the attire of the new Army, including the sky-blue uniforms of the Luftwaffe, which few had seen before. At Hitler's side was Field Marshal von Mackensen, the last surviving field marshal of the Kaiser's Army, colorfully attired in the uniform of the Death's-Head Hussars. Strong lights played on the stage, where young officers stood like marble statues holding upright the nation's war flags. Behind them on an enormous curtain hung an immense silver-and-black Iron Cross. Ostensibly this was a ceremony to honor Germany's war dead. It turned out to be a jubilant celebration of the death of Versailles and the rebirth of the conscript German Army.

The generals, one could see by their faces, were immensely pleased. Like everyone else they had been taken by surprise, for Hitler, who had spent the previous days at his mountain retreat at Berchtesgaden, had not bothered to apprise them of his thoughts. According to General von Manstein's later testimony at Nuremberg, he and his commanding officer, of Wehrkreis III (the Third Military District) in Berlin, General von Witzleben, first heard of Hitler's decision over the radio on March 16. The General Staff would have preferred a smaller army to begin with.

The General Staff, had it been asked [Manstein testified], would have proposed twenty-one divisions . . . The figure of thirty-six divisions was due to a spontaneous decision of Hitler.[10]

There now took place a series of empty gestures of warning to Hitler by the other powers. The British, the French and the Italians met at

Stresa on April 11, condemned Germany's action and reiterated their support of Austria's independence and the Locarno Treaty. The Council of the League of Nations at Geneva also expressed its displeasure at Hitler's precipitate action and duly appointed a committee to suggest steps which might impede him the next time. France, recognizing that Germany would never join an Eastern Locarno, hastily signed a pact of mutual assistance with Russia, and Moscow made a similar treaty with Czechoslovakia.

In the headlines this closing of ranks against Germany sounded somewhat ominous and even impressed a number of men in the German Foreign Office and in the Army, but apparently not Hitler. After all, he had gotten away with his gamble. Still, it would not do to rest on his laurels. It was time, he decided, to pull out the stops again on his love of peace and to see whether the new unity of the powers arrayed against him might not be undermined and breached after all.

On the evening of May 21* he delivered another "peace" speech to the Reichstag—perhaps the most eloquent and certainly one of the cleverest and most misleading of his Reichstag orations this writer, who sat through most of them, ever heard him make. Hitler was in a relaxed mood and exuded a spirit not only of confidence but—to the surprise of his listeners—of tolerance and conciliation. There was no resentment or defiance toward the nations which had condemned his scrapping of the military clauses of Versailles. Instead there were assurances that all he wanted was peace and understanding based on justice for all. He rejected the very idea of war; it was senseless, it was useless, as well as a horror.

The blood shed on the European continent in the course of the last three hundred years bears no proportion to the national result of the events. In the end France has remained France, Germany Germany, Poland Poland, and Italy Italy. What dynastic egotism, political passion and patriotic blindness have attained in the way of apparently far-reaching political changes by shedding rivers of blood has, as regards national feeling, done no more than touched the skin of the nations. It has not substantially altered their fundamental characters. If these states had applied merely a fraction of their sacrifices to wiser purposes the success would certainly have been greater and more permanent.

---

* Earlier that day Hitler had promulgated the secret Reich Defense Law, putting Dr. Schacht, as we have seen, in charge of war economy and thoroughly reorganizing the armed forces. The Reichswehr of Weimar days became the Wehrmacht. Hitler, as Fuehrer and Chancellor, was Supreme Commander of the Armed Forces (Wehrmacht) and Blomberg, the Minister of Defense, was designated as Minister of War with the additional title of Commander in Chief of the Armed Forces—the only general in Germany who ever held that rank. Each of the three services had its own commander in chief and its own general staff. The camouflage name of "Truppenamt" in the Army was dropped for the real thing and its head, General Beck, assumed the title of Chief of the General Staff. But this title did not denote what it did in the Kaiser's time, when the General Staff Chief was actually the Commander in Chief of the German Army under the warlord.

Germany, Hitler proclaimed, had not the slightest thought of conquering other peoples.

Our racial theory regards every war for the subjection and domination of an alien people as a proceeding which sooner or later changes and weakens the victor internally, and eventually brings about his defeat . . . As there is no longer any unoccupied space in Europe, every victory . . . can at best result in a quantitative increase in the number of the inhabitants of a country. But if the nations attach so much importance to that they can achieve it without tears in a simpler and more natural way—[by] a sound social policy, by increasing the readiness of a nation to have children.

No! National Socialist Germany wants peace because of its fundamental convictions. And it wants peace also owing to the realization of the simple primitive fact that no war would be likely essentially to alter the distress in Europe . . . The principal effect of every war is to destroy the flower of the nation . . .

Germany needs peace and desires peace!

He kept hammering away at the point. At the end he made thirteen specific proposals for maintaining the peace which seemed so admirable that they created a deep and favorable impression not only in Germany but in all of Europe. He prefaced them with a reminder:

Germany has solemnly recognized and guaranteed France her frontiers as determined after the Saar plebiscite . . . We thereby finally renounced all claims to Alsace-Lorraine, a land for which we have fought two great wars . . . Without taking the past into account Germany has concluded a nonaggression pact with Poland . . . We shall adhere to it unconditionally. . . . We recognize Poland as the home of a great and nationally conscious people.

As for Austria:

Germany neither intends nor wishes to interfere in the internal affairs of Austria, to annex Austria, or to conclude an Anschluss.

Hitler's thirteen points were quite comprehensive. Germany could not return to Geneva until the League divested itself of the Versailles Treaty. When that was done and full equality of all nations recognized, he implied, Germany would rejoin the League. Germany, however, would "unconditionally respect" the nonmilitary clauses of the Versailles Treaty, "including the territorial provisions. In particular it will uphold and fulfill all obligations arising out of the Locarno Treaty." Hitler also pledged Germany to abide by the demilitarization of the Rhineland. Though willing "at any time" to participate in a system of collective security, Germany preferred bilateral agreements and was ready to conclude nonaggression pacts with its neighbor states. It was also prepared to agree to British and French proposals for supplementing the Locarno Treaty with an air accord.

As for disarmament, Hitler was ready to go the limit:

> The German government is ready to agree to any limitation which leads to abolition of the heaviest arms, especially suited for aggression, such [as] the heaviest artillery and the heaviest tanks . . . Germany declares herself ready to agree to any limitation whatsoever of the caliber of artillery, battleships, cruisers and torpedo boats. In like manner, the German government is ready to agree to the limitation of tonnage for submarines, or to their complete abolition . . .

In this connection Hitler held out a special bait for Great Britain. He was willing to limit the new German Navy to 35 per cent of the British naval forces; that, he added, would still leave the Germans 15 per cent below the French in naval tonnage. To the objections raised abroad that this would be only the beginning of German demands, Hitler answered, "For Germany, this demand is final and abiding."

A little after ten in the evening, Hitler came to his peroration:

> Whoever lights the torch of war in Europe can wish for nothing but chaos. We, however, live in the firm conviction that in our time will be fulfilled not the decline but the renaissance of the West. That Germany may make an imperishable contribution to this great work is our proud hope and our unshakable belief.[11]

These were honeyed words of peace, reason and conciliation, and in the Western democracies of Europe, where the people and their governments desperately yearned for the continuance of peace on any reasonable basis, on almost any basis, they were lapped up. The most influential newspaper in the British Isles, the *Times* of London, welcomed them with almost hysterical joy.

> . . . The speech turns out to be reasonable, straightforward and comprehensive. No one who reads it with an impartial mind can doubt that the points of policy laid down by Herr Hitler may fairly constitute the basis of a complete settlement with Germany—a free, equal and strong Germany instead of the prostrate Germany upon whom peace was imposed sixteen years ago . . .
>
> It is to be hoped that the speech will be taken everywhere as a sincere and well-considered utterance meaning precisely what it says.[12]

This great journal, one of the chief glories of English journalism, would play, like the Chamberlain government, a dubious role in the disastrous British appeasement of Hitler. But to this writer, at least, it had even less excuse than the government, for in its Berlin correspondent, Norman Ebbutt, it had, until he was expelled on August 16, 1937, a source of information about Hitler's doings and purposes that was much more revealing than that provided by other foreign correspondents or foreign diplomats, including the British. Though much that he wrote for the *Times* from Berlin in those days was not published,* as he often complained to this writer and as was later confirmed, the *Times* editors must have read *all* of his dispatches and have been in the position therefore of knowing what was really going on in Nazi Germany and how hollow Hitler's grandiose promises were.

The British government, no less than the *Times,* was ready and anxious to accept Hitler's proposals as "sincere" and "well-considered"—especially the one by which Germany would agree to a Navy 35 per cent the size of Britain's.

Hitler had shrewdly thrown out a hint to Sir John Simon, when the British Foreign Secretary and Eden made their postponed visit to him at the end of March, that a naval agreement might easily be worked out between the two powers which would guarantee English superiority. Now on May 21 he had made a public and specific offer—a German fleet of only 35 per cent of the tonnage of the British—and he had added in his speech some especially friendly words for England. "Germany," he had said, "has not the intention or the necessity or the means to participate in any new naval rivalry"—an allusion, which apparently was not lost on the English, to the days before 1914 when Tirpitz, enthusiastically backed by Wilhelm II, was building up a high-seas fleet to match England's. "The German government," continued Hitler, "recognizes the overpowering vital importance, and therewith the justification, of a dominating protection for the British Empire on the sea . . . The German government has the straightforward intention to find and maintain a relationship with the British people and state which will prevent for all time a repetition of the only struggle there has been between the two nations." Hitler had expressed similar sentiments in *Mein Kampf,* where he had stressed that one of the Kaiser's greatest mistakes had been his enmity toward England and his absurd attempt to rival the British in naval power.

With incredible naïveté and speed, the British government fell for Hitler's bait. Ribbentrop, who had now become Hitler's messenger boy for foreign errands, was invited to come to London in June for naval talks. Vain and tactless, he told the British that Hitler's offer was not subject to negotiation; they must take it or leave it. The British took it. Without consulting their allies of the Stresa front, France and Italy, which were

---

* "I do my utmost, night after night, to keep out of the paper anything that might hurt their [German] susceptibilities," Geoffrey Dawson, the editor of the *Times,* wrote on May 23, 1937, to his Geneva correspondent, H. G. Daniels, who had preceded Ebbutt in Berlin. "I can really think of nothing that has been printed now for many months past to which they could possibly take exception as unfair comment." (John Evelyn Wrench, *Geoffrey Dawson and Our Times.*)

also naval powers and much concerned over German rearmament and German flouting of the military clauses of Versailles, and without even informing the League of Nations, which was supposed to uphold the 1919 peace treaties, they proceeded, for what they thought was a private advantage, to wipe out the naval restrictions of Versailles.

For it was obvious to the most simple mind in Berlin that by agreeing to Germany's building a navy a third as large as the British, the London government was giving Hitler free rein to build up a navy as fast as was physically possible—one that would tax the capacity of his shipyards and steel mills for at least ten years. It was thus not a limitation on German rearmament but an encouragement to expand it, in the naval arm, as rapidly as Germany could find the means to do so.

To add insult to the injury already done France, the British government, in fulfillment of a promise to Hitler, refused to tell her closest ally what kind of ships and how many Great Britain had agreed that Germany should build, except that the German submarine tonnage—the building of submarines in Germany was specifically forbidden by Versailles—would be 60 per cent of Britain's and, if exceptional circumstances arose, might be 100 per cent.[13] Actually the Anglo–German agreement authorized the Germans to build five battleships, whose tonnage and armament would be greater than that of anything the British had afloat, though the official figures were faked to deceive London—twenty-one cruisers and sixty-four destroyers. Not all of them were built or completed by the outbreak of the war, but enough of them, with the U-boats, were ready to cause Britain disastrous losses in the first years of the second war.

Mussolini took due notice of the "perfidy of Albion." Two could play at the game of appeasing Hitler. Moreover, England's cynical attitude of disregarding the Versailles Treaty encouraged him in the belief that London might not take too seriously the flouting of the Covenant of the League of Nations. On October 3, 1935, in defiance of the Covenant, his armies invaded the ancient mountain kingdom of Abyssinia. The League, led by Great Britain and supported halfheartedly by France, which saw that Germany was the greater danger in the long run, promptly voted sanctions. But they were only partial sanctions, timidly enforced. They did not prevent Mussolini from conquering Ethiopia but they did destroy the friendship of Fascist Italy with Britain and France and bring an end to the Stresa front against Nazi Germany.

Who stood the most to gain from this chain of events but Adolf Hitler? On October 4, the day after the Italian invasion began, I spent the day in the Wilhelmstrasse talking with a number of party and government officials. A diary note that evening summed up how quickly and well the Germans had sized up the situation:

The Wilhelmstrasse is delighted. Either Mussolini will stumble and get himself so heavily involved in Africa that he will be greatly weakened in Europe, whereupon Hitler can seize Austria, hitherto protected by the Duce; or he will win, defying France and Britain, and thereupon be ripe for a tie-up with Hitler against the Western democracies. Either way Hitler wins.[14]

This would soon be demonstrated.

A COUP IN THE RHINELAND

In his Reichstag "peace" speech of May 21, 1935, which, as we have seen, had so impressed the world and, above all, Great Britain, Hitler had mentioned that "an element of legal insecurity" had been brought into the Locarno Pact as a result of the mutual-assistance pact which had been signed between Russia and France on March 2 in Paris and on March 14 in Moscow, but which up to the end of the year had not been ratified by the French Parliament. The German Foreign Office called this "element" to the attention of Paris in a formal note to the French government.

On November 21, François-Poncet, the French ambassador, had a talk with Hitler in which the Fuehrer launched "into a long tirade" against the Franco–Soviet Pact. François-Poncet reported to Paris he was convinced that Hitler intended to use the pact as an excuse to occupy the demilitarized zone of the Rhineland. "Hitler's sole hesitancy," he added, "is now concerned with the appropriate moment to act."[15]

François-Poncet, probably the best-informed ambassador in Berlin, knew what he was talking about, though he was undoubtedly unaware that as early as the previous spring, on May 2, nineteen days before Hitler's assurances in the Reichstag that he would respect the Locarno Pact and the territorial clauses of Versailles, General von Blomberg had issued his first directive to the three armed services to prepare plans for the reoccupation of the demilitarized Rhineland. The code name *Schulung* was given to the operation, it was to be "executed by a surprise blow at lightning speed" and its planning was to be so secret that "only the very smallest number of officers should be informed." In fact, in the interests of secrecy, Blomberg wrote out the order in handwriting.[16]

On June 16 further discussion of the move into the Rhineland took place at the tenth meeting of the Working Committee of the Reich Defense Council, during which a Colonel Alfred Jodl, who had just become head of the Home Defense Department, reported on the plans and emphasized the need for the strictest secrecy. Nothing should be committed to writing that was not absolutely necessary, he warned, and he added that "without exception such material must be kept in safes."[17]

All through the winter of 1935–36 Hitler bided his time. France and Britain, he could not help but note, were preoccupied with stopping Italy's aggression in Abyssinia, but Mussolini seemed to be getting by with it. Despite its much-publicized sanctions, the League of Nations was proving itself impotent to halt a determined aggressor. In Paris the French Parliament seemed to be in no hurry to ratify the pact with the Soviet Union; the growing sentiment in the Right was all against it. Apparently Hitler

thought there was a good chance of the French Chamber or Senate rejecting the alliance with Moscow. In that case he would have to look for another excuse for *Schulung*. But the pact came before the Chamber on
February 11 and it was approved on the twenty-seventh by a vote of 353
to 164. Two days later, on March 1, Hitler reached his decision, somewhat
to the consternation of the generals, most of whom were convinced that
the French would make mincemeat of the small German forces which had
been gathered for the move into the Rhineland. Nevertheless, on the next
day, March 2, 1936, in obedience to his master's instructions, Blomberg
issued formal orders for the occupation of the Rhineland. It was, he told
the senior commanders of the armed forces, to be a "surprise move."
Blomberg expected it to be a "peaceful operation." If it turned out that
it was not—that is, that the French would fight—the Commander in Chief
reserved the "right to decide on any military countermeasures."[18] Actually, as I learned six days later and as would be confirmed from the
testimony of the generals at Nuremberg, Blomberg already had in mind
what those countermeasures would be: a hasty retreat back over the
Rhine!

But the French, their nation already paralyzed by internal strife and
the people sinking into defeatism, did not know this when a small token
force of German troops paraded across the Rhine bridges at dawn on
March 7 and entered the demilitarized zone.* At 10 A.M. Neurath, the
compliant Foreign Minister, called in the ambassadors of France, Britain
and Italy, apprised them of the news from the Rhineland and handed them
a formal note denouncing the Locarno Treaty, which Hitler had just
broken—and proposing new plans for peace! "Hitler struck his adversary in the face," François-Poncet wryly observed, "and as he did so declared: 'I bring you proposals for peace!' "[20]

Indeed, two hours later the Fuehrer was standing at the rostrum of the
Reichstag before a delirious audience, expounding on his desire for peace
and his latest ideas of how to maintain it. I went over to the Kroll Opera
House to see the spectacle, which I shall never forget, for it was both fascinating and gruesome. After a long harangue about the evils of Versailles
and the threat of Bolshevism, Hitler calmly announced that France's pact
with Russia had invalidated the Locarno Treaty, which, unlike that of
Versailles, Germany had freely signed. The scene that followed I noted
down in my diary that evening.

"Germany no longer feels bound by the Locarno Treaty [Hitler said]. In the
interest of the primitive rights of its people to the security of their frontier and
the safeguarding of their defense, the German government has re-established,

---

* According to Jodl's testimony at Nuremberg, only three battalions crossed the
Rhine, making for Aachen, Trier and Saarbruecken, and only one division was
employed in the occupation of the entire territory. Allied intelligence estimates
were considerably larger: 35,000 men, or approximately three divisions. Hitler
commented later, "The fact was, I had only four brigades."[19]

as from today, the absolute and unrestricted sovereignty of the Reich in the demilitarized zone!"

Now the six hundred deputies, personal appointees all of Hitler, little men with big bodies and bulging necks and cropped hair and pouched bellies and brown uniforms and heavy boots . . . leap to their feet like automatons, their right arms upstretched in the Nazi salute, and scream "Heils" . . . Hitler raises his hand for silence. . . . He says in a deep, resonant voice, "Men of the German Reichstag!" The silence is utter.

"In this historic hour, when, in the Reich's western provinces, German troops are at this minute marching into their future peacetime garrisons, we all unite in two sacred vows."

He can go no further. It is news to this "parliamentary" mob that German soldiers are already on the move into the Rhineland. All the militarism in their German blood surges to their heads. They spring, yelling and crying, to their feet . . . Their hands are raised in slavish salute, their faces now contorted with hysteria, their mouths wide open, shouting, shouting, their eyes, burning with fanaticism, glued on the new god, the Messiah. The Messiah plays his role superbly. His head lowered, as if in all humbleness, he waits patiently for silence. Then his voice, still low, but choking with emotion, utters the two vows:

"First, we swear to yield to no force whatever in restoration of the honor of our people . . . Secondly, we pledge that now, more than ever, we shall strive for an understanding between the European peoples, especially for one with our Western neighbor nations . . . We have no territorial demands to make in Europe! . . . Germany will never break the peace!"

It was a long time before the cheering stopped . . . A few generals made their way out. Behind their smiles, however, you could not help detecting a nervousness . . . I ran into General von Blomberg . . . His face was white, his cheeks twitching.[21]

And with reason. The Minister of Defense, who five days before had issued in his own handwriting the order to march, was losing his nerve. The next day I learned that he had given orders for his troops to withdraw across the Rhine should the French move to oppose them. But the French never made the slightest move. François-Poncet says that after his warning of the previous November, the French High Command had asked the government what it would do in case the ambassador proved right. The answer was, he says, that the government would take the matter up with the League of Nations.[22] Actually, when the blow occurred,* it was the French government which wanted to act and the French General Staff which held back. "General Gamelin," François-Poncet declares, "advised that a war operation, however limited, entailed unpredictable risks and could not be undertaken without decreeing a general mobiliza-

---

* Despite François-Poncet's warning of the previous fall, Germany's action apparently came as a complete surprise to the French and British governments and their general staffs.

tion."[23] The most General Gamelin, the Chief of the General Staff, would do—and did—was concentrate thirteen divisions near the German frontier, but merely to reinforce the Maginot Line. Even this was enough to throw a scare into the German High Command. Blomberg, backed by Jodl and most of the officers at the top, wanted to pull back the three battalions that had crossed the Rhine. As Jodl testified at Nuremberg, "Considering the situation we were in, the French covering army could have blown us to pieces."[24]

It could have—and had it, that almost certainly would have been the end of Hitler, after which history might have taken quite a different and brighter turn than it did, for the dictator could never have survived such a fiasco. Hitler himself admitted as much. "A retreat on our part," he conceded later, "would have spelled collapse."[25] It was Hitler's iron nerves alone, which now, as during many crises that lay ahead, saved the situation and, confounding the reluctant generals, brought success. But it was no easy moment for him.

"The forty-eight hours after the march into the Rhineland," Paul Schmidt, his interpreter, heard him later say, "were the most nerve-racking in my life. If the French had then marched into the Rhineland, we would have had to withdraw with our tails between our legs, for the military resources at our disposal would have been wholly inadequate for even a moderate resistance."[26]

Confident that the French would not march, he bluntly turned down all suggestions for pulling back by the wavering High Command. General Beck, Chief of the General Staff, wanted the Fuehrer to at least soften the blow by proclaiming that he would not fortify the area west of the Rhine— a suggestion, Jodl later testified, "which the Fuehrer turned down very bluntly"—for obvious reasons, as we shall see.[27] Blomberg's proposal to withdraw, Hitler later told General von Rundstedt, was nothing less than an act of cowardice.[28]

"What would have happened," Hitler exclaimed in a bull session with his cronies at headquarters on the evening of March 27, 1942, in recalling the Rhineland coup, "if anybody other than myself had been at the head of the Reich! Anyone you care to mention would have lost his nerve. I was obliged to lie, and what saved us was my unshakable obstinacy and my amazing aplomb."[29]

It was true, but it must also be recorded that he was aided not only by the hesitations of the French but by the supineness of their British allies. The French Foreign Minister, Pierre Étienne Flandin, flew to London on March 11 and begged the British government to back France in a military counteraction in the Rhineland. His pleas were unavailing. Britain would not risk war even though Allied superiority over the Germans was overwhelming. As Lord Lothian remarked, "The Germans, after all, are only going into their own back garden." Even before the French arrived in London, Anthony Eden, who had become Foreign Secretary in the previous December, had told the House of Commons, on March 9, "Occupation of the Rhineland by the Reichswehr deals a heavy blow to the principle of the sanctity of treaties. Fortunately," he added, "we have no reason to suppose that Germany's present action threatens hostilities."[30]

And yet France was entitled, under the terms of the Locarno Treaty, to take military action against the presence of German troops in the demilitarized zone, and Britain was obligated by that treaty to back her with her own armed forces. The abortive London conversations were a confirmation to Hitler that he had gotten away with his latest gamble.

The British not only shied away from the risk of war but once again they took seriously the latest installment of Hitler's "peace" proposals. In the notes handed to the three ambassadors on March 7 and in his speech to the Reichstag, Hitler had offered to sign a twenty-five-year nonaggression pact with Belgium and France, to be guaranteed by Britain and Italy; to conclude similar nonaggression pacts with Germany's neighbors on the east; to agree to the demilitarization of *both* sides of the Franco–German frontier; and, finally, to return to the League of Nations. Hitler's sincerity might have been judged by his proposal to demilitarize *both* sides of the Franco–German border, since it would have forced France to scrap her Maginot Line, her last protection against a surprise German attack.

In London, the esteemed *Times,* while deploring Hitler's precipitate action in invading the Rhineland, headed its leading editorial "A Chance to Rebuild."

In retrospect, it is easy to see that Hitler's successful gamble in the Rhineland brought him a victory more staggering and more fatal in its immense consequences than could be comprehended at the time. At home it fortified his popularity* and his power, raising them to heights which no German ruler of the past had ever enjoyed. It assured his ascendancy over his generals, who had hesitated and weakened at a moment of crisis when he had held firm. It taught them that in foreign politics and even in military affairs his judgment was superior to theirs. They had feared that the French would fight; he knew better. And finally, and above all, the Rhineland occupation, small as it was as a military operation, opened the way, as only Hitler (and Churchill, alone, in England) seemed to realize, to vast new opportunities in a Europe which was not only shaken

---

* On March 7 Hitler had dissolved the Reichstag and called for a new "election" and a referendum on his move into the Rhineland. According to the official figures of the voting on March 29, some 99 per cent of the 45,453,691 registered voters went to the polls, and 98.8 per cent of them approved Hitler's action. Foreign correspondents who visited the polling places found some irregularities—especially, open instead of secret voting—and there was no doubt that some Germans feared (with justification, as we have seen) that a *Nein* vote might be discovered by the Gestapo. Dr. Hugo Eckener told this writer that on his new Zeppelin *Hindenburg,* which Goebbels had ordered to cruise over German cities as a publicity stunt, the *Ja* vote, which was announced by the Propaganda Minister as forty-two, outnumbered the total number of persons aboard by two. Nevertheless, this observer, who covered the "election" from one corner of the Reich to the other, has no doubt that the vote of approval for Hitler's coup was overwhelming. And why not? The junking of Versailles and the appearance of German soldiers marching again into what was, after all, German territory were things that almost all Germans naturally approved. The "No" vote was given as 540,211.

but whose strategic situation was irrevocably changed by the parading of three German battalions across the Rhine bridges.

Conversely, it is equally easy to see, in retrospect, that France's failure to repel the Wehrmacht battalions and Britain's failure to back her in what would have been nothing more than a police action was a disaster for the West from which sprang all the later ones of even greater magnitude. In March 1936 the two Western democracies were given their last chance to halt, without the risk of a serious war, the rise of a militarized, aggressive, totalitarian Germany and, in fact—as we have seen Hitler admitting— bring the Nazi dictator and his regime tumbling down. They let the chance slip by.

For France, it was the beginning of the end. Her allies in the East, Russia, Poland, Czechoslovakia, Rumania and Yugoslavia, suddenly were faced with the fact that France would not fight against German aggression to preserve the security system which the French government itself had taken the lead in so laboriously building up. But more than that. These Eastern allies began to realize that even if France were not so supine, she would soon not be able to lend them much assistance because of Germany's feverish construction of a West Wall behind the Franco–German border. The erection of this fortress line, they saw, would quickly change the strategic map of Europe, to their detriment. They could scarcely expect a France which did not dare, with her one hundred divisions, to repel three German battalions, to bleed her young manhood against impregnable German fortifications while the Wehrmacht attacked in the East. But even if the unexpected took place, it would be futile. Henceforth the French could tie down in the West only a small part of the growing German Army. The rest would be free for operations against Germany's Eastern neighbors.

The value of the Rhineland fortifications to Hitler's strategy was conveyed to William C. Bullitt, the American ambassador to France, when he called on the German Foreign Minister in Berlin on May 18, 1936.

Von Neurath said [Bullitt reported to the State Department] that it was the policy of the German Government to do nothing active in foreign affairs until "the Rhineland had been digested." He explained that he meant that until the German fortifications had been constructed on the French and Belgian frontiers, the German Government would do everything possible to prevent rather than encourage an outbreak by the Nazis in Austria and would pursue a quiet line with regard to Czechoslovakia. "As soon as our fortifications are constructed and the countries of Central Europe realize that France cannot enter German territory at will, all those countries will begin to feel very differently about their foreign policies and a new constellation will develop," he said.[31]

This development now began.

"As I stood at the grave of my predecessor [the murdered Dollfuss]," Dr. Schuschnigg related in his memoirs, "I knew that in order to save

Austrian independence I had to embark on a course of appeasement . . .
Everything had to be avoided which could give Germany a pretext for
intervention and everything had to be done to secure in some way Hitler's
toleration of the status quo."[32]

The new and youthful Austrian Chancellor had been encouraged by
Hitler's public declaration to the Reichstag on May 21, 1935, that "Germany neither intends nor wishes to interfere in the internal affairs of
Austria, to annex Austria or to conclude an Anschluss"; and he had been
reassured by the reiteration at Stresa by Italy, France and Britain of their
determination to help safeguard Austria's independence. Then Mussolini,
Austria's principal protector since 1933, had become bogged down in
Abyssinia and had broken with France and Britain. When the Germans
marched into the Rhineland and began to fortify it, Dr. Schuschnigg
realized that some appeasement of Hitler was due. He began negotiating
a new treaty with the wily German minister in Vienna, Papen, who,
though the Nazis had come within an ace of murdering him during the
June purge, had nevertheless gone to work on his arrival in Austria in
the late summer of 1934, after the Nazi assassination of Dollfuss, to undermine Austria's independence and capture Hitler's native land for the
Leader. "National Socialism must and will overpower the new Austrian
ideology," he had written Hitler on July 27, 1935, in giving an account
of his first year of service in Vienna.[33]

In its published text the Austro–German agreement signed on July 11,
1936, seemed to show an unusual amount of generosity and tolerance on
the part of Hitler. Germany reaffirmed its recognition of Austria's sovereignty and the promise not to interfere in the internal affairs of its neighbor. In return, Austria pledged that in its foreign policy it would always
act on the principle that it acknowledged itself to be "a German state."

But there were secret clauses in the treaty,[34] and in them Schuschnigg
made concessions which would lead him—and his little country—to their
doom. He agreed secretly to amnesty Nazi political prisoners in Austria
and to appoint representatives of the "so-called 'National Opposition' "—
a euphemism for Nazis or Nazi sympathizers—to positions of "political
responsibility." This was equivalent to allowing Hitler to set up a Trojan
horse in Austria. Into it would crawl shortly Seyss-Inquart, a Viennese
lawyer, who will cut a certain figure in the subsequent narrative.

Although Papen had obtained Hitler's approval of the text of the
treaty, making a personal visit to Berlin for the purpose early in July, the
Fuehrer was furious with his envoy when the latter telephoned him on
July 16 to notify him that the agreement had been signed.

Hitler's reaction astonished me [Papen later wrote]. Instead of expressing
his gratification, he broke into a flood of abuse. I had misled him, he said, into
making exaggerated concessions . . . The whole thing was a trap.[35]

As it turned out, it was a trap for Schuschnigg, not for Hitler.
The signing of the Austro–German treaty was a sign that Mussolini had

lost his grip on Austria. It might have been expected that this would worsen the relations between the two fascist dictators. But just the opposite occurred—due to events which now, in 1936, played into Hitler's hands.

On May 2, 1936, Italian forces entered the Abyssinian capital, Addis Ababa, and on July 4 the League of Nations formally capitulated and called off its sanctions against Italy. Two weeks later, on July 16, Franco staged a military revolt in Spain and civil war broke out.

Hitler, as was his custom at that time of year, was taking in the opera at the Wagner Festival at Bayreuth. On the night of July 22, after he had returned from the theater, a German businessman from Morocco, accompanied by the local Nazi leader, arrived in Bayreuth with an urgent letter from Franco. The rebel leader needed planes and other assistance. Hitler immediately summoned Goering and General von Blomberg, who happened to be in Bayreuth, and that very evening the decision was taken to give support to the Spanish rebellion.[36]

Though German aid to Franco never equaled that given by Italy, which dispatched between sixty and seventy thousand troops as well as vast supplies of arms and planes, it was considerable. The Germans estimated later that they spent half a billion marks on the venture[37] besides furnishing planes, tanks, technicians and the Condor Legion, an Air Force unit which distinguished itself by the obliteration of the Spanish town of Guernica and its civilian inhabitants. Relative to Germany's own massive rearmament it was not much, but it paid handsome dividends to Hitler.

It gave France a third unfriendly fascist power on its borders. It exacerbated the internal strife in France between Right and Left and thus weakened Germany's principal rival in the West. Above all it rendered impossible a *rapprochement* of Britain and France with Italy, which the Paris and London governments had hoped for after the termination of the Abyssinian War, and thus drove Mussolini into the arms of Hitler.

From the very beginning the Fuehrer's Spanish policy was shrewd, calculated and far-seeing. A perusal of the captured German documents makes plain that one of Hitler's purposes was to *prolong* the Spanish Civil War in order to keep the Western democracies and Italy at loggerheads and draw Mussolini toward him.* As early as December 1936, Ulrich von Hassell, the German ambassador in Rome, who had not yet achieved that recognition of Nazi aims and practices which he later obtained and which would cost him his life, was reporting to the Wilhelmstrasse:

---

* More than a year later, on November 5, 1937, Hitler would reiterate his Spanish policy in a confidential talk with his generals and his Foreign Minister. "A hundred per cent victory for Franco," he told them, was "not desirable from the German point of view. Rather we are interested in a continuance of the war and in keeping up the tension in the Mediterranean."[38]

The role played by the Spanish conflict as regards Italy's relations with France and England could be similar to that of the Abyssinian conflict, bringing out clearly the actual, opposing interests of the powers and thus preventing Italy from being drawn into the net of the Western powers and used for their machinations. The struggle for dominant political influence in Spain lays bare the natural opposition between Italy and France; at the same time the position of Italy as a power in the western Mediterranean comes into competition with that of Britain. All the more clearly will Italy recognize the advisability of confronting the Western powers shoulder to shoulder with Germany.[39]

It was these circumstances which gave birth to the Rome–Berlin Axis. On October 24, after conferences with Neurath in Berlin, Count Galeazzo Ciano, Mussolini's son-in-law and Foreign Minister, made the first of his many pilgrimages to Berchtesgaden. He found the German dictator in a friendly and expansive mood. Mussolini, Hitler declared, was "the leading statesman in the world, to whom none may even remotely compare himself." Together, Italy and Germany could conquer not only "Bolshevism" but the West. Including England! The British, Hitler thought, might eventually seek an accommodation with a united Italy and Germany. If not, the two powers, acting together, could easily dispose of her. "German and Italian rearmament," Hitler reminded Ciano, "is proceeding much more rapidly than rearmament can in England . . . In three years Germany will be ready . . ."[40]

The date is interesting. Three years hence would be the fall of 1939.

In Berlin on October 21, Ciano and Neurath had signed a secret protocol which outlined a common policy for Germany and Italy in foreign affairs. In a speech at Milan a few days later (November 1) Mussolini publicly referred to it without divulging the contents, as an agreement which constituted an "Axis"—around which the other European powers "may work together." It would become a famous—and, for the Duce, a fatal—word.

With Mussolini in the bag, Hitler turned his attentions elsewhere. In August 1936 he had appointed Ribbentrop as German ambassador in London in an effort to explore the possibility of a settlement with England—on his own terms. Incompetent and lazy, vain as a peacock, arrogant and without humor, Ribbentrop was the worst possible choice for such a post, as Goering realized. "When I criticized Ribbentrop's qualifications to handle British problems," he later declared, "the Fuehrer pointed out to me that Ribbentrop knew 'Lord So and So' and 'Minister So and So.' To which I replied: 'Yes, but the difficulty is that they know Ribbentrop.' "[41]

It is true that Ribbentrop, unattractive a figure though he was, was not without influential friends in London. Mrs. Simpson, the friend of the King, was believed in Berlin to be one of these. But Ribbentrop's initial efforts in his new post were discouraging and in November he flew back to Berlin to conclude some non-British business he had been dabbling in.

On November 25 he signed the Anti-Comintern Pact with Japan, in which, he told the correspondents (of whom this writer was one) without batting an eye, Germany and Japan had joined together to defend *Western* civilization. On the surface this pact seemed to be nothing more than a propaganda trick by which Germany and Japan could win world support by exploiting the universal dislike for Communism and the general distrust of the Comintern. But in this treaty too there was a secret protocol, specifically directed against Russia. In case of an unprovoked attack by the Soviet Union against Germany or Japan, the two nations agreed to consult on what measures to take "to safeguard their common interests" and also to "take no measures which would tend to ease the situation of the Soviet Union." It was also agreed that neither nation would make any political treaties with Russia contrary to the spirit of the agreement without mutual consent.[42]

It would not be very long before Germany broke the agreement and accused Japan—unjustifiably—of not observing it. But the pact did serve a certain propaganda purpose among the world's gullible and it brought together for the first time the three have-not and aggressor nations. Italy signed it the following year.

On January 30, 1937, Hitler addressed the Reichstag, proclaiming "the withdrawal of the German signature" from the Versailles Treaty—an empty but typical gesture, since the treaty was by now dead as a doornail—and reviewing with pride the record of his four years in office. He could be pardoned for his pride, for it was an impressive record in both domestic and foreign affairs. He had, as we have seen, abolished unemployment, created a boom in business, built up a powerful Army, Navy and Air Force, provided them with considerable armaments and the promise of more on a massive scale. He had singlehandedly broken the fetters of Versailles and bluffed his way into occupying the Rhineland. Completely isolated at first, he had found a loyal ally in Mussolini and another in Franco, and he had detached Poland from France. Most important of all, perhaps, he had released the dynamic energy of the German people, reawakening their confidence in the nation and their sense of its mission as a great and expanding world power.

Everyone could see the contrast between this thriving, martial, boldly led new Germany and the decadent democracies in the West, whose confusions and vacillations seemed to increase with each new month of the calendar. Though they were alarmed, Britain and France had not lifted a finger to prevent Hitler from violating the peace treaty by rearming Germany and by reoccupying the Rhineland; they had been unable to stop Mussolini in Abyssinia. And now, as the year 1937 began, they were cutting a sorry figure by their futile gestures to prevent Germany and Italy from determining the outcome of the Spanish Civil War. Everyone knew what Italy and Germany were doing in Spain to assure Franco's victory. Yet the governments of London and Paris continued for years to engage in empty diplomatic negotiations with Berlin and Rome to assure "nonintervention" in Spain. It was a sport which seems to have amused the German dictator and which certainly increased his contempt for the stumbling political leaders of France and Britain—"little worms," he would shortly call them on a historic occasion when he again humbled the two Western democracies with the greatest of ease.

Neither Great Britain and France, their governments and their peoples, nor the majority of the German people seemed to realize as 1937 began that almost all that Hitler had done in his first four years was a preparation for war. This writer can testify from personal observation that right up to September 1, 1939, the German people were convinced that Hitler would get what he wanted—and what they wanted—without recourse to war. But among the elite who were running Germany, or serving it in the key positions, there could have been no doubt what Hitler's objective was. As the four-year "trial" period of Nazi rule, as Hitler called it, approached an end, Goering, who in September 1936 had been put in charge of the Four-Year Plan, bluntly stated what was coming in a secret speech to industrialists and high officials in Berlin.

The battle we are now approaching [he said] demands a colossal measure of production capacity. No limit on rearmament can be visualized. The only alternatives are victory or destruction . . . We live in a time when the final battle is in sight. We are already on the threshold of mobilization and we are already at war. All that is lacking is the actual shooting.[43]

Goering's warning was given on December 17, 1936. Within eleven months, as we shall shortly see, Hitler made his fateful and inalterable decision to go to war.

1937: "NO SURPRISES"

In his address to the robots of the Reichstag on January 30, 1937, Hitler proclaimed, "The time of so-called surprises has been ended."

And in truth, there were no weekend surprises during 1937.* The year for Germany was one of consolidation and further preparation for the objectives which in November the Fuehrer would at last lay down to a handful of his highest officers. It was a year devoted to forging armaments, training troops, trying out the new Air Force in Spain,† developing

---

* Wilhelmstrasse officials used to say jokingly that Hitler pulled his surprises on Saturdays because he had been told that British officials took the weekend off in the country.

† In his testimony at Nuremberg on March 14, 1946, Goering spoke proudly of the opportunities which the Spanish Civil War gave for testing "my young Luftwaffe. With the permission of the Fuehrer I sent a large part of my transport fleet and a number of experimental fighter units, bombers and antiaircraft guns; and in that way I had an opportunity to ascertain, under combat conditions, whether the material was equal to the task. In order that the personnel, too, might gather a certain experience, I saw to it that there was a continuous flow [so] that new people were constantly being sent and others recalled."[44]

ersatz gasoline and rubber, cementing the Rome–Berlin Axis and watching for further weak spots in Paris, London and Vienna.

All through the first months of 1937, Hitler sent important emissaries to Rome to cultivate Mussolini. The Germans were somewhat uneasy over Italy's flirtation with Britain (on January 2 Ciano had signed a "gentleman's agreement" with the British government in which the two countries recognized each other's vital interests in the Mediterranean) and they realized that the question of Austria was still a touchy subject in Rome. When Goering saw the Duce on January 15 and bluntly spoke of the inevitability of the Anschluss with Austria, the excitable Italian dictator, according to the German interpreter, Paul Schmidt, shook his head violently, and Ambassador von Hassell reported to Berlin that Goering's statement on Austria "had met with a cool reception." In June Neurath hastened to assure the Duce that Germany would abide by its July 11 pact with Austria. Only in the case of an attempted restoration of the Hapsburgs would the Germans take stern action.

Thus placated on Austria and still smarting from the opposition of France and Britain to almost all of his ambitions—in Ethiopia, in Spain, in the Mediterranean—Mussolini accepted an invitation from Hitler to visit Germany, and on September 25, 1937, outfitted in a new uniform created especially for the occasion, he crossed the Alps into the Third Reich. Feted and flattered as a conquering hero by Hitler and his aides, Mussolini could not then know how fateful a journey this was, the first of many to Hitler's side which were to lead to a progressive weakening of his own position and finally to a disastrous end. Hitler's purpose was not to engage in further diplomatic conversations with his guest but to impress him with Germany's strength and thus play on Mussolini's obsession to cast his lot with the winning side. The Duce was rushed from one side of Germany to the other: to parades of the S.S. and the troops, to Army maneuvers in Mecklenburg, to the roaring armament factories in the Ruhr.

His visit was climaxed by a celebration in Berlin on September 28 which visibly impressed him. A gigantic crowd of one million persons was gathered on the Maifeld to hear the two fascist dictators speak their pieces. Mussolini, orating in German, was carried away by the deafening applause—and by Hitler's flattering words. The Duce, said the Fuehrer, was "one of those lonely men of the ages on whom history is not tested, but who themselves are the makers of history." I remember that a severe thunderstorm broke over the field before Mussolini had finished his oration and that in the confusion of the scattering mob the S.S. security arrangements broke down and the proud Duce, drenched to the skin and sorely put, was forced to make his way back to his headquarters alone and as best he could. However, this untoward experience did not dampen Mussolini's enthusiasm to be a partner of this new, powerful Germany, and the next day, after reviewing a military parade of Army, Navy and Air Force detachments, he returned to Rome convinced that his future lay at the side of Hitler.

It was not surprising, then, that a month later when Ribbentrop journeyed to Rome to obtain Mussolini's signature for the Anti-Comintern Pact, a ceremony held on November 6, he was told by the Duce of Italy's declining interest in the independence of Austria. "Let events [in Austria] take their natural course," Mussolini said. This was the go-ahead for which Hitler had been waiting.

Another ruler became impressed by Nazi Germany's growing power. When Hitler broke the Locarno Treaty and, in occupying the Rhineland, placed German troops on the Belgian border, King Leopold withdrew his country from the Locarno Pact and from its alliance with Britain and France and proclaimed that henceforth Belgium would follow a strict course of neutrality. This was a serious blow to the collective defense of the West, but in April 1937 Britain and France accepted it—an action for which they, as well as Belgium, would soon pay dearly.

At the end of May the Wilhelmstrasse had watched with interest the retirement of Stanley Baldwin as Prime Minister of Great Britain and the accession of Neville Chamberlain to that post. The Germans were pleased to hear that the new British Prime Minister would take a more active part in foreign affairs than had his predecessor and that he was determined to reach, if possible, an understanding with Nazi Germany. What sort of understanding would be acceptable to Hitler was outlined in a secret memorandum of November 10, written by Baron von Weizsaecker, then head of the Political Department of the German Foreign Office.

From England we want colonies and freedom of action in the East . . . The British need for tranquillity is great. It would be profitable to find out what England would be willing to pay for such tranquillity.[45]

An occasion for finding out what England would pay arose in November when Lord Halifax, with Mr. Chamberlain's enthusiastic approval, made the pilgrimage to Berchtesgaden to see Hitler. On November 19 they held a long conversation, and in the lengthy secret German memorandum on it drawn up by the German Foreign Office[46] three points emerge: Chamberlain was most anxious for a settlement with Germany and proposed talks between the two countries on a cabinet level; Britain wanted a general European settlement, in return for which she was prepared to make concessions to Hitler as regards colonies and Eastern Europe; Hitler was not greatly interested at the moment in an Anglo–German accord.

In view of the rather negative outcome of the talk, it was surprising to the Germans that the British seemed to be encouraged by it.* It would

---

* Chamberlain wrote in his diary: "The German visit [of Halifax] was from my point of view a great success because it achieved its object, that of creating an atmosphere in which it is possible to discuss with Germany the practical questions involved in a European settlement." (Keith Feiling, *The Life of Neville Chamberlain,* p. 332.)

Halifax himself seems to have been taken in by Hitler. In a written report to have been a much greater surprise to the British government had it known of a highly secret meeting which Hitler had held in Berlin with his military chiefs and his Foreign Minister exactly fourteen days before his conversation with Lord Halifax.

THE FATEFUL DECISION OF NOVEMBER 5, 1937

An indication of things to come and of the preparations that must be made to meet them had been given the commanders in chief of the three armed forces on June 24, 1937, by Field Marshal von Blomberg in a directive marked "Top Secret," of which only four copies were made.[47] "The general political situation," the Minister of War and Commander in Chief of the Armed Forces informed the three service chiefs, "justifies the supposition that Germany need not consider an attack from any side." Neither the Western Powers nor Russia, he said, had any desire for war, nor were they prepared for it.

"Nevertheless," the directive continued, "the politically fluid world situation, which does not preclude surprising incidents, demands constant preparedness for war on the part of the German armed forces . . . to make possible the military exploitation of politically favorable opportunities should they occur. Preparations of the armed forces for a possible war in the mobilization period 1937–38 must be made with this in mind."

What possible war, since Germany need not fear an attack "from any side"? Blomberg was quite specific. There were two eventualities for war (*Kriegsfalle*) "for which plans are being drafted":

I. War on two fronts with the main struggle in the West. (Strategic Concentration "*Rot.*")

II. War on two fronts with the main struggle in the Southeast. (Strategic Concentration "*Gruen.*")

The "assumption" in the first case was that the French might stage a surprise attack on Germany, in which case the Germans would employ their main forces in the West. This operation was given the code name "Red" (*Rot*).*

---

the Foreign Office he said: "The German Chancellor and others gave the impression that they were not likely to embark on adventures involving force or at least war." To Chamberlain Halifax reported orally, says Charles C. Tansill, that Hitler "was not bent on early adventures, partly because they might be unprofitable, and partly because he was busy building up Germany internally . . . Goering had assured him that not one drop of German blood would be shed in Europe unless Germany was absolutely forced to do it. The Germans gave him [Halifax] the impression . . . of intending to achieve their aims in orderly fashion." (Tansill, *Back Door to War*, pp. 365–66.)

* This is the first of many such code names for German military plans which we shall meet in the ensuing narrative. The Germans used the word *Fall*, literally "Case" (*Fall Rot, Fall Gruen*—Case Red, Case Green—the code names for opera-

For the second eventuality:

The war in the East can begin with a surprise German operation against Czechoslovakia in order to parry the imminent attack of a superior enemy coalition. The necessary conditions to justify such an action politically and in the eyes of international law must be created *beforehand*. [Emphasis by Blomberg.]

Czechoslovakia, the directive stressed, must be "eliminated from the very beginning" and occupied.

There were also three cases where "special preparations" were to be made:

I. Armed intervention against Austria. (Special Case "Otto.")
II. Warlike complications with Red Spain. (Special Case "Richard.")
III. England, Poland, Lithuania take part in a war against us. (Extension of "Red/Green.")

Case Otto is a code name that will appear with some frequency in these pages. "Otto" stood for Otto of Hapsburg, the young pretender to the Austrian throne, then living in Belgium. In Blomberg's June directive Case Otto was summarized as follows:

The object of this operation—armed intervention in Austria in the event of her restoring the Monarchy—will be to compel Austria by armed force to give up a restoration.

Making use of the domestic political dissension of the Austrian people, there will be a march to this end in the general direction of Vienna, and any resistance will be broken.

A note of caution, almost of despair, creeps into this revealing document at the end. There are no illusions about Britain. "England," it warns, "will employ all her available economic and military resources against us." Should she join Poland and Lithuania, the directive acknowledges, "our military position would be worsened to an unbearable, even hopeless, extent. The political leaders will therefore do everything to keep these countries neutral, above all England."

Although the directive was signed by Blomberg it is obvious that it came from his master in the Reich Chancellery. To that nerve center of the Third Reich in the Wilhelmstrasse in Berlin there came on the after-

---

tions in the West and against Czechoslovakia, respectively) and in the beginning, according to the arguments of the German generals in Nuremberg, it was merely the designation commonly used by all military commands for plans to cover hypothetical situations. But as will become obvious in the course of these pages, the term, as the Germans used it, soon became a designation for a plan of armed aggression. The word "Operation" would probably be a more accurate rendering of *Fall* than the word "Case." However, for the sake of convenience, the author will go along with the word "Case."

noon of November 5, 1937, to receive further elucidation from the Fuehrer six individuals: Field Marshal von Blomberg, Minister of War and Commander in Chief of the Armed Forces; Colonel General Baron von Fritsch, Commander in Chief of the Army; Admiral Dr. Raeder, Commander in Chief of the Navy; Colonel General Goering, Commander in Chief of the Air Force; Baron von Neurath, Foreign Minister; and Colonel Hossbach, military adjutant to the Fuehrer. Hossbach is not a familiar name in these pages, nor will it become one. But in the darkening hours of that November day the young colonel played an important role. He took notes of what Hitler said and five days later wrote them up in a highly secret memorandum, thus recording for history—his account showed up at Nuremberg among the captured documents[48]—the decisive turning point in the life of the Third Reich.

The meeting began at 4:15 P.M. and lasted until 8:30, with Hitler doing most of the talking. What he had to say, he began, was the fruit of "thorough deliberation and the experiences of four and a half years of power." He explained that he regarded the remarks he was about to make as of such importance that, in the event of his death, they should be regarded as his last will and testament.

"The aim of German policy," he said, "was to make secure and to preserve the racial community and to enlarge it. It was therefore a question of space [*Lebensraum*]." The Germans, he laid it down, had "the right to a greater living space than other peoples . . . Germany's future was therefore wholly conditional upon the solving of the need for space."*

Where? Not in some far-off African or Asian colonies, but in the heart of Europe "in immediate proximity to the Reich." The question for Germany was, Where could she achieve the greatest gain at the lowest cost?

The history of all ages—the Roman Empire and the British Empire—had proved that expansion could only be carried out by breaking down resistance and taking risks; setbacks were inevitable. There had never . . . been spaces without a master, and there were none today; the attacker always comes up against a possessor.

---

* From here on, the reader will note that what obviously is indirect discourse has been put within quotation marks or in quotations in the form of extracts. Almost all the German records of the remarks of Hitler and of others in private talks were written down in the third person as indirect discourse, though frequently they abruptly slipped into direct, first-person discourse without any change of punctuation. This question posed a problem for American English.

Because I wanted to preserve the accuracy of the original document and the exact wording used or recorded, I decided it was best to refrain from tampering with these accounts by rendering them into first-person direct discourse or by excluding them from within quotation marks. In the latter case it would have looked as though I were indulging in liberal paraphrasing when I was not.

It is largely a matter in the German records of verb tenses being changed by the actual recorders from present to past and of changing the first-person pronoun to third-person. If this is borne in mind there will not be, I believe, any confusion.

Two "hate-inspired" countries, Hitler declared, stood in Germany's way: Britain and France. Both countries were opposed "to any further strengthening of Germany's position." The Fuehrer did not believe that the British Empire was "unshakable." In fact, he saw many weaknesses in it, and he proceeded to elaborate them: the troubles with Ireland and India, the rivalry with Japan in the Far East and with Italy in the Mediterranean. France's position, he thought, "was more favorable than that of Britain . . . but France was going to be confronted with internal political difficulties." Nonetheless, Britain, France and Russia must be considered as "power factors in our political calculations."

Therefore:

Germany's problem could be solved only by means of force, and this was never without attendant risk . . . If one accepts as the basis of the following exposition the resort to force, with its attendant risks, then there remain to be answered the questions "when" and "where." There were three cases to be dealt with:

Case I: Period 1943–45

After this date only a change for the worse, from our point of view, could be expected. The equipment of the Army, Navy and Airforce . . . was nearly completed. Equipment and armament were modern; in further delay there lay the danger of their obsolescence. In particular, the secrecy of "special weapons" could not be preserved forever . . . Our relative strength would decrease in relation to the rearmament . . . by the rest of the world . . . Besides, the world was expecting our attack and was increasing its countermeasures from year to year. It was while the rest of the world was increasing its defenses that we were obliged to take the offensive.

Nobody knew today what the situation would be in the years 1943–45. One thing only was certain, that we could not wait longer.

If the Fuehrer was still living, it was his unalterable resolve to solve Germany's problem of space at the latest by 1943–45. The necessity for action before 1943–45 would arise in Cases II and III.

Case II

If internal strife in France should develop into such a domestic crisis as to absorb the French Army completely and render it incapable of use for war against Germany, then the time for action against the Czechs had come.

Case III

If France is so embroiled by a war with another state that she cannot "proceed" against Germany. . . .

Our first objective . . . must be to overthrow Czechoslovakia and Austria simultaneously in order to remove the threat to our flank in any possible operation against the West . . . If the Czechs were overthrown and a common German–Hungarian frontier achieved, a neutral attitude on the part of Poland could be the more certainly counted upon in the event of a Franco–German conflict.

But what would France, Britain, Italy and Russia do? Hitler went into the answer to that question in considerable detail. He believed "that almost certainly Britain, and probably France, had already tacitly written off the Czechs. Difficulties connected with the Empire and the prospect of being once more entangled in a protracted European war were decisive considerations for Britain against participation in a war against Germany. Britain's attitude would certainly not be without influence on that of France. An attack by France without British support, and with the prospect of the offensive being brought to a standstill on our western fortifications, was hardly probable. Nor was a French march through Belgium and Holland without British support to be expected . . . It would of course be necessary to maintain a strong defense on our western frontier during the prosecution of our attack on the Czechs and Austria."

Hitler then outlined some of the advantages of the "annexation of Czechoslovakia and Austria": better strategic frontiers for Germany, the freeing of military forces "for other purposes," acquisition of some twelve million "Germans," additional foodstuffs for five to six million Germans in the Reich, and manpower for twelve new Army divisions.

He had forgotten to mention what Italy and Russia might do, and he now returned to them. He doubted whether the Soviet Union would intervene, "in view of Japan's attitude." Italy would not object "to the elimination of the Czechs" but it was still a question as to her attitude if Austria was also taken. It depended "essentially on whether the Duce were still alive."

Hitler's supposition for Case III was that France would become embroiled in a war with Italy—a conflict that he counted upon. That was the reason, he explained, for his policy in trying to prolong the Spanish Civil War; it kept Italy embroiled with France and Britain. He saw a war between them "coming definitely nearer." In fact, he said, he was "resolved to take advantage of it, whenever it happened, even as early as 1938"— which was just two months away. He was certain that Italy, with a little German help in raw materials, could stand off Britain and France.

If Germany made use of this war to settle the Czech and Austrian questions, it was to be assumed that Britain—herself at war with Italy—would decide not to act against Germany. Without British support, a warlike action by France against Germany was not to be expected.

The time for our attack on the Czechs and Austria must be made dependent on the course of the Anglo–French–Italian war . . . This favorable situation . . . would not occur again . . . The descent upon the Czechs would have to be carried out with "lightning speed."

Thus as evening darkened Berlin on that autumn day of November 5, 1937—the meeting broke up at eight-fifteen—the die was cast. Hitler had communicated his irrevocable decision to go to war. To the handful of men who would have to direct it there could no longer be any doubt. The dictator had said it all ten years before in *Mein Kampf,* had said that

Germany must have *Lebensraum* in the East and must be prepared to use force to obtain it; but then he had been only an obscure agitator and his book, as Field Marshal von Blomberg later said, had been regarded by the soldiers—as by so many others—as "a piece of propaganda" whose "large circulation was due to forced sales."

But now the Wehrmacht chiefs and the Foreign Minister were confronted with specific dates for actual aggression against two neighboring countries—an action which they were sure would bring on a European war. They must be ready by the following year, 1938, and at the latest by 1943–45.

The realization stunned them. Not, so far as the Hossbach records show, because they were struck down by the immorality of their Leader's proposals but for more practical reasons: Germany was not ready for a big war; to provoke one now would risk disaster.

On those grounds Blomberg, Fritsch and Neurath dared to speak up and question the Fuehrer's pronouncement. Within three months all of the three were out of office and Hitler, relieved of their opposition, such as it was—and it was the last he was to suffer in his presence during the Third Reich—set out on the road of the conqueror to fulfill his destiny. In the beginning, it was an easier road than he—or anyone else—had foreseen.

10

STRANGE, FATEFUL INTERLUDE: THE FALL

OF BLOMBERG, FRITSCH, NEURATH

AND SCHACHT

THE DECISION TO USE armed force against Austria and Czechoslovakia even if it involved Germany in a war with Great Britain and France, which Hitler laid down on November 5, came as such a shock to his Foreign Minister that Baron von Neurath, easygoing, complacent and morally weak though he was, suffered several heart attacks.[1]

"I was extremely upset at Hitler's speech," he later told the Nuremberg tribunal, "because it knocked the bottom out of the whole foreign policy which I had consistently pursued."[2] In this frame of mind, and despite his heart attacks, he sought out General von Fritsch and General Beck, Chief of the General Staff, two days later and discussed with them what could be done "to get Hitler to change his ideas." The impression on Beck of Hitler's harangue, according to Colonel Hossbach, who informed him of it, had been "shattering." It was agreed that Fritsch should again remonstrate with the Fuehrer at their next appointment, pointing out to him the military considerations which made his plans inadvisable, while Neurath would follow up by again stressing to Hitler the political dangers. As for Beck, he immediately committed to paper a devastating critique of Hitler's plans, which apparently he showed to no one—the first sign of a fatal flaw in the mind and character of this estimable general who at first had welcomed the advent of Nazism and who, in the end, would give his life in an abortive effort to destroy it.

General von Fritsch saw Hitler on November 9. There is no record of their talk but it may be presumed that the Commander in Chief of the Army repeated his military arguments against Hitler's plans and that he got nowhere. The Fuehrer was in no mood to brook opposition either from the generals or from his Foreign Minister. He refused to receive Neurath and took off for a long rest at his mountain retreat at Berchtesgaden. It was not until the middle of January that the stricken Neurath was able to arrange an appointment with the Leader.

On that occasion I tried to show him [Neurath later testified at Nuremberg] that his policy would lead to a world war, and that I would have no part in it . . . I called his attention to the danger of war and to the serious warnings of the generals . . . When despite all my arguments he still held to his opinions I told him that he would have to find another Foreign Minister . . .³

Though Neurath did not then know it, that was precisely what Hitler had decided to do. In a fortnight he would celebrate the fifth anniversary of his coming to power and he intended to mark it by cleaning house not only in the Foreign Office but in the Army, those two citadels of upper-class "reaction" which he secretly distrusted, which he felt had never completely accepted him nor really understood his aims and which, as Blomberg, Fritsch and Neurath had shown on the evening of November 5, stood in the way of realizing his ambitions. The last two gentlemen in particular, and perhaps even the accommodating Blomberg, to whom he owed so much, would have to follow the inimitable Dr. Schacht into retirement.

For the crafty financier, the early enthusiast for Nazism and backer of Hitler, had already fallen.

Schacht, as we have seen, had devoted his energies and his wizardry to financing Hitler's speedy rearmament. As Plenipotentiary for War Economy, as well as Minister of Economics, he had concocted any number of fancy schemes, including the use of the printing press, to raise the money for the new Army, Navy and Air Force and to pay the armament bills. But there was a limit beyond which the country could not go without becoming bankrupt, and by 1936 he believed Germany was approaching that limit. He warned Hitler, Goering and Blomberg, but to little avail, though the War Minister for a time sided with him. With Goering's appointment in September 1936 as Plenipotentiary for the Four-Year Plan, a farfetched scheme to make Germany self-sufficient in four years—a goal which Schacht regarded as impossible—the Luftwaffe chief became, in fact, the economic dictator of Germany. To a man as vain and ambitious* and as contemptuous of Goering's ignorance of economics as Schacht was, this made his own position untenable and after months of violent controversy between the two strong-minded men Schacht asked the Fuehrer to place the further direction of economic policies solely in his rival's hand and to allow him to resign his post in the cabinet. To add to his discouragement had been the attitude of many of the nation's leading industrialists and businessmen, who, as he later recounted, "crowded into Goering's anteroom in the hope of getting orders when I was still trying to make the voice of reason heard."⁴

To make the voice of reason heard in the frenzied atmosphere of Nazi Germany in 1937 was an impossible task, as Schacht realized, and after a further exchange of blows with Goering during the summer in which he

---

* The astute French ambassador, François-Poncet, who knew him well, says in his book *The Fateful Years* (p. 221) that at one time Schacht had hoped to succeed Hindenburg as President, and even Hitler, "should things go ill with the Fuehrer."

denounced as unsound "your foreign-exchange policy, your policy regarding production and your financial policy," he traveled down to the Obersalzberg in August to submit his formal resignation to Hitler. The Fuehrer was loath to accept it in view of the unfavorable reaction both at home and abroad which the departure of Schacht would almost certainly bring, but the battered Minister was adamant and Hitler finally agreed to release him at the end of two months. On September 5 Schacht went on leave, and his resignation was formally accepted on December 8.

At Hitler's insistence Schacht remained in the cabinet as Minister without Portfolio and retained the presidency of the Reichsbank, thus preserving appearances and blunting the shock to German and world opinion. His influence as a brake on Hitler's feverish rearmament for war, however, had come to an end, though by remaining in the cabinet and at the Reichsbank he continued to lend the aura of his name and reputation to Hitler's purposes. Indeed, he would shortly endorse publicly and enthusiastically the Leader's first gangster act of naked aggression, for, like the generals and the other conservatives who had played such a key role in turning over Germany to the Nazis, he was slow to awaken to the facts of life.

Goering took over temporarily the Ministry of Economics, but one evening in mid-January 1938 Hitler ran into Walther Funk at the opera in Berlin and casually informed him that he would be Schacht's successor. The official appointment of this greasy, dwarfish, servile nonentity who, it will be remembered, had played a certain role in interesting business leaders in Hitler in the early Thirties, was held up, however. For there now burst upon the Third Reich a two-headed crisis in the Army which was precipitated by, among all things, certain matters pertaining to sex, both normal and abnormal, and which played directly into the hands of Hitler, enabling him to deal a blow to the old aristocratic military hierarchy from which it never recovered, with dire consequences not only for the Army, which thereby lost the last vestiges of independence which it had guarded so zealously during the Hohenzollern Empire and the Republic, but eventually for Germany and the world.

THE FALL OF FIELD MARSHAL VON BLOMBERG

"What influence a woman, even without realizing it, can exert on the history of a country and thereby on the world!" Colonel Alfred Jodl exclaimed in his diary on January 26, 1938. "One has the feeling of living in a fateful hour for the German people."[5]

The woman this brilliant young staff officer referred to was Fräulein Erna Gruhn, and as the year 1937 approached its end she must have regarded herself as the last person in Germany who could possibly propel, as Jodl declared, the German people into a fateful crisis and exercise a profound influence on their history. Perhaps only in the eerie, psychopathic world in which the inner circle of the Third Reich moved at this time with such frenzy would it have been possible.

Fräulein Gruhn was the secretary of Blomberg and toward the end of 1937 he felt sufficiently enamored of her to suggest marriage. His first wife, the daughter of a retired Army officer, whom he had married in 1904, had died in 1932. His five children in the meantime had grown up (his youngest daughter had married the oldest son of General Keitel, his protégé, in 1937) and, tiring of his somewhat lonely widowerhood, he decided the time had come to remarry. Realizing that for the senior officer of the German Army to wed a commoner would not go down well with the haughty, aristocratic officer corps, he sought out Goering for advice. Goering could see no objection to the marriage—had he himself not married, after the death of his first wife, a divorced actress? There was no place in the Third Reich for the stodgy social prejudices of the officer corps. Goering not only approved what Blomberg had in mind; he declared himself ready to smooth matters over with Hitler, if that were necessary, and to help in any other way. As it happened, there was another way he could be helpful. There was a rival lover involved, the Field Marshal confided. To Goering that was no problem. Such nuisances in other cases had been carted off to concentration camp. Probably out of consideration for the old-fashioned morals of the Field Marshal, Goering, however, offered to ship the troublesome rival off to South America, which he did.

Still, Blomberg felt troubled. On December 15, 1937, Jodl made a curious entry in his diary: "The General Field Marshal [Blomberg] in a high state of excitement. Reason not known. Apparently a personal matter. He retired for eight days to an unknown place."[6]

On December 22 Blomberg reappeared to deliver the funeral oration for General Ludendorff at the Feldherrnhalle in Munich. Hitler was there, but declined to speak. The World War hero had refused to have anything to do with him ever since he had fled from in front of the Feldherrnhalle after the volley of bullets during the Beer Hall Putsch. After the funeral Blomberg broached the matter of his proposed marriage to Hitler. The Fuehrer, to his relief, gave it his blessing.

The wedding took place on January 12, 1938, and Hitler and Goering were present as the principal witnesses. Hardly had the bridal pair taken off for Italy on their honeymoon than the storm broke. The rigid officer corps might have absorbed the shock of their Field Marshal marrying his stenographer, but they were not prepared to accept his marriage to a woman with a past such as now began to come to light in all its horrific details.

At first there were only rumors. Anonymous telephone calls began to be received by stiff-necked generals from giggling girls, apparently calling from unsavory cafés and night clubs, congratulating the Army for having accepted one of their number. At police headquarters in Berlin a police inspector, checking on the rumors, came upon a file marked "Erna Gruhn." Horrified, he took it to the police chief, Count von Helldorf.

The count, a roughneck veteran of the *Freikorps* and the brawling days of the S.A., was horrified too. For the dossier showed that the bride of the Field Marshal and Commander in Chief had a police record as a prostitute and had been convicted of having posed for pornographic photographs. The young Frau Field Marshal, it developed, had grown up in a massage salon run by her mother which, as sometimes happened in Berlin, was merely a camouflage for a brothel.

It was obviously Helldorf's duty to pass along the damaging dossier to his superior, the chief of the German police, Himmler. But ardent Nazi though he was, he had formerly been a member of the Army officer corps himself and had absorbed some of its traditions. He knew that Himmler, who had been feuding with the Army High Command for more than a year and was now coming to be regarded by it as more of a sinister threat than Roehm had been, would use the file to blackmail the Field Marshal and make him his tool against the conservative generals. Courageously, Helldorf took the police papers to General Keitel instead. He apparently was convinced that Keitel, who owed his recent rise in the Army to Blomberg, to whom he was attached by family ties, would arrange for the officer corps itself to handle the affair and also would warn his chief of the peril he was in. But Keitel, an arrogant and ambitious man, though of feeble mind and moral character, had no intention of risking his career by getting into trouble with the party and the S.S. Instead of passing on the papers to the Army chief, General von Fritsch, he gave them back to Helldorf with the suggestion that he show them to Goering.

No one could have been more pleased to possess them than Goering, for it was obvious that Blomberg now would have to go and logical, he thought, that he himself should succeed him as Commander in Chief of the Wehrmacht—a goal he had long had in mind. Blomberg interrupted his honeymoon in Italy to return to Germany for the funeral of his mother and on January 20, still unmindful of what was brewing, appeared at his office in the War Ministry to resume his duties.

But not for long. On January 25 Goering brought the explosive documents to Hitler, who had just returned from Berchtesgaden, and the Fuehrer blew up. His Field Marshal had deceived him and made him, who was an official witness at the wedding, look like a fool. Goering quickly agreed with him and at noon went off to see Blomberg personally and break the news to him. The Field Marshal appears to have been overwhelmed by the revelations about his bride and offered to divorce her at once. But this, Goering politely explained, would not be enough. The Army Command itself was demanding his resignation; as Jodl's diary of two days later reveals, the Chief of the General Staff, General Beck, had informed Keitel that "one cannot tolerate the highest-ranking soldier marrying a whore." On January 25, Jodl learned through Keitel that Hitler had dismissed his Field Marshal. Two days later the sixty-year-old fallen officer left Berlin for Capri to resume his honeymoon.

To this idyllic island he was pursued by his naval adjutant, who provided the final grotesque touch to this singular tragi-comedy. Admiral Raeder had dispatched this aide, Lieutenant von Wangenheim, to demand of Blomberg that for the sake of the honor of the officer corps he divorce his wife. The junior naval officer was an arrogant and extremely zealous

young man and when he arrived in the presence of the honeymooning
Field Marshal he exceeded his instructions. Instead of asking for a divorce
he suggested that his former chief do the honorable thing, whereupon he
attempted to thrust a revolver into Blomberg's hand. Despite his fall,
however, the Field Marshal seemed to have retained a zest for life—
obviously he was still enamored of his bride notwithstanding all that had
happened. He declined to take the proffered weapon, remarking, as he
immediately wrote to Keitel, that he and the young naval officer "apparently had quite different views and standards of life."[7]

After all, the Fuehrer had held out to him the prospect of further employment at the highest level as soon as the storm blew over. According
to Jodl's diary, Hitler told Blomberg during the interview in which he
dismissed him that "as soon as Germany's hour comes, you will again be
by my side, and everything that has happened in the past will be forgotten."[8] Indeed, Blomberg wrote in his unpublished memoirs that Hitler,
at their final meeting, promised him "with the greatest emphasis" that he
would be given the supreme command of the armed forces in the event
of war.[9]

Like so many other promises of Hitler, this one was not kept. Field
Marshal von Blomberg's name was stricken forever from the Army rolls,
and not even when the war came and he offered his services was he restored to duty in any capacity. After their return to Germany Blomberg
and his wife settled in the Bavarian village of Wiessee, where they lived in
complete obscurity until the end of the war. As was the case of a former
English King of the same era he remained to the end loyal to the wife who
had brought his downfall. That end came with his death on March 13,
1946, in Nuremberg jail, where he was waiting, a pitiful, emaciated man,
to testify in the trial.

THE FALL OF GENERAL FREIHERR WERNER
VON FRITSCH

Colonel General Freiherr Werner von Fritsch, the Commander in Chief
of the Army and a gifted and unbending officer of the old school ("a
typical General Staff character," Admiral Raeder called him) was the
obvious candidate to succeed Blomberg as Minister of War and Commander in Chief of the Armed Forces. But Goering himself, as we have
seen, had his eye on the top post, and there were some who believed that
he had deliberately pushed Blomberg into his marriage with a woman
whose unfortunate past he may have had prior knowledge of, in order to
clear the way for himself. If this was true, Blomberg did not know it, for
during his farewell interview with Hitler on January 27 he at first suggested Goering as his successor. The Fuehrer, however, knew his old
Nazi henchman better than anyone else; Goering, he said, was too self-
indulgent and lacked both patience and diligence. Nor did he favor
General von Fritsch, whose opposition to his grandiose plans on November
5 he had not liked or forgotten. Moreover, Fritsch's hostility to the Nazi

Party and especially to the S.S. had never been concealed—a circumstance which not only had attracted the attention of the Fuehrer but had provoked in Heinrich Himmler, the S.S. leader and chief of police, a growing determination to overthrow this formidable antagonist who led the Army.*

Himmler's opportunity now came, or, rather, he created it by setting in motion a frame-up so outrageous that it is difficult to believe that it could have happened—at least in 1938—even in the gangster-ridden world of the S.S. and the National Socialist Party, or that the German Army, which after all did have its traditions, would have stood for it. Coming on the heels of the Blomberg scandal, it set off a second and much more explosive bomb which rocked the officer corps to its foundation and settled its fate.

On January 25, the day on which Goering was showing Hitler the police record of Blomberg's bride, he also spread before the Fuehrer an even more damaging document. This had been conveniently provided by Himmler and his principal aide, Heydrich, chief of the S.D., the S.S. Security Service, and it purported to show that General von Fritsch had been guilty of homosexual offenses under Section 175 of the German criminal code and that he had been paying blackmail to an ex-convict since 1935 to hush the matter up. The Gestapo papers seemed so conclusive that Hitler was inclined to believe the charge, and Blomberg, perhaps venting his resentment at Fritsch for the severe attitude the Army had taken toward him because of his marriage, did nothing to dissuade him. Fritsch, he confided, was not a "woman's man," and he added that the General, a lifelong bachelor, might well have "succumbed to weakness."

Colonel Hossbach, the Fuehrer's adjutant, who was present when the Gestapo file was shown, was horrified and, in defiance of Hitler's orders that he was to say nothing to Fritsch, went immediately to the Army commander's apartment to inform him of the charge and to warn him of the dire trouble he was in.† The taciturn Prussian nobleman was stupefied. "A lot of stinking lies!" he blurted out. When he had calmed down he assured his brother officer on his word of honor that the charges were utterly baseless. Early the next morning Hossbach, fearless of the consequences, told Hitler of his meeting with Fritsch, reported the General's categorical denial of the accusations and urged that the Fuehrer

---

* On March 1, 1935, the day Germany took over the Saar, I stood next to Fritsch in the reviewing stand at Saarbruecken for some time before the parade started. Although he scarcely knew me, except as one of the many American correspondents in Berlin, he poured out a running fire of sarcastic remarks about the S.S., the party and various Nazi leaders from Hitler on down. He did not disguise his contempt for them all. See *Berlin Diary*, p. 27.

† This cost Hossbach his job two days later, but not, as some feared, his life. He was restored to the Army General Staff, rose during the war to the rank of General of the Infantry and commanded the Fourth Army on the Russian front until abruptly dismissed by Hitler by telephone on January 28, 1945, for withdrawing his troops in defiance of the Fuehrer's orders.

give him a hearing and the opportunity of personally denying his guilt.

To this Hitler, to Hossbach's surprise, assented, and the Commander in Chief of the German Army was summoned to the Chancellery late on the evening of the same day. He was there to undergo an experience for which his long training as an aristocrat, an officer and a gentleman had scarcely prepared him. The meeting took place in the Chancellery library and this time Himmler as well as Goering was present. After Hitler had summed up the charges, Fritsch gave his word of honor as an officer that they were completely untrue. But such assurances no longer had much value in the Third Reich and now Himmler, who had been waiting for three years for this moment, introduced a shuffling, degenerate-looking figure from a side door. He must have been one of the strangest, if not the most disreputable, figures ever let into the offices of the Chancellor of Germany. His name was Hans Schmidt and he had a long prison record dating back to his first sentence to a boy's reformatory. His chief weakness, it developed, had been spying on homosexuals and then blackmailing them. He now professed to recognize General von Fritsch as the Army officer whom he had caught in a homosexual offense in a dark alley near the Potsdam railroad station in Berlin with an underworld character by the name of "Bavarian Joe."* For years, Schmidt insisted to the three most powerful figures in Germany, this officer had paid him blackmail to keep quiet, the payments only ceasing when the law again clamped him behind the bars of a penitentiary.

General Freiherr von Fritsch was too outraged to answer. The spectacle of the head of the German State, the successor of Hindenburg and the Hohenzollerns, introducing such a shady character in such a place for such a purpose was too much for him. His speechlessness only helped to convince Hitler that he was guilty and the Fuehrer asked for his resignation. This Fritsch declined to give, demanding in turn a trial by a military court of honor. But Hitler had no intention of allowing the military caste to take over the case, at least for the moment. This was a heaven-sent opportunity, which he would not let pass, to smash the opposition of the generals who would not bend to his will and genius. He then and there ordered Fritsch to go on indefinite leave, which was equivalent to his suspension as Commander in Chief of the Army. The next day Hitler conferred with Keitel about a successor not only to Blomberg but to Fritsch. Jodl, whose chief source of information was Keitel, began sprinkling his diary with entries which indicated that a drastic shake-up not only in the Army Command but in the whole organization of the armed forces was being worked out which would at last bring the military to heel.

Would the senior generals surrender their power, which though by no means absolute was the last that remained outside the grip of Hitler? When Fritsch returned to his apartment in the Bendlerstrasse from the ordeal in the Chancellery library he conferred with General Beck, the

---

* The name is supplied by Gisevius in *To the Bitter End*, p. 229.

Chief of the Army General Staff. Some English historians[10] have recounted that Beck urged him to carry out a military putsch at once against the Hitler government, and that Fritsch declined. But Wolfgang Foerster, the German biographer of Beck, who had the General's personal papers at his disposal, states merely that on the fateful evening Beck saw first Hitler, who apprised him of the grave charges, then Fritsch, who denied them, and that finally, late on the same evening, he hurried back to Hitler to demand only that the Army commander be given a chance to clear himself before a military court of honor. Beck too, his biographer makes clear, had not yet attained that understanding of the rulers of the Third Reich which was later to come to him—when it was too late. Some days later, when it was also too late, when not only Blomberg and Fritsch were gone but sixteen of the senior generals retired and forty-four others transferred to lesser commands, Fritsch and his closest associates, of whom Beck was one, did seriously consider military countermeasures. But they quickly abandoned such dangerous thoughts. "It was clear to these men," Foerster says, "that a military putsch would mean civil war and was by no means sure of success." Then, as always, the German generals wanted to be sure of winning before taking any great risks. They feared, as this German writer states, that not only would Goering's Air Force and Admiral Raeder's Navy oppose them, since both commanders were completely under the Fuehrer's spell, but that the Army itself might not fully support its fallen Commander in Chief.[11]

However, one last chance was given the ranking Army officers to deal a blow in their turn to Hitler. A preliminary investigation conducted by the Army in collaboration with the Ministry of Justice quickly established that General von Fritsch was the innocent victim of a Gestapo frame-up initiated by Himmler and Heydrich. It was found that the ex-convict Schmidt had indeed caught an Army officer in an unnatural act in the shadows of the Potsdam Station and had successfully blackmailed him for years. But his name was Frisch, not Fritsch, and he was a bedridden retired cavalry officer listed in the Army rolls as Rittmeister von Frisch. This the Gestapo had known, but it had arrested Schmidt and threatened him with death unless he pointed the finger to the Commander in Chief of the Army. The ailing Rittmeister also was taken into custody by the secret police so as to prevent him from talking, but both he and Schmidt were eventually wrested from the Gestapo's clutches by the Army and kept in a safe place until they could testify at the court-martial of Fritsch.

The old leaders of the Army were jubilant. Not only would their Commander in Chief be vindicated and restored to his leadership of the Army. The machinations of the S.S. and the Gestapo, of those two unscrupulous men, Himmler and Heydrich, who held such unbridled power in the country, would be exposed and they and the S.S. would go the way of Roehm and the S.A. four years before. It would be a blow too to the party and to Hitler himself; it would shake the foundations of the Third Reich so violently that the Fuehrer himself might topple over. If he tried to cover up the crime, the Army itself, with a clear conscience, now that the truth was known, would take matters in its own hands. But once again, as so often in the past five years, the generals were outsmarted by the former Austrian corporal and then utterly defeated by fate, which the Leader, if not they, knew how to take advantage of for his own ends.

All through the last week of January 1938 a tension, reminiscent of that of late June 1934, gripped Berlin. Again the capital seethed with rumors. Hitler had dismissed the two top men in the Army, for reasons unknown. The generals were in revolt. They were plotting a military putsch. Ambassador François-Poncet heard that Fritsch, who had invited him to dinner for February 2 and then canceled the invitation, had been arrested. There were reports that the Army planned to surround the Reichstag, when it met to hear Hitler's fifth-anniversary speech on January 30, and arrest the entire Nazi government and its hand-picked deputies. Credence of such reports grew when it was announced that the meeting of the Reichstag had been indefinitely postponed. The German dictator was obviously in difficulties. He had met his match at last in the unbending senior generals of the German Army. Or so the latter must have thought, but they were in error.

On February 4, 1938, the German cabinet met for what was to prove the last time. Whatever difficulties Hitler had experienced, he now resolved them in a manner which eliminated those who stood in his way, not only in the Army but in the Foreign Office. A decree which he hastily put through the cabinet that day and which was announced to the nation and the world on the radio shortly before midnight began:

"From now on I take over personally the command of the whole armed forces."

As head of state, Hitler of course had been the Supreme Commander of the Armed Forces, but now he took over Blomberg's office of Commander in Chief and abolished the War Ministry, over which the now moon-struck bridegroom had also presided. In its place was created the organization which was to become familiar to the world during World War II, the High Command of the Armed Forces (Oberkommando der Wehrmacht, or OKW), to which the three fighting services, the Army, the Navy and the Air Force, were subordinated. Hitler was its Supreme Commander, and under him was a chief of staff, with the high-sounding title of "Chief of the High Command of the Armed Forces"—a post which went to the toady Keitel, who managed to keep it to the end.

To assuage the wounded feelings of Goering, who had been confident of succeeding Blomberg, Hitler named him a Field Marshal, which made him the ranking officer of the Reich and apparently pleased him no end. To calm the uneasiness of the public, Hitler announced that Blomberg and Fritsch had resigned "for reasons of health." Thus Fritsch was got rid of once and for all even before his trial by a military court of honor, which Hitler knew would exonerate him. This seemed particularly outrageous to the senior generals but there was nothing they could do about it, for they were sent into the discard in the same decree. Sixteen of them, including Generals von Rundstedt, von Leeb, von Witzleben, von Kluge and von Kleist, were relieved of their commands, and forty-four others, who were regarded as less than enthusiastic in their devotion to Nazism, were transferred.

As Fritsch's successor to command the Army, Hitler, after some hesitation, picked General Walther von Brauchitsch, who enjoyed a good reputation among the generals but who was to prove as weak and as compliant as Blomberg when it came to standing up to the mercurial temperament of Hitler. For a few days during the crisis it appeared that a problem of sex would prove Brauchitsch's undoing as it had that of Blomberg and Fritsch. For this officer was on the point of getting a divorce, an action frowned upon by the military aristocracy. The ever curious Jodl noted the complication in his diary. On Sunday, January 30, he recorded that Keitel had called in Brauchitsch's son "in order to send him to his mother (he is to get her assent to the divorce)," and a couple of days later he reported a meeting of Brauchitsch and Keitel with Goering "for a discussion of the family situation." Goering, who seemed to have made himself an arbiter of the sex difficulties of the generals, promised to look into the matter. On the same day, Jodl further noted, "the son of Br. returns with a very dignified letter from his mother." The inference was that she would not stand in her husband's way. Nor would Goering and Hitler disapprove of a divorce, which the new commander of the Army actually obtained a few months after assuming his new post. For both of them knew that Frau Charlotte Schmidt, the woman he wanted to marry, was, as Ulrich von Hassell said, "a two hundred per cent rabid Nazi." The marriage took place in the following autumn and was to prove, as Jodl might have noted again, another instance of the influence of a woman on history.*

Hitler's house cleaning of February 4 was not confined to the generals. He also swept Neurath out of the Foreign Office, replacing him with the shallow and compliant Ribbentrop.† Two veteran career diplomats, Ulrich von Hassell, the ambassador in Rome, and Herbert von Dirksen, the ambassador in Tokyo, were relieved, as was Papen in Vienna. The

---

* According to Milton Shulman (*Defeat in the West*, p. 10), Hitler himself intervened with the first Frau von Brauchitsch in order to obtain her consent to the divorce and helped provide a financial settlement for her, thus putting the Army Commander in Chief under personal obligation to him. Shulman gives as his source a Canadian Army intelligence report.

† To divert attention from the military crisis and to save something of Neurath's prestige both at home and abroad, Hitler, at Goering's suggestion, created the so-called Secret Cabinet Council (Geheimer Kabinettsrat) whose purpose, said the Fuehrer's February 4 decree, was to furnish him "guidance in the conduct of foreign policy." Neurath was appointed its president, and its members included Keitel and the chiefs of the three armed services as well as the most important members of the ordinary cabinet and of the party. Goebbels' propaganda machine gave it much fanfare, making it look as if it were a supercabinet and that Neurath actually had been promoted. Actually the Secret Cabinet Council was pure fiction. It never existed. As Goering testified at Nuremberg, "There was, to be sure, no such cabinet in existence, but the expression would sound quite nice and everyone would imagine that it meant something . . . I declare under oath that this Secret Cabinet Council never met at all, not even for a minute."[12]

weakling Funk was formally named as the successor of Schacht as Minister of Economics.

The next day, February 5, there were screaming headlines in the *Voelkischer Beobachter:* STRONGEST CONCENTRATION OF ALL POWERS IN THE FUEHRER'S HANDS! For once, the leading daily Nazi newspaper did not exaggerate.

February 4, 1938, is a major turning point in the history of the Third Reich, a milestone on its road to war. On that date the Nazi revolution, it might be said, was completed. The last of the conservatives who stood in the way of Hitler's embarking upon the course which he had long determined to follow, once Germany was sufficiently armed, were swept away. Blomberg, Fritsch and Neurath had been put in office by Hindenburg and the old-school conservatives to act as a brake upon Nazi excesses, and Schacht had joined them. But in the struggle for control of the foreign and economic policy and the military power of Germany they proved to be no match for Hitler. They had neither the moral strength nor the political shrewdness to stand up to him, let alone to triumph over him. Schacht quit. Neurath stepped aside. Blomberg, under pressure from his own brother generals, resigned. Fritsch, though he was framed in gangster fashion, accepted his dismissal without a gesture of defiance. Sixteen top generals meekly accepted theirs—and his. There was talk in the officer corps of a military putsch, but only talk. Hitler's contempt for the Prussian officer caste, which he held till the end of his life, proved quite justified. It had accepted with scarcely a murmur the officially condoned murder of Generals von Schleicher and von Bredow. It was swallowing supinely now the cashiering of its senior officers. Was not Berlin swarming with younger generals eager to replace them, eager to serve him? Where was the vaunted solidarity of the Army officers? Was it not a myth?

For five years up to this winter day of February 4, 1938, the Army had possessed the physical power to overthrow Hitler and the Third Reich. When it learned on November 5, 1937, where he was leading it and the nation, why did it not attempt to do so? Fritsch himself gave the answer after his fall. On Sunday, December 18, 1938, he entertained the deposed Ambassador von Hassell at his manor house at Achterberg, near Soltau, which the Army had put at his disposal after his retirement. Hassell noted down in his diary "the substance of his views":

"This man—Hitler—is Germany's destiny for good and for evil. If he now goes over the abyss—which Fritsch believes he will—he will drag us all down with him. There is nothing we can do."[13]

With foreign, economic and military policy concentrated in his hands and the armed forces directly under his command, Hitler now proceeded on his way. Having got rid of Fritsch without giving him the opportunity of clearing his name, he belatedly afforded him the opportunity by setting up a military court of honor to hear the case. Field Marshal Goering presided and at his side were the commanders in chief of the Army and

Navy, General von Brauchitsch and Admiral Raeder, and two professional judges of the Supreme War Tribunal.

The trial, from which the press and the public were excluded, began in Berlin on March 10, 1938, and was suddenly suspended before the day was over. Late on the previous night news had come from Austria which sent the Fuehrer into one of his greatest tantrums.* Field Marshal Goering and General von Brauchitsch were urgently needed elsewhere.

---

* When Papen arrived at the Chancellery in Berlin thirty-six hours later he found Hitler still "in a state bordering on hysteria." (Papen, *Memoirs*, p. 428.)

11

ANSCHLUSS: THE RAPE OF AUSTRIA

Toward the end of 1937, due to a change of jobs from newspaper to radio reporting, my headquarters were transferred from Berlin to Vienna, which I had come to know as a youthful correspondent a decade before. Though I would spend most of the period of the next three crucial years in Germany, my new assignment, which was to cover continental Europe, gave me a certain perspective of the Third Reich and, as it happened, set me down in those very neighboring countries which were to be victims of Hitler's aggression just prior to and during the time the aggression took place. I roved back and forth in those days between Germany and the country that for the moment was the object of Hitler's fury and so gathered a firsthand experience of the events which are now to be described and which led inexorably to the greatest and bloodiest war in man's experience. Though we observed these happenings at first hand, it is amazing how little we really knew of how they came about. The plottings and maneuvers, the treachery, the fateful decisions and moments of indecision, and the dramatic encounters of the principal participants which shaped the course of events took place in secret beneath the surface, hidden from the prying eyes of foreign diplomats, journalists and spies, and thus for years remained largely unknown to all but a few who took part in them.

We have had to wait for the maze of secret documents and the testimony of the surviving leading actors in the drama, most of whom were not free at the time—many landed in Nazi concentration camps—to tell their story. What follows, therefore, in the ensuing pages is based largely on the mass of factual evidence which has been accumulated since 1945. But it was perhaps helpful for a narrator of such a history as this to have been personally present at its main crises and turning points. Thus, it happened that I was in Vienna on the memorable night of March 11–12, 1938, when Austria ceased to exist.

For more than a month the beautiful baroque capital by the Danube, whose inhabitants were more attractive, more genial, more gifted in enjoying life, such as it was, than any people I had ever known, had been prey to deep anxieties. Dr. Kurt von Schuschnigg, the Austrian Chancellor, would later recall the period between February 12 and March 11 as "The Four Weeks' Agony." Since the Austro–German agreement of July 11, 1936, in which Schuschnigg, in a secret annex to the treaty, had made far-reaching concessions to the Austrian Nazis,* Franz von Papen, Hitler's special ambassador in Vienna, had been continuing his labors to undermine the independence of Austria and bring about its union with Nazi Germany. In a long report to the Fuehrer at the end of 1936, he had reported on his progress and a year later had done the same, this time stressing "that only by subjecting the Federal Chancellor [Schuschnigg] to the strongest possible pressure can further progress be made."[1] His advice, though scarcely needed, was soon to be taken more literally than even he could conceive.

Throughout 1937, the Austrian Nazis, financed and egged on by Berlin, had stepped up their campaign of terror. Bombings took place nearly every day in some part of the country, and in the mountain provinces massive and often violent Nazi demonstrations weakened the government's position. Plans were uncovered disclosing that Nazi thugs were preparing to bump off Schuschnigg as they had his predecessor. Finally on January 25, 1938, Austrian police raided the Vienna headquarters of a group called the Committee of Seven, which had been set up to bring about peace between the Nazis and the Austrian government, but which in reality served as the central office of the illegal Nazi underground. There they found documents initialed by Rudolf Hess, the Fuehrer's deputy, which made it clear that the Austrian Nazis were to stage an open revolt in the spring of 1938 and that when Schuschnigg attempted to put it down, the German Army would enter Austria to prevent "German blood from being shed by Germans." According to Papen, one of the documents called for his own murder or that of his military attaché, Lieutenant General Muff, by local Nazis so as to provide an excuse for German intervention.[2]

If the debonair Papen was less than amused to learn that he was marked—for the second time—for assassination by Nazi roughnecks on orders from party leaders in Berlin, he was also distressed by a telephone call which came to him at the German Legation in Vienna on the evening of February 4. State Secretary Hans Lammers was on the line from the Chancellery in Berlin to inform him that his special mission in Austria had ended. He had been fired, along with Neurath, Fritsch and several others.

"I was almost speechless with astonishment," Papen later remembered.[3] He recovered sufficiently to realize that Hitler evidently had decided on more drastic action in Austria, now that he had rid himself of Neurath, Fritsch and Blomberg. In fact, Papen recovered sufficiently to decide to do "something unusual for a diplomat," as he put it. He resolved to deposit copies of all his correspondence with Hitler "in a safe place,"

---

* See above, p. 296.

which turned out to be Switzerland. "The defamatory campaigns of the Third Reich," he says, "were only too well known to me." As we have seen, they had almost cost him his life in June 1934.

Papen's dismissal was also a warning to Schuschnigg. He had not fully trusted the suave former cavalry officer, but he was quick to see that Hitler must have something worse in mind than inflicting on him the wily ambassador, who at least was a devout Catholic, as was he, and a gentleman. In the last few months the course of European diplomacy had not favored Austria. Mussolini had drawn closer to Hitler since the establishment of the Rome–Berlin Axis and was not so concerned about maintaining the little country's independence as he had been at the time of the murder of Dollfuss, when he had rushed four divisions to the Brenner Pass to frighten the Fuehrer. Neither Britain, freshly embarked under Chamberlain upon a policy of appeasing Hitler, nor France, beset by grave internal political strife, had recently shown much interest in defending Austria's independence should Hitler strike. And now, with Papen, had gone the conservative leaders of the German Army and Foreign Office, who had exercised some restraining influence on Hitler's towering ambitions. Schuschnigg, who was a narrow-minded man but, within his limits, an intelligent one, and who was quite well informed, had few illusions about his worsening situation. The time had come, as he felt it had come after the Nazis slew Dollfuss, to further appease the German dictator.

Papen, discharged from office though he was, offered an opportunity. Never a man to resent a slap in the face if it came from above, he had hurried to Hitler the very day after his dismissal "to obtain some picture of what was going on." At Berchtesgaden on February 5, he found the Fuehrer "exhausted and distrait" from his struggle with the generals. But Hitler's recuperative powers were considerable, and soon the cashiered envoy was interesting him in a proposal that he had already broached to him a fortnight before when they had met in Berlin: Why not have it out with Schuschnigg personally? Why not invite him to come to Berchtesgaden for a personal talk? Hitler found the idea interesting. Unmindful of the fact that he had just fired Papen, he ordered him to return to Vienna and arrange the meeting.

Schuschnigg readily assented to it, but, weak as his position was, laid down certain conditions. He must be informed in advance of the precise points which Hitler wanted to discuss, and he must be assured beforehand that the agreement of July 11, 1936, in which Germany promised to respect Austria's independence and not to interfere in her internal affairs, would be maintained. Furthermore, the communiqué at the end of the meeting must reaffirm that both countries would continue to abide by the 1936 treaty. Schuschnigg wanted to take no chances in bearding the lion in his den. Papen hurried off to Obersalzberg to confer with Hitler and returned with the Fuehrer's assurance that the 1936 agreement would remain unchanged and that he merely wanted to discuss "such misunderstandings and points of friction as have persisted" since it was signed. This was not as precise as the Austrian Chancellor had requested, but he said he was satisfied with the answer. The meeting was set for the morning of February 12,* and on the evening of February 11 Schuschnigg, accompanied by his Undersecretary for Foreign Affairs, Guido Schmidt, set off by special train in the strictest secrecy for Salzburg, whence he would drive by car over the border to Hitler's mountain retreat on the following morning. It was to prove a fateful journey.

THE MEETING AT BERCHTESGADEN: FEBRUARY 12, 1938

Papen showed up at the frontier to greet his Austrian visitors and in the frosty winter morning air seemed to be, Schuschnigg thought, "in the very best of humor." Hitler, he assured his guests, was in an excellent mood this day. And then came the first warning note. The Fuehrer, Papen said genially, hoped Dr. Schuschnigg would not mind the presence at the Berghof of three generals who had arrived quite by chance: Keitel, the new Chief of OKW, Reichenau, who commanded the Army forces on the Bavarian–Austrian frontier, and Sperrle, who was in charge of the Air Force in this area.

Papen later remembered of his guests that this was "a piece of information that seemed little to their taste." Schuschnigg says he told the ambassador he would not mind, especially since he had "not much choice in the matter." A Jesuit-trained intellectual, he was getting on his guard.

Even so, he was not prepared for what now took place. Hitler, wearing the brown tunic of a storm trooper, with black trousers, and flanked by the three generals, greeted the Austrian Chancellor and his aide on the steps of the villa. Schuschnigg felt it was a friendly but formal greeting. In a few moments he found himself alone with the German dictator in the spacious second-floor study whose great picture windows looked out upon the stately, snow-capped Alps and on Austria, the birthplace of both these men, beyond.

Kurt von Schuschnigg, forty-one years old, was, as all who have known him would agree, a man of impeccable Old World Austrian manners, and it was not unnatural for him to begin the conversation with a graceful tidbit about the magnificent view, the fine weather that day, and a flattering word about this room having been, no doubt, the scene of many decisive

---

* Which happened to be the fourth anniversary of the slaughter of the Austrian Social Democrats by the Dollfuss government, of which Schuschnigg was a member. On February 12, 1934, seventeen thousand government troops and fascist militia had turned artillery on the workers' flats in Vienna, killing a thousand men, women and children and wounding three or four thousand more. Democratic political freedom was stamped out and Austria thereafter was ruled first by Dollfuss and then by Schuschnigg as a clerical-fascist dictatorship. It was certainly milder than the Nazi variety, as those of us who worked in both Berlin and Vienna in those days can testify. Nevertheless it deprived the Austrian people of their political freedom and subjected them to more repression than they had known under the Hapsburgs in the last decades of the monarchy. The author has discussed this more fully in *Midcentury Journey.*

conferences. Adolf Hitler cut him short: "We did not gather here to speak of the fine view or of the weather." Then the storm broke. As the Austrian Chancellor later testified, the ensuing two-hour "conversation was somewhat unilateral."*

You have done everything to avoid a friendly policy [Hitler fumed] . . . The whole history of Austria is just one uninterrupted act of high treason. That was so in the past and is no better today. This historical paradox must now reach its long-overdue end. And I can tell you right now, Herr Schuschnigg, that I am absolutely determined to make an end of all this. The German Reich is one of the great powers, and nobody will raise his voice if it settles its border problems.

Shocked at Hitler's outburst, the quiet-mannered Austrian Chancellor tried to remain conciliatory and yet stand his ground. He said he differed from his host on the question of Austria's role in German history. "Austria's contribution in this respect," he maintained, "is considerable."

HITLER: Absolutely zero. I am telling you, absolutely zero. Every national idea was sabotaged by Austria throughout history; and indeed all this sabotage was the chief activity of the Hapsburgs and the Catholic Church.†

SCHUSCHNIGG: All the same, Herr Reichskanzler, many an Austrian contribution cannot possibly be separated from the general picture of German culture. Take for instance a man like Beethoven . . .

HITLER: Oh—Beethoven? Let me tell you that Beethoven came from the lower Rhineland.

SCHUSCHNIGG: Yet Austria was the country of his choice, as it was for so many others . . .

HITLER: That's as may be. I am telling you once more that things cannot go on in this way. I have a historic mission, and this mission I will fulfill because Providence has destined me to do so . . . who is not with me will be crushed . . . I have chosen the most difficult road that any German ever took; I have made the greatest achievement in the history of Germany, greater than any other German. And not by force, mind you. I am carried along by the love of my people . . .

SCHUSCHNIGG: Herr Reichskanzler, I am quite willing to believe that.

---

* Later Dr. Schuschnigg wrote down from memory an account of what he calls the "significant passages" of the one-sided conversation, and though it is therefore not a verbatim record it rings true to anyone who has heard and studied Hitler's countless utterances and its substance is verified not only by all that happened subsequently but by others who were present at the Berghof that day, notably Papen, Jodl and Guido Schmidt. I have followed Schuschnigg's account given in his book *Austrian Requiem* and in his Nuremberg affidavit on the meeting.[4]
† It is evident that Hitler's warped version of Austro-German history, which, as we have seen in earlier chapters, was picked up in his youth at Linz and Vienna, remained unchanged.

After an hour of this, Schuschnigg asked his antagonist to enumerate his complaints. "We will do everything," he said, "to remove obstacles to a better understanding, as far as it is possible."

HITLER: That is what you say, Herr Schuschnigg. But I am telling you that I am going to solve the so-called Austrian problem one way or the other.

He then launched into a tirade against Austria for fortifying its border against Germany, a charge that Schuschnigg denied.

HITLER: Listen, you don't really think you can move a single stone in Austria without my hearing about it the next day, do you? . . . I have only to give an order, and in one single night all your ridiculous defense mechanisms will be blown to bits. You don't seriously believe that you can stop me for half an hour, do you? . . . I would very much like to save Austria from such a fate, because such an action would mean blood. After the Army, my S.A. and Austrian Legion would move in, and nobody can stop their just revenge—not even I.

After these threats, Hitler reminded Schuschnigg (rudely addressing him always by his name instead of by his title, as diplomatic courtesy called for) of Austria's isolation and consequent helplessness.

HITLER: Don't think for one moment that anybody on earth is going to thwart my decisions. Italy? I see eye to eye with Mussolini . . . England? England will not move one finger for Austria . . . And France?

France, he said, could have stopped Germany in the Rhineland "and then we would have had to retreat. But now it is too late for France." Finally:

HITLER: I give you once more, and for the last time, the opportunity to come to terms, Herr Schuschnigg. Either we find a solution now or else events will take their course . . . Think it over, Herr Schuschnigg, think it over well. I can only wait until this afternoon . . .

What exactly were the German Chancellor's terms? Schuschnigg asked. "We can discuss that this afternoon," Hitler said.

During lunch Hitler appeared to be, Schuschnigg observed somewhat to his surprise, "in excellent spirits." His monologue dwelt on horses and houses. He was going to build the greatest skyscrapers the world had ever seen. "The Americans will see," he remarked to Schuschnigg, "that Germany is building bigger and better buildings than the United States." As for the harried Austrian Chancellor, Papen noted that he appeared "worried and preoccupied." A chain cigarette smoker, he had not been allowed to smoke in Hitler's presence. But after coffee in an adjoining room, Hitler excused himself and Schuschnigg was able for the first time to snatch a smoke. He was also able to tell his Foreign Undersecretary, Guido Schmidt, the bad news. It was soon to grow worse.

After cooling their heels for two hours in a small anteroom, the two Austrians were ushered into the presence of Ribbentrop, the new German Foreign Minister, and of Papen. Ribbentrop presented them with a two-page typewritten draft of an "agreement" and remarked that they were Hitler's final demands and that the Fuehrer would not permit discussion of them. They must be signed forthwith. Schuschnigg says he felt relieved to have at least something definite from Hitler. But as he perused the document his relief evaporated. For here was a German ultimatum calling on him, in effect, to turn the Austrian government over to the Nazis within one week.

The ban against the Austrian Nazi Party was to be lifted, all Nazis in jail were to be amnestied and the pro-Nazi Viennese lawyer Dr. Seyss-Inquart was to be made Minister of the Interior, with authority over the police and security. Another pro-Nazi, Glaise-Horstenau, was to be appointed Minister of War, and the Austrian and German armies were to establish closer relations by a number of measures, including the systematic exchange of one hundred officers. "Preparations will be made," the final demand read, "for the assimilation of the Austrian into the German economic system. For this purpose Dr. Fischboeck [a pro-Nazi] will be appointed Minister of Finance."[5]

Schuschnigg, as he later wrote, realized at once that to accept the ultimatum would mean the end of Austria's independence.

Ribbentrop advised me to accept the demands at once. I protested, and referred him to my previous agreement with von Papen, made prior to coming to Berchtesgaden, and made clear to Ribbentrop that I was not prepared to be confronted with such unreasonable demands . . .[6]

But was Schuschnigg prepared to accept them? That he was not prepared to be confronted with them was obvious even to a dullard such as Ribbentrop. The question was: Would he sign them? In this difficult and decisive moment the young Austrian Chancellor began to weaken. He inquired lamely, according to his own account, "whether we could count on the good will of Germany, whether the Reich government had at least the intention to keep its side of the bargain."[7] He says he received an answer "in the affirmative."

Then Papen went to work on him. The slippery ambassador admits to his "amazement" when he read the ultimatum. It was an "unwarrantable interference in Austrian sovereignty." Schuschnigg says Papen apologized to him and expressed his "complete surprise" at the terms. Nevertheless, he advised the Austrian Chancellor to sign them.

He furthermore informed me that I could be assured that Hitler would take care that, if I signed, and acceded to these demands, from that time on Germany would remain loyal to this agreement and that there would be no further difficulties for Austria.[8]

Schuschnigg, it would appear from the above statements, the last given in an affidavit at Nuremberg, was not only weakening but letting his naïveté get the best of him.

He had one last chance to make a stand. He was summoned again to Hitler. He found the Fuehrer pacing excitedly up and down in his study.

HITLER: Herr Schuschnigg . . . here is the draft of the document. There is nothing to be discussed. I will not change one single iota. You will either sign it as it is and fulfill my demands within three days, or I will order the march into Austria.[9]

Schuschnigg capitulated. He told Hitler he was willing to sign. But he reminded him that under the Austrian constitution only the President of the Republic had the legal power to accept such an agreement and carry it out. Therefore, while he was willing to appeal to the President to accept it, he could give no guarantee.

"You have to guarantee it!" Hitler shouted.

"I could not possibly, Herr Reichskanzler," Schuschnigg says he replied.[10]

At this answer [Schuschnigg later recounted] Hitler seemed to lose his self-control. He ran to the doors, opened them, and shouted, "General Keitel!" Then turning back to me, he said, "I shall have you called later."[11]

This was pure bluff, but the harassed Austrian Chancellor, who had been made aware of the presence of the generals all day, did not perhaps know it. Papen relates that Keitel told later of how Hitler greeted him with a broad grin when he rushed in and asked for orders. "There are no orders," Hitler chuckled. "I just wanted to have you here."

But Schuschnigg and Dr. Schmidt, waiting outside the Fuehrer's study, were impressed. Schmidt whispered that he would not be surprised if the both of them were arrested within the next five minutes. Thirty minutes later Schuschnigg was again ushered into the presence of Hitler.

I have decided to change my mind—for the first time in my life [Hitler said]. But I warn you this is your very last chance. I have given you three additional days to carry out the agreement.[12]

That was the extent of the German dictator's concessions, and though the wording of the final draft was somewhat softened, the changes, as Schuschnigg later testified, were inconsequential. Schuschnigg signed. It was Austria's death warrant.

The behavior of men under duress differs according to their character and is often puzzling. That Schuschnigg, a veteran despite his comparative youth of the rough and tumble of politics which had seen his predecessor murdered by the Nazis, was a brave man few would doubt. Yet his capitulation to Hitler on February 11, 1938, under the terrible threat of armed attack has left a residue of unresolved doubts among his fellow countrymen and the observers and historians of this fateful period. Was surrender necessary? Was there no alternative? It would be a rash man who would argue that Britain and France, in view of their subsequent behavior in the face of Hitler's aggressions, might have come to the aid of Austria had Hitler then and there marched in. But up to this moment Hitler had not yet broken across the German borders nor had he prepared his own people and the world for any such act of wanton aggression. The German Army itself was scarcely prepared for a war should France and Britain intervene. In a few weeks Austria, as a result of the Berchtesgaden "agreement," would be softened up by the local Nazis and German machinations to a point where Hitler could take it with much less risk of foreign intervention than on February 11. Schuschnigg himself, as he later wrote, recognized that acceptance of Hitler's terms meant "nothing else but the complete end of the independence of the Austrian government."

Perhaps he was in a daze from his ordeal. After signing away his country's independence at the point of a gun he indulged in a strange conversation with Hitler which he himself later recorded in his book. "Does the Herr Reichskanzler," he asked, "believe that the various crises in the world today can be solved in a peaceful manner?" The Fuehrer answered fatuously that they could—"if my advice were followed." Whereupon Schuschnigg said, apparently with no sign of sarcasm, "At the moment the state of the world looks rather promising, don't you think?"[13]

Such an utterance at such a moment seems incredible, but that is what the beaten Austrian Chancellor says he said. Hitler had one more humiliation to administer to him. When Schuschnigg suggested that in the press release of their meeting mention be made that their discussion reaffirmed the July 1936 agreement, Hitler exclaimed, "Oh, no! First you have to fulfill the conditions of our agreement. This is what is going to the press: 'Today the Fuehrer and Reichskanzler conferred with the Austrian Bundeskanzler at the Berghof.' That's all."

Declining the Fuehrer's invitation to stay for dinner, Schuschnigg and Schmidt drove down from the mountains to Salzburg. It was a gray and foggy winter night. The ubiquitous Papen accompanied them as far as the frontier and was somewhat uncomfortable in what he terms the "oppressive silence." He could not refrain from trying to cheer his Austrian friends up.

"Well, now," he exclaimed to them, "you have seen what the Fuehrer can be like at times! But the next time I am sure it will be different. You know, the Fuehrer can be absolutely charming."*

---

* Papen's version (see his *Memoirs*, p. 420) is somewhat different, but that of Schuschnigg rings more true.

THE FOUR WEEKS' AGONY:
FEBRUARY 12–MARCH 11, 1938

Hitler had given Schuschnigg four days—until Tuesday, February 15 —to send him a "binding reply" that he would carry out the ultimatum, and an additional three days—until February 18—to fulfill its specific terms. Schuschnigg returned to Vienna on the morning of February 12 and immediately sought out President Miklas. Wilhelm Miklas was a plodding, mediocre man of whom the Viennese said that his chief accomplishment in life had been to father a large brood of children. But there was in him a certain peasant solidity, and in this crisis at the end of fifty-two years as a state official he was to display more courage than any other Austrian. He was willing to make certain concessions to Hitler such as amnestying the Austrian Nazis, but he balked at putting Seyss-Inquart in charge of the police and the Army. Papen duly reported this to Berlin on the evening of February 14. He said Schuschnigg hoped "to overcome the resistance of the President by tomorrow."

At 7:30 that same evening Hitler approved orders drawn up by General Keitel to put military pressure on Austria.

Spread false, but quite credible news, which may lead to the conclusion of military preparations against Austria.[14]

As a matter of fact, Schuschnigg had hardly departed from Berchtesgaden when the Fuehrer began shamming military action in order to see that the Austrian Chancellor did as he was told. Jodl jotted it all down in his diary.

February 13. In the afternoon General K[eitel] asks Admiral C[anaris]* and myself to come to his apartment. He tells us that the Fuehrer's order is that military pressure by shamming military action should be kept up until the 15th. Proposals for these measures are drafted and submitted to the Fuehrer by telephone for approval.

February 14. The effect is quick and strong. In Austria the impression is created that Germany is undertaking serious military preparations.[15]

General Jodl was not exaggerating. Before the threat of armed invasion President Miklas gave in and on the last day of grace, February 15, Schuschnigg formally advised Ambassador von Papen that the Berchtesgaden agreement would be carried out before February 18. On February 16 the Austrian government announced a general amnesty for Nazis, including those convicted in the murder of Dollfuss, and made public the reorganized cabinet, in which Arthur Seyss-Inquart was named Minister of Security. The next day this Nazi Minister hurried off to Berlin to see Hitler and receive his orders.

---

* Wilhelm Canaris was head of the Intelligence Bureau (Abwehr) of OKW.

Seyss-Inquart, the first of the quislings, was a pleasant-mannered, intelligent young Viennese lawyer who since 1918 had been possessed with a burning desire to see Austria joined with Germany. This was a popular notion in the first years after the war. Indeed, on November 12, 1918, the day after the armistice, the Provisional National Assembly in Vienna, which had just overthrown the Hapsburg monarchy and proclaimed the Austrian Republic, had tried to effect an Anschluss by affirming that "German Austria is a component part of the German Republic." The victorious Allies had not allowed it and by the time Hitler came to power in 1933 there was no doubt that the majority of Austrians were against their little country's joining with Nazi Germany. But to Seyss-Inquart, as he said at his trial in Nuremberg, the Nazis stood unflinchingly for the Anschluss and for this reason he gave them his support. He did not join the party and took no part in its rowdy excesses. He played the role, rather, of a respectable front for the Austrian Nazis, and after the July 1936 agreement, when he was appointed State Councilor, he concentrated his efforts, aided by Papen and other German officials and agents, in burrowing from within. Strangely, both Schuschnigg and Miklas seem to have trusted him almost to the end. Later Miklas, a devout Catholic as was Schuschnigg, confessed that he was favorably impressed by the fact that Seyss was "a diligent churchgoer." The man's Catholicism and also the circumstance that he, like Schuschnigg, had served in a Tyrolean *Kaiserjaeger* regiment during the First World War, in which he was severely wounded, seems to have been the basis of the trust which the Austrian Chancellor had for him. Schuschnigg, unfortunately, had a fatal inability to judge a man on more substantial grounds. Perhaps he thought he could keep his new Nazi Minister in line by simple bribes. He himself tells in his book of the magic effect of $500 on Seyss-Inquart a year before when he threatened to resign as State Councilor and then reconsidered on the receipt of this paltry sum. But Hitler had the bigger prizes to dazzle before the ambitious young lawyer, as Schuschnigg was soon to learn.

On February 20 Hitler made his long-expected speech to the Reichstag, which had been postponed from January 30 because of the Blomberg–Fritsch crisis and his own machinations against Austria. Though he spoke warmly of Schuschnigg's "understanding" and of his "warmhearted willingness" to bring about a closer understanding between Austria and Germany—a piece of humbug which impressed Prime Minister Chamberlain —the Fuehrer issued a warning which, however much lost on London, did not fall upon deaf ears in Vienna—and in Prague.

Over ten million Germans live in two of the states adjoining our frontiers . . . There must be no doubt about one thing. Political separation from the Reich may not lead to deprivation of rights—that is, the general rights of self-determination. It is unbearable for a world power to know there are racial comrades at its side who are constantly being afflicted with the severest suffering for their sympathy or unity with the whole nation, its destiny and its *Weltanschauung*. To the interests of the German Reich belong the protection of those German peoples who are not in a position to secure along our frontiers their political and spiritual freedom by their own efforts.[16]

That was blunt, public notice that henceforth Hitler regarded the future of the seven million Austrians and the three million Sudeten Germans in Czechoslovakia as the affair of the Third Reich.

Schuschnigg answered Hitler four days later—on February 24—in a speech to the Austrian Bundestag, whose members, like those of the German Reichstag, were hand-picked by a one-party dictatorial regime. Though conciliatory toward Germany, Schuschnigg emphasized that Austria had gone to the very limit of concessions "where we must call a halt and say: 'Thus far and no further.' " Austria, he said, would never vol·untarily give up its independence, and he ended with a stirring call: "Red-White-Red [the Austrian national colors] until we're dead!" (The expression also rhymes in German.)

"The twenty-fourth of February," Schuschnigg wrote after the war, "was for me the crucial date." He awaited anxiously the Fuehrer's reaction to his defiant speech. Papen telegraphed to Berlin the next day advising the Foreign Office that the speech should not be taken too seriously. Schuschnigg, he said, had expressed his rather strong nationalist feelings in order to retrieve his domestic position; there were plots in Vienna to overthrow him because of his concessions at Berchtesgaden. In the meantime, Papen informed Berlin, "the work of Seyss-Inquart . . . is proceeding according to plan."[17] The next day Papen, his long years of devious work in Austria nearing fruition, took formal leave of the Austrian Chancellor and set off for Kitzbuehl to do some skiing.

Hitler's speech of February 20, which had been broadcast by the Austrian radio network, had set off a series of massive Nazi demonstrations throughout Austria. On February 24, during the broadcast of Schuschnigg's reply, a wild mob of twenty thousand Nazis in Graz had invaded the town square, torn down the loudspeakers, hauled down the Austrian flag and raised the swastika banner of Germany. With Seyss-Inquart in personal command of the police, no effort was made to curb the Nazi outbreaks. Schuschnigg's government was breaking down. Not only political but economic chaos was setting in. There were large withdrawals of accounts from the banks both from abroad and by the local people. Cancellation of orders from uneasy foreign firms poured into Vienna. The foreign tourists, one of the main props of the Austrian economy, were being frightened away. Toscanini cabled from New York that he was canceling his appearance at the Salzburg Festival, which drew tens of thousands of tourists each summer, "because of political developments in Austria." The situation was becoming so desperate that Otto of Hapsburg, the exiled youthful pretender to the throne, sent a letter from his home in Belgium and, as Schuschnigg later revealed, implored him on his old oath of allegiance as a former officer of the Imperial Army to appoint him as Chancellor if he thought such a step might save Austria.

In his desperation Schuschnigg turned to the Austrian workers whose free trade unions and political party, the Social Democrats, he had kept suppressed after Dollfuss had brutally smashed them in 1934. These people had represented 42 per cent of the Austrian electorate, and if at any time during the past four years the Chancellor had been able to see beyond the narrow horizons of his own clerical-fascist dictatorship and had enlisted their support for a moderate, anti-Nazi democratic coalition the Nazis, a relatively small minority, could have been easily handled. But Schuschnigg had lacked the stature to take such a step. A decent, upright man as a human being, he had become possessed, as had certain others in Europe, with a contempt for Western democracy and a passion for authoritarian one-party rule.

Out of the factories and the prisons, from which many of them recently had been released along with the Nazis, the Social Democrats came in a body on March 4 to respond to the Chancellor's call. Despite all that had happened they said they were ready to help the government defend the nation's independence. All they asked was what the Chancellor had already conceded to the Nazis: the right to have their own political party and preach their own principles. Schuschnigg agreed, but it was too late.

On March 3 the always well-informed General Jodl noted in his diary: "The Austrian question is becoming critical. 100 officers shall be dispatched here. The Fuehrer wants to see them personally. They should not see to it that the Austrian armed forces will fight better against us, but rather that they do not fight at all."

At this crucial moment, Schuschnigg decided to make one more final, desperate move which he had been mulling over in his mind since the last days of February when the Nazis began to take over in the provinces. He would hold a plebiscite. He would ask the Austrian people whether they were for a "free, independent, social, Christian and united Austria—*Ja oder Nein?*"*

I felt that the moment for a clear decision had come [he wrote later]. It seemed irresponsible to wait with fettered hands until, in the course of some weeks, we should be gagged as well. The gamble now was for stakes which demanded the ultimate and supreme effort.[19]

Shortly after his return from Berchtesgaden, Schuschnigg had apprised Mussolini, Austria's protector, of Hitler's threats and had received an immediate reply from the Duce that Italy's position on Austria remained un-

---

* According to the testimony of President Miklas during a trial of an Austrian Nazi in Vienna after the war, the plebiscite was suggested to Schuschnigg by France. Papen in his memoirs suggests that the French minister in Vienna, M. Puaux, a close personal friend of the Chancellor, was the "father of the plebiscite idea." He concedes, however, that Schuschnigg certainly adopted it on his own responsibility.[18]

changed. Now on March 7 he sent his military attaché in Rome to Mussolini to inform him that in view of events he "was probably going to have to resort to a plebiscite." The Italian dictator answered that it was a mistake —"*C'è un errore!*" He advised Schuschnigg to hold to his previous course. Things were improving; an impending relaxation of relations between Rome and London would do much to ease the pressure. It was the last Schuschnigg ever heard from Mussolini.

On the evening of March 9, Schuschnigg announced in a speech at Innsbruck that a plebiscite would be held in four days—on Sunday, March 13. The unexpected news sent Adolf Hitler into a fit of fury. Jodl's diary entry of March 10 described the initial reaction in Berlin:

By surprise and without consulting his Ministers, Schuschnigg ordered a plebiscite for Sunday, March 13 . . .

Fuehrer is determined not to tolerate it. The same night, March 9 to 10, he calls for Goering. General v. Reichenau is called back from Cairo Olympic Committee. General v. Schobert [commander of the Munich Military District on the Austrian border] is ordered to come, as well as [Austrian] Minister Glaise-Horstenau, who is . . . in the Palatinate . . . Ribbentrop is being detained in London. Neurath takes over the Foreign Office.[20]

The next day, Thursday, March 10, there was a great bustle in Berlin. Hitler had decided on a military occupation of Austria and there is no doubt that his generals were taken by surprise. If Schuschnigg's plebiscite on Sunday were to be prevented by force the Army would have to move into Austria by Saturday, and there were no plans for such a hasty move. Hitler summoned Keitel for 10 A.M., but before hurrying to the Fuehrer the General conferred with Jodl and General Max von Viebahn, chief of the Fuehrungsstab (Operations Staff) of OKW. The resourceful Jodl remembered Special Case Otto which had been drawn up to counter an attempt to place Otto of Hapsburg on the Austrian throne. Since it was the only plan that existed for military action against Austria, Hitler decided it would have to do. "Prepare Case Otto," he ordered.

Keitel raced back to OKW headquarters in the Bendlerstrasse to confer with General Beck, Chief of the General Staff. When he asked for details of the Otto plan, Beck replied, "We have prepared nothing, nothing has been done, nothing at all." Beck in turn was summoned to the Reich Chancellery. Seizing General von Manstein, who was about to leave Berlin to take up a divisional post, he drove with him over to see Hitler, who told them the Army must be ready to march into Austria by Saturday. Neither of the generals offered any objection to this proposal for armed aggression. They were merely concerned with the difficulty of improvising military action on such short notice. Manstein, returning to the Bendlerstrasse, set to work to draft the necessary orders, finishing his task within five hours, at 6 P.M. At 6:30 P.M., according to Jodl's diary, mobilization orders went out to three Army corps and the Air Force. At 2 A.M. the next morning, March 11, Hitler issued Directive Number One for Operation Otto. Such was his haste that he neglected to sign it, and his signature was not obtained until 1 P.M.

TOP SECRET

1. If other measures prove unsuccessful, I intend to invade Austria with armed forces to establish constitutional conditions and to prevent further outrages against the pro-German population.

2. The whole operation will be directed by myself. . . .

4. The forces of the Army and Air Force detailed for this operation must be ready for invasion on March 12, 1938, at the latest by 12:00 hours . . .

5. The behavior of the troops must give the impression that we do not want to wage war against our Austrian brothers. . . . Therefore any provocation is to be avoided. If, however, resistance is offered it must be broken ruthlessly by force of arms. . . .[21]

A few hours later Jodl issued supplemental "top-secret" orders on behalf of the Chief of the Supreme Command of the Armed Forces:

1. If Czechoslovakian troops or militia units are encountered in Austria, they are to be regarded as hostile.

2. The Italians are everywhere to be treated as friends, especially as Mussolini has declared himself disinterested in the solution of the Austrian question.[22]

Hitler had been worried about Mussolini. On the afternoon of March 10, as soon as he had decided on military invasion, he had sent off by special plane Prince Philip of Hesse, with a letter to the Duce (dated March 11) informing him of the action he contemplated and asking for the Italian dictator's understanding. The letter, a tissue of lies concerning his treatment of Schuschnigg and conditions in Austria, which he assured the Duce were "approaching a state of anarchy," began with such a fraudulent argument that Hitler had it omitted when the letter was later published in Germany.* He stated that Austria and Czechoslovakia were plotting to restore the Hapsburgs and preparing "to throw the weight of a mass of at least twenty million men against Germany." He then outlined his demands to Schuschnigg, which, he assured Mussolini, "were more than moderate," told of Schuschnigg's failure to carry them out and spoke of the "mockery" of "a so-called plebiscite."

In my responsibility as Fuehrer and Chancellor of the German Reich and likewise as a son of this soil, I can no longer remain passive in the face of these developments.

I am now determined to restore law and order in my homeland and enable

---

* The stricken passages were found after the war in the archives of the Italian Foreign Ministry.

the people to decide their own fate according to their judgment in an unmistakable, clear and open manner. . . .

Whatever the manner may be in which this plebiscite is to be carried out, I now wish solemnly to assure Your Excellency, as the Duce of Fascist Italy:

1. Consider this step only as one of national self-defense and therefore as an act that any man of character would do in the same way, were he in my position. You too, Excellency, could not act differently if the fate of Italians were at stake. . . .

2. In a critical hour for Italy I proved to you the steadfastness of my sympathy. Do not doubt that in the future there will be no change in this respect.

3. Whatever the consequences of the coming events may be, I have drawn a definite boundary between Germany and France and now draw one just as definite between Italy and us. It is the Brenner . . .*

Always in friendship,

Yours,

ADOLF HITLER[23]

THE COLLAPSE OF SCHUSCHNIGG

Unmindful of the feverish goings on over the border in the Third Reich, Dr. Schuschnigg went to bed on the evening of March 10 firmly convinced, as he later testified, that the plebiscite would be a success for Austria and that the Nazis "would present no formidable obstacle."† Indeed, that evening Dr. Seyss-Inquart had assured him that he would support the plebiscite and even broadcast a speech in its favor.

At half past five on the morning of Friday, March 11, the Austrian Chancellor was wakened by the ringing of the telephone at his bedside. Dr. Skubl, the Austrian chief of police, was speaking. The Germans had closed the border at Salzburg, he said. Rail traffic between the two countries had been halted. German troops were reported concentrating on the Austrian frontier.

By 6:15 Schuschnigg was on his way to his office at the Ballhausplatz,

---

* Drawing the frontier at the Brenner was a sop to Mussolini. It meant that Hitler would not be asking for the return of the southern Tyrol, which was taken from Austria and awarded to Italy at Versailles.

† In all fairness, it should be pointed out that Schuschnigg's plebiscite was scarcely more free or democratic than those perpetrated by Hitler in Germany. Since there had been no free elections in Austria since 1933, there were no up-to-date polling lists. Only those persons above twenty-four were eligible to vote. Only four days' notice of the plebiscite had been given to the public, so there was no time for campaigning even if the opposition groups, the Nazis and the Social Democrats, had been free to do so. The Social Democrats undoubtedly would have voted *Ja*, since they regarded Schuschnigg as a lesser evil than Hitler and moreover had been promised the restoration of political freedom. There is no question that their vote would have given Schuschnigg a victory.

but he decided to stop first at St. Stephen's Cathedral. There in the first
dim light of dawn while early mass was being read he sat restlessly in his
pew thinking of the ominous message from the chief of police. "I was not
quite sure what it meant," he later recalled. "I only knew that it would
bring some change." He gazed at the candles burning in front of the image
of Our Lady of Perpetual Succor, looked furtively around and then made
the sign of the cross, as countless Viennese had done before this figure in
past times of stress.

At the Chancellery all was quiet; not even any disturbing dispatches
had arrived during the night from Austria's diplomats abroad. He called
police headquarters and asked that as a precautionary measure a police
cordon be thrown around the Inner City and the government buildings.
He also convoked his cabinet colleagues. Only Seyss-Inquart failed to
show up. Schuschnigg could not locate him anywhere. Actually the Nazi
Minister was out at the Vienna airport. Papen, summarily summoned to
Berlin the night before, had departed by special plane at 6 A.M. and Seyss
had seen him off. Now the Number One quisling was waiting for the Number Two—Glaise-Horstenau, like Seyss a minister in Schuschnigg's cabinet, like him already deep in treason, who was due to arrive from Berlin
with Hitler's orders on what they were to do about the plebiscite.

The orders were to call it off, and these were duly presented to Schuschnigg by the two gentlemen at 10 A.M. along with the information that Hitler was furious. After several hours of consultations with President Miklas, his cabinet colleagues and Dr. Skubl, Schuschnigg agreed to cancel
the plebiscite. The police chief had reluctantly told him that the police,
liberally sprinkled with Nazis who had been restored to their posts in accordance with the Berchtesgaden ultimatum, could no longer be counted
on by the government. On the other hand, Schuschnigg felt sure that the
Army and the militia of the Patriotic Front—the official authoritarian
party in Austria—would fight. But at this crucial moment Schuschnigg
decided—he says, in fact, that his mind had long been made up on the
matter—that he would not offer resistance to Hitler if it meant spilling
German blood. Hitler was quite willing to do this, but Schuschnigg shrank
back from the very prospect.

At 2 P.M. he called in Seyss-Inquart and told him that he was calling
off the plebiscite. The gentle Judas immediately made for the telephone to
inform Goering in Berlin. But in the Nazi scheme of things one concession
from a yielding opponent must lead quickly to another. Goering and Hitler then and there began raising the ante. The minute-by-minute account
of how this was done, of the threats and the swindles employed, was recorded—ironically enough—by Goering's own Forschungsamt, the "Institute for Research," which took down and transcribed twenty-seven
telephone conversations from the Field Marshal's office beginning at 2:45
P.M. on March 11. The documents were found in the German Air Ministry after the war and constitute an illuminating record of how Austria's
fate was settled by telephone from Berlin during the next few critical
hours.[24]

During Seyss's first call to Goering at 2:45 P.M. the Field Marshal told him that Schuschnigg's cancellation of the plebiscite was not enough and that after talking with Hitler he would call him back. This he did at 3:05. Schuschnigg, he ordered, must resign, and Seyss-Inquart must be named Chancellor within two hours. Goering also told Seyss then to "send the telegram to the Fuehrer, as agreed upon." This is the first mention of a telegram that was to pop up throughout the frantic events of the next few hours and which would be used to perpetrate the swindle by which Hitler justified his aggression to the German people and to the foreign offices of the world.

Wilhelm Keppler, Hitler's special agent in Austria, arriving in the afternoon from Berlin to take charge in Papen's absence, had shown Seyss-Inquart the text of a telegram he was to send the Fuehrer. It requested the dispatch of German troops to Austria to put down disorder. In his Nuremberg affidavit, Seyss declared that he refused to send such a wire since there were no disorders. Keppler, insisting that it would have to be done, hurried to the Austrian Chancellery, where he was brazen enough to set up an emergency office along with Seyss and Glaise-Horstenau. Why Schuschnigg allowed such interlopers and traitors to establish themselves physically in the seat of the Austrian government at this critical hour is incomprehensible, but he did. Later he remembered the Chancellery as looking "like a disturbed beehive," with Seyss-Inquart and Glaise-Horstenau holding "court" in one corner "and around them a busy coming and going of strange-looking men"; but apparently it never occurred to the courteous but dazed Chancellor to throw them out.

He had made up his mind to yield to Hitler's pressure and resign. While still closeted with Seyss he had put through a telephone call to Mussolini, but the Duce was not immediately available and a few minutes later Schuschnigg canceled the call. To ask for Mussolini's help, he decided, "would be a waste of time." Even Austria's pompous protector was deserting her in the hour of need. A few minutes later, when Schuschnigg was trying to talk President Miklas into accepting his resignation, a message came from the Foreign Office: "The Italian government declares that it could give no advice under the circumstances, in case such advice should be asked for."[25]

President Wilhelm Miklas was not a great man, but he was a stubborn, upright one. He reluctantly accepted Schuschnigg's resignation but he refused to make Seyss-Inquart his successor. "That is quite impossible," he said. "We will not be coerced." He instructed Schuschnigg to inform the Germans that their ultimatum was refused.[26]

This was promptly reported by Seyss-Inquart to Goering at 5:30 P.M.

SEYSS-INQUART: The President has accepted the resignation [of Schuschnigg] . . . I suggested he entrust the Chancellorship to me . . . but he would like to entrust a man like Ender . . .

GOERING: Well, that won't do! Under no circumstances! The President has to be informed immediately that he has to turn the powers of the Federal Chancellor over to you and to accept the cabinet as it was arranged.

There was an interruption at this point. Seyss-Inquart put a Dr. Muehl-mann, a shadowy Austrian Nazi whom Schuschnigg had noticed lurking in the background at Berchtesgaden and who was a personal friend of Goering, on the line.

MUEHLMANN: The President still refuses persistently to give his consent. We three National Socialists went to speak to him personally . . . He would not even let us see him. So far, it looks as if he were not willing to give in.

GOERING: Give me Seyss. [To Seyss] Now, remember the following: You go immediately together with Lieutenant General Muff [the German military attaché] and tell the President that if the conditions are not accepted immediately, the troops which are already advancing to the frontier will march in tonight along the whole line, and Austria will cease to exist . . . Tell him there is no time now for any joke. The situation now is that tonight the invasion will begin from all the corners of Austria. The invasion will be stopped and the troops held on the border only if we are informed by seven-thirty that Miklas has entrusted you with the Federal Chancellorship . . . Then call out the National Socialists all over the country. They should now be in the streets. So remember, a report must be given by seven-thirty. If Miklas could not understand it in four hours, we shall make him understand it now in four minutes.

But still the resolute President held out.

At 6:30 Goering was back on the phone to Keppler and Seyss-Inquart. Both reported that President Miklas refused to go along with them.

GOERING: Well, then, Seyss-Inquart has to dismiss him! Just go upstairs again and tell him plainly that Seyss will call on the National Socialist guards and in five minutes the troops will march in on my order.

After this order General Muff and Keppler presented to the President a second military ultimatum threatening that if he did not yield within an hour, by 7:30, German troops would march into Austria. "I informed the two gentlemen," Miklas testified later, "that I refused the ultimatum . . . and that Austria alone determines who is to be the head of government."

By this time the Austrian Nazis had gained control of the streets as well as of the Chancellery. About six that evening, returning from the hospital where my wife was fighting for her life after a difficult childbirth which had ended with a Caesarean operation, I had emerged from the subway at the Karlsplatz to find myself engulfed in a shouting, hysterical Nazi mob which was sweeping toward the Inner City. These contorted faces I had seen before, at the Nuremberg party rallies. They were yelling, "Sieg Heil! Sieg Heil! Heil Hitler! Heil Hitler! Hang Schuschnigg! Hang Schuschnigg!"

The police, whom only a few hours before I had seen disperse a small Nazi group without any trouble, were standing by, grinning.

Schuschnigg heard the tramp and the shouts of the mob, and the sounds impressed him. He hurried to the President's office to make a final plea. But, he says:

President Miklas was adamant. He would not appoint a Nazi as Austrian Chancellor. On my insistence that he appoint Seyss-Inquart he said again: "You all desert me now, all of you." But I saw no other possibility than Seyss-Inquart. With the little hope I had left I clung to all the promises he had made me, I clung to his personal reputation as a practicing Catholic and an honest man.[27]

Schuschnigg clung to his illusions to the last.

The fallen Chancellor then proposed that he make a farewell broadcast and explain why he had resigned. He says that Miklas agreed, though the President would later dispute it. It was the most moving broadcast I have ever heard. The microphone was set up some five paces from where Dollfuss had been shot to death by the Nazis.

. . . The German government [Schuschnigg said] today handed to President Miklas an ultimatum, with a time limit, ordering him to nominate as Chancellor a person designated by the German government . . . otherwise German troops would invade Austria.

I declare before the world that the reports launched in Germany concerning disorders by the workers, the shedding of streams of blood and the creation of a situation beyond the control of the Austrian government are lies from A to Z. President Miklas has asked me to tell the people of Austria that we have yielded to force since we are not prepared even in this terrible hour to shed blood. We have decided to order the troops to offer no resistance.*

So I take leave of the Austrian people with a German word of farewell, uttered from the depth of my heart: God protect Austria!

---

* In his postwar testimony already referred to, Miklas denied that he asked Schuschnigg to say any such thing or that he even agreed that the broadcast should be made. Contrary to what the retiring Chancellor said, the President was not yet ready to yield to force. "Things have not gone so far that we must capitulate," he says he told Schuschnigg. He had just turned down the second German ultimatum. He was standing firm. But Schuschnigg's broadcast did help to undermine his position and force his hand. As we shall see, the obstinate old President held out for several hours more before capitulating. On March 13, he refused to sign the Anschluss law snuffing out Austria's independent existence which Seyss-Inquart, at Hitler's insistence, promulgated. Though he surrendered the functions of his office to the Nazi Chancellor for as long as he was prevented from carrying them out, he maintained that he never formally resigned as President. "It would have been too cowardly," he later explained to a Vienna court. This did not prevent Seyss-Inquart from announcing officially on March 13 that "the President, upon request of the Chancellor," had "resigned from his office" and that his "affairs" were transferred to the Chancellor.[28]

The Chancellor might take leave but the stubborn President was not yet ready to. Goering learned this when he phoned General Muff shortly after Schuschnigg's broadcast. "The best thing will be if Miklas resigns," Goering told him.

"Yes, but he won't," Muff rejoined. "It was very dramatic. I spoke to him almost fifteen minutes. He declared that under no circumstances will he yield to force."

"So? He will not give in to force?" Goering could not believe the words.

"He does not yield to force," the General repeated.

"So he just wants to be kicked out?"

"Yes," said Muff. "He is staying put."

"Well, with fourteen children," Goering laughed, "a man has to stay put. Anyway, tell Seyss to take over."

There was still the matter of the telegram which Hitler wanted in order to justify his invasion. The Fuehrer, according to Papen, who had joined him at the Chancellery in Berlin, was now "in a state bordering on hysteria." The stubborn Austrian President was fouling up his plans. So was Seyss-Inquart, because of his failure to send the telegram calling on Hitler to send troops into Austria to quell disorder. Exasperated beyond enduring, Hitler flashed the invasion order at 8:45 P.M. on the evening of March 11.* Three minutes later, at 8:48, Goering was on the phone to Keppler in Vienna.

Listen carefully. The following telegram should be sent here by Seyss-Inquart. Take the notes.

"The provisional Austrian Government, which after the resignation of the Schuschnigg Government considers it its task to establish peace and order in Austria, sends to the German Government the urgent request to support it in the task and to help it to prevent bloodshed. For this purpose it asks the German Government to send German troops as soon as possible."

Keppler assured the Field Marshal he would show Seyss-Inquart the text of the "telegram" immediately.

"Well," Goering said, "he does not even have to send the telegram. All he needs to do is say 'Agreed.' "

One hour later Keppler called back Berlin. "Tell the Field Marshal," he said, "that Seyss-Inquart agrees."†

---

* Marked "Top Secret" and identified as Directive No. 2 of Operation Otto, it read in part: "The demands of the German ultimatum to the Austrian government have not been fulfilled . . . To avoid further bloodshed in Austrian cities, the entry of the German armed forces into Austria will commence, according to Directive No. 1, at daybreak of March 12. I expect the set objectives to be reached by exerting all forces to the full as quickly as possible. (Signed) Adolf Hitler."[29]

† Actually, Seyss-Inquart tried until long after midnight to get Hitler to call off the German invasion. A German Foreign Office memorandum reveals that at 2:10 A.M. on March 12 General Muff telephoned Berlin and stated that on the instructions of Chancellor Seyss-Inquart he was requesting that "the alerted troops should remain on, but not cross, the border." Keppler also came on the telephone

Thus it was that when I passed through Berlin the next day I found a screaming headline in the *Voelkischer Beobachter:* GERMAN AUSTRIA SAVED FROM CHAOS. There were incredible stories hatched up by Goebbels describing Red disorders—fighting, shooting, pillaging—in the main streets of Vienna. And there was the text of the telegram, issued by D.N.B., the official German news agency, which said that it had been dispatched by Seyss-Inquart to Hitler the night before. Actually two copies of the "telegram," just as Goering had dictated it, were found in the German Foreign Office archives at the end of the war. Papen later explained how they got there. They were concocted, he says, sometime later by the German Minister of Posts and Telegraph and deposited in the government files.

Hitler had waited anxiously throughout the frenzied afternoon and evening not only for President Miklas to capitulate but for some word from Mussolini. The silence of Austria's protector was becoming ominous. At 10:25 P.M. Prince Philip of Hesse called the Chancellery from Rome. Hitler himself grabbed the telephone. Goering's technicians recorded the conversation that followed:

PRINCE: I have just come back from the Palazzo Venezia. The Duce accepted the whole thing in a very friendly manner. He sends you his regards. . . . Schuschnigg gave him the news . . . Mussolini said that Austria would be immaterial to him.

Hitler was beside himself with relief and joy.

HITLER: Then, please tell Mussolini I will never forget him for this!
PRINCE: Yes, sir.
HITLER: Never, never, never, no matter what happens! I am ready to make a quite different agreement with him.
PRINCE: Yes, sir. I told him that too.
HITLER: As soon as the Austrian affair has been settled I shall be ready to go with him through thick and thin—through anything!
PRINCE: Yes, my Fuehrer.
HITLER: Listen! I shall make any agreement. I am no longer in fear of the terrible position which would have existed militarily in case we had gotten into a conflict. You may tell him that I do thank him from the bottom of my heart. Never, never shall I forget it.
PRINCE: Yes, my Fuehrer.
HITLER: I shall never forget him for this, no matter what happens. If he should ever need any help or be in any danger, he can be convinced that I shall stick to him whatever may happen, even if the whole world gangs up on him.
PRINCE: Yes, my Fuehrer.

to support the request. General Muff, a decent man and an officer of the old school, seems to have been embarrassed by his role in Vienna. When he was informed by Berlin that Hitler declined to halt his troops he replied that he "regretted this message."[30]

And what stand were Great Britain and France and the League of Nations taking at this critical moment to halt Germany's aggression against a peaceful neighboring country? None. For the moment France was again without a government. On Thursday, March 10, Premier Chautemps and his cabinet had resigned. All through the crucial day of Friday, March 11, when Goering was telephoning his ultimatums to Vienna, there was no one in Paris who could act. It was not until the Anschluss had been proclaimed on the thirteenth that a French government was formed under Léon Blum.

And Britain? On February 20, a week after Schuschnigg had capitulated at Berchtesgaden, Foreign Secretary Anthony Eden had resigned, principally because of his opposition to further appeasement of Mussolini by Prime Minister Chamberlain. He was replaced by Lord Halifax. This change was welcomed in Berlin. So was Chamberlain's statement to the Commons after the Berchtesgaden ultimatum. The German Embassy in London reported fully on it in a dispatch to Berlin on March 4.[31] Chamberlain was quoted as saying that "what happened [at Berchtesgaden] was merely that two statesmen had agreed upon certain measures for the improvement of relations between their two countries . . . It appeared hardly possible to insist that just because two statesmen had agreed on certain domestic changes in one of two countries—changes desirable in the interest of relations between them—the one country had renounced its independence in favor of the other. On the contrary, the Federal Chancellor's speech of February 24 contained nothing that might convey the impression that the Federal Chancellor [Schuschnigg] himself believed in the surrender of the independence of his country."

In view of the fact that the British Legation in Vienna, as I myself learned at the time, had provided Chamberlain with the details of Hitler's Berchtesgaden ultimatum to Schuschnigg, this speech, which was made to the Commons on March 2, is astounding.* But it was pleasing to Hitler. He knew that he could march into Austria without getting into complications with Britain. On March 9, Ribbentrop, the new German Foreign Minister, had arrived in London to wind up his affairs at the embassy, where he had been ambassador. He had long talks with Chamberlain, Halifax, the King and the Archbishop of Canterbury. His impressions of the British Prime Minister and Foreign Secretary, he reported back to Berlin, were "very good." After a long conference with Lord Halifax, Ribbentrop reported directly to Hitler on March 10 as to what Britain would do "if the Austrian question cannot be settled peacefully." Basically he was convinced from his London talks "that England will do nothing in regard to Austria."[33]

On Friday, March 11, Ribbentrop was lunching at Downing Street with

---

* In his testimony at Nuremberg Guido Schmidt swore that both he and Schuschnigg informed the envoys of the "Big Powers" of Hitler's ultimatum "in detail."[32] Moreover, the Vienna correspondents of the *Times* and the *Daily Telegraph* of London, to my knowledge, also telephoned their respective newspapers a full and accurate report.

the Prime Minister and his associates when a Foreign Office messenger broke in with urgent dispatches for Chamberlain telling of the startling news from Vienna. Only a few minutes before, Chamberlain had asked Ribbentrop to inform the Fuehrer "of his sincere wish and firm determination to clear up German-British relations." Now, at the receipt of the sour news from Austria, the statesmen adjourned to the Prime Minister's study, where Chamberlain read to the uncomfortable German Foreign Minister two telegrams from the British Legation in Vienna telling of Hitler's ultimatum. "The discussion," Ribbentrop reported to Hitler, "took place in a tense atmosphere and the usually calm Lord Halifax was more excited than Chamberlain, who outwardly at least appeared calm and cool-headed." Ribbentrop expressed doubts about "the truth of the reports" and this seems to have calmed down his British hosts, for "our leave-taking," he reported, "was entirely amiable, and even Halifax was calm again."*[34]

Chamberlain's reaction to the dispatches from Vienna was to instruct Ambassador Henderson in Berlin to pen a note to Acting Foreign Minister von Neurath stating that if the report of the German ultimatum to Austria was correct, "His Majesty's Government feel bound to register a protest in the strongest terms."[35] But a formal diplomatic protest at this late hour was the least of Hitler's worries. The next day, March 12, while German troops were streaming into Austria, Neurath returned a contemptuous reply,[36] declaring that Austro–German relations were the exclusive concern of the German people and not of the British government, and repeating the lies that there had been no German ultimatum to Austria and that troops had been dispatched only in answer to "urgent" appeals from the newly formed Austrian government. He referred the British ambassador to the telegram, "already published in the German press."†

Hitler's only serious worry on the evening of March 11 had been over Mussolini's reaction to his aggression,‡ but there was some concern in Berlin too as to what Czechoslovakia might do. However, the indefati-

---

* Churchill has given an amusing description of this luncheon in *The Gathering Storm* (pp. 271–72).

† The lies were repeated in a circular telegram dispatched by Baron von Weizsaecker of the Foreign Office March 12 to German envoys abroad for "information and orientation of your conversations." Weizsaecker stated that Schuschnigg's declaration concerning a German ultimatum "was sheer fabrication" and went on to inform his diplomats abroad: "The truth was that the question of sending military forces . . . was first raised in the well-known telegram of the newly formed Austrian government. In view of the imminent danger of civil war, the Reich government decided to comply with this appeal."[37] Thus the German Foreign Office lied not only to foreign diplomats but to its own. In a long and ineffectual book written after the war Weizsaecker, like so many other Germans who served Hitler, maintained that he was anti-Nazi all along.

‡ In his testimony at Nuremberg on August 9, 1946, Field Marshal von Manstein emphasized that "at the time when Hitler gave us the orders for Austria his chief worry was not so much that there might be interference on the part of the Western Powers, but his only worry was as to how Italy would behave, because it appeared that Italy always sided with Austria and the Hapsburgs."[38]

gable Goering quickly cleared this up. Busy though he was at the telephone directing the coup in Vienna, he managed to slip over during the evening to the Haus der Flieger, where he was official host to a thousand high-ranking officials and diplomats, who were being entertained at a glittering soiree by the orchestra, the singers and the ballet of the State Opera. When the Czech minister in Berlin, Dr. Mastny, arrived at the gala fete he was immediately taken aside by the bemedaled Field Marshal, who told him on his word of honor that Czechoslovakia had nothing to fear from Germany, that the entry of the Reich's troops into Austria was "nothing more than a family affair" and that Hitler wanted to improve relations with Prague. In return he asked for assurances that the Czechs would not mobilize. Dr. Mastny left the reception, telephoned to his Foreign Minister in Prague, and returned to the hall to tell Goering that his country was not mobilizing and that Czechoslovakia had no intention of trying to interfere with events in Austria. Goering was relieved and repeated his assurances, adding that he was authorized to back them up by Hitler's word too.

It may have been that even the astute Czech President, Eduard Beneš, did not have time to realize that evening that Austria's end meant Czecho-slovakia's as well. There were some in Europe that weekend who thought the Czech government was shortsighted, who argued that in view of the disastrous strategic position in which Czechoslovakia would be left by the Nazi occupation of Austria—with German troops surrounding her on three sides—and considering too that her intervention to help save Austria might have brought Russia, France and Britain, as well as the League of Nations, into a conflict with the Third Reich which the Germans were in no condition to meet, the Czechs should have acted on the night of March 11. But subsequent events, which shortly will be chronicled here, surely demolish any such argument. A little later when the two big Western democracies and the League had a better opportunity of stopping Hitler they shrank from it. Anyway, at no time on the eventful day did Schusch-nigg make a formal appeal to London, Paris, Prague or Geneva. Perhaps, as his memoirs indicate, he thought this would be a waste of time. Presi-dent Miklas, on the other hand, was under the impression, as he later testi-fied, that the Austrian government, which immediately had informed Paris and London of the German ultimatum, was continuing "conversations" with the French and British governments throughout the afternoon in order to ascertain their "frame of mind."

When it became clear that their "frame of mind" was to do nothing more than utter empty protests President Miklas, a little before midnight, gave in. He appointed Seyss-Inquart Chancellor and accepted his list of cabi-net ministers. "I was completely abandoned both at home and abroad," he commented bitterly later.

Having issued a grandiose proclamation to the German people in which he justified his aggression with his usual contempt for the truth and prom-ised that the Austrian people would choose their future in "a real plebiscite"—Goebbels read it over the German and Austrian radio stations at noon on March 12—Hitler set off for his native land. He received a tumultuous welcome. At every village, hastily decorated in his honor, there were cheering crowds. During the afternoon he reached his first goal, Linz, where he had spent his school days. The reception there was delirious and Hitler was deeply touched. The next day, after getting off a telegram to Mussolini—"I shall never forget you for this!"—he laid a wreath on the graves of his parents at Leonding and then returned to Linz to make a speech:

When years ago I went forth from this town I bore within me precisely the same profession of faith which today fills my heart. Judge the depth of my emotion when after so many years I have been able to bring that profession of faith to its fulfillment. If Providence once called me forth from this town to be the leader of the Reich, it must in so doing have charged me with a mission, and that mission could only be to restore my dear homeland to the German Reich. I have believed in this mission, I have lived and fought for it, and I believe I have now fulfilled it.

On the afternoon of the twelfth, Seyss-Inquart, accompanied by Himmler, had flown to Linz to meet Hitler and had proudly proclaimed that Article 88 of the Treaty of St. Germain, which proclaimed Austria's independence as inalienable and made the League of Nations its guarantor, had been voided. To Hitler, carried away by the enthusiasm of the Austrian crowds, this was not enough. He ordered Dr. Wilhelm Stuckart, an undersecretary in the Ministry of the Interior who had been rushed by his Minister, Frick, to Vienna to draft a law making Hitler President of Austria, to come at once to Linz. Somewhat to the surprise of this legal expert, the Fuehrer instructed him, as he later deposed at Nuremberg, to "draft a law providing for a total Anschluss."[39]

This draft Stuckart presented to the newly formed Austrian government in Vienna on Sunday, March 13, the day on which Schuschnigg's plebiscite was to have been held. President Miklas, as we have seen, refused to sign it, but Seyss-Inquart, who had taken over the President's powers, did and late that evening flew back to Linz to present it to the Fuehrer. It proclaimed the end of Austria. "Austria," it began, "is a province of the German Reich." Hitler shed tears of joy, Seyss-Inquart later recalled.[40] The so-called Anschluss law was also promulgated the same day at Linz by the German government and signed by Hitler, Goering, Ribbentrop, Frick and Hess. It provided for "a free and secret plebiscite" on April 10 in which the Austrians could determine "the question of reunion with the German Reich." The Reich Germans, Hitler announced on March 18, were also to have a plebiscite on the Anschluss, along with new elections to the Reichstag.

Hitler did not make his triumphal entry into Vienna, where he had lived so long as a tramp, until the afternoon of Monday, March 14. He was delayed by two unforeseen developments. Despite the delirium of the Austrians at the prospect of seeing the Fuehrer in the capital, Himmler asked for an extra day to perfect security arrangements. He was already carrying out the arrest of thousands of "unreliables"—within a few weeks the number would reach 79,000 in Vienna alone. Also the vaunted German panzer units had broken down long before they got within sight of Vienna's hills. According to Jodl, some 70 per cent of the armored vehicles were stranded on the road from Salzburg and Passau to Vienna, though General Guderian, who commanded the panzer troops, later contended that only 30 per cent of his forces became stalled. At any rate, Hitler was furious at the delay. He remained in Vienna only overnight, putting up at the Hotel Imperial.

Still, this triumphant return to the former imperial capital which he felt had rejected him and condemned him in his youth to a starved and miserable gutter life and which was now acclaiming him with such tumultuous jubilation could not have failed to revive his spirits. The ubiquitous Papen, rushing by plane from Berlin to Vienna to get in on the festivities, found Hitler in the reviewing stand opposite the Hofburg, the ancient palace of the Hapsburgs. "I can only describe him," Papen later wrote, "as being in a state of ecstasy."*

He remained in this state during most of the next four weeks, when he traversed Germany and Austria from one end to the other whipping up public fervor for a big *Ja* vote in favor of the Anschluss. But in his exuberant speeches he missed no opportunity to vilify Schuschnigg or to peddle the by now shopworn lies about how the Anschluss was achieved. In his address to the Reichstag on March 18 he asserted that Schuschnigg

---

* Yet underneath the ecstasy, and unnoticed by the shallow Papen, there may have burned in Hitler a feeling of revenge for a city and a people which had not appreciated him as a young man and which at heart he despised. This in part may have accounted for his brief stay. Though a few weeks later he would publicly say to the burgomaster of Vienna, "Be assured that this city is in my eyes a pearl—I will bring it into a setting which is worthy of it," this was probably more electioneering propaganda than an expression of his inner feelings. These feelings were revealed to Baldur von Schirach, the Nazi Governor and Gauleiter of Vienna during the war, at a heated meeting at the Berghof in 1943. Describing it during his testimony at Nuremberg, Schirach said:

> Then the Fuehrer began with, I might say, incredible and unlimited hatred to speak against the people of Vienna. . . . At four o'clock in the morning Hitler suddenly said something which I should now like to repeat for historical reasons. He said: "Vienna should never have been admitted into the Union of the Greater Germany." Hitler never loved Vienna. He hated its people.[41]

Papen's own festive spirits on March 14 were spoiled that same day when he learned that Wilhelm von Ketteler, his close friend and aide at the German Legation, had disappeared under circumstances which indicated foul play by the Gestapo. Three years before, another friend and collaborator at the legation, Baron Tschirschky, had fled to England to escape certain death from the S.S. At the end of April Ketteler's body was fished out of the Danube, where Gestapo thugs in Vienna had thrown it after murdering him.

had "broken his word" by his "election forgery," adding that "only a crazy, blinded man" could have behaved in such a manner. On March 25 at Koenigsberg the "election forgery" had become in Hitler's mind "this ridiculous comedy." Letters had been found, Hitler claimed, proving that Schuschnigg had deliberately double-crossed him by seeking delays in augmenting the Berchtesgaden agreement until "a more propitious hour to stir up foreign countries against Germany."

In Koenigsberg Hitler also answered the taunts of the foreign press at his use of brutal force and his trickery in having proclaimed the Anschluss without even waiting for the decision of the plebiscite:

> Certain foreign newspapers have said that we fell on Austria with brutal methods. I can only say: even in death they cannot stop lying. I have in the course of my political struggle won much love from my people, but when I crossed the former frontier [into Austria] there met me such a stream of love as I have never experienced. Not as tyrants have we come, but as liberators . . . Under the force of this impression I decided not to wait until April tenth but to effect the unification forthwith . . .

If this sounded less than logical—or honest—to foreign ears, there is no doubt that it made a great impression on the Germans. When at the conclusion of his Reichstag speech Hitler implored, in a voice choked with emotion, "German people, give me another four years so that I can now exploit the accomplished union for the benefit of all!" he received an ovation so overwhelming that it dwarfed all his former triumphs at this tribune.

The Fuehrer wound up his election campaign in Vienna on April 9, on the eve of the polling. The man who had once tramped the pavements of this city as a vagabond, unwashed and empty-bellied, who but four years before had assumed in Germany the powers of the Hohenzollern kings and had now taken upon himself those of the Hapsburg emperors, was full of a sense of God-given mission.

> I believe that it was God's will to send a youth from here into the Reich, to let him grow up, to raise him to be the leader of the nation so as to enable him to lead back his homeland into the Reich.
>
> There is a higher ordering and we all are nothing else than its agents. When on March 9 Herr Schuschnigg broke his agreement, then in that second I felt that now the call of Providence had come to me. And that which then took place in three days was only conceivable as the fulfillment of the wish and the will of this Providence.
>
> In three days the Lord has smitten them! . . . And to me the grace was given on the day of the betrayal to be able to unite my homeland with the Reich! . . .
>
> I would now give thanks to Him who let me return to my homeland in order that I might now lead it into my German Reich! Tomorrow may every

German recognize the hour and measure its import and bow in humility before the Almighty, who in a few weeks has wrought a miracle upon us!

That a majority of Austrians, who undoubtedly would have said *Ja* to Schuschnigg on March 13, would say the same to Hitler on April 10 was a foregone conclusion. Many of them sincerely believed that ultimate union with any kind of Germany, even a Nazi Germany, was a desirable and inevitable end, that Austria, cut off from its vast Slavic and Hungarian hinterland in 1918, could not in the long run exist decently by itself, that it could only survive as part of the German Reich. In addition to these Austrians were the fanatical Nazis whose ranks were swelling rapidly with jobseekers and jobholders attracted by success and anxious to improve their position. Many Catholics in this overwhelmingly Catholic country were undoubtedly swayed by a widely publicized statement of Cardinal Innitzer welcoming Nazism to Austria and urging a *Ja* vote.*

In a fair and honest election in which the Social Democrats and Schuschnigg's Christian Socials would have had freedom to campaign openly the plebiscite, in my opinion, might have been close. As it was, it took a very brave Austrian to vote No. As in Germany, and not without reason, the voters feared that their failure to cast an affirmative ballot might be found out. In the polling station which I visited in Vienna that Sunday afternoon, wide slits in the corner of the polling booths gave the Nazi election committee sitting a few feet away a good view of how one voted. In the country districts few bothered—or dared—to cast their ballots in the secrecy of the booth; they voted openly for all to see. I happened to broadcast at seven-thirty that evening, a half hour after the polls had closed, when few votes had yet been counted. A Nazi official assured me before the broadcast that the Austrians were voting 99 per cent *Ja*. That was the figure officially given later—99.08 per cent in Greater Germany, 99.75 in Austria.

And so Austria, as Austria, passed for a moment out of history, its very name suppressed by the revengeful Austrian who had now joined it to Germany. The ancient German word for Austria, Oesterreich, was abolished. Austria became the Ostmark and soon even that name was dropped and Berlin administered the country by *Gaue* (districts) which corresponded roughly to the historic *Laender* such as Tyrol, Salzburg, Styria and Carinthia. Vienna became just another city of the Reich, a provincial district administrative center, withering away. The former Austrian tramp become dictator had wiped his native land off the map and deprived its once glittering capital of its last shred of glory and importance. Disillusionment among the Austrians was inevitable.

---

* A few months later, on October 8, the cardinal's palace opposite St. Stephen's Cathedral was sacked by Nazi hooligans. Too late Innitzer had learned what National Socialism was, and had spoken out in a sermon against the Nazi persecution of his Church.

For the first few weeks the behavior of the Vienna Nazis was worse than anything I had seen in Germany. There was an orgy of sadism. Day after day large numbers of Jewish men and women could be seen scrubbing Schuschnigg signs off the sidewalk and cleaning the gutters. While they worked on their hands and knees with jeering storm troopers standing over them, crowds gathered to taunt them. Hundreds of Jews, men and women, were picked off the streets and put to work cleaning public latrines and the toilets of the barracks where the S.A. and the S.S. were quartered. Tens of thousands more were jailed. Their worldly possessions were confiscated or stolen. I myself, from our apartment in the Plosslgasse, watched squads of S.S. men carting off silver, tapestries, paintings and other loot from the Rothschild palace next door. Baron Louis de Rothschild himself was later able to buy his way out of Vienna by turning over his steel mills to the Hermann Goering Works. Perhaps half of the city's 180,000 Jews managed, by the time the war started, to purchase their freedom to emigrate by handing over what they owned to the Nazis.

This lucrative trade in human freedom was handled by a special organization set up under the S.S. by Heydrich, the "Office for Jewish Emigration," which became the sole Nazi agency authorized to issue permits to Jews to leave the country. Administered from the beginning to the end by an Austrian Nazi, a native of Hitler's home town of Linz by the name of Karl Adolf Eichmann, it was to become eventually an agency not of emigration but of extermination and to organize the slaughter of more than four million persons, mostly Jews. Himmler and Heydrich also took advantage of their stay in Austria during the first weeks of the Anschluss to set up a huge concentration camp at Mauthausen, on the north bank of the Danube near Enns. It was too much trouble to continue to transport thousands of Austrians to the concentration camps of Germany. Austria, Himmler decided, needed one of its own. Before the Third Reich tumbled to its fall the non-Austrian prisoners were to outnumber the local inmates and Mauthausen was to achieve the dubious record as the German concentration camp (the *extermination* camps in the East were something else) with the largest number of officially listed executions—35,318 in the six and a half years of its existence.

Despite the Gestapo terror led by Himmler and Heydrich after the Anschluss Germans flocked by the hundreds of thousands to Austria, where they could pay with their marks for sumptuous meals not available in Germany for years and for bargain-priced vacations amid Austria's matchless mountains and lakes. German businessmen and bankers poured in to buy up the concerns of dispossessed Jews and anti-Nazis at a fraction of their value. Among the smiling visitors was the inimitable Dr. Schacht, who, despite his quarrels with Hitler, was still a minister (without portfolio) in the Reich cabinet, still the president of the Reichsbank, and who was overjoyed with the Anschluss. Arriving to take over the Austrian National Bank on behalf of the Reichsbank even before the plebiscite, he addressed the staff of the Austrian bank on March 21. Ridiculing the foreign press for criticizing Hitler's methods of effecting the union, Dr,

Schacht stoutly defended the methods, arguing that the Anschluss was "the consequence of countless perfidies and brutal acts of violence which foreign countries have practiced against us.

"Thank God . . . Adolf Hitler has created a communion of German will and German thought. He bolstered it up with the newly strengthened Wehrmacht and he then finally gave the external form to the inner union between Germany and Austria. . . .

"Not a single person will find a future with us who is not wholeheartedly for Adolf Hitler . . . The Reichsbank will always be nothing but National Socialist or I shall cease to be its manager."

Whereupon Dr. Schacht administered to the Austrian staff an oath to be "faithful and obedient to the Fuehrer."

"A scoundrel he who breaks it!" Dr. Schacht cried, and then led his audience in the bellowing of a triple "Sieg Heil!"[42]

In the meantime Dr. Schuschnigg had been arrested and subjected to treatment so degrading that it is difficult to believe that it was not prescribed by Hitler himself. Kept under house arrest from March 12 until May 28, during which time the Gestapo contrived to prevent him from getting any sleep by the most petty devices, he was then taken to Gestapo headquarters at the Hotel Metropole in Vienna, where he was incarcerated in a tiny room on the fifth floor for the next seventeen months. There, with the towel issued to him for his personal use, he was forced to clean the quarters, washbasins, slop buckets and latrines of the S.S. guards and perform other various menial tasks thought up by the Gestapo. By March 11, the first anniversary of his fall, he had lost fifty-eight pounds, but the S.S. doctor reported that his condition was excellent. The years of solitary confinement and then of life "among the living dead" in some of the worst of the German concentration camps such as Dachau and Sachsenhausen that followed have been described by Dr. Schuschnigg in his book.*

Shortly after his arrest he was allowed to marry by proxy the former Countess Vera Czernin, whose marriage had been annulled by an ecclesiastical court,† and in the last war years she was permitted to share his existence in the concentration camps along with their child, who was born in 1941. How they survived the nightmare of imprisonment is a miracle. Toward the end they were joined by a number of other distinguished victims of Hitler's wrath such as Dr. Schacht, Léon Blum, the former French Premier, and Madame Blum, Pastor Niemoeller, a host of high-ranking generals and Prince Philip of Hesse, whose wife, Princess Mafalda, the daughter of the King of Italy, had been done to death by the S.S. at Buchen-

---

* *Austrian Requiem.*
† At this time Schuschnigg was a widower.

wald in 1944 as part of the Fuehrer's revenge for Victor Emmanuel's desertion to the Allied side.

On May 1, 1945, the eminent group of prisoners, who had been hastily evacuated from Dachau and transported southward to keep them from being liberated by the Americans advancing from the West, arrived at a village high in the mountains of southern Tyrol. The Gestapo officers showed Schuschnigg a list of those who, on Himmler's orders, were to be done away with before they fell into the hands of the Allies. Schuschnigg noted his own name and that of his wife, "neatly printed." His spirits fell. To have survived so much so long—and then to be bumped off at the last minute!

On May 4, however, Schuschnigg was able to write in his diary:

> At two o'clock this afternoon, alarm! The Americans!
> An American detachment takes over the hotel.
> We are free!

Without firing a shot and without interference from Great Britain, France and Russia, whose military forces could have overwhelmed him, Hitler had added seven million subjects to the Reich and gained a strategic position of immense value to his future plans. Not only did his armies flank Czechoslovakia on three sides but he now possessed in Vienna the gateway to Southeast Europe. As the capital of the old Austro-Hungarian Empire, Vienna had long stood at the center of the communications and the trading systems of Central and Southeast Europe. Now that nerve center was in German hands.

Perhaps most important to Hitler was the demonstration again that neither Britain nor France would lift a finger to stop him. On March 14 Chamberlain had addressed the Commons on Hitler's *fait accompli* in Austria, and the German Embassy in London had got off to Berlin a succession of urgent telegrams on the course of the debate. There was not much for Hitler to fear. "The hard fact is," Chamberlain declared, "that nothing could have arrested what actually has happened [in Austria]— unless this country and other countries had been prepared to use force."

The British Prime Minister, it became clear to Hitler, was unwilling not only to employ force but even to concert with the other Big Powers about halting Germany's future moves. On March 17 the Soviet government had proposed a conference of powers, within or without the League of Nations, to consider means of seeing that there was no further German aggression. Chamberlain took a chilly view of any such meeting and on March 24, in the House of Commons, publicly rejected it. "The inevitable consequence of any such action," he said, "would be to aggravate the tendency towards the establishment of exclusive groups of nations which must . . . be inimical to the prospects of European peace." Apparently he overlooked, or did not take seriously, the Rome–Berlin Axis or the tripartite Anti-Comintern Pact of Germany, Italy and Japan.

In the same speech Chamberlain announced a decision of his government which must have been even more pleasing to Hitler. He bluntly rejected the suggestion not only that Britain should give a guarantee to come to the aid of Czechoslovakia in case she were attacked but also that Britain should support France if the French were called upon to implement their obligations under the Franco–Czech pact. This forthright statement eased Hitler's problems considerably. He now knew that Britain would also stand by when he took on his next victim. If Britain held back would not France also? As his secret papers of the next few months make clear, he was sure of it. And he knew that, by the terms of the Russian pacts with France and Czechoslovakia, the Soviet Union was not obliged to come to the aid of the Czechs until the French moved first. Such knowledge was all that he needed to enable him to go ahead at once with his plans.

The reluctant German generals, Hitler could assume after the success of the Anschluss, would no longer stand in his way. If he had any doubts at all on this, they were removed by the denouement of the Fritsch affair.

As we have seen,* General von Fritsch's trial before a military court of honor on charges of homosexualism had been abruptly suspended on its opening day, March 10, when Field Marshal Goering and the commanders of the Army and Navy were convoked by Hitler to handle more urgent affairs in connection with Austria. The trial resumed on March 17, but in view of what had happened in the interval it was bound to be anti-climactic. A few weeks before, the senior generals had been confident that when the military court exposed the unbelievable machinations of Himmler and Heydrich against Fritsch not only would their fallen Commander in Chief be restored to his post in the Army but the S.S., perhaps even the Third Reich, possibly even Adolf Hitler, would be shaken to a fall. Vain and empty hope! On February 4, as has been recounted, Hitler had smashed the dreams of the old officer corps by taking over command of the armed forces himself and cashiering Fritsch and most of the high-ranking generals around him. Now he had conquered Austria without a shot. After this astounding triumph, nobody in Germany, not even the old generals, had much thought for General von Fritsch.

True, he was quickly cleared. After some browbeating from Goering, who could now pose as the fairest of judges, the blackmailing ex-convict, Schmidt, broke down in court and confessed that the Gestapo had threatened his life unless he implicated General von Fritsch—a threat, incidentally, which was carried out anyway a few days later—and that the similarity of names between Fritsch and Rittmeister von Frisch, whom he had actually blackmailed for homosexualism, had led to the frame-up. No attempt was made by Fritsch or the Army to expose the Gestapo's real role, nor the personal guilt of Himmler and Heydrich in cooking up the false charges. On the second day, March 18, the trial was concluded with the inevitable verdict: "Proven not guilty as charged, and acquitted."

---

* See previous chapter.

It was a personal exoneration for General von Fritsch but it did not restore him to his command, nor the Army to its former position of some independence in the Third Reich. Since the trial was held *in camera,* the public knew nothing of it or of the issues involved. On March 25 Hitler sent a telegram to Fritsch congratulating him on his "recovery of health." That was all.

The deposed General, who had declined to point an accusing finger at Himmler in court, now made a final futile gesture. He challenged the Gestapo chief to a duel. The challenge, drawn up in strict accordance with the old military code of honor by General Beck himself, was given to General von Rundstedt, as the senior ranking Army officer, to deliver to the head of the S.S. But Rundstedt got cold feet, carried it around in his pocket for weeks and in the end forgot it.

General von Fritsch, and all he stood for, soon faded out of German life. But what did he stand for in the end? In December he was writing his friend Baroness Margot von Schutzbar a letter which indicated the pathetic confusion into which he, like so many of the other generals, had fallen.

It is really strange that so many people should regard the future with increasing fears, in spite of the Fuehrer's indisputable successes during the past years . . .

Soon after the war I came to the conclusion that we should have to be victorious in three battles if Germany were to become powerful again:

1. The battle against the working class—Hitler has won this.

2. Against the Catholic Church, perhaps better expressed against Ultramontanism, and

3. Against the Jews.

We are in the midst of these battles and the one against the Jews is the most difficult. I hope everyone realizes the intricacies of this campaign.[43]

On August 7, 1939, as the war clouds darkened, he wrote the Baroness: "For me there is, neither in peace nor in war, any part in Herr Hitler's Germany. I shall accompany my regiment only as a target, because I cannot stay at home."

That is what he did. On August 11, 1938, he had been named colonel in chief of his old regiment, the 12th Artillery Regiment, a purely honorary title. On September 22, 1939, he was the target of a Polish machine gunner before beleaguered Warsaw, and four days later he was buried with full military honors in Berlin on a cold, rainy, dark morning, one of the dreariest days, according to my diary, I ever lived through in the capital.

With Fritsch's discharge as Commander in Chief of the German Army twenty months before, Hitler had won, as we have seen, a complete victory over the last citadel of possible opposition in Germany, the old, traditional Army officer caste. Now, in the spring of 1938, by his clever coup in Austria, he had further established his hold on the Army, demonstrating his bold leadership and emphasizing that he alone would make the decisions in foreign policy and that it was the Army's role merely to supply the force, or the threat of force. Moreover, he had given the Army, without the sacrifice of a man, a strategic position which rendered Czechoslovakia militarily indefensible. There was no time to lose in taking advantage of it.

On April 21, eleven days after the Nazi plebiscite on Austria, Hitler called in General Keitel, Chief of the High Command of the Armed Forces, to discuss Case Green.

12

THE ROAD TO MUNICH

C ASE GREEN WAS THE CODE NAME of the plan for a surprise attack on
Czechoslovakia. It had first been drawn up, as we have seen, on June
24, 1937, by Field Marshal von Blomberg, and Hitler had elaborated on
it in his lecture to the generals on November 5, admonishing them that
"the descent upon the Czechs" would have to be "carried out with lightning
speed" and that it might take place "as early as 1938."*

Obviously, the easy conquest of Austria now made Case Green a matter
of some urgency; the plan must be brought up to date and preparations for
carrying it out begun. It was for this purpose that Hitler summoned
Keitel on April 21, 1938. On the following day, Major Rudolf Schmundt,
the Fuehrer's new military aide, prepared a summary of the discussion,
which was divided into three parts: "political aspects," "military conclusions" and "propaganda."[1]

Hitler rejected the "idea of strategic attack out of the blue without cause
or possibility of justification" because of "hostile world opinion which
might lead to a critical situation." He thought a second alternative, "action
after a period of diplomatic discussions which gradually lead to a crisis
and to war," was "undesirable because Czech (Green) security measures
will have been taken." The Fuehrer preferred, at the moment at least, a
third alternative: "Lightning action based on an incident (for example,
the murder of the German minister in the course of an anti-German
demonstration)."† Such an "incident," it will be remembered, was at one
time planned to justify a German invasion of Austria, when Papen was
to have been the victim. In Hitler's gangster world German envoys abroad
were certainly expendable.

The German warlord, as he now was—since he had taken over personal command of the armed forces—emphasized to General Keitel the
necessity of speed in the operations.

---

* See above, pp. 303–08.
† The parentheses are in the original.

The first four days of military action are, politically speaking, decisive. In the absence of outstanding military successes, a European crisis is certain to rise. *Faits accomplis* must convince foreign powers of the hopelessness of military intervention.

As for the propaganda side of the war, it was not yet time to call in Dr. Goebbels. Hitler merely discussed leaflets "for the conduct of the Germans in Czechoslovakia" and those which would contain "threats to intimidate the Czechs."

The Republic of Czechoslovakia, which Hitler was now determined to destroy, was the creation of the peace treaties, so hateful to the Germans, after the First World War. It was also the handiwork of two remarkable Czech intellectuals, Tomáš Garrigue Masaryk, a self-educated son of a coachman, who became a noted savant and the country's first President; and Eduard Beneš, son of a peasant, who worked his way through the University of Prague and three French institutions of higher learning, and who after serving almost continually as Foreign Minister became the second President on the retirement of Masaryk in 1935. Carved out of the Hapsburg Empire, which in the sixteenth century had acquired the ancient Kingdom of Bohemia, Czechoslovakia developed during the years that followed its founding in 1918 into the most democratic, progressive, enlightened and prosperous state in Central Europe.

But by its very make-up of several different nationalities it was gripped from the beginning by a domestic problem which over twenty years it had not been able entirely to solve. This was the question of its minorities. Within the country lived one million Hungarians, half a million Ruthenians and three and a quarter million Sudeten Germans. These peoples looked longingly toward their "mother" countries, Hungary, Russia, and Germany respectively, though the Sudeteners had never belonged to the German Reich (except as a part of the loosely formed Holy Roman Empire) but only to Austria. At the least, these minorities desired more autonomy than they had been given.

Even the Slovaks, who formed a quarter of the ten million Czechoslovaks, wanted some measure of autonomy. Although racially and linguistically closely related to the Czechs, the Slovaks had developed differently—historically, culturally and economically—largely due to their centuries-old domination by Hungary. An agreement between Czech and Slovak émigrés in America signed in Pittsburgh on May 30, 1918, had provided for the Slovaks' having their own government, parliament and courts. But the government in Prague had not felt bound by this agreement and had not kept it.

To be sure, compared to minorities in most other countries even in the West, even in America, those in Czechoslovakia were not badly off. They enjoyed not only full democratic and civil rights—including the right to vote—but to a certain extent were given their own schools and allowed to maintain their own cultural institutions. Leaders of the minority political parties often served as ministers in the central government. Nevertheless, the Czechs, not fully recovered from the effects of centuries of oppression by the Austrians, left a great deal to be desired in solving the minorities problem. They were often chauvinistic and frequently tactless. I recall from my own earlier visits to the country the deep resentment in Slovakia against the imprisonment of Dr. Vojtech Tuka, at that time a respected professor, who had been sentenced to fifteen years' confinement "for treason," though it was doubtful that he was guilty of more than working for Slovak autonomy. Above all, the minority groups felt that the Czechoslovak government had not honored the promises made by Masaryk and Beneš to the Paris Peace Conference in 1919 to establish a cantonal system similar to that of Switzerland.

Ironically enough, in view of what is now to be set down here, the Sudeten Germans had fared tolerably well in the Czechoslovak state—certainly better than any other minority in the country and better than the German minorities in Poland or in Fascist Italy. They resented the petty tyrannies of local Czech officials and the discrimination against them that sometimes occurred in Prague. They found it difficult to adjust to the loss of their former dominance in Bohemia and Moravia under the Hapsburgs. But lying in compact groups along the northwestern and southwestern parts of the new Republic, where most of the industry of the country was concentrated, they prospered and as the years went by they gradually reached a state of relative harmony with the Czechs, continuing always to press for more autonomy and more respect for their linguistic and cultural rights. Until the rise of Hitler, there was no serious political movement which asked for more. The Social Democrats and other democratic parties received most of the Sudeten votes.

Then in 1933, when Hitler became Chancellor, the virus of National Socialism struck the Sudeten Germans. In that year was formed the Sudeten German Party (S.D.P.) under the leadership of a mild-mannered gymnastics teacher by the name of Konrad Henlein. By 1935, the party was being secretly subsidized by the German Foreign Office to the amount of 15,000 marks a month.[2] Within a couple of years it had captured the majority of the Sudeten Germans, only the Social Democrats and the Communists remaining outside it. By the time of the Anschluss Henlein's party, which for three years had been taking its orders from Berlin, was ready to do the bidding of Adolf Hitler.

To receive this bidding, Henlein sped to Berlin a fortnight after the annexation of Austria and on March 28 was closeted with Hitler for three hours, Ribbentrop and Hess also being present. Hitler's instructions, as revealed in a Foreign Office memorandum, were that "demands should be made by the Sudeten German Party which are unacceptable to the Czech government." As Henlein himself summarized the Fuehrer's views, "We must always demand so much that we can never be satisfied."[3]

Thus, the plight of the German minority in Czechoslovakia was for Hitler merely a pretext, as Danzig was to be a year later in regard to Poland, for cooking up a stew in a land he coveted, undermining it, confusing and misleading its friends and concealing his real purpose. What that purpose was he had made clear in his November 5 harangue to the military leaders and in the initial directives of Case Green: to destroy the Czechoslovak state and to grab its territories and inhabitants for the Third Reich. Despite what had happened in Austria, the leaders of France and Great Britain did not grasp this. All through the spring and summer, indeed almost to the end, Prime Minister Chamberlain and Premier Daladier apparently sincerely believed, along with most of the rest of the world, that all Hitler wanted was justice for his kinsfolk in Czechoslovakia.

In fact, as the spring days grew warmer the British and French governments went out of their way to pressure the Czech government to grant far-reaching concessions to the Sudeten Germans. On May 3 the new German ambassador in London, Herbert von Dirksen, was reporting to Berlin that Lord Halifax had informed him of a *démarche* the British government would shortly make in Prague "which would aim at inducing Beneš to show the utmost measure of accommodation to the Sudeten Germans."[4] Four days later, on May 7, the British and French ministers in Prague made their *démarche,* urging the Czech government "to go to the utmost limit," as the German minister reported to Berlin, to meet the Sudeten demands. Hitler and Ribbentrop seemed quite pleased to find that the British and French governments were so concerned with aiding them.

Concealment of German aims, however, was more than ever necessary at this stage. On May 12 Henlein paid a secret visit to the Wilhelmstrasse in Berlin and received instructions from Ribbentrop on how to bamboozle the British when he arrived in London that evening to see Sir Robert Vansittart, chief diplomatic adviser to the Foreign Secretary, and other British officials. A memorandum by Weizsaecker laid down the line to be taken: "Henlein will deny in London that he is acting on instructions from Berlin . . . Finally, Henlein will speak of the progressive disintegration of the Czech political structure, in order to discourage those circles which consider that their intervention on behalf of this structure may still be of use."[5] On the same day the German minister in Prague was wiring Ribbentrop about the need of precaution to cover his legation in its work of handing over money and instructions to the Sudeten German Party.

Hugh R. Wilson, the American ambassador in Berlin, called on Weizsaecker on May 14 to discuss the Sudeten crisis and was told of German fears that Czech authorities were deliberately provoking a European crisis in order to try to prevent the "disintegration of Czechoslovakia." Two days later, on May 16, Major Schmundt got off an urgent and "most secret" telegram to OKW headquarters on behalf of Hitler, who was resting at Obersalzberg, asking how many divisions on the Czech frontier were "ready to march within twelve hours, in the case of mobilization." Lieutenant Colonel Zeitzler, of the OKW staff, replied immediately, "Twelve." This did not satisfy Hitler. "Please send the numbers of the divisions," he asked. And the answer came back, listing ten infantry divisions by their numbers and adding one armored and one mountain division.[6]

Hitler was getting restless for action. The next day, the seventeenth, he was inquiring of OKW for precise information on the fortifications which the Czechs had constructed in the Sudeten mountains on their borders. These were known as the Czech Maginot Line. Zeitzler replied from Berlin on the same day with a long and "most secret" telegram informing the Fuehrer in considerable detail of the Czech defense works. He made it clear that they were fairly formidable.[7]

THE FIRST CRISIS: MAY 1938

The weekend which began on Friday, May 20, developed into a critical one and would later be remembered as the "May crisis." During the ensuing forty-eight hours, the governments in London, Paris, Prague and Moscow were panicked into the belief that Europe stood nearer to war than it had at any time since the summer of 1914. This may have been largely due to the possibility that new plans for a German attack on Czechoslovakia, which were drawn up for Hitler by OKW and presented to him on that Friday, leaked out. At any rate, it was believed at least in Prague and London that Hitler was about to launch aggression against Czechoslovakia. In this belief the Czechs began to mobilize and Britain, France and Russia displayed a firmness and a unity in the face of what their governments feared to be an imminent German threat which they were not to show again until a new world war had almost destroyed them.

On Friday, May 20, General Keitel dispatched to Hitler at the Obersalzberg a new draft of Case Green which he and his staff had been working on since the Fuehrer had laid down the general lines for it in their meeting on April 21. In an obsequious letter to the Leader attached to the new plan, Keitel explained that it took into account "the situation created by the incorporation of Austria into the German Reich" and that it would not be discussed with the commanders in chief of the three armed services until "you, my Fuehrer," approved it and signed it.

The new directive for "Green," dated Berlin, May 20, 1938, is an interesting and significant document. It is a model of the kind of Nazi planning for aggression with which the world later became acquainted.

It is not my intention [it began] to smash Czechoslovakia by military action in the immediate future without provocation, unless an unavoidable development . . . *within* [emphasis in the original] Czechoslovakia forces the issue, or political events in Europe create a particularly favorable opportunity which may perhaps never recur.[8]

Three "political possibilities for commencing the operation" are considered. The first, "a sudden attack without convenient outward excuse," is rejected.

Operations preferably will be launched, either:

(a) after a period of increasing diplomatic controversies and tension linked with military preparations, which will be exploited so as to shift the war guilt on the enemy.

(b) by lightning action as the result of a serious incident which will subject Germany to unbearable provocation and which, in the eyes of at least a part of world opinion, affords the moral justification for military measures.

Case (b) is more favorable, both from a military and a political point of view.

As for the military operation itself, it was to attain such a success within four days that it would "demonstrate to enemy states which may wish to intervene the hopelessness of the Czech military position and also provide an incentive to those states which have territorial claims upon Czechoslovakia to join in immediately against her." Those states were Hungary and Poland, and the plan counted on their intervention. Whether France would honor its obligations to the Czechs was considered doubtful, but "attempts by Russia to give Czechoslovakia military support are to be expected."

The German High Command, or at least Keitel and Hitler, were so confident that the French would not fight that only a "minimum strength is to be provided as a rear cover in the west" and it was emphasized that "the whole weight of all forces must be employed in the invasion of Czechoslovakia." The "task of the bulk of the Army," aided by the Luftwaffe, was "to smash the Czechoslovak Army and to occupy Bohemia and Moravia as quickly as possible."

It was to be total war, and for the first time in the planning of German soldiers the value of what the directive calls "propaganda warfare" and "economic warfare" is emphasized and their employment woven into the over-all military plan of attack.

Propaganda warfare [emphasis in the original] must on the one hand intimidate the Czechs by means of threats and wear down their power of resistance; on the other hand it must give the national minorities indications as to how to support our military operations and influence the neutrals in our favor.

Economic warfare has the task of employing all available economic resources to hasten the final collapse of the Czechs . . . In the course of military operations it is important to help to increase the total economic war effort by rapidly collecting information about important factories and setting them going again as soon as possible. For this reason the sparing—as far as military operations permit—of Czech industrial and engineering establishments may be of decisive importance to us.

This model for Nazi aggression was to remain essentially unchanged and to be used with staggering success until an aroused world much later woke up to it.

Shortly after noon on May 20, the German minister in Prague sent an "urgent and most secret" wire to Berlin reporting that the Czech Foreign Minister had just informed him by telephone that his government was "perturbed by reports of concentration of [German] troops in Saxony." He had replied, he said, "that there were absolutely no grounds for anxiety," but he requested Berlin to inform him immediately what, if anything, was up.

This was the first of a series of feverish diplomatic exchanges that weekend which shook Europe with a fear that Hitler was about to move again and that this time a general war would follow. The basis for the information received by British and Czech intelligence that German troops were concentrating on the Czech border has never, so far as I know, come to light. To a Europe still under the shock of the German military occupation of Austria there were several straws in the wind. On May 19 a newspaper in Leipzig had published a report of German troop movements. Henlein, the Sudeten Fuehrer, had announced the breaking off of his party's negotiations with the Czech government on May 9 and it was known that on his return from London on the fourteenth he had stopped off at Berchtesgaden to see Hitler and that he was still there. There were shooting affrays in the Sudetenland. And all through May Dr. Goebbels' propaganda war—featuring wild stories of "Czech terror" against the Sudeten Germans—had been stepped up. The tension seemed to be reaching a climax.

Though there was some movement of German troops in connection with spring maneuvers, particularly in the eastern regions, no evidence was ever found from the captured German documents indicating any sudden, new concentration of armed forces on the Czech border at this moment. On the contrary, two German Foreign Office papers dated May 21 contain confidential assurances to the Wilhelmstrasse from Colonel Jodl of the OKW that there had been no such concentrations either in Silesia or in Lower Austria. There had been nothing, Jodl asserted in messages not intended for foreign perusal, "apart from peacetime maneuvers."[9] It was not that the Czech border was denuded of German troops. As we have seen, on May 16 Hitler had been informed by OKW, in answer to his urgent request for information, that there were twelve German divisions on the Czech frontier "ready to march within twelve hours."

Could it have been that Czech or British intelligence got wind of the telegrams which exchanged this information? And that they learned of the new directive for "Green" which Keitel dispatched for Hitler's approval on May 20? For on the next day the Czech Chief of Staff, General Krejci, told the German military attaché in Prague, Colonel Toussaint, that he had "irrefutable proof that in Saxony a concentration of from eight to ten [German] divisions had taken place."[10] The figures on the number of divisions were not far from correct, even if the information on the manner of their deployment was somewhat inaccurate. At any rate, on the afternoon of May 20, following an emergency cabinet session at Hradschin Palace in Prague presided over by President Beneš, the Czechs decided on an immediate partial mobilization. One class was called to the colors and certain technical reservists were mobilized. The Czech government, in contrast to the Austrian two months before, did not intend to give up without a fight.

The Czech mobilization, partial though it was, sent Adolf Hitler into a fit of fury, and his feelings were not assuaged by the dispatches that arrived for him at Obersalzberg from the German Foreign Office in Berlin telling of continual calls by the British and French ambassadors warning Germany that aggression against Czechoslovakia meant a European war.

The Germans had never been subjected to such strenuous and persistent diplomatic pressure as the British employed on this weekend. Sir Nevile Henderson, the British ambassador, who had been sent to Berlin by Prime Minister Chamberlain to apply his skills as a professional diplomat to the appeasement of Hitler and who applied them to the utmost, called repeatedly at the German Foreign Office to inquire about German troop movements and to advise caution. There is no doubt that he was egged on by Lord Halifax and the British Foreign Office, for Henderson, a suave, debonair diplomat, had little sympathy with the Czechs, as all who knew him in Berlin were aware. He saw Ribbentrop twice on May 21 and on the next day, though it was a Sunday, called on State Secretary von Weizsaecker—Ribbentrop having been hastily convoked to Hitler's presence at Obersalzberg—to deliver a personal message from Halifax stressing the gravity of the situation. In London, the British Foreign Secretary also called in the German ambassador on the Sabbath and emphasized how grave the moment was.

In all these British communications the Germans did not fail to note, as Ambassador von Dirksen pointed out in a dispatch after seeing Halifax, that the British government, while certain that France would go to the aid of Czechoslovakia, did not affirm that Britain would too. The furthest the British would go was to warn, as Dirksen says Halifax did, that "in the event of a European conflict it was impossible to foresee whether Britain would not be drawn into it."[11] As a matter of fact, this was as far as Chamberlain's government would ever go—until it was too late to stop Hitler. It was this writer's impression in Berlin from that moment until the end that had Chamberlain frankly told Hitler that Britain would do what it ultimately did in the face of Nazi aggression, the Fuehrer would never have embarked on the adventures which brought on the Second World War—an impression which has been immensely strengthened by the study of the secret German documents. This was the well-meaning Prime Minister's fatal mistake.

Adolf Hitler, brooding fitfully in his mountain retreat above Berchtesgaden, felt deeply humiliated by the Czechs and by the support given them in London, Paris and even Moscow, and nothing could have put the German dictator in a blacker, uglier mood. His fury was all the more intense because he was accused, prematurely, of being on the point of committing an aggression which he indeed intended to commit. That very weekend he had gone over the new plan for "Green" submitted by Keitel. But it could not be carried out at once. Swallowing his pride, he ordered the Foreign Office in Berlin to inform the Czech envoy on Monday, May 23, that Germany had no aggressive intentions toward Czechoslovakia and that the reports of German troop concentrations on her borders were without foundation. In Prague, London, Paris and Moscow the government leaders breathed a sigh of relief. The crisis had been mastered. Hitler had been given a lesson. He must now know he could not get away with aggression as easily as he had done in Austria.

Little did these statesmen know the Nazi dictator.

After sulking at Obersalzberg a few more days, during which there grew within him a burning rage to get even with Czechoslovakia and particularly with President Beneš, who, he believed, had deliberately humiliated him, he suddenly appeared in Berlin on May 28 and convoked the ranking officers of the Wehrmacht to the Chancellery to hear a momentous decision. He himself told of it in a speech to the Reichstag eight months later:

I resolved to solve once and for all, and this radically, the Sudeten question. On May 28, I ordered:

1. That preparations should be made for military action against this state by October 2.

2. That the construction of our western defenses should be greatly extended and speeded up . . .

The immediate mobilization of 96 divisions was planned, to begin with . . .[12]

To his assembled confederates, Goering, Keitel, Brauchitsch, Beck, Admiral Raeder, Ribbentrop and Neurath, he thundered, "It is my unshakable will that Czechoslovakia shall be wiped off the map!"[13] Case Green was again brought out and again revised.

Jodl's diary traces what had been going on in Hitler's feverish, vindictive mind.

The intention of the Fuehrer not to activate the Czech problem as yet is changed because of the Czech strategic troop concentration of May 21, which occurs without any German threat and without the slightest cause for it. Because of Germany's self-restraint, its consequences lead to a loss of prestige of the Fuehrer, which he is not willing to take again. Therefore, the new directive for "Green" is issued on May 30.[14]

The details of the new directive on Case Green which Hitler signed on May 30 do not differ essentially from those of the version submitted to Hitler nine days before. But there are two significant changes. Instead of the opening sentence of May 21, which read: "It is not my intention to smash Czechoslovakia in the near future," the new directive began: "*It is my unalterable decision to smash Czechoslovakia by military action in the near future.*"

What the "near future" meant was explained by Keitel in a covering letter. "Green's execution," he ordered, "must be assured by October 1, 1938, at the latest."[15]

It was a date which Hitler would adhere to through thick and thin, through crisis after crisis, and at the brink of war, without flinching.

WAVERING OF THE GENERALS

After noting in his diary on May 30 that Hitler had signed the new directive for "Green" and that because of its demand for "an immediate breakthrough into Czechoslovakia right on X Day . . . the previous intentions of the Army must be changed considerably," Jodl added the following sentence:

The whole contrast becomes acute once more between the Fuehrer's intuition that we *must* do it this year and the opinion of the Army that we cannot do it as yet because most certainly the Western powers will interfere and we are not as yet equal to them.[16]

The perceptive Wehrmacht staff officer had put his finger on a new rift between Hitler and some of the highest-ranking generals of the Army. The opposition to the Fuehrer's grandiose plans for aggression was led by General Ludwig Beck, Chief of the Army General Staff, who henceforth would assume the leadership of such resistance as there was to Hitler in the Third Reich. Later this sensitive, intelligent, decent but indecisive general would base his struggle against the Nazi dictator on broad grounds. As late as the spring of 1938, however, after more than four years of National Socialism, Beck opposed the Fuehrer only on the narrower professional grounds that Germany was not yet strong enough to take on the Western Powers and perhaps Russia as well.

Beck, as we have seen, had welcomed Hitler's coming to power and had publicly acclaimed the Fuehrer for re-establishing the conscript German Army in defiance of Versailles. As far back as 1930, it will be remembered from earlier pages, Beck, then an obscure regimental commander, had gone out of his way to defend three of his subalterns on a treason charge that they were fomenting Nazism in the armed forces and, in fact, had testified in their favor before the Supreme Court after Hitler had appeared on the stand and warned that when he came to power "heads would roll." It was not the Fuehrer's aggression against Austria—which Beck had supported—but the rolling of General von Fritsch's head after the Gestapo frame-up which seems to have cleared his mind. Swept of its cobwebs it began to perceive that Hitler's policy of deliberately risking war with Britain, France and Russia against the advice of the top generals would, if carried out, be the ruin of Germany.

Beck had got wind of Hitler's meeting with Keitel on April 21 in which the Wehrmacht was instructed to hasten plans for attacking Czechoslovakia, and on May 5 he wrote out the first of a series of memoranda for General von Brauchitsch, the new Commander in Chief of the Army, strenuously opposing any such action.[17] They are brilliant papers, blunt as to unpleasant facts and full of solid reasoning and logic. Although Beck overestimated the strength of will of Britain and France, the political shrewdness of their leaders and the power of the French Army, and in the end proved wrong on the outcome of the Czech problem, his long-range predictions turned out, so far as Germany was concerned, to be deadly accurate.

Beck was convinced, he wrote in his May 5 memorandum, that a German attack on Czechoslovakia would provoke a European war in which Britain, France and Russia would oppose Germany and in which the United States would be the arsenal of the Western democracies. Germany simply could not win such a war. Its lack of raw materials alone made victory impossible. In fact, he contended, Germany's "military-economic situation is worse than it was in 1917–18," when the collapse of the Kaiser's armies began.

On May 28, Beck was among the generals convoked to the Reich Chancellery after the "May crisis" to hear Hitler storm that he intended to wipe Czechoslovakia off the map the coming autumn. He took careful notes of the Fuehrer's harangue and two days later, on the very day that Hitler was signing the new directive for "Green," which fixed the date for the attack as October 1, penned another and sharper memorandum to Brauchitsch criticizing Hitler's program point by point. To make sure that his cautious Commander in Chief fully understood it, Beck read it to him personally. At the end he emphasized to the unhappy and somewhat shallow Brauchitsch that there was a crisis in the "top military hierarchy" which had already led to anarchy and that if it was not mastered the fate of the Army, indeed of Germany, would be "black." A few days later, on June 3, Beck got off another memorandum to Brauchitsch in which he declared that the new directive for "Green" was "militarily unsound" and that the Army General Staff rejected it.

Hitler, however, pressed forward with it. The captured "Green" file discloses how frenzied he grew as the summer proceeded. The usual autumn troop maneuvers, he orders, must be moved forward so that the Army will be in trim for the attack. Special exercises must be held "in the taking of fortifications by surprise attack." General Keitel is informed that "the Fuehrer repeatedly emphasized the necessity of pressing forward more rapidly the fortification work in the west." On June 9, Hitler asks for more information on Czech armament and receives immediately a detailed report on every conceivable weapon, large and small, used by the Czechs. On the same day he asks, "Are the Czech fortifications still occupied in reduced strength?" In his mountain retreat, where he is spending the summer, surrounded by his toadies, his spirits rise and fall as he toys with war. On June 18 he issues a new "General Guiding Directive" to "Green."

There is no danger of a preventive war against Germany . . . I will decide
to take action against Czechoslovakia only if I am firmly convinced . . . that
France will not march and that therefore England will not intervene.

On July 7, however, Hitler is laying down "considerations" of what to
do *if* France and Britain intervene. "The prime consideration," he says,
"is to hold the western fortifications" until Czechoslovakia is smashed and
troops can be rushed to the Western front. The fact that there are no
troops available to hold the western fortifications does not intrude itself
upon his feverish thinking. He advises that "Russia is most likely to intervene" and by now he is not so sure that Poland may not too. These
eventualities must be met, but he does not say how.

Apparently Hitler, somewhat isolated at Obersalzberg, has not yet
heard the rumblings of dissent in the upper echelons of the Army General
Staff. Despite Beck's pestering of Brauchitsch with his memoranda, the
General Staff Chief began to realize by midsummer that his unstable
Commander in Chief was not bringing his opinions to the notice of the
Fuehrer. By the middle of July Beck therefore determined to make one
last desperate effort to bring matters to a head, one way or the other. On
July 16 he penned his last memorandum to Brauchitsch. He demanded
that the Army tell Hitler to halt his preparations for war.

In full consciousness of the magnitude of such a step but also of my
responsibilities I feel it my duty to urgently ask that the Supreme Commander
of the Armed Forces [Hitler] call off his preparations for war, and abandon the
intention of solving the Czech question by force until the military situation is
fundamentally changed. For the present I consider it hopeless, and this view
is shared by all the higher officers of the General Staff.

Beck took his memorandum personally to Brauchitsch and augmented
it orally with further proposals for unified action on the part of the Army
generals should Hitler prove recalcitrant. Specifically, he proposed that
in that case the ranking generals should all resign at once. And for the
first time in the Third Reich, he raised a question which later haunted the
Nuremberg trials: Did an officer have a higher allegiance than the one to
the Fuehrer? At Nuremberg dozens of generals excused their war crimes
by answering in the negative. They had to obey orders, they said. But
Beck on July 16 held a different view, which he was to press, unsuccessfully
for the most part, to the end. There were "limits," he said, to one's
allegiance to the Supreme Commander where conscience, knowledge and
responsibility forbade carrying out an order. The generals, he felt, had
reached those limits. If Hitler insisted on war, they should resign in a
body. In that case, he argued, a war was impossible, since there would be
nobody to lead the armies.

The Chief of the German Army General Staff was now aroused as he
had never been before in his lifetime. The scales were falling from his eyes.

What was at stake for the German nation, he saw at last, was more than just the thwarting of a hysterical head of state bent, out of pique, on attacking a small neighboring nation at the risk of a big war. The whole folly of the Third Reich, its tyranny, its terror, its corruption, its contempt for the old Christian virtues, suddenly dawned on this once pro-Nazi general. Three days later, on July 19, he went again to Brauchitsch to speak of this revelation.

Not only, he insisted, must the generals go on strike to prevent Hitler from starting a war, but they must help clean up the Third Reich. The German people and the Fuehrer himself must be freed from the terror of the S.S. and the Nazi party bosses. A state and society ruled by law must be restored. Beck summed up his reform program:

> For the Fuehrer, against war, against boss rule, peace with the Church, free expression of opinion, an end to the Cheka terror, restoration of justice, reduction of contributions to the party by one half, no more building of palaces, housing for the common people and more Prussian probity and simplicity.

Beck was too naïve politically to realize that Hitler, more than any other single man, was responsible for the very conditions in Germany which now revolted him. However, Beck's immediate task was to continue to browbeat the hesitant Brauchitsch into presenting an ultimatum on behalf of the Army to Hitler calling on him to stop his preparations for war. To further this purpose he arranged a secret meeting of the commanding generals for August 4. He prepared a ringing speech that the Army Commander in Chief was to read, rallying the senior generals behind him in a common insistence that there be no Nazi adventures leading to armed conflict. Alas for Beck, Brauchitsch lacked the courage to read it. Beck had to be content with reading his own memorandum of July 16, which left a deep impression on most of the generals. But no decisive action was taken and the meeting of the top brass of the German Army broke up without their having had the courage to call Hitler to count, as their predecessors once had done with the Hohenzollern emperors and the Reich Chancellors.

Brauchitsch did summon up enough courage to show Beck's July 16 memorandum to Hitler. Hitler's response was to call in not the resisting ranking generals, who were behind it, but the officers just below them, the Army and Air Force staff chiefs of various commands who formed a younger set on which he believed he could count after he had treated it to his persuasive oratory. Summoned to the Berghof on August 10—Hitler had scarcely budged from his mountain villa all summer—they were treated after dinner to a speech that, according to Jodl, who was present and who described it in his faithful diary, lasted nearly three hours. But on this occasion the eloquence of the Fuehrer was not so persuasive as he had hoped. Both Jodl and Manstein, who was also present, later told of "a most serious and unpleasant clash" between General von Wietersheim and Hitler. Wietersheim was the ranking officer at the gathering and as designate chief of staff of the Army of the West under General Wilhelm Adam he dared to speak up about the key problem which Hitler and the OKW were dodging: that with almost all of the military forces committed to the blow against Czechoslovakia, Germany was defenseless in the west and would be overrun by the French. In fact, he reported, the West Wall could not be held for more than three weeks.

The Fuehrer [Jodl recounted in his diary] becomes furious and flames up, bursting into the remark that in such a case the whole Army would not be good for anything. "I say to you, Herr General [Hitler shouted back], the position will be held not only for three weeks but for three years!"[18]

With what, he did not say. On August 4, General Adam had reported to the meeting of senior generals that in the west he would have only five active divisions and that they would be overwhelmed by the French. Wietersheim presumably gave the same figure to Hitler, but the Fuehrer would not listen. Jodl, keen staff officer though he was, was now so much under the spell of the Leader that he left the meeting deeply depressed that the generals did not seem to understand Hitler's genius.

The cause of this despondent opinion [Wietersheim's], which unfortunately is held very widely within the Army General Staff, is based on various grounds.

First of all, it [the General Staff] is restrained by old memories and feels itself responsible for political decisions instead of obeying and carrying out its military assignments. Admittedly it does the last with traditional devotion but the vigor of the soul is lacking because in the end it does not believe in the genius of the Fuehrer. And one does perhaps compare him with Charles XII.

And just as certain as water flows downhill there stems from this defeatism [Miesmacherei] not only an immense political damage—for everyone is talking about the opposition between the opinions of the generals and those of the Fuehrer—but a danger for the morale of the troops. But I have no doubt that the Fuehrer will be able to boost the morale of the people when the right moment comes.[19]

Jodl might have added that Hitler would be able, too, to quell revolt among the generals. As Manstein told the tribunal at Nuremberg in 1946, this meeting was the last at which Hitler permitted any questions or discussions from the military.[20] At the Jueterbog military review on August 15, Hitler reiterated to the generals that he was determined "to solve the Czech question by force" and no officer dared—or was permitted—to say a word to oppose him.

Beck saw that he was defeated, largely by the spinelessness of his own brother officers, and on August 18 he resigned as Chief of the Army General Staff. He tried to induce Brauchitsch to follow suit, but the

Army commander was now coming under Hitler's hypnotic power, no doubt aided by the Nazi enthusiasms of the woman who was about to become his second wife.* As Hassell said of him, "Brauchitsch hitches his collar a notch higher and says: 'I am a soldier; it is my duty to obey.' "[21]

Ordinarily the resignation of a chief of the Army General Staff in the midst of a crisis, and especially of one so highly respected as was General Beck, would have caused a storm in military circles and even given rise to repercussions abroad. But here again Hitler showed his craftiness. Though he accepted Beck's resignation at once, and with great relief, he forbade any mention of it in the press or even in the official government and military gazettes and ordered the retired General and his fellow officers to keep it to themselves. It would not do to let the British and French governments get wind of dissension at the top of the German Army at this critical juncture and it is possible that Paris and London did not hear of the matter until the end of October, when it was officially announced in Berlin. Had they heard, one could speculate, history might have taken a different turning; the appeasement of the Fuehrer might not have been carried so far.

Beck himself, out of a sense of patriotism and loyalty to the Army, made no effort to bring the news of his quitting to the public's attention. He was disillusioned, though, that not a single general officer among those who had agreed with him and backed him in his opposition to war felt called upon to follow his example and resign. He did not try to persuade them. He was, as Hassell later said of him, "pure Clausewitz, without a spark of Bluecher or Yorck"[22]—a man of principles and thought, but not of action. He felt that Brauchitsch, as Commander in Chief of the Army, had let him down at a decisive moment in German history, and this embittered him. Beck's biographer and friend noted years later the General's "deep bitterness" whenever he spoke of his old commander. On such occasions he would shake with emotion and mutter, "Brauchitsch left me in the lurch."[23]

Beck's successor as Chief of the Army General Staff—though his appointment was kept a secret by Hitler for several weeks, until the end of the crisis—was Franz Halder, fifty-four years old, who came from an old Bavarian military family and whose father had been a general. Himself trained as an artilleryman, he had served as a young officer on the staff of Crown Prince Rupprecht in the First World War. Though a friend of Roehm in the first postwar Munich days, which might have made him somewhat suspect in Berlin, he had risen rapidly in the Army and for the past year had served as Beck's deputy. In fact, Beck recommended him to Brauchitsch as his successor, for he was certain that his deputy shared his views.

Halder became the first Bavarian and the first Catholic ever to become Chief of the German General Staff—a severe break with the old Protes-

---

* General von Brauchitsch received his divorce during the summer and on September 24 married Frau Charlotte Schmidt.

tant Prussian tradition of the officer corps. A man of wide intellectual interests, with a special bent for mathematics and botany (my own first impression of him was that he looked like a university professor of mathematics or science) and a devout Christian, there was no doubt that he had the mind and the spirit to be a true successor to Beck. The question was whether, like his departed chief, he lacked the knack of taking decisive action at the proper moment. And whether, if he did not lack it, at that moment he had the character to disregard his oath of allegiance to the Fuehrer and move resolutely against him. For Halder, like Beck, though not at first a member of a growing conspiracy against Hitler, knew about it and apparently, again like Beck, was willing to back it. As the new Chief of the General Staff, he became the key figure in the first serious plot to overthrow the dictator of the Third Reich.

BIRTH OF A CONSPIRACY AGAINST HITLER

After five and a half years of National Socialism it was evident to the few Germans who opposed Hitler that only the Army possessed the physical strength to overthrow him. The workers, the middle and upper classes, even if they had wanted to, had no means of doing it. They had no organization outside of the Nazi party groups and they were, of course, unarmed. Though much would later be written about the German "resistance" movement, it remained from the beginning to the end a small and feeble thing, led, to be sure, by a handful of courageous and decent men, but lacking followers.

The very maintenance of its bare existence was, admittedly, difficult in a police state dominated by terror and spying. Moreover, how could a tiny group—or even a large group, had there been one—rise up in revolt against the machine guns, the tanks, the flame throwers of the S.S.?

In the beginning, what opposition there was to Hitler sprang from among the civilians; the generals, as we have seen, were only too pleased with a system which had shattered the restrictions of the Versailles Treaty and given them the heady and traditional task of building up a great army once again. Ironically, the principal civilians who emerged to lead the opposition had served the Fuehrer in important posts, most of them with an initial enthusiasm for Nazism which dampened only when it began to dawn on them in 1937 that Hitler was leading Germany toward a war which it was almost sure to lose.

One of the earliest of these to see the light was Carl Goerdeler, the mayor of Leipzig, who, first appointed Price Controller by Bruening, had continued in that job for three years under Hitler. A conservative and a monarchist at heart, a devout Protestant, able, energetic and intelligent, but also indiscreet and headstrong, he broke with the Nazis in 1936 over their anti-Semitism and their frenzied rearmament and, resigning both his posts, went to work with heart and soul in opposition to Hitler. One of his first acts was to journey to France, England and the United States in 1937 to discreetly warn of the peril of Nazi Germany.

The light came a little later to two other eventual conspirators, Johannes Popitz, Prussian Minister of Finance, and Dr. Schacht. Both had received the Nazi Party's highest decoration, the Golden Badge of Honor, for their services in shaping Germany's economy for war purposes. Both had begun to wake up to what Hitler's real goal was in 1938. Neither of them seems to have been fully trusted by the inner circle of the opposition because of their past and their character. Schacht was too opportunist, and Hassell remarked in his diary that the Reichsbank president had a capacity "for talking one way and acting another," an opinion, he says, that was shared by Generals Beck and von Fritsch. Popitz was brilliant but unstable. A fine Greek scholar as well as eminent economist, he, along with General Beck and Hassell, was a member of the Wednesday Club, a group of sixteen intellectuals who gathered once a week to discuss philosophy, history, art, science and literature and who as time went on—or ran out—formed one of the centers of the opposition.

Ulrich von Hassell became a sort of foreign-affairs adviser to the resistance leaders. His dispatches as ambassador in Rome during the Abyssinian War and the Spanish Civil War, as we have seen, had been full of advice to Berlin on how to keep Italy embroiled with France and Britain and therefore on the side of Germany. Later he came to fear that war with France and Britain would be fatal to Germany and that even a German alliance with Italy would be too. Far too cultivated to have anything but contempt for the vulgarism of National Socialism, he did not, however, voluntarily give up serving the regime. He was kicked out of the diplomatic service in the big military, political and Foreign Office shake-up which Hitler engineered on February 4, 1938. A member of an old Hanover noble family, married to the daughter of Grand Admiral von Tirpitz, the founder of the German Navy, and a gentleman of the old school to his finger tips, Hassell, like so many others of his class, seems to have needed the shock of being cast out by the Nazis before he became much interested in doing anything to bring them down. Once this had happened, this sensitive, intelligent, uneasy man devoted himself to that task and in the end, as we shall see, sacrificed his life to it, meeting a barbarous end.

There were others, lesser known and mostly younger, who had opposed the Nazis from the beginning and who gradually came together to form various resistance circles. One of the leading intellects of one group was Ewald von Kleist, a gentleman farmer and a descendant of the great poet. He worked closely with Ernst Niekisch, a former Social Democrat and editor of *Widerstand* (Resistance), and with Fabian von Schlabrendorff, a young lawyer, who was the great-grandson of Queen Victoria's private physician and confidential adviser, Baron von Stockmar. There were former trade-union leaders such as Julius Leber, Jakob Kaiser and Wilhelm Leuschner. Two Gestapo officials, Artur Nebe, the head of the criminal police, and Bernd Gisevius, a young career police officer, became valuable aides as the conspiracies developed. The latter became the darling of the American prosecution at Nuremberg and wrote a book which sheds much light on the anti-Hitler plots, though most historians take the book and the author with more than a grain of salt.

There were a number of sons of venerable families in Germany: Count Helmuth von Moltke, great-grandnephew of the famous Field Marshal, who later formed a resistance group of young idealists known as the Kreisau Circle; Count Albrecht Bernstorff, nephew of the German ambassador in Washington during the First World War; Freiherr Karl Ludwig von Guttenberg, editor of a fearless Catholic monthly; and Pastor Dietrich Bonhoeffer, a descendant of eminent Protestant clergymen on both sides of his family, who regarded Hitler as Antichrist and who believed it a Christian duty to "eliminate him."

Nearly all of these brave men would persevere until, after being caught and tortured, they were executed by rope or by ax or merely murdered by the S.S.

For a good long time this tiny nucleus of civilian resistance had little success in interesting the Army in its work. As Field Marshal von Blomberg testified at Nuremberg, "Before 1938–39 German generals did not oppose Hitler. There was no reason to oppose him, since he produced the results they desired." There was some contact between Goerdeler and General von Hammerstein, but the former Commander in Chief of the German Army had been in retirement since 1934 and had little influence among the active generals. Early in the regime Schlabrendorff had got in touch with Colonel Hans Oster, chief assistant to Admiral Canaris in the Abwehr, the Intelligence Bureau of OKW, and found him to be not only a staunch anti-Nazi but willing to try to bridge the gulf between the military and civilians. However, it was not until the winter of 1937–38, when the generals were subjected to the successive shocks engendered by Hitler's decision to go to war, his shake-up of the military command, which he himself took over, and his shabby treatment of General von Fritsch, that some of them became aware of the danger to Germany of the Nazi dictator. The resignation of General Beck toward the end of August 1938, as the Czech crisis grew more menacing, provided a further awakening, and though none of his fellow officers followed him into retirement as he had hoped, it immediately became evident that the fallen Chief of the General Staff was the one person around whom both the recalcitrant generals and the civilian resistance leaders could rally. Both groups respected and trusted him.

Another consideration became evident to both of them. To stop Hitler, force would now be necessary, and only the Army possessed it. But who in the Army could muster it? Not Hammerstein and not even Beck, since they were in retirement. What was needed, it was realized, was to bring in generals who at the moment had actual command of troops in and around Berlin and who thus could act effectively on short notice. General Halder, the new Chief of the Army General Staff, had no actual forces under his command. General von Brauchitsch had the whole Army, but he was not fully trusted. His authority would be useful but he could be brought in only, the conspirators felt, at the last minute.

As it happened, certain key generals who were willing to help were quickly discovered and initiated into the budding conspiracy. Three of them held commands which were vital to the success of the venture: General Erwin von Witzleben, commander of the all-important Wehrkreis III, which comprised Berlin and the surrounding areas; General Count Erich von Brockdorff-Ahlefeld, commander of the Potsdam garrison, which was made up of the 23rd Infantry Division; and General Erich Hoepner, who commanded an armored division in Thuringia which could, if necessary, repulse any S.S. troops attempting to relieve Berlin from Munich.

The plan of the conspirators, as it developed toward the end of August, was to seize Hitler as soon as he had issued the final order to attack Czechoslovakia and hale him before one of his own People's Courts on the charge that he had tried recklessly to hurl Germany into a European war and was therefore no longer competent to govern. In the meantime, for a short interim, there would be a military dictatorship followed by a provisional government presided over by some eminent civilian. In due course a conservative democratic government would be formed.

There were two considerations on which the success of the coup depended and which involved the two key conspirators, General Halder and General Beck. The first was timing. Halder had arranged with OKW that he personally be given forty-eight hours' notice of Hitler's final order to attack Czechoslovakia. This would give him the time to put the plot into execution before the troops could cross the Czech frontier. Thus he would be able not only to arrest Hitler but to prevent the fatal step that would lead to war.

The second factor was that Beck must be able to convince the generals beforehand and the German people later (during the proposed trial of Hitler) that an attack on Czechoslovakia would bring in Britain and France and thus precipitate a European war, for which Germany was not prepared and which it would certainly lose. This had been the burden of his memoranda all summer and it was the basis of all that he was now prepared to do: to preserve Germany from a European conflict which he believed would destroy her—by overthrowing Hitler.

Alas for Beck, and for the future of most of the world, it was Hitler and not the recently resigned Chief of the General Staff who proved to have the shrewder view of the possibilities of a big war. Beck, a cultivated European with a sense of history, could not conceive that Britain and France would willfully sacrifice their self-interest by not intervening in case of a German attack on Czechoslovakia. He had a sense of history but not of contemporary politics. Hitler had. For some time now he had felt himself reinforced in his judgment that Prime Minister Chamberlain would sacrifice the Czechs rather than go to war and that, in such a case, France would not fulfill her treaty obligations to Prague.

The Wilhelmstrasse had not failed to notice dispatches published in the New York newspapers as far back as May 14 in which their London correspondents had reported an "off-the-record" luncheon talk with Chamberlain at Lady Astor's. The British Prime Minister, the journalists reported, had said that neither Britain nor France nor probably Russia would come to the aid of Czechoslovakia in the case of a German attack, that the Czech state could not exist in its present form and that Britain favored, in the interest of peace, turning over the Sudetenland to Germany. Despite angry questions in the House of Commons, the Germans noted, Chamberlain had not denied the veracity of the American dispatches.

On June 1, the Prime Minister had spoken, partly off the record, to British correspondents, and two days later the *Times* had published the first of its leaders which were to help undermine the Czech position; it had urged the Czech government to grant "self-determination" to the country's minorities "even if it should mean their secession from Czechoslovakia" and for the first time it had suggested plebiscites as a means of determining what the Sudetens and the others desired. A few days later the German Embassy in London informed Berlin that the *Times* editorial was based on Chamberlain's off-the-record remarks and that it reflected his views. On June 8 Ambassador von Dirksen told the Wilhelmstrasse that the Chamberlain government would be willing to see the Sudeten areas separated from Czechoslovakia providing it was done after a plebiscite and "not interrupted by forcible measures on the part of Germany."[24]

All this must have been pleasing for Hitler to hear. The news from Moscow also was not bad. By the end of June Friedrich Werner Count von der Schulenburg, the German ambassador to Russia, was advising Berlin that the Soviet Union was "hardly likely to march in defense of a bourgeois state," i.e., Czechoslovakia.[25] By August 3, Ribbentrop was informing the major German diplomatic missions abroad that there was little fear of intervention over Czechoslovakia by Britain, France or Russia.[26]

It was on that day, August 3, that Chamberlain had packed off Lord Runciman to Czechoslovakia on a curious mission to act as a "mediator" in the Sudeten crisis. I happened to be in Prague the day of his arrival and after attending his press conference and talking with members of his party remarked in my diary that "Runciman's whole mission smells." Its very announcement in the House of Commons on July 26 had been accompanied by a piece of prevaricating by Chamberlain himself which must have been unique in the experience of the British Parliament. The Prime Minister had said that he was sending Runciman "in response to a request from the government of Czechoslovakia." The truth was that Runciman had been forced down the throat of the Czech government by Chamberlain. But there was an underlying and bigger falsehood. Everyone, including Chamberlain, knew that Runciman's mission to "mediate" between the Czech government and the Sudeten leaders was impossible and absurd. They knew that Henlein, the Sudeten leader, was not a free agent and could not negotiate, and that the dispute now was between Prague and Berlin. My diary notes for the first evening and subsequent days make it clear that the Czechs knew perfectly well that Runciman had been sent by Chamberlain to pave the way for the handing over of the Sudetenland to Hitler. It was a shabby diplomatic trick.

And now the summer of 1938 was almost over. Runciman puttered about in the Sudetenland and in Prague, making ever more friendly gestures to the Sudeten Germans and increasing demands on the Czech government to grant them what they wanted. Hitler, his generals and his Foreign Minister were frantically busy. On August 23, the Fuehrer entertained aboard the liner *Patria* in Kiel Bay during naval maneuvers the Regent of Hungary, Admiral Horthy, and the members of the Hungarian government. If they wanted to get in on the Czech feast, Hitler told them, they must hurry. "He who wants to sit at the table," he put it, "must at least help in the kitchen."[27] The Italian ambassador, Bernardo Attolico, was also a guest on the ship. But when he pressed Ribbentrop for the date of "the German move against Czechoslovakia" so that Mussolini could be prepared, the German Foreign Minister gave an evasive answer. The Germans, it was plain, did not quite trust the discretion of their Fascist ally. Of Poland they were now sure. All through the summer Ambassador von Moltke in Warsaw was reporting to Berlin that not only would Poland decline to help Czechoslovakia by allowing Russia to send troops and planes through or over her territory but Colonel Józef Beck, the Polish Foreign Minister, was casting covetous eyes on a slice of Czech territory, the Teschen area. Beck already was exhibiting that fatal shortsightedness, so widely shared in Europe that summer, which in the end would prove more disastrous than he could possibly imagine.

At OKW (the High Command of the Armed Forces) and at OKH (the High Command of the Army) there was incessant activity. Final plans were being drawn up to have the armed forces ready for the push-off into Czechoslovakia by October 1. On August 24, Colonel Jodl at OKW wrote an urgent memorandum for Hitler stressing that "the fixing of the *exact* time for the 'incident' which will give Germany provocation for military intervention is most important." The timing of X Day, he explained, depended on it.

No advance measures [he went on] may be taken before X minus 1 for which there is not an innocent explanation, as otherwise we shall appear to have manufactured the incident. . . . If for technical reasons the *evening hours* should be considered desirable for the incident, then the following day cannot be X Day, but it must be the day after that . . . It is the purpose of these notes to point out what a great interest the Wehrmacht has in the incident and that it must be informed of the Fuehrer's intention in good time—insofar as the Abwehr Section is not also charged with organizing the incident.[28]

The expert preparations for the onslaught on Czechoslovakia were obviously in fine shape by the summer's end. But what about the defense of the west, should the French honor their word to the Czechs and attack? On August 26 Hitler set off for a tour of the western fortifications accompanied by Jodl, Dr. Todt, the engineer in charge of building the West Wall, Himmler and various party officials. On August 27 General Wilhelm Adam, a blunt and able Bavarian who was in command of the west, joined the party and in the next couple of days witnessed how intoxicated the Fuehrer became at the triumphal reception he was given by the Rhinelanders. Adam himself was not impressed; in fact, he was alarmed, and on the twenty-ninth in a surprising scene in Hitler's private car he abruptly demanded to speak with the Fuehrer alone. Not without sneers, according to the General's later report, Hitler dismissed Himmler and his other party cronies. Adam did not waste words. He declared that despite all the fanfare about the West Wall he could not possibly hold it with the troops at his disposal. Hitler became hysterical and launched into a long harangue about how he had made Germany stronger than Britain and France together.

"The man who doesn't hold these fortifications," Hitler shouted, "is a scoundrel!"*

Nevertheless doubts on this score were rising in the minds of generals other than Adam. On September 3, Hitler convoked the chiefs of OKW and OKH, Keitel and Brauchitsch, to the Berghof. Field units, it was agreed, were to be moved into position along the Czech border on September 28. But OKW must know when X Day was by noon on September 27. Hitler was not satisfied with the operational plan for "Green" and ordered that it be changed in several respects. From the notes of this meeting kept by Major Schmundt it is clear that Brauchitsch at least—for Keitel was too much the toady to speak up—again raised the question of how they were going to hold out in the west. Hitler fobbed him off with the assurance that he had given orders for speeding up the western fortifications.[30]

On September 8 General Heinrich von Stuelpnagel saw Jodl and the latter noted in his diary the General's pessimism regarding the military position in the west. It was becoming clear to both of them that Hitler, his spirits whipped up by the fanaticism of the Nuremberg Party Rally, which had just opened, was going ahead with the invasion of Czechoslovakia whether France intervened or not. "I must admit," wrote the usually optimistic Jodl, "that I am worried too."

The next day, September 9, Hitler convoked Keitel, Brauchitsch and Halder to Nuremberg for a conference which began at 10 P.M., lasted until 4 o'clock the next morning and, as Keitel later confided to Jodl, who in turn confided it to his diary, was exceedingly stormy. Halder found himself in the ticklish position—for the key man in the plot to overthrow Hit-

---

* Hitler, according to Jodl's diary, used the word *Hundsfott,* a stronger word.[29] Telford Taylor, in *Sword and Swastika,* gives a fuller account based on General Adam's unpublished memoirs.

ler the moment he gave the word to attack—of having to explain in great detail the General Staff's plan for the campaign in Czechoslovakia, and in the uncomfortable position, as it developed, of seeing Hitler tear it to shreds and dress down not only him but Brauchitsch for their timidity and their military incapabilities.[31] Keitel, Jodl noted on the thirteenth, was "terribly shaken" by his experience at Nuremberg and by the evidence of "defeatism" at the top of the German Army.

Accusations are made to the Fuehrer about the defeatism in the High Command of the Army . . . Keitel declares that he will not tolerate any officer in OKW indulging in criticism, unsteady thoughts and defeatism . . . The Fuehrer knows that the Commander of the Army [Brauchitsch] has asked his commanding generals to support him in order to open the Fuehrer's eyes about the adventure which he has resolved to risk. He himself [Brauchitsch] has no more influence with the Fuehrer.

Thus a cold and frosty atmosphere prevailed in Nuremberg and it is highly unfortunate that the Fuehrer has the whole nation behind him with the exception of the leading generals of the Army.

All of this greatly saddened the aspiring young Jodl, who had hitched his star to Hitler.

Only by actions can [these generals] honorably repair the damage which they have caused through lack of strength of mind and lack of obedience. It is the same problem as in 1914. There is only one example of disobedience in the Army and that is of the generals and in the end it springs from their arrogance. They can no longer believe and no longer obey because they do not recognize the Fuehrer's genius. Many of them still see in him the corporal of the World War but not the greatest statesman since Bismarck.[32]

In his talk with Jodl on September 8, General von Stuelpnagel, who held the post of Oberquartiermeister I in the Army High Command, and who was in on the Halder conspiracy, had asked for written assurances from OKW that the Army High Command would receive notice of Hitler's order for the attack on Czechoslovakia five days in advance. Jodl had answered that because of the uncertainties of the weather two days' notice was all that could be guaranteed. This, however, was enough for the conspirators.

But they needed assurances of another kind—whether, after all, they had been right in their assumption that Britain and France would go to war against Germany if Hitler carried out his resolve to attack Czechoslovakia. For this purpose they had decided to send trustworthy agents to London not only to find out what the British government intended to do but, if necessary, to try to influence its decision by informing it that Hitler had decided to attack the Czechs on a certain date in the fall, and that the General Staff, which knew the date, opposed it and was prepared to take the most decisive action to prevent it if Britain stood firm against Hitler to the last.

The first such emissary of the plotters, selected by Colonel Oster of the Abwehr, was Ewald von Kleist, who arrived in London on August 18. Ambassador Henderson in Berlin, who was already anxious to give Hitler whatever he wanted in Czechoslovakia, advised the British Foreign Office that "it would be unwise for him [Kleist] to be received in official quarters."* Nevertheless Sir Robert Vansittart, chief diplomatic adviser to the Foreign Secretary and one of the leading opponents in London of the appeasement of Hitler, saw Kleist on the afternoon of his arrival, and Winston Churchill, still in the political wilderness in Britain, received him the next day. To both men, who were impressed by their visitor's sobriety and sincerity, Kleist repeated what he had been instructed to tell, stressing that Hitler had set a date for aggression against the Czechs and that the generals, most of whom opposed him, would act, but that further British appeasement of Hitler would cut the ground from under their feet. If Britain and France would declare publicly that they would not stand idly by while Hitler threw his armies into Czechoslovakia and if some prominent British statesmen would issue a solemn warning to Germany of the consequences of Nazi aggression, then the German generals, for their part, would act to stop Hitler.[34]

Churchill gave Kleist a ringing letter to take back to Germany to bolster his colleagues:

I am sure that the crossing of the frontier of Czechoslovakia by German armies or aviation in force will bring about renewal of the World War. I am as certain as I was at the end of July, 1914, that England will march with France . . . Do not, I pray you, be misled upon this point . . .†

Vansittart took Kleist's warning seriously enough to submit immediately a report on it to both the British Prime Minister and the Foreign

_____
* According to a German Foreign Office memorandum of August 6, Henderson, at a private party, had remarked to the Germans present "that Great Britain would not think of risking even one sailor or airman for Czechoslovakia, and that any reasonable solution would be agreed to so long as it were not attempted by force."[33]
† Kleist returned to Berlin on August 23 and showed Churchill's letter to Beck, Halder, Hammerstein, Canaris, Oster and others in the plot. In *Nemesis of Power* (p. 413), Wheeler-Bennett writes that, according to private information given him after the war by Fabian von Schlabrendorff, Canaris made two copies of the letter, one for himself and one for Beck, and Kleist hid the original in his country house at Schmenzin in Pomerania. It was discovered there by the Gestapo after the July 20, 1944, attempt on Hitler's life and contributed to Kleist's death sentence before a People's Court, which was passed and carried out on April 16, 1945. Actually the contents of Churchill's letter became known to the German authorities much sooner than the conspirators could have imagined. I found it in a German Foreign Office memorandum which, though undated, is known to have been submitted on September 6, 1938. It is marked: "Extract from a letter of Winston Churchill to a German confidant."[35]

Secretary, and though Chamberlain, writing to Lord Halifax, said he was inclined "to discount a good deal of what he [Kleist] says," he added: "I don't feel sure that we ought not to do something."[36] What he did was to summon Ambassador Henderson, in the wake of some publicity, to London on August 28 "for consultations."

He instructed his ambassador in Berlin to do two things: convey a sober warning to Hitler and, secondly, prepare secretly a "personal contact" between himself and the Fuehrer. According to his own story, Henderson persuaded the Prime Minister to drop the first request.[37] As for the second, Henderson was only too glad to try to carry it out.*

This was the first step toward Munich and Hitler's greatest bloodless victory.

Ignorant of this turning in Chamberlain's course, the conspirators in Berlin made further attempts to warn the British government. On August 21, Colonel Oster sent an agent to inform the British military attaché in Berlin of Hitler's intention to invade Czechoslovakia at the end of September. "If by firm action abroad Hitler can be forced at the eleventh hour to renounce his present intentions, he will be unable to survive the blow," he told the British. "Similarly, if it comes to war the immediate intervention by France and England will bring about the downfall of the regime." Sir Nevile Henderson dutifully forwarded this warning to London, but described it "as clearly biased and largely propaganda." The blinkers on the eyes of the debonair British ambassador seemed to grow larger and thicker as the crisis mounted.

General Halder had a feeling that the conspirators were not getting their message through effectively enough to the British, and on September 2 he sent his own emissary, a retired Army officer, Lieutenant Colonel Hans Boehm-Tettelbach, to London to make contact with the British War Office and Military Intelligence. Though, according to his own story, the colonel saw several important personages in London, he does not seem to have made much of an impression on them.

Finally, the plotters resorted to using the German Foreign Office and the embassy in London in a last desperate effort to induce the British to remain firm. Counselor of the embassy and chargé d'affaires was Theodor Kordt, whose younger brother, Erich, was chief of Ribbentrop's secretariat in the German Foreign Office. The brothers were protégés of Baron von Weizsaecker, the principal State Secretary and undoubtedly the brains of the Foreign Office, a man who after the war made a great fuss of his alleged anti-Nazism but who served Hitler and Ribbentrop well almost to the end. It is clear, however, from captured Foreign Office documents,

---

* "I honestly believe," the ambassador had written Lord Halifax from Berlin on July 18, "the moment has come for Prague to get a real twist of the screw . . . If Beneš cannot satisfy Henlein, he can satisfy no Sudeten leader . . . We have got to be disagreeable to the Czechs."[38] It seems inconceivable that even Henderson did not know by this time that Henlein was a mere tool of Hitler and had been ordered by him to keep increasing his demands to such an extent that Beneš could not possibly "satisfy" him. See above, p. 359

that at this time he opposed aggression against Czechoslovakia on the same grounds as those of the generals: that it would lead to a lost war. With Weizsaecker's connivance, and after consultations with Beck, Halder and Goerdeler, it was agreed that Theodor Kordt should sound a last warning to Downing Street. As counselor of the embassy his visits to the British authorities would not be suspect.

The information he brought on the evening of September 5 to Sir Horace Wilson, Chamberlain's confidential adviser, seemed so important and urgent that this official spirited him by a back way to Downing Street and the chambers of the British Foreign Secretary. There he bluntly informed Lord Halifax that Hitler was planning to order a general mobilization on September 16, that the attack on Czechoslovakia had been fixed for October 1 at the latest, that the German Army was preparing to strike against Hitler the moment the final order for attack was given and that it would succeed if Britain and France held firm. Halifax was also warned that Hitler's speech closing the Nuremberg Party Rally on September 12 would be explosive and might precipitate a showdown over Czechoslovakia and that that would be the moment for Britain to stand up against the dictator.[39]

Kordt, too, despite his continuous personal contact with Downing Street and his frankness on this occasion with the Foreign Secretary, did not know what was in the London wind. But he got a good idea, as did everyone else, two days later, on September 7, when the *Times* of London published a famous leader:

It might be worth while for the Czechoslovak Government to consider whether they should exclude altogether the project, which has found favor in some quarters, of making Czechoslovakia a more homogeneous State by the secession of that fringe of alien populations who are contiguous to the nation with which they are united by race . . . The advantages to Czechoslovakia of becoming a homogeneous State might conceivably outweigh the obvious disadvantages of losing the Sudeten German district of the borderland.

There was no mention in the editorial of the obvious fact that by ceding the Sudetenland to Germany the Czechs would lose both the natural mountain defenses of Bohemia and their "Maginot Line" of fortifications and be henceforth defenseless against Nazi Germany.

Though the British Foreign Office was quick to deny that the *Times* leader represented the views of the government, Kordt telegraphed Berlin the next day that it was possible that "it derived from a suggestion which reached the *Times* editorial staff from the Prime Minister's entourage." Possible indeed!

In these crisis-ridden years that have followed World War II it is difficult to recall the dark and almost unbearable tension that gripped the capitals of Europe as the Nuremberg Party Rally, which had begun on

September 6, approached its climax on September 12, when Hitler was scheduled to make his closing speech and expected to proclaim to the world his final decision for peace or war with Czechoslovakia. I was in Prague, the focus of the crisis, that week, and it seemed strange that the Czech capital, despite the violence unleashed by the Germans in the Sudetenland, the threats from Berlin, the pressure of the British and French governments to yield, and the fear that they might leave Czechoslovakia in the lurch, was the calmest of all—at least outwardly.

On September 5, President Beneš, realizing that a decisive step on his part was necessary to save the peace, convoked the Sudeten leaders Kundt and Sebekovsky to Hradschin Palace and told them to write out their full demands. Whatever they were he would accept them. "My God," exclaimed the deputy Sudeten leader, Karl Hermann Frank, the next day, "they have given us everything." But that was the last thing the Sudeten politicians and their bosses in Berlin wanted. On September 7 Henlein, on instructions from Germany, broke off all negotiations with the Czech government. A shabby excuse about alleged Czech police excesses at Moravská-Ostrava was given.

On September 10, Goering made a bellicose speech at the Nuremberg Party Rally. "A petty segment of Europe is harassing the human race . . . This miserable pygmy race [the Czechs] is oppressing a cultured people, and behind it is Moscow and the eternal mask of the Jew devil." But Beneš' broadcast of the same day took no notice of Goering's diatribe; it was a quiet and dignified appeal for calm, good will and mutual trust.

Underneath the surface, though, the Czechs were tense. I ran into Dr. Beneš in the hall of the Czech Broadcasting House after his broadcast and noted that his face was grave and that he seemed to be fully aware of the terrible position he was in. The Wilson railroad station and the airport were full of Jews scrambling desperately to find transportation to safer parts. That weekend gas masks were distributed to the populace. The word from Paris was that the French government was beginning to panic at the prospect of war, and the London dispatches indicated that Chamberlain was contemplating desperate measures to meet Hitler's demands —at the expense of the Czechs, of course.

And so all Europe waited for Hitler's word on September 12 from Nuremberg. Though brutal and bombastic, and dripping with venom against the Czech state and especially against the Czech President, the Fuehrer's speech, made to a delirious mass of Nazi fanatics gathered in the huge stadium on the last night of the party rally, was not a declaration of war. He reserved his decision—publicly at least, for, as we know from the captured German documents, he had already set October 1 for the attack across the Czech frontier. He simply demanded that the Czech government give "justice" to the Sudeten Germans. If it didn't, Germany would have to see to it that it did.

The repercussions to Hitler's outburst were considerable. In the Sudetenland it inspired a revolt which after two days of savage fighting the

Czech government put down by rushing in troops and declaring martial law. Henlein slipped over the border to Germany proclaiming that the only solution now was the ceding of the Sudeten areas to Germany.

This was the solution which, as we have seen, was gaining favor in London, but before it could be furthered the agreement of France had to be obtained. The day following Hitler's speech, September 13, the French cabinet sat all day, remaining hopelessly divided on whether it should honor its obligations to Czechoslovakia in case of a German attack, which it believed imminent. That evening the British ambassador in Paris, Sir Eric Phipps, was fetched from the Opéra Comique for an urgent conference with Prime Minister Daladier. The latter appealed to Chamberlain to try at once to make the best bargain he could with the German dictator.

Mr. Chamberlain, it may be surmised, needed little urging. At eleven o'clock that same night the British Prime Minister got off an urgent message to Hitler:

In view of the increasingly critical situation I propose to come over at once to see you with a view to trying to find a peaceful solution. I propose to come across by air and am ready to start tomorrow.

Please indicate earliest time at which you can see me and suggest place of meeting. I should be grateful for a very early reply.[40]

Two hours before, the German chargé d'affaires in London, Theodor Kordt, had wired Berlin that Chamberlain's press secretary had informed him that the Prime Minister "was prepared to examine far-reaching German proposals, including plebiscite, to take part in carrying them out, and to advocate them in public."[41]

The surrender that was to culminate in Munich had begun.

CHAMBERLAIN AT BERCHTESGADEN:
SEPTEMBER 15, 1938

"Good heavens!" ("*Ich bin vom Himmel gefallen!*") Hitler exclaimed when he read Chamberlain's message.[42] He was astounded but highly pleased that the man who presided over the destinies of the mighty British Empire should come pleading to him, and flattered that a man who was sixty-nine years old and had never traveled in an airplane before should make the long seven hours' flight to Berchtesgaden at the farthest extremity of Germany. Hitler had not had even the grace to suggest a meeting place on the Rhine, which would have shortened the trip by half.

Whatever the enthusiasm of the English,* who seemed to believe that

---

* Even the severest critics of Chamberlain's foreign policy in the British press and in Parliament warmly applauded the Prime Minister for going to Berchtesgaden. The Poet Laureate, John Masefield, composed a poem, a paean of praise, entitled "Neville Chamberlain," which was published in the *Times* September 16.

the Prime Minister was making the long journey to do what Mr. Asquith and Sir Edward Grey had failed to do in 1914—warn Germany that any aggression against a small power would bring not only France but Britain into war against it—Hitler realized, as the confidential German papers and subsequent events make clear, that Chamberlain's action was a god-send to him. Already apprised by the German Embassy in London that the British leader was prepared to advocate "far-reaching German pro-posals," the Fuehrer felt fairly certain that Chamberlain's visit was a fur-ther assurance that, as he had believed all along, Britain and France would not intervene on behalf of Czechoslovakia. The Prime Minister had not been with him more than an hour or so before this estimate of the situa-tion became a certainty.

In the beginning there was a diplomatic skirmish, though Hitler, as was his custom, did most of the talking.[43] Chamberlain had landed at the Munich airport at noon on September 15, driven in an open car to the railroad station and there boarded a special train for the three-hour rail journey to Berchtesgaden. He did not fail to notice train after train of German troops and artillery passing on the opposite track. Hitler did not meet his train at Berchtesgaden, but waited on the top steps of the Berghof to greet his distinguished visitor. It had begun to rain, Dr. Schmidt, the German interpreter, later remembered, the sky darkened and clouds hid the mountains. It was now 4 P.M. and Chamberlain had been on his way since dawn.

After tea Hitler and Chamberlain mounted the steps to Hitler's study on the second floor, the very room where the dictator had received Schuschnigg seven months before. At the urging of Ambassador Hender-son, Ribbentrop was left out of the conversation, an exclusion which so irritated the vain Foreign Minister that the next day he refused to give Schmidt's notes on the conference to the Prime Minister—a singular but typical discourtesy—and Chamberlain thereafter was forced to rely on his memory of what he and Hitler had said.

Hitler began the conversation, as he did his speeches, with a long ha-rangue about all that he had done for the German people, for peace, and for an Anglo–German *rapprochement*. There was now one problem he was determined to solve "one way or another." The three million Germans in Czechoslovakia must "return" to the Reich.*

He did not wish [as Schmidt's official account puts it] that any doubts should arise as to his absolute determination not to tolerate any longer that a small, second-rate country should treat the mighty thousand-year-old German Reich as something inferior . . . He was forty-nine years old, and if Germany were to become involved in a world war over the Czechoslovak question, he wished to lead his country through the crisis in the full strength of manhood . . . He

---

* Both in his talk with Hitler and in his report to the Commons, Chamberlain, whose knowledge of German history does not appear to have been very wide, ac-cepted this false use of the word "return." The Sudeten Germans had belonged to Austria, but never to Germany.

would, of course, be sorry if a world war should result from this problem. This danger, however, was incapable of making him falter in his determination : . . . He would face any war, even a world war, for this. The rest of the world might do what it liked. He would not yield one single step.

Chamberlain, who had scarcely been able to get a word in, was a man of immense patience, but there were limits to it. At this juncture he interrupted to say, "If the Fuehrer is determined to settle this matter by force without waiting even for a discussion between ourselves, why did he let me come? I have wasted my time."

The German dictator was not accustomed to such an interruption—no German at this date would dare to make one—and Chamberlain's retort appears to have had its effect. Hitler calmed down. He thought they could go "into the question whether perhaps a peaceful settlement was still possible after all." And then he sprang his proposal.

Would Britain agree to a secession of the Sudeten region, or would she not? . . . A secession on the basis of the right of self-determination?

The proposal did not shock Chamberlain. Indeed, he expressed satisfaction that they "had now got down to the crux of the matter." According to Chamberlain's own account, from memory, he replied that he could not commit himself until he had consulted his cabinet and the French. According to Schmidt's version, taken from his own shorthand notes made while he was interpreting, Chamberlain did say that, but added that *"he could state personally that he recognized the principle of the detachment of the Sudeten areas . . . He wished to return to England to report to the Government and secure their approval of his personal attitude."*

From this surrender at Berchtesgaden, all else ensued.

That it came as no surprise to the Germans is obvious. At the very moment of the Berchtesgaden meeting Henlein was penning a secret letter to Hitler from Eger, dated September 15, just before he fled across the border to Germany:

My Fuehrer:

I informed the British [Runciman] delegation yesterday that the basis for further negotiations could . . . only be the achievement of a union with the Reich.

It is probable that Chamberlain will propose such a union.[44]

The next day, September 16, the German Foreign Office sent confidential telegrams to its embassies in Washington and several other capitals.

Fuehrer told Chamberlain yesterday he was finally resolved to put an end in one way or another to the intolerable conditions in Sudetenland within a very short time. Autonomy for Sudeten Germans is no longer being considered, but only cession of the region to Germany. Chamberlain has indicated personal approval. He is now consulting British Cabinet and is in communication with Paris. Further meeting between Fuehrer and Chamberlain planned for very near future.[45]

Toward the end of their conference Chamberlain had extracted a promise from Hitler that he would take no military action until they had again conferred. In this period the Prime Minister had great confidence in the Fuehrer's word, remarking privately a day or two later, "In spite of the hardness and ruthlessness I thought I saw in his face, I got the impression that here was a man who could be relied upon when he had given his word."[46]

While the British leader was entertaining these comforting illusions Hitler went ahead with his military and political plans for the invasion of Czechoslovakia. Colonel Jodl, on behalf of OKW, worked out with the Propaganda Ministry what he described in his diary as "joint preparations for refutation of our own violations of international law." It was to be a rough war, at least on the part of the Germans, and Dr. Goebbels' job was to justify Nazi excesses. The plan for his lies was worked out in great detail.[47] On September 17 Hitler assigned an OKW staff officer to help Henlein, who was now operating from new headquarters at a castle at Dondorf, outside Bayreuth, to organize the Sudeten Free Corps. It was to be armed with Austrian weapons and its orders from the Fuehrer were to maintain "disturbances and clashes" with the Czechs.

September 18, a day on which Chamberlain occupied himself with rallying his cabinet and the French to his policy of surrender, was a busy one for Hitler and his generals. The jumping-off schedule for five armies, the Second, Eighth, Tenth, Twelfth and Fourteenth, comprising thirty-six divisions, including three armored, was sent out. Hitler also confirmed the selection of the commanding officers for ten armies. General Adam, despite his obstreperousness, was left in over-all command in the west. Surprisingly, two of the plotters were recalled from retirement and named to lead armies: General Beck the First Army, and General von Hammerstein the Fourth Army.

Political preparations for the final blow against Czechoslovakia also continued. The captured German Foreign Office documents abound with reports of increasing German pressure on Hungary and Poland to get in on the spoils. Even the Slovaks were brought in to stir up the brew. On September 20 Henlein urged them to formulate their demands for autonomy "more sharply." On the same day Hitler received Prime Minister Imredy and Foreign Minister Kanya of Hungary and gave them a dressing down for the hesitancy shown in Budapest. A Foreign Office memorandum gives a lengthy report on the meeting.

First of all, the Fuehrer reproached the Hungarian gentlemen for the undecided attitude of Hungary. He, the Fuehrer, was determined to settle the

Czech question even at the risk of a world war . . . He was convinced [however] that neither England nor France would intervene. It was Hungary's last opportunity to join in. If she did not, he would not be in a position to put in a word for Hungarian interests. In his opinion, the best thing would be to destroy Czechoslovakia . . .

He presented two demands to the Hungarians: (1) that Hungary should make an immediate demand for a plebiscite in the territories which she claimed, and (2) that she should not guarantee any proposed new frontiers for Czechoslovakia.[48]

Come what might with Chamberlain, Hitler, as he made clear to the Hungarians, had no intention of allowing even a rump Czechoslovakia to long exist. As to the British Prime Minister:

The Fuehrer declared that he would present the German demands to Chamberlain with brutal frankness. In his opinion, action by the Army would provide the only satisfactory solution. There was, however, a danger of the Czechs submitting to every demand.

It was a danger that was to haunt the dictator in all the subsequent meetings with the unsuspecting British Prime Minister.

Egged on by Berlin, the Polish government on September 21 demanded of the Czechs a plebiscite in the Teschen district, where there was a large Polish minority, and moved troops to the frontier of the area. The next day the Hungarian government followed suit. On that day, too, September 22, the Sudeten Free Corps, supported by German S.S. detachments, occupied the Czech frontier towns of Asch and Eger, which jutted into German territory.

September 22, in fact, was a tense day throughout Europe, for on that morning Chamberlain had again set out for Germany to confer with Hitler. It is now necessary to glance briefly at what the Prime Minister had been up to in London during the interval between his visits to the Fuehrer.

On his return to London on the evening of September 16, Chamberlain called a cabinet meeting to acquaint his ministers with Hitler's demands. Lord Runciman was summoned from Prague to make his recommendations. They were astonishing. Runciman, in his zeal to appease the Germans, went further than Hitler. He advocated transferring the predominantly Sudeten territories to Germany without bothering about a plebiscite. He strongly recommended the stifling of all criticism of Germany in Czechoslovakia "by parties or persons" through legal measures. He demanded that Czechoslovakia, even though deprived of her mountain barrier and fortifications—and thus left helpless—should nevertheless "so remodel her foreign relations as to give assurances to her neighbors that she will in no circumstances attack them or enter into any aggressive action against them arising from obligations to other States." For even Runciman to be concerned at this hour with the danger of aggression from a rump Czech state against Nazi Germany seems incredible, but his fantastic recommendations apparently made a deep impression on the British cabinet and bolstered Chamberlain's intention to meet Hitler's demands.*

Premier Daladier and his Foreign Minister, Georges Bonnet, arrived in London on September 18, for consultations with the British cabinet. No thought was given to bringing the Czechs in. The British and the French, anxious to avoid war at any cost, lost little time in agreeing on joint proposals which the Czechs would have to accept. All territories inhabited more than 50 per cent by Sudeten Germans must be turned over to Germany to assure "the maintenance of peace and the safety of Czechoslovakia's vital interests." In return Britain and France agreed to join in "an international guarantee of the new boundaries . . . against unprovoked aggression." Such a guarantee would supplant the mutual-assistance treaties which the Czech state had with France and Russia. This was an easy way out for the French, and led by Bonnet, who, as the course of events would show, was determined to outdo Chamberlain in the appeasement of Hitler, they seized upon it. And then there was the cant.

Both the French and British governments [they told the Czechs in a formal note] recognize how great is the sacrifice thus required of the Czechoslovak Government in the cause of peace. But because that cause is common both to Europe in general and in particular to Czechoslovakia herself they have felt it their duty jointly to set forth frankly the conditions essential to secure it.

Also, they were in a hurry. The German dictator could not wait.

The Prime Minister must resume conversations with Herr Hitler not later than Wednesday [September 22], and earlier if possible. We therefore feel we must ask for your reply at the earliest possible moment.[49]

And so at noon on September 19 the British and French ministers in Prague jointly presented the Anglo–French proposals to the Czech government. They were rejected the next day in a dignified note which explained—prophetically—that to accept them would put Czechoslovakia "sooner or later under the complete domination of Germany." After reminding France of her treaty obligations and also of the consequences to the French position in Europe should the Czechs yield, the reply offered

---

* Though the main points of Runciman's recommendations were presented to the cabinet on the evening of September 16, the report itself was not officially made until the twenty-first, and not published until the twenty-eighth, when events had made it only of academic interest. Wheeler-Bennett points out that certain parts of the report give the impression of having been written after September 21. When Runciman left Prague on the morning of September 16, no one, not even Hitler or the Sudeten leaders, had gone so far as to suggest that the Sudetenland be turned over to Germany without a plebiscite. (Wheeler-Bennett, *Munich*, pp. 111–12. The text of the Runciman report is in the British White Paper, Cmd. 5847, No. 1.)

to submit the whole Sudeten question to arbitration under the terms of the German–Czech treaty of October 16, 1925.*

But the British and French were in no mood to allow such a matter as the sanctity of treaties to interfere with the course they had set. No sooner was the note of rejection received by the Anglo–French envoys in Prague at 5 P.M. on the twentieth than the British minister, Sir Basil Newton, warned the Czech Foreign Minister, Dr. Kamil Krofta, that if the Czech government adhered to it Britain would disinterest herself in the fate of the country. M. de Lacroix, the French minister, associated himself with this statement on behalf of France.

In London and Paris, in the meantime, the Czech note was received with ill grace. Chamberlain called a meeting of his inner cabinet and a telephone link with Paris was set up for conversations with Daladier and Bonnet throughout the evening. It was agreed that both governments should subject Prague to further pressure. The Czechs must be told that if they held out they could expect no help from France or Britain.

By this time President Beneš realized that he was being deserted by his supposed friends. He made one final effort to rally at least France. Shortly after 8 P.M. on the twentieth he had Dr. Krofta put the vital question to Lacroix: Would France honor her word to Czechoslovakia in case of a German attack or would she not? And when at 2:15 on the morning of September 21 Newton and Lacroix got Beneš out of bed, bade him withdraw his note of rejection and declared that unless this were done and the Anglo–French proposals were accepted Czechoslovakia would have to fight Germany alone, the President asked the French minister to put it in writing. Probably he had already given up, but he had an eye on history.†

All through the next day, September 21, Beneš, aching from fatigue, from the lack of sleep and from the contemplation of treachery and disaster, consulted with his cabinet, party leaders and the Army High Command. They had shown courage in the face of enemy threats but they began to crumble at the desertion of their friends and allies. What about Russia? As it happened, the Soviet Foreign Commissar, Litvinov, was making a speech that very day at Geneva reiterating that the Soviet Union would stand by its treaty with Czechoslovakia. Beneš called in the Russian minister in Prague, who backed up what his Foreign Commissar had said. Alas for the Czechs, they realized that the pact with Russia called for the Soviets to come to their aid *on condition* that France did the same. And France had reneged.

---

* It is worth noting that neither the British nor the French government published the text of this Czech note when they later issued the documents justifying their policies which led up to Munich.

† The treachery of Bonnet at this juncture is too involved to be related in a history of Germany. Among other things, he contrived to convince the French and British cabinet ministers of the falsehood that the Czech government wanted the French to state they would not fight for Czechoslovakia so that it would have a good excuse for capitulating. For the story, see Wheeler-Bennett's *Munich;* Herbert Ripka, *Munich, Before and After;* Pertinax, *The Grave Diggers of France.*

Late in the afternoon of September 21, the Czech government capitulated and accepted the Anglo–French plan. "We had no other choice, because we were left alone," a government communiqué explained bitterly. Privately, Beneš put it more succinctly: "We have been basely betrayed." The next day the cabinet resigned and General Jan Sirovy, the Inspector General of the Army, became the head of a new "government of national concentration."

CHAMBERLAIN AT GODESBERG: SEPTEMBER 22–23

Though Chamberlain was bringing to Hitler all that he had asked for at their Berchtesgaden meeting, both men were uneasy as they met at the little Rhine town of Godesberg on the afternoon of September 22. The German chargé d'affaires, after seeing the Prime Minister off at the London airport, had rushed off a wire to Berlin: "Chamberlain and his party have left under a heavy load of anxiety . . . Unquestionably opposition is growing to Chamberlain's policy."

Hitler was in a highly nervous state. On the morning of the twenty-second I was having breakfast on the terrace of the Hotel Dreesen, where the talks were to take place, when Hitler strode past on his way down to the riverbank to inspect his yacht. He seemed to have a peculiar tic. Every few steps he cocked his right shoulder nervously, his left leg snapping up as he did so. He had ugly, black patches under his eyes. He seemed to be, as I noted in my diary that evening, on the edge of a nervous breakdown. "*Teppichfresser!*" muttered my German companion, an editor who secretly despised the Nazis. And he explained that Hitler had been in such a maniacal mood over the Czechs the last few days that on more than one occasion he had lost control of himself completely, hurling himself to the floor and chewing the edge of the carpet. Hence the term "carpet eater." The evening before, while talking with some of the party hacks at the Dreesen, I had heard the expression applied to the Fuehrer— in whispers, of course.[50]

Despite his misgivings about the growing opposition to his policies at home, Mr. Chamberlain appeared to be in excellent spirits when he arrived at Godesberg and drove through streets decorated not only with the swastika but with the Union Jack to his headquarters at the Petershof, a castlelike hotel on the summit of the Petersberg, high above the opposite (right) bank of the Rhine. He had come to fulfill everything that Hitler had demanded at Berchtesgaden, and even more. There remained only the details to work out and for this purpose he had brought along, in addition to Sir Horace Wilson and William Strang (the latter a Foreign Office expert on Eastern Europe), the head of the drafting and legal department of the Foreign Office, Sir William Malkin.

Late in the afternoon the Prime Minister crossed the Rhine by ferry to the Hotel Dreesen* where Hitler awaited him. For once, at the start at least, Chamberlain did all the talking. For what must have been more than an hour, judging by Dr. Schmidt's lengthy notes of the meeting,[51] the Prime Minister, after explaining that following "laborious negotiations" he had won over not only the British and French cabinets but the Czech government to accept the Fuehrer's demands, proceeded to outline in great detail the means by which they could be implemented. Accepting Runciman's advice, he was now prepared to see the Sudetenland turned over to Germany *without* a plebiscite. As to the mixed areas, their future could be determined by a commission of three members, a German, a Czech and one neutral. Furthermore, Czechoslovakia's mutual-assistance treaties with France and Russia, which were so distasteful to the Fuehrer, would be replaced by an international guarantee against an unprovoked attack on Czechoslovakia, which in the future "would have to be completely neutral."

It all seemed so simple, so reasonable, so logical to the peace-loving British businessman become British Prime Minister. He paused with evident self-satisfaction, as one eyewitness recorded, for Hitler's reaction.

"Do I understand that the British, French and Czech governments have agreed to the transfer of the Sudetenland from Czechoslovakia to Germany?" Hitler asked.† He was astounded as he later told Chamberlain, that the concessions to him had gone so far and so fast.

"Yes," replied the Prime Minister, smiling.

"I am terribly sorry," Hitler said, "but after the events of the last few days, this plan is no longer of any use."

Chamberlain, Dr. Schmidt later remembered, sat up with a start. His owllike face flushed with surprise and anger. But apparently not with resentment that Hitler had deceived him, that Hitler, like a common blackmailer, was upping his demands at the very moment they were being accepted. The Prime Minister described his own feelings at this moment in a report to the Commons a few days later:

I do not want the House to think that Hitler was deliberately deceiving me— I do not think so for one moment—but, for me, I expected that when I got

---

* It was from this hotel, run by Herr Dreesen, an early Nazi crony of Hitler, that the Fuehrer had set out on the night of June 29–30, 1934, to kill Roehm and carry out the Blood Purge. The Nazi leader had often sought out the hotel as a place of refuge where he could collect his thoughts and resolve his hesitations.
† Hitler knew that the Czechs had accepted the Anglo–French proposals. Jodl noted in his diary that at 11:30 A.M. on September 21, the day before Chamberlain arrived in Godesberg, he had received a telephone call from the Fuehrer's adjutant: "The Fuehrer has received news five minutes ago that Prague is said to have accepted unconditionally." At 12:45 Jodl noted, "Department heads are informed to continue preparation for 'Green,' but nevertheless to get ready for everything necessary for a peaceful penetration."[52] It is possible, however, that Hitler did not know the terms of the Anglo–French plan until the Prime Minister explained them to him.

back to Godesberg I had only to discuss quietly with him the proposals that I had brought with me; and it was a profound shock to me when I was told . . . that these proposals were not acceptable . . .

Chamberlain saw the house of peace which he had so "laboriously" built up at the expense of the Czechs collapsing like a stack of cards. He was, he told Hitler, "both disappointed and puzzled. He could rightly say that the Fuehrer had got from him what he had demanded."

In order to achieve this he [Chamberlain] had risked his whole political career . . . He was being accused by certain circles in Great Britain of having sold and betrayed Czechoslovakia, of having yielded to the dictators, and on leaving England that morning he actually had been booed.

But the Fuehrer was unmoved by the personal plight of the British Prime Minister. The Sudeten area, he demanded, must be *occupied* by Germany at once. The problem "must be completely and finally solved by October first, at the latest." He had a map handy to indicate what territories must be ceded immediately.

And so, his mind "full of foreboding," as he later told the Commons, Chamberlain withdrew across the Rhine "to consider what I was to do." There seemed so little hope that evening that after he had consulted with his own cabinet colleagues and with members of the French government by telephone it was agreed that London and Paris should inform the Czech government the next day that they could not "continue to take the responsibility of advising them not to mobilize."*

At 7:20 that evening General Keitel telephoned Army headquarters from Godesberg: "Date (of X Day) cannot yet be ascertained. Continue preparations according to plan. If Case Green occurs, it will not be before September 30. If it occurs sooner, it will probably be improvised."[53]

For Adolf Hitler himself was caught in a dilemma. Though Chamberlain did not know it, the Fuehrer's real objective, as he had laid it down in his OKW directive after the May crisis, was "to destroy Czechoslovakia by military action." To accept the Anglo–French plan, which the Czechs already had agreed to, however reluctantly, would not only give Hitler his Sudeten Germans but would effectively destroy the Czech state, since it would be left defenseless. But it would not be by military action, and the Fuehrer was determined not only to humiliate President Beneš and the Czech government, which had so offended him in May, but to expose the spinelessness of the Western powers. For that, at least a *military occupation* was necessary. It could be bloodless, as was the military occupation of Austria, but it must take place. He must have at least that much revenge on the upstart Czechs.

There was no further contact between the two men on the evening of September 22. But after sleeping on the problem and spending the early

---

* Czech mobilization began at 10:30 P.M. on September 23.

morning pacing his balcony overlooking the Rhine, Chamberlain sat down following breakfast and wrote a letter to Hitler. He would submit the new German demands to the Czechs but he did not think they would be accepted. In fact, he had no doubt that the Czechs would forcibly resist an immediate occupation by German troops. But he was willing to suggest to Prague, since all parties had agreed on the transfer of the Sudeten area to Germany, that the Sudeten Germans themselves maintain law and order in their area until it was turned over to the Reich.

To such a compromise Hitler would not listen. After keeping the Prime Minister waiting throughout most of the day he finally replied by note with a bitter tirade, again rehearsing all the wrongs the Czechs had done to Germans, again refusing to modify his position and concluding that war "now appears to be the case." Chamberlain's answer was brief. He asked Hitler to put his new demands in writing, "together with a map," and undertook "as mediator" to send them to Prague. "I do not see that I can perform any further service here," he concluded. "I propose therefore to return to England."

Before doing so he came over once again to the Dreesen for a final meeting with Hitler which began at 10:30 on the evening of September 23. Hitler presented his demands in the form of a memorandum with an accompanying map. Chamberlain found himself confronted with a new time limit. The Czechs were to begin the evacuation of the ceded territory by 8 A.M. on September 26—two days hence—and complete it by September 28.

"But this is nothing less than an ultimatum!" Chamberlain exclaimed.

"Nothing of the sort," Hitler shot back. When Chamberlain retorted that the German word *Diktat* applied to it, Hitler answered, "It is not a *Diktat* at all. Look, the document is headed by the word 'Memorandum.' "

At this moment an adjutant brought in an urgent message for the Fuehrer. He glanced at it and tossed it to Schmidt, who was interpreting. "Read this to Mr. Chamberlain."

Schmidt did. "Beneš has just announced over the radio a general mobilization in Czechoslovakia."

The room, Schmidt recalled afterward, was deadly still. Then Hitler spoke: "Now, of course, the whole affair is settled. The Czechs will not dream of ceding any territory to Germany."

Chamberlain, according to the Schmidt minutes, disagreed. In fact, there followed a furious argument.

The Czechs had mobilized first [said Hitler]. Chamberlain contradicted this. Germany had mobilized first . . . The Fuehrer denied that Germany had mobilized.

And so the talks continued into the early-morning hours. Finally, after Chamberlain had inquired whether the German memorandum "was really his last word" and Hitler had replied that it was indeed, the Prime Minister answered that there was no point in continuing the conversations. He had done his utmost; his efforts had failed. He was going away with a heavy heart, for the hopes with which he had come to Germany were destroyed.

The German dictator did not want Chamberlain to get off the hook. He responded with a "concession."

"You are one of the few men for whom I have ever done such a thing," he said breezily. "I am prepared to set one single date for the Czech evacuation—October first—if that will facilitate your task." And so saying, he took a pencil and changed the dates himself. This, of course, was no concession at all. October 1 had been X Day all along.*

But it seems to have impressed the Prime Minister. "He fully appreciated," Schmidt recorded him as saying, "the Fuehrer's consideration on the point." Nevertheless, he added, he was not in a position to accept or reject the proposals; he could only transmit them.

The ice, however, had been broken, and as the meeting broke up at 1:30 A.M. the two men seemed, despite all that had happened, to be closer together personally than at any time since they had first met. I myself, from a vantage point twenty-five feet away in the porter's booth, where I had set up a temporary broadcasting studio, watched them say their farewells near the door of the hotel. I was struck by their cordiality to each other. Schmidt took down the words which I could not hear.

Chamberlain bid a hearty farewell to the Fuehrer. He said he had the feeling that a relationship of confidence had grown up between himself and the Fuehrer as a result of the conversations of the last few days . . . He did not cease to hope that the present difficult crisis would be overcome, and then he would be glad to discuss other problems still outstanding with the Fuehrer in the same spirit.

The Fuehrer thanked Chamberlain for his words and told him that he had similar hopes. As he had already stated several times, the Czech problem was the last territorial demand which he had to make in Europe.

This renunciation of further land grabs seems to have impressed the departing Prime Minister too, for in his subsequent report to the House of Commons he stressed that Hitler had made it "with great earnestness."

When Chamberlain arrived at his hotel toward 2 A.M. he was asked by a journalist, "Is the position hopeless, sir?"

---

* The memorandum called for the withdrawal of all Czech armed forces, including the police, etc., by October 1 from large areas indicated on a map with red shading. A plebiscite was to determine the future of further areas shaded in green. All military installations in the evacuated territories were to be left intact. All commercial and transport materials, "especially the rolling stock of the railway system," were to be handed over to the Germans undamaged. "Finally, no foodstuffs, goods, cattle, raw material, etc., are to be removed."[54] The hundreds of thousands of Czechs in the Sudetenland were not to be allowed to take with them even their household goods or the family cow.

"I would not like to say that," the Prime Minister answered. "It is up to the Czechs now."[55]

It did not occur to him, it is evident, that it was up to the Germans, with their outrageous demands, too.

In fact, no sooner had the Prime Minister returned to London on September 24 than he attempted to do the very thing he had informed Hitler he would not do: persuade the British cabinet to accept the new Nazi demands. But now he ran into unexpected opposition. Duff Cooper, the First Lord of the Admiralty, firmly opposed him. Surprisingly, so did Lord Halifax, though very reluctantly. Chamberlain could not carry his cabinet. Nor could he persuade the French government, which on the twenty-fourth rejected the Godesberg memorandum and on the same day ordered a partial mobilization.

When the French ministers, headed by Premier Daladier, arrived in London on Sunday, September 25, the two governments were apprised of the formal rejection of the Godesberg proposals by the Czech government.* There was nothing for the French to do but affirm that they would honor their word and come to the aid of Czechoslovakia if attacked. But they had to know what Britain would do. Finally cornered, or so it seemed, Chamberlain agreed to inform Hitler that if France became engaged in war with Germany as a result of her treaty obligations to the Czechs, Britain would feel obliged to support her.

But first he would make one last appeal to the German dictator. Hitler was scheduled to make a speech at the Sportpalast in Berlin on September 26. In order to induce him not to burn his bridges Chamberlain once again dashed off a personal letter to Hitler and on the afternoon of the twenty-sixth rushed it to Berlin by his faithful aide, Sir Horace Wilson, who sped to the German capital by special plane.

On the departure of Chamberlain from the Dreesen in the early-morning hours of September 24, the Germans had been plunged into gloom. Now that war seemed to face them, some of them, at least, did not like it. I lingered in the hotel lobby for some time over a late supper. Goering, Goebbels, Ribbentrop, General Keitel and lesser men stood around earnestly talking. They seemed dazed at the prospect of war.

In Berlin later that day I found hopes reviving. In the Wilhelmstrasse the feeling was that since Chamberlain, with all the authority of the British Prime Minister, had agreed to present Hitler's new demands to Prague, it must be assumed that the British leader supported Hitler's proposals. As we have seen, the assumption was quite correct—so far as it went.

Sunday, September 25, was a lovely day of Indian summer in Berlin, warm and sunny, and since it undoubtedly would be the last such weekend that autumn, half of the population flocked to the lakes and woods that surround the capital. Despite reports of Hitler's rage at hearing that the

---

* The Czech reply is a moving and prophetic document. The Godesberg proposals, it said, "deprive us of every safeguard for our national existence."[56]

Godesberg ultimatum was being rejected in Paris, London and Prague, there was no feeling of great crisis, certainly no war fever, in Berlin. "Hard to believe there will be war," I noted in my diary that evening.*

On the Monday following there was a sudden change for the worse. At 5 P.M. Sir Horace Wilson, accompanied by Ambassador Henderson and Ivone Kirkpatrick, First Secretary of the British Embassy, arrived at the Chancellery bearing Chamberlain's letter.[57] They found Hitler in an ugly mood—probably he was already working himself down to a proper level for his Sportpalast speech three hours hence.

When Dr. Schmidt began to translate the letter, which stated that the Czech government had informed the Prime Minister that the Godesberg memorandum was "wholly unacceptable," just as he had warned at Godesberg, Hitler, according to Schmidt, suddenly leaped up, shouting, "There's no sense at all in negotiating further!" and bounded for the door.[58]

It was a painful scene, says the German interpreter. "For the first and only time in my presence, Hitler completely lost his head." And according to the British present, the Fuehrer, who soon stamped back to his chair, kept further interrupting the reading of the letter by screaming, "The Germans are being treated like niggers . . . On October first I shall have Czechoslovakia where I want her. If France and England decide to strike, let them . . . I do not care a pfennig."

Chamberlain had proposed that since the Czechs were willing to give Hitler what he wanted, the Sudeten areas, a meeting of Czech and German representatives be called immediately to settle "by agreement the way in which the territory is to be handed over." He added that he was willing to have British representatives sit in at the meeting. Hitler's response was that he would negotiate details with the Czechs if they accepted in advance the Godesberg memorandum (which they had just rejected) and agreed to a German occupation of the Sudetenland by October 1. He must have an affirmative reply, he said, within forty-four hours—by 2 P.M. on September 28.

That evening Hitler burned his bridges, or so it seemed to those of us who listened in amazement to his mad outburst at the jammed Sportpalast in Berlin. Shouting and shrieking in the worst paroxysm I had ever seen him in, he venomously hurled personal insults at "Herr Beneš," declared that the issue of war or peace was now up to the Czech President and that, in any case, he would have the Sudetenland by October 1. Carried away as he was by his angry torrent of words and the ringing cheers of the crowd, he was shrewd enough to throw a sop to the British Prime Minister. He thanked him for his efforts for peace and reiterated that this was his last territorial claim in Europe. "We want no Czechs!" he muttered contemptuously.

---

* At the conclusion of the Godesberg talks, the British and French correspondents —and the chief European correspondent of the New York *Times,* who was an English citizen—had scurried off for the French, Belgian and Dutch frontiers, none of them wishing to be interned in case of war.

Throughout the harangue I sat in a balcony just above Hitler, trying with no great success to broadcast a running translation of his words. That night in my diary I noted:

. . . For the first time in all the years I've observed him he seemed tonight to have completely lost control of himself. When he sat down, Goebbels sprang up and shouted into the microphone: "One thing is sure: 1918 will never be repeated!" Hitler looked up to him, a wild, eager expression in his eyes, as if those were the words which he had been searching for all evening and hadn't quite found. He leaped to his feet and with a fanatical fire in his eyes that I shall never forget brought his right hand, after a grand sweep, pounding down on the table, and yelled with all the power in his mighty lungs: "*Ja!*" Then he slumped into his chair exhausted.

He was fully recovered when he received Sir Horace Wilson for the second time the next noon, September 27. The special envoy, a man with no diplomatic training but who was as anxious as the Prime Minister, if not more so, to give Hitler the Sudetenland if the dictator would only accept it peacefully, called Hitler's attention to a special statement issued by Chamberlain in London shortly after midnight in response to the Fuehrer's Sportpalast speech. In view of the Chancellor's lack of faith in Czech promises, the British government, Chamberlain said, would regard itself "as morally responsible" for seeing that the Czech promises were carried out "fairly, fully and with all reasonable promptitude." He trusted that the Chancellor would not reject this proposal.

But Hitler showed no interest in it. He had, he said, no further message for Mr. Chamberlain. It was now up to the Czechs. They could accept or reject his demands. If they rejected them, he shouted angrily, "I shall destroy Czechoslovakia!" He kept repeating the threat with obvious relish.

Apparently that was too much even for the accommodating Wilson, who rose to his feet and said, "In that case, I am entrusted by the Prime Minister to make the following statement: 'If France, in fulfillment of her treaty obligations, should become actively engaged in hostilities against Germany, the United Kingdom would feel obliged to support France.'"

"I can only take note of that position," Hitler replied with some heat. "It means that if France elects to attack Germany, England will feel obliged to attack her also."

When Sir Horace replied that he had not said that, that it was up to Hitler, after all, whether there would be peace or war, the Fuehrer, working himself up by now to a fine lather, shouted, "If France and England strike, let them do so! It's a matter of complete indifference to me. Today is Tuesday; by next Monday we shall be at war."

According to Schmidt's official notes on the meeting, Wilson apparently wished to continue the conversation, but was advised by Ambassador Henderson to desist. This did not prevent the inexperienced special envoy from getting in a word with the Fuehrer alone as the meeting broke up.

"I shall try to make these Czechs sensible,"* he assured Hitler, and the latter replied that he "would welcome that." Perhaps, the Fuehrer must have thought, Chamberlain could still be coaxed to go further in making the Czechs "sensible." That evening, in fact, he sat down and dictated to the Prime Minister a shrewdly worded letter.

There were well-grounded reasons for writing it. Much had happened in Berlin—and elsewhere—during that day, September 27.

At 1 P.M., shortly after Wilson's departure, Hitler issued a "most secret" order directing assault units comprising some twenty-one reinforced regiments, or seven divisions, to move forward from their training areas to the jumping-off points on the Czech frontier. "They must be ready," said the order, "to begin action against 'Green' on September 30, the decision having been made one day previously by twelve noon." A few hours later a further concealed mobilization was ordered by the Fuehrer. Among other measures, five new divisions were mobilized for the west.[59]

But even as Hitler went ahead with his military moves, there were developments during the day which made him hesitate. In order to stir up some war fever among the populace Hitler ordered a parade of a motorized division through the capital at dusk—an hour when hundreds of thousands of Berliners would be pouring out of their offices onto the streets. It turned out to be a terrible fiasco—at least for the Supreme Commander. The good people of Berlin simply did not want to be reminded of war. In my diary that night I noted down the surprising scene.

I went out to the corner of the Linden where the column [of troops] was turning down the Wilhelmstrasse, expecting to see a tremendous demonstration. I pictured the scenes I had read of in 1914 when the cheering throngs on this same street tossed flowers at the marching soldiers, and the girls ran up and kissed them . . . But today they ducked into the subways, refused to look on, and the handful that did stood at the curb in utter silence . . . It has been the most striking demonstration against war I've ever seen.

At the urging of a policeman I walked down the Wilhelmstrasse to the Reichskanzlerplatz, where Hitler stood on a balcony of the Chancellery reviewing the troops.

. . . There weren't two hundred people there. Hitler looked grim, then angry, and soon went inside, leaving his troops to parade by unreviewed. What I've seen tonight almost rekindles a little faith in the German people. They are dead set against war.

Within the Chancellery there was further bad news—this from abroad. There was a dispatch from Budapest saying that Yugoslavia and Rumania

---

* Wilson's assurance is given in English in the original of Schmidt's German notes.

had informed the Hungarian government that they would move against Hungary militarily if she attacked Czechoslovakia. That would spread the war to the Balkans, something Hitler did not want.

The news from Paris was graver. From the German military attaché there came a telegram marked "Very Urgent" and addressed not only to the Foreign Ministry but to OKW and the General Staff. It warned that France's partial mobilization was so much like a total one "that I reckon with the completion of the deployment of the first 65 divisions on the German frontier by the sixth day of mobilization." Against such a force the Germans had, as Hitler knew, barely a dozen divisions, half of them reserve units of doubtful value. Furthermore, wired the German military attaché, "it appears probable that in the event of belligerent measures by Germany . . . an immediate attack will take place, in all probability from Lower Alsace and from Lorraine in the direction of Mainz."

Finally, this German officer informed Berlin, the Italians were doing absolutely nothing to pin down French troops on the Franco–Italian frontier.[60] Mussolini, the valiant ally, seemed to be letting Hitler down in a crucial hour.

And then, the President of the United States and the King of Sweden were butting in. The day before, on the twenty-sixth, Roosevelt had addressed an appeal to Hitler to help keep the peace, and though Hitler had answered it within twenty-four hours, saying that peace depended solely on the Czechs, there came another message from the American President during the course of this day, Wednesday the twenty-seventh, suggesting an immediate conference of all the nations directly interested and implying that if war broke out the world would hold Hitler responsible.[61]

The King of Sweden, staunch friend of Germany, as he had proved during the 1914–18 war, was more frank. During the afternoon a dispatch arrived in Berlin from the German minister in Stockholm saying that the King had hastily summoned him and told him that unless Hitler extended his time limit of October 1 by ten days world war would inevitably break out, Germany would be solely to blame for it and moreover just as inevitably would lose it "in view of the present combination of the Powers." In the cool, neutral air of Stockholm, the shrewd King was able to assess at least the military situation more objectively than the heads of government in Berlin, London and Paris.

President Roosevelt, as perhaps was necessary in view of American sentiment, had weakened his two appeals for peace by stressing that the United States would not intervene in a war nor even assume any obligations "in the conduct of the present negotiations." The German ambassador in Washington, Hans Dieckhoff, therefore thought it necessary to get off a "very urgent" cable to Berlin during the day. He warned that if Hitler resorted to force and was opposed by Britain he had reason to assume "that the whole weight of the United States [would] be thrown into the scale on the side of Britain." And the ambassador, usually a timid man when it came to standing up to the Fuehrer, added, "I consider it my duty to emphasize this very strongly." He did not want the German government to stumble into the same mistaken assumptions it had made about America in 1914.

And Prague? Was there any sign of weakening there? In the evening came a telegram from Colonel Toussaint, the German military attaché, to OKW: "Calm in Prague. Last mobilization measures carried out . . . Total estimated call-up is 1,000,000; field army 800,000 . . ."[62] That was as many trained men as Germany had for two fronts. Together the Czechs and the French outnumbered the Germans by more than two to one.

Faced with these facts and developments and no doubt mindful of Wilson's parting words and of Chamberlain's character and of Chamberlain's utter fear of war, Hitler sat down early on that evening of September 27 to dictate a letter to the Prime Minister. Dr. Schmidt, who was called in to translate it into English, got the feeling that the dictator was shrinking back "from the extreme step." Whether Hitler knew that the order was going out that evening for the mobilization of the British fleet cannot be established. Admiral Raeder arranged to see the Fuehrer at 10 P.M., and it is possible that the German Navy learned of the British move, which was made at 8 P.M. and publicly announced at 11:38 P.M., and that Raeder informed Hitler by telephone. At any rate, when the Admiral arrived he appealed to the Fuehrer not to go to war.

What Hitler did know at this moment was that Prague was defiant, Paris rapidly mobilizing, London stiffening, his own people apathetic, his leading generals dead against him, and that his ultimatum on the Godesberg proposals expired at 2 P.M. the next day.

His letter was beautifully calculated to appeal to Chamberlain. Moderate in tone, it denied that his proposals would "rob Czechoslovakia of every guarantee of its existence" or that his troops would fail to stop at the demarcation lines. He was ready to negotiate details with the Czechs; he was ready to "give a formal guarantee for the remainder of Czechoslovakia." The Czechs were holding out simply because they hoped, with the help of England and France, to start a European war. Nevertheless, he did not slam the door on the last hopes of peace.

I must leave it to your judgment [he concluded] whether, in view of these facts, you consider that you should continue your effort . . . to spoil such maneuvers and bring the Government in Prague to reason at the very last hour.[63]

THE ELEVENTH HOUR

Hitler's letter, telegraphed urgently to London, reached Chamberlain at 10:30 on the night of September 27. It came at the end of a busy day for the Prime Minister.

The disquieting news which Sir Horace Wilson, who arrived in London early in the afternoon, brought from his second conference with Hitler spurred Chamberlain and his inner cabinet to action. It was decided to mobilize the fleet, call up the Auxiliary Air Force and declare a state of emergency. Already trenches were being dug in the parks and squares for protection against bombing, and the evacuation of London's school children had begun.

Also, the Prime Minister promptly sent off a message to President Beneš in Prague warning that his information from Berlin "makes it clear that the German Army will receive orders to cross the Czechoslovak frontier immediately if, by tomorrow [September 28] at 2 P.M. the Czechoslovak Government have not accepted the German conditions." But having honorably warned the Czechs, Chamberlain could not refrain from admonishing them, in the last part of his message, "that Bohemia would be overrun by the German Army and nothing which another Power or Powers could do would be able to save your country and your people from such a fate. This remains true whatever the result of a world war might be."

Thus Chamberlain was putting the responsibility for peace or war no longer on Hitler but on Beneš. And he was giving a military opinion which even the German generals, as we have seen, held as irresponsible. However, he did add, at the end of his message, that he would not assume the responsibility of telling the Czechs what they must now do. It was up to them.

But was it? Beneš had not had time to reply to the telegram when a second one arrived in which Chamberlain did endeavor to tell the Czech government what to do. He proposed that the Czechs accept a limited German military occupation on October 1—of Egerland and Asch, outside the Czech fortifications—and that a German–Czech–British boundary commission then quickly establish the rest of the areas to be turned over to the Germans.* And the Prime Minister added a further warning:

The only alternative to this plan would be an invasion and a dismemberment of the country by force, and Czechoslovakia, though a conflict might arise which would lead to incalculable loss of life, could not be reconstituted in her frontiers whatever the result of the conflict may be.[64]

The Czechs were thus warned by their friends (France associated herself with these latest proposals) that even if they and their allies defeated the Germans in a war, Czechoslovakia would have to give up the Sudetenland to Germany. The inference was plain: Why plunge Europe into a war, since the Sudetenland is lost to you anyway?

---

* These proposals were also transmitted by Ambassador Henderson to the German Foreign Office at 11 P.M. with the request that they be immediately submitted to Hitler

This business out of the way, the Prime Minister broadcast to the nation at 8:30 P.M.:

How horrible, fantastic, incredible it is that we should be digging trenches . . . here because of a quarrel in a faraway country between people of whom we know nothing! . . .

Hitler had got the "substance of what he wanted." Britain had offered to guarantee that the Czechs would accept it and carry it out.

I would not hesitate to pay even a third visit to Germany if I thought it would do any good . . .

However much we may sympathize with a small nation confronted by a big and powerful neighbor, we cannot in all circumstances undertake to involve the whole British Empire in a war simply on her account. If we have to fight it must be on larger issues than that . . .

I am myself a man of peace to the very depths of my soul. Armed conflict between nations is a nightmare to me; but, if I were convinced that any nation had made up its mind to dominate the world by fear of force, I should feel that it must be resisted. Under such a domination, life for people who believe in liberty would not be worth living; but war is a fearful thing, and we must be very clear, before we embark on it, that it is really the great issues that are at stake.

Wheeler-Bennett has recorded that after listening to this broadcast most people in Britain went to bed that night believing that Britain and Germany would be at war within twenty-four hours.[65] But the good people did not know what was happening at Downing Street still later that evening.

At 10:30 P.M. came Hitler's letter. It was a straw which the Prime Minister eagerly grasped. To the Fuehrer he replied:

After reading your letter, I feel certain that you can get all essentials without war, and without delay. I am ready to come to Berlin myself at once to discuss arrangements for transfer with you and representatives of the Czech Government, together with representatives of France and Italy, if you desire. I feel convinced we can reach agreement in a week. I cannot believe that you will take responsibility of starting a world war which may end civilization for the sake of a few days delay in settling this long-standing problem.[66]

A telegram also went out to Mussolini asking him to urge the Fuehrer's acceptance of this plan and to agree to being represented at the suggested meeting.

The idea of a conference had been in the back of the Prime Minister's mind for some time. As far back as July, Sir Nevile Henderson had suggested it on his own in a dispatch to London. He had proposed that four powers, Germany, Italy, Britain and France, settle the Sudeten problem. But both the ambassador and the Prime Minister had been reminded by the British Foreign Office that it would be difficult to exclude other powers from participating in such a conference.[67] The "other powers" were Russia, which had a pact of mutual assistance with Prague, and Czechoslovakia. Chamberlain had returned from Godesberg convinced—quite correctly—that Hitler would never consent to any meeting which included the Soviet Union. Nor did the Prime Minister himself desire the presence of the Russians. Though it was obvious to the smallest mind in Britain that in case of war with Germany, Soviet participation on the side of the West would be of immense value, as Churchill repeatedly tried to point out to the head of the British government, this was a view which seems to have escaped the Prime Minister. He had, as we have seen, turned down the Russian proposal for a conference after the Anschluss to discuss means of opposing further German aggression. Despite Moscow's guarantee to Czechoslovakia and the fact that right up to this moment Litvinov was proclaiming that Russia would honor it, Chamberlain had no intention of allowing the Soviets to interfere with his resolve to keep the peace by giving Hitler the Sudetenland.

But until Wednesday, September 28, he had not yet gone so far in his thinking as to exclude the Czechs from a conference. Indeed, on the twenty-fifth, after Prague had rejected Hitler's Godesberg demands, the Prime Minister had called in Jan Masaryk, the Czech ambassador in London, and proposed that Czechoslovakia should agree to negotiations at "an international conference in which Germany, Czechoslovakia and other powers could participate." On the following day the Czech government had accepted the idea. And, as we have just seen, in his message to Hitler late on the night of the twenty-seventh Chamberlain had specified that "representatives of Czechoslovakia" should be included in his proposed conference of Germany, Italy, France and Great Britain.

"BLACK WEDNESDAY" AND THE HALDER PLOT AGAINST HITLER

Deep gloom hung over Berlin, Prague, London and Paris as "Black Wednesday," September 28, dawned. War seemed inevitable.

"A Great War can hardly be avoided any longer," Jodl quoted Goering as saying that morning. "It may last seven years, and we will win it."[68]

In London the digging of trenches, the evacuation of school children, the emptying of hospitals, continued. In Paris there was a scramble for the choked trains leaving the city, and the motor traffic out of the capital was jammed. There were similar scenes in western Germany. Jodl jotted in his diary that morning reports of German refugees fleeing from the border regions. At 2 P.M. Hitler's time limit for Czechoslovakia's acceptance of the Godesberg proposals would run out. There was no sign from Prague that they would be accepted. There were, however, certain other signs: great activity in the Wilhelmstrasse; a frantic coming and going of the French, British and Italian ambassadors. But of these the general public and indeed the German generals remained ignorant.

To some of the generals and to General Halder, Chief of the General Staff, above all, the time had come to carry out their plot to remove Hitler and save the Fatherland from plunging into a European war which they felt it was doomed to lose. All through September the conspirators, according to the later accounts of the survivors,* had been busy working out their plans.

General Halder was in close touch with Colonel Oster and his chief at the Abwehr, Admiral Canaris, who tried to keep him abreast of Hitler's political moves and of foreign intelligence. The plotters, as we have seen, had warned London of Hitler's resolve to attack Czechoslovakia by the end of September and had begged the British government to make clear that Britain, along with France, would answer German aggression by armed force. For some months General von Witzleben, who commanded the Berlin Military District, and who would have to furnish most of the troops to carry out the coup, had been hesitant because he suspected that London and Paris had secretly given Hitler a free hand in the East and would therefore not go to war over Czechoslovakia—a view shared by several other generals and one which Hitler and Ribbentrop had encouraged. If this were true, the plot to depose Hitler, in the opinion of generals such as Witzleben and Halder, was senseless. For, at this stage of the Third Reich, they were concerned only with getting rid of the Fuehrer in order to avert a European war which Germany had no chance of winning. If there were really no risk of a big war, if Chamberlain were going to give Hitler what he wanted in Czechoslovakia without a war, then they saw no point in trying to carry out a revolt.

To assure the generals that Britain and France meant business, Colonel Oster and Gisevius arranged for General Halder and General von Witzleben to meet Schacht, who, besides having prestige with the military hierarchy as the man who financed German rearmament and who still was in the cabinet, was considered an expert on British affairs. Schacht assured them that the British would fight if Hitler resorted to arms against the Czechs.

The news that had reached Erich Kordt, one of the conspirators, in the German Foreign Office late on the night of September 13, that Chamberlain urgently proposed "to come over at once by air" to seek a peaceful solution of the Czech crisis, had caused consternation in the camp

---

* These include firsthand accounts by Halder, Gisevius and Schacht.[69] Each of them contains much that is confusing and contradictory, and on some points they contradict each other. It must be remembered that all three of these men, who had begun by serving the Nazi regime, were anxious after the war to prove their opposition to Hitler and their love of peace.

Erich Kordt, chief of Ribbentrop's secretariat in the Foreign Office, also was an important participant in the plot who survived the war. At Nuremberg he drew up a long memorandum about events in September 1938, which was made available to this writer.

of the plotters. They had counted on Hitler's returning to Berlin from the Nuremberg Party Rally on the fourteenth and, according to Kordt, had planned to carry out the putsch on that day or the next. But the Fuehrer did not return to the capital.* Instead, he went to Munich and on the fourteenth continued on to Berchtesgaden, where he awaited the visit of the British Prime Minister the next day.

There were double grounds for the feeling of utter frustration among the plotters. Their plans could be carried out only if Hitler were in Berlin, and they had been confident that, since the Nuremberg rally had only sharpened the Czech crisis, he would certainly return immediately to the capital. In the second place, although some of the members of the conspiracy complacently assumed, as did the people of Britain, that Chamberlain was flying to Berchtesgaden to warn Hitler not to make the mistake that Wilhelm II had made in 1914 as to what Great Britain would do in the case of German aggression, Kordt knew better. He had seen the text of Chamberlain's urgent message explaining to Hitler that he wanted to see him "with a view to trying to find a peaceful solution." Furthermore, he had seen the telegram from his brother, Theodor Kordt, counselor of the German Embassy in London, that day, confiding that the Prime Minister was prepared to go a long way to meet Hitler's demands in the Sudetenland.†

"The effect on our plans," says Kordt, "was bound to be disastrous. It would have been absurd to stage a putsch to overthrow Hitler at a moment when the British Prime Minister was coming to Germany to discuss with Hitler 'the peace of the world.' "

However, on the evening of September 15, according to Erich Kordt, Dr. Paul Schmidt, who was in on the conspiracy, and who, as we have seen, acted as sole interpreter—and sole witness—at the Hitler–Chamberlain talk, informed him "by prearranged code" that the Fuehrer was still determined to conquer the whole of Czechoslovakia and that he had put forward to Chamberlain impossible demands "in the hope that they would be refused." This intelligence revived the spirits of the conspirators. Kordt informed Colonel Oster of it the same evening and it was decided to go ahead with the plans as soon as Hitler returned to

---

* There is considerable confusion among the historians and even among the conspirators about Hitler's whereabouts on September 13 and 14. Churchill, basing his account on a memorandum of General Halder, states that Hitler arrived in Berlin from Berchtesgaden "on the morning of September 14" and that Halder and Witzleben, on learning of it, "decided to strike at 8 that same evening." They called the operation off, according to this account, when they learned at 4 P.M. that Chamberlain was flying to Berchtesgaden. (Churchill, *The Gathering Storm*, p. 312.) But Halder's memory—and hence Churchill's account—is certainly in error. Hitler's daily schedule book, now in the Library of Congress, has several entries showing that he spent the thirteenth and fourteenth in Munich, where, among other things, he conferred with Ribbentrop at Bormann's home and visited the Sonnenwinkel, a cabaret, departing for the Obersalzberg at the end of the day of the fourteenth.

† See above, p. 384.

Berlin. "But first of all," Oster said, "we must get the bird back into his cage in Berlin."

The bird flew back to his "cage" from the Godesberg talks on the afternoon of September 24. On the morning of "Black Wednesday," the twenty-eighth, Hitler had been in Berlin for nearly four days. On the twenty-sixth he apparently had burned his bridges in his outburst at the Sportpalast. On the twenty-seventh he had sent Sir Horace Wilson back to London empty-handed, and the British government's reaction had been to mobilize the fleet and warn Prague to expect an immediate German attack. During the day he had also, as we have seen, ordered the "assault units" to take their combat positions on the Czech frontier and be ready for "action" on September 30—three days hence.

What were the conspirators waiting for? All the conditions they themselves had set had now been fulfilled. Hitler was in Berlin. He was determined to go to war. He had set the date for the attack on Czechoslovakia as September 30—two days away now. Either the putsch must be made at once, or it would be too late to overthrow the dictator and stop the war.

Kordt declares that during the day of September 27 the plotters set a definite date for action: September 29. Gisevius, in his testimony on the stand at Nuremberg and also in his book, claims that the generals—Halder and Witzleben—decided to act immediately on September 28 after they got a copy of Hitler's "defiant letter" with its "insulting demand" to Chamberlain of the night before.

Oster received a copy of this defiant letter [Gisevius says] late that night [September 27], and on the morning of September 28 I took the copy to Witzleben. Witzleben went to Halder with it. Now, at last, the Chief of the General Staff had his desired, unequivocal proof that Hitler was not bluffing, that he wanted war.

Tears of indignation ran down Halder's cheeks . . . Witzleben insisted that now it was time to take action. He persuaded Halder to go to see Brauchitsch. After a while Halder returned to say that he had good news: Brauchitsch was also outraged and would probably take part in the Putsch.[70]

But either the text of the letter had been altered in the copying or the generals misunderstood it, for, as we have seen, it was so moderate in tone, so full of promises to "negotiate details with the Czechs" and to "give a formal guarantee for the remainder of Czechoslovakia," so conciliatory in suggesting to Chamberlain that he might continue his efforts, that the Prime Minister, after reading it, had immediately telegraphed Hitler suggesting a Big-Power conference to settle the details and at the same time wired Mussolini asking his support for such a proposal.

Of this eleventh-hour effort at appeasement the generals apparently had no knowledge, but General von Brauchitsch, the Commander in Chief of the Army, may have had some inkling. According to Gisevius, Witzleben telephoned Brauchitsch from Halder's office, told him that all was ready and pleaded with him to lead the revolt himself. But the Army commander was noncommittal. He informed Halder and Witzleben that he would first have to go over to the Fuehrer's Chancellery to see for himself whether the generals had assessed the situation correctly. Gisevius says that Witzleben rushed back to his military headquarters.

"Gisevius," he declared excitedly, "the time has come!"

At eleven o'clock that morning of September 28 the phone rang at Kordt's desk in the Foreign Office. Ciano was on the line from Rome and wanted urgently to speak to the German Foreign Minister. Ribbentrop was not available—he was at the Reich Chancellery—so the Italian Foreign Minister asked to be put through to his ambassador, Bernardo Attolico. The Germans listened in and recorded the call. It developed that Mussolini, and not his son-in-law, wanted to do the talking.

MUSSOLINI: This is the Duce speaking. Can you hear me?
ATTOLICO: Yes, I hear you.
MUSSOLINI: Ask immediately for an interview with the Chancellor. Tell him the British government asked me through Lord Perth* to mediate in the Sudeten question. The point of difference is very small. Tell the Chancellor that I and Fascist Italy stand behind him. He must decide. But tell him I favor accepting the suggestion. You hear me?
ATTOLICO: Yes, I hear you.
MUSSOLINI: Hurry![71]

Out of breath, his face flushed with excitement (as Dr. Schmidt, the interpreter, noted), Ambassador Attolico arrived at the Chancellery to find that the French ambassador was already closeted with Hitler. M. François-Poncet had had a hard time getting there. Very late the night before, Bonnet, the French Foreign Minister, who was now intent on going Chamberlain one better, had telephoned his ambassador in Berlin and instructed him to see Hitler at the earliest possible moment and present a French proposal for surrendering the Sudetenland which went much further than the British plan. Whereas the Prime Minister's proposal, delivered to Hitler at 11 P.M. on September 27, offered Hitler the occupation of Zone I of the Sudetenland by October 1—a mere token occupation of a tiny enclave—the French now proposed to hand over three large zones, which comprised most of the disputed territory, by October 1.

It was a tempting offer, but the French ambassador had great difficulty in making it. He phoned at 8 A.M. on September 28 for an appointment with the Chancellor and when no response had been received by ten o'clock rushed his military attaché off to the Army General Staff to inform the German generals of the offer which he was as yet unable to deliver. He enlisted the aid of the British ambassador. Sir Nevile Henderson, who was only too ready to oblige anyone who might help prevent a war—at

* The British ambassador in Rome.

any cost—telephoned Goering, and the Field Marshal said he would try to make the appointment. As a matter of fact, Henderson was trying to make one for himself, for he had been instructed to present to Hitler "a final personal message from the Prime Minister," the one which Chamberlain had drafted late the night before,* assuring Hitler that he could get everything he wanted "without war, and without delay," and proposing a conference of the powers to work out the details.[72]

Hitler received François-Poncet at 11:15 A.M. The ambassador found him nervous and tense. Brandishing a map which he had hastily drawn up and which showed the large chunks of Czech territory which Czechoslovakia's principal ally was now prepared to hand over to Hitler on a platter, the French ambassador urged the Fuehrer to accept the French proposals and spare Europe from war. Despite Ribbentrop's negative comments, which François-Poncet says he dealt "roundly" with, Hitler was impressed—especially, as Dr. Schmidt noted, by the ambassador's map, with its generous markings.

At 11:40 the interview was suddenly interrupted by a messenger who announced that Attolico had just arrived with an urgent message for the Fuehrer from Mussolini. Hitler left the room, with Schmidt, to greet the panting Italian ambassador.

"I have an urgent message to you from the Duce!" Attolico, who had a naturally hoarse voice, shouted from some distance off.[73] After delivering it, he added that Mussolini begged the Fuehrer to refrain from mobilization.

It was at this moment, says Schmidt, the only surviving eyewitness of the scene, that the decision for peace was made. It was now just noon, two hours before the time limit on Hitler's ultimatum to the Czechs ran out.

"Tell the Duce," Hitler said, with obvious relief, to Attolico, "that I accept his proposal."[74]

The rest of the day was anticlimactic. Ambassador Henderson followed Attolico and François-Poncet to the Fuehrer's presence.

"At the request of my great friend and ally, Mussolini," Hitler told Henderson, "I have postponed mobilizing my troops for twenty-four hours."† He would give his decision on other matters, such as the proposed conference of the powers, after he had again consulted Mussolini.[75]

There followed much telephoning between Berlin and Rome—Schmidt says the two fascist dictators talked directly once. A few minutes before 2 P.M. on September 28, just as his ultimatum was to expire, Hitler made up his mind and invitations were hastily issued to the heads of government of Great Britain, France and Italy to meet the Fuehrer at Munich at noon on the following day to settle the Czech question. No invitation was sent to Prague or Moscow. Russia, the coguarantor of Czechoslo-

---

* See above, p. 403.
† As we have seen, Hitler already had mobilized all the troops available.

vakia's integrity in case of a German attack, was not to be allowed to interfere. The Czechs were not even asked to be present at their own death sentence.

In his memoirs Sir Nevile Henderson gave most of the credit for saving the peace at this moment to Mussolini, and in this he has been backed by most of the historians who have written of this chapter in European history.* But surely this is being overgenerous. Italy was the weakest of the Big Powers in Europe and her military strength was so negligible that the German generals, as their papers make clear, treated it as a joke. Great Britain and France were the only powers that counted in German calculations. And it was the British Prime Minister who, from the start, had sought to convince Hitler that he could get the Sudetenland without a war. Chamberlain, not Mussolini, made Munich possible, and thus preserved the peace for exactly eleven months. The cost of such a feat to his own country and to its allies and friends will be considered later, but it was, by any accounting, as it turned out, almost beyond bearing.

At five minutes to three on "Black Wednesday," which now appeared less dark than it had in the bleak morning hours, the British Prime Minister had begun to address the House of Commons in London, giving a detailed account of the Czech crisis and of the part which he and his government had played in trying to solve it. The situation he depicted was still uncertain, but it had improved. Mussolini, he said, had succeeded in getting Hitler to postpone mobilization for twenty-four hours. It was now 4:15, and Chamberlain had been speaking for an hour and twenty minutes and was nearing the end of his speech. At this point he was interrupted. Sir John Simon, the Chancellor of the Exchequer, passed him a paper which had been handed down to the Treasury front bench by Lord Halifax, who had been sitting in the peers' gallery.

Whatever view honorable members may have had about Signor Mussolini [Chamberlain was saying] I believe that everyone will welcome his gesture . . . for peace.

The Prime Minister paused, glanced at the paper, and smiled.

That is not all. I have something further to say to the House yet. I have now been informed by Herr Hitler that he invites me to meet him at Munich tomorrow morning. He has also invited Signor Mussolini and Monsieur Daladier. Signor Mussolini has accepted and I have no doubt Monsieur Daladier will accept. I need not say what my answer will be . . .

There was no need. The ancient chamber, the Mother of Parliaments, reacted with a mass hysteria without precedent in its long history. There

* Alan Bullock (*Hitler—A Study in Tyranny,* p. 428) says: "Almost certainly it was Mussolini's intervention which turned the scale."

was wild shouting and a wild throwing of order papers into the air and many were in tears and one voice was heard above the tumult which seemed to express the deep sentiments of all: "Thank God for the Prime Minister!"

Jan Masaryk, the Czech minister, the son of the founding father of the Czechoslovak Republic, looked on from the diplomatic gallery, unable to believe his eyes. Later he called on the Prime Minister and the Foreign Secretary in Downing Street to find out whether his country, which would have to make all the sacrifices, would be invited to Munich. Chamberlain and Halifax answered that it would not, that Hitler would not stand for it. Masaryk gazed at the two God-fearing Englishmen and struggled to keep control of himself.

"If you have sacrificed my nation to preserve the peace of the world," he finally said, "I will be the first to applaud you. But if not, gentlemen, God help your souls!"[76]

And what of the conspirators, the generals and the civilians, General Halder and General von Witzleben, Schacht and Gisevius and Kordt, and the rest, who shortly before noon on that fateful day had believed, as Witzleben said, that their time had come? The answer can be given briefly in their own words—spoken much later when all was over and they were anxious to prove to the world how opposed they had been to Hitler and his catastrophic follies which had brought Germany to utter ruin after a long and murderous war.

Neville Chamberlain, they all claimed, was the villain! By agreeing to come to Munich he had forced them at the very last minute to call off their plans to overthrow Hitler and the Nazi regime!

On February 25, 1946, as the long Nuremberg trial neared its end, General Halder was interrogated privately by Captain Sam Harris, a young New York attorney on the staff of the American prosecution.

It had been planned [Halder said] to occupy by military force the Reich Chancellery and those government offices, particularly ministries, which were administered by party members and close supporters of Hitler, with the express intention of avoiding bloodshed and then trying the group before the whole German nation . . . On the day [September 28] Witzleben came to see me in my office during the noon hour. We discussed the matter. He requested that I give him the order of execution. We discussed other details—how much time he needed, etc. During this discussion, the news came that the British Prime Minister and the French Premier had agreed to come to Hitler for further talks. This happened in the presence of Witzleben. I therefore took back the order of execution because, owing to this fact, the entire basis for the action had been taken away . . .

We were firmly convinced that we would be successful. But now came Mr. Chamberlain and with one stroke the danger of war was averted . . . The critical hour for force was avoided . . . One could only wait in case a new chance should come . . .

"Do I understand you to say that if Chamberlain had not come to Munich, your plan would have been executed, and Hitler would have been deposed?" asked Captain Harris.

"I can only say the plan would have been executed," General Halder replied. "I do not know if it would have been successful."[77]

Dr. Schacht, who at Nuremberg and in his postwar books clearly exaggerated the importance of his role in the various conspiracies against Hitler, also blamed Chamberlain for the failure of the Germans to carry out the plot on September 28:

It is quite clear from the later course of history that this first attempt at a *coup d'etat* by Witzleben and myself was the only one which could have brought a real turning point in Germany's fate. It was the only attempt which was planned and prepared in good time . . . In the autumn of 1938 it was still possible to count on bringing Hitler to trial before the Supreme Court, but all subsequent efforts to get rid of him necessarily involved attempts on his life . . . I had made preparations for a *coup d'etat* in good time and I had brought them·to within an ace of success. History had decided against me. The intervention of foreign statesmen was something I could not possibly have taken into account.[78]

And Gisevius, who was Schacht's stoutest champion on the witness stand at Nuremberg, added:

The impossible had happened. Chamberlain and Daladier were flying to Munich. Our revolt was done for. For a few hours I went on imagining that we could revolt anyway. But Witzleben soon demonstrated to me that the troops would never revolt against the victorious Fuehrer . . . Chamberlain saved Hitler.[79]

Did he? Or was this merely an excuse of the German civilians and generals for their failure to act?

In his interrogation at Nuremberg Halder explained to Captain Harris that there were three conditions for a successful "revolutionary action":

The first condition is a clear and resolute leadership. The second condition is the readiness of the masses of the people to follow the idea of the revolution. The third condition is the right choice of time. According to our views, the first condition of a clear resolute leadership was there. The second condition we thought fulfilled too, because . . . the German people did not want war. Therefore the nation was ready to consent to a revolutionary act for fear of war. The third condition—the right choice of time—was good because we had to expect within forty-eight hours the order for carrying out a military action. Therefore we were firmly convinced that we would be successful.

But now came Mr. Chamberlain and with one stroke the danger of war was avoided.

One can doubt that General Halder's first condition was ever fulfilled, as he claimed. For had there been "clear and resolute leadership" why should the generals have hesitated for four days? They had on tap the military force to easily sweep Hitler and his regime aside: Witzleben had a whole army corps—the IIIrd—in and around Berlin, Brockdorff-Ahlefeldt had a crack infantry division in nearby Potsdam, Hoefner had a panzer division to the south, and the two ranking police officers in the capital, Count von Helldorf and Count von der Schulenburg, had a large force of well-armed police to help out. All of these officers, according to the plotters themselves, were but waiting for the word from Halder to spring into action with overwhelming armed force. And the population of Berlin, scared to death that Hitler was about to bring on a war, would have—so far as this writer could, at first hand, judge them—spontaneously backed the coup.

Whether Halder and Witzleben would have *finally* acted had Chamberlain not agreed to come to Munich is a question that can never be answered with any degree of finality. Given the peculiar attitude of these generals at this time which made them concerned with overthrowing Hitler not in order to bring an end to the tyranny and terror of his regime but merely to avert a lost war, it is possible that they might have acted had not the Munich Conference been arranged. The information necessary to establish how well the plot was hatched, how ready the armed forces were to march and how near Halder and Witzleben really came to giving the order to act has so far been lacking. We have only the statements of a handful of participants who after the war were anxious to prove their opposition to National Socialism, and what they have said and written in self-defense is often conflicting and confusing.*

If, as the conspirators claim, their plans were on the point of being carried out, the announcement of Chamberlain's trip to Munich certainly cut the ground from underneath their feet. The generals could scarcely have arrested Hitler and tried him as a war criminal when it was obvious that he was about to achieve an important conquest without war.

What is certain among all these uncertainties—and here Dr. Schacht must be conceded his point—is that such a golden opportunity never again presented itself to the German opposition to dispose of Hitler, bring a swift end to the Third Reich and save Germany and the world from war. The Germans, if one may risk a generalization, have a weakness for blaming foreigners for their failures. The responsibility of Chamberlain and Halifax, of Daladier and Bonnet, for Munich and thus for all the disastrous consequences which ensued is overwhelming. But they may be pardoned

---

* For example, the explanation for the failure of the revolt given by General Georg Thomas, the brilliant chief of the Economic and Armaments Branch of OKW, and one of the conspirators: "The execution of this enterprise was unfortunately frustrated because, according to the view of the commanding general appointed for the task [Witzleben], the younger officers were found to be unreliable for a political action of this kind." See his paper, "Gedanken und Ereignisse," published in the December 1945 number of the *Schweizerische Monatshefte*.

to some extent for not taking very seriously the warnings of a "revolt" of a group of German generals and civilians most of whom had served Hitler with great ability up to this moment. They, or at least some of their advisers in London and Paris, may have recalled the bleak facts of recent German history: that the Army had helped put the former Austrian corporal into power, had been delighted at the opportunities he gave it to rearm, had apparently not objected to the destruction of individual freedom under National Socialism or done anything about the murder of its own General von Schleicher or the removal, on a dastardly frame-up, of its commanding officer, General von Fritsch; and—recently—had gone along with the rape of Austria, indeed had supplied the military force to carry it out. Whatever blame may be heaped on the archappeasers in London and Paris, and great it undoubtedly is, the fact remains that the German generals themselves, and their civilian coconspirators, failed at an opportune moment to act on their own.

THE SURRENDER AT MUNICH: SEPTEMBER 29–30, 1938

In this baroque Bavarian city where in the murky back rooms of rundown little cafés he had made his lowly start as a politician and in whose streets he had suffered the fiasco of the Beer Hall Putsch, Adolf Hitler greeted, like a conqueror, the heads of governments of Great Britain, France and Italy at half past noon on September 29.

Very early that morning he had gone to Kufstein on the former Austro–German frontier to meet Mussolini and set up a basis for common action at the conference. In the train coming up to Munich Hitler was in a bellicose mood, explaining to the Duce over maps how he intended to "liquidate" Czechoslovakia. Either the talks beginning that day must be immediately successful, he said, or he would resort to arms. "Besides," Ciano, who was present, quotes the Fuehrer as adding, "the time will come when we shall have to fight side by side against France and England." Mussolini agreed.[80]

Chamberlain made no similar effort to see Daladier beforehand to work out a joint strategy for the two Western democracies with which to confront the two fascist dictators. Indeed, it became evident to many of us in contact with the British and French delegations in Munich as the day progressed that Chamberlain had come to Munich absolutely determined that no one, certainly not the Czechs and not even the French, should stand in the way of his reaching a quick agreement with Hitler.* In the case of Daladier, who went around all day as if in a daze, no precaution was necessary, but the determined Prime Minister took no risks.

---

* At 6:45 the evening before, Chamberlain had sent a message to President Beneš informing him officially of the meeting at Munich. "I shall have the interests of Czechoslovakia," he stated, "fully in mind . . . I go there [to Munich] with the intention of trying to find accommodation between the positions of the German and Czechoslovak governments." Beneš had immediately replied, "I beg that nothing may be done at Munich without Czechoslovakia being heard."[81]

The talks, which began at 12:45 P.M. in the so-called Fuehrerhaus in the Koenigsplatz, were anticlimactic and constituted little more than a mere formality of rendering to Hitler exactly what he wanted when he wanted it. Dr. Schmidt, the indomitable interpreter, who was called upon to function in three languages, German, French and English, noticed from the beginning "an atmosphere of general good will." Ambassador Henderson later remembered that "at no stage of the conversations did they become heated." No one presided. The proceedings unfolded informally, and judging by the German minutes of the meeting[82] which came to light after the war, the British Prime Minister and the French Premier fairly fell over themselves to agree with Hitler. Even when he made the following opening statement:

He had now declared in his speech at the Sportpalast that he would in any case march in on October 1. He had received the answer that this action would have the character of an act of violence. Hence the task arose to absolve this action from such a character. Action must, however, be taken at once.

The conferees got down to business when Mussolini, speaking third in turn—Daladier was left to the last—said that "in order to bring about a practical solution of the problem" he had brought with him a definite written proposal. Its origins are interesting and remained unknown to Chamberlain, I believe, to his death. From the memoirs of François-Poncet and Henderson it is obvious that they too were ignorant of them. In fact, the story only became known long after the violent deaths of the two dictators.

What the Duce now fobbed off as his own compromise plan had been hastily drafted the day before in the German Foreign Office in Berlin by Goering, Neurath and Weizsaecker behind the back of Foreign Minister von Ribbentrop, whose judgment the three men did not trust. Goering took it to Hitler, who said it might do, and then it was hurriedly translated into French by Dr. Schmidt and passed along to the Italian ambassador, Attolico, who telephoned the text of it to the Italian dictator in Rome just before he entrained for Munich. Thus it was that the "Italian proposals," which provided the informal conference not only with its sole agenda but with the basic terms which eventually became the Munich Agreement, were in fact German proposals concocted in Berlin.*

This must have seemed fairly obvious from the text, which closely fol-

---

* Erich Kordt recounted the German origins of Mussolini's proposals in his testimony before U.S. Military Tribunal IV at Nuremberg on June 4, 1948, in the case of *U.S.A.* v. *Ernst Weizsaecker. Documents on German Foreign Policy,* II, p. 1005, gives a summary from the official trial transcript. Kordt also tells the story in his book *Wahn und Wirklichkeit,* pp. 129–31. Dr. Schmidt (*Hitler's Interpreter,* p. 111) substantiates Kordt's account and remarks that translating the Duce's proposals "was easy" because he had already translated them the day before in Berlin. Ciano, the Italian Foreign Minister, in a diary entry of September 29–30 from Munich, tells of Mussolini producing his document "which in fact had been telephoned to us by our Embassy the previous evening, as expressing the desires of the German Government." (*Ciano's Hidden Diary, 1937–38,* p. 167.)

lowed Hitler's rejected Godesberg demands; but it was not obvious to Daladier and Chamberlain or to their ambassadors in Berlin, who now attended them. The Premier, according to the German minutes, "welcomed the Duce's proposal, which had been made in an objective and realistic spirit," and the Prime Minister "also welcomed the Duce's proposal and declared that he himself had conceived of a solution on the lines of this proposal." As for Ambassador Henderson, as he later wrote, he thought Mussolini "had tactfully put forward as his own a combination of Hitler's and the Anglo–French proposals"; while Ambassador François-Poncet got the impression that the conferees were working on a British memorandum "drawn up by Horace Wilson."[83] So easily were the British and French statesmen and diplomats, bent on appeasement at any cost, deceived!

With the "Italian" proposals so warmly welcomed by all present, there remained but a few details to iron out. Chamberlain, as perhaps might have been expected from an ex-businessman and former Chancellor of the Exchequer, wanted to know who would compensate the Czech government for the public property which would pass to Germany in the Sudetenland. Hitler, who, according to François-Poncet, appeared somewhat pale and worried, and annoyed because he could not follow, as Mussolini could, the talk in French and English, replied heatedly there would be no compensation. When the Prime Minister objected to the stipulation that the Czechs moving out of the Sudetenland could not even take their cattle (this had been one of the Godesberg demands)—exclaiming, "Does this mean that the farmers will be expelled but that their cattle will be retained?"—Hitler exploded.

"Our time is too valuable to be wasted on such trivialities!" he shouted at Chamberlain.[84] The Prime Minister dropped the matter.

He did insist at first that a Czech representative ought to be present, or at least, as he put it, be "available." His country, he said, "could naturally undertake no guarantee that the [Sudeten] territory would be evacuated by October 10 [as Mussolini had proposed] if no assurance of this was forthcoming from the Czech government." Daladier gave him lukewarm support. The French government, he said, "would in no wise tolerate procrastination in this matter by the Czech government," but he thought "the presence of a Czech representative, who could be consulted, if necessary, would be an advantage."

But Hitler was adamant. He would permit no Czechs in his presence. Daladier meekly gave in, but Chamberlain finally won a small concession. It was agreed that a Czech representative might make himself available "in the next room," as the Prime Minister proposed.

And indeed during the afternoon session two Czech representatives, Dr. Vojtech Mastny, the Czech minister in Berlin, and Dr. Hubert Masarik, from the Prague Foreign Office, did arrive and were coolly ushered into an adjoining room. There, after they had been left from 2 P.M. to 7 to cool their heels, the roof figuratively fell in on them. At the latter hour Frank Ashton-Gwatkin, who had been a member of the Runciman mission and was now on Chamberlain's staff, came to break the bad news to them. A general agreement had been reached, the details of which he could not yet give to them; but it was much "harsher" than the Franco–British proposals. When Masarik asked if the Czechs couldn't be heard, the Englishman answered, as the Czech representative later reported to his government, "that I seemed to ignore how difficult was the situation of the Great Powers, and that I could not understand how hard it had been to negotiate with Hitler."

At 10 P.M. the two unhappy Czechs were taken to Sir Horace Wilson, the Prime Minister's faithful adviser. On behalf of Chamberlain, Wilson informed them of the main points in the four-power agreement and handed them a map of the Sudeten areas which were to be evacuated by the Czechs at once. When the two envoys attempted to protest, the British official cut them short. He had nothing more to say, he stated, and promptly left the room. The Czechs continued to protest to Ashton-Gwatkin, who had remained with them, but to no avail.

"If you do not accept," he admonished them, as he prepared to go, "you will have to settle your affairs with the Germans absolutely alone. Perhaps the French may tell you this more gently, but you can believe me that they share our views. They are disinterested."

This was the truth, wretched though it must have sounded to the two Czech emissaries. Shortly after 1 A.M. on September 30* Hitler, Chamberlain, Mussolini and Daladier, in that order, affixed their signatures to the Munich Agreement providing for the German Army to begin its march into Czechoslovakia on October 1, as the Fuehrer had always said it would, and to complete the occupation of the Sudetenland by October 10. Hitler had got what had been refused him at Godesberg.

There remained the painful matter—painful at least to the victims—

---

* The agreement was dated September 29, though not actually signed until the early-morning hours of September 30. It stipulated that the German occupation "of the predominantly German territory" should be carried out by German troops in four stages, from October 1 through October 7. The remaining territory, after being delimited by the "International Commission," would be occupied "by October 10." The commission was to consist of representatives of the four Big Powers and Czechoslovakia. Britain, France and Italy agreed "that the evacuation of the territory shall be completed by October 10, without any existing installations having been destroyed, and that the Czechoslovak Government will be held responsible for carrying out the evacuation without damage to the said installations."

Further, the "International Commission" would arrange for plebiscites, "not later than the end of November," in the regions where the ethnographical character was in doubt and would make the final determination of the new frontiers. In an annex to the accord, Britain and France declared that "they stand by their offer . . . relating to an international guarantee of the new boundaries of the Czechoslovak State against unprovoked aggression. When the question of the Polish and Hungarian minorities . . . has been settled, Germany and Italy, for their part, will give a guarantee to Czechoslovakia."[85]

The pledge of plebiscites was never carried out. Neither Germany nor Italy ever gave the guarantee to Czechoslovakia against aggression, even after the matter of the Polish and Hungarian minorities was settled, and, as we shall see, Britain and France declined to honor their guarantee.

of informing the Czechs of what they had to give up and how soon. Hitler and Mussolini were not interested in this part of the ceremony and withdrew, leaving the task to the representatives of Czechoslovakia's ally, France, and of Great Britain. The scene was vividly described by Masarik, in his official report to the Czech Foreign Office.

At 1:30 A.M. we were taken into the hall where the conference had been held. There were present Mr. Chamberlain, M. Daladier, Sir Horace Wilson, M. Léger [secretary general of the French Foreign Office], Mr. Ashton-Gwatkin, Dr. Mastny and myself. The atmosphere was oppressive; sentence was about to be passed. The French, obviously nervous, seemed anxious to preserve French prestige before the court. Mr. Chamberlain, in a long introductory speech, referred to the Agreement and gave the text to Dr. Mastny . . .

The Czechs began to ask several questions, but

Mr. Chamberlain was yawning continuously, without making any effort to conceal his yawns. I asked MM. Daladier and Léger whether they expected a declaration or answer of our Government to the Agreement. M. Daladier was noticeably nervous. M. Léger replied that the four statesmen had not much time. He added hurriedly and with superficial casualness that no answer was required from us, that they regarded the plan as accepted, that our Government had that very day, at the latest at 3 P.M., to send its representative to Berlin to the sitting of the Commission, and finally that the Czechoslovak officer who was to be sent would have to be in Berlin on Saturday in order to fix the details for the evacuation of the first zone. The atmosphere, he said, was beginning to become dangerous for the whole world.

He spoke to us harshly enough. This was a Frenchman . . . Mr. Chamberlain did not conceal his weariness. They gave us a second slightly corrected map. Then they finished with us, and we could go.[86]

I remember from that fateful night the light of victory in Hitler's eyes as he strutted down the broad steps of the Fuehrerhaus after the meeting, the cockiness of Mussolini, laced in his special militia uniform, the yawns of Chamberlain and his air of pleasant sleepiness as he returned to the Regina Palace Hotel.

Daladier [I wrote in my diary that night], on the other hand, looked a completely beaten and broken man. He came over to the Regina to say good-bye to Chamberlain. . . . Someone asked, or started to ask: "Monsieur le Président, are you satisfied with the agreement?" He turned as if to say something, but he was too tired and defeated and the words did not come out and he stumbled out the door in silence.[87]

Chamberlain was not through conferring with Hitler about the peace of the world. Early the next morning, September 30, refreshed by a few hours of sleep and pleased with his labors of the previous day, he sought out the Fuehrer at his private apartment in Munich to discuss further the state of Europe and to secure a small concession which he apparently thought would improve his political position at home.

According to Dr. Schmidt, who acted as interpreter and who was the sole witness of this unexpected meeting, Hitler was pale and moody. He listened absent-mindedly as the exuberant head of the British government expressed his confidence that Germany would "adopt a generous attitude in the implementation of the Munich Agreement" and renewed his hope that the Czechs would not be "so unreasonable as to make difficulties" and that, if they did make them, Hitler would not bomb Prague "with the dreadful losses among the civilian population which it would entail." This was only the beginning of a long and rambling discourse which would seem incredible coming from a British Prime Minister, even one who had made so abject a surrender to the German dictator the night before, had it not been recorded by Dr. Schmidt in an official Foreign Office memorandum. Even today, when one reads this captured document, it seems difficult to believe.

But the British leader's opening remarks were only the prelude to what was to come. After what must have seemed to the morose German dictator an interminable exposition by Chamberlain in proposing further cooperation in bringing an end to the Spanish Civil War (which German and Italian "volunteers" were winning for Franco), in furthering disarmament, world economic prosperity, political peace in Europe and even a solution of the Russian problem, the Prime Minister drew out of his pocket a sheet of paper on which he had written something which he hoped they would both sign and release for immediate publication.

We, the German Fuehrer and Chancellor, and the British Prime Minister [it read], have had a further meeting today and are agreed in recognizing that the question of Anglo–German relations is of the first importance for the two countries and for Europe.

We regard the agreement signed last night and the Anglo–German Naval Agreement as symbolic of the desire of our two peoples never to go to war with one another again.

We are resolved that the method of consultation shall be the method adopted to deal with any other questions that may concern our two countries, and we are determined to continue our efforts to remove possible sources of difference, and thus to contribute to assure the peace of Europe.

Hitler read the declaration and quickly signed it, much to Chamberlain's satisfaction, as Dr. Schmidt noted in his official report. The interpreter's impression was that the Fuehrer agreed to it "with a certain reluctance . . . only to please Chamberlain," who, he recounts further, "thanked the Fuehrer warmly . . . and underlined the great psychological effect which he expected from this document."

The deluded British Prime Minister did not know, of course, that, as the secret German and Italian documents would reveal much later, Hitler

and Mussolini had already agreed at this very meeting in Munich that in
time they would have to fight "side by side" against Great Britain. Nor,
as we shall shortly see, did he divine much else that already was fermenting
in Hitler's lugubrious mind.[88]

Chamberlain returned to London—as did Daladier to Paris—in triumph. Brandishing the declaration which he had signed with Hitler, the
jubilant Prime Minister faced a large crowd that pressed into Downing
Street. After listening to shouts of "Good old Neville!" and a lusty singing of "For He's a Jolly Good Fellow," Chamberlain smilingly spoke a few
words from a second-story window in Number 10.

"My good friends," he said, "this is the second time in our history that
there has come back from Germany to Downing Street peace with honor.*
I believe it is peace in our time."

The *Times* declared that "no conqueror returning from a victory on the
battlefield has come adorned with nobler laurels." There was a spontaneous movement to raise a "National Fund of Thanksgiving" in Chamberlain's honor, which he graciously turned down. Only Duff Cooper, the
First Lord of the Admiralty, resigned from the cabinet, and when in the
ensuing Commons debate Winston Churchill, still a voice in the wilderness, began to utter his memorable words, "We have sustained a total,
unmitigated defeat," he was forced to pause, as he later recorded, until
the storm of protest against such a remark had subsided.

The mood in Prague was naturally quite different. At 6:20 A.M. on
September 30, the German chargé d'affaires had routed the Czech Foreign Minister, Dr. Krofta, out of bed and handed him the text of the
Munich Agreement together with a request that Czechoslovakia send two
representatives to the first meeting of the "International Commission,"
which was to supervise the execution of the accord, at 5 P.M. in Berlin.

For President Beneš, who conferred all morning at the Hradschin Palace with the political and military leaders, there was no alternative but to
submit. Britain and France had not only deserted his country but would
now back Hitler in the use of armed force should he turn down the terms
of Munich. At ten minutes to one, Czechoslovakia surrendered, "under
protest to the world," as the official statement put it. "We were abandoned. We stand alone," General Sirovy, the new Premier, explained bitterly in a broadcast to the Czechoslovak people at 5 P.M.

To the very last Britain and France maintained their pressure on the
country they had seduced and betrayed. During the day the British,
French and Italian ministers went to see Dr. Krofta to make sure that
there was no last-minute revolt of the Czechs against the surrender. The
German chargé, Dr. Hencke, in a dispatch to Berlin described the scene.

The French Minister's attempt to address words of condolence to Krofta was
cut short by the Foreign Minister's remark: "We have been forced into this

---

* The reference is to Disraeli's return from the Congress of Berlin in 1878.

situation; now everything is at an end; today it is our turn, tomorrow it will be the turn of others." The British Minister succeeded with difficulty in saying that Chamberlain had done his utmost; he received the same answer as the French Minister. The Foreign Minister was a completely broken man and intimated only one wish: that the three Ministers should quickly leave the room.[89]

President Beneš resigned on October 5 on the insistence of Berlin and, when it became evident that his life was in danger, flew to England and exile. He was replaced provisionally by General Sirovy. On November 30, Dr. Emil Hácha, the Chief Justice of the Supreme Court, a well-intentioned but weak and senile man of sixty-six, was selected by the National Assembly to be President of what remained of Czecho-Slovakia, which was now officially spelled with a hyphen.

What Chamberlain and Daladier at Munich had neglected to give Germany in Czechoslovakia the so-called "International Commission" proceeded to hand over. This hastily formed body consisted of the Italian, British and French ambassadors and the Czech minister in Berlin and Baron von Weizsaecker, the State Secretary in the German Foreign Office. Every dispute over additional territory for the Germans was settled in their favor, more than once under the threat from Hitler and OKW to resort to armed force. Finally, on October 13, the commission voted to dispense with the plebiscites which the Munich Agreement had called for in the disputed regions. There was no need for them.

The Poles and the Hungarians, after threatening military action against the helpless nation, now swept down, like vultures, to get a slice of Czechoslovak territory. Poland, at the insistence of Foreign Minister Józef Beck, who for the next twelve months will be a leading character in this narrative, took some 650 square miles of territory around Teschen, comprising a population of 228,000 inhabitants, of whom 133,000 were Czechs. Hungary got a larger slice in the award meted out on November 2 by Ribbentrop and Ciano: 7,500 square miles, with a population of 500,000 Magyars and 272,000 Slovaks.

Moreover, the truncated and now defenseless country was forced by Berlin to install a pro-German government of obvious fascist tendencies. It was clear that from now on the Czechoslovak nation existed at the mercy of the Leader of the Third Reich.

THE CONSEQUENCES OF MUNICH

Under the terms of the Munich Agreement Hitler got substantially what he had demanded at Godesberg, and the "International Commission," bowing to his threats, gave him considerably more. The final settlement of November 20, 1938, forced Czechoslovakia to cede to Germany 11,000 square miles of territory in which dwelt 2,800,000 Sudeten Germans and 800,000 Czechs. Within this area lay all the vast Czech fortifications which hitherto had formed the most formidable defensive line in Europe, with the possible exception of the Maginot Line in France.

But that was not all. Czechoslovakia's entire system of rail, road, telephone and telegraph communications was disrupted. According to German figures, the dismembered country lost 66 per cent of its coal, 80 per cent of its lignite, 86 per cent of its chemicals, 80 per cent of its cement, 80 per cent of its textiles, 70 per cent of its iron and steel, 70 per cent of its electric power and 40 per cent of its timber. A prosperous industrial nation was split up and bankrupted overnight.

No wonder that Jodl could write joyfully in his diary on the night of Munich:

The Pact of Munich is signed. Czechoslovakia as a power is out . . . The genius of the Fuehrer and his determination not to shun even a World War have again won the victory without the use of force. The hope remains that the incredulous, the weak and the doubtful people have been converted, and will remain that way.[90]

Many of the doubtful were converted and the few who were not were plunged into despair. The generals such as Beck, Halder and Witzleben and their civilian advisers had again been proved wrong. Hitler had got what he wanted, had achieved another great conquest, without firing a shot. His prestige soared to new heights. No one who was in Germany in the days after Munich, as this writer was, can forget the rapture of the German people. They were relieved that war had been averted; they were elated and swollen with pride at Hitler's bloodless victory, not only over Czechoslovakia but over Great Britain and France. Within the short space of six months, they reminded you, Hitler had conquered Austria and the Sudetenland, adding ten million inhabitants to the Third Reich and a vast strategic territory which opened the way for German domination of southeastern Europe. And without the loss of a single German life! With the instinct of a genius rare in German history he had divined not only the weaknesses of the smaller states in Central Europe but those of the two principal Western democracies, Britain and France, and forced them to bend to his will. He had invented and used with staggering success a new strategy and technique of *political warfare,* which made actual war unnecessary.

In scarcely four and a half years this man of lowly origins had catapulted a disarmed, chaotic, nearly bankrupt Germany, the weakest of the big powers in Europe, to a position where she was regarded as the mightiest nation of the Old World, before which all the others, Britain even and France, trembled. At no step in this dizzy ascent had the victorious powers of Versailles dared to try to stop her, even when they had the power to do so. Indeed at Munich, which registered the greatest conquest of all, Britain and France had gone out of their way to support her. And what must have amazed Hitler most of all—it certainly astounded General

Beck, Hassell and others in their small circle of opposition—was that none of the men who dominated the governments of Britain and France ("little worms," as the Fuehrer contemptuously spoke of them in private after Munich) realized the consequences of their inability to react with any force to one after the other of the Nazi leader's aggressive moves.

Winston Churchill, in England, alone seemed to understand. No one stated the consequences of Munich more succinctly than he in his speech to the Commons of October 5:

> We have sustained a total and unmitigated defeat . . . We are in the midst of a disaster of the first magnitude. The road down the Danube . . . the road to the Black Sea has been opened . . . All the countries of Mittel Europa and the Danube valley, one after another, will be drawn in the vast system of Nazi politics . . . radiating from Berlin . . . And do not suppose that this is the end. It is only the beginning . . .

But Churchill was not in the government and his words went unheeded.

Was the Franco–British surrender at Munich necessary? Was Adolf Hitler not bluffing?

The answer, paradoxically, to both questions, we now know, is No. All the generals close to Hitler who survived the war agree that had it not been for Munich Hitler would have attacked Czechoslovakia on October 1, 1938, and they presume that, whatever momentary hesitations there might have been in London, Paris and Moscow, in the end Britain, France and Russia would have been drawn into the war.

And—what is most important to this history at this point—the German generals agree unanimously that Germany would have lost the war, and in short order. The argument of the supporters of Chamberlain and Daladier—and they were in the great majority at the time—that Munich saved the West not only from war but from defeat in war and, incidentally, preserved London and Paris from being wiped out by the Luftwaffe's murderous bombing has been impressively refuted, so far as concern the last two points, by those in a position to know best: the German generals, and especially those generals who were closest to Hitler and who supported him from beginning to end the most fanatically.

The leading light among the latter was General Keitel, chief of OKW, toady to Hitler and constantly at his side. When asked on the stand at the Nuremberg trial what the reaction of the German generals was to Munich he replied:

> We were extraordinarily happy that it had not come to a military operation because . . . we had always been of the opinion that our means of attack against the frontier fortifications of Czechoslovakia were insufficient. From a purely military point of view we lacked the means for an attack which involved the piercing of the frontier fortifications.[91]

It has always been assumed by Allied military experts that the German Army would have romped through Czechoslovakia. But to the testimony of Keitel that this would not have been the case must be added that of Field Marshal von Manstein, who became one of the most brilliant of the German field commanders. When he, in his turn, testified at Nuremberg (unlike Keitel and Jodl, he was not on trial for his life) on the German position at the time of Munich, he explained:

If a war had broken out, neither our western border nor our Polish frontier could really have been effectively defended by us, and there is no doubt whatsoever that had Czechoslovakia defended herself, we would have been held up by her fortifications, for we did not have the means to break through.[92]*

Jodl, the "brains" of OKW, put it this way when he took the stand in his own defense at Nuremberg:

It was out of the question, with five fighting divisions and seven reserve divisions in the western fortifications, which were nothing but a large construction site, to hold out against 100 French divisions. That was militarily impossible.[93]

If, as these German generals concede, Hitler's army lacked the means of penetrating the Czech fortifications, and Germany, in the face of France's overwhelming strength in the west, was in a "militarily impossible" situation, and further, since, as we have seen, there was such grave dissension among the generals that the Chief of the Army General Staff was prepared to overthrow the Fuehrer in order to avert a hopeless war— why, then, did not the French and British general staffs know this? Or did they? And if they did, how could the heads of government of Britain and France be forced at Munich into sacrificing so much of their nations' vital interests? In seeking answers to such questions we confront one of the mysteries of the Munich time which has not yet been cleared up. Even Churchill, concerned as he is with military affairs, scarcely touches on it in his massive memoirs.

It is inconceivable that the British and French general staffs and the two governments did not know of the opposition of the German Army General Staff to a European war. For, as already noted here, the conspirators in Berlin warned the British of this through at least four channels in August and September and, as we know, the matter came to the attention of

---

* Even Hitler became at least partly convinced of this after he had inspected the Czech fortress line. He later told Dr. Carl Burckhardt, League of Nations High Commissioner of Danzig, "When after Munich we were in a position to examine Czechoslovak military strength from within, what we saw of it greatly disturbed us; we had run a serious danger. The plan prepared by the Czech generals was formidable. I now understand why my generals urged restraint." (Pertinax, *The Grave Diggers of France*, p. 5.)

Chamberlain himself. By early September Paris and London must have learned of the resignation of General Beck and of the obvious consequences to the German Army of the rebellion of its most eminent and gifted leader.

It was generally conceded in Berlin at this time that British and French military intelligence was fairly good. It is extremely difficult to believe that the military chiefs in London and Paris did not know of the obvious weaknesses of the German Army and Air Force and of their inability to fight a two-front war. What doubts could the Chief of Staff of the French Army, General Gamelin, have—despite his inbred caution, which was monumental—that with nearly one hundred divisions he could overwhelm the five regular and seven reserve German divisions in the west and sweep easily and swiftly deep into Germany?

On the whole, as he later recounted,[94] Gamelin had few doubts. On September 12, the day on which Hitler was thundering his threats against Czechoslovakia at the closing session of the Nuremberg rally, the French generalissimo had assured Premier Daladier that if war came "the democratic nations would dictate the peace." He says he backed it up with a letter expressing the reasons for his optimism. On September 26, at the height of the Czech crisis following the Godesberg meeting, Gamelin, who had accompanied the French government leaders to London, repeated his assurances to Chamberlain and tried to substantiate them with an analysis of the military situation calculated to buck up not only the British Prime Minister but his own wavering Premier. In this attempt, apparently, he failed. Finally, just before Daladier flew to Munich, Gamelin outlined to him the limits of territorial concessions in the Sudetenland which could be made without endangering French security. The main Czech fortifications, as well as the rail trunk lines, certain strategic branch lines and the principal defense industries must not be given to Germany. Above all, he added, the Germans must not be permitted to cut off the Moravian Gap. Good advice, if Czechoslovakia was to be of any use to France in a war with Germany, but, as we have seen, Daladier was not the man to act on it.

A good deal was said at the time of Munich that one reason for Chamberlain's surrender was his fear that London would be obliterated by German bombing, and there is no doubt that the French were jittery at the awful prospect of their beautiful capital being destroyed from the air. But from what is now known of the Luftwaffe's strength at this moment, the Londoners and the Parisians, as well as the Prime Minister and the Premier, were unduly alarmed. The German Air Force, like the Army, was concentrated against Czechoslovakia and therefore, like the Army, was incapable of serious action in the West. Even if a few German bombers could have been spared to attack London and Paris it is highly doubtful that they would have reached their targets. Weak as the British and French fighter defenses were, the Germans could not have given their bombers fighter protection, if they had had the planes. Their fighter bases were too far away.

It has also been argued—most positively by Ambassadors François-

Poncet and Henderson—that Munich gave the two Western democracies nearly a year to catch up with the Germans in rearmament. The facts belie such an argument. As Churchill, backed up by every serious Allied military historian, has written, "The year's breathing space said to be 'gained' by Munich left Britain and France in a much worse position compared to Hitler's Germany than they had been at the Munich crisis."[95] As we shall see, all the German military calculations a year later bear this out, and subsequent events, of course, remove any doubts whatsoever.

In retrospect, and with the knowledge we now have from the secret German documents and from the postwar testimony of the Germans themselves, the following summing up, which was impossible to make in the days of Munich, may be given:

Germany was in no position to go to war on October 1, 1938, against Czechoslovakia *and* France and Britain, not to mention Russia. Had she done so, she would have been quickly and easily defeated, and that would have been the end of Hitler and the Third Reich. If a European war had been averted at the last moment by the intercession of the German Army, Hitler might have been overthrown by Halder and Witzleben and their confederates carrying out their plan to arrest him as soon as he had given the final order for the attack on Czechoslovakia.

By publicly boasting that he would march into the Sudetenland by October 1 "in any case," Hitler had put himself far out on a limb. He was in the "untenable position" which General Beck had foreseen. Had he, after all his categorical threats and declarations, tried to crawl back from the limb on his own, he scarcely could have survived for long, dictatorships being what they are and his dictatorship, in particular, being what it was. It would have been extremely difficult, if not impossible, for him to have backed down, and had he tried to do so his loss of prestige in Europe, among his own people and, above all, with his generals would, most likely, have proved fatal.

Chamberlain's stubborn, fanatical insistence on giving Hitler what he wanted, his trips to Berchtesgaden and Godesberg and finally the fateful journey to Munich rescued Hitler from his limb and strengthened his position in Europe, in Germany, in the Army, beyond anything that could have been imagined a few weeks before. It also added immeasurably to the power of the Third Reich vis-à-vis the Western democracies and the Soviet Union.

For France, Munich was a disaster, and it is beyond understanding that this was not fully realized in Paris. Her military position in Europe was destroyed. Because her Army, when the Reich was fully mobilized, could never be much more than half the size of that of Germany, which had nearly twice her population, and because her ability to produce arms was also less, France had laboriously built up her alliances with the smaller powers in the East on the other flank of Germany—and of Italy: Czechoslovakia, Poland, Yugoslavia and Rumania, which, together, had the military potential of a Big Power. The loss now of thirty-five well-trained, well-armed Czech divisions, deployed behind their strong mountain fortifications and holding down an even larger German force, was a crippling one to the French Army. But that was not all. After Munich how could France's remaining allies in Eastern Europe have any confidence in her written word? What value now were alliances with France? The answer in Warsaw, Bucharest and Belgrade was: Not much; and there was a scramble in these capitals to make the best deal possible, while there was still time, with the Nazi conqueror.

And if not a scramble, there was a stir in Moscow. Though the Soviet Union was militarily allied to both Czechoslovakia and France, the French government had gone along with Germany and Britain, without protest, in excluding Russia from Munich. It was a snub which Stalin did not forget and which was to cost the two Western democracies dearly in the months to come. On October 3, four days after Munich, the counselor of the German Embassy in Moscow, Werner von Tippelskirch, reported to Berlin on the "consequences" of Munich for Soviet policy. He thought Stalin "would draw conclusions"; he was certain the Soviet Union would "reconsider her foreign policy," become less friendly to her ally France and "more positive" toward Germany. As a matter of fact, the German diplomat thought that "the present circumstances offer favorable opportunities for a new and wider German economic agreement with the Soviet Union."[96] This is the first mention in the secret German archives of a change in the wind that now began to stir, however faintly, over Berlin and Moscow and which, within a year, would have momentous consequences.

Despite his staggering victory and the humiliation he administered not only to Czechoslovakia but to the Western democracies, Hitler was disappointed with the results of Munich. "That fellow [Chamberlain]," Schacht heard him exclaim to his S.S. entourage on his return to Berlin, "has spoiled my entry into Prague!"[97] That was what he really had wanted all along, as he had constantly confided to his generals since his lecture to them on November 5 of the previous year. The conquest of Austria and Czechoslovakia, he had explained then, was to be but the preliminary for a major drive for *Lebensraum* in the East and a military settlement with France in the West. As he had told the Hungarian Prime Minister on September 20, the best thing was "to destroy Czechoslovakia." This, he had said, would "provide the only satisfactory solution." He was only afraid of the "danger" that the Czechs might submit to all of his demands.*

Now Mr. Chamberlain, grasping his much-publicized umbrella, had come to Munich and forced the Czechs to submit to all his demands and thereby had deprived him of his military conquest. Such, it is evident from the record, were Hitler's tortuous thoughts after Munich. "It was clear to me from the first moment," he later confided to his generals, "that I could not be satisfied with the Sudeten-German territory. That was only a partial solution."[98]

A few days after Munich the German dictator set in motion plans to achieve a total solution.

---

* See above, p. 388.

13

CZECHOSLOVAKIA CEASES TO EXIST

WITHIN TEN DAYS of affixing his signature to the Munich Agreement—
before even the peaceful military occupation of the Sudetenland had
been completed—Adolf Hitler got off an urgent top-secret message to
General Keitel, Chief of OKW.

1. What reinforcements are necessary in the present situation to break all
Czech resistance in Bohemia and Moravia?
2. How much time is required for the regrouping or moving up of new
forces?
3. How much time will be required for the same purpose if it is executed
after the intended demobilization and return measures?
4. How much time would be required to achieve the state of readiness of
October 1?[1]

Keitel shot back to the Fuehrer on October 11 a telegram giving detailed
answers. Not much time and not very many reinforcements would be
necessary. There were already twenty-four divisions, including three
armored and four motorized, in the Sudeten area. "OKW believes,"
Keitel stated, "that it would be possible to commence operations without
reinforcements, in view of the present signs of weakness in Czech
resistance."[2]

Thus assured, Hitler communicated his thoughts to his military chiefs
ten days later.

TOP SECRET   Berlin, October 21, 1938

The future tasks for the armed forces and the preparations for the conduct
of war resulting from these tasks will be laid down by me in a later directive.

Until this directive comes into force the armed forces must be prepared at
all times for the following eventualities:

1. The securing of the frontiers of Germany.
2. The liquidation of the remainder of Czechoslovakia.
3. The occupation of the Memel district.

Memel, a Baltic port of some forty thousand inhabitants, had been lost by Germany to Lithuania after Versailles. Since Lithuania was smaller and weaker than Austria and Czechoslovakia, the seizure of the town presented no problem to the Wehrmacht and in this directive Hitler merely mentioned that it would be "annexed." As for Czechoslovakia:

> It must be possible to smash at any time the remainder of Czechoslovakia if her policy should become hostile toward Germany.
>
> The preparations to be made by the armed forces for this contingency will be considerably smaller in extent than those for "Green"; they must, however, guarantee a considerably higher state of preparedness since planned mobilization measures have been dispensed with. The organization, order of battle and state of readiness of the units earmarked for that purpose are in peacetime to be so arranged for a surprise assault that Czechoslovakia herself will be deprived of all possibility of organized resistance. The object is the swift occupation of Bohemia and Moravia and the cutting off of Slovakia.[3]

Slovakia, of course, could be cut off by political means, which might make the use of German troops unnecessary. For this purpose the German Foreign Office was put to work. All through the first days of October, Ribbentrop and his aides urged the Hungarians to press for their share of the spoils in Slovakia. But when Hungary, which hardly needed German prodding to whet its greedy appetite, spoke of taking Slovakia outright, the Wilhelmstrasse put its foot down. It had other plans for the future of this land. The Prague government had already, immediately after Munich, granted Slovakia a far-reaching autonomy. The German Foreign Office advised "tolerating" this solution for the moment. But for the future the German thinking was summed up by Dr. Ernst Woermann, director of the Political Department of the Foreign Office, in a memorandum of October 7. "An independent Slovakia," he wrote, "would be weak constitutionally and would therefore best further the German need for penetration and settlement in the East."[4]

Here is a new turning point for the Third Reich. For the first time Hitler is on the verge of setting out to conquer non-Germanic lands. Over the last six weeks he had been assuring Chamberlain, in private and in public, that the Sudetenland was his last territorial demand in Europe. And though the British Prime Minister was gullible almost beyond comprehension in accepting Hitler's word, there was some ground for his believing that the German dictator would halt when he had digested the Germans who previously had dwelt outside the Reich's frontier and were now within it. Had not the Fuehrer repeatedly said that he wanted no Czechs in the Third Reich? Had he not in *Mein Kampf* and in countless public speeches reiterated the Nazi theory that a Germany, to be strong, must be racially pure and therefore must not take in foreign, and especially Slav, peoples? He had. But also—and perhaps this was forgotten in London—he had preached in many a turgid page in *Mein Kampf* that

Germany's future lay in conquering *Lebensraum* in the East. For more than a millennium this space had been occupied by the Slavs.

THE WEEK OF THE BROKEN GLASS

In the autumn of 1938 another turning point for Nazi Germany was reached. It took place during what was later called in party circles the "Week of the Broken Glass."

On November 7, a seventeen-year-old German Jewish refugee by the name of Herschel Grynszpan shot and mortally wounded the third secretary of the German Embassy in Paris, Ernst vom Rath. The youth's father had been among ten thousand Jews deported to Poland in boxcars shortly before, and it was to revenge this and the general persecution of Jews in Nazi Germany that he went to the German Embassy intending to kill the ambassador, Count Johannes von Welczeck. But the young third secretary was sent out to see what he wanted, and was shot. There was irony in Rath's death, because he had been shadowed by the Gestapo as a result of his anti-Nazi attitude; for one thing, he had never shared the anti-Semitic aberrations of the rulers of his country.

On the night of November 9–10, shortly after the party bosses, led by Hitler and Goering, had concluded the annual celebration of the Beer Hall Putsch in Munich, the worst pogrom that had yet taken place in the Third Reich occurred. According to Dr. Goebbels and the German press, which he controlled, it was a "spontaneous" demonstration of the German people in reaction to the news of the murder in Paris. But after the war, documents came to light which show how "spontaneous" it was.[5] They are among the most illuminating—and gruesome—secret papers of the prewar Nazi era.

On the evening of November 9, according to a secret report made by the chief party judge, Major Walther Buch, Dr. Goebbels issued instructions that "spontaneous demonstrations" were to be "organized and executed" during the night. But the real organizer was Reinhard Heydrich, the sinister thirty-four-year-old Number Two man, after Himmler, in the S.S., who ran the Security Service (S.D.) and the Gestapo. His teletyped orders during the evening are among the captured German documents.

At 1:20 A.M. on November 10 he flashed an urgent teletype message to all headquarters and stations of the state police and the S.D. instructing them to get together with party and S.S. leaders "to discuss the organization of the demonstrations."

a. Only such measures should be taken which do not involve danger to German life or property. (For instance synagogues are to be burned down only when there is no danger of fire to the surroundings.)*

---

* The parentheses are in the original.

b. Business and private apartments of Jews may be destroyed but not looted. . . .

d. . . . 2. The demonstrations which are going to take place should not be hindered by the police . . .

     5. As many Jews, especially rich ones, are to be arrested as can be accommodated in the existing prisons . . . Upon their arrest, the appropriate concentration camps should be contacted immediately, in order to confine them in these camps as soon as possible.

It was a night of horror throughout Germany. Synagogues, Jewish homes and shops went up in flames and several Jews, men, women and children, were shot or otherwise slain while trying to escape burning to death. A preliminary confidential report was made by Heydrich to Goering on the following day, November 11.

The extent of the destruction of Jewish shops and houses cannot yet be verified by figures . . . 815 shops destroyed, 171 dwelling houses set on fire or destroyed only indicate a fraction of the actual damage so far as arson is concerned . . . 119 synagogues were set on fire, and another 76 completely destroyed . . . 20,000 Jews were arrested. 36 deaths were reported and those seriously injured were also numbered at 36. Those killed and injured are Jews. . . .

The ultimate number of murders of Jews that night is believed to have been several times the preliminary figure. Heydrich himself a day after his preliminary report gave the number of Jewish shops looted as 7,500. There were also some cases of rape, which Major Buch's party court, judging by its own report, considered worse than murder, since they violated the Nuremberg racial laws which forbade sexual intercourse between Gentiles and Jews. Such offenders were expelled from the party and turned over to the civil courts. Party members who simply murdered Jews "cannot be punished," Major Buch argued, since they had merely carried out orders. On that point he was quite blunt. "The public, down to the last man," he wrote, "realizes that political drives like those of November 9 were organized and directed by the party, whether this is admitted or not."*

Murder and arson and pillage were not the only tribulations suffered by innocent German Jews as the result of the murder of Rath in Paris. The Jews had to pay for the destruction of their own property. Insurance

---

* Major Buch's report gives an authentic picture of justice in the Third Reich. "In the following cases of killing Jews," one part reads, "proceedings were suspended or minor punishments were pronounced." He then cites a large number of such "cases," giving the names of the murdered and the murderers. "Party Member Fruehling, August, because of shooting of the Jewish couple Goldberg and because of shooting of the Jew Sinasohn . . . Party Members Behring, Willi, and Heike, Josef, because of the shooting of the Jew Rosenbaum and the Jewess Zwienicki . . . Party Members Schmidt, Heinrich, and Meckler, Ernst, because of drowning the Jew Ilsoffer . . . ," etc.

monies due them were confiscated by the State. Moreover, they were subjected, collectively, to a fine of one billion marks as punishment, as Goering put it, "for their abominable crimes, etc." These additional penalties were assessed at a grotesque meeting of a dozen German cabinet ministers and ranking officials presided over by the corpulent Field Marshal on November 12, a partial stenographic record of which survives.

A number of German insurance firms faced bankruptcy if they were to make good the policies on gutted buildings (most of which, though they harbored Jewish shops, were owned by Gentiles) and damaged goods. The destruction in broken window glass alone came to five million marks ($1,250,000) as a Herr Hilgard, who had been called in to speak for the insurance companies, reminded Goering; and most of the glass replacements would have to be imported from abroad in foreign exchange, of which Germany was very short.

"This cannot continue!" exclaimed Goering, who, among other things, was the czar of the German economy. "We won't be able to last, with all this. Impossible!" And turning to Heydrich, he shouted, "I wish you had killed two hundred Jews instead of destroying so many valuables!"*

"Thirty-five were killed," Heydrich answered, in self-defense.

Not all the conversation, of which the partial stenographic record runs to ten thousand words, was so deadly serious. Goering and Goebbels had a lot of fun arguing about subjecting the Jews to further indignities. The Propaganda Minister said the Jews would be made to clean up and level off the debris of the synagogues; the sites would then be turned into parking lots. He insisted that the Jews be excluded from everything: schools, theaters, movies, resorts, public beaches, parks, even from the German forests. He proposed that there be special railway coaches and compartments for the Jews, but that they be made available only after all Aryans were seated.

"Well, if the train is overcrowded," Goering laughed, "we'll kick the Jew out and make him sit all alone all the way in the toilet."

When Goebbels, in all seriousness, demanded that the Jews be forbidden to enter the forests, Goering replied, "We shall give the Jews a certain part of the forest and see to it that various animals that look damned much like Jews—the elk has a crooked nose like theirs—get there also and become acclimated."

In such talk, and much more like it, did the leaders of the Third Reich while away the time in the crucial year of 1938.

But the question of who was to pay for the 25 million marks' worth of damage caused by a pogrom instigated and organized by the State was a fairly serious one, especially to Goering, who now had become responsible for the economic well-being of Nazi Germany. Hilgard, on behalf of the insurance companies, pointed out that if their policies were not honored to the Jews, the confidence of the people, both at home and abroad, in

---

* When asked during cross-examination by Mr. Justice Jackson at Nuremberg whether he had actually said this, Goering replied, "Yes, this was said in a moment of bad temper and excitement . . . It was not meant seriously."[6]

German insurance would be forfeited. On the other hand, he did not see how many of the smaller companies could pay up without going broke.

This problem was quickly solved by Goering. The insurance companies would pay the Jews in full, but the sums would be confiscated by the State and the insurers reimbursed for a part of their losses. This did not satisfy Herr Hilgard, who, judging by the record of the meeting, must have felt that he had fallen in with a bunch of lunatics.

GOERING: The Jew shall get the refund from the insurance company but the refund will be confiscated. There will remain some profit for the insurance companies, since they won't have to make good for all the damage. Herr Hilgard, you may consider yourself damned lucky.

HILGARD: I have no reason to. The fact that we won't have to pay for all the damage, you call a profit!

The Field Marshal was not accustomed to such talk and he quickly squelched the bewildered businessman.

GOERING: Just a moment! If you are legally bound to pay five millions and all of a sudden an angel in my somewhat corpulent shape appears before you and tells you that you may keep one million, for heaven's sake isn't that a profit? I should like to go fifty-fifty with you, or whatever you call it. I have only to look at you. Your whole body seethes with satisfaction. You are getting a big rake-off!

The insurance executive was slow to see the point.

HILGARD: All the insurance companies are the losers. That is so, and remains so. Nobody can tell me differently.

GOERING: Then why don't you take care of it that a few windows less are being smashed!

The Field Marshal had had enough of this commercial-minded man. Herr Hilgard was dismissed, disappearing into the limbo of history.

A representative of the Foreign Office dared to suggest that American public opinion be considered in taking further measures against the Jews.* This inspired an outburst from Goering: "That country of scoundrels! . . . That gangster state!"

---

* The American ambassador in Berlin, Hugh Wilson, was recalled by President Roosevelt on November 14, two days after Goering's meeting, "for consultations," and never returned to his post. The German ambassador in Washington, Hans Dieckhoff, who on that day reported to Berlin that "a hurricane is raging here" as the result of the German pogrom, was recalled on November 18 and likewise never returned. On November 30, Hans Thomsen, the German chargé d'affaires in Washington, advised Berlin by code that "in view of the strained relations and the lack of security for secret material" in the embassy, the "secret political files" be removed to Berlin. "The files," he said, "are so bulky that they cannot be destroyed quickly enough should the necessity arise."[7]

After further lengthy discussion it was agreed to solve the Jewish question in the following manner: eliminate the Jews from the German economy; transfer all Jewish business enterprises and property, including jewelry and works of art, to Aryan hands with some compensation in bonds from which the Jews could use the interest but not the capital. The matter of excluding Jews from schools, resorts, parks, forests, etc., and of either expelling them after they had been deprived of all their property or confining them to German ghettos where they would be impressed as forced labor, was left for further consideration by a committee.

As Heydrich put it toward the close of the meeting: "In spite of the elimination of the Jews from economic life, the main problem remains, namely, to kick the Jew out of Germany." Count Schwerin von Krosigk, the Minister of Finance, the former Rhodes scholar who prided himself on representing the "traditional and decent Germany" in the Nazi government, agreed "that we will have to do everything to shove the Jews into foreign countries." As for the ghettos, this German nobleman said meekly, "I don't imagine the prospect of the ghetto is very nice. The idea of the ghetto is not a very agreeable one."

At 2:30 P.M.—after nearly four hours—Goering brought the meeting to a close.

I shall close the meeting with these words: German Jewry shall, as punishment for their abominable crimes, et cetera, have to make a contribution for one billion marks. That will work. The swine won't commit another murder. Incidentally, I would like to say that I would not like to be a Jew in Germany.

Much worse was to be inflicted on the Jews by this man and this State and its Fuehrer in the course of time, and a brief time it turned out to be. On the flaming, riotous night of November 9, 1938, the Third Reich had deliberately turned down a dark and savage road from which there was to be no return. A good many Jews had been murdered and tortured and robbed before, but these crimes, except for those which took place in the concentration camps, had been committed mostly by brown-shirted rowdies acting out of their own sadism and greed while the State authorities looked on, or looked the other way. Now the German government itself had organized and carried out a vast pogrom. The killings, the looting, the burning of synagogues and houses and shops on the night of November 9 were its doing. So were the official decrees, duly published in the official gazette, the *Reichsgesetzblatt*—three of them on the day of Goering's meeting—which fined the Jewish community a billion marks, eliminated them from the economy, robbed them of what was left of their property and drove them toward the ghetto—and worse.

World opinion was shocked and revolted by such barbarity in a nation which boasted a centuries-old Christian and humanist culture. Hitler, in turn, was enraged by the world reaction and convinced himself that it merely proved the power and scope of "the Jewish world conspiracy."

In retrospect, it is easy to see that the horrors inflicted upon the Jews of Germany on November 9 and the harsh and brutal measures taken against them immediately afterward were portents of a fatal weakening which in the end would bring the dictator, his regime and his nation down in utter ruin. The evidences of Hitler's megalomania we have seen permeating hundreds of pages of this narrative. But until now he had usually been able to hold it in check at critical stages in his rise and in that of his country. At such moments his genius for acting not only boldly, but usually only after a careful calculation of the consequences, had won him one crashing success after another. But now, as November 9 and its aftermath clearly showed, Hitler was losing his self-control. His megalomania was getting the upper hand. The stenographic record of the Goering meeting on November 12 reveals that it was Hitler who, in the final analysis, was responsible for the holocaust of that November evening; it was he who gave the necessary approval to launch it; he who pressed Goering to go ahead with the elimination of the Jews from German life. From now on the absolute master of the Third Reich would show little of that restraint which had saved him so often before. And though his genius and that of his country would lead to further startling conquests, the poisonous seeds of eventual self-destruction for the dictator and his land had now been sown.

Hitler's sickness was contagious; the nation was catching it, as if it were a virus. Individually, as this writer can testify from personal experience, many Germans were as horrified by the November 9 inferno as were Americans and Englishmen and other foreigners. But neither the leaders of the Christian churches nor the generals nor any other representatives of the "good" Germany spoke out at once in open protest. They bowed to what General von Fritsch called "the inevitable," or "Germany's destiny."

The atmosphere of Munich soon was dissipated. At Saarbruecken, at Weimar, at Munich, Hitler delivered petulant speeches that fall warning the outside world and particularly the British to mind their own business and to quit concerning themselves "with the fate of Germans within the frontiers of the Reich." That fate, he thundered, was exclusively Germany's affair. It could not be long before even Neville Chamberlain would be awakened to the nature of the German government which he had gone so far to appease. Gradually, as the eventful year of 1938 gave way to ominous 1939, the Prime Minister got wind of what the Fuehrer whom he had tried so hard to personally accommodate in the interest of European peace was up to behind the scenes.*

---

* On January 28, 1939, Lord Halifax secretly warned President Roosevelt that "as early as November 1938, there were indications which gradually became more definite that Hitler was planning a further foreign adventure for the spring of 1939." The British Foreign Secretary said that "reports indicate that Hitler, encouraged by Ribbentrop, Himmler and others, is considering an attack on the Western Powers as a preliminary to subsequent action in the East."[8]

Not long after Munich Ribbentrop journeyed to Rome. His mind was "fixed" on war, Ciano noted in his diary of October 28.[9]

The Fuehrer [the German Foreign Minister told Mussolini and Ciano] is convinced that we must inevitably count on a war with the Western democracies in the course of a few years, perhaps three or four . . . The Czech crisis has shown our power! We have the advantage of the initiative and are masters of the situation. We cannot be attacked. The military situation is excellent: as from September [1939] we could face a war with the great democracies.*

To the young Italian Foreign Minister, Ribbentrop was "vain, frivolous, and loquacious," and in so describing him in his diary he added, "The Duce says you only have to look at his head to see that he has a small brain." The German Foreign Minister had come to Rome to persuade Mussolini to sign a military alliance between Germany, Japan and Italy, a draft of which had been given the Italians at Munich; but Mussolini stalled for time. He was not yet ready, Ciano noted, to shut the door on Britain and France.

Hitler himself toyed that autumn with the idea of trying to detach France from her ally over the Channel. When on October 18 he received the French ambassador, François-Poncet, for a farewell visit in the eerie fastness of Eagle's Nest, high above Berchtesgaden on a mountaintop,† he broke out into a bitter attack on Great Britain. The ambassador found the Fuehrer pale, his face drawn with fatigue, but not too tired to inveigh against Albion. Britain re-echoed "with threats and calls to arms." She was selfish and took on "superior" airs. It was the British who were destroying the spirit of Munich. And so on. France was different. Hitler said he wanted more friendly and close relations with her. To prove it, he was willing to sign at once a pact of friendship, guaranteeing their present frontiers (and thus again renouncing any German claims to Alsace-Lorraine) and proposing to settle any future differences by consultation.

The pact was duly signed in Paris on December 6, 1938, by the German and French foreign ministers. France, by that time, had somewhat re-

---

* A German version of Ribbentrop's talk with Ciano in Rome on October 28, drawn up by Dr. Schmidt, confirms Ribbentrop's bellicose attitude and quotes him as saying that Germany and Italy must prepare for "armed conflict with the Western democracies . . . here and now." At this meeting Ribbentrop also assured Ciano that Munich had revealed the strength of the isolationists in the U.S.A. "so that there is nothing to fear from America."[10]

† This fantastic retreat, built at great cost over three years, was difficult to reach. Ten miles of a hairpin road, cut into the mountainside, led up to a long underground passageway, drilled into the rock, from which an elevator carried one 370 feet to the cabin perched at an elevation of over 6,000 feet on the summit of a mountain. It afforded a breath-taking panorama of the Alps. Salzburg could be seen in the distance. Describing it later, François-Poncet wondered, "Was this edifice the work of a normal mind or of one tormented by megalomania and haunted by visions of domination and solitude?"

covered from the defeatist panic of the Munich days. The writer happened to be in Paris on the day the paper was signed and noted the frosty atmosphere. When Ribbentrop drove through the streets they were completely deserted, and several cabinet ministers and other leading figures in the French political and literary worlds, including the eminent presidents of the Senate and the Chamber, MM. Jeanneney and Herriot respectively, refused to attend the social functions accorded the Nazi visitor.

From this meeting of Bonnet and Ribbentrop stemmed a misunderstanding which was to play a certain part in future events. The German Foreign Minister claimed that Bonnet had assured him that after Munich France was no longer interested in Eastern Europe and he subsequently interpreted this as meaning that the French would give Germany a free hand in this region, especially in regard to rump Czechoslovakia and Poland. Bonnet denied this. According to Schmidt's minutes of the meeting, Bonnet declared, in answer to Ribbentrop's demand that Germany's sphere of influence in the East be recognized, that "conditions had changed fundamentally since Munich."[11] This ambiguous remark was soon stretched by the slippery German Foreign Minister into the flat statement, which he passed along to Hitler, that "at Paris Bonnet had declared he was no longer interested in questions concerning the East." France's swift surrender at Munich had already convinced the Fuehrer of this. It was not quite true.

SLOVAKIA "WINS" ITS "INDEPENDENCE"

What had happened to the German guarantee of the rest of Czechoslovakia which Hitler had solemnly promised at Munich to give? When the new French ambassador in Berlin, Robert Coulondre, inquired of Weizsaecker on December 21, 1938, the State Secretary replied that the destiny of Czechoslovakia lay in the hands of Germany and that he rejected the idea of a British–French guarantee. As far back as October 14, when the new Czech Foreign Minister, František Chvalkovsky, had come humbly begging for crumbs at the hand of Hitler in Munich and had inquired whether Germany was going to join Britain and France in the guarantee of his country's shrunken frontiers, the Fuehrer replied sneeringly that "the British and French guarantees were worthless . . . and that the only effective guarantee was that by Germany."[12]

Yet, as 1939 began, it was still not forthcoming. The reason was simple. The Fuehrer had no intention of giving it. Such a guarantee would have interfered with the plans which he had begun to lay immediately after Munich. Soon there would be no Czechoslovakia to guarantee. To start with, Slovakia would be induced to break away.

A few days after Munich, on October 17, Goering had received two Slovak leaders, Ferdinand Durcansky and Mach, and the leader of the German minority in Slovakia, Franz Karmasin. Durcansky, who was

Deputy Prime Minister of the newly appointed autonomous Slovakia, assured the Field Marshal that what the Slovaks really wanted was "complete independence, with very close political, economic and military ties with Germany." In a secret Foreign Office memorandum of the same date it was noted that Goering had decided that independence for Slovakia must be supported. "A Czech State minus Slovakia is even more completely at our mercy. Air base in Slovakia for operation against the East very important."[13] Such were Goering's thoughts on the matter in mid-October.

We must here attempt to follow a double thread in the German plan: to detach Slovakia from Prague, and to prepare for the liquidation of what remained of the state by the military occupation of the Czech lands, Bohemia and Moravia. On October 21, 1938, as we have seen, Hitler had directed the Wehrmacht to be ready to carry out that liquidation.* On December 17, General Keitel issued what he called a "supplement to Directive of October 21":

TOP SECRET

With reference to the "liquidation of the Rump Czech State," the Fuehrer has given the following orders:

The operation is to be prepared on the assumption that no resistance worth mentioning is to be expected.

To the outside world it must clearly appear that it is merely a peaceful action and not a warlike undertaking.

The action must therefore be carried out by the peacetime armed forces *only*, without reinforcement by mobilization . . .[14]

Try as it might to please Hitler, the new pro-German government of Czechoslovakia began to realize as the new year began that the country's goose was cooked. Just before Christmas, 1938, the Czech cabinet, in order to further appease the Fuehrer, had dissolved the Communist Party and suspended all Jewish teachers in German schools. On January 12, 1939, Foreign Minister Chvalkovsky, in a message to the German Foreign Office, stressed that his government "will endeavor to prove its loyalty and good will by far-reaching fulfillment of Germany's wishes." On the same day he brought to the attention of the German chargé in Prague the spreading rumors "that the incorporation of Czechoslovakia into the Reich was imminent."[15]

To see if even the pieces could be saved Chvalkovsky finally prevailed upon Hitler to receive him in Berlin on January 21. It turned out to be a painful scene, though not as painful for the Czechs as one that would shortly follow. The Czech Foreign Minister groveled before the mighty

---

* On November 24, Hitler issued another secret directive instructing the Wehrmacht to make preparations for the military occupation of Danzig, but that will be taken up later. Already the Fuehrer was looking beyond the final conquest of Czechoslovakia.

German dictator, who was in one of his most bullying moods. Czechoslovakia, said Hitler, had been saved from catastrophe by "Germany's moderation." Nevertheless, unless the Czechs showed a different spirit, he would "annihilate" them. They must forget their "history," which was "schoolboy nonsense," and do as the Germans bade. That was their only salvation. Specifically, Czechoslovakia must leave the League of Nations, drastically reduce the size of her Army—"because it did not count anyway"—join the Anti-Comintern Pact, accept German direction of her foreign policy, make a preferential trade agreement with Germany, one condition of which was that no new Czech industries could be established without German consent,* dismiss all officials and editors not friendly to the Reich and, finally, outlaw the Jews, as Germany had done under its Nuremberg Laws. ("With us, the Jews will be destroyed," Hitler told his visitor.) On the same day Chvalkovsky received further demands from Ribbentrop, who threatened "catastrophic consequences" unless the Czechs immediately mended their ways and did as they were told. The German Foreign Minister, so much the lackey in the presence of Hitler but a boor and a bully with anyone over whom he had the upper hand, bade Chvalkovsky not to mention the new German demands to the British and French but just to go ahead and carry them out.[17]

And to do so without worrying about any German guarantee of the Czech frontiers! Apparently there had been little worry about this in Paris and London. Four months had gone by since Munich, and still Hitler had not honored his word to add Germany's guarantee to that given by Britain and France. Finally on February 8 an Anglo–French *note verbale* was presented in Berlin stating that the two governments "would now be glad to learn the views of the German Government as to the best way of giving effect to the understanding reached at Munich in regard to the guarantee of Czechoslovakia."[18]

Hitler himself, as the captured German Foreign Office documents establish, drafted the reply, which was not made until February 28. It said that the time had not yet come for a German guarantee. Germany would have to "await first a clarification of the internal development of Czechoslovakia."[19]

The Fuehrer already was shaping that "internal development" toward an obvious end. On February 12 he received at the Chancellery in Berlin Dr. Vojtech Tuka, one of the Slovak leaders, whose long imprisonment had embittered him against the Czechs.† Addressing Hitler as "my

---

* Hitler also demanded that the Czechoslovak National Bank turn over part of its gold reserve to the Reichsbank. The sum requested was 391.2 million Czech crowns in gold. On February 18 Goering wrote the German Foreign Office: "In view of the increasingly difficult currency position, I must insist most strongly that the 30 to 40 million Reichsmarks in gold [from the Czech National Bank] which are involved come into our possession very shortly; they are urgently required for the execution of important orders of the Fuehrer."[16]
† See above, p. 359.

Fuehrer," as the secret German memorandum of the talk emphasizes, Dr. Tuka begged the German dictator to make Slovakia independent and free. "I lay the destiny of my people in your hands, my Fuehrer," he declared. "My people await their complete liberation from you."

Hitler's reply was somewhat evasive. He said that unfortunately he had not understood the Slovak problem. Had he known the Slovaks wanted to be independent he would have arranged it at Munich. It would be "a comfort to him to know that Slovakia was independent . . . He could guarantee an independent Slovakia at any time, even today . . ." These were comforting words to Professor Tuka too.[20] "This," he said later, "was the greatest day of my life."

The curtain on the next act of the Czechoslovak tragedy could now go up. By another one of those ironies with which this narrative history is so full, it was the Czechs in Prague who forced the curtain up a little prematurely. By the beginning of March 1939 they were caught in a terrible dilemma. The separatist movements in Slovakia and Ruthenia, fomented, as we have seen, by the German government (and in Ruthenia also by Hungary, which was hungry to annex that little land) had reached such a state that unless they were squelched Czechoslovakia would break up. In that case Hitler would surely occupy Prague. If the separatists were put down by the central government, then the Fuehrer, just as certainly, would take advantage of the resulting disturbance to also march into Prague.

The Czech government, after much hesitation and only after the provocation became unbearable, chose the second alternative. On March 6, Dr. Hácha, the President of Czechoslovakia, dismissed the autonomous Ruthenian government from office, and on the night of March 9–10 the autonomous Slovakian government. The next day he ordered the arrest of Monsignor Tiso, the Slovak Premier, Dr. Tuka and Durcansky and proclaimed martial law in Slovakia. The one courageous move of this government, which had become so servile to Berlin, quickly turned into a disaster which destroyed it.

The swift action by the tottering Prague government caught Berlin by surprise. Goering had gone off to sunny San Remo for a vacation. Hitler was on the point of leaving for Vienna to celebrate the first anniversary of the Anschluss. But now the master improviser went feverishly to work. On March 11, he decided to take Bohemia and Moravia by ultimatum. The text was drafted that day on Hitler's orders by General Keitel and sent to the German Foreign Office. It called upon the Czechs to submit to military occupation without resistance.[21] For the moment, however, it remained a "top military secret."

It was now time for Hitler to "liberate" Slovakia. Karol Sidor, who had represented the autonomous Slovak government at Prague, was named by President Hácha to be the new Premier of it in place of Monsignor Tiso. Returning to Bratislava, the Slovak seat of government, on Saturday,

March 11, Sidor called a meeting of his new cabinet. At ten o'clock in the evening the session of the Slovak government was interrupted by strange and unexpected visitors. Seyss-Inquart, the quisling Nazi Governor of Austria, and Josef Buerckel, the Nazi Gauleiter of Austria, accompanied by five German generals, pushed their way into the meeting and told the cabinet ministers to proclaim the independence of Slovakia at once. Unless they did, Hitler, who had decided to settle the question of Slovakia definitely and now, would disinterest himself in the fate of Slovakia.[22]

Sidor, who opposed severing all links with the Czechs, stalled for time, but the next morning Monsignor Tiso, who had escaped from a monastery where he supposedly was under house arrest, demanded a cabinet meeting, though he was no longer himself in the cabinet. To forestall further interruptions by high German officials and generals, Sidor called the meeting in his own apartment, and when this became unsafe—for German storm troopers were taking over the town—he adjourned it to the offices of a local newspaper. There Tiso informed him that he had just received a telegram from Buerckel inviting him to go at once to see the Fuehrer in Berlin. If he refused the invitation, Buerckel threatened, two German divisions across the Danube from Bratislava would march in and Slovakia would be divided up between Germany and Hungary. Arriving in Vienna the next morning, Monday, March 13, with the intention of proceeding to Berlin by train, the chubby little prelate* was packed into a plane by the Germans and flown to the presence of Hitler. For the Fuehrer, there was no time to waste.

When Tiso and Durcansky arrived at the Chancellery in Berlin at 7:40 on the evening of March 13, they found Hitler flanked not only by Ribbentrop but by his two top generals, Brauchitsch, Commander in Chief of the German Army, and Keitel, Chief of OKW. Though they may not have realized it, the Slovaks also found the Fuehrer in a characteristic mood. Here again, thanks to the captured confidential minutes of the meeting, we may peer into the weird mind of the German dictator, rapidly giving way to megalomania, and watch him spinning his fantastic lies and uttering his dire threats in a manner and to an extent which he no doubt was sure would never come to public attention.[23]

"Czechoslovakia," he said, "owed it only to Germany that she had not been mutilated further." The Reich had exhibited "the greatest self-control." Yet the Czechs had not appreciated this. "During recent weeks," he went on, working himself up easily to a fine lather, "conditions have become impossible. The old Beneš spirit has come to life again."

The Slovaks had also disappointed him. After Munich he had "fallen

---

* Monsignor Tiso, as this writer recalls him, was almost as broad as he was high. He was an enormous eater. "When I get worked up," he once told Dr. Paul Schmidt, "I eat half a pound of ham, and that soothes my nerves." He was to die on the gallows. Arrested by American Army authorities on June 8, 1945, and turned over to the newly restored Czechoslovakia, he was condemned to death on April 15, 1947, after a trial lasting four months, and was executed on April 18.

out" with his friends the Hungarians by not permitting them to grab
Slovakia. He had thought Slovakia wanted to be independent.

He had now summoned Tiso in order to clear up this question *in a very short
time.** . . . The question was: Did Slovakia want to lead an independent existence or not? . . . It was a question not of days but of hours. If Slovakia
wished to become independent he would support and even guarantee it . . .
If she hesitated or refused to be separated from Prague, he would leave the fate
of Slovakia to events for which he was no longer responsible.

At this point, the German minutes reveal, Ribbentrop "handed to the
Fuehrer a report just received announcing Hungarian troop movements
on the Slovak frontier. The Fuehrer read this report, told Tiso of its
contents, and expressed the hope that Slovakia would reach a decision
soon."

Tiso did not give his decision then. He asked the Fuehrer to "pardon
him if, under the impact of the Chancellor's words, he could make no
definite decision at once." But the Slovaks, he quickly added, "would
prove themselves worthy of the Fuehrer's benevolence."

This they did in a conference which continued far into the night at the
Foreign Ministry. According to the Nuremberg testimony of Keppler,
who had been Hitler's secret agent in Bratislava, as he had been the year
before in Vienna on the eve of the Anschluss, the Germans helped Tiso
draft a telegram, which the "Premier" was to send as soon as he returned
to Bratislava, proclaiming Slovakia's independence and urgently requesting the Fuehrer to take over the protection of the new state.[24] It is
reminiscent of the "telegram" dictated by Goering just a year before in
which Seyss-Inquart was to appeal to Hitler to send German troops to
Austria. By this time the Nazi "telegram" technique had been perfected.
The telegram, considerably abridged, was duly dispatched by Tiso on
March 16, and Hitler immediately replied that he would be glad to "take
over the protection of the Slovak State."

At the Foreign Office that night Ribbentrop also drafted the Slovak
proclamation of "independence" and had it translated into Slovak in time
for Tiso to take it back to Bratislava, where the "Premier" read it—in
slightly altered form, as one German agent reported—to Parliament on
the following day, Tuesday, March 14. Attempts by several Slovak
deputies to at least discuss it were squelched by Karmasin, the leader of
the German minority, who warned that German troops would occupy
the country if there was any delay in proclaiming independence. Faced
with this threat the doubting deputies gave in.

Thus was "independent" Slovakia born on March 14, 1939. Though
British diplomatic representatives were quick to inform London as to the
manner of its birth, Chamberlain, as we shall see, was just as quick to

---

* Italics in the original German minutes.

use Slovakia's "secession" as an excuse for Britain not to honor its guarantee of Czechoslovakia after Hitler, on that very evening, March 14, acted to finish what had been left undone at Munich.

The life of the Czechoslovak Republic of Masaryk and Beneš had now run out. And once again the harassed leaders in Prague played into Hitler's hands to set up the final act of their country's tragedy. The aging, bewildered President Hácha asked to be received by the Fuehrer.* Hitler graciously consented. It gave him an opportunity to set the stage for one of the most brazen acts of his entire career.

Consider how well the dictator had already arranged the set as he waited on the afternoon of March 14 for the President of Czechoslovakia to arrive. The proclamations of independence of Slovakia and Ruthenia, which he had so skillfully engineered, left Prague with only the Czech core of Bohemia and Moravia. Had not Czechoslovakia in reality ceased to exist—the nation whose frontiers Britain and France had guaranteed against aggression? Chamberlain and Daladier, his partners at Munich where the guarantee had been solemnly given, already had their "out." That they would take it he had no doubt—and he was right. That disposed of any danger of foreign intervention. But to make doubly sure—to see to it that his next move looked quite legal and legitimate by the vague standards of international law, at least on paper—he would force the weak and senile Hácha, who had begged to see him, to accept the very solution which he had intended to achieve by military force. And in so doing he could make it appear—he, who, alone in Europe, had mastered the new technique of bloodless conquest, as the Anschluss and Munich had proved—that the President of Czechoslovakia had actually and formally asked for it. The niceties of "legality," which he had perfected so well in taking over power in Germany, would be preserved in the conquest of a non-Germanic land.

Hitler had also set the stage to fool the German and other gullible people in Europe. For several days now German provocateurs had been trying to stir up trouble in various Czech towns, Prague, Bruenn and Iglau. They had not had much success because, as the German Legation in Prague reported, the Czech "police have been instructed to take no action against Germans, even in cases of provocation."[26] But this failure did not prevent Dr. Goebbels from whipping up the German press into a frenzy over invented acts of terror by the Czechs against the poor Germans. As the French ambassador, M. Coulondre, informed Paris,

---

* There is a difference of opinion on this point. Some historians have contended that the Germans forced Hácha to come to Berlin. They probably base this contention on a dispatch of the French ambassador in Berlin, who said he had learned this "from a reliable source." But the German Foreign Office documents, subsequently discovered, make it clear that the initiative came from Hácha. He first requested an interview with Hitler on March 13, through the German Legation in Prague, and repeated the request on the morning of the fourteenth. Hitler agreed to it that afternoon.[25]

they were the same stories with the same headlines which Dr. Goebbels had concocted during the Sudeten crisis—down to the pregnant German woman struck down by Czech beasts and the general "*Blutbad*" ("blood bath") to which the defenseless Germans were being subjected by the Czech barbarians. Hitler could assure the proud German people that their kinsmen would not remain unprotected for long.

Such was the situation and such were Hitler's plans, we now know from the German archives, as the train bearing President Hácha and his Foreign Minister, Chvalkovsky, drew into the Anhalt Station in Berlin at 10:40 on the evening of March 14. Because of a heart condition the President had been unable to fly.

THE ORDEAL OF DR. HÁCHA

The German protocol was perfect. The Czech President was accorded all the formal honors due to a head of state. There was a military guard of honor at the station, where the German Foreign Minister himself greeted the distinguished visitor and slipped his daughter a fine bouquet of flowers. At the swank Adlon Hotel, where the party was put up in the best suite, there were chocolates for Miss Hácha—a personal gift of Adolf Hitler, who believed that everyone else shared his craving for sweets. And when the aged President and his Foreign Minister arrived at the Chancellery he was given a salute by an S.S. guard of honor.

They were not summoned to Hitler's presence until 1:15 A.M. Hácha must have known what was in store for him. Before his train had left Czech territory he learned from Prague that German troops had already occupied Moravská-Ostrava, an important Czech industrial town, and were poised all along the perimeter of Bohemia and Moravia to strike. And he saw at once, as he entered the Fuehrer's study in the early-morning hour, that, besides Ribbentrop and Weizsaecker, Field Marshal Goering, who had been urgently recalled from his holiday at San Remo, and General Keitel stood at Hitler's side. Most probably, as he went into this lion's den, he did not notice that Hitler's physician, the quack Dr. Theodor Morell, was on tap. But the doctor was, and for good reason.

The secret German minutes of the meeting reveal a pitiful scene at the very outset. The unhappy Dr. Hácha, despite his background as a respected judge of the Supreme Court, shed all human dignity by groveling before the swaggering German Fuehrer. Perhaps the President thought that only in this way could he appeal to Hitler's generosity and save something for his people; but regardless of his motive, his words, as the Germans recorded them for their confidential archives, nauseate the reader even so long afterward as today. He himself, Hácha assured Hitler, had never mixed in politics. He had rarely seen the founders of the Czechoslovak Republic, Masaryk and Beneš, and what he had seen of them he did not like. Their regime, he said, was "alien" to him—"so alien that immediately after the change of regime [after Munich] he had asked himself whether it was a good thing for Czechoslovakia to be an independent state at all."

He was convinced that the destiny of Czechoslovakia lay in the Fuehrer's hands, and he believed it was in safekeeping in such hands . . . Then he came to what affected him most, the fate of his people. He felt that it was precisely the Fuehrer who would understand his holding the view that Czechoslovakia had the right to live a national life . . . Czechoslovakia was being blamed because there still existed many supporters of the Beneš system . . . The Government was trying by every means to silence them. This was about all he had to say.

Adolf Hitler then said all there was to say. After rehearsing all the alleged wrongs which the Czechoslovakia of Masaryk and Beneš had done to Germans and Germany, and reiterating that unfortunately the Czechs had not changed since Munich, he came to the point.

He had come to the conclusion that this journey by the President, despite his advanced years, might be of great benefit to his country because it was only a matter of hours now before Germany intervened . . . He harbored no enmity against any nation . . . That the Rump State of Czechoslovakia existed at all was attributable only to his loyal attitude . . . In the autumn he had not wished to draw the final conclusions because he had thought a coexistence possible, but he had left no doubt that if the Beneš tendencies did not disappear completely he would destroy this state completely.

They had not disappeared, and he gave "examples."

And so last Sunday, March 12, the die was cast . . . *He had given the order for the invasion by the German troops and for the incorporation of Czechoslovakia into the German Reich.**

"Hácha and Chvalkovsky," noted Dr. Schmidt, "sat as though turned to stone. Only their eyes showed that they were alive." But Hitler was not quite through. He must humble his guests with threats of Teutonic terror.

The German Army [Hitler continued] had already marched in today, and at a barracks where resistance was offered it had been ruthlessly broken.

Tomorrow morning at six o'clock the German Army was to enter Czechia from all sides and the German Air Force would occupy the Czech airfields. There were two possibilities. The first was that the entry of German troops might develop into fighting. In that case, resistance would be broken by brute force. The other possibility was that the entry of the German troops would

---

* The emphasis is in the German original.

take place in a peaceful manner, in which case it would be easy for the Fuehrer to accord Czechoslovakia a generous way of life of her own, autonomy, and a certain measure of national freedom.

He was doing all this not from hatred but in order to protect Germany. If last autumn Czechoslovakia had not given in, the Czech people would have been exterminated. No one would have prevented him doing it. If it came to a fight . . . in two days the Czech Army would cease to exist. Naturally, some Germans would be killed too and this would engender a hatred which would compel him, in self-preservation, not to concede autonomy. The world would not care a jot about this. He sympathized with the Czech people when he read the foreign press. It gave him the impression which might be summed up in the German proverb: "The Moor has done his duty; the Moor can go." . . .

That was why he had asked Hácha to come here. This was the last good turn he could render the Czech people . . . Perhaps Hácha's visit might prevent the worst . . .

The hours were passing. At six o'clock the troops would march in. He was almost ashamed to say it, but for every Czech battalion there was a German division. He would like now to advise him [Hácha] to withdraw with Chvalkovsky and discuss what was to be done.

What was to be done? The broken old President did not have to withdraw to decide that. He told Hitler at once, "The position is quite clear. Resistance would be folly." But how, he asked—since it was now a little after 2 A.M.—could he, in the space of four hours, arrange to restrain the whole Czech people from offering resistance? The Fuehrer replied that he had better consult with his companions. The German military machine was already in motion and could not be stopped. Hácha should get in touch at once with Prague. "It was a grave decision," the German minutes report Hitler as saying, "but he saw dawning the possibility of a long period of peace between the two peoples. Should the decision be otherwise, he saw the annihilation of Czechoslovakia."

With these words, he dismissed his guests for the time being. It was 2:15 A.M. In an adjoining room Goering and Ribbentrop stepped up the pressure on the two victims. According to the French ambassador, who in an official dispatch to Paris depicted the scene as he got it from what he believed to be an authentic source, Hácha and Chvalkovsky protested against the outrage to their nation. They declared they would not sign the document of surrender. Were they to do so they would be forever cursed by their people.

The German ministers [Goering and Ribbentrop] were pitiless [M. Coulondre wrote in his dispatch]. They literally hunted Dr. Hácha and M. Chvalkovsky round the table on which the documents were lying, thrusting them continually before them, pushing pens into their hands, incessantly repeating that if they continued in their refusal, half of Prague would lie in ruins from bombing within two hours, and that this would be only the beginning. Hundreds of bombers were waiting the order to take off, and they would receive that order at six in the morning if the signatures were not forthcoming.*

At this point, Dr. Schmidt, who seems to have managed to be present whenever and wherever the drama of the Third Reich reached a climax, heard Goering shouting for Dr. Morell.

"Hácha has fainted!" Goering cried out.

For a moment the Nazi bullies feared that the prostrate Czech President might die on their hands and, as Schmidt says, "that the whole world will say tomorrow that he was murdered at the Chancellery." Dr. Morell's specialty was injections—much later he would almost kill Hitler with them—and he now applied the needle to Dr. Hácha and brought him back to consciousness. The President was revived sufficiently to be able to grasp the telephone which the Germans thrust into his hand and talk to his government in Prague over a special line which Ribbentrop had ordered rigged up. He apprised the Czech cabinet of what had happened and advised surrender. Then, somewhat further restored by a second injection from the needle of Dr. Morell, the President of the expiring Republic stumbled back into the presence of Adolf Hitler to sign his country's death warrant. It was now five minutes to four in the morning of March 15, 1939.

The text had been prepared "beforehand by Hitler," Schmidt recounts, and during Hácha's fainting spells the German interpreter had been busy copying the official communiqué, which had also been written up "beforehand," and which Hácha and Chvalkovsky were also forced to sign. It read as follows:

Berlin, March 15, 1939

At their request, the Fuehrer today received the Czechoslovak President, Dr. Hácha, and the Czechoslovak Foreign Minister, Dr. Chvalkovsky, in Berlin in the presence of Foreign Minister von Ribbentrop. At the meeting the serious situation created by the events of recent weeks in the present Czechoslovak territory was examined with complete frankness.

The conviction was unanimously expressed on both sides that the aim of all efforts must be the safeguarding of calm, order and peace in this part of Central Europe. The Czechoslovak President declared that, in order to serve this object and to achieve ultimate pacification, he confidently placed the fate of the Czech people and country in the hands of the Fuehrer of the German Reich. The Fuehrer accepted this declaration and expressed his intention of taking the Czech people under the protection of the German Reich and of

---

* On the stand in Nuremberg, Goering admitted that he told Hácha, "I should be sorry if I had to bomb beautiful Prague." He really didn't intend to carry out the threat—"that would not have been necessary," he explained. "But a point like that, I thought, might serve as an argument and accelerate the whole matter."[27]

guaranteeing them an autonomous development of their ethnic life as suited to their character.

Hitler's chicanery had reached, perhaps, its summit.

According to one of his woman secretaries, Hitler rushed from the signing into his office, embraced all the women present and exclaimed, "Children! This is the greatest day of my life! I shall go down in history as the greatest German!"

It did not occur to him—how could it?—that the end of Czechoslovakia might be the beginning of the end of Germany. From this dawn of March 15, 1939—the Ides of March—the road to war, to defeat, to disaster, as we now know, stretched just ahead. It would be a short road and as straight as a line could be. And once on it, and hurtling down it, Hitler, like Alexander and Napoleon before him, could not stop.[28]

At 6 A.M. on March 15 German troops poured into Bohemia and Moravia. They met no resistance, and by evening Hitler was able to make the triumphant entry into Prague which he felt Chamberlain had cheated him of at Munich. Before leaving Berlin he had issued a grandiose proclamation to the German people, repeating the tiresome lies about the "wild excesses" and "terror" of the Czechs which he had been forced to bring an end to, and proudly proclaiming, "Czechoslovakia has ceased to exist!"

That night he slept in Hradschin Castle, the ancient seat of the kings of Bohemia high above the River Moldau where more recently the despised Masaryk and Beneš had lived and worked for the first democracy Central Europe had ever known. The Fuehrer's revenge was complete, and that it was sweet he showed in the series of proclamations which he issued. He had paid off all the burning resentments against the Czechs which had obsessed him as an Austrian in his vagabond days in Vienna three decades before and which had flamed anew when Beneš dared to oppose him, the all-powerful German dictator, over the past year.

The next day, from Hradschin Castle, he proclaimed the Protectorate of Bohemia and Moravia, which though it professed to provide "autonomy and self-government" for the Czechs brought them, by its very language, completely under the German heel. All power was given to the "Reich Protector" and to his Secretary of State and his Head of the Civil Administration, who were to be appointed by the Fuehrer. To placate outraged public opinion in Britain and France, Hitler brought the "moderate" Neurath out of cold storage and named him Protector.* The two top Sudeten leaders, Konrad Henlein and the gangster Karl Hermann Frank, were given an opportunity to get revenge on the Czechs by being ap-

---

* On the stand at Nuremberg, Neurath stated that he was taken by "complete surprise" when Hitler named him Protector, and that he had "misgivings" about taking the job. However, he says, he took it when Hitler explained that by this appointment he wanted to assure Britain and France "that he did not wish to carry on a policy hostile to Czechoslovakia."[29]

pointed Head of the Civil Administration and Secretary of State respectively. It was not long before Himmler, as boss of the German police, got a stranglehold on the protectorate. To do his work, he made the notorious Frank chief of police of the protectorate and ranking S.S. officer.*

For a thousand years [Hitler said in his proclamation of the protectorate] the provinces of Bohemia and Moravia formed part of the *Lebensraum* of the German people . . . Czechoslovakia showed its inherent inability to survive and has therefore now fallen a victim to actual dissolution. The German Reich cannot tolerate continuous disturbances in these areas . . . Therefore the German Reich, in keeping with the law of self-preservation, is now resolved to intervene decisively to rebuild the foundations of a reasonable order in Central Europe. For in the thousand years of its history it has already proved that, thanks to the greatness and the qualities of the German people, it alone is called upon to undertake this task.

A long night of German savagery now settled over Prague and the Czech lands.

On March 16, Hitler took Slovakia too under his benevolent protection in response to a "telegram," actually composed in Berlin, as we have seen, from Premier Tiso. German troops quickly entered Slovakia to do the "protecting." On March 18, Hitler was in Vienna to approve the "Treaty of Protection," which, as signed on March 23 in Berlin by Ribbentrop and Dr. Tuka, contained a secret protocol giving Germany exclusive rights to exploit the Slovak economy.[30]

As for Ruthenia, which had formed the eastern tip of Czechoslovakia, its independence as the "Republic of Carpatho-Ukraine," proclaimed on March 14, lasted just twenty-four hours. Its appeal to Hitler for "protection" was in vain. Hitler had already awarded this territory to Hungary. In the captured Foreign Office archives there is an interesting letter in the handwriting of Miklós Horthy, Regent of Hungary, addressed to Adolf Hitler on March 13.

YOUR EXCELLENCY: Heartfelt thanks! I cannot express how happy I am, for this headwater region [Ruthenia] is for Hungary—I dislike using big words— a *vital question.* . . . We are tackling the matter with enthusiasm. The plans are already laid. On Thursday, the 16th, a frontier incident will take place, to be followed Saturday by the big thrust.[31]

---

* It might be of interest to skip ahead here and note what happened to some of the characters in the drama just recounted. Frank was sentenced to death by a postwar Czech court and publicly hanged near Prague on May 22, 1946. Henlein committed suicide after his arrest by Czech resistance forces in 1945. Chvalkovsky, who became the representative of the protectorate in Berlin, was killed in an Allied bombing there in 1944. Hácha was arrested by the Czechs on May 14, 1945, but died before he could be tried.

As things turned out, there was no need for an "incident." Hungarian troops simply moved into Ruthenia at 6 A.M. on March 15, timing their entry with that of the Germans to the west, and on the following day the territory was formally annexed by Hungary.

Thus by the end of the day of March 15, which had started in Berlin at 1:15 A.M. when Hácha arrived at the Chancellery, Czechoslovakia, as Hitler said, had ceased to exist.

Neither Britain nor France made the slightest move to save it, though at Munich they had solemnly guaranteed Czechoslovakia against aggression.

Since that meeting not only Hitler but Mussolini had reached the conclusion that the British had become so weak and their Prime Minister, as a consequence, so accommodating that they need pay little further attention to London. On January 11, 1939, Chamberlain, accompanied by Lord Halifax, had journeyed to Rome to seek improvement in Anglo–Italian relations. This writer happened to be at the station in Rome when the two Englishmen arrived and noted in his diary the "fine smirk" on Mussolini's face as he greeted his guests. "When Mussolini passed me," I noted as the party left the station, "he was joking with his son-in-law [Ciano], passing wisecracks."[32] I could not, of course, catch what he was saying, but later Ciano, in his diary, revealed the gist of it.

Arrival of Chamberlain. [Ciano wrote on January 11 and 12] . . . How far apart we are from these people! It is another world. We were talking about it after dinner with the Duce. "These men are not made of the same stuff," he was saying, "as the Francis Drakes and the other magnificent adventurers who created the Empire. These, after all, are the tired sons of a long line of rich men, and they will lose their Empire."

The British do not want to fight. They try to draw back as slowly as possible, but they do not fight . . . Our conversations with the British have ended. Nothing was accomplished. I have telephoned Ribbentrop that the visit was "a big lemonade" [a farce]. . . .

I accompanied the Duce to the station on the departure of Chamberlain [Ciano wrote on January 14]. . . . Chamberlain's eyes filled with tears when the train started moving and his countrymen began singing "For He's a Jolly Good Fellow." "What is this little song?" the Duce asked.[33]

Though during the Sudeten crisis Hitler had been solicitous of Chamberlain's views, there is not a word in the captured German papers to indicate that thereafter he cared a whit what the Prime Minister thought of his destroying the rest of Czechoslovakia despite the British guarantee— and, for that matter, despite the Munich Agreement. On March 14, as Hitler waited in Berlin to humble Hácha, and as angry questions were raised in the House of Commons in London about Germany's engineering Slovakia's "secession" and about its effect on Britain's guarantee to Prague against aggression, Chamberlain replied heatedly, "No such aggression has taken place."

But the next day, March 15, after it had taken place, the Prime Minister used the proclamation of Slovakia's "independence" as an excuse not to honor his country's word. "The effect of this declaration," he explained, "put an end by internal disruption to the State whose frontier we had proposed to guarantee. His Majesty's Government cannot accordingly hold themselves any longer bound by this obligation."

Hitler's strategy had thus worked to perfection. He had given Chamberlain his out and the Prime Minister had taken it.

It is interesting that the Prime Minister did not even wish to accuse Hitler of breaking his word. "I have so often heard charges of breach of faith bandied about which did not seem to me to be founded upon sufficient premises," he said, "that I do not wish to associate myself today with any charges of that character." He had not one word of reproach for the Fuehrer, not even for his treatment of Hácha and the shabby swindle which obviously—even if the details were still unknown—had been perpetrated at the Reich Chancellery on the early morning of this day, March 15.

No wonder that the British protest that day, if it could be called that,* was so tepid, and that the Germans treated it—and subsequent Anglo–French complaints—with so much arrogance and contempt.

His Majesty's Government have no desire to interfere unnecessarily in a matter with which other Governments may be more directly concerned. . . . They are, however, as the German Government will surely appreciate, deeply concerned for the success of all efforts to restore confidence and a relaxation of tension in Europe. They would deplore any action in Central Europe which would cause a setback to the growth of this general confidence . . .[34]

There was not a word in this note, which was delivered on March 15 by Ambassador Henderson to Ribbentrop as an official message from Lord Halifax, about the specific events of the day.

The French were at least specific. Robert Coulondre, the new ambassador of France in Berlin, shared neither his British colleague's illusions about Nazism nor Henderson's disdain of the Czechs. On the morning of the fifteenth he demanded an interview with Ribbentrop, but the vain and vindictive German Foreign Minister was already on his way to Prague, intending to share in Hitler's humiliation of a beaten people. State Secretary von Weizsaecker received Coulondre, instead, at noon. The ambassador lost no time in saying what Chamberlain and Henderson were not yet ready to say: that by its military intervention in Bohemia and Moravia, Germany had violated both the Munich Agreement and the Franco–German declaration of December 6. Baron von Weizsaecker, who later

---

* On March 16 Chamberlain told the Commons that "so far" no protest had been lodged with the German government.

was to insist that he had been stoutly anti-Nazi all along, was in an arrogant mood that would have done credit to Ribbentrop. According to his own memorandum of the meeting,

I spoke rather sharply to the Ambassador and told him not to mention the Munich Agreement, which he alleged had been violated, and not to give us any lectures . . . I told him that in view of the agreement reached last night with the Czech government I could see no reason for any *démarche* by the French ambassador . . . and that I was sure he would find fresh instructions when he returned to his Embassy, and these would set his mind at rest.[35]

Three days later, on March 18, when the British and French governments, in deference to outraged public opinion at home, finally got around to making formal protests to the Reich, Weizsaecker fairly outdid his master, Ribbentrop, in his insolence—again on his own evidence. In a memorandum found in the German Foreign Office files, he tells with evident glee how he refused even to accept the formal French note of protest.

I immediately replaced the Note in its envelope and thrust it back at the Ambassador with the remark that I categorically refused to accept from him any protest regarding the Czecho-Slovak affair. Nor would I take note of the communication, and I would advise M. Coulondre to urge his government to revise the draft . . .[36]

Coulondre, unlike Henderson at this period, was not an envoy who could be browbeaten by the Germans. He retorted that his government's note had been written after due consideration and that he had no intention of asking for it to be revised. When the State Secretary continued to refuse to accept the document, the ambassador reminded him of common diplomatic practice and insisted that France had a perfect right to make known its views to the German government. Finally Weizsaecker, according to his own account, left the note lying on his desk, explaining that he "would regard it as transmitted to us through the post." But before he arrived at this impudent gesture, he got the following off his mind:

From the legal point of view there existed a Declaration which had come about between the Fuehrer and the President of the Czecho-Slovak State. The Czech President, at his own request, had come to Berlin and had then immediately declared that he wished to place the fate of his country in the Fuehrer's hands. I could not imagine that the French Government were more Catholic than the Pope and intended meddling in things which had been duly settled between Berlin and Prague.*

---

* Coulondre's version of the interview is given in the *French Yellow Book* (No. 78, pp. 102–3, in the French edition). He confirms Weizsaecker's account. Later, at his trial in Nuremberg, the State Secretary argued that in his memoranda of such meetings he had purposely exaggerated his Nazi sentiments in order to cover his real anti-Nazi activities. But Coulondre's account of the meeting is only one piece of evidence that Weizsaecker did not exaggerate at all.

Weizsaecker behaved quite differently to the accommodating British ambassador, who transmitted his government's protest late on the afternoon of March 18. Great Britain now held that it could not "but regard the events of the past few days as a complete repudiation of the Munich Agreement" and that the "German military actions" were "devoid of any basis of legality." Weizsaecker, in recording it, noted that the British note did not go as far in this respect as the French protest, which said that France "would not recognize the legality of the German occupation."

Henderson had gone to see Weizsaecker on March 17 to inform him of his recall to London for "consultations" and, according to the State Secretary, had sounded him out "for arguments which he could give Chamberlain for use against the latter's political opposition . . . Henderson explained that there was no direct British interest in the Czechoslovak territory. His—Henderson's—anxieties were more for the future."[37]

Even Hitler's destruction of Czechoslovakia apparently had not awakened the British ambassador to the nature of the government he was accredited to, nor did he seem aware of what was happening that day to the government which he represented.

For, suddenly and unexpectedly, Neville Chamberlain, on March 17, two days after Hitler extinguished Czechoslovakia, had experienced a great awakening. It had not come without some prodding. Greatly to his surprise, most of the British press (even the *Times,* but not the *Daily Mail*) and the House of Commons had reacted violently to Hitler's latest aggression. More serious, many of his own backers in Parliament and half of the cabinet had revolted against any further appeasement of Hitler. Lord Halifax, especially, as the German ambassador informed Berlin, had insisted that the Prime Minister recognize what had happened and abruptly change his course.[38] It dawned on Chamberlain that his own position as head of government and leader of the Conservative Party was in jeopardy.

His radical change of mind came abruptly. As late as the evening of March 16, Sir John Simon, on behalf of the government, had made a speech in the Commons which was so cynical in regard to the Czechs, and so much in the "Munich spirit," that according to press accounts it aroused the House to "a pitch of anger rarely seen." The next day, on the eve of his seventieth birthday, Chamberlain was scheduled to make a speech in his home city of Birmingham. He had drafted an address on domestic matters with special emphasis on the social services. On the afternoon train going up to Birmingham, according to an account given this writer by French diplomatic sources, Chamberlain finally made his decision. He jettisoned his prepared speech and quickly jotted down notes for one of quite a different kind.

To all of Britain and indeed to large parts of the world, for the speech was broadcast, Chamberlain apologized for "the very restrained and cautious . . . somewhat cool and objective statement" which he had felt obliged to make in the Commons two days before. "I hope to correct that statement tonight," he said.

The Prime Minister at last saw that Adolf Hitler had deceived him. He recapitulated the Fuehrer's various assurances that the Sudetenland had been his last territorial demand in Europe and that he "wanted no Czechs." Now Hitler had gone back on them—"he has taken the law into his own hands."

Now we are told that this seizure of territory has been necessitated by disturbances in Czechoslovakia. . . . If there were disorders, were they not fomented from without? . . . Is this the end of an old adventure or is it the beginning of a new? Is this the last attack upon a small State or is it to be followed by others? Is this, in effect, a step in the direction of an attempt to dominate the world by force? . . . While I am not prepared to engage this country by new and unspecified commitments operating under conditions which cannot now be foreseen, yet no greater mistake could be made than to suppose that because it believes war to be a senseless and cruel thing, this nation has so lost its fiber that it will not take part to the utmost of its power in resisting such a challenge if it ever were made.

This was an abrupt and fateful turning point for Chamberlain and for Britain, and Hitler was so warned the very next day by the astute German ambassador in London. "It would be wrong," Herbert von Dirksen notified the German Foreign Office in a lengthy report on March 18, "to cherish any illusions that a fundamental change has not taken place in Britain's attitude to Germany."[39]

It was obvious to anyone who had read *Mein Kampf,* who glanced at a map and saw the new positions of the German Army in Slovakia, who had wind of certain German diplomatic moves since Munich, or who had pondered the dynamics of Hitler's bloodless conquests of Austria and Czechoslovakia in the past twelve months, just which of the "small states" would be next on the Fuehrer's list. Chamberlain, like almost everyone else, knew perfectly well.

On March 31, sixteen days after Hitler entered Prague, the Prime Minister told the House of Commons:

In the event of any action which clearly threatened Polish independence and which the Polish Government accordingly considered it vital to resist with their national forces, His Majesty's Government would feel themselves bound at once to lend the Polish Government all support in their power. They have given the Polish Government an assurance to this effect. I may add that the French Government have authorized me to make it plain that they stand in the same position in this matter.

The turn of Poland had come.

14

THE TURN OF POLAND

O N OCTOBER 24, 1938, less than a month after Munich, Ribbentrop was host to Józef Lipski, the Polish ambassador in Berlin, at a three-hour lunch at the Grand Hotel in Berchtesgaden. Poland, like Germany and indeed in connivance with her, had just seized a strip of Czech territory. The luncheon talk proceeded, as a German Foreign Office memorandum stressed, "in a very friendly atmosphere."[1]

Nevertheless, the Nazi Foreign Minister lost little time in getting down to business. The time had come, he said, for a general settlement between Poland and Germany. It was necessary, first of all, he continued, "to speak with Poland about Danzig." It should "revert" to Germany. Also, Ribbentrop said, the Reich wished to build a super motor highway and a double-track railroad across the Polish Corridor to connect Germany with Danzig and East Prussia. Both would have to enjoy extraterritorial rights. Finally, Hitler wished Poland to join the Anti-Comintern Pact against Russia. In return for all these concessions, Germany would be willing to extend the Polish–German treaty by from ten to twenty years and guarantee Poland's frontiers.

Ribbentrop emphasized he was broaching these problems "in strict confidence." He suggested that the ambassador make his report to Foreign Minister Beck "orally—since otherwise there was great danger of its leaking out, especially to the press." Lipski promised to report to Warsaw but warned Ribbentrop that personally he saw "no possibility" of the return of Danzig to Germany. He further reminded the German Foreign Minister of two recent occasions—November 5, 1937, and January 14, 1938—when Hitler had personally assured the Poles that he would not support any change in the Danzig Statute.[2] Ribbentrop replied that he did not wish an answer now, but advised the Poles "to think it over."

The government in Warsaw did not need much time to collect its thoughts. A week later, on October 31, Foreign Minister Beck dispatched detailed instructions to his ambassador in Berlin on how to answer the Germans. But it was not until November 19 that the latter was able to secure an interview with Ribbentrop—the Nazis obviously wanted the Poles to consider well their response. It was negative. As a gesture of understanding, Poland was willing to replace the League of Nations' guarantee of Danzig with a German–Polish agreement about the status of the Free City.

"Any other solution," Beck wrote in a memorandum which Lipski read to Ribbentrop, "and in particular any attempt to incorporate the Free City into the Reich, must inevitably lead to conflict." And he added that Marshal Pilsudski, the late dictator of Poland, had warned the Germans in 1934, during the negotiations for a nonaggression pact, that "the Danzig question was a sure criterion for estimating Germany's intentions toward Poland."

Such a reply was not to Ribbentrop's taste. "He regretted the position taken by Beck" and advised the Poles that it was "worth the trouble to give serious consideration to the German proposals."[3]

Hitler's response to Poland's rebuff on Danzig was more drastic. On November 24, five days after the Ribbentrop–Lipski meeting, he issued another directive to the commanders in chief of the armed forces.

TOP SECRET

The Fuehrer has ordered: Apart from the three contingencies mentioned in the instructions of 10/21/38* preparations are also to be made to enable the Free State of Danzig to be occupied by German troops by surprise.

The preparations will be made on the following basis: Condition is a *quasi-revolutionary* occupation of Danzig, exploiting a politically favorable situation, *not a war against Poland*.† . . .

The troops to be employed for this purpose must not simultaneously be earmarked for the occupation of the Memelland, so that both operations can, if necessary, take place simultaneously. The *Navy* will support the Army's operation by attack from the sea . . . The plans of the branches of the armed forces are to be submitted by January 10, 1939.

Though Beck had just warned that an attempt by Germany to take Danzig would lead "inevitably" to conflict, Hitler now convinced himself that it could be done without a war. Local Nazis controlled Danzig and they took their orders, as had the Sudeteners, from Berlin. It would not be difficult to stir up a "quasi-revolutionary" situation there.

Thus, as 1938 approached its end, the year that had seen the bloodless occupation of Austria and the Sudetenland, Hitler was preoccupied with further conquest: the remainder of Czechoslovakia, Memel, and Danzig. It had been easy to humble Schuschnigg and Beneš. Now it was Józef Beck's turn.

---

* See above, p. 428. The three "contingencies" were the liquidation of the rest of Czechoslovakia, occupation of Memel and protection of the Reich's frontiers.
† Italics in the original.

Yet, when the Fuehrer received the Polish Foreign Minister at Berchtesgaden shortly after New Year's—on January 5, 1939—he was not yet prepared to give him the treatment which he had meted out to Schuschnigg and was shortly to apply to President Hácha. The rest of Czechoslovakia would have to be liquidated first. Hitler, as the secret Polish and German minutes of the meeting make clear, was in one of his more conciliatory moods. He was "quite ready," he began, "to be at Beck's service." Was there anything "special," he asked, on the Polish Foreign Minister's mind? Beck replied that Danzig was on his mind. It became obvious that it had also been on Hitler's.

"Danzig is German," the Fuehrer reminded his guest, "will always remain German, and will sooner or later become part of Germany." He could give the assurance, however, that "no *fait accompli* would be engineered in Danzig."

He wanted Danzig and he wanted a German highway and railroad across the Corridor. If he and Beck would "depart from old patterns and seek solutions along entirely new lines," he was sure they could reach an agreement which would do justice to both countries.

Beck was not so sure. Though, as he confided to Ribbentrop the next day, he did not want to be too blunt with the Fuehrer, he had replied that "the Danzig problem was a very difficult one." He did not see in the Chancellor's suggestion any "equivalent" for Poland. Hitler thereupon pointed out the "great advantage" to Poland "of having her frontier with Germany, including the Corridor, secured by treaty." This apparently did not impress Beck, but in the end he agreed to think the problem over further.[4]

After mulling it over that night, the Polish Foreign Minister had a talk with Ribbentrop the next day in Munich. He requested him to inform the Fuehrer that whereas all his previous talks with the Germans had filled him with optimism, he was today, after his meeting with Hitler, "for the first time in a pessimistic mood." Particularly in regard to Danzig, as it had been raised by the Chancellor, he "saw no possibility whatever of agreement."[5]

It had taken Colonel Beck, like so many others who have figured in these pages, some time to awaken and to arrive at such a pessimistic view. Like most Poles, he was violently anti-Russian. Moreover, he disliked the French, for whom he had nursed a grudge since 1923, when, as Polish military attaché in Paris, he had been expelled for allegedly selling documents relating to the French Army. Perhaps it had been natural for this man, who had become Polish Foreign Minister in November 1932, to turn to Germany. For the Nazi dictatorship he had felt a warm sympathy from the beginning, and over the past six years he had striven to bring his country closer to the Third Reich and to weaken its traditional ties with France.

Of all the countries that lay on the borders of Germany, Poland had, in the long run, the most to fear. Of all the countries, it had been the most

blind to the German danger. No other provision of the Versailles Treaty
had been resented by the Germans as much as that which established the
Corridor, giving Poland access to the sea—and cutting off East Prussia
from the Reich. The detachment of the old Hanseatic port of Danzig
from Germany and its creation as a free city under the supervision of the
League of Nations, but dominated economically by Poland, had equally
outraged German public opinion. Even the weak and peaceful Weimar
Republic had never accepted what it regarded as the Polish mutilation of
the German Reich. As far back as 1922, General von Seeckt, as we have
seen,* had defined the German Army's attitude.

Poland's existence is intolerable and incompatible with the essential conditions of Germany's life. Poland must go and will go—as a result of her own
internal weaknesses and of action by Russia—with our aid . . . The obliteration of Poland must be one of the fundamental drives of German policy . . .
[and] is attainable by means of, and with the help of, Russia.

Prophetic words!
The Germans forgot—or perhaps did not wish to remember—that
almost all of the German land awarded Poland at Versailles, including the
provinces of Posen and Polish Pomerania (Pomorze), which formed the
Corridor, had been grabbed by Prussia at the time of the partitions when
Prussia, Russia and Austria had destroyed the Polish nation. For more
than a millennium it had been inhabited by Poles—and, to a large extent,
it still was.
No nation re-created by Versailles had had such a rough time as Poland.
In the first turbulent years of its rebirth it had waged aggressive war against
Russia, Lithuania, Germany and even Czechoslovakia—in the last instance over the coal-rich Teschen area. Deprived of their political freedom
for a century and a half and thus without modern experience in self-rule,
the Poles were unable to establish stable government or to begin to solve
their economic and agrarian problems. In 1926 Marshal Pilsudski, the
hero of the 1918 revolution, had marched on Warsaw, seized control of
the government and, though an old-time Socialist, had gradually replaced
a chaotic democratic regime with his own dictatorship. One of his last
acts, before his death in 1935, was to sign a treaty of nonaggression with
Hitler. This took place on January 26, 1934, and, as has been recounted,†
was one of the first steps in the undermining of France's system of alliances
with Germany's Eastern neighbors and in the weakening of the League of
Nations and its concept of collective security. After Pilsudski's death,
Poland was largely governed by a small band of "colonels," leaders of
Pilsudski's old Polish Legion which had fought against Russia during the
First World War. At the head of these was Marshal Smigly-Rydz, a

* See above, p. 212.
† See above, pp. 212–13.

capable soldier but in no way a statesman. Foreign policy drifted into the hands of Colonel Beck. From 1934 on, it became increasingly pro-German.

This was bound to be a policy of suicide. And indeed when one considers Poland's position in post-Versailles Europe it is difficult to escape the conclusion that the Poles in the nineteen thirties, as on occasions in the centuries before, were driven by some fateful flaw in their national character toward self-destruction and that in this period, as sometimes formerly, they were their own worst enemies. As long as Danzig and the Corridor existed as they were, there could be no lasting peace between Poland and Nazi Germany. Nor was Poland strong enough to afford the luxury of being at odds with both her giant neighbors, Russia and Germany. Her relations with the Soviet Union had been uniformly bad since 1920, when Poland had attacked Russia, already weakened by the World War and the civil war, and a savage conflict had followed.*

Seizing an opportunity to gain the friendship of a country so stoutly anti-Russian and at the same time to detach her from Geneva and Paris, thus undermining the system of Versailles, Hitler had taken the initiative in bringing about the Polish–German pact of 1934. It was not a popular move in Germany. The German Army, which had been pro-Russian and anti-Polish since the days of Seeckt, resented it. But it served Hitler admirably for the time being. Poland's sympathetic friendship helped him to get first things done first: the reoccupation of the Rhineland, the destruction of independent Austria and Czechoslovakia. On all of these steps, which strengthened Germany, weakened the West and threatened the East, Beck and his fellow colonels in Warsaw looked on benevolently and with utter and inexplicable blindness.

If the Polish Foreign Minister at the very start of the new year had, as he said, been plunged into a pessimistic mood by Hitler's demands, his spirits sank much lower with the coming of spring. Though in his anniversary speech to the Reichstag on January 30, 1939, Hitler spoke in warm terms of "the friendship between Germany and Poland" and declared that it was "one of the reassuring factors in the political life in Europe," Ribbentrop had talked with more frankness when he paid a state visit to Warsaw four days before. He again raised with Beck the question of Hitler's demands concerning Danzig and communications through the Corridor, insisting that they were "extremely moderate." But neither on these questions nor on his insistence that Poland join the Anti-Comintern Pact against the Soviet Union did the German Foreign Minister get a

---

* As a result of that war, Poland pushed its eastern boundary 150 miles east of the ethnographic Curzon Line, at the expense of the Soviet Union—a frontier which transferred four and a half million Ukrainians and one and a half million White Russians to Polish rule. Thus Poland's western and eastern borders were unacceptable to Germany and Russia respectively—a fact which seems to have been lost sight of in the Western democracies when Berlin and Moscow began to draw together in the summer of 1939.

satisfactory answer.[6] Colonel Beck was becoming wary of his friends. As a matter of fact, he was beginning to squirm. On February 26, the German ambassador in Warsaw informed Berlin that Beck had taken the initiative in getting himself invited to visit London at the end of March and that he might go on to Paris afterward. Though it was late in the day, Poland, as Moltke put it in his dispatch, "desires to get in touch with the Western democracies . . . [for] fear that a conflict might arise with Germany over Danzig."[7] With Beck too, as with so many others who had tried to appease the ravenous appetite of Adolf Hitler, the scales were falling from the eyes.

They fell completely and forever on March 15 when Hitler occupied Bohemia and Moravia and sent his troops to protect "independent" Slovakia. Poland woke up that morning to find itself flanked in the south along the Slovak border, as it already was in the north on the frontiers of Pomerania and East Prussia, by the German Army. Its military position had overnight become untenable.

March 21, 1939, is a day to be remembered in the story of Europe's march toward war.

There was intense diplomatic activity that day in Berlin, Warsaw and London. The President of the French Republic, accompanied by Foreign Minister Bonnet, arrived in the British capital for a state visit. To the French Chamberlain suggested that their two countries join Poland and the Soviet Union in a formal declaration stating that the four nations would consult immediately about steps to halt further aggression in Europe. Three days before, Litvinov had proposed—as he had just a year before, after the Anschluss—a European conference, this time of France, Britain, Poland, Russia, Rumania and Turkey, which would join together to stop Hitler. But the British Prime Minister had found the idea "premature." He was highly distrustful of Moscow and thought a "declaration" by the four powers, including the Soviet Union, was as far as he could go.*

His proposal was presented to Beck in Warsaw by the British ambassador on the same day, March 21, and received a somewhat cool reception, as far as including the Russians was concerned. The Polish Foreign Minister was even more distrustful of the Soviet Union than Chamberlain and, moreover, shared the Prime Minister's views about the worthlessness of Russian military aid. He was to hold these views, unflinchingly, right up to the moment of disaster.

But the most fateful event of this day of March 21 for Poland took place in Berlin. Ribbentrop invited the Polish ambassador to call on him at noon. For the first time, as Lipski noted in a subsequent report, the

---

* "I must confess," Chamberlain wrote in a private letter on March 26, "to the most profound distrust of Russia. I have no belief whatever in her ability to maintain an effective offensive, even if she wanted to. And I distrust her motives . . . Moreover, she is both hated and suspected by many of the smaller states, notably by Poland, Rumania and Finland." (Feiling, *The Life of Neville Chamberlain,* p. 603.)

Foreign Minister was not only cool toward him but aggressive. The Fuehrer, he warned, "was becoming increasingly amazed at Poland's attitude." Germany wanted a satisfactory reply to her demands for Danzig and a highway and railroad through the Corridor. This was a condition for continued friendly Polish–German relations. "Poland must realize," Ribbentrop laid it down, "that she could not take a middle course between Russia and Germany." Her only salvation was "a reasonable relationship with Germany and her Fuehrer." That included a joint "anti-Soviet policy." Moreover, the Fuehrer desired Beck "to pay an early visit to Berlin." In the meantime, Ribbentrop strongly advised the Polish ambassador to hurry to Warsaw and explain to his Foreign Minister in person what the situation was. "He advised," Lipski informed Beck, "that the talk [with Hitler] should not be delayed, lest the Chancellor should come to the conclusion that Poland was rejecting all his offers."[8]

A SLIGHT AGGRESSION BY THE BY

Before leaving the Wilhelmstrasse, Lipski had asked Ribbentrop whether he could tell him anything about his conversation with the Foreign Minister of Lithuania. The German replied that they had discussed the Memel question, "which called for a solution."

As a matter of fact, Ribbentrop had received the Lithuanian Foreign Minister, Juozas Urbays, who was passing through Berlin after a trip to Rome, on the previous day and demanded that Lithuania hand back the Memel district to Germany forthwith. Otherwise "the Fuehrer would act with lightning speed." The Lithuanians, he warned, must not deceive themselves by expecting "some kind of help from abroad."[9]

Actually, some months before, on December 12, 1938, the French ambassador and the British chargé d'affaires had called the attention of the German government to reports that the German population of Memel was planning a revolt and had asked it to use its influence to see that the Memel Statute, guaranteed by both Britain and France, was respected. The Foreign Office reply had expressed "surprise and astonishment" at the Anglo–French *démarche,* and Ribbentrop had ordered that if there were any further such steps the two embassies should be told "that we had really expected that the French and British would finally become tired of meddling in Germany's affairs."[10]

For some time the German government and particularly the party and S.S. leaders had been organizing the Germans of Memel along lines with which we are now familiar from the Austrian and Sudeten affairs. The German armed forces had also been called in to co-operate and, as we have seen,* three weeks after Munich Hitler had ordered his military chiefs to prepare, along with the liquidation of the remainder of Czechoslovakia, the occupation of Memel. Since the Navy had had no opportu-

---

* See above, pp. 428–29.

nity for glory in the march-in to landlocked Austria and Sudetenland, Hitler decided that Memel should be taken from the sea. In November, naval plans for the venture were drawn up under the code name "Transport Exercise Stettin." Hitler and Admiral Raeder were so keen on this little display of naval might that they actually put to sea from Swinemuende aboard the pocket battleship *Deutschland* for Memel on March 22, exactly a week after the Fuehrer's triumphant entry into Prague, before defenseless Lithuania had time to capitulate to a German ultimatum.

On March 21, Weizsaecker, who much later would proclaim his distaste for the brutality of Nazi methods, notified the Lithuanian government that "there was no time to lose" and that its plenipotentiaries must come to Berlin "by special plane tomorrow" to sign away to Germany the district of Memel. The Lithuanians had obediently arrived late in the afternoon of March 22, but despite German pressure administered in person by Ribbentrop, egged on by a seasick Hitler aboard his battleship at sea, they took their time about capitulating. Twice during the night, the captured German documents reveal, the Fuehrer got off urgent radiograms from the *Deutschland* to Ribbentrop asking whether the Lithuanians had surrendered, as requested. The dictator and his Admiral had to know whether they must shoot their way into the port of Memel. Finally, at 1:30 A.M. on March 23, Ribbentrop was able to transmit by radio to his master the news that the Lithuanians had signed.[11]

At 2:30 in the afternoon of the twenty-third, Hitler made another of his triumphant entries into a newly occupied city and at the Stadttheater in Memel again addressed a delirious "liberated" German throng. Another provision of the Versailles Treaty had been torn up. Another bloodless conquest had been made. Although the Fuehrer could not know it, it was to be the last.

THE HEAT ON POLAND

The German annexation of the Memelland came as "a very unpleasant surprise" to the Polish government, as the German ambassador to Poland, Hans-Adolf von Moltke, reported to Berlin from Warsaw on the following day. "The main reason for this," he added, "is that it is generally feared that now it will be the turn of Danzig and the Corridor."[12] He also informed the German Foreign Office that Polish reservists were being called up. The next day, March 25, Admiral Canaris, chief of the Abwehr, reported that Poland had mobilized three classes and was concentrating troops around Danzig. General Keitel did not believe this showed "any aggressive intentions on the part of the Poles," but the Army General Staff, he noted, "took a somewhat more serious view."[13]

Hitler returned to Berlin from Memel on March 24 and on the next day had a long talk with General von Brauchitsch, the Commander in Chief of the Army. From the latter's confidential memorandum of the conversation it appears that the Leader had not yet made up his mind exactly how to proceed against Poland.[14] In fact, his turbulent brain seemed to be full of contradictions. Ambassador Lipski was due back on the next day, March 26, and the Fuehrer did not want to see him.

Lipski will return from Warsaw on Sunday, March 26 [Brauchitsch noted]. He was commissioned to ask whether Poland would be prepared to come to some terms with regard to Danzig. The Fuehrer left during the night of March 25: he does not wish to be here when Lipski returns. Ribbentrop shall negotiate at first. The Fuehrer does not wish, though, to solve the Danzig problem by force. He would not like to drive Poland into the arms of Great Britain by doing so.

A military occupation of Danzig would have to be taken into consideration only if Lipski gives a hint that the Polish Government could not take the responsibility toward their own people to cede Danzig voluntarily and the solution would be made easier for them by a *fait accompli.*

This is an interesting insight into Hitler's mind and character at this moment. Three months before, he had personally assured Beck that there would be no German *fait accompli* in Danzig. Yet he remembered that the Polish Foreign Minister had stressed that the Polish people would never stand for turning over Danzig to Germany. If the Germans merely seized it, would not this *fait accompli* make it easier for the Polish government to accept it? Hitherto Hitler had been a genius at sizing up the weaknesses of his foreign opponents and taking advantage of them, but here, for almost the first time, his judgment has begun to falter. The "colonels" who governed Poland were a mediocre and muddling lot, but the last thing they wanted, or would accept, was a *fait accompli* in Danzig.

The Free City was uppermost in Hitler's mind, but he was also thinking beyond it, just as he had done in regard to Czechoslovakia after Munich had given him the Sudetenland.

For the time being [Brauchitsch noted], the Fuehrer does not intend to solve the Polish question. However, it should be worked on. A solution in the near future would have to be based on especially favorable political conditions. In that case Poland shall be knocked down so completely that it need not be taken into account as a political factor for the next few decades. The Fuehrer has in mind as such a solution a borderline advanced from the eastern border of East Prussia to the eastern tip of Upper Silesia.

Brauchitsch well knew what that border signified. It was Germany's prewar eastern frontier, which Versailles had destroyed, and which had prevailed as long as there was no Poland.

If Hitler had any doubts as to what the Polish reply would be they were dissipated when Ambassador Lipski returned to Berlin on Sunday, March 26, and presented his country's answer in the form of a written memorandum.[15] Ribbentrop read it at once, rejected it, stormed about Polish mobilization measures and warned the envoy "of possible consequences."

He also declared that any violation of Danzig territory by Polish troops would be regarded as aggression against the Reich.

Poland's written response, while couched in conciliatory language, was a firm rejection of the German demands. It expressed willingness to discuss further means of facilitating German rail and road traffic across the Corridor but refused to consider making such communications extraterritorial. As for Danzig, Poland was willing to replace the League of Nations status by a Polish–German guarantee but not to see the Free City become a part of Germany.

Nazi Germany by this time was not accustomed to see a smaller nation turning down its demands, and Ribbentrop remarked to Lipski that "it reminded him of certain risky steps taken by another state"—an obvious reference to Czechoslovakia, which Poland had helped Hitler to dismember. It must have been equally obvious to Lipski, when he was summoned again to the Foreign Office the next day by Ribbentrop, that the Third Reich would now resort to the same tactics against Poland which had been used so successfully against Austria and Czechoslovakia. The Nazi Foreign Minister raged at the alleged persecution of the German minority in Poland, which, he said, had created "a disastrous impression in Germany."

In conclusion, the [German] Foreign Minister remarked that he could no longer understand the Polish Government . . . The proposals transmitted yesterday by the Polish Ambassador could not be regarded as a basis for a settlement. Relations between the two countries were therefore rapidly deteriorating.[16]

Warsaw was not so easily intimidated as Vienna and Prague. The next day, March 28, Beck sent for the German ambassador and told him, in answer to Ribbentrop's declaration that a Polish coup against Danzig would signify a *casus belli,* that he in turn was forced to state that any attempt by Germany or the Nazi Danzig Senate to alter the status of the Free City would be regarded by Poland as a *casus belli.*

"You want to negotiate at the point of a bayonet!" exclaimed the ambassador.

"This is your own method," Beck replied.[17]

The reawakened Polish Foreign Minister could afford to stand up to Berlin more firmly than Beneš had been able to do, for he knew that the British government, which a year before had been anxious to help Hitler obtain his demands against Czechoslovakia, was now taking precisely the opposite course in regard to Poland. Beck himself had torpedoed the British proposal for a four-power declaration, declaring that Poland refused to associate itself with Russia in any manner. Instead, on March 22, he had suggested to Sir Howard Kennard, the British ambassador in Warsaw, the immediate conclusion of a secret Anglo–Polish agreement for consultation in case of a threatened attack by a third power. But, alarmed by German troop movements adjacent to Danzig and the Corridor and by British intelligence concerning German demands on Poland (which the tricky Beck had denied to the British), Chamberlain and Halifax wanted to go further than mere "consultations."

On the evening of March 30, Kennard presented to Beck an Anglo–French proposal for mutual-assistance pacts in case of German aggression.* But even this step was overtaken by events. Fresh reports of the possibility of an imminent German attack on Poland prompted the British government on the same evening to ask Beck whether he had any objection to an interim unilateral British guarantee of Poland's independence. Chamberlain had to know by the morrow, as he wished to answer a parliamentary question on the subject. Beck—his sense of relief may be imagined—had no objection. In fact, he told Kennard, he "agreed without hesitation."[19]

The next day, March 31, as we have seen, Chamberlain made his historic declaration in the House of Commons that Britain and France "would lend the Polish Government all support in their power" if Poland were attacked and resisted.†

To anyone in Berlin that weekend when March 1939 came to an end, as this writer happened to be, the sudden British unilateral guarantee of Poland seemed incomprehensible, however welcome it might be in the lands to the west and the east of Germany. Time after time, as we have seen, in 1936 when the Germans marched into the demilitarized Rhineland, in 1938 when they took Austria and threatened a European war to take the Sudetenland, even a fortnight before, when they grabbed Czechoslovakia, Great Britain and France, backed by Russia, could have taken action to stop Hitler at very little cost to themselves. But the peace-hungry Chamberlain had shied away from such moves. Not only that: he had gone out of his way, he had risked, as he said, his political career to help Adolf Hitler get what he wanted in the neighboring lands. He had done nothing to save the independence of Austria. He had consorted with the German dictator to destroy the independence of Czechoslovakia, the only truly democratic nation on Germany's eastern borders and the only one which was a friend of the West and which supported the League of Nations and the idea of collective security. He had not even considered the military value to the *West* of Czechoslovakia's thirty-five well-trained, well-

---

* In the telegram of instructions to Kennard[18] it was made clear that Russia was to be left out in the cold. "It is becoming clear," it said, "that our attempts to consolidate the situation will be frustrated if the Soviet Union is openly associated with the initiation of the scheme. Recent telegrams from a number of His Majesty's Missions abroad have warned us that the inclusion of Russia would not only jeopardise the success of our constructive effort but also tend to consolidate the relations of the parties to the Anti-Comintern Pact, as well as excite anxiety among a number of friendly governments."
† See above, p. 454.

armed divisions entrenched behind their strong mountain fortifications at a time when Britain could put only two divisions in France and when the German Army was incapable of fighting on two fronts and, according to the German generals, even incapable of penetrating the Czech defenses.

Now overnight, in his understandably bitter reaction to Hitler's occupation of the rest of Czechoslovakia, Chamberlain, after having deliberately and recklessly thrown so much away, had undertaken to unilaterally guarantee an Eastern country run by a junta of politically inept "colonels" who up to this moment had closely collaborated with Hitler, who like hyenas had joined the Germans in the carving up of Czechoslovakia and whose country had been rendered militarily indefensible by the very German conquests which Britain and Poland had helped the Reich to achieve.* And he had taken this eleventh-hour risk without bothering to enlist the aid of Russia, whose proposals for joint action against further Nazi aggression he had twice turned down within the year.

Finally, he had done exactly what for more than a year he had stoutly asserted that Britain would never do: he had left to another nation the decision whether his country would go to war.

Nevertheless, the Prime Minister's precipitate step, belated as it was, presented Adolf Hitler with an entirely new situation. From now on, apparently, Britain would stand in the way of his committing further aggression. He could no longer use the technique of taking one nation at a time while the Western democracies stood aside debating what to do. Moreover, Chamberlain's move appeared to be the first serious step toward forming a coalition of powers against Germany which, unless it were successfully countered, might bring again that very encirclement which had been the nightmare of the Reich since Bismarck.

CASE WHITE

The news of Chamberlain's guarantee of Poland threw the German dictator into one of his characteristic rages. He happened to be with Ad-

---

* Chamberlain could not have been ignorant of Poland's military weakness. Colonel Sword, the British military attaché in Warsaw, had sent to London a week before, on March 22, a long report on the disastrous strategic position of Poland, "bounded on three sides by Germany," and on the deficiencies of the Polish armed forces, especially in modern arms and equipment.[20]

On April 6, while Colonel Beck was in London discussing a mutual-assistance pact, Colonel Sword and also the British air attaché in Warsaw, Group Captain Vachell, sent fresh reports which were even less hopeful. Vachell emphasized that during the next twelve months the Polish Air Force would have "no more than about 600 aircraft, many of which are no match for German aircraft." Sword reported that the Polish Army and Air Force were both so lacking in modern equipment that they could put up only a limited resistance to an all-out German attack. Ambassador Kennard, summing up his attachés' reports, informed London that the Poles would be unable to defend the Corridor or the western frontier against Germany and would have to fall back on the Vistula in the heart of Poland. "A friendly Russia," he added, was "thus of paramount importance" for Poland.[21]

miral Canaris, chief of the Abwehr, and according to the latter he stormed about the room, pounding his fists on the marble table top, his face contorted with fury, and shouting against the British, "I'll cook them a stew they'll choke on!"[22]

The next day, April 1, he spoke at Wilhelmshaven at the launching of the battleship *Tirpitz* and was in such a belligerent mood that apparently he did not quite trust himself, for at the last moment he ordered that the direct radio broadcast of his speech be canceled; he directed that it be rebroadcast later from recordings, which could be edited.* Even the rebroadcast version was spotted with warnings to Britain and Poland.

If they [the Western Allies] expect the Germany of today to sit patiently by until the very last day while they create satellite States and set them against Germany, then they are mistaking the Germany of today for the Germany of before the war.

He who declares himself ready to pull the chestnuts out of the fire for these powers must realize he burns his fingers. . . .

When they say in other countries that they will arm and will keep arming still more, I can tell those statesmen only this: "Me you will never tire out!" I am determined to continue on this road.

Hitler, as his cancellation of the direct broadcast showed, was cautious enough not to provoke foreign opinion too much. It was reported in Berlin that day that he would denounce the Anglo–German naval treaty as his first reply to Chamberlain. But in his speech he merely declared that if Great Britain no longer wished to adhere to it, Germany "would accept this very calmly."

As so often before, Hitler ended on an old familiar note of peace: "Germany has no intention of attacking other people . . . Out of this conviction I decided three weeks ago to name the coming party rally the 'Party Convention of Peace' "—a slogan, which as the summer of 1939 developed, became more and more ironic.

That was for public consumption. In the greatest of secrecy Hitler gave his real answer to Chamberlain and Colonel Beck two days later, on April 3. It was contained in a top-secret directive to the armed forces, of which only five copies were made, inaugurating "Case White." This was

---

* Actually, the relay of the broadcast to the American radio networks was cut off after Hitler had begun to speak. This led to reports in New York that he had been assassinated. I was in the control room of the short-wave section of the German Broadcasting Company in Berlin, looking after the relay to the Columbia Broadcasting System in New York, when the broadcast was suddenly shut off. To my protests, German officials answered that the order had come from Hitler himself. Within fifteen minutes CBS was telephoning me from New York to check on the assassination report. I could easily deny it because through an open telephone circuit to Wilhelmshaven I could hear Hitler shouting his speech. It would have been difficult to shoot the Fuehrer that day because he spoke behind a bulletproof glass enclosure.

a code name which was to loom large in the subsequent history of the world.

TOP SECRET

Case White

The present attitude of Poland requires . . . the initiation of military preparations to remove, if necessary, any threat from this direction forever.

1. Political Requirements and Aims

. . . The aim will be to destroy Polish military strength and create in the East a situation which satisfies the requirements of national defense. The Free State of Danzig will be proclaimed a part of the Reich territory at the outbreak of hostilities, at the latest.

The political leaders consider it their task in this case to isolate Poland if possible, that is to say, to limit the war to Poland only.

The development of increasing internal crises in France and the resulting British cautiousness might produce such a situation in the not too distant future.

Intervention by Russia . . . cannot be expected to be of any use to Poland . . . Italy's attitude is determined by the Rome–Berlin Axis.

2. Military Conclusions

The great objectives in the building up of the German armed forces will continue to be determined by the antagonism of the Western democracies. "Case White" constitutes only a precautionary complement to these preparations . . .

The isolation of Poland will be all the more easily maintained, even after the outbreak of hostilities, if we succeed in starting the war with sudden, heavy blows and in gaining rapid successes . . .

3. Tasks of the Armed Forces

The task of the Wehrmacht is to destroy the Polish armed forces. To this end a surprise attack is to be aimed at and prepared.

As for Danzig:

Surprise occupation of Danzig may become possible independently of "Case White" by exploiting a favorable political situation . . . Occupation by the Army will be carried out from East Prussia. The Navy will support the action of the Army by intervention from the sea.

Case White is a lengthy document with several "enclosures," "annexes" and "special orders," most of which were reissued as a whole on April 11 and of course added to later as the time for hostilities approached. But already on April 3, Hitler appended the following directives to Case White:

1. Preparations must be made in such a way that the operation can be carried out at any time from September 1, 1939, onward.

As in the case of the date Hitler gave long in advance for getting the Sudetenland—October 1, 1938—this more important date of September 1, 1939, would also be kept.

2. The High Command of the Armed Forces [OKW] is charged with drawing up a precise timetable for "Case White" and is to arrange for synchronized timing between the three branches of the Wehrmacht.

3. The plans of the branches of the Wehrmacht and the details for the timetable must be submitted to OKW by May 1, 1939.[23]

The question now was whether Hitler could wear down the Poles to the point of accepting his demands, as he had done with the Austrians and (with Chamberlain's help) the Czechs, or whether Poland would hold its ground and resist Nazi aggression if it came, and if so, with what. This writer spent the first week of April in Poland in search of answers. They were, as far as he could see, that the Poles would not give in to Hitler's threats, would fight if their land were invaded, but that militarily and politically they were in a disastrous position. Their Air Force was obsolete, their Army cumbersome, their strategic position—surrounded by the Germans on three sides—almost hopeless. Moreover, the strengthening of Germany's West Wall made an Anglo–French offensive against Germany in case Poland were attacked extremely difficult. And finally it became obvious that the headstrong Polish "colonels" would never consent to receiving Russian help even if the Germans were at the gates of Warsaw.

Events now moved quickly. On April 6 Colonel Beck signed an agreement with Great Britain in London transforming the unilateral British guarantee into a temporary pact of mutual assistance. A permanent treaty, it was announced, would be signed as soon as the details had been worked out.

The next day, April 7, Mussolini sent his troops into Albania and added the conquest of that mountainous little country to that of Ethiopia. It gave him a springboard against Greece and Yugoslavia and in the tense atmosphere of Europe served to make more jittery the small countries which dared to defy the Axis. As the German Foreign Office papers make clear, it was done with the complete approval of Germany, which was informed of the step in advance. On April 13, France and Britain countered with a guarantee to Greece and Rumania. The two sides were beginning to line up. In the middle of April, Goering arrived in Rome and much to Ribbentrop's annoyance had two long talks with Mussolini, on the fifteenth and sixteenth.[24] They agreed that they "needed two or three years" to prepare for "a general conflict," but Goering declared that if war came sooner "the Axis was in a very strong position" and "could defeat any likely opponents."

Mention was made of an appeal from President Roosevelt which had arrived in Rome and Berlin on April 15. The Duce, according to Ciano, had at first refused to read it and Goering declared that it was not worth answering. Mussolini thought it "a result of infantile paralysis," but Goering's impression was that "Roosevelt was suffering from an incipient mental disease." In his telegram to Hitler and Mussolini the President of the United States had addressed a blunt question:

Are you willing to give assurance that your armed forces will not attack or invade the territory of the following independent nations?

There had followed a list of thirty-one countries, including Poland, the Baltic States, Russia, Denmark, the Netherlands, Belgium, France and Britain. The President hoped that such a guarantee of nonaggression could be given for "ten years at the least" or "a quarter of a century, if we dare look that far ahead." If it were given, he promised American participation in world-wide "discussions" to relieve the world from "the crushing burden of armament" and to open up avenues of international trade.

"You have repeatedly asserted," he reminded Hitler, "that you and the German people have no desire for war. If this is true there need be no war."

In the light of what now is known, this seemed like a naïve appeal, but the Fuehrer found it embarrassing enough to let it be known that he would reply to it—not directly, but in a speech to a specially convoked session of the Reichstag on April 28.

In the meantime, as the captured German Foreign Office papers reveal, the Wilhelmstrasse in a circular telegram of April 17 put two questions of its own to all the states mentioned by Roosevelt except Poland, Russia, Britain and France: Did they feel themselves in any way threatened by Germany? Had they authorized Roosevelt to make his proposal?

"We are in no doubt," Ribbentrop wired his various envoys in the countries concerned, "that both questions will be answered in the negative, but nevertheless, for special reasons, we should like to have authentic confirmation at once." The "special reasons" would become evident when Hitler spoke on April 28.

By April 22 the German Foreign Office was able to draw up a report for the Fuehrer that most of the countries, including Yugoslavia, Belgium, Denmark, Norway, the Netherlands and Luxembourg "have answered both questions in the negative"—a reply which would soon show what an innocent view their governments took of the Third Reich. From Rumania, however, came a tart answer that the "Reich Government were themselves in a position to know whether a threat might arise." Little Latvia up in the Baltic did not at first understand what answer was expected of it, but the Foreign Office soon put it right. On April 18 Weizsaecker rang up his minister in Riga

to tell him we were unable to understand the answer of the Latvian Foreign Minister to our question about the Roosevelt telegram. While practically all the other governments have already answered, and naturally in the negative, M. Munters treated this ridiculous American propaganda as a question on which he wished to consult his cabinet. If M. Munters did not answer "no" to our question right away, we should have to add Latvia to those countries which made themselves into willing accomplices of Mr. Roosevelt. I said that I assumed that a word on these lines by Herr von Kotze [the German minister] would be enough to obtain the obvious answer from him.[25]

It was.

HITLER'S REPLY TO ROOSEVELT

The replies were potent ammunition for Hitler, and he made masterly use of them as he swung into his speech to the Reichstag on the pleasant spring day of April 28, 1939. It was, I believe, the longest major public speech he ever made, taking more than two hours to deliver. In many ways, especially in the power of its appeal to Germans and to the friends of Nazi Germany abroad, it was probably the most brilliant oration he ever gave, certainly the greatest this writer ever heard from him. For sheer eloquence, craftiness, irony, sarcasm and hypocrisy, it reached a new level that he was never to approach again. And though prepared for German ears, it was broadcast not only on all German radio stations but on hundreds of others throughout the world; in the United States it was carried by the major networks. Never before or afterward was there such a world-wide audience as he had that day.*

The speech began, after the usual introductory dissertation on the iniquities of Versailles and the many injustices and long suffering heaped upon the German people by it, with an answer first to Great Britain and Poland which shook an uneasy Europe.

After declaring his feeling of admiration and friendship for England and then attacking it for its distrust of him and its new "policy of encirclement" of Germany, he denounced the Anglo–German Naval Treaty of 1935. "The basis for it," he said, "has been removed."

Likewise with Poland. He made known his proposal to Poland concerning Danzig and the Corridor (which had been kept secret), called it "the greatest imaginable concession in the interests of European peace" and informed the Reichstag that the Polish government had rejected this "one and only offer."

---

* On the day of the speech Weizsaecker wired Hans Thomsen, German chargé in Washington, instructing him to give the Fuehrer's address the widest possible publicity in the United States and assuring him that extra funds would be provided for the purpose. On May 1 Thomsen replied, "Interest in speech surpasses anything so far known. I have therefore directed that the English text printed here is to be sent . . . to tens of thousands of addressees of all classes and callings, in accordance with the agreed plan. Claim for costs to follow."[26]

I have regretted this incomprehensible attitude of the Polish Government
. . . The worst is that now Poland, like Czechoslovakia a year ago, believes,
under pressure of a lying international campaign, that it must call up troops,
although Germany has not called up a single man and had not thought of
proceeding in any way against Poland. This is in itself very regrettable, and
posterity will one day decide whether it was really right to refuse this suggestion,
made this once by me . . . a truly unique compromise . . .

Reports that Germany intended to attack Poland, Hitler went on, were
"mere inventions of the international press." (Not one of the tens of millions of persons listening could know that only three weeks before he had
given written orders to his armed forces to prepare for the destruction of
Poland by September 1, "at the latest.") The inventions of the press, he
continued, had led Poland to make its agreement with Great Britain
which, "under certain circumstances, would compel Poland to take military action against Germany." Therefore, Poland had broken the Polish–
German nonaggression pact! "Therefore, I look upon the agreement . . .
as having been unilaterally infringed by Poland and thereby no longer in
existence."

Having himself unilaterally torn up two formal treaties, Hitler then
told the Reichstag that he was willing to negotiate replacements for them!
"I can but welcome such an idea," he exclaimed. "No one would be happier than I at the prospect." This was an old trick he had pulled often before when he had broken a treaty, as we have seen, but though he probably
did not know it, it would no longer work.

Hitler next turned to President Roosevelt, and here the German dictator reached the summit of his oratory. To a normal ear, to be sure, it
reeked with hypocrisy and deception. But to the hand-picked members
of the Reichstag, and to millions of Germans, its masterly sarcasm and
irony were a delight. The paunchy deputies rocked with raucous laughter
as the Fuehrer uttered with increasing effect his seemingly endless ridicule
of the American President. One by one he took up the points of Roosevelt's telegram, paused, almost smiled, and then, like a schoolmaster, uttered in a low voice one word, "Answer"—and gave it. (This writer can
still, in his mind, see Hitler pausing time after time to say quietly, "*Antwort*," while above the rostrum in the President's chair Goering tried ineffectually to stifle a snicker and the members of the Reichstag prepared,
as soon as the *Antwort* was given, to roar and laugh.)

Mr. Roosevelt declares that it is clear to him that all international problems
can be solved at the council table.

Answer: . . . I would be very happy if these problems could really find
their solution at the council table. My skepticism, however, is based on the
fact that it was America herself who gave sharpest expression to her mistrust
in the effectiveness of conferences. For the greatest conference of all time
was the League of Nations . . . representing all the peoples of the world,
created in accordance with the will of an American President. The first State,

however, that shrank from this endeavor was the United States . . . It was not until after years of purposeless participation that I resolved to follow the example of America. . . .

The freedom of North America was not achieved at the conference table any more than the conflict between the North and the South was decided there. I will say nothing about the innumerable struggles which finally led to the subjugation of the North American continent as a whole.

I mention all this only in order to show that your view, Mr. Roosevelt, although undoubtedly deserving of all honor, finds no confirmation in the history of your own country or of the rest of the world.

Germany, Hitler reminded the President, had once gone to a conference—at Versailles—not to discuss but to be told what to do: its representatives "were subjected to even greater degradations than can ever have been inflicted on the chieftains of the Sioux tribes."

Hitler finally got to the core of his answer to the President's request that he give assurances not to attack any of thirty-one nations.

Answer: How has Mr. Roosevelt learned which nations consider themselves threatened by German policy and which do not? Or is Mr. Roosevelt in a position, in spite of the enormous amount of work which must rest upon him in his own country, to recognize of his own accord all these inner spiritual and mental impressions of other peoples and their governments?

Finally, Mr. Roosevelt asks that assurance be given him that the German armed forces will not attack, and above all, not invade the territory or possessions of the following independent nations . . .

Hitler then read out slowly the name of each country and as he intoned the names, I remember, the laughter in the Reichstag grew. Not one member, no one in Berlin, I believe, including this writer, noticed that he slyly left out Poland.

Hitler now pulled the ace out of the pack, or so he must have thought.

Answer: I have taken the trouble to ascertain from the States mentioned, firstly, whether they feel themselves threatened, and secondly and above all, whether this inquiry by the American President was addressed to us at their suggestion, or at any rate, with their consent.

The reply was in all cases negative . . . It is true that I could not cause inquiries to be made of certain of the States and nations mentioned because they themselves—as for example, Syria—are at present not in possession of their freedom, but are occupied and consequently deprived of their rights by the military agents of democratic States.

Apart from this fact, however, all States bordering on Germany have received much more binding assurances . . . than Mr. Roosevelt asked from me in his curious telegram. . . .

I must draw Mr. Roosevelt's attention to one or two historical errors. He mentioned Ireland, for instance, and asks for a statement that Germany will not attack Ireland. Now, I have just read a speech by De Valera, the Irish Taoiseach,* in which, strangely enough, and contrary to Mr. Roosevelt's opinion, he does not charge Germany with oppressing Ireland but he reproaches England with subjecting Ireland to continuous aggression . . .

In the same way, the fact has obviously escaped Mr. Roosevelt's notice that Palestine is at present occupied not by German troops but by the English; and that the country is having its liberty restricted by the most brutal resort to force . . .

Nevertheless, said Hitler, he was prepared "to give each of the States named an assurance of the kind desired by Mr. Roosevelt." But more than that! His eyes lit up.

I should not like to let this opportunity pass without giving above all to the President of the United States an assurance regarding those territories which would, after all, give him most cause for apprehension, namely the United States itself and the other States of the American continent.

I here solemnly declare that all the assertions which have been circulated in any way concerning an intended German attack or invasion on or in American territory are rank frauds and gross untruths, quite apart from the fact that such assertions, as far as the military possibilities are concerned, could have their origin only in a stupid imagination.

The Reichstag rocked with laughter; Hitler did not crack a smile, maintaining with great effect his solemn mien.

And then came the peroration—the most eloquent for German ears, I believe, he ever made.

Mr. Roosevelt! I fully understand that the vastness of your nation and the immense wealth of your country allow you to feel responsible for the history of the whole world and for the history of all nations. I, sir, am placed in a much more modest and smaller sphere . . .

I once took over a State which was faced by complete ruin, thanks to its trust in the promises of the rest of the world and to the bad regime of democratic governments . . . I have conquered chaos in Germany, re-established order and enormously increased production . . . developed traffic, caused mighty roads to be built and canals to be dug, called into being gigantic new factories and at the same time endeavored to further the education and culture of our people.

I have succeeded in finding useful work once more for the whole of the seven million unemployed . . . Not only have I united the German people politically, but I have also rearmed them. I have also endeavored to destroy sheet

---

* Hitler was careful to use the Gaelic word for Prime Minister.

by sheet that treaty which in its four hundred and forty-eight articles contains the vilest oppression which peoples and human beings have ever been expected to put up with.

I have brought back to the Reich provinces stolen from us in 1919. I have led back to their native country millions of Germans who were torn away from us and were in misery . . . and, Mr. Roosevelt, without spilling blood and without bringing to my people, and consequently to others, the misery of war . . .

You, Mr. Roosevelt, have a much easier task in comparison. You became President of the United States in 1933 when I became Chancellor of the Reich. From the very outset you stepped to the head of one of the largest and wealthiest States in the world . . . Conditions prevailing in your country are on such a large scale that you can find time and leisure to give your attention to universal problems . . . Your concerns and suggestions cover a much larger and wider area than mine, because my world, Mr. Roosevelt, in which Providence has placed me and for which I am therefore obliged to work, is unfortunately much smaller, although for me it is more precious than anything else, for it is limited to my people!

I believe however that this is the way in which I can be of the most service to that for which we are all concerned, namely, the justice, well-being, progress and peace of the whole community.

In the hoodwinking of the German people, this speech was Hitler's greatest masterpiece. But as one traveled about Europe in the proceeding days it was easy to see that, unlike a number of Hitler's previous orations, this one no longer fooled the people or the governments abroad. In contrast to the Germans, they were able to see through the maze of deceptions. And they realized that the German Fuehrer, for all his masterful oratory, though scoring off Roosevelt, had not really answered the President's fundamental questions: Had he finished with aggression? Would he attack Poland?

As it turned out, this was the last great peacetime public speech of Hitler's life. The former Austrian waif had come as far in this world as was possible by the genius of his oratory. From now on he was to try to make his niche in history as a warrior.

Retiring for the summer to his mountain retreat at Berchtesgaden, Hitler did not publicly respond to the Polish answer to him which was given on May 5 in a speech by Colonel Beck to Parliament and in an official government memorandum presented to Germany on that date. The Polish statement and Beck's speech constituted a dignified, conciliatory but also firm reply.

It is clear [it said] that negotiations, in which one State formulates demands and the other is obliged to accept those demands unaltered, are not negotiations.

THE INTERVENTION OF RUSSIA: I

In his speech to the Reichstag on April 28, Hitler had omitted his customary attack on the Soviet Union. There was not a word about Russia. Colonel Beck, in his reply, had mentioned "various other hints" made by Germany "which went much further than the subjects of discussion" and reserved the right "to return to this matter, if necessary"—a veiled but obvious reference to Germany's previous efforts to induce Poland to join the Anti-Comintern Pact against Russia. Though Beck did not know it, nor did Chamberlain, those anti-Russian efforts were now being abandoned. Fresh ideas were beginning to germinate in Berlin and Moscow.

It is difficult to ascertain exactly when the first moves were made in the two capitals toward an understanding between Nazi Germany and the Soviet Union which was to lead to such immense consequences for the world. One of the first slight changes in the wind, as has already been noted,* took place as far back as October 3, 1938, four days after Munich, when the counselor of the German Embassy in Moscow informed Berlin that Stalin would draw certain conclusions from the Sudeten settlement, from which he had been excluded, and might well become "more positive" toward Germany. The diplomat strongly advocated a "wider" economic collaboration between the two countries and renewed his appeal in a second dispatch a week later.[27] Toward the end of October, the German ambassador in Moscow, Friedrich Werner Count von der Schulenburg, notified the German Foreign Office that it was his "intention in the immediate future to approach Molotov, the Chairman of the Council of the People's Commissars, in an attempt to reach a settlement of the questions disturbing German–Soviet relations."[28] The ambassador would hardly have conceived such an intention on his own, in view of Hitler's previous extremely hostile attitude toward Moscow. The hint must have come from Berlin.

That it did becomes clear from a study of the captured Foreign Office archives. The first step, in the German view, was to improve trade between the two countries. A Foreign Office memorandum of November 4, 1938, reveals "an emphatic demand from Field Marshal Goering's office at least to try to reactivate our Russian trade, especially insofar as Russian raw materials are concerned."[29] The Russo–German economic agreements expired at the end of the year and the Wilhelmstrasse files are full of material showing the ups and downs experienced in negotiating a renewal. The two sides were highly suspicious of each other but were vaguely drawing closer together. On December 22, there were lengthy talks in Moscow between Russian trade officials and Germany's crack economic troubleshooter, Julius Schnurre.

Shortly after the New Year, the Soviet ambassador in Berlin, Alexei Merekalov, made one of his infrequent trips to the Wilhelmstrasse to inform it "of the Soviet Union's desire to begin a new era in German–Soviet

---

* See above, p. 427.

economic relations." And for a few weeks there were promising talks, but by February 1939 they had pretty much broken down, ostensibly over whether the main negotiations should be conducted in Moscow or Berlin. But the real reason was revealed in a memorandum of the director of the Economic Policy Department of the German Foreign Office on March 11, 1939: Though Germany was hungry for Russia's raw materials and Goering was constantly demanding that they be obtained, the Reich simply could not supply the Soviet Union with the goods which would have to be exchanged. The director thought the "rupture of negotiations" was "extremely regrettable in view of Germany's raw-materials position."[30]

But if the first attempt to draw nearer in their economic relations had failed for the time being, there were other straws in the wind. On March 10, 1939, Stalin made a long speech at the first session of the Eighteenth Party Congress in Moscow. Three days later the attentive Schulenburg filed a long report on it to Berlin. He thought it "noteworthy that Stalin's irony and criticism were directed in considerably sharper degree against Britain than against the so-called aggressor States, and in particular, Germany." The ambassador underlined Stalin's remarks that "the weakness of the democratic powers . . . was evident from the fact that they had abandoned the principle of collective security and had turned to a policy of nonintervention and neutrality. Underlying this policy was the wish to divert the aggressor States to other victims." And he quoted further the Soviet dictator's accusations that the Western Allies were

pushing the Germans further eastward, promising them an easy prey and saying: "Just start a war with the Bolsheviks, everything else will take care of itself. This looks very much like encouragement . . . It looks as if the purpose . . . was to engender the fury of the Soviet Union against Germany . . . and to provoke a conflict with Germany without apparent reasons. . . .

In conclusion Stalin formulated the guiding principles:

1. To continue to pursue a policy of peace and consolidation of economic relations with all countries.
2. . . . Not to let our country be drawn into conflict by warmongers, whose custom it is to let others pull their chestnuts out of the fire.[31]

This was a plain warning from the man who made all the ultimate decisions in Russia that the Soviet Union did not intend to be maneuvered into a war with Nazi Germany in order to spare Britain and France; and if it was ignored in London, it was at least noticed in Berlin.*

---

* Though an Associated Press dispatch from Moscow (published in the New York *Times* March 12) reported that Stalin's condemnation of efforts to embroil Russia in a war with Germany had led to talk in diplomatic circles in Moscow of the possibility of a *rapprochement* between the Soviet Union and Germany, Sir William Seeds, the British ambassador, apparently did not participate in any such talk. In his dispatch reporting Stalin's speech Seeds made no mention of such a possi-

Still, it is evident from Stalin's speech and from the various diplomatic exchanges which shortly took place that Soviet foreign policy, while cautious, was still very much open. Three days after the Nazi occupation of Czechoslovakia on March 15, the Russian government proposed, as we have seen,* a six-power conference to discuss means of preventing further aggression, and Chamberlain turned it down as "premature."† That was on March 18. Two days later an official communiqué in Moscow, which the German ambassador there hurriedly wired to Berlin, denied that the Soviet Union had offered Poland and Rumania assistance "in the event of their becoming the victims of aggression." Reason: "Neither Poland nor Rumania had approached the Soviet government for assistance or informed [it] of any danger threatening them."[34]

The British government's unilateral guarantee of Poland of March 31 may have helped to convince Stalin that Great Britain preferred an alliance with the Poles to one with the Russians and that Chamberlain was intent, as he had been at the time of Munich, on keeping the Soviet Union out of the European concert of powers.[35]

In this situation the Germans and Italians began to glimpse certain opportunities. Goering, who now had an important influence on Hitler in foreign affairs, saw Mussolini in Rome on April 16 and called the Duce's attention to Stalin's recent speech to the Communist Party Congress. He had been impressed by the Soviet dictator's statement that "the Russians would not allow themselves to be used as cannon fodder for the capitalist powers." He said he "would ask the Fuehrer whether it would not be possible to put out feelers cautiously to Russia . . . with a view to *rapprochement*." And he reminded Mussolini that there had been "absolutely no mention of Russia in the Fuehrer's latest speeches." The Duce, according to the confidential German memorandum of the meeting, warmly welcomed the idea of a *rapprochement* of the Axis Powers with the

---

bility. One Western diplomat, Joseph E. Davies, former American ambassador in Moscow, who was now stationed in Brussels, did draw the proper conclusions from Stalin's speech. "It is a most significant statement," he noted in his diary on March 11. "It bears the earmarks of a definite warning to the British and French governments that the Soviets are getting tired of 'nonrealistic' opposition to the aggressors. This . . . is really ominous for the negotiations . . . between the British Foreign Office and the Soviet Union. It certainly is the most significant danger signal that I have yet seen." On March 21 he wrote to Senator Key Pittman: ". . . Hitler is making a desperate effort to alienate Stalin from France and Britain. Unless the British and French wake up, I am afraid he will succeed."[32]

* See above, p. 460.

† In explaining to the Soviet ambassador in London, Ivan Maisky, on March 19 why the Russian proposal for a conference, preferably at Bucharest, was "not acceptable," Lord Halifax said that no Minister of the Crown could be spared for the moment to go to Bucharest. It is obvious that this rebuff soured the Russians in the subsequent negotiations with the British and French. Maisky later told Robert Boothby, a Conservative M.P., that the rejection of the Russian proposal had been "another smashing blow at the policy of effective collective security" and that it had decided the fate of Litvinov.[33]

Soviet Union. The Italian dictator too had sensed a change in Moscow; he thought a *rapprochement* could be "effected with comparative ease."

The object [said Mussolini] would be to induce Russia to react coolly and unfavorably to Britain's efforts at encirclement, on the lines of Stalin's speech . . . Moreover, in their ideological struggle against plutocracy and capitalism the Axis Powers had, to a certain extent, the same objectives as the Russian regime.[36]

This was a radical turn in Axis policy, and no doubt it would have surprised Chamberlain had he learned of it. Perhaps it would have surprised Litvinov too.

On the very day of this discussion between Goering and Mussolini, April 16, the Soviet Foreign Commissar received the British ambassador in Moscow and made a formal proposal for a triple pact of mutual assistance between Great Britain, France and the Soviet Union. It called for a military convention between the three powers to enforce the pact and a guarantee by the signatories, to be joined by Poland, if it desired, of all the nations in Central and Eastern Europe which felt themselves menaced by Nazi Germany. It was Litvinov's last bid for an alliance against the Third Reich, and the Russian Foreign Minister, who had staked his career on a policy of stopping Hitler by collective action, must have thought that at last he would succeed in uniting the Western democracies with Russia for that purpose. As Churchill said in a speech on May 4, complaining that the Russian offer had not yet been accepted in London, "there is no means of maintaining an Eastern front against Nazi aggression without the active aid of Russia." No other power in Eastern Europe, certainly not Poland, possessed the military strength to maintain a front in that region. Yet the Russian proposal caused consternation in London and Paris.

Even before it was rejected, however, Stalin made his first serious move to play the other side of the street.

The day after Litvinov made his far-reaching offer to the British ambassador in Moscow, on April 17, the Soviet ambassador in Berlin paid a visit to Weizsaecker at the German Foreign Office. It was the first call, the State Secretary noted in a memorandum, that Merekalov had made on him since he assumed his post nearly a year before. After some preliminary remarks about German–Russian economic relations, the ambassador turned to politics and

asked me point-blank [Weizsaecker wrote] what I thought of German–Russian relations . . . The Ambassador spoke somewhat as follows:

Russian policy had always followed a straight course. Ideological differences had had very little adverse effect on relations between Russia and Italy and need not disturb those with Germany either. Russia had not exploited the present friction between Germany and the Western democracies against us, neither did she wish to do that. As far as Russia was concerned, there was no reason why she should not live on a normal footing with us, and out of normal relations could grow increasingly improved relations.

With this remark, toward which he had been steering the conversation, M. Merekalov ended the talk. He intends to visit Moscow in a day or two.[37]

In the Russian capital, to which the Soviet ambassador returned, there was something up.

It came out on May 3. On that date, tucked away on the back page of the Soviet newspapers in a column called "News in Brief," appeared a small item: "M. Litvinov has been released from the Office of Foreign Commissar at his own request." He was replaced by Vyacheslav Molotov, Chairman of the Council of the People's Commissars.

The German chargé d'affaires reported the change to Berlin the next day.

The sudden change has caused the greatest surprise here, as Litvinov was in the midst of negotiations with the British delegation, had appeared in close proximity to Stalin at the parade on May 1 . . .

Since Litvinov had received the British Ambassador as recently as May 2 and had even been mentioned in the press yesterday as a guest of honor at the parade, it seems that his dismissal must be due to a spontaneous decision by Stalin. . . . At the last Party Congress Stalin urged caution lest the Soviet Union be dragged into conflicts. Molotov, who is not a Jew, has the reputation of being the "most intimate friend and closest collaborator" of Stalin. His appointment is obviously intended to provide a guarantee that foreign policy will be conducted strictly on lines laid down by Stalin.[38]

The significance of Litvinov's abrupt dismissal was obvious to all. It meant a sharp and violent turning in Soviet foreign policy. Litvinov had been the archapostle of collective security, of strengthening the power of the League of Nations, of seeking Russian security against Nazi Germany by a military alliance with Great Britain and France. Chamberlain's hesitations about such an alliance were fatal to the Russian Foreign Commissar. In Stalin's judgment—and his was the only one which counted in Moscow—Litvinov's policies had failed. Moreover, they threatened to land the Soviet Union in a war with Germany which the Western democracies might well contrive to stay out of. It was time, Stalin concluded, to try a new tack.* If Chamberlain could appease Hitler, could not the

---

* If some credence can be cautiously given to the published journal of Litvinov (*Notes for a Journal*), Stalin had been contemplating such a change since Munich, from which the Soviet Union had been excluded. Toward the end of 1938, according to an entry in this journal, Stalin told Litvinov that "we are prepared to come to an agreement with the Germans . . . and also to render Poland harmless." In January 1939 the Foreign Commissar noted: "It would appear they have decided to remove me." In the same entry he reveals that all his communications with the Soviet Embassy in Berlin must now go through Stalin and that Ambassador Merekalov, on Stalin's instructions, is about to begin negotiations with Weizsaecker in

Russian dictator? The fact that Litvinov, a Jew, was replaced by Molotov, who, as the German Embassy had emphasized in its dispatch to Berlin, was not, might be expected to have a certain impact in high Nazi circles.

To see that the significance of the change was not lost on the Germans, Georgi Astakhov, the Soviet chargé d'affaires, brought the matter up on May 5 when he conferred with Dr. Julius Schnurre, the German Foreign Office expert on East European economic affairs.

Astakhov touched upon the dismissal of Litvinov [Schnurre reported] and tried . . . to learn whether this event would cause a change in our attitude toward the Soviet Union. He stressed the great importance of the personality of Molotov, who was by no means a specialist in foreign policy but who would have all the greater importance for future Soviet foreign policy.[39]

The chargé also invited the Germans to resume the trade negotiations which had been broken off in February.

The British government did not reply until May 8 to the Soviet proposals of April 16 for a military alliance. The response was a virtual rejection. It strengthened suspicions in Moscow that Chamberlain was not willing to make a military pact with Russia to prevent Hitler from taking Poland.

It is not surprising, then, that the Russians intensified their approach to the Germans. On May 17 Astakhov again saw Schnurre at the Foreign Office and after discussing problems of trade turned to larger matters.

Astakhov stated [Schnurre reported] that there were no conflicts in foreign policy between Germany and the Soviet Union and that therefore there was no reason for any enmity between the two countries. It was true that in the Soviet Union there was a distinct feeling of being menaced by Germany. It would undoubtedly be possible to eliminate this feeling of being menaced and the distrust in Moscow . . . In reply to my incidental question he commented on the Anglo–Soviet negotiations to the effect that, as they stood at the moment, the result desired by Britain would hardly materialize.[40]

Three days later, on May 20, Ambassador von der Schulenburg had a long talk with Molotov in Moscow. The newly appointed Commissar for Foreign Affairs was in a "most friendly" mood and informed the German envoy that economic negotiations between the two countries could be resumed if the *necessary political bases* for them were created. This was a new approach from the Kremlin but it was made cautiously by the cagey Molotov. When Schulenburg asked him what he meant by "political bases" the Russian replied that this was something both governments

---

order to let Hitler know "in effect: 'We couldn't come to an agreement until now, but now we can.' " The *Journal* is a somewhat dubious book. Professor Edward Hallett Carr, a British authority on the Soviet Union, investigated it and found that though undoubtedly it had been touched up to a point where some of it was "pure fiction," a large part of it fairly represents Litvinov's outlook.

would have to think about. All the ambassador's efforts to draw out the wily Foreign Commissar were in vain. "He is known," Schulenburg reminded Berlin, "for his somewhat stubborn manner." On his way out of the Russian Foreign Office, the ambassador dropped in on Vladimir Potemkin, the Soviet Deputy Commissar for Foreign Affairs, and told him he had not been able to find out what Molotov wanted of a political nature. "I asked Herr Potemkin," Schulenburg reported, "to find out."[41]

The renewed contacts between Berlin and Moscow did not escape the watchful eyes of the French ambassador in the German capital. As early as May 7, four days after Litvinov's dismissal, M. Coulondre was informing the French Foreign Minister that, according to information given him by a close confidant of the Fuehrer, Germany was seeking an understanding with Russia which would result in, among other things, a fourth partition of Poland. Two days later the French ambassador got off another telegram to Paris telling of new rumors in Berlin "that Germany had made, or was going to make, to Russia proposals aimed at a partition of Poland."[42]

THE PACT OF STEEL

Although the top brass of the Wehrmacht had a low opinion of Italian military power, Hitler now pressed for a military alliance with Italy, which Mussolini had been in no hurry to conclude. Staff talks between the two high commands began in April and Keitel reported to OKW his "impression" that neither the Italian fighting services nor Italian rearmament were in very good shape. A war, he thought, would have to be decided quickly, or the Italians would be out of it.[43]

By mid-April, as his diary shows,[44] Ciano was alarmed by increasing signs that Germany might attack Poland at any moment and precipitate a European war for which Italy was not prepared. When, on April 20, Ambassador Attolico in Berlin wired Rome that German action against Poland was "imminent" Ciano urged him to hasten arrangements for his meeting with Ribbentrop so that Italy would not be caught napping.

The two foreign ministers met at Milan on May 6. Ciano had arrived with written instructions from Mussolini to emphasize to the Germans that Italy wished to avoid war for at least three years. To the Italian's surprise, Ribbentrop agreed that Germany wished to keep the peace for that long too. In fact, Ciano found the German Foreign Minister "for the first time" in a "pleasantly calm state of mind." They reviewed the situation in Europe, agreed on improving Axis relations with the Soviet Union and adjourned for a gala dinner.

When after dinner Mussolini telephoned to see how the talks had gone, and Ciano replied that they had gone well, the Duce had a sudden brain storm. He asked his son-in-law to release to the press a communiqué saying that Germany and Italy had decided to conclude a military alliance. Ribbentrop at first hesitated. He finally agreed to put the matter up to

Hitler, and the Fuehrer, when reached by telephone, readily agreed to Mussolini's suggestion.[45]

Thus, on a sudden impulse, after more than a year of hesitation, Mussolini committed himself irrevocably to Hitler's fortunes. This was one of the first signs that the Italian dictator, like the German, was beginning to lose that iron self-control which up until this year of 1939 had enabled them both to pursue their own national interests with ice-cold clarity. The consequences for Mussolini would soon prove disastrous.

The "Pact of Steel," as it came to be known, was duly signed with considerable pomp at the Reich Chancellery in Berlin on May 22. Ciano had bestowed on Ribbentrop the Collar of the Annunziata, which not only made Goering furious but, as the Italian Foreign Minister noticed, brought tears to his eyes. In fact, the plump Field Marshal had made quite a scene, complaining that the collar really should have been awarded to him since it was he who had really promoted the alliance.

"I promised Mackensen [the German ambassador in Rome]," Ciano reported, "that I would try to get Goering a collar."

Ciano found Hitler looking "very well, quite serene, less aggressive," though he seemed a little older and his eyes more deeply wrinkled, probably from lack of sleep.* The Fuehrer was in the best of spirits as he watched the two foreign ministers sign the document.

It was a bluntly worded military alliance and its aggressive nature was underlined by a sentence in the preamble which Hitler had insisted on putting in declaring that the two nations, "united by the inner affinity of their ideologies . . . are resolved to act side by side and with united forces *to secure their living space.*" The core of the treaty was Article III.

If contrary to the wishes and hopes of the High Contracting Parties it should happen that one of them became involved in warlike complications with another Power or Powers, the other High Contracting Party would immediately come to its assistance as an ally and support it with all its military forces on land, at sea and in the air.

Article V provided that in the event of war neither nation would conclude a separate armistice or peace.[46]

In the beginning, as it would turn out, Mussolini did not honor the first, nor, at the end, did Italy abide by the second.

---

* Ciano's diary for May 22 is full of titbits about Hitler and his weird entourage. Frau Goebbels complained that the Fuehrer kept his friends up all night and exclaimed, "It is always Hitler who talks! He repeats himself and bores his guests." Ciano also heard hints "of the Fuehrer's tender feelings for a beautiful girl. She is twenty years old, with beautiful quiet eyes, regular features and a magnificent body. Her name is Sigrid von Lappus. They see each other frequently and intimately." (*The Ciano Diaries*, p. 85.) Ciano, a great man with the ladies himself, was obviously intrigued. Apparently he had not yet heard of Eva Braun, Hitler's mistress, who was rarely permitted at this time to come to Berlin.

HITLER BURNS HIS BOATS: MAY 23, 1939

The day after the signing of the Pact of Steel, on May 23, Hitler summoned his military chiefs to the study in the Chancellery in Berlin and told them bluntly that further successes could not be won without the shedding of blood and that war therefore was inevitable.

This was a somewhat larger gathering than a similar one on November 5, 1937, when the Fuehrer had first imparted his decision to go to war to the commanders in chief of the three armed services.* Altogether fourteen officers were present, including Field Marshal Goering, Grand Admiral Raeder (as he now was), General von Brauchitsch, General Halder, General Keitel, General Erhard Milch, Inspector General of the Luftwaffe, and Rear Admiral Otto Schniewind, naval Chief of Staff. The Fuehrer's adjutant, Lieutenant Colonel Rudolf Schmundt, was also present and, luckily for history, took notes. His minutes of the meeting are among the captured German documents. Apparently Hitler's words on this occasion were regarded as such a top secret that no copies of the minutes were made; the one we have is in Schmundt's own handwriting.[47]

It is one of the most revealing and important of the secret papers which depict Hitler's road to war. Here, before the handful of men who will have to direct the military forces in an armed conflict, Hitler cuts through his own propaganda and diplomatic deceit and utters the truth about why he must attack Poland and, if necessary, take on Great Britain and France as well. He predicts with uncanny accuracy the course the war will take—at least in its first year. And yet for all its bluntness his discourse—for the dictator did all the talking—discloses more uncertainty and confusion of mind than he has shown up to this point. Above all, Britain and the British continue to baffle him, as they did to the end of his life.

But about the coming of war and his aims in launching it he is clear and precise, and no general or admiral could have left the Chancellery on May 23 without knowing exactly what was coming at the summer's end. Germany's economic problems, he began, could only be solved by obtaining more *Lebensraum* in Europe, and "this is impossible without invading other countries or attacking other people's possessions."

Further successes can no longer be attained without the shedding of blood . . .

Danzig is not the subject of the dispute at all. It is a question of expanding our living space in the East, of securing our food supplies and also of solving the problem of the Baltic States. . . . There is no other possibility in Europe . . . If fate forces us into a showdown with the West it is invaluable to possess a large area in the East. In wartime we shall be even less able to rely on record harvests than in peacetime.

Besides, Hitler adds, the population of non-German territories in the

---

* See above, p. 305.

East will be available as a source of labor—an early hint of the slave labor program he was later to put into effect.

The choice of the first victim was obvious.

There is no question of sparing Poland and we are left with the decision: *To attack Poland at the first suitable opportunity.**

We cannot expect a repetition of the Czech affair. There will be war. Our task is to isolate Poland. Success in isolating her will be decisive.

So there will be war. With an "isolated" Poland alone? Here the Fuehrer is not so clear. In fact, he becomes confused and contradictory. He must reserve to himself, he says, the final order to strike.

It must not come to a simultaneous showdown with the West—France and England.

If it is not certain that a German–Polish conflict will not lead to war with the West, then the fight must be primarily against England and France.

Fundamentally therefore: Conflict with Poland—beginning with an attack on Poland—will only be successful if the West keeps out of it.

If that is not possible it is better to fall upon the West and to finish off Poland at the same time.

In the face of such rapid-fire contradictions the generals must have winced, perhaps prying their monocles loose, though there is no evidence in the Schmundt minutes that this happened or that anyone in the select audience even dared to ask a question to straighten matters out.

Hitler next turned to Russia. "It is not ruled out," he said, "that Russia might disinterest herself in the destruction of Poland." On the other hand, if the Soviet Union allied herself to Britain and France, that "would lead me to attack England and France with a few devastating blows." That would mean committing the same mistake Wilhelm II made in 1914, but though in this lecture Hitler drew several lessons from the World War he did not draw this one. His thoughts now turned toward Great Britain.

The Fuehrer doubts the possibility of a peaceful settlement with England. It is necessary to be prepared for the showdown. England sees in our development the establishment of a hegemony which would weaken England. Therefore England is our enemy, and the conflict with England is a matter of life and death.

What will this conflict be like?†

England cannot finish off Germany with a few powerful blows and force us down. It is of decisive importance for England to carry the war as near as

---

* Emphasis in the original.
† Emphasis in the original.

possible to the Ruhr. French blood will not be spared. (West Wall!) The duration of our existence is dependent on possession of the Ruhr.

Having decided to follow the Kaiser in one mistake—attacking France and England if they lined up with Russia—Hitler now announced that he would follow the Emperor in another matter which eventually had proved disastrous to Germany.

The Dutch and Belgian air bases must be militarily occupied. Declarations of neutrality can be ignored. If England wants to intervene in the Polish war, we must make a lightning attack on Holland. We must aim at establishing a new line of defense on Dutch territory as far as the Zuyder Zee. The war with England and France will be a war of life and death.

The idea that we can get off cheaply is dangerous; there is no such possibility. We must then burn our boats and it will no longer be a question of right or wrong but of to be or not to be for eighty million people.

Though he had just announced that Germany would attack Poland "at the first suitable opportunity" and though his listeners knew that almost all of Germany's military strength was being concentrated on that objective, Hitler, as he rambled on, could not keep his thoughts off Great Britain.

"England," he emphasized, "is the driving force against Germany." Whereupon he discussed her strengths and weaknesses.

The Britisher himself is proud, brave, tough, dogged and a gifted organizer. He knows how to exploit every new development. He has the love of adventure and the courage of the Nordic race . . .

England is a world power in herself. Constant for three hundred years. Increased by alliances. This power is not only something concrete but must also be considered as psychological force, embracing the entire world.

Add to this immeasurable wealth and the solvency that goes with it.

Geopolitical security and protection by a strong sea power and courageous air force.

But Britain, Hitler reminded his hearers, also had her weaknesses, and he proceeded to enumerate them.

If in the last war we had had two more battleships and two more cruisers and had begun the Battle of Jutland in the morning, the British fleet would have been defeated and England brought to her knees.* It would have meant the end of the World War. In former times . . . to conquer England it was necessary to invade her. England could feed herself. Today she no longer can.

The moment England is cut off from her supplies she is forced to capitulate. Imports of food and fuel oil are dependent on naval protection.

---

* Hitler's understanding of the Battle of Jutland was obviously faulty.

Luftwaffe attacks on England will not force her to capitulate. But if the fleet is annihilated instant capitulation results. There is no doubt that a surprise attack might lead to a quick decision.

A surprise attack with what? Surely Admiral Raeder must have thought that Hitler was talking through his hat. Under the so-called Z Plan, promulgated at the end of 1938, German naval strength would only begin to approach that of the British by 1945. At the moment, in the spring of 1939, Germany did not have the heavy ships to sink the British Navy, even by a surprise attack.

Perhaps Britain could be brought down by other means. Here Hitler came down to earth again and outlined a strategic plan which a year later, in fact, would be carried out with amazing success.

The aim must be to deal the enemy a smashing or a finally decisive blow right at the start. Considerations of right or wrong, or of treaties, do not enter into the matter. This will be possible only when we do not "slide" into a war with England on account of Poland.

Preparations must be made for a *long war as well as* for a surprise *attack*, and every possible intervention by England on the Continent must be smashed.

The Army must occupy the positions important for the fleet and the Luftwaffe. If we succeed in occupying and securing Holland and Belgium, as well as defeating France, the basis for a successful war against England has been created.

The Luftwaffe can then closely blockade England from western France and the fleet undertake the wider blockade with submarines.

That is precisely what would be done a little more than a year later. Another decisive strategic plan, which the Fuehrer emphasized on May 23, would also be carried out. At the beginning of the last war, had the German Army executed a wheeling movement toward the Channel ports instead of toward Paris, the end, he said, would have been different. Perhaps it would have been. At any rate he would try it in 1940.

"The aim," Hitler concluded, apparently forgetting all about Poland for the moment, "will always be to force England to her knees."

There was one final consideration.

Secrecy is the decisive prerequisite for success. Our objectives must be kept secret from both Italy and Japan.

Even Hitler's own Army General Staff, whose Chief, General Halder, sat there listening, was not to be trusted entirely. "Our studies," the Fuehrer laid down, "must not be left to the General Staff. Secrecy would then no longer be assured." He ordered that a small planning staff in OKW be set up to work out the military plans.

On May 23, 1939, then, Hitler, as he himself said, burned his boats. There would be war. Germany needed *Lebensraum* in the East. To get it Poland would be attacked at the first opportunity. Danzig had nothing to do with it. That was merely an excuse. Britain stood in the way; she was the real driving force against Germany. Very well, she would be taken on too, and France. It would be a life-and-death struggle.

When the Fuehrer had first outlined his plans for aggression to the military chiefs, on November 5, 1937, Field Marshal von Blomberg and General von Fritsch had protested—at least on the grounds that Germany was too weak to fight a European war.* During the following summer General Beck had resigned as Chief of the Army General Staff for the same reason. But on May 23, 1939, not a single general or admiral, so far as the record shows, raised his voice to question the wisdom of Hitler's course.

Their job, as they saw it, was not to question but to blindly obey. Already they had been applying their considerable talents to working out plans for military aggression. On May 7, Colonel Guenther Blumentritt of the Army General Staff, who with Generals von Rundstedt and von Manstein formed a small "Working Staff," submitted an estimate of the situation for Case White. Actually it was a plan for the conquest of Poland. It was an imaginative and daring plan, and it would be followed with very few changes.[48]

Admiral Raeder came through with naval plans for Case White in a top-secret directive signed May 16.[49] Since Poland had only a few miles of coast on the Baltic west of Danzig and possessed only a small navy, no difficulties were expected. France and Britain were the Admiral's chief concern. The entrance to the Baltic was to be protected by submarines, and the two pocket battleships and the two battleships, with the "remaining" submarines, were to prepare for "war in the Atlantic." According to the instructions of the Fuehrer, the Navy had to be prepared to carry out its part of "White" by September 1 but Raeder urged his commanders to hasten plans because "due to the latest political developments" action might come sooner.[50]

As May 1939 came to an end German preparations for going to war by the end of the summer were well along. The great armament works were humming, turning out guns, tanks, planes and warships. The able staffs of the Army, Navy and Air Force had reached the final stage of planning. The ranks were being swelled by new men called up for "summer training." Hitler could be pleased with what he had accomplished.

The day after the Fuehrer's lecture to the military chiefs, on May 24, General Georg Thomas, head of the Economic and Armaments Branch of OKW, summed up that accomplishment in a confidential lecture to the staff of the Foreign Office. Whereas it had taken the Imperial Army,

---

* See above, p. 308.

Thomas reminded his listeners, sixteen years—from 1898 to 1914—to increase its strength from forty-three to fifty divisions, the Army of the Third Reich had jumped from seven to fifty-one divisions in just four years. Among them were five heavy armored divisions and four light ones, a "modern battle cavalry" such as no other nation possessed. The Navy had built up from practically nothing a fleet of two battleships of 26,000 tons,* two heavy cruisers, seventeen destroyers and forty-seven submarines. It had already launched two battleships of 35,000 tons, one aircraft carrier, four heavy cruisers, five destroyers and seven submarines, and was planning to launch a great many more ships. From absolutely nothing, the Luftwaffe had built up a force of twenty-one squadrons with a personnel of 260,000 men. The armament industry, General Thomas said, was already producing more than it had during the peak of the last war and its output in most fields far exceeded that of any other country. In fact, total German rearmament, the General declared, was "probably unique in the world."

Formidable as German military power was becoming at the beginning of the summer of 1939, the prospect of success in the war which Hitler was planning for the early fall depended on what kind of a war it was. Germany was still not strong enough, and probably would never be, to take on France, Britain *and* Russia in addition to Poland. As the fateful summer commenced, all depended on the Fuehrer's ability to limit the war—above all, to keep Russia from forming the military alliance with the West which Litvinov, just before his fall, had proposed and which Chamberlain, though he had at first seemed to reject it, was, by May's end, again mulling over.

THE INTERVENTION OF RUSSIA: II

In a debate in the House of Commons on May 19, the British Prime Minister had again taken a cool and even disdainful view, as Churchill thought, of the Russian proposals. Somewhat wearily he had explained to the House that "there is a sort of veil, a sort of wall, between the two Governments which it is extremely difficult to penetrate." Churchill, on the other hand, backed by Lloyd George, argued that Moscow had made "a fair offer . . . more simple, more direct, more effective" than Chamberlain's own proposals. He begged His Majesty's Government "to get some brutal truths into their heads. Without an effective Eastern front, there

---

* In giving these tonnages for German battleships, General Thomas was deceiving even the Foreign Office. An interesting German naval document[51] dated more than a year before, February 18, 1938, notes that false figures on battleship tonnage had been furnished the British government under the Anglo–German naval agreement. It states that the actual tonnage of the 26,000-ton ships was 31,300 tons; that of the 35,000-ton battleships (the top level in the British and American navies) was actually 41,700 tons. It is a curious example of Nazi deceit.

can be no satisfactory defense in the West, and without Russia there can be no effective Eastern front."

Bowing to the storm of criticism from all sides, Chamberlain on May 27 finally instructed the British ambassador in Moscow to agree to begin discussions of a pact of mutual assistance, a military convention and guarantees to the countries threatened by Hitler.* Ambassador von Dirksen in London advised the German Foreign Office that the British government had taken the step "with the greatest reluctance." Furthermore, Dirksen divulged what was perhaps the primary reason for Chamberlain's move. The British Foreign Office, he reported urgently to Berlin, had got wind of "German feelers in Moscow" and was "afraid that Germany might succeed in keeping Soviet Russia neutral or even inducing her to adopt benevolent neutrality. That would have meant the complete collapse of the encirclement action."[53]

On the last day of May, Molotov made his first public speech as Commissar for Foreign Affairs in an address to the Supreme Council of the U.S.S.R. He castigated the Western democracies for their hesitation and declared that if they were serious in joining Russia to stop aggression they must get down to brass tacks and come to an agreement on three main points:

1. Conclude a tripartite mutual-assistance pact of a purely defensive character.

2. Guarantee the states of Central and Eastern Europe, including *all* European states bordering on the Soviet Union.

3. Conclude a definite agreement on the form and scope of the immediate and effective aid to be afforded each other and the smaller states threatened by aggression.

Molotov also declared that the talks with the West did not mean that Russia would forego "business relations on a practical footing" with Germany and Italy. In fact, he said that "it was not out of the question" that commercial negotiations with Germany could be resumed. Ambassador von der Schulenburg, in reporting the speech to Berlin, pointed out that Molotov had indicated that Russia was still prepared to conclude a treaty with Britain and France "on condition that all her demands are accepted," but that it was now evident from the address that it would take a long time before any real agreement was reached. He pointed out that Molotov had "avoided sallies against Germany and showed readiness to continue the talks begun in Berlin and Moscow."[54]

This readiness was now suddenly shared by Hitler in Berlin.

During the last ten days of May, Hitler and his advisers blew hot and cold over the thorny question of making advances to Moscow in order to thwart the Anglo–Russian negotiations. It was felt in Berlin that Molotov

---

* On May 27, the British ambassador and the French chargé d'affaires in Moscow presented Molotov with an Anglo–French draft of the proposed pact. To the surprise of the Western envoys, Molotov took a very cool view of it.[52]

in his talk with Ambassador von der Schulenburg on May 20* had thrown cold water on Germany's approaches, and on the following day, May 21, Weizsaecker wired the ambassador that in view of what the Foreign Commissar had said "we must now sit tight and wait to see if the Russians will speak more openly."[55]

But Hitler, having fixed September 1 for his attack on Poland, could not afford to sit tight. On or about May 25, Weizsaecker and Friedrich Gaus, director of the Legal Department of the German Foreign Office, were summoned to Ribbentrop's country house at Sonnenburg and, according to Gaus's affidavit submitted at Nuremberg,† informed that the Fuehrer wanted "to establish more tolerable relations between Germany and the Soviet Union." Draft instructions to Schulenburg were drawn up by Ribbentrop outlining in considerable detail the new line he was to take with Molotov, whom he was asked to see "as soon as possible." This draft is among the captured German Foreign Office documents.[56]

It was shown to Hitler, according to a notation on the document, on May 26. It is a revealing paper. It discloses that by this date the German Foreign Office was convinced that the Anglo–Russian negotiations would be successfully concluded unless Germany intervened decisively. Ribbentrop therefore proposed that Schulenburg tell Molotov the following:

A real opposition of interests in foreign affairs does not exist between Germany and Soviet Russia . . . The time has come to consider a pacification and normalization of German–Soviet Russian foreign relations . . . The Italo-German alliance is not directed against the Soviet Union. It is exclusively directed against the Anglo–French combination . . .

If against our wishes it should come to hostilities with Poland, we are firmly convinced that even this need not in any way lead to a clash of interests with Soviet Russia. We can even go so far as to say that when settling the German–Polish question—in whatever way this is done—we would take Russian interests into account as far as possible.

Next the danger to Russia of an alliance with Great Britain was to be pointed up.

We are unable to see what could really induce the Soviet Union to play an active part in the game of the British policy of encirclement . . . This would mean Russia undertaking a one-sided liability without any really valuable British *quid pro quo* . . . Britain is by no means in a position to offer Russia

---

* See above, pp. 481–82.
† The affidavit was rejected as evidence by the tribunal and is not published in the *Nazi Conspiracy and Aggression* or *Trial of the Major War Criminals* volumes of the Nuremberg evidence. This does not detract from its authenticity. All material dealing with Nazi–Soviet collaboration during this period was handled gingerly by the tribunal, one of whose four judges was a Russian.

a really valuable *quid pro quo,* no matter how the treaties may be formulated. All assistance in Europe is rendered impossible by the West Wall . . . We are therefore convinced that Britain will once more remain faithful to her traditional policy of letting other powers pull her chestnuts out of the fire.

Schulenburg also was to emphasize that Germany had "no aggressive intentions against Russia." Finally, he was instructed to tell Molotov that Germany was ready to discuss with the Soviet Union not only economic questions but "a return to normal in political relations."

Hitler thought the draft went too far and ordered it held up. The Fuehrer, according to Gaus, had been impressed by Chamberlain's optimistic statement of two days before, May 24, when the Prime Minister had told the House of Commons that as the result of new British proposals he hoped that full agreement with Russia could be reached "at an early date." What Hitler feared was a rebuff. He did not abandon the idea of a *rapprochement* with Moscow but decided that for the time being a more cautious approach would be best.

The backing and filling which took place in the Fuehrer's mind during the last week of May is documented in the captured German Foreign Office papers. On or about the twenty-fifth—the exact day is not quite certain—he had suddenly come out for pushing talks with the Soviet Union in order to thwart the Anglo–Russian negotiations. Schulenburg was to see Molotov at once for that purpose. But Ribbentrop's instructions to him, which were shown Hitler on the twenty-sixth, were never sent. The Fuehrer canceled them. That evening Weizsaecker wired Schulenburg advising him to maintain an "attitude of complete reserve—you personally should not make any move until further notice."[57]

This telegram and a letter which the State Secretary wrote the ambassador in Moscow on May 27 but did not mail until May 30, when a significant postscript was added, go far to explaining the hesitations in Berlin.[58] Weizsaecker, writing on the twenty-seventh, informed Schulenburg that it was the opinion in Berlin that an Anglo–Russian agreement would "not be easy to prevent" and that Germany hesitated to intervene decisively against it for fear of provoking "a peal of Tartar laughter" in Moscow. Also, the State Secretary revealed, both Japan and Italy had been cool toward Germany's proposed move in Moscow, and the reserve of her allies had helped to influence the decision in Berlin to sit tight. "Thus," he concluded, "we now want to wait and see how deeply Moscow and Paris–London mutually engage themselves."

For some reason Weizsaecker did not post his letter at once; perhaps he felt that Hitler had not yet fully made up his mind. When he did mail it on May 30, he added a postscript:

P.S. To my above lines I must add that, with the approval of the Fuehrer, an approach is nonetheless now to be made to the Russians, though a very much modified one, and this by means of a conversation which I am to hold today with the Russian chargé d'affaires.

This talk with Georgi Astakhov did not get very far, but it represented for the Germans a new start. Weizsaecker's pretext for calling in the Russian chargé was to discuss the future of the Soviet trade delegation in Prague, which the Russians were anxious to maintain. Around this subject the two diplomats sparred to find out what was in each other's mind. Weizsaecker said he agreed with Molotov that political and economic questions could not be entirely separated and expressed interest in the "normalization of relations between Soviet Russia and Germany." Astakhov asserted that Molotov had no "intention of barring the door against further Russo–German discussions."

Cautious as both men were, the Germans were encouraged. At 10:40 o'clock that evening of May 30 Weizsaecker got off a "most urgent" telegram[59] to Schulenburg in Moscow:

Contrary to the tactics hitherto planned we have now, after all, decided to make a certain degree of contact with the Soviet Union.*

It may have been that a long secret memorandum which Mussolini penned to Hitler on May 30 strengthened the Fuehrer's resolve to turn to the Soviet Union, however cautiously. As the summer commenced, the Duce's doubts mounted as to the advisability of an early conflict. He was convinced, he wrote Hitler, that "war between the plutocratic, self-seeking conservative nations" and the Axis was "inevitable." But—"Italy requires a period of preparation which may extend until the end of 1942 . . . Only from 1943 onward will an effort by war have the greatest prospects of success." After enumerating several reasons why "Italy needs a period of peace," the Duce concluded: "For all these reasons Italy does not wish to hasten a European war, although she is convinced of the inevitability of such a war."[60]

Hitler, who had not taken his good friend and ally into his confidence about the date of September 1 which he had set for attacking Poland, replied that he had read the secret memorandum "with the greatest interest" and suggested that the two leaders meet for discussions sometime in the future. In the meantime the Fuehrer decided to see if a crack could

---

* In *Nazi–Soviet Relations*, a volume of German Foreign Office documents on that subject published by the U.S. State Department in 1949, the English translation of the telegram came out much stronger. The key sentence was given as: "We have now decided to undertake definite negotiations with the Soviet Union." This has led many historians, including Churchill, to conclude that this telegram of May 30 marked the decisive turning point in Hitler's efforts to make a deal with Moscow. That turning point came later. As Weizsaecker pointed out in the May 30 postscript to his letter to Schulenburg, the German approach, which Hitler had approved, was to be "a very much modified one."

be made in the Kremlin wall. All through June preliminary talks concerning a new trade agreement were held in Moscow between the German Embassy and Anastas Mikoyan, the Russian Commissar for Foreign Trade.

The Soviet government was still highly suspicious of Berlin. As Schulenburg reported toward the end of the month (June 27), the Kremlin believed the Germans, in pressing for a trade agreement, wished to torpedo the Russian negotiations with Britain and France. "They are afraid," he wired Berlin, "that as soon as we have gained this advantage we might let the negotiations peter out."[61]

On June 28 Schulenburg had a long talk with Molotov which proceeded, he told Berlin in a "secret and urgent" telegram, "in a friendly manner." Nevertheless, when the German ambassador referred assuringly to the nonaggression treaties which Germany had just concluded with the Baltic States,* the Soviet Foreign Commissar tartly replied that "he must doubt the permanence of such treaties after the experiences which Poland had had." Summing up the talk, Schulenburg concluded:

My impression is that the Soviet Government is greatly interested in learning our political views and in maintaining contact with us. Although there was no mistaking the strong distrust evident in all that Molotov said, he nevertheless described a normalization of relations with Germany as being desirable and possible.[62]

The ambassador requested telegraphic instructions as to his next move. Schulenburg was one of the last survivors of the Seeckt, Maltzan and Brockdorff-Rantzau school which had insisted on a German *rapprochement* with Soviet Russia after 1919 and which had brought it about at Rapallo. As his dispatches throughout 1939 make clear, he sincerely sought to restore the close relations which had existed during the Weimar Republic. But like so many other German career diplomats of the old school he little understood Hitler.

Suddenly on June 29 Hitler, from his mountain retreat at Berchtesgaden, ordered the talks with the Russians broken off.

Berchtesgaden, June 29, 1939

. . . The Fuehrer has decided as follows:

The Russians are to be informed that we have seen from their attitude that they are making the continuation of further talks dependent on the acceptance of the basis for our economic discussions as fixed in January. Since this basis

---

* To try to forestall an Anglo–French–Russian guarantee of Latvia and Estonia, which bordered on the Soviet Union, Germany had hastily signed nonaggression pacts with these two Baltic States on June 7. Even before this, on May 31, Germany had pushed through a similar pact with Denmark, which, considering recent events, appears to have given the Danes an astonishing sense of security.

was not acceptable to us, we would not be interested in a resumption of the economic discussions with Russia at present.

The Fuehrer has agreed that this answer be delayed for a few days.[63]

Actually, the substance of it was telegraphed to the German Embassy in Moscow the next day.

The Foreign Minister [Weizsaecker wired] . . . is of the opinion that in the political field enough has been said until further instructions and that for the moment the talks should not be taken up again by us.

Concerning the possible economic negotiations with the Russian Government, the deliberations here have not yet been concluded. In this field too you are requested for the time being to take no further action, but to await instructions.[64]

There is no clue in the secret German documents which explains Hitler's sudden change of mind. The Russians already had begun to compromise on their proposals of January and February. And Schnurre had warned on June 15 that a breakdown in the economic negotiations would be a setback for Germany both economically and politically.

Nor could the rocky course of the Anglo–French–Soviet negotiations have so discouraged Hitler as to lead him to such a decision. He knew from the reports of the German Embassy in Moscow that Russia and the Western Powers were deadlocked over the question of guarantees to Poland, Rumania and the Baltic States. Poland and Rumania were happy to be guaranteed by Britain and France, which could scarcely help them in the event of German aggression except by the indirect means of setting up a Western front. But they refused to accept a Russian guarantee or even to allow for Soviet troops to pass through their territories to meet a German attack. Latvia, Estonia and Finland also stoutly declined to accept any Russian guarantee, an attitude which, as the German Foreign Office papers later revealed, was encouraged by Germany in the form of dire threats should they weaken in their resolve.

In this impasse Molotov suggested at the beginning of June that Great Britain send its Foreign Secretary to Moscow to take part in the negotiations. Apparently in the Russian view this would not only help to break the deadlock but would show that Britain was in earnest in arriving at an agreement with Russia. Lord Halifax declined to go.* Anthony Eden, who was at least a former Foreign Secretary, offered to go in his place, but Chamberlain turned him down. It was decided, instead, to send William Strang, a capable career official in the Foreign Office who had previously

---

* According to the British Foreign Office papers, Halifax told Maisky on June 8 that he had thought of suggesting to the Prime Minister that he should go to Moscow, "but it was really impossible to get away." Maisky, on June 12, after Strang had left, suggested to Halifax that it would be a good idea for the Foreign Secretary to go to Moscow "when things were quieter," but Halifax again stressed the impossibility of his being absent from London "for the present."[65]

served in the Moscow Embassy and spoke Russian but was little known either in his own country or outside of it. The appointment of so subordinate an official to head such an important mission and to negotiate directly with Molotov and Stalin was a signal to the Russians, they later said, that Chamberlain still did not take very seriously the business of building an alliance to stop Hitler.

Strang arrived in Moscow on June 14, but though he participated in eleven Anglo–French meetings with Molotov, his appearance had little effect on the course of Anglo–Soviet negotiations. A fortnight later, on June 29, Russian suspicion and irritation was publicly displayed in an article in *Pravda* by Andrei Zhdanov under the headline, "British and French Governments Do Not Want a Treaty on the Basis of Equality for the Soviet Union." Though purporting to write "as a private individual and not committing the Soviet Government," Zhdanov was not only a member of the Politburo and president of the Foreign Affairs Committee of the Soviet Parliament but, as Schulenburg emphasized to Berlin in reporting on the matter, "one of Stalin's confidants [whose] article was doubtless written on orders from above."

It seems to me [Zhdanov wrote] that the British and French Governments are not out for a real agreement acceptable to the U.S.S.R. but only for talks about an agreement in order to demonstrate before the public opinion of their own countries the alleged unyielding attitude of the U.S.S.R. and thus facilitate the conclusion of an agreement with the aggressors. The next few days will show whether this is so or not.[66]

Stalin's distrust of Britain and France and his suspicion that the Western Allies might in the end make a deal with Hitler, as they had the year before at Munich, was thus publicized for all the world to ponder. Ambassador von der Schulenburg, pondering it, suggested to Berlin that one purpose of the article was "to lay the blame on Britain and France for the possible breakdown of the negotiations."[67]

PLANS FOR TOTAL WAR

Still Adolf Hitler did not rise to the Russian bait. Perhaps it was because all during June he was busy at Berchtesgaden supervising the completion of military plans to invade Poland at the summer's end.

By June 15 he had General von Brauchitsch's top-secret plan for the operations of the Army against Poland.[68] "The object of the operation," the Commander in Chief of the Army, echoing his master, declared, "is to destroy the Polish armed forces. The political leadership demands that the war should be begun by heavy surprise blows and lead to quick successes. The intention of the Army High Command is to prevent a regular mobilization and concentration of the Polish Army by a surprise invasion of Polish territory and to destroy the mass of the Polish Army, which is expected to be west of the Vistula–Narew line, by a concentric attack from Silesia on the one side and from Pomerania–East Prussia on the other."

To carry out his plan, Brauchitsch set up two army groups—Army Group South, consisting of the Eighth, Tenth and Fourteenth armies, and Army Group North, made up of the Third and Fourth armies. The southern army group, under the command of General von Rundstedt, was to attack from Silesia "in the general direction of Warsaw, scatter opposing Polish forces and occupy as early as possible with forces as strong as possible the Vistula on *both* sides of Warsaw with the aim of destroying the Polish forces still holding out in western Poland in co-operation with Army Group North." The first mission of the latter group was "to establish connection between the Reich and East Prussia" by driving across the Corridor. Detailed objectives of the various armies were outlined as well as those for the Air Force and Navy. Danzig, said Brauchitsch, would be declared German territory on the first day of hostilities and would be secured by local forces under German command.

A supplemental directive issued at the same time stipulated that the order of deployment for "White" would be put into operation on August 20. "All preparations," it laid down, "must be concluded by that date."[69]

A week later, on June 22, General Keitel submitted to Hitler a "preliminary timetable for Case White."[70] The Fuehrer, after studying it, agreed with it "in the main" but ordered that "so as not to disquiet the population by calling up reserves on a larger scale than usual . . . civilian establishments, employers or other private persons who make inquiries should be told that men are being called up for the autumn maneuvers." Also Hitler stipulated that "for reasons of security, the clearing of hospitals in the frontier area which the Supreme Command of the Army proposed should take place from the middle of July must not be carried out."

The war which Hitler was planning to launch would be total war and would require not only military mobilization but a total mobilization of all the resources of the nation. To co-ordinate this immense effort a meeting of the Reich Defense Council was convoked the next day, on June 23, under the chairmanship of Goering. Some thirty-five ranking officials, civil and military, including Keitel, Raeder, Halder, Thomas and Milch for the armed forces and the Ministers of the Interior, Economics, Finance and Transport, as well as Himmler, were present. It was only the second meeting of the Council but, as Goering explained, the body was convoked only to make the most important decisions and he left no doubt in the minds of his hearers, as the captured secret minutes of the session reveal, that war was near and that much remained to be done about manpower for industry and agriculture and about many other matters relating to total mobilization.[71]

Goering informed the Council that Hitler had decided to draft some seven million men. To augment the labor supply Dr. Funk, the Minister of Economics, was to arrange "what work is to be given to prisoners of war and to the inmates of prisons and concentration camps." Himmler chimed in to say that "greater use will be made of the concentration camps in wartime." And Goering added that "hundreds of thousands of workers from the Czech protectorate are to be employed under supervision in Germany, particularly in agriculture, and housed in hutments." Already, it was obvious, the Nazi program for slave labor was taking shape.

Dr. Frick, the Minister of the Interior, promised to "save labor in the public administration" and enlivened the proceedings by admitting that under the Nazi regime the number of bureaucrats had increased "from twenty to forty fold—an impossible state of affairs." A committee was set up to correct this lamentable situation.

An even more pessimistic report was made by Colonel Rudolf Gercke, chief of the Transport Department of the Army General Staff. *"In the transportation sphere,"* he declared bluntly, *"Germany is at the moment not ready for war."*

Whether the German transportation facilities would be equal to their task depended, of course, on whether the war was confined to Poland. If it had to be fought in the West against France and Great Britain it was feared that the transport system would simply not be adequate. In July two emergency meetings of the Defense Council were called "in order to bring the West Wall, by August 25 at the latest, into the optimum condition of preparedness with the material that can be obtained by that time by an extreme effort." High officials of Krupp and the steel cartel were enlisted to try to scrape up the necessary metal to complete the armament of the western fortifications. For on their impregnancy, the Germans knew, depended whether the Anglo–French armies would be inclined to mount a serious attack on western Germany while the Wehrmacht was preoccupied in Poland.

Though Hitler, with unusual frankness, had told his generals on May 23 that Danzig was not the cause of the dispute with Poland at all, it seemed for a few weeks at midsummer that the Free City might be the powder keg which any day would set off the explosion of war. For some time the Germans had been smuggling into Danzig arms and Regular Army officers to train the local defense guard in their use.* The arms and officers came in across the border from East Prussia, and in order to keep closer watch on them the Poles increased the number of their customs officials and frontier guards. The local Danzig authorities, now operating exclusively on orders from Berlin, countered by trying to prevent the Polish officials from carrying out their duties.

---

* On June 19 the High Command of the Army had informed the Foreign Office that 168 German Army officers "have been granted permission to travel through the Free State of Danzig in civilian clothes on a tour for study purposes." Early in July General Keitel inquired of the Foreign Office "whether it is politically advisable to show in public the twelve light and four heavy guns which are in Danzig and to let exercises be carried out with them, or whether it is better to conceal the presence of these guns."[72] How the Germans succeeded in smuggling in heavy artillery past the Polish inspectors is not revealed in the German papers.

The conflict reached a crisis on August 4 when the Polish diplomatic representative in Danzig informed the local authorities that the Polish customs inspectors had been given orders to carry out their functions "with arms" and that any attempt by the Danzigers to hamper them would be regarded "as an act of violence" against Polish officials, and that in such a case the Polish government would "retaliate without delay against the Free City."

This was a further sign to Hitler that the Poles could not be intimidated and it was reinforced by the opinion of the German ambassador in Warsaw, who on July 6 telegraphed Berlin that there was "hardly any doubt" that Poland would fight "if there was a clear violation" of her rights in Danzig. We know from a marginal note on the telegram in Ribbentrop's handwriting that it was shown the Fuehrer.[73]

Hitler was furious. The next day, August 7, he summoned Albert Forster, the Nazi Gauleiter of Danzig, to Berchtesgaden and told him that he had reached the extreme limit of his patience with the Poles. Angry notes were exchanged between Berlin and Warsaw—so violent in tone that neither side dared to make them public. On the ninth, the Reich government warned Poland that a repetition of its ultimatum to Danzig "would lead to an aggravation of German–Polish relations . . . for which the German Government must disclaim all responsibility." The next day the Polish government replied tartly

that they will continue to react as hitherto to any attempt by the authorities of the Free City to impair the rights and interests which Poland enjoys in Danzig, and will do so by such means and measures as they alone may deem appropriate, and that they will regard any intervention by the Reich Government . . . as an act of aggression.[74]

No small nation which stood in Hitler's way had ever used such language. When on the following day, August 11, the Fuehrer received Carl Burckhardt, a Swiss, who was League of Nations High Commissioner at Danzig and who had gone more than halfway to meet the German demands there, he was in an ugly mood. He told his visitor that "if the slightest thing was attempted by the Poles, he would fall upon them like lightning with all the powerful arms at his disposal, of which the Poles had not the slightest idea."

M. Burckhardt said [the High Commissioner later reported] that that would lead to a general conflict. Herr Hitler replied that if he had to make war he would rather do it today than tomorrow, that he would not conduct it like the Germany of Wilhelm II, who had always had scruples about the full use of every weapon, and that he would fight without mercy up to the extreme limit.[75]

Against whom? Against Poland certainly. Against Britain and France, if necessary. Against Russia too? With regard to the Soviet Union, Hitler had finally made up his mind.

THE INTERVENTION OF RUSSIA: III

A fresh initiative had come from the Russians.

On July 18, E. Babarin, the Soviet trade representative in Berlin, accompanied by two aides, called on Julius Schnurre at the German Foreign Office and informed him that Russia would like to extend and intensify German–Soviet economic relations. He brought along a detailed memorandum for a trade agreement calling for a greatly increased exchange of goods between the two countries and declared that if a few differences between the two parties were clarified he was empowered to sign a trade treaty in Berlin. The Germans, as Dr. Schnurre's confidential memorandum of the meeting shows, were rather pleased. Such a treaty, Schnurre noted, "will not fail to have its effect at least in Poland and Britain."[76] Four days later, on July 22, the Russian press announced in Moscow that Soviet–German trade negotiations had been resumed in Berlin.

On the same day Weizsaecker rather exuberantly wired Ambassador von der Schulenburg in Moscow some interesting new instructions. As to the trade negotiations, he informed the ambassador, "we will act here in a markedly forthcoming manner, since a conclusion, and this at the earliest possible moment, is desired here for general reasons. As far as the purely political aspect of our conversations with the Russians is concerned," he added, "we regard the period of waiting stipulated for you in our telegram [of June 30]* as having expired. You are therefore empowered to pick up the threads again there, without in any way pressing the matter."[77]

They were, in fact, picked up four days later, on July 26, in Berlin. Dr. Schnurre was instructed by Ribbentrop to dine Astakhov, the Soviet chargé, and Babarin at a swank Berlin restaurant and sound them out. The two Russians needed little sounding. As Schnurre noted in his confidential memorandum of the meeting, "the Russians stayed until about 12:30 A.M." and talked "in a very lively and interested manner about the political and economic problems of interest to us."

Astakhov, with the warm approval of Babarin, declared that a Soviet–German political *rapprochement* corresponded to the vital interests of the two countries. In Moscow, he said, they had never quite understood why Nazi Germany had been so antagonistic to the Soviet Union. The German diplomat, in response, explained that "German policy in the East had now taken an entirely different course."

On our part there could be no question of menacing the Soviet Union. Our aims were in an entirely different direction . . . German policy was aimed

---

* See above, p. 495.

at Britain . . . I could imagine a far-reaching arrangement of mutual interests with due consideration for vital Russian problems.

However, this possibility would be barred the moment the Soviet Union aligned itself with Britain against Germany. The time for an understanding between Germany and the Soviet Union was opportune now, but would no longer be so after the conclusion of a pact with London.

What could Britain offer Russia? At best, participation in a European war and the hostility of Germany. What could we offer against this? Neutrality and keeping out of a possible European conflict and, if Moscow wished, a German–Russian understanding on mutual interests which, just as in former times, would work out to the advantage of both countries . . . Controversial problems [between Germany and Russia] did not, in my opinion, exist anywhere along the line from the Baltic Sea to the Black Sea and to the Far East. In addition, despite all the divergencies in their views of life, there was one thing common to the ideology of Germany, Italy and the Soviet Union: opposition to the capitalist democracies in the West.[78]

Thus in the late-evening hours of July 26 in a small Berlin restaurant over good food and wine partaken by second-string diplomats was Germany's first serious bid for a deal with Soviet Russia made. The new line which Schnurre took had been given him by Ribbentrop himself. Astakhov was pleased to hear it. He promised Schnurre that he would report it at once to Moscow.

In the Wilhelmstrasse the Germans waited impatiently to see what the reaction in the Soviet capital would be. Three days later, on July 29, Weizsaecker sent a secret dispatch by courier to Schulenburg in Moscow.

It would be important for us to know whether the remarks made to Astakhov and Babarin have met with any response in Moscow. If you see an opportunity of arranging a further conversation with Molotov, please sound him out on the same lines. If this results in Molotov abandoning the reserve he has so far maintained you could go a step further . . . This applies in particular to the Polish problem. We would be prepared, however the Polish problem may develop . . . to safeguard all Soviet interests and to come to an understanding with the Government in Moscow. In the Baltic question, too, if the talks took a positive course, the idea could be advanced of so adjusting our attitude to the Baltic States as to respect vital Soviet interests in the Baltic Sea.[79]

Two days later, on July 31, the State Secretary wired Schulenburg "urgent and secret":

With reference to our dispatch of July 29, arriving in Moscow by courier today:

Please report by telegram the date and time of your next interview with Molotov as soon as it is fixed.

We are anxious for an early interview.[80]

For the first time a note of urgency crept into the dispatches from Berlin to Moscow.

There was good reason for Berlin's sense of urgency. On July 23, France and Britain had finally agreed to Russia's proposal that military-staff talks be held at once to draw up a military convention which would spell out specifically how Hitler's armies were to be met by the three nations. Although Chamberlain did not announce this agreement until July 31, when he made it to the House of Commons, the Germans got wind of it earlier. On July 28 Ambassador von Welczeck in Paris wired Berlin that he had learned from "an unusually well-informed source" that France and Britain were dispatching military missions to Moscow and that the French group would be headed by General Doumenc, whom he described as being "a particularly capable officer" and a former Deputy Chief of Staff under General Maxime Weygand.[81] It was the German ambassador's impression, as he stated in a supplementary dispatch two days later, that Paris and London had agreed to military-staff talks as a last means of preventing the adjournment of the Moscow negotiations.[82]

It was a well-founded impression. As the confidential British Foreign Office papers make clear, the political talks in Moscow had reached an impasse by the last week in July largely over the impossibility of reaching a definition of "indirect aggression." To the British and French the Russian interpretation of that term was so broad that it might be used to justify Soviet intervention in Finland and the Baltic States even if there were no serious Nazi threat, and to this London at least—the French were prepared to be more accommodating—would not agree.

Also, on June 2 the Russians had insisted that a military agreement setting down in detail the "methods, form and extent" of the military help which the three countries were to give each other should come into force at the same time as the mutual-assistance pact itself. The Western Powers, which did not think highly of Russia's military prowess,* tried to put Molotov off. They would only agree to starting staff talks after the political agreement had been signed. But the Russians were adamant. When the British tried to strike a bargain, offering on July 17 to begin staff conversations at once if the Soviet Union would yield on its insistence on signing political and military agreements simultaneously and also—for

---

* The British High Command, like the German later, grossly underestimated the potential strength of the Red Army. This may have been due in large part to the reports it received from its military attachés in Moscow. On March 6, for instance, Colonel Firebrace, the military attaché, and Wing Commander Hallawell, the air attaché, had filed long reports to London to the effect that while the defensive capabilities of the Red Army and Air Force were considerable they were incapable of mounting a serious offensive. Hallawell thought that the Russian Air Force, "like the Army, is likely to be brought to a standstill as much by the collapse of essential services as by enemy action." Firebrace found that the purge of higher officers had severely weakened the Red Army. But he did point out to London that "the Red Army considers war inevitable and is undoubtedly being strenuously prepared for it."[88]

good measure—accept the British definition of "indirect aggression," Molotov answered with a blunt rejection. Unless the French and British agreed to political and military agreements in one package, he said, there was no point in continuing the negotiations. This Russian threat to end the talks caused consternation in Paris, which seems to have been more acutely aware than London of the course of Soviet–Nazi flirtations, and it was largely due to French pressure that the British government, on August 23, while refusing to accept the Russian proposals on "indirect aggression," reluctantly agreed to negotiate a military convention.[84]

Chamberlain was less than lukewarm to the whole business of staff talks.* On August 1 Ambassador von Dirksen in London informed Berlin that the military negotiations with the Russians were "regarded skeptically" in British government circles.

This is borne out [he wrote] by the composition of the British Military Mission.† The Admiral . . . is practically on the retired list and was never on the Naval Staff. The General is also purely a combat officer. The Air Marshal is outstanding as a pilot and an instructor, but not as a strategist. This seems to indicate that the task of the Military Mission is rather to ascertain the fighting value of the Soviet forces than to conclude agreements on operations . . . The Wehrmacht attachés are agreed in observing a surprising skepticism in British military circles about the forthcoming talks with the Soviet armed forces.[86]

Indeed, so skeptical was the British government that it neglected to give Admiral Drax written authority to negotiate—an oversight, if it was that, which Marshal Voroshilov complained about when the staff officers first met. The Admiral's credentials did not arrive until August 21, when they were no longer of use.

But if Admiral Drax had no written credentials he certainly had secret written instructions as to the course he was to take in the military talks in Moscow. As the British Foreign Office papers much later revealed, the Admiral was admonished to "go very slowly with the [military] conversations, watching the progress of the political negotiations," until a political

---

* Strang, negotiating with Molotov in Moscow, was even cooler. "It is, indeed, extraordinary," he wrote the Foreign Office on July 20, "that we should be expected to talk military secrets with the Soviet Government before we are sure that they will be our allies."

The Russian view was just the opposite and was put by Molotov to the Anglo–French negotiators on July 27: "The important point was to see how many divisions each party would contribute to the common cause and where they would be located."[85] Before the Russians committed themselves politically they wanted to know how much military help they could expect from the West.

† The British mission consisted of Admiral Sir Reginald Plunkett-Ernle-Erle-Drax, who had been Commander in Chief, Plymouth, 1935–1938, Air Marshal Sir Charles Burnett and Major General Heywood.

agreement had been concluded.[87] It was explained to him that confidential military information could not be imparted to the Russians until the political pact was signed.

But since the political conversations had been suspended on August 2 and Molotov had made it clear that he would not assent to their being renewed until the military talks had made some progress, the conclusion can scarcely be escaped that the Chamberlain government was quite prepared to take its time in spelling out the military obligations of each country in the proposed mutual-assistance pact.* In fact the confidential British Foreign Office documents leave little doubt that, by the beginning of August, Chamberlain and Halifax had almost given up hope of reaching an agreement with the Soviet Union to stop Hitler but thought that if they stretched out the staff negotiations in Moscow this might somehow deter the German dictator from taking, during the next four weeks, the fatal step toward war.†

In contrast to the British and French, the Russians placed on their military mission the highest officers of their armed forces: Marshal Voroshilov, who was Commissar for Defense, General Shaposhnikov, Chief of the General Staff of the Red Army, and the commanders in chief of the Navy and Air Force. The Russians could not help noting that whereas the British had sent the Chief of the Imperial General Staff, General Sir Edmund Ironside, to Warsaw in July for military talks with the Polish General Staff, they did not consider sending this ranking British officer to Moscow.

It cannot be said that the Anglo–French military missions were exactly rushed to Moscow. A plane would have got them there in a day. But they were sent on a slow boat—a passenger-cargo vessel—which took as long to get them to Russia as the *Queen Mary* could have conveyed them to America. They sailed for Leningrad on August 5 and did not arrive in Moscow until August 11.

By that time it was too late. Hitler had beaten them to it.

---

* A conclusion reached by Arnold Toynbee and his collaborators in their book, *The Eve of War, 1939,* based largely on the British Foreign Office documents. See p. 482.

† On August 16, Air Marshal Sir Charles Burnett wrcte to London from Moscow: "I understand it is the Government's policy to prolong negotiations as long as possible if we cannot get acceptance of a treaty." Seeds, the British ambassador in Moscow, had wired London on July 24, the day after his government agreed to staff talks: "I am not optimistic as to the success of military conversations, nor do I think they can in any case be rapidly concluded, but to begin with them now would give a healthy shock to the Axis Powers and a fillip to our friends, while they might be prolonged sufficiently to tide over the next dangerous few months."[88] In view of what Anglo–French intelligence knew of the meetings of Molotov with the German ambassador, of German efforts to interest Russia in a new partition of Poland—which Coulondre had warned Paris of as early as May 7 (see above, p. 482), of massive German troop concentrations on the Polish border, and of Hitler's intentions, this British trust in stalling in Moscow is somewhat startling.

While the British and French military officers were waiting for their slow boat to Leningrad the Germans were acting swiftly. August 3 was a crucial day in Berlin and Moscow.

At 12:58 P.M. on that day Foreign Minister von Ribbentrop, who invariably left the sending of telegrams to State Secretary von Weizsaecker, got off on his own a wire marked "Secret—Most Urgent" to Schulenburg in Moscow.

Yesterday I had a lengthy conversation with Astakhov, on which a telegram follows.

I expressed the *German* wish for remolding German–Russian relations and stated that from the Baltic to the Black Sea there was no problem which could not be solved to our mutual satisfaction. In response to Astakhov's desire for more concrete conversations on topical questions . . . I declared myself ready for such conversations if the Soviet Government would inform me through Astakhov that they also desired to place German–Russian relations on a new and definitive basis.[89]

It was known at the Foreign Office that Schulenburg was seeing Molotov later in the day. An hour after Ribbentrop's telegram was dispatched, Weizsaecker got off one of his own, also marked "Secret—Most Urgent."

In view of the political situation and in the interests of speed, we are anxious, without prejudice to your conversation with Molotov today, to continue in more concrete terms in Berlin the conversations on harmonizing German–Soviet intentions. To this end Schnurre will receive Astakhov today and will tell him that we would be ready for a continuation on more concrete terms.[90]

Though Ribbentrop's sudden desire for "concrete" talks on everything from the Baltic to the Black Sea must have surprised the Russians—at one point, as he informed Schulenburg in his following telegram which was sent at 3:47 P.M., he "dropped a gentle hint [to Astakhov] at our coming to an understanding with Russia on the fate of Poland"—the Foreign Minister emphasized to his ambassador in Moscow that he had told the Russian chargé that "we were in no hurry."[91]

This was bluff, and the sharp-minded Soviet chargé called it when he saw Schnurre at the Foreign Office at 12:45 P.M. He remarked that while Schnurre seemed to be in a hurry, the German Foreign Minister the previous day "had shown no such urgency." Schnurre rose to the occasion.

I told M. Astakhov [he noted in a secret memorandum][92] that though the Foreign Minister last night had not shown any urgency to the Soviet Government, we nevertheless thought it expedient to make use of *the next few days**

---

* Emphasis in the original document.

for continuing the conversations in order to establish a basis as quickly as possible.

For the Germans, then, it had come down to a matter of the next few days. Astakhov told Schnurre that he had received "a provisional answer" from Molotov to the German suggestions. It was largely negative. While Moscow too desired an improvement in relations, "Molotov said," he reported, "that so far nothing concrete was known of Germany's attitude."

The Soviet Foreign Commissar conveyed his ideas directly to Schulenburg in Moscow that evening. The ambassador reported in a long dispatch filed shortly after midnight[93] that in a talk lasting an hour and a quarter Molotov had "abandoned his habitual reserve and appeared unusually open." There seems no doubt of that. For after Schulenburg had reiterated Germany's view that no differences existed between the two countries "from the Baltic to the Black Sea" and reaffirmed the German wish to "come to an understanding," the unbending Russian Minister enumerated some of the hostile acts that the Reich had committed against the Soviet Union: the Anti-Comintern Pact, support of Japan against Russia and the exclusion of the Soviets from Munich.

"How," asked Molotov, "could the new German statements be reconciled with these three points? Proofs of a changed attitude of the German Government were for the present still lacking."

Schulenburg seems to have been somewhat discouraged.

My general impression [he telegraphed Berlin] is that the Soviet Government are at present determined to conclude an agreement with Britain and France, if they fulfill all Soviet wishes . . . I believe that my statements made an impression on Molotov; it will nevertheless require considerable effort on our part to cause a reversal in the Soviet Government's course.

Knowledgeable though the veteran German diplomat was about Russian affairs, he obviously overestimated the progress in Moscow of the British and French negotiators. Nor did he yet realize the lengths to which Berlin was now prepared to go to make the "considerable effort" which he thought was necessary to reverse the course of Soviet diplomacy.

In the Wilhelmstrasse confidence grew that this could be accomplished. With Russia neutralized, Britain and France either would not fight for Poland or, if they did, would easily be held on the western fortifications until the Poles were quickly liquidated and the German Army could turn its full strength on the West.

The astute French chargé d'affaires in Berlin, Jacques Tarbé de St.-Hardouin, noticed the change of atmosphere in the German capital. On the very day, August 3, when there was so much Soviet–German diplomatic activity in Berlin and Moscow, he reported to Paris: "In the course of the last week a very definite change in the political atmosphere has been observed in Berlin . . . The period of embarrassment, hesitation, inclination to temporization or even to appeasement has been succeeded among the Nazi leaders by a new phase."[94]

THE HESITATION OF GERMANY'S ALLIES

It was different with Germany's allies, Italy and Hungary. As the summer progressed, the governments in Budapest and Rome became increasingly fearful that their countries would be drawn into Hitler's war on Germany's side.

On July 24 Count Teleki, Premier of Hungary, addressed identical letters to Hitler and Mussolini informing them that "in the event of a general conflict Hungary will make her policy conform to the policy of the Axis." Having gone so far, he then pulled back. On the same day he wrote the two dictators a second letter stating that "in order to prevent any possible misinterpretation of my letter of July 24, I . . . repeat that Hungary could not, on moral grounds, be in a position to take armed action against Poland."[95]

The second letter from Budapest threw Hitler into one of his accustomed rages. When he received Count Csáky, the Hungarian Foreign Minister, at Obersalzberg on August 8, in the presence of Ribbentrop, he opened the conversation by stating that he had been "shocked" at the Hungarian Prime Minister's letter. He emphasized, according to the confidential memorandum drawn up for the Foreign Office, that he had never expected help from Hungary—or from any other state—"in the event of a German–Polish conflict." Count Teleki's letter, he added, "was impossible." And he reminded his Hungarian guest that it was due to Germany's generosity that Hungary had been able to regain so much territory at the expense of Czechoslovakia. Were Germany to be defeated in war, he said, "Hungary would be automatically smashed too."

The German memorandum of this conversation, which is among the captured Foreign Office documents, reveals Hitler's state of mind as the fateful month of August got under way. Poland, he said, presented no military problem at all for Germany. Nevertheless, he was reckoning from the start with a war on two fronts. "No power in the world," he boasted, "could penetrate Germany's western fortifications. Nobody in all my life has been able to frighten me, and that goes for Britain. Nor will I succumb to the oft-predicted nervous breakdown." As for Russia:

The Soviet Government would not fight against us . . . The Soviets would not repeat the Czar's mistake and bleed to death for Britain. They would, however, try to enrich themselves, possibly at the expense of the Baltic States or Poland, without engaging in military action themselves.

So effective was Hitler's harangue that at the end of a second talk held the same day Count Csáky requested him "to regard the two letters written by Teleki as not having been written." He said he would also make the same request of Mussolini.

For some weeks the Duce had been worrying and fretting about the danger of the Fuehrer dragging Italy into war. Attolico, his ambassador in Berlin, had been sending increasingly alarming reports about Hitler's determination to attack Poland.* Since early June Mussolini had been pressing for another meeting with Hitler and in July it was fixed for August 4 at the Brenner. On July 24 he presented to Hitler through Attolico "certain basic principles" for their discussion. If the Fuehrer considered war "inevitable," then Italy would stand by her side. But the Duce reminded him that a war with Poland could not be localized; it would become a European conflict. Mussolini did not think that this was the time for the Axis to start such a war. He proposed instead "a constructive peaceful policy over several years," with Germany settling her differences with Poland and Italy hers with France by diplomatic negotiation. He went further. He suggested another international conference of the Big Powers.[97]

The Fuehrer's reaction, as Ciano noted in his diary on July 26, was unfavorable, and Mussolini decided it might be best to postpone his meeting with Hitler.[98] He proposed instead, on August 7, that the foreign ministers of the two countries meet immediately. Ciano's diary notes during these days indicate the growing uneasiness in Rome. On August 6 he wrote:

We must find some way out. By following the Germans we shall go to war and enter it under the least favorable conditions for the Axis, and especially for Italy. Our gold reserves are reduced to almost nothing, as well as our stocks of metals . . . We must avoid war. I propose to the Duce the idea of my meeting with Ribbentrop . . . during which I would attempt to continue discussion of Mussolini's project for a world conference.

---

* Typical was a vivid report Attolico sent of a talk he had with Ribbentrop on July 6. If Poland dared to attack Danzig, the Nazi Foreign Minister told him, Germany would settle the Danzig question in forty-eight hours—at Warsaw! If France were to intervene over Danzig, and so precipitate a general war, let her; Germany would like nothing better. France would be "annihilated"; Britain, if she stirred, would be bringing destruction on the British Empire. Russia? There was going to be a Russian–German treaty, and Russia was not going to march. America? One speech of the Fuehrer's had been enough to rout Roosevelt; and Americans would not stir anyway. Fear of Japan would keep America quiet.

I listened [Attolico reported] in wondering silence, while Ribbentrop drew this picture of the war *ad usum Germaniae* which his imagination has now established indelibly in his head . . . He can see nothing but his version—which is a really amazing one—of an assured German victory in every field and against all comers . . . At the end, I observed that, according to my understanding, there was complete agreement between the Duce and the Fuehrer that Italy and Germany were preparing for a war that was *not* to be immediate.[96]

But the astute Attolico did not believe that at all. All through July his dispatches warned of imminent German action in Poland.

August 9.—Ribbentrop has approved the idea of our meeting. I decided to leave tomorrow night in order to meet him at Salzburg. The Duce is anxious that I prove to the Germans, by documentary evidence, that the outbreak of war at this time would be folly.

August 10.—The Duce is more than ever convinced of the necessity of delaying the conflict. He himself has worked out the outline of a report concerning the meeting at Salzburg which ends with an allusion to international negotiations to settle the problems that so dangerously disturb European life.

Before letting me go he recommends that I shall frankly inform the Germans that we must avoid a conflict with Poland since it will be impossible to localize it, and a general war would be disastrous for everybody.[99]

Armed with such commendable but, in the circumstances, naïve thoughts and recommendations, the youthful Fascist Foreign Minister set out for Germany, where during the next three days—August 11, 12 and 13—he received from Ribbentrop and especially from Hitler the shock of his life.

CIANO AT SALZBURG AND OBERSALZBERG: AUGUST 11, 12, 13

For some ten hours on August 11, Ciano conferred with Ribbentrop at the latter's estate at Fuschl, outside Salzburg, which the Nazi Foreign Minister had taken from an Austrian monarchist who, conveniently, had been put away in a concentration camp. The hot-blooded Italian found the atmosphere, as he later reported, cold and gloomy. During dinner at the White Horse Inn at St. Wolfgang not a word was exchanged between the two. It was scarcely necessary. Ribbentrop had informed his visitor earlier in the day that the decision to attack Poland was implacable.

"Well, Ribbentrop," Ciano says he asked, "what do you want? The Corridor or Danzig?"

"Not that any more," Ribbentrop replied, gazing at him with his cold, metallic eyes. "We want war!"

Ciano's arguments that a Polish conflict could not be localized, that if Poland were attacked the Western democracies would fight, were bluntly rejected. The day before Christmas Eve four years later—1943—when Ciano lay in Cell 27 of the Verona jail waiting execution at the instigation of the Germans, he still remembered that chilling day of August 11 at Fuschl and Salzburg. Ribbentrop, he wrote in his very last diary entry on December 23, 1943, had bet him "during one of those gloomy meals at the Oesterreichischer Hof in Salzburg" a collection of old German armor against an Italian painting that France and Britain would remain neutral —a bet, he remarks ruefully, which was never paid.[100]

Ciano moved on to Obersalzberg, where Hitler during two meetings on August 12 and 13 reiterated that France and Britain would not fight.

In contrast to the Nazi Foreign Minister, the Fuehrer was cordial, but he was equally implacable in his determination to go to war. This is evident not only from Ciano's reports but from the confidential German minutes of the meeting, which are among the captured documents.[101] The Italian Minister found Hitler standing before a large table covered with military staff maps. He began by explaining the strength of Germany's West Wall. It was, he said, impenetrable. Besides, he added scornfully, Britain could put only three divisions into France. France would have considerably more, but since Poland would be defeated "in a very short time," Germany could then concentrate 100 divisions in the west "for the life-and-death struggle which would then commence."

But would it? A few moments later, annoyed by Ciano's initial response, the Fuehrer was contradicting himself. The Italian Minister, as he had promised himself, spoke up to Hitler. According to the German minutes, he expressed "Italy's great surprise at the entirely unexpected gravity of the situation." Germany, he complained, had not kept her ally informed. "On the contrary," he said, "the Reich Foreign Minister had stated [at Milan and Berlin in May] that the Danzig question would be settled in due course." When Ciano went on to declare that a conflict with Poland would spread into a European war his host interrupted to say that he differed.

"I personally," said Hitler, "am absolutely convinced that the Western democracies will, in the last resort, recoil from unleashing a general war." To which Ciano replied (the German minutes add) "that he hoped the Fuehrer would prove right but he did not believe it." The Italian Foreign Minister then outlined in great detail Italy's weaknesses, and from his tale of woe, as the Germans recorded it, Hitler must have been finally convinced that Italy would be of little help to him in the coming war.* One of Mussolini's reasons, Ciano said, for wanting to postpone the war was that he "attached great importance to holding, according to plan, the World Exhibition of 1942"—a remark that must have astounded the Fuehrer, lost as he was in his military maps and calculations. He must have been equally astounded when Ciano naïvely produced the text of a communiqué, which he urged to be published, stating that the meeting of the Axis ministers had "reaffirmed the peaceful intentions of their governments" and their belief that peace could be maintained "through normal diplomatic negotiations." Ciano explained that the Duce had in mind a peace conference of the chief European nations but that out of deference to "the Fuehrer's misgivings" he would settle for ordinary diplomatic negotiations.

Hitler did not, the first day, turn down completely the idea of a conference but reminded Ciano that "Russia could no longer be excluded

---

* At one point, Ribbentrop, with obvious exasperation, told Ciano, "We don't need you!"; to which Ciano replied, "The future will show." (From General Halder's unpublished diary, entry of August 14.[102] Halder says he got it through Weizsaecker.)

from future meetings of the powers." This was the first mention of the Soviet Union but it was not the last.

Finally when Ciano tried to pin his host down as to the date of the attack on Poland Hitler replied that because of the autumn rains, which would render useless his armored and motorized divisions in a country with few paved roads, the "settlement with Poland would have to be made one way or the other by the end of August."

At last Ciano had the date. Or the last possible date, for a moment later Hitler was storming that if the Poles offered any fresh provocation he was determined "to attack Poland within forty-eight hours." Therefore, he added, "a move against Poland must be expected any moment." That outburst ended the first day's talks except for Hitler's promise to think over the Italian proposals.

Having given them twenty-four hours' thought, he told Ciano the next day that it would be better if no communiqué of any kind were issued about their talks.* Because of the expected bad weather in the fall

it was of decisive importance, firstly [he said], that within the shortest possible time Poland should make her intentions plain, and secondly, that no further acts of provocation of any sort should be tolerated by Germany.

When Ciano inquired as to "what the shortest possible time" was, Hitler replied, "By the end of August at the latest." While it would take only a fortnight, he explained, to defeat Poland, the "final liquidation" would require a further two to four weeks—a remarkable forecast of timing, as it turned out.

Finally, at the end, Hitler uttered his customary flattery of Mussolini, whom Ciano must have convinced him he could no longer count on. He personally felt fortunate, he declared, "to live at a time when, apart from himself, there was another statesman living who would stand out in history as a great and unique figure. It was a source of great personal happiness that he could be a friend of this man. When the hour struck for the

---

* Though the German minutes explicitly state that Ciano agreed with Hitler "that no communiqué should be issued at the conclusion of the conversation," the Germans immediately double-crossed their Italian ally. D.N.B., the official German news agency, issued a communiqué two hours after Ciano's departure and without any consultation whatever with the Italians, that the talks had covered all the problems of the day—with particular attention to Danzig—and had resulted in a "hundred per cent" agreement. So much so, the communiqué added, that not a single problem had been left in suspense, and therefore there would be no further meetings, because there was no occasion for them. Attolico was furious. He protested to the Germans, accusing them of bad faith. He tipped off Henderson that war was imminent. And in an angry dispatch to Rome he described the German communique as "Machiavellian," pointed out that it was deliberately done to bind Italy to Germany after the latter's attack on Poland and pleaded that Mussolini should be firm with Hitler in demanding German fulfillment of the "consultation" provisions of the Pact of Steel and under these provisions insist on a month's grace to settle the Danzig question through diplomatic channels.[103]

common fight he would always be found at the side of the Duce, come what may."

However much the strutting Mussolini might be impressed by such words, his son-in-law was not. "I return to Rome," he wrote in his diary on August 13, after the second meeting with Hitler, "completely disgusted with the Germans, with their leader, with their way of doing things. They have betrayed us and lied to us. Now they are dragging us into an adventure which we have not wanted and which might compromise the regime and the country as a whole."

But Italy at the moment was the least of Hitler's concerns. His thoughts were concentrating on Russia. Toward the end of the meeting with Ciano, on August 12, a "telegram from Moscow," as the German minutes put it, was handed to the Fuehrer. The conversation was interrupted for a few moments while Hitler and Ribbentrop perused it. They then informed Ciano of its contents.

"The Russians," Hitler said, "have agreed to a German political negotiator being sent to Moscow."

15

THE NAZI–SOVIET PACT

THE "TELEGRAM FROM MOSCOW" whose contents Hitler disclosed to Ciano at Obersalzberg on the afternoon of August 12 appears to have been, like certain previous "telegrams" which have figured in this narrative, of doubtful origin. No such wire from the Russian capital has been found in the German archives. Schulenburg did send a telegram to Berlin from Moscow on the twelfth, but it merely reported the arrival of the Franco–British military missions and the friendly toasts exchanged between the Russians and their guests.

Yet there was some basis for the "telegram" with which Hitler and Ribbentrop had so obviously tried to impress Ciano. On August 12 a teleprint was sent to Obersalzberg from the Wilhelmstrasse reporting the results of a call which the Russian chargé had made on Schnurre in Berlin on that day. Astakhov informed the Foreign Office official that Molotov was now ready to discuss the questions raised by the Germans, including Poland and other political matters. The Soviet government proposed Moscow as the place of these negotiations. But, Astakhov made it clear, they were not to be hurried. He stressed, Schnurre noted in his report, which apparently was rushed to Obersalzberg, "that the chief emphasis in his instructions from Molotov lay in the phrase 'by degrees' . . . The discussions could be undertaken only by degrees."[1]

But Adolf Hitler could not wait for negotiations with Russia "by degrees." As he had just revealed to a shocked Ciano, he had set the last possible date for the onslaught on Poland for September 1, and it was now almost the middle of August. If he were to successfully sabotage the Anglo–French parleys with the Russians and swing his own deal with Stalin, it had to be done quickly—not by stages but in one big leap.

Monday, August 14, was another crucial day. While Ambassador von der Schulenburg, who obviously had not yet been taken fully into the confidence of Hitler and Ribbentrop, was writing Weizsaecker from Moscow advising him that Molotov was "a strange man and a difficult character" and that "I am still of the opinion that any hasty measures in our relations with the Soviet Union should be avoided," he was being sent a "most urgent" telegram from Berlin.[2] It came from Ribbentrop and it was dispatched from the Wilhelmstrasse (the Foreign Minister was still at Fuschl) at 10:53 P.M. on August 14. It directed the German ambassador to call upon Molotov and read him a long communication "verbatim."

This, finally, was Hitler's great bid. German–Russian relations, said Ribbentrop, had "come to a historic turning point . . . There exist no real conflicts of interests between Germany and Russia . . . It has gone well with both countries previously when they were friends and badly when they were enemies."

The crisis which has been produced in Polish–German relations by English policy [Ribbentrop continued] and the attempts at an alliance which are bound up with that policy, make a speedy clarification of German–Russian relations necessary. Otherwise matters . . . might take a turn which would deprive both Governments of the possibility of restoring German–Russian friendship and in due course clarifying jointly territorial questions in Eastern Europe. The leadership of both countries, therefore, should not allow the situation to drift, but should take action at the proper time. It would be fatal if, through mutual ignorance of views and intentions, the two peoples should finally drift apart.

The German Foreign Minister, "in the name of the Fuehrer," was therefore prepared to act in proper time.

As we have been informed, the Soviet Government also feel the desire for a clarification of German–Russian relations. Since, however, according to previous experience this clarification can be achieved only slowly through the usual diplomatic channels, I am prepared to make a short visit to Moscow in order, in the name of the Fuehrer, to set forth the Fuehrer's views to M. Stalin. In my view, only through such a direct discussion can a change be brought about, and it should not be impossible thereby to lay the foundations for a final settlement of German–Russian relations.

The British Foreign Secretary had not been willing to go to Moscow, but now the German Foreign Minister was not only willing but anxious to go—a contrast which the Nazis calculated quite correctly would make an impression on the suspicious Stalin.* The Germans saw that it was highly important to get their message through to the Russian dictator himself. Ribbentrop therefore added an "annex" to his urgent telegram.

I request [Ribbentrop advised Schulenburg] that you do not give M. Molotov these instructions in writing, but that they reach M. Stalin in as exact a form as possible and I authorize you, if the occasion arises, to request from M. Molotov on my behalf an audience with M. Stalin, so that you may be able to

---

* See p. 523.

make this important communication directly to him also. In addition to a conference with Molotov, a detailed discussion with Stalin would be a condition for my making the trip.[3]

There was a scarcely disguised bait in the Foreign Minister's proposal which the Germans, not without reason, must have thought the Kremlin would rise to. Reiterating that "there is no question between the Baltic Sea and the Black Sea which cannot be settled to the complete satisfaction of both counties," Ribbentrop specified "the Baltic States, Poland, southeastern questions, etc." And he spoke of the necessity of "clarifying jointly territorial questions of Eastern Europe."

Germany was ready to divide up Eastern Europe, including Poland, with the Soviet Union. This was a bid which Britain and France could not—and, obviously, if they could, would not—match. And having made it, Hitler, apparently confident that it would not be turned down, once more—on the same day, August 14—called in the commanders in chief of his armed forces to listen to him lecture on the plans and prospects for war.

THE MILITARY CONFERENCE AT OBERSALZBERG: AUGUST 14*

"The great drama," Hitler told his select listeners, "is now approaching its climax." While political and military successes could not be had without taking risks, he was certain that Great Britain and France would not fight. For one thing, Britain "has no leaders of real caliber. The men I got to know at Munich are not the kind that start a new world war." As at previous meetings with his military chiefs, the Fuehrer could not keep his mind off England and he spoke in considerable detail of her strengths and weaknesses, especially the latter.

England [Halder noted down the words], unlike in 1914, will not allow herself to blunder into a war lasting for years . . . Such is the fate of rich coun-

---

* The only source found for what happened at this meeting is in the unpublished diary of General Halder, Chief of the Army General Staff. It is the first entry, August 14, 1939. Halder kept his diary in Gabelsberger shorthand and it is an immensely valuable record of the most confidential military and political goings on in Nazi Germany from August 14, 1939, to September 24, 1942, when he was dismissed from his post. The Obersalzberg entry consists of Halder's shorthand notes jotted down while Hitler spoke and a summary which he added at the end. It is strange that no American or British publisher has published the Halder diary. The writer had access to the German longhand version of it, transcribed by Halder himself, during the writing of this volume. Hitler's daily record book confirms the date of this meeting and adds that besides the commanders in chief, Brauchitsch, Goering and Raeder, Dr. Todt, the engineer who built the West Wall, also was present.

tries . . . Not even England has the money nowadays to fight a world war. What should England fight for? You don't get yourself killed for an ally.

What military measures, Hitler asked, could Britain and France undertake?

Drive against the West Wall unlikely [he answered]. A northward swing through Belgium and Holland will not bring speedy victory. None of this would help the Poles.

All these factors argue against England and France entering the war . . . There is nothing to force them into it. The men of Munich will not take the risk . . . English and French general staffs take a very sober view of the prospects of an armed conflict and advise against it. . . .

All this supports the conviction that while England may talk big, even recall her Ambassador, perhaps put a complete embargo on trade, she is sure not to resort to armed intervention in the conflict.

So Poland, probably, could be taken on alone, but she would have to be defeated "within a week or two," Hitler explained, so that the world could be convinced of her collapse and not try to save her.

Hitler was not quite ready to tell his generals just how far he was going that very day to make a deal with Russia, though it would have immensely pleased them, convinced as they were that Germany could not fight a major war on two fronts. But he told them enough to whet their appetite for more.

"Russia," he said, "is not in the least disposed to pull chestnuts out of the fire." He explained the "loose contacts" with Moscow which had started with the trade negotiations. He was now considering whether "a negotiator should go to Moscow and whether this should be a prominent figure." The Soviet Union, he declared, felt under no obligation to the West. The Russians understood the destruction of Poland. They were interested in a "delimitation of spheres of interest." The Fuehrer was "inclined to meet them halfway."

In all of Halder's voluminous shorthand notes on the meeting there is no mention that he, the Chief of the Army's General Staff, or General von Brauchitsch, its Commander in Chief, or Goering questioned the Fuehrer's course in leading Germany into a European conflict—for despite Hitler's confidence it was by no means certain that France and Britain would not fight nor that Russia would stay out. In fact, exactly a week before, Goering had received a direct warning that the British would certainly fight if Germany attacked Poland.

Early in July a Swedish friend of his, Birger Dahlerus, had tried to convince him that British public opinion would not stand for further Nazi aggression and when the Luftwaffe chief expressed his doubts had arranged for him to meet privately with a group of seven British businessmen on August 7 in Schleswig-Holstein, near the Danish border, where

Dahlerus had a house. The British businessmen, both orally and in a written memorandum, did their best to persuade Goering that Great Britain would stand by its treaty obligations with Poland should Germany attack. Whether they succeeded is doubtful, though Dahlerus, a businessman himself, thought so.* This curious Swede, who was to play a certain role as a peacemaker between Germany and Britain in the next hectic weeks, certainly had high connections in Berlin and London. He had access to Downing Street, where on July 20 he had been received by Lord Halifax, with whom he discussed the coming meeting of British businessmen with Goering; and soon he would be called in by Hitler and Chamberlain themselves. But, though well-meaning in his quest to save the peace, he was naïve and, as a diplomat, dreadfully amateurish. Years later at Nuremberg, Sir David Maxwell-Fyfe, in a devastating cross-examination, led the Swedish diplomatic interloper to admit sadly that he had been badly misled by Goering and Hitler.[4]

And why did not General Halder, who had been the ringleader in the plot eleven months before to remove Hitler, speak up on August 14 to oppose the Fuehrer's determination to go to war? Or, if he thought that useless, why did he not renew plans to get rid of the dictator on the same grounds as just before Munich: that a war now would be disastrous for Germany? Much later, in his interrogation at Nuremberg, Halder would explain that even at mid-August 1939 he simply did not believe that Hitler would, in the end, risk war, regardless of what he said.[5] Also, a diary entry of August 15, the day after the meeting with Hitler at the Berghof, shows that Halder did not believe that France and Britain would risk war either.

As for Brauchitsch, he was not the man to question what the Fuehrer planned to do. Hassell, who on August 15 learned of the military conference at the Obersalzberg from Gisevius, got word through to the Army chief that he was "absolutely convinced" that Britain and France would intervene if Germany invaded Poland. "Nothing can be done with him," Hassell noted sadly in his diary. "Either he is afraid or he doesn't understand what it is all about. . . . Nothing is to be hoped for from the generals . . . Only a few have kept clear heads: Halder, Canaris, Thomas."[6]

Only General Thomas, the brilliant head of the Economic and Armaments Branch of OKW, dared to openly challenge the Fuehrer. A few days after the August 14 military conference, following a discussion with the now largely inactive conspirators Goerdeler, Beck and Schacht, Gen-

---

* Dahlerus told the Nuremberg tribunal on March 19, 1946, when he was on the stand as a witness for Goering, that the Field Marshal had assured the British businessmen "on his word of honor" that he would do everything in his power to avert war. But Goering's state of mind at this time may have been more accurately expressed in a statement he made two days after seeing the British visitors. In boasting about the Luftwaffe's air defenses, he said, "The Ruhr will not be subjected to a single bomb. If an enemy bomber reaches the Ruhr, my name is not Hermann Goering: you can call me Meier!"—a boast he was soon to rue.

eral Thomas drew up a memorandum and personally read it to General
Keitel, the Chief of OKW. A quick war and a quick peace were a complete illusion, he argued. An attack on Poland would unleash a world
war and Germany lacked the raw materials and the food supplies to fight
it. But Keitel, whose only ideas were those he absorbed from Hitler,
scoffed at the very idea of a big war. Britain was too decadent, France too
degenerate, America too uninterested, to fight for Poland, he said.[7]

And so as the second half of August 1939 began, the German military
chiefs pushed forward with their plans to annihilate Poland and to protect the western Reich just in case the democracies, contrary to all evidence, did intervene. On August 15 the annual Nuremberg Party Rally,
which Hitler on April 1 had proclaimed as the "Party Rally of Peace" and
which was scheduled to begin the first week in September, was secretly
canceled. A quarter of a million men were called up for the armies of the
west. Advance mobilization orders to the railways were given. Plans were
made to move Army headquarters to Zossen, east of Berlin. And on the
same day, August 15, the Navy reported that the pocket battleships *Graf
Spee* and *Deutschland* and twenty-one submarines were ready to sail for
their stations in the Atlantic.

On August 17 General Halder made a strange entry in his diary: "Canaris checked with Section I [Operations]. Himmler, Heydrich, Obersalzberg: 150 Polish uniforms with accessories for Upper Silesia."

What did it mean? It was only after the war that it became clear. It
concerned one of the most bizarre incidents ever arranged by the Nazis.
Just as Hitler and his Army chiefs, it will be remembered, had considered
cooking up an "incident," such as the assassination of the German minister, in order to justify their invading Austria and Czechoslovakia, so now
they concerned themselves, as time began to run out, with concocting
an incident which would, at least in their opinion, justify before the world
the planned aggression against Poland.

The code name was "Operation Himmler" and the idea was quite
simple—and crude. The S.S.-Gestapo would stage a faked attack on the
German radio station at Gleiwitz, near the Polish border, using condemned concentration camp inmates outfitted in Polish Army uniforms.
Thus Poland could be blamed for attacking Germany. Early in August
Admiral Canaris, chief of the Abwehr Section of OKW, had received an
order from Hitler himself to deliver to Himmler and Heydrich 150 Polish
uniforms and some Polish small arms. This struck him as a strange business and on August 17 he asked General Keitel about it. While the spineless OKW Chief declared he did not think much of "actions of this kind,"
he nevertheless told the Admiral that "nothing could be done," since the
order had come from the Fuehrer.[8] Repelled though he was, Canaris
obeyed his instructions and turned the uniforms over to Heydrich.

The chief of the S.D. chose as the man to carry out the operation a
young S.S. secret-service veteran by the name of Alfred Helmut Naujocks.

This was not the first of such assignments given this weird individual nor would it be the last. Early in March of 1939, shortly before the German occupation of Czechoslovakia, Naujocks, at Heydrich's instigation, had busied himself running explosives into Slovakia, where they were used, as he later testified, to "create incidents."

Alfred Naujocks was a typical product of the S.S.-Gestapo, a sort of intellectual gangster. He had studied engineering at Kiel University, where he got his first taste of brawling with anti-Nazis; on one occasion he had his nose bashed in by Communists. He had joined the S.S. in 1931 and was attached to the S.D. from its inception in 1934. Like so many other young men around Heydrich he dabbled in what passed as intellectual pursuits in the S.S.—"history" and "philosophy" especially— while rapidly emerging as a tough young man (Skorzeny was another) who could be entrusted with the carrying out of the less savory projects dreamed up by Himmler and Heydrich.* On October 19, 1944, Naujocks deserted to the Americans and at Nuremberg a year later made a number of sworn affidavits, in one of which he preserved for history the account of the "incident" which Hitler used to justify his attack on Poland.

On or about August 10, 1939, the chief of the S.D., Heydrich, personally ordered me to simulate an attack on the radio station near Gleiwitz near the Polish border [Naujocks related in an affidavit signed in Nuremberg November 20, 1945] and to make it appear that the attacking force consisted of Poles. Heydrich said: "Practical proof is needed for these attacks of the Poles for the foreign press as well as for German propaganda." . . .

My instructions were to seize the radio station and to hold it long enough to permit a Polish-speaking German who would be put at my disposal to broadcast a speech in Polish. Heydrich told me that this speech should state that the time had come for conflict between Germans and Poles . . . Heydrich also told me that he expected an attack on Poland by Germany in a few days.

I went to Gleiwitz and waited there fourteen days . . . Between the 25th and 31st of August, I went to see Heinrich Mueller, head of the Gestapo, who was then nearby at Oppeln. In my presence, Mueller discussed with a man

---

* Naujocks had a hand in the "Venlo Incident," which will be recounted further on. He was involved in an undertaking to disguise German soldiers in Dutch and Belgian frontier guard uniforms at the time of the invasion of the West in May 1940. Early in the war, he managed a section of the S.D. which forged passports and while thus employed proposed "Operation Bernhard," a fantastic plan to drop forged British banknotes over England. Heydrich eventually tired of him and forced him to serve in the ranks of an S.S. regiment in Russia, where he was wounded. In 1944 Naujocks turned up in Belgium as an economic administrator, but his principal job at that time appears to have been to carry out in Denmark the murder of a number of members of the Danish resistance movement. He probably deserted to the American Army in Belgium to save his neck. In fact, he had a charmed life. Held as a war criminal, he made a dramatic escape from a special camp in Germany for war criminals in 1946 and thus escaped trial. At the time of writing, he has never been apprehended or heard of. An account of his escape is given in Schaumburg-Lippe, *Zwischen Krone und Kerker.*

named Mehlhorn* plans for another border incident, in which it should be made to appear that Polish soldiers were attacking German troops . . . Mueller stated that he had 12 to 13 condemned criminals who were to be dressed in Polish uniforms and left dead on the ground of the scene of the incident to show they had been killed while attacking. For this purpose they were to be given fatal injections by a doctor employed by Heydrich. Then they were also to be given gunshot wounds. After the incident members of the press and other persons were to be taken to the spot of the incident . . .

Mueller told me he had an order from Heydrich to make one of those criminals available to me for the action at Gleiwitz. The code name by which he referred to these criminals was "Canned Goods."[9]

While Himmler, Heydrich and Mueller, at Hitler's command, were arranging for the use of "Canned Goods" to fake an excuse for Germany's aggression against Poland, the Fuehrer made his first decisive move to deploy his armed forces for a possibly bigger war. On August 19—another fateful day—orders to sail were issued to the German Navy. Twenty-one submarines were directed to put out for positions north and northwest of the British Isles, the pocket battleship *Graf Spee* to depart for waters off the Brazilian coast and her sister ship, the *Deutschland,* to take a position athwart the British sea lanes in the North Atlantic.†

The date of the order to dispatch the warships for possible action against Britain is significant. For on August 19, after a hectic week of frantic appeals from Berlin, the Soviet government finally gave Hitler the answer he wanted.

THE NAZI–SOVIET TALKS: AUGUST 15–21, 1939

Ambassador von der Schulenburg saw Molotov at 8 P.M. on August 15 and, as instructed, read to him Ribbentrop's urgent telegram stating that the Reich Foreign Minister was prepared to come to Moscow to settle Soviet–German relations. According to a "most urgent, secret" telegram which the German envoy got off to Berlin later that night, the Soviet Foreign Commissar received the information "with the greatest interest" and "warmly welcomed German intentions of improving relations with the Soviet Union." However, expert diplomatic poker player that he was, Molotov gave no sign of being in a hurry. Such a trip as Ribbentrop

---

* S.S. Oberfuehrer Dr. Mehlhorn, who administered the S.D. under Heydrich. Schellenberg, in his memoirs (*The Labyrinth*, pp. 48–50), recounts that Mehlhorn told him on August 26 that he had been put in charge of staging the faked attack at Gleiwitz but that Mehlhorn got out of it by feigning illness. Mehlhorn's stomach grew stronger in later years. During the war he was a notable instigator of Gestapo terror in Poland.

† The submarines sailed between August 19 and 23, the *Graf Spee* on the twenty-first and the *Deutschland* on the twenty-fourth.

proposed, he suggested, "required adequate preparation in order that the exchange of opinions might lead to results."

What results? The wily Russian dropped some hints. Would the German government, he asked, be interested in a nonaggression pact between the two countries? Would it be prepared to use its influence with Japan to improve ʻSoviet–Japanese relations and "eliminate border conflicts"?—a reference to an undeclared war which had raged all summer on the Manchurian–Mongolian frontier. Finally, Molotov asked, how did Germany feel about a joint guarantee of the Baltic States?

All such matters, he concluded, "must be discussed in concrete terms so that, should the German Foreign Minister come here, it will not be a matter of an exchange of opinions but of making concrete decisions." And he stressed again that "adequate preparation of the problems is indispensable."[10]

The first suggestion, then, for a Nazi–Soviet nonaggression pact came from the Russians—at the very moment they were negotiating with France and Great Britain to go to war, if necessary, to oppose further German aggression.* Hitler was more than willing to discuss such a pact "in concrete terms," since its conclusion would keep Russia out of the war and enable him to attack Poland without fear of Soviet intervention. And with Russia out of the conflict he was convinced that Britain and France would get cold feet.

Molotov's suggestions were just what he had hoped for; they were more specific and went further than anything which he had dared to propose. There was only one difficulty. With August running out he could not wait for the slow Soviet tempo which was indicated by Molotov's insistence on "adequate preparation" for the Foreign Minister's visit to Moscow. Schulenburg's report on his conversation with Molotov was telephoned by the Wilhelmstrasse to Ribbentrop at Fuschl at 6:40 A.M. on August 16 and he hurried across the mountain to seek further instruction from the Fuehrer at Obersalzberg. By early afternoon they had drawn up a reply to Molotov and it was rushed off on the teleprinter to Weizsaecker in Berlin with instructions to wire it "most urgent" to Moscow immediately.[12]

The Nazi dictator accepted the Soviet suggestions unconditionally. Schulenburg was directed by Ribbentrop to see Molotov again and inform him

that Germany is prepared to conclude a nonaggression pact with the Soviet Union and, if the Soviet Government so desire, one which would be undenounceable for a term of twenty-five years. Further, Germany is ready to guarantee the Baltic States jointly with the Soviet Union. Finally, Germany

---

* The British government soon learned of this. On August 17 Sumner Welles, the U.S. Undersecretary of State, informed the British ambassador in Washington of Molotov's suggestions to Schulenburg. The American ambassador in Moscow had wired them to Washington the day before and they were deadly accurate.[11] Ambassador Steinhardt had seen Molotov on August 16.

is prepared to exercise influence for an improvement and consolidation of Russian–Japanese relations.

All pretense was now dropped that the Reich government was not in a hurry to conclude a deal with Moscow.

The Fuehrer [Ribbentrop's telegram continued] is of the opinion that, in view of the present situation and of the possibility of the occurrence any day of serious events (please at this point explain to M. Molotov that Germany is determined not to endure Polish provocation indefinitely), a basic and rapid clarification of German–Russian relations, and of each country's attitude to the questions of the moment, is desirable.

For these reasons I am prepared to come by airplane to Moscow at any time after Friday, August 18, to deal, on the basis of full powers from the Fuehrer, with the entire complex of German–Russian relations and, if the occasion arises, to sign the appropriate treaties.

Again Ribbentrop added an "annex" of personal instructions to his ambassador.

I request that you again read these instructions word for word to Molotov and ask for the views of the Russian Government and of M. Stalin immediately. Entirely confidentially, it is added for your guidance that it would be of very special interest to us if my Moscow trip could take place at the end of this week or the beginning of next week.

The next day, on their mountaintop, Hitler and Ribbentrop waited impatiently for the response from Moscow. Telegraphic communication between Berlin and Moscow was by no means instantaneous—a condition of affairs which did not seem to be realized in the rarefied atmosphere of the Bavarian Alps. By noon of the seventeenth, Ribbentrop was wiring Schulenburg "most urgent" requesting "a report by telegram regarding the time when you made your request to be received by Molotov and the time for which the conversation has been arranged."[13] By dinnertime the harassed ambassador was replying, also "most urgent," that he had only received the Foreign Minister's telegram at eleven the night before, that it was by then too late to conduct any diplomatic business and that first thing in the morning of today, August 17, he had made an appointment with Molotov for 8 P.M.[14]

For the now frantic Nazi leaders it turned out to be a disappointing meeting. Conscious of Hitler's eagerness and no doubt fully aware of the reasons for it, the Russian Foreign Commissar played with the Germans, teasing and taunting them. After Schulenburg had read to him Ribbentrop's telegram, Molotov, taking little note of its contents, produced the Soviet government's written reply to the Reich Foreign Minister's first communication of August 15.

Beginning acidly with a reminder of the Nazi government's previous hostility to Soviet Russia, it explained "that until very recently the Soviet Government have proceeded on the assumption that the German Government are seeking occasion for clashes with the Soviet Union . . . Not to mention the fact that the German Government, by means of the so-called Anti-Comintern Pact, were endeavoring to create, and have created, the united front of a number of States against the Soviet Union." It was for this reason, the note explained, that Russia "was participating in the organization of a defensive front against [German] aggression."

If, however [the note continued], the German Government now undertake a change from the old policy in the direction of a serious improvement in political relations with the Soviet Union, the Soviet Government can only welcome such a change, and are, for their part, prepared to revise their policy in the sense of a serious improvement in respect of Germany.

But, the Russian note insisted, it must be "by serious and practical steps"—not in one big leap, as Ribbentrop proposed.

What steps?

The first step: conclusion of a trade and credit agreement.

The second step, "to be taken shortly thereafter": conclusion of a non-aggression pact.

Simultaneously with the second step, the Soviets demanded the "conclusion of a special protocol defining the interests of the contracting parties in this or that question of foreign policy." This was more than a hint that in regard to dividing up Eastern Europe at least, Moscow was receptive to the German view that a deal was possible.

As for the proposed visit of Ribbentrop, Molotov declared that the Soviet government was "highly gratified" with the idea, "since the dispatch of such an eminent politician and statesman emphasized how serious were the intentions of the German Government. This stood," he added, "in noteworthy contrast to England, which, in the person of Strang, had sent only an official of second-class rank to Moscow. However, the journey by the German Foreign Minister required thorough preparation. The Soviet Government did not like the publicity that such a journey would cause. They preferred to do practical work without much fuss."[15]

Molotov made no mention of Ribbentrop's urgent, specific proposal that he come to Moscow over the weekend, and Schulenburg, perhaps somewhat taken aback by the course of the interview, did not press the matter.

The next day, after the ambassador's report had been received, Ribbentrop did. Hitler, it is obvious, was now growing desperate. From his summer headquarters on the Obersalzberg there went out on the evening of August 18 a further "most urgent" telegram to Schulenburg signed by Ribbentrop. It arrived at the German Embassy in Moscow at 5:45 A.M. on the nineteenth and directed the ambassador to "arrange immediately another conversation with M. Molotov and do everything possible to see that it takes place without any delay." There was no time to lose. "I ask you," Ribbentrop wired, "to speak to M. Molotov as follows":

> . . . We, too, under normal circumstances, would naturally be ready to pursue a realignment of German–Russian relations through diplomatic channels, and to carry it out in the customary way. But the present unusual situation makes it necessary, in the opinion of the Fuehrer, to employ a different method which would lead to quick results.
>
> German–Polish relations are becoming more acute from day to day. We have to take into account that incidents might occur any day that would make the outbreak of open conflict unavoidable . . . The Fuehrer considers it necessary that we be not taken by surprise by the outbreak of a German–Polish conflict while we are striving for a clarification of German–Russian relations. He therefore considers a previous clarification necessary, if only to be able to take into account Russian interests in case of such a conflict, which would, of course, be difficult without such a clarification.

The ambassador was to say that the "first stage" in the consultations mentioned by Molotov, the conclusion of the trade agreement, had been concluded in Berlin this very day (August 18) and that it was now time to "attack" the second stage. To do this the German Foreign Minister proposed his "immediate departure for Moscow," to which he would come "with full powers from the Fuehrer, authorizing me to settle fully and conclusively the total complex of problems." In Moscow, Ribbentrop added, he would "be in a position . . . to take Russian wishes into account."

What wishes? The Germans now no longer beat around the bush.

> I should also be in a position [Ribbentrop continued] to sign a special protocol regulating the interests of both parties in questions of foreign policy of one kind or another; for instance, the settlement of spheres of interest in the Baltic area. Such a settlement will only be possible, however, in an oral discussion.

This time the ambassador must not take a Russian "No."

> Please emphasize [Ribbentrop concluded] that German foreign policy has today reached a historic turning point . . . Please press for a rapid realization of my journey and oppose appropriately any fresh Russian objections. In this connection you must keep in mind the decisive fact that an early outbreak of open German–Polish conflict is possible and that we, therefore, have the greatest interest in having my visit to Moscow take place immediately.[16]

August 19 was the decisive day. Orders for the German submarines and pocket battleships to sail for British waters were being held up until word came from Moscow. The warships would have to get off at once if they were to reach their appointed stations by Hitler's target date for the beginning of the war, September 1—only thirteen days away. The two great army groups designated for the onslaught on Poland would have to be deployed immediately.

The tension in Berlin and especially on the Obersalzberg, where Hitler and Ribbentrop waited nervously for Moscow's decision, was becoming almost unbearable. The Foreign Office dispatches and memoranda that day disclosed the jittery feelings in the Wilhelmstrasse. Dr. Schnurre reported that the discussions with the Russians on the trade agreement had ended the previous evening "with complete agreement" but that the Soviets were stalling on signing it. The signature, he said, was to have taken place at noon this day, August 19, but at noon the Russians had telephoned saying they had to await instructions from Moscow. "It is obvious," Schnurre reported, "that they have received instructions from Moscow to delay the conclusion of the treaty for political reasons."[17] From the Obersalzberg, Ribbentrop wired Schulenburg "most urgent" to be sure to report anything Molotov said or any sign of "Russian intentions" by telegram, but the only wire received from the ambassador during the day was the text of a denial by Tass, the Soviet news agency, in Moscow that the negotiations between the Russian and Anglo–French military delegations had become snarled over the Far East. However, the Tass *démenti* added that there were differences between the delegations on "entirely different matters." This was a signal to Hitler that there was still time—and hope.

And then at 7:10 P.M. on August 19 came the anxiously awaited telegram:

SECRET

MOST URGENT

The Soviet Government agree to the Reich Foreign Minister coming to Moscow one week after the announcement of the signature of the economic agreement. Molotov stated that if the conclusion of the economic agreement is made public tomorrow, the Reich Foreign Minister could arrive in Moscow on August 26 or 27.

Molotov handed me a draft of a nonaggression pact.

A detailed account of the two conversations I had with Molotov today, as well as the text of the Soviet draft, follows by telegram at once.

SCHULENBURG[18]

The first talk in the Kremlin, which began at 2 P.M. on the nineteenth and lasted an hour, did not, the ambassador reported, go very well. The Russians, it seemed, could not be stampeded into receiving Hitler's Foreign Minister. "Molotov persisted in his opinion," Schulenburg wired, "that for the present it was not possible even approximately to fix the time of the journey since thorough preparations would be required . . . To the reasons I repeatedly and very emphatically advanced for the need of

haste, Molotov rejoined that, so far, not even the first step—the concluding of the economic agreement—had been taken. First of all, the economic
agreement had to be signed and published, and achieve its effect abroad.
Then would come the turn of the nonaggression pact and protocol.

"Molotov remained apparently unaffected by my protests, so that the
first conversation closed with a declaration by Molotov that he had
imparted to me the views of the Soviet Government and had nothing to
add to them."

But he had something, shortly.

"Hardly half an hour after the conversation had ended," Schulenburg
reported, "Molotov sent me word asking me to call on him again at the
Kremlin at 4:30 P.M. He apologized for putting me to the trouble and
explained that he had reported to the Soviet Government."

Whereupon the Foreign Commissar handed the surprised but happy
ambassador a draft of the nonaggression pact and told him that Ribbentrop
could arrive in Moscow on August 26 or 27 if the trade treaty were signed
and made public tomorrow.

"Molotov did not give reasons," Schulenburg added in his telegram,
"for his sudden change of mind. I assume that Stalin intervened."[19]

The assumption was undoubtedly correct. According to Churchill, the
Soviet intention to sign a pact with Germany was announced to the
Politburo by Stalin on the evening of August 19.[20] A little earlier that
day—between 3 P.M. and 4:30 P.M.—it is clear from Schulenburg's dispatch, he had communicated his fateful decision to Molotov.

Exactly three years later, in August 1942, "in the early hours of the
morning," as Churchill later reported, the Soviet dictator gave to the
British Prime Minister, then on a mission to Moscow, some of the reasons
for his brazen move.[21]

We formed the impression [said Stalin] that the British and French
Governments were not resolved to go to war if Poland were attacked, but that
they hoped the diplomatic line-up of Britain, France and Russia would deter
Hitler. We were sure it would not. "How many divisions," Stalin had asked,
"will France send against Germany on mobilization?" The answer was:
"About a hundred." He then asked: "How many will England send?" The
answer was: "Two, and two more later." "Ah, two, and two more later,"
Stalin had repeated. "Do you know," he asked, "how many divisions we shall
have to put on the Russian front if we go to war with Germany?" There was
a pause. "More than three hundred."

In his dispatch reporting the outcome of his conversations with Molotov
on August 19, Schulenburg had added that his attempt to induce the
Foreign Commissar to accept an earlier date for Ribbentrop's journey to
Moscow "was, unfortunately, unsuccessful."

But for the Germans it had to be made successful. The whole timetable for the invasion of Poland, indeed the question of whether the attack could take place at all in the brief interval before the autumn rains, depended upon it. If Ribbentrop were not received in Moscow before August 26 or 27 and then if the Russians stalled a bit, as the Germans feared, the target date of September 1 could not be kept.

At this crucial stage, Adolf Hitler himself intervened with Stalin. Swallowing his pride, he personally begged the Soviet dictator, whom he had so often and for so long maligned, to receive his Foreign Minister in Moscow at once. His telegram to Stalin was rushed off to Moscow at 6:45 P.M. on Sunday, August 20, just twelve hours after the receipt of Schulenburg's dispatch. The Fuehrer instructed the ambassador to hand it to Molotov "at once."

M. STALIN, Moscow,

I sincerely welcome the signing of the new German–Soviet Commercial Agreement as the first step in the reshaping of German–Soviet relations.*

The conclusion of a nonaggression pact with the Soviet Union means to me the establishment of German policy for a long time. Germany thereby resumes a political course that was beneficial to both States during bygone centuries . . .

I accept the draft of the nonaggression pact that your Foreign Minister, M. Molotov, handed over, but consider it urgently necessary to clarify the questions connected with it as soon as possible.

The substance of the supplementary protocol desired by the Soviet Union can, I am convinced, be clarified in the shortest possible time if a responsible German statesman can come to Moscow himself to negotiate. Otherwise the Government of the Reich are not clear as to how the supplementary protocol could be cleared up and settled in a short time.

The tension between Germany and Poland has become intolerable . . . A crisis may arise any day. Germany is determined from now on to look after the interests of the Reich with all the means at her disposal.

In my opinion, it is desirable in view of the intentions of the two States to enter into a new relationship to each other, not to lose any time. I therefore again propose that you receive my Foreign Minister on Tuesday, August 22, but at the latest on Wednesday, August 23. The Reich Foreign Minister has the fullest powers to draw up and sign the nonaggression pact as well as the protocol. A longer stay by the Foreign Minister in Moscow than one to two days at most is impossible in view of the international situation. I should be glad to receive your early answer.

ADOLF HITLER[22]

During the next twenty-four hours, from the evening of Sunday, August 20, when Hitler's appeal to Stalin went out over the wires to Moscow, until

---

* It was signed in Berlin at 2 A.M. on Sunday, August 20.

the following evening, the Fuehrer was in a state bordering on collapse. He could not sleep. In the middle of the night he telephoned Goering to tell of his worries about Stalin's reaction to his message and to fret over the delays in Moscow. At 3 A.M. on the twenty-first, the Foreign Office received a "most urgent" wire from Schulenburg saying that Hitler's telegram, of which Weizsaecker had advised him earlier, had not yet arrived. "Official telegrams from Berlin to Moscow," the ambassador reminded the Foreign Office, "take four to five hours, inclusive of two hours' difference in time. To this must be added the time for deciphering."23 At 10:15 A.M. on Monday, August 21, the anxious Ribbentrop got off an urgent wire to Schulenburg: "Please do your utmost to ensure that the journey materializes. Date as in telegram."24 Shortly after noon, the ambassador advised Berlin: "I am to see Molotov at 3 P.M. today."25

Finally, at 9:35 P.M. on August 21, Stalin's reply came over the wires in Berlin.

To the Chancellor of the German Reich,
A. Hitler:

I thank you for the letter. I hope that the German–Soviet nonaggression pact will bring about a decided turn for the better in the political relations between our countries.

The peoples of our countries need peaceful relations with each other. The assent of the German Government to the conclusion of a nonaggression pact provides the foundation for eliminating the political tension and for the establishment of peace and collaboration between our countries.

The Soviet Government have instructed me to inform you that they agree to Herr von Ribbentrop's arriving in Moscow on August 23.

J. Stalin26

For sheer cynicism the Nazi dictator had met his match in the Soviet despot. The way was now open to them to get together to dot the *i*'s and cross the *t*'s on one of the crudest deals of this shabby epoch.

Stalin's reply was transmitted to the Fuehrer at the Berghof at 10:30 P.M. A few minutes later, this writer remembers—shortly after 11 P.M.— a musical program on the German radio was suddenly interrupted and a voice came on to announce, "The Reich government and the Soviet government have agreed to conclude a pact of nonaggression with each other. The Reich Minister for Foreign Affairs will arrive in Moscow on Wednesday, August 23, for the conclusion of the negotiations."

The next day, August 22, 1939, Hitler, having been assured by Stalin himself that Russia would be a friendly neutral, once more convoked his top military commanders to the Obersalzberg, lectured them on his own greatness and on the need for them to wage war brutally and without pity and apprised them that he probably would order the attack on Poland to begin four days hence, on Saturday, August 26—six days ahead of schedule. Stalin, the Fuehrer's mortal enemy, had made this possible.

THE MILITARY CONFERENCE OF AUGUST 22, 1939

The generals found Hitler in one of his most arrogant and uncompromising moods.* "I have called you together," he told them, "to give you a picture of the political situation in order that you may have some insight into the individual factors on which I have based my irrevocable decision to act and in order to strengthen your confidence. After that we shall discuss military details." First of all, he said, there were two personal considerations.

My own personality and that of Mussolini.

Essentially, all depends on me, on my existence, because of my political talents. Furthermore, the fact that probably no one will ever again have the confidence of the whole German people as I have. There will probably never again in the future be a man with more authority than I have. My existence is therefore a factor of great value. But I can be eliminated at any time by a criminal or a lunatic.

The second personal factor is the Duce. His existence is also decisive. If something happens to him, Italy's loyalty to the alliance will no longer be certain. The Italian Court is fundamentally opposed to the Duce.

Franco too was a help. He would assure Spain's "benevolent neutrality." As for "the other side," he assured his listeners, "there is no outstanding personality in England or France."

For what must have been a period of several hours, broken only by a late lunch, the demonic dictator rambled on, and there is no evidence from the records that a single general, admiral or Air Force commander dared

---

* No official minutes of Hitler's harangue have been found, but several records of it, two of them made by high-ranking officers from notes jotted down during the meeting, have come to light. One by Admiral Hermann Boehm, Chief of the High Seas Fleet, was submitted at Nuremberg in Admiral Raeder's defense and is published in the original German in *TMWC*, XLI, pp. 16–25. General Halder made voluminous notes in his unique Gabelsberger shorthand, and an English translation of them from his diary entry of August 22 is published in *DGFP*, VII, pp. 557–59. The chief document of the session used by the prosecution as evidence in the Nuremberg trial was an unsigned memorandum in two parts from the OKW files which were captured by American troops at Saalfelden in the Austrian Tyrol. It is printed in English translation in *NCA*, III, pp. 581–86 (Nuremberg Document 798-PS), 665–66 (N.D. 1014-PS), and also in *DGFP*, VII, pp. 200–6. The original German text of the two-part memorandum is, of course, in the *TMWC* volumes. It makes Hitler's language somewhat more lively than do Admiral Boehm and General Halder. But all three versions are similar in content and there can be no doubt of their authenticity. At Nuremberg there was some doubt about a fourth account of Hitler's speech, listed as N.D. C-3 (*NCA*, VII, pp. 752–54), and though it was referred to in the proceedings the prosecution did not submit it in evidence. While it undoubtedly rings true, it may have been embellished a little by persons who were not present at the meeting at the Berghof. In piecing together Hitler's remarks I have used the records of Boehm and Halder and the unsigned memorandum submitted at Nuremberg as evidence.

to interrupt him to question his judgment or even to challenge his lies. He had made his decision in the spring, he said, that a conflict with Poland was inevitable, but he had thought that first he would turn against the West. In that case, however, it became "clear" to him that Poland would attack Germany. Therefore she must be liquidated now.

The time to fight a war, anyway, had come.

For us it is easy to make the decision. We have nothing to lose; we can only gain. Our economic situation is such that we cannot hold out more than a few years. Goering can confirm this. We have no other choice, we must act . . .

Besides the personal factor, the political situation is favorable to us; in the Mediterranean, rivalry among Italy, France and England; in the Orient, tension . . .

England is in great danger. France's position has also deteriorated. Decline in birth rate . . . Yugoslavia carries the germ of collapse . . . Rumania is weaker than before . . . Since Kemal's death, Turkey has been ruled by small minds, unsteady, weak men.

All these fortunate circumstances will not prevail in two to three years. No one knows how long I shall live. Therefore a showdown, which it would not be safe to put off for four to five years, had better take place now.

Such was the Nazi Leader's fervid reasoning.

He thought it "highly probable" that the West would not fight, but the risk nevertheless had to be accepted. Had he not taken risks—in occupying the Rhineland when the generals wanted to pull back, in taking Austria, the Sudetenland and the rest of Czechoslovakia? "Hannibal at Cannae, Frederick the Great at Leuthen, and Hindenburg and Ludendorff at Tannenberg," he said, "took chances. So now we also must take risks which can only be mastered by iron determination." There must be no weakening.

It has done much damage that many reluctant Germans in high places spoke and wrote to Englishmen after the solution of the Czech question. The Fuehrer carried his point when you lost your nerve and capitulated too soon.

Halder, Witzleben and Thomas and perhaps other generals who had been in on the Munich conspiracy must have winced at this. Hitler obviously knew more than they had realized.

At any rate, it was now time for them all to show their fighting qualities. Hitler had created Greater Germany, he reminded them, "by political bluff." It had now become necessary to "test the military machine. The Army must experience actual battle before the big final showdown in the West." Poland offered such an opportunity.

Coming back to England and France:

The West has only two possibilities to fight against us:

1. Blockade: It will not be effective because of our self-sufficiency and our sources of aid in the East.

2. Attack from the West from the Maginot Line. I consider this impossible. Another possibility is the violation of Dutch, Belgium and Swiss neutrality. England and France will not violate the neutrality of these countries. Actually they cannot help Poland.

Would it be a long war?

No one is counting on a long war. If Herr von Brauchitsch had told me that I would need four years to conquer Poland I would have replied, It cannot be done. It is nonsense to say that England wants to wage a long war.

Having disposed, to his own satisfaction, at least, of Poland, Britain and France, Hitler pulled out his ace card. He turned to Russia.

The enemy had another hope, that Russia would become our enemy after the conquest of Poland. The enemy did not count on my great power of resolution. Our enemies are little worms. I saw them at Munich.

I was convinced that Stalin would never accept the English offer. Only a blind optimist could believe that Stalin would be so crazy as not to see through England's intentions. Russia has no interest in maintaining Poland . . . Litvinov's dismissal was decisive. It came to me like a cannon shot as a sign of a change in Moscow toward the Western Powers.

I brought about the change toward Russia gradually. In connection with the commercial treaty we got into political conversations. Finally a proposition came from the Russians for a nonaggression treaty. Four days ago I took a special step which brought it about that Russia announced yesterday that she is ready to sign. The personal contact with Stalin is established. The day after tomorrow Ribbentrop will conclude the treaty. Now Poland is in the position in which I wanted her . . . A beginning has been made for the destruction of England's hegemony. The way is open for the soldier, now that I have made the political preparations.

The way would be open for the soldiers, that is, if Chamberlain didn't pull another Munich. "I am only afraid," Hitler told his warriors, "that some *Schweinehund** will make a proposal for mediation."

At this point the meeting broke up for lunch, but not until Goering had expressed thanks to the Fuehrer for pointing the way and had assured him that the armed services would do their duty.†

---

* "Dirty dog."

† According to the account in Nuremberg Document C-3 (see footnote above, p. 529), Goering jumped up on the table and gave "bloodthirsty thanks and bloody promises. He danced around like a savage. The few doubtful ones remained silent." This description greatly nettled Goering during an interrogation at Nuremberg on August 28 and 29, 1945. "I dispute the fact that I stood on the

The afternoon lecture was devoted by Hitler mainly to bucking up his military chiefs and trying to steel them for the task ahead. The rough jottings of all three records of the talk indicate its nature.

The most iron determination on our part. No shrinking back from anything. Everyone must hold the view that we have been determined to fight the Western powers right from the start. A life-and-death struggle . . . A long period of peace would not do us any good . . . A manly bearing . . . We have the better men . . . On the opposite side they are weaker . . . In 1918 the nation collapsed because the spiritual prerequisites were insufficient. Frederick the Great endured only because of his fortitude.

The destruction of Poland has priority. The aim is to eliminate active forces, not to reach a definite line. Even if war breaks out in the West, the destruction of Poland remains the primary objective. A quick decision, in view of the season.

I shall give a propagandist reason for starting the war—never mind whether it is plausible or not. The victor will not be asked afterward whether he told the truth or not. In starting and waging a war it is not right that matters, but victory.

Close your hearts to pity! Act brutally! Eighty million people must obtain what is their right . . . The stronger man is right . . . Be harsh and remorseless! Be steeled against all signs of compassion! . . . Whoever has pondered over this world order knows that its meaning lies in the success of the best by means of force . . .

Having thundered such Nietzschean exhortations, the Fuehrer, who had worked himself up to a fine fit of Teutonic fury, calmed down and delivered a few directives for the campaign ahead. Speed was essential. He had "unshakable faith" in the German soldier. If any crises developed they would be due solely to the commanders' losing their nerve. The first aim was to drive wedges from the southeast to the Vistula, and from the north to the Narew and the Vistula. Military operations, he insisted, must not be influenced by what he might do with Poland after her defeat. As to that he was vague. The new German frontier, he said, would be based on "sound principles." Possibly he would set up a small Polish buffer state between Germany and Russia.

The order for the start of hostilities, Hitler concluded, would be given later, probably for Saturday morning, August 26.

The next day, the twenty-third, after a meeting of the OKW section chiefs, General Halder noted in his diary: "Y Day definitely set for the 26th (Saturday)."

---

table," Goering said. "I want you to know that the speech was made in the great hall of Hitler's private house. I did not have the habit of jumping on tables in private homes. That would have been an attitude completely inconsistent with that of a German officer."

"Well, the fact is," Colonel John H. Amen, the American interrogator, said at this point, "that you led the applause after the speech, didn't you?"

"Yes, but not on the table," Goering rejoined.[27]

ALLIED STALEMATE IN MOSCOW

By the middle of August the military conversations in Moscow between the Western democracies and the Soviet Union had come to a virtual standstill—and for this the intransigence of the Poles was largely to blame. The Anglo–French military missions, it will be remembered, after taking a slow boat to Leningrad, had arrived in Moscow on August 11, exactly one week after the frustrated Mr. Strang had left the Russian capital, obviously relieved to be able to turn over to the generals and admirals the difficult and unpleasant job of trying to negotiate with the Russians.*

What now had to be worked out hurriedly was a military convention which would spell out in detail just how and where, and with what, Nazi armed force could be met. But as the confidential British minutes of the day-to-day military conversations and the reports of the British negotiators reveal[29] the Anglo–French military team had been sent to Moscow to discuss not details but rather "general principles." The Russians, however, insisted on getting down at once to hard, specific and—in the Allied view—awkward facts, and Voroshilov's response to the Allied declaration of principles made at the first meeting by General Doumenc was that they were "too abstract and immaterial and do not oblige anyone to do anything . . . We are not gathered here," he declared coolly, "to make abstract declarations, but to work out a complete military convention."

The Soviet Marshal posed some very definite questions: Was there any treaty which defined what action Poland would take? How many British troops could reinforce the French Army on the outbreak of the war? What would Belgium do? The answers he got were not very reassuring. Doumenc said he had no knowledge of Polish plans. General Heywood answered that the British envisaged "a first contingent of sixteen divisions, ready for service in the early stages of a war, followed later by a second contingent of sixteen divisions." Pressed by Voroshilov to reveal how many British troops there would be immediately on the outbreak of war, Heywood replied, "At the moment there are five regular divisions and one mechanized division in England." These paltry figures came as an unpleasant surprise to the Russians, who were prepared, they said, to deploy 120 infantry divisions against an aggressor in the west at the very outbreak of hostilities.

As for Belgium, General Doumenc answered the Russian question by saying that "French troops cannot enter unless and until they are asked to, but France is ready to answer any call."

This reply led to the crucial question before the military negotiators in Moscow and one which the British and French had been anxious to avoid. During the very first meeting and again at a critical session on August 14, Marshal Voroshilov insisted that the essential question was whether Poland was willing to permit Soviet troops to enter her territory to meet

---

* "A humiliating experience," Strang had called it in a dispatch to the Foreign Office on July 20.[28]

the Germans. If not, how could the Allies prevent the German Army from quickly overrunning Poland? Specifically—on the fourteenth—he asked, "Do the British and French general staffs think that the Red Army can move across Poland, and in particular through the Vilna gap and across Galicia in order to make contact with the enemy?"

This was the core of the matter. As Seeds wired London, the Russians had now

raised the fundamental problem, on which the military talks will succeed or fail and which has indeed been at the bottom of all our difficulties since the very beginning of the political conversations, namely, how to reach any useful agreement with the Soviet Union as long as this country's neighbors maintain a sort of boycott which is only to be broken . . . when it is too late.

If the question came up—and how could it help coming up?—Admiral Drax had been instructed by the British government on how to handle it. The instructions, revealed in the confidential British papers, seem unbelievably naïve when read today. The "line of argument" he was to take in view of the refusal of Poland and Rumania "even to consider plans for possible co-operation" was:

An invasion of Poland and Rumania would greatly alter their outlook. Moreover, it would be greatly to Russia's disadvantage that Germany should occupy a position right up to the Russian frontier . . . It is in Russia's own interest therefore that she should have plans ready to help both Poland and Rumania should these countries be invaded.

If the Russians propose that the British and French governments should communicate to the Polish, Roumanian or Baltic States proposals involving co-operation with the Soviet Government or General Staff, the Delegation should not commit themselves but refer home.

And this is what they did.

At the August 14 session Voroshilov demanded "straightforward answers" to his questions. "Without an exact and unequivocal answer," he said, "continuance of the military conversations would be useless . . . The Soviet Military Mission," he added, "cannot recommend to its Government to take part in an enterprise so obviously doomed to failure."

From Paris General Gamelin counseled General Doumenc to try to steer the Russians off the subject. But they were not to be put off.[30]

The meeting of August 14, as General Doumenc later reported, was dramatic. The British and French delegates were cornered and they knew it. They tried to evade the issue as best they could. Drax and Doumenc asserted they were sure the Poles and Rumanians would ask for Russian aid as soon as they were attacked. Doumenc was confident they would "implore the Marshal to support them." Drax thought it was "inconceivable" that they should not ask for Soviet help. He added—not very diplomatically, it would seem—that "if they did not ask for help when necessary and allow themselves to be overrun, it may be expected that they would become German provinces." This was the last thing the Russians wanted, for it meant the presence of the Nazi armies on the Soviet border, and Voroshilov made a special point of the Admiral's unfortunate remark.

Finally, the uncomfortable Anglo–French representatives contended that Voroshilov had raised political questions which they were not competent to handle. Drax declared that since Poland was a sovereign state, its government would first have to sanction the entry of Russian troops. But since this was a political matter, it would have to be settled by the governments. He suggested that the Soviet government put its questions to the Polish government. The Russian delegation agreed that this was a political matter. But it insisted that the British and French governments must put the question to the Poles and pressure them to come to reason.

Were the Russians, in view of their dealings with the Germans at this moment, negotiating in good faith with the Franco–British military representatives? Or did they, as the British and French foreign offices, not to mention Admiral Drax, later concluded, insist on the right to deploy their troops through Poland merely to stall the talks until they saw whether they could make a deal with Hitler?*

In the beginning, the British and French confidential sources reveal, the Western Allies did think that the Soviet military delegation was negotiating in good faith—in fact, that it took its job much too seriously. On August 13, after two days of staff talks, Ambassador Seeds wired London that the Russian military chiefs seemed really "to be out for business." As a result, Admiral Drax's instructions to "go very slowly" were changed and on August 15 he was told by the British government to support Doumenc in bringing the military talks to a conclusion "as soon as possible." His restrictions on confiding confidential military information to the Russians were partially lifted.

Unlike the British Admiral's original instructions to stall, those given General Doumenc by Premier Daladier personally had been to try to conclude a military convention with Russia at the earliest possible moment. Despite British fears of leaks to the Germans, Doumenc on the second day of the meetings had confided to the Russians such "highly secret figures," as he termed them, on the strength of the French Army that the

---

* The timing is important. Molotov did not receive the Nazi proposal that Ribbentrop come to Moscow until the evening of August 15. (See above, p. 520.) And though he did not accept it definitely he did hint that Russia would be interested in a nonaggression pact with Germany, which of course would have made negotiation of a military alliance with France and Britain superfluous. The best conclusion this writer can come to is that, as of August 14, when Voroshilov demanded an "unequivocal answer" to the question of allowing Soviet troops to meet the Germans in Poland, the Kremlin still had an open mind as to which side to join. Unfortunately the Russian documents, which could clear up this crucial question, have not been published. At any rate, Stalin does not seem to have made his final decision until the afternoon of August 19. (See above, p. 526.)

Soviet members promised "to forget" them as soon as the meeting was concluded.

As late as August 17, after he and Drax had waited vainly for three days for instructions from their governments as to how to reply to the Polish question, General Doumenc telegraphed Paris: "The U.S.S.R. wants a military pact . . . She does not want us to give her a piece of paper without substantial undertakings. Marshal Voroshilov has stated that all problems . . . would be tackled without difficulty as soon as what he called the crucial question was settled." Doumenc strongly urged Paris to get Warsaw to agree to accepting Russian help.

Contrary to a widespread belief at the time, not only in Moscow but in the Western capitals, that the British and French governments did nothing to induce the Poles to agree to Soviet troops meeting the Germans on Polish soil, it is clear from documents recently released that London and Paris went quite far—but not quite far enough. It is also clear that the Poles reacted with unbelievable stupidity.[31]

On August 18, after the first Anglo–French attempt was made in Warsaw to open the eyes of the Poles, Foreign Minister Beck told the French ambassador, Léon Noël, that the Russians were "of no military value," and General Stachiewicz, Chief of the Polish General Staff, backed him up by declaring that he saw "no benefit to be gained by Red Army troops operating in Poland."

The next day both the British and French ambassadors saw Beck again and urged him to agree to the Russian proposal. The Polish Foreign Minister stalled, but promised to give them a formal reply the next day. The Anglo–French *démarche* in Warsaw came as the result of a conversation earlier on the nineteenth in Paris between Bonnet, the French Foreign Minister, and the British chargé d'affaires. Somewhat to the Briton's surprise, this archappeaser of Hitler was now quite aroused at the prospect of losing Russia as an ally because of Polish stubbornness.

It would be disastrous [Bonnet told him] if, in consequence of a Polish refusal, the Russian negotiations were to break down . . . It was an untenable position for the Poles to take up in refusing the only immediate efficacious help that could reach them in the event of a German attack. It would put the British and French Governments in an almost impossible position if we had to ask our respective countries to go to war in defense of Poland, which had refused this help.

If this were so—and there is no doubt that it was—why then did not the British and French governments at this crucial moment put the ultimate pressure on Warsaw and simply say that unless the Polish government agreed to accept Russian help Britain and France could see no use of themselves going to war to aid Poland? The formal Anglo–Polish mutual-security treaty had not yet been signed. Could Warsaw's acceptance of Russian military backing not be made a condition of concluding that pact?*

In his talk with the British chargé in Paris on August 19, Bonnet suggested this, but the government in London frowned upon such a "maneuver," as Downing Street called it. To such an extreme Chamberlain and Halifax would not go.

On the morning of August 20 the Polish Chief of Staff informed the British military attaché in Warsaw that "in no case would the admission of Soviet troops into Poland be agreed to." And that evening Beck formally rejected the Anglo–French request. The same evening Halifax, through his ambassador in Warsaw, urged the Polish Foreign Minister to reconsider, emphasizing in strong terms that the Polish stand was "wrecking" the military talks in Moscow. But Beck was obdurate. "I do not admit," he told the French ambassador, "that there can be any kind of discussion whatsoever concerning the use of part of our territory by foreign troops. We have not got a military agreement with the U.S.S.R. We do not want one."

Desperate at such a display of blind stubbornness on the part of the Polish government, Premier Daladier, according to an account he gave to the French Constituent Assembly on July 18, 1946, took matters in his own hands. After once more appealing to the Poles to be realistic, he telegraphed General Doumenc on the morning of August 21 authorizing him to sign a military convention with Russia on the best terms he could get, with the provision, however, that it must be approved by the French government. The French ambassador, Paul-Émile Naggiar, was at the same time instructed by Bonnet, according to the latter's subsequent account, to tell Molotov that France agreed "in principle" to the passage of Soviet troops through Poland if the Germans attacked.

But this was only an idle gesture, as long as the Poles had not agreed—and, as we know now, a futile gesture in view of the state of Russo–German dealings. Doumenc did not receive Daladier's telegram until late in the evening of August 21. When he brought it to the attention of Voroshilov on the evening of the next day—the eve of Ribbentrop's departure for Moscow—the Soviet Marshal was highly skeptical. He demanded to see the French General's authorization for saying—as Doumenc had—that the French government had empowered him to sign a military pact permitting the passage of Russian troops through Poland. Doumenc, obviously, declined. Voroshilov next wanted to know what

---

* Lloyd George, in a speech in the Commons on April 3, four days after Chamberlain's unilateral guarantee to Poland had been announced, had urged the British government to make such a condition. "If we are going in without the help of Russia we are walking into a trap. It is the only country whose armies can get there [to Poland]. . . . I cannot understand why, before committing ourselves to this tremendous enterprise, we did not secure beforehand the adhesion of Russia . . . If Russia has not been brought into this matter because of certain feelings the Poles have that they do not want the Russians there, it is for us to declare the conditions, and unless the Poles are prepared to accept the only conditions with which we can successfully help them, the responsibility must be theirs."

the British response was and whether the consent of Poland had been obtained. These were embarrassing questions and Doumenc merely answered that he had no information.

But neither the questions nor the answers had by this time any reality. They were being put too late. Ribbentrop was already on his way to Moscow. The trip had been announced publicly the night before, and also its purpose: to conclude a nonaggression pact between Nazi Germany and the Soviet Union.

Voroshilov, who seems to have developed a genuine liking for the French General, tried gently to let him know that their contacts were about to end.

I fear one thing [Voroshilov said]. The French and English sides have allowed the political and military discussions to drag on too long. That is why we must not exclude the possibility, during this time, of certain political events.*

RIBBENTROP IN MOSCOW: AUGUST 23, 1939

Those "certain political events" now took place.

Armed with full powers in writing from Hitler to conclude a nonaggression treaty "and other agreements" with the Soviet Union, which would become effective as soon as they were signed, Ribbentrop set off by plane for Moscow on August 22. The large German party spent the night at Koenigsberg in East Prussia, where the Nazi Foreign Minister, according to Dr. Schmidt, worked throughout the night, constantly telephoning to Berlin and Berchtesgaden and making copious notes for his talks with Stalin and Molotov.

The two large Condor transport planes carrying the German delegation

---

* At a session of the military delegates the morning before, on August 21, Voroshilov had demanded the indefinite adjournment of the talks on the excuse that he and his colleagues would be busy with the autumn maneuvers. To the Anglo–French protests at such a delay the Marshal had answered, "The intentions of the Soviet Delegation were, and still are, to agree on the organization of military co-operation of the armed forces of the three parties . . . The U.S.S.R., not having a common frontier with Germany, can give help to France, Britain, Poland and Rumania, only on condition that her troops are given rights of passage across Polish and Rumanian territory . . . The Soviet forces cannot co-operate with the armed forces of Britain and France if they are not allowed onto Polish and Rumanian territory . . . The Soviet Military Delegation cannot picture to itself how the governments and general staffs of Britain and France, in sending their missions to the U.S.S.R. . . . could not have given them some directives on such an elementary matter . . . This can only show that there are reasons to doubt their desire to come to serious and effective co-operation with the U.S.S.R."

The logic of the Marshal's military argument was sound and the failure of the French and especially the British governments to answer it would prove disastrous. But to have repeated it—with all the rest of the statement—on this late date, August 21, when Voroshilov could not have been ignorant of Stalin's decision of August 19, was deceitful.

arrived in Moscow at noon on August 23, and after a hasty meal at the embassy Ribbentrop hurried off to the Kremlin to confront the Soviet dictator and his Foreign Commissar. This first meeting lasted three hours and, as Ribbentrop advised Hitler by "most urgent" wire, it went well for the Germans.[32] Judging by the Foreign Minister's dispatch, there was no trouble at all in reaching agreement on the terms of a nonaggression pact which would keep the Soviet Union out of Hitler's war. In fact the only difficulty, he reported, was a distinctly minor one concerning the division of spoils. The Russians, he said, were demanding that Germany recognize the small ports of Libau and Windau in Latvia "as being in their sphere of interest." Since all of Latvia was to be placed on the Soviet side of the line dividing the interests of the two powers, this demand presented no problem and Hitler quickly agreed. Ribbentrop also advised the Fuehrer after the first conference that "the signing of a secret protocol on the delimitation of mutual spheres of interest in the whole Eastern area is contemplated."

The whole works—the nonaggression treaty and the secret protocol—were signed at a second meeting at the Kremlin later that evening. So easily had the Germans and Russians come to agreement that this convivial session, which lasted into the small hours of the following morning, was taken up mostly not by any hard bargaining but with a warm and friendly discussion of the state of the world, country by country, and with the inevitable, effusive toasts customary at gala gatherings in the Kremlin. A secret German memorandum by a member of the German delegation who was present has recorded the incredible scene.[33]

To Stalin's questions about the ambitions of Germany's partners, Italy and Japan, Ribbentrop gave breezy, reassuring answers. As to England the Soviet dictator and the Nazi Foreign Minister, who was now on his best behavior, found themselves at once in accord. The British military mission in Moscow, Stalin confided to his guest, "had never told the Soviet government what it really wanted." Ribbentrop responded by emphasizing that Britain had always tried to disrupt good relations between Germany and the Soviet Union. "England is weak," he boasted, "and wants to let others fight for her presumptuous claim to world dominion."

"Stalin eagerly concurred," says the German memorandum, and he remarked: "If England dominated the world, that was due to the stupidity of the other countries that always let themselves be bluffed."

By this time the Soviet ruler and Hitler's Foreign Minister were getting along so splendidly that mention of the Anti-Comintern Pact no longer embarrassed them. Ribbentrop explained again that the pact had been directed not against Russia but against the Western democracies. Stalin interposed to remark that "the Anti-Comintern had in fact frightened principally the City of London [i.e., the British financiers] and the English shopkeepers."

At this juncture, the German memorandum reveals, Ribbentrop felt himself in such good humor at Stalin's accommodating manner that he even tried to crack a joke or two—a remarkable feat for so humorless a man.

The Reich Foreign Minister [the memorandum continues] remarked jokingly that M. Stalin was surely less frightened by the Anti-Comintern Pact than the City of London and the English shopkeepers. What the German people thought of this matter was evident from a joke, which had originated with the Berliners, well known for their wit and humor, that Stalin will yet join the Anti-Comintern Pact himself.

Finally the Nazi Foreign Minister dwelt on how warmly the German people welcomed an understanding with Russia. "M. Stalin replied," says the German record, "that he really believed this. The Germans desired peace."
Such hokum grew worse as the time for toasts arrived.

M. Stalin spontaneously proposed a toast to the Fuehrer:
"I know how much the German nation loves its Fuehrer. I should therefore like to drink to his health."
M. Molotov drank to the health of the Reich Foreign Minister . . . MM. Molotov and Stalin drank repeatedly to the Nonaggression Pact, the new era of German–Russian relations, and to the German nation.
The Reich Foreign Minister in turn proposed a toast to M. Stalin, toasts to the Soviet Government, and to a favorable development of relations between Germany and the Soviet Union.

And yet despite such warm exchanges between those who until recently had been such mortal enemies, Stalin appears to have had mental reservations about the Nazis' keeping the pact. As Ribbentrop was leaving, he took him aside and said, "The Soviet Government take the new pact very seriously. He could guarantee on his word of honor that the Soviet Union would not betray its partner."
What had the new partners signed?
The published treaty carried an undertaking that neither power would attack the other. Should one of them become "the object of belligerent action" by a third power, the other party would "in no manner lend its support to this Third Power." Nor would either Germany or Russia "join any grouping of Powers whatsoever which is aimed directly or indirectly at the other Party."*

---

* The wording of the essential articles is almost identical to that of a Soviet draft which Molotov handed Schulenburg on August 19 and which Hitler, in his telegram to Stalin, said he accepted. The Russian draft had specified that the nonaggression treaty would be valid only if a "special protocol" were signed simultaneously and made an integral part of the pact.[34]
According to Friedrich Gaus, who participated at the evening meeting, a high-falutin preamble which Ribbentrop wanted to insert stressing the formation of

Thus Hitler got what he specifically wanted: an immediate agreement by the Soviet Union not to join Britain and France if they honored their treaty obligations to come to the aid of Poland in case she were attacked.*

The price he paid was set down in the "Secret Additional Protocol" to the treaty:

On the occasion of the signature of the Nonaggression Treaty between Germany and the Soviet Union the undersigned plenipotentiaries discussed in strictly confidential conversations the question of the delimitation of their respective spheres of interest in Eastern Europe.

1. In the event of a territorial and political transformation in the territories belonging to the Baltic States (Finland, Estonia, Latvia, Lithuania), the northern frontier of Lithuania shall represent the frontier of the spheres of interest both of Germany and the U.S.S.R.

2. In the event of a territorial and political transformation of the territories belonging to the Polish State, the spheres of interest of both Germany and the U.S.S.R. shall be bounded approximately by the line of the rivers Narew, Vistula and San.

The question whether the interests of both Parties make the maintenance of an independent Polish State appear desirable and how the frontiers of this State should be drawn can be definitely determined only in the course of further political developments.

In any case both Governments will resolve this question by means of a friendly understanding.

Once again Germany and Russia, as in the days of the German kings and Russian emperors, had agreed to partition Poland. And Hitler had given Stalin a free hand in the eastern Baltic.

Finally, in Southeastern Europe, the Russians emphasized their interest in Bessarabia, which the Soviet Union had lost to Rumania in 1919, and the Germans declared their disinterest in this territory—a concession Ribbentrop later was to regret.

"This protocol," the document concluded, "will be treated by both parties as strictly secret."[36]

As a matter of fact, its contents became known only after the war with the capture of the secret German archives.

On the following day, August 24, while the jubilant Ribbentrop was winging his way back to Berlin, the Allied military missions in Moscow requested to see Voroshilov. Admiral Drax had actually sent an urgent

---

friendly Soviet–German relations was thrown out at the insistence of Stalin. The Soviet dictator complained that "the Soviet government could not suddenly present to the public assurances of friendship after they had been covered with pails of manure by the Nazi government for six years."[35]

* Article VII provided for the treaty to enter into force immediately upon signature. Formal ratification in two such totalitarian states was, to be sure, a mere formality. But it would take a few days. Hitler had insisted on this provision.

letter to the Marshal requesting his views on the continuation of their talks.

Voroshilov gave them to the British and French military staffs at 1 P.M. the next day, August 25. "In view of the changed political situation," he said, "no useful purpose can be served in continuing the conversations."

Two years later, when German troops were pouring into Russia in violation of the pact, Stalin would still justify his odious deal with Hitler, made behind the backs of the Anglo–French military delegations which had come to negotiate in Moscow. "We secured peace for our country for one and a half years," he boasted in a broadcast to the Russian people on July 3, 1941, "as well as an opportunity of preparing our forces for defense if fascist Germany risked attacking our country in defiance of the pact. This was a definite gain for our country and a loss for fascist Germany."

But was it? The point has been debated ever since. That the sordid, secret deal gave Stalin the same breathing space—*peredyshka*—which Czar Alexander I had secured from Napoleon at Tilsit in 1807 and Lenin from the Germans at Brest Litovsk in 1917 was obvious. Within a short time it also gave the Soviet Union an advanced defensive position against Germany beyond the existing Russian frontiers, including bases in the Baltic States and Finland—at the expense of the Poles, Latvians, Estonians and Finns. And most important of all, as the official Soviet *History of Diplomacy* later emphasized, it assured the Kremlin that if Russia were later attacked by Germany the Western Powers would already be irrevocably committed against the Third Reich and the Soviet Union would not stand alone against the German might as Stalin had feared throughout the summer of 1939.

All this undoubtedly is true. But there is another side to the argument. By the time Hitler got around to attacking Russia, the armies of Poland and France and the British Expeditionary Force on the Continent had been destroyed and Germany had the resources of all of Europe to draw upon and no Western front to tie her hands. All through 1941, 1942 and 1943 Stalin was to complain bitterly that there was no second front in Europe against Germany and that Russia was forced to bear the brunt of containing almost the entire German Army. In 1939–40, there was a Western front to draw off the German forces. And Poland could not have been overrun in a fortnight if the Russians had backed her instead of stabbing her in the back. Moreover, there might not have been any war at all if Hitler had known he must take on Russia as well as Poland, England and France. Even the politically timid German generals, if one can judge from their later testimony at Nuremberg, might have put their foot down against embarking on war against such a formidable coalition. Toward the end of May, according to the French ambassador in Berlin, both Keitel and Brauchitsch had warned Hitler that Germany had little chance of winning a war in which Russia participated on the enemy side.

No statesmen, not even dictators, can foretell the course of events over the long run. It is arguable, as Churchill has argued, that cold-blooded as Stalin's move was in making a deal with Hitler, it was also "at the moment realistic in a high degree."[37] Stalin's first and primary consideration, as was that of any other head of government, was his nation's security. He was convinced in the summer of 1939, as he later told Churchill, that Hitler was going to war. He was determined that Russia should not be maneuvered into the disastrous position of having to face the German Army alone. If a foolproof alliance with the West proved impossible, then why not turn to Hitler, who suddenly was knocking at his door?

By the end of July 1939, Stalin had become convinced, it is obvious, not only that France and Britain did not want a binding alliance but that the objective of the Chamberlain government in Britain was to induce Hitler to make his wars in Eastern Europe. He seems to have been intensely skeptical that Britain would honor its guarantee to Poland any more than France had kept its obligations to Czechoslovakia. And everything that had happened in the West for the past two years tended to increase his suspicions: the rejection by Chamberlain of Soviet proposals, after the Anschluss and after the Nazi occupation of Czechoslovakia, for conferences to draw up plans to halt further Nazi aggression; Chamberlain's appeasement of Hitler at Munich, from which Russia had been excluded; the delays and hesitations of Chamberlain in negotiating a defensive alliance against Germany as the fateful summer days of 1939 ticked by.

One thing was certain—to almost everyone but Chamberlain. The bankruptcy of Anglo–French diplomacy, which had faltered and tottered whenever Hitler made a move, was now complete.* Step by step, the two Western democracies had retreated: when Hitler defied them by declaring conscription in 1935, when he occupied the Rhineland in 1936, when he took Austria in 1938 and in the same year demanded and got the Sudetenland; and they had sat by weakly when he occupied the rest of Czechoslovakia in March 1939. With the Soviet Union on their side, they still might have dissuaded the German dictator from launching war or, if that failed, have fairly quickly defeated him in an armed conflict. But they had allowed this last opportunity to slip out of their hands.† Now, at the worst

---

* And of Polish diplomacy too. Ambassador Noël reported Foreign Minister Beck's reaction to the signing of the Nazi–Soviet Pact in a dispatch to Paris: "Beck is quite unperturbed and does not seem in the slightest worried. He believes that, in substance, very little has changed."

† Despite many warnings, as we have seen, that Hitler was courting the Kremlin. On June 1, M. Coulondre, the French ambassador in Berlin, had informed Bonnet, the French Foreign Minister, that Russia was looming larger and larger in Hitler's thoughts. "Hitler will risk war," Coulondre wrote, "if he does not have to fight Russia. On the other hand, if he knows he has to fight her too he will draw back rather than expose his country, his party and himself to ruin." The ambassador urged the prompt conclusion of the Anglo–French negotiations in Moscow and advised Paris that the British ambassador in Berlin had made a similar appeal to his government in London. (*French Yellow Book*, Fr. ed., pp. 180–81.)

On August 15, both Coulondre and Henderson saw Weizsaecker at the Foreign possible time in the worst possible circumstances, they were committed to come to the aid of Poland when she was attacked.

The recriminations in London and Paris against the double-dealing of Stalin were loud and bitter. The Soviet despot for years had cried out at the "fascist beasts" and called for all peace-loving states to band together to halt Nazi aggression. Now he had made himself an accessory to it. The Kremlin could argue, as it did, that the Soviet Union had only done what Britain and France had done the year before at Munich: bought peace and the time to rearm against Germany at the expense of a small state. If Chamberlain was right and honorable in appeasing Hitler in September 1938 by sacrificing Czechoslovakia, was Stalin wrong and dishonorable in appeasing the Fuehrer a year later at the expense of Poland, which had shunned Soviet help anyway?

Stalin's cynical and secret deal with Hitler to divide up Poland and to obtain a free hand to gobble up Latvia, Estonia, Finland and Bessarabia was not known outside Berlin and Moscow, but it would soon become evident from Soviet acts, and it would shock most of the world even at this late date. The Russians might say, as they did, that they were only repossessing territories which had been taken away from them at the end of the First World War. But the peoples of these lands were not Russian and had shown no desire to return to Russia. Only force, which the Soviets had eschewed in the heyday of Litvinov, could make them return.

Since joining the League of Nations the Soviet Union had built up a certain moral force as the champion of peace and the leading opponent of fascist aggression. Now that moral capital had been utterly dissipated.

Above all, by assenting to a shoddy deal with Nazi Germany, Stalin had given the signal for the commencement of a war that almost certainly would develop into a world conflict. This he certainly knew.* As things turned out, it was the greatest blunder of his life.

Office. The British ambassador informed London that the State Secretary was confident that the Soviet Union "would in the end join in sharing the Polish spoils." (*British Blue Book,* p. 91.) And Coulondre, after his talk with Weizsaecker, wired Paris: "It is necessary at all costs to come to some solution of the Russian talks as soon as possible." (*French Yellow Book,* p. 282.)

Throughout June and July, Laurence Steinhardt, the American ambassador in Moscow, had also sent warnings of an impending Soviet–Nazi deal, which President Roosevelt passed on to the British, French and Polish embassies. As early as July 5, when Soviet Ambassador Constantine Oumansky left for a leave in Russia, he carried with him a message from Roosevelt to Stalin "that if his government joined up with Hitler, it was as certain as that the night followed day that as soon as Hitler had conquered France he would turn on Russia." (Joseph E. Davies, *Mission to Moscow,* p. 450.) The President's warning was cabled to Steinhardt with instructions to repeat it to Molotov, which the ambassador did on August 16. (*U.S. Diplomatic Papers, 1939,* I, pp. 296–99.)

* Years before, Hitler had written prophetically in *Mein Kampf:* "The very fact of the conclusion of an alliance with Russia embodies a plan for the next war. Its outcome would be the end of Germany." (See p. 660 of the Houghton Mifflin edition, 1943.)

16

THE LAST DAYS OF PEACE

T HE BRITISH GOVERNMENT had not waited idly for the formal signing of the Nazi–Soviet Pact in Moscow. The announcement in Berlin on the late evening of August 21 that Ribbentrop was flying to Moscow to conclude a German–Russian agreement stirred the British cabinet to action. It met at 3 P.M. on the twenty-second and issued a communiqué stating categorically that a Soviet–Nazi nonaggression pact "would in no way affect their obligation to Poland, which they have repeatedly stated in public and which they are determined to fulfill." At the same time Parliament was summoned to meet on August 24 to pass the Emergency Powers (Defense) Bill, and certain precautionary mobilization measures were taken.

Though the cabinet statement was as clear as words could make it, Chamberlain wanted Hitler to have no doubts about it. Immediately after the cabinet meeting broke up he wrote a personal letter to the Fuehrer.

. . . Apparently the announcement of a German–Soviet Agreement is taken in some quarters in Berlin to indicate that intervention by Great Britain on behalf of Poland is no longer a contingency that need be reckoned with. No greater mistake could be made. Whatever may prove to be the nature of the German–Soviet Agreement, it cannot alter Great Britain's obligation to Poland . . .

It has been alleged that, if His Majesty's Government had made their position more clear in 1914, the great catastrophe would have been avoided. Whether or not there is any force in that allegation, His Majesty's Government are resolved that on this occasion there shall be no such tragic misunderstanding.

If the case should arise, they are resolved, and prepared, to employ without delay all the forces at their command, and it is impossible to foresee the end of hostilities once engaged . . .[1]

Having, as he added, "thus made our position perfectly clear," the Prime Minister again appealed to Hitler to seek a peaceful solution of his differences with Poland and once more offered the British government's co-operation in helping to obtain it.

The letter, which Ambassador Henderson, flying down from Berlin, delivered to Hitler shortly after 1 P.M. on August 23 at Berchtesgaden, threw the Nazi dictator into a violent rage. "Hitler was excitable and uncompromising," Henderson wired Lord Halifax. "His language was violent and exaggerated both as regards England and Poland."[2] Henderson's report of the meeting and the German Foreign Office memorandum on it—the latter among the captured Nazi papers—agree on the nature of Hitler's tirade. England, he stormed, was responsible for Poland's intransigence just as it had been responsible for Czechoslovakia's unreasonable attitude the year before. Tens of thousands of *Volksdeutsche* in Poland were being persecuted. There were even, he claimed, six cases of castration—a subject that obsessed him. He could stand it no more. Any further persecution of Germans by the Poles would bring immediate action.

I contested every point [Henderson wired Halifax] and kept calling his statements inaccurate but the only effect was to launch him on some fresh tirade.

Finally Hitler agreed to give a written answer to the Prime Minister's letter in two hours' time, and Henderson withdrew to Salzburg for a little respite.* Later in the afternoon Hitler sent for him and handed him his reply. In contrast to the first meeting, the Fuehrer, Henderson reported to London, "was quite calm and never raised his voice."

He was, he said [Henderson reported], fifty years old; he preferred war now to when he would be fifty-five or sixty.

The megalomania of the German dictator, declaiming on his mountaintop, comes out even more forcibly in the German minutes of the meeting. After quoting him as preferring to make war at fifty rather than later, they add:

England [Hitler said] would do well to realize that as a front-line soldier he knew what war was and would utilize every means available. It was surely quite clear to everyone that the World War [i.e., 1914–1918] would not have been lost if he had been Chancellor at the time.

Hitler's reply to Chamberlain was a mixture of all the stale lies and exaggerations which he had been bellowing to foreigners and his own people since the Poles dared to stand up to him. Germany, he said, did not seek a conflict with Great Britain. It had been prepared all along to discuss the questions of Danzig and the Corridor with the Poles "on the basis of a

---

* "Hardly had the door shut on the Ambassador," Weizsaecker, who was present, later noted, "than Hitler slapped himself on the thigh, laughed and said: 'Chamberlain won't survive that conversation; his Cabinet will fall this evening.'" (Weizsaecker, *Memoirs,* p. 203.)

proposal of truly unparalleled magnanimity." But the unconditional guarantee of Poland by Britain had only encouraged the Poles "to unloosen a wave of appalling terrorism against the one and a half million German inhabitants living in Poland." Such "atrocities" he declared, "are terrible for the victims but intolerable for a Great Power such as the German Reich." Germany would no longer tolerate them.

Finally he took note of the Prime Minister's assurance that Great Britain would honor its commitments to Poland and assured him "that it can make no change in the determination of the Reich Government to safeguard the interests of the Reich . . . Germany, if attacked by England, will be found prepared and determined."[3]

What had this exchange of letters accomplished? Hitler now had a solemn assurance from Chamberlain that Britain would go to war if Germany attacked Poland. The Prime Minister had the Fuehrer's word that it would make no difference. But, as the events of the next hectic eight days would show, neither man believed on August 23 that he had heard the last word from the other.

This was especially true of Hitler. Buoyed up by the good news from Moscow and confident that, despite what Chamberlain had just written him, Great Britain and, in its wake, France would have second thoughts about honoring their obligations to Poland after the defection of Russia, the Fuehrer on the evening of August 23, as Henderson was flying back to Berlin, set the date for the onslaught on Poland: Saturday, August 26, at 4:30 A.M.

"There will be no more orders regarding Y Day and X Hour," General Halder noted in his diary. *"Everything is to roll automatically."*

But the Chief of the Army General Staff was wrong. On August 25 two events occurred which made Adolf Hitler shrink back from the abyss less than twenty-four hours before his troops were scheduled to break across the Polish frontier. One originated in London, the other in Rome.

On the morning of August 25, Hitler, who on the previous day had returned to Berlin to welcome Ribbentrop back from Moscow and receive a firsthand report on the Russians, got off a letter to Mussolini. It contained a belated explanation as to why he had not been able to keep his Axis partner informed of his negotiations with the Soviet Union. (He had "no idea," he said, that they would go so far so fast.) And he declared that the Russo–German pact "must be regarded as the greatest possible gain for the Axis."

But the real purpose of the letter, whose text is among the captured documents, was to warn the Duce that a German attack on Poland was liable to take place at any moment, though Hitler refrained from giving his friend and ally the exact date which he had set. "In case of intolerable events in Poland," he said, "I shall act immediately . . . In these circumstances no one can say what the next hour may bring." Hitler did not specifically ask for Italy's help. That was, by the terms of the Italo–German alliance, supposed to be automatic. He contented himself with expressing the hope for Italy's understanding.[4] Nevertheless, he was anxious for an immediate answer. The letter was telephoned by Ribbentrop personally to the German ambassador in Rome and reached the Duce at 3:20 P.M.

In the meantime, at 1:30 P.M., the Fuehrer had received Ambassador Henderson at the Chancellery. His resolve to destroy Poland had in no way lessened but he was more anxious than he had been two days before, when he had talked with Henderson at Berchtesgaden, to make one last attempt to keep Britain out of the war.* The ambassador found the Fuehrer, as he reported to London, "absolutely calm and normal and [he] spoke with great earnestness and apparent sincerity." Despite all his experience of the past year Henderson could not, even at this late date, see through the "sincerity" of the German Leader. For what Hitler had to say was quite preposterous. He "accepted" the British Empire, he told the ambassador, and was ready "to pledge himself personally to its continued existence and to commit the power of the German Reich for this."

He desired [Hitler explained] to make a move toward England which should be as decisive as the move towards Russia . . . The Fuehrer is ready to conclude agreements with England which would not only guarantee the existence of the British Empire in all circumstances so far as Germany is concerned, but would also if necessary assure the British Empire of German assistance regardless of where such assistance should be necessary.

He would also be ready, he added, "to accept a reasonable limitation of armaments" and to regard the Reich's western frontiers as final. At one point, according to Henderson, Hitler lapsed into a typical display of sentimental hogwash, though the ambassador did not describe it as that when he recounted it in his dispatch to London. The Fuehrer stated

that he was by nature an artist, not a politician, and that once the Polish question was settled he would end his life as an artist and not as a warmonger.

But the dictator ended on another note.

The Fuehrer repeated [says the verbal statement drawn up by the Germans for Henderson] that he is a man of great decisions . . . and that this is his last offer. If they [the British government] reject these ideas, there will be war.

In the course of the interview Hitler repeatedly pointed out that his "large comprehensive offer" to Britain, as he described it, was subject to one condition: that it would take effect only "*after* the solution of the German–Polish problem." When Henderson kept insisting that Britain could not consider his offer unless it meant at the same time a peaceful

---

* According to Erich Kordt (*Wahn und Wirklichkeit*, p. 192) Hitler was so excited by his triumph in Moscow that on the morning of August 25 he asked his press bureau for news of the cabinet crises in Paris and London. He thought both governments must fall. He was brought down to earth by being told of the firm speeches of Chamberlain and Halifax in Parliament the day before.

settlement with Poland, Hitler replied, "If you think it useless then do not send my offer at all."

However, the ambassador had scarcely returned to the embassy a few steps up the Wilhelmstrasse from the Chancellery before Dr. Schmidt was knocking at the door with a written copy of Hitler's remarks—with considerable deletions—coupled with a message from the Fuehrer begging Henderson to urge the British government "to take the offer very seriously" and suggesting that he himself fly to London with it, for which purpose a German plane would be at his disposal.[5]

It was rarely easy, as readers who have got this far in this book are aware, to penetrate the strange and fantastic workings of Hitler's fevered mind. His ridiculous "offer" of August 25 to guarantee the British Empire was obviously a brain storm of the moment, for he had not mentioned it two days before when he discussed Chamberlain's letter with Henderson and composed a reply to it. Even making allowances for the dictator's aberrations, it is difficult to believe that he himself took it as seriously as he made out to the British ambassador. Besides, how could the British government, as he requested, be asked to take it "very seriously" when Chamberlain would scarcely have time to read it before the Nazi armies hurtled into Poland at dawn on the morrow—the X Day which still held?

But behind the "offer," no doubt, was a serious purpose. Hitler apparently believed that Chamberlain, like Stalin, wanted an out by which he could keep his country out of war.* He had purchased Stalin's benevolent neutrality two days before by offering Russia a free hand in Eastern Europe "from the Baltic to the Black Sea." Could he not buy Britain's nonintervention by assuring the Prime Minister that the Third Reich would never, like the Hohenzollern Germany, become a threat to the British Empire? What Hitler did not realize, nor Stalin—to the latter's awful cost—was that to Chamberlain, his eyes open at long last, Germany's domination of the European continent would be the greatest of all threats to the British Empire—as indeed it would be to the Soviet Russian Empire. For centuries, as Hitler had noted in *Mein Kampf,* the first imperative of British foreign policy had been to prevent any single nation from dominating the Continent.

At 5:30 P.M. Hitler received the French ambassador but had little of importance to say to him beyond repeating that "Polish provocation of the Reich" could no longer be endured, that he would not attack France but that if France entered the conflict he would fight her to the end. Whereupon he started to dismiss the French envoy by rising from his chair. But Coulondre had something to say to the Fuehrer of the Third Reich and he insisted on saying it. He told him on his word of honor as a

---

* Or if not out of war, out of any serious participation in it. General Halder intimates this in a recapitulation of the "sequence of events" of August 25 in a diary entry made later, on August 28. Noting that at 1:30 P.M. on the twenty-fifth Hitler saw Henderson, Halder added: "Fuehrer would not take it amiss if England were to wage a sham war."

soldier that he had not the least doubt "that if Poland is attacked France will be at the side of Poland with all its forces."

"It is painful to me," Hitler replied, "to think of having to fight your country, but that does not depend on me. Please say that to Monsieur Daladier."[6]

It was now 6 P.M. of August 25 in Berlin. Tension in the capital had been building up all day. Since early afternoon all radio, telegraph and telephone communication with the outside world had been cut off on orders from the Wilhelmstrasse. The night before, the last of the British and French correspondents and nonofficial civilians had hurriedly left for the nearest frontier. During the day of the twenty-fifth, a Friday, it became known that the German Foreign Office had wired the embassies and consulates in Poland, France and Britain requesting that German citizens be asked to leave by the quickest route. My own diary notes for August 24–25 recall the feverish atmosphere in Berlin. The weather was warm and sultry and everyone seemed to be on edge. All through the sprawling city antiaircraft guns were being set up, and bombers flew continually overhead in the direction of Poland. "It looks like war," I scribbled on the evening of the twenty-fourth; "War is imminent," I repeated the next day, and on both nights, I remember, the Germans we saw in the Wilhelmstrasse whispered that Hitler had ordered the soldiers to march into Poland at dawn.

Their orders, we now know, were to attack at 4:30 on Saturday morning, August 26.* And up until 6 P.M. on the twenty-fifth nothing that had happened during the day, certainly not the personal assurances of Ambassadors Henderson and Coulondre that Britain and France would surely honor their commitments to Poland, had budged Adolf Hitler from his resolve to go ahead with his aggression on schedule. But about 6 P.M., or shortly afterward, there arrived news from London and Rome that made this man of apparently unshakable will hesitate.

It is not quite clear from the confidential German records and the postwar testimony of the Wilhelmstrasse officials at just what time Hitler learned of the signing in London of the formal Anglo–Polish treaty which transformed Britain's unilateral guarantee of Poland into a pact of mutual assistance.† There is some evidence in Halder's diary and in the German

---

* Although Hitler's standing orders, which had not been canceled, called for the attack on this day and hour and, as Halder said, were "automatic," a number of German writers have reported that the Fuehrer gave specific orders a few minutes after 3 P.M. to launch *Fall Weiss* the following morning. (See Weizsaecker, *Memoirs;* Kordt, *Wahn und Wirklichkeit;* and Walther Hofer, *War Premeditated, 1939.*) Hofer says the order was given at 3:02 P.M. and cites as his source General von Vormann, who was present at the Chancellery when it was issued. No official record of this has been found in the German documents.

† There was a secret protocol to this treaty which stated that the "European Power" mentioned in Article I, whose aggression would bring about mutual military assistance, was Germany. This saved the British government from the disastrous step of having to declare war on the Soviet Union when the Red Army, in cahoots with the Germans, invaded eastern Poland.

Naval Register that the Wilhelmstrasse got wind at noon on August 25 that the pact would be signed during the day. The General Staff Chief notes that at 12 noon he got a call from OKW asking what was the latest deadline for postponement of the decision to attack and that he replied: 3 P.M. The Naval Register also mentions that news of the Anglo–Polish pact and of "information from the Duce" was received at noon.[7] But this is impossible. Word from Mussolini did not arrive, according to a German notation on the document, until "about 6 P.M." And Hitler could not have learned of the signing of the Anglo–Polish treaty in London until about that time, since this event only took place at 5:35 P.M.—and, at that, barely fifteen minutes after the Polish ambassador in London, Count Edward Raczyński, had received permission from his Foreign Minister in Warsaw over the telephone to affix his signature.*

Whatever time he received it—and around 6 P.M. is an accurate guess—Hitler was moved by the news from London. This could well be Britain's answer to his "offer," the terms of which must have reached London by now. It meant that he had failed in his bid to buy off the British as he had bought off the Russians. Dr. Schmidt, who was in Hitler's office when the report arrived, remembered later that the Fuehrer, after reading it, sat brooding at his desk.[8]

MUSSOLINI GETS COLD FEET

His brooding was interrupted very shortly by equally bad news from Rome. Throughout the afternoon the German dictator had waited with "unconcealed impatience," as Dr. Schmidt describes it, for the Duce's reply to his letter. The Italian ambassador, Attolico, was summoned to the Chancellery at 3 P.M., shortly after Henderson had departed, but he could only inform the Fuehrer that no answer had been received as yet. By this time Hitler's nerves were so strained that he sent Ribbentrop out to get Ciano on the long-distance telephone, but the Foreign Minister was unable to get through to him. Attolico, Schmidt says, was dismissed "with scant courtesy."[9]

For some days Hitler had been receiving warnings from Rome that his Axis partner might go back on him at the crucial moment of the attack on Poland, and this intelligence was not without foundation. No sooner had Ciano returned from his disillusioning meetings with Hitler and Ribbentrop on August 11 to 13, than he set to work to turn Mussolini against the Germans—an action which did not escape the watchful eyes of the German Embassy in Rome. The Fascist Foreign Minister's diary traces the ups and downs of his efforts to make the Italian dictator see the light and disassocia e himself, in time, from Hitler's war.[10] On the evening of his return from Berchtesgaden on August 13, Ciano saw the

---

* Germany did not observe summer time, as did Great Britain. Therefore the one-hour difference in time between Berlin and London was canceled out.

Duce and after describing his talks with Hitler and Ribbentrop tried to convince his chief that the Germans "have betrayed us and lied to us" and "are dragging us into an adventure."

The Duce's reactions are varied [Ciano noted in his diary that night]. At first he agrees with me. Then he says that honor compels him to march with Germany. Finally, he states that he wants his part of the booty in Croatia and Dalmatia.

August 14.—I find Mussolini worried. I do not hesitate to arouse in him every possible anti-German reaction by every means in my power. I speak to him of his diminished prestige and his playing the role of second fiddle. And, finally, I turn over to him documents which prove the bad faith of the Germans on the Polish question. The alliance was based on premises which they now deny; they are traitors and we must not have any scruples in ditching them. But Mussolini still has many scruples.

On the next day, Ciano talked it out with Mussolini for six hours.

August 15.—The Duce . . . is convinced that we must not march blindly with the Germans. However . . . he wants time to prepare the break with Germany . . . He is more and more convinced that the democracies will fight . . . This time it means war. And we cannot engage in war because our plight does not permit us to do so.

August 18.—A conversation with the Duce in the morning; his usual shifting feelings. He still thinks it possible that the democracies will not march and that Germany might do good business cheaply, from which business he does not want to be excluded. Then, too, he fears Hitler's rage. He believes that a denunciation of the pact or something like it might induce Hitler to abandon the Polish question in order to square accounts with Italy. All this makes him nervous and disturbed.

August 20.—The Duce made an about-face. He wants to support Germany at any cost in the conflict which is now close at hand . . . Conference between Mussolini, myself, and Attolico. [The ambassador had returned from Berlin to Rome for consultations.] This is the substance: It is already too late to go back on the Germans . . . The press of the whole world would say that Italy is cowardly . . . I try to debate the matter but it is useless now. Mussolini holds very stubbornly to his idea . . .

August 21.—Today I have spoken very clearly . . . When I entered the room Mussolini confirmed his decision to go along with the Germans. "You, Duce, cannot and must not do it . . . I went to Salzburg in order to adopt a common line of action. I found myself face to face with a *Diktat.* The Germans, not ourselves, have betrayed the alliance . . . Tear up the pact. Throw it in Hitler's face! . . ."

The upshot of this conference was that Ciano should seek a meeting with Ribbentrop for the next day at the Brenner and inform him that Italy would stay out of a conflict provoked by a German attack on Poland. Ribbentrop was not available for several hours when Ciano put in a call for him at noon, but at 5:30 he finally came on the line. The Nazi Foreign Minister could not give Ciano an immediate answer about meeting on the Brenner on such quick notice, because he was "waiting for an important message from Moscow" and would call back later. This he did at 10:30 P.M.

August 22.—Last evening at 10:30 a new act opened [Ciano recorded in his diary]. Ribbentrop telephoned that he would prefer to see me in Innsbruck rather than at the frontier, because he was to leave later for Moscow to sign a political pact with the Soviet Government.

This was news, and of the most startling kind, to Ciano and Mussolini. They decided that a meeting of the two foreign ministers "would no longer be timely." Once more their German ally had shown its contempt for them by not letting them know about the deal with Moscow.

The hesitations of the Duce, the anti-German feelings of Ciano and the possibility that Italy might crawl out of its obligations under Article III of the Pact of Steel, which called for the automatic participation in war of one party if the other party "became involved in hostilities with another Power," became known in Berlin before Ribbentrop set off for Moscow on August 22.

On August 20, Count Massimo Magistrati, the Italian chargé d'affaires in Berlin, called on Weizsaecker at the Foreign Office and revealed "an Italian state of mind which, although it does not surprise me," the State Secretary informed Ribbentrop in a confidential memorandum,[11] "must in my opinion definitely be considered." What Magistrati brought to the attention of Weizsaecker was that since Germany had not adhered to the terms of the alliance, which called for close contact and consultation on major questions, and had treated its conflict with Poland as an exclusively German problem, "Germany was thus forgoing Italy's armed assistance." And if contrary to the German view the Polish conflict developed into a big war, Italy did not consider that the "prerequisites" of the alliance existed. In brief, Italy was seeking an out.

Two days later, on August 23, a further warning was received in Berlin from Ambassador Hans Georg von Mackensen in Rome. He wrote to Weizsaecker on what had been happening "behind the scenes." The letter, according to a marginal note in Weizsaecker's handwriting on the captured document, was "submitted to the Fuehrer." It must have opened his eyes. The Italian position, following a series of meetings between Mussolini, Ciano and Attolico, was, Mackensen reported, that if Germany invaded Poland she would violate the Pact of Steel, which was based on an agreement to refrain from war until 1942. Furthermore, contrary to the German view, Mussolini was sure that if Germany attacked Poland both Britain and France would intervene—"and the

United States too after a few months." While Germany remained on the defensive in the west the French and British,

in the Duce's opinion, would descend on Italy with all the forces at their disposal. In this situation Italy would have to bear the whole brunt of the war in order to give the Reich the opportunity of liquidating the affair in the East . . .[12]

It was with these warnings in mind that Hitler got off his letter to Mussolini on the morning of August 25 and waited all day, with mounting impatience, for an answer. Shortly after midnight of the day before, Ribbentrop, after an evening recounting to the Fuehrer the details of his triumph in Moscow, rang up Ciano to warn him, "at the instigation of the Fuehrer," of the "extreme gravity of the situation due to Polish provocations."* A note by Weizsaecker reveals that the call was made to "prevent the Italians from being able to speak of unexpected developments."

By the time Ambassador Mackensen handed Mussolini Hitler's letter at the Palazzo Venezia in Rome at 3:20 P.M. on August 25, the Duce, then, knew that the German attack on Poland was about to take place. Unlike Hitler, he was certain that Great Britain and France would immediately enter the war, with catastrophic consequences for Italy, whose Navy was no match for the British Mediterranean Fleet and whose Army would be overwhelmed by the French.† According to a dispatch which Mackensen got off to Berlin at 10:25 P.M. describing the meeting, Mussolini, after carefully reading the letter twice in his presence, declared that he was "in complete agreement" about the Nazi–Soviet Pact and that he realized that an "armed conflict with Poland could no longer be avoided." Finally—"and this he emphasized expressly," Mackensen reported—"he stood beside us unconditionally and with all his resources."[13]

But this was not what the Duce wrote the Fuehrer, unbeknownst to the German ambassador, the text of which was hurriedly telephoned by Ciano to Attolico, who had returned to his post in Berlin and who "about 6 P.M." arrived at the Chancellery to deliver it in person to Adolf Hitler.

---

* It must be kept in mind that the "Polish provocations" which Hitler and Ribbentrop harped on in their meetings and diplomatic exchanges with the British, French, Russians and Italians during these days, and the news of which was published under flaming headlines in the controlled Nazi press, were almost entirely invented by the Germans. Most of the provoking in Poland was done, on orders from Berlin, by the Germans. The captured German documents are replete with evidence on this.
† The day before, on August 24, Ciano had visited the King at his summer residence in Piedmont, and the aging ruler, who had been shunted to the sidelines by Mussolini, spoke contemptuously of the country's armed services. "The Army is in a pitiful state," Ciano quotes him as saying. "Even the defense of our frontier is insufficient. He has made thirty-two inspections and is convinced that the French can go through it with great ease. The officers of the Italian Army are not qualified for the job, and our equipment is old and obsolete." (*Ciano Diaries*, p. 127.)

It struck the Fuehrer, according to Schmidt, who was present, like a bombshell. After expressing his "complete approval" of the Nazi–Soviet Pact and his "understanding concerning Poland," Mussolini came to the main point.

As for the *practical* attitude of Italy in case of military action [Mussolini wrote, and the emphasis is his], my point of view is as follows:

If Germany attacks Poland and the conflict remains localized, Italy will afford Germany every form of political and economic assistance which is requested of her.

If Germany attacks Poland* and the latter's allies open a counterattack against Germany, I inform you in advance that it will be opportune for me not to take the *initiative* in military operations in view of the *present* state of Italian war preparations, of which we have repeatedly and in good time informed you, Fuehrer, and Herr von Ribbentrop.

Our intervention can, nevertheless, take place at once if Germany delivers to us immediately the military supplies and the raw materials to resist the attack which the French and English would predominantly direct against us.

At our meetings the war was envisaged for 1942, and by that time I would have been ready on land, on sea and in the air, according to the plans which had been concerted.

I am furthermore of the opinion that the purely military measures which have already been taken, and other measures to be taken later, will immobilize, in Europe and Africa, considerable French and British forces.

I consider it my bounden duty as a loyal friend to tell you the whole truth and inform you beforehand about the real situation. Not to do so might have unpleasant consequences for us all. This is my view, and since within a short time I must summon the highest governmental bodies, I beg you to let me know yours.

MUSSOLINI†[15]

---

* In the German translation of Mussolini's letter found in the Foreign Office archives after the war, and which I have used here, the word "Germany" has been crossed out here and the word "Poland" typed above it, making it read: "If Poland attacks . . ." In the Italian original, published after the war by the Italian government, the passage reads "*Se la Germania attacca la Polonia.*" It is strange that the Nazis falsified even the secret documents deposited in their official government archives.[14]

† As if Mussolini's letter were not bad enough medicine for Hitler, a number of German writers, mostly observers at first hand of the dramatic events of the last days of peace, have published an imaginary text of this letter of the Duce to the Fuehrer. Erich Kordt, one of the anti-Nazi conspirators, who was head of the secretariat at the Foreign Office, was the first to commit this faked version to print in his book, *Wahn und Wirklichkeit*, published in Stuttgart in 1947. Kordt dropped it in his second edition but other writers continued to copy it from the first edition. It shows up in Peter Kleist's *Zwischen Hitler und Stalin,* published in 1950, and even in the English translation of Paul Schmidt's memoirs published in New York and London in 1951. Yet the authentic text was published in Italy in 1946 and an English translation in the State Department's *Nazi–Soviet Relations* in 1948. Dr. Schmidt, who was with Hitler when he received the letter from Attolico, quotes the letter as saying, "In one of the most painful moments of my life, I have to inform

So though Russia was in the bag as a friendly neutral instead of a belligerent, Germany's ally of the Pact of Steel was out of it—and this on the very day that Britain had seemed to commit herself irrevocably by signing a mutual-assistance pact with Poland against German aggression. Hitler read the Duce's letter, told Attolico he would answer it immediately and icily dismissed the Italian envoy.

"The Italians are behaving just as they did in 1914," Dr. Schmidt overheard Hitler remark bitterly after Attolico had left, and that evening the Chancellery echoed with unkind words about the "disloyal Axis partner." But words were not enough. The German Army was scheduled to hop off against Poland in nine hours, for it was now 6:30 P.M. of August 25 and the invasion was set to begin at 4:30 A.M. on August 26. The Nazi dictator had to decide at once whether, in view of the news from London and Rome, to go ahead with it or postpone or cancel it.

Schmidt, accompanying Attolico out of Hitler's study, bumped into General Keitel rushing to the presence of the Fuehrer. A few minutes later the General hurried out, crying excitedly to his adjutant, "The order to advance must be delayed again!"

Hitler, pushed into a corner by Mussolini and Chamberlain, had swiftly made his decision. "Fuehrer considerably shaken," Halder noted in his diary, and then continued:

7:30 P.M.—Treaty between Poland and England ratified. No opening of hostilities. All troop movements to be stopped, even near the frontier if not otherwise possible.

8:35 P.M.—Keitel confirms. Canaris: Telephone restrictions lifted on England and France. Confirms development of events.

The German Naval Register gives a more concise account of the postponement, along with the reasons:

August 25:—Case White already started will be stopped at 20:30 (8:30 P.M.) because of changed political conditions. (Mutual-Assistance Pact England–Poland of August 25, noon, and information from Duce that he would be true to his word but has to ask for large supply of raw materials.)[16]

Three of the chief defendants at Nuremberg submitted, under interrogation, their version of the postponement of the attack.[17] Ribbentrop claimed that when he heard about the Anglo–Polish pact and "heard" that

---

you that Italy is not ready for war. According to what the responsible heads of the services tell me, the gasoline supplies of the Italian Air Force are so low that they would last only for three weeks of fighting. The position is the same with regard to supplies for the Army, and supplies of raw materials . . . Please understand my situation." For an amusing note on the faking of this letter, see Namier, *In the Nazi Era,* p. 5.

"military steps were being taken against Poland" (as if he didn't know all along about the attack) he went "at once" to the Fuehrer and urged him to call off the invasion of Poland, to which "the Fuehrer at once agreed." This is surely entirely untrue.

But the testimony of Keitel and Goering at least seemed more honest. "I was suddenly called to Hitler at the Chancellery," Keitel recounted on the stand at Nuremberg, "and he said to me, 'Stop everything at once. Get Brauchitsch immediately. I need time for negotiations.'"

That Hitler still believed at this late hour that he could negotiate his way out of his impasse was confirmed by Goering during a pretrial interrogation at Nuremberg.

On the day that England gave her official guarantee to Poland the Fuehrer called me on the telephone and told me that he had stopped the planned invasion of Poland. I asked him whether this was just temporary or for good. He said, "No, I will have to see whether we can eliminate British intervention."

Though Mussolini's last-minute defection was a heavy blow to Hitler, it is obvious from the above testimony that Britain's action in signing a mutual-assistance treaty with Poland was the stronger influence in inducing the German leader to postpone the attack. Yet it is strange that after Ambassador Henderson on this very day had again warned him that Britain would fight if Poland were attacked and that after the British government had now solemnly given its word to that effect in a formal treaty, he still believed he could, as he told Goering, "eliminate British intervention." It is likely that his experience with Chamberlain at Munich led him to believe that the Prime Minister again would capitulate if a way out could be concocted. But again it is strange that a man who had previously shown such insight into foreign politics did not know of the changes in Chamberlain and in the British position. After all, Hitler himself had provoked them.

It took some doing to halt the German Army on the evening of August 25, for many units were already on the move. In East Prussia the order calling off the attack reached General Petzel's I Corps at 9:37 P.M. and only the frantic efforts of several officers who were rushed out to the forward detachments succeeded in stopping the troops. The motorized columns of General von Kleist's corps to the south had begun to move at dusk up to the Polish frontier. They were halted on the border by a staff officer who made a quick landing in a small scouting plane on the frontier. In a few sectors the orders did not arrive until after the shooting began, but since the Germans had been provoking incidents all along the border for several days the Polish General Staff apparently did not suspect what had really happened. It did report on August 26 that numerous "German bands" had crossed the border and attacked blockhouses and customs posts with machine guns and hand grenades and that "in one case it was a Regular Army detachment."

JOY AND CONFUSION OF THE "CONSPIRATORS"

The news on the evening of August 25 that Hitler had called off the attack on Poland caused great jubilation among the conspiratorial members of the Abwehr. Colonel Oster gave Schacht and Gisevius the news, exclaiming, "The Fuehrer is done for," and the next morning Admiral Canaris was even more in the clouds. "Hitler," Canaris declared, "will never survive this blow. Peace has been saved for the next twenty years." Both men thought there was no further need of bothering to overthrow the Nazi dictator; he was finished.

For several weeks as the fateful summer approached its end the conspirators, as they conceived themselves, had again been busy, though with what purpose exactly it is difficult to comprehend. Goerdeler, Adam von Trott, Helmuth von Moltke, Fabian von Schlabrendorff and Rudolf Pechel had all made the pilgrimage to London and there had informed not only Chamberlain and Halifax but Churchill and other British leaders that Hitler planned to attack Poland at the end of August. These German opponents of the Fuehrer could see for themselves that Britain, right up to its umbrella-carrying Chamberlain, had changed since the days of Munich, and that the one condition they themselves had made the year before to their resolve to get rid of Hitler, namely that Britain and France declare they would oppose any further Nazi aggression by armed force, had now been fulfilled. What more did they want? It is not clear from the records they have left, and one gathers the impression that they did not quite know themselves. Well-meaning though they were, they were gripped by utter confusion and a paralyzing sense of futility. Hitler's hold on Germany—on the Army, the police, the government, the people—was too complete to be loosened or undermined by anything they could think of doing.

On August 15, Hassell visited Dr. Schacht at his new bachelor quarters in Berlin. The dismissed Minister of Economics had just returned from a six-month journey to India and Burma. "Schacht's view is," Hassell wrote in his diary, "that we can do nothing but keep our eyes open and wait, that things will follow their inevitable course." Hassell himself told Gisevius the same day, according to his own diary entry, that he "too was in favor of postponing direct action for the moment."

But what "direct action" was there to be put off? General Halder, keen as Hitler to smash Poland, was not at the moment interested in getting rid of the dictator. General von Witzleben, who was to have led the troops in the overthrow of the Fuehrer the year before, was now in command of an army group in the west and was, therefore, in no position to act in Berlin, even if he had wished to. But did he have any such wish? Gisevius visited him at his headquarters, found him listening to the BBC radio news from London and soon realized that the General was interested merely in finding out what was going on.

As for General Halder, he was preoccupied with last-minute plans for the onslaught on Poland, to the exclusion of any treasonable thoughts about getting rid of Hitler. When interrogated after the war—on February 26, 1946—at Nuremberg, he was exceedingly fuzzy about why he and the other supposed enemies of the Nazi regime had done nothing in the last days of August to depose the Fuehrer and thus save Germany from involvement in war. "There was no possibility," he said. Why? Because General von Witzleben had been transferred to the west. Without Witzleben the Army could not act.

What about the German people? When Captain Sam Harris, the American interrogator, reminding Halder that he had said the German people were opposed to war, asked, "If Hitler were irrevocably committed to war, why couldn't you count on the support of the people before the invasion of Poland?" Halder replied, "You must excuse me if I smile. If I hear the word 'irrevocably' connected with Hitler, I must say that nothing was irrevocable." And the General Staff Chief went on to explain that as late as August 22, after Hitler had revealed to his generals at the meeting on the Obersalzberg his "irrevocable" resolve to attack Poland and fight the West if necessary, he himself did not believe that the Fuehrer would do what he said he would do.[18] In the light of Halder's own diary entries for this period, this is an astonishing statement indeed. But it is typical not only of Halder but of most of the other conspirators.

Where was General Beck, Halder's predecessor as Chief of the Army General Staff and the acknowledged leader of the conspirators? According to Gisevius, Beck wrote a letter to General von Brauchitsch but the Army Commander in Chief did not even acknowledge it. Next, Gisevius says, Beck had a long talk with Halder, who agreed with him that a big war would be the ruin of Germany but thought "Hitler would never permit a world war" and that therefore there was no need at the moment to try to overthrow him.[19]

On August 14, Hassell dined alone with Beck, and recorded their feeling of frustration in his diary.

> Beck [is] a most cultured, attractive and intelligent man. Unfortunately, he has a very low opinion of the leading people in the Army. For that reason he could see no place there where we could gain a foothold. He is firmly convinced of the vicious character of the policies of the Third Reich.[20]

The convictions of Beck—and of the others around him—were high and noble, but as Adolf Hitler prepared to hurl Germany into war not one of these estimable Germans did anything to halt him. The task was obviously difficult and perhaps, at this late hour, impossible to fulfill. But they did not even attempt it.

General Thomas, perhaps, tried. Following up his memorandum to Keitel which he had personally read to the OKW Chief at the middle of August,* he called on him again on Sunday, August 27, and, according to

---

* See above, pp. 517–18.

his own account, "handed him graphically illustrated statistical evidence
. . . [which] demonstrated clearly the tremendous military-economic
superiority of the Western Powers and the tribulation we would face."
Keitel, with unaccustomed courage, showed the material to Hitler, who
replied that he did not share General Thomas' "anxiety over the danger
of a world war, especially since he had now got the Soviet Union on his
side."[21]

Thus ended the attempts of the "conspirators" to prevent Hitler from
launching World War II, except for the feeble last-minute efforts of Dr.
Schacht, of which the canny financier made much in his own defense at
the Nuremberg trial. On his return from India in August he wrote letters
to Hitler, Goering and Ribbentrop—at the fateful moment none of the
opposition leaders seem to have gone beyond writing letters and memoranda—but, to his "very great surprise," as he said later, received no
replies. Next he decided to go to Zossen, a few miles southeast of Berlin,
where the Army High Command had set up headquarters for the Polish
campaign, and personally confront General von Brauchitsch. To tell him
what? On the witness stand at Nuremberg Schacht explained that he
intended to tell the Army chief that it would be unconstitutional for
Germany to go to war without the approval of the Reichstag! It was
therefore the duty of the Army Commander in Chief to respect his oath
to the constitution!

Alas, Dr. Schacht never got to see Brauchitsch. He was warned by
Canaris that if he came to Zossen the Army commander "would probably
have us arrested immediately"—a fate that did not seem attractive to this
former supporter of Hitler.[22] But the real reason Schacht did not go to
Zossen on his ridiculous errand (it would have been child's play for Hitler
to get the rubber-stamp Reichstag to approve his war had he wanted to
bother with such a formality) was stated by Gisevius when he took the
witness stand on behalf of Schacht at Nuremberg. It seems that Schacht
planned to go to Zossen on August 25 and called off the trip when Hitler
on that evening called off the attack on Poland scheduled for the next
day. Three days later, according to the testimony of Gisevius, Schacht
again decided to carry out his mission at Zossen but Canaris informed him
it was too late.[23] It wasn't that the "conspirators" missed the bus; they
never arrived at the bus station to try to catch it.

As ineffective as the handful of anti-Nazi Germans in staying Hitler's
hand were the various neutral world leaders who now appealed to the
Fuehrer to avert war. On August 24, President Roosevelt sent urgent
messages to Hitler and the President of Poland pressing them to settle
their differences without resorting to arms. President Mościcki, in a
dignified reply the following day, reminded Roosevelt that it was not
Poland which was "formulating demands and demanding concessions"
but that nevertheless it was willing to settle its disputes with Germany by
direct negotiation or by conciliation, as the American President had
urged. Hitler did not reply (Roosevelt had reminded him that he had not

answered the President's appeal to him of last April) and on the next day, August 25, Roosevelt sent a second message, informing Hitler of Mościcki's conciliatory response, and beseeching him to "agree to the pacific means of settlement accepted by the Government of Poland."

To the second letter there was no answer either, although on the evening of August 26 Weizsaecker summoned the American chargé d'affaires in Berlin, Alexander C. Kirk, and asked him to tell the President that the Fuehrer had received the two telegrams and had placed them "in the hands of the Foreign Minister for consideration by the government."

The Pope took to the air on August 24 to make a broadcast appeal for peace, beseeching "by the blood of Christ . . . the strong [to] hear us that they may not become weak through injustice . . . [and] if they desire that their power may not be a destruction." On the afternoon of August 31 the Pope sent identical notes to the governments of Germany, Poland, Italy and the two Western Powers "beseeching, in the name of God, the German and Polish Governments . . . to avoid any incident," begging the British, French and Italian governments to support his appeal and adding:

The Pope is unwilling to abandon hope that pending negotiations may lead to a just pacific solution.

His Holiness, like almost everyone else in the world, did not realize that the "pending negotiations" were but a propaganda trick by Hitler to justify his aggression. Actually, as shortly will be shown, there were no bona fide negotiations, pending or otherwise, on that last afternoon of the peace.

A few days earlier, on August 23, the King of the Belgians, in the name of the rulers of the "Oslo" powers (Belgium, the Netherlands, Luxembourg, Finland and the three Scandinavian states), had also broadcast a moving appeal for peace, calling "on the men who are responsible for the course of events to submit their disputes and their claims to open negotiation." On August 28 the King of the Belgians and the Queen of the Netherlands jointly offered their good offices "in the hope of averting war."[24]

Noble in form and in intent as all these neutral appeals were, there is something unreal and pathetic about them when reread today. It was as if the President of the United States, the Pope and the rulers of the small Northern European democracies lived on a different planet from that of the Third Reich and had no more understanding of what was going on in Berlin than of what might be transpiring on Mars. This ignorance of the mind and character and purposes of Adolf Hitler, and indeed of the Germans, who, with a few exceptions, were ready to follow him blindly no matter where nor how, regardless of morals, ethics, honor, or the Christian concept of humanity, was to cost the peoples led by Roosevelt and the monarchs of Belgium, Holland, Luxembourg, Norway and Denmark dearly in the months to come.

Those of us who were in Berlin during those last few tense days of peace and who were attempting to report the news to the outside world knew very little either of what was going on in the Wilhelmstrasse, where the Chancellery and the Foreign Office were, or in the Bendlerstrasse, where the military had their offices. We followed as best we could the frantic comings and goings in the Wilhelmstrasse. We sifted daily an avalanche of rumors, tips and "plants." We caught the mood of the people in the street and of the government officials, party leaders, diplomats and soldiers of our acquaintance. But what was said at Ambassador Henderson's frequent and often stormy interviews with Hitler and Ribbentrop, what was written between Hitler and Chamberlain, between Hitler and Mussolini, between Hitler and Stalin, what was talked about between Ribbentrop and Molotov and between Ribbentrop and Ciano, what was contained in all the secret, coded dispatches humming over the wires between the stumbling, harassed diplomats and foreign-office officials, and all the moves which the military chiefs were planning or making—of all this we and the general public remained almost completely ignorant at the time.

A few things, of course, we, and the public, knew. The Nazi–Soviet Pact was trumpeted to the skies by the Germans, though the secret protocol dividing up Poland and the rest of Eastern Europe remained unknown until after the war. We knew that even before it was signed Henderson had flown to Berchtesgaden to emphasize to Hitler that the pact would not prevent Britain from honoring its guarantee to Poland. As the last week of August began we felt in Berlin that war was inevitable —unless there was another Munich—and that it would come within a few days. By August 25 the last of the British and French civilians had skipped out. The next day the big Nazi rally at Tannenberg scheduled for August 27, at which Hitler was to have spoken, was publicly called off, as was the annual party convention at Nuremberg (the "Party Rally of Peace," Hitler had officially called it), due to convene the first week of September. On August 27 the government announced that rationing of food, soap, shoes, textiles and coal would begin on the following day. This announcement, I remember, above all others, woke up the German people to the imminence of war, and their grumbling about it was very audible. On Monday, August 28, the Berliners watched troops pouring through the city toward the east. They were being transported in moving vans, grocery trucks and every other sort of vehicle that could be scraped up.

That too must have alerted the man in the street as to what was up. The weekend, I remember, had been hot and sultry and most of the Berliners, regardless of how near war was, had betaken themselves to the lakes and the woods which surround the capital. Returning to the city Sunday evening, they learned from the radio that there had been a secret, unofficial meeting of the Reichstag at the Chancellery. A D.N.B. communiqué stated that the "Fuehrer outlined the gravity of the situation"—this was the first the German public had been told by Hitler that the hour was grave. No details of the meeting were given and no one outside of the Reichstag members and of Hitler's entourage could know of the mood the Nazi dictator was in that day. Halder's diary of August 28 supplied—much later—one account, given him by Colonel Oster of the Abwehr.

Conference at Reich Chancellery at 5:30 P.M. Reichstag and several Party notables . . . Situation very grave. Determined to solve Eastern question one way or another. Minimum demands: return of Danzig, settling of Corridor question. Maximum demands: "Depending on military situation." If minimum demands not satisfied, then war: Brutal! He will himself be on front line. The Duce's attitude served our best interests.

War very difficult, perhaps hopeless; "As long as I am alive there will be no talk of capitulation." Soviet Pact widely misunderstood by Party. A pact with Satan to cast out the Devil . . . "Applause on proper cues, but thin."

Personal impression of Fuehrer: exhausted, haggard, croaking voice, preoccupied. "Keeps himself completely surrounded now by his S.S. advisers."

In Berlin too a foreign observer could watch the way the press, under Goebbels' expert direction, was swindling the gullible German people. For six years, since the Nazi "co-ordination" of the daily newspapers, which had meant the destruction of a free press, the citizens had been cut off from the truth of what was going on in the world. For a time the Swiss German-language newspapers from Zurich and Basel could be purchased at the leading newsstands in Germany and these presented objective news. But in recent years their sale in the Reich had been either prohibited or limited to a few copies. For Germans who could read English or French, there were occasionally a few copies of the London and Paris journals available, though not enough to reach more than a handful of persons.

"How completely isolated a world the German people live in," I noted in my diary on August 10, 1939. "A glance at the newspapers yesterday and today reminds you of it." I had returned to Germany from a brief leave in Washington, New York and Paris, and coming up in the train from my home in Switzerland two days before I had bought a batch of Berlin and Rhineland newspapers. They quickly propelled one back to the cockeyed world of Nazism, which was as unlike the world I had just left as if it had been on another planet. I noted further on August 10, after I had arrived in Berlin:

Whereas all the rest of the world considers that the peace is about to be broken by Germany, that it is Germany that is threatening to attack Poland . . . here in Germany, in the world the local newspapers create, the very reverse is maintained . . . What the Nazi papers are proclaiming is this: that it is Poland which is disturbing the peace of Europe; Poland which is threatening Germany with armed invasion . . .

"POLAND, LOOK OUT!" warns the *B.Z.* headline, adding: "ANSWER TO POLAND, THE RUNNER-AMOK [AMOKLÄUFFER] AGAINST PEACE AND RIGHT IN EUROPE!"

Or the headline in *Der Fuehrer,* daily paper of Karlsruhe, which I bought on the train: "WARSAW THREATENS BOMBARDMENT OF DANZIG—UNBELIEVABLE AGITATION OF THE POLISH ARCHMADNESS [POLNISCHEN GROESSENWAHSN]!"

You ask: But the German people can't possibly believe these lies? Then you talk to them. So many do.

By Saturday, August 26, the date originally set by Hitler for the attack on Poland, Goebbels' press campaign had reached its climax. I noted in my diary some of the headlines.

The *B.Z.:* "COMPLETE CHAOS IN POLAND—GERMAN FAMILIES FLEE—POLISH SOLDIERS PUSH TO EDGE OF GERMAN BORDER!" The *12-Uhr Blatt:* "THIS PLAYING WITH FIRE GOING TOO FAR—THREE GERMAN PASSENGER PLANES SHOT AT BY POLES—IN CORRIDOR MANY GERMAN FARMHOUSES IN FLAMES!"

On my way to Broadcast House at midnight I picked up the Sunday edition (August 27) of the *Voelkischer Beobachter.* Across the whole top of the front page were inch-high headlines:

WHOLE OF POLAND IN WAR FEVER! 1,500,000 MEN MOBILIZED! UNINTERRUPTED TROOP TRANSPORT TOWARD THE FRONTIER! CHAOS IN UPPER SILESIA!

There was no mention, of course, of any German mobilization, though, as we have seen, Germany had been mobilized for a fortnight.

THE LAST SIX DAYS OF PEACE

After recovering from the cold douche of Mussolini's letter which had arrived early in the evening of August 25 and which, along with the news of the signing of the Anglo–Polish alliance, had caused him to postpone the attack on Poland scheduled for the next day, Hitler got off a curt note to the Duce asking him "what implements of war and raw materials you require and within what time" in order that Italy could "enter a major European conflict." The letter was telephoned by Ribbentrop personally to the German ambassador in Rome at 7:40 P.M. and handed to the Italian dictator at 9:30 P.M.[25]

The next morning, in Rome, Mussolini had a meeting with the chiefs of the Italian armed services to draw up a list of his minimum requirements for a war lasting twelve months. In the words of Ciano, who helped draw it up, it was "enough to kill a bull—if a bull could read it."[26] It included seven million tons of petroleum, six million tons of coal, two million tons of steel, one million tons of timber and a long list of other items down to 600 tons of molybdenum, 400 tons of titanium, and twenty tons of zirconium. In addition Mussolini demanded 150 antiaircraft batteries to protect the Italian industrial area in the north, which was but a few minutes' flying time from French air bases, a circumstance which he reminded Hitler of in a letter which he now composed. This message was telephoned by Ciano to Attolico in Berlin shortly after noon on August 26 and immediately delivered to Hitler.[27]

It contained more than a swollen list of materials needed. By now the deflated Fascist leader was obviously determined to wriggle out of his obligations to the Third Reich, and the Fuehrer, after reading this second letter, could no longer have the slightest doubt of it.

FUEHRER [Mussolini wrote his comrade], I would not have sent you this list, or else it would have contained a smaller number of items and much lower figures, if I had had the time agreed upon beforehand to accumulate stocks and to speed up the tempo of autarchy.

It is my duty to tell you that unless I am certain of receiving these supplies, the sacrifices I should call on the Italian people to make . . . could well be in vain and could compromise your cause along with my own.

On his own hook, Ambassador Attolico, who was opposed to war, and especially to Italy's joining Germany in it if it came, emphasized to Hitler, when he delivered the message, "that all material must be in Italy *before* the beginning of hostilities" and that this demand was "decisive."*

Mussolini was still hoping for another Munich. He added a paragraph to his note, declaring that if the Fuehrer thought there was still "any possibility whatsoever of a solution in the political field" he was ready, as before, to give his German colleague his full support. Despite their close personal relations and their Pact of Steel and all the noisy demonstrations of solidarity they had given in the past years, the fact remains that even at this eleventh hour Hitler had not confided to Mussolini his true aim, the destruction of Poland, and that the Italian partner remained quite ignorant of it. Only at the end of this day, the twenty-sixth, was this gulf between them finally bridged.

---

* This caused added resentment in Berlin and some confusion in Rome which Ciano had to straighten out. Attolico told Ciano later he had deliberately insisted on complete deliveries *before* hostilities "in order to discourage the Germans from meeting our requests." To deliver thirteen million tons of supplies in a few days was, of course, utterly impossible, and Mussolini apologized to Ambassador von Mackensen for the "misunderstanding," remarking that "even the Almighty Himself could not transport such quantities here in a few days. It had never occurred to him to make such an absurd request."[28]

Within three hours on August 26, Hitler sent a long reply to the Duce's message. Ribbentrop again telephoned it, at 3:08 P.M., to Ambassador von Mackensen in Rome, who rushed it to Mussolini shortly after 5 P.M. While some of Italy's requirements such as coal and steel, Hitler said, could be met in full, many others could not. In any case, Attolico's insistence that the materials must be supplied before the outbreak of hostilities was "impossible."

And now, finally, Hitler took his friend and ally into his confidence as to his real and immediate aims.

As neither France nor Britain can achieve any decisive successes in the West, and as Germany, as a result of the Agreement with Russia, will have all her forces free in the East after the defeat of Poland . . . I do not shrink from solving the Eastern question even at the risk of complications in the West.

Duce, I understand your position, and would only ask you to try to achieve the pinning down of Anglo–French forces by active propaganda and suitable military demonstrations such as you have already proposed to me.[29]

This is the first evidence in the German documents that, twenty-four hours after he had canceled the onslaught on Poland, Hitler had recovered his confidence and was going ahead with his plans, "even at the risk" of war with the West.

The same evening, August 26, Mussolini made somewhat of an effort to still dissuade him. He wrote again to the Fuehrer, Ciano again telephoned it to Attolico and it reached the Reich Chancellery just before 7 P.M.

FUEHRER:

I believe that the misunderstanding into which Attolico involuntarily fell was cleared up immediately . . . That which I asked of you, except for the antiaircraft batteries, was to be delivered in the course of twelve months. But even though the misunderstanding has been cleared up, it is evident that it is impossible for you to assist me materially in filling the large gaps which the wars in Ethiopia and Spain have made in Italian armaments.

I will therefore adopt the attitude which you advise, at least during the initial phase of the conflict, thereby immobilizing the maximum Franco–British forces, as is already happening, while I shall speed up military preparations to the utmost possible extent.

But the anguished Duce—anguished at cutting such a sorry figure at such a crucial moment—still thought that the possibilities of another Munich should be looked into.

. . . I venture to insist anew [he continued] and not at all from considerations of a pacifist character foreign to my nature, but by reason of the interests of our two peoples and our two regimes, on the opportunity for a political solution which I regard as still possible and such a one as will give full moral and material satisfaction to Germany.[30]

The Italian dictator was, as the records now make clear, striving for peace because he was not ready for war. But his role greatly disturbed him. "I leave you to imagine," he declared to Hitler in this last of the exchange of messages on August 26, "my state of mind in finding myself compelled by forces beyond my control not to afford you real solidarity at the moment of action." Ciano noted in his diary after this busy day that "the Duce is really out of his wits. His military instinct and his sense of honor were leading him to war. Reason has now stopped him. But this hurts him very much . . . Now he has had to confront the hard truth. And this, for the Duce, is a great blow."

After such a plentiful exchange of letters, Hitler was now resigned to Mussolini's leaving him in the lurch. Late on the night of August 26 he got off one more note to his Axis partner. It was dispatched by telegram from Berlin at 12:10 A.M. on August 27 and reached Mussolini that morning at 9 o'clock.

DUCE:

I have received your communication on your final attitude. I respect the reasons and motives which led you to take this decision. In certain circumstances it can nevertheless work out well.

In my opinion, however, the prerequisite is that, at least until the outbreak of the struggle, the world should have no idea of the attitude Italy intends to adopt. I therefore cordially request you to support my struggle psychologically with your press or by other means. I would also ask you, Duce, if you possibly can, by demonstrative military measures, at least to compel Britain and France to tie down certain of their forces, or at all events to leave them in uncertainty.

But, Duce, the most important thing is this: If, as I have said, it should come to a major war, the issue in the East will be decided before the two Western Powers can score a success. Then, this winter, at latest in the spring, I shall attack in the West with forces which will be at least equal to those of France and Britain . . .

I must now ask a great favor of you, Duce. In this difficult struggle you and your people can best help me by sending me Italian workers, for both industrial and agricultural purposes . . . In specially commending this request of mine to your generosity, I thank you for all the efforts you have made for our common cause.

ADOLF HITLER[31]

The Duce replied meekly late in the afternoon that the world would "not know before the outbreak of hostilities what the attitude of Italy is"— he would keep the secret well. He would also tie down as many Anglo-

French military and naval forces as possible and he would send Hitler the Italian workers he requested.[32] Earlier in the day he had repeated to Ambassador von Mackensen "in forceful terms," as the latter reported to Berlin, "that he still believed it possible to attain all our objectives without resort to war" and had added that he would again bring this aspect up in his letter to the Fuehrer.[33] But he did not. For the moment he seemed too discouraged to even mention it again.

Although France would provide almost the entire Allied army on Germany's western border if war were suddenly to come, and although, in the initial weeks, it would far outnumber the German forces there, Hitler seemed unconcerned as August began to run out about what the French would do. On August 26, Premier Daladier dispatched to him a moving and eloquent letter reminding him of what France would do; it would fight if Poland were attacked.

Unless you attribute to the French people [Daladier wrote] a conception of national honor less high than that which I myself recognize in the German people, you cannot doubt that France will be true to her solemn promises to other nations, such as Poland . . .

After appealing to Hitler to seek a pacific solution of his dispute with Poland, Daladier added:

If the blood of France and of Germany flows again, as it did twenty-five years ago, in a longer and even more murderous war, each of the two peoples will fight with confidence in its own victory, but the most certain victors will be the forces of destruction and barbarism.[34]

Ambassador Coulondre, in presenting the Premier's letter, added a passionate verbal and personal appeal of his own, adjuring Hitler "in the name of humanity and for the repose of his own conscience not to let pass this last chance of a peaceful solution." But the ambassador had the "sadness" to report to Paris that Daladier's letter had not moved the Fuehrer—"he stands pat."

Hitler's reply to the French Premier the next day was cleverly calculated to play on the reluctance of Frenchmen to "die for Danzig," though he did not use the phrase—that was left for the French appeasers. Germany had renounced all territorial claims on France after the return of the Saar, Hitler declared; there was therefore no reason why they should go to war. If they did, it was not his fault and it would be "very painful" to him.

That was the extent of the diplomatic contact between Germany and France during the last week of peace. Coulondre did not see Hitler after the meeting on August 26 until all was over. The country that concerned the German Chancellor the most at this juncture was Great Britain. As Hitler had told Goering on the evening of August 25, when he postponed the move into Poland, he wanted to see whether he could "eliminate British intervention."

GERMANY AND GREAT BRITAIN AT THE ELEVENTH HOUR

"Fuehrer considerably shaken," General Halder had noted in his diary on August 25 after the news from Rome and London had induced Hitler to draw back from the precipice of war. But the next afternoon the General Staff Chief noticed an abrupt change in the Leader. "Fuehrer very calm and clear," he jotted down in his diary at 3:22 P.M. There was a reason for this and the General's journal gives it. "Get everything ready for morning of 7th Mobilization Day. Attack starts September 1." The order was telephoned by Hitler to the Army High Command.

Hitler, then, would have his war with Poland. That was settled. In the meantime he would do everything he could to keep the British out. Halder's diary notes convey the thinking of the Fuehrer and his entourage during the decisive day of August 26.

Rumor has it that England is disposed to consider comprehensive proposal.* Details when Henderson returns. According to another rumor England stresses that she herself must declare that Poland's vital interests are threatened. In France more and more representations to the government against war . . .

Plan: We demand Danzig, corridor through Corridor, and plebiscite on the same basis as Saar. England will perhaps accept. Poland probably not. *Wedge between them.*[35]

The emphasis is Halder's and there is no doubt that it accurately reflects up to a point what was in Hitler's mind. He would contrive to drive a *wedge* between Poland and Britain and give Chamberlain an excuse to get out of his pledge to Warsaw. Having ordered the Army to be ready to march on September 1, he waited to hear from London about his grandiose offer to "guarantee" the British Empire.

He now had two contacts with the British government outside of the German Embassy in London, whose ambassador (Dirksen) was on leave, and which played no part in the frenzied eleventh-hour negotiations. One contact was official, through Ambassador Henderson, who had flown to London in a special German plane on the morning of Saturday, August 26, with the Fuehrer's proposals. The other was unofficial, surreptitious and, as it turned out, quite amateurish, through Goering's Swedish friend, the peripatetic Birger Dahlerus, who had flown to London from Berlin

---

* *I.e.,* Hitler's offer of August 25 to "guarantee" the British Empire.

with a message for the British government from the Luftwaffe chief on the previous day.

"At this time," Goering related later during an interrogation at Nuremberg, "I was in touch with Halifax by a special courier outside the regular diplomatic channels."*[36] It was to the British Foreign Secretary in London that the Swedish "courier" made his way at 6:30 P.M. on Friday, August 25. Dahlerus had been summoned to Berlin from Stockholm the day before by Goering, who informed him that despite the Nazi–Soviet Pact, which had been signed the preceding night, Germany wanted an "understanding" with Great Britain. He put one of his own planes at the Swede's disposal so that he could rush to London to apprise Lord Halifax of this remarkable fact.

The Foreign Secretary, who an hour before had signed the Anglo–Polish mutual-assistance pact, thanked Dahlerus for his efforts and informed him that Henderson had just conferred with Hitler in Berlin and was flying to London with the Fuehrer's latest proposals and that since official channels of communication between Berlin and London had now been reopened he did not think the services of the Swedish intermediary would be needed any longer. But they soon proved to be. Telephoning Goering later that evening to report on his conference with Halifax, Dahlerus was informed by the Field Marshal that the situation had deteriorated as the result of the signing of the Anglo–Polish treaty and that probably only a conference between representatives of Britain and Germany could save the peace. As he later testified at Nuremberg, Goering, like Mussolini, had in mind another Munich.

Late the same night the indefatigable Swede informed the British Foreign Office of his talk with Goering, and the next morning he was invited to confer again with Halifax. This time he persuaded the British Foreign Secretary to write a letter to Goering, whom he described as the one German who might prevent war. Couched in general terms, the letter was brief and noncommittal. It merely reiterated Britain's desire to reach a peaceful settlement and stressed the need "to have a few days" to achieve it.†

---

* "Ribbentrop knew nothing whatsoever about Dahlerus being sent," Goering testified on the stand at Nuremberg. "I never discussed the matter of Dahlerus with Ribbentrop. He did not know at all that Dahlerus went back and forth between me and the British government."[37] But Goering kept Hitler informed.

† The text is published in *Documents on British Foreign Policy*, Third Series, Vol. VII, p. 283. It was omitted from all published British records until the above volume came out in 1954, an omission much commented upon by British historians. Dahlerus is not mentioned in the *British Blue Book* of documents concerning the outbreak of the war nor in Henderson's *Final Report* nor even in Henderson's book *Failure of a Mission*, though in the book the Swedish intermediary is referred to as "a source in touch with Goering." In Henderson's dispatches and in those from other members of the British Embassy which have now been published, Dahlerus and his activities play a fairly prominent part, as they do in various memoranda of the British Foreign Office.

The role of this singular Swedish businessman in trying to save the peace was a well-kept secret and both the Wilhelmstrasse and Downing Street went to con-

Nevertheless it struck the fat Field Marshal as being of the "greatest importance." Dahlerus had delivered it to him that evening (August 26), as he was traveling in his special train to his Luftwaffe headquarters at Oranienburg outside Berlin. The train was stopped at the next station, an automobile was commandeered and the two men raced to the Chancellery, where they arrived at midnight. The Chancellery was dark. Hitler had gone to bed. But Goering insisted on arousing him. Up to this moment Dahlerus, like so many others, believed that Hitler was not an unreasonable man and that he might accept a peaceful settlement, as he had the year before at Munich. The Swede was now to confront for the first time the weird fantasies and the terrible temper of the charismatic dictator.[38] It was a shattering experience.

Hitler took no notice of the letter which Dahlerus had brought from Halifax and which had seemed important enough to Goering to have the Fuehrer waked up in the middle of the night. Instead, for twenty minutes he lectured the Swede on his early struggles, his great achievements and all his attempts to come to an understanding with the British. Next, when Dahlerus had got in a word about his having once lived in England as a worker, the Chancellor questioned him about the strange island and its strange people whom he had tried so vainly to understand. There followed a long and somewhat technical lecture on Germany's military might. By this time, Dahlerus says, he thought his visit "would not prove useful." In the end, however, the Swede seized an opportunity to tell his host something about the British as he had come to know them.

Hitler listened without interrupting me . . . but then suddenly got up, and, becoming very excited and nervous, walked up and down saying, as though to himself, that Germany was irresistible . . . Suddenly he stopped in the middle of the room and stood there staring. His voice was blurred, and his behavior that of a completely abnormal person. He spoke in staccato phrases: "If there should be war, then I shall build U-boats, build U-boats, U-boats, U-boats, U-boats." His voice became more indistinct and finally one could not follow him at all. Then he pulled himself together, raised his voice as though addressing a large audience and shrieked: "I shall build airplanes, build airplanes, airplanes, airplanes, and I shall annihilate my enemies." He seemed more like a phantom from a storybook than a real person. I stared at him in amazement and turned to see how Goering was reacting, but he did not turn a hair.

---

siderable lengths to keep his movements hidden from the correspondents and neutral diplomats, who, to the best of my knowledge, knew absolutely nothing of them until Dahlerus testified at Nuremberg on March 19, 1946. His book, *The Last Attempt*, was published in Swedish in 1945, at the end of the war, but the English edition did not come out until 1948 and there remained a further interval of six years before his role was officially confirmed, so to speak, by the documents in Vol. VII of the *DBrFP* series. The German Foreign Office documents for August do not mention Dahlerus, except in one routine memorandum reporting receipt of a message from the Lufthansa airline that "Dahlerus, a gentleman from the 'Foreign Office,'" was arriving in Berlin August 26 on one of its planes. He does appear, however, in some later papers.

Finally the excited Chancellor strode up to his guest and said, "Herr Dahlerus, you who know England so well, can you give me any reason for my perpetual failure to come to an agreement with her?" Dahlerus confesses that he "hesitated at first" to answer but then replied that in his personal opinion the British "lack of confidence in him and in his Government was the reason."

"Idiots!" Dahlerus says Hitler stormed back, flinging out his right arm and striking his breast with his left hand. "Have I ever told a lie in my life?"

The Nazi dictator thereupon calmed down, there was a discussion of Hitler's proposals made through Henderson and it was finally settled that Dahlerus should fly back to London with a further offer to the British government. Goering objected to committing it to writing and the accommodating Swede was told he must, instead, commit it to memory. It contained six points:

1. Germany wanted a pact or alliance with Britain.
2. Britain was to help Germany obtain Danzig and the Corridor, but Poland was to have a free harbor in Danzig, to retain the Baltic port of Gdynia and a corridor to it.
3. Germany would guarantee the new Polish frontiers.
4. Germany was to have her colonies, or their equivalent, returned to her.
5. Guarantees were to be given for the German minority in Poland.
6. Germany was to pledge herself to defend the British Empire.

With these proposals imprinted in his memory, Dahlerus flew to London on the morning of Sunday, August 27, and shortly after noon was whisked by a roundabout route so as to avoid the snooping press reporters and ushered into the presence of Chamberlain, Lord Halifax, Sir Horace Wilson and Sir Alexander Cadogan. It was obvious that the British government now took the Swedish courier quite seriously.

He had brought with him some hastily scribbled notes jotted down in the plane describing his meeting with Hitler and Goering the night before. In these notes he assured the two leading members of the British cabinet who now scanned his memorandum that during the interview Hitler had been "calm and composed." Although no record of this extraordinary Sabbath meeting has been found in the Foreign Office archives, it has been reconstructed in the volume of Foreign Office papers (Volume VII, Third Series) from data furnished by Lord Halifax and Cadogan and from the emissary's memorandum. The British version differs somewhat from that given by Dahlerus in his book and at Nuremberg, but taking the various accounts together what follows seems as accurate a report as we shall ever get.

Chamberlain and Halifax saw at once that they were faced with two sets of proposals from Hitler, the one given to Henderson and the other now brought by Dahlerus, and that they differed. Whereas the first had proposed to guarantee the British Empire after Hitler had settled accounts with Poland, the second seemed to suggest that the Fuehrer was ready to negotiate through the British for the return of Danzig and the Corridor, after which he would "guarantee" Poland's new boundaries. This was an old refrain to Chamberlain, after his disillusioning experiences with Hitler over Czechoslovakia, and he was skeptical of the Fuehrer's offer as Dahlerus outlined it. He told the Swede that he saw "no prospect of a settlement on these terms; the Poles might concede Danzig, but they would fight rather than surrender the Corridor."

Finally it was agreed that Dahlerus should return to Berlin immediately with an initial and unofficial reply to Hitler and report back to London on Hitler's reception of it before the official response was drawn up and sent to Berlin with Henderson the next evening. As Halifax put it (according to the British version), "the issues might be somewhat confused as a result of these informal and secret communications through M. Dahlerus. It was [therefore] desirable to make it clear that when Dahlerus returned to Berlin that night he went, not to carry the answer of His Majesty's Government, but rather to prepare the way for the main communication" which Henderson would bring.[39]

So important had this unknown Swedish businessman become as an intermediary in the negotiations between the governments of the two most powerful nations in Europe that, according to his own account, he told the Prime Minister and the Foreign Secretary at this critical juncture that "they should keep Henderson in London until Monday [the next day] so that the answer could be given after they had been informed how Hitler regarded the English standpoint."[40]

And what was the English standpoint, as Dahlerus was to present it to Hitler? There is some confusion about it. According to Halifax's own rough notes of his verbal instructions to Dahlerus, the British standpoint was merely this:

i. Solemn assurance of desire for good understanding between G. and Gt.B. [The initials are Halifax's.] Not a single member of the Govt. who thinks different. *ii.* Gt.B. bound to honor her obligations to Poland. *iii.* German–Polish differences must be settled peacefully.[41]

According to Dahlerus, the unofficial British reply entrusted to him was more comprehensive.

Naturally, Point 6, the offer to defend the British Empire, was rejected. Similarly they did not want to have any discussion on colonies as long as Germany was mobilized. With regard to the Polish boundaries, they wanted them to be guaranteed by the five great powers. Concerning the Corridor, they proposed that negotiations with Poland be undertaken immediately. As to the first point [of Hitler's proposals] England was willing in principle to come to an agreement with Germany.[42]

Dahlerus flew back to Berlin Sunday evening and saw Goering shortly before midnight. The Field Marshal did not consider the British reply "very favorable." But after seeing Hitler at midnight, Goering rang up Dahlerus at his hotel at 1 A.M. and said that the Chancellor would "accept the English standpoint" provided the official version to be brought by Henderson Monday evening was in agreement with it.

Goering was pleased, and Dahlerus even more so. The Swede woke up Sir George Ogilvie Forbes, the counselor of the British Embassy, at 2 A.M. to give him the glad tidings. Not only to do that but—such had his position become, at least in his own mind—to advise the British government what to say in its official reply. That note, which Henderson would be bringing later on this Monday, August 28, must contain an undertaking, Dahlerus emphasized, that Britain would persuade Poland to negotiate with Germany directly and immediately.

Dahlerus has just telephoned [read a later dispatch from Forbes on August 28] from Goering's office following suggestions which he considers most important.

1. British reply to Hitler should not contain any reference to Roosevelt plan.*

2. Hitler suspects Poles will try to avoid negotiations. Reply should therefore contain clear statement that the Poles have been strongly advised to immediately establish contact with Germany and negotiate.†[43]

Throughout the day the now confident Swede not only heaped advice on Forbes, who dutifully wired it to London, but himself telephoned the British Foreign Office with a message for Halifax containing further suggestions.

At this critical moment in world history the amateur Swedish diplomat had indeed become the pivotal point between Berlin and London. At 2 P.M. on August 28, Halifax, who had been apprised both from his Berlin embassy and from Dahlerus' telephone call to the Foreign Office of the Swede's urgent advice, wired the British ambassador in Warsaw, Sir Howard Kennard, to see Foreign Minister Beck "at once" and get him to authorize the British government to inform Hitler "that Poland is ready to enter at once into direct discussion with Germany." The Foreign Secretary was in a hurry. He wanted to include the authorization in the official reply to Hitler which Henderson was waiting to carry back to

---

* Presumably President Roosevelt's message to Hitler on August 24 and 25 urging direct negotiations between Germany and Poland.

† Dahlerus, it must be pointed out in all fairness, was not so pro-German as some of his messages seem to imply. On the night of this same Monday, after two hours with Goering at Luftwaffe headquarters at Oranienburg, he rang up Forbes to tell him, "German Army will be in final position of attack on Poland during night of Wednesday–Thursday, August 30–31." Forbes got this intelligence off to London as quickly as possible.

Berlin this same day. He urged his ambassador in Warsaw to telephone Beck's reply. Late in the afternoon Beck gave the requested authorization and it was hastily inserted in the British note.[44]

Henderson arrived back in Berlin with it on the evening of August 28, and after being received at the Chancellery by an S.S. guard of honor, which presented arms and rolled its drums (the formal diplomatic pretensions were preserved to the end), he was ushered into the presence of Hitler, to whom he handed a German translation of the note, at 10:30 P.M. The Chancellor read it at once.

The British government "entirely agreed" with him, the communication said, that there must "first" be a settlement of the differences between Germany and Poland. "Everything, however," it added, "turns upon the nature of the settlement and the method by which it is to be reached." On this matter, the note said, the Chancellor had been "silent." Hitler's offer to "guarantee" the British Empire was gently declined. The British government "could not, for any advantage offered to Great Britain, acquiesce in a settlement which put in jeopardy the independence of a State to whom they had given their guarantee."

That guarantee would be honored, but because the British government was "scrupulous" concerning its obligations to Poland the Chancellor must not think it was not anxious for an equitable settlement.

It follows that the next step should be the initiation of direct discussions between the German and Polish Governments on a basis . . . of safeguarding Poland's essential interests and the securing of the settlement by an international guarantee.

They [the British government] have already received a definite assurance from the Polish Government that they are prepared to enter into discussions on this basis, and H. M. Government hope the German Government would also be willing to agree to this course.

. . . A just settlement . . . between Germany and Poland may open the way to world peace. Failure to reach it would ruin the hopes of an understanding between Germany and Great Britain, would bring the two countries into conflict and might well plunge the whole world into war. Such an outcome would be a calamity without parallel in history.[45]

When Hitler had finished reading the communication, Henderson began to elaborate on it from notes, he told the Fuehrer, which he had made during his conversations with Chamberlain and Halifax. It was the only meeting with Hitler, he said later, in which he, the ambassador, did most of the talking. The gist of his remarks was that Britain wanted Germany's friendship, it wanted peace, but it would fight if Hitler attacked Poland. The Fuehrer, who was by no means silent, replied by expatiating on the crimes of Poland and on his own "generous" offers for a peaceful settlement with her, which would not be repeated. In fact today "nothing less than the return of Danzig and the whole of the Corridor would satisfy him, together with a rectification in Silesia, where ninety per cent of the population voted for Germany at the postwar plebiscite." This was not true nor was Hitler's rejoinder a moment later that a million Germans had been driven out of the Corridor after 1918. There had been only 385,000 Germans there, according to the German census of 1910, but by this time, of course, the Nazi dictator expected everyone to swallow his lies. For the last time in his crumbling mission to Berlin, the British ambassador swallowed a good deal, for, as he declared in his *Final Report,* "Herr Hitler on this occasion was again friendly and reasonable and appeared to be not dissatisfied with the answer which I had brought to him."

"In the end I asked him two straight questions," Henderson wired London at 2:35 A.M. in a long dispatch describing the interview.[46]

Was he willing to negotiate direct with the Poles, and was he ready to discuss the question of an exchange of populations? He replied in the affirmative as regards the latter (though I have no doubt that he was thinking at the same time of a rectification of frontiers).

As to the first point, he would first have to give "careful consideration" to the whole British note. At this point, Henderson recounted in his dispatch, the Chancellor turned to Ribbentrop and said, "We must summon Goering to discuss it with him." Hitler promised a written reply to the British communication on the next day, Tuesday, August 29.

"Conversation was conducted," Henderson emphasized to Halifax, "in quite a friendly atmosphere in spite of absolute firmness on both sides." Probably Henderson, despite all of his personal experience with his host, did not quite appreciate why Hitler had made the atmosphere so friendly. The Fuehrer was still resolved to go to war that very weekend against Poland; he was still hopeful, despite all the British government and Henderson had said, of keeping Britain out of it.

Apparently, Hitler, encouraged by the obsequious and ignorant Ribbentrop, simply could not believe that the British meant what they said, though he said he did.

The next day Henderson added a postscript to his long dispatch.

Hitler insisted that he was not bluffing, and that people would make a big mistake if they believed that he was. I replied that I was fully aware of the fact and that we were not bluffing either. Herr Hitler stated that he fully realized that.[47]

He said so, but did he realize it? For in his reply on August 29 he deliberately tried to trick the British government in a way which he must have thought would enable him to eat his cake and have it too.

The British reply and Hitler's first reaction to it generated a burst of optimism in Berlin, especially in Goering's camp, where the inimitable Dahlerus now spent most of his time. At 1:30 in the morning of August 29 the Swede received a telephone call from one of the Field Marshal's adjutants, who was calling from the Chancellery, where Hitler, Ribbentrop and Goering had pondered the British note after Henderson's departure. The word to Dahlerus from his German friend was that the British reply "was highly satisfactory and that there was every hope that the threat of war was past."

Dahlerus conveyed the good news by long-distance telephone to the British Foreign Office later that morning, informing Halifax that "Hitler and Goering considered that there was now a definite possibility of a peaceful settlement." At 10:50 A.M. Dahlerus saw Goering, who greeted him effusively, pumped his hand warmly and exclaimed, "There will be peace! Peace is secured!" Fortified with such happy assurances, the Swedish courier made immediately for the British Embassy to let Henderson, whom he had not yet personally met, in on the glad tidings. According to the ambassador's dispatch describing this encounter, Dahlerus reported that the Germans were highly optimistic. They "agreed" with the "main point" of the British reply. Hitler, Dahlerus said, was asking "only" for Danzig and the Corridor—not the whole Corridor but just a small one along the railroad tracks to Danzig. In fact, Dahlerus reported, the Fuehrer was prepared to be "most reasonable. He would go a long way to meet the Poles."[48]

Sir Nevile Henderson, on whom some light was finally dawning, was not so sure. He told his visitor, according to the latter, that one could not believe a word that Hitler said and the same went for Dahlerus' friend, Hermann Goering, who had lied to the ambassador "heaps of times." Hitler, in the opinion of Henderson, was playing a dishonest and ruthless game.

But the Swede, now at the very center of affairs, could not be persuaded —his awakening was to come even after Henderson's. Just to make sure that the ambassador's inexplicable pessimism did not jeopardize his own efforts, he again telephoned the British Foreign Office at 7:10 P.M. to leave a message for Halifax that there would be "no difficulties in the German reply." But, advised the Swede, the British government should tell the Poles "to behave properly."[49]

Five minutes later, at 7:15 o'clock on the evening of August 29, Henderson arrived at the Chancellery to receive from the Fuehrer Germany's actual reply. It soon became evident how hollow had been the optimism of Goering and his Swedish friend. The meeting, as the ambassador advised Halifax immediately afterward, "was of a stormy character and Herr Hitler was far less reasonable than yesterday."

The formal, written German note itself reiterated the Reich's desire for friendship with Great Britain but emphasized that "it could not be bought at the price of a renunciation of vital German interests." After a long and familiar rehearsal of Polish misdeeds, provocations and "barbaric actions of maltreatment which cry to heaven," the note presented Hitler's demands officially and in writing for the first time: return of Danzig and the Corridor, and the safeguarding of Germans in Poland. To eliminate "present conditions," it added, "there no longer remain days, still less weeks, but perhaps only hours."

Germany, the communication continued, could no longer share the British view that a solution could be reached by direct negotiations with Poland. However, "solely" to please the British government and in the interests of Anglo–German friendship, Germany was ready "to accept the British proposal and enter into direct negotiations" with Poland. "In the event of a territorial rearrangement in Poland," the German government could not give guarantees without the agreement of the Soviet Union. (The British government, of course, did not know of the secret protocol of the Nazi–Soviet Pact dividing up Poland.) "For the rest, in making these proposals," the note declared, "the German Government never had any intention of touching Poland's vital interests or questioning the existence of an independent Polish State."

And then, at the very end, came the trap.

The German Government accordingly agree to accept the British Government's offer of their good offices in securing the dispatch to Berlin of a Polish emissary with full powers. They count on the arrival of this emissary on Wednesday, August 30, 1939.

The German Government will immediately draw up proposals for a solution acceptable to themselves and will, if possible, place these at the disposal of the British Government before the arrival of the Polish negotiator.[50]

Henderson read through the note while Hitler and Ribbentrop watched him and said nothing until he came to the passage saying that the Germans expected the arrival of a Polish emissary with full powers on the following day.

"That sounds like an ultimatum," he commented, but Hitler and Ribbentrop strenuously denied it. They merely wished to stress, they said, "the urgency of the moment when two fully mobilized armies were standing face to face."

The ambassador, no doubt mindful of the reception accorded by Hitler to Schuschnigg and Hácha, says he asked whether if a Polish plenipotentiary did come he would be "well received" and the discussions "conducted on a footing of complete equality."

"Of course," Hitler answered.

There followed an acrimonious discussion provoked at one point by Hitler's "gratuitous" remark, as Henderson put it, that the ambassador did not "care a row of pins" how many Germans were being slaughtered in Poland. To this Henderson says he made a "heated retort."*

"I left the Reich Chancellery that evening filled with the gloomiest forebodings," Henderson recounted later in his memoirs, though he does

---

* "I proceeded to outshout Hitler," Henderson wired Halifax the next day. ". . . I added a good deal more shouting at the top of my voice."[51] This temperamental display was not mentioned in earlier British documents.

not seem to have mentioned this in his dispatches which he got off to London that night. "My soldiers," Hitler had told him, "are asking me, 'Yes or no?' " They had already lost a week and they could not afford to lose another "lest the rainy season in Poland be added to their enemies."

Nevertheless it is evident from the ambassador's official reports and from his book that he did not quite comprehend the nature of Hitler's trap until the next day, when another trap was sprung and the Fuehrer's trickery became clear. The dictator's game seems quite obvious from the text of his formal note. He demanded on the evening of August 29 that an emissary with full powers to negotiate show up in Berlin the next day. There can be no doubt that he had in mind inflicting on him the treatment he had accorded the Austrian Chancellor and the Czechoslovak President under what he thought were similar circumstances. If the Poles, as he was quite sure, did not rush the emissary to Berlin, or even if they did and the negotiator declined to accept Hitler's terms, then Poland could be blamed for refusing a "peaceful settlement" and Britain and France might be induced not to come to its aid when attacked. Primitive, but simple and clear.*

But on the night of August 29 Henderson did not see it so clearly. While he was still working on his dispatches to London describing his meeting with Hitler he invited the Polish ambassador to come over to the embassy. He filled him in on the German note and his talk with Hitler and, by his own account, "impressed on him the need for immediate action. I implored him, in Poland's own interests, to urge his Government to nominate without any delay someone to represent them in the proposed negotiations."[52]

In the London Foreign Office, heads were cooler. At 2 A.M. on August 29, Halifax, after pondering the German reply and Henderson's account of the meeting with Hitler, wired the ambassador that while careful consideration would be given the German note, it was "of course unreasonable to expect that we can produce a Polish representative in Berlin today, and German Government must not expect this."[53] The diplomats and Foreign Office officials were now laboring frantically around the clock and Henderson conveyed this message to the Wilhelmstrasse at 4:30 A.M.

He conveyed four further messages from London during the day, August 30. One was a personal note from Chamberlain to Hitler advising him that the German reply was being considered "with all urgency" and that it would be answered later in the afternoon. In the meantime the Prime Minister urged the German government, as he said he had the Polish government, to avoid frontier incidents. For the rest, he "welcomed the evidence in the exchanges of views which are taking place of

---

* General Halder put Hitler's game succinctly in a diary entry of August 29: "Fuehrer hopes to drive wedge between British, French and Poles. Strategy: Raise a barrage of demographic and democratic demands . . . The Poles will come to Berlin on August 30. On August 31 the negotiations will blow up. On September 1, start to use force."

the desire for an Anglo–German understanding."[54] The second message
was in similar terms from Halifax. A third from the Foreign Secretary
spoke of reports of German sabotage in Poland and asked the Germans
to refrain from such activities. The fourth message from Halifax, dispatched at 6:50 P.M., reflected a stiffening of both the Foreign Office and
the British ambassador in Berlin.

On further reflection, Henderson had got off a wire to London earlier
in the day:

> While I still recommend that the Polish Government should swallow this
> eleventh-hour effort to establish direct contact with Hitler, even if it be only
> to convince the world that they were prepared to make their own sacrifice for
> preservation of peace, one can only conclude from the German reply that
> Hitler is determined to achieve his ends by so-called peaceful fair means if he
> can, but by force if he cannot.[55]

By this time even Henderson had no more stomach for another Munich.
The Poles had never considered one—for themselves. At 10 A.M. that
morning of August 30, the British ambassador in Warsaw had wired
Halifax that he felt sure "that it would be impossible to induce the Polish
Government to send M. Beck or any other representative immediately to
Berlin to discuss a settlement on the basis proposed by Hitler. They
would sooner fight and perish rather than submit to such humiliation,
especially after the examples of Czechoslovakia, Lithuania and Austria."
He suggested that if negotiations were to be "between equals" they must
take place in some neutral country.[56]

His own stiffening attitude thus reinforced from his ambassadors in
Berlin and Warsaw, Halifax wired Henderson that the British government
could not "advise" the Poles to comply with Hitler's demand that an
emissary with full powers come to Berlin. It was, said the Foreign
Secretary, "wholly unreasonable."

> Could you not suggest [Halifax added] to German Government that they
> adopt the normal procedure, when their proposals are ready, of inviting the
> Polish Ambassador to call and handing proposals to him for transmission to
> Warsaw and inviting suggestions as to conduct of negotiations.[57]

The promised British reply to Hitler's latest note was delivered to
Ribbentrop by Henderson at midnight on August 30–31. There now
ensued a highly dramatic meeting which Dr. Schmidt, the only observer
present, later described as "the stormiest I have ever experienced during
my twenty-three years as interpreter."[58]

"I must tell you," the ambassador wired Halifax immediately afterward, "that Ribbentrop's whole demeanor during an unpleasant interview
was aping Hitler at his worst." And in his *Final Report* three weeks later

Henderson recalled the German Foreign Minister's "intense hostility, which increased in violence as I made each communication in turn. He kept leaping from his chair in a state of great excitement and asking if I had anything more to say. I kept replying that I had." According to Schmidt, Henderson was also aroused from his chair. At one point, says this sole eyewitness, both men leaped from their seats and glared at each other so angrily that the German interpreter thought they were coming to blows.

But what is important for history is not the grotesqueness of this meeting between the German Minister for Foreign Affairs and His Majesty's Ambassador in Berlin at midnight of August 30–31, but a development, during the tempestuous interview, which produced Hitler's final act of trickery and completed, when it was too late, the education of Sir Nevile Henderson insofar as the Third Reich was concerned.

Ribbentrop scarcely glanced at the British reply or listened to Henderson's attempted explanation of it.* When Henderson ventured to ask for the German proposals for a Polish settlement, which had been promised the British in Hitler's last note, Ribbentrop retorted contemptuously that it was now too late since the Polish emissary had not arrived by midnight. However, the Germans had drawn up proposals and Ribbentrop now proceeded to read them.

He read them in German "at top speed, or rather gabbled to me as fast as he could, in a tone of utmost annoyance," Henderson reported.

Of the sixteen articles I was able to gather the gist of six or seven, but it would have been quite impossible to guarantee even the exact accuracy of these without a careful study of the text itself. When he had finished I accordingly asked him to let me see it. Ribbentrop refused categorically, threw the document with a contemptuous gesture on the table and said that it was now out of date since no Polish emissary had arrived by midnight.†

---

* Though couched in conciliatory terms, the British note was firm. His Majesty's Government, it said, "reciprocated" the German desire for improved relations, but "they could not sacrifice the interests of other friends in order to obtain that improvement." They fully understood, it continued, that the German government could not "sacrifice Germany's vital interests, but the Polish Government are in the same position." The British government must make "an express reservation" regarding Hitler's terms and, while urging direct negotiations between Berlin and Warsaw, considered that "it would be impracticable to establish contact so early as today." (Text in *British Blue Book*, pp. 142–43.)

† Ribbentrop, who, it seemed to this writer, cut the sorriest figure of all the chief defendants at the Nuremberg trial—and made the weakest defense—claimed on the stand that Hitler, who, he said, "personally dictated" the sixteen points, had "expressly forbidden me to let these proposals out of my hands." Why, he did not say and was not asked on cross-examination. "Hitler told me," Ribbentrop conceded, "that I might communicate to the British Ambassador only the substance of them, if I thought it advisable. I did a little more than that: I read all the proposals from the beginning to the end."[59] Dr. Schmidt denies that Ribbentrop read the text of the proposals in German so fast that it would have been impossible for Henderson to grasp them. He says the Foreign Minister did not "particularly

It may have been out of date, since the Germans chose to make it so, but what is important is that these German "proposals" were never meant to be taken seriously or indeed to be taken at all. In fact they were a hoax. They were a sham to fool the German people and, if possible, world opinion into believing that Hitler had attempted at the last minute to reach a reasonable settlement of his claims against Poland. The Fuehrer admitted as much. Dr. Schmidt later heard him say, "I needed an alibi, especially with the German people, to show them that I had done every-thing to maintain peace. This explains my generous offer about the settlement of the Danzig and Corridor questions."*

Compared to his demands of recent days, they *were* generous, astonish-ingly so. In them Hitler demanded only that Danzig be returned to Ger-many. The future of the Corridor would be decided by a plebiscite, and then only after a period of twelve months when tempers had calmed down. Poland would keep the port of Gdynia. Whoever received the Corridor in the plebiscite would grant the other party extraterritorial highway and railroad routes through it—this was a reversion to his "offer" of the previous spring. There was to be an exchange of populations and full rights accorded to nationals of one country in the other.

One may speculate that had these proposals been offered seriously they would undoubtedly have formed at least the basis of negotiations between Germany and Poland and might well have spared the world its second great war in a generation. They were broadcast to the German people at 9 P.M. on August 31, eight and one half hours after Hitler had issued the final orders for the attack on Poland, and, so far as I could judge in Berlin, they succeeded in their aim of fooling the German people. They certainly fooled this writer, who was deeply impressed by their reasonable-ness when he heard them over the radio, and who said so in his broadcast to America on that last night of the peace.

Henderson returned to His Majesty's Embassy that night of August 30–31, convinced, as he later said, "that the last hope for peace had vanished." Still, he kept trying. He roused the Polish ambassador out of bed at 2 A.M., invited him to hurry over to the embassy, gave him "an objective and studiously moderate account" of his conversation with Ribbentrop, mentioned the cession of Danzig and the plebiscite in the Corridor as the two main points in the German proposals, stated that so far as he could gather "they were not too unreasonable" and suggested

---

hurry over them." Henderson, Schmidt says, was "not exactly a master of German" and he might have been more effective in these crucial talks had he used his native language. Ribbentrop's English was excellent, but he refused to speak it during these parleys.[60]

* The text of the sixteen proposals was telegraphed to the German chargé d'affaires in London at 9:15 P.M. on August 30, four hours before Ribbentrop "gabbled" them to Henderson. But the German envoy in London was instructed that they were to "be kept strictly secret and not to be communicated to anyone else until further instructions."[61] Hitler in his note of the previous day, it will be remembered, had promised to place them at the disposal of the British government before the arrival of the Polish negotiator.

that Lipski recommend to his government that they should propose at once a meeting between Field Marshals Smigly-Rydz and Goering. "I felt obliged to add," says Henderson, "that I could not conceive of the success of any negotiations if they were conducted by Herr von Ribbentrop."*[62]

In the meantime the tireless Dahlerus had not been inactive. At 10 P.M. on August 29, Goering had summoned him to his home and informed him of the "unsatisfactory course" of the meeting just finished between Hitler, Ribbentrop and Henderson. The corpulent Field Marshal was in one of his hysterical moods and treated his Swedish friend to a violent outburst against the Poles and the British. Then he calmed down, assured his visitor that the Fuehrer was already at work drawing up a "magnanimous" (*"grosszuegig"*) offer to Poland in which the only clear-cut demand would be the return of Danzig and generously leaving the future of the Corridor to be decided by a plebiscite "under international control." Dahlerus mildly inquired about the size of the plebiscite area, whereupon Goering tore a page out of an old atlas and with colored pencils shaded off the "Polish" and "German" parts, including in the latter not only prewar Prussian Poland but the industrial city of Lódz, which was sixty miles east of the 1914 frontier. The Swedish interloper could not help but notice the "rapidity and the recklessness" with which such important decisions were made in the Third Reich. However, he agreed to Goering's request that he fly immediately back to London, emphasize to the British government that Hitler still wanted peace and hint that as proof of it the Fuehrer was already drawing up a most generous offer to Poland.

Dahlerus, who seems to have been incapable of fatigue, flew off to London at 4 A.M. August 30 and, changing cars several times on the drive in from Heston to the city to throw the newspaper reporters off the track (apparently no journalist even knew of his existence), arrived at Downing Street at 10:30 A.M., where he was immediately received by Chamberlain, Halifax, Wilson and Cadogan.

But by now the three British architects of Munich (Cadogan, a permanent Foreign Office official, had always been impervious to Nazi charms) could no longer be taken in by Hitler and Goering, nor were they much impressed by Dahlerus' efforts. The well-meaning Swede found them "highly mistrustful" of both Nazi leaders and "inclined to assume that nothing would now prevent Hitler from declaring war on Poland." Moreover, the British government, it was made plain to the Swedish mediator,

---

* In a dispatch to Halifax filed at 5:15 A.M. (August 31), Henderson reported that he had also advised Lipski "in the very strongest terms" to "ring up" Ribbentrop and ask for the German proposals so that he could communicate them to the Polish government. Lipski said he would first have to talk with Warsaw. "The Polish Ambassador," Henderson added, "promised to telephone at once to his Government, but he is so inert or so handicapped by instructions of his Government that I cannot rely on his action being very effective."[63]

had not fallen for Hitler's trickery in demanding that a Polish plenipotentiary show up in Berlin within twenty-four hours.

But Dahlerus, like Henderson in Berlin, kept on trying. He telephoned
Goering in Berlin, suggested that the Polish–German delegates meet
"outside Germany" and received the summary answer that "Hitler was
in Berlin" and the meeting would have to take place there.

So the Swedish go-between accomplished nothing by this flight. By
midnight he was back in Berlin, where, it must be said, he had another
opportunity to be at least helpful. He reached Goering's headquarters at
half past midnight to find the Luftwaffe chief once more in an expansive
mood. The Fuehrer, said Goering, had just handed Henderson through
Ribbentrop a "democratic, fair and workable offer" to Poland. Dahlerus,
who seems to have been sobered by his meeting in Downing Street, called
up Forbes at the British Embassy to check and learned that Ribbentrop
had "gabbled" the terms so fast that Henderson had not been able to fully
grasp them and that the ambassador had been refused a copy of the text.
Dahlerus says he told Goering that this was no way "to treat the ambassador of an empire like Great Britain" and suggested that the Field
Marshal, who had a copy of the sixteen points, permit him to telephone
the text to the British Embassy. After some hesitation Goering acquiesced.*

In such a way, at the instigation of an unknown Swedish businessman
in connivance with the chief of the Air Force, were Hitler and Ribbentrop
circumvented and the British informed of the German "proposals" to
Poland. Perhaps by this time the Field Marshal, who was by no means
unintelligent or inexperienced in the handling of foreign affairs, saw more
quickly than the Fuehrer and his fawning Foreign Minister certain advantages which might be gained by finally letting the British in on the secret.

To make doubly sure that Henderson got it correctly, Goering dispatched Dahlerus to the British Embassy at 10 A.M. of Thursday, August
31, with a typed copy of the sixteen points. Henderson was still trying to
persuade the Polish ambassador to establish the "desired contact" with
the Germans. At 8 A.M. he had once more urged this on Lipski, this time
over the telephone, warning him that unless Poland acted by noon there
would be war.† Shortly after Dahlerus had arrived with the text of the
German proposals, Henderson dispatched him, along with Forbes, to the

---

* On the stand at Nuremberg Goering claimed that in turning over the text of
Hitler's "offer" to the British Embassy he was taking "an enormous risk, since the
Fuehrer had forbidden this information being made public. Only I," Goering told
the tribunal, "could take that risk."[64]
† Even the levelheaded French ambassador supported his British colleague in this.
Henderson had telephoned him at 9 A.M. to say that if the Poles did not agree by
noon to sending a plenipotentiary to Berlin the German Army would begin its
attack. Coulondre went immediately to the Polish Embassy and urged Lipski to
telephone his government, asking authorization to make immediate contact with
the Germans "as a plenipotentiary." (*French Yellow Book*, French edition, pp.
366–67.)

Polish Embassy. Lipski, who had never heard of Dahlerus, was somewhat confused at meeting the Swede—he was by this time, like most of the key diplomats in Berlin, strained and dead tired—and became irritated when Dahlerus urged him to go immediately to Goering and accept the Fuehrer's offer. Requesting the Swede to dictate the sixteen points to a secretary in an adjoining room, he expressed his annoyance to Forbes for bringing in a "stranger" at this late date on so serious a matter. The harassed Polish ambassador must have been depressed too at the pressure which Henderson was bringing on him and his government to negotiate immediately on the basis of an offer which he had just received quite unofficially and surreptitiously, but which the British envoy, as he had told Lipski the night before, thought was not "on the whole too unreasonable."* He did not know that Henderson's view was not endorsed by Downing Street. What he did know was that he had no intention of taking the advice of an unknown Swede, even though he had been sent to him by the British ambassador, and of going to Goering to accept Hitler's "offer," even if he had been empowered to do so, which he was not.†

---

* By now, that is before noon of August 31, Henderson, striving desperately for peace at almost any price, had convinced himself that the German terms were quite reasonable and even moderate. And though Ribbentrop had told him the previous midnight that the German proposals were "out of date, since no Polish emissary had arrived," and though the Polish government had not yet even seen them, and though they were, in sum, a hoax, Henderson kept urging Halifax all day to put pressure on the Poles to send a plenipotentiary, as Hitler had demanded, and kept stressing the reasonableness of the Fuehrer's sixteen points.

At 12:30 P.M. (on August 31) Henderson wired Halifax "urging" him to "insist" to Poland that Lipski ask the German government for the German proposals for urgent communication to his government "with a view to dispatching a plenipotentiary. The terms sound moderate to me," Henderson contended. "This is no Munich . . . Poland will never get such good terms again . . ."

At the same time Henderson wrote a long letter to Halifax: ". . . The German proposals do not endanger the independence of Poland . . . She is likely to get a worse deal later . . ."

Still keeping at it, Henderson wired Halifax at 12:30 A.M. on September 1, four hours before the German attack was scheduled to begin (though he did not know this): "German proposals . . . are not unreasonable . . . I submit that on German offer war would be completely unjustifiable." He urged again that the British government pressure the Poles "in unmistakable language" to state "their intention to send a plenipotentiary to Berlin."

The British ambassador in Warsaw took a different view. He wired to Halifax on August 31: "H. M. Ambassador at Berlin appears to consider German terms reasonable. I fear that I cannot agree with him from point of view of Warsaw."[65]

† There was another somewhat weird diplomatic episode this last day of peace which deserves a footnote. Dahlerus returned from the visit with Lipski to the British Embassy, where from Henderson's office he put through at midday a telephone call to Sir Horace Wilson at the British Foreign Office in London. He told Wilson that the German proposals were "extremely liberal" but that the Polish ambassador had just rejected them. "It is clear," he said, "that the Poles are obstructing the possibilities of negotiations."

At this moment Wilson heard certain noises on the long-distance line which sounded to him as though the Germans were listening in. He tried to end the conversation, but Dahlerus persisted in rambling on about the unreasonableness of

THE LAST DAY OF PEACE

Having got the Germans and Poles to agree to direct negotiations, as they thought, the British and French governments, though highly skeptical of Hitler, had concentrated their efforts on trying to bring such talks about. In this Britain took the lead, supported diplomatically in Berlin and especially in Warsaw by France. Although the British did not advise the Poles to accept Hitler's ultimatum and fetch an emissary with full powers to Berlin on August 30, holding that such a demand was, as Halifax had wired Henderson, "wholly unreasonable," they did urge Colonel Beck to declare that he was prepared to negotiate with Berlin "without delay." This was the substance of a message which Halifax got off to his ambassador in Warsaw late on the night of August 30. Kennard was to inform Beck of the contents of the British note to Germany which Henderson was presenting to Ribbentrop, assure him that Britain would stand by its commitments to Poland, but stress the importance of Poland's agreeing to direct discussions with Germany at once.

We regard it as most important [Halifax telegraphed] from the point of view of the internal situation in Germany and of world opinion that, so long as the German Government profess themselves ready to negotiate, no opportunity should be given them for placing the blame for a conflict on Poland.[67]

Kennard saw Beck at midnight and the Polish Foreign Minister promised to consult his government and give him a "considered reply" by midday on August 31. Kennard's dispatch describing this interview reached the British Foreign Office at 8 A.M. and Halifax was not entirely satisfied with it. At noon—it was now the last day of August—he wired Kennard that he should "concert" with his French colleague in Warsaw (Léon Nöel, the French ambassador) and suggest to the Polish government

that they should now make known to the German Government, preferably direct, but if not, through us, that they have been made aware of our last reply to German Government and that they confirm their acceptance of the principle of direct discussions.

French Government fear that German Government might take advantage of silence on part of Polish Government.[68]

Lord Halifax was still uneasy about his Polish allies, and less than two hours later, at 1:45 P.M., he again wired Kennard:

---

the Poles. "I again told Dahlerus," Sir Horace noted in a Foreign Office memorandum, "to shut up, but as he did not I put down the receiver."

Wilson reported this indiscretion, committed in the very office of H. M. Ambassador in Berlin, to his superiors. At 1 P.M., less than an hour later, Halifax wired Henderson in code: "You really must be careful of use of telephone. D's conversation [Dahlerus was always referred to in the messages between the Foreign Office and the Berlin Embassy as "D"] at midday from Embassy was most indiscreet and has certainly been heard by the Germans."[66]

Please at once inform Polish Government and advise them, in view of fact that they have accepted principle of direct discussions, immediately to instruct Polish Ambassador in Berlin to say to German Government that, if latter have any proposals, he is ready to transmit them to his Government so that they may at once consider them and make suggestions for early discussions.[69]

But shortly before this telegram was dispatched, Beck, in response to the *démarche* of the midnight before, had already informed the British ambassador in a written note that the Polish government "confirm their readiness . . . for a direct exchange of views with the German Government" and had orally assured him that he was instructing Lipski to seek an interview with Ribbentrop to say that "Poland had accepted the British proposals." When Kennard asked Beck what Lipski would do if Ribbentrop handed over the German proposals, the Foreign Minister replied that his ambassador in Berlin would not be authorized to accept them as, "in view of past experience, it might be accompanied by some sort of an ultimatum." The important thing, said Beck, was to re-establish contact "and then details should be discussed as to where, with whom and on what basis negotiations should be commenced." In the light of the "past experience" which the once pro-Nazi Polish Foreign Minister mentioned, this was not an unreasonable view. Beck added, Kennard wired London, that "if invited to go to Berlin he would of course not go, as he had no intention of being treated like President Hácha."[70]

Actually Beck did not send to Lipski quite those instructions. Instead of saying that Poland "accepted" the British proposals, Lipski was told to tell the Germans that Poland "was favorably considering" the British suggestions and would make a formal reply "during the next few hours at the latest."

There was more to Beck's instructions to Lipski than that and the Germans, having solved the Polish ciphers, knew it.

For a simple and good reason that will soon become apparent, the Germans were not anxious to receive the Polish ambassador in Berlin. It was too late. At 1 P.M., a few minutes after he had received his telegraphic instructions from Warsaw, Lipski requested an interview with Ribbentrop for the purpose of presenting a communication from his government. After cooling his heels for a couple of hours he received a telephone call from Weizsaecker asking, on behalf of the German Foreign Minister, whether he was coming as an emissary with full power "or in some other capacity."

"I replied," Lipski reported later in his final report,[71] "that I was asking for an interview as Ambassador, to present a declaration from my Government."

Another long wait followed. At 5 P.M. Attolico called on Ribbentrop and communicated the "urgent desire of the Duce" that the Fuehrer should receive Lipski "to establish in this way at least the minimum contact necessary for the avoidance of a final breach." The German Foreign Minister promised to "transmit" the Duce's wishes to the Fuehrer.[72]

This was not the first call the Italian ambassador had made in the Wilhelmstrasse on this last day of August in order to try to save the peace. At 9 that morning Attolico had advised Rome that the situation was "desperate" and that unless "something new comes up there will be war in a few hours." In Rome Mussolini and Ciano put their heads together to find something new. The first result was that Ciano telephoned Halifax to say that Mussolini could not intervene unless he were able to produce for Hitler a "fat prize: Danzig." The British Foreign Secretary did not rise to the bait. He told Ciano the first thing to be done was to establish direct contact between the Germans and the Poles through Lipski.

Thus at 11:30 A.M. Attolico saw Weizsaecker at the German Foreign Office and apprised him that Mussolini was in contact with London and had suggested the return of Danzig as a first step toward a German–Polish settlement, and that the Duce needed a certain "margin of time" to perfect his plan for peace. In the meantime, couldn't the German government receive Lipski?

Lipski was received by Ribbentrop at 6:15 P.M., more than five hours after he had requested the interview. It did not last long. The ambassador, despite his fatigue and his worn nerves, behaved with dignity. He read to the Nazi Foreign Minister a written communication.

Last night the Polish Government were informed by the British Government of an exchange of views with the Reich Government as to a possibility of direct negotiations between the Polish and German Governments.

The Polish Government are favorably considering the British Government's suggestion, and will make them a formal reply on the subject during the next few hours.

"I added," said Lipski later, "that I had been trying to present this declaration since 1 P.M." When Ribbentrop asked him whether he had come as an emissary empowered to negotiate, the ambassador replied that, "for the time being," he had only been instructed to remit the communication which he had just read, whereupon he handed it to the Foreign Minister. He had expected, Ribbentrop said, that Lipski would come as a "fully empowered delegate," and when the ambassador again declared that he had no such role he was dismissed. Ribbentrop said he would inform the Fuehrer.[73]

"On my return to the embassy," Lipski later related, "I found myself unable to communicate with Warsaw, as the Germans had cut my telephone."

The questions of Weizsaecker and Ribbentrop as to the ambassador's status as a negotiator were purely formal, with an eye, no doubt, for the record, for ever since noon, when Lipski's communication had been received by telegram from Warsaw, the Germans had known that he was not coming, as they had demanded, as a plenipotentiary. They had decoded the telegram immediately. A copy had been sent to Goering, who showed it to Dahlerus and instructed him to take it posthaste to Henderson so that the British government, as the Field Marshal later explained on the stand at Nuremberg, "should find out as quickly as possible how intransigent the Polish attitude was." Goering read to the tribunal the secret instructions to Lipski, which were that the ambassador should refrain from conducting official negotiations "under any circumstances" and should insist that he had "no plenipotentiary powers" and that he was merely empowered to deliver the official communication of his government. In his testimony, the Field Marshal made much of this during his vain effort to convince the Nuremberg judges that Poland had "sabotaged" Hitler's last bid for peace and that, as he said, he, Goering, did not want war and had done everything he could to prevent it. But Goering's veracity was only a shade above Ribbentrop's and one example of this was his further assertion to the court that only after Lipski's visit to the Wilhelmstrasse at 6:15 P.M. on August 31 did Hitler decide "on invasion the next day."

The truth was quite otherwise. In fact, all these scrambling eleventh-hour moves of the weary and exhausted diplomats, and of the overwrought men who directed them on the afternoon and evening of that last day of August 1939, were but a flailing of the air, completely futile, and, in the case of the Germans, entirely and purposely deceptive.

For at half after noon on August 31, before Lord Halifax had urged the Poles to be more accommodating and before Lipski had called on Ribbentrop and before the Germans had made publicly known their "generous" proposals to Poland and before Mussolini had tried to intervene, Adolf Hitler had taken his final decision and issued the decisive order that was to throw the planet into its bloodiest war.

SUPREME COMMANDER OF THE ARMED FORCES
MOST SECRET

Berlin, August 31, 1939

Directive No. 1 for the Conduct of the War

1. Now that all the *political possibilities* of disposing by peaceful means of a situation on the Eastern Frontier which is intolerable for Germany *are* exhausted, I have determined on a *solution by force.**

2. The *attack on Poland* is to be carried out in accordance with the preparations made for Case White, with the alterations which result, where the Army is concerned, from the fact that it has in the meantime almost completed its dispositions.

Allotment of tasks and the operational target remain unchanged.

Date of attack: September 1, 1939.

Time of attack: 4:45 A.M. [Inserted in red pencil.]

This timing also applies to the operation at Gdynia, Bay of Danzig and the Dirschau Bridge.

---

* The emphasis is in the original German text.

3. In the *West* it is important that the responsibility for the opening of hostilities should rest squarely on England and France. For the time being insignificant frontier violations should be met by purely local action.

The neutrality of Holland, Belgium, Luxembourg and Switzerland, to which we have given assurances, must be scrupulously observed.

On land, the German Western Frontier is not to be crossed without my express permission.

At sea, the same applies for all warlike actions or actions which could be regarded as such.*

4. *If Britain and France open hostilities* against Germany, it is the task of the Wehrmacht formations operating in the West to conserve their forces as much as possible and thus maintain the conditions for a victorious conclusion of the operations against Poland. Within these limits enemy forces and their military-economic resources are to be damaged as much as possible. Orders to go over to the attack I reserve, in any case, to myself.

The Army will hold the West Wall and make preparations to prevent its being outflanked in the north through violation of Belgian or Dutch territory by the Western powers . . .

The Navy will carry on warfare against merchant shipping, directed mainly at England . . . The Air Force is, in the first place, to prevent the French and British Air Forces from attacking the German Army and the German *Lebensraum.*

In conducting the war against England, preparations are to be made for the use of the Luftwaffe in disrupting British supplies by sea, the armaments industry, and the transport of troops to France. A favorable opportunity is to be taken for an effective attack on massed British naval units, especially against battleships and aircraft carriers. Attacks against London are reserved for my decision.

Preparations are to be made for attacks against the British mainland, bearing in mind that partial success with insufficient forces is in all circumstances to be avoided.

ADOLF HITLER[74]

Shortly after noon on August 31, then, Hitler formally and in writing directed the attack on Poland to begin at dawn the next day. As his first war directive indicates, he was still not quite sure what Britain and France would do. He would refrain from attacking them first. If they took hostile action, he was prepared to meet it. Perhaps, as Halder had indicated in his diary entry of August 28, the British would go through the motions of honoring their obligation to Poland and "wage a sham war." If so, the Fuehrer would not take it "amiss."

Probably the Nazi dictator made his fateful decision a little earlier than

---

* A marginal note in the directive clears up this ambiguous point—"Thus, Atlantic forces will for the time being remain in a waiting position."

12:30 P.M. on the last day of August. At 6:40 P.M. on the previous day Halder jotted in his diary a communication from Lieutenant Colonel Curt Siewert, adjutant of General von Brauchitsch: "Make all preparations so that attack can begin at 4:30 A.M. on September 1. Should negotiations in London require postponement, then September 2. In that case we shall be notified before 3 P.M. tomorrow. . . . Fuehrer: either September 1 or 2. All off after September 2." Because of the autumn rains, the attack had to begin at once or be called off altogether.

Very early on the morning of August 31, while Hitler still claimed he was waiting for the Polish emissary, the German Army received its orders. At 6:30 A.M. Halder jotted down: "Word from the Reich Chancellery that jump-off order has been given for September 1." At 11:30: "Gen. Stuelpnagel reports on fixing of time of attack for 0445 [4:45 A.M.]. Intervention of West said to be unavoidable; in spite of this Fuehrer has decided to attack." An hour later the formal Directive No. 1 was issued.

There was, I remember, an eerie atmosphere that day in Berlin; everyone seemed to be going around in a daze. At 7:25 in the morning Weizsaecker had telephoned Ulrich von Hassell, one of the "conspirators," and asked him to hurry over to see him. The State Secretary saw only one last hope: that Henderson should persuade Lipski and his government to send a Polish plenipotentiary at once or at least to announce the intention of dispatching one. Could the unemployed Hassell see his friend Henderson at once and also Goering to this end? Hassell tried. He saw Henderson twice and Goering once. But veteran diplomat and, now, anti-Nazi that he was, he did not seem to realize that events had outstripped such puny efforts. Nor did he grasp the extent of his own confusions and of those of Weizsaecker and all the "good" Germans who, of course, wanted peace—on German terms. For it must have been obvious to them on August 31 that there would be war unless either Hitler or the Poles backed down, and that there was not the slightest possibility of the one or the other capitulating. And yet, as Hassell's diary entry for this day makes clear, he expected the Poles to back down and to follow the same disastrous route which the Austrians and Czechs had taken.

When Henderson tried to point out to Hassell that the "chief difficulty" was in German methods, in the way they were trying to order the Poles around "like stupid little boys," Hassell retorted "that the persistent silence of the Poles was also objectionable." He added that "everything depended on Lipski putting in an appearance—not to ask questions but to declare his willingness to negotiate." Even to Hassell the Poles, who were threatened with imminent attack on trumped-up Nazi charges, were not supposed to ask questions. And when the former ambassador summed up his "final conclusions" about the outbreak of the war, though he blamed Hitler and Ribbentrop for "knowingly taking the risk of war with the Western Powers," he also heaped much responsibility on the Poles and even on the British and French. "The Poles, for their part," he wrote, "with Polish conceit and Slavic aimlessness, confident of English and

French support, had missed every remaining chance of avoiding war." One can only ask what chance they missed except to surrender to Hitler's full demands. "The Government in London," Hassell added, ". . . gave up the race in the very last days and adopted a kind of devil-may-care attitude. France went through the same stages, only with much more hesitation. Mussolini did all in his power to avoid war."[75] If an educated, cultivated and experienced diplomat such as Hassell could be so woolly in his thinking is it any wonder that it was easy for Hitler to take in the mass of the German people?

There now followed during the waning afternoon of the last day of peace a somewhat grotesque interlude. In view of what is now known about the decisions of the day it might have been thought that the Commander in Chief of the Luftwaffe, which was to carry out far-flung air operations against Poland beginning at dawn on the morrow, would be a very busy Field Marshal. On the contrary. Dahlerus took him out to lunch at the Hotel Esplanade and plied him with good food and drink. The cognac was of such high quality that Goering insisted on lugging away two bottles of it when he left. Having got the Field Marshal into the proper humor, Dahlerus proposed that he invite Henderson for a talk. After receiving Hitler's permission, he did so, inviting him and Forbes to his house for tea at 5 P.M. Dahlerus (whose presence is not mentioned by Henderson in his *Final Report* or in his book) says that he suggested that Goering, on behalf of Germany, meet a Polish emissary in Holland and that Henderson promised to submit the proposal to London. The British ambassador's version of the tea talk, given in his *Final Report,* was that Goering "talked for two hours of the iniquities of the Poles and about Herr Hitler's and his own desire for friendship with England. It was a conversation which led to nowhere . . . My general impression was that it constituted a final but forlorn effort on his part to detach Britain from the Poles . . . I augured the worst from the fact that he was in a position at such a moment to give me so much of his time . . . He could scarcely have afforded at such a moment to spare time in conversation if it did not mean that everything down to the last detail was now ready for action."

The third and most piquant description of this bizarre tea party was given by Forbes in answer to a questionnaire from Goering's lawyer at Nuremberg.

The atmosphere was negative and desperate, though friendly . . . Goering's statement to the British ambassador was: If the Poles should not give in, Germany would crush them like lice, and if Britain should decide to declare war, he would regret it greatly, but it would be most imprudent of Britain.[76]

Later in the evening Henderson, according to his own account, drafted a dispatch to London saying "that it would be quite useless for me to make any further suggestions since they would now only be outstripped by events and that the only course remaining to us was to show our inflexible determination to resist force by force."*

Sir Nevile Henderson's disillusionment seemed complete. Despite all his strenuous efforts over the years to appease the insatiable Nazi dictator, his mission to Germany, as he called it, had failed. In the fading hours of August's last day this shallow, debonair Englishman whose personal diplomacy in Berlin had been so disastrously blind tried to face up to the shattering collapse of his vain hopes and abortive plans. And though he would suffer one more typical, incredible lapse the next day, the first day of war, an ancient truth was dawning on him: that there were times and circumstances when, as he at last said, force must be met by force.†

As darkness settled over Europe on the evening of August 31, 1939, and a million and a half German troops began moving forward to their final positions on the Polish border for the jump-off at dawn, all that remained for Hitler to do was to perpetrate some propaganda trickery to prepare the German people for the shock of aggressive war.

The people were in need of the treatment which Hitler, abetted by Goebbels and Himmler, had become so expert in applying. I had been about in the streets of Berlin, talking with the ordinary people, and that morning noted in my diary: "Everybody against the war. People talking openly. How can a country go into a major war with a population so dead against it?" Despite all my experience in the Third Reich I asked such a naïve question! Hitler knew the answer very well. Had he not the week before on his Bavarian mountaintop promised the generals that he would "give a propagandist reason for starting the war" and admonished them not to "mind whether it was plausible or not"? "The victor," he had told them, "will not be asked afterward whether he told the truth or not. In starting and waging a war it is not right that matters, but victory."

At 9 P.M., as we have seen, all German radio stations broadcast the Fuehrer's Polish peace proposals which, as they were read over the air,

---

* He may have drafted it that evening but he did not send it to London until 3:45 P.M. the next day, nearly twelve hours after the German attack on Poland had begun. It followed several of his telegrams, which like it were telephoned to London—so that transmission was simultaneous—reporting the outbreak of hostilities. It read: "Mutual distrust of Germans and Poles is so complete that I do not feel I can usefully acquiesce [*sic*] in any further suggestions from here, which would only once again be outstripped by events or lead to nothing as the result of methods followed or of considerations of honor and prestige.

"Last hope lies in inflexible determination on our part to resist force by force."[77]
† Since friends who have read this section have expressed doubts about this writer's objectivity in dealing with Henderson, perhaps another's view of the British ambassador in Berlin should be given. Sir L. B. Namier, the British historian, has summed up Henderson as follows: "Conceited, vain, self-opinionated, rigidly adhering to his preconceived ideas, he poured out telegrams, dispatches and letters in unbelievable numbers and of formidable length, repeating a hundred times the same ill-founded views and ideas. Obtuse enough to be a menace and not stupid enough to be innocuous, he proved *un homme néfaste*." (Namier, *In the Nazi Era*, p. 162.)

seemed so reasonable to this misled correspondent. The fact that Hitler had never presented them to the Poles nor even, except in a vague and unofficial manner, to the British, and then less than twenty-four hours before, was brushed over. In fact, in a lengthy statement explaining to the German people how their government had exhausted every diplomatic means to preserve the peace the Chancellor, no doubt aided by Goebbels, showed that he had lost none of his touch for masterly deceit. After the British government on August 28, it said, had offered its mediation between Germany and Poland, the German government on the next day had replied that,

in spite of being skeptical of the desire of the Polish Government to come to an understanding, they declared themselves ready in the interests of peace to accept the British mediation or suggestion . . . They considered it necessary . . . if the danger of a catastrophe was to be avoided that action must be taken readily and without delay. They declared themselves ready to receive a personage appointed by the Polish Government up to the evening of August 30, with the proviso that the latter was empowered not only to discuss but to conduct and conclude negotiations.

Instead of a statement regarding the arrival of an authorized personage, the first answer the Government of the Reich received to their readiness for an understanding was the news of the Polish mobilization . . .

The Reich Government cannot be expected continually not only to emphasize their willingness to start negotiations, but actually to be ready to do so, while being from the Polish side merely put off with empty subterfuges and meaningless declarations.

It has once more been made clear as a result of a *démarche* which has meanwhile been made by the Polish Ambassador that the latter himself has no plenary powers either to enter into any discussion or even to negotiate.

The Fuehrer and the German Government have thus waited two days in vain for the arrival of a Polish negotiator.

In these circumstances the German Government regard their proposals as having this time too been . . . rejected, although they considered that these proposals, in the form in which they were made known to the British Government also, were more than loyal, fair and practicable.

Good propaganda, to be effective, as Hitler and Goebbels had learned from experience, needs more than words. It needs deeds, however much they may have to be fabricated. Having convinced the German people (and of this the writer can testify from personal observation) that the Poles had rejected the Fuehrer's generous peace offer, there remained only the concocting of a deed which would "prove" that not Germany but Poland had attacked first.

For this last shady business, it will be remembered, the Germans, at Hitler's direction, had made careful preparation.* For six days Alfred

---

* See above, pp. 518–20.

Naujocks, the intellectual S.S. ruffian, had been waiting at Gleiwitz on the Polish border to carry out a simulated Polish attack on the German radio station there. The plan had been revised. S.S. men outfitted in Polish Army uniforms were to do the shooting, and drugged concentration camp inmates were to be left dying as "casualties"—this last delectable part of the operation had, as we have seen, the expressive code name "Canned Goods." There were to be several such faked "Polish attacks" but the principal one was to be on the radio station at Gleiwitz.

At noon on August 31 [Naujocks related in his Nuremberg affidavit] I received from Heydrich the code word for the attack which was to take place at 8 o'clock that evening. Heydrich said: "In order to carry out this attack report to Mueller for Canned Goods." I did this and gave Mueller instructions to deliver the man near the radio station. I received this man and had him laid down at the entrance to the station. He was alive but completely unconscious. I tried to open his eyes. I could not recognize by his eyes that he was alive, only by his breathing. I did not see the gun wounds but a lot of blood was smeared across his face. He was in civilian clothes.

We seized the radio station, as ordered, broadcast a speech of three to four minutes over an emergency transmitter,* fired some pistol shots and left.†[79]

Berlin that evening was largely shut off from the outside world, except for outgoing press dispatches and broadcasts which reported the Fuehrer's "offer" to Poland and the German allegations of Polish "attacks" on German territory. I tried to get through on the telephone to Warsaw, London and Paris but was told that communications with these capitals were cut. Berlin itself was quite normal in appearance. There had been no evacuation of women and children, as there had been in Paris and London, nor any sandbagging of storefront windows, as was reported from the other capitals. Toward 4 A.M. on September 1, after my last broadcast, I drove back from Broadcasting House to the Adlon Hotel. There was no traffic. The houses were dark. The people were asleep and perhaps—for all I knew—had gone to bed hoping for the best, for peace.

Hitler himself had been in fine fettle all day. At 6 P.M. on August 31 General Halder noted in his diary, "Fuehrer calm; has slept well . . .

---

* The speech in Polish had been outlined by Heydrich to Naujocks. It contained inflammatory statements against Germany and declared that the Poles were attacking. See above, p. 519.

† The "Polish attack" at Gleiwitz was used by Hitler in his speech to the Reichstag the next day and was cited as justification for the Nazi aggression by Ribbentrop, Weizsaecker and other members of the Foreign Office in their propaganda. The New York *Times* and other newspapers reported it, as well as similar incidents, in their issues of September 1, 1939. It remains only to be added that according to the testimony at Nuremberg of General Lahousen, of the Abwehr, all the S.S. men who wore Polish uniforms in the simulated attacks that evening were, as the General put it, "put out of the way."[78]

Decision against evacuation [in the west] shows that he expects France and England will not take action."*

Admiral Canaris, chief of the Abwehr in OKW and one of the key anti-Nazi conspirators, was in a different mood. Though Hitler was carrying Germany into war, an action which the Canaris circle had supposedly sworn to prevent by getting rid of the dictator, there was no conspiracy in being now that the moment for it had arrived.

Later in the afternoon Gisevius had been summoned to OKW head-quarters by Colonel Oster. This nerve center of Germany's military might was humming with activity. Canaris drew Gisevius down a dimly lit corridor. In a voice choked with emotion he said:

"This means the end of Germany."[81]

---

* During the day Hitler found time to send a telegram to the Duke of Windsor at Antibes, France.

> Berlin, August 31, 1939
>
> I thank you for your telegram of August 27. You may rest assured that my attitude toward Britain and my desire to avoid another war between our peoples remain unchanged. It depends on Britain, however, whether my wishes for the future development of German–British relations can be realized.
>
> ADOLF HITLER[80]

This is the first mention of the former King of England, but by no means the last, in the captured German documents. Subsequently, for a time, as will be recorded further on, the Duke of Windsor loomed large in certain calculations of Hitler and Ribbentrop..

17

THE LAUNCHING OF WORLD WAR II

AT DAYBREAK on September 1, 1939, the very date which Hitler had set in his first directive for "Case White" back on April 3, the German armies poured across the Polish frontier and converged on Warsaw from the north, south and west.

Overhead German warplanes roared toward their targets: Polish troop columns and ammunition dumps, bridges, railroads and open cities. Within a few minutes they were giving the Poles, soldiers and civilians alike, the first taste of sudden death and destruction from the skies ever experienced on any great scale on the earth and thereby inaugurating a terror which would become dreadfully familiar to hundreds of millions of men, women and children in Europe and Asia during the next six years, and whose shadow, after the nuclear bombs came, would haunt all mankind with the threat of utter extinction.

It was a gray, somewhat sultry morning in Berlin, with clouds hanging low over the city, giving it some protection from hostile bombers, which were feared but never came.

The people in the streets, I noticed, were apathetic despite the immensity of the news which had greeted them from their radios and from the extra editions of the morning newspapers.* Across the street from the Adlon Hotel the morning shift of laborers had gone to work on the new I. G. Farben building just as if nothing had happened, and when newsboys came by shouting their extras no one laid down his tools to buy one. Perhaps, it occurred to me, the German people were simply dazed at waking up on this first morning of September to find themselves in a war which they had been sure the Fuehrer somehow would avoid. They could not quite believe it, now that it had come.

What a contrast, one could not help thinking, between this gray apathy and the way the Germans had gone to war in 1914. Then there had been a wild enthusiasm. The crowds in the streets had staged delirious demon-

---

* Hitler's proclamation to the Army announcing the opening of hostilities was broadcast over the German radio at 5:40 A.M., and the newspaper extras were on the street shortly after. See below, p. 599.

strations, tossed flowers at the marching troops and frantically cheered the Kaiser and Supreme Warlord, Wilhelm II.

There were no such demonstrations this time for the troops or for the Nazi warlord, who shortly before 10 A.M. drove from the Chancellery to the Reichstag through empty streets to address the nation on the momentous happenings which he himself, deliberately and cold-bloodedly, had just provoked. Even the robot members of the Reichstag, party hacks, for the most part, whom Hitler had appointed, failed to respond with much enthusiasm as the dictator launched into his explanation of why Germany found itself on this morning engaged in war. There was far less cheering than on previous and less important occasions when the Leader had declaimed from this tribune in the ornate hall of the Kroll Opera House.

Though truculent at times he seemed strangely on the defensive, and throughout the speech, I thought as I listened, ran a curious strain, as though he himself were dazed at the fix he had got himself into and felt a little desperate about it. His explanation of why his Italian ally had reneged on its automatic obligations to come to his aid did not seem to go over even with this hand-picked audience.

I should like [he said] here above all to thank Italy, which throughout has supported us, but you will understand that for the carrying out of this struggle we do not intend to appeal for foreign help. We will carry out this task ourselves.

Having lied so often on his way to power and in his consolidation of power, Hitler could not refrain at this serious moment in history from thundering a few more lies to the gullible German people in justification of his wanton act.

You know the endless attempts I made for a peaceful clarification and understanding of the problem of Austria, and later of the problem of the Sudetenland, Bohemia and Moravia. It was all in vain . . .

In my talks with Polish statesmen . . . I formulated at last the German proposals and . . . there is nothing more modest or loyal than these proposals. I should like to say this to the world. I alone was in the position to make such proposals, for I know very well that in doing so I brought myself into opposition to millions of Germans. These proposals have been refused. . . .

For two whole days I sat with my Government and waited to see whether it was convenient for the Polish Government to send a plenipotentiary or not . . . But I am wrongly judged if my love of peace and my patience are mistaken for weakness or even cowardice . . . I can no longer find any willingness on the part of the Polish Government to conduct serious negotiations with us . . . I have therefore resolved to speak to Poland in the same language that Poland for months past has used toward us . . .

This night for the first time Polish regular soldiers fired on our own territory. Since 5:45 A.M. we have been returning the fire, and from now on bombs will be met with bombs.

Thus was the faked German attack on the German radio station at Gleiwitz, which, as we have seen, was carried out by S.S. men in Polish uniforms under the direction of Naujocks, used by the Chancellor of Germany as justification of his cold-blooded aggression against Poland. And indeed in its first communiqués the German High Command referred to its military operations as a "counterattack." Even Weizsaecker did his best to perpetrate this shabby swindle. During the day he got off a circular telegram from the Foreign Office to all German diplomatic missions abroad advising them on the line they were to take.

In defense against Polish attacks, German troops moved into action against Poland at dawn today. This action is for the present not to be described as war, but merely as engagements which have been brought about by Polish attacks.[1]

Even the German soldiers, who could see for themselves who had done the attacking on the Polish border, were bombarded with Hitler's lie. In a grandiose proclamation to the German Army on September 1, the Fuehrer said:

The Polish State has refused the peaceful settlement of relations which I desired, and has appealed to arms . . . A series of violations of the frontier, intolerable to a great Power, prove that Poland is no longer willing to respect the frontier of the Reich.

In order to put an end to this lunacy, I have no other choice than to meet force with force from now on.

Only once that day did Hitler utter the truth.

I am asking of no German man [he told the Reichstag] more than I myself was ready throughout four years to do . . . I am from now on just the first soldier of the German Reich. I have once more put on that coat that was most sacred and dear to me. I will not take it off again until victory is secured, or I will not survive the outcome.

In the end, this once, he would prove as good as his word. But no German I met in Berlin that day noticed that what the Leader was saying quite bluntly was that he could not face, not take, defeat should it come.

In his speech Hitler named Goering as his successor should anything happen to him. Hess, he added, would be next in line. "Should anything happen to Hess," Hitler advised, "then by law the Senate will be called and will choose from its midst the most worthy—that is to say, the bravest —successor." What law? What Senate? Neither existed!

Hitler's relatively subdued manner at the Reichstag gave way to another and uglier mood as soon as he had returned to the Chancellery. The ubiquitous Dahlerus, in tow of Goering, found him there in an "exceedingly nervous and very agitated" state.

He told me [the Swedish mediator later testified] he had all along suspected that England wanted the war. He told me further that he would crush Poland and annex the whole country . . .

He grew more and more excited, and began to wave his arms as he shouted in my face: "If England wants to fight for a year, I shall fight for a year; if England wants to fight two years, I shall fight two years . . ." He paused and then yelled, his voice rising to a shrill scream and his arms milling wildly: "If England wants to fight for three years, I shall fight for three years . . ."

The movements of his body now began to follow those of his arms, and when he finally bellowed: "*Und wenn es erforderlich ist, will ich zehn Jahre kaempfen*" ("And if necessary, I will fight for ten years") he brandished his fist and bent down so that it nearly touched the floor.[2]

Yet for all his hysteria Hitler was by no means convinced that he would have to fight Great Britain at all. It was now past noon, German armored columns were already several miles inside Poland and advancing rapidly and most of Poland's cities, including Warsaw, had been bombed with considerable civilian casualties. But there was not a word from London or Paris that Britain and France were in any hurry to honor their word to Poland.

Their course seemed clear, but Dahlerus and Henderson appeared to be doing their best to confuse it.

At 10:30 A.M. the British ambassador telephoned a message to Halifax.

I understand [he said] that the Poles blew up the Dirschau bridge during the night.* And that fighting took place with the Danzigers. On receipt of this news, Hitler gave orders for the Poles to be driven back from the border line and to Goering for destruction of the Polish Air Force along the frontier.

Only at the end of his dispatch did Henderson add:

This information comes from Goering himself.
Hitler may ask to see me after Reichstag as a last effort to save the peace.[3]

What peace? Peace for Britain? For six hours Germany had been waging war—with all its military might—against Britain's ally.

---

* The German operation to seize the Dirschau bridge over the Vistula before the Poles could blow it up had been planned early in the summer and appears constantly in the papers for "Case White." It was specifically ordered in Hitler's Directive No. 1 on August 31. Actually the operation failed, partly because early-morning fog hampered the dropping of paratroopers who were to seize the bridge. The Poles succeeded in blowing it up just in time.

Hitler did not send for Henderson after his Reichstag speech, and the ambassador, who had accommodatingly passed along to London Goering's lies about the Poles beginning the attack, became discouraged—but not completely discouraged. At 10:50 A.M. he telephoned a further message to Halifax. A new idea had sprung up in his fertile but confused mind.

I feel it my duty [he reported], however little prospect there may be of its realization, to express the belief that the only possible hope now for peace would be for Marshal Smigly-Rydz to announce his readiness to come immediately to Germany to discuss as soldier and plenipotentiary the whole question with Field Marshal Goering.[4]

It does not seem to have occurred to this singular British ambassador that Marshal Smigly-Rydz might have his hands full trying to repel the massive and unprovoked German attack, or that if he could break off and did come to Berlin as a "plenipotentiary" it would be equivalent, under the circumstances, to surrender. The Poles might be quickly beaten but they would not surrender.

Dahlerus was even more active than Henderson during this first day of the German attack on Poland. At 8 A.M. he had gone to see Goering, who told him that "war had broken out because the Poles had attacked the radio station at Gleiwitz and blown up a bridge near Dirschau." The Swede immediately rang up the Foreign Office in London with the news.

"I informed somebody," he later testified in cross-examination at Nuremberg, "that according to the information I had received the Poles had attacked, and they naturally wondered what was happening to me when I gave that information."[5] But after all, it was only what H. M. Ambassador in Berlin would be telephoning a couple of hours later.

A confidential British Foreign Office memorandum records the Swede's call at 9:05 A.M. Aping Goering, Dahlerus insisted to London that "the Poles are sabotaging everything," and that he had "evidence they never meant to attempt to negotiate."[6]

At half after noon Dahlerus was on the long-distance phone again to the Foreign Office in London, and this time got Cadogan. He again blamed the Poles for sabotaging the peace by blowing the Dirschau bridge and suggested that he once again fly to London with Forbes. But the stern and unappeasing Cadogan had had about enough of Dahlerus now that the war which he had tried to prevent had come. He told the Swede that "nothing could now be done."

But Cadogan was merely the permanent Undersecretary for Foreign Affairs, not even a member of the cabinet. Dahlerus insisted that his request be submitted to the cabinet itself, informing Cadogan haughtily that he would ring back in an hour. This he did, and got his answer.

Any idea of mediation [Cadogan said] while German troops are invading Poland is quite out of the question. The only way in which a world war can be stopped is (one) that hostilities be suspended, and (two) that German troops be immediately withdrawn from Polish territory.[7]

At 10 A.M. the Polish ambassador in London, Count Raczyński, had called on Lord Halifax and officially communicated to him the news of the German aggression, adding that "it was a plain case as provided for by the treaty." The Foreign Secretary answered that he had no doubt of the facts. At 10:50 he summoned the German chargé d'affaires, Theodor Kordt, to the Foreign Office and asked him if he had any information. Kordt replied that he had neither information about a German attack on Poland nor any instructions. Halifax then declared that the reports which he had received "create a very serious situation." But further than that he did not go. Kordt telephoned this information to Berlin at 11:45 A.M.

By noon, then, Hitler had reason to hope that Britain, though it considered the situation serious, might not go to war after all. But the hope was soon to be dashed.

At 7:15 P.M. a member of the British Embassy in Berlin telephoned the German Foreign Office and requested Ribbentrop to receive Henderson and Coulondre "on a matter of urgency as soon as possible." The French Embassy made a similar request a few minutes later. Ribbentrop, having declined to meet the two ambassadors together, received Henderson at 9 P.M. and Coulondre an hour later. From the British ambassador he was handed a formal note from the British government.

. . . Unless the German Government are prepared [it said] to give His Majesty's Government satisfactory assurances that the German Government have suspended all aggressive action against Poland and are prepared promptly to withdraw their forces from Polish territory, His Majesty's Government will without hesitation fulfill their obligation to Poland.[8]

The French communication was in identical words.

To both ambassadors Ribbentrop replied that he would transmit their notes to Hitler, whereupon he launched into a lengthy dissertation declaring that "there was no question of German aggression" but of Polish aggression and repeating the by now somewhat stale lie that "regular" Polish troops had attacked German soil on the previous day. Still, the diplomatic niceties were maintained. Sir Nevile Henderson did not fail to note in his dispatch that night describing the meeting that Ribbentrop had been "courteous and polite." As the ambassador prepared to take his leave an argument arose as to whether the German Foreign Minister had gabbled the text of the German "proposals" to Poland at their stormy meeting two evenings before. Henderson said he had; Ribbentrop said he had read them "slowly and clearly and even given oral explanations of the main points so that he could suppose Henderson had understood everything." It was an argument that would never be settled—but what difference did it make now?[9]

On the night of September 1, as the German armies penetrated further into Poland and the Luftwaffe bombed and bombed, Hitler knew from the Anglo–French notes that unless he stopped his armies and quickly withdrew them—which was unthinkable—he had a world war on his hands. Or did he still hope that night that his luck—his Munich luck—might hold? For his friend Mussolini, frightened by the advent of war and fearing that an overwhelming Anglo–French naval and military force might strike against Italy, was desperately trying to arrange another Munich.

THE LAST-MINUTE INTERVENTION OF MUSSOLINI

As late as August 26, it will be remembered, the Duce, in ducking out of Italy's obligations under the Pact of Steel, had insisted to the Fuehrer that there was still a possibility of "a political solution" which would give "full moral and material satisfaction to Germany."* Hitler had not bothered to argue the matter with his friend and ally, and this had discouraged the junior partner in the Axis. Nevertheless on August 31, as we have seen, Mussolini and Ciano, after being advised by their ambassador in Berlin that the situation had become desperate, had urged Hitler at least to see the Polish ambassador, Lipski, and had informed him that they were trying to get the British government to agree to the return of Danzig "as a first step" in peace negotiations.†

But it was too late for Hitler to be tempted by such small bait. Danzig was a mere pretense, as the Fuehrer had told his generals. What he wanted was to destroy Poland. But the Duce did not know this. On the morning of September 1, he himself was confronted with the choice of immediately declaring Italy's neutrality or risking an attack by Britain and France. Ciano's diary entries make clear what a nightmare this prospect was for his deflated father-in-law.‡

Early on the morning of September 1 the unhappy Italian dictator personally telephoned Ambassador Attolico in Berlin and, in the words of Ciano, "urged him to entreat Hitler to send him a telegram releasing him from the obligations of the alliance."[11] The Fuehrer quickly and even graciously obliged. Just before he left for the Reichstag, at 9:40 A.M., he got off a telegram to his friend which was telephoned through to the German Embassy in Rome to save time.

---

* See above, pp. 566–67.
† See above, p. 588.
‡ Actually Mussolini's decision was conveyed to Britain the night before. At 11:15 P.M. on August 31 the Foreign Office received a message from Sir Percy Loraine in Rome: "Decision of the Italian Government is taken. Italy will not fight against either England or France . . . This communication made to me by Ciano at 21:15 [9:15 P.M.] under seal of secrecy."[10]

That evening the Italians had been given a scare by the British cutting off all telephone communication with Rome after 8 P.M. Ciano feared it might be the prelude to an Anglo–French attack.

DUCE:

I thank you most cordially for the diplomatic and political support which you have been giving recently to Germany and her just cause. I am convinced that we can carry out the task imposed upon us with the military forces of Germany. I do not therefore expect to need Italy's military support in these circumstances. I also thank you, Duce, for everything which you will do in future for the common cause of Fascism and National Socialism.

ADOLF HITLER[*12]

At 12:45 P.M., after having addressed the Reichstag and after having, apparently, recovered from the effects of his outburst to Dahlerus, Hitler was moved to send a further message to Mussolini. Declaring that he had been prepared to solve the Polish problem "by negotiation" and that "for two whole days I have waited in vain for a Polish negotiator" and that "last night alone there were fourteen more cases of frontier violation" and that consequently he had "now decided to answer force with force," he again expressed his gratitude to his welshing partner.

I thank you, Duce, for all your efforts. I thank you in particular also for your offers of mediation. But from the start I was skeptical about these attempts because the Polish Government, if they had had even the slightest intention of solving the matter amicably, could have done so at any time. But they refused . . .

For this reason, Duce, I did not want to expose you to the danger of assuming the role of mediator which, in view of the Polish Government's intransigent attitude, would in all probability have been in vain . . .

ADOLF HITLER[13]

But Mussolini, prompted by Ciano, made one last desperate effort to expose himself to the danger of being a mediator. Already on the previous day, shortly after noon, Ciano had proposed to the British and French ambassadors in Rome that, if their governments agreed, Mussolini would invite Germany to a conference on September 5 for the purpose of "examining the clauses of the Treaty of Versailles which are the cause of the present troubles."

It might have been thought that the news of the German invasion of Poland the next morning would have rendered Mussolini's proposal superfluous. But to the Italian's surprise Georges Bonnet, the French Foreign Minister and master appeaser, telephoned François-Poncet, who was now the ambassador of France in Rome, at 11:45 A.M. on September 1 and asked him to tell Ciano that the French government welcomed such a conference provided that it did not try to deal with problems of countries

---

* At 4:30 P.M., following a meeting of the Council of Ministers in Rome, the Italian radio broadcast the Council's announcement "to the Italian people that Italy will take no initiative in the way of military operations." Immediately afterward Hitler's message to Mussolini releasing Italy from its obligations was broadcast.

not represented and that it did not restrict itself to seeking "partial and provisional solutions for limited and immediate problems." Bonnet made no mention of any withdrawal of German troops or even of their halting, as a condition for such a conference.[14]*

But the British were insistent upon that condition and succeeded in carrying the badly'divided French cabinet along with them so that identical warning notes could be delivered in Berlin on the evening of September 1. Since the text of those notes giving notice that Britain and France would go to war unless the German troops were withdrawn from Poland was made public the same evening, it is interesting that Mussolini, now clutching desperately at every straw—or even at straws which were not there—went ahead the next morning in a further appeal to Hitler just as if he, the Duce, did not take the Anglo–French warnings at face value.

September 2, as Henderson noted in his *Final Report,* was a day of suspense.† He and Coulondre waited anxiously for Hitler's reply to their notes, but none came. Shortly after midday Attolico, somewhat out of breath, arrived at the British Embassy and told Henderson he must know one thing immediately: Was the British note of the previous evening an ultimatum or not?

"I told him," Henderson later wrote, "that I had been authorized to tell the Minister of Foreign Affairs if he had asked me—which he had not done—that it was not an ultimatum but a warning."[16]

Having received his answer, the Italian ambassador hastened down the Wilhelmstrasse to the German Foreign Office. Attolico had arrived at 10 o'clock that morning at the Wilhelmstrasse with a communication from Mussolini and, being told that Ribbentrop was unwell, handed it to Weizsaecker.

September 2, 1939

For purposes of information, Italy wishes to make known, naturally leaving any decision to the Fuehrer, that she still has the possibility of getting France, Britain and Poland to agree to a conference on the following bases:

1. An armistice, which leaves the armies *where* [emphasis in the original] they now are.

2. Convening of the conference within two to three days.

---

* Twice during the afternoon of September 1, Bonnet instructed Noël, the French ambassador in Warsaw, to ask Beck if Poland would accept the Italian proposal for a conference. Later that evening he received his reply: "We are in the midst of war as the result of unprovoked aggression. It is no longer a question of a conference but of common action which the Allies should take to resist." Bonnet's messages and Beck's reply are in the *French Yellow Book.*

The British government did not associate itself with Bonnet's efforts. A Foreign Office memorandum signed by R. M. Makins notes that the British government "was neither consulted nor informed of this *démarche.*"[15]

† The previous afternoon, on instructions from Halifax, Henderson had burned his ciphers and confidential documents and officially requested the United States chargé d'affaires "to be good enough to take charge of British interests in the event of war." (*British Blue Book,* p. 21.)

3. Settlement of the Polish–German dispute, which, as matters stand today, would certainly be favorable to Germany.

The idea, which originally emanated from the Duce, is now supported particularly by France.*

Danzig is already German, and Germany has already in her hands pledges which guarantee her the greater part of her claims. Moreover, Germany has already had her "moral satisfaction." If she accepted the proposal for a conference she would achieve all her aims and at the same time avoid a war, which even now looks like becoming general and of extremely long duration.

The Duce does not want to insist, but it is of the greatest moment to him that the above should be immediately brought to the attention of Herr von Ribbentrop and the Fuehrer.[17]

No wonder that when Ribbentrop, who had quickly recovered from his indisposition, saw Attolico at 12:30 P.M., he pointed out that the Duce's proposal could not be "reconciled" with the Anglo–French notes of the evening before, which had "the character of an ultimatum."

The Italian ambassador, who was as anxious as his chief to avoid a world war and certainly more sincere, interrupted Ribbentrop to say that the British and French declarations "had been superseded by the latest communication from the Duce." Attolico, of course, had no authority whatsoever to make such a statement, which was not true, but at this late hour he probably thought he could lose nothing by being reckless. When the German Foreign Minister expressed his doubts, Attolico stuck to his view.

The French and British declarations [he said] no longer came into consideration. Count Ciano had telephoned only at 8:30 this morning, that is to say at a time when the declarations had already been given out on the radio in Italy. It followed that the two declarations must be considered as superseded. Count Ciano stated moreover that France in particular was greatly in favor of the Duce's proposal. The pressure comes at the moment from France but England will follow.[18]

Ribbentrop remained skeptical. He had just discussed Mussolini's proposal with Hitler, he said, and what the Fuehrer wanted to know was: Were the Anglo–French notes ultimata? The Foreign Minister finally agreed to Attolico's suggestion that the Italian envoy should immediately consult Henderson and Coulondre to find out.

That was the reason for Attolico's call at the British Embassy. "I can still see Attolico, no longer in his first youth," Schmidt, who acted as interpreter, wrote later, "running out of Ribbentrop's room and down the

---

* Ciano claims that the note was sent as the result of "French pressure." (*Ciano Diaries*, p. 136.) But this is surely misleading. Though Bonnet was doing all he could to get a conference, Mussolini was pushing the proposal even more desperately.

steps to consult Henderson and Coulondre . . . A half hour later Attolico came running back, as breathless as he had left."[19]

Regaining his breath, the Italian ambassador reported that Henderson had just told him the British note was not an ultimatum. Ribbentrop replied that while "a German reply to the Anglo–French declarations could only be negative the Fuehrer was examining the Duce's proposals and, if Rome confirmed that there had been no question of an ultimatum in the Anglo–French declaration, would draft an answer in a day or two." When Attolico pressed for an earlier answer, Ribbentrop finally agreed to reply by noon the next day, Sunday, September 3.

Meantime in Rome Mussolini's hopes were being smashed. At 2 P.M. Ciano received the British and French ambassadors and in their presence telephoned to both Halifax and Bonnet and informed them of Attolico's talks with the German Foreign Minister. Bonnet was effusive as usual and, according to his own account (in the *French Yellow Book*), warmly thanked Ciano for his efforts on behalf of peace. Halifax was sterner. He confirmed that the British note was not an ultimatum—one marvels at the splitting of hairs among the statesmen over a single word, for the Anglo–French declarations spoke for themselves unequivocably—but added that in his own view the British could not accept Mussolini's proposal for a conference unless the German armies withdrew from Poland, a matter on which Bonnet again was silent. Halifax promised to telephone Ciano the decision of the British cabinet on that.

The decision came shortly after 7 P.M. Britain accepted the Duce's offer on condition that Hitler pull back his troops to the German frontier. The Italian Foreign Minister realized that Hitler would never accept this and that "nothing more could be done," as he put it in his diary.

It isn't my business [he added] to give Hitler advice that he would reject decisively and maybe with contempt. I tell this to Halifax, to the two ambassadors and to the Duce, and finally I telephone to Berlin that unless the Germans advise us to the contrary we shall let the conversations lapse. The last note of hope has died.[20]

And so at 8:50 P.M. on September 2 the weary and crushed Attolico once more made his way to the Wilhelmstrasse in Berlin. This time Ribbentrop received him in the Chancellery, where he was in conference with Hitler. A captured Foreign Office memo records the scene.

The Italian Ambassador brought the Foreign Minister the information that the British were not prepared to enter into negotiations on the basis of the Italian proposal of mediation. The British demanded, before starting negotiations, the immediate withdrawal of all German troops from the occupied Polish areas and from Danzig . . .

In conclusion the Italian Ambassador stated that the Duce now considered his mediation proposal as no longer in being. The Foreign Minister received the communication from the Italian Ambassador without comment.[21]

Not a word of thanks to the tireless Attolico for all his efforts! Only the contempt of silence toward an ally who was trying to cheat Germany of its Polish spoils.

The last slight possibility of averting World War II had now been exhausted. This apparently was obvious to all except one actor in the drama. At 9 P.M. the pusillanimous Bonnet telephoned Ciano, confirmed once more that the French note to Germany did not have the "character of an ultimatum" and reiterated that the French government was prepared to wait until noon of September 3—the next day—for a German response. However, "in order for the conference to achieve favorable results," Bonnet told Ciano, the French government agreed with the British that German troops must "evacuate" Poland. This was the first time Bonnet had mentioned this—and now only because the British had insisted upon it. Ciano replied that he did not think the Reich government would accept this condition. But Bonnet would not give up. He sought during the night a final escape from France's obligations to the now battered and beleaguered Poland. Ciano recounts this bizarre move in the first paragraph of his diary entry for September 3.

During the night I was awakened by the Ministry because Bonnet had asked Guariglia [the Italian ambassador in Paris] if we could not at least obtain a symbolic withdrawal of German forces from Poland . . . I throw the proposal in the wastebasket without informing the Duce. But this shows that France is moving toward the great test without enthusiasm and full of uncertainty.[22]

THE POLISH WAR BECOMES WORLD WAR II

Sunday, September 3, 1939, in Berlin was a lovely, end-of-the-summer day. The sun was shining, the air was balmy—"the sort of day," I noted in my diary, "the Berliner loves to spend in the woods or on the lakes nearby."

As it dawned a telegram arrived at the British Embassy from Lord Halifax for Sir Nevile Henderson, instructing him to seek an interview with the German Foreign Minister at 9 A.M. and convey a communication the text of which was then given.

The Chamberlain government had reached the end of the road. Some thirty-two hours before, it had informed Hitler that unless Germany withdrew its troops from Poland, Britain would go to war. There had been no answer, and now the British government was determined to make good its word. On the previous day it had feared, as Charles Corbin, the French ambassador in London, had informed the hesitant Bonnet at 2:30 P.M., that Hitler was deliberately delaying his reply in order to grab as much Polish territory as possible, after which, having secured Danzig, the Corridor and other areas, he might make a "magnanimous" peace proposal based on his sixteen points of August 31.[23]

To avoid that trap Halifax had proposed to the French that unless the German government gave a favorable reply within a few hours to the Anglo–French communications of September 1, the two Western nations should declare themselves at war with Germany. Following a British cabinet meeting on the afternoon of September 2, when a definite decision was made, Halifax suggested specifically that the two allies present an ultimatum to Berlin that very midnight which would expire at 6 A.M. on September 3.[24] Bonnet would not hear of any such precipitate action.

Indeed, the badly divided French cabinet had had a difficult time over the past week reaching a decision to honor France's obligations to Poland —and to Britain—in the first place. On the dark day of August 23, overwhelmed by the news that Ribbentrop had arrived in Moscow to conclude a Nazi–Soviet nonaggression pact, Bonnet had persuaded Daladier to call a meeting of the Council of National Defense to consider what France should do.* Besides Premier Daladier and Bonnet, it was attended by the ministers of the three armed services, General Gamelin, the chiefs of the Navy and Air Force and four additional generals—twelve in all.

The minutes state that Daladier posed three questions:

1. Can France remain inactive while Poland and Rumania (or one of them) are being wiped off the map of Europe?
2. What means has she of opposing it?
3. What measures should be taken now?

Bonnet himself, after explaining the grave turn of events, posed a question which was to remain uppermost in his mind to the last:

Taking stock of the situation, had we better remain faithful to our engagements and enter the war forthwith, or should we reconsider our attitude and profit by the respite thus gained? . . . The answer to this question is essentially of a military character.

When thus handed the ball, Gamelin and Admiral Darlan answered

that the Army and Navy were ready. In the early stages of the conflict they can do little against Germany. But the French mobilization by itself would bring some relief to Poland by tying down some considerable German units at our frontier.

. . . General Gamelin, asked how long Poland and Rumania could resist,

---

* The minutes of the meeting, drawn up by General Decamp, chief of Premier Daladier's military cabinet, came to light at the Riom trial. The paper was never submitted to other members of the meeting for correction, and General Gamelin in his book, *Servir,* claims it was so abbreviated as to be misleading. Still, even the timid generalissimo confirms its main outlines.

says that he believes Poland would honorably resist, which would prevent the bulk of the German forces from turning against France before next spring; by then Great Britain would be by her side.*

After a great deal of talk the French finally reached a decision, which was duly recorded in the minutes of the meeting.

In the course of the discussion it is pointed out that if we are stronger a few months hence, Germany will have gained even more, for she will have the Polish and Rumanian resources at her disposal.

Therefore France has no choice.

The only solution . . . is to adhere to our engagements to Poland assumed before negotiations were started with the U.S.S.R.

Having made up its mind, the French government began to act. Following this meeting on August 23, the *alerte* was sounded, which placed all frontier troops in their war stations. The next day 360,000 reservists were called up. On August 31 the cabinet published a communiqué saying France would "firmly fulfill" its obligations. And the next day, the first day of the German attack on Poland, Bonnet was persuaded by Halifax to associate France with Britain in the warning to Berlin that both countries would honor their word to their ally.

But on September 2, when the British pressed for an ultimatum to be presented to Hitler at midnight, General Gamelin and the French General Staff held back. After all, it was the French who alone would have to do the fighting if the Germans immediately attacked in the West. There would not be a single British trooper to aid them. The General Staff insisted on a further forty-eight hours in which to carry out the general mobilization unhindered.

At 6 P.M. Halifax telephoned Sir Eric Phipps, the British ambassador in Paris: "Forty-eight hours is impossible for British Government. The French attitude is very embarrassing to H. M. Government."

It was to become dangerously so a couple of hours later when Chamberlain rose to address a House of Commons whose majority of members, re-

---

* In his book, *Servir*, Gamelin admits that he hesitated to call attention to some of France's military weaknesses because he did not trust Bonnet. He quotes Daladier as later telling him, "You did right. If you had exposed them, the Germans would have known about them the next day."

Gamelin also claimed (in his book) that he did point out at this conference the weakness of France's military position. He says he explained that if Germany "annihilated Poland" and then threw her whole weight against the French, France would be in a "difficult" situation. "In this case," he said, "it would no longer be possible for France to enter upon the struggle . . . By spring, with the help of British troops and American equipment I hoped we should be in a position to fight a defensive battle (of course if necessary). I added that we could not hope for victory except in a long war. It had *always* been my opinion that we should not be able to assume the offensive in less than about two years . . . that is, in 1941–2."

The French generalissimo's timid views explain a good deal of subsequent history.

gardless of party, was impatient at the British delay in honoring its obligations. Their patience became almost exhausted after the Prime Minister spoke. He informed the House that no reply had yet come from Berlin. Unless it did, and contained a German assurance of withdrawal from Poland, the government would "be bound to take action." If the Germans did agree to withdraw, the British government, he said, would "be willing to regard the position as being the same as it was before the German forces crossed the Polish frontier." In the meantime, he said, the government was in communication with France about a time limit to their warning to Germany.

After thirty-nine hours of war in Poland the House of Commons was in no mood for such dilatory tactics. A smell of Munich seemed to emanate from the government bench. "Speak for England!" cried Leopold Amery from the Conservative benches as the acting leader of the Labor Opposition, Arthur Greenwood, got up to talk.

"I wonder how long we are prepared to vacillate," said Greenwood, "at a time when Britain and all that Britain stands for, and human civilization, are in peril . . . We must march with the French . . ."

That was the trouble. It was proving difficult at this moment to get the French to march. But so disturbed was Chamberlain at the angry mood of the House that he intervened in the sharp debate to plead that it took time to synchronize "thoughts and actions" by telephone with Paris. "I should be horrified if the House thought for one moment," he added, "that the statement that I have made to them betrayed the slightest weakening either of this Government or of the French Government." He said he understood the French government was "in session at this moment" and that a communication would be received from it "in the next few hours." At any rate, he tried to assure the aroused members, "I anticipate that there is only one answer I shall be able to give the House tomorrow . . . and I trust the House . . . will believe me that I speak in complete good faith . . ."

The inexorable approach of the greatest ordeal in British history was announced, as Namier later wrote, "in a singularly halting manner."

Chamberlain well understood, as the confidential British papers make clear, that he was in deep trouble with his own people and that at this critical moment for his country his own government was in danger of being overthrown.

As soon as he left the Commons he rang up Daladier. The time is recorded as 9:50 P.M. and Cadogan, listening in, made a minute of it for the record.

CHAMBERLAIN: The situation here is very grave . . . There has been an angry scene in the House . . . if France were to insist on forty-eight hours to run from midday tomorrow, it would be impossible for the Government to hold the situation here.

The Prime Minister said he quite realized that it is France who must bear the burden of a German attack. But he was convinced some step must be taken this evening.

He proposed a compromise . . . An ultimatum at 8 A.M. tomorrow . . . expiring at noon. . . .

Daladier replied that unless British bombers were ready to act at once it would be better for French to delay, if possible, for some hours attacks on German armies.

Less than an hour later, at 10:30 P.M., Halifax rang up Bonnet. He urged the French to agree to the British compromise, an ultimatum to be presented in Berlin at 8 A.M. on the morrow (September 3) and to expire at noon. The French Foreign Minister not only would not agree, he protested to Halifax that the British insistence on such speed would create a "deplorable impression." He demanded that London wait at least until noon before presenting any ultimatum to Hitler.

HALIFAX: It is impossible for H. M. Government to wait until that hour . . . It is very doubtful whether the [British] Government could hold the position here.

The House of Commons was to meet at noon, on Sunday, September 3, and it was obvious to Chamberlain and Halifax from the mood of Saturday evening's session that in order to survive they would have to give Parliament the answer it demanded. At 2 o'clock the next morning the French ambassador in London, Corbin, warned Bonnet that the Chamberlain cabinet risked overthrow if it could not give Parliament definite word. Halifax, at the close of his telephone conversation with Bonnet, therefore informed him that Britain proposed "to act on its own."

The telegram of Halifax to Henderson reached Berlin about 4 A.M.* The communication he was to make to the German government at 9 A.M. on Sunday, September 3, recalled the British note of September 1 in which Great Britain declared its intention of fulfilling its obligations to Poland unless German troops were promptly withdrawn.

---

* The Foreign Secretary had sent Henderson two warning telegrams during the night. The first, dispatched at 11:50 P.M., read:

I may have to send you instructions tonight to make an immediate communication to the German Government. Please be ready to act. You had better warn the Minister for Foreign Affairs that you may have to ask to see him at any moment.

It would seem from this telegram that the British government had not quite made up its mind to go it alone despite the French. But thirty-five minutes later, at 12:25 A.M. on September 3, Halifax wired Henderson:

You should ask for an appointment with M.F.A. [Minister for Foreign Affairs] at 9 A.M. Sunday morning. Instructions will follow.[25]

The decisive telegram from Halifax is dated 5 A.M., London time. Henderson, in his *Final Report,* says he received it 4 A.M.

Although this communication [it continued] was made more than 24 hours ago, no reply has been received but German attacks upon Poland have been continued and intensified. I have accordingly the honor to inform you that, unless not later than 11 A.M., British summer time, today September 3, satisfactory assurances to the above effect have been given by the German Government and have reached His Majesty's Government in London, a state of war will exist between the two countries as from that hour.[26]*

In the early predawn Sabbath hours Henderson found it difficult to make contact with the Wilhelmstrasse. He was told that Ribbentrop would not be "available" at 9 A.M. on the Sunday but that he could leave his communication with the official interpreter, Dr. Schmidt.

On this historic day Dr. Schmidt overslept, and, rushing to the Foreign Office by taxi, he saw the British ambassador already mounting the steps to the Foreign Office as he arrived. Ducking in by a side door, Schmidt managed to slip into Ribbentrop's office just at the stroke of 9 o'clock, in time to receive Henderson on the dot. "He came in looking very serious," Schmidt later recounted, "shook hands, but declined my invitation to be seated, remaining solemnly standing in the middle of the room."[28] He read out the British ultimatum, handed Schmidt a copy, and bade him goodby.

The official interpreter hastened down the Wilhelmstrasse to the Chancellery with the document. Outside the Fuehrer's office he found most members of the cabinet and several ranking party officials collected about and "anxiously awaiting" his news.

When I entered the next room [Schmidt later recounted] Hitler was sitting at his desk and Ribbentrop stood by the window. Both looked up expectantly as I came in. I stopped at some distance from Hitler's desk, and then slowly translated the British ultimatum. When I finished there was complete silence.

Hitler sat immobile, gazing before him . . . After an interval which seemed an age, he turned to Ribbentrop, who had remained standing by the window. "What now?" asked Hitler with a savage look, as though implying that his Foreign Minister had misled him about England's probable reaction.

Ribbentrop answered quietly: "I assume that the French will hand in a similar ultimatum within the hour."[29]

His duty performed, Schmidt withdrew, stopping in the outer room to apprise the others of what had happened. They too were silent for a moment. Then:

Goering turned to me and said: "If we lose this war, then God have mercy on us!"

---

* Halifax sent an additional wire, also dated 5 A.M., informing the ambassador that Coulondre "will not make a similar communication to the German Government until midday today (Sunday)." He did not know what the French time limit would be but thought it "likely" to be anything between six and nine hours.[27]

Goebbels stood in a corner by himself, downcast and self-absorbed. Everywhere in the room I saw looks of grave concern.[30]

In the meantime the inimitable Dahlerus had been making his last amateurish effort to avoid the inevitable. At 8 A.M. Forbes had informed him of the British ultimatum which was being presented an hour later. He hastened out to Luftwaffe headquarters to see Goering and, according to his later account on the stand at Nuremberg, appealed to him to see to it that the German reply to the ultimatum was "reasonable." He further suggested that the Field Marshal himself, before 11 o'clock, declare himself prepared to fly to London "to negotiate." In his book the Swedish businessman claims that Goering accepted the suggestion and telephoned to Hitler, who also agreed. There is no mention of this in the German papers, and Dr. Schmidt makes it clear that Goering, a few minutes after 9 o'clock, was not at his headquarters but at the Chancellery in the Fuehrer's anteroom.

At any rate, there is no doubt that the Swedish intermediary telephoned the British Foreign Office—not once but twice. In the first call, at 10:15 A.M., he took it upon himself to inform the British government that the German reply to its ultimatum was "on the way" and that the Germans were still "most anxious to satisfy the British Government and to give satisfactory assurances not to violate the independence of Poland."(!) He hoped London would consider Hitler's response "in the most favorable light."[31]

Half an hour later, at 10:50 A.M.—ten minutes before the ultimatum ran out—Dahlerus was once more on the long-distance line to the Foreign Office in London, this time to present his proposal that Goering, with Hitler's assent, fly immediately to the British capital. He did not realize that it was past time for such diplomatic antics, but he was soon made to. He was given an uncompromising answer from Halifax. His proposal could not be entertained. The German government had been asked a definite question, "and presumably they would be sending a definite answer." H. M. Government could not wait for further discussion with Goering.[32]

Whereupon Dahlerus hung up and disappeared into the limbo of history until he reappeared, briefly, after the war at Nuremberg—and in his book—to recount his bizarre attempt to save world peace.* He had meant well, he had striven for peace; for a few moments he had found himself in the center of the dazzling stage of world history. But as happened to almost everyone else, the confusion had been too great for him to see clearly; and as he would admit at Nuremberg, he had at no time realized how much he had been taken in by the Germans.

---

* He reappeared for a moment on September 24 when he met with Forbes at Oslo "to ascertain," as he told the Nuremberg tribunal before he was shut off, "if there was still a possibility of averting a world war."[33]

Shortly after 11 A.M., when the time limit in the British ultimatum had run out, Ribbentrop, who had declined to see the British ambassador two hours before, sent for him in order to hand him Germany's reply. The German government, it said, refused "to receive or accept, let alone to fulfill" the British ultimatum. There followed a lengthy and shabby propaganda statement obviously hastily concocted by Hitler and Ribbentrop during the intervening two hours. Designed to fool the easily fooled German people, it rehearsed all the lies with which we are now familiar, including the one about the Polish "attacks" on German territory, blamed Britain for all that had happened, and rejected attempts "to force Germany to recall their forces which are lined up for the defense of the Reich." It declared, falsely, that Germany had accepted Mussolini's eleventh-hour proposals for peace and pointed out that Britain had rejected them. And after all of Chamberlain's appeasement of Hitler it accused the British government of "preaching the destruction and extermination of the German people."*

Henderson read the document ("this completely false representation of events," as he later called it) and remarked "It would be left to history to judge where the blame really lay." Ribbentrop retorted that "history had already proved the facts."

I was standing in the Wilhelmstrasse before the Chancellery about noon when the loudspeakers suddenly announced that Great Britain had declared herself at war with Germany.† Some 250 people—no more—were standing there in the sun. They listened attentively to the announcement. When it was finished, there was not a murmur. They just stood there. Stunned. It was difficult for them to comprehend that Hitler had led them into a world war.

Soon, though it was the Sabbath, the newsboys were crying their extras. In fact, I noticed, they were giving the papers away. I took one. It was the *Deutsche Allgemeine Zeitung,* its headlines marching in large type across the page:

---

* So shoddy was this hastily prepared note that it ended with this sentence: "The intention, communicated to us by order of the British Government by Mr. King-Hall, of carrying the destruction of the German people even further than was done through the Versailles Treaty, is taken note of by us, and we shall therefore answer any aggressive action on the part of England with the same weapons and in the same form." The British government had, of course, never presented to Germany any intentions of Stephen King-Hall, a retired naval officer, whose newsletters were a purely private venture. In fact, Henderson had protested to the Foreign Office against the circulation of King-Hall's publication in Germany and the British government had requested the editor to desist.

† In London at 11:15 A.M. Halifax had handed the German chargé d'affaires a formal note stating that since no German assurances had been received by 11 A.M., "I have the honor to inform you that a state of war exists between the two countries as from 11 A.M. today, September 3."

BRITISH ULTIMATUM TURNED DOWN

ENGLAND DECLARES A STATE OF WAR
WITH GERMANY

BRITISH NOTE DEMANDS WITHDRAWAL
OF OUR TROOPS IN THE EAST

THE FUEHRER LEAVING TODAY FOR THE FRONT

The headline over the official account read as though it had been dictated by Ribbentrop.

GERMAN MEMORANDUM PROVES
ENGLAND'S GUILT

"Proved" though it may have been to a people as easily swindled as the Germans, it aroused no ill feelings toward the British during the day. When I passed the British Embassy, from whose premises Henderson and his staff were moving to the Hotel Adlon around the corner, a lone *Schupo* paced up and down before the building. He had nothing to do but saunter back and forth.

The French held out a little longer. Bonnet played for time until the last moment, clinging stubbornly to the hope that Mussolini might still swing a deal with Hitler which would let France off the hook. He even pleaded with the Belgian ambassador to get King Leopold to use his influence with Mussolini to influence Hitler. All day Saturday, September 2, he argued with his own cabinet, as he did with the British, that he had "promised" Ciano to wait until noon of September 3 for the German answer to the Anglo–French warning notes of September 1, and that he could not go back on his word. He had, to be sure, given this assurance to the Italian Foreign Minister over the phone—but not until 9 o'clock on the evening of September 2.* By that time the Duce's proposal for a conference was as dead as stone, as Ciano had tried to tell him. And by that hour, too, the British were pleading with him to present a joint ultimatum to Berlin at midnight.

Shortly before midnight on September 2, the French government finally reached a decision. At precisely midnight, Bonnet wired Coulondre at Berlin that in the morning he would forward the terms of a "new *démarche*" to be made "at noon to the Wilhelmstrasse."†

---

* See above, p. 608.
† But even after that, it will be remembered (see above, p. 608), Bonnet made a last-minute effort to keep France out of the war by proposing, during the night, to the Italians that they get Hitler to make a "symbolic" withdrawal from Poland.

This he did, at 10:20 A.M. on Sunday, September 3—forty minutes before the British ultimatum ran out. The French ultimatum was similarly worded except that in case of a negative reply France declared that she would fulfill her obligations to Poland "which are known to the German government"—even at this final juncture Bonnet held out against a formal declaration of war.

In the official *French Yellow Book* the text of the French ultimatum wired to Coulondre gives 5 P.M. as the time limit for the German response. But this was not the hour set in the original telegram. At 8:45 A.M. Ambassador Phipps had notified Halifax from Paris: "Bonnet tells me French time limit will only expire at 5 o'clock Monday morning [September 4]." That was the time given in Bonnet's telegram.

Though it represented a concession wrung by Daladier early Sunday morning from the French General Staff, which had insisted on a full forty-eight hours from the time the ultimatum was given Berlin at noon, it still irritated the British government, whose displeasure was communicated to Paris in no uncertain terms during the forenoon. Premier Daladier therefore made one last appeal to the military. He called in General Colston, of the General Staff, at 11:30 A.M. and urged a shorter deadline. The General reluctantly agreed to move it up by twelve hours to 5 P.M.

Thus it was that just as Coulondre was leaving the French Embassy in Berlin for the Wilhelmstrasse, Bonnet got through to him on the telephone and instructed him to make the necessary change in the zero hour.[34]

Ribbentrop was not available to the French ambassador at the noon hour. He was taking part in a little ceremony at the Chancellery, where the new Soviet ambassador, Alexander Shkvarzev, was being warmly received by the Fuehrer—an occasion that lent a bizarre note to this historic Sabbath in Berlin. Coulondre, insistent on following the letter of his instructions to call at the Wilhelmstrasse at precisely twelve noon, was therefore received by Weizsaecker. To the ambassador's inquiry as to whether the State Secretary was empowered to give a "satisfactory" answer to the French, Weizsaecker replied that he was not in a position to give him "any kind of reply."

There now followed at this solemn moment a minor diplomatic comedy. When Coulondre attempted to treat Weizsaecker's response as the negative German reply which he fully anticipated and to hand to the State Secretary France's formal ultimatum, the latter declined to accept it. He suggested that the ambassador "be good enough to be patient a little longer and see the Foreign Minister personally." Thus rebuffed—and not for the first time—Coulondre cooled his heels for nearly half an hour. At 12:30 P.M. he was conducted to the Chancellery to see Ribbentrop.[35]

Though the Nazi Foreign Minister knew what the ambassador's mission was, he could not let the opportunity, the very last such one, slip by without treating the French envoy to one of his customary prevarications of history. After remarking that Mussolini, in presenting his last-minute peace proposal, had emphasized that France approved it, Ribbentrop declared that "Germany had informed the Duce yesterday that she also was prepared to agree to the proposal. Later in the day," Ribbentrop added, "the Duce reported that his proposal had been wrecked by the intransigence of the British Government."

But Coulondre, over the past months, had heard enough of Ribbentrop's falsifications. After listening a little longer to the Nazi Foreign Minister, who had gone on to say that he would regret it if France followed Great Britain and that Germany had no intention of attacking France, the ambassador got in the question he had come to ask: Did the Foreign Minister's remarks mean that the response of the German government to the French communication of September 1 was negative?

"*Ja,*" replied Ribbentrop.

The ambassador then handed the Foreign Minister France's ultimatum, prefacing it with a remark that "for the last time" he must emphasize the "heavy responsibility of the Reich Government" in attacking Poland "without a declaration of war" and in refusing the Anglo–French request that German troops be withdrawn.

"Then France will be the aggressor," Ribbentrop said.

"History will be the judge of that," Coulondre replied.

On that Sunday in Berlin all the participants in the final act of the drama seemed intent on calling upon the judgment of history.

Although France was mobilizing an army which would have overwhelming superiority for the time being over the German forces in the west, it was Great Britain, whose army at the moment was negligible, which loomed in Hitler's feverish mind as the main enemy and as the antagonist who was almost entirely responsible for the pass in which he found himself as September 3, 1939, began to wane and pass into history. This was made clear in the two grandiose proclamations which he issued during the afternoon to the German people and to the Army of the West. His bitter resentment and hysterical anger at the British burst forth.

Great Britain [he said in an "Appeal to the German People"] has for centuries pursued the aim of rendering the peoples of Europe defenseless against the British policy of world conquest . . . [and] claimed the right to attack on threadbare pretexts and destroy that European state which at the moment seemed most dangerous . . .

We ourselves have been witnesses of the policy of encirclement . . . carried on by Great Britain against Germany since before the war . . . The British war inciters . . . oppressed the German people under the Versailles *Diktat* . . .

Soldiers of the Western Army! [Hitler said in an appeal to the troops who for many weeks could only face the French Army] . . . Great Britain has pursued the policy of Germany's encirclement . . . The British Government, driven on by those warmongers whom we knew in the last war, have resolved to let fall their mask and to proclaim war on a threadbare pretext . . .

There was not a word about France.

In London at six minutes past noon, Chamberlain addressed the House of Commons and informed it that Britain was now at war with Germany. Though Hitler, on September 1, had forbidden listening to foreign broadcasts on the pain of death, we picked up in Berlin the words of the Prime Minister as quoted over the BBC. To those of us who had seen him risking his political life at Godesberg and Munich to appease Hitler, his words were poignant.

This is a sad day for all of us, and to none is it sadder than to me. Everything that I have worked for, everything that I have believed in during my public life, has crashed into ruins. There is only one thing left for me to do: that is, to devote what strength and powers I have to forwarding the victory of the cause for which we have to sacrifice so much . . . I trust I may live to see the day when Hitlerism has been destroyed and a liberated Europe has been re-established.

Chamberlain was fated not to live to see that day. He died, a broken man—though still a member of the cabinet—on November 9, 1940. In view of all that has been written about him in these pages it seems only fitting to quote what was said of him by Churchill, whom he had excluded from the affairs of the British nation for so long and who on May 10, 1940, succeeded him as Prime Minister. Paying tribute to his memory in the Commons on November 12, 1940, Churchill said:

. . . It fell to Neville Chamberlain in one of the supreme crises of the world to be contradicted by events, to be disappointed in his hopes, and to be deceived and cheated by a wicked man. But what were these hopes in which he was disappointed? What were these wishes in which he was frustrated? What was that faith that was abused? They were surely among the most noble and benevolent instincts of the human heart—the love of peace, the toil for peace, the strife for peace, the pursuit of peace, even at great peril and certainly in utter disdain of popularity or clamor.

His diplomacy having failed to keep Britain and France out of the war, Hitler turned his attention during the afternoon of September 3 to military matters. He issued Top-Secret Directive No. 2 for the Conduct of the War. Despite the Anglo–French war declarations, it said, "the German war objective remains for the time being the speedy and victorious conclusion of the operations against Poland . . . In the West the opening of hostilities is to be left to the enemy . . . Against Britain, naval offensive operations are permitted." The Luftwaffe was not to attack even British naval forces unless the British opened similar attacks on German targets—and then only "if prospects of success are particularly favorable." The conversion of the whole of German industry to "war economy" was ordered.[36]

At 9 o'clock in the evening Hitler and Ribbentrop left Berlin in separate special trains for General Headquarters in the East. But not before they had made two more diplomatic moves. Britain and France were now at war with Germany. But there were the two other great European powers, whose support had made Hitler's venture possible, to consider: Italy, the ally, which had reneged at the last moment, and Soviet Russia, which, though distrusted by the Nazi dictator, had obliged him by making his gamble on war seem worth the taking.

Just before leaving the capital, Hitler got off another letter to Mussolini. It was dispatched by wire at 8:51 P.M., nine minutes before the Fuehrer's special train pulled out of the station. Though not entirely frank nor devoid of deceit it gives the best picture we shall probably ever have of the mind of Adolf Hitler as he set out for the first time from the darkened capital of the Third Reich to assume his role as Supreme German Warlord. It is among the captured Nazi papers.

DUCE:

I must first thank you for your last attempt at mediation. I would have been ready to accept, but only on condition that some possibility could have been found to give me certain guarantees that the conference would be successful. For the German troops have been engaged for two days in an extraordinarily rapid advance into Poland. It would have been impossible to allow blood which was there sacrificed to be squandered through diplomatic intrigue.

Nevertheless, I believe that a way could have been found if England had not been determined from the outset to let it come to war in any case. I did not yield to England's threats because, Duce, I no longer believe that peace could have been maintained for more than six months or, shall we say, a year. In these circumstances, I considered that the present moment was, in spite of everything, more suitable for making a stand.

. . . The Polish Army will collapse in a very short time. Whether it would have been possible to achieve this quick success in another year or two is, I must say, very doubtful in my opinion. England and France would have gone on arming their allies to such an extent that the decisive technical superiority of the German Wehrmacht could not have been in evidence in the same way. I am aware, Duce, that the struggle in which I am engaging is a struggle for life and death . . . But I am also aware that such a struggle cannot in the end be avoided, and that the moment for resistance must be chosen with icy deliberation so that the likelihood of success is assured; and in this success, Duce, my faith is as firm as a rock.

Next came words of warning to Mussolini.

You kindly assured me recently that you believe you can help in some fields. I accept this in advance with sincere thanks. But I also believe that, even if we now march down separate paths, destiny will yet bind us one to the other. If National Socialist Germany were to be destroyed by the Western democracies, Fascist Italy also would face a hard future. I personally was always aware that the futures of our two regimes were bound up, and I know that you, Duce, are of exactly the same opinion.

After recounting the initial German victories in Poland, Hitler concluded:

. . . In the West I shall remain on the defensive. France can shed her blood there first. The moment will then come when we can pit ourselves there also against the enemy with the whole strength of the nation.

Please accept once more my thanks, Duce, for all the support you have given me in the past, and which I ask you not to refuse me in the future either.

ADOLF HITLER[37]

Hitler's disappointment that Italy did not honor her word, even after Britain and France had honored theirs by declaring war on this day, was kept under tight control. A friendly Italy, even though nonbelligerent, could still be helpful to him.

But even more helpful could be Russia.

Already on the first day of the German attack on Poland the Soviet government, as the secret Nazi papers would later reveal, had rendered the German Luftwaffe a signal service. Very early on that morning the Chief of the General Staff of the Air Force, General Hans Jeschonnek, had rung up the German Embassy in Moscow to say that in order to give his pilots navigational aid in the bombing of Poland—"urgent navigation tests," he called it—he would appreciate it if the Russian radio station at Minsk would continually identify itself. By afternoon Ambassador von der Schulenburg was able to inform Berlin that the Soviet government was "prepared to meet your wishes." The Russians agreed to introduce a station identification as often as possible in the programs over their transmitter and to extend the broadcasting time of the Minsk station by two hours so as to aid the German flyers late at night.[38]

But as they prepared to leave Berlin late on September 3 Hitler and Ribbentrop had in mind much more substantial Russian military help for their conquest of Poland. At 6:50 P.M., Ribbentrop got off a "most urgent" telegram to the embassy in Moscow. It was marked "Top Secret" and began: "Exclusive for the Ambassador. For the Head of Mission or his representative personally. Special security handling. To be decoded by himself. Most secret."

In the greatest of secrecy the Germans invited the Soviet Union to join in the attack on Poland!

We definitely expect to have beaten the Polish Army decisively in a few weeks. We should then keep the territory that was fixed at Moscow as a

German sphere of interest under military occupation. We should naturally, however, for military reasons, have to continue to take action against such Polish military forces as are at that time located in the Polish territory belonging to the Russian sphere of interest.

Please discuss this at once with Molotov and see if the Soviet Union does not consider it desirable for Russian forces to move at the proper time against Polish forces in the Russian sphere of interest and for their part to occupy this territory. In our estimation this would be not only a relief for us, but also be in the sense of the Moscow agreements and in the Soviet interest as well.[39]

That such a cynical move by the Soviet Union would be a "relief" to Hitler and Ribbentrop is obvious. It would not only avoid misunderstandings and friction between the Germans and the Russians in dividing up the spoils but would take some of the onus of the Nazi aggression in Poland off Germany and place it on the Soviet Union. If they shared the booty, why should they not share the blame?

The most gloomy German of any consequence in Berlin that Sunday noon after it became known that Britain was in the war was Grand Admiral Erich Raeder, Commander in Chief of the German Navy. For him the war had come four or five years too soon. By 1944–45, the Navy's Z Plan would have been completed, giving Germany a sizable fleet with which to confront the British. But this was September 3, 1939, and Raeder knew, even if Hitler wouldn't listen to him, that he had neither the surface ships nor even the submarines to wage effective war against Great Britain.

Confiding to his diary, the Admiral wrote:

Today the war against France and England broke out, the war which, according to the Fuehrer's previous assertions, we had no need to expect before 1944. The Fuehrer believed up to the last minute that it could be avoided, even if this meant postponing a final settlement of the Polish question. . . .

As far as the Navy is concerned, obviously it is in no way very adequately equipped for the great struggle with Great Britain . . . the submarine arm is still much too weak to have any *decisive* effect on the war. The surface forces, moreover, are so inferior in number and strength to those of the British Fleet that, even at full strength, they can do no more than show that they know how to die gallantly . . .[40]

Nevertheless at 9 P.M. on September 3, 1939, at the moment Hitler was departing Berlin, the German Navy struck. Without warning, the submarine *U-30* torpedoed and sank the British liner *Athenia* some two hundred miles west of the Hebrides as it was en route from Liverpool to Montreal with 1,400 passengers, of whom 112, including twenty-eight Americans, lost their lives.

World War II had begun.

Book Four

✠ ✠ ✠

WAR: EARLY VICTORIES AND THE TURNING POINT

18

THE FALL OF POLAND

At ten o'clock on the morning of September 5, 1939, General Halder had a talk with General von Brauchitsch, the Commander in Chief of the German Army, and General von Bock, who led Army Group North. After sizing up the situation as it looked to them at the beginning of the fifth day of the German attack on Poland they agreed, as Halder wrote in his diary, that "the enemy is practically beaten."

By the evening of the previous day the battle for the Corridor had ended with the junction of General von Kluge's Fourth Army, pushing eastward from Pomerania, and General von Kuechler's Third Army, driving westward from East Prussia. It was in this battle that General Heinz Guderian first made a name for himself with his tanks. At one point, racing east across the Corridor, they had been counterattacked by the Pomorska Brigade of cavalry, and this writer, coming upon the scene a few days later, saw the sickening evidence of the carnage. It was symbolic of the brief Polish campaign.

Horses against tanks! The cavalryman's long lance against the tank's long cannon! Brave and valiant and foolhardy though they were, the Poles were simply overwhelmed by the German onslaught. This was their—and the world's—first experience of the blitzkrieg: the sudden surprise attack; the fighter planes and bombers roaring overhead, reconnoitering, attacking, spreading flame and terror; the Stukas screaming as they dove; the tanks, whole divisions of them, breaking through and thrusting forward thirty or forty miles in a day; self-propelled, rapid-firing heavy guns rolling forty miles an hour down even the rutty Polish roads; the incredible speed of even the infantry, of the whole vast army of a million and a half men on motorized wheels, directed and co-ordinated through a maze of electronic communications consisting of intricate radio, telephone and telegraphic networks. This was a monstrous mechanized juggernaut such as the earth had never seen.

Within forty-eight hours the Polish Air Force was destroyed, most of its five hundred first-line planes having been blown up by German bombing on their home airfields before they could take off. Installations were burned and most of the ground crews were killed or wounded. Cracow, the second city of Poland, fell on September 6. That night the Polish government fled from Warsaw to Lublin. The next day Halder busied himself with plans to begin transferring troops to the Western front, though he could detect no activity there. On the afternoon of September 8 the 4th Panzer Division reached the outskirts of the Polish capital, while directly south of the city, rolling up from Silesia and Slovakia, Reichenau's Tenth Army captured Kielce and List's Fourteenth Army arrived at Sandomierz, at the junction of the Vistula and San rivers.

In one week the Polish Army had been vanquished. Most of its thirty-five divisions—all that there had been time to mobilize—had been either shattered or caught in a vast pincers movement that closed in around Warsaw. There now remained for the Germans the "second phase": tightening the noose around the dazed and disorganized Polish units which were surrounded and destroying them, and completing a second and larger pincers movement a hundred miles to the east which would trap the remaining Polish formations west of Brest Litovsk and the River Bug.

This phase began September 9 and ended on September 17. The left wing of Bock's Army Group North headed for Brest Litovsk, which Guderian's XIXth Corps reached on the fourteenth and captured two days later. On September 17 it met patrols of List's Fourteenth Army fifty miles south of Brest Litovsk at Wlodawa, closing the second great pincers there. The "counterattack," as Guderian later observed, had come to a "definite conclusion" on September 17. All Polish forces, except for a handful on the Russian border, were surrounded. Pockets of Polish troops in the Warsaw triangle and farther west near Posen held out valiantly, but they were doomed. The Polish government, or what was left of it, after being unceasingly bombed and strafed by the Luftwaffe reached a village on the Rumanian frontier on the fifteenth. For it and the proud nation all was over, except the dying in the ranks of the units which still, with incredible fortitude, held out.

It was now time for the Russians to move in on the stricken country to grab a share of the spoils.

THE RUSSIANS INVADE POLAND

The Kremlin in Moscow, like every other seat of government, had been taken by surprise at the rapidity with which the German armies hurtled through Poland. On September 5 Molotov, in giving a formal written reply to the Nazi suggestion that Russia attack Poland from the east, stated that this would be done "at a suitable time" but that "this time has not yet come." He thought that "excessive haste" might injure the Soviet "cause" but he insisted that even though the Germans got there first they must scrupulously observe the "line of demarcation" in Poland agreed upon in the secret clauses of the Nazi–Soviet Pact.[1] Russian suspicion of the Germans was already evident. So was the feeling in the Kremlin that the German conquest of Poland might take quite a long time.

But shortly after midnight of September 8, after a German armored division had reached the outskirts of Warsaw, Ribbentrop wired "urgent" a "top secret" message to Schulenburg in Moscow stating that operations in Poland were "progressing even beyond our expectations" and that in these circumstances Germany would like to know the "military intentions of the Soviet Government."[2] By 4:10 P.M. the next day Molotov had replied that Russia would move militarily "within the next few days." Earlier in the day the Soviet Foreign Commissar had officially congratulated the Germans "on the entry of German troops into Warsaw."[3]

On September 10, Molotov and Ambassador von der Schulenburg got into a fine snafu. After declaring that the Soviet government had been taken "completely by surprise by the unexpectedly rapid German military successes" and that the Soviet Union was consequently in "a difficult situation," the Foreign Commissar touched on the excuse which the Kremlin would have to give for its own aggression in Poland. This was, as Schulenburg wired Berlin "most urgent" and "top secret,"

that Poland was falling apart and that it was necessary for the Soviet Union, in consequence, to come to the aid of the Ukrainians and the White Russians "threatened" by Germany. This argument [said Molotov] was necessary to make the intervention of the Soviet Union plausible to the masses and at the same time avoid giving the Soviet Union the appearance of an aggressor.

Furthermore, Molotov complained that General von Brauchitsch had just been quoted by D.N.B. as saying that "military action was no longer necessary on the German eastern border." If that were so, if the war was over, Russia, said Molotov, "could not start a new war." He was very displeased about the whole situation.[4] To further complicate matters he summoned Schulenburg to the Kremlin on September 14 and after informing him that the Red Army would march sooner than they had anticipated demanded to know when Warsaw would fall. In order to justify their move the Russians must wait on the capture of the Polish capital.[5]

The Commissar had raised some embarrassing questions. When would Warsaw fall? How did the Germans like being blamed for Russian intervention? On the evening of September 15 Ribbentrop dispatched a "most urgent," a "top secret" message to Molotov through the German ambassador, answering them. Warsaw, he said, would be occupied "in the next few days." Germany would "welcome the Soviet military operation now." As to the Russian excuse blaming Germany for it, this "was out of the question . . . contrary to the true German intentions . . . would be in contradiction to the arrangements made in Moscow and finally . . . would make the two States appear as enemies before the whole world." He ended by asking the Soviet government to set "the day and the hour" for their attack on Poland.[6]

This was done the next evening and two dispatches of Schulenburg, which are among the captured German papers, telling how it was done give a revealing picture of the Kremlin's deceit.

I saw Molotov at 6 P.M. [Schulenburg wired on September 16]. Molotov declared that military intervention by the Soviet Union was imminent— perhaps even tomorrow or the day after. Stalin was at present in consultation with the military leaders . . .

Molotov added that . . . the Soviet Government intended to justify its procedure as follows: The Polish State had disintegrated and no longer existed; therefore, all agreements concluded with Poland were void: third powers might try to profit by the chaos which had arisen; the Soviet Government considered itself obligated to intervene to protect its Ukrainian and White Russian brothers and make it possible for these unfortunate people to work in peace.

Since Germany could be the only possible "third power" in question, Schulenburg objected.

Molotov conceded that the proposed argument of the Soviet Government contained a note that was jarring to German sensibilities but asked us in view of the difficult situation of the Soviet Government not to stumble over this piece of straw. The Soviet Government unfortunately saw no possibility of any other motivation, since the Soviet Union had heretofore not bothered about the plight of its minorities in Poland and had to justify abroad, in some way or other, its present intervention.[7]

At 5:20 P.M. on September 17, Schulenburg got off another "most urgent" and "top secret" wire to Berlin.

Stalin received me at 2 o'clock . . . and declared that the Red Army would cross the Soviet border at 6 o'clock . . . Soviet planes would begin today to bomb the district east of Lwów (Lemberg).

When Schulenburg objected to three points in the Soviet communiqué the Russian dictator "with the utmost readiness" altered the text.[8]

Thus it was that on the shabby pretext that because Poland had ceased to exist and therefore the Polish–Soviet nonaggression pact had also ceased to exist and because it was necessary to protect its own interests and those of the Ukrainian and White Russian minorities, the Soviet Union trampled over a prostrate Poland beginning on the morning of September 17. To add insult to injury the Polish ambassador in Moscow was informed that Russia would maintain strict neutrality in the Polish conflict! The next day, September 18, Soviet troops met the Germans at Brest Litovsk, where exactly twenty-one years before a newborn Bolshevik government had gone back on its country's ties with the Western Allies and had received from the German Army, and accepted, separate peace terms of great harshness.

And yet though they were now accomplices of Nazi Germany in wiping ancient Poland off the map, the Russians were at once distrustful of their new comrades. At his meeting with the German ambassador on the eve of the Soviet aggression, Stalin had expressed his doubts, as Schulenburg duly notified Berlin, whether the German High Command would stand by the Moscow agreements and withdraw to the line that had been agreed upon. The ambassador tried to reassure him but apparently with no great success. "In view of Stalin's well-known attitude of mistrust," Schulenburg wired Berlin, "I would be gratified if I were authorized to make a further declaration of such a nature as to remove his last doubts."[9] The next day, September 19, Ribbentrop telegraphed the ambassador authorizing him to "tell Stalin that the agreements which I made at Moscow will, of course, be kept, and that they are regarded by us as the foundation stone of the new friendly relations between Germany and the Soviet Union."[10]

Nevertheless friction between the two unnatural partners continued. On September 17 there was disagreement over the text of a joint communiqué which would "justify" the Russo–German destruction of Poland. Stalin objected to the German version because "it presented the facts all too frankly." Whereupon he wrote out his own version, a masterpiece of subterfuge, and forced the Germans to accept it. It stated that the joint aim of Germany and Russia was "to restore peace and order in Poland, which has been destroyed by the disintegration of the Polish State, and to help the Polish people to establish new conditions for its political life." For cynicism Hitler had met his match in Stalin.

At first both dictators seem to have considered setting up a rump Polish state on the order of Napoleon's Grand Duchy of Warsaw in order to mollify world public opinion. But on September 19 Molotov disclosed that the Bolsheviks were having second thoughts on that. After angrily protesting to Schulenburg that the German generals were disregarding the Moscow agreement by trying to grab territory that should go to Russia, he came to the main point.

> Molotov hinted [Schulenburg wired Berlin] that the original inclination entertained by the Soviet Government and Stalin personally to permit the existence of a residual Poland had given way to the inclination to partition Poland along the Pissa–Narew–Vistula–San Line. The Soviet Government wishes to commence negotiations on this matter at once.[11]

Thus the initiative to partition Poland completely, to deny the Polish people any independent existence of their own whatsoever, came from the Russians. But the Germans did not need much urging to agree. On September 23 Ribbentrop wired Schulenburg instructing him to tell Molotov that the "Russian idea of a border line along the well-known four-rivers line coincides with the view of the Reich Government." He proposed to again fly to Moscow to work out the details of that as well as of "the definitive structure of the Polish area."[12]

Stalin now took personal charge of the negotiations, and his German allies learned, as his British and American allies later would also learn, what a tough, cynical and opportunistic bargainer he was. The Soviet dictator summoned Schulenburg to the Kremlin at 8 P.M. on September 25 and the ambassador's dispatch later that evening warned Berlin of some stern realities and of some chickens that were coming home to roost.

Stalin stated . . . he considered it wrong to leave an independent residual Poland. He proposed that from the territory to the east of the demarcation line, all the Province of Warsaw which extends to the Bug should be added to our share. In return we should waive our claim to Lithuania.

Stalin . . . added that if we consented, the Soviet Union would immediately take up the solution of the problem of the Baltic countries in accordance with the [secret] Protocol of August 23, and expected in this matter the unstinting support of the German Government. Stalin expressly indicated Estonia, Latvia and Lithuania, but did not mention Finland.[13]

This was a shrewd and hard bargain. Stalin was offering to trade two Polish provinces, which the Germans had already captured, for the Baltic States. He was taking advantage of the great service he had rendered Hitler—making it possible for him to attack Poland—to get everything he could for Russia while the getting was good. Moreover, he was proposing that the Germans take over the mass of the Polish people. As a Russian, he well knew what centuries of history had taught: that the Poles would never peacefully submit to the loss of their independence. Let them be a headache for the Germans, not the Russians! In the meantime he would get the Baltic States, which had been taken from Russia after the First World War and whose geographical position offered the Soviet Union great protection against surprise attack by his German ally.

Ribbentrop arrived by plane in Moscow for the second time at 6 P.M. on September 28, and before proceeding to the Kremlin he had time to read two telegrams from Berlin which apprised him of what the Russians were up to. They were messages forwarded from the German minister at Tallinn, who reported that the Estonian government had just informed him that the Soviet Union had demanded, "under the gravest threat of imminent attack," military and air bases in Estonia.[14] Later that night, after a long conference with Stalin and Molotov, Ribbentrop wired Hitler that "this very night" a pact was being concluded which would put two Red Army divisions and an Air Force brigade "on Estonian territory, without, however, abolishing the Estonian system of government at this time." But the Fuehrer, an experienced hand at this sort of thing, knew how fleeting Estonia's time would be. The very next day Ribbentrop was informed that Hitler had ordered the evacuation of the 86,000 Volksdeutsche in Estonia *and* Latvia.[15]

Stalin was presenting his bill and Hitler, for the time being at least, had to pay it. He was instantly abandoning not only Estonia but Latvia, both of which, he had agreed in the Nazi–Soviet Pact, belonged in the Soviet sphere of interest. Before the day was up he was also giving up Lithuania, on Germany's northeastern border, which, according to the secret clauses of the Moscow Pact, belonged in the Reich's sphere.

Stalin had presented the Germans two choices in the meeting with Ribbentrop, which began at 10 P.M. on September 27 and lasted until 1 A.M. They were, as he had suggested to Schulenburg on the twenty-fifth: acceptance of the original line of demarcation in Poland along the Pissa, Narew, Vistula and San rivers, with Germany getting Lithuania; or yielding Lithuania to Russia in return for more Polish territory (the province of Lublin and the lands to the east of Warsaw) which would give the Germans almost all of the Polish people. Stalin strongly urged the second choice and Ribbentrop in a long telegram to Hitler filed at 4 A.M. on September 28 put it up to Hitler, who agreed.

Dividing up Eastern Europe took quite a bit of intricate drawing of maps, and after three and a half more hours of negotiations on the afternoon of September 28, followed by a state banquet at the Kremlin, Stalin and Molotov excused themselves in order to confer with a Latvian delegation they had summoned to Moscow. Ribbentrop dashed off to the opera house to take in an act of *Swan Lake,* returning to the Kremlin at midnight for further consultations about maps and other things. At 5 A.M. Molotov and Ribbentrop put their signatures to a new pact officially called the "German–Soviet Boundary and Friendship Treaty" while Stalin once more beamed on, as a German official later reported, "with obvious satisfaction."* He had reason to.[17]

The Treaty itself, which was made public, announced the boundary of the "respective national interests" of the two countries in "the former Polish state" and stated that within their acquired territories they would re-establish "peace and order" and "assure the people living there a peaceful life in keeping with their national character."

But, as with the previous Nazi–Soviet deal, there were "secret protocols"—three of them, of which two contained the meat of the agreement. One added Lithuania to the Soviet "sphere of influence," and the provinces of Lublin and Eastern Warsaw to the German. The second was short and to the point.

Both parties will tolerate in their territories no Polish agitation which affects the territories of the other party. They will suppress in their territories all beginnings of such agitation and inform each other concerning suitable measures for this purpose.

---

* This official, Andor Hencke, Understate Secretary in the Foreign Office, who had served for many years in the embassy at Moscow, wrote a detailed and amusing account of the talks. It was the only German record made of the second day's conferences.[16]

So Poland, like Austria and Czechoslovakia before it, disappeared from the map of Europe. But this time Adolf Hitler was aided and abetted in his obliteration of a country by the Union of Soviet Socialist Republics, which had posed for so long as the champion of the oppressed peoples. This was the fourth partition of Poland by Germany and Russia* (Austria had participated in the others), and while it lasted it was to be by far the most ruthless and pitiless. In the secret protocol of September 28† Hitler and Stalin agreed to institute in Poland a regime of terror designed to brutally suppress Polish freedom, culture and national life.

Hitler fought and won the war in Poland, but the greater winner was Stalin, whose troops scarcely fired a shot.‡ The Soviet Union got nearly half of Poland and a stranglehold on the Baltic States. It blocked Germany more solidly than ever from two of its main long-term objectives: Ukrainian wheat and Rumanian oil, both badly needed if Germany was to survive the British blockade. Even Poland's oil region of Borislav–Drogobycz, which Hitler desired, was claimed successfully by Stalin, who graciously agreed to sell the Germans the equivalent of the area's annual production.

Why did Hitler pay such a high price to the Russians? It is true that he had agreed to it in August in order to keep the Soviet Union out of the Allied camp and out of the war. But he had never been a stickler for keeping agreements and now, with Poland conquered by an incomparable feat of German arms, he might have been expected to welsh, as the Army urged, on the August 23 pact. If Stalin objected, the Fuehrer could threaten him with attack by the most powerful army in the world, as the Polish campaign had just proved it to be. Or could he? Not while the British and French stood at arms in the West. To deal with Britain and France he must keep his rear free. This, as subsequent utterances of his would make clear, was the reason why he allowed Stalin to strike such a hard bargain. But he did not forget the Soviet dictator's harsh dealings as he now turned his attention to the Western front.

---

* Arnold Toynbee, in his various writings, calls it the fifth partition.
† Though signed at 5 A.M. September 29, the treaty is officially dated September 28.
‡ German casualties in Poland were officially given as 10,572 killed, 30,322 wounded and 3,400 missing.

19

SITZKRIEG IN THE WEST

NOTHING MUCH had happened there. Hardly a shot had been fired. The German man in the street was beginning to call it the "sit-down war"—*Sitzkrieg*. In the West it would soon be dubbed the "phony war." Here was "the strongest army in the world [the French]," as the British General J. F. C. Fuller would put it, "facing no more than twenty-six [German] divisions, sitting still and sheltering behind steel and concrete while a quixotically valiant ally was being exterminated!"[1]

Were the Germans surprised? Hardly. In Halder's very first diary entry, that of August 14, the Chief of the Army General Staff had composed a detailed estimate of the situation in the West if Germany attacked Poland. He considered a French offensive "not very likely." He was sure that France would not send its army through Belgium "against Belgian wishes." His conclusion was that the French would remain on the defensive. On September 7, with the Polish Army already doomed, Halder, as has been noted, was already occupied with plans to transfer German divisions to the west.

That evening he noted down the results of a conference which Brauchitsch had had during the afternoon with Hitler.

Operation in the West not yet clear. Some indications that there is no real intention of waging a war . . . French cabinet lacks heroic caliber. Also from Britain first hints of sobering reflection.

Two days later Hitler issued Directive No. 3 for the Conduct of the War, ordering arrangements to be made for Army and Air Force units to be sent from Poland to the west. But not necessarily to fight. "Even after the irresolute opening of hostilities by Great Britain . . . and France my express command," the directive laid it down, "must be obtained in each of the following cases: Every time our ground forces [or] . . . one of our planes cross the western borders; [and] for every air attack on Britain."[2]

What had France and Britain promised Poland to do in case she were attacked? The British guarantee was general. But the French was specific. It was laid down in the Franco–Polish Military Convention of May 19, 1939. In this it was agreed that the French would "progressively launch offensive operations against limited objectives toward the third day after General Mobilization Day." General mobilization had been proclaimed September 1. But further, it was agreed that "as soon as the principal German effort develops against Poland, France will launch an offensive action against Germany with the bulk of her forces, starting on the fifteenth day after the first day of the general French mobilization." When the Deputy Chief of the Polish General Staff, Colonel Jaklincz, had asked how many French troops would be available for this major offensive, General Gamelin had replied that there would be about thirty-five to thirty-eight divisions.[3]

But by August 23, as the German attack on Poland became imminent, the timid French generalissimo was telling his government, as we have seen,* that he could not possibly mount a serious offensive "in less than about two years . . . in 1941–2"—assuming, he had added, that France by that time had the "help of British troops and American equipment."

In the first weeks of the war, to be sure, Britain had pitifully few troops to send to France. By October 11, three weeks after the fighting was over in Poland, it had four divisions—158,000 men—in France. "A symbolic contribution," Churchill called it, and Fuller noted that the first British casualty—a corporal shot dead on patrol—did not occur until December 9. "So bloodless a war," Fuller comments, "had not been seen since the Battles of Molinella and Zagonara."†

In retrospect at Nuremberg the German generals agreed that by failing to attack in the West during the Polish campaign the Western Allies had missed a golden opportunity.

The success against Poland was only possible [said General Halder] by almost completely baring our Western border. If the French had seen the logic of the situation and had used the engagement of the German forces in Poland, they would have been able to cross the Rhine without our being able to prevent it and would have threatened the Ruhr area, which was the most decisive factor of the German conduct of the war.[4]

---

* See above, p. 610n.
† On October 9 this writer journeyed by rail up the east bank of the Rhine where for a hundred miles it forms the Franco–German frontier and noted in his diary: "No sign of war and the train crew told me not a shot had been fired on this front since the war began . . . We could see the French bunkers and at many places great mats behind which the French were building fortifications. Identical picture on the German side. The troops . . . went about their business in full sight and range of each other . . . The Germans were hauling up guns and supplies on the railroad line, but the French did not disturb them. Queer kind of war." (*Berlin Diary,* p. 234.)

. . . . If we did not collapse in 1939 [said General Jodl] that was due only to the fact that during the Polish campaign the approximately 110 French and British divisions in the West were held completely inactive against the 23 German divisions.[5]

And General Keitel, Chief of the OKW, added this testimony:

We soldiers had always expected an attack by France during the Polish campaign, and were very surprised that nothing happened . . . A French attack would have encountered only a German military screen, not a real defense.[6]

Why then did not the French Army (the first two British divisions were not deployed until the first week of October), which had overwhelming superiority over the German forces in the west, attack, as General Gamelin and the French government had promised in writing it would?

There were many reasons: the defeatism in the French High Command, the government and the people; the memories of how France had been bled white in the First World War and a determination not to suffer such slaughter again if it could be avoided; the realization by mid-September that the Polish armies were so badly defeated that the Germans would soon be able to move superior forces to the west and thus probably wipe out any initial French advances; the fear of German superiority in arms and in the air. Indeed, the French government had insisted from the start that the British Air Force should not bomb targets in Germany for fear of reprisal on French factories, though an all-out bombing of the Ruhr, the industrial heart of the Reich, might well have been disastrous to the Germans. It was the one great worry of the German generals in September, as many of them later admitted.

Fundamentally the answer to the question of why France did not attack Germany in September was probably best stated by Churchill. "This battle," he wrote, "had been lost some years before."[7] At Munich in 1938; at the time of the reoccupation of the Rhineland in 1936; the year before when Hitler proclaimed a conscript army in defiance of Versailles. The price of those sorry Allied failures to act had now to be paid, though it seems to have been thought in Paris and London that payment might somehow be evaded by inaction.

At sea there was action.

The German Navy was not put under such wraps as the Army in the west, and during the first week of hostilities it sank eleven British ships with a total tonnage of 64,595 tons, which was nearly half the weekly tonnage sunk at the peak of German submarine warfare in April 1917 when Great Britain had been brought to the brink of disaster. British losses tapered off thereafter: 53,561 tons the second week, 12,750 the third week and only 4,646 the fourth week—for a total during September of twenty-six ships of 135,552 tons sunk by U-boats and three ships of 16,488 tons by mines.*

There was a reason, unknown to the British, for the sharp tapering off. On September 7, Admiral Raeder had a long conference with Hitler. The Fuehrer, jubilant over his initial victories in Poland and the failure of the French to attack in the west, advised the Navy to go more slowly. France was showing "political and military restraint"; the British were proving "hesitant." In view of this situation it was decided that submarines in the Atlantic would spare all passenger ships without exception and refrain altogether from attacking the French, and that the pocket battleships *Deutschland* in the North Atlantic and the *Graf Spee* in the South Atlantic should withdraw to their "waiting" stations for the time being. The "general policy," Raeder noted in his diary, would be "to exercise restraint until the political situation in the West has become clearer, which will take about a week."[8]

THE SINKING OF THE *ATHENIA*

There was one other decision agreed upon by Hitler and Raeder at the meeting on September 7. The Admiral noted it in his diary: "No attempt shall be made to solve the *Athenia* affair until the submarines return home."

The war at sea, as we have noted, had begun ten hours after Britain's declaration of war when the British liner *Athenia,* jammed with some 1,400 passengers, was torpedoed without warning at 9 P.M. on September 3 some two hundred miles west of the Hebrides, with the loss of 112 lives, including twenty-eight Americans. The German Propaganda Ministry checked the first reports from London with the Naval High Command, was told that there were no U-boats in the vicinity and promptly denied that the ship had been sunk by the Germans. The disaster was most embarrassing to Hitler and the Naval Command and at first they did not believe the British reports. Strict orders had been given to all submarine commanders to observe the Hague Convention, which forbade attacking a ship without warning. Since all U-boats maintained radio silence, there

---

* Churchill, then First Lord of the Admiralty, disclosed the general figures in the House of Commons on September 26. He gives the corrected official figures in his memoirs. He also told the House that six or seven U-boats had been sunk, but actually, as he also notes in his book, the figure was later learned to be only two.

Churchill's speech was marked by an amusing anecdote in which he told how a U-boat commander had signaled him personally the position of a British ship he had just sunk and urged that rescue should be sent. "I was in some doubt to what address I should direct a reply," Churchill said. "However, he is now in our hands." But he wasn't. This writer interviewed the submarine skipper, Captain Herbert Schultze, in Berlin two days later in a broadcast to America. He produced from his logbook his message to Churchill. (See Churchill, *The Gathering Storm,* pp. 436–37; *Berlin Diary,* pp. 225–27.)

was no means of immediately checking what had happened.* That did not prevent the controlled Nazi press from charging, within a couple of days, that the British had torpedoed their own ship in order to provoke the United States into coming into the war.

The Wilhelmstrasse was indeed concerned with American reaction to a disaster that had caused the deaths of twenty-eight United States citizens. The day after the sinking Weizsaecker sent for the American chargé, Alexander Kirk, and denied that a German submarine had done it. No German craft was in the vicinity, he emphasized. That evening, according to his later testimony at Nuremberg, the State Secretary sought out Raeder, reminded him of how the German sinking of the *Lusitania* during the First World War had helped bring America into it and urged that "everything should be done" to avoid provoking the United States. The Admiral assured him that "no German U-boat could have been involved."[9]

At the urging of Ribbentrop, Admiral Raeder invited the American naval attaché to come to see him on September 16 and stated that he had now received reports from all the submarines, "as a result of which it was definitely established that the *Athenia* had not been sunk by a German U-boat." He asked him to so inform his government, which the attaché promptly did.†[10]

The Grand Admiral had not quite told the truth. Not all the submarines which were at sea on September 3 had yet returned to port. Among those that had not was the *U-30,* commanded by Oberleutnant Lemp, which did not dock in home waters until September 27. It was met by Admiral Karl Doenitz, commander of submarines, who years later at Nuremberg described the meeting and finally revealed the truth about who sank the *Athenia.*

I met the captain, Oberleutnant Lemp, on the lockside at Wilhelmshaven as the boat was entering harbor, and he asked permission to speak to me in private. I noticed immediately that he was looking very unhappy and he told me at once that he thought he was responsible for the sinking of the *Athenia* in the North Channel area. In accordance with my previous instructions he had been keeping a sharp lookout for possible armed merchant cruisers in the approaches to the British Isles, and had torpedoed a ship he afterward identified as the *Athenia* from wireless broadcasts, under the impression that she was an armed merchant cruiser on patrol . . .

I dispatched Lemp at once by air to report to the Naval War Staff (SKL) at Berlin; in the meantime I ordered complete secrecy as a provisional measure. Later the same day, or early on the following day, I received an order from Kapitaen zur See Fricke that:

1. *The affair was to be kept a total secret.*

---

* The next day, September 4, all U-boats were signaled: "By order of the Fuehrer, on no account are operations to be carried out against passenger steamers, even when under escort."

† Apparently not in code. A copy of the naval attaché's cable to Washington showed up in the German naval papers at Nuremberg.

2. The High Command of the Navy (OKM) *considered* that a court-martial was not necessary, as they were satisfied that the captain had acted in good faith.

3. *Political explanations would be handled by OKM.**

I had had no part whatsoever in the political events in which the Fuehrer claimed that no U-boat had sunk the *Athenia*.[11]

But Doenitz, who must have suspected the truth all along, for otherwise he would not have been at the dock to greet the returning *U-30*, did have a part in altering the submarine's log and his own diary so as to erase any telltale evidence of the truth. In fact, as he admitted at Nuremberg, he himself ordered any mention of the *Athenia* stricken from the *U-30*'s log and deleted it from his own diary. He swore the vessel's crew to absolute secrecy.†

The military high commands of all nations no doubt have skeletons in their closets during the course of war, and it was understandable if not laudable that Hitler, as Admiral Raeder testified at Nuremberg, insisted that the *Athenia* affair be kept secret, especially since the Naval Command had acted in good faith in at first denying German responsibility and would have been greatly embarrassed to have to admit it later. But Hitler did not stop there. On the evening of Sunday, October 22, Propaganda Minister Goebbels personally took to the air—this writer well remembers the broadcast—and accused Churchill of having sunk the *Athenia*. The next day the official Nazi newspaper, the *Voelkischer Beobachter,* ran a front-page story under the headline CHURCHILL SANK THE "ATHENIA" and stating that the First Lord of the Admiralty had planted a time bomb in the ship's hold. At Nuremberg it was established that the Fuehrer had personally ordered the broadcast and the article—and also that though Raeder, Doenitz and Weizsaecker were highly displeased at such a brazen lie, they dared not do anything about it.[13]

This spinelessness on the part of the admirals and the self-styled anti-Nazi leader in the Foreign Office, which was fully shared by the generals, whenever the demonic Nazi warlord cracked down, was to lead to one of the darkest pages in German history.

HITLER PROPOSES PEACE

"Tonight the press talks openly of peace," I noted in my diary September 20. "All the Germans I've talked to today are dead sure we shall have peace within a month. They are in high spirits."

* The italics are the Admiral's.
† The officers, including Lemp, and some of the crew were transferred to the *U-110* and went down with her on May 9, 1941. One member of the crew was wounded by aircraft fire a few days after the sinking of the *Athenia*. He was disembarked at Reykjavik, Iceland, under pledge of the strictest secrecy, later taken to a POW camp in Canada, and after the war signed an affidavit giving the facts. The Germans appear to have been worried that he would "talk," but he didn't until the war's end.[12]

The afternoon before at the ornate Guild Hall in Danzig I had heard Hitler make his first speech since his Reichstag address of September 1 started off the war. Though he was in a rage because he had been balked from making this speech at Warsaw, whose garrison still gallantly held out, and dripped venom every time he mentioned Great Britain, he made a slight gesture toward peace. "I have no war aims against Britain and France," he said. "My sympathies are with the French poilu. What he is fighting for he does not know." And he called upon the Almighty, "who now has blessed our arms, to give other peoples comprehension of how useless this war will be . . . and to cause reflection on the blessings of peace."

On September 26, the day before Warsaw fell, the German press and radio launched a big peace offensive. The line, I recorded in my diary, was: "Why do France and Britain want to fight now? Nothing to fight about. Germany wants nothing in the West."

A couple of days later, Russia, fast devouring its share of Poland, joined in the peace offensive. Along with the signing of the German–Soviet Boundary and Friendship Treaty, with its secret clauses dividing up Eastern Europe, Molotov and Ribbentrop concocted and signed at Moscow on September 28 a ringing declaration for peace.

The governments of Germany and Russia, it said, after having

definitely settled the problems arising from the disintegration of the Polish state and created a firm foundation for a lasting peace in Eastern Europe, mutually express their conviction that it would serve the true interests of all peoples to put an end to the state of war between Germany and England and France. Both governments will therefore direct their common efforts . . . toward attaining this goal as soon as possible.

Should, however, the efforts of the two governments remain fruitless, this would demonstrate the fact that England and France are responsible for the continuation of the war . . .

Did Hitler want peace, or did he want to continue the war and, with Soviet help, push the responsibility for its continuance on the Western Allies? Perhaps he did not quite know himself, although he was pretty certain.

On September 26 he had a long talk with Dahlerus, who had by no means given up the quest for peace. Two days before, the indefatigable Swede had seen his old friend Ogilvie Forbes at Oslo, where the former counselor of the Berlin embassy was now serving in a similar capacity in the British Legation in the Norwegian capital. Dahlerus reported to Hitler, according to a confidential memorandum of Dr. Schmidt,[14] that Forbes had told him the British government was looking for peace. The only question was: How could the British save face?

"If the British actually want peace," Hitler replied, "they can have it in two weeks—without losing face."

They would have to reconcile themselves, said the Fuehrer, to the fact "that Poland cannot rise again." Beyond that he was prepared, he declared, to guarantee the status quo "of the rest of Europe," including guarantees of the "security" of Britain, France and the Low Countries. There followed a discussion of how to launch the peace talks. Hitler suggested that Mussolini do it. Dahlerus thought the Queen of the Netherlands might be more "neutral." Goering, who was also present, suggested that representatives of Britain and Germany first meet secretly in Holland and then, if they made progress, the Queen could invite both countries to armistice talks. Hitler, who several times professed himself as skeptical regarding "the British will to peace," finally agreed to the Swede's proposal that he "go to England the very next day in order to send out feelers in the direction indicated."

"The British can have peace if they want it," Hitler told Dahlerus as he left, "but they will have to hurry."

That was one trend in the Fuehrer's thinking. He expressed another to his generals. The day before, on September 25, an entry in Halder's diary mentions receipt of "word on Fuehrer's plan to attack in the West." On September 27, the day after he had assured Dahlerus that he was ready to make peace with Britain, Hitler convoked the commanders in chief of the Wehrmacht to the Chancellery and informed them of his decision to "attack in the West as soon as possible, since the Franco–British army is not yet prepared." According to Brauchitsch he even set a date for the attack: November 12.[15] No doubt Hitler was fired that day by the news that Warsaw had finally capitulated. He probably thought that France, at least, could be brought to her knees as easily as Poland, though two days later Halder made a diary note to "explain" to the Fuehrer that "technique of Polish campaign no recipe for the West. No good against a well-knit army."

Perhaps Ciano penetrated Hitler's mind best when he had a long talk with the Chancellor in Berlin on October 1. The young Italian Foreign Minister, who by now thoroughly detested the Germans but had to keep up appearances, found the Fuehrer in a confident mood. As he outlined his plans, his eyes "flashed in a sinister fashion whenever he talked about his ways and means of fighting," Ciano observed. Summing up his impressions, the Italian visitor wrote:

. . . Today to offer his people a solid peace after a great victory is perhaps an aim which still tempts Hitler. But if in order to reach it he had to sacrifice, even to the smallest degree, what seems to him the legitimate fruits of his victory, he would then a thousand times prefer battle.*[16]

---

* Mussolini did not share Hitler's confidence in victory, which Ciano reported to him. He thought the British and French "would hold firm . . . Why hide it?" Ciano wrote in his diary October 3, "he [Mussolini] is somewhat bitter about Hitler's sudden rise to fame." (*Ciano Diaries*, p. 155.)

To me as I sat in the Reichstag beginning at noon on October 6 and listened to Hitler utter his appeal for peace, it seemed like an old gramophone record being replayed for the fifth or sixth time. How often before I had heard him from this same rostrum, after his latest conquest, and in the same apparent tone of earnestness and sincerity, propose what sounded—if you overlooked his latest victim—like a decent and reasonable peace. He did so again this crisp, sunny autumn day, with his usual eloquence and hypocrisy. It was a long speech—one of the most lengthy public utterances he ever made—but toward the end, after more than an hour of typical distortions of history and a boastful account of the feat of German arms in Poland ("this ridiculous state") he came to his proposals for peace and the reasons therefore.

My chief endeavor has been to rid our relations with France of all trace of ill will and render them tolerable for both nations . . . Germany has no further claims against France . . . I have refused even to mention the problem of Alsace-Lorraine . . . I have always expressed to France my desire to bury forever our ancient enmity and bring together these two nations, both of which have such glorious pasts . . .

And Britain?

I have devoted no less effort to the achievement of Anglo–German understanding, nay, more than that, of an Anglo–German friendship. At no time and in no place have I ever acted contrary to British interests . . . I believe even today that there can only be real peace in Europe and throughout the world if Germany and England come to an understanding.

And peace?

Why should this war in the West be fought? For restoration of Poland? Poland of the Versailles Treaty will never rise again . . . The question of re-establishment of the Polish State is a problem which will not be solved by war in the West but exclusively by Russia and Germany . . . It would be senseless to annihilate millions of men and to destroy property worth millions in order to reconstruct a State which at its very birth was termed an abortion by all those not of Polish extraction.

What other reason exists? . . .

If this war is really to be waged only in order to give Germany a new regime . . . then millions of human lives will be sacrificed in vain . . . No, this war in the West cannot settle any problems . . .

There were problems to be solved. Hitler trotted out a whole list of them: "formation of a Polish State" (which he had already agreed with the Russians should not exist); "solution and settlement of the Jewish problem"; colonies for Germany; revival of international trade; "an unconditionally guaranteed peace"; reduction of armaments; "regulation of air warfare, poison gas, submarines, etc."; and settlement of minority problems in Europe.

To "achieve these great ends" he proposed a conference of the leading European nations "after the most thorough preparation."

It is impossible [he continued] that such a conference, which is to determine the fate of this continent for many years to come, could carry on its deliberations while cannon are thundering or mobilized armies are bringing pressure to bear upon it.

If, however, these problems must be solved sooner or later, then it would be more sensible to tackle the solution before millions of men are first uselessly sent to death and billions of riches destroyed. Continuation of the present state of affairs in the West is unthinkable. Each day will soon demand increasing sacrifices . . . The national wealth of Europe will be scattered in the form of shells and the vigor of every nation will be sapped on the battlefields . . .

One thing is certain. In the course of world history there have never been two victors, but very often only losers. May those peoples and their leaders who are of the same opinion now make their reply. And let those who consider war to be the better solution reject my outstretched hand.

He was thinking of Churchill.

If, however, the opinions of Messrs. Churchill and followers should prevail, this statement will have been my last. Then we shall fight . . . There will never be another November, 1918, in German history.

It seemed to me highly doubtful, as I wrote in my diary on my return from the Reichstag, that the British and French would listen to these vague proposals "for five minutes." But the Germans were optimistic. On my way to broadcast that evening I picked up an early edition of Hitler's own paper, the *Voelkischer Beobachter*. The flamboyant headlines said:

GERMANY'S WILL FOR PEACE—NO WAR AIMS AGAINST FRANCE AND ENGLAND —NO MORE REVISION CLAIMS EXCEPT COLONIES—REDUCTION OF ARMAMENTS—CO-OPERATION WITH ALL NATIONS OF EUROPE—PROPOSAL FOR A CONFERENCE

The Wilhelmstrasse, it is now known from the secret German documents, was encouraged to believe by the reports it was getting from Paris through the Spanish and Italian ambassadors there that the French had no stomach for continuing the war. As early as September 8, the Spanish ambassador was tipping the Germans off that Bonnet, "in view of the great unpopularity of the war in France, is endeavoring to bring about an understanding as soon as the operations in Poland are concluded. There are certain indications that he is in contact with Mussolini to that end."[17]

On October 2, Attolico handed Weizsaecker the text of the latest message from the Italian ambassador in Paris, stating that the majority of the French cabinet were in favor of a peace conference and it was now mainly a question of "enabling France and England to save face." Apparently, though, Premier Daladier did not belong to the majority.*[18]

This was good intelligence. On October 7, Daladier answered Hitler. He declared that France would not lay down her arms until guarantees for a "real peace and general security" were obtained. But Hitler was more interested in hearing from Chamberlain than from the French Premier. On October 10, on the occasion of a brief address at the Sportpalast inaugurating Winterhilfe, Winter Relief, he again stressed his "readiness for peace." Germany, he added, "has no cause for war against the Western Powers."

Chamberlain's reply came on October 12. It was a cold douche to the German people, if not to Hitler.† Addressing the House of Commons, the Prime Minister termed Hitler's proposals "vague and uncertain" and noted that "they contain no suggestions for righting the wrongs done to Czechoslovakia and Poland." No reliance, he said, could be put on the promises "of the present German Government." If it wanted peace, "acts —not words alone—must be forthcoming." He called for "convincing proof" from Hitler that he really wanted peace.

The man of Munich could no longer be fooled by Hitler's promises. The next day, October 13, an official German statement declared that Chamberlain, by turning down Hitler's offer of peace, had deliberately chosen war. Now the Nazi dictator had his excuse.

Actually, as we now know from the captured German documents, Hitler had not waited for the Prime Minister's reply before ordering preparations for an immediate assault in the West. On October 10 he called in his military chiefs, read them a long memorandum on the state of the war and the world and threw at them Directive No. 6 for the Conduct of the War.[20]

The Fuehrer's insistence toward the end of September that an attack be mounted in the West as soon as possible had thrown the Army High Command into a fit. Brauchitsch and Halder, aided by several other generals, had consorted to prove to the Leader that an immediate offensive was out

---

* A little later, on November 16, the Italians informed the Germans that according to their information from Paris, "Marshal Pétain is regarded as the advocate of a peace policy in France . . . If the question of peace should become more acute in France, Pétain will play a role."[19] This appears to be the first indication to the Germans that Pétain might prove useful to them later on.

† The day before, on October 11, there had been a peace riot in Berlin. Early in the morning a broadcast on the Berlin radio wave length announced that the British government had fallen and that there would be an immediate armistice. There was great rejoicing in the capital as the rumor spread. Old women in the vegetable markets tossed their cabbages into the air, wrecked their stands in sheer joy and made for the nearest pub to toast the peace with *Schnaps*.

of the question. It would take several months, they said, to refit the tanks used in Poland. General Thomas furnished figures to show that Germany had a monthly steel deficit of 600,000 tons. General von Stuelpnagel, the Quartermaster General, reported there was ammunition on hand only "for about one third of our divisions for fourteen combat days"—certainly not long enough to win a battle against the French. But the Fuehrer would not listen to his Army Commander in Chief and his Chief of the General Staff when they presented a formal report to him on Army deficiencies on October 7. General Jodl, the leading yes man on OKW, next to Keitel, warned Halder "that a very severe crisis is in the making" because of the Army's opposition to an offensive in the West and that the Fuehrer was "bitter because the soldiers do not obey him."

It was against this background that Hitler convoked the generals at 11 A.M. on October 10. They were not asked for their advice. Directive No. 6, dated the day before, told them what to do:

TOP SECRET

If it should become apparent in the near future that England, and under England's leadership, also France, are not willing to make an end of the war, I am determined to act vigorously and aggressively without great delay . . .

Therefore I give the following orders:

a. Preparations are to be made for an attacking operation . . . through the areas of Luxembourg, Belgium and Holland. This attack must be carried out . . . at as early a date as possible.

b. The purpose will be to defeat as strong a part of the French operational army as possible, as well as allies fighting by its side, and at the same time to gain as large an area as possible in Holland, Belgium and northern France as a base for conducting a promising air and sea war against England . . .

I request the Commanders in Chief to give me, as soon as possible, detailed reports of their plans on the basis of this directive and to keep me currently informed . . .

The secret memorandum, also dated October 9, which Hitler read out to his military chiefs before presenting them the directive is one of the most impressive papers the former Austrian corporal ever wrote. It showed not only a grasp of history, from the German viewpoint, and of military strategy and tactics which is remarkable but, as a little later would be proved, a prophetic sense of how the war in the West would develop and with what results. The struggle between Germany and the Western Powers, which, he said, had been going on since the dissolution of the First German Reich by the Treaty of Muenster (Westphalia) in 1648 "would have to be fought out one way or the other." However, after the great victory in Poland, "there would be no objection to ending the war immediately" providing the gains in Poland were not "jeopardized."

It is not the object of this memorandum to study the possibilities in this direction or even to take them into consideration. I shall confine myself exclusively to the other case: the necessity to continue the fight . . . The German war aim is the final military dispatch of the West, that is, the destruction of the power and ability of the Western Powers ever again to be able to oppose the state consolidation and further development of the German people in Europe.

As far as the outside world is concerned, this eternal aim will have to undergo various propaganda adjustments . . . This does not alter the war aim. It is and remains the destruction of our Western enemies.

The generals had objected to haste in taking the offensive in the West. Time, however, he told them, was on the enemy's side. The Polish victories, he reminded them, were possible because Germany really had only one front. That situation still held—but for how long?

By no treaty or pact can a lasting neutrality of Soviet Russia be insured with certainty. At present all reasons speak against Russia's departure from neutrality. In eight months, one year, or even several years, this may be altered. The trifling significance of treaties has been proved on all sides in recent years. The greatest safeguard against any Russian attack lies . . . in a prompt demonstration of German strength.

As for Italy, the "hope of Italian support for Germany" was dependent largely on whether Mussolini lived and on whether there were further German successes to entice the Duce. Here too time was a factor, as it was with Belgium and Holland, which could be compelled by Britain and France to give up their neutrality—something Germany could not afford to wait for. Even with the United States, "time is to be viewed as working against Germany."

There were great dangers to Germany, Hitler admitted, in a long war, and he enumerated several of them. Friendly and unfriendly neutrals (he seems to have been thinking mainly of Russia, Italy and the U.S.A.) might be drawn to the opposite side, as they were in the First World War. Also, he said, Germany's "limited food and raw-material basis" would make it difficult to find "the means for carrying on the war." The greatest danger, he said, was the vulnerability of the Ruhr. If this heart of German industrial production were hit, it would "lead to the collapse of the German war economy and thus of the capacity to resist."

It must be admitted that in this memorandum the former corporal showed an astonishing grasp of military strategy and tactics, accompanied though it was by a typical lack of morals. There are several pages about the new tactics developed by the tanks and planes in Poland, and a detailed analysis of how these tactics can work in the West and just where. The chief thing, he said, was to avoid the positional warfare of 1914–18. The armored divisions must be used for the crucial breakthrough.

They are not to be lost among the maze of endless rows of houses in Belgian towns. It is not necessary for them to attack towns at all, but . . . to maintain the flow of the army's advance, to prevent fronts from becoming stable by massed drives through identified weakly held positions.

This was a deadly accurate forecast of how the war in the West would be fought, and when one reads it one wonders why no one on the Allied side had similar insights.

This goes too for Hitler's strategy. "The only possible area of attack," he said, was through Luxembourg, Belgium and Holland. There must be two military objectives first in mind: to destroy the Dutch, Belgian, French and British armies and thereby to gain positions on the Channel and the North Sea from which the Luftwaffe could be "brutally employed" against Britain.

Above all, he said, returning to tactics, improvise!

The peculiar nature of this campaign may make it necessary to resort to improvisations to the utmost, to concentrate attacking or defending forces at certain points in more than normal proportion (for example, tank or antitank forces) and in subnormal concentrations at others.

As for the time of the attack, Hitler told his reluctant generals, "the start cannot take place too early. It is to take place in all circumstances (if at all possible) this autumn."

The German admirals, unlike the generals, had not needed any prodding from Hitler to take the offensive, outmatched though their Navy was by the British. In fact all through the last days of September and the first days of October Raeder pleaded with the Fuehrer to take the wraps off the Navy. This was gradually done. On September 17 a German U-boat torpedoed the British aircraft carrier *Courageous* off southwest Ireland. On September 27 Raeder ordered the pocket battleships *Deutschland* and *Graf Spee* to leave their waiting areas and start attacking British shipping. By the middle of October they had accounted for seven British merchantmen and taken in prize the American ship *City of Flint*.

On October 14, the German U-boat *U-47*, commanded by Oberleutnant Guenther Prien, penetrated the seemingly impenetrable defenses of Scapa Flow, the great British naval base, and torpedoed and sank the battleship *Royal Oak* as it lay at anchor, with a loss of 786 officers and men. It was a notable achievement, exploited to the full by Dr. Goebbels in his propaganda, and it enhanced the Navy in the mind of Hitler.

The generals remained, however, a problem. Despite his long and considered memorandum to them and the issuance of Directive No. 6 to get ready for an imminent attack in the West, they stalled. It wasn't that they had any moral scruples against violating Belgium and Holland; they simply were highly doubtful of success at this time. There was one exception.

General Wilhelm Ritter von Leeb, commander of Army Group C opposing the French on the Rhine and along the Maginot Line, not only was skeptical of victory in the West; he, alone so far as the available records reveal, opposed attacking neutral Belgium and Holland at least partly on moral grounds. The day after Hitler's meeting with the generals, on October 11, Leeb composed a long memorandum himself, which he sent to Brauchitsch and other generals. The whole world, he wrote, would turn against Germany,

which for the second time within 25 years assaults neutral Belgium! Germany, whose government solemnly vouched for and promised the preservation of and respect for this neutrality only a few weeks ago!

Finally, after detailing military arguments against an attack in the West, he appealed for peace. "The entire nation," he said, "is longing for peace."[21]

But Hitler by this time was longing for war, for battle, and he was fed up with what he thought to be the unpardonable timidity of his generals. On October 14 Brauchitsch and Halder put their heads together in a lengthy conference. The Army chief saw "three possibilities: Attack. Wait and see. Fundamental changes." Halder noted them in his diary that day and, after the war, explained that "fundamental changes" meant "the removal of Hitler." But the weak Brauchitsch thought such a drastic measure was "essentially negative and tends to render us vulnerable." They decided that none of the three possibilities offered "prospects of decisive successes." The only thing to do was to work further on Hitler.

Brauchitsch saw the Fuehrer again on October 17, but his arguments, he told Halder, were without effect. The situation was "hopeless." Hitler informed him curtly, as Halder wrote in his diary that day, that "the British will be ready to talk only after a beating. We must get at them as quickly as possible. Date between November 15 and 20 at the latest."

There were further conferences with the Nazi warlord, who finally laid down the law to the generals on October 27. After a ceremony conferring on fourteen of them the Knight's Cross of the Iron Cross, the Fuehrer got down to the business of the attack in the West. When Brauchitsch tried to argue that the Army would not be ready for a month, not before November 26, Hitler answered that this was "much too late." The attack, he ordered, would begin on November 12. Brauchitsch and Halder retired from the meeting feeling battered and defeated. That night they tried to console one another. "Brauchitsch tired and dejected," Halder noted in his diary.

THE ZOSSEN "CONSPIRACY" TO OVERTHROW HITLER

The time had now come for the conspirators to spring to action once more, or so they thought. The unhappy Brauchitsch and Halder were faced with the stern alternatives of either carrying out the third of the "possibilities" they had seen on October 14—the removal of Hitler—or organizing an attack in the West which they thought would be disastrous for Germany. Both the military and civilian "plotters," suddenly come to life, were urging the first alternative.

They had already been balked once since the start of the war. General von Hammerstein, recalled temporarily from his long retirement on the eve of the attack on Poland, had been given a command in the west. During the first week of the war he had urged Hitler to visit his headquarters in order to show that he was not neglecting that front while conquering Poland. Actually Hammerstein, an implacable foe of Hitler, planned to arrest him. Fabian von Schlabrendorff had already tipped Ogilvie Forbes on this plot the day Britain declared war, on September 3, at a hasty meeting in the Adlon Hotel in Berlin. But the Fuehrer had smelled a rat, had declined to visit the former Commander in Chief of the Army and shortly thereafter had sacked him.[22]

The conspirators continued to maintain contact with the British. Having failed to take any action to prevent Hitler from destroying Poland, they had concentrated their efforts on trying to keep the war from spreading to the West. The civilian members realized that, more than before, the Army was the only organization in the Reich which possessed the means of stopping Hitler: its power and importance had vastly increased with general mobilization and the lightning victory in Poland. But its expanded size, as Halder tried to explain to the civilians, also was a handicap. The officers' ranks had been swollen with reserve officers many of whom were fanatical Nazis; and the mass of the troops were thoroughly indoctrinated with Nazism. It would be difficult, Halder pointed out— he was a great man to emphasize difficulties, whether to friend or foe— to find an army formation which could be trusted to move against the Fuehrer.

There was another consideration which the generals pointed out and which the men in mufti fully appreciated. If they were to stage a revolt against Hitler with the accompanying confusion in the Army as well as the country, might not the British and French take advantage of it to break through in the west, occupy Germany and mete out a harsh peace to the German people—even though they had got rid of their criminal leader? It was necessary therefore to keep in contact with the British in order to come to a clear understanding that the Allies would not take such an advantage of a German anti-Nazi coup.

Several channels were used. One was developed through the Vatican by Dr. Josef Mueller, a leading Munich lawyer, a devout Catholic, a man of such great physical bulk and tremendous energy and toughness that he had been dubbed in his youth "Joe the Ox"—*Ochsensepp*. Early in October, with the connivance of Colonel Oster of the Abwehr, Mueller had journeyed to Rome and at the Vatican had established contact with the British minister to the Holy See. According to German sources, he succeeded in obtaining not only an assurance from the British but the agreement of the Pope to act as an intermediary between a new anti-Nazi German regime and Britain.[23]

The other contact was in Berne, Switzerland. There Weizsaecker had installed Theodor Kordt, until recently the German chargé in London, as an attaché in the German Legation and it was in the Swiss capital that he saw on occasion an Englishman, Dr. Philip Conwell-Evans, whose professorship at the German University of Koenigsberg had made him both an expert on Nazism and to some extent a sympathizer with it. In the latter part of October Conwell-Evans brought to Kordt what the latter later described as a solemn promise by Chamberlain to deal justly and understandingly with a future anti-Nazi German government. Actually the Britisher had only brought extracts from Chamberlain's speech to the Commons in which, while rejecting Hitler's peace proposals, the Prime Minister had declared that Britain had no desire to "exclude from her rightful place in Europe a Germany which will live in amity and confidence with other nations." Though this statement and others in the speech of a friendly nature toward the German people had been broadcast from London and presumably picked up by the conspirators, they hailed the "pledge" brought by the unofficial British representative to Berne as of the utmost importance. With this and the British assurances they thought they had through the Vatican, the conspirators turned hopefully to the German generals. Hopefully, but also desperately. "Our only hope of salvation," Weizsaecker told Hassell on October 17, "lies in a military *coup d'état*. But how?"

Time was short. The German attack through Belgium and Holland was scheduled to begin on November 12. The plot had to be carried out before that date. As Hassell warned the others, it would be impossible to get a "decent peace" *after* Germany had violated Belgium.

There are several accounts from the participants as to what happened next, or rather why nothing much happened, and they are conflicting and confusing. General Halder, the Chief of the Army General Staff, was again the key figure, as he had been at the time of Munich. But he blew hot and cold, was hesitant and confused. In his interrogation at Nuremberg he explained that the "Field Army" could not stage the revolt because it had a "fully armed enemy in front of it." He says he appealed to the "Home Army," which was not up against the enemy, to act but the most he could get from its commander, General Friedrich (Fritz) Fromm, was an understanding that "as a soldier"[24] he would execute any order from Brauchitsch.

But Brauchitsch was even more wishy-washy than his General Staff Chief. "If Brauchitsch hasn't enough force of character," General Beck told Halder, "to make a decision, then you must make the decision and present him with a *fait accompli*." But Halder insisted that since Brauchitsch was the Commander in Chief of the Army, the final responsibility was his. Thus the buck was continually passed. "Halder," Hassell mourned in his diary at the end of October, "is not equal to the situation either in caliber or in authority." As for Brauchitsch, he was, as Beck said, "a sixth-grader." Still the conspirators, led this time by General Thomas, the economic expert of the Army, and Colonel Oster of the Abwehr, worked on Halder, who finally agreed, they thought, to stage a putsch as soon as Hitler gave the final order for the attack in the West. Halder himself says it was still conditional on Brauchitsch's making the final decision. At any rate, on November 3, according to Colonel Hans Groscurth of OKW, a confidant of both Halder and Oster, Halder sent word to General Beck and Goerdeler, two of the chief conspirators, to hold themselves in readiness from November 5 on. Zossen, the headquarters of both the Army Command and the General Staff, became a hotbed of conspiratorial activity.

November 5 was a key date. On that day the movement of troops to their jump-off points opposite Holland, Belgium and Luxembourg was to begin. Also on that day, Brauchitsch had an appointment for a showdown with Hitler. He and Halder had visited the top army commands in the west on November 2 and 3 and fortified themselves with the negative opinions of the field commanders. "None of the higher headquarters," Halder confided to his diary, "thinks the offensive . . . has any prospect of success." Thus amply supplied with arguments from the generals on the Western front as well as his own and Halder's and Thomas', which were assembled in a memorandum, and carrying for good measure a "countermemorandum," as Halder calls it, replying to Hitler's memorandum of October 9, the Commander in Chief of the German Army drove over to the Chancellery in Berlin on November 5 determined to talk the Fuehrer out of his offensive in the West. If Brauchitsch were unsuccessful, he would then join the conspiracy to remove the dictator—or so the conspirators understood. They were in a high state of excitement—and optimism. Goerdeler, according to Gisevius, was already drawing up a cabinet list for the provisional anti-Nazi government and had to be restrained by the more sober Beck. Schacht alone was highly skeptical. "Just you watch," he warned. "Hitler will smell a rat and won't make any decision at all tomorrow."

They were all, as usual, wrong.

Brauchitsch, as might have been expected, got nowhere with his memoranda or his reports from the front-line commanders or his own arguments. When he stressed the bad weather in the West at this time of year, Hitler retorted that it was as bad for the enemy as for the Germans and moreover that it might be no better in the spring. Finally in desperation the spineless Army chief informed the Fuehrer that the morale of the troops in the west was similar to that in 1917–18, when there was defeatism, insubordination and even mutiny in the German Army.

At hearing this, Hitler, according to Halder (whose diary is the principal source for this highly secret meeting), flew into a rage. "In what units," he demanded to know, "have there been any cases of lack of discipline? What happened? Where?" He would fly there himself tomorrow. Poor Brauchitsch, as Halder notes, had deliberately exaggerated "in order to deter Hitler," and he now felt the full force of the Leader's uncontrolled wrath. "What action has been taken by the Army Command?" the

Fuehrer shouted. "How many death sentences have been carried out?" The truth was, Hitler stormed, that "the Army did not want to fight."

"Any further conversation was impossible," Brauchitsch told the tribunal at Nuremberg in recalling his unhappy experience. "So I left." Others remembered that he staggered into headquarters at Zossen, eighteen miles away, in such a state of shock that he was unable at first to give a coherent account of what had happened.

That was the end of the "Zossen Conspiracy." It had failed as ignobly as the "Halder Plot" at the time of Munich. Each time the conditions laid down by the plotters in order to enable them to act had been fulfilled. This time Hitler had stuck to his decision to attack on November 12. In fact, after the stricken Brauchitsch had left his presence he had the order reconfirmed by telephone to Zossen. When Halder asked that it be sent in writing, he was immediately obliged. Thus the conspirators had in writing the evidence which they had said they needed in order to overthrow Hitler—the order for an attack which they thought would bring disaster to Germany. But they did nothing further except to panic. There was a great scramble to burn incriminating papers and cover up traces. Only Colonel Oster seems to have kept his head. He sent a warning to the Belgian and Dutch legations in Berlin to expect an attack on the morning of November 12.[25] Then he set out for the Western front on a fruitless expedition to see if he could again interest General von Witzleben in bumping off Hitler. The generals, Witzleben included, knew when they were beaten. The former corporal had once again triumphed over them with the greatest of ease. A few days later Rundstedt, commanding Army Group A, called in his corps and divisional commanders to discuss details of the attack. While still doubting its success he advised his generals to bury their doubts. "The Army," he said, "has been given its task, and it will fulfill that task!"

The day after provoking Brauchitsch to the edge of a nervous breakdown Hitler busied himself with composing the texts of proclamations to the Dutch and Belgian people justifying his attack on them. Halder noted the pretext: "French march into Belgium."

But on the next day, November 7, to the relief of the generals, Hitler postponed the date of the attack.

TOP SECRET

Berlin, November 7, 1939

. . . The Fuehrer and Supreme Commander of the Armed Forces, after hearing reports on the meteorological and the railway transport situation, has ordered:

A-day is postponed by three days. The next decision will be made at 6 P.M. on November 9, 1939.

KEITEL

This was the first of fourteen postponements ordered by Hitler throughout the fall and winter, copies of which were found in the OKW archives at the end of the war.[26] They show that at no time did the Fuehrer abandon for one moment his decision to attack in the West; he merely put off the date from week to week. On November 9, the attack was postponed to November 19; on November 13, to November 22; and so on, with five or six days' notice being given each time, and usually the weather stated as the reason. Probably the Fuehrer was, to some extent, deferring to the generals. Probably he got it through his head that the Army was not ready. Certainly the strategic and tactical plans had not been fully worked out, for he was always tinkering with them.

There may have been other reasons for Hitler's first postponement of the offensive. On November 7, the day the decision was made, the Germans had been considerably embarrassed by a joint declaration of the King of the Belgians and the Queen of the Netherlands, offering, "before the war in Western Europe begins in full violence," to mediate a peace. In such circumstances it would have been difficult to convince anyone, as Hitler was attempting to do in the proclamations he was drafting, that the German Army was moving into the two Low Countries because it had learned the French Army was about to march into Belgium.

Also Hitler may have got wind that his attack on the neutral little country of Belgium would not have the benefit of surprise, on which he had counted. At the end of October, Goerdeler had journeyed to Brussels with a secret message from Weizsaecker urging the German ambassador, Buelow-Schwante, to privately warn the King of the "extreme gravity of the situation." This the ambassador did and shortly thereafter King Leopold rushed to The Hague to consult with the Queen and draw up their declaration. But the Belgians had more specific information. Some of it came from Oster, as we have seen. On November 8, Buelow-Schwante wired Berlin a warning that King Leopold had told the Dutch Queen that he had "exact information" of a German military build-up on the Belgian frontier which pointed toward a German offensive through Belgium "in two or three days."[27]

Then on the evening of November 8 and the afternoon of the following day there occurred two strange events—a bomb explosion that just missed killing Hitler and the kidnaping by the S.S. of two British agents in Holland near the German border—which at first distracted the Nazi warlord from his plans for attacking the West and yet in the end bolstered his prestige in Germany while frightening the Zossen conspirators, who actually had nothing to do with either happening.

A NAZI KIDNAPING AND A BEERHOUSE BOMB

Twelve minutes after Hitler had finished making his annual speech, on the evening of November 8, to the "Old Guard" party cronies at the Buergerbräukeller in Munich in commemoration of the 1923 Beer Hall Putsch, a shorter speech than usual, a bomb which had been planted in a pillar directly behind the speaker's platform exploded, killing seven persons and wounding sixty-three others. By that time all the important Nazi leaders, with Hitler at their head, had hurriedly left the premises, though it had been their custom in former years to linger over their beers and reminisce with old party comrades about the early putsch.

The next morning Hitler's own paper, the *Voelkischer Beobachter,* alone carried the story of the attempt on the Fuehrer's life. It blamed the "British Secret Service" and even Chamberlain for the foul deed. "The attempted 'assassination,' " I wrote that evening in my diary, "undoubtedly will buck up public opinion behind Hitler and stir up hatred of England . . . Most of us think it smells of another Reichstag fire."

What connection could the British secret service have with it, outside of Goebbel's feverish mind? An attempt was made at once to connect them. An hour or two after the bomb went off in Munich, Heinrich Himmler, chief of the S.S. and the Gestapo, telephoned to one of his rising young S.S. subordinates, Walter Schellenberg, at Duesseldorf and ordered him by command of the Fuehrer, to cross the border into Holland the next day and kidnap two British secret-service agents with whom Schellenberg had been in contact.

Himmler's order led to one of the most bizarre incidents of the war. For more than a month Schellenberg, who, like Alfred Naujocks, was a university-educated intellectual gangster, had been seeing in Holland two British intelligence officers, Captain S. Payne Best and Major R. H. Stevens. To them he posed as "Major Schaemmel," an anti-Nazi officer in OKW (Schellenberg took the name from a living major) and gave a convincing story of how the German generals were determined to overthrow Hitler. What they wanted from the British, he said, were assurances that the London government would deal fairly with the new anti-Nazi regime. Since the British had heard from other sources (as we have seen) of a German military conspiracy, whose members wanted the same kind of assurances, London was interested in developing further contacts with "Major Schaemmel." Best and Stevens provided him with a small radio transmitter and receiving set; there were numerous ensuing communications over the wireless and further meetings in various Dutch towns. By November 7, when the two parties met at Venlo, a Dutch town on the German frontier, the British agents were able to give "Schaemmel" a rather vague message from London to the leaders of the German resistance stating in general terms the basis for a just peace with an anti-Nazi regime. It was agreed that "Schaemmel" should bring one of these leaders, a German general, to Venlo the next day, to begin definitive negotiations. This meeting was put off to the ninth.

Up to this moment the objectives of the two sides were clear. The British were trying to establish direct contact with the German military putschists in order to encourage and aid them. Himmler was attempting to find out through the British who the German plotters were and what their connection was with the enemy secret service. That Himmler and Hitler were already suspicious of some of the generals as well as of men like Oster and Canaris of the Abwehr is clear. But now on the night of November 8, Hitler and Himmler found need of a new objective: Kidnap Best and Stevens and blame these two British secret-service agents for the Buergerbräu bombing!

A familiar character now entered the scene. Alfred Naujocks, who had staged the "Polish attack" on the German radio station at Gleiwitz, showed up in command of a dozen Security Service (S.D.) toughs to help Schellenberg carry out the kidnaping. The deed came off nicely. At 4 P.M. on November 9, while Schellenberg sipped an *apéritif* on the terrace of a café at Venlo, waiting for a rendezvous with Best and Stevens, the two British agents drove up in their Buick, parked it behind the café, and then ran into a hail of bullets from an S.S. car filled with Naujock's ruffians. Lieutenant Klop, a Dutch intelligence officer, who had always accompanied the British pair in their talks with Schellenberg, fell mortally wounded. Best and Stevens were tossed into the S.S. car "like bundles of hay," as Schellenberg later remembered, along with the wounded Klop, and driven speedily across the border into Germany.*[28]

And so on November 21 Himmler announced to the public that the assassination plot against Hitler at the Buergerbräukeller had been solved. It was done at the instigation of the British Intelligence Service, two of whose leaders, Stevens and Best, had been arrested "on the Dutch–German frontier" on the day following the bombing. The actual perpetrator was given as Georg Elser, a German Communist carpenter residing in Munich.

Himmler's detailed account of the crime sounded "fishy" to me, as I wrote in my diary the same day. But his accomplishment was very real. "What Himmler and his gang are up to, obviously," I jotted down, "is to convince the gullible German people that the British government tried to win the war by murdering Hitler and his chief aides."

The mystery of who arranged the bombing has never been completely cleared up. Elser, though not the half-wit that was Marinus van der Lubbe of the Reichstag fire, was a man of limited intelligence though quite sincere. He not only pleaded guilty to making and setting off the bomb, he boasted of it. Though of course he had never met Best and Stevens prior to the

---

* According to the official Dutch account, which came to light after the war, the British car, with Stevens, Best and Klop in it, was towed by the Germans across the frontier, which was only 125 feet away. Starting on November 10, the next day, the Dutch government made nine written requests at frequent intervals for the return of Klop and the Dutch chauffeur of the car and also demanded a German investigation of this violation of Dutch neutrality. No reply was ever made until May 10, when Hitler justified his attack on the Netherlands partly on the grounds that the Venlo affair had proven the complicity of the Dutch with the British secret service. Klop died from his wounds a few days later. Best and Stevens survived five years in Nazi concentration camps.[29]

attempt, he did make the former's acquaintance during long years at the Sachsenhausen concentration camp. There he told the Englishman a long and involved—and not always logical—story.

One day in October at the Dachau concentration camp, where he had been incarcerated since midsummer as a Communist sympathizer, he related, he had been summoned to the office of the camp commandant, where he was introduced to two strangers. They explained the necessity of doing away with some of the Fuehrer's "traitorous" followers by exploding a bomb in the Buergerbräukeller *immediately after* Hitler had made his customary address on the evening of November 8 and had left the hall. The bomb was to be planted in a pillar behind the speakers' platform. Since Elser was a skilled cabinetmaker and electrician and a tinkerer, they suggested that he was the man to do the job. If he did, they would arrange for his escape to Switzerland and for a large sum of money to keep him in comfort there. As a token of their seriousness they promised him better treatment in the camp in the meanwhile: better food, civilian clothes, plenty of cigarettes—for he was a chain smoker—and a carpenter's bench and tools. There Elser constructed a crude but efficient bomb with an eight-day alarm-clock mechanism and a contraption by which the weapon could also be detonated by an electric switch. Elser asserted that he was taken one night early in November to the beer cellar, where he installed his gadget in the well-placed pillar.

On the evening of November 8, at about the time the bomb was set to go off, he was taken by his accomplices, he said, to the Swiss frontier, given a sum of money and—interestingly—a picture postcard of the interior of the beer hall, with the pillar in which he had placed his bomb marked with a cross. But instead of being helped across the frontier—and this seems to have surprised the dim-witted fellow—he was nabbed by the Gestapo, postcard and all. Later he was coached by the Gestapo to implicate Best and Stevens at the coming state trial, in which he would be made the center of attention.*

The trial never came off. We know now that Himmler, for reasons best known to himself, didn't dare to have a trial. We also know—now—that Elser lived on at Sachsenhausen and then Dachau concentration camps, being accorded, apparently on the express orders of Hitler, who had personally gained so much from the bombing, quite humane treatment under the circumstances. But Himmler kept his eye on him to the last. It would

---

* Later at Dachau Elser told a similar story to Pastor Niemoeller, who since has stated his personal conviction that the bombing was sanctioned by Hitler to increase his own popularity and stir up the war fever of the people. It is only fair to add that Gisevius, archenemy of Hitler, Himmler and Schellenberg, believes—as he testified at Nuremberg and in his book—that Elser really attempted to kill Hitler and that there were no Nazi accomplices. Schellenberg, who is less reliable, states that though he was suspicious at first of Himmler and Heydrich, he later concluded, after questioning the carpenter and after reading interrogations made while Elser was first drugged and then hypnotized, that it was a case of a genuine attempt at assassination.

not do to let the carpenter survive the war and live to tell his tale. Shortly before the war ended, on April 16, 1945, the Gestapo announced that Georg Elser had been killed in an Allied bombing attack the previous day. We know now that the Gestapo murdered him.[30]

HITLER TALKS TO HIS GENERALS

Having escaped assassination, or so it was made to seem, and quelled defiance among his generals, Hitler went ahead with his plans for the big attack in the West. On November 20, he issued Directive No. 8 for the Conduct of the War, ordering the maintenance of the "state of alert" so as to "exploit favorable weather conditions immediately," and laying down plans for the destruction of Holland and Belgium. And then to put courage in the fainthearted and arouse them to the proper pitch he thought necessary on the eve of great battles, he summoned the commanding generals and General Staff officers to the Chancellery at noon on November 23.

It was one of the most revealing of the secret pep talks to his principal military chiefs, and thanks to the Allied discovery of some of the OKW files at Flensburg it has been preserved in the form of notes taken by an unidentified participant.[31]

The purpose of this conference [Hitler began] is to give you an idea of the world of my thoughts, which govern me in the face of future events, and to tell you my decisions.

His mind was full of the past, the present and the future, and to this limited group he spoke with brutal frankness and great eloquence, giving a magnificent résumé of all that had gone on in his warped but fertile brain and predicting with deadly accuracy the shape of things to come. But it seems difficult to imagine that anyone who heard it could have had any further doubts that the man who now held the fate of Germany—and the world—in his hands had become beyond question a dangerous megalomaniac.

I had a clear recognition of the probable course of historical events [he said in discussing his early struggles] and the firm will to make brutal decisions . . . As the last factor I must name my own person in all modesty: irreplaceable. Neither a military man nor a civilian could replace me. Assassination attempts may be repeated. I am convinced of the powers of my intellect and of decision . . . No one has ever achieved what I have achieved . . . I have led the German people to a great height, even if the world does hate us now . . . The fate of the Reich depends only on me. I shall act accordingly.

He chided the generals for their doubts when he made his "hard decisions" to leave the League of Nations, decree conscription, occupy the

Rhineland, fortify it and seize Austria. "The number of people who put trust in me," he said, "was very small."

"The next step," he declared in describing his conquests with a cynicism which it is unfortunate that Chamberlain never heard, "was Bohemia, Moravia and Poland."

It was clear to me from the first moment that I could not be satisfied with the Sudeten-German territory. That was only a partial solution. The decision to march into Bohemia was made. Then followed the establishment of the Protectorate and with that the basis for the conquest of Poland was laid, but I was not quite clear at that time whether I should start first against the East and then against the West, or vice versa. By the pressure of events it came first to the fight against Poland. One might accuse me of wanting to fight and fight again. In struggle I see the fate of all beings. Nobody can avoid fighting if he does not want to go under.

The increasing number of [German] people required a larger *Lebensraum*. My goal was to create a rational relation between the number of people and the space for them to live in. The fight must start here. No nation can evade the solution of this problem. Otherwise it must yield and gradually go down . . . No calculated cleverness is of any help here: solution only with the sword. A people unable to produce the strength to fight must withdraw . . .

The trouble with the German leaders of the past, Hitler said, including Bismarck and Moltke, was "insufficient hardness. The solution was possible only by attacking a country at a favorable moment." Failure to realize this brought on the 1914 war "on several fronts. It did not bring a solution of the problem."

Today [Hitler went on] the second act of this drama is being written. For the first time in sixty-seven years we do not have a two-front war to wage . . . But no one can know how long that will remain so . . . Basically I did not organize the armed forces in order not to strike. The decision to strike was always in me.

Thoughts of the present blessings of a one-front war brought the Fuehrer to the question of Russia.

Russia is at present not dangerous. It is weakened by many internal conditions. Moreover, we have the treaty with Russia. Treaties, however, are kept only as long as they serve a purpose. Russia will keep it only as long as Russia herself considers it to be to her benefit . . . Russia still has far-reaching goals, above all the strengthening of her position in the Baltic. *We can oppose Russia only when we are free in the West.*

As for Italy, all depended on Mussolini, "whose death can alter everything . . . Just as the death of Stalin, so the death of the Duce can bring danger to us. How easily the death of a statesman can come I myself have experienced recently." Hitler did not think that the United States was yet dangerous—"because of her neutrality laws"—nor that her aid to the Allies yet amounted to much. Still, time was working for the enemy. "The moment is favorable now; in six months it might not be so any more." Therefore:

My decision is unchangeable. I shall attack France and England at the most favorable and earliest moment. Breach of the neutrality of Belgium and Holland is of no importance. No one will question that when we have won. We shall not justify the breach of neutrality as idiotically as in 1914.

The attack in the West, Hitler told his generals, meant "the end of the World War, not just a single action. It concerns not just a single question but the existence or nonexistence of the nation." Then he swung into his peroration.

The spirit of the great men of our history must hearten us all. Fate demands from us no more than from the great men of German history. As long as I live I shall think only of the victory of my people. I shall shrink from nothing and shall annihilate everyone who is opposed to me . . . I want to annihilate the enemy!

It was a telling speech and so far as is known not a single general raised his voice either to express the doubts which almost all the Army commanders shared about the success of an offensive at this time or to question the immorality of attacking Belgium and Holland, whose neutrality and borders the German government had solemnly guaranteed. According to some of the generals present Hitler's remarks about the poor spirit in the top echelons of the Army and the General Staff were much stronger than in the above account.

Later that day, at 6 P.M., the Nazi warlord sent again for Brauchitsch and Halder and to the former—the General Staff Chief was kept waiting outside the Fuehrer's office like a bad boy—delivered a stern lecture on the "spirit of Zossen." The Army High Command (OKH) was shot through with "defeatism," Hitler charged, and Halder's General Staff had a "stiff-necked attitude which kept it from falling in with the Fuehrer." The beaten Brauchitsch, according to his own account given much later on the stand at Nuremberg, offered his resignation, but Hitler rejected it, reminding him sharply, as the Commander in Chief remembered, "that I had to fulfill my duty and obligation just like every other soldier." That evening Halder scribbled a shorthand note in his diary: "A day of crisis!"[32]

In many ways November 23, 1939, was a milestone. It marked Hitler's final, decisive triumph over the Army, which in the First World War had shunted Emperor Wilhelm II aside and assumed supreme political as well as military authority in Germany. From that day on the onetime Austrian corporal considered not only his political but his military judgment superior to that of his generals and therefore refused to listen to their advice or permit their criticism—with results ultimately disastrous to all.

"A breach had occurred," Brauchitsch told the Nuremberg tribunal in describing the events of November 23, "which was later closed but was never completely mended."

Moreover, Hitler's harangue to the generals that autumn day put a complete damper on any ideas Halder and Brauchitsch might have had, however tepidly, to overthrow the Nazi dictator. He had warned them that he would "annihilate" anyone who stood in his way, and Halder says Hitler had specifically added that he would suppress any opposition to him on the General Staff "with brutal force." Halder, for the moment at least, was not the man to stand up to such terrible threats. When four days later, on November 27, General Thomas went to see him, at the prompting of Schacht and Popitz, and urged him to keep after Brauchitsch to take action against the Fuehrer ("Hitler has to be removed!" Halder later remembered Thomas as saying), the General Staff Chief reminded him of all the "difficulties." He was not yet sure, he said, that Brauchitsch "would take part actively in a *coup d'état.*"[33]

A few days later Halder gave Goerdeler the most ludicrous reasons for not going on with the plans to get rid of the Nazi dictator. Hassell noted them down in his diary. Besides the fact that "one does not rebel when face to face with the enemy," Halder added, according to Hassell, the following points: "We ought to give Hitler this last chance to deliver the German people from the slavery of English capitalism . . . There is no great man available . . . The opposition has not yet matured enough . . . One could not be sure of the younger officers." Hassell himself appealed to Admiral Canaris, one of the original conspirators, to go ahead, but got nowhere. "He has given up hope of resistance from the generals," the former ambassador confided to his diary on November 30, "and thinks it would be useless to try anything more along this line." A little later Hassell noted that "Halder and Brauchitsch are nothing more than caddies to Hitler."[34]

NAZI TERROR IN POLAND: FIRST PHASE

Not many days after the German attack on Poland my diary began to fill with items about the Nazi terror in the conquered land. Later one would learn that many another diary was filling with them too. Hassell on October 19 reported hearing of "the shocking bestialities of the S.S., especially toward the Jews." A little later he was confiding to his diary a story told by a German landlord in the province of Posen.

The last thing he had seen there was a drunken district Party leader who had ordered the prison opened; he had shot five whores, and attempted to rape two others.[35]

On October 18, Halder wrote down in his diary the main points of a talk he had had with General Eduard Wagner, the Quartermaster General, who had conferred with Hitler that day about the future of Poland. That future was to be grim.

We have no intention of rebuilding Poland . . . Not to be a model state by German standards. Polish intelligentsia must be prevented from establishing itself as a governing class. Low standard of living must be conserved. Cheap slaves . . .

Total disorganization must be created! The Reich will give the Governor General the means to carry out this devilish plan.

The Reich did.

A brief account of the beginning of Nazi terror in Poland, as disclosed by the captured German documents and the evidence at the various Nuremberg trials, may now be given. It was but a forerunner to dark and terrible deeds that would eventually be inflicted by the Germans on all the conquered peoples. But from first to last it was worse in Poland than anyplace else. Here Nazi barbarism reached an incredible depth.

Just before the attack on Poland was launched, Hitler had told his generals at the conference on the Obersalzberg on August 22 that things would happen "which would not be to the taste of German generals" and he warned them that they "should not interfere in such matters but restrict themselves to their military duties." He knew whereof he spoke. Both in Berlin and in Poland this writer soon was being overwhelmed with reports of Nazi massacres. So were the generals. On September 10, with the Polish campaign in full swing, Halder noted in his diary an example which soon became widely known in Berlin. Some toughs belonging to an S.S. artillery regiment, having worked fifty Jews all day on a job of bridge repairing, herded them into a synagogue and, as Halder put it, "massacred them." Even General von Kuechler, the commander of the Third Army, who was later to have few qualms, refused to confirm the light sentences of the court-martial meted out to the murderers—one year in prison—on the ground that they were too lenient. But the Army Commander in Chief, Brauchitsch, quashed the sentences altogether though not until Himmler had intervened, with the excuse that they came under a "general amnesty."

The German generals, upright Christians that they considered themselves to be, found the situation embarrassing. On September 12 there was a meeting on the Fuehrer's railroad train between Keitel and Admiral Canaris at which the latter protested against the atrocities in Poland. The lackey Chief of OKW curtly replied that "the Fuehrer has already decided on this matter." If the Army wanted "no part in these occurrences it would have to accept the S.S. and Gestapo as rivals"—that is, it would have to accept S.S. commissars in each military unit "to carry out the exterminations."

I pointed out to General Keitel [Canaris wrote in his diary, which was produced at Nuremberg] that I knew that extensive executions were planned in Poland and that particularly the nobility and the clergy were to be exterminated. Eventually the world would hold the Wehrmacht responsible for these deeds.[36]

Himmler was too clever to let the generals wiggle out of part of the responsibility. On September 19 Heydrich, Himmler's chief assistant, paid a visit to the Army High Command and told General Wagner of S.S. plans for the "housecleaning of [Polish] Jews, intelligentsia, clergy and the nobility." Halder's reaction to such plans was put down in his diary after Wagner had reported to him:

Army insists that "housecleaning" be deferred until Army has withdrawn and the country has been turned over to civil administration. Early December.

This brief diary entry by the Chief of the Army General Staff provides a key to the understanding of the morals of the German generals. They were not going to seriously oppose the "housecleaning"—that is, the wiping out of the Polish Jews, intelligentsia, clergy and nobility. They were merely going to ask that it be "deferred" until they got out of Poland and could escape the responsibility. And, of course, foreign public opinion must be considered. As Halder jotted down in his diary the next day, after a long conference with Brauchitsch about the "housecleaning" in Poland:

Nothing must occur which would afford foreign countries an opportunity to launch any sort of atrocity propaganda based on such incidents. Catholic clergy! Impractical at this time.

The next day, September 21, Heydrich forwarded to the Army High Command a copy of his initial "housecleaning" plans. As a first step the Jews were to be herded into the cities (where it would be easy to round them up for liquidation). "The final solution," he declared, would take some time to achieve and must be kept "strictly secret," but no general who read the confidential memorandum could have doubted that the "final solution" was extermination.[37] Within two years, when it came time to carry it out, it would become one of the most sinister code names bandied about by high German officials to cover one of the most hideous Nazi crimes of the war.

What was left of Poland after Russia seized her share in the east and Germany formally annexed her former provinces and some additional territory in the west was designated by a decree of the Fuehrer of October 12 as the General Government of Poland and Hans Frank appointed as its Governor General, with Seyss-Inquart, the Viennese quisling, as his deputy. Frank was a typical example of the Nazi intellectual gangster.

He had joined the party in 1927, soon after his graduation from law school, and quickly made a reputation as the legal light of the movement. Nimble-minded, energetic, well read not only in the law but in general literature, devoted to the arts and especially to music, he became a power in the legal profession after the Nazis assumed office, serving first as Bavarian Minister of Justice, then Reichsminister without Portfolio and president of the Academy of Law and of the German Bar Association. A dark, dapper, bouncy fellow, father of five children, his intelligence and cultivation partly offset his primitive fanaticism and up to this time made him one of the least repulsive of the men around Hitler. But behind the civilized veneer of the man lay the cold killer. The forty-two-volume journal he kept of his life and works, which showed up at Nuremberg,* was one of the most terrifying documents to come out of the dark Nazi world, portraying the author as an icy, efficient, ruthless, bloodthirsty man. Apparently it omitted none of his barbaric utterances.

"The Poles," he declared the day after he took his new job, "shall be the slaves of the German Reich." When once he heard that Neurath, the "Protector" of Bohemia, had put up posters announcing the execution of seven Czech university students, Frank exclaimed to a Nazi journalist, "If I wished to order that one should hang up posters about every seven Poles shot, there would not be enough forests in Poland with which to make the paper for these posters."[38]

Himmler and Heydrich were assigned by Hitler to liquidate the Jews. Frank's job, besides squeezing food and supplies and forced labor out of Poland, was to liquidate the intelligentsia. The Nazis had a beautiful code name for this operation: "Extraordinary Pacification Action" (*Ausserordenliche Befriedigungsaktion,* or "AB Action," as it came to be known). It took some time for Frank to get it going. It was not until the following late spring, when the big German offensive in the West took the attention of the world from Poland, that he began to achieve results. By May 30, as his own journal shows, he could boast in a pep talk to his police aides of good progress—the lives of "some thousands" of Polish intellectuals taken, or about to be taken.

"I pray you, gentlemen," he asked, "to take the most rigorous measures possible to help us in this task." Confidentially he added that these were "the Fuehrer's orders." Hitler, he said, had expressed it this way:

"The men capable of leadership in Poland must be liquidated. Those following them . . . must be eliminated in their turn. There is no need to burden the Reich with this . . . no need to send these elements to Reich concentration camps."

They would be put out of the way, he said, right there in Poland.[39]

At the meeting, as Frank noted in his journal, the chief of the Security

---

* It was found in May 1945 by Lieutenant Walter Stein of the U.S. Seventh Army in Frank's apartment at the hotel Berghof near Neuhaus in Bavaria.

Police gave a progress report. About two thousand men and several hundred women, he said, had been apprehended "at the beginning of the Extraordinary Pacification Action." Most of them already had been "summarily sentenced"—a Nazi euphemism for liquidation. A second batch of intellectuals was now being rounded up "for summary sentence." Altogether "about 3,500 persons," the most dangerous of the Polish intelligentsia, would thus be taken care of.[40]

Frank did not neglect the Jews, even if the Gestapo had filched the direct task of extermination away from him. His journal is full of his thoughts and accomplishments on the subject. On October 7, 1940, it records a speech he made that day to a Nazi assembly in Poland summing up his first year of effort.

My dear Comrades! . . . I could not eliminate all lice and Jews in only one year. ["Public amused," he notes down at this point.] But in the course of time, and if you help me, this end will be attained.[41]

A fortnight before Christmas of the following year, Frank closed a cabinet session at Cracow, his headquarters, by saying:

As far as the Jews are concerned, I want to tell you quite frankly that they must be done away with in one way or another . . . Gentlemen, I must ask you to rid yourself of all feeling of pity. We must annihilate the Jews.

It was difficult, he admitted, to "shoot or poison the three and a half million Jews in the General Government, but we shall be able to take measures which will lead, somehow, to their annihilation." This was an accurate prediction.[42]

The hounding of Jews and Poles from the homes which they and their families had dwelt in for generations began as soon as the fighting in Poland was over. On October 7, the day after his "peace speech" in the Reichstag, Hitler appointed Himmler to be the head of a new organization, the Reich Commissariat for the Strengthening of German Nationhood, or R.K.F.D.V., for short. It was to carry out the deportation of Poles and Jews first from the Polish provinces annexed outright by Germany and replace them by Germans and *Volksdeutsche,* the latter being Germans of foreign nationality who were streaming in from the threatened Baltic lands and various outlying parts of Poland. Halder had heard of the plan a fortnight before, noting in his diary that "for every German moving into these territories, two people will be expelled to Poland."

On October 9, two days after assuming the latest of his posts, Himmler decreed that 550,000 of the 650,000 Jews living in the annexed Polish provinces, together with all Poles not fit for "assimilation," should be moved into the territory of the General Government, east of the Vistula River. Within a year 1,200,000 Poles and 300,000 Jews had been uprooted and driven to the east. But only 497,000 *Volksdeutsche* had been settled in their place. This was a little better than Halder's ratio: three Poles and Jews expelled to one German settled in their stead.

It was an unusually severe winter, that of 1939–40, as this writer remembers, with heavy snows, and the "resettlement," carried out in zero weather and often during blizzards, actually cost more Jewish and Polish lives than had been lost to Nazi firing squads and gallows. Himmler himself may be cited as authority. Addressing the S.S. Leibstandarte the following summer after the fall of France, he drew a comparison between the deportations which his men were beginning to carry out in the West with what had been accomplished in the East.

[It] happened in Poland in weather forty degrees below zero, where we had to haul away thousands, tens of thousands, hundreds of thousands; where we had to have the toughness—you should hear this, but also forget it immediately —to shoot thousands of leading Poles . . . Gentlemen, it is much easier in many cases to go into combat with a company than to suppress an obstructive population of low cultural level, or to carry out executions or to haul away people or to evict crying and hysterical women.[48]

Already on February 21, 1940, S.S. Oberfuehrer Richard Gluecks, the head of the Concentration Camp Inspectorate, scouting around near Cracow, had informed Himmler that he had found a "suitable site" for a new "quarantine camp" at Auschwitz, a somewhat forlorn and marshy town of twelve thousand inhabitants in which was situated, besides some factories, a former Austrian cavalry barracks. Work was commenced immediately and on June 14 Auschwitz was officially opened as a concentration camp for Polish political prisoners whom the Germans wished to treat with special harshness. It was soon to become a much more sinister place. In the meantime the directors of I. G. Farben, the great German chemical trust, had discovered Auschwitz as a "suitable" site for a new synthetic coal-oil and rubber plant. There not only the construction of new buildings but the operation of the new plant would have the benefit of cheap slave labor.

To superintend the new camp and the supply of slave labor for I. G. Farben there arrived at Auschwitz in the spring of 1940 a gang of the most choice ruffians in the S.S., among them Josef Kramer, who would later become known to the British public as the "Beast of Belsen," and Rudolf Franz Hoess, a convicted murderer who had served five years in prison—he spent most of his adult life as first a convict and then a jailer —and who in 1946, at the age of forty-six, would boast at Nuremberg that at Auschwitz he had superintended the extermination of two and a half million persons, not counting another half million who had been allowed to "succumb to starvation."

For Auschwitz was soon destined to become the most famous of the *extermination* camps—*Vernichtungslager*—which must be distinguished from the *concentration* camps, where a few did survive. It is not without significance for an understanding of the Germans, even the most respectable Germans, under Hitler, that such a distinguished, internationally known firm as I. G. Farben, whose directors were honored as being among the leading businessmen of Germany, God-fearing men all, should deliberately choose this death camp as a suitable place for profitable operations.

FRICTION BETWEEN THE TOTALITARIANS

The Rome–Berlin Axis became squeaky that first fall of the war.

Sharp exchanges at various levels took place over several differences: the failure of the Germans to carry out the evacuation of the *Volksdeutsche* from Italian South Tyrol, which had been agreed upon the previous June; failure of the Germans to supply Italy with a million tons of coal a month; failure of the Italians to ignore the British blockade and supply Germany with raw materials brought through it; Italy's thriving trade with Britain and France, including the sale to them of war materials; Ciano's increasingly anti-German sentiments.

Mussolini, as usual, blew hot and cold, and Ciano recorded his waverings in his diary. On November 9, the Duce had trouble composing a telegram to Hitler congratulating him on his escape from assassination.

He wanted it to be warm, but not too warm, because in his judgment no Italian feels any great joy over the fact that Hitler escaped death—least of all the Duce.

November 20. . . . For Mussolini the idea of Hitler's waging war, and, worse still, winning it, is altogether unbearable.

The day after Christmas the Duce was expressing a "desire for a German defeat" and instructing Ciano to secretly inform Belgium and Holland that they were about to be attacked.* But by New Year's Eve he was talking again of jumping into the war on Hitler's side.

The chief cause of friction between the two Axis Powers was Germany's pro-Russian policy. On November 30, 1939, the Soviet Red Army had attacked Finland and Hitler had been placed in a most humiliating position. Driven out of the Baltic as the price of his pact with Stalin, forced to hurriedly evacuate the German families who had lived there for centuries, he now had to officially condone Russia's unprovoked attack on a little country which had close ties with Germany and whose very independence as a non-Communist nation had been won from the Soviet Union

---

* Ciano conveyed the warning to the Belgian ambassador in Rome on January 2, noting the action in his diary. According to Weizsaecker the Germans intercepted two coded telegrams from the ambassador to Brussels containing the Italian warning and deciphered them.[44]

largely by the intervention of regular German troops in 1918.* It was a bitter pill to swallow, but he swallowed it. Strict instructions were given to German diplomatic missions abroad and to the German press and radio to support Russia's aggression and avoid expressing any sympathy with the Finns.

This may have been the last straw with Mussolini, who had to cope with anti-German demonstrations throughout Italy. At any rate, shortly after the New Year, 1940, on January 3, he unburdened himself in a long letter to the Fuehrer. Never before, and certainly never afterward, was the Duce so frank with Hitler or so ready to give such sharp and unpleasant advice.

He was "profoundly convinced," he said, that Germany, even if assisted by Italy, could never bring Britain and France "to their knees or even divide them. To believe that is to delude oneself. The United States would not permit a total defeat of the democracies." Therefore, now that Hitler had secured his eastern frontier, was it necessary "to risk all—including the regime—and sacrifice the flower of German generations" in order to try to defeat them? Peace could be had, Mussolini suggested, if Germany would allow the existence of "a modest, disarmed Poland, which is exclusively Polish. Unless you are irrevocably resolved to prosecute the war to a finish," he added, "I believe that the creation of a Polish state . . . would be an element that would resolve the war and constitute a condition sufficient for the peace."

But it was Germany's deal with Russia which chiefly concerned the Italian dictator.

. . . Without striking a blow, Russia has in Poland and the Baltic profited from the war. But I, a born revolutionist, tell you that you cannot permanently sacrifice the principles of your Revolution to the tactical exigencies of a certain political moment . . . It is my duty to add that one further step in your relations with Moscow would have catastrophic repercussions in Italy . . .[45]

Mussolini's letter not only was a warning to Hitler of the degeneration of Italo–German relations but it hit a vulnerable target: the Fuehrer's honeymoon with Soviet Russia, which was beginning to get on the nerves of both parties. It had enabled him to launch his war and destroy Poland. It had even given him other benefits. The captured German papers reveal, for instance, one of the best-kept secrets of the war: the Soviet Union's help in providing ports on the Arctic, the Black Sea and the Pa-

---

* On October 9, 1918—this is a little-known, ludicrous tidbit of history—the Finnish Diet, under the impression that Germany was winning the war, elected by a vote of 75 to 25 Prince Friedrich Karl of Hesse to be King of Finland. Allied victory a month later put an end to this fantastic episode.

cific through which Germany could import badly needed raw materials otherwise shut off by the British blockade.

On November 10, 1939, Molotov even agreed to the Soviet government's paying the freight charges on all such goods carried over the Russian railways.[46] Refueling and repair facilities were provided German ships, including submarines, at the Arctic port of Teriberka, east of Murmansk—Molotov thought the latter port "was not isolated enough," whereas Teriberka was "more suited because it was more remote and not visited by foreign ships."[47]

All through the autumn and early winter of 1939 Moscow and Berlin negotiated for increased trade between the two countries. By the end of October Russian deliveries of raw stuffs, especially grain and oil, to Germany were considerable, but the Germans wanted more. However, they were learning that in economics, as well as politics, the Soviets were shrewd and hard bargainers. On November 1, Field Marshal Goering, Grand Admiral Raeder and Colonel General Keitel, "independently of each other," as Weizsaecker noted, protested to the German Foreign Office that the Russians were demanding too much German war material. A month later Keitel was again complaining to Weizsaecker that Russian requirements for German products, especially machine tools for manufacturing munitions, were "growing more and more voluminous and unreasonable."[48]

But if Germany wanted food and oil from Russia, it would have to pay for them in the goods Moscow needed and wanted. So desperate was the blockaded Reich for these necessities from Russia that later, on March 30, 1940, at a crucial moment, Hitler ordered that delivery of war material to the Russians should have priority even over that to the German armed forces.[*50] At one point the Germans threw in the unfinished heavy cruiser *Luetzow* as part of current payments to Moscow. Earlier, on December 15, Admiral Raeder proposed selling the plans and drawings for the *Bismarck,* the world's biggest battleship (45,000 tons), then building, to the Russians if they paid "a very high price."[51]

By the end of 1939 Stalin himself was personally participating in the negotiations at Moscow with the German trade delegation. The German economists found him a formidable trader. In the captured Wilhelmstrasse papers there are long and detailed memoranda of three memorable meetings with the awesome Soviet dictator, who had a grasp of detail that stunned the Germans. Stalin, they found, could not be bluffed or cheated but could be terribly demanding, and at times, as Dr. Schnurre, one of the Nazi negotiators, reported to Berlin, he "became quite agitated." The Soviet Union, Stalin reminded the Germans, had "rendered a very great service to Germany [and] had made enemies by rendering this assistance."

---

* After the conquest of France and the lowlands, Goering informed General Thomas, the economic chief of OKW, "that the Fuehrer desired punctual delivery to the Russians only until the spring of 1941. Later on," he added, "we would have no further interest in completely satisfying the Russian demands."[49]

In return it expected some consideration from Berlin. At one conference at the Kremlin on New Year's Eve, 1939–40,

Stalin characterized the total price of the airplanes as out of the question. It represented a multiplication of the actual prices. If Germany did not wish to deliver the airplanes, he would have preferred to have this openly stated.

At a midnight meeting in the Kremlin on February 8

Stalin requested the Germans to propose suitable prices and not to set them too high, as had happened before. As examples were mentioned the total price of 300 million Reichsmarks for airplanes and the German valuation of the cruiser *Luetzow* at 150 million RM. One should not take advantage of the Soviet Union's good nature.[52]

On February 11, 1940, an intricate trade agreement was finally signed in Moscow providing for an exchange of goods, during the ensuing eighteen months, of a minimum worth of 640 million Reichsmarks. This was in addition to the trade agreed upon during the previous August amounting to roughly 150 millions a year. Russia was to get, besides the cruiser *Luetzow* and the plans of the *Bismarck,* heavy naval guns and other gear and some thirty of Germany's latest warplanes, including the Messerschmitt fighters 109 and 110 and the Ju-88 dive bombers. In addition the Soviets were to receive machines for their oil and electric industries, locomotives, turbines, generators, Diesel engines, ships, machine tools and samples of German artillery, tanks, explosives, chemical-warfare equipment and so on.[53]

What the Germans got the first year was recorded by OKW—one million tons of cereals, half a million tons of wheat, 900,000 tons of oil, 100,000 tons of cotton, 500,000 tons of phosphates, considerable amounts of numerous other vital raw materials and the transit of a million tons of soybeans from Manchuria.[54]

Back in Berlin, Dr. Schnurre, the Foreign Office's economic expert, who had masterminded the trade negotiations for Germany in Moscow, drew up a long memorandum on what he had gained for the Reich. Besides the desperately needed raw materials which Russia would supply, Stalin, he said, had promised "generous help" in acting "as a buyer of metals and raw materials in third countries."

The Agreement [Schnurre concluded] means a wide-open door to the East for us . . . The effects of the British blockade will be decisively weakened.[55]

This was one reason why Hitler swallowed his pride, supported Russia's aggression against Finland, which was very unpopular in Germany, and accepted the threat of Soviet troops and airmen setting up bases in the three Baltic countries (to be eventually used against whom but Germany?). Stalin was helping him to surmount the British blockade. But more important than that, Stalin still afforded him the opportunity of fighting a one-front war, of concentrating all his military might in the west for a knockout blow against France and Britain and the overrunning of Belgium and Holland, after which—well, Hitler had already told his generals what he had in mind.

As early as October 17, 1939, with the Polish campaign scarcely over, he had reminded Keitel that Polish territory

is important to us from a military point of view as an advanced jumping-off point and for strategic concentration of troops. To that end the railroads, roads and communication channels are to be kept in order.[56]

As the momentous year of 1939 approached its end Hitler realized, as he had told his generals in his memorandum of October 9, that Soviet neutrality could not be counted on forever. In eight months or a year, he had said, things might change. And in his harangue to them on November 23 he had emphasized that "we can oppose Russia only when we are free in the West." This was a thought which never left his restless mind.

The fateful year faded into history in a curious and even eerie atmosphere. Though there was world war, there was no fighting on land, and in the skies the big bombers carried only propaganda pamphlets, and badly written ones at that. Only at sea was there actual warfare. U-boats continued to take their toll of British and sometimes neutral shipping in the cruel, icy northern Atlantic.

In the South Atlantic the *Graf Spee,* one of Germany's three pocket battleships, had emerged from its waiting area and in three months had sunk nine British cargo vessels totaling 50,000 tons. Then, a fortnight before the first Christmas of the war, on December 14, 1939, the German public was electrified by the news, splashed in flaming headlines and in bulletins flashed over the radio, of a great victory at sea. The *Graf Spee,* it was said, had engaged three British cruisers on the previous day four hundred miles off Montevideo and put them out of action. But elation soon turned to puzzlement. Three days later the press announced that the pocket battleship had scuttled herself in the Plate estuary just outside the Uruguayan capital. What kind of a victory was that? On December 21, the High Command of the Navy announced that the *Graf Spee*'s commander, Captain Hans Langsdorff, had "followed his ship" and thus "fulfilled like a fighter and hero the expectations of his Fuehrer, the German people and the Navy."

The wretched German people were never told that the *Graf Spee* had been severely damaged by the three British cruisers, which it outgunned,* that it had had to put into Montevideo for repairs, that the Uruguayan

---

* The day before the scuttling Goebbels had made the German press play up a faked dispatch from Montevideo saying the *Graf Spee* had suffered only "superficial damage" and that British reports that it had been severely crippled were "pure lies."

government, in accordance with international law, had allowed it to remain for only seventy-two hours, which was not enough, that the "hero," Captain Langsdorff, rather than risk further battle with the British with his crippled ship, had therefore scuttled it, and that he himself, instead of going down with her, had shot himself two days afterward in a lonely hotel room in Buenos Aires. Nor were they told, of course, that, as General Jodl jotted in his diary on December 18, the Fuehrer was "very angry about the scuttling of *Graf Spee* without a fight" and sent for Admiral Raeder, to whom he gave a dressing down.[57]

On December 12, Hitler issued another top-secret directive postponing the attack in the West and stipulating that a fresh decision would not be made until December 27 and that the earliest date for "A Day" would be January 1, 1940. He advised that Christmas leaves could therefore be granted. According to my diary, Christmas, the high point of the year for Germans, was a bleak one in Berlin that winter, with few presents exchanged, Spartan food, the menfolk away, the streets blacked out, the shutters and curtains drawn tight, and everyone grumbling about the war, the food and the cold.

There was an exchange of Christmas greetings between Hitler and Stalin.

Best wishes [Hitler wired] for your personal well-being as well as for the prosperous future of the peoples of the friendly Soviet Union.

To which Stalin replied:

The friendship of the peoples of Germany and the Soviet Union, cemented by blood, has every reason to be lasting and firm.

In Berlin Ambassador von Hassell used the holidays to confer with his fellow conspirators, Popitz, Goerdeler and General Beck, and on December 30 recorded in his diary the latest plan. It was

to have a number of divisions stop in Berlin "in transit from west to east." Then Witzleben was to appear in Berlin and dissolve the S.S. On the basis of this action Beck would go to Zossen and take the supreme command from Brauchitsch's hands. A doctor would declare Hitler incapable of continuing in office, whereupon he would be taken into custody. Then an appeal would be made to the people along these lines: prevention of further S.S. atrocities, restoration of decency and Christian morality, continuation of the war, but readiness for peace on a reasonable basis . . .

But it was all unreal; all talk. And so confused were the "plotters" that Hassell devoted a long patch of his diary to the consideration of whether they should retain Goering or not!

Goering himself, along with Hitler, Himmler, Goebbels, Ley and other party leaders, used the New Year to issue grandiose proclamations. Ley said, "The Fuehrer is always right! Obey the Fuehrer!" The Fuehrer himself proclaimed that not he but "the Jewish and capitalistic warmongers" had started the war and went on:

United within the country, economically prepared and militarily armed to the highest degree, we enter this most decisive year in German history . . . May the year 1940 bring the decision. It will be, whatever happens, our victory.

On December 27 he had again postponed the attack in the West "by at least a fortnight." On January 10 he ordered it definitely set for January 17 "fifteen minutes before sunrise—8:16 A.M." The Air Force was to begin *its* attack on January 14, three days in advance, its task being to destroy enemy airfields in France, but not in Belgium and Holland. The two little neutral countries were to be kept guessing about their fate until the last moment.

But on January 13 the Nazi warlord suddenly postponed the onslaught again "on account of the meteorological situation." The captured OKW file on D Day in the West is thereafter silent until May 7. Weather may have played a part in the calling off of the attack on January 13. But we now know that two other events were mainly responsible—an unfortunate forced landing of a very special German military plane in Belgium on January 10 and a new opportunity that now appeared to the north.

On the very day, January 10, that Hitler had ordered the attack through Belgium and Holland to begin on the seventeenth, a German military plane flying from Muenster to Cologne became lost in the clouds over Belgium and was forced to land near Mechelen-sur-Meuse. In it was Major Helmut Reinberger, an important Luftwaffe staff officer, and in his briefcase were the German plans, complete with maps, for the attack in the West. As Belgian soldiers closed in, the major made for some nearby bushes and lit a fire to the contents of his briefcase. Attracted by this interesting phenomenon the Belgian soldiers stamped out the flames and retrieved what was left. Taken to military quarters nearby, Reinberger, in a desperate gesture, grabbed the partly burned papers, which a Belgian officer had placed on a table, and threw them into a lighted stove. The Belgian officer quickly snatched them out.

Reinberger promptly reported to Luftwaffe headquarters in Berlin through his embassy in Brussels that he had succeeded in burning down the papers to "insignificant fragments, the size of the palm of his hand." But in Berlin there was consternation in high quarters. Jodl immediately reported to Hitler "on what the enemy may or may not know." But he did not know himself. "If enemy is in possession of all the files," he confided to his diary on January 12, after seeing the Fuehrer, "the situation is catastrophic." That evening Ribbentrop sent a "most urgent" wire to the German Embassy in Brussels asking for an immediate report on the "destruction of the courier baggage." On the morning of January 13, Jodl's diary reveals, there was a conference of Goering with his air attaché in Brussels, who had flown posthaste back to Berlin, and the top Luftwaffe brass. "Result: Dispatch case burned for certain," Jodl recorded.

But this was whistling in the dark, as Jodl's journal makes clear. At 1 P.M. it noted: "Order to Gen. Halder by telephone: All movements to stop."

The same day, the thirteenth, the German ambassador in Brussels was urgently informing Berlin of considerable Belgian troop movements "as a result of alarming reports received by the Belgian General Staff." The next day the ambassador got off another "most urgent" message to Berlin: The Belgians were ordering "Phase D," the next-to-the-last step in mobilization, and calling up two new classes. The reason, he thought, was "reports of German troop movements on the Belgian and Dutch frontiers as well as the content of the partly unburned courier mail found on the German Air Force officer."

By the evening of January 15 doubts had risen in the minds of the top brass in Berlin whether Major Reinberger had really destroyed the incriminating documents as he had claimed. They were "presumably burned," Jodl remarked after another conference on the matter. But on January 17 the Belgian Foreign Minister, Paul-Henri Spaak, sent for the German ambassador and told him flatly, as the latter promptly reported to Berlin, that

the plane which made an emergency landing on January 10 had put into Belgian hands a document of the most extraordinary and serious nature, which contained clear proof of an intention to attack. It was not just an operations plan, but an attack order worked out in every detail, in which only the time remained to be inserted.

The Germans were never quite sure whether Spaak was not bluffing. On the Allied side—the British and French general staffs were given copies of the German plan—there was a tendency to view the German papers as a "plant." Churchill says he vigorously opposed this interpretation and laments that nothing was done about this grave warning. What is certain is that on January 13, the day after Hitler was informed of the affair, he postponed the attack and that by the time it again came up for decision in the spring the whole strategic plan had been fundamentally changed.[58]

But the forced landing in Belgium—and the bad weather—were not the only reasons for putting off the attack. Plans for a daring German assault on two other little neutral states farther to the north had in the meantime been ripening in Berlin and now took priority. The phony war, so far as the Germans were concerned, was coming to an end with the approach of spring.

20

THE CONQUEST OF DENMARK
AND NORWAY

THE INNOCENT-SOUNDING code name for the latest plan of German aggression was *Weseruebung,* or "Weser Exercise." Its origins and development were unique, quite unlike those for unprovoked attack that have filled so large a part of this narrative. It was not the brain child of Hitler, as were all the others, but of an ambitious admiral and a muddled Nazi party hack. It was the only act of German military aggression in which the German Navy played the decisive role. It was also the only one for which OKW did the planning and co-ordinating of the three armed services. In fact, the Army High Command and its General Staff were not even consulted, much to their annoyance, and Goering was not brought into the picture until the last moment—a slight that infuriated the corpulent chief of the Luftwaffe.

The German Navy had long had its eyes on the north. Germany had no direct access to the wide ocean, a geographical fact which had been imprinted on the minds of its naval officers during the First World War. A tight British net across the narrow North Sea, from the Shetland Islands to the coast of Norway, maintained by a mine barrage and a patrol of ships, had bottled up the powerful Imperial Navy, seriously hampered the attempts of U-boats to break out into the North Atlantic, and kept German merchant shipping off the seas. The German High Seas Fleet never reached the high seas. The British naval blockade stifled Imperial Germany in the first war. Between the wars the handful of German naval officers who commanded the country's modestly sized Navy pondered this experience and this geographical fact and came to the conclusion that in any future war with Britain, Germany must try to gain bases in Norway, which would break the British blockade line across the North Sea, open up the broad ocean to German surface and undersea vessels and indeed offer an opportunity for the Reich to reverse the tables and mount an effective blockade of the British Isles.

It was not surprising, then, that at the outbreak of war in 1939 Admiral Rolf Carls, the third-ranking officer in the German Navy and a forceful personality, should start peppering Admiral Raeder, as the latter noted in his diary and testified at Nuremberg, with letters suggesting "the importance of an occupation of the Norwegian coast by Germany."[1] Raeder needed little urging and on October 3, at the end of the Polish campaign, sent a confidential questionnaire to the Naval War Staff asking it to ascertain the possibility of gaining "bases in Norway under the combined pressure of Russia and Germany." Ribbentrop was consulted about Moscow's attitude and replied that "far-reaching support may be expected" from that source. Raeder told his staff that Hitler must be informed as soon as possible about the "possibilities."[2]

On October 10, in the course of a lengthy report to the Fuehrer on naval operations, Raeder suggested the importance of obtaining naval bases in Norway, if necessary with the help of Russia. This—so far as the confidential records show—was the first time the Navy had directly called the matter to the attention of Hitler. Raeder says the Leader "saw at once the significance of the Norwegian problem." He asked him to leave his notes on the subject and promised to give the question some thought. But at the moment the Nazi warlord was preoccupied with launching his attack in the West and with overcoming the hesitations of his generals.* Norway apparently slipped out of his mind.[3]

But it came back in two months—for three reasons.

One was the advent of winter. Germany's very existence depended upon the import of iron ore from Sweden. For the first war year the Germans were counting on eleven million tons of it out of a total annual consumption of fifteen million tons. During the warm-weather months this ore was transported from northern Sweden down the Gulf of Bothnia and across the Baltic to Germany, and presented no problem even in wartime, since the Baltic was effectively barred to British submarines and surface ships. But in the wintertime this shipping lane could not be used because of thick ice. During the cold months the Swedish ore had to be shipped by rail to the nearby Norwegian port of Narvik and brought down the Norwegian coast by ship to Germany. For almost the entire journey German ore vessels could sail within Norway's territorial waters and thereby escape destruction by British naval vessels and bombers.

Thus, as Hitler at first pointed out to the Navy, a neutral Norway had its advantages. It enabled Germany to obtain its lifeblood of iron ore without interference from Britain.

In London, Churchill, then First Lord of the Admiralty, perceived this at once and in the very first weeks of the war attempted to persuade the cabinet to allow him to lay mines in Norwegian territorial waters in order to stop the German iron traffic. But Chamberlain and Halifax were most

---

* It was on October 10 that Hitler had called in his military chiefs, read them a long memorandum on the necessity of an immediate attack in the West and handed them Directive No. 6 ordering preparations for an offensive through Belgium and Holland. (See above, pp. 644–46.)

reluctant to violate Norwegian neutrality, and the proposal was for the time being dropped.[4]

Russia's attack on Finland on November 30, 1939, radically changed the situation in Scandinavia, immensely increasing its strategic importance to both the Western Allies and Germany. France and Britain began to organize an expeditionary force in Scotland to be sent to the aid of the gallant Finns, who, defying all predictions, held out stubbornly against the onslaughts of the Red Army. But it could reach Finland only through Norway and Sweden, and the Germans at once saw that if Allied troops were granted, or took, transit across the northern part of the two Scandinavian lands enough of them would remain, on the excuse of maintaining communications, to completely cut off Germany's supply of Swedish iron ore.* Moreover, the Western Allies would outflank the Reich on the north. Admiral Raeder was not backward in reminding Hitler of these threats.

The chief of the German Navy had now found in Norway itself a valuable ally for his designs in the person of Major Vidkun Abraham Lauritz Quisling, whose name would soon become a synonym in almost all languages for a traitor.

THE EMERGENCE OF VIDKUN QUISLING

Quisling had begun life honorably enough. Born in 1887 of peasant stock, he had graduated first in his class at the Norwegian Military Academy and while still in his twenties had been sent to Petrograd as military attaché. For his services in looking after British interests after diplomatic relations were broken with the Bolshevik government, Great Britain awarded him the C.B.E. At this time he was both pro-British and pro-Bolshevik. He remained in Soviet Russia for some time as assistant to Fridtjof Nansen, the great Norwegian explorer and humanitarian, in Russian relief work.

So impressed had the young Norwegian Army officer been by the success of the Communists in Russia that when he returned to Oslo he offered his services to the Labor Party, which at that time was a member of the Comintern. He proposed that he establish a "Red Guard," but the Labor Party was suspicious of him and his project and turned him down. He then veered to the opposite extreme. After serving as Minister of Defense from 1931 to 1933, he founded in May of the latter year a

---

* It was a correct assumption. It is now known that the Allied Supreme War Council, meeting in Paris on February 5, 1940, decided that in sending an expeditionary force to Finland the Swedish iron fields should be occupied by troops landed at Narvik, which was but a short distance from the mines. (See the author's *The Challenge of Scandinavia*, pp. 115–16n.) Churchill remarks that at the meeting it was decided "incidentally to get control of the Gullivare ore-field." (*The Gathering Storm*, p. 560.)

fascist party called Nasjonal Samling—National Union—appropriating the ideology and tactics of the Nazis, who had just come to power in Germany. But Nazism did not thrive in the fertile democratic soil of Norway. Quisling was unable even to get himself elected to Parliament. Defeated at the polls by his own people, he turned to Nazi Germany.

There he established contact with Alfred Rosenberg, the befuddled official philosopher of the Nazi movement, among whose jobs was that of chief of the party's Office for Foreign Affairs. This Baltic dolt, one of Hitler's earliest mentors, thought he saw possibilities in the Norwegian officer, for one of Rosenberg's pet fantasies was the establishment of a great Nordic Empire from which the Jews and other "impure" races would be excluded and which eventually would dominate the world under Nazi German leadership. From 1933 on, he kept in touch with Quisling and heaped on him his nonsensical philosophy and propaganda.

In June 1939, as the war clouds gathered over Europe, Quisling took the occasion of his attendance at a convention of the Nordic Society at Luebeck to ask Rosenberg for something more than ideological support. According to the latter's confidential reports, which were produced at Nuremberg, Quisling warned Rosenberg of the danger of Britain's getting control of Norway in the event of war and of the advantages to Germany of occupying it. He asked for some substantial aid for his party and press. Rosenberg, a great composer of memoranda, dashed out three of them for Hitler, Goering and Ribbentrop, but the three top men appear to have ignored them—no one in Germany took the "official philosopher" very seriously. Rosenberg himself was able to arrange at least for a fortnight's training course in Germany in August for twenty-five of Quisling's husky storm troopers.

During the first months of the war Admiral Raeder—or so he testified at Nuremberg—had no contact with Rosenberg, whom he scarcely knew, and none with Quisling, of whom he had never heard. But immediately after the Russian attack on Finland Raeder began to get reports from his naval attaché at Oslo, Captain Richard Schreiber, of imminent Allied landings in Norway. He mentioned these to Hitler on December 8 and advised him flatly, "It is important to occupy Norway."[5]

Shortly afterward Rosenberg dashed off a memorandum (undated) to Admiral Raeder "regarding visit of Privy Councilor Quisling—Norway." The Norwegian conspirator had arrived in Berlin and Rosenberg thought Raeder ought to be told who he was and what he was up to. Quisling, he said, had many sympathizers among key officers in the Norwegian Army and, as proof, had shown him a recent letter from Colonel Konrad Sundlo, the commanding officer at Narvik, characterizing Norway's Prime Minister as a "blockhead" and one of his chief ministers as "an old soak" and declaring his willingness to "risk his bones for the national uprising." Later Colonel Sundlo did not risk his bones to defend his country against aggression.

Actually, Rosenberg informed Raeder, Quisling had a plan for a coup.

It must have fallen upon sympathetic ears in Berlin, for it was copied from the Anschluss. A number of Quisling's storm troopers would be hurriedly trained in Germany "by experienced and diehard National Socialists who are practiced in such operations." The pupils, once back in Norway, would seize strategic points in Oslo,

and at the same time the German Navy with contingents of the German Army will have to put in an appearance at a prearranged bay outside Oslo in answer to a special summons from the new Norwegian Government.

It was the Anschluss tactic all over again, with Quisling playing the part of Seyss-Inquart.

Quisling has no doubt [Rosenberg added] that such a coup . . . would meet with the approval of those sections of the Army with which he now has connections . . . As regards the King, he believes that he would accept such a *fait accompli.*

Quisling's estimate of the number of German troops needed for the operation coincides with the German estimates.[6]

Admiral Raeder saw Quisling on December 11, the meeting being arranged through Rosenberg by one Viljam Hagelin, a Norwegian businessman whose affairs kept him largely in Germany and who was Quisling's chief liaison there. Hagelin and Quisling told Raeder a mouthful and he duly recorded it in the confidential naval archives.

Quisling stated . . . a British landing is planned in the vicinity of Stavanger, and Christiansand is proposed as a possible British base. The present Norwegian Government as well as the Parliament and the whole foreign policy are controlled by the well-known Jew, Hambro [Carl Hambro, the President of the Storting], a great friend of Hore-Belisha . . . The dangers to Germany arising from a British occupation were depicted in great detail . . .

To anticipate a British move, Quisling proposed to place "the necessary bases at the disposal of the German Armed Forces. In the whole coastal area men in important positions (railway, post office, communications) have already been bought for this purpose." He and Hagelin had come to Berlin to establish "clear-cut relations with Germany for the future . . . Conferences are desired for discussion of combined action, transfer of troops to Oslo, etc."[7]

Raeder, as he later testified at Nuremberg, was impressed and told his two visitors that he would confer with the Fuehrer and inform them of the results. This he did the next day at a meeting at which Keitel and Jodl were also present. The Navy Commander in Chief (whose report on this conference is among the captured documents) informed Hitler that Quisling had made "a reliable impression" on him. He then outlined the main points the Norwegians had made, emphasizing Quisling's "good connections with officers in the Norwegian Army" and his readiness "to take over the government by a political coup and ask Germany for aid." All present agreed that a British occupation of Norway could not be countenanced, but Raeder, become suddenly cautious, pointed out that a German occupation "would naturally occasion strong British countermeasures . . . and the German Navy is not yet prepared to cope with them for any length of time. In the event of occupation this is a weak spot." On the other hand, Raeder suggested that OKW

be permitted to make plans with Quisling for preparing and executing the occupation either:

a. by friendly methods, i.e., the German Armed Forces are called upon by Norway, or

b. by force.

Hitler was not quite ready to go so far at the moment. He replied that he first wanted to speak to Quisling personally "in order to form an impression of him."[8]

This he did the very next day, December 14, Raeder personally escorting the two Norwegian traitors to the Chancellery. Although no record of this meeting has been found, Quisling obviously impressed the German dictator,* as he had the Navy chief, for that evening Hitler ordered OKW to work out a draft plan in consultation with Quisling. Halder heard that it would also include action against Denmark.[10]

Hitler saw Quisling again on December 16 and 18, despite his preoccupation with the bad news about the *Graf Spee*. The naval setback, however, seems to have added to his cautiousness about a Scandinavian adventure which would depend first of all on the Navy. According to Rosenberg, the Fuehrer emphasized to his visitor that "the most preferable attitude for Norway would be . . . complete neutrality." However, if the British were preparing to enter Norway the Germans would have to beat them to it. In the meantime he would provide Quisling with funds to combat British propaganda and strengthen his own pro-German movement. An initial sum of 200,000 gold marks was allotted in January, with the promise of 10,000 pounds sterling per month for three months beginning on March 15.[11]

Shortly before Christmas Rosenberg dispatched a special agent, Hans-Wilhelm Scheidt, to Norway to work with Quisling, and over the holidays the handful of officers at OKW who were in the know began working on "Study North," as the plans were first called. In the Navy opinion was

---

* He had not impressed the German minister in Oslo, Dr. Curt Bräuer, who twice in December warned Berlin that Quisling "need not be taken seriously . . . his influence and prospects are . . . very slight."[9] For his frankness and reluctance to play Hitler's game, the minister was quickly to pay.

divided. Raeder was convinced that Britain intended to move into Norway in the near future. The Operations Division of the Naval War Staff disagreed, and in its confidential war diary for January 13, 1940, their differences were aired.[12]

The Operations Division does *not* believe an imminent British occupation of Norway is probable . . . [It] considers, however, that an occupation of Norway by Germany, if no British action is to be feared, would be a dangerous undertaking.

The Naval War Staff therefore concluded "that the most favorable solution is definitely the maintenance of the status quo" and emphasized that this would permit the continued use of Norwegian territorial waters for the ore traffic "in perfect safety."

Hitler was displeased with both the hesitations of the Navy and the results of Study North, which OKW presented to him the middle of January. On January 27 he had Keitel issue a top-secret directive stating that further work on "North" be continued under the Fuehrer's "personal and immediate supervision" and directing Keitel to take charge of all preparations. A small working staff composed of one representative from each of the three armed services was to be set up in OKW and henceforth the operation was to have the code name *Weseruebung.*[13]

This step seems to have marked the end of the Fuehrer's hesitations about occupying Norway, but if there were any lingering doubts in his mind they were dispelled by an incident which occurred in Norwegian waters on February 17.

An auxiliary supply ship of the *Graf Spee,* the *Altmark,* had managed to slip back through the British blockade and on February 14 was discovered by a British scouting plane proceeding southward in Norwegian territorial waters toward Germany. The British government knew that aboard it were three hundred captured British seamen from the ships sunk by the *Graf Spee.* They were being taken to Germany as prisoners of war. Norwegian naval officers had made a cursory inspection of the *Altmark,* found that it had no prisoners aboard and was unarmed, and given it clearance to proceed on to Germany. Now Churchill, who knew otherwise, personally ordered a British destroyer flotilla to go into Norwegian waters, board the German vessel and liberate the prisoners.

The British destroyer *Cossack,* commanded by Captain Philip Vian, carried out the mission on the night of February 16–17 in Jösing Fjord, where the *Altmark* had sought safety. After a scuffle in which four Germans were killed and five wounded, the British boarding party liberated 299 seamen, who had been locked in storerooms and in an empty oil tank to avoid their detection by the Norwegians.

The Norwegian government made a vehement protest to Britain about this violation of its territorial waters, but Chamberlain replied in the Commons that Norway itself had violated international law by allowing its waters to be used by the Germans to convey British prisoners to a German prison.

For Hitler this was the last straw. It convinced him that the Norwegians would not seriously oppose a British display of force in their own territorial waters. He was also furious, as Jodl noted in his diary, that the members of the *Graf Spee* crew aboard the *Altmark* had not put up a stiffer fight— "no resistance, no British losses." On February 19, Jodl's diary discloses, Hitler "pressed energetically" for the completion of plans for *Weseruebung*. "Equip ships. Put units in readiness," he told Jodl. They still lacked an officer to lead the enterprise and Jodl reminded Hitler that it was time to appoint a general and his staff for this purpose.

Keitel suggested an officer who had fought with General von der Goltz's division in Finland at the end of the First World War, General Nikolaus von Falkenhorst, who now commanded an army corps in the west, and Hitler, who had overlooked the little matter of a commander for the northern adventure, immediately sent for him. Though the General came from an old Silesian military family by the name of Jastrzembski, which he had changed to Falkenhorst (in German, "falcon's eyrie"), he was personally unknown to the Fuehrer.

Falkenhorst later described in an interrogation at Nuremberg their first meeting at the Chancellery on the morning of February 21, which was not without its amusing aspects. Falkenhorst had never even heard of the "North" operation and this was the first time he had faced the Nazi warlord, who apparently did not awe him as he had all the other generals.

I was made to sit down [he recounted at Nuremberg]. Then I had to tell the Fuehrer about the operations in Finland in 1918 . . . He said: "Sit down and just tell me how it was," and I did.

Then we got up and he led me to a table that was covered with maps. He said: ". . . The Reich Government has knowledge that the British intend to make a landing in Norway . . ."

Falkenhorst said he got the impression from Hitler that it was the *Altmark* incident which had influenced the Leader the most to "carry out the plan now." And the General, to his surprise, found himself appointed then and there to do the carrying out as commander in chief. The Army, Hitler added, would put five divisions at his disposal. The idea was to seize the main Norwegian ports.

At noon the warlord dismissed Falkenhorst and told him to report back at 5 P.M. with his plans for the occupation of Norway.

I went out and bought a Baedeker, a travel guide [Falkenhorst explained at Nuremberg], in order to find out just what Norway was like. I didn't have any idea . . . Then I went to my hotel room and I worked on this Baedeker . . . At 5 P.M. I went back to the Fuehrer.[14]

The General's plans, worked out from an old Baedeker—he was never shown the plans worked out by OKW—were, as can be imagined, somewhat sketchy, but they seem to have satisfied Hitler. One division was to be allotted to each of Norway's five principal harbors, Oslo, Stavanger, Bergen, Trondheim and Narvik. "There wasn't much else you could do," Falkenhorst said later, "because they were the large harbors." After being sworn to secrecy and urged "to hurry up," the General was again dismissed and thereupon set to work.

Of all these goings on, Brauchitsch and Halder, busy preparing the offensive on the Western front, were largely ignorant until Falkenhorst called on the Army General Staff Chief on February 26 and demanded some troops, especially mountain units, to carry out his operation. Halder was not very co-operative; in fact, he was indignant and asked for more information on what was up and what was needed. "Not a single word on this matter has been exchanged between the Fuehrer and Brauchitsch," Halder exclaimed in his diary. "That must be recorded for the history of the war!"

However, Hitler, full of contempt as he was for the old-line generals and especially for his General Staff Chief, was not to be put off. On March 29 he enthusiastically approved Falkenhorst's plans, including his acquisition of two mountain divisions, and moreover declared that more troops would be necessary because he wanted "a strong force at Copenhagen." Denmark had definitely been added to the list of Hitler's victims; the Air Force had its eyes on bases there to be used against Britain.

The next day, March 1, Hitler issued the formal directive for Weser Exercise.

MOST SECRET

TOP SECRET

The development of the situation in Scandinavia requires the making of all preparations for the occupation of Denmark and Norway. This operation should prevent British encroachment on Scandinavia and the Baltic. Further it should guarantee our ore base in Sweden and give our Navy and the Air Force a wider starting line against Britain . . .

In view of our military and political power in comparison with that of the Scandinavian States, the force to be employed in "Weser Exercise" will be kept as small as possible. The numerical weakness will be balanced by daring actions and surprise execution.

On principle, we will do our utmost to make the operation appear as a *peaceful* occupation, the object of which is the military protection of the neutrality of the Scandinavian States. Corresponding demands will be transmitted to the Governments at the beginning of the occupation. If necessary, demonstrations by the Navy and Air Force will provide the necessary emphasis. If, in spite of this, resistance should be met, all military means will be used to crush it . . . The crossing of the Danish border and the landings in Norway must take place *simultaneously* . . .

It is most important that the Scandinavian States as well as the Western opponents should be *taken by surprise* . . . The troops may be acquainted with the actual objectives only after putting to sea . . .[15]

That very evening, March 1, there was "fury" at the Army High Command, Jodl reported, because of Hitler's demands for troops for the northern operation. The next day Goering "raged" at Keitel and went to complain to Hitler. The fat Field Marshal was furious at having been left out of the secret so long and because the Luftwaffe had been put under Falkenhorst's command. Threatened by a serious jurisdictional dispute, Hitler convoked the heads of the three armed services to the Chancellery on March 5 to smooth matters out, but it was difficult.

Field Marshal [Goering] vents his spleen [Jodl wrote in his diary] because he was not consulted beforehand. He dominates the discussion and tries to prove that all previous preparations are good for nothing.

The Fuehrer mollified him by some small concessions, and plans raced forward. As early as February 21, according to his diary, Halder had got the impression that the attack on Denmark and Norway would not begin until after the offensive in the West had been launched and "carried to a certain point." Hitler himself had been in doubt which operation to begin first and raised the question with Jodl on February 26. Jodl's advice was to keep the two operations quite separate and Hitler agreed, "if it were possible."

On March 3 he decided that Weser Exercise would precede "Case Yellow" (the code name for attack in the West) and expressed "very sharply" to Jodl "the necessity of prompt and strong action in Norway." By this time the courageous but outmanned and outgunned Finnish Army was facing disaster from a massive Russian offensive and there were well-founded reports that the Anglo–French expeditionary corps was about to embark from its bases in Scotland for Norway and march across that country and Sweden to Finland to try to save the Finns.* The threat of this was the main reason for Hitler's hurry.

---

* On March 7 General Ironside, Chief of the British General Staff, informed Marshal Mannerheim that an Allied expeditionary force of 57,000 men was ready to come to the aid of the Finns and that the first division, of 15,000 troops, could reach Finland by the end of March if Norway and Sweden would allow them transit. Actually five days before, on March 2, as Mannerheim knew, both Norway and Sweden had again turned down the Franco–British request for transit privileges. This did not prevent Premier Daladier on March 8 from scolding the Finns for not *officially* asking for Allied troops and from intimating that the Allied forces would be sent regardless of Norwegian and Swedish protests. But Mannerheim was not to be fooled, and, having advised his government to sue for peace while the Finnish Army was still intact and undefeated, he approved the immediate dispatch of a peace delegation to Moscow on March 8. The Finnish Commander in Chief seems to have been skeptical of the French zeal for fighting on the Finnish front rather

But on March 12 the Russo–Finnish War suddenly ended with Finland accepting Russia's harsh terms for peace. While this was generally welcomed in Berlin because it freed Germany from its unpopular championship of the Russians against the Finns and also brought an end, for the moment, of the Soviet drive to take over the Baltic, it nevertheless embarrassed Hitler so far as his own Scandinavian venture was concerned. As Jodl confided to his diary, it made the "motivation" for the occupation of Norway and Denmark "difficult." "Conclusion of peace between Finland and Russia," he noted on March 12, "deprives England, but us too, of any political basis to occupy Norway."

In fact, Hitler was now hard put to find an excuse. On March 13 the faithful Jodl recorded that the Fuehrer was "still looking for some justification." The next day: "Fuehrer has not yet decided how to justify the 'Weser Exercise.' " To make matters worse, Admiral Raeder began to get cold feet. He was "in doubt whether it was still important to play at preventive war (?) in Norway."[16]

For the moment Hitler hesitated. Two other problems had in the meantime arisen: (1) how to handle Sumner Welles, the United States Undersecretary of State, who had arrived in Berlin March 1 on a mission from President Roosevelt to see if there was any chance of ending the war before the slaughter began in the West; and (2) how to placate the neglected, offended Italian ally. Hitler had not yet bothered to answer Mussolini's defiant letter of January 3, and relations between Berlin and Rome had distinctly cooled. Now Sumner Welles, the Germans believed, and with some reason, had come to Europe to try to detach Italy from the creaky Axis and persuade her, at any event, not to enter the war on Germany's side if the conflict continued. Various warnings had reached Berlin from Rome that it was time something were done to keep the sulking Duce in line.

HITLER MEETS WITH SUMNER WELLES AND MUSSOLINI

Hitler's ignorance of the United States, as well as that of Goering and Ribbentrop, was abysmal.* And though their policy at this time was to

---

than on their own front in France. (See *The Memoirs of Marshal Mannerheim.*)

One can only speculate on the utter confusion which would have resulted among the belligerents had the Franco–British expeditionary corps ever arrived in Finland and fought the Russians. In little more than a year Germany would be at war with Russia, in which case the enemies in the West would have been allies in the East!

* Examples of Hitler's weird views on America have been given in earlier chapters, but in the captured Foreign Office documents there is a revealing paper on the Fuehrer's state of mind at this very moment. On March 12 Hitler had a long talk with Colin Ross, a German "expert" on the United States, who had recently returned from a lecture trip in America, where he had contributed his mite to Nazi propaganda. When Ross remarked that an "imperialist tendency" prevailed in the

try to keep America out of the war, they, like their predecessors in Berlin in 1914, did not take the Yankee nation seriously as even a potential military power. As early as October 1, 1939, the German military attaché in Washington, General Friedrich von Boetticher, advised OKW in Berlin not to worry about any possible American expeditionary force in Europe. On December 1 he further informed his military superiors in Berlin that American armament was simply inadequate "for an aggressive war policy" and added that the General Staff in Washington "in contrast to the State Department's sterile policy of hatred and the impulsive policy of Roosevelt—often based on an overestimation of American military power—still has understanding for Germany and her conduct of the war." In his first dispatch Boetticher had noted that "Lindbergh and the famous flyer Rickenbacker" were advocating keeping America out of the war. By December 1, however, despite his low estimate of American military power, he warned OKW that "the United States will still enter the war if it considers that the Western Hemisphere is threatened."[18]

Hans Thomsen, the German chargé d'affaires in Washington, did his best to impart some facts about the U.S.A. to his ignorant Foreign Minister in Berlin. On September 18, as the Polish campaign neared its end, he warned the Wilhelmstrasse that "the sympathies of the overwhelming majority of the American people are with our enemies, and America is convinced of Germany's war guilt." In the same dispatch he pointed out the dire consequences of any attempts by Germany to carry out sabotage in America and requested that there be no such sabotage "in any manner whatsoever."[19]

The request evidently was not taken very seriously in Berlin, for on January 25, 1940, Thomsen was wiring Berlin:

I have learned that a German-American, von Hausberger, and a German citizen, Walter, both of New York, are alleged to be planning acts of sabotage

---

United States, Hitler asked (according to the shorthand notes of Dr. Schmidt) "whether this imperialist tendency did not strengthen the desire for the *Anschluss* of Canada to the United States, and thus produce an anti-English attitude."

It must be admitted that Hitler's advisers on the U.S.A. were not very helpful in shedding light on their subject. At this same interview, Ross, in trying to answer Hitler's questions as to why America was so anti-German, gave the following answers, among others:

. . . An additional factor in hatred against Germany . . . is the monstrous power of Jewry, directing with a really fantastic cleverness and organizational skill the struggle against everything German and National Socialist . . .

Colin Ross then talked about Roosevelt, whom he believes to be an enemy of the Fuehrer for reasons of pure personal jealousy and also on account of his personal lust for power . . . He had come to power the same year as the Fuehrer and he had to watch the latter carrying out his great plans, while he, Roosevelt . . . had not reached his goal. He too had ideas of dictatorship which in some respects were very similar to National Socialist ideas. Yet precisely this realization that the Fuehrer had attained his goal, while he had not, gave to his pathological ambition the desire to act upon the stage of world history as the Fuehrer's rival . . .

After Herr Colin Ross had taken his leave, the Fuehrer remarked that Ross was a very intelligent man who certainly had many good ideas.[17]

against the American armament industry by direction of the German Abwehr. Von Hausberger is supposed to have detonators hidden in his dwelling.

Thomsen asked Berlin to desist, declaring that

there is no surer way of driving America into the war than by resorting again to a course of action which drove America into the ranks of our enemies once before in the World War and, incidentally, did not in the least impede the war industries of the United States.

Besides, he added, "both individuals are unfitted in every respect to act as agents of the Abwehr."*

Since November 1938, when Roosevelt had recalled the American ambassador in Berlin in protest against the officially sponsored Nazi pogrom against the Jews, neither country had been represented in the other by an ambassador. Trade had dwindled to a mere trickle, largely as the result of American boycotts, and was now completely shut down by the British blockade. On November 4, 1939, the arms embargo was lifted, following votes in the Senate and the House, thus opening the way for the United States to supply the Western Allies with arms. It was against this background of rapidly deteriorating relations that Sumner Welles arrived in Berlin on March 1, 1940.

The day before, on February 29—it was a leap year—Hitler had taken the unusual step of issuing a secret "Directive for the Conversations with Mr. Sumner Welles."[20] It called for "reserve" on the German side and advised that "as far as possible Mr. Welles be allowed to do the talking." It then laid down five points for the guidance of all the top officials who were to receive the special American envoy. The principal German argument was to be that Germany had not declared war on Britain and France but vice versa; that the Fuehrer had offered them peace in October and that they had rejected it; that Germany accepted the challenge; that the war aims of Britain and France were "the destruction of the German State," and that Germany therefore had no alternative but to continue the war.

A discussion [Hitler concluded] of concrete political questions, such as the question of a future Polish state, is to be avoided as much as possible. In case [he] brings up subjects of this kind, the reply should be that such questions are

---

* Weizsaecker replied that Canaris himself had assured him that neither of the men mentioned by Thomsen was an agent of the Abwehr. But no good secret service admits these things. Other Foreign Office papers reveal that on January 24 an Abwehr agent left Buenos Aires with instructions to report to Fritz von Hausberger at Weehawken, N.J., "for instructions in our speciality." Another agent had been sent from the same place to New York in December to gather information on American aircraft factories and arms shipments to the Allies. Thomsen himself reported on February 20 the arrival of Baron Konstantin von Maydell, a Baltic German of Estonian citizenship, who had told the German Embassy in Washington that he was on a sabotage mission for the Abwehr.

decided by me. It is self-evident that it is entirely out of the question to discuss the subject of Austria and the Protectorate of Bohemia and Moravia . . .

All statements are to be avoided which could be interpreted . . . to mean that Germany is in any way interested at present in discussing possibilities of peace. I request, rather, that Mr. Sumner Welles not be given the slightest reason to doubt that Germany is determined to end this war victoriously . . .

Not only Ribbentrop and Goering but the Leader himself followed the directive to a letter when they saw Welles separately on March 1, 3 and 2, respectively. Judging by the' lengthy minutes of the talks kept by Dr. Schmidt (which are among the captured documents), the American diplomat, a somewhat taciturn and cynical man, must have got the impression that he had landed in a lunatic asylum—if he could believe his ears. Each of the Big Three Nazis bombarded Welles with the most grotesque perversions of history, in which facts were fantastically twisted and even the simplest of words lost all meaning.* Hitler, who on March 1 had issued his directive for *Weseruebung,* received Welles the next day and insisted that the Allied war aim was "annihilation," that of Germany "peace." He lectured his visitor on all he had done to maintain peace with England and France.

Shortly before the outbreak of the war the British Ambassador had sat exactly where Sumner Welles was now sitting, and the Fuehrer had made him the greatest offer of his life.

All his offers to the British had been rejected and now Britain was out to destroy Germany. Hitler therefore believed "that the conflict would have to be fought to a finish . . . there was no other solution than a life-and-death struggle."

No wonder that Welles confided to Weizsaecker and repeated to Goering that if Germany were determined to win a military victory in the West then his trip to Europe "was pointless . . . and there was nothing more for him to say."[21]†

---

* "Before God and the world," Goering exclaimed to Welles, "he, the Field Marshal, could state that Germany had not desired the war. It had been forced upon her . . . But what was Germany to do when the others wanted to destroy her?"

† A quite unofficial American peacemaker was also in Berlin at this time: James D. Mooney, a vice-president of General Motors. He had been in Berlin, as I recall, shortly before or after the outbreak of the war, trying like that other amateur in diplomacy, Dahlerus, though without the latter's connections to save the peace. The day after Welles left Berlin, on March 4, 1940, Hitler received Mooney, who told him, according to a captured German record of the meeting, that President Roosevelt was "more friendly and sympathetic" to Germany "than was generally believed in Berlin" and that the President was prepared to act as "moderator" in bringing the belligerents together. Hitler merely repeated what he had told Welles two days before.

On March 11 Thomsen sent to Berlin a confidential memorandum prepared for

Though he had emphasized in his talks with the Germans that what he heard from the European statesmen on this trip was for the ears of Roosevelt only, Welles thought it wise to be sufficiently indiscreet to tell both Hitler and Goering that he had had a "long, constructive and helpful" talk with Mussolini and that the Duce thought "there was still a possibility of bringing about a firm and lasting peace in Europe." If these were the Italian dictator's thoughts, then it was time, the Germans realized, to correct them. Peace yes, but only after a resounding German victory in the West.

Hitler's failure to answer Mussolini's letter of January 3 had filled the Duce with mounting annoyance. All through the month Ambassador Attolico was inquiring of Ribbentrop when a reply might be expected and hinting that Italy's relations with France and Britain—and their trade, to boot—were improving.

This trade, which included Italian sales of war materials, aggravated the Germans, who constantly protested in Rome that it was unduly aiding the Western Allies. Ambassador von Mackensen kept reporting his "grave anxieties" to his friend Weizsaecker and the latter himself was afraid that Mussolini's unanswered letter, if it were "disregarded" much longer, would give the Duce "freedom of action"—he and Italy might be lost for good.[23]

Then on March 1 Hitler received a break. The British announced that they were cutting off shipments of German coal by sea via Rotterdam to Italy. This was a heavy blow to the Italian economy and threw the Duce into a rage against the British and warmed his feelings toward the Germans, who promptly promised to find the means of delivering their coal by rail. Taking advantage of this circumstance, Hitler got off a long letter to Mussolini on March 8, which Ribbentrop delivered personally in Rome two days later.[24]

It made no apologies for its belatedness, but was cordial in tone and went into considerable detail about the Fuehrer's thoughts and policies on almost every conceivable subject, being more wordy than any previous letter of Hitler's to his Italian partner. It defended the Nazi alliance with Russia, the abandonment of the Finns, the failure to leave even a rump Poland.

> If I had withdrawn the German troops from the General Government this would not have brought about a pacification of Poland, but a hideous chaos. And the Church would not have been able to exercise its function in praise of the Lord, but the priests would have had their heads chopped off . . .

him by an unnamed American informant declaring that Mooney "was more or less pro-German." The General Motors executive was certainly taken in by the Germans. Thomsen's memorandum states that Mooney had informed Roosevelt on the basis of an earlier talk with Hitler that the Fuehrer "was desirous of peace and wished to prevent the bloodshed of a spring campaign." Hans Dieckhoff, the recalled German ambassador to the United States, who was whiling away his time in Berlin, saw Mooney immediately after the latter's interview with Hitler and reported to the Foreign Office that the American businessman was "rather verbose" and that "I cannot believe that the Mooney initiative has any great importance."[22]

As for the visit of Sumner Welles, Hitler continued, it had achieved nothing. He was still determined to attack in the West. He realized "that the coming battle will not be a walkover but the fiercest struggle in Germany's history . . . a battle for life or death."

And then Hitler made his pitch to Mussolini to get into the war.

I believe, Duce, that there can be no doubt that the outcome of this war will also decide the future of Italy . . . You will some day be confronted by the very opponents who are fighting Germany today . . . I, too, see the destinies of our two countries, our peoples, our revolutions and our regimes indissolubly joined with each other . . .

And, finally, let me assure you that in spite of everything I believe that sooner or later fate will force us after all to fight side by side, that is, that you will likewise not escape this clash of arms, no matter how the individual aspects of the situation may develop today, and that your place will then more than ever be at our side, just as mine will be at yours.

Mussolini was flattered by the letter and at once assured Ribbentrop that he agreed that his place was at Hitler's side "on the firing line." The Nazi Foreign Minister, on his part, lost no time in buttering up his host. The Fuehrer, he said, was "deeply aroused by the latest British measures to block the shipment of coal from Germany to Italy by sea." How much coal did the Italians need? From 500,000 to 700,000 tons a month, Mussolini replied. Germany was now prepared, Ribbentrop answered glibly, to furnish a million tons a month and would provide most of the cars to haul it.

There were two lengthy meetings between the two, with Ciano present, on March 11 and 12, and Dr. Schmidt's shorthand minutes reveal that Ribbentrop was at his most flatulent.[25] Though there were more important things to talk about, he produced captured Polish diplomatic dispatches from the Western capitals to show "the monstrous war guilt of the United States."

The Foreign Minister explained that these documents showed specifically the sinister role of the American Ambassadors Bullitt [Paris], Kennedy [London] and Drexel Biddle [Warsaw] . . . They gave an intimation of the machinations of that Jewish-plutocratic clique whose influence, through Morgan and Rockefeller, reached all the way up to Roosevelt.

For several hours the arrogant Nazi Foreign Minister raved on, displaying his customary ignorance of world affairs, emphasizing the common destiny of the two fascist nations and stressing that Hitler would soon attack in the West, "beat the French Army in the course of the summer" and drive the British from the Continent "before fall." Mussolini mostly listened, only occasionally interjecting a remark whose sarcasm apparently escaped the Nazi Minister. When, for example, Ribbentrop pompously

declared that "Stalin had renounced the idea of world revolution," the
Duce retorted, according to Schmidt's notes, "Do you really believe that?"
When Ribbentrop explained that "there was not a single German soldier
who did not believe that victory would be won this year," Mussolini interjected, "That is an extremely interesting remark." That evening Ciano
noted in his diary:

After the interview, when we were left alone, Mussolini says that he does
not believe in the German offensive nor in a complete German success.

The Italian dictator had promised to give his own views at the meeting
the next day and Ribbentrop was somewhat uneasy as to what they might
be, wiring Hitler that he had been unable to obtain a "hint as to the Duce's
thoughts."
He need not have worried. The next day Mussolini was a completely
different man. He had quite suddenly, as Schmidt noted, "turned completely prowar." It was not a question, he told his visitor, of whether Italy
would enter the war on Germany's side, but when. The question of timing
was "extremely delicate, for he ought not to intervene until all his preparations were complete, so as not to burden his partner."

In any event he had to state at this time with all distinctness that Italy was
in no position financially to sustain a long war. He could not afford to spend
a billion lire a day, as England and France were doing.

This remark seems to have set Ribbentrop back for a moment and he
tried to pin the Duce down on a date for Italy's entry into the war, but the
latter was wary of committing himself. "The moment would come," he
said, "when a definition of Italy's relations with France and England, i.e.,
a break wi h these countries, would occur." It would be easy, he added, to
"provoke" such a rupture. Though he persisted, Ribbentrop could not get
a definite date. Obviously Hitler himself would have to intervene personally for that. The Nazi Foreign Minister thereupon suggested a meeting at the Brenner between the two men for the latter part of March, after
the nineteenth, to which Mussolini readily agreed. Ribbentrop, incidentally, had not breathed a word about Hitler's plans to occupy Denmark and
Norway. There were some secrets you did not mention to an ally, even
while pressing for it to join you.
Though he had not succeeded in getting Mussolini to agree to a date,
Ribbentrop had lured the Duce into a commitment to enter the war. "If
he wanted to reinforce the Axis," Ciano lamented in his diary, "he has
succeeded." When Sumner Welles, after visiting Berlin, Paris and London,
returned to Rome and saw Mussolini again on March 16, he found him a
changed man.

He seemed to have thrown off some great weight [Welles wrote later] . . .
I have often wondered whether, during the two weeks which had elapsed since

my first visit to Rome, he had not determined to cross the Rubicon, and during Ribbentrop's visit had not decided to force Italy into the war.[26]

Welles need not have wondered.

As soon as Ribbentrop had departed Rome in his special train the anguished Italian dictator was prey to second thoughts. "He fears," Ciano jotted in his diary on March 12, "that he has gone too far in his commitment to fight against the Allies. He would now like to dissuade Hitler from his land offensive, and this he hopes to achieve at the meeting at the Brenner Pass." But Ciano, limited as he was, knew better. "It cannot be denied," he added in his diary, "that the Duce is fascinated by Hitler, a fascination which involves something deeply rooted in his make-up. The Fuehrer will get more out of the Duce than Ribbentrop was able to get." This was true—with reservations, as shortly will be seen.

No sooner had he returned to Berlin than Ribbentrop telephoned Ciano —on March 13—asking that the Brenner meeting be set earlier than contemplated, for March 18. "The Germans are unbearable," Mussolini exploded. "They don't give one time to breathe or to think matters over." Nevertheless, he agreed to the date.

The Duce was nervous [Ciano recorded in his diary that day]. Until now he has lived under the illusion that a real war would not be waged. The prospect of an imminent clash in which he might remain an outsider disturbs him and, to use his words, humiliates him.[27]

It was snowing when the respective trains of the two dictators drew in on the morning of March 18, 1940, at the little frontier station at the Brenner Pass below the lofty snow-mantled Alps. The meeting, as a sop to Mussolini, took place in the Duce's private railroad car, but Hitler did almost all the talking. Ciano summed up the conference in his diary that evening.

The conference is more a monologue . . . Hitler talks all the time . . . Mussolini listens to him with interest and with deference. He speaks little and confirms his intention to move with Germany. He reserves to himself only the choice of the right moment.

He realized, Mussolini said, when he was finally able to get in a word, that it was "impossible to remain neutral until the end of the war." Co-operation with England and France was "inconceivable. We hate them. Therefore Italy's entry into the war is inevitable." Hitler had spent more than an hour trying to convince him of that—if Italy did not want to be left out in the cold and, as he added, become "a second-rate power."[28] But having answered the main question to the Fuehrer's satisfaction. the Duce immediately began to hedge.

The great problem, however, was the date . . . One condition for this would have to be fulfilled. Italy would have to be "very well prepared" . . . Italy's financial position did not allow her to wage a protracted war . . .

He was asking the Fuehrer whether there would be any danger for Germany if the offensive were delayed. He did not believe there was such a danger . . . he would [then] have finished his military preparations in three to four months, and would not be in the embarrassing position of seeing his comrade fighting and himself limited to making demonstrations . . . He wanted to do something more and he was not now in a position to do it.

The Nazi warlord had no intention of postponing his attack in the West and said so. But he had a "few theoretical ideas" which might solve Mussolini's difficulty of making a frontal attack on mountainous southern France, since that conflict, he realized, "would cost a great deal of blood." Why not, he suggested, supply a strong Italian force which together with German troops would advance along the Swiss frontier toward the Rhone Valley "in order to turn the Franco–Italian Alpine front from the rear." Before this, of course, the main German armies would have rolled back the French and British in the north. Hitler was obviously trying to make it easy for the Italians.

When the enemy has been smashed [in northern France] the moment would come [Hitler continued] for Italy to intervene actively, not at the most difficult point on the Alpine front, but elsewhere . . .

The war will be decided in France. Once France is disposed of, Italy will be mistress of the Mediterranean and England will have to make peace.

Mussolini, it must be said, was not slow at seizing upon this glittering prospect of getting so much after the Germans had done all the hard fighting.

The Duce replied that once Germany had made a victorious advance he would intervene immediately . . . he would lose no time . . . when the Allies were so shaken by the German attack that it needed only a second blow to bring them to their knees.

On the other hand,

If Germany's progress was slow, the Duce said that then he would wait.

This crude, cowardly bargain seems not to have unduly bothered Hitler. If Mussolini was personally attracted to him, as Ciano said, by "something deeply rooted in his make-up," it might be said that the attraction was mutual, for the same mysterious reasons. Disloyal as he had been to some of his closest associates, a number of whom he had had murdered, such as Roehm and Strasser, Hitler maintained a strange and unusual loyalty to his ridiculous Italian partner that did not weaken, that indeed was strengthened when adversity and then disaster overtook the strutting, sawdust Roman Caesar. It is one of the interesting paradoxes of this narrative.

At any rate, for what it was worth—and few Germans besides Hitler, especially among the generals, thought it was worth very much—Italy's entrance into the war had now at last been solemnly promised. The Nazi warlord could turn his thoughts again to new and imminent conquests. Of the most imminent one—in the north—he did not breathe a word to his friend and ally.

THE CONSPIRATORS AGAIN FRUSTRATED

Once more the anti-Nazi plotters tried to persuade the generals to depose the Leader—this time before he could launch his new aggression in the north, of which they had got wind. What the civilian conspirators again wanted was assurance from the British government that it would make peace with an anti-Nazi German regime, and, being what they were, they were insistent that in any settlement the new Reich government be allowed to keep most of Hitler's territorial gains: Austria, the Sudetenland and the 1914 frontier in Poland, though this last had only been obtained in the past by the wiping out of the Polish nation.

It was with such a proposal that Hassell, with considerable personal courage, journeyed to Arosa, Switzerland, on February 21, 1940, to confer with a British contact whom he calls "Mr. X" in his diary and who was a certain J. Lonsdale Bryans. They conferred in the greatest secrecy at four meetings on February 22 and 23. Bryans, who had cut a certain figure in the diplomatic society of Rome, was another of those self-appointed and somewhat amateurish negotiators for peace who have turned up in this narrative. He had contacts in Downing Street, and Hassell, once they had met, was personally impressed by him. After the fiasco of the attempt of Major Stevens and Captain Best in Holland to get in touch with the German conspirators, the British were somewhat skeptical of the whole business, and when Bryans pressed Hassell for some reliable information as to whom he was speaking for the German envoy became cagey.

"I am not in a position to name the men who are backing me," Hassell retorted. "I can only assure you that a statement from Halifax would get to the right people."[29]

Hassell then outlined the views of the German "opposition": it was realized that Hitler had to be overthrown "before major military operations are undertaken"; that this must be "an exclusively German affair"; that there must be "some authoritative English statement" about how a new anti-Nazi regime in Berlin would be treated and that "the principal obstacle to any change in regime is the story of 1918, that is, German anxiety lest things develop as they did then, after the Kaiser was sacrificed." Hassell and his friends wanted guarantees that if they got rid of Hitler

Germany would be treated more generously than it was after the Germans had got rid of Wilhelm II.

He thereupon handed over to Bryans a memorandum which he himself had drawn up in English. It is a wooly document, though full of noble sentiments about a future world based "on the principles of Christian ethics, justice and law, social welfare and liberty of thought and conscience." The greatest danger of continuing "this mad war," Hassell wrote, was "a bolshevization of Europe"—he considered that worse than the continuance of Nazism. And his main condition for peace was that the new Germany be left with almost all of Hitler's conquests, which he enumerated. The German acquisition of Austria and the Sudetenland could not even be discussed in any proposed peace; and Germany would have to have the 1914 frontier with Poland, which, of course, though he did not say so, was actually the 1914 frontier with Russia, since Poland had not been allowed to exist in 1914.

Bryans agreed that speedy action was necessary in view of the imminence of the German offensive in the West and promised to deliver Hassell's memorandum to Lord Halifax. Hassell returned to Berlin to acquaint his fellow plotters with his latest move. Although they hoped for the best from Hassell's "Mr. X" they were more concerned at the moment with the so-called "X Report" which Hans von Dohnanyi, one of the members of the group in the Abwehr, had drawn up on the basis of Dr. Mueller's contact with the British at the Vatican.* It declared that the Pope was ready to intervene with Britain for reasonable peace terms with a new anti-Nazi German government, and it is a measure of the views of these opponents of Hitler that one of their terms, which they claimed the Holy Father would back, was "the settlement of the Eastern question in favor of Germany." The demonic Nazi dictator had obtained a settlement in the East "in favor of Germany" by armed aggression; the good German conspirators wanted the same thing handed to them by the British with the Pope's blessings.

The X Report loomed very large in the minds of the plotters that winter of 1939–40. At the end of October General Thomas had shown it to Brauchitsch with the intention of bucking up the Army Commander in Chief in his efforts to dissuade Hitler from launching the offensive in the West that fall. But Brauchitsch did not appreciate such encouragement. In fact, he threatened to have General Thomas arrested if he brought the matter up again. It was "plain high treason," he barked at him.

Now, with a fresh Nazi aggression in the offing, Thomas took the X Report to General Halder in the hope that *he* might act on it. But this was a vain hope. As the General Staff Chief told Goerdeler, one of the most active of the conspirators—who had also begged him to take the lead, since the spineless Brauchitsch would not—he could not at this time justify breaking his oath as a soldier to the Fuehrer. Besides:

England and France had declared war on us, and one had to see it through.

* See above, p. 648.

A peace of compromise was senseless. Only in the greatest emergency could one take the action desired by Goerdeler.

"*Also, doch!*" exclaimed Hassell in his diary on April 6, 1940, in recounting Halder's state of mind as explained to him by Goerdeler. "Halder," the diarist added, "who had begun to weep during the discussion of his responsibility, gave the impression of a weak man with shattered nerves."

The accuracy of such an impression is to be doubted. When one goes over Halder's diary for the first week of April, cluttered as it is with hundreds of detailed entries about preparations for the gigantic offensive in the West, which he was helping to mastermind, this writer at least gets the impression that the General Staff Chief was in a buoyant mood as he conferred with the field commanders and checked the final plans for the greatest and most daring military operation in German history. There is no hint in his journal of treasonable thoughts or of any wrestling with his conscience. Though he has misgivings about the attack on Denmark and Norway, they are based purely on military grounds, and there is not a word of moral doubt about Nazi aggression against the four small neutral countries whose frontiers Germany had solemnly guaranteed and whom Halder knew Germany was about to attack, and against two of whom, Belgium and Holland, he himself had taken a leading part in drafting the plans.

So ended the latest attempt of the "good Germans" to oust Hitler before it was too late. It was the last opportunity they would have to obtain a generous peace. The generals, as Brauchitsch and Halder had made clear, were not interested in a negotiated peace. They were thinking now, as was the Fuehrer, of a dictated peace—dictated after German victory. Not until the chances of that had gone glimmering did they seriously return to their old and treasonable thoughts, which had been so strong at Munich and at Zossen, of removing their mad dictator. This state of mind and character must be remembered in view of subsequent events and of subsequent spinning of myths.

THE TAKING OF DENMARK AND NORWAY

Hitler's preparations for the conquest of Denmark and Norway have been called by many writers one of the best-kept secrets of the war, but it has seemed to this author that the two Scandinavian countries and even the British were caught napping not because they were not warned of what was coming but because they did not believe the warnings in time.

Ten days before disaster struck, Colonel Oster of the Abwehr warned a close friend of his, Colonel J. G. Sas, the Dutch military attaché in Berlin, of the German plans for *Weseruebung* and Sas immediately informed the Danish naval attaché, Captain Kjölsen.[30] But the complacent Danish government would not believe its own naval attaché, and when on April 4 the Danish minister in Berlin sent Kjölsen scurrying to Copenhagen to repeat the warning in person his intelligence was still not taken seriously. Even on the eve of catastrophe, on the evening of March 8, after news had been received of the torpedoing of a German transport laden with troops off the south coast of Norway—just north of Denmark—and the Danes had seen with their own eyes a great German naval armada sailing north between their islands, the King of Denmark had dismissed with a smile a remark at the dinner table that his country was in danger.

"He really didn't believe that," a Guards officer who was present later reported. In fact, this officer related, the King had proceeded after dinner to the Royal Theater in a "confident and happy" frame of mind.[31]

Already in March the Norwegian government had received warnings from its legation in Berlin and from the Swedes about a German concentration of troops and naval vessels in the North Sea and Baltic ports and on April 5 definite intelligence arrived from Berlin of imminent German landings on the southern coast of Norway. But the complacent cabinet in Oslo remained skeptical. Not even on the seventh, when several large German war vessels were *sighted* proceeding up the Norwegian coast and reports arrived of British planes strafing a German battle fleet off the mouth of the Skagerrak, not even on April 8, when the British Admiralty informed the Legation of Norway in London that a strong German naval force had been discovered approaching Narvik and the newspapers in Oslo were reporting that German soldiers rescued from the transport *Rio de Janeiro,* torpedoed that day off the Norwegian coast at Lillesand by a Polish submarine, had declared they were en route to Bergen to help defend it against the British—not even then did the Norwegian government consider it necessary to take such obvious steps as mobilizing the Army, fully manning the forts guarding the harbors, blocking the airfield runways, or, most important of all, mining the easily mined narrow water approaches to the capital and the main cities. Had it done these things history might have taken a different turning.

Ominous news, as Churchill puts it, had begun filtering into London by the first of April, and on April 3 the British War Cabinet discussed the latest intelligence, above all from Stockholm, which told of the Germans collecting sizable military forces in its northern ports with the objective of moving into Scandinavia. But the news does not seem to have been taken very seriously. Two days later, on April 5, when the first wave of German naval supply ships was already at sea, Prime Minister Chamberlain proclaimed in a speech that Hitler, by failing to attack in the West when the British and French were unprepared, had "missed the bus"—a phrase he was very shortly to rue.*

The British government at this moment, according to Churchill, was inclined to believe that the German build-up in the Baltic and North Sea

---

* The first three German supply ships had sailed for Narvik at 2 A.M. on April 3. Germany's largest tanker left Murmansk for Narvik on April 6, with the connivance of the Russians, who obligingly furnished the cargo of oil.

ports was being done merely to enable Hitler to deliver a counterstroke in case the British, in mining Norwegian waters to cut off the ore shipments from Narvik, also occupied that port and perhaps others to the south.

As a matter of fact, the British government was contemplating such an occupation. After seven months of frustration Churchill, First Lord of the Admiralty, had finally succeeded in getting the approval of the War Cabinet and the Allied Supreme War Council to mine the Norwegian Leads on April 8—an action called "Wilfred." Since it seemed likely that the Germans would react violently to the mortal blow of having their iron ore shipments from Narvik blocked, it was decided that a small Anglo–French force should be dispatched to Narvik and advance to the nearby Swedish frontier. Other contingents would be landed at Trondheim, Bergen and Stavanger farther south in order, as Churchill explained, "to deny these bases to the enemy." This was known as "Plan R-4."[32]

Thus during the first week of April, while German troops were being loaded on various warships for the passage to Norway, British troops, though in much fewer numbers, were being embarked on transports in the Clyde and on cruisers in the Forth for the same destination.

On the afternoon of April 2, Hitler, after a long conference with Goering, Raeder and Falkenhorst, issued a formal directive ordering *Weseruebung* to begin at 5:15 A.M. on April 9. At the same time he issued another directive stipulating that "the escape of the Kings of Denmark and Norway from their countries at the time of the occupation must be prevented by all means."[33] Also on the same day OKW let the Foreign Office in on the secret. A lengthy directive was presented to Ribbentrop instructing him to prepare the diplomatic measures for inducing Denmark and Norway to surrender without a fight as soon as the German armed forces had arrived and to concoct some kind of justification for Hitler's latest aggression.[34]

But trickery was not to be confined to the Foreign Office. The Navy was also to make use of it. On April 3, with the departure of the first vessels, Jodl reflected in his diary on the problem of how deceit could be used to hoodwink the Norwegians in case they became suspicious of the presence of so many German men-of-war in their vicinity. Actually this little matter had already been worked out by the Navy. It had instructed its warships and transports to try to pass as British craft—even if it were necessary to fly the Union Jack! Secret German naval commands laid down detailed orders for "Deception and Camouflage in the Invasion of Norway."[35]

MOST SECRET

Behavior During Entrance into the Harbor

All ships darkened . . . The disguise as British craft must be kept as long as possible. All challenges in Morse by Norwegian ships will be answered in English. In answer, something like the following will be chosen:

"Calling at Bergen for a short visit. No hostile intent."

. . . Challenges to be answered with names of British warships:

Koeln—H.M.S. *Cairo*.

Koenigsberg—H.M.S. *Calcutta*. . . . (etc.)

Arrangements are to be made to enable British war flags to be illuminated . . .

For Bergen . . . Following is laid down as guiding principle should one of our own units find itself compelled to answer the challenge of passing craft:

To challenge: (in case of the *Koeln*) H.M.S. *Cairo*.

To order to stop: "(1) Please repeat last signal. (2) Impossible to understand your signal."

In case of a warning shot: "Stop firing. British ship. Good friend."

In case of an inquiry as to destination and purpose: "Going Bergen. Chasing German steamers."*

And so on April 9, 1940, at 5:20 A.M. precisely (4:20 A.M. in Denmark), an hour before dawn, the German envoys at Copenhagen and Oslo, having routed the respective foreign ministers out of bed exactly twenty minutes before (Ribbentrop had insisted on a strict timetable in co-ordination with the arrival at that hour of the German troops), presented to the Danish and Norwegian governments a German ultimatum demanding that they accept on the instant, and without resistance, the "protection of the Reich." The ultimatum was perhaps the most brazen document yet composed by Hitler and Ribbentrop, who were such masters and by now so experienced in diplomatic deceit.[37]

After declaring that the Reich had come to the aid of Denmark and Norway to protect them against an Anglo–French occupation, the memorandum stated:

The German troops therefore do not set foot on Norwegian soil as enemies. The German High Command does not intend to make use of the points occupied by German troops as bases for operations against England as long as it is not forced to . . . On the contrary, German military operations aim exclusively at protecting the north against the proposed occupation of Norwegian bases by Anglo–French forces . . .

. . . In the spirit of the good relations between Germany and Norway which have existed hitherto, the Reich Government declares to the Royal Norwegian Government that Germany has no intention of infringing by her measures the territorial integrity and political independence of the Kingdom of Norway now or in the future . . .

The Reich Government therefore expects that the Norwegian Government and the Norwegian people will . . . offer no resistance to it. Any resistance

---

* On the stand at Nuremberg, Grand Admiral Raeder justified such tactics on the ground that they were a legitimate "ruse of war against which, from the legal point of view, no objection can be made."[36]

would have to be, and would be, broken by all possible means . . . and would therefore lead only to absolutely useless bloodshed. . . .

German expectations proved justified as regards Denmark but not Norway. This became known in the Wilhelmstrasse with the receipt of the first urgent messages from the respective ministers to those countries. The German envoy in Copenhagen wired Ribbentrop at 8:34 A.M. that the Danes had "accepted all our demands [though] registering a protest." Minister Curt Bräuer in Oslo had a quite different report to make. At 5:52 A.M., just thirty-two minutes after he had delivered the German ultimatum, he wired Berlin the quick response of the Norwegian government: "We will not submit voluntarily: the struggle is already under way."[38]

The arrogant Ribbentrop was outraged.* At 10:55 he wired Bräuer "most urgent": "You will once more impress on the Government there that Norwegian resistance is completely senseless."

This the unhappy German envoy could no longer do. The Norwegian King, government and members of Parliament had by this time fled the capital for the mountains in the north. However hopeless the odds, they were determined to resist. In fact, resistance had already begun in some places, though not in all, with the arrival of German ships out of the night.

The Danes were in a more hopeless position. Their pleasant little island country was incapable of defense. It was too small, too flat, and the largest part, Jutland, lay open by land to Hitler's panzers. There were no mountains for the King and the government to flee to as there were in Norway, nor could any help be expected from Britain. It has been said that the Danes were too civilized to fight in such circumstances; at any rate, they did not. General W. W. Pryor, the Army Commander in Chief, almost alone pleaded for resistance, but he was overruled by Premier Thorvald Stauning, Foreign Minister Edvard Munch, and the King, who, when the bad news began coming in on April 8, refused his pleas for mobilization. For reasons which remain obscure to this writer, even after an investigation in Copenhagen, the Navy never fired a shot, either from its ships or from its shore batteries, even when German troop ships passed under the noses of its guns and could have been blown to bits. The Army

---

* This writer had rarely seen the Nazi Foreign Minister more insufferable than he was that morning. He strutted into a specially convoked press conference at the Foreign Office, garbed in a flashy field-gray uniform and looking, I noted in my diary, "as if he owned the earth." He snapped, "The Fuehrer has given his answer . . . Germany has occupied Danish and Norwegian soil in order to protect those countries from the Allies, and will defend their true neutrality until the end of the war. Thus an honored part of Europe has been saved from certain downfall."

The Berlin press was also something to see that day. The *Boersen Zeitung:* "England goes cold-bloodedly over the dead bodies of small peoples. Germany protects the weak states from the English highway robbers . . . Norway ought to see the righteousness of Germany's action, which was taken to ensure the freedom of the Norwegian people." Hitler's own paper, the *Voelkischer Beobachter*, carried this banner line: GERMANY SAVES SCANDINAVIA!

fought a few skirmishes in Jutland, the Royal Guard fired a few shots around the royal palace in the capital and suffered a few men wounded. By the time the Danes had finished their hearty breakfasts it was all over. The King, on the advice of his government but against that of General Pryor, capitulated and ordered what slight resistance there was to cease.

The plans to take Denmark by surprise and deceit, as the captured German Army records show, had been prepared with meticulous care. General Kurt Himer, chief of staff of the task force for Denmark, had arrived by train in civilian clothes in Copenhagen on April 7 to reconnoiter the capital and make the necessary arrangements for a suitable pier to dock the troopship *Hansestadt Danzig* and a truck to handle the moving of a few supplies and a radio transmitter. The commander of the battalion—all that was considered necessary to capture a great city—had also been in Copenhagen in civilian clothes a couple of days before to get the layout of the land.

It was not so strange, therefore, that the plans of the General and the battalion major were carried out with scarcely a hitch. The troopship arrived off Copenhagen shortly before dawn, passed without challenge the guns of the fort guarding the harbor and those of the Danish patrol vessels and tied up neatly at the Langelinie Pier in the heart of the city, only a stone's throw from the Citadel, the headquarters of the Danish Army, and but a short distance from Amalienborg Palace, where the King resided. Both were quickly seized by the lone battalion with no resistance worth mentioning.

Upstairs in the palace, amidst the rattle of scattered shots, the King conferred with his ministers. The latter were all for nonresistance. Only General Pryor begged to be allowed to put up a fight. At the very least he demanded that the King should leave for the nearest military camp at Høvelte to escape capture. But the King agreed with his ministers. The monarch, according to one eyewitness, asked "whether our soldiers had fought long enough"—and Pryor retorted that they had not.*[39]

General Himer became restless at the delay. He telephoned headquarters for the combined operation, which had been set up at Hamburg— the Danish authorities had not thought of cutting the telephone lines to Germany—and, according to his own story,[40] asked for some bombers to zoom over Copenhagen "in order to force the Danes to accept." The conversation was in code and the Luftwaffe understood that Himer was calling for an actual bombing, which it promised to carry out forthwith—an error which was finally corrected just in time. General Himer says the bombers "roaring over the Danish capital did not fail to make their impression: the Government accepted the German requests."

There was some difficulty in finding means of broadcasting the government's capitulation to the Danish troops, because the local radio stations were not yet on the air at such an early hour. This was solved by broad-

---

* Total Danish casualties throughout the realm were thirteen killed and twenty-three wounded. The Germans suffered some twenty casualties.

casting it on the Danish wave length over the transmitter which the German battalion had brought along with it and for which General Himer had thoughtfully dug up a truck to haul it to the Citadel.

At 2 o'clock that afternoon General Himer, accompanied by the German minister, Cecil von Renthe-Fink, called on the King of Denmark, who was no longer sovereign but did not yet realize it. Himer left a record of the interview in the secret Army archives.

The seventy-year-old King appeared inwardly shattered, although he preserved outward appearances perfectly and maintained absolute dignity during the audience. His whole body trembled. He declared that he and his government would do everything possible to keep peace and order in the country and to eliminate any friction between the German troops and the country. He wished to spare his country further misfortune and misery.

General Himer replied that personally he very much regretted coming to the King on such a mission, but that he was only doing his duty as a soldier . . . We came as friends, etc. When the King then asked whether he might keep his bodyguard, General Himer replied . . . that the Fuehrer would doubtless permit him to retain them. He had no doubt about it.

The King was visibly relieved at hearing this. During the course of the audience . . . the King became more at ease, and at its conclusion addressed General Himer with the words: "General, may I, as an old soldier, tell you something? As soldier to soldier? You Germans have done the incredible again! One must admit that it is magnificent work!"

For nearly four years, until the tide of war had changed, the Danish King and his people, a good-natured, civilized and happy-go-lucky race, offered very little trouble to the Germans. Denmark became known as the "model protectorate." The monarch, the government, the courts, even the Parliament and the press, were at first allowed a surprising amount of freedom by their conquerors. Not even Denmark's seven thousand Jews were molested—for a time. But the Danes, later than most of the other conquered peoples, finally came to the realization that further "loyal cooperation," as they called it, with their Teutonic tyrants, whose brutality increased with the years and with the worsening fortunes of war, was impossible—if they were to retain any shred of self-respect and honor. They also began to see that Germany might not win the war after all and that little Denmark was not inexorably condemned, as so many had feared at first, to be a vassal state in Hitler's unspeakable New Order. Then resistance began.

THE NORWEGIANS RESIST

It began in Norway from the outset, though certainly not everywhere. At Narvik, the port and railhead of the iron ore line from Sweden, Colonel

Konrad Sundlo, in command of the local garrison, who, as we have seen, was a fanatical follower of Quisling,* surrendered to the Germans without firing a shot. The naval commander was of a different caliber. With the approach of ten German destroyers at the mouth of the long fjord, the *Eidsvold,* one of two ancient ironclads in the harbor, fired a warning shot and signaled to the destroyers to identify themselves. Rear Admiral Fritz Bonte, commanding the German destroyer flotilla, answered by sending an officer in a launch to the Norwegian vessel to demand surrender. There now followed a bit of German treachery, though German naval officers later defended it with the argument that in war necessity knows no law. When the officer in the launch signaled the German Admiral that the Norwegians had said they would resist, Bonte waited only until his launch got out of the way and then quickly blew up the *Eidsvold* with torpedoes. The second Norwegian ironclad, the *Norge,* then opened fire but was quickly dispatched. Three hundred Norwegian sailors—almost the entire crews of the two vessels—perished. By 8 A.M. Narvik was in the hands of the Germans, taken by ten destroyers which had slipped through a formidable British fleet, and occupied by a mere two battalions of Nazi troops under the command of Brigadier General Eduard Dietl, an old Bavarian crony of Hitler since the days of the Beer Hall Putsch, who was to prove himself a resourceful and courageous commander when the going at Narvik got rough, as it did beginning the next day.

Trondheim, halfway down the long Norwegian west coast, was taken by the Germans almost as easily. The harbor batteries failed to fire on the German naval ships, led by the heavy cruiser *Hipper,* as they came up the long fjord, and the troops aboard that ship and four destroyers were conveniently disembarked at the city's piers without interference. Some forts held out for a few hours and the nearby airfield at Vaernes for two days, but this resistance did not affect the occupation of a fine harbor suitable for the largest naval ships as well as submarines and the railhead of a line that ran across north-central Norway to Sweden and over which the Germans expected, and with reason, to receive supplies should the British cut them off at sea.

Bergen, the second port and city of Norway, lying some three hundred miles down the coast from Trondheim and connected with Oslo, the capital, by railway, put up some resistance. The batteries guarding the harbor badly damaged the cruiser *Koenigsberg* and an auxiliary ship, but troops from other vessels landed safely and occupied the city before noon. It was at Bergen that the first direct British aid for the stunned Norwegians arrived. In the afternoon fifteen naval dive bombers sank the *Koenigsberg,* the first ship of that size ever to go down as the result of an air attack. Outside the harbor the British had a powerful fleet of four cruisers and seven destroyers which could have overwhelmed the smaller German naval force. It was about to enter the harbor when it received orders from

* See above, p. 676.

the Admiralty to cancel the attack because of the risk of mines and bombing from the air, a decision which Churchill, who concurred in it, later regretted. This was the first sign of caution and of half measures which
would cost the British dearly in the next crucial days.

Sola airfield, near the port of Stavanger on the southwest coast, was
taken by German parachute troops after the Norwegian machine gun
emplacements—there was no real antiaircraft protection—were silenced.
This was Norway's biggest airfield and strategically of the highest importance to the Luftwaffe, since from here bombers could range not only
against the British fleet along the Norwegian coast but against the chief
British naval bases in northern Britain. Its seizure gave the Germans immediate air superiority in Norway and spelled the doom of any attempt by
the British to land sizable forces.

Kristiansand on the south coast put up considerable resistance to the
Germans, its shore batteries twice driving off a German fleet led by the
light cruiser *Karlsruhe*. But the forts were quickly reduced by Luftwaffe
bombing and the port was occupied by midafternoon. The *Karlsruhe,*
however, on leaving port that evening was torpedoed by a British submarine and so badly damaged that it had to be sunk.

By noon, then, or shortly afterward, the five principal Norwegian cities
and ports and the one big airfield along the west and south coasts that ran
for 1,500 miles from the Skagerrak to the Arctic were in German hands.
They had been taken by a handful of troops conveyed by a Navy vastly
inferior to that of the British. Daring, deceit and surprise had brought
Hitler a resounding victory at very little cost.

But at Oslo, the main prize, his military force and his diplomacy had
run into unexpected trouble.

All through the chilly night of April 8–9, a gay welcoming party from
the German Legation, led by Captain Schreiber, the naval attaché, and
joined occasionally by the busy Dr. Bräuer, the minister, stood at the
quayside in Oslo Harbor waiting for the arrival of a German fleet and troop
transports. A junior German naval attaché was darting about the bay in
a motorboat waiting to act as pilot for the fleet, headed by the pocket
battleship *Leutzow* (its name changed from *Deutschland* because Hitler
did not want to risk losing a ship by that name) and the brand-new heavy
cruiser *Bluecher,* flagship of the squadron.

They waited in vain. The big ships never arrived. They had been challenged at the entrance to the fifty-mile-long Oslo Fjord by the Norwegian
mine layer *Olav Trygverson,* which sank a German torpedo boat and damaged the light cruiser *Emden*. After landing a small force to subdue the
shore batteries the German squadron, however, continued on its way up
the fjord. At a point some fifteen miles south of Oslo where the waters
narrowed to fifteen miles, further trouble developed. Here stood the ancient fortress of Oskarsborg, whose defenders were more alert than the
Germans suspected. Just before dawn the fort's 28-centimeter Krupp guns
opened fire on the *Luetzow* and the *Bluecher,* and torpedoes were also

launched from the shore. The 10,000-ton *Bluecher,* ablaze and torn by the explosions of its ammunition, went down, with the loss of 1,600 men, including several Gestapo and administrative officials (and all their papers) who were to arrest the King and the government and take over the administration of the capital. The *Luetzow* was also damaged but not completely disabled. Rear Admiral Oskar Kummetz, commander of the squadron, and General Erwin Engelbrecht, who led the 163rd Infantry Division, who were on the *Bluecher,* managed to swim ashore, where they were made prisoners by the Norwegians. Whereupon the crippled German fleet turned back for the moment to lick its wounds. It had failed in its mission to take the main German objective, the capital of Norway. It did not get there until the next day.

Oslo, in fact, fell to little more than a phantom German force dropped from the air at the local, undefended airport. The catastrophic news from the other seaports and the pounding of the guns fifteen miles down the Oslo Fjord had sent the Norwegian royal family, the government and members of Parliament scurrying on a special train from the capital at 9:30 A.M. for Hamar, eighty miles to the north. Twenty motor trucks laden with the gold of the Bank of Norway and three more with the secret papers of the Foreign Office got away at the same hour. Thus the gallant action of the garrison at Oskarsborg had foiled Hitler's plans to get his hands on the Norwegian King, government and gold.

But Oslo was left in complete bewilderment. There were some Norwegian troops there, but they were not put into a state for defense. Above all, nothing was done to block the airport at nearby Fornebu, which could have been done with a few old automobiles parked along the runway and about the field. Late on the previous night Captain Spiller, the German air attaché in Oslo, had stationed himself there to welcome the airborne troops, which were to come in after the Navy had reached the city. When the ships failed to arrive a frantic radio message was sent from the legation to Berlin apprising it of the unexpected and unhappy situation. The response was immediate. Soon parachute and airborne infantry troops were being landed at Fornebu. By noon about five companies had been assembled. As they were only lightly armed, the available Norwegian troops in the capital could have easily destroyed them. But for reasons never yet made clear—so great was the confusion in Oslo—they were not mustered, much less deployed, and the token German infantry force *marched* into the capital behind a blaring, if makeshift, military band. Thus the last of Norway's cities fell. But not Norway; not yet.

On the afternoon of April 9, the Storting, the Norwegian Parliament, met at Hamar with only five of the two hundred members missing, but adjourned at 7:30 P.M. when news was received that German troops were approaching and moved on to Elverum, a few miles to the east toward the Swedish border. Dr. Bräuer, pressed by Ribbentrop, was demanding an immediate audience with the King, and the Norwegian Prime Minister had assented on condition that German troops withdraw to a safe distance south. This the German minister would not agree to.

Indeed, at this moment a further piece of Nazi treachery was in the making. Captain Spiller, the air attaché, had set out from the Fornebu airport for Hamar with two companies of German parachutists to capture the recalcitrant King and government. It seemed to them more of a lark than anything else. Since Norwegian troops had not fired a shot to prevent the German entry into Oslo, Spiller expected no resistance at Hamar. In fact the two companies, traveling on commandeered autobuses, were making a pleasant sightseeing jaunt of it. But they did not reckon with a Norwegian Army officer who acted quite unlike so many of the others. Colonel Ruge, Inspector General of Infantry, who had accompanied the King northward, had insisted on providing some sort of protection to the fugitive government and had set up a roadblock near Hamar with two battalions of infantry which he had hastily rounded up. The German buses were stopped and in a skirmish which followed Spiller was mortally wounded. After suffering further casualties the Germans fell back all the way to Oslo.

The next day, Dr. Bräuer set out from Oslo alone along the same road to see the King. An old-school professional diplomat, the German minister did not relish his role, but Ribbentrop had kept after him relentlessly to talk the King and the government into surrender. Bräuer's difficult task had been further complicated by certain political events which had just taken place in Oslo. On the preceding evening Quisling had finally bestirred himself, once the capital was firmly in German hands, stormed into the radio station and broadcast a proclamation naming himself as head of a new government and ordering all Norwegian resistance to the Germans to halt immediately. Though Bräuer could not yet grasp it— and Berlin could never, even later, understand it—this treasonable act doomed the German efforts to induce Norway to surrender. And paradoxically, though it was a moment of national shame for the Norwegian people, the treason of Quisling rallied the stunned Norwegians to a resistance which was to become formidable and heroic.

Dr. Bräuer met Haakon VII, the only king in the twentieth century who had been elected to the throne by popular vote and the first monarch Norway had had of its own for five centuries,* in a schoolhouse at the little town of Elverum at 3 P.M. on April 10. From a talk this writer later had with the monarch and from a perusal of both the Norwegian records and Dr. Bräuer's secret report (which is among the captured German Foreign Office documents) it is possible to give an account of what hap-

---

* Norway had been a part of Denmark for four centuries and of Sweden for a further century, regaining its complete independence only in 1905, when it broke away from its union with Sweden and the people elected Prince Carl of Denmark as King of Norway. He assumed the name of Haakon VII. Haakon VI had died in 1380. Haakon VII was a brother of Christian X of Denmark, who surrendered so promptly to the Germans on the morning of April 9, 1940.

pened. After considerable reluctance the King had agreed to receive the German envoy in the presence of his Foreign Minister, Dr. Halvdan Koht. When Bräuer insisted on seeing Haakon at first alone the King, with the agreement of Koht, finally consented.

The German minister, acting on instructions, alternately flattered and tried to intimidate the King. Germany wanted to preserve the dynasty. It was merely asking Haakon to do what his brother had done the day before in Copenhagen. It was folly to resist the Wehrmacht. Only useless slaughter for the Norwegians would ensue. The King was asked to approve the government of Quisling and return to Oslo. Haakon, a salty, democratic man and a great stickler, even at this disastrous moment, for constitutional procedure, tried to explain to the German diplomat that in Norway the King did not make political decisions; that was exclusively the business of the government, which he would now consult. Koht then joined the conversation and it was agreed that the government's answer would be telephoned to Bräuer at some point on his way back to Oslo.

For Haakon, who, though he could not make the political decision could surely influence it, there was but one answer to the Germans. Retiring to a modest inn in the village of Nybergsund near Elverum—just in case the Germans, with Bräuer gone, tried to capture him in another surprise attack—he assembled the members of the government as Council of State.

. . . For my part [he told them] I cannot accept the German demands. It would conflict with all that I have considered to be my duty as King of Norway since I came to this country nearly thirty-five years ago . . . I do not want the decision of the government to be influenced by or based upon this statement. But . . . I cannot appoint Quisling Prime Minister, a man in whom I know neither our people . . . nor its representatives in the Storting have any confidence at all.

If therefore the government should decide to accept the German demands—and I fully understand the reasons in favor of it, considering the impending danger of war in which so many young Norwegians will have to give their lives—if so, *abdication* will be the only course open to me.[41]

The government, though there may have been some waverers up to this moment, could not be less courageous than the King, and it quickly rallied behind him. By the time Brauer got to Eidsvold, halfway back to Oslo, Koht was on the telephone line to him with the Norwegian reply. The German minister telephoned it immediately to the legation in Oslo, where it was sped to Berlin.

The King will name no government headed by Quisling and this decision was made upon the unanimous advice of the Government. To my specific question, Foreign Minister Koht replied: "Resistance will continue as long as possible."[42]

That evening from a feeble little rural radio station nearby, the only means of communication to the outside world available, the Norwegian government flung down the gauntlet to the mighty Third Reich. It announced its decision not to accept the German demands and called upon the people—there were only three million of them—to resist the invaders. The King formally associated himself with the appeal.

But the Nazi conquerors could not quite bring themselves to believe that the Norwegians meant what they said. Two more attempts were made to dissuade the King. On the morning of April 11 an emissary of Quisling, a Captain Irgens, arrived to urge the monarch to return to the capital. He promised that Quisling would serve him loyally. His proposal was dismissed with silent contempt.

In the afternoon an urgent message came from Bräuer, requesting a further audience with the King to talk over "certain proposals." The hard-pressed German envoy had been instructed by Ribbentrop to tell the monarch that he "wanted to give the Norwegian people one last chance of a reasonable agreement."* This time Dr. Koht, after consulting the King, replied that if the German minister had "certain proposals" he could communicate them to the Foreign Minister.

The Nazi reaction to this rebuff by such a small and now helpless country was immediate and in character. The Germans had failed, first, to capture the King and the members of the government and, then, to persuade them to surrender. Now the Germans tried to kill them. Late on April 11, the Luftwaffe was sent out to give the village of Nybergsund the full treatment. The Nazi flyers demolished it with explosive and incendiary bombs and then machine-gunned those who tried to escape the burning ruins. The Germans apparently believed at first that they had succeeded in massacring the King and the members of the government. The diary of a German airman, later captured in northern Norway, had this entry for April 11: "Nybergsund. *Oslo Regierung. Alles vernichtet.*" (Oslo government. Completely wiped out.)

The village had been, but not the King and the government. With the approach of the Nazi bombers they had taken refuge in a nearby wood. Standing in snow up to their knees, they had watched the Luftwaffe reduce the modest cottages of the hamlet to ruins. They now faced a choice of either moving on to the nearby Swedish border and asylum in neutral Sweden or pushing north into their own mountains, still deep in the spring snow. They decided to move on up the rugged Gudbrands Valley, which led past Hamar and Lillehammer and through the mountains to Åndalsnes

---

* There is an ominous hint of further treachery in Ribbentrop's secret instructions. Bräuer was told to try to arrange the meeting "at a point between Oslo and the King's present place of residence. For obvious reasons he, Bräuer, would have to discuss this move fully with General von Falkenhorst and would then also have to inform the latter of the meeting place agreed upon." Gaus, who telephoned Ribbentrop's instructions, reported that "Herr Bräuer clearly understood the meaning of the instructions." One cannot help but think that had the King gone to this meeting, Falkenhorst's troops would have grabbed him.[43]

on the northwest coast, a hundred miles southwest of Trondheim. Along the route they might organize the still dazed and scattered Norwegian forces for further resistance. And there was some hope that British troops might eventually arrive to help them.

THE BATTLES FOR NORWAY

In the far north at Narvik the British Navy already had reacted sharply to the surprise German occupation. It had been, as Churchill, who was in charge of it, admitted, "completely outwitted" by the Germans. Now in the north at least, out of range of the German land-based bombers, it went over to the offensive. On the morning of April 10, twenty-four hours after ten German destroyers had taken Narvik and disembarked Dietl's troops, a force of five British destroyers entered Narvik harbor, sank two of the five German destroyers then in the port, damaged the other three and sank all the German cargo vessels except one. In this action the German naval commander, Rear Admiral Bonte, was killed. On leaving the harbor, however, the British ships ran into the five remaining German destroyers emerging from nearby fjords. The German craft were heavier gunned and sank one British destroyer, forced the beaching of another on which the British commander, Captain Warburton-Lee, was mortally wounded, and damaged a third. Three of the five British destroyers managed to make the open sea where, in retiring, they sank a large German freighter, laden with ammunition, which was approaching the port.

At noon on April 13 the British, this time with the battleship *Warspite,* a survivor of the First World War Battle of Jutland, leading a flotilla of destroyers, returned to Narvik and wiped out the remaining German war vessels. Vice-Admiral W. J. Whitworth, the commanding officer, in wire-lessing the Admiralty of his action urged that since the German troops on shore had been stunned and disorganized—Dietl and his men had in fact taken to the hills—Narvik be occupied at once "by the main landing force." Unfortunately for the Allies, the British Army commander, Major General P. J. Mackesy, was an exceedingly cautious officer and, arriving the very next day with an advance contingent of three infantry battalions, decided not to risk a landing at Narvik but to disembark his troops at Harstad, thirty-five miles to the north, which was in the hands of the Norwegians. This was a costly error.

In the light of the fact that they had prepared a small expeditionary corps for Norway, the British were unaccountably slow in getting their troops under way. On the afternoon of April 8, after news was received of the movement of German fleet units up the Norwegian coast, the British Navy hurriedly *disembarked* the troops that had already been loaded on shipboard for the possible occupation of Stavanger, Bergen, Trondheim and Narvik, on the ground that every ship would be needed for naval action. By the time the British land forces were re-embarked all those port cities were in German hands. And by the time they reached central Norway they were doomed, as were the British naval ships which were to cover them, by the Luftwaffe's control of the air.

By April 20, one British brigade, reinforced by three battalions of French Chasseurs Alpins, had been landed at Namsos, a small port eighty miles northeast of Trondheim, and a second British brigade had been put ashore at Åndalsnes, a hundred miles to the southwest of Trondheim, which was thus to be attacked from north and south. But lacking field artillery, antiaircraft guns and air support, their bases pounded night and day by German bombers which blocked the further landing of supplies or reinforcements, neither force ever seriously threatened Trondheim. The Åndalsnes brigade, after meeting a Norwegian unit at Dombas, a rail junction sixty miles to the east, abandoned the proposed attack northward toward Trondheim and pushed southeast down the Gudbrandsdal in order to aid the Norwegian troops which, under the energetic command of Colonel Ruge, had been slowing up the main German drive coming up the valley from Oslo.

At Lillehammer, north of Hamar, the first engagement of the war between British and German troops took place on April 21, but it was no match. The ship laden with the British brigade's artillery had been sunk and there were only rifles and machine guns with which to oppose a strong German force armed with artillery and light tanks. Even worse, the British infantry, lacking air support, was incessantly pounded by Luftwaffe planes operating from nearby Norwegian airfields. Lillehammer fell after a twenty-four-hour battle and the British and Norwegian forces began a retreat of 140 miles up the valley railway to Åndalsnes, halting here and there to fight a rear-guard action·which slowed the Germans but never stopped them. On the nights of April 30 and May 1 the British forces were evacuated from Åndalsnes and on May 2 the Anglo–French contingent from Namsos, considerable feats in themselves, for both harbors were blazing shambles from continuous German bombing. On the night of April 29 the King of Norway and the members of his government were taken aboard the British cruiser *Glasgow* at Molde, across the Romsdalsfjord from Åndalsnes, itself also a shambles from Luftwaffe bombing, and conveyed to Tromsö, far above the Arctic Circle and north of Narvik, where on May Day the provisional capital was set up.

By then the southern half of Norway, comprising all the cities and main towns, had been irretrievably lost. But northern Norway seemed secure. On May 28 an Allied force of 25,000 men, including two brigades of Norwegians, a brigade of Poles and two battalions of the French Foreign Legion, had driven the greatly outnumbered Germans out of Narvik. There seemed no reason to doubt that Hitler would be deprived of both his iron ore and his objective of occupying all of Norway and making the Norwegian government capitulate. But by this time the Wehrmacht had struck with stunning force on the Western front and every Allied soldier was needed to plug the gap. Narvik was abandoned, the Allied troops were hastily re-embarked, and General Dietl, who had held out in a wild mountainous tract near the Swedish border, reoccupied the port on June 8 and four days later accepted the surrender of the persevering and gallant Colonel Ruge and his bewildered, resentful Norwegian troops, who felt they had been left in the lurch by the British. King Haakon and his government were taken aboard the cruiser *Devonshire* at Tromsö on June 7 and departed for London and five years of bitter exile.* In Berlin Dietl was promoted to Major General, awarded the Ritterkreuz and hailed by Hitler as the *Sieger von Narvik.*

Despite his amazing successes the Fuehrer had had his bad moments during the Norwegian campaign. General Jodl's diary is crammed with terse entries recounting a succession of the warlord's nervous crises. "Terrible excitement," he noted on April 14 after news had been received of the wiping out of the German naval forces at Narvik. On April 17 Hitler had a fit of hysteria about the loss of Narvik; he demanded that General Dietl's troops there be evacuated by air—an impossibility. "Each piece of bad news," Jodl scribbled that day in his diary, "leads to the worst fears." And two days later: "Renewed crisis. Political action has failed. Envoy Bräuer is recalled. According to the Fuehrer, force has to be used . . .† The conferences at the Chancellery in Berlin that day, April 19, became so embittered, with the heads of the three services blaming each other for

---

* Quisling did not last long in his first attempt to govern Norway. Six days after he had proclaimed himself Prime Minister, on April 15, the Germans kicked him out and appointed an Administrative Council of six leading Norwegian citizens, including Bishop Eivind Berggrav, head of the Lutheran Church of Norway, and Paal Berg, the President of the Supreme Court. It was mostly the doing of Berg, an eminent and scrappy jurist who later became the secret head of the Norwegian resistance movement. On April 24 Hitler appointed Josef Terboven, a tough young Nazi gauleiter, to be Reich Commissar for Norway, and it was he who actually governed the country, with increasing brutality, during the occupation. Bräuer, who had opposed Quisling from the beginning, was recalled on April 17, retired from the diplomatic service, and sent to the Western front as a soldier. The Germans reinstated Quisling as Prime Minister in 1942, but though his unpopularity among the people was immense, his power was nil despite his best efforts to serve his German masters.

At the end of the war Quisling was tried for treason and after an exhaustive trial sentenced to death and executed on October 24, 1945. Terboven committed suicide rather than face capture. Knut Hamsun, the great Norwegian novelist, who had openly collaborated with the Germans, singing their praises, was indicted for treason, but the charges were dropped on the grounds of his old age and senility. He was, however, tried and convicted for "profiting from the Nazi regime," and fined $65,000. He died on February 19, 1952, at the age of ninety-three. General von Falkenhorst was tried as a war criminal before a mixed British and Norwegian military court on charges of having handed over captured Allied commandos to the S.S. for execution. He was sentenced to death on August 2, 1946, but the sentence was commuted to life imprisonment.

† On April 13, General von Falkenhorst, no doubt goaded by Hitler, who was in a fury because of Norwegian resistance, signed an order providing for taking as hostages twenty of the most distinguished citizens of Oslo, including Bishop Berggrav and Paal Berg, who, in the words of Minister Bräuer, "were to be shot in the event of the continued resistance or attempted sabotage."[44]

the delays, that even the lackey Keitel stalked out of the room. "Chaos of leadership is again threatening," Jodl noted. And on April 22 he added: "Fuehrer is increasingly worried about the English landings."

On April 23 the slow progress of the German forces moving up from Oslo toward Trondheim and Åndalsnes caused the "excitement to grow," as Jodl put it, but the next day the news was better and from that day it continued to grow more rosy. By the twenty-sixth the warlord was in such fine fettle that at 3:30 in the morning, during an all-night session with his military advisers, he told them he intended to start "Yellow" between May 1 and 7. "Yellow" was the code name for the attack in the West across Holland and Belgium. Though on April 29 Hitler was again "worried about Trondheim," the next day he was "happy with joy" at the news that a battle group from Oslo had reached the city. He could at last turn his attention back to the West. On May 1 he ordered that preparations for the big attack there be ready by May 5.

The Wehrmacht commanders—Goering, Brauchitsch, Halder, Keitel, Jodl, Raeder and the rest—had for the first time had a foretaste during the Norwegian campaign of how their demonic Leader cracked under the strain of even minor setbacks in battle. It was a weakness which would grow on him when, after a series of further astonishing military successes, the tide of war changed, and it would contribute mightily to the eventual debacle of the Third Reich.

Still, any way one looked at it, the quick conquest of Denmark and Norway had been an important victory for Hitler and a discouraging defeat for the British. It secured the winter iron ore route, gave added protection to the entrance to the Baltic, allowed the daring German Navy to break out into the North Atlantic and provided them with excellent port facilities there for submarines and surface ships in the sea war against Britain. It brought Hitler air bases hundreds of miles closer to the main enemy. And perhaps most important of all it immensely enhanced the military prestige of the Third Reich and correspondingly diminished that of the Western Allies. Nazi Germany seemed invincible. Austria, Czechoslovakia, Poland and now Denmark and Norway had succumbed easily to Hitler's force, or threat of force, and not even the help of two major allies in the West had been, in the latter cases, of the slightest avail. The wave of the future, as an eminent American woman wrote, seemed to belong to Hitler and Nazism.

For the remaining neutral states Hitler's latest conquest was also a terrifying lesson. Obviously neutrality no longer offered protection to the little democratic nations trying to survive in a totalitarian-dominated world. Finland had just found that out, and now Norway and Denmark. They had themselves to blame for being so blind, for declining to accept in good time—before the actual aggression—the help of friendly world powers.

I trust this fact [Churchill told Commons on April 11] will be meditated upon by other countries who may tomorrow, or a week hence, *or a month hence,* find themselves the victims of an equally elaborately worked-out staff plan for their destruction and enslavement.[45]

He was obviously thinking of Holland and Belgium, but even in their case, though there would be a month of grace, no such meditation began.*

There were military lessons, too, to be learned from Hitler's lightning conquest of the two Scandinavian countries. The most significant was the importance of air power and its superiority over naval power when land bases for bombers and fighters were near. Hardly less important was an old lesson, that victory often goes to the daring and the imaginative. The German Navy and Air Force had been both, and Dietl at Narvik had shown a resourcefulness of the German Army which the Allies had lacked.

There was one military result of the Scandinavian adventure which could not be evaluated at once, if only because it was not possible to look very far into the future. The losses in men in Norway on both sides were light. The Germans suffered 1,317 killed, 2,375 missing and 1,604 wounded, a total of 5,296 casualties; those of the Norwegians, French and British were slightly less than 5,000. The British lost one aircraft carrier, one cruiser and seven destroyers and the Poles and the French one destroyer each. German naval losses were comparably much heavier: ten out of twenty destroyers, three of eight cruisers, while the battle cruisers *Scharnhorst* and *Gneisenau* and the pocket battleship *Luetzow* were damaged so severely that they were out of action for several months. Hitler had no fleet worthy of mention for the coming events of the summer. When the time to invade Britain came, as it did so shortly, this proved to be an insurmountable handicap.

---

* The Swedes, caught between Russia in Finland and the Baltic countries and Germany in possession of adjoining Denmark and Norway, meditated and decided there was no choice except to cling to their precarious neutrality and go down fighting if they were attacked. They had placated the Soviet Union by refusing to allow Allied troops transit to Finland, and now under great pressure they placated Germany. Though Sweden had sent an impressive stock of arms to Finland, it refused to sell Norway either arms or gasoline when it was attacked. All through April the Germans demanded that Sweden allow the transit of troops to Narvik to relieve Dietl, but this was refused until the end of hostilities, although a train of medical personnel and supplies was allowed through. On June 19, fearing a direct attack by Germany, Sweden gave in to Hitler's pressure and agreed to permit the transport over Swedish railways of Nazi troops and war material to Norway on condition that the number of troops moving in each direction should balance so that the German garrisons in Norway would not be strengthened by the arrangement.

This was of immense help to Germany. By transporting fresh troops and war material by land through Sweden Hitler avoided the risk of having them sunk at sea by the British. In the first six months of the accord, some 140,000 German troops in Norway were exchanged and the German forces there greatly strengthened by supplies. Later, just before the German onslaught on Russia, Sweden permitted the Nazi High Command to transport an entire army division, fully armed, from Norway across Sweden to Finland to be used to attack the Soviet Union. What it had refused the Allies the year before it accorded to Nazi Germany. For details of German pressure on Sweden and for the text of the exchange of letters between King Gustav V and Hitler, see *Documents on German Foreign Policy,* IX. The author has covered the subject more thoroughly in *The Challenge of Scandinavia.*

The possible consequences of the severe crippling of the German Navy, however, did not enter the Fuehrer's thoughts as, at the beginning of May, with Denmark and Norway now added to his long list of conquests, he worked with his eager generals—for they had now shed their misgivings of the previous autumn—on the last-minute preparations for what they were confident would be the greatest conquest of all.

21

VICTORY IN THE WEST

SHORTLY AFTER DAWN on the fine spring day of May 10, 1940, the ambassador of Belgium and the minister of the Netherlands in Berlin were summoned to the Wilhelmstrasse and informed by Ribbentrop that German troops were entering their countries to safeguard their neutrality against an imminent attack by the Anglo–French armies—the same shabby excuse that had been made just a month before with Denmark and Norway. A formal German ultimatum called upon the two governments to see to it that no resistance was offered. If it were, it would be crushed by all means and the responsibility for the bloodshed would "be borne exclusively by the Royal Belgian and the Royal Netherlands Government."

In Brussels and The Hague, as previously in Copenhagen and Oslo, the German envoys made their way to the respective foreign offices with similar messages. Ironically enough, the bearer of the ultimatum in The Hague was Count Julius von Zech-Burkersroda, the German minister, who was a son-in-law of Bethmann-Hollweg, the Kaiser's Chancellor, who in 1914 had publicly called Germany's guarantee of Belgian neutrality, which the Hohenzollern Reich had just violated, "a scrap of paper."

At the Foreign Ministry in Brussels, while German bombers roared overhead and the explosion of their bombs on nearby airfields rattled the windows, Buelow-Schwante, the German ambassador, started to take a paper from his pocket as he entered the Foreign Minister's office. Paul-Henri Spaak stopped him.

"I beg your pardon, Mr. Ambassador. I will speak first."

The German Army [Spaak said, not attempting to hold back his feeling of outrage] has just attacked our country. This is the second time in twenty-five years that Germany has committed a criminal aggression against a neutral and loyal Belgium. What has happened is perhaps even more odious than the aggression of 1914. No ultimatum, no note, no protest of any kind has ever been placed before the Belgian Government. It is through the attack itself that Belgium has learned that Germany has violated the undertakings given

713

by her . . . The German Reich will be held responsible by history. Belgium is resolved to defend herself.

The unhappy German diplomat then began to read the formal German ultimatum, but Spaak cut him short. "Hand me the document," he said. "I should like to spare you so painful a task."[1]

The Third Reich had given the two small Low Countries guarantees of their neutrality almost without number. The independence and neutrality of Belgium had been guaranteed "perpetually" by the five great European powers in 1839, a pact that was observed for seventy-five years until Germany broke it in 1914. The Weimar Republic had promised never to take up arms against Belgium, and Hitler, after he came to power, continually reaffirmed that policy and gave similar assurances to the Netherlands. On January 30, 1937, after he had repudiated the Locarno Treaty, the Nazi Chancellor publicly proclaimed:

The German Government has further given the assurance to Belgium and Holland that it is prepared to recognize and to guarantee the inviolability and neutrality of these territories.

Frightened by the remilitarization of the Third Reich and its reoccupation of the Rhineland in the spring of 1936, Belgium, which wisely had abandoned neutrality after 1918, again sought refuge in it. On April 24, 1937, Britain and France released her from the obligations of Locarno and on October 13 of that year Germany officially and solemnly confirmed

its determination that in no circumstances will it impair the inviolability and integrity [of Belgium] and that it will at all times respect Belgian territory . . . and [be] prepared to assist Belgium should she be subjected to an attack . . .

From that day on there is a familiar counterpoint in Hitler's solemn public assurances to the Low Countries and his private admonitions to his generals. On August 24, 1938, in regard to one of the papers drawn up for him for Case Green, the plan for the attack on Czechoslovakia, he spoke of the "extraordinary advantage" to Germany if Belgium and Holland were occupied and asked the Army's opinion "as to the conditions under which an occupation of this area could be carried out and how long it would take." On April 28, 1939, in his reply to Roosevelt, Hitler again stressed the "binding declarations" which he had given to the Netherlands and Belgium, among others. Less than a month later, on May 23, the Fuehrer, as has been noted, was telling his generals that "the Dutch and Belgian air bases must be occupied by armed force . . . with lightning speed. Declarations of neutrality must be ignored."

He had not yet started his war, but his plans were ready. On August 22, a week before he launched the war by attacking Poland, he conferred with his generals about the "possibility" of violating Dutch and Belgian neutrality. "England and France," he said, "will not violate the neutrality of these countries." Four days later, on August 26, he ordered his envoys in Brussels and The Hague to inform the respective governments that in the event of an outbreak of war "Germany will in no circumstances impair the inviolability of Belgium and Holland," an assurance which he repeated publicly on October 6, after the conclusion of the Polish campaign. The very next day, October 7, General von Brauchitsch advised his army group commanders, at Hitler's prompting,

to make all preparations for immediate invasion of Dutch and Belgian territory, if the political situation so demands.[2]

Two days later, on October 9, in Directive No. 6, Hitler ordered:

Preparations are to be made for an attacking operation . . . through Luxembourg, Belgium and Holland. This attack must be carried out as soon and as forcefully as possible . . . The object of this attack is to acquire as great an area of Holland, Belgium and northern France as possible.[3]

The Belgians and Dutch, of course, were not privy to Hitler's secret orders. Nevertheless they did receive warnings of what was in store for them. A number of them have already been noted: Colonel Oster, one of the anti-Nazi conspirators, warned the Dutch and Belgian military attachés in Berlin on November 5 to expect the German attack on November 12, which was then the target date. At the end of October Goerdeler, another one of the conspirators, had gone to Brussels at the instigation of Weizsaecker, to warn the Belgians of an imminent attack. And shortly after the New Year, on January 10, 1940, Hitler's plans for the offensive in the West had fallen into the hands of the Belgians when an officer carrying them had made a forced landing in Belgium.*

By that time the Dutch and Belgian general staffs knew from their own border intelligence that the Germans were concentrating some fifty divisions on their frontiers. They also had the benefit of an unusual source of information in the German capital. This "source" was Colonel G. J. Sas, the Netherland's military attaché in Berlin. Sas was a close personal friend of Colonel Oster and often dined with him at the latter's home in the secluded suburb of Zehlendorf—a practice facilitated, once the war broke out, by the blackout, whose cover enabled a number of persons in Berlin at that time, German and foreign, to get about on various subversive missions without much fear of detection. It was Sas whom Oster tipped off early in November about the German onslaught then set for November 12, and he gave the attaché a new warning in January. The fact that neither attack came off somewhat lessened the credibility of Sas in The Hague and in Brussels, where the fact that Hitler had actually set dates for his aggression and then postponed them naturally was not known. However the ten days' warning that Sas got through Oster of the invasion

---

* See above, pp. 651, 652, 671–72, respectively.

of Norway and Denmark and his prediction of the exact date seems to have restored his prestige at home.

On May 3, Oster told Sas flatly that the German attack in the West through the Netherlands and Belgium would begin on May 10, and the military attaché promptly informed his government. The next day The Hague received confirmation of this from its envoy at the Vatican. The Dutch immediately passed the word along to the Belgians. May 5 was a Sunday and as the week began to unfold it became pretty obvious to all of us in Berlin that the blow in the West would fall within a few days. Tension mounted in the capital. By May 8 I was cabling my New York office to hold one of our correspondents in Amsterdam instead of shipping him off to Norway, where the war had ended anyway, and that evening the military censors allowed me to hint in my broadcast that there would soon be action in the West, including Holland and Belgium.

On the evening of May 9 Oster and Sas dined together for what would prove the last time. The German officer confirmed that the final order had been given to launch the attack in the West at dawn the next day. Just to make sure that there were no last-minute changes Oster dropped by OKW headquarters in the Bendlerstrasse after dinner. There had been no changes. "The swine has gone to the Western front," Oster told Sas. The "swine" was Hitler. Sas informed the Belgian military attaché and then went to his own legation and put through a call to The Hague. A special code for this moment already had been arranged and Sas spoke some seemingly innocuous words which conveyed the message "Tomorrow, at dawn. Hold tight!"[4]

Strangely enough, the two Big Powers in the West, Britain and France, were caught napping. Their general staffs discounted the alarming reports from Brussels and The Hague. London itself was preoccupied with a three-day cabinet crisis which was resolved only on the evening of May 10 by the replacement of Chamberlain by Churchill as Prime Minister. The first the French and British headquarters heard of the German onslaught was when the peace of the spring predawn was broken by the roar of German bombers and the screech of Stuka dive bombers overhead, followed shortly afterward, as daylight broke, by frantic appeals for help from the Dutch and Belgian governments which had held the Allies at arm's length for eight months instead of concerting with them for a common defense.

Nevertheless the Allied plan to meet the main German attack in Belgium went ahead for the first couple of days almost without a hitch. A great Anglo–French army rushed northeastward from the Franco–Belgian border to man the main Belgian defense line along the Dyle and Meuse rivers east of Brussels. As it happened, this was just what the German High Command wanted. This massive Allied wheeling movement played directly into its hands. Though they did not know it the Anglo–French armies sped directly into a trap that, when sprung, would soon prove to be utterly disastrous.

THE RIVAL PLANS

The original German plan of attack in the West had been drastically changed since it fell into the hands of the Belgians and, as the Germans suspected, of the French and British, in January. *Fall Gelb* (Case Yellow), as the operation was called, had been hastily concocted in the fall of 1939 by the Army High Command under the pressure of Hitler's order to launch the offensive in the West by mid-November. There is much dispute among military historians and indeed among the German generals themselves whether this first plan was a modified version of the old Schlieffen plan or not; Halder and Guderian have maintained that it was. It called for the main German drive on the right flank through Belgium and northern France, with the object of occupying the Channel ports. It fell short of the famous Schlieffen plan, which had failed by an ace of success in 1914 and which provided not only for the capture of the Channel ports but for a continuation of a great wheeling movement which would bring the German right-wing armies through Belgium and northern France and across the Seine, after which they would turn east below Paris and encircle and destroy the remaining French forces. Its purpose had been to quickly put an end to armed French resistance so that Germany, in 1914, could then turn on Russia with the great bulk of its military might.

But in 1939–40 Hitler did not have to worry about a Russian front. Nevertheless his objective was more limited. In the first phase of the campaign, at any rate, he planned not to knock out the French Army but to roll it back and occupy the Channel coast, thus cutting off Britain from its ally and at the same time securing air and naval bases from which he could harass and blockade the British Isles. It is obvious from his various harangues to the generals at this time that he thought that after such a defeat Britain and France would be inclined to make peace and leave him free to turn his attention once more to the East.

Even before the original plan for *Fall Gelb* had fallen into the hands of the enemy it was anticipated by the Allied Supreme Command. On November 17 the Allied Supreme War Council, meeting in Paris, had adopted "Plan D," which, in the event of a German attack through Belgium, called for the French First and Ninth armies and the British Expeditionary Force to dash forward to the principal Belgian defense line on the Dyle and Meuse rivers from Antwerp through Louvain, Namur and Givet to Mézières. A few days before, the French and British general staffs, in a series of secret meetings with the Belgian High Command, had received the latter's assurance that it would strengthen the defenses on that line and make its main stand there. But the Belgians, still clinging to the illusions of neutrality which fortified their hope that they yet might be spared involvement in war, would not go further. The British chiefs of staff argued that there would not be time to deploy the Allied forces so far forward once the Germans had attacked, but they went along with Plan D at the urging of General Gamelin.

At the end of November the Allies added a scheme to rush General

Henri Giraud's Seventh Army up the Channel coast to help the Dutch north of Antwerp in case the Netherlands was also attacked. Thus a German attempt to sweep through Belgium—and perhaps Holland—to flank the Maginot Line would be met very early in the game by the entire B.E.F., the bulk of the French Army, the twenty-two divisions of the Belgians and the ten divisions of the Dutch—a force numerically equal, as it turned out, to that of the Germans.

It was to avoid such a head-on clash and at the same time to trap the British and French armies that would speed forward so far that General Erich von Manstein (born Lewinski), chief of staff of Rundstedt's Army Group A on the Western front, proposed a radical change in *Fall Gelb*. Manstein was a gifted and imaginative staff officer of relatively junior rank, but during the winter he succeeded in getting his bold idea put before Hitler over the initial opposition of Brauchitsch, Halder and a number of other generals. Manstein's proposal was that the main German assault should be launched in the center through the Ardennes with a massive armored force which would then cross the Meuse just north of Sedan and break out into the open country and race to the Channel at Abbeville.

Hitler, always attracted by daring and even reckless solutions, was interested. Rundstedt pushed the idea relentlessly not only because he believed in it but because it would give his Army Group A the decisive role in the offensive. Although Halder's personal dislike of Manstein and certain professional jealousies among some of the generals who outranked him led to Manstein's transfer from his staff post to the command of an infantry corps at the end of January, he had an opportunity to expound his unorthodox views to Hitler personally at a dinner given for a number of new corps commanders in Berlin on February 17. He argued that an armored strike through the Ardennes would hit the Allies where they least expected it, since their generals probably, like most of the Germans, considered this hilly, wooded country unsuitable for tanks. A feint by the right wing of the German forces would bring the British and French armies rushing pell-mell into Belgium. Then by cracking through the French at Sedan and heading west along the north bank of the Somme for the Channel, the Germans would entrap the major Anglo–French forces as well as the Belgian Army.

It was a daring plan, not without its risks, as several generals, including Jodl, emphasized. But by now Hitler, who considered himself a military genius, practically believed that it was his own idea and his enthusiasm for it mounted. Halder, who had at first dismissed it as a crackpot idea, also began to embrace it and indeed, with the help of his General Staff officers, considerably improved it. On February 24, 1940, it was formally adopted in a new OKW directive and the generals were told to redeploy their troops by March 7. Somewhere along the line, incidentally, the plan for the conquest of the Netherlands, which had been dropped from *Fall Gelb* in a revision on October 29, 1939, was reinstated on November 14 at the urging of the Luftwaffe, which wanted the Dutch airfields for use against

Britain and which offered to supply a large batch of airborne troops for this minor but somewhat complicated operation. On such considerations are the fates of little nations sometimes decided.[5]

And so as the campaign in Norway approached its victorious conclusion and the first warm days of the beginning of May arrived, the Germans, with the most powerful army the world had ever seen up to that moment, stood poised to strike in the West. In mere numbers the two sides were evenly matched—136 German divisions against 135 divisions of the French, British, Belgian and Dutch. The defenders had the advantage of vast defensive fortifications: the impenetrable Maginot Line in the south, the extensive line of Belgian forts in the middle and fortified water lines in Holland in the north. Even in the number of tanks, the Allies matched the Germans. But they had not concentrated them as had the latter. And because of the aberration of the Dutch and Belgians for neutrality there had been no staff consultations by which the defenders could pool their plans and resources to the best advantage. The Germans had a unified command, the initiative of the attacker, no moral scruples against aggression, a contagious confidence in themselves and a daring plan. They had had experience in battle in Poland. There they had tested their new tactics and their new weapons in combat. They knew the value of the dive bomber and the mass use of tanks. And they knew, as Hitler had never ceased to point out, that the French, though they would be defending their own soil, had no heart in what lay ahead.

Notwithstanding their confidence and determination, the German High Command, as the secret records make clear, suffered some moments of panic as the zero hour drew near—or at least Hitler, the Supreme Commander, did. General Jodl jotted them down in his diary. Hitler ordered several last-minute postponements of the jump-off, which on May 1 he had set for May 5. On May 3 he put it off until May 6 on account of the weather but perhaps also in part because the Foreign Office didn't think his proposed justification for violating the neutrality of Belgium and Holland was good enough. The next day he set May 7 as X Day and on the following day postponed it again until Wednesday, May 8. "Fuehrer has finished justification for Case Yellow," Jodl noted. Belgium and the Netherlands were to be accused of having acted most unneutrally.

May 7. Fuehrer railroad train was scheduled to leave Finkenkrug at 16:38 hours [Jodl's diary continued]. But weather remains uncertain and therefore the order [for the attack] is rescinded . . . Fuehrer greatly agitated about new postponement as there is danger of treachery. Talk of the Belgian Envoy to the Vatican with Brussels permits the deduction that treason has been committed by a German personality who left Berlin for Rome on April 29 . . .

May 8. Alarming news from Holland. Canceling of furloughs, evacuations, roadblocks, other mobilization methods . . . Fuehrer does not want to wait any longer. Goering wants postponement until the 10th, at least . . . Fuehrer is very agitated; then he consents to postponement until May 10, which he says is against his intuition. But not one day longer . . .

May 9. Fuehrer decides on attack for May 10 for sure. Departure with Fuehrer train at 17:00 hours from Finkenkrug. After report that weather situation will be favorable on the 10th, the code word "Danzig" is given at 21:00 hours.

Hitler, accompanied by Keitel, Jodl and others of the OKW staff, arrived at headquarters, which he had named Felsennest (Eyrie), near Muenstereifel just as dawn was breaking on May 10. Twenty-five miles to the west German forces were hurtling over the Belgian frontier. Along a front of 175 miles, from the North Sea to the Maginot Line, Nazi troops broke across the borders of three small neutral states, Holland, Belgium and Luxembourg, in brutal violation of the German word, solemnly and repeatedly given.

THE SIX WEEKS' WAR: MAY 10–JUNE 25, 1940

For the Dutch it was a five-day war, and indeed in that brief period the fate of Belgium, France and the British Expeditionary Force was sealed. For the Germans everything went according to the book, or even better than the book, in the unfolding both of strategy and of tactics. Their success exceeded the fondest hopes of Hitler. His generals were confounded by the lightning rapidity and the extent of their own victories. As for the Allied leaders, they were quickly paralyzed by developments they had not faintly expected and could not—in the utter confusion that ensued—comprehend.

Winston Churchill himself, who had taken over as Prime Minister on the first day of battle, was dumfounded. He was awakened at half past seven on the morning of May 15 by a telephone call from Premier Paul Reynaud in Paris, who told him in an excited voice, "We have been defeated! We are beaten!" Churchill refused to believe it. The great French Army vanquished in a week? It was impossible. "I did not comprehend," he wrote later, "the violence of the revolution effected since the last war by the incursion of a mass of fast-moving armor."[6]

Tanks—seven divisions of them concentrated at one point, the weakest position in the Western defenses, for the big breakthrough—that was what did it. That and the Stuka dive bombers and the parachutists and the airborne troops who landed far behind the Allied lines or on the top of their seemingly impregnable forts and wrought havoc.

And yet we who were in Berlin wondered why these German tactics should have come as such a shattering surprise to the Allied leaders. Had not Hitler's troops demonstrated their effectiveness in the campaign against Poland? There the great breakthroughs which had surrounded or destroyed the Polish armies within a week had been achieved by the massing of armor after the Stukas had softened up resistance. Parachutists and airborne troops had not done well in Poland even on the very limited scale with which they were used; they had failed to capture intact the key bridges. But in Norway, a month before the onslaught in the West, they had been prodigious, capturing Oslo and all the airfields, and reinforcing the isolated small groups that had been landed by sea at Stavanger, Bergen, Trondheim and Narvik and thereby enabling them to hold out. Hadn't the Allied commanders studied these campaigns and learned their lessons?

THE CONQUEST OF THE NETHERLANDS

Only one division of panzers could be spared by the Germans for the conquest of the Netherlands, which was accomplished in five days largely by parachutists and by troops landed by air transports behind the great flooded water lines which many in Berlin had believed would hold the Germans up for weeks. To the bewildered Dutch was reserved the experience of being subjected to the first large-scale airborne attack in the history of warfare. Considering their unpreparedness for such an ordeal and the complete surprise by which they were taken they did better than was realized at the time.

The first objective of the Germans was to land a strong force by air on the flying fields near The Hague, occupy the capital at once and capture the Queen and the government, as they had tried to do just a month before with the Norwegians. But at The Hague, as at Oslo, the plan failed, though due to different circumstances. Recovering from their initial surprise and confusion, Dutch infantry, supported by artillery, was able to drive the Germans—two regiments strong—from the three airfields surrounding The Hague by the evening of May 10. This saved the capital and the government momentarily, but it tied down the Dutch reserves, which were desperately needed elsewhere.

The key to the German plan was the seizure by airborne troops of the bridges just south of Rotterdam over the Nieuwe Maas and those farther southeast over the two estuaries of the Maas (Meuse) at Dordrecht and Moerdijk. It was over these bridges that General Georg von Kuechler's Eighteenth Army driving from the German border nearly a hundred miles away hoped to force his way into Fortress Holland. In no other way could this entrenched place, lying behind formidable water barriers and comprising The Hague, Amsterdam, Utretcht, Rotterdam and Leyden, be taken easily and quickly.

The bridges were seized on the morning of May 10 by airborne units —including one company that landed on the river at Rotterdam in antiquated seaplanes—before the surprised Dutch guards could blow them. Desperate efforts were made by improvised Netherlands units to drive the Germans away and they almost succeeded. But the Germans hung on tenuously until the morning of May 12, when the one armored division assigned to Kuechler arrived, having smashed through the Grebbe–Peel

Line, a fortified front to the east strengthened by a number of water barriers, on which the Dutch had hoped to hold out for several days.

There was some hope that the Germans might be stopped short of the Moerdijk bridges by General Giraud's French Seventh Army, which had raced up from the Channel and reached Tilburg on the afternoon of May 11. But the French, like the hard-pressed Dutch, lacked air support, armor, and antitank and antiaircraft guns, and were easily pushed back to Breda. This opened the way for the German 9th Panzer Division to cross the bridges at Moerdijk and Dordrecht and, on the afternoon of May 12, arrive at the south bank of the Nieuwe Maas across from Rotterdam, where the German airborne troops still held the bridges.

But the tanks could not get across the Rotterdam bridges. The Dutch in the meantime had sealed them off at the northern ends. By the morning of May 14, then, the situation for the Netherlands was desperate but not hopeless. Fortress Holland had not been cracked. The strong German airborne forces around The Hague had been either captured or dispersed into nearby villages. Rotterdam still held. The German High Command, anxious to pull the armored division and supporting troops out of Holland to exploit a new opportunity which had just been opened to the south in France, was not happy. Indeed, on the morning of the fourteenth Hitler issued Directive No. 11 stating: "The power of resistance of the Dutch Army has proved to be stronger than was anticipated. Political as well as military considerations require that this resistance be broken *speedily*." How? He commanded that detachments of the Air Force be taken from the Sixth Army front in Belgium "to facilitate the rapid conquest of Fortress Holland."[7]

Specifically he and Goering ordered a heavy bombing of Rotterdam. The Dutch would be induced to surrender by a dose of Nazi terror—the kind that had been applied the autumn before at beleaguered Warsaw.

On the morning of May 14 a German staff officer from the XXXIXth Corps had crossed the bridge at Rotterdam under a white flag and demanded the surrender of the city. He warned that unless it capitulated it would be bombed. While surrender negotiations were under way—a Dutch officer had come to German headquarters near the bridge to discuss the details and was returning with the German terms—bombers appeared and wiped out the heart of the great city. Some eight hundred persons, almost entirely civilians, were massacred, several thousand wounded and 78,000 made homeless.* This bit of treachery, this act of calculated ruthlessness, would long be remembered by the Dutch, though at Nuremberg both Goering and Kesselring of the Luftwaffe defended it on the grounds that Rotterdam was not an open city but stoutly defended by the Dutch. Both denied that they knew that surrender negotiations were going

---

* It was first reported and long believed that from 25,000 to 30,000 Dutch were killed, and this is the figure given in the 1953 edition of the *Encyclopaedia Britannica*. However, at Nuremberg the Dutch government gave the figure as 814 killed.[8]

on when they dispatched the bombers, though there is strong evidence from German Army archives that they did.*[9] At any rate, OKW made no excuses at the time. I myself heard over the Berlin radio on the evening of May 14 a special OKW communiqué:

Under the tremendous impression of the attacks of German dive bombers and the imminent attack of German tanks, the city of Rotterdam has capitulated and thus saved itself from destruction.

Rotterdam surrendered, and then the Dutch armed forces. Queen Wilhelmina and the government members had fled to London on two British destroyers. At dusk on May 14 General H. G. Winkelmann, the Commander in Chief of the Dutch forces, ordered his troops to lay down their arms and at 11 A.M. on the next day he signed the official capitulation. Within five days it was all over. The fighting, that is. For five years a night of savage German terror would henceforth darken this raped, civilized little land.

THE FALL OF BELGIUM AND THE TRAPPING
OF THE ANGLO–FRENCH ARMIES

By the time the Dutch had surrendered, the die was cast for Belgium, France and the British Expeditionary Force. May 14, though it was only the fifth day of the attack, was the fatal day. The previous evening German armor had secured four bridgeheads across the steeply banked and heavily wooded Meuse River from Dinant to Sedan, captured the latter city, which had been the scene of Napoleon III's surrender to Moltke in 1870 and the end of the Third Empire, and gravely threatened the center of the Allied lines and the hinge on which the flower of the British and French armies had so quickly wheeled into Belgium.

The next day, May 14, the avalanche broke. An army of tanks unprecedented in warfare for size, concentration, mobility and striking power, which when it had started through the Ardennes Forest from the German frontier on May 10 stretched in three columns back for a hundred miles far behind the Rhine, broke through the French Ninth and Second armies and headed swiftly for the Channel, behind the Allied forces in Belgium. This was a formidable and frightening juggernaut. Preceded by waves of Stuka dive bombers, which softened up the French defensive positions, swarming with combat engineers who launched rubber boats and threw up pontoon bridges to get across the rivers and canals, each panzer division possessed of its own self-propelled artillery and of one brigade of motorized infantry, and the armored corps closely followed by divisions of motorized infantry to hold the positions opened up by the

---

* There were no criminal convictions at Nuremberg for the bombing of Rotterdam.

tanks, this phalanx of steel and fire could not be stopped by any means in the hands of the bewildered defenders. On both sides of Dinant on the Meuse the French gave way to General Hermann Hoth's XVth Armored Corps, one of whose two tank divisions was commanded by a daring young brigadier general, Erwin Rommel. Farther south along the river, at Monthermé, the same pattern was being executed by General Georg-Hans Reinhardt's XLIst Armored Corps of two tank divisions.

But it was around Sedan, of disastrous memory to the French, that the greatest blow fell. Here on the morning of May 14 two tank divisions of General Heinz Guderian's XIXth Armored Corps* poured across a hastily constructed pontoon bridge set up during the night over the Meuse and struck toward the west. Though French armor and British bombers tried desperately to destroy the bridge—forty of seventy-one R.A.F. planes were shot down in one single attack, mostly by flak, and seventy French tanks were destroyed—they could not damage it. By evening the German bridgehead at Sedan was thirty miles wide and fifteen miles deep and the French forces in the vital center of the Allied line were shattered. Those who were not surrounded and made prisoners were in disorderly retreat. The Franco–British armies to the north, as well as the twenty-two divisions of Belgians, were placed in dire danger of being cut off.

The first couple of days had gone fairly well for the Allies, or so they thought. To Churchill, plunging with new zest into his fresh responsibilities as Prime Minister, "up until the night of the twelfth," as he later wrote, "there was no reason to suppose that the operations were not going well."[10] Gamelin, the generalissimo of the Allied forces, was highly pleased with the situation. The evening before, the best and largest part of the French forces, the First, Seventh and Ninth armies, along with the B.E.F., nine divisions strong under Lord Gort, had joined the Belgians, as planned, on a strong defensive line running along the Dyle River from Antwerp through Louvain to Wavre and thence across the Gembloux gap to Namur and south along the Meuse to Sedan. Between the formidable Belgian fortress of Namur and Antwerp, on a front of only sixty miles, the Allies actually outnumbered the oncoming Germans, having some thirty-six divisions against the twenty in Reichenau's Sixth Army.

The Belgians, though they had fought well along the reaches of their northeast frontier, had not held out there as long as had been expected, certainly not as long as in 1914. They, like the Dutch to the north of them, had simply not been able to cope with the revolutionary new tactics of the Wehrmacht. Here, as in Holland, the Germans seized the vital bridges by the daring use of a handful of specially trained troops landed silently at dawn in gliders. They overpowered the guards at two of the three bridges over the Albert Canal behind Maastricht before the defenders could throw the switches that were supposed to blow them.

---

* The two armored corps of Reinhardt and Guderian made up General Ewald von Kleist's panzer group, which consisted of five tank divisions and three motorized infantry divisions.

They had even greater success in capturing Fort Eben Emael, which commanded the junction of the Meuse River and the Albert Canal. This modern, strategically located fortress was regarded by both the Allies and the Germans as the most impregnable fortification in Europe, stronger than anything the French had built in the Maginot Line or the Germans in the West Wall. Constructed in a series of steel-and-concrete galleries deep underground, its gun turrets protected by heavy armor and manned by 1,200 men, it was expected to hold out indefinitely against the pounding of the heaviest bombs and artillery shells. It fell in thirty hours to eighty German soldiers who under the command of a sergeant had landed in nine gliders on its roof and whose total casualties amounted to six killed and nineteen wounded. In Berlin, I remember, OKW made the enterprise look very mysterious, announcing in a special communiqué on the evening of May 11 that Fort Eben Emael had been taken by a "new method of attack," an announcement that caused rumors to spread—and Dr. Goebbels was delighted to fan them—that the Germans had a deadly new "secret weapon," perhaps a nerve gas that temporarily paralyzed the defenders.

The truth was much more prosaic. With their usual flair for minute preparation, the Germans during the winter of 1939–40 had erected at Hildesheim a replica of the fort and of the bridges across the Albert Canal and had trained some four hundred glider troops on how to take them. Three groups were to capture the three bridges, the fourth Eben Emael. This last unit of eighty men landed on the top of the fortress and placed a specially prepared "hollow" explosive in the armored gun turrets which not only put them out of action but spread flames and gas in the chambers below. Portable flame throwers were also used at the gun portals and observation openings. Within an hour the Germans were able to penetrate the upper galleries, render the light and heavy guns of the great fort useless and blind its observation posts. Belgian infantry behind the fortification tried vainly to dislodge the tiny band of attackers but they were driven off by Stuka attacks and by reinforcements of parachutists. By the morning of May 11 advance panzer units, which had raced over the two intact bridges to the north, arrived at the fort and surrounded it, and, after further Stuka bombings and hand-to-hand fighting in the underground tunnels, a white flag was hoisted at noon and the 1,200 dazed Belgian defenders filed out and surrendered.[11]

This feat, along with the capture of the bridges and the violence of the attack mounted by General von Reichenau's Sixth Army, which was sustained by General Hoepner's XVIth Armored Corps of two tank divisions and one mechanized infantry division, convinced the Allied High Command that now, as in 1914, the brunt of the German offensive was being carried out by the enemy's right wing and that they had taken the proper means to stop it. In fact, as late as the evening of May 15 the Belgian, British and French forces were holding firm on the Dyle line from Antwerp to Namur.

This was just what the German High Command wanted. It had now become possible for it to spring the Manstein plan and deliver the haymaker in the center. General Halder, the Chief of the Army General Staff, saw the situation—and his opportunities—very clearly on the evening of May 13.

North of Namur [he wrote in his diary] we can count on a completed concentration of some 24 British and French and about 15 Belgian divisions. Against this our Sixth Army has 15 divisions on the front and six in reserve . . . We are strong enough there to fend off any enemy attack. No need to bring up any more forces. South of Namur we face a weaker enemy. About half our strength. Outcome of Meuse attack will decide if, when and where we will be able to exploit this superiority. The enemy has no force worth mentioning behind this front.

No force worth mentioning *behind* this front, which, the next day, was broken?

On May 16 Prime Minister Churchill flew to Paris to find out. By the afternoon, when he drove to the Quai d'Orsay to see Premier Reynaud and General Gamelin, German spearheads were sixty miles west of Sedan, rolling along the undefended open country. Nothing very much stood between them and Paris, or between them and the Channel, but Churchill did not know this. "Where is the strategic reserve?" he asked Gamelin and, breaking into French, "*Où est la masse de manœuvre?*" The Commander in Chief of the Allied armies turned to him with a shake of the head and a shrug and answered, "*Aucune*—there is none."*

"I was dumbfounded," Churchill later related. It was unheard of that a great army, when attacked, held no troops in reserve. "I admit," says Churchill, "that this was one of the greatest surprises I have had in my life."[12]

It was scarcely less a surprise to the German High Command, or at least to Hitler and the generals at OKW if not to Halder. Twice during this campaign in the West, which the Fuehrer himself directed, he hesitated. The first occasion was on May 17 when a crisis of nerves overcame him. That morning Guderian, who was a third of the way to the Channel with his panzer corps, received an order to halt in his tracks. Intelligence had been received from the Luftwaffe that the French were mounting a great counterattack to cut off the thin armored German wedges which extended westward from Sedan. Hitler conferred hastily with his Army Commander in Chief, Brauchitsch, and with Halder. He was certain that a serious French threat was developing from the south. Rundstedt, commander of Army Group A, the main force which had launched the breakthrough over the Meuse, backed him up when they conferred later in the day. He expected, he said, "a great surprise counteroffensive by strong French forces from the Verdun and Châlons-sur-Marne areas."

---

* After the war Gamelin stated that his reply was not "There is none," but "There is no longer any." (*L'Aurore*, Paris, November 21, 1949.)

The specter of a second Marne rose in Hitler's feverish mind. "I am keeping an eye on this," he wrote Mussolini the next day. "The miracle of the Marne of 1914 will not be repeated!"[13]

A very unpleasant day [Halder noted in his diary the evening of May 17]. The Fuehrer is terribly nervous. He is worried over his own success, will risk nothing and insists on restraining us. Puts forward the excuse that it is all because of his concern with the left flank . . . [He] has brought only bewilderment and doubts.

The Nazi warlord showed no improvement during the next day despite the avalanche of news about the French collapse. Halder recorded the crisis in his diary of the eighteenth:

The Fuehrer has an unaccountable worry about the south flank. He rages and screams that we are on the way to ruining the whole operation and that we are courting the danger of a defeat. He won't have any part in continuing the drive westward, let alone southwest, and clings always to the idea of a thrust to the northwest. This is the subject of a most unpleasant dispute between the Fuehrer on the one side and Brauchitsch and me on the other.

General Jodl of OKW, for whom the Fuehrer was nearly always right, also noted the discord at the top.

Day of great tension [he wrote on the eighteenth]. The Commander in Chief of the Army [Brauchitsch] has not carried out the intention of building up as quickly as possible a new flanking position to the south . . . Brauchitsch and Halder are called immediately and ordered peremptorily to adopt the necessary measures immediately.

But Halder had been right; the French had no forces with which to stage a counterattack from the south. And though the panzer divisions, chafing at the bit as they were, received orders to do no more than proceed with "a reconnaissance in force" this was all they needed to press toward the Channel. By the morning of May 19 a mighty wedge of seven armored divisions, driving relentlessly westward north of the Somme River past the storied scenes of battle of the First World War, was only some fifty miles from the Channel. On the evening of May 20, to the surprise of Hitler's headquarters, the 2nd Panzer Division reached Abbeville at the mouth of the Somme. The Belgians, the B.E.F. and three French armies were trapped.

Fuehrer is beside himself with joy [Jodl scribbled in his diary that night]. Talks in words of highest appreciation of the German Army and its leadership. Is working on the peace treaty, which shall express the tenor: return of territory robbed over the last 400 years from the German people, and of other values . . .

A special memorandum is in the files containing the emotion-choked words of the Fuehrer when receiving the telephone report from the Commander in Chief of the Army about the capture of Abbeville.

The only hope of the Allies to extricate themselves from this disastrous encirclement was for the armies in Belgium to immediately turn south-west, disengage themselves from the German Sixth Army attacking them there, fight their way across the German armored wedge that stretched across northern France to the sea and join up with fresh French forces pushing northward from the Somme. This was in fact what General Gamelin ordered on the morning of May 19, but he was replaced that evening by General Maxime Weygand, who immediately canceled the order. Weygand, who had a formidable military reputation gained in the First World War, wanted to confer first with the Allied commanders in Belgium before deciding what to do. As a result, three days were lost before Weygand came up with precisely the same plan as his predecessor. The delay proved costly. There were still forty French, British and Belgian battle-tested divisions in the north, and had they struck south across the thin armored German line on May 19 as Gamelin ordered, they might have succeeded in breaking through. By the time they moved, communications between the various national commands had become chaotic and the several Allied armies, hard pressed as they were, began to act at cross-purposes. At any rate, the Weygand plan existed only in the General's mind; no French troops ever moved up from the Somme.

In the meantime the German High Command had thrown in all the infantry troops that could be rushed up to strengthen the armored gap and enlarge it. By May 24 Guderian's tanks, driving up the Channel from Abbeville, had captured Boulogne and surrounded Calais, the two main ports, and reached Gravelines, some twenty miles down the coast from Dunkirk. The front in Belgium had moved southwestward as the Allies attempted to detach themselves there. By the 24th, then, the British, French and Belgian armies in the north were compressed into a relatively small triangle with its base along the Channel from Gravelines to Terneuzen and its apex at Valenciennes, some seventy miles inland. There was now no hope of breaking out of the trap. The only hope, and it seemed a slim one, was possible evacuation by sea from Dunkirk.

It was at this juncture, on May 24, that the German armor, now within sight of Dunkirk and poised along the Aa Canal between Gravelines and St.-Omer for the final kill, received a strange—and to the soldiers in the field inexplicable—order to halt their advance. It was the first of the German High Command's major mistakes in World War II and became a subject of violent controversy, not only between the German generals themselves but among the military historians, as to who was responsible and why. We shall return to that question in a moment in the light of a mass of material now available. Whatever the reasons for this stop order, it provided a miraculous reprieve to the Allies, and especially to the British, leading as it did to the miracle of Dunkirk. But it did not save the Belgians.

THE CAPITULATION OF KING LEOPOLD

King Leopold III of the Belgians surrendered early on the morning of May 28. The headstrong young ruler, who had taken his country out of its alliance with France and Britain into a foolish neutrality, who had refused to restore the alliance even during the months when he knew the Germans were preparing a massive assault across his border, who at the last moment, after Hitler had struck, called on the French and British for military succor and received it, now deserted them in a desperate hour, opening the dyke for German divisions to pour through on the flank of the sorely pressed Anglo–French troops. Moreover, he did it, as Churchill told the Commons on June 4, "without prior consultation, with the least possible notice, without the advice of his ministers and upon his own personal act."

Actually he did it *against* the unanimous advice of his government, which he was constitutionally sworn to follow. At 5 A.M. on May 25 there was a showdown meeting at the King's headquarters between the monarch and three members of the cabinet, including the Prime Minister and the Foreign Minister. They urged him for the last time not to surrender personally and become a prisoner of the Germans, for if he did he "would be degraded to the role of Hácha" in Prague. They also reminded him that he was head of state as well as Commander in Chief, and that if matters came to the worst he could exercise his first office in exile, as the Queen of Holland and the King of Norway had decided to do, until eventual Allied victory came.

"I have decided to stay," Leopold answered. "The cause of the Allies is lost."[14]

At 5 P.M. on May 27 he dispatched General Derousseaux, Deputy Chief of the Belgian General Staff, to the Germans to ask for a truce. At 10 o'clock the General brought back the German terms: "The Fuehrer demands that arms be laid down unconditionally." The King accepted unconditional surrender at 11 P.M. and proposed that fighting cease at 4 A.M., which it did.

Leopold's capitulation was angrily denounced by Premier Reynaud of France in a violent broadcast, and Belgian Premier Pierlot, also broadcasting from Paris but in a more dignified tone, informed the Belgian people that the King had acted against the unanimous advice of the government, broken his links with the people and was no longer in a position to govern, and that the Belgian government in exile would continue the struggle. Churchill when he spoke in the House on May 28 reserved judgment on Leopold's action but on June 4 joined in the general criticism.

The controversy raged long after the war was over. Leopold's defenders, and there were many in and outside Belgium, believed that he had done he right and honorable thing in sharing the fate of his soldiers and of the Belgian people. And they made much of the claim that the King acted not as chief of state but as Commander in Chief of the Belgian Army in surrendering.

That the battered Belgian troops were in desperate straits by May 27 there is no dispute. Valiantly they had agreed to extend their front in order to free the British and French to fight their way south. And that extended front was fast collapsing though the Belgians fought doggedly. Also Leopold was not told that on May 26 Lord Gort had received orders from London to withdraw to Dunkirk and save what he could of the B.E.F. That is one side of the argument, but there is another. The Belgian Army was under the over-all Allied Command and Leopold made a separate peace without consulting it. In his defense it has been pointed out that on May 27 at 12:30 P.M. he telegraphed Gort that he soon would "be forced to capitulate to avoid a collapse." But the British commander, who was ex'remely busy and constantly on the move, did not receive it. He later testified that he first heard of the surrender only shortly after 11 P.M. on May 27 and found himself "suddenly faced with an open gap of twenty miles between Ypres and the sea through which enemy armored forces might reach the beaches."[15] To General Weygand, who was the King s superior military commander, the news arrived by telegram from French liaison at Belgian headquarters a little after 6 P.M. and it hit him, he later said, "like a bolt out of the blue. There had been no warning . . ."[16]

Finally, even as Commander in Chief of the armed forces, Leopold in this constitutional, democratic monarchy was bound to accept the advice of his government. Neither in that role nor certainly as chief of state did he have the authority to surrender on his own. In the end the Belgian people, as was proper, passed judgment on their sovereign. He was not recalled to the throne from Switzerland, where he took refuge at the war's end, until five years after it was over. When the call came, on July 20, 1950, after 57 per cent of those voting in a referendum had approved it, his return provoked such a violent reaction among the populace that civil war threatened to break out. He soon abdicated in favor of his son.

Whatever may be said of Leopold's behavior, there should be no dispute—though there has been*—about the magnificent way his Army fought. For a few days in May I followed Reichenau's Sixth Army through Belgium and saw for myself the tenacity with which the Belgians struggled against insuperable odds. Not once did they break under the unmerciful and unopposed bombing of the Luftwaffe or when the German armor tried to cut through them. This could not be said of certain other Allied

---

* From, among others, General Sir Alan Brooke, who commanded the British IInd Corps and later became Field Marshal Lord Alanbrooke, Chief of the Imperial General Staff. See Sir Arthur Bryant, *The Turn of the Tide,* based on Alanbrooke's diaries.

troops in that campaign. The Belgians held out for eighteen days and would have held out much longer had not they, like the B.E.F. and the French northern armies, been caught in a trap which was not of their making.

MIRACLE AT DUNKIRK

Ever since May 20, when Guderian's tanks broke through to Abbeville on the sea, the British Admiralty, on the personal orders of Churchill, had been rounding up shipping for a possible evacuation of the B.E.F. and other Allied forces from the Channel ports. Noncombatant personnel and other "useless mouths" began to be ferried across the narrow sea to England at once. By May 24, as we have seen, the Belgian front to the north was near collapse, and to the south the German armor, striking up the coast from Abbeville, after taking Boulogne and enveloping Calais, had reached the Aa Canal only twenty miles from Dunkirk. In between were caught the Belgian Army, the nine divisions of the B.E.F. and ten divisions of the French First Army. Though the terrain on the southern end of the pocket was bad tank country, being crisscrossed with canals, ditches and flooded areas, Guderian's and Reinhardt's panzer corps already had five bridgeheads across the main barrier, the Aa Canal, between Gravelines on the sea and St.-Omer, and were poised for the knockout blow which would hammer the Allied armies against the anvil of the advancing German Sixth and Eighteenth armies pushing down from the northeast and utterly destroy them.

Suddenly on the evening of May 24 came the peremptory order from the High Command, issued at the insistence of Hitler with the prompting of Rundstedt and Goering but over the violent objections of Brauchitsch and Halder, that the tank forces should halt on the canal line and attempt no further advance. This furnished Lord Gort an unexpected and vital reprieve which he and the British Navy and Air Force made the most of and which, as Rundstedt later perceived and said, led "to one of the great turning points of the war."

How did this inexplicable stop order on the threshold of what seemed certain to be the greatest German victory of the campaign come about? What were the reasons for it? And who was responsible? The questions have provoked one of the greatest arguments of the war, among the German generals involved and among the historians. The generals, led by Rundstedt and Halder, have put the blame exclusively on Hitler. Churchill added further fuel to the controversy in the second volume of his war memoirs by contending that the initiative for the order came from Rundstedt and not Hitler and citing as evidence the war diaries of Rundstedt's own headquarters. In the maze of conflicting and contradictory testimony it has been difficult to ascertain the facts. In the course of preparing this chapter the author wrote General Halder himself for further elucidation and promptly received a courteous and detailed reply. On the basis of this and much other evidence now in, certain conclusions may be drawn and the controversy settled, if not conclusively, at least fairly convincingly.

As for responsibility for the famous order, Rundstedt, despite his later assertions to the contrary, must share it with Hitler. The Fuehrer visited the General's Army Group A headquarters at Charleville on the morning of May 24. Rundstedt proposed that the panzer divisions on the canal line before Dunkirk be halted until more infantry could be brought up.* Hitler agreed, observing that the armor should be conserved for later operations against the French south of the Somme. Moreover, he declared that if the pocket in which the Allies were entrapped became too small it would hamper the activities of the Luftwaffe. Probably Rundstedt, with the approval of the Fuehrer, issued the stop order at once, for Churchill notes that the B.E.F. intercepted a German radio message giving orders to that effect at 11:42 that morning.[17] Hitler and Rundstedt were at that moment in conference.

At any rate, that evening Hitler issued the formal order from OKW, both Jodl and Halder noting it in their diaries. The General Staff Chief was most unhappy.

Our left wing, consisting of armor and motorized forces [he wrote in his diary], will thus be stopped dead in its tracks on the direct orders of the Fuehrer! Finishing off the encircled enemy army is to be left to the Air Force!

This exclamation mark of contempt indicates that Goering had intervened with Hitler, and it is now known that he did. He offered to liquidate the entrapped enemy troops with his Air Force alone! The reasons for his

---

* This fact, established from the records of Rundstedt's own headquarters, did not prevent the General from making several statements after the war which put the blame entirely on Hitler. "If I had had my way," he told Major Milton Shulman, a Canadian intelligence officer, "the English would not have got off so lightly at Dunkirk. But my hands were tied by direct orders from Hitler himself. While the English were clambering into the ships off the beaches, I was kept uselessly outside the port unable to move . . . I sat outside the town, watching the English escape, while my tanks and infantry were prohibited from moving. This incredible blunder was due to Hitler's personal idea of generalship." (Shulman, *Defeat in the West*, pp. 42–43.)

To a commission of the International Military Tribunal at Nuremberg on June 20, 1946 (mimeographed transcript, p. 1490), Rundstedt added: "That was a very big mistake of the Commander . . . How angry we leaders were at that time is indescribable." Rundstedt made similar declarations to Liddell Hart (*The German Generals Talk*, pp. 112–13) and to the Nuremberg Military Tribunal in the trial of *United States v. Leeb* (pp. 3350–53, 3931–32, of the mimeographed transcript).

Telford Taylor in *The March of Conquest* and Major L. F. Ellis in *The War in France and Flanders, 1939–40* have analyzed the German Army records of the incident and drawn conclusions that somewhat differ. Ellis' book is the official British account of the campaign and contains both British and German documents. Taylor, who spent four years as an American prosecutor at the Nuremberg trials, is an authority on the German documents.

ambitious and vain proposal were given the writer in the letter from Halder on July 19, 1957.

> During the following days [i.e., after May 24] it became known that Hitler's decision was mainly influenced by Goering. To the dictator the rapid movement of the Army, whose risks and prospects of success he did not understand because of his lack of military schooling, became almost sinister. He was constantly oppressed by a feeling of anxiety that a reversal loomed . . .
>
> Goering, who knew his Fuehrer well, took advantage of this anxiety. He offered to fight the rest of the great battle of encirclement alone with his Luftwaffe, thus eliminating the risk of having to use the valuable panzer formations. He made this proposal . . . for a reason which was characteristic of the unscrupulously ambitious Goering. He wanted to secure for *his* Air Force, after the surprisingly smooth operations of the Army up to then, the decisive final act in the great battle and thus gain the glory of success before the whole world.

General Halder then tells in his letter of an account given him by Brauchitsch after a talk which the latter had with the Luftwaffe Generals Milch and Kesselring in Nuremberg jail in January 1946, in which the Air Force officers declared

> that Goering at that time [May 1940] emphasized to Hitler that if the great victory in battle then developing could be claimed exclusively by the Army generals, the prestige of the Fuehrer in the German homeland would be damaged beyond repair. That could be prevented only if the Luftwaffe and not the Army carried out the decisive battle.

It is fairly clear, then, that Hitler's idea, prompted by Goering and Rundstedt but strenuously opposed by Brauchitsch and Halder, was to let the Air Force and Bock's Army Group B, which, without any armor to speak of, was slowly driving back the Belgians and British southwest to the Channel, mop up the enemy troops in the pocket. Rundstedt's Army Group A, with some seven tank divisions, halted on the water lines west and south of Dunkirk, would merely stand pat and keep the enemy hemmed in. But neither the Luftwaffe nor Bock's army group proved able to achieve their objectives. On the morning of May 26, Halder was fuming in his diary that "these orders from the top just make no sense . . . The tanks are stopped as if they were paralyzed."

Finally, on the evening of May 26, Hitler rescinded the stop order and agreed that, in view of Bock's slow advance in Belgium and the movement of transports off the coast, the armored forces could resume their advance on Dunkirk. By then it was late; the cornered enemy had had time to strengthen his defenses and behind them was beginning to slip away to sea.

We now know that there were political reasons too for Hitler's fatal order. Halder had noted in his diary on May 25, a day, he says, that started "off with one of those painful wrangles between Brauchitsch and the Fuehrer on the next moves in the battle of encirclement," that

now *political* command has formed the fixed idea that the battle of decision must not be fought on Flemish soil, but rather in northern France.

This entry puzzled me and when I wrote to the former General Staff Chief I asked him if he could recall Hitler's *political* reasons for wanting to finish this battle in northern France rather than in Belgium. Halder recalled them very well. "According to my still quite lively memory," he replied, "Hitler, in our talks at the time, supported his reasons for the stop order with two main lines of thought. The first were military reasons: the unsuitable nature of the terrain for tanks, the resulting high losses which would weaken the impending attack on the rest of France, and so on." Then, writes Halder, the Fuehrer cited

a second reason which he knew that we, as soldiers, could not argue against since it was political and not military.

This second reason was that for political reasons he did not want the decisive final battle, which inevitably would cause great damage to the population, to take place in territory inhabited by the Flemish people. He had the intention, he said, of making an independent National Socialist region out of the territory inhabited by the German-descended Flemish, thereby binding them close to Germany. His supporters on Flemish soil had been active in this direction for a long time; he had promised them to keep their land free from the damage of war. If he did not keep this promise now, their confidence in him would be severely damaged. That would be a political disadvantage for Germany which he, as the politically responsible leader, must avoid.

Absurd? If this seems to be another of Hitler's sudden aberrations (Halder writes that he and Brauchitsch were "not convinced by this reasoning"), other political consideration which he confided to other generals were more sane—and important. Describing after the war Hitler's meeting with Rundstedt on May 24, General Guenther Blumentritt, the latter's chief of operations, told Liddell Hart, the British military writer:

Hitler was in very good humor . . . and gave us his opinion that the war would be finished in six weeks. After that he wished to conclude a reasonable peace with France and then the way would be free for an agreement with Britain . . .

He then astonished us by speaking with admiration of the British Empire, of the necessity for its existence, and of the civilization that Britain had brought into the world . . . He said that all he wanted from Britain was that she should acknowledge Germany's position on the continent. The return of Germany's colonies would be desirable but not essential . . . He concluded by saying that his aim was to make peace with Britain on a basis that she would regard as compatible with her honor to accept.[18]

Such thoughts Hitler was to express often during the next few weeks to his generals, to Ciano and Mussolini and finally in public. Ciano was astonished a month later to find the Nazi dictator, then at the zenith of his success, harping about the importance of maintaining the British Empire as "a factor in world equilibrium,"[19] and on July 13 Halder, in his diary, described the Fuehrer as sorely puzzled over Britain's failure to accept peace. To bring England to her knees by force, he told his generals that day, "would not benefit Germany . . . only Japan, the United States and others."

It may be, then, though some doubt it, that Hitler restrained his armored forces before Dunkirk in order to spare Britain a bitter humiliation and thereby facilitate a peace settlement. It would have to be, as he said, a peace in which the British left Germany free to turn once more eastward, this time against Russia. London would have to recognize, as he also said, the Third Reich's domination of the Continent. For the next couple of months Hitler would be confident that such a peace was within his grasp. No more now than in all the years before did he comprehend the character of the British nation or the kind of world its leaders and its people were determined to fight for—to the end.

Nor did he and his generals, ignorant of the sea as they were—and remained—dream that the sea-minded British could evacuate a third of a million men from a small battered port and from the exposed beaches right under their noses.

At three minutes before seven on the evening of May 26, shortly after Hitler's stop order had been canceled, the British Admiralty signaled the beginning of "Operation Dynamo," as the Dunkirk evacuation was called. That night the German armor resumed its attack on the port from the west and south, but now the panzers found it hard going. Lord Gort had had time to deploy against them three infantry divisions with heavy artillery support. The tanks made little progress. In the meantime the evacuation began. An armada of 850 vessels of all sizes, shapes and methods of propulsion, from cruisers and destroyers to small sailboats and Dutch *skoots,* many of them manned by civilian volunteers from the English coastal towns, converged on Dunkirk. The first day, May 27, they took off 7,669 troops; the next day, 17,804; the following day, 47,310; and on May 30, 53,823, for a total of 126,606 during the first four days. This was far more than the Admiralty had hoped to get out. When the operation began it counted on evacuating only about 45,000 men in the two days' time it then thought it would have.

It was not until this fourth day of Operation Dynamo, on May 30, that the German High Command woke up to what was happening. For four days the communiqués of OKW had been reiterating that the encircled enemy armies were doomed. A communiqué of May 29, which I noted in my diary, stated flatly: "The fate of the French army in Artois is sealed . . . The British army, which has been compressed into the territory . . . around Dunkirk, is also going to its destruction before our concentric attack."

But it wasn't; it was going to sea. Without its heavy arms and equipment, to be sure, but with the certainty that the men would live to fight another day.

As late as the morning of May 30, Halder confided confidentially in his diary that "the disintegration of the enemy which we have encircled continues." Some of the British, he conceded, were "fighting with tooth and nail:" the others were "fleeing to the coast and trying to get across the Channel on anything that floats. *Le Débâcle,*" he concluded, alluding to Zola's famous novel of the French collapse in the Franco–Prussian War.

By afternoon, after a session with Brauchitsch, the General Staff Chief had awakened to the significance of the swarms of miserable little boats on which the British were fleeing.

Brauchitsch is angry . . . The pocket would have been closed at the coast if only our armor had not been held back. The bad weather has grounded the Luftwaffe and we must now stand by and watch countless thousands of the enemy get away to England right under our noses.

That was, in fact, what they watched. Despite increased pressure which was immediately applied by the Germans on all sides of the pocket, the British lines held and more troops were evacuated. The next day, May 31, was the biggest day of all. Some 68,000 men were embarked for England, a third of them from the beaches, the rest from the Dunkirk harbor. A total of 194,620 men had now been taken out, more than four times the number originally hoped for.

Where was the famed Luftwaffe? Part of the time, as Halder noted, it was grounded by bad weather. The rest of the time it encountered unexpected opposition from the Royal Air Force, which from bases just across the Channel successfully challenged it for the first time.* Though outnumbered, the new British Spitfires proved more than a match for the Messerschmitts and they mowed down the cumbersome German bombers. On a few occasions Goering's planes arrived over Dunkirk between British sorties and did such extensive damage to the port that for a time it was unusable and the troops had to be lifted exclusively from the beaches. The Luftwaffe also pressed several strong attacks on the shipping and ac-

---

* A good many of the exhausted Tommies on the beaches, who underwent severe bombings, were not aware of this, since the air clashes were often above the clouds or some distance away. They knew only that they had been bombed and strafed all the way back from eastern Belgium to Dunkirk, and they felt their Air Force had let them down. When they reached the home ports some of them insulted men in the blue R.A.F. uniforms. Churchill was much aggrieved at this and went out of his way to put them right when he spoke in the House on June 4. The deliverance at Dunkirk, he said, "was gained by the Air Force."

counted for most of the 243—out of 861—vessels sunk. But it failed to achieve what Goering had promised Hitler: the annihilation of the B.E.F. On June 1, when it carried out its heaviest attack (and suffered its heaviest losses—each side lost thirty planes), sinking three British destroyers and a number of small transports, the second-highest day's total was evacuated —64,429 men. By dawn of the next day, only 4,000 British troops remained in the perimeter, protected by 100,000 French who now manned the defenses.

Medium German artillery had in the meantime come within range and daytime evacuation operations had to be abandoned. The Luftwaffe at that time did not operate after dark and during the nights of June 2 and 3 the remainder of the B.E.F. and 60,000 French troops were successfully brought out. Dunkirk, still defended stubbornly by 40,000 French soldiers, held out until the morning of June 4. By that day 338,226 British and French soldiers had escaped the German clutches. They were no longer an army; most of them, understandably, were for the moment in a pitiful shape. But they were battle-tried; they knew that if properly armed and adequately covered from the air they could stand up to the Germans. Most of them, when the balance in armament was achieved, would prove it—and on beaches not far down the Channel coast from where they had been rescued.

A deliverance Dunkirk was to the British. But Churchill reminded them in the House on June 4 that "wars are not won by evacuations." The predicament of Great Britain was indeed grim, more dangerous than it had been since the Norman landings nearly a millennium before. It had no army to defend the islands. The Air Force had been greatly weakened in France. Only the Navy remained, and the Norwegian campaign had shown how vulnerable the big fighting ships were to land-based aircraft. Now the Luftwaffe bombers were based but five or ten minutes away across the narrow Channel. France, to be sure, still held out below the Somme and the Aisne. But its best troops and armament had been lost in Belgium and in northern France, its small and obsolescent Air Force had been largely destroyed, and its two most illustrious generals, Marshal Pétain and General Weygand, who now began to dominate the shaky government, had no more stomach for battle against such a superior foe.

These dismal facts were very much on the mind of Winston Churchill when he rose in the House of Commons on June 4, 1940, while the last transports from Dunkirk were being unloaded, determined, as he wrote later, to show not only his own people but the world—and especially the U.S.A.—"that our resolve to fight on was based on serious grounds." It was on this occasion that he uttered his famous peroration, which will be long remembered and will surely rank with the greatest ever made down the ages:

Even though large tracts of Europe and many old and famous States have fallen or may fall into the grip of the Gestapo and all the odious apparatus of

Nazi rule, we shall not flag or fail. We shall go on to the end, we shall fight in France, we shall fight in the seas and oceans, we shall fight with growing confidence and growing strength in the air, we shall defend our island, whatever the cost may be, we shall fight on the beaches, we shall fight on the landing grounds, we shall fight in the fields and in the streets, we shall fight in the hills; we shall never surrender, and even if, which I do not for a moment believe, this island or a large part of it were subjugated and starving, then our Empire beyond the seas, armed and guarded by the British Fleet, would carry on the struggle, until, in God's good time, the New World, with all its power and might, steps forth to the rescue and the liberation of the Old.

THE COLLAPSE OF FRANCE

The determination of the British to fight on does not seem to have troubled Hitler's thoughts. He was sure they would see the light after he had finished off France, which he now proceeded to do. The morning after Dunkirk fell, on June 5, the Germans launched a massive assault on the Somme and soon they were attacking in overwhelming strength all along a 400-mile front that stretched across France from Abbeville to the Upper Rhine. The French were doomed. Against 143 German divisions, including ten armored, they could deploy only 65 divisions, most of them second-rate, for the best units and most of the armor had been expended in Belgium. Little was left of the weak French Air Force. The British could contribute but one infantry division, which had been in the Saar, and parts of an armored division. The R.A.F. could spare few planes for this battle unless it were to leave the British Isles themselves defenseless. Finally, the French High Command, now dominated by Pétain and Weygand, had become sodden with defeatism. Nevertheless some French units fought with great bravery and tenacity, temporarily stopping even the German armor here and there, and standing up resolutely to the incessant pounding of the Luftwaffe.

But it was an unequal struggle. In "victorious confusion," as Telford Taylor has aptly put it, the German troops surged across France like a tidal wave, the confusion coming because there were so many of them and they were moving so fast and often getting in each other's way.[20] On June 10 the French government hastily departed Paris and on June 14 the great city, the glory of France, which was undefended, was occupied by General von Kuechler's Eighteenth Army. The swastika was immediately hoisted on the Eiffel Tower. On June 16, Premier Reynaud, whose government had fled to Bordeaux, resigned and was replaced by Pétain, who the next day asked the Germans, through the Spanish ambassador, for an armistice.* Hitler replied the same day that he would first have to con-

---

* On this day, June 17, 1940, the exiled Kaiser sent from Doorn, in occupied Holland, a telegram of congratulations to Hitler, whom he had for so long scorned as a vulgar upstart. It was found among the captured Nazi papers.

Under the deeply moving impression of the capitulation of France I consult his ally, Mussolini. For this strutting warrior, after making sure that the French armies were hopelessly beaten, had, like a jackal, hopped into the war on June 10, to try to get in on the spoils.

THE DUCE PLUNGES HIS SMALL DAGGER
INTO FRANCE'S BACK

Despite his preoccupation with the unfolding of the Battle of the West, Hitler had found time to write Mussolini at surprisingly frequent intervals, keeping him informed of the mounting German victories.

After the first letter on May 7, apprising the Duce that he was attacking Belgium and Holland "to ensure their neutrality" and saying he would keep his friend informed of his progress so that the Duce could make his own decisions in time, there were further ones on May 13, 18 and 25, each more detailed and enthusiastic than the other.[22] Though the generals, as Halder's diary confirms, couldn't have cared less what Italy did—whether it came into the war or not—the Fuehrer for some reason attached importance to Italian intervention. As soon as the Netherlands and Belgium had surrendered and the Anglo–French northern armies had been smashed and the surviving British troops began taking to the boats at Dunkirk, Mussolini decided to slither into the war. He informed Hitler by letter on May 30 that the date would be June 5. Hitler replied immediately that he was "most profoundly moved."

If there could still be anything which could strengthen my unshakable belief in the victorious outcome of this war [Hitler wrote on May 31] it was your statement . . . The mere fact of your entering the war is an element calculated to deal the front of our enemies a staggering blow.

The Fuehrer asked his ally, however, to postpone his date for three days—he wanted to knock out the rest of the French Air Force first, he said—and Mussolini obliged by setting it back five days, to June 10. Hostilities, the Duce said, would begin the following day.

---

gratulate you and the whole German Wehrmacht on the mighty victory granted by God, in the words of the Emperor Wilhelm the Great in 1870: "What a turn of events brought about by divine dispensation."

In all German hearts there echoes the Leuthen chorale sung by the victors of Leuthen, the soldiers of the Great King: "Now thank we all our God!"

Hitler, who believed that the mighty victory was due more to himself than to God, drafted a restrained reply, but whether it was ever sent is not indicated in the documents.[21]

The Fuehrer had been furious a little earlier when he learned that a German unit which overran Doorn had posted a guard of honor around the exiled Emperor's residence. Hitler ordered the guard removed and Doorn posted as out of bounds to all German soldiers. Wilhelm II died at Doorn on June 4, 1941, and was buried there. His death, Hassell noted in his diary (p. 200), "went almost unnoticed" in Germany. Hitler and Goebbels saw to that.

They did not amount to much. By June 18, when Hitler summoned his junior partner to Munich to discuss an armistice with France, some thirty-two Italian divisions, after a week of "fighting," had been unable to budge a scanty French force of six divisions on the Alpine front and farther south along the Riviera, though the defenders were now threatened by assault in the rear from the Germans sweeping down the Rhone Valley.* On June 21 Ciano noted in his diary:

Mussolini is quite humiliated because our troops have not moved a step forward. Even today they have not succeeded in advancing and have halted in front of the first French fortification which put up some resistance.[23]

The hollowness of Mussolini's boasted military might was exposed at the very beginning and this put the deflated Italian dictator in a dour mood as he and Ciano set out by train on the evening of June 17 to confer with Hitler about the armistice with France.

Mussolini dissatisfied [Ciano wrote in his diary]. This sudden peace disquiets him. During the trip we speak at length in order to clarify conditions under which the armistice is to be granted to the French. The Duce . . . would like to go so far as the total occupation of French territory and demands the surrender of the French fleet. But he is aware that his opinion has only a consultative value. The war has been won by Hitler without any active military participation on the part of Italy, and it is Hitler who will have the last word. This naturally disturbs and saddens Mussolini.

The mildness of the Fuehrer's "last word" came as a distinct shock to the Italians when they conferred with the Nazi warlord at the Fuehrerhaus at Munich where Chamberlain and Daladier had been so accommodating to the two dictators regarding Czechoslovakia less than two years before. The secret German memorandum of the meeting[24] makes clear that Hitler was determined above all not to allow the French fleet to fall into the hands of the British. He was also concerned lest the French government flee to North Africa or to London and continue the war. For that reason the armistice terms—the final terms of peace might be something else—would have to be moderate, designed to keep "a French government functioning on French soil" and "the French fleet neutralized." He abruptly dismissed Mussolini's demands for the Italian occupation of the Rhone Valley, including Toulon (the great French Mediterranean naval base, where most of the fleet was concentrated) and Marseilles, and the disarmament of Corsica, Tunisia and Djibouti. The last town, the

---

* The defeatist French High Command forbade any offensive action against Italy. On June 14 a French naval squadron bombarded factories, oil tanks and refineries near Genoa, but Admiral Darlan prohibited any further action of this kind. When the R.A.F. tried to send bombers from the airfield at Marseilles to attack Milan and Turin the French drove trucks onto the field and prevented the planes from taking off.

gateway to Italian-held Ethiopia, was thrown in by Ciano, the German notes say, "in an undertone."

Even the bellicose Ribbentrop, Ciano found, was "exceptionally moderate and calm, and in favor of peace." The warrior Mussolini was "very much embarrassed," his son-in-law noted.

He feels that his role is secondary . . . In truth, the Duce fears that the hour of peace is growing near and sees fading once again that unattainable dream of his life: glory on the field of battle.[25]

Mussolini was unable even to get Hitler to agree to joint armistice negotiations with the French. The Fuehrer was not going to share his triumph at a very historic spot (he declined to name it to his friend) with this Johnny-come-lately. But he promised the Duce that his armistice with France would not come into effect until the French had also signed one with Italy.

Mussolini left Munich bitter and frustrated, but Ciano had been very favorably impressed by a side of Hitler which his diaries make clear he had not previously seen or suspected.

From all that he [Hitler] says [he wrote in his diary as they returned to Rome] it is clear that he wants to act quickly to end it all. Hitler is now the gambler, who has made a big scoop and would like to get up from the table, risking nothing more. Today he speaks with a reserve and a perspicacity which, after such a victory, are really astonishing. I cannot be accused of excessive tenderness toward him, but today I truly admire him.[26]

THE SECOND ARMISTICE AT COMPIEGNE

I followed the German Army into Paris that June, always the loveliest of months in the majestic capital, which was now stricken, and on June 19 got wind of where Hitler was going to lay down his terms for the armistice which Pétain had requested two days before. It was to be on the same spot where the German Empire had capitulated to France and her allies on November 11, 1918: in the little clearing in the woods at Compiègne. There the Nazi warlord would get his revenge, and the place itself would add to the sweetness of it for him. On May 20, a bare ten days after the great offensive in the West had started and on the day the German tanks reached Abbeville, the idea had come to him. Jodl noted it in his diary that day: "Fuehrer is working on the peace treaty . . . First negotiations in the Forest of Compiègne." Late on the afternoon of June 19 I drove out there and found German Army engineers demolishing the wall of the museum where the old *wagon-lit* of Marshal Foch, in which the 1918 armistice was signed, had been preserved. By the time I left, the engineers, working with pneumatic drills, had torn the wall down and were pulling the car out to the tracks in the center of the clearing on the exact spot, they said, where it had stood at 5 A.M. on November 11, 1918, when at the dictation of Foch the German emissaries put their signatures to the armistice.

And so it was that on the afternoon of June 21 I stood by the edge of the forest at Compiègne to observe the latest and greatest of Hitler's triumphs, of which, in the course of my work, I had seen so many over the last turbulent years. It was one of the loveliest summer days I ever remember in France. A warm June sun beat down on the stately trees—elms, oaks, cypresses and pines—casting pleasant shadows on the wooded avenues leading to the little circular clearing. At 3:15 P.M. precisely, Hitler arrived in his big Mercedes, accompanied by Goering, Brauchitsch, Keitel, Raeder, Ribbentrop and Hess, all in their various uniforms, and Goering, the lone Field Marshal of the Reich, fiddling with his field marshal's baton. They alighted from their automobiles some two hundred yards away, in front of the Alsace-Lorraine statue, which was draped with German war flags so that the Fuehrer could not see (though I remembered from previous visits in happier days) the large sword, the sword of the victorious Allies of 1918, sticking through a limp eagle representing the German Empire of the Hohenzollerns. Hitler glanced at the monument and strode on.

I observed his face [I wrote in my diary]. It was grave, solemn, yet brimming with revenge. There was also in it, as in his springy step, a note of the triumphant conqueror, the defier of the world. There was something else . . . a sort of scornful, inner joy at being present at this great reversal of fate—a reversal he himself had wrought.

When he reached the little opening in the forest and his personal standard had been run up in the center of it, his attention was attracted by a great granite block which stood some three feet above the ground.

Hitler, followed by the others, walks slowly over to it [I am quoting my diary], steps up, and reads the inscription engraved (in French) in great high letters:

"HERE ON THE ELEVENTH OF NOVEMBER 1918 SUCCUMBED THE CRIMINAL PRIDE OF THE GERMAN EMPIRE—VANQUISHED BY THE FREE PEOPLES WHICH IT TRIED TO ENSLAVE."

Hitler reads it and Goering reads it. They all read it, standing there in the June sun and the silence. I look for the expression in Hitler's face. I am but fifty yards from him and see him through my glasses as though he were directly in front of me. I have seen that face many times at the great moments of his life. But today! It is afire with scorn, anger, hate, revenge, triumph.

He steps off the monument and contrives to make even this gesture a masterpiece of contempt. He glances back at it, contemptuous, angry—angry, you almost feel, because he cannot wipe out the awful, provoking lettering with one sweep of his high Prussian boot.* He glances slowly around the clearing, and now, as his eyes meet ours, you grasp the depth of his hatred. But there is triumph there too—revengeful, triumphant hate. Suddenly, as though his face were not giving quite complete expression to his feelings, he throws his whole body into harmony with his mood. He swiftly snaps his hands on his hips, arches his shoulders, plants his feet wide apart. It is a magnificent gesture of defiance, of burning contempt for this place now and all that it has stood for in the twenty-two years since it witnessed the humbling of the German Empire.

Hitler and his party then entered the armistice railway car, the Fuehrer seating himself in the chair occupied by Foch in 1918. Five minutes later the French delegation arrived, headed by General Charles Huntziger, commander of the Second Army at Sedan, and made up of an admiral, an Air Force general and one civilian, Léon Noël, the former ambassador to Poland, who was now witnessing his second debacle wrought by German arms. They looked shattered, but retained a tragic dignity. They had not been told that they would be led to this proud French shrine to undergo such a humiliation, and the shock was no doubt just what Hitler had calculated. As Halder wrote in his diary that evening after being given an eyewitness account by Brauchitsch:

> The French had no warning that they would be handed the terms at the very site of the negotiations in 1918. They were apparently shaken by this arrangement and at first inclined to be sullen.

Perhaps it was natural, even for a German so cultivated as Halder, or Brauchitsch, to mistake solemn dignity for sullenness. The French, one saw at once, were certainly dazed. Yet, contrary to the reports at the time, they tried, as we now know from the official German minutes of the meetings found among the captured Nazi secret papers,[27] to soften the harsher portions of the Fuehrer's terms and to eliminate those which they thought were dishonorable. But they tried in vain.

Hitler and his entourage left the *wagon-lit* as soon as General Keitel had read the preamble of the armistice terms to the French, leaving the negotiations in the hands of his OKW Chief, but allowing him no leeway in departing from the conditions which he himself had laid down.

Huntziger told the Germans at once, as soon as he had read them, that they were "hard and merciless," much worse than those which France had handed Germany here in 1918. Moreover, if "another country beyond the Alps, which had not defeated France (Huntziger was too contemptuous of Italy even to name her), advanced similar demands France would in no circumstances submit. She would fight to the bitter end . . .

---

* It was blown up three days later, at Hitler's command.

It was therefore impossible for him to put his signature to the German armistice agreement . . ."

General Jodl, the Number Two officer at OKW, who presided temporarily at this moment, had not expected such defiant words from a hopelessly beaten foe and replied that though he could not help express his "understanding" for what Huntziger had said about the Italians nevertheless he had no power to change the Fuehrer's terms. All he could do, he said, was "to give explanations and clear up obscure points." The French would have to take the armistice document or leave it, as it was.

The Germans had been annoyed that the French delegation had arrived without authority to conclude an armistice except with the express agreement of the government at Bordeaux. By a miracle of engineering and perhaps with some luck they succeeded in setting up a telephone connection from the old sleeping car right through the battle lines, where the fighting still continued, to Bordeaux. The French delegates were authorized to use it to transmit the text of the armistice terms and to discuss it with their government. Dr. Schmidt, who served as interpreter, was directed to listen in on the tapped conversations from an Army communications van a few yards away behind a clump of trees. The next day I myself contrived to hear the German recording of part of the conversation between Huntziger and General Weygand.

To the credit of the latter, who bears a grave responsibility for French defeatism and the final surrender and the break with Britain, it must be recorded that he at least strenuously objected to many of the German demands. One of the most odious of them obligated the French to turn over to the Reich all anti-Nazi German refugees in France and in her territories. Weygand called this dishonorable in view of the French tradition of the right of asylum, but when it was discussed the next day the arrogant Keitel would not listen to its being deleted. "The German émigrés," he shouted, were "the greatest warmongers." They had "betrayed their own people." They must be handed over "at all costs." The French made no protest against a clause which stated that all their nationals caught fighting with another country against Germany would be treated as "francs-tireurs"—that is, immediately shot. This was aimed against De Gaulle, who was already trying to organize a Free French force in Britain, and both Weygand and Keitel knew it was a crude violation of the primitive rules of war. Nor did the French question a paragraph which provided for all prisoners of war to remain in captivity until the conclusion of peace. Weygand was sure the British would be conquered within three weeks and the French POWs thereafter released. Thus he condemned a million and a half Frenchmen to war prison camps for five years.

The crux of the armistice treaty was the disposal of the French Navy. Churchill, as France tottered, had offered to release her from her pledge not to make a separate peace if the French Navy were directed to sail for British ports. Hitler was determined that this should not take place; he fully realized, as he told Mussolini on June 18, that it would immeasurably strengthen Britain. With so much at stake he had to make a concession, or at least a promise, to the beaten foe. The armistice agreement stipulated that the French fleet would be demobilized and disarmed and the ships laid up in their home ports. In return for this

the German Government solemnly declares to the French Government that it does not intend to use for its own purposes in the war the French fleet which is in ports under German supervision. Furthermore, they solemnly and expressly declare that they have no intention of raising any claim to the French war fleet at the time of the conclusion of peace.

Like almost all of Hitler's promises, this one too would be broken.

Finally, Hitler left the French government an unoccupied zone in the south and southeast in which it ostensibly was free to govern. This was an astute move. It would not only divide France itself geographically and administratively; it would make difficult if not impossible the formation of a French government-in-exile and quash any plans of the politicians in Bordeaux to move the seat of government to French North Africa—a design which almost succeeded, being defeated in the end not by the Germans but by the French defeatists: Pétain, Weygand, Laval and their supporters. Moreover, Hitler knew that the men who had now seized control of the French government at Bordeaux were enemies of French democracy and might be expected to be co-operative in helping him set up the Nazi New Order in Europe.

Yet on the second day of the armistice negotiations at Compiègne the French delegates continued to bicker and delay. One reason for the delay was that Huntziger insisted that Weygand give him not an authorization to sign but an order—no one in France wanted to take the responsibility. Finally, at 6:30 P.M. Keitel issued an ultimatum. The French must accept or reject the German armistice terms within an hour. Within the hour the French government capitulated. At 6:50 P.M. on June 22, 1940, Huntziger and Keitel signed the armistice treaty.*

I listened to the last scene as it was picked up by the hidden microphones in the *wagon-lit*. Just before he signed, the French General, his voice quivering, said he wished to make a personal statement. I took it down in French, as he spoke.

I declare that the French Government has ordered me to sign these terms of armistice . . . Forced by the fate of arms to cease the struggle in which we were engaged on the side of the Allies, France sees imposed on her very hard conditions. France has the right to expect in the future negotiations that Germany show a spirit which will permit the two great neighboring countries to live and work in peace.

---

* It was stipulated that it would go into effect as soon as the Franco–Italian armistice was signed, and that hostilities would cease six hours after that event.

Those negotiations—for a peace treaty—would never take place, but the spirit which the Nazi Third Reich would have shown, if they had, soon became evident as the occupation became harsher and the pressure on the servile Pétain regime increased. France was now destined to become a German vassal, as Pétain, Weygand and Laval apparently believed—and accepted.

A light rain began to fall as the delegates left the armistice car and drove away. Down the road through the woods you could see an unbroken line of refugees making their way home on weary feet, on bicycles, on carts, a few fortunate ones on old trucks. I walked out to the clearing. A gang of German Army engineers, shouting lustily, had already started to move the old *wagon-lit*.

"Where to?" I asked.

"To Berlin," they said.*

The Franco–Italian armistice was signed in Rome two days later. Mussolini was able to occupy only what his troops had conquered, which meant a few hundred yards of French territory, and to impose a fifty-mile demilitarized zone opposite him in France and Tunisia. The armistice was signed at 7:35 P.M. on June 24. Six hours later the guns in France lapsed into silence.

France, which had held out unbeaten for four years the last time, was out of the war after six weeks. German troops stood guard over most of Europe, from the North Cape above the Arctic Circle to Bordeaux, from the English Channel to the River Bug in eastern Poland. Adolf Hitler had reached the pinnacle. The former Austrian waif, who had been the first to unite the Germans in a truly national State, this corporal of the First World War, had now become the greatest of German conquerors. All that stood between him and the establishment of German hegemony in Europe under his dictatorship was one indomitable Englishman, Winston Churchill, and the determined people Churchill led, who did not recognize defeat when it stared them in the face and who now stood alone, virtually unarmed, their island home besieged by the mightiest military machine the world had ever seen.

HITLER PLAYS FOR PEACE

Ten days after the German onslaught on the West began, on the evening German tanks reached Abbeville, General Jodl, after describing in his diary how the Fuehrer was "beside himself with joy," added: ". . . is working on the peace treaty . . . Britain can get a separate peace any time after restitution of the colonies." That was May 20. For several weeks thereafter Hitler seems to have had no doubts that, with France

---

* It arrived there July 8. Ironically, it was destroyed in an Allied bombing of Berlin later in the war.

knocked out, Britain would be anxious to make peace. His terms, from the German point of view, seemed most generous, considering the beating the British had taken in Norway and in France. He had expounded them to General von Rundstedt on May 24, expressing his admiration of the British Empire and stressing the "necessity" for its existence. All he wanted from London, he said, was a free hand on the Continent.

So certain was he that the British would agree to this that even after the fall of France he made no plans for continuing the war against Britain, and the vaunted General Staff, which supposedly planned with Prussian thoroughness for every contingency far in advance, did not bother to furnish him any. Halder, the Chief of the General Staff, made no mention of the subject at this time in his voluminous diary entries. He was more disturbed about Russian threats in the Balkans and the Baltic than about the British.

Indeed, why should Great Britain fight on alone against helpless odds? Especially when it could get a peace that would leave it, unlike France, Poland and all the other defeated lands, unscathed, intact and free? This was a question asked everywhere except in Downing Street, where, as Churchill later revealed, it was never even discussed, because the answer was taken for granted.[28] But the German dictator did not know this, and when Churchill began to state it publicly—that Britain was not quitting— Hitler apparently did not believe it. Not even when on June 4, after the evacuation from Dunkirk, the Prime Minister had made his resounding speech about fighting on in the hills and on the beaches; not even when on June 18, after Pétain had asked for an armistice, Churchill reiterated in the Commons Britain's "inflexible resolve to continue the war" and in another one of his eloquent and memorable perorations concluded:

Let us therefore brace ourselves to our duties, and so bear ourselves that, if the British Empire and its Commonwealth last for a thousand years, men will say: "This was their finest hour."

These could be merely soaring words from a gifted orator, and so Hitler, a dazzling orator himself, must have thought. He must have been encouraged too by soundings in neutral capitals and by the appeals for ending the war that now emanated from them. On June 28 a confidential message arrived for Hitler from the Pope—analogous communications were addressed to Mussolini and Churchill—offering his mediation for "a just and honorable peace" and declaring that before initiating this step he wished to ascertain confidentially how it would be received.[29] The King of Sweden was also active in proposing peace to both London and Berlin.

In the United States the German Embassy, under the direction of Hans Thomsen, the chargé d'affaires, was spending every dollar it could lay its hands on to support the isolationists in keeping America out of the war and thus discourage Britain from continuing it. The captured German

Foreign Office documents are full of messages from Thomsen reporting on the embassy's efforts to sway American public opinion in Hitler's favor. The party conventions were being held that summer and Thomsen was bending every effort to influence their foreign-policy planks, especially that of the Republicans.

On June 12, for example, he cabled Berlin in code "most urgent, top secret" that a "well-known Republican Congressman," who was working "closely" with the German Embassy, had offered, for $3,000, to invite fifty isolationist Republican Congressmen to the Republican convention "so that they may work on the delegates in favor of an isolationist foreign policy." The same individual, Thomsen reported, wanted $30,000 to help pay for full-page advertisements in the American newspapers, to be headed "Keep America Out of the War!"*[30]

The next day Thomsen was wiring Berlin about a new project he said he was negotiating through an American literary agent to have five well-known American writers write books "from which I await great results." For this project he needed $20,000, a sum Ribbentrop okayed a few days later.†[31]

One of Hitler's first public utterances about his hopes for peace with Britain had been given Karl von Wiegand, a Hearst correspondent, and published in the New York *Journal-American* on June 14. A fortnight later Thomsen informed the German Foreign Office that he had printed 100,000 extra copies of the interview and that

I was able furthermore through a confidential agent to induce the isolationist Representative Thorkelson [Republican of Montana] to have the Fuehrer interview inserted in the *Congressional Record* of June 22. This assures the interview once more the widest distribution.[33]

The Nazi Embassy in Washington grasped at every straw. At one point during the summer its press attaché was forwarding what he said was a suggestion of Fulton Lewis, Jr., the radio commentator, whom he de-

---

* Such an advertisement appeared in the New York *Times* June 25, 1940.
† By July 5, 1940, Thomsen had become so apprehensive about his payments that he cabled Berlin for permission to destroy all receipts and accounts:

> The payments . . . are made to the recipients through trusted go-betweens, but in the circumstances it is obvious that no receipts can be expected . . . Such receipts or memoranda would fall into the hands of the American Secret Service if the Embassy were suddenly to be seized by American authorities, and despite all camouflage, by the fact of their existence alone, they would mean political ruin and have other grave consequences for our political friends, who are probably known to our enemies . . .
>
> I therefore request that the Embassy be authorized to destroy these receipts and statements and henceforth dispense with making them, as also with keeping accounts of such payments.

This telegraphic report has been destroyed.[32]

scribed as an admirer of "Germany and the Fuehrer and a highly respected American journalist."

The Fuehrer should address telegrams to Roosevelt . . . reading approximately as follows: "You, Mr. Roosevelt, have repeatedly appealed to me and always expressed the wish that a sanguinary war be avoided. I did not declare war on England; on the contrary I always stressed that I did not wish to destroy the British Empire. My repeated requests to Churchill to be reasonable and to arrive at an honorable peace treaty were stubbornly rejected by Churchill. I am aware that England will suffer severely when I order total war to be launched against the British Isles. I ask you therefore to approach Churchill on your part and prevail upon him to abandon his senseless obstinacy." Lewis added that Roosevelt would, of course, make a rude and spiteful reply; that would make no difference. Such an appeal would surely make a profound impression on the North American people and especially in South America . . .[34]

Adolf Hitler did not take Mr. Lewis' purported advice, but the Foreign Office in Berlin cabled to ask how important the radio commentator was in America. Thomsen replied that Lewis had "enjoyed a particular success of late . . . [but that] on the other hand, in contrast to some leading American commentators, no political importance is to be attached to L."*[35]

---

* The doings of the German Embassy in Washington at this period, as disclosed in its own dispatches which are published in *Documents on German Foreign Policy*, would furnish the material for a revealing book. One is struck by the tendency of the German diplomats to tell the Nazi dictator pretty much what he wanted to hear —a practice common among representatives of totalitarian lands. Two officers of OKW told me in Berlin that the High Command, or at least the General Staff, was highly suspicious of the objectivity of the reports from the Washington embassy and that they had established their own military intelligence in the United States.

They were not served very well by General Friedrich von Boetticher, the German military attaché in Washington, if one can judge by his dispatches included in the *DGFP* volumes. He never tired of warning OKW and the general staffs of the Army and Air Force to whom his messages were addressed, that America was controlled by the Jews and the Freemasons, which was exactly what Hitler thought. Boetticher also overestimated the influence of the isolationists in American politics, especially of Colonel Charles A. Lindbergh, who emerges in his dispatches as his great hero. An extract or two indicates the tenor of his reports.

July 20, 1940: . . . As the exponent of the Jews, who especially through Freemasonry control the broad masses of the American people, Roosevelt wants England to continue fighting and the war to be prolonged . . . The circle about Lindbergh has become aware of this development and now tries at least to impede the fatal control of American policy by the Jews . . . I have repeatedly reported on the mean and vicious campaign against Lindbergh, whom the Jews fear as their most potent adversary . . . [*DGFP*, X, pp. 254–55.]

August 6, 1940: . . . The background of Lindbergh's re-emergence in public and the campaign against him.

The Jewish element now controls key positions in the American armed forces, after having in the last weeks filled the posts of Secretary of War, Assistant Secre-

Churchill himself, as he related later in his memoirs, was somewhat troubled by the peace feelers emanating through Sweden, the United States and the Vatican and, convinced that Hitler was trying to make the most of them, took stern measures to counter them. Informed that the German chargé in Washington, Thomsen, had been attempting to talk with the British ambassador there, he cabled that "Lord Lothian should be told on no account to make any reply to the German Chargé d'Affaires' message."[36]

To the King of Sweden, who had urged Great Britain to accept a peace settlement, the grim Prime Minister drafted a strong reply.

. . . Before any such requests or proposals could even be considered, it would be necessary that effective guarantees by deeds, not words, should be forthcoming from Germany which would ensure the restoration of the free and independent life of Czechoslovakia, Poland, Norway, Denmark, Holland, Belgium and above all, France . . .*[37]

---

tary of War, and Secretary of the Navy with subservient individuals and attached a leading and very influential Jew, "Colonel" Julius Ochs-Adler, as secretary to the Secretary of War.

The forces opposing the Jewish element and the present policy of the United States have been mentioned in my reports, taking account also of the importance of the General Staff. The greatly gifted Lindbergh, whose connections reach very far, is much the most important of them all. The Jewish element and Roosevelt fear the spiritual and, particularly, the moral superiority and purity of this man.

On Sunday [August 4] Lindbergh delivered a blow that will hurt the Jews. He . . . stressed that America should strive for sincere collaboration with Germany with a view to peace and the preservation of Western culture. Several hours later, the aged General Pershing, who has long been a puppet in the hands of Roosevelt, which means of the Jews, read over the radio a declaration, foisted upon him by the wire-pullers, to the effect that America would be imperiled by England's defeat . . .

The chorus of the Jewish element casting suspicion on Lindbergh in the press, and his denunciation by a Senator . . . Lucas, who spoke against Lindbergh over the radio Monday night at Roosevelt's behest . . . as a "fifth columnist," that is, a traitor, merely serve to underline the fear of the spiritual power of this man, about whose progress I have reported since the beginning of the war and in whose great importance for future German–American relations I believe. [*DGFP*, X, pp. 413–15.]

On September 18, Thomsen, in a further report, gave an account of a confidential conversation he said had taken place between Lindbergh and several American General Staff officers. Lindbergh gave it as his opinion that England would soon collapse before German air attacks. The General Staff officers, however, held that Germany's air strength was not sufficient to force a decision. (*DGFP*, X, pp. 413–15.)

On October 19, 1938, three weeks after Munich, Lindbergh had been awarded— and had accepted—the "Service Cross of the German Eagle with Star." This was, I believe, the second highest German decoration, usually conferred on distinguished foreigners who, in the official words of the citations, "deserved well of the Reich."
* There are in the *DGFP* volumes several dispatches to the German Foreign Office about alleged contacts with various British diplomats and personages, sometimes direct, sometimes through neutrals such as the Franco Spaniards. Prince Max von Hohenlohe, the Sudeten-German Anglophile, reported to Berlin on his conversa-

That was the nub of Churchill's case and apparently no one in London dreamt of compromising it by concluding a peace that would preserve Britain but permanently enslave the countries Hitler had conquered. But this was not comprehended in Berlin, where, as I recall those summer days, everyone, especially in the Wilhelmstrasse and the Bendlerstrasse, was confident that the war was as good as over.

All through the last fortnight of June and the first days of July, Hitler waited for word from London that the British government was ready to throw in the sponge and conclude peace. On July 1 he told the new Italian ambassador, Dino Alfieri,* that he "could not conceive of anyone in England still seriously believing in victory."[38] Nothing had been done in the High Command about continuing the war against Britain.

But the next day, July 2, the first directive on that subject was finally issued by OKW. It was a hesitant order.

The Fuehrer and Supreme Commander has decided:
That a landing in England is possible, providing that air superiority can be attained and certain other necessary conditions fulfilled. The date of commencement is still undecided. All preparations to be begun immediately.

Hitler's lukewarm feeling about the operation and his belief that it would not be necessary is reflected in the concluding paragraph of the directive.

All preparations must be undertaken on the basis that the invasion is still only a plan, and has not yet been decided upon.[39]

When Ciano saw the Fuehrer in Berlin on July 7, he got the impression, as he noted in his diary, that the Nazi warlord was having trouble making up his mind.

---

tions with the British minister in Switzerland, Sir David Kelly, and with the Aga Khan. He claimed the latter had asked him to relay the following message to the Fuehrer:

The Khedive of Egypt, who is also here, had agreed with him that on the day when the Fuehrer puts up for the night in Windsor, they would drink a bottle of champagne together . . . If Germany or Italy were thinking of taking over India, he would place himself at our disposal . . . The struggle against England was not a struggle against the English people but against the Jews. Churchill had been for years in their pay and the King was too weak and limited . . . If he were to go with these ideas to England, Churchill would lock him up. . . . [*DGFP*, X, pp. 294–95.]

It must be kept in mind that these are German reports and may not be true at all, but they are what Hitler had to go on. The Nazi plan to enlist the Duke of Windsor, indeed the plot to kidnap him and then try to use him, as disclosed in the Foreign Office secret papers, is noted later.

* Attolico had been replaced by Alfieri at the instigation of Ribbentrop in May.

He is rather inclined to continue the struggle and to unleash a storm of wrath and of steel upon the English. But the final decision has not been reached, and it is for this reason that he is delaying his speech, of which, as he himself puts it, he wants to weigh every word.[40]

On July 11 Hitler began assembling his military chiefs on the Obersalzberg to see how they felt about the matter. Admiral Raeder, whose Navy would have to ferry an invading army across the Channel, had a long talk with the Fuehrer on that date. Neither of them was eager to come to grips with the problem—in fact, they spent most of their time together discussing the matter of developing the naval bases at Trondheim and Narvik in Norway.

The Supreme Commander, judging by Raeder's confidential report of the meeting,[41] was in a subdued mood. He asked the Admiral whether he thought his planned speech to the Reichstag "would be effective." Raeder replied that it would be, especially if it were preceded by a "concentrated" bombing attack on Britain. The Admiral, who reminded his chief that the R.A.F. was carrying out "damaging attacks" on the principal German naval bases at Wilhelmshaven, Hamburg and Kiel, thought the Luftwaffe ought to get busy immediately on Britain. But on the question of invasion, the Navy Commander in Chief was distinctly cool. He urgently advised that it be attempted "only as a last resort to force Britain to sue for peace."

He [Raeder] is convinced that Britain can be made to ask for peace simply by cutting off her import trade by means of submarine warfare, air attacks on convoys and heavy air attacks on her main centers. . . .

The C. in C., Navy [Raeder], cannot for his part therefore advocate an invasion of Britain as he did in the case of Norway . . .

Whereupon the Admiral launched into a long and detailed explanation of all the difficulties involved in such an invasion, which must have been most discouraging to Hitler. Discouraging but perhaps also convincing. For Raeder reports that "the Fuehrer also views invasion as a last resort." Two days later, on July 13, the generals arrived at the Berghof above Berchtesgaden to confer with the Supreme Commander. They found him still baffled by the British. "The Fuehrer," Halder jotted in his diary that evening, "is obsessed with the question why England does not yet want to take the road to peace." But now, for the first time, one of the reasons had begun to dawn on him. Halder noted it.

He sees, just as we do, the solution of this question in the fact that England is still setting her hope in Russia. Thus he too expects that England will have to be compelled by force to make peace. He does not like to do such a thing, however. Reasons: If we smash England militarily, the British Empire will disintegrate. Germany, however, would not profit from this. With German blood we would achieve something from which only Japan, America and others will derive profit.

On the same day, July 13, Hitler wrote Mussolini, declining with thanks the Duce's offer to furnish Italian troops and aircraft for the invasion of Britain. It is clear from this letter that the Fuehrer was at last beginning to make up his mind. The strange British simply wouldn't listen to reason.

I have made to Britain so many offers of agreement, even of co-operation, and have been treated so shabbily [he wrote] that I am now convinced that any new appeal to reason would meet with a similar rejection. For in that country at present it is not reason that rules . . .[42]

Three days later, on July 16, the warlord finally reached a decision. He issued "Directive No. 16 on the Preparation of a Landing Operation against England."[43]

TOP SECRET

Fuehrer's Headquarters
July 16, 1940

Since England, despite her militarily hopeless situation, still shows no sign of willingness to come to terms, I have decided to prepare a landing operation against England, and if necessary to carry it out.

The aim of this operation is to eliminate the English homeland as a base for the carrying on of the war against Germany, and, if it should become necessary, to occupy it completely.

The code name for the assault was to be "Sea Lion." Preparations for it were to be completed by mid-August.

"If necessary to carry it out." Despite his growing instinct that it would be necessary, he was not quite sure, as the directive shows. The "if" was still a big one as Adolf Hitler rose in the Reichstag on the evening of July 19 to make his final peace offer to Britain. It was the last of his great Reichstag speeches and the last of so many in this place down the years that this writer would hear. It was also one of his best. I put down my impressions of it that same evening.

The Hitler we saw in the Reichstag tonight was the conqueror and conscious of it, and yet so wonderful an actor, so magnificent a handler of the German mind, that he mixed superbly the full confidence of the conqueror with the humbleness which always goes down so well with the masses when they know a man is on top. His voice was lower tonight; he rarely shouted as he usually does; and he did not once cry out hysterically as I've seen him do so often from this rostrum.

To be sure, his long speech was swollen with falsifications of history and liberally sprinkled with personal insults of Churchill. But it was moderate in tone, considering the glittering circumstances, and shrewdly conceived to win the support not only of his own people but of the neutrals and to give the masses in England something to think about.

From Britain [he said] I now hear only a single cry—not of the people but of the politicians—that the war must go on! I do not know whether these politicians already have a correct idea of what the continuation of this struggle will be like. They do, it is true, declare that they will carry on with the war and that, even if Great Britain should perish, they would carry on from Canada. I can hardly believe that they mean by this that the people of Britain are to go to Canada. Presumably only those gentlemen interested in the continuation of their war will go there. The people, I am afraid, will have to remain in Britain and . . . will certainly regard the war with other eyes than their so-called leaders in Canada.

Believe me, gentlemen, I feel a deep disgust for this type of unscrupulous politician who wrecks whole nations. It almost causes me pain to think that I should have been selected by fate to deal the final blow to the structure which these men have already set tottering . . . Mr. Churchill . . . no doubt will already be in Canada, where the money and children of those principally interested in the war have already been sent. For millions of other people, however, great suffering will begin. Mr. Churchill ought perhaps, for once, to believe me when I prophesy that a great Empire will be destroyed—an Empire which it was never my intention to destroy or even to harm . . .

Having thus tilted at the dogged Prime Minister and attempted to detach the British people from him, Hitler came to the point of his lengthy speech.

In this hour I feel it to be my duty before my own conscience to appeal once more to reason and common sense in Great Britain as much as elsewhere. I consider myself in a position to make this appeal since I am not the vanquished begging favors, but the victor speaking in the name of reason.

I can see no reason why this war must go on. *

---

* There was a colorful scene and one unprecedented in German history when Hitler suddenly broke off his speech in the middle to award field marshals' batons to twelve generals and a special king-size one to Goering, who was given the newly created rank of Reich Marshal of the Greater German Reich, which put him above all the others. He was also awarded the Grand Cross of the Iron Cross, the only one given during the entire war. Halder was passed over in this avalanche of field marshal awards, being merely promoted one grade, from lieutenant general to general. This promiscuous award of field-marshalships—the Kaiser had named only five field marshals from the officer corps during all of World War I and not even Ludendorff had been made one—undoubtedly helped to stifle any latent opposition to Hitler among the generals such as had threatened to remove him on at least three occasions

He was not more specific than that. He made no concrete suggestions for peace terms, no mention of what was to happen to the hundred million people now under the Nazi yoke in the conquered countries. But there were few if any in the Reichstag that evening who believed that it was necessary at this stage to go into the details. I mingled with a good many officials and officers at the close of the session and not one of them had the slightest doubt, as they said, that the British would accept what they really believed was a very generous and even magnanimous offer from the Fuehrer. They were not for long to be deceived.

I drove directly to the Rundfunk to make a broadcast report of the speech to the United States. I had hardly arrived at Broadcasting House when I picked up a BBC broadcast in German from London. It was giving the British answer to Hitler already—within the hour. It was a determined *No!**

Junior officers from the High Command and officials from various ministries were sitting around the room listening with rapt attention. Their faces fell. They could not believe their ears. "Can you make it out?" one of them shouted to me. He seemed dazed. "Can you understand those British fools?" he continued to bellow. "To turn down peace now? They're crazy!"

The same evening Ciano† heard the reaction to the crazy English on a much higher level in Berlin than mine. "Late in the evening," he noted in his diary, "when the first cold English reactions to the speech arrive, a sense of ill-concealed disappointment spreads among the Germans." The effect on Mussolini, according to Ciano, was just the opposite.

He . . . defines it "a much too cunning speech." He fears that the English may find in it a pretext to begin negotiations. That would be sad for Mussolini, because now more than ever he wants war.[44]

The Duce, as Churchill later remarked, "need not have fretted himself. He was not to be denied all the war he wanted."[45]

---

in the past. In achieving this and in debasing the value of the highest military rank by raising so many to it, Hitler acted shrewdly to tighten his hold over the generals. Nine Army generals were promoted to field marshal: Brauchitsch, Keitel, Rundstedt, Bock, Leeb, List, Kluge, Witzleben and Reichenau; and three Luftwaffe officers: Milch, Kesselring and Sperrle.

* Churchill later declared that this immediate and brusque rejection of Hitler's peace offer was made "by the BBC without any prompting from H. M. Government as soon as Hitler's speech was heard over the radio." (Churchill, *Their Finest Hour,* p. 260.)

† The Italian Foreign Minister had behaved like a clown during the Reichstag session, bobbing up and down like a jack-in-the-box to give the Fascist salute every time Hitler paused for breath. I also noticed Quisling, a pig-eyed little man, crouching in a corner seat in the first balcony. He had come to Berlin to beg the Fuehrer to reinstate him in power in Oslo.

"As a manuever calculated to rally the German people for the fight against Britain," I wrote in my diary that night, "Hitler's speech was a masterpiece. For the German people will now say: 'Hitler offers England peace, and no strings attached. He says he sees no reason why this war should go on. If it does, it's England's fault.' "

And was that not the principal reason for giving it, three days after he had issued Directive No. 16 to prepare the invasion of Britain? He admitted as much—beforehand—to two Italian confidants, Alfieri and Ciano. On July 1 he had told the ambassador:

. . . It was always a good tactic to make the enemy responsible in the eyes of public opinion in Germany and abroad for the future course of events. This strengthened one's own morale and weakened that of the enemy. An operation such as the one Germany was planning would be very bloody . . . Therefore one must convince public opinion that everything had first been done to avoid this horror . . .

In his speech of October 6 [when he had offered peace to the West at the conclusion of the Polish campaign—W.L.S.] he had likewise been guided by the thought of making the opposing side responsible for all subsequent developments. He had thereby won the war, as it were, before it had really started. Now again he intended for psychological reasons to buttress morale, so to speak, for the action about to be taken.[46]

A week later, on July 8, Hitler confided to Ciano that

he would stage another demonstration so that in case the war should continue—which he thought was the only real possibility that came into question—he might achieve a psychological effect among the English people . . . Perhaps it would be possible by a skillful appeal to the English people to isolate the English Government still further in England.[47]

It did not prove possible. The speech of July 19 worked with the German people, but not with the British. On July 22 Lord Halifax in a broadcast made the rejection of Hitler's peace offer official. Though it had been expected, it somehow jolted the Wilhelmstrasse, where I found many angry faces that afternoon. "Lord Halifax," the official government spokesman told us, "has refused to accept the peace offer of the Fuehrer. Gentlemen, there will be war!"

It was easier said than done. In truth neither Hitler, the High Command nor the general staffs of the Army, Navy and Air Force had ever seriously considered how a war with Great Britain could be fought and won. Now in the midsummer of 1940 they did not know what to do with their glittering success; they had no plans and scarcely any will for exploiting the greatest military victories in the history of their soldiering nation. This is one of the great paradoxes of the Third Reich. At the very moment when Hitler stood at the zenith of his military power, with most of the European Continent at his feet, his victorious armies stretched from the Pyrenees to the Arctic Circle, from the Atlantic to beyond the Vistula, rested now and ready for further action, he had no idea how to go on and bring the war to a victorious conclusion. Nor had his generals, twelve of whom now bandied field marshals' batons.

There is, of course, a reason for this, although it was not clear to us at the time. The Germans, despite their vaunted military talents, lacked any grand strategic concept. Their horizons were limited—they had always been limited—to *land warfare* against the neighboring nations on the European Continent. Hitler himself had a horror of the sea* and his great captains almost a total ignorance of it. They were land-minded, not sea-minded. And though their armies could have crushed in a week the feeble land forces of Britain if they had only been able to come to grips with them, even the narrow waters of the Dover Straits which separated the two—so narrow that you can see across to the opposite shore—loomed in their minds, as the splendid summer began to wane, as an obstacle they knew not how to overcome.

There was of course another alternative open to the Germans. They might bring Britain down by striking across the Mediterranean with their Italian ally, taking Gibraltar at its western opening and in the east driving on from Italy's bases in North Africa through Egypt and over the canal to Iran, severing one of the Empire's main life lines. But this necessitated vast operations overseas at distances far from home bases, and in 1940 it seemed beyond the scope of the German imagination.

Thus at the height of dizzy success Hitler and his captains hesitated. They had not thought out the next step and how it was to be carried through. This fateful neglect would prove to be one of the great turning points of the war and indeed of the short life of the Third Reich and of the meteoric career of Adolf Hitler. Failure, after so many stupendous victories, was now to set in. But this, to be sure, could not be foreseen as beleaguered Britain, now holding out alone, girded herself with what small means she had for the German onslaught at the summer's end.

---

* "On land I am a hero, but on water I am a coward," he told Rundstedt once. (Shulman, *Defeat in the West*, p. 50.)

22

OPERATION SEA LION: THE THWARTED

INVASION OF BRITAIN

"THE FINAL GERMAN VICTORY over England is now only a question of time," General Jodl, Chief of Operations at OKW, wrote on June 30, 1940. "Enemy offensive operations on a large scale are no longer possible."

Hitler's favorite strategist was in a confident and complacent mood. France had capitulated the week before, leaving Britain alone and apparently helpless. On June 15 Hitler had informed the generals that he wanted the Army partially demobilized—from 160 to 120 divisions. "The assumption behind this," Halder noted in his diary that day, "is that the task of the Army is fulfilled. The Air Force and Navy will be given the mission of carrying on alone the war against England."

In truth, the Army showed little interest in it. Nor was the Fuehrer himself much concerned. On June 17 Colonel Walter Warlimont, Jodl's deputy, informed the Navy that "with regard to the landing in Britain, the Fuehrer . . . has not up to now expressed such an intention . . . Therefore, even at this time, no preparatory work of any kind [has] been carried out in OKW."[1] Four days later, on June 21, at the very moment Hitler was entering the armistice car at Compiègne to humble the French, the Navy was informed that the "Army General Staff is not concerning itself with the question of England. Considers execution impossible. Does not know how operation is to be conducted from southern area . . . General Staff rejects the operation."[2]

None of the gifted planners in any of the three German armed services knew how Britain was to be invaded, though it was the Navy, not unnaturally, which had first given the matter some thought. As far back as November 15, 1939, when Hitler was trying vainly to buck up his generals to launch an attack in the West, Raeder instructed the Naval War Staff to examine "the possibility of invading England, a possibility arising if certain conditions are fulfilled by the further course of the war."[3] It was the first time in history that any German military staff had been asked even to consider such an action. It seems likely that Raeder took this step largely because he wanted to anticipate any sudden aberration of his unpredictable Leader. There is no record that Hitler was consulted or knew anything about it. The furthest his thoughts went at this time was to get airfields and naval bases in Holland, Belgium and France for the tightening of the blockade against the British Isles.

By December 1939, the Army and Luftwaffe high commands were also giving some thought to the problem of invading Britain. Rather nebulous ideas of the three services were exchanged, but they did not get very far. In January 1940, the Navy and Air Force rejected an Army plan as unrealistic. To the Navy it did not take into account British naval power; to the Luftwaffe it underestimated the R.A.F. "In conclusion," remarked the Luftwaffe General Staff in a communication to OKH, "a combined operation with a landing in England as its object must be rejected."[4] Later, as we shall see, Goering and his aides were to take a quite contrary view.

The first mention in the German records that Hitler was even facing the possibility of invading Britain was on May 21, the day after the armored forces drove through to the sea at Abbeville. Raeder discussed "in private" with the Fuehrer "the possibility of a later landing in England." The source of this information is Admiral Raeder,[5] whose Navy was not sharing in the glory of the astounding victories of the Army and Air Force in the West and who, understandably, was seeking means of bringing his service back into the picture. But Hitler's thoughts were on the battle of encirclement to the north and on the Somme front then forming to the south. He did not trouble his generals with matters beyond these two immediate tasks.

The naval officers, however, with little else to do, continued to study the problem of invasion, and by May 27 Rear Admiral Kurt Fricke, Chief of the Naval War Staff Operations Division, came up with a fresh plan entitled *Studie England*. Preliminary work was also begun on rounding up shipping and developing landing craft, the latter of which the Germany Navy was entirely bereft. In this connection Dr. Gottfried Feder, the economic crank who had helped Hitler draft the party program in the early Munich days and who was now a State Secretary in the Ministry of Economics, where his crackpot ideas were given short shrift, produced plans for what he called a "war crocodile." This was a sort of self-propelled barge made of concrete which could carry a company of two hundred men with full equipment or several tanks or pieces of artillery, roll up on any beach and provide cover for the disembarking troops and vehicles. It was taken quite seriously by the Naval Command and even by Halder, who mentioned it in his diary, and was discussed at length by Hitler and Raeder on June 20. But nothing came of it in the end.

To the admirals nothing seemed to be coming of an invasion of the British Isles as June approached its end. Following his appearance at Compiègne on June 21, Hitler went off with some old cronies to do the sights of Paris briefly* and then to visit the battlefields, not of this war but of the first war, where he had served as a dispatch runner. With him was his tough top sergeant of those days, Max Amann, now a millionaire Nazi publisher. The future course of the war—specifically, how to continue the fight against Britain—seemed the least of his concerns, or perhaps it was merely that he believed that this little matter was already settled, since the British would now come to "reason" and make peace.

Hitler did not return to his new headquarters, Tannenberg, west of Freudenstadt in the Black Forest, until the twenty-ninth of June. The next day, coming down to earth, he mulled over Jodl's paper on what to do next. It was entitled "The Continuation of the War against England."[6] Though Jodl was second only to Keitel at OKW in his fanatical belief in the Fuehrer's genius, he was, when left alone, usually a prudent strategist. But now he shared the general view at Supreme Headquarters that the war was won and almost over. If Britain didn't realize it, a little more force would have to be supplied to remind her. For the "siege" of England, his memorandum proposed three steps: intensification of the German air and sea war against British shipping, storage depots, factories and the R.A.F.; "terror attacks against the centers of population"; "a landing of troops with the objective of occupying England."

Jodl recognized that "the fight against the British Air Force must have top priority." But, on the whole, he thought this as well as other aspects of the assault could be carried out with little trouble.

Together with propaganda and periodic terror attacks, announced as reprisals, this increasing weakening of the basis of food supply *will paralyze and finally break the will of the people to resist, and thereby force its government to capitulate.*†

As for a landing, it could

only be contemplated after Germany has gained control of the air. A landing, therefore, should not have as its objective the military conquest of England, a task that could be left to the Air Force and Navy. Its aim should rather be to administer the deathblow [*Todesstoss*] to an England already economically paralyzed and no longer capable of fighting in the air, if this is still necessary.‡

However, thought Jodl, all this might not be necessary.

---

* And to gaze down at the tomb of Napoleon at the Invalides. "That," he told his faithful photographer, Heinrich Hoffmann, "was the greatest and finest moment of my life."
† The emphasis is Jodl's.
‡ Jodl also suggested the possibility of "extending the war to the periphery"—that is, attacking the British Empire with the help not only of Italy but of Japan, Spain and Russia.

Since England can no longer fight for victory, but only for the preservation of its possessions and its world prestige she should, according to all predictions, be inclined to make peace when she learns that she can still get it now at relatively little cost.

This was what Hitler thought too and he immediately set to work on his peace speech for the Reichstag. In the meantime, as we have seen, he ordered (July 2) some preliminary planning for a landing and on July 16, when no word of "reason" had come from London, issued Directive No. 16 for Sea Lion. At last, after more than six weeks of hesitation, it was decided to invade Britain, "if necessary." This, as Hitler and his generals belatedly began to realize, would have to be a major military operation, not without its risks and depending for success on whether the Luftwaffe and the Navy could prepare the way for the troops against a far superior British Navy and a by no means negligible enemy Air Force.

Was Sea Lion a serious plan? And was it seriously intended that it should be carried out?

To this day many have doubted it and they have been reinforced in their opinions by the chorus from the German generals after the war. Rundstedt, who was in command of the invasion, told Allied investigators in 1945:

The proposed invasion of England was nonsense, because adequate ships were not available . . . We looked upon the whole thing as a sort of game because it was obvious that no invasion was possible when our Navy was not in a position to cover a crossing of the Channel or carry reinforcements. Nor was the German Air Force capable of taking on these functions if the Navy failed . . . I was always very skeptical about the whole affair . . . I have a feeling that the Fuehrer never really wanted to invade England. He never had sufficient courage . . . He definitely hoped that the English would make peace . . .[7]

Blumentritt, Rundstedt's chief of operations, expressed similar views to Liddell Hart after the war, claiming that "among ourselves we talked of it [Sea Lion] as a bluff."[8]

I myself spent a few days at the middle of August on the Channel, snooping about from Antwerp to Boulogne in search of the invasion army. On August 15, at Calais and at Cap Gris-Nez, we saw swarms of German bombers and fighters heading over the Channel toward England on what turned out to be the first massive air assault. And while it was evident that the Luftwaffe was going all out, the lack of shipping and especially of invasion barges in the ports and in the canals and rivers behind them left me with the impression that the Germans *were* bluffing. They simply did not have the means, so far as I could see, of getting their troops across the Channel.

But one reporter can see very little of a war and we know now that the

Germans did not begin to assemble the invasion fleet until September 1. As for the generals, anyone who read their interrogations or listened to them on cross-examination at the Nuremberg trials learned to take their postwar testimony with more than a grain of salt.* The trickiness of man's memory is always considerable and the German generals were no exception to this rule. Also they had many axes to grind, one of the foremost being to discredit Hitler's military leadership. Indeed, their principal theme, expounded at dreary length in their memoirs and in their interrogations and trial testimony, was that if they had been left to make the decisions Hitler never would have led the Third Reich to defeat.

Unfortunately for them, but fortunately for posterity and the truth, the mountainous secret German military files leave no doubt that Hitler's plan to invade Britain in the early fall of 1940 was deadly serious and that, though given to many hesitations, the Nazi dictator seriously intended to carry it out if there were any reasonable chance of success. Its ultimate fate was settled not by any lack of determination or effort but by the fortunes of war, which now, for the first time, began to turn against him.

On July 17, the day after Directive No. 16 was issued to prepare the invasion and two days before the Fuehrer's "peace" speech in the Reichstag, the Army High Command (OKH) allocated the forces for Sea Lion and ordered thirteen picked divisions to the jumping-off places on the Channel coast for the first wave of the invasion. On the same day the Army Command completed its detailed plan for a landing on a broad front on the south coast of England.

The main thrust here, as in the Battle of France, would be carried out by Field Marshal von Rundstedt (as he would be titled on July 19) as commander of Army Group A. Six infantry divisions of General Ernst Busch's Sixteenth Army were to embark from the Pas de Calais and hit the beaches between Ramsgate and Bexhill. Four divisions of General Adolf Strauss's Ninth Army would cross the Channel from the area of Le Havre and land between Brighton and the Isle of Wight. Farther to the west three divisions of Field Marshal von Reichenau's Sixth Army (from Field Marshal von Bock's Army Group B), taking off from the Cherbourg peninsula, would be put ashore in Lyme Bay, between Weymouth and Lyme Regis. Altogether 90,000 men would form the first wave; by the third day the High Command planned on putting ashore a total of 260,000 men. Airborne forces would help out after being dropped at Lyme Bay and other areas. An armored force of no less than six panzer divisions, reinforced by three motorized divisions, would follow in the second wave and in a few days it was planned to have ashore a total of thirty-nine divisions plus two airborne divisions.

Their task was as follows. After the bridgeheads had been secured, the

---

* Even so astute a military critic as Liddell Hart neglected always to do so, and this neglect mars his book *The German Generals Talk*. Talk they did, but not always with very good memories or even very truthfully.

divisions of Army Group A in the southeast would push forward to the first objective, a line running between Gravesend and Southampton. Reichenau's Sixth Army would advance north to Bristol, cutting off Devon and Cornwall. The second objective would be a line between Maldon on the east coast north of the Thames estuary to the Severn River, blocking off Wales. "Heavy battles with strong British forces" were expected to develop at about the time the Germans reached their first objective. But they would be quickly won, London surrounded, and the drive northward resumed.[9] Brauchitsch told Raeder on July 17 that the whole operation would be finished in a month and would be relatively easy.*[10]

But Raeder and the Naval High Command were skeptical. An operation of such size on such a broad front—it stretched over two hundred miles from Ramsgate to Lyme Bay—was simply beyond the means of the German Navy to convoy and protect. Raeder so informed OKW two days later and brought it up again on July 21 when Hitler summoned him, Brauchitsch and General Hans Jeschonnek (Chief of the Luftwaffe General Staff) to a meeting in Berlin. The Fuehrer was still confused about "what is going on in England." He appreciated the Navy's difficulties but stressed the importance of ending the war as soon as possible. For the invasion forty divisions would be necessary, he said, and the "main operation" would have to be completed by September 15. On the whole the warlord was in an optimistic mood despite Churchill's refusal at that very moment to heed his peace appeal.

England's situation is hopeless [Halder noted Hitler as saying]. The war has been won by us. A reversal of the prospects of success is impossible.[11]

But the Navy, faced with the appalling task of transporting a large army across the choppy Channel in the face of a vastly stronger British Navy and of an enemy Air Force that seemed still rather active, was not so sure. On July 29 the Naval War Staff drew up a memorandum advising

---

* German intelligence overestimated British strength on the ground throughout July, August and September by about eight divisions. Early in July the German General Staff estimated British strength at from fifteen to twenty divisions "of fighting value." Actually there were twenty-nine divisions in England at this time but not more than half a dozen of much "fighting value," as they had practically no armor or artillery. But contrary to widespread belief at the time, which has lingered to this day, the British Army by the middle of September would have been a match for the German divisions then allocated for the first wave of invasion. By that time it had ready to meet an attack on the south coast a force of sixteen well-trained divisions, of which three were armored, with four divisions plus an armored brigade covering the east coast from the Thames to the Wash. This represented a remarkable recovery after the debacle at Dunkirk, which had left Britain virtually defenseless on land in June.

British intelligence of the German plans was extremely faulty and for the first three months of the invasion threat almost completely wrong. Throughout the summer, Churchill and his military advisers remained convinced that the Germans would make their main landing attempt on the east coast and it was here that the bulk of the British land forces were concentrated until September.

"against undertaking the operation this year" and proposing that "it be considered in May 1941 or thereafter."[12]

Hitler, however, insisted on considering it on July 31, 1940, when he again summoned his military chiefs, this time to his villa on the Obersalzberg. Besides Raeder, Keitel and Jodl were there from OKW and Brauchitsch and Halder from the Army High Command. The Grand Admiral, as he now was, did most of the talking. He was not in a very hopeful mood.

September 15, he said, would be the earliest date for Sea Lion to begin, and then only if there were no "unforeseen circumstances due to the weather or the enemy." When Hitler inquired about the weather problem Raeder responded with a lecture on the subject that grew quite eloquent and certainly forbidding. Except for the first fortnight in October the weather, he explained, was "generally bad" in the Channel and the North Sea; light fog came in the middle of that month and heavy fog at the end. But that was only part of the weather problem. "The operation," he declared, "can be carried out only if the sea is *calm*." If the water were rough, the barges would sink and even the big ships would be helpless, since they could not unload supplies. The Admiral grew gloomier with every minute that he contemplated what lay ahead.

Even if the first wave crosses successfully [he went on] under favorable weather conditions, there is *no* guarantee that the same favorable weather will carry through the second and third waves . . . As a matter of fact, we must realize that no traffic worth mentioning will be able to cross for several days, until certain harbors can be utilized.

That would leave the Army in a fine pickle, stranded on the beaches without supplies and reinforcements. Raeder now came to the main point of the differences between the Army and the Navy. The Army wanted a broad front from the Straits of Dover to Lyme Bay. But the Navy simply couldn't provide the ships necessary for such an operation against the expected strong reaction of the British Navy and Air Force. Raeder therefore argued strongly that the front be shortened—to run only from the Dover Straits to Eastbourne. The Admiral saved his clincher for the end.

"*All things considered,*" he said, "*the best time for the operation would be May 1941.*"

But Hitler did not want to wait that long. He conceded that "naturally" there was nothing they could do about the weather. But they had to consider the consequences of losing time. The German Navy would not be any stronger vis-à-vis the British Navy by spring. The British Army at the moment was in poor shape. But give it another eight to ten months and it would have from thirty to thirty-five divisions, which was a considerable force in the restricted area of the proposed invasion. Therefore his decision (according to the confidential notes made by both Raeder and Halder)[13] was as follows:

Diversions in Africa should be studied. But the decisive result can be achieved only by an attack on England. An attempt must therefore be made to prepare the operation for September 15, 1940 . . . The decision as to whether the operation is to take place in September or is to be delayed until May 1941, will be made after the Air Force has made concentrated attacks on southern England for one week. If the effect of the air attacks is such that the enemy air force, harbors and naval forces, etc. are heavily damaged, Operation Sea Lion will be carried out in 1940. Otherwise it is to be postponed until May 1941.

All now depended on the Luftwaffe.

The next day, August 1, Hitler issued as a consequence two directives from OKW, one signed by himself, the other by Keitel.

Fuehrer's Headquarters
August 1, 1940

TOP SECRET

Directive No. 17 for the Conduct of Air and Naval Warfare against England

In order to establish the conditions necessary for the final conquest of England, I intend to continue the air and naval war against the English homeland more intensively than heretofore.

To this end I issue the following orders:

1. The German Air Force is to overcome the British Air Force with all means at its disposal and as soon as possible . . .

2. After gaining temporary or local air superiority the air war is to be carried out against harbors, especially against establishments connected with food supply . . . Attacks on the harbors of the south coast are to be undertaken on the smallest scale possible, in view of our intended operations. . . .

4. The Luftwaffe is to stand by in force for Operation Sea Lion.

5. I reserve for myself the decision on terror attacks as a means of reprisal.

6. The intensified air war may commence on or after August 6 . . . The Navy is authorized to begin the projected intensified naval warfare at the same time.

ADOLF HITLER[14]

The directive signed by Keitel on behalf of Hitler the same day read in part:

TOP SECRET

Operation Sea Lion

The C. in C., Navy, having reported on July 31 that the necessary preparations for Sea Lion could not be completed before September 15, the Fuehrer has ordered:

Preparations for Sea Lion are to be continued and completed by the Army and Air Force by September 15.

Eight to fourteen days after the launching of the air offensive against Britain, scheduled to begin about August 5, the Fuehrer will decide whether the invasion will take place this year or not; his decision will depend largely on the outcome of the air offensive . . .

In spite of the Navy's warning that it can guarantee only the defense of a narrow strip of coast (as far west as Eastbourne), preparations are to be continued for the attack on a broad basis, as originally planned . . .[15]

The last paragraph only served to inflame the feud between the Army and Navy over the question of a long or a short invasion front. A fortnight before, the Naval War Staff had estimated that to fulfill the demands of the Army for landing 100,000 men with equipment and supplies in the first wave, along a 200-mile front from Ramsgate to Lyme Bay, would necessitate rounding up 1,722 barges, 1,161 motorboats, 471 tugs and 155 transports. Even if it were possible to assemble such a vast amount of shipping, Raeder told Hitler on July 25, it would wreck the German economy, since taking away so many barges and tugs would destroy the whole inland-waterway transportation system, on which the economic life of the country largely depended.[16] At any rate, Raeder made it clear, the protection of such an armada trying to supply such a broad front against the certain attacks of the British Navy and Air Force was beyond the powers of the German naval forces. At one point the Naval War Staff warned the Army that if it insisted on the broad front, the Navy might lose *all* of its ships.

But the Army persisted. Overestimating British strength as it did, it argued that to land on a narrow front would confront the attackers with a "superior" British land force. On August 7 there was a showdown between the two services when Halder met his opposite number in the Navy, Admiral Schniewind, the Chief of the Naval War Staff. There was a sharp and dramatic clash.

"I utterly reject the Navy's proposal," the Army General Staff Chief, usually a very calm man, fumed. "From the point of view of the Army I regard it as complete suicide. I might just as well put the troops that have landed straight through a sausage machine!"

According to the Naval War Staff's record of the meeting* Schniewind replied that it would be "equally suicidal" to attempt to transport the troops for such a broad front as the Army desired, "in view of British naval supremacy."

It was a cruel dilemma. If a broad front with the large number of

---

* In his diary entry that evening Halder did not quote himself as above. He declared, however, that "the talk led only to the confirmation of an unbridgeable gap." The Navy, he said, was "afraid of the British High Seas Fleet and maintained that a defense against this danger by the Luftwaffe was impossible." Obviously by this time the German Navy, if not the Army, had few illusions about the striking power of Goering's Air Force.

troops to man it was attempted, the whole German expedition might be sunk at sea by the British Navy. If a short front, with correspondingly fewer troops, was adopted, the invaders might be hurled back into the sea by the British Army. On August 10 Brauchitsch, the Commander in Chief of the Army, informed OKW that he "could not accept" a landing between Folkestone and Eastbourne. However, he was willing, albeit "very reluctantly," to abandon the landing at Lyme Bay in order to shorten the front and meet the Navy halfway.

This was not enough for the hardheaded admirals, and their caution and stubbornness were beginning to have an effect at OKW. On August 13 Jodl drafted an "appreciation" of the situation, laying down five conditions for the success of Sea Lion that seemingly would have struck the generals and admirals as almost ludicrous had their dilemma not been so serious. First, he said, the British Navy would have to be eliminated from the south coast, and second, the R.A.F. would have to be eliminated from the British skies. The other conditions concerned the landing of troops in a strength and with a rapidity that were obviously far beyond the Navy's powers. If these conditions were not fulfilled, he considered the landing "an act of desperation which would have to be carried out in a desperate situation, but which we have no cause to carry out now."[17]

If the Navy's fears were spreading to Jodl, the OKW Operations Chief's hesitations were having their effect on Hitler. All through the war the Fuehrer leaned much more heavily on Jodl than on the Chief of OKW, the spineless, dull-minded Keitel. It is not surprising, then, that on August 13, when Raeder saw the Supreme Commander in Berlin and requested a decision on the broad versus the narrow front, Hitler was inclined to agree with the Navy on the smaller operation. He promised to make a definite ruling the next day after he had seen the Commander in Chief of the Army.[18] After hearing Brauchitsch's views on the fourteenth, Hitler finally made up his mind, and on the sixteenth an OKW directive signed by Keitel declared that the Fuehrer had decided to abandon the landing in Lyme Bay, which Reichenau's Sixth Army was to have made. Preparations for landings on the narrower front on September 15 were to be continued, but now, for the first time, the Fuehrer's own doubts crept into a secret directive. "Final orders," it added, "will not be given until the situation is clear." The new order, however, was somewhat of a compromise. For a further directive that day enlarged the narrower front.

Main crossing to be on narrow front. Simultaneous landing of four to five thousand troops at Brighton by motorboats and the same number of airborne troops at Deal-Ramsgate. In addition, on D-minus-1 Day the Luftwaffe is to make a strong attack on London, which would cause the population to flee from the city and block the roads.[19]

Although Halder on August 23 was scribbling a shorthand note in his diary that "on this basis, an attack has no chance of success this year," a directive on August 27 over Keitel's signature laid down final plans for landings in four main areas on the south coast between Folkestone and Selsey Bill, just east of Portsmouth, with the first objective, as before, a line running between Portsmouth and the Thames, east of London at Gravesend, to be reached as soon as the beachheads had been connected and organized and the troops could strike north. At the same time orders were given to get ready to carry out certain deception maneuvers, of which the principal one was "Autumn Journey" (*Herbstreise*). This called for a large-scale feint against Britain's east coast, where, as has been noted, Churchill and his military advisers were still expecting the main invasion blow to fall. For this purpose four large liners, including Germany's largest, *Europa* and *Bremen,* and ten additional transports, escorted by four cruisers, were to put out from the southern Norwegian ports and the Heligoland Bight on D-minus-2 Day and head for the English coast between Aberdeen and Newcastle. The transports would be empty and the whole expedition would turn back as darkness fell, repeating the maneuver the next day.[20]

On August 30 Brauchitsch gave out a lengthy order of instructions for the landings, but the generals who received it must have wondered how much heart their Army chief now had in the undertaking. He entitled it "Instruction for the *Preparation* of Operation Sea Lion"—rather late in the game to be ordering preparations for an operation that he commanded must be carried out from September 15. "The order for execution," he added, "depends on the political situation"—a condition that must have puzzled the unpolitical generals.[21]

On September 1 the movement of shipping from Germany's North Sea ports toward the embarkation harbors on the Channel began, and two days later, on September 3, came a further directive from OKW.

The earliest day for the sailing of the invasion fleet has been fixed as September 20, and that of the landing for September 21.

Orders for the launching of the attack will be given D-minus-10 Day, presumably therefore on September 11.

Final commands will be given at the latest on D-minus-3 Day, at midday.

All preparations must remain liable to cancellation 24 hours before zero hour.

KEITEL[22]

This sounded like business. But the sound was deceptive. On September 6 Raeder had another long session with Hitler. "The Fuehrer's decision to land in England," the Admiral recorded in the Naval Staff War Diary that night, "is still by no means settled, as he is firmly convinced that Britain's defeat will be achieved even without the 'landing.' " Actually, as Raeder's long recording of the talk shows, the Fuehrer discoursed at length about almost everything except Sea Lion: about Norway, Gibraltar, Suez, "the problem of the U.S.A.," the treatment of the French colonies and his fantastic views about the establishment of a "North Germanic Union."[23]

If Churchill and his military chiefs had only got wind of this remarkable conference the code word "Cromwell" might not have been sent out in England on the evening of the next day, September 7, signifying "Invasion imminent" and causing no end of confusion, the endless ringing of church bells by the Home Guard, the blowing of several bridges by Royal Engineers and the needless casualties suffered by those stumbling over hastily laid mines.*

But on the late afternoon of Saturday, September 7, the Germans had begun their first massive bombing of London, carried out by 625 bombers pro ected by 648 fighters. It was the most devastating attack from the air ever delivered up to that day on a city—the bombings of Warsaw and Rotterdam were pinpricks beside it—and by early evening the whole dock-side area of the great city was a mass of flames and every railway line to the south, so vital to the defense against invasion, was blocked. In the circumstances, many in London believed that this murderous bombing was the prelude to immediate German landings, and it was because of this more than anything else that the alert, "Invasion imminent," was sent out. As will shortly be seen, this savage bombing of London on September 7, though setting off a premature warning and causing much damage, marked a decisive turning point in the Battle of Britain, the first great decisive struggle in the air the earth had ever experienced, which was now rapidly approaching its climax.

The time for Hitler to make his fatal decision to launch the invasion or not to launch it was also drawing near. It was to be made, as the September 3 directive stipulated, on September 11, giving the armed services ten days to carry out the preliminaries. But on the tenth Hitler decided to postpone his decision until the fourteenth. There seem to have been at least two reasons for the delay. One was the belief at OKW that the bombing of London was causing so much destruction, both to property and to British morale, that an invasion might not be necessary.†

The other reason arose from the difficulties the German Navy was

---

* Churchill says that neither he nor the chiefs of staff were "aware" that the decisive code word Cromwell had been given. It was sent out by Headquarters of the Home Forces. (*Their Finest Hour*, p. 312.) But four days later, on September 11, the Prime Minister did broadcast a warning that if the invasion were going to take place it could not "be long delayed. Therefore," he said, "we must regard the next week or so as a very important period in our history. It ranks with the days when the Spanish Armada was approaching the Channel, and Drake was finishing his game of bowls; or when Nelson stood between us and Napoleon's Grand Army at Boulogne."

† The Germans were greatly impressed by reports from the embassy in Washington, which relayed information received there from London and embroidered on it. The American General Staff was said to believe that Britain couldn't hold out much longer. According to Lieutenant Colonel von Lossberg (*Im Wehrmacht Fuehrungsstab*, p. 91) Hitler seriously expected a revolution to break out in Britain. Lossberg was an Army representative on OKW.

beginning to experience in assembling its shipping. Besides the weather, which the naval authorities reported on September 10 as being "completely abnormal and unstable," the R.A.F., which Goering had promised to destroy, and the British Navy were increasingly interfering with the concentration of the invasion fleet. That same day the Naval War Staff warned of the "danger" of British air and naval attacks on German transport movements, which it said had "undoubtedly been successful." Two days later, on September 12, H.Q. of Naval Group West sent an ominous message to Berlin:

Interruptions caused by the enemy's air forces, long-range artillery and light naval forces have, for the first time, assumed major significance. The harbors at Ostend, Dunkirk, Calais and Boulogne cannot be used as night anchorages for shipping because of the danger of English bombings and shelling. Units of the British Fleet are now able to operate almost unmolested in the Channel. Owing to these difficulties further delays are expected in the assembly of the invasion fleet.

The next day matters grew worse. British light naval forces bombarded the chief Channel invasion ports, Ostend, Calais, Boulogne and Cherbourg, while the R.A.F. sank eighty barges in Ostend Harbor. In Berlin that day Hitler conferred with his service chiefs at lunch. He thought the air war was going very well and declared that he had no intention of running the risk of invasion.[24] In fact, Jodl got the impression from the Fuehrer's remarks that he had "apparently decided to abandon Sea Lion completely," an impression which was accurate for that day, as Hitler confirmed the following day—when, however, he again changed his mind.

Both Raeder and Halder have left confidential notes of the meeting of the Fuehrer with his commanders in chief in Berlin on September 14.[25] The Admiral managed to slip Hitler a memorandum before the session opened, setting forth the Navy's opinion that

the present air situation does not provide conditions for carrying out the operation [Sea Lion], as the risk is still too great.

At the beginning of the conference, the Nazi warlord displayed a somewhat negative mood and his thoughts were marred by contradictions. He would not give the order to launch the invasion, but neither would he call it off as, Raeder noted in the Naval War Diary, "he apparently had planned to do on September 13."

What were the reasons for his latest change of mind? Halder recorded them in some detail.

A successful landing [the Fuehrer argued] followed by an occupation would end the war in a short time. England would starve. A landing need not necessarily be carried out within a specified time . . . But a long war is not desirable. We have already achieved everything that we need.

British hopes in Russia and America, Hitler said, had not materialized. Russia was not going to bleed for Britain. America's rearmament would not be fully effective until 1945. As for the moment, the "quickest solution would be a landing in England. The Navy has achieved the necessary conditions. The operations of the Luftwaffe are above all praise. Four or five days of decent weather would bring the decisive results . . . We have a good chance of bringing England to her knees."

What was wrong, then? Why hesitate any longer in launching the invasion?

The trouble was, Hitler conceded:

The enemy recovers again and again . . . Enemy fighters have not yet been completely eliminated. Our own reports of successes do not give a completely reliable picture, although the enemy has been severely damaged.

On the whole, then, Hitler declared, "in spite of all of our successes *the prerequisite conditions for Operation Sea Lion have not yet been realized.*" (The emphasis is Halder's.)

Hitler summed up his reflections.

1. Successful landing means victory, but for this we must obtain complete air superiority.

2. Bad weather has so far prevented our attaining complete air superiority.

3. All other factors are in order.

Decision therefore: The operation will not be renounced yet.

Having come to that negative conclusion, Hitler thereupon gave way to soaring hopes that the Luftwaffe might still bring off the victory that so tantalizingly and so narrowly continued to evade him. "The air attacks up to now," he said, "have had a tremendous effect, though perhaps chiefly on the nerves. Even if victory in the air is only achieved in ten or twelve days the English may yet be seized by mass hysteria."

To help bring that about, Jeschonnek of the Air Force begged to be allowed to bomb London's residential districts, since, he said, there was no sign of "mass panic" in London while these areas were being spared. Admiral Raeder enthusiastically supported some terror bombing. Hitler, however, thought concentration on military objectives was more important. "Bombing with the object of causing a mass panic," he said, "must be left to the last."

Admiral Raeder's enthusiasm for terror bombing seems to have been due mainly to his lack of enthusiasm for the landings. He now intervened to stress again the "great risks" involved. The situation in the air, he pointed out, could hardly improve before the projected dates of September 24–27 for the landing; therefore they must be abandoned "until October 8 or 24."

But this was practically to call off the invasion altogether, as Hitler realized, and he ruled that he would hold up his decision on the landings only until September 17—three days hence—so that they still might take place on September 27. If not feasible then, he would have to think about the October dates. A Supreme Command directive was thereupon issued.

> Berlin
> September 14, 1940
>
> TOP SECRET
>
> . . . The Fuehrer has decided:
>
> The start of Operation Sea Lion is again postponed. A new order follows September 17. All preparations are to be continued.
>
> The air attacks against London are to be continued and the target area expanded against military and other vital installations (e.g., railway stations).
>
> Terror attacks against purely residential areas are reserved for use as an ultimate means of pressure.[26]

Thus though Hitler had put off for three days a decision on the invasion he had by no means abandoned it. Give the Luftwaffe another few days to finish off the R.A.F. and demoralize London, and the landing then could take place. It would bring final victory. So once again all depended on Goering's vaunted Air Force. It would make, in fact, its supreme effort the very next day.

The Navy's opinion of the Luftwaffe, however, grew hourly worse. On the evening of the crucial conference in Berlin the German Naval War Staff reported severe R.A.F. bombings of the invasion ports, from Antwerp to Boulogne.

> . . . In Antwerp . . . considerable casualties are inflicted on transports— five transport steamers in port heavily damaged; one barge sunk, two cranes destroyed, an ammunition train blown up, several sheds burning.

The next night was even worse, the Navy reporting "strong enemy air attacks on the entire coastal area between Le Havre and Antwerp." An S.O.S. was sent out by the sailors for more antiaircraft protection of the invasion ports. On September 17 the Naval Staff reported:

> The R.A.F. are still by no means defeated: on the contrary they are showing increasing activity in their attacks on the Channel ports and in their mounting interference with the assembly movements.*[27]

---

* On September 16, according to a German authority, R.A.F. bombers surprised a large invasion training exercise and inflicted heavy losses in men and landing vessels. This gave rise to many reports in Germany and elsewhere on the Continent

That night there was a full moon and the British night bombers made the most of it. The German Naval War Staff reported "very considerable losses" of the shipping which now jammed the invasion ports. At Dunkirk eighty-four barges were sunk or damaged, and from Cherbourg to Den Helder the Navy reported, among other depressing items, a 500-ton ammunition store blown up, a rations depot burned out, various steamers and torpedo boats sunk and many casualties to personnel suffered. This severe bombing plus bombardment from heavy guns across the Channel made it necessary, the Navy Staff reported, to disperse the naval and transport vessels already concentrated on the Channel and to stop further movement of shipping to the invasion ports.

Otherwise [it said] with energetic enemy action such casualties will occur in the course of time that the execution of the operation on the scale previously envisaged will in any case be problematic.[28]

It had already become so.
In the German Naval War Diary there is a laconic entry for September 17.

The enemy Air Force is still by no means defeated. On the contrary, it shows increasing activity. The weather situation as a whole does not permit us to expect a period of calm . . . *The Fuehrer therefore decides to postpone "Sea Lion" indefinitely.*[29]

The emphasis is the Navy's.

Adolf Hitler, after so many years of dazzling successes, had at last met failure. For nearly a month thereafter the pretense was kept up that the invasion might still take place that autumn, but it was a case of whistling in the dark. On September 19 the Fuehrer formally ordered the further assembling of the invasion fleet to be stopped and the shipping already in the ports to be dispersed "so that the loss of shipping space caused by enemy air attacks may be reduced to a minimum."
But it was impossible to maintain even a dispersed armada and all the troops and guns and tanks and supplies that had been assembled to cross over the Channel for an invasion that had been postponed indefinitely. "This state of affairs," Halder exclaimed in his diary September 28, "drag-

---

that the Germans had actually attempted a landing and been repulsed by the British. (Georg W. Feuchter, *Geschichte des Luftkriegs*, p. 176.) I heard such a "report" on the night of September 16 in Geneva, Switzerland, where I was taking a few days off. On September 18 and again on the next day I saw two long ambulance trains unloading wounded soldiers in the suburbs of Berlin. From the bandages, I concluded the wounds were mostly burns. There had been no fighting anywhere for three months on land.

On September 21, confidential German Navy papers recorded that 21 transports and 214 barges—some 12 per cent of the total assembled for the invasion—had been lost or damaged. (*Fuehrer Conferences on Naval Affairs*, p. 102.)

ging out the continued existence of Sea Lion, is unbearable." When Ciano and Mussolini met the Fuehrer on the Brenner on October 4, the Italian Foreign Minister observed in his diary that "there is no longer any talk about a landing in the British Isles." Hitler's setback put his partner, Mussolini, in the best mood he had been in for ages. "Rarely have I seen the Duce in such good humor . . . as at the Brenner Pass today," Ciano noted.[30]

Already both the Navy and the Army were pressing the Fuehrer for a decision to call off Sea Lion altogether. The Army General Staff pointed out to him that the holding of the troops on the Channel "under constant British air attacks led to continual casualties."

Finally on October 12, the Nazi warlord formally admitted failure and called off the invasion until spring, if then. A formal directive was issued.

> Fuehrer's Headquarters
> October 12, 1940

TOP SECRET

The Fuehrer has decided that from now on until the spring, preparations for "Sea Lion" shall be continued solely for the purpose of maintaining political and military pressure on England.

Should the invasion be reconsidered in the spring or early summer of 1941, orders for a renewal of operational readiness will be issued later . . .

The Army was commanded to release its Sea Lion formations "for other duties or for employment on other fronts." The Navy was instructed to "take all measures to release personnel and shipping space." But both services were to camouflage their moves. "The British," Hitler laid it down, "must continue to believe that we are preparing an attack on a broad front."[31]

What had happened to make Adolf Hitler finally give in?

Two things: the fatal course of the Battle of Britain in the air, and the turning of his thoughts once more eastward, to Russia.

THE BATTLE OF BRITAIN

Goering's great air offensive against Britain, Operation Eagle (*Adler-angriffe*), had been launched on August 15 with the objective of driving the British Air Force from the skies and thus achieving the one condition on which the launching of the invasion depended. The fat Reich Marshal, as he now was, had no doubts about victory. By mid-July he was confident that British fighter defenses in southern England could be smashed within four days by an all-out assault, thus opening the way for the invasion. To destroy the R.A.F. completely would take a little longer, Goering told the Army High Command: from two to four weeks.[32] In fact, the bemedaled German Air Force chief thought that the Luftwaffe alone could bring Britain to her knees and that an invasion by land forces probably would not be necessary.

To obtain this mighty objective he had three great air fleets (*Luftflotten*): Number 2 under Field Marshal Kesselring, operating from the Low Countries and northern France, Number 3 under Field Marshal Sperrle, based on northern France, and Number 5 under General Stumpff, stationed in Norway and Denmark. The first two had a total of 929 fighters, 875 bombers and 316 dive bombers; Number 5 was much smaller, with 123 bombers and 34 twin-engined ME-110 fighters. Against this vast force the R.A.F. had for the air defense of the realm at the beginning of August between 700 and 800 fighters.

Throughout July the Luftwaffe gradually stepped up its attacks on British shipping in the Channel and on Britain's southern ports. This was a probing operation. Though it was necessary to clear the narrow waters of British ships before an invasion could begin, the main object of these preliminary air assaults was to lure the British fighters to battle. This failed. The R.A.F. Command shrewdly declined to commit more than a fraction of its fighters, and as a result considerable damage was done to shipping and to some of the ports. Four destroyers and eighteen merchant ships were sunk, but this preliminary sparring cost the Luftwaffe 296 aircraft destroyed and 135 damaged. The R.A.F. lost 148 fighters.

On August 12, Goering gave orders to launch Eagle the next day. As a curtain raiser heavy attacks were made on the twelfth on enemy radar stations, five of which were actually hit and damaged and one knocked out, but the Germans at this stage did not realize how vital to Britain's defenses radar was and did not pursue the attack. On the thirteenth and fourteenth the Germans put in the air some 1,500 aircraft, mostly against R.A.F. fighter fields, and though they claimed five of them had been "completely destroyed" the damage was actually negligible and the Luftwaffe lost forty-seven planes against thirteen for the R.A.F.*

August 15 brought the first great battle in the skies. The Germans threw in the bulk of their planes from all three air fleets, flying 801 bombing and 1,149 fighter sorties. Luftflotten 5, operating from Scandinavia, met disaster. By sending some 800 planes in a massive attack on the south coast the Germans had expected to find the northeast coast defenseless. But a force of a hundred bombers, escorted by thirty-four twin-engined ME-110 fighters, was surprised by seven squadrons of Hurricanes and Spitfires as it approached the Tyneside and severely mauled. Thirty German planes, mostly bombers, were shot down without loss to the defenders. That was the end of Air Fleet 5 in the Battle of Britain. It never returned to it.

In the south of England that day the Germans were more successful. They launched four massive attacks, one of which was able to penetrate

---

* The Luftwaffe claimed 134 British craft against a loss of 34. From that date on both sides grossly overestimated the damage they did the other.

almost to London. Four aircraft factories at Croydon were hit and five R.A.F. fighter fields damaged. In all, the Germans lost seventy-five planes, against thirty-four for the R.A.F.* At this rate, despite their numerical superiority, the Germans could scarcely hope to drive the R.A.F. from the skies.

Now Goering made the first of his two tactical errors. The skill of British Fighter Command in committing its planes to battle against vastly superior attacking forces was based on its shrewd use of radar. From the moment they took off from their bases in Western Europe the German aircraft were spotted on British radar screens, and their course so accurately plotted that Fighter Command knew exactly where and when they could best be attacked. This was something new in warfare and it puzzled the Germans, who were far behind the British in the development and use of this electronic device.

We realized [Adolf Galland, the famous German fighter ace, later testified] that the R.A.F. fighter squadrons must be controlled from the ground by some new procedure because we heard commands skillfully and accurately directing Spitfires and Hurricanes on to German formations . . . For us this radar and fighter control was a surprise and a very bitter one.[33]

Yet the attack on British radar stations which on August 12 had been so damaging had not been continued and on August 15, the day of his first major setback, Goering called them off entirely, declaring: "It is doubtful whether there is any point in continuing the attacks on radar stations, since not one of those attacked has so far been put out of action."

A second key to the successful defense of the skies over southern England was the sector station. This was the underground nerve center from which the Hurricanes and Spitfires were guided by radiotelephone into battle on the basis of the latest intelligence from radar, from ground observation posts and from pilots in the air. The Germans, as Galland noted, could hear the constant chatter over the air waves between the sector stations and the pilots aloft and finally began to understand the importance of these ground control centers. On August 24 they switched their tactics to the destruction of the sector stations, seven of which on the airfields around London were crucial to the protection of the south of England and of the capital itself. This was a blow against the very vitals of Britain's air defenses.

Until that day the battle had appeared to be going against the Luftwaffe. On August 17 it lost seventy-one aircraft against the R.A.F.'s twenty-seven. The slow Stuka dive bomber, which had helped to pave the way for the Army's victories in Poland and in the West, was proving to be a

---

* In London that evening an official communiqué reported 182 German planes shot down and 43 more probably destroyed. This gave a great fillip to British morale in general and to that of the hard-pressed fighter pilots in particular.

sitting duck for British fighters and on that day, August 17, was withdrawn by Goering from the battle, reducing the German bombing force by a third. Between August 19 and 23 there was a five-day lull in the air due to bad weather. Goering, reviewing the situation at Karinhall, his country show place near Berlin, on the nineteenth, ordered that as soon as the weather improved, the Luftwaffe was to concentrate its attacks exclusively on the Royal Air Force.

"We have reached the decisive period of the air war against England," he declared. "The vital task is the defeat of the enemy air force. Our first aim is to destroy the enemy's fighters."[34]

From August 24 to September 6 the Germans sent over an average of a thousand planes a day to achieve this end. For once the Reich Marshal was right. The Battle of Britain had entered its decisive stage. Though the R.A.F. pilots, already strained from a month of flying several sorties a day, put up a valiant fight, the German preponderance in sheer numbers began to tell. Five forward fighter fields in the south of England were extensively damaged and, what was worse, six of the seven key sector stations were so severely bombed that the whole communications system seemed to be on the verge of being knocked out. This threatened disaster to Britain.

Worst of all, the pace was beginning to tell on the R.A.F. fighter defense. In the crucial fortnight between August 23 and September 6 the British lost 466 fighters destroyed or badly damaged, and though they did not know it at the time the Luftwaffe losses were less: 385 aircraft, of which 214 were fighters and 138 bombers. Moreover, the R.A.F. had lost 103 pilots killed and 128 seriously wounded—a quarter of all those available.

"The scales," as Churchill later wrote, "had tilted against Fighter Command . . . There was much anxiety." A few more weeks of this and Britain would have had no organized defense of its skies. The invasion would almost certainly succeed.

And then suddenly Goering made his second tactical error, this one comparable in its consequences to Hitler's calling off the armored attack on Dunkirk on May 24. It saved the battered, reeling R.A.F. and marked one of the major turning points of history's first great battle in the air.

With the British fighter defense suffering losses in the air and on the ground which it could not for long sustain, the Luftwaffe switched its attack on September 7 to massive night bombings of London. The R.A.F. fighters were reprieved.

What had happened in the German camp to cause this change in tactics which was destined to prove so fatal to the ambitions of Hitler and Goering? The answer is full of irony.

To begin with, there was a minor navigational error by the pilots of a dozen German bombers on the night of August 23. Directed to drop their loads on aircraft factories and oil tanks on the outskirts of London, they missed their mark and dropped bombs on the center of the capital, blowing up some homes and killing some civilians. The British thought it was deliberate and as retaliation bombed Berlin the next evening.

It didn't amount to much. There was a dense cloud cover over Berlin that night and only about half of the eighty-one R.A.F. bombers dispatched found the target. Material damage was negligible. But the effect on German morale was tremendous. *For this was the first time that bombs had ever fallen on Berlin.*

The Berliners are stunned [I wrote in my diary the next day, August 26]. They did not think it could ever happen. When this war began, Goering assured them it couldn't . . . They believed him. Their disillusionment today therefore is all the greater. You have to see their faces to measure it.

Berlin was well defended by two great rings of antiaircraft and for three hours while the visiting bombers droned above the clouds, which prevented the hundreds of searchlight batteries from picking them up, the flak fire was the most intense I had ever seen. But not a single plane was brought down. The British also dropped a few leaflets saying that "the war which Hitler started will go on, and it will last as long as Hitler does." This was good propaganda, but the thud of exploding bombs was better.

The R.A.F. came over in greater force on the night of August 28–29 and, as I noted in my diary, "*for the first time killed Germans in the capital of the Reich.*" The official count was ten killed and twenty-nine wounded. The Nazi bigwigs were outraged. Goebbels, who had ordered the press to publish only a few lines on the first attack, now gave instructions to cry out at the "brutality" of the British flyers in attacking the defenseless women and children of Berlin. Most of the capital's dailies carried the same headline: COWARDLY BRITISH ATTACK. Two nights later, after the third raid, the headlines read: BRITISH AIR PIRATES OVER BERLIN!

The main effect of a week of constant British night bombings [I wrote in my diary on September 1] has been to spread great disillusionment among the people and sow doubt in their minds . . . Actually the bombings have not been very deadly.

September 1 was the first anniversary of the beginning of the war. I noted the mood of the people, aside from their frayed nerves at having been robbed of their sleep and frightened by the surprise bombings and the terrific din of the flak.

In this year German arms have achieved victories never equaled even in the brilliant military history of this aggressive, militaristic nation. And yet the war is not yet over or won. And it was on this aspect that people's minds were concentrated today. They long for peace. And they want it before the winter comes.

Hitler deemed it necessary to address them on September 4 on the occasion of the opening of the Winterhilfe campaign at the Sportpalast. His appearance there was kept secret to the last moment, apparently out of fear that enemy planes might take advantage of the cloud cover and break up the meeting, though it was held in the afternoon, an hour before dark.

I have rarely seen the Nazi dictator in a more sarcastic mood or so given to what the German people regarded as humor, though Hitler was essentially a humorless man. He described Churchill as "that noted war correspondent." For "a character like Duff Cooper," he said, "there is no word in conventional German. Only the Bavarians have a word that adequately describes this type of man, and that is *Krampfhenne*," which might be translated as "a nervous old hen."

The babbling of Mr. Churchill or of Mr. Eden [he said]—reverence for old age forbids the mention of Mr. Chamberlain—doesn't mean a thing to the German people. At best, it makes them laugh.

And Hitler proceeded to make his audience, which consisted mostly of women nurses and social workers, laugh—and then applaud hysterically. He was faced with the problem of answering two questions uppermost in the minds of the German people: When would Britain be invaded, and what would be done about the night bombings of Berlin and other German cities? As to the first:

In England they're filled with curiosity and keep asking, "Why doesn't he come?" Be calm. Be calm. He's coming! He's coming!

His listeners found that crack very funny, but they also believed that it was an unequivocal pledge. As to the bombings, he began by a typical falsification and ended with a dire threat:

Just now . . . Mr. Churchill is demonstrating his new brain child, the night air raid. Mr. Churchill is carrying out these raids not because they promise to be highly effective, but because his Air Force cannot fly over Germany in daylight . . . whereas German planes are over English soil every day . . . Whenever the Englishman sees a light, he drops a bomb . . . on residential districts, farms and villages.

And then came the threat.

For three months I did not answer because I believed that such madness would be stopped. Mr. Churchill took this for a sign of weakness. We are now answering night for night.

When the British Air Force drops two or three or four thousand kilograms of bombs, then we will in one night drop 150-, 230-, 300- or 400,000 kilograms.

At this point, according to my diary, Hitler had to pause because of the hysterical applause of the German women listeners.

"When they declare," Hitler continued, "that they will increase their attacks on our cities, then we will *raze* their cities to the ground." At this, I noted, the young ladies were quite beside themselves and applauded phrenetically. When they had recovered, he added, "We will stop the handiwork of these night air pirates, so help us God!"

On hearing this, I also noted, "the young German women hopped to their feet and, their breasts heaving, screamed their approval!"

"The hour will come," Hitler concluded, "when one of us will break, and it will not be National Socialist Germany!" At this, I finally noted, "the raving maidens kept their heads sufficiently to break their wild shouts of joy with a chorus of 'Never! Never!' "

Ciano in Rome, listening to the broadcast, which was made from records some hours later, confessed to being perplexed. "Hitler must be nervous," he concluded.[35]

His nerves were a factor in the fatal decision to switch the Luftwaffe's winning daylight attacks on the R.A.F. to massive night bombings of London. This was a political as well as a military decision, made in part to revenge the bombings of Berlin and other German cities (which were but pinpricks compared to what the Luftwaffe was doing to Britain's cities) and to destroy the will of the British to resist by *razing* their capital. If it succeeded, and Hitler and Goebbels had no doubt it would, an invasion might not be necessary.

And so on the late afternoon of September 7 the great air attack on London began. The Germans threw in, as we have seen,* 625 bombers and 648 fighters. At about 5 P.M. that Saturday the first wave of 320 bombers, protected by every fighter the Germans had, flew up the Thames and began to drop their bombs on Woolwich Arsenal, various gas works, power stations, depots and mile upon mile of docks. The whole vast area was soon a mass of flames. At one locality, Silvertown, the population was surrounded by fire and had to be evacuated by water. At 8:10 P.M., after dark, a second wave of 250 bombers arrived and resumed the attack, which was kept up by successive waves until dawn at 4:30 on Sunday morning. The next evening at 7:30, the attack was renewed by two hundred bombers and continued throughout the night. Some 842 persons were killed and 2,347 wounded, according to the official British historian, during these first two nights, and vast damage was inflicted on the sprawling city.[36] The assault went on all the following week, night after night.†

And then, stimulated by its successes, or what it thought were such, the Luftwaffe decided to carry out a great daylight assault on the battered, burning capital. This led on Sunday, September 15, to one of the decisive battles of the war.

---

* Above, p. 769.
† At this time night defenses had not yet been perfected and the German losses were negligible.

Some two hundred German bombers, escorted by three times as many fighters, appeared over the Channel about midday, headed for London. Fighter Command had watched the assembling of the attackers on its radar screens and was ready. The Germans were intercepted before they approached the capital, and though some planes got through, many were dispersed and others shot down before they could deliver their bomb load. Two hours later an even stronger German formation returned and was routed. Though the British claimed to have shot down 185 Luftwaffe planes, the actual figure, as learned after the war from the Berlin archives, was much lower—fifty-six, but thirty-four of these were bombers. The R.A.F. lost only twenty-six aircraft.

The day had shown that the Luftwaffe could not for the moment, anyway, now that it had given Fighter Command a week to recover, carry out a successful major daylight attack on Britain. That being so, the prospect of an effective landing was dim. September 15 therefore was a turning point, "the crux," as Churchill later judged, of the Battle of Britain. Though Goering the next day, in ordering a change of tactics that provided for the use of bombers in daylight no longer to bomb but merely to serve as decoys for British fighters, boasted that the enemy's fighters "ought to be finished off within four or five days,"[37] Hitler and the Army and Navy commanders knew better and two days after the decisive air battle, on September 17, as has been noted, the Fuehrer called off Sea Lion indefinitely.

Although London was to take a terrible pounding for fifty-seven consecutive nights from September 7 to November 3 from a daily average of two hundred bombers, so that it seemed certain to Churchill, as he later revealed, that the city would soon be reduced to a rubble heap, and though most of Britain's other cities, Coventry above all, were to suffer great damage throughout that grim fall and winter, British morale did not collapse nor armament production fall off, as Hitler had so confidently expected. Just the opposite. Aircraft factories in England, one of the prime targets of the Luftwaffe bombers, actually outproduced the Germans in 1940 by 9,924 to 8,070 planes. Hitler's bomber losses over England had been so severe that they could never be made up, and in fact the Luftwaffe, as the German confidential records make clear, never fully recovered from the blow it received in the skies over Britain that late summer and fall.

The German Navy, crippled by the losses off Norway in the early spring, was unable, as its chiefs admitted all along, to provide the sea power for an invasion of Britain. Without this, and without air supremacy, the German Army was helpless to move across the narrow Channel waters. For the first time in the war Hitler had been stopped, his plans of further conquest frustrated, and just at the moment, as we have seen, when he was certain that final victory had been achieved.

He had never conceived—nor had anyone else up to that time—that a decisive battle could be decided in the air. Nor perhaps did he yet realize as the dark winter settled over Europe that a handful of British fighter pilots, by thwarting his invasion, had preserved England as a great base for the possible reconquest of the Continent from the west at a later date. His thoughts were perforce turning elsewhere; in fact, as we shall see, had already turned.

Britain was saved. For nearly a thousand years it had successfully defended itself by sea power. Just in time, its leaders, a very few of them, despite all the bungling (of which these pages have been so replete) in the interwar years, had recognized that air power had become decisive in the mid-twentieth century and the little fighter plane and its pilot the chief shield for defense. As Churchill told the Commons in another memorable peroration on August 20, when the battle in the skies still raged and its outcome was in doubt, "never in the field of human conflict was so much owed by so many to so few."

IF THE INVASION HAD SUCCEEDED

The Nazi German occupation of Britain would not have been a gentle affair. The captured German papers leave no doubt of that. On September 9 Brauchitsch, the Commander in Chief of the Army, signed a directive providing that "the able-bodied male population between the ages of seventeen and forty-five [in Britain] will, unless the local situation calls for an exceptional ruling, be interned and dispatched to the Continent." Orders to this effect were sent out a few days later by the Quartermaster General, in OKH, to the Ninth and Sixteenth armies, which were assembled for the invasion. In no other conquered country, not even in Poland, had the Germans begun with such a drastic step. Brauchitsch's instructions were headed "Orders Concerning the Organization and Function of Military Government in England" and went into considerable detail. They seem designed to ensure the systematic plunder of the island and the terrorization of its inhabitants. A special "Military Economic Staff England" was set up on July 27 to achieve the first aim. Everything but normal household stocks was to be confiscated at once. Hostages would be taken. Anybody posting a placard the Germans didn't like would be liable to immediate execution, and a similar penalty was provided for those who failed to turn in firearms or radio sets within twenty-four hours.

But the real terror was to be meted out by Himmler and the S.S. For this the dreaded R.S.H.A.,* under Heydrich, was put in charge. The man who was designated to direct its activities on the spot from London was a certain S.S. colonel, Professor Dr. Franz Six, another of the peculiar intellectual gangsters who in the Nazi time were somehow attracted to the service of Himmler's secret police. Professor Six had left his post as dean

---

* R.S.H.A., the initials of the Reich Central Security Office (Reichssicherheitshauptamt), which, as has been noted, took over control in 1939 of the Gestapo, the Criminal Police and the Security Service, or S.D.

of the economic faculty of Berlin University to join Heydrich's S.D., where he specialized in "scientific matters," the weirder side of which cast such a spell over the bespectacled Heinrich Himmler and his fellow thugs. What the British people missed by not having Dr. Six in their presence may be judged by his later career in Russia, where he was active in the S.S. Einsatzgruppen, which distinguished themselves in wholesale massacres there, one of the professor's specialties being to ferret out captured Soviet political commissars for execution.*

On August 1, the R.S.H.A. captured archives reveal, Goering told Heydrich to get busy. The S.S. Security Police and the S.D. (Security Service) were to

commence their activities simultaneously with the military invasion in order to seize and combat effectively the numerous important organizations and societies in England which are hostile to Germany.

On September 17, which, ironically, was the date on which Hitler postponed the invasion indefinitely, Professor Six was formally appointed to his new post in England by Heydrich and told:

Your task is to combat, with the requisite means, all anti-German organizations, institutions, and opposition groups which can be seized in England, to prevent the removal of all available material and to centralize and safeguard it for future exploitation. I designate London as the location of your headquarters . . . and I authorize you to set up small *Einsatzgruppen* in other parts of Great Britain as the situation dictates and the necessity arises.

Actually, already in August Heydrich had organized six *Einsatzkommando* for Britain which were to operate from headquarters in London, Bristol, Birmingham, Liverpool, Manchester and Edinburgh—or in Glasgow, if the Forth Bridge was found blown up. They were to carry out Nazi terror; to begin with, they were to arrest all those on the "Special Search List, G.B. [Great Britain]," which in May had been hurriedly and carelessly compiled by Walter Schellenberg, another one of Himmler's bright young university graduates, who was then chief of Amt (Bureau) IV E— Counterespionage—of R.S.H.A. Or so Schellenberg later claimed, though at this time he was mainly occupied in Lisbon, Portugal, on a bizarre mission to kidnap the Duke of Windsor.

The Special Search List, G.B. (*die Sonderfahndungsliste, G.B.*) is among the more amusing "invasion" documents found in the Himmler papers, though of course it was not meant to be. It contains the names of some 2,300 prominent persons in Great Britain, not all of them English,

---

* Dr. Six was sentenced in 1948 at Nuremberg as a war criminal to twenty years in prison, but was released in 1952.

whom the Gestapo thought it important to incarcerate at once. Churchill is there, naturally, along with members of the cabinet and o her well-known politicians of all parties. Leading editors, publishers and reporters, including two former *Times* correspondents in Berlin, Norman Ebbutt and Douglas Reed, whose dispatches had displeased the Nazis, are on the list. British authors claim special attention. Shaw's name is conspicuously absent, but H. G. Wells is there along with such writers as Virginia Woolf, E. M. Forster, Aldous Huxley, J. B. Priestley, Stephen Spender, C. P. Snow, Noel Coward, Rebecca West, Sir Philip Gibbs and Norman Angell. The scholars were not omitted either. Among them: Gilbert Murray, Bertrand Russell, Harold Laski, Beatrice Webb and J. B. S. Haldane.

The Gestapo also intended to take advantage of its sojourn in England to round up both foreign and German émigrés. Paderewski, Freud* and Chaim Weizmann were on its list, as well as Beneš, the President, and Jan Masaryk, the Foreign Minister, of the Czechoslovak government in exile. Of the German refugees there were, among many others, two former personal friends of Hitler who had turned on him: Hermann Rauschning and Putzi Hanfstaengl. Many English names were so badly misspelled as to make them almost unrecognizable and sometimes bizarre identifications were attached, as the one for Lady Bonham Carter, who was also listed as "Lady Carter-Bonham" and described not only as "born, Violet Asquith," but as "an Encirclement lady politician." After each name was marked the bureau of R.S.H.A. which was to handle that person. Churchill was to be placed in the hands of Amt VI—Foreign Intelligence—but most were to be handed over to Amt IV—the Gestapo.†

This Nazi Black Book actually formed a supplement to a supposedly highly secret handbook called *Informationsheft,* which Schellenberg also claims to have written, and whose purpose seems to have been to aid the conquerors in looting Britain and stamping out anti-German institutions there. It is even more amusing than the Search List. Among the dangerous institutions, besides the Masonic lodges and Jewish organizations, which deserved "special attention" by R.S.H.A., were the "public schools" (in England, the private schools), the Church of England, which was described as "a powerful tool of British imperial politics," and the Boy Scouts, which was put down as "an excellent source of information for the British Intelligence Service." Its revered leader and founder, Lord Baden-Powell, was to be immediately arrested.

Had the invasion been attempted the Germans would not have been received gently by the British. Churchill later confessed that he had often wondered what would have happened. Of this much he was certain:

---

* The famous psychoanalyst had died in London in 1939.
† A number of Americans are on the arrest list, including Bernard Baruch, John Gunther, Paul Robeson, Louis Fischer, Daniel de Luce (the A.P. correspondent, who is listed under the D's as "Daniel, de Luce—U.S.A. correspondent") and M. W. Fodor, the Chicago *Daily News* correspondent, who was well known for his anti-Nazi writings.

The massacre would have been on both sides grim and great. There would have been neither mercy nor quarter. They would have used terror, and we were prepared to go all lengths.[38]

He does not say specifically to what lengths, but Peter Fleming in his book on Sea Lion gives one of them. The British had decided, he says, as a last resort and if all other conventional methods of defense failed, to attack the German beachheads with mustard gas, sprayed from low-flying airplanes. It was a painful decision, taken not without much soul searching at the highest level; and as Fleming comments, the decision was "surrounded by secrecy at the time and ever since."[39]

This particular massacre on which Churchill speculates, the unleashing of this kind of terror which the Gestapo planned, did not take place at this time in this place—for reasons which have been set down in this chapter. But in less than a year, in another part of Europe, the Germans were to unleash horrors on a scale never before experienced.

Already, even before the invasion of Britain was abandoned, Adolf Hitler had come to a decision. He would turn on Russia in the following spring.

POSTSCRIPT: THE NAZI PLOT TO KIDNAP THE DUKE AND DUCHESS OF WINDSOR

More amusing than important, but not without its insight into the ludicrous side of the rulers of the Third Reich that summer of their great conquests, is the story of the Nazi plot to kidnap the Duke and Duchess of Windsor and induce the former King of England to work with Hitler for a peace settlement with Great Britain. The evolution of the fantastic plan is told at length in the captured German Foreign Office documents[40] and touched on by Walter Schellenberg, the youthful S.S.-S.D. chief who was designated to carry it out, in his memoirs.[41]

The idea, Schellenberg was told by Ribbentrop, was Hitler's. The Nazi Foreign Minister embraced it with all the enthusiasm to which his abysmal ignorance often drove him, and the German Foreign Office and its diplomatic representatives in Spain and Portugal were forced to waste a great deal of time on it during the climactic summer of 1940.

After the fall of France in June 1940, the Duke, who had been a member of the British military mission with the French Army High Command, made his way with the Duchess to Spain to escape capture by the Germans. On June 23 the German ambassador in Madrid, Eberhard von Stohrer, a career diplomat, telegraphed Berlin:

The Spanish Foreign Minister requests advice with regard to the treatment of the Duke and Duchess of Windsor who were to arrive in Madrid today, apparently en route to England by way of Lisbon. The Foreign Minister assumes that we might perhaps be interested in detaining the Duke here and possibly establishing contact with him. Please telegraph instructions.

Ribbentrop shot back instructions by wire the next day. He suggested that the Windsors be "detained for a couple of weeks in Spain" but warned that it must not appear "that the suggestion came from Germany." On the following day, June 25, Stohrer replied: "The [Spanish] Foreign Minister promised me to do everything possible to detain Windsor here for a time." The Foreign Minister, Colonel Juan Beigbeder y Atienza, saw the Duke and reported on his talk to the German ambassador, who informed Berlin by "top secret" telegram of July 2 that Windsor would not return to England unless his wife were recognized as a member of the royal family and he himself given a position of importance. Otherwise he would settle in Spain in a castle promised him by the Franco government.

Windsor has expressed himself to the Foreign Minister and other acquaintances [the ambassador added] against Churchill and against this war.

The Windsors proceeded to Lisbon early in July and on July 11 the German minister there informed Ribbentrop that the Duke had been named Governor of the Bahamas but "intends to postpone his departure there as long as possible . . . in hope of a turn of events favorable to him."

He is convinced [the minister added] that if he had remained on the throne war would have been avoided, and he characterized himself as a firm supporter of a peaceful arrangement with Germany. The Duke definitely believes that continued severe bombing would make England ready for peace.

This intelligence spurred the arrogant German Foreign Minister to get off from his special train at Fuschl a telegram marked "Very Urgent, Top Secret" to the German Embassy in Madrid late on the evening of the same day, July 11. He wanted the Duke to be prevented from going to the Bahamas by being brought back to Spain, preferably by his Spanish friends. "After their return to Spain," Ribbentrop advised, "the Duke and his wife must be persuaded or compelled to remain on Spanish territory." If necessary Spain could "intern" him as an English officer and treat him "as a military fugitive."

At a suitable occasion [Ribbentrop further advised] the Duke must be informed that Germany wants peace with the English people, that the Churchill clique stands in the way of it, and that it would be a good thing if the Duke would hold himself in readiness for further developments. Germany is determined to force England to peace by every means of power and upon this happening would be prepared to accommodate any desire expressed by the Duke, especially with a view to the assumption of the English throne by the Duke and Duchess. If the Duke should have other plans, but be prepared to co-operate in the establishment of good relations between Germany and England, we would likewise be prepared to assure him and his wife of a subsistence which would permit him . . . to lead a life suitable for a king.*

The fatuous Nazi Minister, whose experience as German ambassador in London had taught him little about the English, added that he had information that the "British Secret Service" was going to "do away" with the Duke as soon as it got him to the Bahamas.

The next day, July 12, the German ambassador in Madrid saw Ramón Serrano Suñer, Spanish Minister of the Interior and brother-in-law of Franco, who promised to get the Generalissimo in on the plot and carry out the following plan. The Spanish government would send to Lisbon an old friend of the Duke, Miguel Primo de Rivera, Madrid leader of the Falange and son of a former Spanish dictator. Rivera would invite the Duke to Spain for some hunting and also to confer with the government about Anglo–Spanish relations. Suñer would inform the Duke about the British secret-service plot to bump him off.

The Minister [the German ambassador informed Berlin] will then add an invitation to the Duke and Duchess to accept Spanish hospitality, and possibly financial assistance as well. Possibly also the departure of the Duke could be prevented in some other way. In this whole plan we remain completely in the background.

Rivera, according to the German papers, returned from Lisbon to Madrid after his first visit with the Windsors on July 16 and brought a message to the Spanish Foreign Minister, who passed it along to the German ambassador, who, in turn, flashed it to Berlin. Churchill, the message said, had designated the Duke as Governor of the Bahamas "in a very cool and categorical letter" and ordered him to proceed to his post at once. Should he fail to do so, "Churchill has threatened Windsor with a court-martial." The Spanish government agreed, the dispatch added, "to warn the Duke most urgently once more against taking up the post."

Rivera was back from a second visit to Lisbon on July 22, and the next day the German ambassador in Madrid duly reported on his findings in a "most urgent, top secret" telegram to Ribbentrop.

He had two long conversations with the Duke of Windsor; at the last one the Duchess was present also. The Duke expressed himself very freely . . . Politically he was more and more distant from the King and the present British Government. The Duke and Duchess have less fear of the King, who was quite foolish, than of the shrewd Queen, who was intriguing skillfully against the Duke and particularly against the Duchess.

---

* Fifty million Swiss francs, deposited in Switzerland, Ribbentrop told Schellenberg, adding that "the Fuehrer is quite ready to go to a higher figure."

The Duke was considering making a public statement . . . disavowing present English policy and breaking with his brother . . . The Duke and Duchess said they very much desired to return to Spain.

To facilitate this, the ambassador had arranged with Suñer, the telegram added, to send another Spanish emissary to Portugal "to persuade the Duke to leave Lisbon, as if for a long excursion in an automobile, and then to cross the border at a place which has been arranged, where the Spanish secret police will see that there is a safe crossing of the frontier."

Two days later the ambassador added further information from Rivera in an "urgent and strictly confidential" telegram to Ribbentrop.

When he gave the Duke the advice not to go to the Bahamas, but to return to Spain, since the Duke was likely to be called upon to play an important role in English policy and possibly to ascend the English throne, both the Duke and Duchess gave evidence of astonishment. Both . . . replied that according to the English constitution this would not be possible after the abdication. When the confidential emissary then expressed his expectation that the course of the war might bring about changes even in the English constitution, the Duchess especially became very pensive.

In this dispatch the German ambassador reminded Ribbentrop that Rivera did not know of "any German interest in the matter." The young Spaniard apparently believed he was acting for his own government.

By the last week in July, the Nazi plan to kidnap the Windsors had been drawn up. Walter Schellenberg was assigned personally by Hitler to carry it out. He had flown from Berlin to Madrid, conferred with the German ambassador there, and gone on to Portugal to begin work. On July 26 the ambassador was able to file a long "most urgent and top secret" dispatch to Ribbentrop outlining the plot.

. . . A firm intention by the Duke and Duchess to return to Spain can be assumed. To strengthen this intention the second confidential emissary was sent off today with a letter to the Duke very skillfully composed; as an enclosure to it was attached the very precisely prepared plan for carrying out the crossing of the frontier.

According to this plan the Duke and his wife should set out officially for a summer vacation in the mountains at a place near the Spanish frontier, in order to cross over at a precisely designated place at a particular time in the course of a hunting trip. Since the Duke is without passports, the Portuguese frontier official in charge there will be won over.

At the time set according to plan, the first confidential emissary [Primo de Rivera] is to be staying at the frontier with Spanish forces suitably placed in order to guarantee safety.

Schellenberg, with his group, is operating out of Lisbon in closest relation to the same purpose.

For this purpose, the journey to the place of the summer vacation, as well as the vacation itself, will be shadowed with the help of a trustworthy Portuguese police chief . . .

At the exact moment of the crossing of the frontier as scheduled the Schellenberg group is to take over the security arrangements on the Portuguese side of the frontier and continue thus into Spain as a direct escort which is to be unobtrusively changed from time to time.

For the security of the entire plan, the [Spanish] Minister has selected another confidential agent, a woman, who can make contact if necessary with the second confidential agent and can also, if necessary, get information to the Schellenberg group.

In case there should be an emergency as a result of action by the British Intelligence Service preparations are being made whereby the Duke and Duchess can reach Spain by plane. In this case, as in the execution of the first plan, the chief requisite is to obtain willingness to leave by psychologically adroit influence upon the pronounced English mentality of the Duke, without giving the impression of flight, through exploiting anxiety about the British Intelligence Service and the prospect of free political activity from Spanish soil.

In addition to the protection in Lisbon, it is being considered in case of necessity to induce willingness to leave by a suitable scare maneuver to be charged to the British Intelligence Service.

Such was the Nazi plan to kidnap the Windsors. It had a typical German clumsiness, and it was handicapped by the customary German inability to understand "the English mentality of the Duke."

The "scare maneuvers" were duly carried out by Schellenberg. One night he arranged for some stone-throwing against the windows of the Windsors' villa and then circulated rumors among the servants that it had been done by the "British Secret Service." He had a bouquet delivered to the Duchess with a card: "Beware of the machinations of the British Secret Service. From a Portuguese friend who has your interests at heart." And in an official report to Berlin he reported that "a firing of shots (harmless breaking of the bedroom window) scheduled for the night of July 30 was omitted, since the psychological effect on the Duchess would only have been to increase her desire to depart."

Time was getting short. On July 30 Schellenberg reported the arrival in Lisbon of Sir Walter Monckton, an old friend of the Duke and an important official in the British government. His mission was obviously to get the Windsors speeding toward the Bahamas as soon as possible. On the same day the German ambassador in Madrid was telegraphing Ribbentrop "most urgent, top secret" that a German agent in Lisbon had just informed him that the Duke and Duchess were planning to depart on August 1—two days hence. In view of this information he asked Ribbentrop "whether we should not, to some extent, emerge from our reserve." According to German intelligence, the ambassador continued, the Duke had expressed to his host, the Portuguese banker Ricardo do Espirito

Santo Silva, "a desire to come in contact with the Fuehrer." Why not arrange for a meeting between Windsor and Hitler?

The next day, July 31, the ambassador was again wiring Ribbentrop "most urgent and top secret," telling him that according to the Spanish emissary, who had just returned from seeing the Windsors in Lisbon, the Duke and Duchess, while "strongly impressed by reports of English intrigues against them and the danger of their personal safety," apparently were planning to sail on August 1, though Windsor was trying "to conceal the true date." The Spanish Minister of the Interior, the ambassador added, was going to make "a last effort to prevent the Duke and Duchess from leaving."

The news that the Windsors might be leaving so soon alarmed Ribbentrop and from his special train at Fuschl he got off a "most urgent, top secret" telegram to the German minister in Lisbon late on the afternoon of the same day, July 31. He asked that the Duke be informed through his Portuguese banker host of the following:

Basically Germany wants peace with the English people. The Churchill clique stands in the way of this peace. Following the rejection of the Fuehrer's last appeal to reason, Germany is now determined to force England to make peace by every means in her power. It would be a good thing if the Duke were to keep himself prepared for further developments. In such case Germany would be willing to co-operate most closely with the Duke and to clear the way for any desire expressed by the Duke and Duchess . . . Should the Duke and Duchess have other intentions, but be ready to collaborate in the establishment of a good relationship between Germany and England, Germany is likewise prepared to co-operate with the Duke and to arrange the future of the Ducal couple in accordance with their wishes. The Portuguese confidant, with whom the Duke is living, should make the most earnest effort to prevent his departure tomorrow, since reliable reports are in our possession to the effect that Churchill intends to get the Duke into his power in the Bahamas in order to keep him there permanently, and also because the establishment of contact at an appropriate moment with the Duke on the Bahama Islands would present the greatest difficulty for us . . .

The German Foreign Minister's urgent message reached the legation in Lisbon shortly before midnight. The German minister saw Senhor Espirito Santo Silva during the course of the night and urged him to pass the word on to his distinguished guest. This the banker did on the morning of August 1 and according to a dispatch of the legation the Duke was deeply impressed.

The Duke paid tribute to the Fuehrer's desire for peace, which was in complete agreement with his own point of view. He was firmly convinced that if he had been King it would never have come to war. To the appeal made to him to co-operate at a suitable time in the establishment of peace he agreed gladly. However, at the present time he must follow the official orders of his

Government. Disobedience would disclose his intentions prematurely, bring about a scandal, and deprive him of his prestige in England. He was also convinced that the present moment was too early for him to come forward, since there was as yet no inclination in England for an approach to Germany. However, as soon as this frame of mind changed he would be ready to return immediately . . . Either England would yet call upon him, which he considered to be entirely possible, or Germany would express the desire to negotiate with him. In both cases he was prepared for any personal sacrifice and would make himself available without the slightest personal ambition.

He would remain in continuing communication with his previous host and had agreed with him upon a code word, upon receiving which he would immediately come back over.

To the consternation of the Germans, the Duke and Duchess sailed on the evening of August 1 on the American liner *Excalibur*. In a final report on the failure of his mission made in a long telegram "to the Foreign Minister [Ribbentrop] personally" on the following day, Schellenberg declared that he had done everything possible right up to the last moment to prevent the departure. A brother of Franco, who was the Spanish ambassador in Lisbon, was prevailed upon to make a last-minute appeal to the Windsors not to go. The automobile carrying the ducal baggage was "sabotaged," Schellenberg claimed, so that the luggage arrived at the ship late. The Germans spread rumors that a time bomb had been planted aboard the ship. Portuguese officials delayed the sailing time until they had searched the liner from top to bottom.

Nevertheless, the Windsors departed that evening. The Nazi plot had failed. Schellenberg, in his final report to Ribbentrop, blamed it on the influence of Monckton, on the collapse of "the Spanish plan" and on "the Duke's mentality."

There is one last paper on the plot in the captured files of the German Foreign Minister. On August 15 the German minister in Lisbon wired Berlin: "The confidant has just received a telegram from the Duke from Bermuda, asking him to send a communication as soon as action was advisable. Should any answer be made?"

No answer has been found in the Wilhelmstrasse papers. By the middle of August, Hitler had decided to conquer Great Britain by armed force. There was no need to find a new King for England. The island, like all the other conquered territory, would be ruled from Berlin. Or so Hitler thought.

So much for this curious tale, as told by the secret German documents and added to by Schellenberg, who was the least reliable of men—though it is difficult to believe that he invented his own role, which he admits was a ridiculous one, out of whole cloth.

In a statement made through his London solicitors on August 1, 1957, after the German documents were released for publication, the Duke branded the communications between Ribbentrop and the German ambassadors in Spain and Portugal as "complete fabrications and, in part, gross distortions of the truth." Windsor explained that while in Lisbon in 1940, waiting to sail for the Bahamas, "certain people," whom he discovered to be pro-Nazi sympathizers, made definite efforts to persuade him to return to Spain and not assume his post as governor.

"It was even suggested to me that there would be a personal risk to the Duchess and myself if we were to proceed to the Bahamas," he said. "At no time did I ever entertain any thought of complying with such a suggestion, which I treated with the contempt it deserved."

The British Foreign Office issued a formal statement declaring that the Duke never wavered in his loyalty to Great Britain during the war.[42]

23

BARBAROSSA: THE TURN OF RUSSIA

WHILE HITLER WAS BUSY that summer of 1940 directing the conquest of the West, Stalin was taking advantage of the Fuehrer's preoccupations by moving into the Baltic States and reaching down into the Balkans.

On the surface all was friendly between the two great dictatorships. Molotov, acting for Stalin, lost no opportunity to praise and flatter the Germans on every occasion of a new act of aggression or a fresh conquest. When Germany invaded Norway and Denmark on April 9, 1940, the Soviet Foreign Commissar hastened to tell Ambassador von der Schulenburg in Moscow that very morning that "the Soviet Government understood the measures which were forced on Germany." "We wish Germany," said Molotov, "complete success in her defensive measures."[1]

A month later, when the German ambassador called on Molotov to inform him officially of the Wehrmacht's attack in the West, which Ribbentrop had instructed his envoy to explain "was forced upon Germany by the impending Anglo–French push on the Ruhr by way of Belgium and Holland," the Soviet statesman again expressed his pleasure. "Molotov received the communication in an understanding spirit," Schulenburg wired Berlin, "and added that he realized that Germany must protect herself against Anglo–French attack. He had no doubt of our success."[2]

On June 17, the day France asked for an armistice, Molotov summoned Schulenburg to his office "and expressed the warmest congratulations of the Soviet Government on the splendid success of the German Wehrmacht."

The Foreign Commissar had something else to say, and this did not sound quite so pleasant in German ears. He informed the German envoy, as the latter wired Berlin "most urgent," of "the Soviet action against the Baltic States," adding—and one can almost see the gleam in Molotov's eyes—"that it had become necessary to put an end to all the intrigues by which England and France had tried to sow discord and mistrust between Germany and the Soviet Union in the Baltic States."[3] To put an end to such "discord" the Soviet government, Molotov added, had dispatched "special emissaries" to the three Baltic countries. They were, in fact, three of Stalin's best hatchetmen: Dekanozov, who was sent to Lithuania; Vishinsky, to Latvia; Zhdanov, to Estonia.

They carried out their assignments with the thoroughness which one would expect from this trio, especially the latter two individuals. Already on June 14, the day German troops entered Paris, the Soviet government had sent a nine-hour ultimatum to Lithuania demanding the resignation of its government, the arrest of some of its key officials and the right to send in as many Red Army troops as it pleased. Though the Lithuanian government accepted the ultimatum, Moscow deemed its acceptance "unsatisfactory," and the next day, June 15, Soviet troops occupied the country, the only one of the Baltic States to border on Germany. During the next couple of days similar Soviet ultimatums were dispatched to Latvia and Estonia, after which they were similarly overrun by the Red Army.

Stalin could be as crude and as ruthless in these matters as Hitler—and even more cynical. The press having been suppressed, the political leaders arrested and all parties but the Communist declared illegal, "elections" were staged by the Russians in all three countries on July 14, and after the respective parliaments thus "elected" had voted for the incorporation of their lands into the Soviet Union, the Supreme Soviet (Parliament) of Russia "admitted" them into the motherland: Lithuania on August 3, Latvia on August 5, Estonia on August 6.

Adolf Hitler was humiliated, but, busy as he was trying to organize the invasion of Britain, could do nothing about it. The letters from the envoys of the three Baltic States in Berlin protesting Russian aggression were returned to them by order of Ribbentrop. To further humble the Germans Molotov brusquely told them on August 11 to "liquidate" their legations in Kaunas, Riga and Tallinn within a fortnight and close down their Baltic consulates by September 1.

The seizure of the Baltic States did not satisfy Stalin's appetite. The surprisingly quick collapse of the Anglo–French armies spurred him on to get as much as he could while the getting was good. He obviously thought there was little time to lose. On June 23, the day after the French formally capitulated and signed the armistice at Compiègne, Molotov again called in the Nazi ambassador in Moscow and told him that "the solution of the Bessarabian question brooked no further delay. The Soviet government was determined to use force, should the Rumanian government decline a peaceful agreement." It expected Germany, Molotov added, "not to hinder but to support the Soviets in their action." Moreover, "the Soviet claim likewise extended to Bucovina."[4] Bessarabia had been taken by Rumania from Russia at the end of the First World War, but Bucovina had never belonged to it, having been under Austria until Rumania grabbed it in 1919. At the negotiations in Moscow for the Nazi-Soviet Pact, Ribbentrop, as he now reminded Hitler, who had questioned him about it, had been forced to give Bessarabia to the Russian sphere of interest. But he had never given away Bucovina.

There was some alarm in Berlin, which spread to OKW headquarters in the West. The Wehrmacht was desperately dependent on Rumanian oil and Germany needed the foodstuffs and fodder it also got from this Balkan country. These would be lost if the Red Army occupied Rumania. Some time back, on May 23, at the height of the Battle of France, the Rumanian General Staff had sent an S.O.S. to OKW informing it that Soviet troops were concentrating on the border. Jodl summed up the reaction at Hitler's headquarters in his diary the next day: "Situation in East becomes threatening because of Russian concentration of force against Bessarabia."

On the night of June 26 Russia delivered an ultimatum to Rumania demanding the ceding to it of Bessarabia and northern Bucovina and insisting on a reply the next day. Ribbentrop, in panic, dashed off instructions from his special train to his minister in Bucharest telling him to advise the Rumanian government to yield, which it did on June 27. Soviet troops marched into the newly acquired territories the next day and Berlin breathed a sigh of relief that at least the rich sources of oil and food had not been cut off by Russia's grabbing the whole of Rumania.

It is clear from his acts and from the secret German papers that though Stalin was out to get all he could in Eastern Europe while the Germans were tied down in the West, he did not wish or contemplate a break with Hitler.

Toward the end of June Churchill had tried to warn Stalin in a personal letter of the danger of the German conquests to Russia as well as to Britain.[5] The Soviet dictator did not bother to answer; probably, like almost everyone else, he thought Britain was finished. So he tattled to the Germans what the British government was up to. Sir Stafford Cripps, a left-wing Labor Party leader, whom the Prime Minister had rushed to Moscow as the new British ambassador in the hope of striking a more responsive chord among the Bolsheviks—a forlorn hope, as he later ruefully admitted—was received by Stalin early in July in an interview that Churchill described as "formal and frigid." On July 13 Molotov, on Stalin's instructions, handed the German ambassador a written memorandum of this confidential conversation.

It is an interesting document. It reveals, as no other source does, the severe limitations of the Soviet dictator in his cold calculations of foreign affairs. Schulenburg sped it to Berlin "most urgent" and, of course, "secret," and Ribbentrop was so grateful for its contents that he told the Soviet government he "greatly appreciated this information." Cripps had pressed Stalin, the memorandum said, for his attitude on this principal question, among others:

The British Government was convinced that Germany was striving for hegemony in Europe . . . This was dangerous to the Soviet Union as well as England. Therefore both countries ought to agree on a common policy of self-protection against Germany and on the re-establishment of the European balance of power . . .

Stalin's answers are given as follows:

He did not see any danger of the hegemony of any one country in Europe and still less any danger that Europe might be engulfed by Germany. Stalin observed the policy of Germany, and knew several leading German statesmen well. He had not discovered any desire on their part to engulf European countries. Stalin was not of the opinion that German military successes menaced the Soviet Union and her friendly relations with Germany . . .[6]

Such staggering smugness, such abysmal ignorance leave one breathless. The Russian tyrant did not know, of course, the secrets of Hitler's turgid mind, but the Fuehrer's past behavior, his known ambitions and the unexpectedly rapid Nazi conquests ought to have been enough to warn him of the dire danger the Soviet Union was now in. But, incomprehensibly, they were not enough.

From the captured Nazi documents and from the testimony of many leading German figures in the great drama that was being played over the vast expanse of Western Europe that year, it is plain that at the very moment of Stalin's monumental complacency Hitler had in fact been mulling over in his mind the idea of turning on the Soviet Union and destroying her.

The basic idea went back much further, at least fifteen years—to *Mein Kampf.*

And so we National Socialists [Hitler wrote] take up where we broke off six hundred years ago. We stop the endless German movement toward the south and west of Europe and turn our gaze toward the lands of the East . . . When we speak of new territory in Europe today we must think principally of Russia and her border vassal states. Destiny itself seems to wish to point out the way to us here . . . This colossal empire in the East is ripe for dissolution, and the end of the Jewish domination in Russia will also be the end of Russia as a state.[7]

This idea lay like bedrock in Hitler's mind, and his pact with Stalin had not changed it at all, but merely postponed acting on it. And but briefly. In fact, less than two months after the deal was signed and had been utilized to destroy Poland the Fuehrer instructed the Army that the conquered Polish territory was to be regarded "as an assembly area for future German operations." The date was October 18, 1939, and Halder recorded it that day in his diary.

Five weeks later, on November 23, when he harangued his reluctant generals about attacking in the West, Russia was by no means out of his mind. *"We can oppose Russia,"* he declared, *"only when we are free in the West."* At that time the two-front war, the nightmare of German generals for a century, was very much on Hitler's mind, and he spoke of it at length on this occasion. He would not repeat the mistake of former German rulers; he would continue to see to it that the Army had one front at a time.

It was only natural, then, that with the fall of France, the chasing of the British Army across the Channel and the prospects of Britain's imminent collapse, Hitler's thoughts should turn once again to Russia. For he now supposed himself to be free in the West and thereby to have achieved the one condition he had laid down in order to be in a position to "oppose Russia." The rapidity with which Stalin seized the Baltic States and the two Rumanian provinces in June spurred Hitler to a decision.

The moment of its making can now be traced. Jodl says that the "fundamental decision" was taken "as far back as during the Western Campaign."[8] Colonel Walter Warlimont, Jodl's deputy at OKW, remembers that on July 29 Jodl announced at a meeting of Operations Staff officers that "Hitler intended to attack the U.S.S.R. in the spring of 1941." Sometime previous to this meeting, Jodl related, Hitler had told Keitel "that he intended to launch the attack against the U.S.S.R. during the fall of 1940." But this was too much even for Keitel and he had argued Hitler out of it by contending that not only the bad weather in the autumn but the difficulties of transferring the bulk of the Army from the West to the East made it impossible. By the time of this conference on July 29, Warlimont relates, "the date for the intended attack [against Russia] had been moved back to the spring of 1941."[9]

Only a week before, we know from Halder's diary,[10] the Fuehrer had still held to a possible campaign in Russia for the autumn if Britain were not invaded. At a military conference in Berlin on July 21 he told Brauchitsch to get busy on the preparations for it. That the Army Commander in Chief and his General Staff already had given the problem some thought—but not enough thought—is evident from his response to Hitler. Brauchitsch told the Leader that the campaign "would last four to six weeks" and that the aim would be "to defeat the Russian Army or at least to occupy enough Russian territory so that Soviet bombers could not reach Berlin or the Silesian industrial area while, on the other hand, the Luftwaffe bombers could reach all important objectives in the Soviet Union." Brauchitsch thought that from eighty to a hundred German divisions could do the job; he assessed Russian strength as "fifty to seventy-five good divisions." Halder's notes on what Brauchitsch told him of the meeting show that Hitler had been stung by Stalin's grabs in the East, that he thought the Soviet dictator was "coquetting with England" in order to encourage her to hold out, but that he had seen no signs that Russia was preparing to enter the war against Germany.

At a further conference at the Berghof on the last day of July 1940, the receding prospects of an invasion of Britain prompted Hitler to announce for the first time to his Army chiefs his decision on Russia. Halder was personally present this time and jotted down his shorthand notes of exactly what the warlord said.[11] They reveal not only that Hitler had made a definite decision to attack Russia in the following spring but that he had already worked out in his mind the major strategic aims.

Britain's hope [Hitler said] lies in Russia and America. If that hope in Russia is destroyed then it will be destroyed for America too because elimination of Russia will enormously increase Japan's power in the Far East.

The more he thought of it the more convinced he was, Hitler said, that Britain's stubborn determination to continue the war was due to its counting on the Soviet Union.

Something strange [he explained] has happened in Britain! The British were already completely down.* Now they are back on their feet. Intercepted conversations. Russia unpleasantly disturbed by the swift developments in Western Europe.

Russia needs only to hint to England that she does not wish to see Germany too strong and the English, like a drowning man, will regain hope that the situation in six to eight months will have completely changed.

But if Russia is smashed, Britain's last hope will be shattered. Then Germany will be master of Europe and the Balkans.

Decision: In view of these considerations Russia must be liquidated. Spring, 1941.

The sooner Russia is smashed, the better.†

The Nazi warlord then elaborated on his strategic plans which, it was obvious to the generals, had been ripening in his mind for some time despite all his preoccupations with the fighting in the West. The operation, he said, would be worth carrying out only if its aim was to shatter the Soviet nation in one great blow. Conquering a lot of Russian territory would not be enough. "Wiping out of the very power to exist of Russia! That is the goal!" Hitler emphasized. There would be two initial drives: one in the south to Kiev and the Dnieper River, the second in the north up through the Baltic States and then toward Moscow. There the two armies would make a junction. After that a special operation, if necessary, to secure the Baku oil fields. The very thought of such new conquests excited Hitler; he already had in mind what he would do with them. He would annex outright, he said, the Ukraine, White Russia and the Baltic States and extend Finland's territory to the White Sea. For the whole operation he would allot 120 divisions, keeping sixty divisions for the defense of the West and Scandinavia. The attack, he laid it down, would begin in May 1941 and would take five months to carry through. It would be finished by winter. He would have preferred, he said, to do it this year but this had not proved possible.

---

* Halder uses the English word "down" here in the German text.
† The emphasis in the report is Halder's.

The next day, August 1, Halder went to work on the plans with his General Staff. Though he would later claim to have opposed the whole idea of an attack on Russia as insane, his diary entry for this day discloses him full of enthusiasm as he applied himself to the challenging new task.

Planning now went ahead with typical German thoroughness on three levels: that of the Army General Staff, of Warlimont's Operations Staff at OKW, of General Thomas' Economic and Armaments Branch of OKW. Thomas was instructed on August 14 by Goering that Hitler desired deliveries of ordered goods to the Russians "only till spring of 1941."* In the meantime his office was to make a detailed survey of Soviet industry, transportation and oil centers both as a guide to targets and later on as an aid for administering Russia.

A few days before, on August 9, Warlimont had got out his first directive for preparing the deployment areas in the East for the jump-off against the Russians. The code name for this was *Aufbau Ost*—"Build-up East." On August 26, Hitler ordered ten infantry and two armored divisions to be sent from the West to Poland. The panzer units, he stipulated, were to be concentrated in southeastern Poland so that they could intervene to protect the Rumanian oil fields.[13] The transfer of large bodies of troops to the East† could not be done without exciting Stalin's easily aroused suspicions if he learned of it, and the Germans went to great lengths to see that he didn't. Since some movements were bound to be detected, General Ernst Koestring, the German military attaché in Moscow, was instructed to inform the Soviet General Staff that it was merely a question of replacing older men, who were being released to industry, by younger men. On September 6, Jodl got out a directive outlining in considerable detail the means of camouflage and deception. "These regroupings," he laid it down, "must not create the impression in Russia that we are preparing an offensive in the East."[14]

So that the armed services should not rest on their laurels after the great victories of the summer, Hitler issued on November 12, 1940, a comprehensive top-secret directive outlining new military tasks all over Europe and beyond. We shall come back to some of them. What concerns us here is that portion dealing with the Soviet Union.

Political discussions have been initiated with the aim of clarifying Russia's attitude for the time being. Irrespective of the results of these discussions, all

---

* In his report on this Thomas stresses how punctual Soviet deliveries of goods to Germany were at this time. In fact, he says, they continued to be "right up to the start of the attack," and observes, not without amusement, that "even during the last few days, shipments of India rubber from the Far East were completed [by the Russians] over express transit trains"—presumably over the Trans-Siberian Railway.[12]

† The Germans had kept only seven divisions in Poland, two of which were transferred to the West during the spring campaign. The troops there, Halder cracked, were scarcely enough to maintain the customs service. If Stalin had attacked Germany in June 1940, the Red Army probably could have got to Berlin before any serious resistance was organized.

preparations for the East which have already been verbally ordered will be continued. Instructions on this will follow, as soon as the general outline of the Army's operational plans have been submitted to, and approved by, me.[15]

As a matter of fact, on that very day, November 12, Molotov arrived in Berlin to continue with Hitler himself those political discussions.

MOLOTOV IN BERLIN

Relations between Berlin and Moscow had for some months been souring. It was one thing for Stalin and Hitler to double-cross third parties, but quite another when they began to double-cross each other. Hitler had been helpless to prevent the Russians from grabbing the Baltic States and the two Rumanian provinces of Bessarabia and northern Bucovina, and his frustration only added to his growing resentment. The Russian drive westward would have to be stopped and first of all in Rumania, whose oil resources were of vital importance to a Germany which, because of the British blockade, could no longer import petroleum by sea.

To complicate Hitler's problem, Hungary and Bulgaria too demanded slices of Rumanian territory. Hungary, in fact, as the summer of 1940 approached its end, prepared to go to war in order to win back Transylvania, which Rumania had taken from her after the First World War. Such a war, Hitler realized, would cut off Germany from her main source of crude oil and probably bring the Russians in to occupy all of Rumania and rob the Reich permanently of Rumanian oil.

By August 28 the situation had become so threatening that Hitler ordered five panzer and three motorized divisions plus parachute and airborne troops to make ready to seize the Rumanian oil fields on September 1.[16] That same day he conferred with Ribbentrop and Ciano at the Berghof and then dispatched them to Vienna, where they were to lay down the law to the foreign ministers of Hungary and Rumania and make them accept Axis arbitration. This mission was accomplished without much trouble after Ribbentrop had browbeaten both sides. On August 30 at the Belvedere Palace in Vienna the Hungarians and Rumanians accepted the Axis settlement. When Mihai Manoilescu, the Rumanian Foreign Minister, saw the map stipulating that about one half of Transylvania should go to Hungary, he fainted, falling across the table at which the signing of the agreement was taking place, and regaining consciousness only after physicians had worked over him with camphor.*[17] Ostensibly for her reasonableness but really to give Hitler a legal excuse for his

---

* It cost King Carol his throne. On September 6 he abdicated in favor of his eighteen-year-old son, Michael, and fled with his red-haired mistress, Magda Lupescu, in a ten-car special train filled with what might be described as "loot" across Yugoslavia to Switzerland. General Ion Antonescu, chief of the fascist "Iron Guard" and a friend of Hitler, became dictator.

further plans, Rumania received from Germany and Italy a guarantee of what was left of her territory.*

Light on the Fuehrer's further plans came to his intimates three weeks later. On September 20, in a top-secret directive, Hitler ordered the sending of "military missions" to Rumania.

To the world their tasks will be to guide friendly Rumania in organizing and instructing her forces.

The real tasks—which must not become apparent either to the Rumanians or to our own troops—will be:

To protect the oil district . . .

To prepare for deployment from Rumanian bases of German and Rumanian forces in case a war with Soviet Russia is forced upon us.[18]

That would take care of the southern flank of a new front he was beginning to picture in his mind.

The Vienna award and especially the German guarantee of Rumania's remaining territory went down badly in Moscow, which had not been consulted. When Schulenburg called on Molotov on September 1 to present a windy memorandum from Ribbentrop attempting to explain—and justify—what had taken place in Vienna, the Foreign Commissar, the ambassador reported, "was reserved, in contrast to his usual manner." He was not too reserved, however, to lodge a strong verbal protest. He accused the German government of violating Article III of the Nazi–Soviet Pact, which called for consultation, and of presenting Russia with "accomplished facts" which conflicted with German assurances about "questions of common interests."[19] The thieves, as is almost inevitable in such cases, had begun to quarrel over the spoils.

Recriminations became more heated in the following days. On September 3 Ribbentrop telegraphed a long memorandum to Moscow denying that Germany had violated the Moscow Pact and accusing Russia of having done just that by gobbling up the Baltic States and two Rumanian provinces without consulting Berlin. The memorandum was couched in strong language and the Russians replied to it on September 21 with equally stern words—by this time both sides were putting their cases in writing. The Soviet answer reiterated that Germany had broken the pact, warned that Russia still had many interests in Rumania and concluded with a sarcastic proposal that if the article calling for consultation involved "certain inconveniences and restrictions" for the Reich the Soviet government was ready to amend or delete this clause of the treaty.[20]

The Kremlin's suspicions of Hitler were further aroused by two events in September. On the sixteenth, Ribbentrop wired Schulenburg to call on Molotov and "casually" inform him that German reinforcements for northern Norway were going to be sent by way of Finland. A few days later, on September 25, the Nazi Foreign Minister got off another telegram to the embassy in Moscow, this time addressed to the chargé, Schulenburg

---

* Minus southern Dobrudja, which Rumania was forced to cede to Bulgaria.

having returned to Germany on leave. It was a most confidential message, being marked "Strictly Secret—State Secret," and directing that its instructions were to be carried out only if on the next day the chargé received from Berlin by wire or telephone a special code word.[21]

He was to inform Molotov that "in the next few days" Japan, Italy and Germany were going to sign in Berlin a military alliance. It was not to be directed against Russia—a specific article would say that.

This alliance [Ribbentrop stated] is directed exclusively against American warmongers. To be sure this is, as usual, not expressly stated in the treaty, but can be unmistakably inferred from its terms . . . Its exclusive purpose is to bring the elements pressing for America's entry into the war to their senses by conclusively demonstrating to them that if they enter the present struggle they will automatically have to deal with the three great powers as adversaries.[22]

The chilly Soviet Foreign Commissar, whose suspicions of the Germans were now growing like flowers in June, was highly skeptical when Werner von Tippelskirch, the chargé, brought him this news on the evening of September 26. He said immediately, with that pedantic attention to detail which so annoyed all with whom he negotiated, friend or foe, that according to Article IV of the Moscow Pact the Soviet government was entitled to see the text of this tripartite military alliance *before it was signed,* including, he added, the text of "any secret protocols."

Molotov also wanted to know more about the German agreement with Finland for the transport of troops through that country, which he had heard of mostly through the press, he said, including a United Press dispatch from Berlin. During the last three days, Molotov added, Moscow had received reports of the landing of German forces in at least three Finnish ports, "without having been informed thereof by Germany."

The Soviet Government [Molotov continued] wished to receive the text of the agreement on the passage of troops through Finland, including its secret portions . . . and to be informed as to the object of the agreement, against whom it was directed, and the purposes that were being served thereby.[23]

The Russians had to be mollified—even the obtuse Ribbentrop could see that—and on October 2 he telegraphed to Moscow what he said was the text of the agreement with Finland. He also reiterated that the Tripartite Pact, which in the meantime had been signed,* was not directed

---

* It was signed in Berlin on September 27, 1940, in a comic-opera setting and ceremony which I have described elsewhere (*Berlin Diary,* pp. 532–37). In Articles 1 and 2, respectively, Japan recognized "the leadership of Germany and Italy in the establishment of a new order in Europe," and the two countries recognized Japan's leadership for the same in Greater East Asia. Article 3 provided for mutual assistance should any one of the powers be attacked by the United States, though America was not specifically mentioned, only defined. To me, as I wrote in my diary that day in Berlin, the most significant thing about the pact was that it meant that Hitler

against the Soviet Union and solemnly declared that "there were no secret protocols nor any other secret agreements."[24] After instructing Tippelskirch on October 7 to inform Molotov "incidentally" that a German "military mission" was being sent to Rumania and after receiving Molotov's skeptical reaction to this further news ("How many troops are you sending to Rumania?" the Foreign Commissar had demanded to know),[25] Ribbentrop on October 13 got off a long letter to Stalin in an attempt to quiet Soviet uneasiness about Germany.[26]

It is, as might be expected, a fatuous and at the same time arrogant epistle, abounding in nonsense and lies and subterfuge. England is blamed for the war and all its aftermaths thus far, but one thing is sure: "The war as such has been won by us. It is only a question of how long it will be before England . . . admits to collapse." The German moves against Russia in Finland and Rumania as well as the Tripartite Pact are explained as really a boon to Russia. In the meantime British diplomacy and British secret agents are trying to stir up trouble between Russia and Germany. To frustrate them, why not send Molotov to Berlin, Ribbentrop asked Stalin, so that the Fuehrer could "explain personally his views regarding the future molding of relations between our two countries"?

Ribbentrop gave a sly hint what those views were: *nothing less than dividing up the world among the four totalitarian powers.*

It appears to be the mission of the Four Powers [he said]—*the Soviet Union, Italy, Japan and Germany—to adopt a long-range policy . . . by delimitation of their interests on a world-wide scale.*

The emphasis is Ribbentrop's.

There was some delay in the German Embassy in Moscow in getting this letter to its destination, which made Ribbentrop livid with rage and inspired an angry telegram from him to Schulenburg demanding to know why his letter had not been delivered until the seventeenth and why, "in keeping with the importance of its contents," it was not delivered to Stalin personally—Schulenburg had handed it to Molotov.[27] Stalin replied on October 22, in a remarkably cordial tone. "Molotov admits," he wrote, "that he is under obligation to pay you a visit in Berlin. He hereby accepts your invitation."[28] Stalin's geniality must have been only a mask. Schulenburg wired Berlin a few days later that the Russians were protesting the refusal of Germany to deliver war material while at the same time shipping arms to Finland. "This is the first time," Schulenburg advised Berlin, "that our deliveries of arms to Finland have been mentioned by the Soviets."[29]

A dark, drizzling day, and Molotov arrived, his reception being extremely stiff and formal. Driving up the Linden to the Soviet Embassy, he looked to

---

was now reconciled to a long war. Ciano, who signed the pact for Italy, came to the same conclusion (*Ciano Diaries,* p. 296). Also, despite the disclaimer, the pact was, and was meant to be, a warning to the Soviet Union.

me like a plugging, provincial schoolmaster. But to have survived in the cutthroat competition of the Kremlin he must have something. The Germans talk glibly of letting Moscow have that old Russian dream, the Bosporus and the Dardanelles, while they will take the rest of the Balkans: Rumania, Yugoslavia and Bulgaria . . .

Thus began my diary entry in Berlin on November 12, 1940. The glib talk of the Germans was accurate enough, as far as it went. Today we know much more about this strange and—as it turned out—fateful meeting, thanks to the capture of the Foreign Office documents, in which one finds the confidential German minutes of the two-day sessions, all but one of them kept by the ubiquitous Dr. Schmidt.*[30]

At the first meeting between the two foreign ministers, during the forenoon of November 12, Ribbentrop was in one of his most vapid and arrogant moods but Molotov quickly saw through him and sized up what the German game was. "England," Ribbentrop began, "is beaten and it is only a question of time when she will finally admit her defeat . . . The beginning of the end has now arrived for the British Empire." The British, it was true, were hoping for aid from America, but "the entry of the United States into the war is of no consequence at all for Germany. Germany and Italy will never again allow an Anglo–Saxon to land on the European Continent . . . This is no military problem at all . . . The Axis Powers are, therefore, not considering how they can win the war, but rather how rapidly they can end the war which is already won."

This being so, Ribbentrop explained, the time had come for the four powers, Russia, Germany, Italy and Japan, to define their "spheres of interest." The Fuehrer, he said, had concluded that all four countries would naturally expand "in a southerly direction." Japan had already turned south, as had Italy, while Germany, after the establishment of the "New Order" in Western Europe, would find her additional *Lebensraum* in (of all places!) "Central Africa." Ribbentrop said he "wondered" if Russia would also not "turn to the south for the natural outlet to the open sea which was so important for her."

"Which sea?" Molotov interjected icily.

This was an awkward but crucial question, as the Germans would learn during the next thirty-six hours of ceaseless conversations with this stubborn, prosaic, precise Bolshevik. The interruption floored Ribbentrop for a moment and he could not think of an answer. Instead, he rambled on about "the great changes that would take place all over the world after the war" and gabbled that the important thing was that "both partners to the German–Russian pact had together done some good business" and "would continue to do some business." But when Molotov insisted on an

---

* Their accuracy on this occasion was later confirmed by Stalin, though not intentionally. Churchill says he received an account of Molotov's talks in Berlin from Stalin in August 1942 "which in no essential differs from the German record," though it was "more pithy." (Churchill, *Their Finest Hour*, pp. 585–86.)

answer to his simple question, Ribbentrop finally replied by suggesting that "in the long run the most advantageous access to the sea for Russia could be found in the direction of the Persian Gulf and the Arabian Sea."

Molotov sat there, says Dr. Schmidt, who was present taking notes, "with an impenetrable expression."[31] He said very little, except to comment at the end that "precision and vigilance" were necessary in delimiting spheres of interest, "particularly between Germany and Russia." The wily Soviet negotiator was saving his ammunition for Hitler, whom he saw in the afternoon. For the all-powerful Nazi warlord it turned out to be quite a surprising, nerve-racking, frustrating and even unique experience.

Hitler was just as vague as his Foreign Minister and even more grandiose. As soon as the weather improved, he began by saying, Germany would strike "the final blow against England." There was, to be sure, "the problem of America." But the United States could not "endanger the freedom of other nations before 1970 or 1980 . . . It had no business either in Europe, in Africa or in Asia"—an assertion which Molotov broke in to say he was in agreement with. But he was not in agreement with much else that Hitler said. After the Nazi leader had finished a lengthy exposition of pleasant generalities, stressing that there were no fundamental differences between the two countries in the pursuit of their respective aspirations and in their common drive toward "access to the ocean," Molotov replied that "the statements of the Fuehrer had been of a general nature." He would now, he said, set forth the ideas of Stalin, who on his departure from Moscow had given him "exact instructions." Whereupon he hurled the book at the German dictator who, as the minutes make clear, was scarcely prepared for it.

"The questions hailed down upon Hitler," Schmidt afterward recalled. "No foreign visitor had ever spoken to him in this way in my presence."[32]

What was Germany up to in Finland? Molotov wanted to know. What was the meaning of the New Order in Europe and in Asia, and what role would the U.S.S.R. be given in it? What was the "significance" of the Tripartite Pact? "Moreover," he continued, "there are issues to be clarified regarding Russia's Balkan and Black Sea interests with respect to Bulgaria, Rumania and Turkey." He would like, he said, to hear some answers and "explanations."

Hitler, perhaps for the first time in his life, was too taken aback to answer. He proposed that they adjourn "in view of a possible air-raid alarm," promising to go into a detailed discussion the next day.

A showdown had been postponed but not prevented, and the next morning when Hitler and Molotov resumed their talks the Russian Commissar was relentless. To begin with, about Finland, over which the two men soon became embroiled in a bitter and caustic dispute. Molotov demanded that Germany get its troops out of Finland. Hitler denied that "Finland was occupied by German troops." They were merely being sent *through* Finland to Norway. But he wanted to know "whether Russia intended to go to war against Finland." According to the German minutes,

Molotov "answered this question somewhat evasively," and Hitler was not satisfied.

"There must be no war in the Baltic," Hitler insisted. "It would put a heavy strain on German–Russian relations," a threat which he added to a moment later by saying that such a strain might bring "unforeseeable consequences." What more did the Soviet Union want in Finland, anyway? Hitler wanted to know, and his visitor answered that it wanted a "settlement on the same scale as in Bessarabia"—which meant outright annexation. Hitler's reaction to this must have perturbed even the imperturbable Russian, who hastened to ask the Fuehrer's "opinion on that."

The dictator in turn was somewhat evasive, replying that he could only repeat that "there must be no war with Finland because such a conflict might have far-reaching repercussions."

"A new factor has been introduced into the discussion by this position," Molotov retorted.

So heated had the dispute become that Ribbentrop, who must have become thoroughly frightened by this time, broke in to say, according to the German minutes, "that there was actually no reason at all for making an issue of the Finnish question. Perhaps it was merely a misunderstanding."

Hitler took advantage of this timely intervention to quickly change the subject. Could not the Russians be tempted by the unlimited plunder soon to be available with the collapse of the British Empire?

"Let us turn to more important problems," he said.

After the conquest of England [he declared] the British Empire would be apportioned as a gigantic world-wide estate in bankruptcy of forty million square kilometers. In this bankrupt estate there would be for Russia access to the ice-free and really open ocean. Thus far, a minority of forty-five million Englishmen had ruled six hundred million inhabitants of the British Empire. He was about to crush this minority . . . Under these circumstances there arose world-wide perspectives . . . All the countries which could possibly be interested in the bankrupt estate would have to stop all controversies among themselves and concern themselves exclusively with the partition of the British Empire. This applied to Germany, France, Italy, Russia and Japan.

The chilly, impassive Russian guest did not appear to be moved by such glittering "world-wide perspectives," nor was he as convinced as the Germans—a point he later rubbed in—that the British Empire would soon be there for the taking. He wanted, he said, to discuss problems "closer to Europe." Turkey, for instance, and Bulgaria and Rumania.

"The Soviet Government," he said, "is of the opinion that the German guarantee of Rumania is aimed against the interests of Soviet Russia—if one may express oneself so bluntly." He had been expressing himself bluntly all day, to the growing annoyance of his hosts, and now he pressed on. He demanded that Germany "revoke" this guarantee. Hitler declined.

All right, Molotov persisted, in view of Moscow's interest in the

Straits, what would Germany say "if Russia gave Bulgaria . . . a guarantee under exactly the same conditions as Germany and Italy had given one to Rumania"?

One can almost see Hitler's dark frown. He inquired whether Bulgaria had asked for such a guarantee, as had Rumania? "He (the Fuehrer)," the German memorandum quotes him as adding, "did not know of any request by Bulgaria." At any rate, he would first have to consult Mussolini before giving the Russians a more definite answer to their question. And he added ominously that if Germany "were perchance looking for sources of friction with Russia, she would not need the Straits for that."

But the Fuehrer, usually so talkative, had no more stomach for talk with this impossible Russian.

"At this point in the conversation," say the German minutes, "the Fuehrer called attention to the late hour and stated that in view of the possibility of English air attacks it would be better to break off the talk now, since the main issues had probably been sufficiently discussed."

That night Molotov gave a gala banquet to his hosts at the Russian Embassy on Unter den Linden. Hitler, apparently exhausted and still irritated by the afternoon's ordeal, did not put in an appearance.

The British did. I had wondered why their bombers had not appeared over Berlin, as they had almost every recent night, to remind the Soviet Commissar on his first evening in the capital that, whatever the Germans told him, Britain was still in the war, and kicking. Some of us, I confess, had waited hopefully for the planes, but they had not come. Officials in the Wilhelmstrasse, who had feared the worst, were visibly relieved. But not for long.

On the evening of November 13, the British came over early.* It gets dark in Berlin about 4 P.M. at this time of year, and shortly after 9 o'clock the air-raid sirens began to whine and then you could hear the thunder of the flak guns and, in between, the hum of the bombers overhead. According to Dr. Schmidt, who was at the banquet in the Soviet Embassy, Molotov had just proposed a friendly toast and Ribbentrop had risen to his feet to reply when the air-raid warning was sounded and the guests scattered to shelter. I remember the hurrying and scurrying down the Linden and around the corner at the Wilhelmstrasse as Germans and Russians made for the underground shelter of the Foreign Ministry. Some of the officials, Dr. Schmidt among them, ducked into the Adlon Hotel, from in front of which some of us were watching, and were unable to get to the impromptu meeting which the two foreign ministers now held in the underground depths of the Foreign Office. The minutes of this meeting were therefore taken, in the enforced absence of Dr. Schmidt, by Gustav Hilger, counselor of the German Embassy in Moscow, who had acted as one of the interpreters during the conference.

---

* Churchill says the air raid was timed for this occasion. "We had heard of the conference beforehand," he later wrote, "and though not invited to join in the discussion did not wish to be entirely left out of the proceedings." (Churchill, *Their Finest Hour,* p. 584.)

While the British bombers cruised overhead in the night and the anti-aircraft guns fired away ineffectively at them, the slippery Nazi Foreign Minister tried one last time to take the Russians in. Out of his pocket he pulled a draft of an agreement which, in substance, transformed the Tripartite Pact into a four-power pact, with Russia as the fourth member. Molotov listened patiently while Ribbentrop read it through.

Article II was the core. In it Germany, Italy, Japan and the Soviet Union undertook "to respect each other's natural spheres of influence." Any disputes concerning them would be settled "in an amicable way." The two fascist countries and Japan agreed to "recognize the present extent of the possessions of the Soviet Union and will respect it." All four countries, in Article III, agreed not to join or support any combination "directed against one of the Four Powers."

The agreement itself, Ribbentrop proposed, would be made public, but not, of course, its secret protocols, which he next proceeded to read. The most important one defined each country's "territorial aspirations." Russia's was to "center south of the national territory of the Soviet Union in the direction of the Indian Ocean."

Molotov did not rise to the bait. The proposed treaty was obviously an attempt to divert Russia from its historic pressure westward, down the Baltic, into the Balkans and through the Straits to the Mediterranean, where inevitably it would clash with the greedy designs of Germany and Italy. The U.S.S.R. was not, at least at the moment, interested in the Indian Ocean, which lay far away. What it was interested in at the moment, Molotov replied, was Europe and the Turkish Straits. "Consequently," he added, "paper agreements will not suffice for the Soviet Union; she would have to insist on effective guarantees of her security."

The questions which interested the Soviet Union [he elaborated] concerned not only Turkey but Bulgaria . . . But the fate of Rumania and Hungary was also of interest to the U.S.S.R. and could not be immaterial to her under any circumstances. It would further interest the Soviet Government to learn what the Axis contemplated with regard to Yugoslavia and Greece, and likewise, what Germany intended with regard to Poland . . . The Soviet Government was also interested in the question of Swedish neutrality . . . Besides, there existed the question of the passages out of the Baltic Sea . . .

The untiring, poker-faced Soviet Foreign Commissar left nothing out and Ribbentrop, who felt himself being buried under the avalanche of questions—for at this point Molotov said he would "appreciate it" if his guest made answer to them—protested that he was being "interrogated too closely."

He could only repeat again and again [he replied weakly] that the decisive question was whether the Soviet Union was prepared and in a position to co-operate with us in the great liquidation of the British Empire.

Molotov was ready with a cutting retort. Hilger duly noted it in the minutes.

In his reply Molotov stated that the Germans were assuming that the war against England had already actually been won. If therefore [as Hitler had maintained] Germany was waging a life-and-death struggle against England, he could only construe this as meaning that Germany was fighting "for life" and England "for death."

This sarcasm may have gone over the head of Ribbentrop, a man of monumental denseness, but Molotov took no chances. To the German's constant reiteration that Britain was finished, the Commissar finally replied, "If that is so, why are we in this shelter, and whose are these bombs which fall?"*

From this wearing experience with Moscow's tough bargainer and from further evidence that came a fortnight later of Stalin's increasingly rapacious appetite, Hitler drew his final conclusions.

It must be set down here that the Soviet dictator, his subsequent claims to the contrary notwithstanding, now accepted Hitler's offer to join the fascist camp, though at a stiffer price than had been offered in Berlin. On November 26, scarcely two weeks after Molotov had returned from Germany, he informed the German ambassador in Moscow that Russia was prepared to join the four-power pact, subject to the following conditions:

1. That German troops are immediately withdrawn from Finland, which . . . belongs to the Soviet Union's sphere of influence . . .

2. That within the next few months the security of the Soviet Union in the Straits is assured by the conclusion of a mutual-assistance pact between the U.S.S.R. and Bulgaria . . . and by the establishment of a base for land and naval forces by the Soviet Union within range of the Bosporus and the Dardanelles by means of a long-term lease.

3. That the area south of Batum and Baku in the general direction of the Persian Gulf is recognized as the center of the aspirations of the Soviet Union.

4. That Japan renounce her rights to concessions for coal and oil in northern Sakhalin.[33]

In all Stalin asked for five, instead of two, secret protocols embodying his new proposals and, for good measure, asked that, should Turkey prove difficult about Russian bases controlling the Straits, the four powers take *military* measures against her.

The proposals constituted a price higher than Hitler was willing even to consider. He had tried to keep Russia out of Europe, but now Stalin was

---

* Molotov's parting shot is given by Churchill, to whom it was related by Stalin later in the war. (Churchill, *Their Finest Hour*, p. 586.)

demanding Finland, Bulgaria, control of the Straits and, in effect, the Arabian and Persian oil fields, which normally supplied Europe with most of its oil. The Russians did not even mention the Indian Ocean, which the Fuehrer had tried to fob off as the center of "aspirations" for the U.S.S.R.

"Stalin is clever and cunning," Hitler told his top military chiefs. "He demands more and more. He's a cold-blooded blackmailer. A German victory has become unbearable for Russia. Therefore: she must be brought to her knees as soon as possible."[34]

The great cold-blooded Nazi blackmailer had met his match, and the realization infuriated him. At the beginning of December he told Halder to bring him the Army General Staff's plan for the onslaught on the Soviet Union. On December 5 Halder and Brauchitsch dutifully brought it to him, and at the end of a four-hour conference he approved it. Both the captured OKW War Diary and Halder's own confidential journal contain a report on this crucial meeting.[35] The Nazi warlord stressed that the Red Army must be broken through both north and south of the Pripet Marshes, surrounded and annihilated "as in Poland." Moscow, he told Halder, "was not important." The important thing was to destroy the "life force" of Russia. Rumania and Finland were to join in the attack, but not Hungary. General Dietl's mountain division at Narvik was to be transported across northern Sweden to Finland for an attack on the Soviet arctic region.* Altogether some "120 to 130 divisions" were allotted for the big campaign.

In its report on this conference, as in previous references to the plan to attack Russia, General Halder's diary employs the code name "Otto." Less than a fortnight later, on December 18, 1940, the code name by which it will go down in history was substituted. On this day Hitler crossed the Rubicon. He issued Directive No. 21. It was headed "Operation Barbarossa." It began:

TOP SECRET

The Fuehrer's Headquarters

December 18, 1940

The German Armed Forces must be prepared to *crush Soviet Russia in a quick campaign* before the end of the war against England.† For this purpose the *Army* will have to employ all available units with the reservation that the occupied territories will have to be safeguarded against surprise attacks . . .

Preparations . . . are to be completed by May 15, 1941. Great caution has to be exercised that the intention of an attack will not be recognized.

---

* Sweden, which had refused transit to the Allies during the Russo–Finnish War, permitted this fully armed division to pass through. Hungary, of course, later joined in the war against Russia.
† The italics are Hitler's.

So the target date was mid-May of the following spring. The "general purpose" of Operation Barbarossa Hitler laid down as follows:

The mass of the Russian *Army* in western Russia is to be destroyed in daring operations by driving forward deep armored wedges, and the retreat of intact, battle-ready troops into the wide spaces of Russia is to be prevented. The ultimate objective of the operation is to establish a defense line against Asiatic Russia from a line running from the Volga River to Archangel.

Hitler's directive then went into considerable detail about the main lines of attack.* The roles of Rumania and Finland were defined. They were to provide the jumping-off areas for attacks on the extreme north and south flanks as well as troops to aid the German forces in these operations. Finland's position was especially important. Various Finnish–German armies were to advance on Leningrad and the Lake Ladoga area, cut the Murmansk rail line, secure the Petsamo nickel mines and occupy the Russian ice-free ports on the Arctic Ocean. Much depended, Hitler admitted, on whether Sweden would permit the transit of German troops from Norway, but he correctly predicted that the Swedes would be accommodating in this.

The main operations were to be divided, Hitler explained, by the Pripet Marshes. The major blow would be delivered north of the swamps with two whole army groups. One would advance up the Baltic States to Leningrad. The other, farther south, would drive through White Russia and then swing north to join the first group, thus trapping what was left of the Soviet forces trying to retreat from the Baltic. Only then, Hitler laid it down, must an offensive against Moscow be undertaken. The Russian capital, which a fortnight before had seemed "unimportant" to Hitler, now assumed more significance. "The capture of this city," he wrote, "means a decisive political and economic victory, beyond the fall of the country's most important railroad junction." And he pointed out that Moscow was not only the main communications center of Russia but its principal producer of armaments.

A third army group would drive south of the marshes through the Ukraine toward Kiev, its principal objective being to roll up and destroy the Soviet forces there west of the Dnieper River. Farther south German–Rumanian troops would protect the flank of the main operation and advance toward Odessa and thence along the Black Sea. Thereafter the Donets basin, where 60 per cent of Soviet industry was concentrated, would be taken.

Such was Hitler's grandiose plan, completed just before the Christmas holidays of 1940, and so well prepared that no essential changes would be

---

* A good many historians have contended that Hitler in this first Barbarossa directive did not go into detail, a misunderstanding due probably to the extremely abbreviated version given in English translation in the *NCA* volumes. But the complete German text given in *TMWC*, XXVI, pp. 47–52 discloses the full details, thus revealing how far advanced the German military plans were at this early date.[36]

made in it. In order to secure secrecy, only nine copies of the directive were made, one for each of the three armed services and the rest to be guarded at OKW headquarters. Even the top field commanders, the directive makes clear, were to be told that the plan was merely for "precaution, in case Russia should change her previous attitude toward us." And Hitler instructed that the number of officers in the secret "be kept as small as possible. Otherwise the danger exists that our preparations will become known and the gravest political and military disadvantages result."

There is no evidence that the generals in the Army's High Command objected to Hitler's decision to turn on the Soviet Union, whose loyal fulfillment of the pact with Germany had made possible their victories in Poland and the West. Later Halder would write derisively of "Hitler's Russian adventure" and claim the Army leaders were against it from the beginning.[37] But there is not a word in his voluminous diary entries for December 1940 which supports him in this. Indeed, he gives the impression of being full of genuine enthusiasm for the "adventure," which he himself, as Chief of the General Staff, had the main responsibility for planning.

At any rate, for Hitler the die was cast, and, though he did not know it, his ultimate fate sealed, by this decision of December 18, 1940. Relieved to have made up his mind at last, as he later revealed, he went off to celebrate the Christmas holidays with the troops and flyers along the English Channel—as far as it was possible for him to get from Russia. Out of his mind too—as far as possible—must have been any thoughts of Charles XII of Sweden and of Napoleon Bonaparte, who after so many glorious conquests not unlike his own, had met disaster in the vast depths of the Russian steppes. How could they be much in his mind? By now, as the record shortly will show, the one-time Vienna waif regarded himself as the greatest conqueror the world had ever seen. Egomania, that fatal disease of all conquerors, was taking hold.

SIX MONTHS OF FRUSTRATION

And yet, after all the tumultuous victories of the spring and early summer of 1940, there had been a frustrating six months for the Nazi conqueror. Not only the final triumph over Britain eluded him but opportunities to deal her a mortal blow in the Mediterranean had been thrown away.

Two days after Christmas Grand Admiral Raeder saw Hitler in Berlin, but he had little Yuletide cheer to offer. "The threat to Britain in the entire eastern Mediterranean, the Near East and in North Africa," he told the Fuehrer, "has been eliminated . . . The decisive action in the Mediterranean for which we had hoped therefore is no longer possible."[38]

Adolf Hitler, balked by a shifty Franco, by the ineptitude of Mussolini and even by the senility of Marshal Pétain, had really missed the bus in the

Mediterranean. Disaster had struck the Italian ally in the Egyptian desert and now in December confronted it in the snowy mountains of Albania. These untoward happenings were also turning points in the war and in the course of history of the Third Reich. They had come about not only because of the weaknesses of Germany's friends and allies, but, in part, because of the Nazi warlord's incapacity to grasp the larger, intercontinental strategy that was called for and that Raeder and even Goering had urged upon him.

Twice in September 1940, on the sixth and the twenty-sixth, the Grand Admiral attempted to open up new vistas in the Fuehrer's mind now that the direct attack on England seemed out of the question. For the second conference Raeder cornered Hitler alone and, without the Army and Air Force officers to muddle the conversation, gave his chief a lengthy lecture on naval strategy and the importance of getting at Britain in other places than over the English Channel.

The British [Raeder said] have always considered the Mediterranean the pivot of their world Empire . . . Italy, surrounded by British power, is fast becoming the main target of attack . . . The Italians have not yet realized the danger when they refuse our help. Germany, however, must wage war against Great Britain with all the means at her disposal and without delay, before the United States is able to intervene effectively. For this reason the Mediterranean question must be cleared up during the winter months.

Cleared up how? The Admiral then got down to brass tacks.

Gibraltar must be taken. The Canary Islands must be secured by the Air Force.
The Suez Canal must be taken.

After Suez, Raeder painted a rosy picture of what then would logically ensue.

An advance from Suez through Palestine and Syria as far as Turkey is necessary. If we reach that point, Turkey will be in our power. The Russian problem will then appear in a different light . . . It is doubtful whether an advance against Russia from the north will be necessary.

Having in his mind driven the British out of the Mediterranean and put Turkey and Russia in Germany's power, Raeder went on to complete the picture. Correctly predicting that Britain, supported by the U.S.A. and the Gaullist forces, eventually would try to get a foothold on Northwest Africa as a basis for subsequent war against the Axis, the Admiral urged that Germany and Vichy France forestall this by securing this strategically important region themselves.

According to Raeder, Hitler agreed with his "general trend of thought" but added that he would have to talk matters over first with Mussolini, Franco and Pétain.[39] This he proceeded to do, though only after much time was lost. He arranged to see the Spanish dictator on October 23, Pétain, who was now the head of a collaborationist government at Vichy, the next day, and the Duce a few days thereafter.

Franco, who owed his triumph in the Spanish Civil War to the massive military aid of Italy and Germany, had, like all his fellow dictators, an inordinate appetite for spoils, especially if they could be gained cheaply. In June, at the moment of France's fall, he had hastily informed Hitler that Spain would enter the war in return for being given most of the vast French African empire, including Morocco and western Algeria, and provided that Germany supplied Spain liberally with arms, gasoline and foodstuffs.[40] It was to give Franco the opportunity to redeem this promise that the Fuehrer arrived in his special train at the Franco–Spanish border town of Hendaye on October 23. But much had happened in the intervening months—Britain had stoutly held out, for one thing—and Hitler was in for an unpleasant surprise.

The crafty Spaniard was not impressed by the Fuehrer's boast that "England already is decisively beaten," nor was he satisfied with Hitler's promise to give Spain territorial compensation in French North Africa "to the extent to which it would be possible to cover France's losses from British colonies." Franco wanted the French African empire, with no strings attached. Hitler's proposal was that Spain enter the war in January 1941, but Franco pointed out the dangers of such precipitate action. Hitler wanted the Spaniards to attack Gibraltar on January 10, with the help of German specialists who had taken the Belgian fort of Eben Emael from the air. Franco replied, with typical Spanish pride, that Gibraltar would have to be taken by Spaniards "alone." And so the two dictators wrangled—for nine hours. According to Dr. Schmidt, who was present here too, Franco spoke on and on in a monotonous singsong voice and Hitler became increasingly exasperated, once springing up, as he had done with Chamberlain, to exclaim that there was no point in continuing the conversations.[41]

"Rather than go through that again," he later told Mussolini, in recounting his ordeal with the Caudillo, "I would prefer to have three or four teeth yanked out."[42]

After nine hours, with time out for dinner in Hitler's special dining car, the talks broke up late in the evening without Franco's having definitely committed himself to come into the war. Hitler left Ribbentrop behind that night to continue the parley with Serrano Suñer, the Spanish Foreign Minister, and to try to get the Spaniards to sign something, at least an agreement to drive the British out of Gibraltar and close to them the western Mediterranean—but to no avail. "That ungrateful coward!" Ribbentrop cursed to Schmidt about Franco the next morning. "He owes us everything and now won't join us!"[43]

Hitler's meeting with Pétain at Montoire the next day went off better. But this was because the aging, defeatist Marshal, the hero of Verdun in the First World War and the perpetrator of the French surrender in the Second, agreed to France's collaboration with her conqueror in one last effort to bring Britain, the late ally, to her knees. In fact, he assented to put down in writing this odious deal.

> The Axis Powers and France have an identical interest in seeing the defeat of England accomplished as soon as possible. Consequently, the French Government will support, within the limits of its ability, the measures which the Axis Powers may take to this end.[44]

In return for this treacherous act, France was to be given in the "New Europe" "the place to which she is entitled," and in Africa she was to receive from the fascist dictators compensation from the British Empire for whatever territory she was forced to cede to others. Both parties agreed to keep the pact "absolutely secret."*

Despite Pétain's dishonorable but vital concessions, Hitler was not satisfied. According to Dr. Schmidt, he had wanted more—nothing less than France's active participation in the war against Britain. On the long journey back to Munich the official interpreter found the Fuehrer disappointed and depressed with the results of his trip. He was to become even more so in Florence, where he arrived on the morning of October 28 to see Mussolini.

They had conferred but three weeks before, on October 4, at the Brenner Pass. Hitler, as usual, had done most of the talking, giving one of his dazzling *tours d'horizon* in which was *not* included any mention that he was sending troops to Rumania, which Italy also coveted. When the Duce learned of this a few days later he was indignant.

> Hitler always faces me with a *fait accompli* [he fumed to Ciano]. This time I am going to pay him back in his own coin. He will find out from the newspapers that I have occupied Greece. In this way the equilibrium will be re-established.[45]

The Duce's ambitions in the Balkans were as rabid as Hitler's and cut across them so that as far back as the middle of August the Germans had warned Rome against any adventures in Yugoslavia and Greece. "It is a complete order to halt all along the line," Ciano noted in his diary on August 17. Mussolini scrapped, for the moment anyway, his plans for further martial glory in the Balkans and confirmed this in a humble letter

---

* Although they did not learn the contents of the secret accord at Montoire, both Churchill and Roosevelt suspected the worst. The King of England sent through American channels a personal appeal to Pétain asking him not to take sides against Britain. President Roosevelt's message to the Marshal was stern and toughly worded and warned him of the dire consequences of Vichy France's betraying Britain. (See William L. Langer, *Our Vichy Gamble*, p. 97. To write this book, Professor Langer had access to German documents that eleven years later have not been released by the British and American governments.)

to Hitler of August 27. But the prospect of a quick, easy conquest of Greece, which would compensate to some extent for his partner's glittering victories, proved too big a temptation for the strutting Fascist Caesar to resist, false though the prospect was.

On October 22 he set the date for a surprise Italian assault on Greece for October 28 and on the same day wrote Hitler a letter (predated October 19) alluding to his contemplated action but making it vague as to the exact nature and date. He feared, Ciano noted that day in his diary, that the Fuehrer might "order" him to halt. Hitler and Ribbentrop got wind of the Duce's plans while they were returning in their respective special trains from France, and at the Fuehrer's orders the Nazi Foreign Minister stopped at the first station in Germany to telephone Ciano in Rome and urge an immediate meeting of the Axis leaders. Mussolini suggested October 28 at Florence and, when his German visitor alighted from the train on the morning of that day, greeted him, his chin up and his eyes full of glee: "Fuehrer, we are on the march! Victorious Italian troops crossed the Greco–Albanian frontier at dawn today!"[46]

According to all accounts, Mussolini greatly enjoyed this revenge on his friend for all the previous occasions when the Nazi dictator had marched into a country without previously confiding to his Italian ally. Hitler was furious. This rash act against a sturdy foe at the worst possible time of year threatened to upset the applecart in the Balkans. The Fuehrer, as he wrote Mussolini a little later, had sped to Florence in the hope of preventing it, but he had arrived too late. According to Schmidt, who was present, the Nazi leader managed to control his rage.

> Hitler went north that afternoon [Schmidt later wrote] with bitterness in his heart. He had been frustrated three times—at Hendaye, at Montoire, and now in Italy. In the lengthy winter evenings of the next few years these long, exacting journeys were a constantly recurring theme of bitter reproaches against ungrateful and unreliable friends, Axis partners and "deceiving" Frenchmen.[47]

Nevertheless he had to do something to prosecute the war against the British, now that the invasion of Britain had proved impossible. Hardly had the Fuehrer returned to Berlin before the need to act was further impressed upon him by the fiasco of the Duce's armies in Greece. Within a week, the "victorious" Italian attack there had been turned into a rout. On November 4 Hitler called a war conference at the Chancellery in Berlin to which he summoned Brauchitsch and Halder from the Army and Keitel and Jodl from OKW. Thanks to Halder's diary and a captured copy of Jodl's report to the Navy on the conference, we know the warlord's decisions, which were embodied in Directive No. 18 issued by Hitler on November 12, the text of which is among the Nuremberg records.[48]

The German Navy's influence on Hitler's strategy became evident, as did the necessity for doing something about the faltering Italian ally. Halder noted the Fuehrer's "lack of confidence" in Italian leadership. As a result it was decided *not* to send any German troops to Libya until Marshal Rodolfo Graziani's army, which in September had advanced sixty miles into Egypt to Sidi Barrâni, had reached Mersa Matrûh, a further seventy-five miles along the coast, which was not expected before Christmas, if then. In the meantime plans were to be made to send a few dive bombers to Egypt to attack the British fleet in Alexandria and mine the Suez Canal.

As for Greece, the Italian attack there, Hitler admitted to his generals, had been a "regrettable blunder" and unfortunately had endangered Germany's position in the Balkans. The British by occupying Crete and Lemnos had achieved air bases from which they could easily bomb the Rumanian oil fields and by sending troops to the Greek mainland threatened the whole German position in the Balkans. To counter this danger Hitler ordered the Army to prepare immediately plans to invade Greece through Bulgaria with a force of at least ten divisions which would be sent first to Rumania. "It is anticipated," he said, "that Russia will remain neutral."

But it was in regard to destroying Britain's position in the western Mediterranean that most of the conference of November 4 and most of the ensuing Directive No. 18 was devoted.

> Gibraltar will be taken [said the directive] and the Straits closed.
> The British will be prevented from gaining a foothold at another point of the Iberian peninsula or the Atlantic islands.

"Felix" was to be the code name for the taking of Gibraltar and the Spanish Canary Islands and the Portuguese Cape Verde Islands. The Navy was also to study the possibility of occupying Portugal's Madeira and the Azores. Portugal itself might have to be occupied. "Operation Isabella" would be the cover name for that, and three German divisions would be assembled on the Spanish–Portuguese frontier to carry it out.

Finally, units of the French fleet and some troops were to be released so that France could defend her possessions in Northwest Africa against the British and De Gaulle. "From this initial task," Hitler said in his directive, "France's participation in the war against England can develop fully."

Hitler's new plans, as enunciated to the generals on November 4 and laid down in the directive a week later, went into considerable military detail—especially on how Gibraltar was to be taken by a daring German stroke—and apparently they impressed his Army chiefs as bold and shrewd. But in reality they were half measures which could not possibly achieve their objectives, and they were based partly on his deceiving his own generals. He assured them on November 4, Halder noted, that he had just received Franco's renewed promise to join Germany in the war, but this, as we have seen, was not quite true. The objectives of driving the British out of the Mediterranean were sound, but the forces allotted to the task were quite insufficient, especially in view of Italy's weaknesses.

The Naval War Staff pointed this out in a toughly worded memorandum which Raeder gave Hitler on November 14.[49] The Italian disaster in Greece—Mussolini's troops had now been hurled back into Albania and were still retreating—had not only greatly improved Britain's strategic position in the Mediterranean, the sailors pointed out, but enhanced British prestige throughout the world. As for the Italian attack on Egypt, the Navy told Hitler flatly: "Italy *will never carry out* the Egyptian offensive.* The Italian leadership is wretched. They have no understanding of the situation. The Italian armed forces have *neither* the leadership nor the military efficiency to carry the required operations in the Mediterranean area to a successful conclusion with the necessary speed and decision."

Therefore, the Navy concluded, this task must be carried out by Germany. The *"fight for the African area,"* it warned Hitler, is "the foremost strategic objective of German warfare as a whole . . . It is of *decisive importance for the outcome of the war."*

But the Nazi dictator was not convinced. He had never been able to envisage the war in the Mediterranean and North Africa as anything but secondary to his main objective. As Admiral Raeder elaborated to him the Navy's strategic conceptions in their meeting on November 14, Hitler retorted that he was "still inclined toward a demonstration with Russia."[50] In fact, he was more inclined than ever, for Molotov had just departed Berlin that morning after so arousing the Fuehrer's ire. When the Admiral next saw his chief a couple of days after Christmas to report on how the bus had been missed in the Mediterranean, Hitler was not unduly perturbed. To Raeder's argument that the victory of Britain over the Italians in Egypt† and the increasing material aid which she was receiving from America necessitated the concentration of all German resources to bring the British down, and that Barbarossa ought to be postponed until "the overthrow of Britain," Hitler turned an almost deaf ear.

"In view of present political developments and especially Russia's

---

* The Navy's italics.
† By this time a ramshackle British desert force of one armored division, an Indian infantry division, two infantry brigades and a Royal Tank regiment—31,000 men in all—had driven an Italian force three times as large out of Egypt and captured 38,000 prisoners at a cost of 133 killed, 387 wounded and 8 missing. The British counteroffensive, under the over-all command of General Sir Archibald Wavell, had begun on December 7 and in four days Marshal Graziani's army was routed. What had started as a five-day limited counterattack continued until February 7, by which time the British had pushed clear across Cyrenaica, a distance of 500 miles, annihilated the entire Italian army of ten divisions in Libya, taken 130,000 prisoners, 1,240 guns and 500 tanks and lost themselves 500 killed, 1,373 wounded and 55 missing. To the skeptical British military writer General J. F. Fuller it was "one of the most audacious campaigns ever fought." (Fuller, *The Second World War,* p. 98.)

The Italian Navy had also been dealt a lethal blow. On the night of November 11–12, bombers from the British carrier *Illustrious* (which the Luftwaffe claimed to have sunk) attacked the Italian fleet at anchor at Taranto and put out of action for many months three battleships and two cruisers. "A black day," Ciano began his diary on November 12. "The British, without warning, have sunk the dreadnought *Cavour* and seriously damaged the battleships *Littorio* and *Duilio.*"

interference in Balkan affairs," Hitler said, "it is necessary to eliminate at all costs the last enemy remaining on the Continent before coming to grips with Britain." From now on to the bitter end he would stick fanatically to this fundamental strategy.

As a sop to his naval chief, Hitler promised to "try once more to influence Franco" so that the attack against Gibraltar could be made and the Mediterranean closed to the British fleet. Actually, he had already dropped the whole idea. On December 11 he had quietly ordered, "Operation Felix will not be carried out as the political conditions no longer exist." Nagged by his own Navy and by the Italians to keep after Franco, Hitler made one final effort, though it was painful to him. On February 6, 1941, he addressed a long letter to the Spanish dictator.

. . . About one thing, Caudillo, there must be clarity: we are fighting a battle of life and death and cannot at this time make any gifts . . .

The battle which Germany and Italy are fighting will determine the destiny of Spain as well. Only in the case of our victory will your present regime continue to exist.[51]

Unfortunately for the Axis, the letter reached the Caudillo on the very day that Marshal Graziani's last forces in Cyrenaica had been wiped out by the British south of Benghazi. Little wonder that when Franco got around to replying—on February 26, 1941—though protesting his "absolute loyalty" to the Axis, he reminded the Nazi leader that recent developments had left "the circumstances of October far behind" and that their understanding of that time had become "outmoded."

For one of the very few times in his stormy life, Adolf Hitler conceded defeat. "The long and short of the tedious Spanish rigmarole," he wrote Mussolini, "is that Spain does not want to enter the war and will not enter it. This is extremely tiresome since it means that for the moment the possibility of striking at Britain in the simplest manner, in her Mediterranean possessions, is eliminated."

Italy, not Spain, however, was the key to defeating Britain in the Mediterranean, but the Duce's creaky empire was not equal to the task of doing it alone and Hitler was not wise enough to give her the means, which he had, to accomplish it. The possibility of striking at Britain either directly across the Channel or indirectly across the broader Mediterranean, he now confessed, had been eliminated "for the moment." Though this was frustrating, the acknowledgment of it brought Hitler relief. He could now turn to matters nearer his heart and mind.

On January 8–9, 1941, he held a council of war at the Berghof above Berchtesgaden, which now lay deep in the winter's snow. The mountain air seems to have cleared his mind, and once more, as the lengthy confidential reports of the meeting by Admiral Raeder and General Halder[52] disclose, his thoughts ranged far and wide as he outlined his grand strategy to his military chiefs. His optimism had returned.

The Fuehrer [Raeder noted] is firmly convinced that the situation in Europe can no longer develop unfavorably for Germany even if we should lose the whole of North Africa. Our position in Europe is so firmly established that the outcome cannot possibly be to our disadvantage . . . The British can hope to win the war only by beating us on the Continent. The Fuehrer is convinced that this is impossible.

It was true, he conceded, that the direct invasion of Britain was "not feasible unless she is crippled to a considerable degree and Germany has complete air superiority." The Navy and Air Force, he said, must concentrate on attacking her shipping lanes and thereby cut off her supplies. Such attacks, he thought, "might lead to victory as early as July or August." In the meantime, he said, "Germany must make herself so strong on the Continent that we can handle a further war against England (and America)." The parentheses are Halder's and their enclosure is significant. This is the first mention in the captured German records that Hitler —at the beginning of 1941—is facing up to the possibility of the entry of the United States into the war against him.

The Nazi warlord then took up the various strategic areas and problems and outlined what he intended to do about them.

The Fuehrer is of the opinion [Raeder wrote] that it is vital for the outcome of the war that Italy does not collapse . . . He is determined to . . . prevent Italy from losing North Africa . . . It would mean a great loss of prestige to the Axis powers . . . He is [therefore] determined to give them support.

At this point he cautioned his military leaders about divulging German plans.

He does *not* wish to inform the Italians of our plans. There is great danger that the Royal Family is transmitting intelligence to Britain!!*

Support for Italy, Hitler declared, would consist of antitank formations and some Luftwaffe squadrons for Libya. More important, he would dispatch an army corps of two and a half divisions to buck up the retreating Italians in Albania—into which the Greeks had now pushed them. In connection with this, "Operation Marita"† would be pushed. The transfer of troops from Rumania to Bulgaria, he ordered, must begin at once so that Marita could commence on March 26. Hitler also spoke at some length of the need to be ready to carry out "Operation Attila"—the German cover names seem almost endless—which he had outlined in a di-

---

* The italics and double exclamation points are Raeder's.
† Operation Marita was promulgated in Directive No. 20 on December 13, 1940. It called for an army of twenty-four divisions to be assembled in Rumania and to descend on Greece through Bulgaria as soon as favorable weather set in. It was signed by Hitler.[53]

rective of December 10, 1940. This was a plan to occupy the rest of France and seize the French fleet at Toulon. He thought now it might have to be carried out soon. "If France becomes troublesome," he declared, "she will have to be crushed completely." This would have been a crude violation of the Compiègne armistice, but no general or admiral, so far as Halder and Raeder noted—or at least recorded—raised the question.

It was at this war conference that Hitler described Stalin as "a cold-blooded blackmailer" and informed his commanders that Russia would have to be brought to her knees "as soon as possible."

If the U.S.A. and Russia should enter the war against Germany [Hitler said, and it was the second time he mentioned that possibility for America], the situation would become very complicated. Hence any possibility for such a threat to develop must be eliminated at the very beginning. If the Russian threat were removed, we could wage war on Britain indefinitely. If Russia collapsed, Japan would be greatly relieved: this in turn would mean increased danger to the U.S.A.

Such were the thoughts of the German dictator on global strategy as 1941 got under way. Two days after the war council, on January 11, he embodied them in Directive No. 22. German reinforcements for Tripoli were to move under "Operation Sunflower"; those for Albania under "Operation Alpine Violets."[54]

"THE WORLD WILL HOLD ITS BREATH!"

Mussolini was summoned by Hitler to the Berghof for January 19 and 20. Shaken and humiliated by the Italian debacles in Egypt and Greece, he had no stomach for this journey. Ciano found him "frowning and nervous" when he boarded his special train, fearful that Hitler, Ribbentrop and the German generals would be insultingly condescending. To make matters worse the Duce took along General Alfredo Guzzoni, Assistant Chief of Staff, whom Ciano in his diary described as a mediocre man with a big paunch and a little dyed wig and whom, he thought, it would be positively humiliating to present to the Germans.

To his surprise and relief, Mussolini found Hitler, who came down to the snow-covered platform of the little station at Puch to greet him, both tactful and cordial and there were no reproaches for Italy's sorry record on the battlefields. He also found his host, as Ciano noted in his diary, in a very anti-Russian mood. For more than two hours on the second day Hitler lectured his Italian guests and an assembly of generals from both countries, and a secret report on it prepared by General Jodl[55] confirms that while the Fuehrer was anxious to be helpful to the Italians in Albania and Libya, his principal thoughts were on Russia.

I don't see great danger coming from *America* [Hitler said] even if she should enter the war. The much greater danger is the gigantic block of Russia. Though we have very favorable political and economic agreements with Russia, I prefer to rely on powerful means at my disposal.

Though he hinted at what he intended to do with his "powerful means," he did not disclose his plans to his partner. These, however, were sufficiently far along to enable the Chief of the Army General Staff, who was responsible for working out the details, to present them to the Supreme Commander at a meeting in Berlin a fortnight later.

This war conference, attended by the top generals of OKW and of the Army High Command (OKH), lasted from noon until 6 P.M. on February 3. And though General Halder, who outlined the Army General Staff's plans, contended later in his book[56] that he and Brauchitsch raised doubts about their own assessment of Soviet military strength and in general opposed Barbarossa as an "adventure," there is not a word in his own diary entry made the same evening or in the highly secret OKW memorandum of the meeting[57] that supports this contention. Indeed, they disclose Halder to have made at first a businesslike estimate of the opposing forces, calculating that while the enemy would have approximately 155 divisions, German strength would be about the same and, as Halder reported, "far superior in quality." Later, when catastrophe set in, Halder and his fellow generals realized that their intelligence on the Red Army had been fantastically faulty. But on February 3, 1941, they did not suspect that. In fact, so convincing was Halder's report on respective strengths and on the strategy to be employed to annihilate the Red armies* that Hitler at the end not only expressed agreement "on the whole" but was so excited by the prospects which the General Staff Chief had raised that he exclaimed:

"When Barbarossa commences, the world will hold its breath and make no comment!"

He could scarcely wait for it to commence. Impatiently he ordered the operation map and the plan of deployment of forces to be sent to him "as soon as possible."

BALKAN PRELUDE

Before Barbarossa could get under way in the spring the southern flank, which lay in the Balkans, had to be secured and built up. By the third week in February 1941, the Germans had massed a formidable army of 680,000 troops in Rumania, which bordered the Ukraine for three hun-

---

* The strategy was essentially that laid down in Directive No. 21 of December 18, 1940. (See pp. 810–11.) Again in comments to Brauchitsch and Halder, Hitler emphasized the importance of "wiping out large sections of the enemy" instead of forcing them to retreat. And he stressed that "the *main aim* [his emphasis] is to gain possession of the Baltic States and Leningrad."

dred miles between the Polish border and the Black Sea.[58] But to the south, Greece still held the Italians at bay and Berlin had reason to believe that British troops from Libya would soon be landed there. Hitler, as the minutes of his numerous conferences at this period make clear, feared that an Allied front above Salonika might be formed which would be more troublesome to Germany than a similar one had been in the First World War, since it would give the British a base from which to bomb the Rumanian oil fields. Moreover, it would jeopardize Barbarossa. In fact, the danger had been foreseen as far back as December 1940, when the first directive for Operation Marita had been issued providing for a strong German attack on Greece through Bulgaria with troops assembled in Rumania.

Bulgaria, whose wrong guess as to the victors in the first war had cost her dearly, now made a similar miscalculation. Believing Hitler's assurances that he had already won the war and bedazzled by the prospect of obtaining Greek territory to the south which would give her access to the Aegean Sea, her government agreed to participate in Marita—at least to the extent of allowing passage of German troops. An agreement to this effect was made secretly on February 8, 1941, between Field Marshal List and the Bulgarian General Staff.[59] On the night of February 28 German Army units crossed the Danube from Rumania and took up strategic positions in Bulgaria, which the next day joined the Tripartite Pact.

The hardier Yugoslavs were not quite so accommodating. But their stubbornness only spurred on the Germans to bring them into camp too. On March 4–5, the Regent, Prince Paul, was summoned in great secrecy to the Berghof by the Fuehrer, given the usual threats and, in addition, offered the bribe of Salonika. On March 25, the Yugoslav Premier, Dragisha Cvetković, and Foreign Minister Aleksander Cincar-Marković, having slipped surreptitiously out of Belgrade the night before to avoid hostile demonstrations or even kidnaping, arrived at Vienna, where in the presence of Hitler and Ribbentrop they signed up Yugoslavia to the Tripartite Pact. Hitler was highly pleased and told Ciano that this would facilitate his attack on Greece. Before leaving Vienna the Yugoslav leaders were given two letters from Ribbentrop confirming Germany's "determination" to respect "the sovereignty and territorial integrity of Yugoslavia at all times" and promising that the Axis would not demand transit rights for its troops across Yugoslavia "during this war."[60] Both agreements were broken by Hitler in what even for him was record time.

The Yugoslav ministers had no sooner returned to Belgrade than they, the government and the Prince Regent were overthrown on the night of March 26–27, by a popular uprising led by a number of top Air Force officers and supported by most of the Army. The youthful heir to the throne, Peter, who had escaped from the surveillance of regency officials by sliding down a rain pipe, was declared King, and though the new regime of General Dušan Simović immediately offered to sign a nonaggression pact with Germany, it was obvious in Berlin that it would not accept the puppet status for Yugoslavia which the Fuehrer had assigned. During the delirious celebrations in Belgrade, in which a crowd spat on the German minister's car, the Serbs had shown where their sympathies lay.

The coup in Belgrade threw Adolf Hitler into one of the wildest rages of his entire life. He took it as a personal affront and in his fury made sudden decisions which would prove utterly disastrous to the fortunes of the Third Reich.

He hurriedly summoned his military chieftains to the Chancellery in Berlin on March 27—the meeting was so hastily called that Brauchitsch, Halder and Ribbentrop arrived late—and raged about the revenge he would take on the Yugoslavs. The Belgrade coup, he said, had endangered both Marita and, even more, Barbarossa. He was therefore determined, "without waiting for possible declarations of loyalty of the new government, to destroy Yugoslavia militarily and as a nation. No diplomatic inquiries will be made," he ordered, "and no ultimatums presented." Yugoslavia, he added, would be crushed with "unmerciful harshness." He ordered Goering then and there to "destroy Belgrade in attacks by waves," with bombers operating from Hungarian air bases. He issued Directive No. 25[61] for the immediate invasion of Yugoslavia and told Keitel and Jodl to work out that very evening the military plans. He instructed Ribbentrop to advise Hungary, Rumania and Italy that they would all get a slice of Yugoslavia, which would be divided up among them, except for a small Croatian puppet state.*

And then, according to an underlined passage in the top-secret OKW notes of the meeting,[62] Hitler announced the most fateful decision of all.

"The beginning of the Barbarossa operation," he told his generals, *"will have to be postponed up to four weeks."*†

This postponement of the attack on Russia in order that the Nazi warlord might vent his personal spite against a small Balkan country which had dared to defy him was probably the most catastrophic single decision in Hitler's career. It is hardly too much to say that by making it that March afternoon in the Chancellery in Berlin during a moment of convulsive rage he tossed away his last golden opportunity to win the war and to make of the Third Reich, which he had created with such stunning if barbarous genius, the greatest empire in German history and himself the master of Europe. Field Marshal von Brauchitsch, the Commander in Chief of the German Army, and General Halder, the gifted Chief of the General Staff, were to recall it with deep bitterness but also with more understanding of its consequences than they showed at the moment of its making, when later the deep snow and subzero temperatures of Russia hit them three or four weeks short of what they thought they needed for final

---

* "The war against Yugoslavia should be very popular in Italy, Hungary and Bulgaria," Hitler sneered. He said he would give the Banat to Hungary, Macedonia to Bulgaria and the Adriatic coast to Italy.

† It had originally been set for May 15 in the first Barbarossa directive of December 18, 1940.

victory. For ever afterward they and their fellow generals would blame that hasty, ill-advised decision of a vain and infuriated man for all the disasters that ensued.

Military Directive No. 25, which the Supreme Commander issued to his generals before the meeting broke up, was a typical Hitlerian document.

The military putsch in Yugoslavia has altered the political situation in the Balkans. Yugoslavia, in spite of her protestations of loyalty, must be considered for the time being as an enemy and therefore crushed as speedily as possible.

It is my intention to force my way into Yugoslavia . . . and to annihilate the Yugoslav Army . . .

Jodl, as Chief of the Operations Staff of OKW, was told to prepare the plans that very night. "I worked the whole night at the Reich Chancellery," Jodl later told the Nuremberg tribunal. "At four o'clock in the morning of March 28, I put an *aide-mémoire* into the hand of General von Rintelen, our liaison officer with the Italian High Command."[63]

For Mussolini, whose sagging armies in Albania were in danger of being taken in the rear by the Yugoslavs, had to be told immediately of the German operational plans and asked to co-operate with them. To make sure that the Duce understood what was expected of him and without waiting for General Jodl to concoct the military plans, Hitler dashed off a letter at midnight of the twenty-seventh and ordered it wired to Rome immediately so that it would reach Mussolini that same night.[64]

Duce, events force me to give you by this quickest means my estimation of the situation and the consequences which may result from it.

From the beginning I have regarded Yugoslavia as a dangerous factor in the controversy with Greece . . . For this reason I have done everything honestly to bring Yugoslavia into our community . . . Unfortunately these endeavors did not meet with success . . . Today's reports leave no doubt as to the imminent turn in the foreign policy of Yugoslavia.

Therefore I have already arranged for all necessary measures . . with military means. Now, I would cordially request you, Duce, not to undertake any further operations in Albania in the course of the next few days. I consider it necessary that you should cover and screen the most important passes from Yugoslavia into Albania with all available forces.

. . . I also consider it necessary, Duce, that you should reinforce your forces on the Italian–Yugoslav front with all available means and with utmost speed.

I also consider it necessary, Duce, that everything which we do and order be shrouded in absolute secrecy . . . These measures will completely lose their value should they become known . . . Duce, should secrecy be observed, then . . . I have no doubt that we will both achieve a success no less than the success in Norway a year ago. This is my unshaken conviction.

Accept my heartfelt and friendly greetings,

Yours,

ADOLF HITLER

For this short-range objective, the Nazi warlord was again right in his prediction, but he seems to have had no inkling how costly his successful revenge on Yugoslavia would be in the long run. At dawn on April 6, his armies in overwhelming strength fell on Yugoslavia and Greece, smashing across the frontiers of Bulgaria, Hungary and Germany itself with all their armor and advancing rapidly against poorly armed defenders dazed by the usual preliminary bombing from the Luftwaffe.

Belgrade itself, as Hitler ordered, was razed to the ground. For three successive days and nights Goering's bombers ranged over the little capital at rooftop level—for the city had no antiaircraft guns—killing 17,000 civilians, wounding many more and reducing the place to a mass of smoldering rubble. "Operation Punishment," Hitler called it, and he obviously was satisfied that his commands had been so effectively carried out. The Yugoslavs, who had not had time to mobilize their tough little army and whose General Staff made the mistake of trying to defend the whole country, were overwhelmed. On April 13 German and Hungarian troops entered what was left of Belgrade and on the seventeenth the remnants of the Yugoslav Army, still twenty-eight divisions strong, surrendered at Sarajevo, the King and the Prime Minister escaping by plane to Greece.

The Greeks, who had humiliated the Italians in six months of fighting, could not stand up to Field Marshal List's Twelfth Army of fifteen divisions, four of which were armored. The British had hurriedly sent to Greece some four divisions from Libya—53,000 men in all—but they, like the Greeks, were overwhelmed by the German panzers and by the murderous strikes of the Luftwaffe. The northern Greek armies surrendered to the Germans and—bitter pill—to the Italians on April 23. Four days later Nazi tanks rattled into Athens and hoisted the swastika over the Acropolis. By this time the British were desperately trying once again to evacuate their troops by sea—a minor Dunkirk and almost as successful.

By the end of April—in three weeks—it was all over except for Crete, which was taken by the Germans from the British in an airborne assault toward the end of May. Where Mussolini had failed so miserably all winter, Hitler had succeeded in a few days in the spring. Though the Duce was relieved to be pulled off the hook, he was humiliated that it had to be done by the Germans. Nor were his feelings assuaged by Italy's disappointing share in the Yugoslav spoils, which Hitler now began to divide up.*

---

* On April 12, 1941, six days after the launching of his attack, Hitler issued a secret directive dividing up Yugoslavia among Germany, Italy, Hungary and Bulgaria. Croatia was created as an autonomous puppet state. The Fuehrer helped himself

The Balkans was not the only place where the Fuehrer pulled his muddling junior partner off the hook. After the annihilation of the Italian armies in Libya Hitler, although reluctantly, had finally consented to sending a light armored division and some Luftwaffe units to North Africa, where he arranged for General Erwin Rommel to be in over-all command of the Italo–German forces. Rommel, a dashing, resourceful tank officer, who had distinguished himself as commander of a panzer division in the Battle of France, was a type of general whom the British had not previously met in the North African desert and he was to prove an immense problem to them for two years. But he was not the only problem. The sizable army and air force which the British had sent to Greece from Libya had greatly weakened them in the desert. At first they were not unduly worried, not even after their intelligence reported the arrival of German armored units in Tripolitania at the end of February. But they should have been.

Rommel, with his German panzer division and two Italian divisions, one of which was armored, struck suddenly at Cyrenaica on the last day of March. In twelve days he recaptured the province, invested Tobruk and reached Bardia, a few miles from the Egyptian border. The entire British position in Egypt and the Suez was again threatened; in fact, with the Germans and Italians in Greece the British hold on the eastern Mediterranean had become gravely endangered.

Another spring, the second of the war, had brought more dazzling German victories, and the predicament of Britain, which now held out alone, battered at home by nightly Luftwaffe bombings, its armies overseas chased out of Greece and Cyrenaica, seemed darker and more hopeless than ever before. Its prestige, so important in a life-and-death struggle where propaganda was so potent a weapon, especially in influencing the United States and Russia, had sunk to a new low point.*

Hitler was not slow or backward in taking advantage of this in a victory

---

liberally, Germany taking territory contiguous to the old Austria and keeping under its occupation all of old Serbia as well as the copper- and coal-mining districts. Italy's grab was left somewhat vague, but it did not amount to much.[65]

* Charles A. Lindbergh, the hero flyer, who had seemed to this writer to have fallen with startling naïveté, during his visits to Germany, to Nazi propaganda boasts, was already consigning Britain to defeat in his speeches to large and enthusiastic audiences in America. On April 23, 1941, at the moment of the Nazi victories in the Balkans and North Africa, he addressed 30,000 persons in New York at the first mass meeting of the newly formed America First Committee. "The British government," he said, "has one last desperate plan: . . . To persuade us to send another American Expeditionary Force to Europe and to share with England militarily, as well as financially, the fiasco of this war." He condemned England for having "encouraged the smaller nations of Europe to fight against hopeless odds." Apparently it did not occur to this man that Yugoslavia and Greece, which Hitler had just crushed, were brutally attacked without provocation, and that they had instinctively tried to defend themselves because they had a sense of honor and because they had courage even in the face of hopeless odds. On April 28 Lindbergh resigned his commission as a colonel in the U.S. Army Air Corps Reserve after President Roosevelt on the twenty-fifth had publicly branded him as a defeatist and an appeaser. The Secretary of War accepted the resignation.

speech to the Reichstag in Berlin on May 4. It consisted mostly of a venomous and sarcastic personal attack on Churchill as the instigator (along with the Jews) of the war and as the man who was masterminding the losing of it.

He is the most bloodthirsty or amateurish strategist in history . . . For over five years this man has been chasing around Europe like a madman in search of something that he could set on fire . . . As a soldier he is a bad politician and as a politician an equally bad soldier . . . The gift Mr. Churchill possesses is the gift to lie with a pious expression on his face and to distort the truth until finally glorious victories are made of the most terrible defeats . . . Churchill, one of the most hopeless dabblers in strategy, thus managed [in Yugoslavia and Greece] to lose two theaters of war at one single blow. In any other country he would be court-martialed . . . His abnormal state of mind can only be explained as symptomatic either of a paralytic disease or of a drunkard's ravings . . .

As to the Yugoslavian coup which had provoked him to such fury, Hitler made no attempt to hide his true feelings.

We were all stunned by that coup, carried through by a handful of bribed conspirators . . . You will understand, gentlemen, that when I heard this I at once gave orders to attack Yugoslavia. *To treat the German Reich in this way is impossible* . . .

Arrogant though he was over his spring victories and especially those over the British, Hitler did not fully realize what a blow they had been to Britain nor how desperate was the predicament of the Empire. On the very day he was addressing the Reichstag, Churchill was writing President Roosevelt about the grave consequences of the loss of Egypt and the Middle East and pleading for America to enter the war. The Prime Minister was in one of the darkest moods he was to know throughout the war.

I adjure you, Mr. President [he wrote], not to underestimate the gravity of the consequences which may follow from a Middle-East collapse.[66]

The German Navy urged the Fuehrer to make the most of this situation. To further improve matters for the Axis, the newly appointed premier of Iraq, Rashid Ali, who was pro-German, had led an attack against the British airbase of Habbaniya, outside Bagdad, and appealed to Hitler for aid in driving the British out of the country. This was at the beginning of May. With Crete conquered by May 27, Admiral Raeder, who had always been lukewarm to Barbarossa, appealed to Hitler on May 30 to prepare a decisive offensive against Egypt and Suez, and Rommel, eager to continue his advance as soon as he had received reinforcements, sent similar pleas from North Africa. "This stroke," Raeder told the Fuehrer, "would be more deadly to the British Empire than the capture of London!" A week later the Admiral handed Hitler a memorandum prepared by the Operations Division of the Naval War Staff which warned that, while Barbarossa "naturally stands in the foreground of the OKW leadership, it must under no circumstances lead to the abandonment of, or to delay in, the conduct of the war in the Mediterranean."[67]

But the Fuehrer already had made up his mind; in fact, he had not changed it since the Christmas holidays when he had promulgated Barbarossa and told Admiral Raeder that Russia must be "eliminated first." His landlocked mind simply did not comprehend the larger strategy advocated by the Navy. Even before Raeder and the Naval Staff pleaded with him at the end of May he laid down the law in Directive No. 30 issued on May 25.[68] He ordered a military mission, a few planes and some arms to be dispatched to Bagdad to help Iraq. "I have decided," he said, "to encourage developments in the Middle East by supporting Iraq." But he saw no further than this small, inadequate step. As for the larger, bold strategy championed by the admirals and Rommel, he declared:

Whether—and if so, by what means—it would be possible afterward to launch an offensive against the Suez Canal and eventually oust the British finally from their position between the Mediterranean and the Persian Gulf cannot be decided until Operation Barbarossa is completed.

The destruction of the Soviet Union came first; all else must wait. This, we can now see, was a staggering blunder. At this moment, the end of May 1941, Hitler, with the use of only a fraction of his forces, could have dealt the British Empire a crushing blow, perhaps a fatal one. No one realized this better than the hard-pressed Churchill. In his message to President Roosevelt on May 4, he had admitted that, were Egypt and the Middle East to be lost, the continuation of the war "would be a hard, long and bleak proposition," even if the United States entered the conflict. But Hitler did not understand this. His blindness is all the more incomprehensible because his Balkan campaign had delayed the commencement of Barbarossa by several weeks and thereby jeopardized it. The conquest of Russia would have to be accomplished in a shorter space of time than originally planned. For there was an inexorable deadline: the Russian winter, which had defeated Charles XII and Napoleon. That gave the Germans only six months to overrun, before the onset of winter, an immense country that had never been conquered from the west. And though June had arrived, the vast army which had been turned southeast into Yugoslavia and Greece had to be brought back great distances to the Soviet frontier over unpaved roads and run-down single-track railway lines that were woefully inadequate to handle so swarming a traffic.

The delay, as things turned out, was fatal. Defenders of Hitler's military genius have contended that the Balkan campaign did not set back the timetable for Barbarossa appreciably and that in any case the postpone-ment was largely due to the late thaw that year which left the roads in Eastern Europe deep in mud until mid-June. But the testimony of the key German generals is otherwise. Field Marshal Friedrich Paulus, whose name will always be associated with Stalingrad, and who at this time was the chief planner of the Russian campaign on the Army General Staff, testi-fied on the stand at Nuremberg that Hitler's decision to destroy Yugo-slavia postponed the beginning of Barbarossa by "about five weeks."[69] The Naval War Diary gives the same length of time.[70] Field Marshal von Rundstedt, who led Army Group South in Russia, told Allied interrogators after the war that because of the Balkan campaign "we began at least four weeks late. That," he added, "was a very costly delay."[71]

At any rate, on April 30, when his armies had completed their conquest of Yugoslavia and Greece, Hitler set the new date for Barbarossa. It was to begin on June 22, 1941.[72]

THE PLANNING OF THE TERROR

No holds were to be barred in the taking of Russia. Hitler insisted that the generals understand this very clearly. Early in March 1941, he con-voked the chiefs of the three armed services and the key Army field com-manders and laid down the law. Halder took down his words.[73]

The war against Russia [Hitler said] will be such that it cannot be conducted in a knightly fashion. This struggle is one of ideologies and racial differences and will have to be conducted with unprecedented, unmerciful and unrelenting harshness. All officers will have to rid themselves of obsolete ideologies. I know that the necessity for such means of waging war is beyond the com-prehension of you generals but . . . I insist absolutely that my orders be executed without contradiction. The commissars are the bearers of ideologies directly opposed to National Socialism. Therefore the commissars will be liquidated. German soldiers guilty of breaking international law . . . will be excused. Russia has not participated in the Hague Convention and therefore has no rights under it.

Thus was the so-called "Commissar Order" issued; it was to be much discussed at the Nuremberg trial when the great moral question was posed to the German generals whether they should have obeyed the orders of the Fuehrer to commit war crimes or obeyed their own consciences.*

---

* "It was the first time I found myself involved in a conflict between my soldierly conceptions and my duty to obey," Field Marshal von Manstein declared on the stand at Nuremberg in discussing the Commissar Order. "Actually, I ought to have obeyed, but I said to myself that as a soldier I could not possibly co-operate in a thing like that. I told the Commander of the Army Group under which I served at that time . . . that I would not carry out such an order, which was against the honor of a soldier."[74]

As a matter of record, the order, of course, was carried out on a large scale.

According to Halder, as he later remembered it, the generals were outraged at this order and, as soon as the meeting was over, protested to their Commander in Chief, Brauchitsch. This spineless Field Marshal* promised that he would "fight against this order in the form it was given." Later, Halder swears, Brauchitsch informed OKW in writing that the officers of the Army "could never execute such orders." But did he?

In his testimony on direct examination at Nuremberg Brauchitsch admitted that he took no such action with Hitler "because nothing in the world could change his attitude." What the head of the Army did, he told the tribunal, was to issue a written order that "discipline in the Army was to be strictly observed along the lines and regulations that applied in the past."

"You did not give any order directly referring to the Commissar Order?" Lord Justice Lawrence, the peppery president of the tribunal, asked Brauchitsch.

"No," he replied. "I could not rescind the order directly."[75]

The old-line Army officers, with their Prussian traditions, were given further occasion to struggle with their consciences by subsequent directives issued in the name of the Fuehrer by General Keitel on May 13. The principal one limited the functions of German courts-martial. They were to give way to a more primitive form of law.

Punishable offenses committed by enemy civilians [in Russia] do not, until further notice, come any longer under the jurisdiction of the courts-martial . . .

Persons suspected of criminal action will be brought at once before an officer. This officer will decide whether they are to be shot.

With regard to *offenses* committed against *enemy civilians by members of the Wehrmacht, prosecution is not obligatory* even where the deed is at the same time a military crime or offense.†

The Army was told to go easy on such offenders, remembering in each case all the harm done to Germany since 1918 by the "Bolsheviki." Courts-martial of German soldiers would be justified only if "maintenance of discipline or security of the Forces call for such a measure." At any rate, the directive concluded, "only those court sentences are confirmed which are in accordance with the political intentions of the High Command."[76] The directive was to "be treated as 'most secret.'"‡

---

* "A man of straw," Hitler later called him. (*Hitler's Secret Conversations*, p. 153.)
† The emphasis is in the original order.
‡ On July 27, 1941, Keitel ordered all copies of this directive of May 13 concerning courts-martial destroyed, though "the validity of the directive," he stipulated, "is not affected by the destruction of the copies." The July 27 order, he added, "would itself be destroyed." But copies of both survived and turned up at Nuremberg to haunt the High Command.

A second directive of the same date signed by Keitel on behalf of Hitler entrusted Himmler with "*special tasks*" for the preparation of the political administration in Russia—"tasks," it said, "which result from the struggle which has to be carried out between two opposing political systems." The Nazi secret-police sadist was delegated to act "independently" of the Army, "under his own responsibility." The generals well knew what the designation of Himmler for "special tasks" meant, though they denied that they did when they took the stand at Nuremberg. Furthermore, the directive said, the occupied areas in Russia were to be sealed off while Himmler went to work. Not even the "highest personalities of the Government and Party," Hitler stipulated, were to be allowed to have a look. The same directive named Goering for the "exploitation of the country and the securing of its economic assets for use by German industry." Incidentally, Hitler also declared in this order that as soon as military operations were concluded Russia would be "divided up into individual states with governments of their own."[78]

Just how this would be done was to be worked out by Alfred Rosenberg, the befuddled Balt and officially the leading Nazi thinker, who had been, as we have seen, one of Hitler's early mentors in the Munich days. On April 20 the Fuehrer appointed him "Commissioner for the Central Control of Questions Connected with the East-European Region" and immediately this Nazi dolt, with a positive genius for misunderstanding history, even the history of Russia, where he was born and educated, went to work to build his castles in his once native land. Rosenberg's voluminous files were captured intact; like his books, they make dreary reading and will not be allowed to impede this narrative, though occasionally they must be referred to because they disclose some of Hitler's plans for Russia.

By early May, Rosenberg had drawn up his first wordy blueprint for what promised to be the greatest German conquest in history. To begin with, European Russia was to be divided up into so-called Reich Commissariats. Russian Poland would become a German protectorate called Ostland, the Ukraine "an independent state in alliance with Germany," Caucasia, with its rich oil fields, would be ruled by a German "plenipotentiary," and the three Baltic States and White Russia would form a German protectorate preparatory to being annexed outright to the Greater German Reich. This last feat, Rosenberg explained in one of the endless memoranda which he showered on Hitler and the generals in order, as he said,

---

Four days before, on July 23, Keitel had issued another order marked "Top Secret":

On July 22, the Fuehrer after receiving the Commander of the Army [Brauchitsch] issued the following order:

In view of the vast size of the occupied areas in the East, the forces available for establishing security will be sufficient only if all resistance is punished not by legal prosecution of the guilty, but by the spreading of such terror by the occupying forces as is alone appropriate to eradicate every inclination to resist amongst the population.[77]

to elucidate "the historical and racial conditions" for his decisions, would be accomplished by Germanizing the racially assimilable Balts and "banishing the undesirable elements." In Latvia and Estonia, he cautioned, "banishment on a large scale will have to be envisaged." Those driven out would be replaced by Germans, preferably war veterans. "The Baltic Sea," he ordained, "must become a Germanic inland sea."[79]

Two days before the troops jumped off, Rosenberg addressed his closest collaborators who were to take over the rule of Russia.

The job of feeding the German people [he said] stands at the top of the list of Germany's claims on the East. The southern [Russian] territories will have to serve . . . for the feeding of the German people.

We see absolutely no reason for any obligation on our part to feed also the Russian people with the products of that surplus territory. We know that this is a harsh necessity, bare of any feelings . . . The future will hold very hard years in store for the Russians.[80]

Very hard years indeed, since the Germans were deliberately planning to starve to death millions of them!

Goering, who had been placed in charge of the economic exploitation of the Soviet Union, made this even clearer than Rosenberg did. In a long directive of May 23, 1941, his Economic Staff, East, laid it down that the surplus food from Russia's black-earth belt in the south must not be diverted to the people in the industrial areas, where, in any case, the industries would be destroyed. The workers and their families in these regions would simply be left to starve—or, if they could, to emigrate to Siberia. Russia's great food production must go to the Germans.

The German Administration in these territories [the directive declared] may well attempt to mitigate the consequences of the famine which undoubtedly will take place and to accelerate the return to primitive agricultural conditions. However, these measures will not avert famine. Any attempt to save the population there from death by starvation by importing surpluses from the black-soil zone would be at the expense of supplies to Europe. It would reduce Germany's staying power in the war, and would undermine Germany's and Europe's power to resist the blockade. This must be clearly and absolutely understood.[81]

How many Russian civilians would die as the result of this deliberate German policy? A meeting of state secretaries on May 2 had already given a general answer. *"There is no doubt,"* a secret memorandum of the conference declared, *"that as a result, many millions of persons will be starved to death if we take out of the country the things necessary for us."*[82] And Goering had said, and Rosenberg, that they would be taken out— that much had to be "clearly and absolutely understood."

Did any German, even one single German, protest against this planned ruthlessness, this well-thought-out scheme to put millions of human beings to death by starvation? In all the memoranda concerning the German directives for the spoliation of Russia, there is no mention of anyone's objecting—as at least some of the generals did in regard to the Commissar Order. These plans were not merely wild and evil fantasies of distorted minds and souls of men such as Hitler, Goering, Himmler and Rosenberg. For weeks and months, it is evident from the records, hundreds of German officials toiled away at their desks in the cheerful light of the warm spring days, adding up figures and composing memoranda which coldly calculated the massacre of millions. By starvation, in this case. Heinrich Himmler, the mild-faced ex-chicken farmer, also sat at his desk at S.S. headquarters in Berlin those days, gazing through his pince-nez at plans for the massacre of other millions in a quicker and more violent way.

Well pleased with the labors of his busy minions, both military and civilian, in planning the onslaught on the Soviet Union, her destruction, her exploitation and the mass murder of her citizenry, Hitler on April 30 set the date for the attack—June 22—made his victory speech in the Reichstag on May 4 and then retired to his favorite haunt, the Berghof above Berchtesgaden, where he could gaze at the splendor of the Alpine mountains, their peaks still covered with spring snow, and contemplate his next conquest, the greatest of all, at which, as he had told his generals, the world would hold its breath.

It was here on the night of Saturday, May 10, 1941, that he received strange and unexpected news which shook him to the bone and forced him, as it did almost everyone else in the Western world, to take his mind for the moment off the war. His closest personal confidant, the deputy leader of the Nazi Party, the second in line to succeed him after Goering, the man who had been his devoted and fanatically loyal follower since 1921 and, since Roehm's murder, the nearest there was to a friend, had literally flown the coop and on his own gone to parley with the enemy!

THE FLIGHT OF RUDOLF HESS

The first report late that evening of May 10 that Rudolf Hess had taken off alone for Scotland in a Messerschmitt-110 fighter plane hit Hitler, as Dr. Schmidt recalled, "as though a bomb had struck the Berghof."[83] General Keitel found the Fuehrer pacing up and down his spacious study pointing a finger at his forehead and mumbling that Hess must have been crazy.[84] "I've got to talk to Goering right away," Hitler shouted. The next morning there was an agitated powwow with Goering and all the party gauleiter as they sought to "figure out"—the words are Keitel's— how to present this embarrassing event to the German public and to the world. Their task was not made easier, Keitel later testified, by the British at first keeping silent about their visitor, and for a time Hitler and his conferees hoped that perhaps Hess had run out of gasoline and fallen into the chilly North Sea and drowned.

The Fuehrer's first information had come in a somewhat incoherent letter from Hess which was delivered by courier a few hours after he took off at 5:45 P.M. on May 10 from Augsburg. "I can't recognize Hess in it. It's a different person. Something must have happened to him—some mental disturbance," Hitler told Keitel. But the Fuehrer was also suspicious. Messerschmitt, from whose company airfield Hess had taken off, was ordered arrested, as were dozens of men on the deputy leader's staff.

If Hitler was mystified by Hess's abrupt departure, so was Churchill by his unexpected arrival.* Stalin was highly suspicious. For the duration of the war, the bizarre incident remained a mystery, and it was cleared up only at the Nuremberg trial, in which Hess was one of the defendants. The facts may be briefly set down.

Hess, always a muddled man though not so doltish as Rosenberg, flew on his own to Britain under the delusion that he could arrange a peace settlement. Though deluded, he was sincere—there seems to be no reason to doubt that. He had met the Duke of Hamilton at the Olympic games in Berlin in 1936, and it was within twelve miles of the Duke's home in Scotland—so efficient was his navigation—that he baled out of his Messerschmitt, parachuted safely to the ground and asked a farmer to take him to the Scottish lord. As it happened, Hamilton, a wing commander in the R.A.F., was on duty that Saturday evening at a sector operations room and had spotted the Messerschmitt plane off the coast as it came in to make a landfall shortly after 10 P.M. An hour later it was reported to him that the plane had crashed in flames, that the pilot, who had baled out and who gave his name as Alfred Horn, had claimed to be on a "special mission" to see the Duke of Hamilton. This meeting was arranged by British authorities for the next morning.

To the Duke, Hess explained that he was on "a mission of humanity and that the Fuehrer did not want to defeat England and wished to stop the fighting." The fact, Hess said, that this was his fourth attempt to fly to Britain—on the three other tries, he had had to turn back because of weather—and that he was, after all, a Reich cabinet minister, showed "his sincerity and Germany's willingness for peace." In this interview, as in later ones with others, Hess was not backward in asserting that Germany would win the war and that if it continued the plight of the British would be terrible. Therefore, his hosts had better take advantage of his presence and negotiate peace. So confident was this Nazi fanatic that the British would sit down and parley with him, that he asked the Duke to request "the King to give him 'parole,' as he had come unarmed and of his own free will."[85] Later he demanded that he be treated with the respect due to a cabinet member.

---

* Churchill has graphically described how he received the news late that Saturday night while visiting in the country and how at first he thought it too fantastic to believe. (*The Grand Alliance*, pp. 50–55.)

The subsequent talks, with one exception, were conducted on the British side by Ivone Kirkpatrick, the knowing former First Secretary of the British Embassy in Berlin, whose confidential reports were later made available at Nuremberg.[86] To this sophisticated student of Nazi Germany Hess, after parroting Hitler's explanations of all the Nazi aggressions, from Austria to Scandinavia and the Lowlands, and having insisted that Britain was responsible for the war and would certainly lose it if she didn't bring a stop to it now, divulged his proposals for peace. They were none other than those which Hitler had urged on Chamberlain—unsuccessfully—on the eve of his attack on Poland: namely, that Britain should give Germany a free hand in Europe in return for Germany's giving Britain "a completely free hand in the Empire." The former German colonies would have to be returned and of course Britain would have to make peace with Italy.

Finally, as we were leaving the room [Kirkpatrick reported], Hess delivered a parting shot. He had forgotten, he declared, to emphasize that the proposal could only be considered on the understanding that it was negotiated by Germany with an English government other than the present one. Mr. Churchill, who had planned the war since 1936, and his colleagues who had lent themselves to his war policy, were not persons with whom the Fuehrer could negotiate.

For a German who had got so far in the jungle warfare within the Nazi Party and then within the Third Reich, Rudolf Hess, as all who knew him could testify, was singularly naïve. He had expected, it is evident from the record of these interviews, to be received immediately as a serious negotiator—if not by Churchill, then by the "opposition party," of which he thought the Duke of Hamilton was one of the leaders. When his contacts with British officialdom continued to be restricted to Kirkpatrick, he grew bellicose and threatening. At an interview on May 14, he pictured to the skeptical diplomat the dire consequences to Britain if she continued the war. There would soon be, he said, a terrible and absolutely complete blockade of the British Isles.

It was fruitless [Kirkpatrick was told by Hess] for anyone here to imagine that England could capitulate and that the war could be waged from the Empire. It was Hitler's intention, in such an eventuality, to continue the blockade of England . . . so that we would have to face the deliberate starvation of the population of these islands.

Hess urged that the conversations, which he had risked so much to bring about, get under way at once. "His own flight," as explained to Kirkpatrick, "was intended to give us a chance of opening conversations without loss of prestige. If we rejected this chance it would be clear proof that we desire no understanding with Germany, and Hitler would be entitled— in fact, it would be his duty—to destroy us utterly and to keep us after the war in a state of permanent subjection." Hess insisted that the number of negotiators be kept small.

As a Reich Minister he could not place himself in the position of being a lone individual subjected to a crossfire of comment and questions from a large number of persons.

On this ridiculous note, the conversations ended, so far as Kirkpatrick was concerned. But—surprisingly—the British cabinet, according to Churchill,[87] "invited" Lord Simon to interview Hess on June 10. According to the Nazi deputy leader's lawyer at Nuremberg, Simon promised that he would bring Hess's peace proposals to the attention of the British government.*[88]

Hess's motives are clear. He sincerely wanted peace with Britain. He had not the shadow of doubt that Germany would win the war and destroy the United Kingdom unless peace were concluded at once. There were, to be sure, other motives. The war had brought his personal eclipse. Running the Nazi Party as Hitler's deputy during the war was dull business and no longer very important. What mattered in Germany now was running the war and foreign affairs. These were the things which engaged the attention of the Fuehrer to the exclusion of almost all else, and which put the limelight on Goering, Ribbentrop, Himmler, Goebbels and the generals. Hess felt frustrated and jealous. How better restore his old position with his beloved Leader and in the country than by pulling off a brilliant and daring stroke of statesmanship such as singlehandedly arranging peace between Germany and Britain?

Finally, the beetle-browed deputy leader, like some of the other Nazi bigwigs—Hitler himself and Himmler—had come to have an abiding belief in astrology. At Nuremberg he confided to the American prison psychiatrist, Dr. Douglas M. Kelley, that late in 1940 one of his astrologers had read in the stars that he was ordained to bring about peace. He also related how his old mentor, Professor Haushofer, the Munich *Geopolitiker,* had seen him in a dream striding through the tapestried halls of English castles, bringing peace between the two great "Nordic" nations.[90] For a man who had never escaped from mental adolescence, this was heady stuff and no doubt helped impel Hess to undertake his weird mission to England.

At Nuremberg one of the British prosecutors suggested still another reason: that Hess flew to England to try to arrange a peace settlement so that Germany would have only a one-front war to fight when she attacked the Soviet Union. The Russian prosecutor told the tribunal that he was sure of it. And so was Joseph Stalin, whose mighty suspicions at this criti-

---

* At Nuremberg Hess told the tribunal that Lord Simon had introduced himself to him as "Dr. Guthrie" and had declared, "I come with the authority of the Government and I shall be willing to discuss with you as far as seems good anything you would wish to state for the information of the Government."[89]

cal time seem to have been concentrated not on Germany, as they should have been, but on Great Britain. The arrival of Hess in Scotland convinced him that there was some deep plot being hatched between Churchill and Hitler which would give Germany the same freedom to strike the Soviet Union which the Russian dictator had given her to assault Poland and the West. When three years later the British Prime Minister, then on his second visit to Moscow, tried to convince Stalin of the truth, he simply did not believe it. It is fairly clear from the interrogations conducted by Kirkpatrick, who tried to draw the Nazi leader out on Hitler's intentions regarding Russia, that either Hess did not know of Barbarossa or, if he did, did not know that it was imminent.

The days following Hess's sudden departure were among the most embarrassing of Hitler's life. He realized that the prestige of his regime had been severely damaged by the flight of his closest collaborator. How was it to be explained to the German people and the outside world? The questioning of the arrested members of Hess's entourage convinced the Fuehrer that there had been no disloyalty toward him and certainly no plot, and that his trusted lieutenant had simply cracked up. It was decided at the Berghof, after the British had confirmed Hess's arrival, to offer this explanation to the public. Soon the German press was dutifully publishing brief accounts that this once great star of National Socialism had become "a deluded, deranged and muddled idealist, ridden with hallucinations traceable to World War [I] injuries."

It seemed [said the official press communiqué] that Party Comrade Hess lived in a state of hallucination, as a result of which he felt he could bring about an understanding between England and Germany . . . This, however, will have no effect on the continuance of the war, which has been forced on the German people.

Privately, Hitler gave orders to have Hess shot at once if he returned,* and publicly he stripped his old comrade of all his offices, replacing him as deputy leader of the party by Martin Bormann, a more sinister and conniving character. The Fuehrer hoped that the bizarre episode would be forgotten as soon as possible; his own thoughts quickly turned again to the attack on Russia, which was not far off.

---

* Hess, a sorry, broken figure at Nuremberg, where for a part of the trial he faked total amnesia (his mind had certainly been shattered), outlived Hitler. He was sentenced to life imprisonment by the International Tribunal, escaping the death sentence largely due to his mental collapse. I have described his appearance there in *End of a Berlin Diary*.

The British treated him as a prisoner of war, releasing him on October 10, 1945, so that he could stand trial at Nuremberg. During his captivity in England, he complained bitterly at being denied "full diplomatic privileges," which he constantly demanded, and his none too balanced mind began to deteriorate and he had long stretches of amnesia. He told Dr. Kelley, however, that he twice tried to kill himself during his internment. He became convinced, he said, that the British were trying to poison him.

THE PLIGHT OF THE KREMLIN

Despite all the evidence of Hitler's intentions—the build-up of German forces in eastern Poland, the presence of a million Nazi troops in the near-by Balkans, the Wehrmacht's conquest of Yugoslavia and Greece and its occupation of Rumania, Bulgaria and Hungary—the men in the Kremlin, Stalin above all, stark realists though they were reputed to be and had been, blindly hoped that Russia somehow would still escape the Nazi tyrant's wrath. Their natural suspicions, of course, could not help but feed on the bare facts, nor could their growing resentment at Hitler's moves in southeastern Europe be suppressed. There is, however, something unreal, almost unbelievable, quite grotesque, in the diplomatic exchanges between Moscow and Berlin in these spring weeks (exhaustively recorded in the captured Nazi documents), in which the Germans tried clumsily to deceive the Kremlin to the last and the Soviet leaders seemed unable to fully grasp reality and act on it in time.

Though they several times protested the entry of German troops into Rumania and Bulgaria and then the attack on Yugoslavia and Greece as a violation of the Nazi–Soviet Pact and a threat to Russian "security interests," the Soviets went out of their way to appease Berlin as the date for the German attack approached. Stalin personally took the lead in this. On April 13, 1941, Ambassador von der Schulenburg telegraphed an interesting dispatch to Berlin recounting how on the departure of the Japanese Foreign Minister, Yosuke Matsuoka, that evening from Moscow, Stalin had shown "a remarkably friendly manner" not only to the Japanese but to the Germans. At the railroad station

Stalin publicly asked for me [Schulenburg wired] . . . and threw his arm around my shoulders: "We must remain friends and you must now do everything to that end!" Somewhat later Stalin turned to the acting German Military Attaché, Colonel Krebs, first made sure that he was a German, and then said to him: "We will remain friends with you—through thick and thin!"[91]

Three days later the German chargé in Moscow, Tippelskirch, wired Berlin stressing that the demonstration at the station showed Stalin's friendliness toward Germany and that this was especially important "in view of the persistently circulating rumors of an imminent conflict between Germany and the Soviet Union."[92] The day before, Tippelskirch had informed Berlin that the Kremlin had accepted "unconditionally," after months of wrangling, the German proposals for the settlement of the border between the two countries from the Igorka River to the Baltic Sea. "The compliant attitude of the Soviet Government," he said, "seems very remarkable."[93] In view of what was brewing in Berlin, it surely was.

In supplying blockaded Germany with important raw materials, the Soviet government continued to be equally compliant. On April 5, 1941, Schnurre, in charge of trade negotiations with Moscow, reported jubilantly to his Nazi masters that after the slowdown in Russian deliveries in January and February 1941, due to the "cooling off of political relations," they had risen "by leaps and bounds in March, especially in grains, petroleum, manganese ore and the nonferrous and precious metals."

Transit traffic through Siberia [he added] is proceeding favorably as usual. At our request the Soviet Government even put a special freight train for rubber at our disposal at the Manchurian border.[94]

Six weeks later, on May 15, Schnurre was reporting that the obliging Russians had put on several special freight trains so that 4,000 tons of badly needed raw rubber could be delivered to Germany over the Siberian railway.

The quantities of raw materials contracted for are being delivered punctually by the Russians, despite the heavy burden this imposes on them . . . I am under the impression that we could make economic demands on Moscow which would even go beyond the scope of the treaty of January 10, demands designed to secure German food and raw-material requirements beyond the extent now contracted for.[95]

German deliveries of machinery to Russia were falling behind, Schnurre observed, but he did not seem to mind, if the Russians didn't. However, he was disturbed on May 15 by another factor. "Great difficulties are created," he complained, "by the countless rumors of an imminent German–Russian conflict," for which he blamed German official sources. Amazingly, the "difficulties," Schnurre explained in a lengthy memorandum to the Foreign Office, did not come from Russia but from German industrial firms, which, he said, were trying "to withdraw" from their contracts with the Russians.

Hitler, it must be noted here, was doing his best to contradict the rumors, but at the same time he was busy trying to convince his generals and top officials that Germany was in growing danger of being attacked by Russia. Though the generals, from their own military intelligence, knew better, so hypnotic was Hitler's spell over them that even after the war Halder, Brauchitsch, Manstein and others (though not Paulus, who seems to have been more honest) contended that a Soviet military build-up on the Polish frontier had become very threatening by the beginning of the summer.

Count von der Schulenburg, who had come home from Moscow on a brief leave, saw Hitler in Berlin on April 28 and tried to convince him of Russia's peaceful intentions. "Russia," he attempted to explain, "is very apprehensive at the rumors predicting a German attack on Russia. I cannot believe," he added, "that Russia will ever attack Germany . . . If Stalin was unable to go with England and France in 1939 when both were still strong, he will certainly not make such a decision today, when France is destroyed and England badly battered. On the contrary, I am convinced that Stalin is prepared to make even further concessions to us."

The Fuehrer feigned skepticism. He had been "forewarned," he said, "by events in Serbia . . . What devil had possessed the Russians," he asked, "to conclude the friendship pact with Yugoslavia?"* He did not believe, it was true, he said, that "Russia could be brought to attack Germany." Nevertheless, he concluded, he was obliged "to be careful." Hitler did not tell his ambassador to the Soviet Union what plans he had in store for that country, and Schulenburg, an honest, decent German of the old school, remained ignorant of them to the last.

Stalin, too, but not of the *signs,* or of the *warnings,* of what Hitler was up to. On April 22 the Soviet government formally protested eighty instances of border violations by Nazi planes which it said had taken place between March 27 and April 18, providing detailed accounts of each. In one case, it said, in a German reconnaissance plane which landed near Rovno on April 15 there was found a camera, rolls of exposed film and a torn topographical map of the western districts of the U.S.S.R., "all of which give evidence of the purpose of the crew of this airplane." Even in protesting the Russians were conciliatory. They had given the border troops, the note said, "the order not to fire on German planes flying over Soviet territory so long as such flights do not occur frequently."[97]

Stalin made further conciliatory moves early in May. To please Hitler he expelled the diplomatic representatives in Moscow of Belgium, Norway, Greece and even Yugoslavia and closed their legations. He recognized the pro-Nazi government of Rashid Ali in Iraq. He kept the Soviet press under the strictest restraint in order to avoid provoking Germany.

These manifestations [Schulenburg wired Berlin on May 12] of the intention of the Stalin Government are calculated . . . to relieve the tension between the Soviet Union and Germany and to create a better atmosphere for the future. We must bear in mind that Stalin personally has always advocated a friendly relationship between Germany and the Soviet Union.[98]

Though Stalin had long been the absolute dictator of the Soviet Union this was the first mention by Schulenburg in his dispatches of the term "Stalin Government." There was good reason. On May 6 Stalin had personally taken over as Chairman of the Council of People's Commissars, or Prime Minister, replacing Molotov, who remained as Foreign Commissar. This was the first time the all-powerful secretary of the Communist Party had taken government office and the general world reaction was that it meant the situation had become so serious for the Soviet Union, especially in its relations with Nazi Germany, that only Stalin could deal with it as the nominal as well as the actual head of government. This in-

---

* On April 5, the day before the German attack on Yugoslavia, the Soviet government had hastily concluded a "Treaty of Nonaggression and Friendship" with the new Yugoslav government, apparently in a frantic attempt to head off Hitler. Molotov had informed Schulenburg of it the night before and the ambassador had exclaimed that "the moment was very unfortunate" and had tried, unsuccessfully, to argue the Russians into at least postponing the signing of the treaty.[96]

terpretation was obvious, but there was another which was not so clear but which the astute German ambassador in Moscow promptly pointed out to Berlin.

Stalin, he reported, was displeased with the deterioration of German–Soviet relations and blamed Molotov's clumsy diplomacy for much of it.

In my opinion [Schulenburg said] it may be assumed with certainty that Stalin has set himself a foreign-policy goal of overwhelming importance . . . which he hopes to attain by his personal efforts. I firmly believe that in an international situation which he considers serious, Stalin has set himself the goal of preserving the Soviet Union from a conflict with Germany.[99]

Did the crafty Soviet dictator not realize by now—the middle of May 1941—that this was an impossible goal, that there was nothing, short of an abject surrender to Hitler, that he could do to attain it? He surely knew the significance of Hitler's conquest of Yugoslavia and Greece, of the presence of large masses of German troops in Rumania and Hungary on his southwest borders, of the Wehrmacht build-up on his western frontier in Poland. The persistent rumors in Moscow itself surely reached him. By the beginning of May what Schulenburg called in a dispatch on the second day of that month "rumors of an imminent German–Russian military showdown" were so rife in the Soviet capital that he and his officials in the German Embassy were having difficulty in combating them.

Please bear in mind [he advised Berlin] that attempts to counteract these rumors here in Moscow must necessarily remain ineffectual if such rumors incessantly reach here from Germany, and if every traveler who comes to Moscow, or travels through Moscow, not only brings these rumors along, but can even confirm them by citing facts.[100]

The veteran ambassador was getting suspicious himself. He was instructed by Berlin to continue to deny the rumors, and to spread it about that not only was there no concentration of German troops on Russia's frontiers but that actually considerable forces (eight divisions, he was told for his "personal information") were being transferred from "east to west."[101] Perhaps these instructions only confirmed the ambassador's uneasiness, since by this time the press throughout the world was beginning to trumpet the German military build-up along the Soviet borders.

But long before this, Stalin had received specific warnings of Hitler's plans, and apparently paid no attention to them. The most serious one came from the government of the United States.

Early in January 1941, the U.S. commercial attaché in Berlin, Sam E. Woods, had sent a confidential report to the State Department stating that he had learned from trustworthy German sources that Hitler was making plans to attack Russia in the spring. It was a long and detailed message, outlining the General Staff plan of attack (which proved to be quite

accurate) and the preparations being made for the economic exploitation
of the Soviet Union, once it was conquered.*

Secretary of State Cordell Hull thought at first that Woods had been
victim of a German "plant." He called in J. Edgar Hoover. The F.B.I.
head read the report and judged it authentic. Woods had named some of
his sources, both in various ministries in Berlin and in the German General
Staff, and on being checked they were adjudged in Washington to be
men who ought to know what was up and anti-Nazi enough to tattle. Despite
the strained relations then existing between the American and Soviet
governments Hull decided to inform the Russians, requesting Undersecretary
of State Sumner Welles to communicate the substance of the report to
Ambassador Constantine Oumansky. This was done on March 20.

> Mr. Oumansky turned very white [Welles later wrote]. He was silent for
> a moment and then merely said: "I fully realize the gravity of the message you
> have given me. My government will be grateful for your confidence and
> I will inform it immediately of our conversation."[102]

If it was grateful, indeed if it ever believed this timely intelligence, it
never communicated any inkling to the American government. In fact,
as Secretary Hull has related in his memoirs, Moscow grew more hostile
and truculent because America's support of Britain made it impossible to
supply Russia with all the materials it demanded. Nevertheless, according
to Hull, the State Department, having received dispatches from its legations
in Bucharest and Stockholm the first week in June stating that Germany
would invade Russia within a fortnight, forwarded copies of them
to Ambassador Steinhardt in Moscow, who turned them over to Molotov.

Churchill too sought to warn Stalin. On April 3 he asked his ambassador
in Moscow, Sir Stafford Cripps, to deliver a personal note to the dictator
pointing out the significance to Russia of German troop movements
in southern Poland which he had learned of through a British agent.

---

* Sam Woods, a genial extrovert whose grasp of world politics and history was not
striking, seems to those of us who knew him and liked him the last man in the
American Embassy in Berlin likely to have come by such crucial intelligence. Some
of his colleagues in the embassy still doubt that he did. But Cordell Hull has confirmed
it in his memoirs and disclosed the details. Woods, the late Secretary of State
relates, had a German friend, an anti-Nazi, who had contacts high in the ministries,
the Reichsbank and the Nazi Party. As early as August 1940, this friend informed
Woods of conferences taking place at Hitler's headquarters concerning preparations
for an attack on the Soviet Union. From then on this informant kept the commercial
attaché *au courant* of what was transpiring both at the General Staff and
among those planning the economic spoliation of Russia. To avoid detection,
Woods met his informant in various movie houses in Berlin and in the darkness received
scribbled notes from him. (See *The Memoirs of Cordell Hull*, II, pp. 967–68.)

I left Berlin in December 1940. George Kennan, the most brilliant Foreign Service
officer at the embassy, who remained there, informs me that the embassy learned
from several sources of the coming attack on Russia. Two or three weeks before
the assault, he says, our consul at Koenigsberg, Kuykendall, relayed a report specifying
correctly the exact day it would begin.

Cripps' delay in delivering the message still vexed Churchill when he wrote about the incident years later in his memoirs.[103]

Before the end of April, Cripps knew the date set for the German attack, and the Germans knew he knew it. On April 24, the German naval attaché in Moscow sent a curt message to the Navy High Command in Berlin:

The British Ambassador predicts June 22 as the day of the outbreak of the war.[104]

This message, which is among the captured Nazi papers, was recorded in the German Naval Diary on the same day, with an exclamation point added at the end.[105] The admirals were surprised at the accuracy of the British envoy's prediction. The poor naval attaché, who, like the ambassador in Moscow, had not been let in on the secret, added in his dispatch that it was "manifestly absurd."

Molotov must have thought so too. A month later, on May 22, he received Schulenburg to discuss various matters. "He was as amiable, self-assured and well-informed as ever," the ambassador reported to Berlin, and again emphasized that Stalin and Molotov, "the two strongest men in the Soviet Union," were striving "above all" to avoid a conflict with Germany.[106]

On one point the usually perspicacious ambassador couldn't have been more wrong. Molotov, at this juncture, was certainly not "well-informed." But neither was the ambassador.

The extent to which the Russian Foreign Commissar was ill-informed was given public expression on June 14, 1941, just a week before the German blow fell. Molotov called in Schulenburg that evening and handed him the text of a Tass statement which, he said, was being broadcast that very night and published in the newspapers the next morning.[107] Blaming Cripps personally for the "widespread rumors of 'an impending war between the U.S.S.R. and Germany' in the English and foreign press," this official statement of the Soviet government branded them as an "obvious absurdity . . . a clumsy propaganda maneuver of the forces arrayed against the Soviet Union and Germany." It added:

In the opinion of Soviet circles the rumors of the intention of Germany . . . to launch an attack against the Soviet Union are completely without foundation.

Even the recent German troop movements from the Balkans to the Soviet frontiers were explained in the communiqué as "having no connection with Soviet–German relations." As for the rumors saying that Russia would attack Germany, they were "false and provocative."

The irony of the Tass communiqué on behalf of the Soviet government is enhanced by two German moves, one on the day of its publication, June 15, the other on the next day.

From Venice, where he was conferring with Ciano, Ribbentrop sent a secret message on June 15 to Budapest warning the Hungarian government "to take steps to secure its frontiers."

In view of the heavy concentration of Russian troops at the German eastern border, the Fuehrer will probably be compelled, by the beginning of July at the latest, to clarify German–Russian relations and in this connection to make certain demands.[108]

The Germans were tipping off the Hungarians, but not their principal ally. When Ciano the next day, during a gondola ride on the canals of Venice, asked Ribbentrop about the rumors of a German attack on Russia, the Nazi Foreign Minister replied:

"Dear Ciano, I cannot tell you anything as yet because every decision is locked in the impenetrable bosom of the Fuehrer. However, one thing is certain: if we attack them, the Russia of Stalin will be erased from the map within eight weeks."*

While the Kremlin was smugly preparing to broadcast to the world on June 14, 1941, that the rumors of a German attack on Russia were an "obvious absurdity," Adolf Hitler that very day was having his final big war conference on Barbarossa with the leading officers of the Wehrmacht. The timetable for the massing of troops in the East and their deployment to the jumping-off positions had been put in operation on May 22. A revised version of the timetable was issued a few days later.[109] It is a long and detailed document and shows that by the beginning of June not only were all plans for the onslaught on Russia complete but the vast and complicated movement of troops, artillery, armor, planes, ships and supplies was well under way and on schedule. A brief item in the Naval War Diary for May 29 states: "The preparatory movements of warships for Barbarossa has begun." Talks with the general staffs of Rumania, Hungary and Finland—the last country anxious now to win back what had been taken from her by the Russians in the winter war—were completed. On June 9 from Berchtesgaden Hitler sent out an order convoking the commanders in chief of the three Armed Services and the top field generals for a final all-day meeting on Barbarossa in Berlin on June 14.

Despite the enormity of the task, not only Hitler but his generals were in a confident mood as they went over last-minute details of the most gigan ic military operation in history—an all-out attack on a front stretch-

---

* This is from the last diary entry of Ciano, made on December 23, 1943, in Cell 27 of the Verona jail, a few days before he was executed. He added that the Italian government learned of the German invasion of Russia a half hour after it began. (*Cian⍥ Diaries*, p. 583.)

ing some 1,500 miles from the Arctic Ocean at Petsamo to the Black Sea. The night before, Brauchitsch had returned to Berlin from an inspection of the build-up in the East. Halder noted in his diary that the Army Commander in Chief was highly pleased. Officers and men, he said, were in top shape and ready.

This last military powwow on June 14 lasted from 11 A.M. until 6:30 P.M. It was broken by lunch at 2 P.M., at which Hitler gave his generals yet another of his fiery, eve-of-the-battle pep talks.[110] According to Halder, it was "a comprehensive political speech," with Hitler stressing that he had to attack Russia because her fall would force England to "give up." But the bloodthirsty Fuehrer must have emphasized something else even more. Keitel told about it during direct examination on the stand at Nuremberg.

The main theme was that this was the decisive battle between two ideologies and that the practices which we knew as soldiers—the only correct ones under international law—had to be measured by completely different standards.

Hitler thereupon, said Keitel, gave various orders for carrying out an unprecedented terror in Russia by "brutal means."

"Did you, or did any other generals, raise objections to these orders?" asked Keitel's own attorney.

"No. I personally made no remonstrances," the General replied. Nor did any of the other generals, he added.*

It is almost inconceivable but nevertheless true that the men in the Kremlin, for all the reputation they had of being suspicious, crafty and hardheaded, and despite all the evidence and all the warnings that stared them in the face, did not realize right up to the last moment that they were to be hit, and with a force which would almost destroy their nation.

At 9:30 on the pleasant summer evening of June 21, 1941, nine hours before the German attack was scheduled to begin, Molotov received the

---

* Hassell confirms this. Writing in his diary two days later, June 16, he remarks: "Brauchitsch and Halder have already agreed to Hitler's tactics [in Russia]. Thus the Army must assume the onus of the murders and burnings which up to now have been confined to the S.S."

At first the anti-Nazi "conspirators" had naïvely believed that Hitler's terror orders for Russia might shock the generals into joining an anti-Nazi revolt. But by June 16 Hassell himself is disillusioned. His diary entry for that date begins:

A series of conferences with Popitz, Goerdeler, Beck and Oster to consider whether certain orders which the Army commanders have received (but which they have not as yet issued) might suffice to open the eyes of the military leaders to the nature of the regime for which they are fighting. These orders concern brutal . . . measures the troops are to take against the Bolsheviks when Russia is invaded.

We came to the conclusion that nothing was to be hoped for now . . . They [the generals] delude themselves . . . Hopeless sergeant majors! [*The Von Hassell Diaries*, pp. 198–99.]

German ambassador at his office in the Kremlin and delivered his "final fatuity."* After mentioning further border violations by German aircraft, which he said he had instructed the Soviet ambassador in Berlin to bring to the attention of Ribbentrop, Molotov turned to another subject, which Schulenburg described in an urgent telegram to the Wilhelmstrasse that same night:

> There were a number of indications [Molotov had told him] that the German Government was dissatisfied with the Soviet Government. Rumors were even current that a war was impending between Germany and the Soviet Union . . . The Soviet Government was unable to understand the reasons for Germany's dissatisfaction . . . He would appreciate it if I could tell him what had brought about the present situation in German–Soviet relations.
>
> I replied [Schulenburg added] that I could not answer his questions, as I lacked the pertinent information.[111]

He was soon to get it.

For on its way to him over the air waves between Berlin and Moscow was a long coded radio message from Ribbentrop, dated June 21, 1941, marked "Very Urgent, State Secret, For the Ambassador Personally," which began:

> Upon receipt of this telegram, all of the cipher material still there is to be destroyed. The radio set is to be put out of commission.
>
> Please inform Herr Molotov at once that you have an urgent communication to make to him . . . Then please make the following declaration to him.

It was a familiar declaration, strewn with all the shopworn lies and fabrications at which Hitler and Ribbentrop had become so expert and which they had concocted so often before to justify each fresh act of unprovoked aggression. Perhaps—at least such is the impression this writer gets in rereading it—it somewhat topped all the previous ones for sheer effrontery and deceit. While Germany had loyally abided by the Nazi–Soviet Pact, it said, Russia had repeatedly broken it. The U.S.S.R. had practiced "sabotage, terrorism and espionage" against Germany. It had "combated the German attempt to set up a stable order in Europe." It had conspired with Britain "for an attack against the German troops in Rumania and Bulgaria." By concentrating "all available Russian forces on a long front from the Baltic to the Black Sea," it had "menaced" the Reich.

> Reports received the last few days [it went on] eliminate the last remaining doubts as to the aggressive character of this Russian concentration . . . In addition, there are reports from England regarding the negotiations of Ambas-

---

* The expression is Churchill's.

sador Cripps for still closer political and military collaboration between England and the Soviet Union.

To sum up, the Government of the Reich declares, therefore, that the Soviet Government, contrary to the obligations it assumed,

1. has not only continued, but even intensified its attempts to undermine Germany and Europe;

2. has adopted a more and more anti-German foreign policy;

3. has concentrated all its forces in readiness at the German border. Thereby the Soviet Government has broken its treaties with Germany and is about to attack Germany from the rear in its struggle for life. The Fuehrer has therefore ordered the German Armed Forces to oppose this threat with all the means at their disposal.[112]

"Please do not enter into any discussion of this communication," Ribbentrop advised his ambassador at the end. What could the shaken and disillusioned Schulenburg, who had devoted the best years of his life to improving German–Russian relations and who knew that the attack on the Soviet Union was unprovoked and without justification, say? Arriving back at the Kremlin just as dawn was breaking, he contented himself with reading the German declaration.* Molotov, stunned at last, listened in silence to the end and then said:

"It is war. Do you believe that we deserved that?"

At the same hour of daybreak a similar scene was taking place in the Wilhelmstrasse in Berlin. All afternoon on June 21, the Soviet ambassador, Vladimir Dekanozov, had been telephoning the Foreign Office asking for an appointment with Ribbentrop so that he could deliver his little protest against further border violations by German planes. He was told that the Nazi Foreign Minister was "out of town." Then at 2 A.M. on the twenty-second he was informed that Ribbentrop would receive him at 4 A.M. at the Foreign Office. There the envoy, who had been a deputy foreign commissar, a hatchetman for Stalin and the troubleshooter who had arranged the taking over of Lithuania, received, like Molotov in Moscow, the shock of his life. Dr. Schmidt, who was present, has described the scene.

I had never seen Ribbentrop so excited as he was in the five minutes before Dekanozov's arrival. He walked up and down his room like a caged animal . . .

---

* Thus ended the veteran ambassador's diplomatic career. Returning to Germany and forced to retire, he joined the opposition circle led by General Beck, Goerdeler, Hassell and others and for a time was marked to become Foreign Minister of an anti-Hitler regime. Hassell reported Schulenburg in 1943 as being willing to cross the Russian lines in order to talk with Stalin about a negotiated peace with an anti-Nazi government in Germany. (*The Von Hassell Diaries*, pp. 321–22.) Schulenburg was arrested and imprisoned after the July 1944 plot against Hitler and executed by the Gestapo on November 10.

Dekanozov was shown in and, obviously not guessing anything was amiss, held out his hand to Ribbentrop. We sat down and . . . Dekanozov proceeded to put on behalf of his Government certain questions that needed clarification. But he had hardly begun before Ribbentrop, with a stony expression, interrupted, saying: "That's not the question now" . . .

The arrogant Nazi Foreign Minister thereupon explained what the question was, gave the ambassador a copy of the memorandum which Schulenburg at that moment was reading out to Molotov, and informed him that German troops were at that instant taking "military countermeasures" on the Soviet frontier. The startled Soviet envoy, says Schmidt, "recovered his composure quickly and expressed his deep regret" at the developments, for which he blamed Germany. "He rose, bowed perfunctorily and left the room without shaking hands."[113]

The Nazi–Soviet honeymoon was over. At 3:30 A.M. on June 22, 1941, a half hour before the closing diplomatic formalities in the Kremlin and the Wilhelmstrasse, the roar of Hitler's guns along hundreds of miles of front had blasted it forever.

There was one other diplomatic prelude to the cannonade. On the afternoon of June 21, Hitler sat down at his desk in his new underground headquarters, Wolfsschanze (Wolf's Lair), near Rastenburg in a gloomy forest of East Prussia, and dictated a long letter to Mussolini. As in the preparation of all his other aggressions he had not trusted his good friend and chief ally enough to let him in on his secret until the last moment. Now, at the eleventh hour, he did. His letter is the most revealing and authentic evidence we have of the reasons for his taking this fatal step, which for so long puzzled the outside world and which was to pave the way for his end and that of the Third Reich. The letter, to be sure, is full of Hitler's customary lies and evasions which he tried to fob off even on his friends. But beneath them, and between them, there emerges his fundamental reasoning and his true—if mistaken—estimate of the world situation as the summer of 1941, the second of the war, officially began.

DUCE!

I am writing this letter to you at a moment when months of anxious deliberation and continuous nerve-racking waiting are ending in the hardest decision of my life.

*The situation:** England has lost this war. Like a drowning person, she grasps at every straw. Nevertheless, some of her hopes are naturally not without a certain logic . . . The destruction of France . . . has directed the glances of the British warmongers continually to the place from which they tried to start the war: to Soviet Russia.

Both countries, Soviet Russia and England, are equally interested in a

* Hitler's emphasis.

Europe . . . rendered prostrate by a long war. Behind these two countries stands the North American Union goading them on. . . .

Hitler next explained that with large Soviet military forces in his rear he could never assemble the strength—"particularly in the air"—to make the all-out attack on Britain which would bring her down.

Really, all available Russian forces are at our border . . . If circumstances should give me cause to employ the German Air Force against England, there is danger that Russia will then begin its strategy of extortion, to which I would have to yield in silence simply from a feeling of air inferiority . . . England will be all the less ready for peace for it will be able to pin its hopes on the Russian partner. Indeed this hope must naturally grow with the progress in preparedness of the Russian armed forces. And behind this is the mass delivery of war material from America which they hope to get in 1942 . . .

I have therefore, after constantly racking my brains, finally reached the decision to cut the noose before it can be drawn tight . . . My over-all view is now as follows:

1. *France* is, as ever, not to be trusted.

2. *North Africa* itself, insofar as your colonies, Duce, are concerned, is probably out of danger until fall.

3. *Spain* is irresolute and—I am afraid—will take sides only when the outcome of the war is decided . . .

5. An attack on *Egypt* before autumn is out of the question . . .

6. Whether or not *America* enters the war is a matter of indifference, inasmuch as she supports our enemy with all the power she is able to mobilize.

7. The situation in England itself is bad; the provision of food and raw materials is growing steadily more difficult. The martial spirit to make war, after all, lives only on hopes. These hopes are based solely on two assumptions: Russia and America. We have no chance of eliminating America. But it does lie in our power to exclude Russia. The elimination of Russia means, at the same time, a tremendous relief for Japan in East Asia, and thereby the possibility of a much stronger threat to American activities through Japanese intervention.

I have decided under these circumstances to put an end to the hypocritical performance in the Kremlin.

Germany, Hitler said, would not need any Italian troops in Russia. (He was not going to share the glory of conquering Russia any more than he had shared the conquest of France.) But Italy, he declared, could "give decisive aid" by strengthening its forces in North Africa and by preparing "to march into France in case of a French violation of the treaty." This was a fine bait for the land-hungry Duce.

So far as the air war on England is concerned, we shall, for a time, remain on the defensive . . .

As for the war in the East, Duce, it will surely be difficult, but I do not entertain a second's doubt as to its great success. I hope, above all, that it will then be possible for us to secure a common food-supply base in the Ukraine which will furnish us such additional supplies as we may need in the future.

Then came the excuse for not tipping off his partner earlier.

If I waited until this moment, Duce, to send you this information, it is because the final decision itself will not be made until 7 o'clock tonight . . .

Whatever may come, Duce, our situation cannot become worse as a result of this step; it can only improve . . . Should England nevertheless not draw any conclusions from the hard facts, then we can, with our rear secured, apply ourselves with increased strength to the dispatching of our enemy.

Finally Hitler described his great feeling of relief at having finally made up his mind.

. . . Let me say one more thing, Duce. Since I struggled through to this decision, I again feel spiritually free. The partnership with the Soviet Union, in spite of the complete sincerity of our efforts to bring about a final conciliation, was nevertheless often very irksome to me, for in some way or other it seemed to me to be a break with my whole origin, my concepts and my former obligations. I am happy now to be relieved of these mental agonies.

With hearty and comradely greetings,

Your
ADOLF HITLER[114]

At 3 o'clock in the morning of June 22, a bare half hour before the German troops jumped off, Ambassador von Bismarck awakened Ciano in Rome to deliver Hitler's long missive, which the Italian Foreign Minister then telephoned to Mussolini, who was resting at his summer place at Riccione. It was not the first time that the Duce had been wakened from his sleep in the middle of the night by a message from his Axis partner, and he resented it. "Not even I disturb my servants at night," Mussolini fretted to Ciano, "but the Germans make me jump out of bed at any hour without the least consideration."[115] Nevertheless, as soon as Mussolini had rubbed the sleep from his eyes he gave orders for an immediate declaration of war on the Soviet Union. He was now completely a prisoner of the Germans. He knew it and resented it. "I hope for only one thing," he told Ciano, "that in this war in the East the Germans lose a lot of feathers."[116] Still, he realized that his own future now depended wholly on German arms. The Germans would win in Russia, he was sure, but he hoped that at least they would get a bloody nose.

He could not know, nor did he suspect, nor did anyone else in the West, on either side, that they would get much worse. On Sunday morning, June 22, the day Napoleon had crossed the Niemen in 1812 on his way to Moscow, and exactly a year after Napoleon's country, France, had capitulated at Compiègne, Adolf Hitler's armored, mechanized and hitherto invincible armies poured across the Niemen and various other rivers and penetrated swiftly into Russia. The Red Army, despite all the warnings and the warning signs, was, as General Halder noted in his diary the first day, "tactically surprised along the entire front."* All the first bridges were captured intact. In fact, says Halder, at most places along the border the Russians were not even deployed for action and were overrun before they could organize resistance. Hundreds of Soviet planes were destroyed on the flying fields.† Within a few days tens of thousands of prisoners began to pour in; whole armies were quickly encircled. It seemed like the *Feldzug in Polen* all over again.

"It is hardly too much to say," the usually cautious Halder noted in his diary on July 3 after going over the latest General Staff reports, "that the *Feldzug* against Russia has been won in fourteen days." In a matter of weeks, he added, it would all be over.

---

* There is a curious notation in Halder's diary that first day. After mentioning that at noon the Russian radio stations, which the Germans were monitoring, had come back on the air he writes: "They have asked Japan to mediate the political and economic differences between Russia and Germany, and remain in active contact with the German Foreign Office." Did Stalin believe—nine hours after the attack—that he somehow might get it called off?

† General Guenther Blumentritt, chief of staff of the Fourth Army, later recalled that a little after midnight on the twenty-first, when the German artillery had already zeroed on its targets, the Berlin–Moscow express train chugged through the German lines on the Bug and across the river into Brest Litovsk "without incident." It struck him as a "weird moment." Almost equally weird to him was that the Russian artillery did not respond even when the assault began. "The Russians," he subsequently wrote, "were taken entirely by surprise on our front." As dawn broke German signal stations picked up the Red Army radio networks. "We are being fired on. What shall we do?" Blumentritt quotes one Russian message as saying. Back came the answer from headquarters: "You must be insane. And why is your signal not in code?" (*The Fatal Decisions*, edited by Seymour Freidin and William Richardson.)

24

A TURN OF THE TIDE

B Y THE BEGINNING of autumn 1941, Hitler believed that Russia was finished.

Within three weeks of the opening of the campaign, Field Marshal von Bock's Army Group Center, with thirty infantry divisions and fifteen panzer or motorized divisions, had pushed 450 miles from Bialystok to Smolensk. Moscow lay but 200 miles farther east along the high road which Napoleon had taken in 1812. To the north Field Marshal von Leeb's army group, twenty-one infantry and six armored divisions strong, was moving rapidly up through the Baltic States toward Leningrad. To the south Field Marshal von Rundstedt's army group of twenty-five infantry, four motorized, four mountain and five panzer divisions was advancing toward the Dnieper River and Kiev, capital of the fertile Ukraine, which Hitler coveted.

So *planmaessig* (according to plan), as the OKW communiqués put it, was the German progress along a thousand-mile front from the Baltic to the Black Sea, and so confident was the Nazi dictator that it would continue at an accelerated pace as one Soviet army after another was surrounded or dispersed, that on July 14, a bare three weeks after the invasion had begun, he issued a directive advising that the strength of the Army could be "considerably reduced in the near future" and that armament production would be concentrated on naval ships and Luftwaffe planes, especially the latter, for the conduct of the war against the last remaining enemy, Britain, and—he added—"against America should the case arise."[1] By the end of September he instructed the High Command to prepare to disband forty infantry divisions so that this additional manpower could be utilized by industry.[2]

Russia's two greatest cities, Leningrad, which Peter the Great had built as the capital on the Baltic, and Moscow, the ancient and now Bolshevik capital, seemed to Hitler about to fall. On September 18 he issued strict orders: "A capitulation of Leningrad or Moscow is not to be

accepted, even if offered."[3] What was to happen to them he made clear
to his commanders in a directive of September 29:

*The Fuehrer has decided to have St. Petersburg [Leningrad] wiped off the
face of the earth.* The further existence of this large city is of no interest once
Soviet Russia is overthrown . . .

The intention is to close in on the city and raze it to the ground by artillery
and by continuous air attack . . .

Requests that the city be taken over will be turned down, for *the problem
of the survival of the population and of supplying it with food is one which
cannot and should not be solved by us.* In this war for existence we have no
interest in keeping even part of this great city's population.†[4]

That same week, on October 3, Hitler returned to Berlin and in an
address to the German people proclaimed the collapse of the Soviet Union.
"I declare today, and I declare it without any reservation," he said, "that
the enemy in the East has been struck down and will never rise again . . .
Behind our troops there already lies a territory twice the size of the
German Reich when I came to power in 1933."

When on October 8, Orel, a key city south of Moscow, fell, Hitler sent
his press chief, Otto Dietrich, flying back to Berlin, to tell the correspondents of the world's leading newspapers there the next day that the last
intact Soviet armies, those of Marshal Timoshenko, defending Moscow,
were locked in two steel German pockets before the capital; that the
southern armies of Marshal Budënny were routed and dispersed; and that
sixty to seventy divisions of Marshal Voroshilov's army were surrounded
in Leningrad.

"For all military purposes," Dietrich concluded smugly, "Soviet Russia
is done with. The British dream of a two-front war is dead."

These public boasts of Hitler and Dietrich were, to say the least, premature.‡ In reality the Russians, despite the surprise with which they
were taken on June 22, their subsequent heavy losses in men and equipment, their rapid withdrawal and the entrapment of some of their best
armies, had begun in July to put up a mounting resistance such as the

---

* Emphasis in the original.
† A few weeks later Goering told Ciano, "This year between twenty and thirty million persons will die of hunger in Russia. Perhaps it is well that it should be so, for
certain nations must be decimated. But even if it were not, nothing can be done
about it. It is obvious that if humanity is condemned to die of hunger, the last to
die will be our two peoples . . . In the camps for Russian prisoners they have begun to eat each other." (*Ciano's Diplomatic Papers,* pp. 464–65.)
‡ Not as premature, however, as the warnings of the American General Staff, which
in July had confidentially informed American editors and Washington correspondents that the collapse of the Soviet Union was only a matter of a few weeks. It is
not surprising that the declarations of Hitler and Dr. Dietrich early in October 1941
were widely believed in the United States and Britain as well as in Germany and
elsewhere.

Wehrmacht had never encountered before. Halder's diary and the reports of such front-line commanders as General Guderian, who led a large panzer group on the central front, began to be peppered—and then laden —with accounts of severe fighting, desperate Russian stands and counter-attacks and heavy casualties to German as well as Soviet troops.

"The conduct of the Russian troops," General Blumentritt wrote later, "even in this first battle [for Minsk] was in striking contrast to the behavior of the Poles and the Western Allies in defeat. Even when encircled the Russians stood their ground and fought."[5] And there proved to be more of them, and with better equipment, than Adolf Hitler had dreamed was possible. Fresh Soviet divisions which German intelligence had no inkling of were continually being thrown into battle. "It is becoming ever clearer," Halder wrote in his diary on August 11, "that we underestimated the strength of the Russian colossus not only in the economic and transportation sphere but above all in the military. At the beginning we reckoned with some 200 enemy divisions and we have already identified 360. When a dozen of them are destroyed the Russians throw in another dozen. On this broad expanse our front is too thin. It has no depth. As a result, the repeated enemy attacks often meet with some success." Rundstedt put it bluntly to Allied interrogators after the war. "I realized," he said, "soon after the attack was begun that everything that had been written about Russia was nonsense."

Several generals, Guderian, Blumentritt and Sepp Dietrich among them, have left reports expressing astonishment at their first encounter with the Russian T-34 tank, of which they had not previously heard and which was so heavily armored that the shells from the German antitank guns bounced harmlessly off it. The appearance of this panzer, Blumentritt said later, marked the beginning of what came to be called the "tank terror." Also, for the first time in the war; the Germans did not have the benefit of overwhelming superiority in the air to protect their ground troops and scout ahead. Despite the heavy losses on the ground in the first day of the campaign and in early combat, Soviet fighter planes kept appearing, like the fresh divisions, out of nowhere. Moreover, the swiftness of the German advance and the lack of suitable airfields in Russia left the German fighter bases too far back to provide effective cover at the front. "At several stages in the advance," General von Kleist later reported, "my panzer forces were handicapped through lack of cover overhead."[6]

There was another German miscalculation about the Russians which Kleist mentioned to Liddell Hart and which, of course, was shared by most of the other peoples of the West that summer.

"Hopes of victory," Kleist said, "were largely built on the prospect that the invasion would produce a political upheaval in Russia . . . Too high hopes were built on the belief that Stalin would be overthrown by his own people if he suffered heavy defeats. The belief was fostered by the Fuehrer's political advisers."[7]

Indeed Hitler had told Jodl, "We have only to kick in the door and the whole rotten structure will come crashing down."

The opportunity to kick in the door seemed to the Fuehrer to be at hand halfway through July when there occurred the first great controversy over strategy in the German High Command and led to a decision by the Fuehrer, over the protests of most of the top generals, which Halder thought proved to be "the greatest strategic blunder of the Eastern campaign." The issue was simple but fundamental. Should Bock's Army Group Center, the most powerful and so far the most successful of the three main German armies, push on the two hundred miles to Moscow from Smolensk, which it had reached on July 16? Or should the original plan, which Hitler had laid down in the December 18 directive, and which called for the main thrusts on the north and south flanks, be adhered to? In other words, was Moscow the prize goal, or Leningrad and the Ukraine?

The Army High Command, led by Brauchitsch and Halder and supported by Bock, whose central army group was moving up the main highway to Moscow, and by Guderian, whose panzer forces were leading it, insisted on an all-out drive for the Soviet capital. There was much more to their argument than merely stressing the psychological value of capturing the enemy capital. Moscow, they pointed out to Hitler, was a vital source of armament production and, even more important, the center of the Russian transportation and communications system. Take it, and the Soviets would not only be deprived of an essential source of arms but would be unable to move troops and supplies to the distant fronts, which thereafter would weaken, wither and collapse.

But there was a final conclusive argument which the generals advanced to the former corporal who was now their Supreme Commander. All their intelligence reports showed that the main Russian forces were now being concentrated before Moscow for an all-out defense of the capital. Just east of Smolensk a Soviet army of half a million men, which had extricated itself from Bock's double envelopment, was digging in to bar further German progress toward the capital.

The center of gravity of Russian strength [Halder wrote in a report prepared for the Allies immediately after the war][8] was therefore in front of Army Group Center . . .

The General Staff had been brought up with the idea that it must be the aim of an operation to defeat the military power of the enemy, and it therefore considered the next and most pressing task to be to defeat the forces of Timoshenko by concentrating all available forces at Army Group Center, to advance on Moscow, to take this nerve center of enemy resistance and to destroy the new enemy formations. The assembly for this attack had to be carried out as soon as possible because the season was advanced. Army Group North was in the meantime to fulfill its original mission and to try to contact the Finns. Army Group South was to advance farther East to tie down the strongest possible enemy force.

. . . After oral discussions between the General Staff and the Supreme

Command [OKW] had failed, the Commander in Chief of the Army [Brauchitsch] submitted a memorandum of the General Staff to Hitler.

This, we learn from Halder's diary, was done on August 18. "The effect," says Halder, "was explosive." Hitler had his hungry eyes on the food belt and industrial areas of the Ukraine and on the Russian oil fields just beyond in the Caucasus. Besides, he thought he saw a golden opportunity to entrap Budënny's armies east of the Dnieper beyond Kiev, which still held out. He also wanted to capture Leningrad and join up with the Finns in the north. To accomplish these twin aims, several infantry and panzer divisions from Army Group Center would have to be detached and sent north and especially south. Moscow could wait.

On August 21, Hitler hurled a new directive at his rebellious General Staff. Halder copied it out word for word in his diary the next day.

The proposals of the Army for the continuation of the operations in the East do not accord with my intentions.

The most important objective to attain before the onset of winter is not the capture of Moscow but the taking of the Crimea, the industrial and coal-mining areas of the Donets basin and the cutting off of Russian oil supplies from the Caucasus. In the north it is the locking up of Leningrad and the union with the Finns.

The Soviet Fifth Army on the Dnieper in the south, whose stubborn resistance had annoyed Hitler for several days, must, he laid it down, be utterly destroyed, the Ukraine and the Crimea occupied, Leningrad surrounded and a junction with the Finns achieved. "Only then," he concluded, "will the conditions be created whereby Timoshenko's army can be attacked and successfully defeated."

Thus [commented Halder bitterly] the aim of defeating decisively the Russian armies in front of Moscow was subordinated to the desire to obtain a valuable industrial area and to advance in the direction of Russian oil . . . Hitler now became obsessed with the idea of capturing both Leningrad and Stalingrad, for he persuaded himself that if these two "holy cities of Communism" were to fall, Russia would collapse.

To add insult to injury to the field marshals and the generals who did not appreciate his strategic genius, Hitler sent what Halder called a "countermemorandum" (to that of the Army of the eighteenth), which the General Staff Chief described as "full of insults," such as stating that the Army High Command was full of "minds fossilized in out-of-date theories."

"Unbearable! Unheard of! The limit!" Halder snorted in his diary the next day. He conferred all afternoon and evening with Field Marshal von

Brauchitsch about the Fuehrer's "inadmissible" mixing into the business of the Army High Command and General Staff, finally proposing that the head of the Army and he himself resign their posts. "Brauchitsch refused," Halder noted, "because it wouldn't be practical and would change nothing." The gutless Field Marshal had already, as on so many other occasions, capitulated to the onetime corporal.

When General Guderian arrived at the Fuehrer's headquarters the next day, August 23, and was egged on by Halder to try to talk Hitler out of his disastrous decision, though the hard-bitten panzer leader needed no urging, he was met by Brauchitsch. "I forbid you," the Army Commander in Chief said, "to mention the question of Moscow to the Fuehrer. The operation to the south has been ordered. The problem now is simply how it is to be carried out. Discussion is pointless."

Nevertheless, when Guderian was ushered into the presence of Hitler— neither Brauchitsch nor Halder accompanied him—he disobeyed orders and argued as strongly as he could for the immediate assault on Moscow.

Hitler let me speak to the end [Guderian later wrote]. He then described in detail the considerations which had led him to make a different decision. He said that the raw materials and agriculture of the Ukraine were vitally necessary for the future prosecution of the war. He spoke of the need of neutralizing the Crimea, "that Soviet aircraft carrier for attacking the Roumanian oil fields." For the first time I heard him use the phrase: "My generals know nothing about the economic aspects of war." . . . He had given strict orders that the attack on Kiev was to be the immediate strategic objective and all actions were to be carried out with that in mind. I here saw for the first time a spectacle with which I was later to become very familiar: all those present— Keitel, Jodl and others—nodded in agreement with every sentence that Hitler uttered, while I was left alone with my point of view . . .[9]

But Halder had at no point in the previous discussions nodded his agreement. When Guderian saw him the next day and reported his failure to get Hitler to change his mind, he says the General Staff Chief "to my amazement suffered a complete nervous collapse, which led him to make accusations and imputations which were utterly unjustified."*

This was the most severe crisis in the German military High Command since the beginning of the war. Worse were to follow, with adversity.

In itself Rundstedt's offensive in the south, made possible by the reinforcement of Guderian's panzer forces and infantry divisions withdrawn from the central front, was, as Guderian put it, a great tactical victory. Kiev itself fell on September 19—German units had already penetrated 150 miles beyond it—and on the twenty-sixth the Battle of Kiev ended

---

* Halder, in his diary of August 24, gives quite a different version. He accuses Guderian of "irresponsibly" changing his mind after seeing Hitler and muses how useless it is to try to change a man's character. If he suffered, as Guderian alleges, "a complete nervous collapse," his pedantic diary notes that day indicate that he quickly recovered.

with the encirclement and surrender of 665,000 Russian prisoners, according to the German claim. To Hitler it was "the greatest battle in the history of the world," but though it was a singular achievement some of his generals were more skeptical of its strategic significance. Bock's armorless army group in the center had been forced to cool its heels for two months along the Desna River just beyond Smolensk. The autumn rains, which would turn the Russian roads into quagmires, were drawing near. And after them—the winter, the cold and the snow.

THE GREAT DRIVE ON MOSCOW

Reluctantly Hitler gave in to the urging of Brauchitsch, Halder and Bock and consented to the resumption of the drive on Moscow. But too late! Halder saw him on the afternoon of September 5 and now the Fuehrer, his mind made up, was in a hurry to get to the Kremlin. "Get started on the central front within eight to ten days," the Supreme Commander ordered. ("Impossible!" Halder exclaimed in his diary.) "Encircle them, beat and destroy them," Hitler added, promising to return to Army Group Center Guderian's panzer group, then still heavily engaged in the Ukraine, and add Reinhardt's tank corps from the Leningrad front. But it was not until the beginning of October that the armored forces could be brought back, refitted and made ready. On October 2 the great offensive was finally launched. "Typhoon" was the code name. A mighty wind, a cyclone, was to hit the Russians, destroy their last fighting forces before Moscow and bring the Soviet Union tumbling down.

But here again the Nazi dictator became a victim of his megalomania. Taking the Russian capital before winter came was not enough. He gave orders that Field Marshal von Leeb in the north was *at the same time* to capture Leningrad, make contact with the Finns beyond the city and drive on and cut the Murmansk railway. Also, at the same time, Rundstedt was to clear the Black Sea coast, take Rostov, seize the Maikop oil fields and push forward to Stalingrad on the Volga, thus severing Stalin's last link with the Caucasus. When Rundstedt tried to explain to Hitler that this meant an advance of more than four hundred miles beyond the Dnieper, with his left flank dangerously exposed, the Supreme Commander told him that the Russians in the south were now incapable of offering serious resistance. Rundstedt, who says that he "laughed aloud" at such ridiculous orders, was soon to find the contrary.

The German drive along the old road which Napoleon had taken to Moscow at first rolled along with all the fury of a typhoon. In the first fortnight of October, in what later Blumentritt called a "textbook battle," the Germans encircled two Soviet armies between Vyazma and Bryansk and claimed to have taken 650,000 prisoners along with 5,000 guns and 1,200 tanks. By October 20 German armored spearheads were within forty miles of Moscow and the Soviet ministries and foreign embassies

were hastily evacuating to Kuibyshev on the Volga. Even the sober
Halder, who had fallen off his horse and broken a collarbone and was
temporarily hospitalized, now believed that with bold leadership and
favorable weather Moscow could be taken before the severe Russian winter
set in.

The fall rains, however, had commenced. *Rasputitza,* the period of
mud, set in. The great army, moving on wheels, was slowed down and
often forced to halt. Tanks had to be withdrawn from battle to pull guns
and ammunition trucks out of the mire. Chains and couplings for this job
were lacking and bundles of rope had to be dropped by Luftwaffe transport
planes which were badly needed for lifting other military supplies. The
rains began in mid-October and, as Guderian later remembered, "the next
few weeks were dominated by the mud." General Blumentritt, chief of
staff of Field Marshal von Kluge's Fourth Army, which was in the thick
of the battle for Moscow, has vividly described the predicament.

The infantryman slithers in the mud, while many teams of horses are needed
to drag each gun forward. All wheeled vehicles sink up to their axles in the
slime. Even tractors can only move with great difficulty. A large portion of
our heavy artillery was soon stuck fast . . . The strain that all this caused our
already exhausted troops can perhaps be imagined.[10]

For the first time there crept into the diary of Halder and the reports of
Guderian, Blumentritt and other German generals signs of doubt and then
of despair. It spread to the lower officers and the troops in the field—or
perhaps it stemmed from them. "And now, when Moscow was already
almost in sight," Blumentritt recalled, "the mood both of commanders and
troops began to change. Enemy resistance stiffened and the fighting became more bitter . . . Many of our companies were reduced to a mere
sixty or seventy men." There was a shortage of serviceable artillery and
tanks. "Winter," he says, "was about to begin, but there was no sign of
winter clothing . . . Far behind the front the first partisan units were
beginning to make their presence felt in the vast forests and swamps.
Supply columns were frequently ambushed . . ."

Now, Blumentritt remembered, the ghosts of the Grand Army, which
had taken this same road to Moscow, and the memory of Napoleon's fate
began to haunt the dreams of the Nazi conquerors. The German generals
began to read, or reread, Caulaincourt's grim account of the French conqueror's disastrous winter in Russia in 1812.

Far to the south, where the weather was a little warmer but the rain
and the mud were just as bad, things were not going well either. Kleist's
tanks had entered Rostov at the mouth of the Don on November 21 amidst
much fanfare from Dr. Goebbels' propaganda band that the "gateway to
the Caucasus" had been opened. It did not remain open very long. Both
Kleist and Rundstedt realized that Rostov could not be held. Five days
later the Russians retook it and the Germans, attacked on both the

northern and southern flanks, were in headlong retreat back fifty miles to the Mius River where Kleist and Rundstedt had wished in the first place to establish a winter line.

The retreat from Rostov is another little turning point in the history of the Third Reich. Here was the first time that any Nazi army had ever suffered a major setback. "Our misfortunes began with Rostov," Guderian afterward commented; "that was the writing on the wall." It cost Field Marshal von Rundstedt, the senior officer in the German Army, his command. As he was retreating to the Mius:

Suddenly an order came to me [he subsequently told Allied interrogators] from the Fuehrer: "Remain where you are, and retreat no further." I immediately wired back: "It is madness to attempt to hold. In the first place the troops cannot do it and in the second place if they do not retreat they will be destroyed. I repeat that this order be rescinded or that you find someone else." That same night the Fuehrer's reply arrived: "I am acceding to your request. Please give up your command."

"I then," said Rundstedt, "went home."*[11]

This mania for ordering distant troops to stand fast no matter what their peril perhaps saved the German Army from complete collapse in the shattering months ahead, though many generals dispute it, but it was to lead to Stalingrad and other disasters and to help seal Hitler's fate.

Heavy snows and subzero temperatures came early that winter in Russia. Guderian noted the first snow on the night of October 6–7, just as the drive on Moscow was being resumed. It reminded him to ask headquarters again for winter clothing, especially for heavy boots and heavy wool socks. On October 12 he recorded the snow as still falling. On November 3 came the first cold wave, the thermometer dropping below the freezing point and continuing to fall. By the seventh Guderian was reporting the first "severe cases of frostbite" in his ranks and on the

---

* "*Groesste Aufregung* (greatest excitement) by the Fuehrer," Halder noted in his diary on November 30 in describing Rundstedt's retreat to the Mius and Hitler's dismissal of the Field Marshal. "The Fuehrer calls in Brauchitsch and hurls reproaches and abuse at him." Halder had begun his diary that day by noting the figures of German casualties up to November 26. "Total losses of the Eastern armies (not counting the sick), 743,112 officers and men—23 per cent of the entire force of 3.2 million."

On December 1, Halder recorded the replacement of Rundstedt by Reichenau, who still commanded the Sixth Army, which he had led in France and which had been having a hard time of it to the north of Kleist's armored divisions, which were retreating from Rostov.

"Reichenau phones the Fuehrer," Halder wrote, "and asks permission to withdraw tonight to the Mius line. Permission is given. So we are exactly where we were yesterday. But time and strength have been sacrificed and Rundstedt lost.

"The health of Brauchitsch," he added, "as the result of the continuing excitement is again causing anxiety." On November 10 Halder had recorded that the Army chief had suffered a severe heart attack.

thirteenth that the temperature had fallen to 8 degrees below zero, Fahrenheit, and that the lack of winter clothing "was becoming increasingly felt." The bitter cold affected guns and machines as well as men.

Ice was causing a lot of trouble [Guderian wrote] since the calks for the tank tracks had not yet arrived. The cold made the telescopic sights useless. In order to start the engines of the tanks fires had to be lit beneath them. Fuel was freezing on occasions and the oil became viscous . . . Each regiment [of the 112th Infantry Division] had already lost some 500 men from frostbite. As a result of the cold the machine guns were no longer able to fire and our 37-mm. antitank guns had proved ineffective against the [Russian] T-34 tank.[12]

"The result," says Guderian, "was a panic which reached as far back as Bogorodsk. This was the first time that such a thing had occurred during the Russian campaign, and it was a warning that the combat ability of our infantry was at an end."

But not only of the infantry. On November 21 Halder scribbled in his diary that Guderian had telephoned to say that his panzer troops "had reached their end." This tough, aggressive tank commander admits that on this very day he decided to visit the commander of Army Group Center, Bock, and request that the orders he had received be changed, since he "could see no way of carrying them out." He was in a deep mood of depression, writing on the same day:

The icy cold, the lack of shelter, the shortage of clothing, the heavy losses of men and equipment, the wretched state of our fuel supplies—all this makes the duties of a commander a misery, and the longer it goes on the more I am crushed by the enormous responsibility I have to bear.[13]

In retrospect Guderian added:

Only he who saw the endless expanse of Russian snow during this winter of our misery and felt the icy wind that blew across it, burying in snow every object in its path; who drove for hour after hour through that no-man's land only at last to find too thin shelter with insufficiently clothed, half-starved men; and who also saw by contrast the well-fed, warmly clad and fresh Siberians, fully equipped for winter fighting . . . can truly judge the events which now occurred.[14]

Those events may now be briefly narrated, but not without first stressing one point: terrible as the Russian winter was and granted that the Soviet troops were naturally better prepared for it than the German, the main factor in what is now to be set down was not the weather but the fierce fighting of the Red Army troops and their indomitable will not to give up. The diary of Halder and the reports of the field commanders, which constantly express amazement at the extent and severity of Russian attacks and counterattacks and despair at the German setbacks and losses, are proof of that. The Nazi generals could not understand why the Russians, considering the nature of their tyrannical regime and the disastrous effects of the first German blows, did not collapse, as had the French and so many others with less excuse.

"With amazement and disappointment," Blumentritt wrote, "we discovered in late October and early November that the beaten Russians seemed quite unaware that as a military force they had almost ceased to exist." Guderian tells of meeting an old retired Czarist general at Orel on the road to Moscow.

"If only you had come twenty years ago [he told the panzer General], we should have welcomed you with open arms. But now it's too late. We were just beginning to get on our feet, and now you arrive and throw us back twenty years so that we will have to start from the beginning all over again. Now we are fighting for Russia and in that cause we are all united."[15]

Yet, as November approached its end amidst fresh blizzards and continued subzero temperatures, Moscow seemed within grasp to Hitler and most of his generals. North, south and west of the capital German armies had reached points within twenty to thirty miles of their goal. To Hitler poring over the map at his headquarters far off in East Prussia the last stretch seemed no distance at all. His armies had advanced five hundred miles; they had only twenty to thirty miles to go. "One final heave," he told Jodl in mid-November, "and we shall triumph." On the telephone to Halder on November 22, Field Marshal von Bock, directing Army Group Center in its final push for Moscow, compared the situation to the Battle of the Marne, "where the last battalion thrown in decided the battle." Despite increased enemy resistance Bock told the General Staff Chief he believed "everything was attainable." By the last day of November he was literally throwing in his last battalion. The final all-out attack on the heart of the Soviet Union was set for the next day, December 1, 1941.

It stumbled on a steely resistance. The greatest tank force ever concentrated on one front: General Hoepner's Fourth Tank Group and General Hermann Hoth's Third Tank Group just north of Moscow and driving south, Guderian's Second Panzer Army just to the south of the capital and pushing north from Tula, Kluge's great Fourth Army in the middle and fighting its way due east through the forests that surrounded the city—on this formidable array were pinned Hitler's high hopes. By December 2 a reconnaissance battalion of the 258th Infantry Division had penetrated to Khimki, a suburb of Moscow, within sight of the spires of the Kremlin, but was driven out the next morning by a few Russian tanks and a motley force of hastily mobilized workers from the city's factories. This was the nearest the German troops ever got to Moscow; it was their first and last glimpse of the Kremlin.

Already on the evening of December 1, Bock, who was now suffering severe stomach cramps, had telephoned Halder to say that he could no longer "operate" with his weakened troops. The General Staff Chief had tried to cheer him on. "One must try," he said, "to bring the enemy down by a last expenditure of force. If that proves impossible then we will have to draw new conclusions." The next day Halder jotted in his diary: "Enemy resistance has reached its peak." On the following day, December 3, Bock was again on the phone to the Chief of the General Staff, who noted his message in his diary:

Spearheads of the Fourth Army again pulled back because the flanks could not come forward . . . The moment must be faced when the strength of our troops is at an end.

When Bock spoke for the first time of going over to the defensive Halder tried to remind him that "the best defense was to stick to the attack."

It was easier said than done, in view of the Russians and the weather. The next day, December 4, Guderian, whose Second Panzer Army had been halted in its attempt to take Moscow from the south, reported that the thermometer had fallen to 31 degrees below zero. The next day it dropped another five degrees. His tanks, he said, were "almost immobilized" and he was threatened on his flanks and in the rear north of Tula.

December 5 was the critical day. Everywhere along the 200-mile semicircular front around Moscow the Germans had been stopped. By evening Guderian was notifying Bock that he was not only stopped but must pull back, and Bock was telephoning Halder that "his strength was at an end," and Brauchitsch was telling his Chief of the General Staff in despair that he was quitting as Commander in Chief of the Army. It was a dark and bitter day for the German generals.

This was the first time [Guderian later wrote] that I had to take a decision of this sort, and none was more difficult . . . Our attack on Moscow had broken down. All the sacrifices and endurance of our brave troops had been in vain. We had suffered a grievous defeat.[16]

At Kluge's Fourth Army headquarters, Blumentritt, the chief of staff, realized that the turning point had been reached. Recalling it later, he wrote: "Our hopes of knocking Russia out of the war in 1941 had been dashed at the very last minute."

The next day, December 6, General Georgi Zhukov, who had replaced Marshal Timoshenko as commander of the central front but six weeks before, struck. On the 200-mile front before Moscow he unleashed seven armies and two cavalry corps—100 divisions in all—consisting of troops that were either fresh or battle-tried and were equipped and trained to fight in the bitter cold and the deep snow. The blow which this relatively unknown general now delivered with such a formidable force of infantry, artillery, tanks, cavalry and planes, which Hitler had not faintly suspected existed, was so sudden and so shattering that the German Army and the Third Reich never fully recovered from it. For a few weeks during the rest of that cold and bitter December and on into January it seemed that the beaten and retreating German armies, their front continually pierced by Soviet breakthroughs, might disintegrate and perish in the Russian snows, as had Napoleon's Grand Army just 130 years before. At several crucial moments it came very close to that. Perhaps it was Hitler's granite will and determination and certainly it was the fortitude of the German soldier that saved the armies of the Third Reich from a complete debacle.

But the failure was great. The Red armies had been crippled but not destroyed. Moscow had not been taken, nor Leningrad nor Stalingrad nor the oil fields of the Caucasus; and the lifelines to Britain and America, to the north and to the south, remained open. For the first time in more than two years of unbroken military victories the armies of Hitler were retreating before a superior force.

That was not all. The failure was greater than that. Halder realized this, at least later. "The myth of the invincibility of the German Army," he wrote, "was broken." There would be more German victories in Russia when another summer came around, but they could never restore the myth. December 6, 1941, then, is another turning point in the short history of the Third Reich and one of the most fateful ones. Hitler's power had reached its zenith; from now on it was to decline, sapped by the growing counterblows of the nations against which he had chosen to make aggressive war.

A drastic shake-up in the German High Command and among the field commanders now took place. As the armies fell back over the icy roads and snowy fields before the Soviet counteroffensive, the heads of the German generals began to roll. Rundstedt, as we have already seen, was relieved of command of the southern armies because he had been forced to retreat from Rostov. Field Marshal von Bock's stomach pains became worse with the setbacks in December and he was replaced on December 18 by Field Marshal von Kluge, whose battered Fourth Army was being pushed back, forever, from the vicinity of Moscow. Even the dashing General Guderian, the originator of massive armored warfare which had so revolutionized modern battle, was cashiered—on Christmas Day—for ordering a retreat without permission from above. General Hoepner, an equally brilliant tank commander, whose Fourth Armored Group had come within sight of Moscow on the north and then been pushed back, was abruptly dismissed by Hitler on the same grounds, stripped of his rank and forbidden to wear a uniform. General Hans Count von Sponeck, who had received the Ritterkreuz for leading the airborne landings at The Hague the year before, received a severer chastisement for pulling back one division of his corps in the Crimea on December 29 after Russian troops had landed by sea behind him. He was not only summarily stripped of his rank but imprisoned, court-martialed and, at the insistence of Hitler, sentenced to death.*

Even the obsequious Keitel was in trouble with the Supreme Commander. Even he had enough sense to see during the first days of December that a general withdrawal around Moscow was necessary in order to avert disaster. But when he got up enough courage to say so to Hitler the latter turned on him and gave him a tongue-lashing, shouting that he was a "blockhead." Jodl found the unhappy OKW Chief a little later sitting at a desk writing out his resignation, a revolver at one side. Jodl quietly removed the weapon and persuaded Keitel—apparently without too much difficulty—to stay on and to continue to swallow the Fuehrer's insults, which he did, with amazing endurance, to the very end.[17]

The strain of leading an army which could not always win under a Supreme Commander who insisted that it always do had brought about renewed heart attacks for Field Marshal von Brauchitsch, and by the time Zhukov's counteroffensive began he was determined to step down as Commander in Chief. He returned to headquarters from a trip to the receding front on December 15 and Halder found him "very beaten down." "Brauchitsch no longer sees any way out," Halder noted in his diary, "for the rescue of the Army from its desperate position." The head of the Army was at the end of his rope. He had asked Hitler on December 7 to relieve him and he renewed the request on December 17. It was formally granted two days later. What the Fuehrer really thought of the man he himself had named to head the Army he told to Goebbels three months later.

> The Fuehrer spoke of him [Brauchitsch] only in terms of contempt [Goebbels wrote in his diary on March 20, 1942]. A vain, cowardly wretch . . . and a nincompoop.[18]

To his cronies Hitler said of Brauchitsch, "He's no soldier; he's a man of straw. If Brauchitsch had remained at his post only for another few weeks, things would have ended in catastrophe."[19]

There was some speculation in Army circles as to who would succeed Brauchitsch, but it was as wide of the mark as the speculation years before as to who would succeed Hindenburg. On December 19 Hitler called in Halder and informed him that he himself was taking over as Commander in Chief of the Army. Halder could stay on as Chief of the General Staff if he wanted to—and he wanted to. But from now on, Hitler made it clear, he was personally running the Army, as he ran almost everything else in Germany.

> This little matter of operational command [Hitler told him] is something anyone can do. The task of the Commander in Chief of the Army is to train

---

* He was not executed until after the July 1944 plot against Hitler, in which he was in no way involved.

the Army in a National Socialist way. I know of no general who could do that, as I want it done. Consequently, I've decided to take over command of the Army myself.[20]

Hitler's triumph over the Prussian officer corps was thus completed. The former Vienna vagabond and ex-corporal was now head of state, Minister of War, Supreme Commander of the Armed Forces and Commander in Chief of the Army. The generals, as Halder complained—in his diary—were now merely postmen purveying Hitler's orders based on Hitler's singular conception of strategy.

Actually the megalomaniacal dictator soon would make himself something even greater, legalizing a power never before held by any man— emperor, king or president—in the experience of the German Reichs. On April 26, 1942, he had his rubber-stamp Reichstag pass a law which gave him absolute power of life and death over every German and simply suspended any laws which might stand in the way of this. The words of the law have to be read to be believed.

. . . In the present war, in which the German people are faced with a struggle for their existence or their annihilation, the Fuehrer must have all the rights postulated by him which serve to further or achieve victory. Therefore —without being bound by existing legal regulations—in his capacity as Leader of the nation, Supreme Commander of the Armed Forces, Head of Government and supreme executive chief, as Supreme Justice and Leader of the Party—the Fuehrer must be in a position to force with all means at his disposal every German, if necessary, whether he be common soldier or officer, low or high official or judge, leading or subordinate official of the party, worker or employer—to fulfill his duties. In case of violation of these duties, the Fuehrer is entitled after conscientious examination, regardless of so-called well-deserved rights, to mete out due punishment and to remove the offender from his post, rank and position without introducing prescribed procedures.[21]

Truly Adolf Hitler had become not only the Leader of Germany but the Law. Not even in medieval times nor further back in the barbarous tribal days had any German arrogated such tyrannical power, nominal and legal as well as actual, to himself.

But even without this added authority, Hitler was absolute master of the Army, of which he had now assumed direct command. Ruthlessly he moved that bitter winter to stem the retreat of his beaten armies and to save them from the fate of Napoleon's troops along the same frozen, snow-bound roads back from Moscow. He forbade any further withdrawals. The German generals have long debated the merits of his stubborn stand— whether it saved the troops from complete disaster or whether it compounded the inevitable heavy losses. Most of the commanders have contended that if they had been given freedom to pull back when their position became untenable they could have saved many men and much equipment and been in a better position to re-form and even counterattack. As it was, whole divisions were frequently overrun or surrounded and cut to pieces when a timely withdrawal would have saved them.

And yet some of the generals later reluctantly admitted that Hitler's iron will in insisting that the armies stand and fight was his greatest accomplishment of the war in that it probably did save his armies from completely disintegrating in the snow. This view is best summed up by General Blumentritt.

Hitler's fanatical order that the troops must hold fast regardless in every position and in the most impossible circumstances was undoubtedly correct. Hitler realized instinctively that any retreat across the snow and ice must, within a few days, lead to the dissolution of the front and that if this happened the Wehrmacht would suffer the same fate that had befallen the *Grande Armée* . . . The withdrawal could only be carried out across the open country since the roads and tracks were blocked with snow. After a few nights this would prove too much for the troops, who would simply lie down and die wherever they found themselves. There were no prepared positions in the rear into which they could be withdrawn, nor any sort of line to which they could hold on.[22]

General von Tippelskirch, a corps commander, agreed.

It was Hitler's one great achievement. At that critical moment the troops were remembering what they had heard about Napoleon's retreat from Moscow, and living under the shadow of it. If they had once begun a retreat, it might have turned into a panic flight.[23]

There was panic in the German Army, not only at the front but far in the rear at headquarters, and it is graphically recorded in Halder's diary. "Very difficult day!" he begins his journal on Christmas Day, 1941, and thereafter into the new year he repeats the words at the head of many a day's entry as he describes each fresh Russian breakthrough and the serious situation of the various armies.

December 29. Another critical day! . . . Dramatic long-distance telephone talk between Fuehrer and Kluge. Fuehrer forbids further withdrawal of northern wing of 4th Army. Very bad crisis by 9th Army where apparently the commanders have lost their heads. At noon an excited call from Kluge. 9th Army wishes to withdraw behind Rzhev . . .

January 2, 1942. A day of wild fighting! . . . Grave crisis by 4th and 9th Armies . . . Russian breakthrough north of Maloyaroslavets tears the front wide open and it's difficult to see at the moment how front can be restored . . . This situation leads Kluge to demand withdrawal of sagging front. Very stormy argument with Fuehrer, who however holds to his stand: The front will remain where it is regardless of consequences . . .

January 3. The situation has become more critical as the result of the breakthrough between Maloyaroslavets and Borovsk. Kuebler* and Bock very excited and demand withdrawal on the north front, which is crumbling. Again a dramatic scene by Fuehrer, who doubts courage of generals to make hard decisions. But troops simply don't hold their ground when it's 30 below zero. Fuehrer orders: He will personally decide if any more withdrawals necessary. . . .

Not the Fuehrer but the Russian Army was by now deciding such matters. Hitler could force the German troops to stand fast and die, but he could no more stop the Soviet advance than King Canute could prevent the tides from coming in. At one moment of panic some of the High Command officers suggested that perhaps the situation could be retrieved by the employment of poison gas. "Colonel Ochsner tries to talk me into beginning gas warfare against the Russians," Halder noted in his diary on January 7. Perhaps it was too cold. At any rate nothing came of the suggestion.

January 8 was "a very critical day," as Halder noted in his journal. "The breakthrough at Sukhinichi [southwest of Moscow] is becoming unbearable for Kluge. He is consequently insisting on withdrawing the 4th Army front." All day long the Field Marshal was on the phone to Hitler and Halder insisting on it. Finally, in the evening the Fuehrer reluctantly consented. Kluge was given permission to withdraw "step by step in order to protect his communications."

Step by step and sometimes more rapidly throughout that grim winter the German armies, which had planned to celebrate Christmas in Moscow, were driven back or forced by Russian encirclements and breakthroughs to retreat. By the end of February they found themselves from 75 to 200 miles from the capital. By the end of that freezing month Halder was noting in his diary the cost in men of the misfired Russian adventure. Total losses up to February 28, he wrote down, were 1,005,636, or 31 per cent of his entire force. Of these 202,251 had been killed, 725,642 wounded and 46,511 were missing. (Casualties from frostbite were 112,627.) This did not include the heavy losses among the Hungarians, Rumanians and Italians in Russia.

With the coming of the spring thaws a lull came over the long front and Hitler and Halder began making plans for bringing up fresh troops and more tanks and guns to resume the offensive—at least on part of the front. Never again would they have the strength to attack all along the vast battle line. The bitter winter's toll and above all Zhukov's counteroffensive doomed that hope.

But Hitler, we now know, had realized long before that his gamble of

---

* General Kuebler had replaced Kluge on December 26 as commander of the Fourth Army when the latter took over Army Group Center. Though a tough soldier, he stood the strain only three weeks and then was relieved by General Heinrici.

conquering Russia—not only in six months but ever—had failed. In a diary entry of November 19, 1941, General Halder notes a long "lecture" of the Fuehrer to several officers of the High Command. Though his armies are only a few miles from Moscow and still driving hard to capture it, Hitler has abandoned hopes of striking Russia down this year and has already turned his thoughts to next year. Halder jotted down the Leader's ideas.

Goals for next year. First of all the Caucasus. Objective: Russia's southern borders. Time: March to April. In the north after the close of this year's campaign, Vologda or Gorki,* but only at the end of May.

Further goals for next year must remain open. They will depend on the capacity of our railroads. The question of later building an "East Wall" also remains open.

No East Wall would be necessary if the Soviet Union were to be destroyed. Halder seems to have mulled over that as he listened to the Supreme Commander go on.

On the whole [he concluded] one gets the impression that Hitler recognizes now that neither side can destroy the other and that this will lead to peace negotiations.

This must have been a rude awakening for the Nazi conqueror who six weeks before in Berlin had made a broadcast declaring "without any reservation" that Russia had been "struck down and would never rise again." His plans had been wrecked, his hopes doomed. They were further dashed a fortnight later, on December 6, when his troops began to be beaten back from the suburbs of Moscow.

The next day, Sunday, December 7, 1941, an event occurred on the other side of the round earth that transformed the European war, which he had so lightly provoked, into a world war, which, though he could not know it, would seal his fate and that of the Third Reich. Japanese bombers attacked Pearl Harbor. The next day† Hitler hurried back by train to Berlin from his headquarters at Wolfsschanze. He had made a solemn secret promise to Japan and the time had come to keep it—or break it.

---

* Vologda, 300 miles northeast of Moscow, controlled the railway to Archangel. Gorki is 300 miles due *east* of the capital.
† Hitler's movements and whereabouts are noted in his daily calendar book, which is among the captured documents.

25

THE TURN OF THE UNITED STATES

Adolf Hitler's reckless promise to Japan had been made during a series of talks in Berlin with Yosuke Matsuoka, the pro-Axis Japanese Foreign Minister, in the spring of 1941 just before the German attack on Russia. The captured German minutes of the meetings enable us to trace the development of another one of Hitler's monumental miscalculations. They and other Nazi documents of the period show the Fuehrer too ignorant, Goering too arrogant and Ribbentrop too stupid to comprehend the potential military strength of the United States—a blunder which had been made in Germany during the First World War by Wilhelm II, Hindenburg and Ludendorff.

There was a basic contradiction from the beginning in Hitler's policy toward America. Though he had only contempt for her military prowess he endeavored during the first two years of the conflict to keep her out of the war. This, as we have seen, was the main task of the German Embassy in Washington, which went to great lengths, including the bribing of Congressmen, attempting to subsidize writers and aiding the America First Committee, to support the American isolationists and thus help to keep America from joining Germany's enemies in the war.

That the United States, as long as it was led by President Roosevelt, stood in the way of Hitler's grandiose plans for world conquest and the dividing up of the planet among the Tripartite powers the Nazi dictator fully understood, as his various private utterances make clear. The American Republic, he saw, would have to be dealt with eventually and, as he said, "severely." But one nation at a time. That had been the secret of his successful strategy thus far. The turn of America would come, but only after Great Britain and the Soviet Union had been struck down. Then, with the aid of Japan and Italy, he would deal with the upstart Americans, who, isolated and alone, would easily succumb to the power of the victorious Axis.

Japan was the key to Hitler's efforts to keep America out of the war until Germany was ready to take her on. Japan, as Ribbentrop pointed out to Mussolini on March 11, 1940, possessed the counterweight to the United States which would prevent the Americans from trying to intervene in Europe against Germany as they had in the first war.[1]

In their wartime dealings with the Japanese, Hitler and Ribbentrop at first stressed the importance of not provoking the United States to abandon her neutrality. By the beginning of 1941 they were exceedingly anxious to draw Japan into the war, not against America, not even against Russia, which they were shortly to attack, but against Britain, which had refused to give in even when apparently beaten. Early in 1941 German pressure on Japan was stepped up. On February 23, Ribbentrop received at his stolen estate at Fuschl, near Salzburg, the fiery and hot-tempered Japanese ambassador, General Hiroshi Oshima, who had often impressed this observer as more Nazi than the Nazis. Though the war, Ribbentrop told his guest, was already won, Japan should come in "as soon as possible —in its own interest," and seize Britain's empire in Asia.

A surprise intervention by Japan [he continued] was bound to keep America out of the war. America, which at present is not armed and would hesitate to expose her Navy to any risks west of Hawaii, could do this even less in such a case. If Japan would otherwise respect the American interests, there would not even be the possibility for Roosevelt to use the argument of lost prestige to make war plausible to the Americans. It was very unlikely that America would declare war if it had to stand by while Japan took the Philippines.

But even if the United States did get involved, Ribbentrop declared, "this would not endanger the final victory of the countries of the Three-Power Pact." The Japanese fleet would easily defeat the American fleet and the war would be brought rapidly to an end with the fall of both Britain and America. This was heady stuff for the fire-eating Japanese envoy and Ribbentrop poured it on. He advised the Japanese to be firm and "use plain language" in their current negotiations in Washington.

Only if the U.S. realized that they were confronting firm determination would they hold back. The people in the U.S. . . . were not willing to sacrifice their sons, and therefore were against any entry into the war. The American people felt instinctively that they were being drawn into war for no reason by Roosevelt and the Jewish wire-pullers. Therefore our policies with the U.S. should be plain and firm . . .

The Nazi Foreign Minister had one warning to give, the one that had failed so dismally with Franco.

If Germany should ever weaken, Japan would find itself confronted by a world coalition within a short time. We were all in the same boat. The fate of both countries was being determined now for centuries to come . . . A defeat of Germany would also mean the end of the Japanese imperialist idea.[2]

To acquaint his military commanders and the top men in the Foreign Office with his new Japanese policy, Hitler issued on March 5, 1941, a top-secret directive entitled "Basic Order No. 24 Regarding Collaboration with Japan."[3]

It must be the *aim* of the collaboration based on the Three-Power Pact to induce Japan as soon as possible *to take active measures in the Far East.* Strong British forces will thereby be tied down, and the center of gravity of the interests of the United States will be diverted to the Pacific . . .

The *common aim* of the conduct of war is to be stressed as forcing England to her knees quickly and thereby keeping the United States out of the war.

The *seizure of Singapore* as the key British position in the Far East would mean a decisive success for the entire conduct of war of the Three Powers.*

Hitler also urged the Japanese seizure of other British naval bases and even American bases "if the entry of the United States into the war cannot be prevented." He concluded by ordering that "the Japanese must not be given any intimation of the Barbarossa operation." The Japanese ally, like the Italian ally, was to be used to further German ambitions, but neither government would be taken into the Fuehrer's confidence regarding his intention to attack Russia.

A fortnight later, on March 18, at a conference with Hitler, Keitel and Jodl, Admiral Raeder strongly urged that Japan be pressed to attack Singapore. The opportunity would never again be so favorable, Raeder explained, what with "the whole English fleet contained, the unpreparedness of the U.S.A. for war against Japan and the inferiority of the U.S. fleet compared to the Japanese." The capture of Singapore, the Admiral said, would "solve all the other Asiatic questions regarding the U.S.A. and England" and would of course enable Japan to avoid war with America, if she wished. There was only one hitch, the Admiral opined, and mention of it must have made Hitler frown. According to naval intelligence, Raeder warned, Japan would move against the British in Southeast Asia only "if Germany proceeds to land in England." There is no record in the Navy minutes of this meeting indicating what reply Hitler made to this remark. Raeder certainly knew that the Supreme Commander had neither plans nor hopes for a landing in England this year. Raeder said something else that the Fuehrer did not respond to. He "recommended" that Matsuoka "be advised regarding the designs on Russia."[4]

The Japanese Foreign Minister was now on his way to Berlin via Siberia and Moscow, uttering bellicose pro-Axis statements, as Secretary of State Hull put it,† along the route. His arrival in the German capital

---

* The italics are Hitler's.

† Hull made the remark to the new Japanese ambassador in Washington, Admiral Nomura, in the presence of Mr. Roosevelt on March 14. Nomura replied that Matsuoka "talked loudly for home consumption because he was ambitious politically." (*The Memoirs of Cordell Hull*, II, pp. 900–01.)

on March 26 came at an awkward moment for Hitler, for that night the pro-German Yugoslav government was overthrown in the Belgrade coup and the Fuehrer was so busy improvising plans to crush the obstreperous Balkan country that he had to postpone seeing the Japanese visitor until the afternoon of the twenty-seventh.

Ribbentrop saw him in the morning, playing over, so to speak, the old gramophone records reserved for such guests on such occasions, though managing to be even more fatuous than usual and not allowing the dapper little Matsuoka to get in a word. The lengthy confidential minutes drawn up by Dr. Schmidt (and now among the captured Foreign Office papers) leave no doubt of that.[5] "The war has already been definitely won by the Axis," Ribbentrop announced, "and it is only a question of time before England admits it." In the next breath he was urging a "quick attack upon Singapore" because it would be "a very decisive factor in the speedy overthrow of England." In the face of such a contradiction the diminutive Japanese visitor did not bat an eye. "He sat there inscrutably," Schmidt later remembered, "in no way revealing how these curious remarks impressed him."[6]

As to America—

There was no doubt [Ribbentrop said] that the British would long since have abandoned the war if Roosevelt had not always given Churchill new hope . . . The Three-Power Pact had above all had the goal of frightening America . . . and of keeping it out of the war . . . America had to be prevented by all possible means from taking an active part in the war and from making its aid to England too effective . . . The capture of Singapore would perhaps be most likely to keep America out of the war because the United States could scarcely risk sending its fleet into Japanese waters . . . Roosevelt would be in a very difficult position . . .

Though Hitler had laid it down that Matsuoka must not be told about the impending German attack on Russia—a necessary precaution to keep the news from leaking out, but nevertheless, as we shall see, one that would have disastrous consequences for Germany—Ribbentrop did drop several broad hints. Relations with the Soviet Union, he told his visitor, were correct but not very friendly. Moreover, should Russia threaten Germany, "the Fuehrer would crush Russia." The Fuehrer was convinced, he added, that if it came to war "there would be in a few months no more Russia."

Matsuoka, says Schmidt, blinked at this and looked alarmed, whereupon Ribbentrop hastened to assure him that he did not believe that "Stalin would pursue an unwise policy." At this juncture, says Schmidt, Ribbentrop was called away by Hitler to discuss the Yugoslav crisis and failed even to return for the official lunch which he was supposed to tender the distinguished visitor.

In the afternoon Hitler, having determined to smash another country

(Yugoslavia), worked on the Japanese Foreign Minister. "England has already lost the war," he began. "It is only a matter of having the intelligence to admit it." Still, the British were grasping at two straws: Russia and America. Toward the Soviet Union Hitler was more circumspect than Ribbentrop had been. He did not believe, he said, that the danger of a war with Russia would arise. After all, Germany had some 160 to 170 divisions "for defense against Russia." As to the United States:

America was confronted by three possibilities: she could arm herself, she could assist England, or she could wage war on another front. If she helped England she could not arm herself. If she abandoned England the latter would be destroyed and America would then find herself fighting the powers of the Three-Power Pact alone. In no case, however, could America wage war on another front.

Therefore, the Fuehrer concluded, "never in the human imagination" could there be a better opportunity for the Japanese to strike in the Pacific than now. "Such a moment," he said, laying it on as thickly as he could, "would never return. It was unique in history." Matsuoka agreed, but reminded Hitler that unfortunately he "did not control Japan. At the moment he could make no pledge on behalf of the Japanese Empire that it would take action."

But Hitler, being absolute dictator, could make a pledge and he made it to Japan—quite casually and without being asked to—on April 4, after Matsuoka had returned to Berlin from seeing Mussolini.* This second meeting took place on the eve of the Nazi attack on two more innocent countries, Yugoslavia and Greece, and the Fuehrer, thirsting for further easy conquests and for revenge on Belgrade, was in one of his warlike moods. While he considered war with the United States "undesirable," he said, he had "already included it in his calculations." But he did not think much of America's military power.†

Germany had made her preparations so that no American could land in Europe. Germany would wage a vigorous war against America with U-boats and the Luftwaffe, and with her greater experience . . . would be more than

---

* Mussolini had told him, he informed Hitler, that "America was the Number One enemy, and Soviet Russia came only in second place."
† Or of anything else about the United States. His weird conception of America—by this time Hitler had come to believe his own Nazi propaganda—was given further exposition in a talk he had with Mussolini at the Russian front late in August 1941. "The Fuehrer," the Italian records quote him indirectly as saying, "gave a detailed account of the Jewish clique which surrounds Roosevelt and exploits the American people. He stated that he could not, for anything in the world, live in a country like the U.S.A., whose conceptions of life are inspired by the most grasping commercialism and which does not love any of the loftiest expressions of the human spirit such as music." (*Ciano's Diplomatic Papers,* pp. 449–52.)

a match for America, entirely apart from the fact that German soldiers were, obviously, far superior to the Americans.

This boast led him to make the fateful pledge. Schmidt recorded it in his minutes:

If Japan got into a conflict with the United States, Germany on her part would take the necessary steps at once.

From Schmidt's notes it is evident that Matsuoka did not quite grasp the significance of what the Fuehrer was promising, so Hitler said it again.

Germany, as he had said, would promptly take part in case of a conflict between Japan and America.*

Hitler paid dearly not only for this assurance, so casually given, but for his deceit in not telling the Japanese about his intention to attack Russia as soon as the Balkans were occupied. Somewhat coyly Matsuoka had asked Ribbentrop during a talk on March 28 whether on his return trip he "should remain in Moscow in order to negotiate with the Russians on the Nonaggression Pact or the Treaty of Neutrality." The dull-witted Nazi Foreign Minister had replied smugly that Matsuoka "if possible should not bring up the question in Moscow since it probably would not altogether fit into the framework of the present situation." He did not quite grasp the significance of what was up. But by the next day it had penetrated his wooden mind and he began the conversations that day by referring to it. First of all he threw in, as casually as Hitler would do on April 4, a German guarantee that if Russia attacked Japan "Germany would strike immediately." He wanted to give this assurance, he said, "so that Japan could push southward toward Singapore without fear of any complications with Russia." When Matsuoka finally admitted that while in Moscow on his way to Berlin he himself had proposed a nonaggression pact with the Soviet Union and hinted that the Russians were favorably inclined toward it, Ribbentrop's mind again became somewhat of a blank. He merely advised that Matsuoka handle the problem in a "superficial way."

But as soon as the Nipponese Foreign Minister was back in Moscow on his trip home, he signed a treaty of neutrality with Stalin which, as Ambassador von der Schulenburg, who foresaw its consequences, wired Berlin, provided for each country to remain neutral in case the other got involved in the war. This was one treaty—it was signed on April 13—which Japan honored to the very last despite subsequent German exhortations that she disregard it. For before the summer of 1941 was out the Nazis would be begging the Japanese to attack not Singapore or Manila but Vladivostok!

At first, however, Hitler did not grasp the significance of the Russo-

---

* The author's italics.

Japanese Neutrality Pact. On April 20 he told Admiral Raeder, who inquired about it, that it had been made "with Germany's acquiescence" and that he welcomed it "because Japan is now restrained from taking action against Vladivostok and should be induced to attack Singapore instead."*[7] At this stage Hitler was confident Germany could destroy Russia during the summer. He did not want Japan to share in this mighty feat any more than he had desired that Italy should share in the conquest of France. And he was absolutely confident that Japanese help would not be needed. Ribbentrop, echoing his master's thoughts, had told Matsuoka on March 29 that if Russia forced Germany "to strike" he would "consider it proper if the Japanese Army were prevented from attacking Russia."

But the views of Hitler and Ribbentrop on this matter changed very suddenly and quite drastically scarcely three months later. Six days after the Nazi armies were flung into Russia, on June 28, 1941, Ribbentrop was cabling the German ambassador in Tokyo, General Eugen Ott, to do everything he could to get the Japanese to promptly attack Soviet Russia in the rear. Ott was advised to appeal to the Japanese appetite for spoils and also to argue that this was the best way of keeping America neutral.

It may be expected [Ribbentrop explained] that the rapid defeat of Soviet Russia—especially should Japan take action in the East—will prove the best argument to convince the United States of the utter futility of entering the war on the side of a Great Britain entirely isolated and confronted by the most powerful alliance in the world.[8]

Matsuoka was in favor of immediately turning on Russia, but his views were not accepted by the government in Tokyo, whose attitude seemed to be that if the Germans were rapidly defeating the Russians, as they claimed, they needed no help from the Japanese. However, Tokyo was not so sure about a lightning Nazi victory and this was the real reason for its stand.

But Ribbentrop persisted. On July 10, when the German offensive in Russia was really beginning to roll and even Halder, as we have seen, thought that victory already had been won, the Nazi Foreign Minister got

---

* News of the signing in Moscow of the Soviet–Japanese neutrality pact caused considerable alarm in Washington, where Roosevelt and Hull were inclined to take a view similar to Hitler's—namely, that the treaty would release Japanese forces earmarked for a possible war with Russia for action farther south against British and perhaps American possessions. Sherwood discloses that on April 13, when the news of the conclusion of the pact was received, the President scrapped a plan for launching aggressive action by U.S. naval ships against German U-boats in the western Atlantic. A new order called merely for American warships to *report* movements of German naval vessels west of Iceland, not to shoot at them. It was considered that the new Japanese–Soviet neutrality agreement made the situation in the Pacific too dangerous to risk too much in the Atlantic. (Robert E. Sherwood, *Roosevelt and Hopkins*, p. 291.)

off from his special train on the Eastern front a new and stronger cable to his ambassador in Tokyo.

Since Russia, as reported by the Japanese ambassador in Moscow, is in effect close to collapse . . . it is simply impossible that Japan does not solve the matter of Vladivostok and the Siberian area as soon as her military preparations are completed . . .

I ask you to employ all available means in further insisting upon Japan's entry into the war against Russia at the soonest possible date . . . The sooner this entry is effected, the better it is. The natural objective still remains that we and Japan join hands on the Trans-Siberian railroad before winter starts.[9]

Such a giddy prospect did not turn the head of even the militaristic Japanese government. Four days later Ambassador Ott replied that he was doing his best to persuade the Japanese to attack Russia as soon as possible, that Matsuoka was all for it, but that he, Ott, had to fight against "great obstacles" in the Tokyo cabinet.[10] As a matter of fact the fire-eating Matsuoka was soon forced out of the cabinet. With his departure, Germany lost, for the time being, its best friend, and though, as we shall see, closer relations were later restored between Berlin and Tokyo they never became close enough to convince the Japanese of the wisdom of helping Germany in the war against Russia. Once more Hitler had been bested at his own game by a wily ally.*

"AVOID INCIDENTS WITH THE U.S.A.!"

With Japan stubbornly refusing to help pull Hitler's chestnuts out of the fire in Russia—the Japanese had their own chestnuts roasting—it became all the more important to Germany that the United States be kept out of the war until the Soviet Union had been conquered, as the Fuehrer was confident that summer of 1941 it would be before winter came.

---

* Ribbentrop kept trying all that fall and several times during the next two years to induce the Japanese to fall upon Russia from the rear, but each time the Tokyo government replied politely, in effect, "So sorry, please."

Hitler himself remained hopeful all through the summer. On August 26 he told Raeder he was "convinced that Japan will carry out the attack on Vladivostok as soon as forces have been assembled. The present aloofness can be explained by the fact that the assembling of forces is to be accomplished undisturbed, and the attack is to come as a surprise."[11]

The Japanese archives reveal how Tokyo evaded the Germans on this embarrassing question. When, for instance, on August 19 Ambassador Ott asked the Japanese Vice-Minister of Foreign Affairs about Japan's intervention against Russia, the latter replied, "For Japan to do a thing like attacking Russia would be a very serious question and would require profound reflection." When on August 30 Ott, who by now was a very irritated ambassador, asked Foreign Minister Admiral Toyoda, "Is there any possibility that Japan may participate in the Russo–German war?" Toyoda replied, "Japan's preparations are now making headway, and it will take more time for their completion."[12]

The German Navy had long chafed under the restraints which Hitler had imposed on its efforts to curtail American shipments to Britain and to cope with the increasing belligerency of U.S. warships toward German U-boats and surface craft operating in the Atlantic. The Nazi admirals, looking further afield than Hitler's landlocked mind was capable of doing, had almost from the first regarded America's entry into the war as inevitable and they had urged the Supreme Commander to prepare for it. Immediately after the fall of France in June 1940, Admiral Raeder, backed by Goering, had urged Hitler to seize not only French West Africa but, more important, the Atlantic islands, including Iceland, the Azores and the Canaries, to prevent the United States from occupying them. Hitler had expressed interest, but he first wanted to invade England and conquer Russia. Then the upstart Americans, their position rendered hopeless, would be taken care of. A top-secret memorandum of Major Freiherr von Falkenstein, of the General Staff, discloses Hitler's views at the end of the summer in 1940.

The Fuehrer is at present occupied with the question of the occupation of the Atlantic Islands with a view to the prosecution of war against America at a later date. Deliberations on this subject are being embarked on here.[13]

It was not a question, then, of whether or not Hitler intended to go to war against the United States but of the *date* he would choose to embark on it. By the following spring the date was beginning to sprout in the Fuehrer's mind. On May 22, 1941, Admiral Raeder conferred with the Supreme Commander and reported ruefully that the Navy "must reject the idea of occupying the Azores." It simply didn't have the strength. But by this time Hitler had warmed to the project and, according to Raeder's confidential notes,[14] replied:

The Fuehrer is still in favor of occupying the Azores in order to be able to operate long-range bombers from there against the U.S.A. The occasion for this may arise by autumn.*

After the fall of the Soviet Union, that is. The turn of the United States would come then. He put this clearly to Raeder when the Admiral saw him just two months later, on July 25, when the offensive in Russia was in full swing. "After the Eastern campaign," Raeder notes him as saying, "he reserves the right to take severe action against the U.S.A."[15] But until then, Hitler emphasized to his Navy chief, he wanted "to avoid having the U.S.A. declare war . . . out of consideration for the Army, which is involved in heavy combat."

Raeder was not satisfied with this stand. In fact, his diary accounts of his meetings with Hitler, which one can now peruse in the captured docu-

---

* The Germans had no long-range bombers capable of reaching the American coast from the Azores—much less getting back—and it is a sign of the warping of Hitler's mind by this time that he conjured up the nonexistent "long-range bombers."

ments, show his growing impatience at the wraps which the Fuehrer had placed on the German Navy. At every interview he sought to change the Leader's mind.

Early that year, on February 4, Raeder submitted a memorandum to Hitler in which the Navy expressed strong doubts about the value of continued American neutrality, as it was working out, to Germany. In fact the admirals argued that America's entry into the war might even prove "advantageous for the German war effort" if Japan thereby became a belligerent on the side of the Axis.[16] But the Nazi dictator was not impressed by the argument.

Raeder was greatly discouraged. The Battle of the Atlantic was at its height and Germany was not winning it. American supplies under the Lend-Lease agreement were pouring into Britain. The Pan-American Neutrality Patrol was making it more and more difficult for the U-boats to be effective. All this Raeder pointed out to Hitler, but without much effect. He saw the Leader again on March 18 and reported that U.S. warships were escorting American convoys bound for Britain as far as Iceland. He demanded authority to attack them without warning. He asked that something be done to prevent the U.S.A. from gaining a foothold in French West Africa. This possibility, he said, "was most dangerous." Hitler listened and said he would discuss these matters with the Foreign Office (of all places!), which was one way of putting the admirals off.[17]

All through the spring and early summer he continued to put them off. On April 20 he refused to listen to Raeder's pleas "for warfare against merchant ships of the U.S.A., according to prize regulations."[18] The first recorded clash between American and German war vessels had occurred on April 10 when the U.S. destroyer *Niblack* dropped depth charges on a German U-boat which showed signs of attacking. On May 22 Raeder was back at the Berghof with a long memorandum suggesting countermeasures to President Roosevelt's unfriendly acts, but he could not move his Supreme Commander.

The Fuehrer [the Admiral noted] considers the attitude of the President of the United States still undecided. Under no circumstances does he wish to cause incidents which would result in U.S. entry into the war.[19]

There was all the more reason to avoid such incidents when the campaign in Russia began, and on June 21, the day before the attack commenced, Hitler emphasized this to Raeder. The Grand Admiral had given him a glowing account of how the *U-253,* spotting the U.S. battleship *Texas* and an accompanying destroyer within the blockade zone in the North Atlantic proclaimed by Germany, had "chased and attempted to attack them" and had added that "where the U.S.A. is concerned firm measures are always more effective than apparent yielding." The Fuehrer agreed with the principle but not with the specific action and once more he admonished the Navy.

The Fuehrer declares in detail that until Operation Barbarossa is well under way he wishes to avoid any incident with the U.S.A. After a few weeks the situation will become clearer, and can be expected to have a favorable effect on the U.S.A. and Japan. America will have less inclination to enter the war due to the threat from Japan which will then increase. If possible, therefore, in the next weeks all attacks on naval vessels in the closed area should cease.

When Raeder attempted to argue that at night it was difficult to distinguish enemy from neutral warships Hitler cut him short by instructing him to issue new orders to avoid incidents with America. As a result the Navy chief sent out orders the same night calling off attacks on *any* naval vessels "inside or outside the closed area" unless they were definitely identified as British. A similar order was given the Luftwaffe.[20]

On July 9, President Roosevelt announced that American forces were taking over the occupation of Iceland from the British. The reaction in Berlin was immediate and violent. Ribbentrop cabled Tokyo that "this intrusion of American military forces in support of England into a territory which has been officially proclaimed by us to be a combat area is in itself an aggression against Germany and Europe."[21]

Raeder hurried to Wolfsschanze, from where the Fuehrer was directing his armies in Russia. He wanted a decision, he said, on "whether the occupation of Iceland by the U.S.A. is to be considered as an entry into the war, or as an act of provocation which should be ignored." As for the German Navy, it considered the American landings in Iceland an act of war and in a two-page memorandum it reminded the Fuehrer of all the other acts of "aggression" against Germany committed by the Roosevelt government. Moreover, the Navy demanded the right to sink American freighters in the convoy area and to attack U.S. warships if the occasion required it.* Hitler refused.

The Fuehrer explains in detail [Raeder's report on the meeting declares] that he is most anxious to postpone the United States' entry into the war for another one or two months. On the one hand the Eastern campaign must be carried on with the entire Air Force . . . which he does not wish to divert even in part; on the other hand, a victorious campaign on the Eastern front will have a tremendous effect on the whole situation and probably on the attitude of the U.S.A. Therefore for the time being he does not wish the existing instructions changed, but rather wants to be sure that incidents will be avoided.

When Raeder argued that his naval commanders could not be held responsible for "a mistake" if American ships were hit, Hitler retorted that at least in regard to war vessels the Navy had better "definitely establish" that they were enemy craft before attacking. To make sure that the

---

* It might be noted here that on the stand at Nuremberg Admiral Raeder insisted that he did everything possible to avoid provoking the United States into war.

admirals understood him correctly the Fuehrer issued a specific order on July 19 stipulating that "in the extended zone of operations U.S. merchant ships, whether single or sailing in English or American convoys and if recognized as such before resort to arms, are not to be attacked." Within the blockade area, which was also recognized by the United States as being out of bounds, American vessels could be attacked, but Hitler specifically laid it down in this order that this war zone "did *not* include the U.S.A.–Iceland sea route." The underlining was Hitler's.[22]

But "mistakes," as Raeder said, were bound to occur. On May 21 a U-boat had sunk the American freighter *Robin Moor* en route to South Africa and at a place well outside the German blockade zone. Two more American merchant vessels were torpedoed toward the end of the summer. On September 4 a German submarine fired two torpedoes at the U.S. destroyer *Greer,* both missing. A week later, on September 11, Roosevelt reacted to this attack in a speech in which he announced that he had given orders to the Navy to "shoot on sight" and warned that Axis warships entering the American defense zone did so "at their peril."

The speech incensed Berlin. In the Nazi press Roosevelt was attacked as "Warmonger Number One." Ribbentrop recalled at Nuremberg that Hitler "was greatly excited." However, by the time Admiral Raeder arrived at the Wolfsschanze headquarters on the Eastern front on the afternoon of September 17 to urge a drastic retaliation to the "shoot-on-sight" order, the Fuehrer had calmed down. To the Admiral's plea that the German Navy at last be released from the restrictions against attacking American ships the Supreme Commander again gave a firm No.

[Since] it appears that the end of September will bring the great decision in the Russian campaign [Raeder's record of the conversation declares], the Fuehrer requests that care be taken to avoid any incidents in the war on merchant shipping before about the middle of October.

"Therefore," Raeder noted sadly, "the Commander in Chief, Navy, and the Commanding Admiral, Submarines [Doenitz], withdraw their suggestions. The submarines are to be informed of the reason for temporarily keeping to the old orders."[23] In view of the circumstances, Hitler was certainly behaving with unaccustomed restraint. But admittedly it was more difficult for the young U-boat commanders, operating in the stormy waters of the North Atlantic and constantly harassed by increasingly effective British antisubmarine measures in which U.S. war vessels sometimes joined, to restrain themselves. Hitler had told Raeder in July that he would never call a submarine skipper to account if he sank an American ship "by mistake." On November 9, in his annual address to the Nazi Old Guard at the familiar beer cellar in Munich, he answered Roosevelt's speech.

President Rooseveit has ordered his ships to shoot the moment they sight German ships. I have ordered German ships *not* to shoot when they sight

American vessels, but to defend themselves when attacked. I will have any German officer court-martialed who fails to defend himself.

And on November 13 he issued a new directive ordering that while engagements with American warships were to be avoided as far as possible German submarines must defend themselves against attack.[24]

They had, of course, already done that. On the night of October 16–17, the U.S. destroyer *Kearny,* coming to the aid of a convoy which was being attacked by German submarines, dropped depth charges on one of them, which retaliated by torpedoing it. Eleven men of the crew were killed. These were the first American casualties in the undeclared war with Germany.* More were to quickly follow. On October 31, the U.S. destroyer *Reuben James* was torpedoed and sunk while on convoy duty, with the loss of 100 men of 145 in its crew, including all its seven officers. Thus, long before the final formalities of declaring war, a shooting war had begun.

JAPAN PLAYS ITS OWN GAME

Japan, as we have seen, had been assigned by Hitler the role not of bringing the United States into the war but of keeping her, at least for the time being, out of it. He knew that if the Japanese took Singapore and threatened India this would not only be a severe blow to the British but would divert America's attention—and some of her energies—from the Atlantic to the Pacific. Even after he began begging the Japanese to attack Vladivostok he saw in this a means not only to help him bring Russia down but to further pressure the United States into remaining neutral. Strangely enough, it never seems to have occurred to him or to anyone else in Germany until very late that Japan had her own fish to fry and that the Japanese might be fearful of embarking on a grand offensive in Southeast Asia against the British and Dutch, not to mention attacking Russia in the rear, until they had secured their own rear by destroying the United States Pacific Fleet. True, the Nazi conqueror had promised Matsuoka that Germany would go to war with America if Japan did, but Matsuoka was no longer in the government, and, besides, Hitler had constantly nagged the Japanese to avoid a direct conflict with America and concentrate on Britain and the Soviet Union, whose resistance was preventing him from winning the war. It did not dawn on the Nazi rulers that Japan might give first priority to a direct challenge to the United States.

---

* "History has recorded who fired the first shot," Roosevelt declared in reference to this incident in a Navy Day speech on October 27. In all fairness it would seem that in dropping depth charges the United States fired the first shot. According to the confidential German Navy records this was not the first such occasion. The official U.S. naval historian confirms that as early as April 10 the *Niblack* (see above, p. 880) attacked a U-boat with depth charges. (Samuel Eliot Morison, *History of the United States Naval Operations in World War II,* Vol. I, p. 57.)

Not that Berlin wanted the Japanese and Americans to reach an under-standing. That would defeat the main purpose of the Tripartite Pact, which was to frighten the Americans into staying out of the war. For once Ribbentrop probably gave an honest and accurate appraisal of the Fuehrer's thoughts on this when he told an interrogator at Nuremberg:

He [Hitler] was afraid that if an arrangement were made between the United States and Japan this would mean, so to speak, the back free for America, and the unexpected attack or entry into the war by the United States would come quicker . . . He was worried about an agreement because there were certain groups in Japan who wanted to come to an arrangement with America.[25]

One member of such a group was Admiral Kichisaburo Nomura, who arrived in Washington in February 1941 as the new Japanese ambassador and whose series of confidential conversations with Cordell Hull which began in March, with the aim of settling peacefully the differences between the two countries, and which continued right up to the end, gave consider-able worry to Berlin.*

In fact, the Germans did their best to sabotage the Washington talks. As early as May 15, 1941, Weizsaecker submitted a memorandum to Ribbentrop pointing out that "any political treaty between Japan and the United States is undesirable at the present" and arguing that unless it were prevented Japan might be lost to the Axis.[26] General Ott, the Nazi ambas-sador in Tokyo, called frequently at the Foreign Office, to warn against the Hull–Nomura negotiations. When, in spite of this, they continued, the Germans switched to a new maneuver of trying to induce the Japanese to make as a condition for their continuation that the United States abandon its aid to Britain and its hostile policies toward Germany.[27]

That was in May. The summer brought a change. In July Hitler was concerned mainly with badgering Japan into attacking the Soviet Union, and that month Secretary Hull broke off the talks with Nomura because the Japanese had invaded French Indochina. They were resumed toward the middle of August when the Japanese government proposed a personal meeting between Premier Prince Konoye and President Roosevelt for the purpose of arriving at a peaceful settlement. This did not please Berlin at all and the indefatigable Ott was soon at the Tokyo Foreign Office express-ing Nazi displeasure with this turn of events. Both Foreign Minister Admiral Toyoda and Vice-Minister Amau told him blandly that the proposed Konoye–Roosevelt talks would merely advance the purpose of the Tripartite Pact, which they reminded him was "to prevent American participation in the war."[28]

In the autumn, as the Hull–Nomura talks continued, the Wilhelmstrasse

---

* "I credit Nomura," Hull wrote later in his memoirs, "with having been honestly sincere in trying to avoid war between his country and mine." (*The Memoirs of Cordell Hull*, II, p. 987.)

switched back to the old tactics of the spring. It insisted in Tokyo that Nomura be instructed to warn the United States that if it continued its unfriendly acts toward the European Axis Germany and Italy might have to declare war, and that in this case Japan, under the terms of the Tripartite Pact, would have to join them. Hitler still did not want America in the war; the move was made, in fact, to bluff Washington into staying out while at the same time affording some relief from American belligerency in the Atlantic.

Secretary Hull learned immediately of this new German pressure, thanks to "Magic," as it was called, which since the end of 1940 had enabled the American government to decode intercepted Japanese cable and wireless messages in Tokyo's most secret ciphers—not only those sent to and from Washington but those to and from Berlin and other capitals. The German demand was cabled by Toyoda to Nomura on October 16, 1941, along with instructions to present a watered-down version to Hull.[29]

That day the Konoye government fell and was replaced by a military cabinet headed by the hotheaded, belligerent General Hideki Tojo. In Berlin General Oshima, a warrior of similar cast, hastened to the Wilhelmstrasse to explain the good news to the German government. Tojo's appearance at the post as Premier meant, the ambassador said, that Japan would draw closer to its Axis partners and that the talks in Washington would cease. Whether on purpose or not, he neglected to tell his Nazi friends what the consequences of the cessation of those talks must be, and that Tojo's appointment therefore meant a good deal more than they suspected: namely, that his new government was determined to go to war with the United States unless the Washington negotiations swiftly ended with President Roosevelt accepting the Japanese terms for a free hand—not to attack Russia but to occupy Southeast Asia. This course had never entered the minds of Ribbentrop and Hitler, who still envisaged Japan as useful and helpful to German interests only if she attacked Siberia and Singapore and frightened Washington into worrying about the Pacific and staying out of the war. The Fuehrer and, of course, his doltish Foreign Minister had never understood that the failure of the Nomura–Hull negotiations in Washington, which they so greatly desired, would bring the very result they had been trying to avoid until the time was ripe: America's entry into the world conflict.*

The sands were now rapidly running out.

On November 15 Saburo Kurusu arrived in Washington as a special ambassador to aid Nomura in the negotiations, but Secretary Hull soon sensed that the diplomat, who as the Japanese envoy in Berlin had signed the Tripartite Pact and was somewhat pro-German, had brought no fresh

---

* Prince Konoye's postwar memoirs reveal that as early as August 4 he was forced to agree to a demand of the Army that if, in his proposed meeting with Roosevelt, the President did not accept Japan's terms, he would walk out of the meeting "with a determination to make war on the United States." (Hull, *Memoirs,* pp. 1025–26.)

proposals with him. His purpose, Hull thought, was to try to persuade Washington to accept the Japanese terms at once or, if that failed, to lull the American government with talk until Japan was ready to strike a heavy surprise blow.[30] On November 19 came the ominous "Winds" message to Nomura from Tokyo, which Hull's cryptographers promptly deciphered. If the Japanese newscaster on the short-wave Tokyo broadcast, which the Embassy picked up daily, inserted the words "East wind, rain," that would mean that the Japanese government had decided on war with America. Nomura was instructed, on receipt of the "Winds" warning, to destroy all his codes and confidential papers.

Now Berlin awoke to what was up. The day before the "Winds" message, on November 18, Ribbentrop was somewhat surprised to receive a request from Tokyo asking Germany to sign a treaty in which the two nations would agree not to conclude a separate peace with common enemies. Just which enemies the Japanese meant was not clear, but the Nazi Foreign Minister obviously hoped that Russia was the first of them. He agreed "in principle" to the proposal, apparently in the comforting belief that Japan at last was about to honor its vague promises to hit the Soviet Union in Siberia. This was most welcome and timely, for the resistance of the Red Army on the broad front was becoming formidable and the Russian winter was setting in—much earlier than had been anticipated. A Japanese attack on Vladivostok and the Pacific maritime provinces might provide that extra ounce of pressure which would bring a Soviet collapse.

Ribbentrop was swiftly disillusioned. On November 23 Ambassador Ott wired him from Tokyo that all indications were that the Japanese were moving south with the intention of occupying Thailand and the Dutch-held Borneo oil fields, and that the Japanese government wanted to know if Germany would make common cause with her if she were to start a war. This information plainly meant that Japan would not strike against Russia but was contemplating "starting a war" with the Netherlands and Britain in the South Pacific which well might embroil her in an armed conflict with the United States. But Ribbentrop and Ott did not grasp the last point. Their exchanges of telegrams during these days show that though they now realized, to their disappointment, that Japan would not attack Russia they believed that her move southward would be against the possessions of the Dutch and British and not those of the United States. Uncle Sam, as Hitler desired, would be kept on the sidelines until his time came.[31]

Nazi misapprehensions were due in large part to the failure at this juncture of the Japanese to take the German government into their confidence as to their fateful decisions regarding America. Secretary Hull, thanks to the "Magic" code breaker, was much better informed. As early as November 5 he knew that the new Foreign Minister, Shigenori Togo, had wired Nomura setting a deadline of November 25 for the signing of an agreement—on Japan's terms—with the American government. The final Japanese proposals were delivered in Washington on November 20. Hull and Roosevelt knew they were final because two days later "Magic" decoded for them a message from Togo to Nomura and Kurusu which said so, while extending the deadline to November 29.

There are reasons beyond your ability to guess [Togo wired his ambassadors] why we wanted to settle Japanese–American relations by the 25th. But if the signing can be completed by the 29th . . . we have decided to wait until that date. This time we mean it, that the deadline absolutely cannot be changed. After that things are automatically going to happen.[32]

November 25, 1941, is a crucial date.

On that day the Japanese carrier task force sailed for Pearl Harbor. In Washington Hull went to the White House to warn the War Council of the danger confronting the country from Japan and to stress to the U.S. Army and Navy chiefs the possibility of Japanese surprise attacks. In Berlin that day there was a somewhat grotesque ceremony in which the three Axis Powers, amid much pomp and ceremony, renewed the Anti-Comintern Pact of 1936—an empty gesture which, as some Germans noted, did absolutely nothing to get Japan into the war against Russia but which afforded the pompous Ribbentrop an opportunity to denounce Roosevelt as the "chief culprit of this war" and to shed crocodile tears for the "truthful, religious . . . American people" betrayed by such an irresponsible leader.

The Nazi Foreign Minister seems to have become intoxicated by his own words. He called in Oshima on the evening of November 28, following a lengthy council of war earlier that day presided over by Hitler, and gave the Japanese ambassador the impression that the German attitude toward the United States, as Oshima promptly radioed Tokyo, had "considerably stiffened." Hitler's policy of doing everything possible to keep America out of the war until Germany was ready to take her on seemed about to be jettisoned. Suddenly Ribbentrop was urging the Japanese to go to war against the United States as well as Britain and promising the backing of the Third Reich. After warning Oshima that "if Japan hesitates . . . all the military might of Britain and the United States will be concentrated against Japan"—a rather silly thesis as long as the European war continued—Ribbentrop added:

As Hitler said today, there are fundamental differences in the very right to exist between Germany and Japan and the United States. We have received advice to the effect that there is practically no hope of the Japanese–U.S. negotiations being concluded successfully because the United States is putting up a stiff front.

If this is indeed the fact of the case, and if Japan reaches a decision to fight Britain and the United States, I am confident that that not only will be in the interest of Germany and Japan jointly, but would bring about favorable results for Japan herself.

The ambassador, a tense little man, was agreeably surprised. But he wanted to be sure he understood correctly.

"Is Your Excellency," he asked, "indicating that a state of actual war is to be established between Germany and the United States?"

Ribbentrop hesitated. Perhaps he had gone too far. "Roosevelt is a fanatic," he replied, "so it is impossible to tell what he would do."

This seemed a strange and unsatisfactory answer to Oshima in view of what the Foreign Minister had said just before, and toward the end of the talk he insisted on coming back to the main point. What would Germany do if the war were actually extended to "countries which have been aiding Britain"?

Should Japan become engaged in a war against the United States [Ribbentrop replied] Germany, of course, would join the war immediately. There is absolutely no possibility of Germany's entering into a separate peace with the United States under such circumstances. The Fuehrer is determined on that point.[33]

This was the flat guarantee for which the Japanese government had been waiting. True, Hitler had given a similar one in the spring to Matsuoka, but it seemed to have been forgotten during the intervening period when he had become vexed at Japan's refusal to join in the war on Russia. All that remained now, so far as the Japanese were concerned, was to get the Germans to put their assurance in writing. General Oshima joyfully filed his report to Tokyo on November 29. Fresh instructions reached him in Berlin the next day. The Washington talks, he was informed, "now stand ruptured—broken."

Will Your Honor [the message directed] therefore immediately interview Chancellor HITLER and Foreign Minister RIBBENTROP and confidentially communicate to them a summary of developments. Say to them that lately England and the United States have taken a provocative attitude, both of them. Say that they are planning to move military forces into various places in East Asia and that we will inevitably have to counter by also moving troops. Say very secretly to them that there is extreme danger that war may suddenly break out between Japan and the Anglo-Saxon nations through some clash of arms and add that the time of the breaking out of that war may come quicker than anyone dreams.*[34]

The Japanese carrier fleet was now well on its way to Pearl Harbor. Tokyo was in a hurry to get Germany to sign. On the same day that Oshima was receiving his new instructions, November 30, the Japanese

---

* Hull says that he received a copy of this message through "Magic." Thus Washington, as well as Berlin, knew by the last day of November that the Japanese might strike against the United States "quicker than anyone dreamt." (Hull, *Memoirs,* p. 1092.)

Foreign Minister was conferring with the German ambassador in Tokyo, to whom he emphasized that the Washington talks had broken down because Japan refused to accede to American demands that she abandon the Tripartite Pact. The Japanese hoped the Germans would appreciate this sacrifice in a common cause.

"Grave decisions are at stake," Togo told General Ott. "The United States is seriously preparing for war . . . Japan is not afraid of a breakdown in negotiations and she hopes that in that case Germany and Italy, according to the Three-Power Agreement, will stand at her side."

I answered [Ott radioed Berlin] that there could be no doubt about Germany's future position. Japanese Foreign Minister thereupon stated that he understood from my words that Germany in such a case would consider her relationship to Japan as that of a community of fate. I answered, according to my opinion, Germany was certainly ready to have mutual agreement between the two countries on this situation.[35]

ON THE EVE OF PEARL HARBOR

General Oshima was a great lover of German–Austrian classical music and despite the gravity and tenseness of the situation he took off for Austria to enjoy a Mozart festival. But he was not permitted to listen to the great Austrian composer's lovely music for long. An urgent call on December 1 brought him rushing back to his embassy in Berlin, where he found new instructions to get busy and sign up Germany on the dotted line. There was no time to lose.

And now, when cornered, Ribbentrop stalled. Apparently realizing fully for the first time the consequences of his rash promises to the Japanese, the Nazi Foreign Minister grew exceedingly cool and evasive. He told Oshima late on the evening of December 1 that he would first have to consult the Fuehrer before making any definite commitment. The Japanese ambassador returned to the Wilhelmstrasse on Wednesday, the third, to press his case but again Ribbentrop put him off. To Oshima's pleas that the situation had become extremely critical the Foreign Minister replied that while he personally was for a written agreement the matter would have to wait until the Fuehrer returned from headquarters later in the week. Actually, as Ciano noted in his diary, not without a sign of glee, Hitler had flown to the southern front in Russia to see General von Kleist, "whose armies continue to fall back under the pressure of an unexpected offensive."

The Japanese, by this time, had also turned to Mussolini, who was not at any front. On December 3 the Japanese ambassador in Rome called on the Duce and formally asked Italy to declare war on the United States, in accordance with the Tripartite Pact, as soon as the conflict with America should begin. The ambassador also wanted a treaty specifying that there would be no separate peace. The Japanese interpreter, Ciano noted in his diary, "was trembling like a leaf." As for the Duce, he was "pleased" to comply, after consultation with Berlin.

The German capital, Ciano found the next day, had grown extremely cautious.

Maybe they will go ahead [he began his diary on December 4] because they can't do otherwise, but the idea of provoking American intervention is less and less liked by the Germans. Mussolini, on the other hand, is happy about it.

Regardless of Ribbentrop's opinion, which Hitler, surprisingly, still paid some attention to, the decision as to whether Germany would give a formal guarantee to Japan could be taken only by the Nazi warlord himself. During the night of December 4–5 the Foreign Minister apparently got the Fuehrer's go-ahead and at 3 A.M. he handed General Oshima a draft of the requested treaty in which Germany would join Japan in war against the United States and agree not to make a separate peace. Having taken the fateful plunge and followed his Leader in reversing a policy that had been clung to stubbornly for two years, he could not refrain from seeing that his Italian ally promptly followed suit.

A night interrupted by Ribbentrop's restiveness [Ciano began his diary on December 5]. After having delayed two days he now hasn't a minute to lose in answering the Japanese, and at 3 o'clock in the morning he sends [Ambassador] Mackensen to my house to submit a plan for a Tripartite Pact of Japanese intervention and the promise not to make a separate peace. They wanted me to wake up the Duce, but I did not do it, and the Duce was very pleased.

The Japanese had a draft treaty, approved by both Hitler and Mussolini, but they did not yet have it signed, and this worried them. They suspected that the Fuehrer was stalling because he wanted a *quid pro quo:* if Germany joined Japan in the war against the United States, Japan would have to join Germany in the war against Russia. In his telegram of instructions to Oshima on November 30, the Japanese Foreign Minister had given some advice on how to handle this ticklish problem if the Germans and Italians raised it.

If [they] question you about our attitude toward the Soviet, say that we have already clarified our attitude toward the Russians in our statement of last July. Say that by our present moves southward we do not mean to relax our pressure against the Soviet and that if Russia joins hands tighter with England and the United States and resists us with hostilities, we are ready to turn upon her with all our might. However, right now, it is to our advantage to stress the south and for the time being we would prefer to refrain from any direct moves in the north.[36]

December 6 came. Zhukov that very day launched his counteroffensive in front of Moscow and the German armies reeled back in the snow and bitter cold. There was all the more reason for Hitler to demand his *quid pro quo*. On this question there was great uneasiness in the Foreign Office in Tokyo. The naval task force was now within flying distance of Pearl Harbor for its carrier planes. So far—miraculously—it had not been discovered by American ships or aircraft. But it might be any moment. A long message was being radioed from Tokyo to Nomura and Kurusu in Washington instructing them to call on Secretary Hull at precisely 1 P.M. the next day, Sunday, December 7, to present Japan's rejection of the latest American proposals, and stressing that the negotiations were "de facto ruptured." In desperation Tokyo turned to Berlin for a written guarantee of German support. The Japanese warlords still did not trust the Germans enough to inform them of the blow against the United States which would fall the next day. But they were more worried than ever that Hitler would refrain from giving his guarantee unless Japan agreed to take on not only the United States and Great Britain but the Soviet Union as well. In this predicament Togo got off a long message to Ambassador Oshima in Berlin urging him to somehow stall the Germans on the Russian matter and not to give in unless it became absolutely necessary. Deluded though they were about their ability to deal with the Americans and the British, the Japanese generals and admirals retained enough sense to realize that they could not fight the Russians at the same time—even with German help. Togo's instructions to Oshima on that fateful Saturday, December 6, which are among the intercepted messages decoded by Secretary Hull's expert decipherers, give an interesting insight into the diplomacy practiced by the Nipponese with the Third Reich at the eleventh hour.

We would like to avoid . . . an armed clash with Russia until strategic circumstances permit it; so get the German government to understand this position of ours and negotiate with them so that at least for the present they will not insist upon exchanging diplomatic notes on this question.

Explain to them at considerable length that insofar as American materials being shipped to Soviet Russia . . . they are neither of high quality nor of large quantity, and that in case we start our war with the United States we will capture all American ships destined for Soviet Russia. Please endeavor to come to an understanding on this line.

However, should Ribbentrop insist upon our giving a guarantee in this matter, since in that case we shall have no other recourse, make a . . . statement to the effect that we would, as a matter of principle, prevent war materials from being shipped from the United States to Soviet Russia via Japanese waters, and get them to agree to a procedure permitting the addition of a statement to the effect that so long as strategic reasons continue to make it necessary for us to keep Soviet Russia from fighting Japan (what I mean is that we cannot capture Soviet ships) we cannot carry this out thoroughly.

In case the German government refuses to agree with [the above] and makes their approval of this question absolutely conditional upon our participation in the war and upon our concluding a treaty against making a separate peace, we have no way but to postpone the conclusion of such a treaty.[37]

The Japanese need not have worried so much. For reasons unknown to the Tokyo militarists, or to anyone else, and which defy logic and understanding, Hitler did not insist on Japan's taking on Russia along with the United States and Britain, though if he had the course of the war conceivably might have been different.

At any rate, the Japanese on this Saturday evening of December 6, 1941, were determined to strike a telling blow against the United States in the Pacific, though no one in Washington or Berlin knew just where or even exactly when. That morning the British Admiralty had tipped off the American government that a large Japanese invasion fleet had been observed heading across the Gulf of Siam for the Isthmus of Kra, which indicated that the Nipponese were striking first at Thailand and perhaps Malaya. At 9 P.M. President Roosevelt got off a personal message to the Emperor of Japan imploring him to join him in finding "ways of dispelling the dark clouds" and at the same time warning him that a thrust of the Japanese military forces into Southeast Asia would create a situation that was "unthinkable." At the Navy Department, intelligence officers drew up their latest report on the location of the major warships of the Japanese Navy. It listed most of them as being in home ports, including all the carriers and other warships of the task force which at that very moment had steamed to within three hundred miles of Pearl Harbor and was tuning up its bombers to take off at dawn.

On that Saturday evening too the Navy Department informed the President and Mr. Hull that the Japanese Embassy was destroying its codes. It had first had to decipher Togo's long message, which had dribbled in all afternoon in fourteen parts. The Navy decoders were also deciphering it as fast as it came in and by 9:30 P.M. a naval officer was at the White House with translations of the first thirteen parts. Mr. Roosevelt, who was with Harry Hopkins in the study, read it and said, "This means war." But exactly when and just where, the message did not say and the President did not know. Even Admiral Nomura did not know. Nor far off in Eastern Europe did Adolf Hitler. He knew less than Roosevelt.

HITLER DECLARES WAR

The Japanese onslaught on the U.S. Pacific Fleet at Pearl Harbor at 7:30 A.M. (local time) on Sunday, December 7, 1941, caught Berlin as completely by surprise as it did Washington. Though Hitler had made an oral promise to Matsuoka that Germany would join Japan in a war against the United States and Ribbentrop had made another to Ambassador

Oshima, the assurance had not yet been signed and the Japanese had not breathed a word to the Germans about Pearl Harbor.* Besides, at this moment, Hitler was fully occupied trying to rally his faltering generals and retreating troops in Russia.

Night had fallen in Berlin when the foreign-broadcast monitoring service first picked up the news of the sneak attack on Pearl Harbor. When an official of the Foreign Office Press Department telephoned Ribbentrop the world-shaking news he at first refused to believe it and was extremely angry at being disturbed. The report was "probably a propaganda trick of the enemy," he said, and ordered that he be left undisturbed until morning.[38] So probably Ribbentrop, for once, told the truth when he testified on the stand at Nuremberg that "this attack came as a complete surprise to us. We had considered the possibility of Japan's attacking Singapore or perhaps Hong Kong, but we never considered an attack on the United States as being to our advantage."[39] However, contrary to what he told the tribunal, he was exceedingly happy about it. Or so he struck Ciano.

A night telephone call from Ribbentrop [Ciano began his diary on December 8]. He is joyful over the Japanese attack on the United States. He is so happy, in fact, that I can't but congratulate him, even though I am not so sure about the advantage . . . Mussolini was [also] happy. For a long time now he has been in favor of clarifying the position between America and the Axis.

At 1 P.M. on Monday, December 8, General Oshima went to the Wilhelmstrasse to get Ribbentrop to clarify Germany's position. He demanded a formal declaration of war on the United States "at once."

Ribbentrop replied [Oshima radioed Tokyo] that Hitler was then in the midst of a conference at general headquarters discussing how the formalities of declaring war could be carried out so as to make a good impression on the German people, and that he would transmit your wish to him at once and do whatever he was able to have it carried out promptly.

The Nazi Foreign Minister also informed the ambassador, according to the latter's message to Tokyo, that on that very morning of the eighth "Hitler issued orders to the German Navy to attack American ships whenever and wherever they may meet them."[40] But the dictator stalled on a declaration of war.†

The Fuehrer, according to the notation in his daily calendar book, hurried back to Berlin on the night of December 8, arriving there at 11 o'clock the next morning. Ribbentrop claimed at Nuremberg that he pointed out

---

* It was long believed by many that Hitler knew in advance the exact hour of the attack on Pearl Harbor, but I have been unable to find a single scrap of evidence in the secret German papers to substantiate it.

† In Tokyo at the same time Foreign Minister Togo was telling Ambassador Ott, "The Japanese Government expects that now Germany too will speedily declare war on the United States."[41]

to the Leader that Germany did not necessarily have to declare war on America under the terms of the Tripartite Pact, since Japan was obviously the aggressor.

The text of the Tripartite Pact bound us to assist Japan only in case of an attack against Japan herself. I went to see the Fuehrer, explained the legal aspect of the situation and told him that, although we welcomed a new ally against England, it meant we had a new opponent to deal with as well . . . if we declared war on the United States.

I told him that according to the stipulation of the Three-Power Pact, since Japan had attacked, we would not have to declare war, formally. The Fuehrer thought this matter over quite a while and then he gave me a very clear decision. "If we don't stand on the side of Japan," he said, "the Pact is politically dead. But that is not the main reason. The chief reason is that the United States already is shooting against our ships. They have been a forceful factor in this war and through their actions have already created a situation of war."

The Fuehrer was of the opinion at that moment that it was quite evident that the United States would now make war against Germany. Therefore he ordered me to hand over the passports to the American representative.[42]

This was a decision that Roosevelt and Hull in Washington had been confidently waiting for. There had been some pressure on them to have Congress declare war on Germany and Italy on December 8 when that step was taken against Japan. But they had decided to wait. The bombing at Pearl Harbor had taken them off one hook and certain information in their possession led them to believe that the headstrong Nazi dictator would take them off a second hook.* They had pondered the intercepted

---

* My own impression in Washington at that moment was that it might be difficult for President Roosevelt to get Congress to declare war on Germany. There seemed to be a strong feeling in both Houses as well as in the Army and Navy that the country ought to concentrate its efforts on defeating Japan and not take on the additional burden of fighting Germany at the same time.

Hans Thomsen, the German chargé in Washington, who, like all the other Nazi envoys abroad, was usually kept ignorant of what Hitler and Ribbentrop were conniving, reported this sentiment to Berlin. Immediately after the President's speech to Congress on the morning of December 8 calling for a declaration of war on Japan Thomsen radioed Berlin: "The fact that he [Roosevelt] did not mention Germany and Italy with one word shows that he will try at first to avoid sharpening the situation in the Atlantic." On the evening of the same day Thomsen got off another dispatch on the subject: "Whether Roosevelt will demand declaration of war on Germany and Italy is uncertain. From the standpoint of the American military leaders it would be logical to avoid everything which could lead to a two-front war." In several dispatches just prior to Pearl Harbor the German chargé had emphasized that the United States simply was not prepared for a two-front war. On December 4 he had radioed the revelations in the Chicago *Tribune* of the "war plans of the American High Command on preparations and prospects for defeating Germany and her allies."

Report confirms [he said] that full participation of America in war is not to be

message of Ambassador Oshima from Berlin to Tokyo on November 29*
in which Ribbentrop had assured the Japanese that Germany would join
Japan if she became "engaged" in a war against the United States. There
was nothing in that assurance which made German aid conditional upon
who was the aggressor. It was a blank check and the Americans had no
doubt that the Japanese were now clamoring in Berlin that it be honored.

It was honored, but only after the Nazi warlord again hesitated. He had
convoked the Reichstag to meet on December 9, the day of his arrival in
Berlin, but he postponed it for two days, until the eleventh. Apparently, as
Ribbentrop later reported, he had made up his mind. He was fed up with
the attacks made by Roosevelt on him and on Nazism; his patience was
exhausted by the warlike acts of the U.S. Navy against German U-boats in
the Atlantic, about which Raeder had continually nagged him for nearly a
year. He had a growing hatred for America and Americans and, what
was worse for him in the long run, a growing tendency to disastrously underestimate the potential strength of the United States.†

At the same time he grossly overestimated Japan's military power. In
fact, he seems to have believed that once the Japanese, whose Navy he believed to be the most powerful in the world, had disposed of the British
and Americans in the Pacific, they would turn on Russia and thus help
him finish his great conquest in the East. He actually told some of his
followers a few months later that he thought Japan's entry into the war had
been "of exceptional value to us, if only because of the date chosen."

It was, in effect, at the moment when the surprises of the Russian winter
were pressing most heavily on the morale of our people, and when everybody
in Germany was oppressed by the certainty that sooner or later the United
States would come into the conflict. Japanese intervention therefore was, from
our point of view, most opportune.[43]

---

expected before July, 1943. Military measures against Japan are of defensive
character.

In his message to Berlin on the evening of December 8, Thomsen stressed that
Pearl Harbor was certain to bring relief to Germany from America's belligerent
activities in the Atlantic.

War with Japan [he reported] means transferring of all energy to America's
own rearmament, a corresponding shrinking of Lend-Lease help and a shifting
of all activity to the Pacific.

For the exchange of dispatches between the Wilhelmstrasse and the German
Embassy in Washington during this period, I am indebted to the State Department,
which gave me access to them. They will be published later in the *Documents on
German Foreign Policy* series.

* See above, p. 888.

† "I don't see much future for the Americans," he told his cronies a month later
during a monologue at headquarters on January 7, 1942. "It's a decayed country.
And they have their racial problem, and the problem of social inequalities . . .
My feelings against Americanism are feelings of hatred and deep repugnance . . .
Everything about the behavior of American society reveals that it's half Judaized,
and the other half Negrified. How can one expect a State like that to hold together
—a country where everything is built on the dollar." (*Hitler's Secret Conversations*, p. 155.)

There is also no doubt that Japan's sneaky and mighty blow against the American fleet at Pearl Harbor kindled his admiration—and all the more so because it was the kind of "surprise" he had been so proud of pulling off so often himself. He expressed this to Ambassador Oshima on December 14 when he awarded him the Grand Cross of the Order of Merit of the German Eagle in gold:

You gave the right declaration of war! This method is the only proper one.

It corresponded, he said, to his "own system."

That is, to negotiate as long as possible. But if one sees that the other is interested only in putting one off, in shaming and humiliating one, and is not willing to come to an agreement, then one should strike—indeed, as hard as possible—and not waste time declaring war. It was heartwarming to him to hear of the first operations of the Japanese. He himself negotiated with infinite patience at times, for example, with Poland and also with Russia. When he then realized that the other did not want to come to an agreement, he struck suddenly and without formalities. He would continue to go this way in the future.[44]

There was one other reason for Hitler's deciding in such haste to add the United States to the formidable list of his enemies. Dr. Schmidt, who was in and out of the Chancellery and Foreign Office that week, put his finger on it: "I got the impression," he later wrote, "that, with his inveterate desire for prestige, Hitler, who was expecting an American declaration of war, wanted to get his declaration in first."[45] The Nazi warlord confirmed this in his speech to the Reichstag on December 11.

"We will always strike first," he told the cheering deputies. "We will always deal the first blow!"

Indeed, Berlin was so fearful on December 10 that America might declare war first that Ribbentrop sternly admonished Thomsen, the German chargé in Washington, about committing any indiscretion which might tip off the State Department to what Hitler planned to do on the following day. In a long radiogram on the tenth the Nazi Foreign Minister filed the text of the declaration he would make in Berlin to the U.S. chargé d'affaires at precisely 2:30 P.M. on December 11. Thomsen was instructed to call on Hull exactly one hour later, at 3:30 P.M. (Berlin time), hand the Secretary of State a copy of the declaration, ask for his passport and turn over Germany's diplomatic representation to Switzerland. At the end of the message Ribbentrop warned Thomsen not to have any contact with the State Department before delivering his note. "We wish to avoid under all circumstances," the warning said, "that the Government there beats us to such a step."

Whatever hesitations led Hitler to postpone the Reichstag session by two days, it is evident from the captured exchange of messages between the Wilhelmstrasse and the German Embassy in Washington, and from other Foreign Office papers, that the Fuehrer actually made his fateful decision to declare war on the United States on December 9, the day he arrived in the capital from headquarters on the Russian front. The Nazi dictator appears to have wanted the two extra days not for further reflection but to prepare carefully his Reichstag speech so that it would make the proper impression on the German people, of whose memories of America's decisive role in the First World War Hitler was quite aware.

Hans Dieçkhoff, who was still officially the German ambassador to the United States but who had been cooling his heels in the Wilhelmstrasse ever since both countries withdrew their chief envoys in the autumn of 1938, was put to work on December 9 to draw up a long list of Roosevelt's anti-German activities for the Fuehrer's Reichstag address.*

Also on December 9 Thomsen in Washington was instructed to burn his secret codes and confidential papers. "Measures carried out as ordered," he flashed to Berlin at 11:30 A.M. on that day. For the first time he became aware of what was going on in Berlin and during the evening tipped the Wilhelmstrasse that apparently the American government knew too. "Believed here," he said, "that within twenty-four hours Germany will declare war on the United States or at least break off diplomatic relations."†

HITLER IN THE REICHSTAG: DECEMBER 11

Hitler's address on December 11 to the robots of the Reichstag in defense of his declaration of war on the United States was devoted mainly to hurling personal insults at Franklin D. Roosevelt, to charging that the President had provoked war in order to cover up the failures of the New Deal and to thundering that "this man alone," backed by the millionaires and the Jews, was "responsible for the Second World War." All the accumulated, pent-up resentment at a man who had stood from the first in his way toward world dominion, who had continually taunted him, who

---

* Dieckhoff, whom Hassell thought "temperamentally submissive," had drawn up just a week before at the request of Ribbentrop a long memorandum entitled "Principles for Influencing American Public Opinion." Among his eleven principles were: "Real danger to America is Roosevelt himself . . . Influence of Jews on Roosevelt (Frankfurter, Baruch, Benjamin Cohen, Samuel Rosenman, Henry Morgenthau, etc.) . . . The slogan for every American mother must be: "I didn't raise my boy to die for Britain!" (From the Foreign Office papers, not yet published.) Some Americans in the State Department and in our embassy in Berlin thought rather highly of Dieckhoff and believed him to be anti-Nazi. My own feeling was that he lacked the guts to be. He served Hitler to the end—from 1943 to 1945 as the Nazi ambassador to Franco Spain.

† Thomsen also urged Berlin to arrest the American correspondents there in retaliation for the arrest of a handful of German newsmen in the United States. A Foreign Office memorandum signed by Undersecretary Ernst Woermann on December 10 declares that all American correspondents in Germany were ordered arrested as "a reprisal." Excepted was Guido Enderis, chief correspondent in Berlin of the New York *Times,* "because," Woermann wrote, "of his proved friendliness to Germany." This may be unfair to the late Enderis, who was in ill health at the time and who mainly for that reason perhaps was not arrested.

had provided massive aid to Britain at a moment when it seemed that battered island nation would fall, and whose Navy was frustrating him in the Atlantic burst forth in violent wrath.

Permit me to define my attitude to that other world, which has its representative in that man who, while our soldiers are fighting in snow and ice, very tactfully likes to make his chats from the fireside, the man who is the main culprit of this war . . .

I will pass over the insulting attacks made by this so-called President against me. That he calls me a gangster is uninteresting. After all, this expression was not coined in Europe but in America, no doubt because such gangsters are lacking here. Apart from this, I cannot be insulted by Roosevelt, for I consider him mad, just as Wilson was . . . First he incites war, then falsifies the causes, then odiously wraps himself in a cloak of Christian hypocrisy and slowly but surely leads mankind to war, not without calling God to witness the honesty of his attack—in the approved manner of an old Freemason . . .

Roosevelt has been guilty of a series of the worst crimes against international law. Illegal seizure of ships and other property of German and Italian nationals was coupled with the threat to, and looting of, those who were deprived of their liberty by being interned. Roosevelt's ever increasing attacks finally went so far that he ordered the American Navy to attack everywhere ships under the German and Italian flags, and to sink them—this in gross violation of international law. American ministers boasted of having destroyed German submarines in this criminal way. German and Italian merchant ships were attacked by American cruisers, captured and their crews imprisoned.

In this way the sincere efforts of Germany and Italy to prevent an extension of the war and to maintain relations with the United States in spite of the unbearable provocations which have been carried on for years by President Roosevelt have been frustrated . . .

What was Roosevelt's motive "to intensify anti-German feeling to the pitch of war"? Hitler asked. He gave two explanations.

I understand only too well that a world-wide distance separates Roosevelt's ideas and my ideas. Roosevelt comes from a rich family and belongs to the class whose path is smoothed in the democracies. I was only the child of a small, poor family and had to fight my way by work and industry. When the Great War came Roosevelt occupied a position where he got to know only its pleasant consequences, enjoyed by those who do business while others bleed. I was only one of those who carried out orders as an ordinary soldier, and naturally returned from the war just as poor as I was in the autumn of 1914. I shared the fate of millions, and Franklin Roosevelt only the fate of the so-called Upper Ten Thousand.

After the war Roosevelt tried his hand at financial speculations. He made profits out of inflation, out of the misery of others, while I . . . lay in a hospital . . .

Hitler continued at some length with this singular comparison before he reached his second point, that Roosevelt had reverted to war to escape the consequences of his failure as President.

National Socialism came to power in Germany in the same year as Roosevelt was elected President . . . He took over a state in a very poor economic condition, and I took over the Reich faced with complete ruin, thanks to democracy . . .

While an unprecedented revival of economic life, culture and art took place in Germany under National Socialist leadership, President Roosevelt did not succeed in bringing about even the slightest improvement in his own country . . . This is not surprising if one bears in mind that the men he had called to support him, or rather, the men who had called him, belonged to the Jewish element, whose interests are all for disintegration and never for order . . .

Roosevelt's New Deal legislation was all wrong. There can be no doubt that a continuation of this economic policy would have undone this President in peacetime, in spite of all his dialectical skill. In a European state he would surely have come eventually before a state court on a charge of deliberate waste of the national wealth; and he would scarcely have escaped at the hands of a civil court on a charge of criminal business methods.

Hitler knew that this assessment of the New Deal was shared, in part at least, by the American isolationists and a considerable portion of the business community and he sought to make the most of it, ignorant of the fact that on Pearl Harbor Day these groups, like all others in America, had rallied to the support of their country.

This fact was realized [he continued, alluding to these groups] and fully appreciated by many Americans, including some of high standing. A threatening opposition was gathering over the head of this man. He guessed that the only salvation for him lay in diverting public attention from home to foreign policy . . . He was strengthened in this by the Jews around him . . . The full diabolical meanness of Jewry rallied around this man, and he stretched out his hands.

Thus began the increasing efforts of the American President to create conflicts . . . For years this man harbored one desire—that a conflict should break out somewhere in the world.

There followed a long recital of Roosevelt's efforts in this direction, beginning with the "quarantine" speech in Chicago in 1937. "Now he [Roosevelt] is seized," Hitler cried at one point, "with fear that if peace is brought about in Europe his squandering of millions of money on armaments will be looked upon as plain fraud, since nobody will attack America —and then he himself must provoke this attack upon his country."

The Nazi dictator seemed relieved that the break had come and he sought to share his sense of relief with the German people.

I think you have all found it a relief now that, at last, one State has been the first to take the step of protesting against this historically unique and shameless ill treatment of truth and of right . . . The fact that the Japanese Government, which has been negotiating for years with this man, has at last become tired of being mocked by him in such an unworthy way fills us all, the German people and, I think, all other decent people in the world, with deep satisfaction . . . The President of the United States ought finally to under-stand—I say this only because of his limited intellect—that we know that the aim of his struggle is to destroy one state after another . . .

As for the German nation, it needs charity neither from Mr. Roosevelt nor from Mr. Churchill, let alone from Mr. Eden. It wants only its rights! It will secure for itself this right to live even if thousands of Churchills and Roose-velts conspire against it . . .

I have therefore arranged for passports to be handed to the American chargé d'affaires today, and the following—[46]

At this point the deputies of the Reichstag leaped to their feet cheering, and the Fuehrer's words were drowned in the bedlam.

Shortly afterward, at 2:30 P.M., Ribbentrop, in one of his most frigid poses, received Leland Morris, the American chargé d'affaires in Berlin, and while keeping him standing read out Germany's declaration of war, handed him a copy and icily dismissed him.

. . . Although Germany for her part [said the declaration] has always strictly observed the rules of international law in her dealings with the United States throughout the present war, the Government of the United States has finally proceeded to overt acts of war against Germany. It has, therefore, virtually created a state of war.

The Reich Government therefore breaks off all diplomatic relations with the United States and declares that under these circumstances brought about by President Roosevelt, Germany too considers herself to be at war with the United States, as from today.[47]

The final act in the day's drama was the signing of a tripartite agreement by Germany, Italy and Japan declaring "their unshakable determination not to lay down arms until the joint war against the United States and England reaches a successful conclusion" and not to conclude a separate peace.

Adolf Hitler, who a bare six months before had faced only a beleaguered Britain in a war which seemed to him as good as won, now, by deliberate choice, had arrayed against him the three greatest industrial powers in the world in a struggle in which military might depended largely, in the long run, on economic strength. Those three enemy countries together also had a great preponderance of manpower over the three Axis nations. Neither Hitler nor his generals nor his admirals seem to have weighed those sober-ing facts on that eventful December day as the year 1941 drew toward a close.

General Halder, the intelligent Chief of the General Staff, did not even note in his diary on December 11 that Germany had declared war on the United States. He mentioned only that in the evening he attended a lecture by a naval captain on the "background of the Japanese–American sea war." The rest of his diary, understandably perhaps, was taken up with the continued bad news from most sectors of the hard-pressed Russian front. There was no room in his thoughts for an eventual day when his weakened armies might also have to confront fresh troops from the New World.

Admiral Raeder actually welcomed Hitler's move. He conferred with the Fuehrer on the following day, December 12. "The situation in the Atlantic," he assured him, "will be eased by Japan's successful intervention." And warming up to his subject he added:

Reports have already been received of the transfer of some [American] battleships from the Atlantic to the Pacific. It is certain that light forces, especially destroyers, will be required in increased numbers in the Pacific. The need for transport ships will be very great, so that a withdrawal of American merchant ships from the Atlantic can be expected. The strain on British merchant shipping will increase.

Hitler, having taken his plunge, and with such reckless bravado, now suddenly was prey to doubts. He had some questions to put to the Grand Admiral. Did he "believe that the enemy will in the near future take steps to occupy the Azores, the Cape Verdes and perhaps even to attack Dakar, in order to win back prestige lost as the result of the setbacks in the Pacific?" Raeder did not think so.

The U.S. [he answered] will have to concentrate all her strength in the Pacific during the next few months. Britain will not want to run any risks after her severe losses of big ships.* It is hardly likely that transport tonnage is available for such occupation tasks or for bringing up supplies.

Hitler had a more important question to pose. "Is there any possibility," he asked, "that the U.S.A. and Britain will abandon East Asia for a time in order to crush Germany and Italy first?" Here again the Grand Admiral was reassuring.

It is improbable [he answered] that the enemy will give up East Asia even temporarily; by so doing Britain would endanger India very seriously, and the U.S. cannot withdraw her fleet from the Pacific as long as the Japanese fleet has the upper hand.

---

* Two days before, on December 10, Japanese planes had sunk two British battleships, the *Prince of Wales* and the *Repulse,* off the coast of Malaya. Coupled with the crippling American losses in battleships at Pearl Harbor on December 7, this blow gave the Japanese fleet complete supremacy in the Pacific, the China Sea and the Indian Ocean. "In all the war," Churchill wrote later of the loss of the two great ships, "I never received a more direct shock."

Raeder further tried to cheer up the Fuehrer by informing him that six "large" submarines were to proceed "as quickly as possible" to the east coast of the United States.[48]

With the situation in Russia being what it was, not to mention that in North Africa, where Rommel was also retreating, the thoughts of the German Supreme Commander and his military chiefs quickly turned from the new enemy, which they were sure would have its hands full in the Pacific far away. Their thoughts were not to return to it before another year had passed, the most fateful year of the war, in which the great turning point would come—irrevocably deciding not only the outcome of the conflict which all through 1941 the Germans had believed almost over, almost won, but the fate of the Third Reich, whose astounding early victories had raised it so quickly to such a giddy height and which Hitler sincerely believed—and said—would flourish for a thousand years.

Halder's scribblings in his diary grew ominous as New Year's, 1942, drew near.

"Another dark day!" he began his journal on December 30, 1941, and again on the last day of the year. The Chief of the German General Staff had a presentiment of terrible things to come.

26

THE GREAT TURNING POINT: 1942—

STALINGRAD AND EL ALAMEIN

THE CONSPIRATORS COME BACK TO LIFE

THE SEVERE SETBACK to Hitler's armies in Russia during the winter of 1941–42 and the cashiering of a number of field marshals and top generals ignited the hopes of the anti-Nazi conspirators again.

They had been unable to interest the leading commanders in a revolt as long as their armies were smashing to one easy victory after another and the glory of German arms and of the German Reich was soaring to the heavens. But now the proud and hitherto invincible soldiers were falling back in the snow and bitter cold before an enemy which had proved their match; casualties in six months had passed the million mark; and a host of the most renowned generals were being summarily dismissed, some of them, such as Hoepner and Sponeck, publicly disgraced, and most of the others humiliated and made scapegoats of by the ruthless dictator.*

"The time is almost ripe," Hassell concluded hopefully in his diary on December 21, 1941. He and his fellow conspirators were sure that the

---

* Among those retired, it will be recalled, were Field Marshal von Brauchitsch, the Commander in Chief of the Army, and Field Marshals von Rundstedt and von Bock, who led the southern and central army groups, respectively, and General Guderian, the genius of the panzer corps. The commander of the army group in the north, Field Marshal von Leeb, soon followed, being relieved of his post on January 18, 1942. The day before, Field Marshal von Reichenau, who had taken over Rundstedt's command, died of a stroke. General Udet of the Luftwaffe shot himself to death on November 17, 1941. Moreover, some thirty-five corps and divisional commanders were replaced during the winter retreat.

This, of course, was only a beginning. Field Marshal von Manstein summed up at Nuremberg what happened to the generals when they started losing battles or finally got up enough courage to oppose Hitler. "Of seventeen field marshals," he told the tribunal, "ten were sent home during the war and three lost their lives as a result of July 20, 1944 [the plot against Hitler—W.L.S.]. Only one field marshal managed to get through the war and keep his position. Of thirty-six full generals [*Generalobersten*] eighteen were sent home, and five died as a result of July 20 or were dishonorably discharged. Only three full generals survived the war in their positions."[1]

Prussian officer corps would react not only to their shabby treatment but to the madness of their Supreme Commander in leading them and their armies to the brink of disaster in the Russian winter. The plotters had long been convinced, as we have seen, that only the generals, in command of troops, had the physical power to overthrow the Nazi tyrant. Now was their chance before it was too late. Timing was all-important. The war, they saw, after the reverses in Russia and the entry of America into the conflict, could no longer be won. But neither was it yet lost. An anti-Nazi government in Berlin could still get peace terms, they thought, which would leave Germany a major power and, perhaps, with at least some of Hitler's gains, such as Austria, the Sudetenland and western Poland.

These thoughts had been very much in their minds at the end of the summer of 1941, even when the prospect of destroying the Soviet Union was still good. The text of the Atlantic Charter, which Churchill and Roosevelt had drawn up on August 19, had come as a heavy blow to them, especially Point 8, which had stipulated that Germany would have to be disarmed after the war pending a general disarmament agreement. To Hassell, Goerdeler, Beck and the other members of their opposition circle this meant that the Allies had no intention of distinguishing between Nazi and anti-Nazi Germans and was "proof," as Hassell put it, "that England and America are not fighting only against Hitler but also want to smash Germany and render her defenseless." Indeed, to this aristocratic former ambassador, now deep in treason against Hitler but determined to get as much as possible for a Germany without Hitler, Point 8, as he noted in his journal, "destroys every reasonable chance for peace."[2]

Disillusioned though they were by the Atlantic Charter, the conspirators seem to have been spurred to action by its promulgation, if only because it impressed them with the necessity of doing away with Hitler while there was yet time for an anti-Nazi regime to bargain advantageously for peace for a Germany which still held most of Europe. They were not adverse to using Hitler's conquests to obtain the most favorable terms for their country. The upshot of a series of talks in Berlin during the last days of August between Hassell, Popitz, Oster, Dohnanyi and General Friedrich Olbricht, chief of staff of the Home Army, was that the "German patriots," as they called themselves, would make "very moderate demands" of the Allies but, to quote Hassell again, "there are certain claims from which they could not desist." What the demands and claims were he does not say; one gathers from other entries in his diary that they amounted to an insistence on Germany's 1914 frontiers in the East plus Austria and the Sudetenland.

But time pressed. After a final conference with his confederates at the end of August, Hassell wrote in his diary: "They were unanimously convinced that it would soon be too late. When our chances for victory are obviously gone or only very slim, there will be nothing more to be done."[3]

There had been some effort to induce key generals on the Eastern front to arrest Hitler during the summer campaign in Russia. But though it inevitably proved ineffectual because the great captains were naturally too absorbed in their initial stunning victories to give any thought to overthrowing the man who had given them the opportunity to achieve them, it did plant some seeds among the military minds that would eventually sprout.

The center of the conspiracy in the Army that summer was in the headquarters of Field Marshal von Bock, whose Army Group Center was driving on Moscow. Major General Henning von Tresckow of Bock's staff, whose early enthusiasm for National Socialism had so soured as to land him in the ranks of the plotters, was the ringleader, and he was assisted by Fabian von Schlabrendorff, his A.D.C., and by two fellow conspirators whom they had planted on Bock as A.D.C.s, Count Hans von Hardenberg and Count Heinrich von Lehndorff, both scions of old and prominent German families.* One of their self-appointed tasks was to work on the Field Marshal and to persuade him to arrest Hitler on one of his visits to the army group's headquarters. But Bock was hard to work on. Though professing to loathe Nazism he had advanced too far under it and was much too vain and ambitious to take any chances at this stage of the game. Once when Tresckow tried to point out to him that the Fuehrer was leading the country to disaster, Bock shouted, "I do not allow the Fuehrer to be attacked!"[4]

Tresckow and his young aide were discouraged but not daunted. They decided to act on their own. When on August 4, 1941, the Fuehrer visited the army group's headquarters at Borisov they planned to seize him as he was driving from the airfield to Bock's quarters. But the plotters were still amateurs at this time and had not counted on the Fuehrer's security arrangements. Surrounded by his own S.S. bodyguards and declining to use one of the army group's automobiles to drive in from the airfield—he had sent ahead his own fleet of cars for this purpose—he gave the two officers no opportunity of getting near him. This fiasco—apparently there were others like it—taught the plotters who were in the Army some lessons. The first was that to get their hands on Hitler was no easy job; he was always well guarded. Another was that to seize him and arrest him might not solve the problem, since the key generals were too cowardly or too confused about their oaths of allegiance to help the opposition to carry on from there. It was about this time, the fall of 1941, that some of the young officers in the Army, many of them civilians in uniform like Schlabrendorff, reluctantly came to the conclusion that the simplest and perhaps the only solution was to kill Hitler. Then the timid generals, released from their personal oaths to the Leader, would go along with the new regime and give it the support of the Army.

But the ringleaders in Berlin were not yet ready to go so far. They were concocting an idiotic plan called "isolated action," which for some reason they thought would satisfy the consciences of the generals about breaking

---

* Lehndorff was executed by the Nazis on September 4, 1944.

their personal oaths to the Fuehrer and at the same time enable them to rid the Reich of Hitler. It is difficult, even today, to follow their minds in this, but the idea was that the top military commanders, both in the East and in the West, would simply, on a prearranged signal, refuse to obey the orders of Hitler as Commander in Chief of the Army. This of course would have been breaking their oath of obedience to the Fuehrer, but the sophists in Berlin pretended not to see that. They explained, at any event, that the real purpose of the scheme was to create confusion, in the midst of which Beck, with the help of detachments of the Home Army in Berlin, would seize power, depose Hitler and outlaw National Socialism.

The Home Army, however, was scarcely a military force but more a motley collection of recruits doing a little basic training before being shipped as replacements to the front. Some top generals in Russia or in the occupation zones who had seasoned troops at their command would have to be won over if the venture were really to succeed. One of them, who had been in on the Halder plot to arrest Hitler at the time of Munich, seemed a natural choice. This was Field Marshal von Witzleben, who was now Commander in Chief in the West. To initiate him and also General Alexander von Falkenhausen, the military commander in Belgium, into the new scheme of things Hassell was sent by the conspirators in mid-January 1942 to confer with the two generals. Already under surveillance by the Gestapo, the former ambassador used the "cover" of a lecture tour, addressing groups of German officers and occupation officials on the subject of "Living Space and Imperialism." In between lectures he conferred privately with Falkenhausen in Brussels and Witzleben in Paris, receiving a favorable impression of both of them, especially of the latter.

Shunted to the sidelines in France while his fellow field marshals were fighting great battles in Russia, Witzleben was thirsting for action. He told Hassell that the idea of "isolated action" was utopian. Direct action to overthrow Hitler was the only solution and he was willing to play a leading part. Probably the best time to strike would be during the summer of 1942 when the German offensive in Russia was resumed. To prepare for The Day he intended to be in top physical trim and would have a minor operation to put him in shape. Unfortunately for the Field Marshal and his co-conspirators this decision had disastrous consequences. Like Frederick the Great—and many others—Witzleben was troubled by hemorrhoids.* The operation to correct this painful and annoying condition was a routine case of surgery, to be sure, but when Witzleben took a brief sick leave in the spring to have it done, Hitler took advantage of the situation to retire the Field Marshal from active service, replacing him with Rundstedt, who had no stomach for conspiring against the Leader who had so recently treated him so shabbily. Thus the plotters found their chief hope in the Army to be a Field Marshal without any troops at his command. Without soldiers no new regime could be established.

---

* The Prussian King often complained about this malady, which he found hampered his mental facilities as well as his physical activities.

The leaders of the conspiracy were greatly disheartened. They kept meeting clandestinely and plotting, but they could not overcome their discouragement. "It seems at the moment," Hassell noted at the end of February 1942, after one of the innumerable meetings, "that nothing can be done about Hitler."[5]

A great deal could be done, however, about straightening out their ideas concerning the kind of government they wanted for Germany after Hitler finally was deposed and about strengthening their helter-skelter and so far quite ineffectual organization so that it could take over that government when the time came.

Most of the resistance leaders, being conservative and well on in years, wanted, for one thing, a restoration of the Hohenzollern monarchy. But for a long time they could not agree on which Hohenzollern prince to hoist on the throne. Popitz, one of the leading civilians in the ring, wanted the Crown Prince, who was anathema to most of the others. Schacht favored the oldest son of the Crown Prince, Prince Wilhelm, and Goerdeler the youngest surviving son of Wilhelm II, Prince Oskar of Prussia. All were in accord that the Kaiser's fourth son, Prince August Wilhelm, or "Auwi," as he was nicknamed, was out of the question since he was a fanatical Nazi and a *Gruppenfuehrer* in the S.S.

By the summer of 1941, however, there was more or less agreement that the most suitable candidate for the throne was Louis-Ferdinand, the second and oldest surviving son of the Crown Prince.* Then just thirty-three, a veteran of five years in the Ford factory at Dearborn, a working employee of the Lufthansa airlines and in contact and in sympathy with the plotters, this personable young man had finally emerged as the most desirable of the Hohenzollerns. He understood the twentieth century, was democratic and intelligent. Moreover, he had an attractive, sensible and courageous wife in Princess Kira, a former Russian Grand Duchess, and—an important point for the conspirators at this stage—he was a personal friend of President Roosevelt, who had invited the couple to stay in the White House during their American honeymoon in 1938.

Hassell and some of his friends were not absolutely convinced that Louis-Ferdinand was an ideal choice. "He lacks many qualities he cannot get along without," Hassell commented wryly in his diary at Christmas time, 1941. But he went along with the others.

Hassell's chief interest was in the form and nature of the future German government, and early the year before he had drawn up, after consultation with General Beck, Goerdeler and Popitz, a program for its interim stage, which he refined in a further draft at the end of 1941.[6] It restored individual freedom and pending the adoption of a permanent constitution provided for the supreme power to rest in the hands of a regent, who, as head of state, would appoint a government and a Council of State. It was

---

* Prince Wilhelm, the oldest son, had died of battle wounds in France on May 26, 1940.

all rather authoritarian and Goerdeler and the few trade-union representatives among the conspirators didn't like it, proposing instead an immediate plebiscite so that the interim regime would have popular backing and give proof of its democratic character. But for the lack of something better Hassell's plan was generally accepted at least as a statement of principles until it was superseded by a liberal and enlightened program drawn up in 1943 under pressure from the Kreisau Circle, led by Count Helmuth von Moltke.

Finally that spring of 1942 the conspirators formally adopted a leader. They had all acknowledged General Beck as such not only because of his intelligence and character but also because of his prestige among the generals, his good name in the country and his reputation abroad. However, they had been so lackadaisical in organizing that they had never actually put him in charge. A few, like Hassell, though full of admiration and respect for the former General Staff Chief, had some doubts about him.

"The principal difficulty with Beck," Hassell wrote in his diary shortly before Christmas, 1941, "is that he is very theoretical. As Popitz says, a man of tactics but little will power." This judgment, as it turned out, was not an ungrounded one and this quirk in the General's temperament and character, this surprising lack of a will to act, was to prove tragic and disastrous in the end.

Nevertheless in March 1942, after a good many secret meetings, the plotters decided, as Hassell reported, that "Beck must hold the strings," and at the end of the month, as the ambassador further noted, "Beck was formally adopted as the head of our group."[7]

Still, the conspiracy remained nebulous and the air of unreality which surrounded even the most active members of it from the first hangs over their endless talk as one tries to follow it at this stage in the records they have left. Hitler, they knew that spring, was planning to resume the offensive in Russia as soon as the ground was dry. This, they felt, could only plunge Germany farther toward the abyss. And yet, though they talked much, they did nothing. On March 28, 1942, Hassell sat in his country house at Ebenhausen and began his diary:

During the last days in Berlin I had detailed discussions with Jessen,* Beck and Goerdeler. Prospects not very good.[8]

How could they be very good? Without even any plans to act. Now. While there was still time.

It was Adolf Hitler who at this unfolding of spring, the third of the war, had plans—and the fierce will to try to carry them out.

---

* Jens Peter Jessen, a professor of economics at the University of Berlin, was one of the brains of the circle. He had become an ardent Nazi during the period between 1931 and 1933 and was one of the few genuine intellectuals in the party. He was quickly disillusioned after 1933 and soon became a fanatical anti-Nazi. Arrested for complicity in the July 20, 1944, plot against Hitler, he was executed at the Ploetzensee prison in Berlin in November of that year.

THE LAST GREAT GERMAN OFFENSIVES OF THE WAR

Although the Fuehrer's folly in refusing to allow the German armies in Russia to retreat in time had led to heavy losses in men and arms, to the demoralization of many commands and to a situation which for a few weeks in January and February 1942 threatened to end in utter catastrophe, there is little doubt that Hitler's fanatical determination to hold on and to stand and fight also helped to stem the Soviet tide. The traditional courage and endurance of the German soldiers did the rest.

By February 20 the Russian offensive from the Baltic to the Black Sea had run out of steam and at the end of March the season of deep mud set in, bringing a relative quiet to the long and bloody front. Both sides were exhausted. A German Army report of March 30, 1942, revealed what a terrible toll had been paid in the winter fighting. Of a total of 162 combat divisions in the East, only eight were ready for offensive missions. The sixteen armored divisions had between them only 140 serviceable tanks— less than the normal number for one division.[9]

While the troops were resting and refitting—indeed long before that, while they were still retreating in the midwinter snows—Hitler, who was now Commander in Chief of the Army as well as Supreme Commander of the Armed Forces, had been busy with plans for the coming summer's offensive. They were not as ambitious as those of the previous year. By now he had sense enough to see that he could not destroy all of the Red armies in a single campaign. This summer he would concentrate the bulk of his forces in the south, conquer the Caucasus oil fields, the Donets industrial basin and the wheat fields of the Kuban and take Stalingrad on the Volga. This would accomplish several prime objectives. It would deprive the Soviets of the oil and much of the food and industry they desperately needed to carry on the war, while giving the Germans the oil and the food resources they were almost as badly in need of.

"If I do not get the oil of Maikop and Grozny," Hitler told General Paulus, the commander of the ill-fated Sixth Army, just before the summer offensive began, "then I must end this war."[10]

Stalin could have said almost the same thing. He too had to have the oil of the Caucasus to stay in the war. That was where the significance of Stalingrad came in. German possession of it would block the last main route via the Caspian Sea and the Volga River over which the oil, as long as the Russians held the wells, could reach central Russia.

Besides oil to propel his planes and tanks and trucks, Hitler needed men to fill out his thinned ranks. Total casualties at the end of the winter fighting were 1,167,835, exclusive of the sick, and there were not enough replacements available to make up for such losses. The High Command turned to Germany's allies—or, rather, satellites—for additional troops. During the winter General Keitel had scurried off to Budapest and Bucharest to drum up Hungarian and Rumanian soldiers—whole divisions of them—for the coming summer. Goering and finally Hitler himself appealed to Mussolini for Italian formations.

Goering arrived in Rome at the end of January 1942 to line up Italian reinforcements for Russia, assuring Mussolini that the Soviet Union would be defeated in 1942 and that Great Britain would lay down her arms in 1943. Ciano found the fat, bemedaled Reich Marshal insufferable. "As usual he is bloated and overbearing," the Italian Foreign Minister noted in his diary on February 2. Two days later:

Goering leaves Rome. We had dinner at the Excelsior Hotel, and during the dinner Goering talked of little else but the jewels he owned. In fact, he had some beautiful rings on his fingers . . . On the way to the station he wore a great sable coat, something between what automobile drivers wore in 1906 and what a high-grade prostitute wears to the opera.[11]

The corruption and corrosion of the Number Two man in the Third Reich was making steady progress.

Mussolini promised Goering to send two Italian divisions to Russia in March if the Germans would give them artillery, but his concern about his ally's defeats on the Eastern front grew to such proportions that Hitler decided it was time for another meeting to explain how strong Germany still was.

This took place on April 29 and 30 at Salzburg, where the Duce and Ciano and their party were put up in the baroque Palace of Klessheim, once the seat of the prince-bishops and now redecorated with hangings, furniture and carpets from France, for which the Italian Foreign Minister suspected the Germans "did not pay too much." Ciano found the Fuehrer looking tired. "The winter months in Russia have borne heavily upon him," he noted in his diary. "I see for the first time that he has many gray hairs."*

There followed the usual German recital sizing up the general situation, with Ribbentrop and Hitler assuring their Italian guests that all was well —in Russia, in North Africa, in the West and on the high seas. The coming offensive in the East, they confided, would be directed against the Caucasus oil fields.

When Russia's sources of oil are exhausted [Ribbentrop said] she will be brought to her knees. Then the British . . . will bow in order to save what remains of the mauled Empire . . .
America is a big bluff . . .

Ciano, listening more or less patiently to his opposite number, got the impression, however, that in regard to what the United States might

---

* Goebbels had seen Hitler a month before at headquarters and expressed shock in his diary at his ailing. "I noted that he has already become quite gray . . . He told me he has had to fight off severe attacks of giddiness . . . The Fuehrer this time truly worries me." He had, Goebbels added, a "physical revulsion against frost and snow . . . What worries and torments the Fuehrer most is that the country is still covered with snow . . ." (*The Goebbels Diaries*, pp. 131–37.)

eventually do it was the Germans who were bluffing and that in reality, when they thought of it, "they feel shivers running down their spines."

It was the Fuehrer who, as always, did most of the talking.

Hitler talks, talks, talks [Ciano wrote in his diary]. Mussolini suffers—he, who is in the habit of talking himself, and who, instead, practically has to keep quiet. On the second day, after lunch, when everything had been said, Hitler talked uninterruptedly for an hour and forty minutes. He omitted absolutely no argument: war and peace, religion and philosophy, art and history. Mussolini automatically looked at his wrist watch . . . The Germans—poor people—have to take it every day, and I am certain there isn't a gesture, a word or a pause, which they don't know by heart. General Jodl, after an epic struggle, finally went to sleep on the divan. Keitel was reeling, but he succeeded in keeping his head up. He was too close to Hitler to let himself go . . .[12]

Despite the avalanche of talk or perhaps because of it, Hitler got the promise of more Italian cannon fodder for the Russian front. So successful were he and Keitel with all the satellites that the German High Command calculated it would have 52 "Allied" divisions available for the summer's task—27 Rumanian, 13 Hungarian, 9 Italian, 2 Slovak and one Spanish. This was one quarter of the combined Axis force in the East. Of the 41 fresh divisions which were to reinforce the southern part of the front, where the main German blow would fall, one half—or 21 divisions —were Hungarian (10), Italian (6) and Rumanian (5). Halder and most of the other generals did not like to stake so much on so many "foreign" divisions whose fighting qualities, in their opinion, were, to put it mildly, questionable. But because of their own shortage of manpower they reluctantly accepted this aid, and this decision was shortly to contribute to the disaster which ensued.

At first, that summer of 1942, the fortunes of the Axis prospered. Even before the jump-off toward the Caucasus and Stalingrad a sensational victory was scored in North Africa. On May 27, 1942, General Rommel had resumed his offensive in the desert.* Striking swiftly with his famed Afrika Korps (two armored divisions and a motorized infantry division) and eight Italian divisions, of which one was armored, he soon had the British desert army reeling back toward the Egyptian frontier. On June 21 he captured Tobruk, the key to the British defenses, which in 1941 had held out for nine months until relieved, and two days later he entered Egypt. By the end of June he was at El Alamein, sixty-five miles from Alexandria and the delta of the Nile. It seemed to many a startled Allied statesman, poring over a map, that nothing could now prevent Rommel

---

* In a savage series of battles with the British in November and December 1941, Rommel's forces had been driven back clear across Cyrenaica to the El Agheila line at its western borders. But bounding back with his customary resilience in January 1942, Rommel recaptured half of the ground lost, in a swift seventeen-day campaign which brought him back to El Gazala, from where the new drive of the end of May 1942 began.

from delivering a fatal blow to the British by conquering Egypt and then, if he were reinforced, sweeping on northeast to capture the great oil fields of the Middle East and then to the Caucasus to meet the German armies in Russia, which already were beginning their advance toward that region from the north.

It was one of the darkest moments of the war for the Allies and correspondingly one of the brightest for the Axis. But Hitler, as we have seen, had never understood global warfare. He did not know how to exploit Rommel's surprising African success. He awarded the daring leader of the Afrika Korps a field marshal's baton but he did not send him supplies or reinforcements.* Under the nagging of Admiral Raeder and the urging of Rommel, the Fuehrer had only reluctantly agreed to send the Afrika Korps and a small German air force to Libya in the first place. But he had done this only to prevent an Italian collapse in North Africa, not because he foresaw the importance of conquering Egypt.

The key to that conquest actually was the small island of Malta, lying in the Mediterranean between Sicily and the Axis bases in Libya. It was from this British bastion that bombers, submarines and surface craft wrought havoc on German and Italian vessels carrying supplies and men to North Africa. In August 1941 some 35 per cent of Rommel's supplies and reinforcements were sunk; in October, 63 per cent. By November 9 Ciano was writing sadly in his diary:

Since September 19 we had given up trying to get convoys through to Libya; every attempt had been paid for at a high price . . . Tonight we tried it again. A convoy of seven ships left, accompanied by two ten-thousand-ton cruisers and ten destroyers . . . All—I mean *all*—our ships were sunk . . . The British returned to their ports [at Malta] after having slaughtered us.[13]

Belatedly the Germans diverted several U-boats from the Battle of the Atlantic to the Mediterranean and Kesselring was given additional squadrons of planes for the bases in Sicily. It was decided to neutralize Malta and destroy, if possible, the British fleet in the eastern Mediterranean. Success was immediate. By the end of 1941 the British had lost three battleships, an aircraft carrier, two cruisers and several destroyers and

---

* Hitler's naming Rommel a field marshal the day after the capture of Tobruk caused Mussolini "much pain" because, as Ciano noted, it accentuated "the German character of the battle." The Duce left immediately for Libya to grab some honors for himself, believing that he could enter Alexandria, Ciano says, "in fifteen days." On July 2 he contacted Hitler by wire about "the question of the future political government of Egypt," proposing Rommel as the military commander and an Italian as "civilian delegate." Hitler replied that he did not consider the matter "urgent." (*Ciano Diaries*, pp. 502–04.)

"Mussolini was waiting impatiently in Derna [behind the front]," General Fritz Bayerlein, chief of staff to Rommel, later recalled, "for the day when he might take the salute at a parade of Axis tanks beneath the shadow of the Pyramids." (*The Fatal Decisions*, ed. Freidin and Richardson, p. 103.)

submarines, and what was left of their fleet was driven to Egyptian bases. Malta had been battered by German bombers day and night for weeks. As a result Axis supplies got through—in January not a ton of shipping was lost—and Rommel was able to build up his forces for the big push into Egypt.

In March Admiral Raeder talked Hitler into approving plans not only for Rommel's offensive toward the Nile (Operation Aïda) but for the capture of Malta by parachute troops (Operation Hercules). The drive from Libya was to begin at the end of May and Malta was to be assaulted in mid-July. But on June 15, while Rommel was in the midst of his initial successes, Hitler postponed the attack on Malta. He could spare neither troops nor planes from the Russian front, he explained to Raeder. A few weeks later he postponed Hercules again, saying it could wait until after the summer offensive in the East had been completed and Rommel had conquered Egypt.[14] Malta could be kept quiet in the meantime, he advised, by continued bombing.

But it was not kept quiet and for this failure either to neutralize it or to capture it the Germans would shortly pay a high price. A large British convoy got through to the besieged island on June 16, and though several warships and freighters were lost this put Malta back in business. Spitfires were flown to the island from the U.S. aircraft carrier *Wasp* and soon drove the attacking Luftwaffe bombers from the skies. Rommel felt the effect. Three quarters of his supply ships thereafter were sunk.

He had reached El Alamein with just thirteen operational tanks.* "Our strength," he wrote in his diary on July 3, "has faded away." And at a moment when the Pyramids were almost in sight, and beyond—the great prize of Egypt and Suez! This was another opportunity lost, and one of the last which Hitler would be afforded by Providence and the fortunes of war.

THE GERMAN SUMMER OFFENSIVE IN RUSSIA: 1942

By the end of the summer of 1942 Adolf Hitler seemed to be once more on top of the world. German U-boats were sinking 700,000 tons of British–American shipping a month in the Atlantic—more than could be replaced in the booming shipyards of the United States, Canada and Scotland. Though the Fuehrer had denuded his forces in the West of most of their troops and tanks and planes in order to finish with Russia, there was no sign that summer that the British and Americans were strong enough to make even a small landing from across the Channel. They had not even risked trying to occupy French-held Northwest Africa, though the weakened French, of divided loyalties, had nothing much with which to

---

* According to General Bayerlein's postwar testimony. He probably exaggerated his losses. Allied intelligence gave Rommel 125 tanks.

stop them even if they attempted to, and the Germans nothing at all except a few submarines and a handful of planes based in Italy and Tripoli.

The British Navy and Air Force had been unable to prevent Germany's two battle cruisers *Scharnhorst* and *Gneisenau* and the heavy cruiser *Prinz Eugen* from dashing up the English Channel in full daylight and making their way safely home from Brest.* Hitler had feared that the British and Americans would certainly try to occupy northern Norway—that was why he had insisted on the dash from Brest so that the three heavy ships there could be used for the defense of Norwegian waters. "Norway," he told Raeder at the end of January 1942, "is the zone of destiny." It had to be defended at all costs. As it turned out, there was no need. The Anglo-Americans had other plans for their limited forces in the West.

On the map the sum of Hitler's conquests by September 1942 looked staggering. The Mediterranean had become practically an Axis lake, with Germany and Italy holding most of the northern shore from Spain to Turkey and the southern shore from Tunisia to within sixty miles of the Nile. In fact, German troops now stood guard from the Norwegian North Cape on the Arctic Ocean to Egypt, from the Atlantic at Brest to the southern reaches of the Volga River on the border of Central Asia.

German troops of the Sixth Army had reached the Volga just north of Stalingrad on August 23. Two days before, the swastika had been hoisted on Mount Elbrus, the highest peak (18,481 feet) in the Caucasus Mountains. The Maikop oil fields, producing annually two and a half million tons of oil, had been captured on August 8, though the Germans found them almost completely destroyed, and by the twenty-fifth Kleist's tanks had arrived at Mozdok, only fifty miles from the main Soviet oil center around Grozny and a bare hundred miles from the Caspian Sea. On the thirty-first Hitler was urging Field Marshal List, commander of the armies in the Caucasus, to scrape up all available forces for the final push to Grozny so that he "could get his hands on the oil fields." On that last day of August, too, Rommel launched his offensive at El Alamein with every hope of breaking through to the Nile.

Although Hitler was never satisfied with the performance of his generals—he had sacked Field Marshal von Bock, who commanded the whole southern offensive, on July 13 and, as Halder's diary reveals, had constantly nagged and cursed most of the other commanders as well as the General Staff for not advancing fast enough—he now believed that the decisive victory was in his grasp. He ordered the Sixth Army and the Fourth Panzer Army to swing north along the Volga, after Stalingrad was taken, in a vast encircling movement which would enable him eventually to advance on central Russia and Moscow from the east as well as from

---

* This had taken place on February 11–12, 1942, and had caught the British by surprise. Only weak naval and aircraft forces were rounded up in time to attack the German fleet and they inflicted little damage. "Vice-Admiral Ciliax [who led the dash]," commented the *Times* of London, "has succeeded where the Duke of Medina Sidonia failed . . . Nothing more mortifying to the pride of sea power has happened in Home Waters since the 17th Century."

the west. He believed the Russians were finished and Halder tells of him at this moment talking of pushing with part of his forces through Iran to the Persian Gulf.[15] Soon he would link up with the Japanese in the Indian Ocean. He had no doubt of the accuracy of a German intelligence report on September 9 that the Russians had used up all their reserves on the entire front. In a conference with Admiral Raeder at the end of August his thoughts were already turning from Russia, which he said he now regarded as a "blockadeproof *Lebensraum*," to the British and Americans, who would soon, he was sure, be brought "to the point of discussing peace terms."[16]

And yet, as General Kurt Zeitzler later recalled, appearances even then, rosy as they were, were deceptive. Almost all the generals in the field, as well as those on the General Staff, saw flaws in the pretty picture. They could be summed up: the Germans simply didn't have the resources—the men or the guns or the tanks or the planes or the means of transportation —to reach the objectives Hitler had insisted on setting. When Rommel tried to tell this to the warlord in respect to Egypt, Hitler ordered him to go on sick leave in the mountains of the Semmering. When Halder and Field Marshal List attempted to do the same in regard to the Russian front, they were cashiered.

Even the rankest amateur strategist could see the growing danger to the German armies in southern Russia as Soviet resistance stiffened in the Caucasus and at Stalingrad and the season of the autumn rains approached. The long northern flank of the Sixth Army was dangerously exposed along the line of the upper Don for 350 miles from Stalingrad to Voronezh. Here Hitler had stationed three satellite armies: the Hungarian Second, south of Voronezh; the Italian Eighth, farther southeast; and the Rumanian Third, on the right at the bend of the Don just west of Stalingrad. Because of the bitter hostility of Rumanians and Hungarians to each other their armies had to be separated by the Italians. In the steppes south of Stalingrad there was a fourth satellite army, the Rumanian Fourth. Aside from their doubtful fighting qualities, all these armies were inadequately equipped, lacking armored power, heavy artillery and mobility. Furthermore, they were spread out very thinly. The Rumanian Third Army held a front of 105 miles with only sixty-nine battalions. But these "allied" armies were all Hitler had. There were not enough German units to fill the gap. And since he believed, as he told Halder, that the Russians were "finished," he did not unduly worry about this exposed and lengthy Don flank.

Yet it was the key to maintaining both the Sixth Army and the Fourth Panzer Army at Stalingrad and Army Group A in the Caucasus. Should the Don flank collapse not only would the German forces at Stalingrad be threatened with encirclement but those in the Caucasus would be cut off. Once more the Nazi warlord had gambled. It was not his first gamble of the summer's campaign.

On July 23, at the height of the offensive, he had made another. The

Russians were in full retreat between the Donets and upper-Don rivers, falling rapidly back toward Stalingrad to the east and toward the lower Don to the south. A decision had to be made. Should the German forces concentrate on taking Stalingrad and blocking the Volga River, or should they deliver their main blow in the Caucasus in quest of Russian oil? Earlier in the month Hitler had pondered this crucial question but had been unable to make up his mind. At first, the smell of oil had tempted him most, and on July 13 he had detached the Fourth Panzer Army from Army Group B, which had been driving down the Don toward the river's bend and Stalingrad just beyond, and sent it south to help Kleist's First Panzer Army get over the lower Don near Rostov and on into the Caucasus toward the oil fields. At that moment the Fourth Panzer Army probably could have raced on to Stalingrad, which was then largely undefended, and easily captured it. By the time Hitler realized his mistake it was too late, and then he compounded his error. When the Fourth Panzer Army was shifted back toward Stalingrad a fortnight later, the Russians had recovered sufficiently to be able to check it; and its departure from the Caucasus front left Kleist too weak to complete his drive to the Grozny oil fields.*

The shifting of this powerful armored unit back to the drive on Stalingrad was one result of the fatal decision which Hitler made on July 23. His fanatical determination to take *both* Stalingrad *and* the Caucasus at the same time, against the advice of Halder and the field commanders, who did not believe it could be done, was embodied in Directive No. 45, which became famous in the annals of the German Army. It was one of the most fateful of Hitler's moves in the war, for in the end, and in a very short time, it resulted in his failing to achieve either objective and led to the most humiliating defeat in the history of German arms, making certain that he could never win the war and that the days of the thousand-year Third Reich were numbered.

General Halder was appalled, and there was a stormy scene at "Werewolf" headquarters in the Ukraine near Vinnitsa to which Hitler had moved on July 16 in order to be nearer the front. The Chief of the General Staff urged that the main forces be concentrated on the taking of Stalingrad and tried to explain that the German Army simply did not possess the strength to carry out two powerful offensives in two different directions. When Hitler retorted that the Russians were "finished," Halder attempted to convince him that, according to the Army's own intelligence, this was far from the case.

---

* Kleist confirmed this to Liddell Hart: "The Fourth Panzer Army . . . could have taken Stalingrad without a fight at the end of July, but was diverted south to help me in crossing the Don. I did not need its aid, and it merely congested the roads I was using. When it turned north again a fortnight later the Russians had gathered just sufficient forces at Stalingrad to check it." By that time Kleist needed the additional tank force. "We could have reached our goal [the Grozny oil] if my forces had not been drawn away . . . to help the attack on Stalingrad," he added. (Liddell Hart, *The German Generals Talk*, pp. 169–71.)

The continual underestimation of enemy possibilities [Halder noted sadly in his diary that evening] takes on grotesque forms and is becoming dangerous. Serious work has become impossible here. Pathological reaction to momentary impressions and a complete lack of capacity to assess the situation and its possibilities give this so-called "leadership" a most peculiar character.

Later the Chief of the General Staff, whose own days at his post were now numbered, would come back to this scene and write:

Hitler's decisions had ceased to have anything in common with the principles of strategy and operations as they have been recognized for generations past. They were the product of a violent nature following its momentary impulses, which recognized no limits to possibility and which made its wish-dreams the father of its acts . . .[17]

As to what he called the Supreme Commander's "pathological over-estimation of his own strength and criminal underestimation of the enemy's," Halder later told a story:

Once when a quite objective report was read to him showing that still in 1942 Stalin would be able to muster from one to one and a quarter million fresh troops in the region north of Stalingrad and west of the Volga, not to mention half a million men in the Caucasus, and which provided proof that Russian output of front-line tanks amounted to at least 1,200 a month, Hitler flew at the man who was reading with clenched fists and foam in the corners of his mouth and forbade him to read any more of such idiotic twaddle.[18]

"You didn't have to have the gift of a prophet," says Halder, "to foresee what would happen when Stalin unleashed those million and a half troops against Stalingrad and the Don flank.* I pointed this out to Hitler very clearly. The result was the dismissal of the Chief of the Army General Staff."

This took place on September 24. Already on the ninth, upon being told by Keitel that Field Marshal List, who had the over-all command of the armies in the Caucasus, had been sacked, Halder learned that he would be the next to go. The Fuehrer, he was told, had become convinced that he "was no longer equal to the psychic demands of his position." Hitler explained this in greater detail to his General Staff Chief at their farewell meeting on the twenty-fourth.

"You and I have been suffering from nerves. Half of my nervous exhaustion is due to you. It is not worth it to go on. We need National

---

* Halder relates that "quite by accident" he came across in the Ukraine about that time a book about Stalin's defeat of General Denikin between the Don bend and Stalingrad during the Russian Civil War. He says the situation then was very similar to that of 1942 and that Stalin exploited "masterfully" Denikin's weak defenses along the Don. "Hence," he adds, "came the changing of the name of the city from 'Tsaritsyn' to 'Stalingrad.'"

Socialist ardor now, not professional ability. I cannot expect this of an officer of the old school such as you."

"So spoke," Halder commented later, "not a responsible warlord but a political fanatic."[19]

And so departed Franz Halder. He was not without his faults, which were similar to those of his predecessor, General Beck, in that his mind was often confused and his will to action paralyzed. And though he had often stood up to Hitler, however ineffectually, he had also, like all of the other Army officers who enjoyed high rank during World War II, gone along with him and for a long time abetted his outrageous aggressions and his conquests. Yet he had retained some of the virtues of more civilized times. He was the last of the old-school General Staff chiefs that the Army of the Third Reich would have.* He was replaced by General Kurt Zeitzler, a younger officer of a different stripe who was serving as chief of staff to Rundstedt in the West, and who endured in the post, which once—especially in the First World War—had been the highest and most powerful in the German Army, as little more than the Fuehrer's office boy until the attempt against the dictator's life in July 1944.†

A change in General Staff chiefs did not change the situation of the German Army, whose twin drives on Stalingrad and the Caucasus had now been halted by stiffening Soviet resistance itself. All through October bitter street fighting continued in Stalingrad itself. The Germans made some progress, from building to building, but with staggering losses, for the rubble of a great city, as everyone who has experienced modern warfare knows, gives many opportunities for stubborn and prolonged defense and the Russians, disputing desperately every foot of the debris, made the most of them. Though Halder and then his successor warned Hitler that the troops in Stalingrad were becoming exhausted, the Supreme Commander insisted that they push on. Fresh divisions were thrown in and were soon ground to pieces in the inferno.

Instead of a means to an end—the end had already been achieved when German formations reached the western banks of the Volga north and south of the city and cut off the river's traffic—Stalingrad had become an end in itself. To Hitler its capture was now a question of personal pres-

---

* The sacking of Halder was a loss not only to the Army but to historians of the Third Reich, for his invaluable diary ends on September 24, 1942. He was eventually arrested, placed in the concentration camp at Dachau along with such illustrious prisoners as Schuschnigg and Schacht and liberated by U.S. forces at Niederdorf, South Tyrol, on April 28, 1945. Since then, up to the time of writing, he has collaborated with the U.S. Army in a number of military historical studies of World War II. His generosity to this writer in answering queries and pointing out sources has already been noted.

† The faithful and fanatically loyal General Jodl, Chief of Operations at OKW, also was in Hitler's doghouse at this time. He had opposed the sacking of Field Marshal List and General Halder and his defense of them sent Hitler into such a rage that for months he refused to shake hands with Jodl or dine with him or any other staff officer. Hitler was on the point of firing Jodl at the end of January 1943 and replacing him with General Paulus, but it was too late. Paulus, as we shall shortly see, was no longer available.

tige. When even Zeitzler got up enough nerve to suggest to the Fuehrer that in view of the danger to the long northern flank along the Don the Sixth Army should be withdrawn from Stalingrad to the elbow of the Don, Hitler flew into a fury. "Where the German soldier sets foot, there he remains!" he stormed.

Despite the hard going and the severe losses, General Paulus, commander of the Sixth Army, informed Hitler by radio on October 25 that he expected to complete the capture of Stalingrad at the latest by November 10. Cheered up by this assurance, Hitler issued orders the next day that the Sixth Army and the Fourth Panzer Army, which was fighting south of the city, should prepare to push north and south along the Volga as soon as Stalingrad had fallen.

It was not that Hitler was ignorant of the threat to the Don flank. The OKW diaries make clear that it caused him considerable worry. The point is that he did not take it seriously enough and that, as a consequence, he did nothing to avert it. Indeed, so confident was he that the situation was well in hand that on the last day of October he, the staff of OKW and the Army General Staff abandoned their headquarters at Vinnitsa in the Ukraine and returned to Wolfsschanze at Rastenburg. The Fuehrer had practically convinced himself that if there were to be any Soviet winter offensive at all it would come on the central and northern fronts. He could handle that better from his quarters in East Prussia.

Hardly had he returned there when bad news reached him from another and more distant front. Field Marshal Rommel's Afrika Korps was in trouble.

THE FIRST BLOW: EL ALAMEIN AND THE ANGLO–AMERICAN LANDINGS

The Desert Fox, as he was called on both sides of the front, had resumed his offensive at El Alamein on August 31 with the intention of rolling up the British Eighth Army and driving on to Alexandria and the Nile. There was a violent battle in the scorching heat on the 40-mile desert front between the sea and the Qattara Depression, but Rommel could not quite make it and on September 3 he broke off the fighting and went over to the defensive. At long last the British army in Egypt had received strong reinforcements in men, guns, tanks and planes (many of the last two from America). It had also received on August 15 two new commanders: an eccentric but gifted general named Sir Bernard Law Montgomery, who took over the Eighth Army, and General Sir Harold Alexander, who was to prove to be a skillful strategist and a brilliant administrator and who now assumed the post of Commander in Chief in the Middle East.

Shortly after his setback Rommel had gone on sick leave on the Semmering in the mountains below Vienna to receive a cure for an infected nose and a swollen liver, and it was there that on the afternoon of October

24 he received a telephone call from Hitler. "Rommel, the news from Africa sounds bad. The situation seems somewhat obscure. Nobody appears to know what has happened to General Stumme.* Do you feel capable of returning to Africa and taking over there again?"[20] Though a sick man, Rommel agreed to return immediately.

By the time he got back to headquarters west of El Alamein on the following evening, the battle, which Montgomery had launched at 9:40 P.M. on October 23, was already lost. The Eighth Army had too many guns, tanks and planes, and though the Italian–German lines still held and Rommel made desperate efforts to shift his battered divisions to stem the various attacks and even to counterattack he realized that his situation was hopeless. He had no reserves: of men, or tanks or oil. The R.A.F., for once, had complete command of the skies and was pounding his troops and armor and remaining supply dumps mercilessly.

On November 2, Montgomery's infantry and armor broke through on the southern sector of the front and began to overrun the Italian divisions there. That evening Rommel radioed Hitler's headquarters in East Prussia two thousand miles away that he could no longer hold out and that he intended to withdraw, while there was still the opportunity, to the Fûka position forty miles to the west.

He had already commenced to do so when a long message came over the air the next day from the Supreme warlord:

To Field Marshal Rommel:

I and the German people are watching the heroic defensive battle waged in Egypt with faithful trust in your powers of leadership and in the bravery of the German–Italian troops under your command. In the situation in which you now find yourself, there can be no other consideration save that of holding fast, of not retreating one step, of throwing every gun and every man into the battle . . . You can show your troops no other way than that which leads to victory or to death.

Adolf Hitler[21]

This idiotic order meant, if obeyed, that the Italo–German armies were condemned to swift annihilation and for the first time in Africa, Bayerlein says, Rommel did not know what to do. After a brief struggle with his conscience he decided, over the protests of General Ritter von Thoma, the actual commander of the German Afrika Korps, who said he was withdrawing in any case,† to obey his Supreme Commander. "I finally com-

---

* Stumme, who was acting commander in the absence of Rommel, had died of a heart attack the first night of the British offensive while fleeing on foot over the desert from a British patrol that had almost captured him.

† The next day, November 4—after telling Bayerlein, "Hitler's order is a piece of unparalleled madness. I can't go along with this any longer"—General von Thoma donned a clean uniform, with the insignia of his rank and his decorations, stood by his burning tank until a British unit arrived, surrendered and in the evening dined with Montgomery at his headquarters mess.

pelled myself to take this decision," Rommel wrote later in his diary, "because I myself have always demanded unconditional obedience from my soldiers and I therefore wished to accept this principle for myself." Later, as a subsequent diary entry declares, he learned better.

Reluctantly Rommel gave the order to halt the withdrawal and at the same time sent off a courier by plane to Hitler to try to explain to him that unless he were permitted to fall back immediately all would be lost. But events were already making that trip unnecessary. On the evening of November 4, at the risk of being court-martialed for disobedience, Rommel decided to save what was left of his forces and retreat to Fûka. Only the remnants of the armored and motorized units could be extricated. The foot soldiers, mostly Italian, were left behind to surrender, as indeed the bulk of them already had done.* On November 5 came a curt message from the Fuehrer: "I agree to the withdrawal of your army into the Fûka position." But that position already had been overrun by Montgomery's tanks. Within fifteen days Rommel had fallen back seven hundred miles to beyond Benghazi with the remnants of his African army—some 25,000 Italians, 10,000 Germans and sixty tanks—and there was no opportunity to stop even there.

This was the beginning of the end for Adolf Hitler, the most decisive battle of the war yet won by his enemies, though a second and even more decisive one was just about to begin on the snowy steppes of southern Russia. But before it did, the Fuehrer was to hear further bad news from North Africa which spelled the doom of the Axis in that part of the world.

Already on November 3, when the first reports had come in of Rommel's disaster, the Fuehrer's headquarters had received word that an Allied armada had been sighted assembling at Gibraltar. No one at OKW could make out what it might be up to. Hitler was inclined to think it was merely another heavily guarded convoy for Malta. This is interesting because more than a fortnight earlier, on October 15, the OKW staff chiefs had discussed several reports about an imminent "Anglo–Saxon landing" in West Africa. The intelligence apparently came from Rome, for Ciano a week before, on October 9, noted in his diary after a talk with the chief of the military secret service that "the Anglo–Saxons are preparing to land in force in North Africa." The news depressed Ciano; he foresaw—correctly, as it turned out—that this would lead inevitably to a direct Allied assault on Italy.

Hitler, preoccupied as he was with the failure of the Russians to cease their infernal resistance, did not take this first intelligence very seriously. At a meeting of OKW on October 15, Jodl suggested that Vichy France be permitted to send reinforcements to North Africa so that the French could repel any Anglo–American landings. The Fuehrer, according to the OKW Diary, turned the suggestion down because it might ruffle the Italians, who were jealous of any move to strengthen France. At the Supreme Com-

---

* Rommel's losses at El Alamein were 59,000 killed, wounded and captured, of whom 34,000 were Germans, out of a total force of 96,000 men.

mander's headquarters the matter appears to have been forgotten until November 3. But on that day, although German agents on the Spanish side of Gibraltar had reported seeing a great Anglo–American fleet gathering there, Hitler was too busy rallying Rommel at El Alamein to bother with what appeared to him to be merely another convoy for Malta.

On November 5, OKW was informed that one British naval force had sailed out of Gibraltar headed east. But it was not until the morning of November 7, twelve hours before American and British troops began landing in North Africa, that Hitler gave the latest intelligence from Gibraltar some thought. The forenoon reports received at his headquarters in East Prussia were that British naval forces in Gibraltar and a vast fleet of transports and warships from the Atlantic had joined up and were steaming east into the Mediterranean. There was a long discussion among the staff officers and the Fuehrer. What did it all mean? What was the objective of such a large naval force? Hitler was now inclined to believe, he said, that the Western Allies might be attempting a major landing with some four or five divisions at Tripoli or Benghazi in order to catch Rommel in the rear. Admiral Krancke, the naval liaison officer at OKW, declared that there could not be more than two enemy divisions at the most. Even so! Something had to be done. Hitler asked that the Luftwaffe in the Mediterranean be immediately reinforced but was told this was impossible "for the moment." Judging by the OKW Diary all that Hitler did that morning was to notify Rundstedt, Commander in Chief in the West, to be ready to carry out "Anton." This was the code word for the occupation of the rest of France.

Whereupon the Supreme Commander, heedless of this ominous news or of the plight of Rommel, who would be trapped if the Anglo–Americans landed behind him, or of the latest intelligence warning of an imminent Russian counteroffensive on the Don in the rear of the Sixth Army at Stalingrad, entrained after lunch on November 7 for Munich, where on the next evening he was scheduled to deliver his annual speech to his old party cronies gathered to celebrate the anniversary of the Beer Hall Putsch!*

The politician in him, as Halder noted, had got the upper hand of the soldier at a critical moment in the war. Supreme Headquarters in East Prussia was left in charge of a colonel, one Freiherr Treusch von Buttlar-Brandenfels. Generals Keitel and Jodl, the chief officers of OKW, went along to participate in the beerhouse festivities. There is something weird and batty about such goings on that take the Supreme warlord, who by now was insisting on directing the war on far-flung fronts down to the divisional or regimental or even battalion level, thousands of miles from the battlefields on an unimportant political errand at a moment when the

---

* I learn from Hitler's captured daily calendar book that the celebration had been moved from the old Buergerbräukeller, where the putsch had taken place, to a more elegant beer hall in Munich, the Loewenbräukeller. The Buergerbräukeller, it will be remembered, had been wrecked by a time bomb which had just missed killing the Fuehrer on the night of November 8, 1939.

house is beginning to fall in. A change in the man, a corrosion, a deterioration has set in, as it already had with Goering who, though his once all-powerful Luftwaffe had been steadily declining, was becoming more and more attached to his jewels and his toy trains, with little time to spare for the ugly realities of a prolonged and increasingly bitter war.

Anglo–American troops under General Eisenhower hit the beaches of Morocco and Algeria at 1:30 A.M. on November 8, 1942, and at 5:30 Ribbentrop was on the phone from Munich to Ciano in Rome to give him the news.

He was rather nervous [Ciano wrote in his diary] and wanted to know what we intended to do. I must confess that, having been caught unawares, I was too sleepy to give a very satisfactory answer.

The Italian Foreign Minister learned from the German Embassy that the officials there were "literally terrified by the blow."

Hitler's special train from East Prussia did not arrive in Munich until 3:40 that afternoon and the first reports he got about the Allied landings in Northwest Africa were optimistic.[22] Everywhere the French, he was told, were putting up stubborn resistance, and at Algiers and Oran they had repulsed the landing attempts. In Algeria, Germany's friend, Admiral Darlan, was organizing the defense with the approval of the Vichy regime. Hitler's first reactions were confused. He ordered the garrison at Crete, which was quite outside the new theater of war, immediately strengthened, explaining that such a step was as important as sending reinforcements to Africa. He instructed the Gestapo to bring Generals Weygand and Giraud* to Vichy and to keep them under surveillance. He asked Field Marshal von Rundstedt to set in action Anton but not to cross the line of demarcation in France until he had further orders. And he requested Ciano† and Pierre Laval, who was now Premier of Vichy France, to meet him in Munich the next day.

For about twenty-four hours Hitler toyed with the idea of trying to make an alliance with France in order to bring her into the war against Britain and America and, at the moment, to strengthen the resolve of the Pétain government to oppose the Allied landings in North Africa. He probably was encouraged in this by the action of Pétain in breaking off diplomatic relations with the United States on the morning of Sunday, November 8, and by the aged French Marshal's statement to the U.S.

---

* General Giraud at that moment was arriving in Algiers. He had escaped from a German POW camp and settled in the south of France, where he was taken off by a British submarine on November 5 and brought to Gibraltar to confer with Eisenhower just before the landings.

† "During the night," Ciano wrote in his diary on November 9, "Ribbentrop telephoned. Either the Duce or I must go to Munich as soon as possible. Laval will also be there. I wake up the Duce. He is not very anxious to leave, especially since he is not feeling very well. I shall go."

chargé d'affaires that his forces would resist the Anglo–American invasion. The OKW Diary for that Sunday emphasizes that Hitler was preoccupied with working out "a far-reaching collaboration with the French." That evening the German representative in Vichy, Krug von Nidda, submitted a proposal to Pétain for a close alliance between Germany and France.[23]

By the next day, following his speech to the party veterans, in which he proclaimed that Stalingrad was "firmly in German hands," the Fuehrer had changed his mind. He told Ciano he had no illusions about the French desire to fight and that he had decided on "the total occupation of France, a landing in Corsica, a bridgehead in Tunisia." This decision, though not the timing, was communicated to Laval when he arrived in Munich by car on November 10. This traitorous Frenchman promptly promised to urge Pétain to accede to the Fuehrer's wishes but suggested that the Germans go ahead with their plans without waiting for the senile old Marshal's approval, which Hitler fully intended to do. Ciano has left a description of the Vichy Premier, who was executed for treason after the war.

Laval, with his white tie and middle-class French peasant attire, is very much out of place in the great salon among so many uniforms. He tries to speak in a familiar tone about his trip and his long sleep in the car, but his words go unheeded. Hitler treats him with frigid courtesy . . .

The poor man could not even imagine the *fait accompli* that the Germans were to place before him. Not a word was said to Laval about the impending action—that the orders to occupy France were being given while he was smoking his cigarette and conversing with various people in the next room. Von Ribbentrop told me that Laval would be informed only the next morning at 8 o'clock that on account of information received during the night Hitler had been obliged to proceed to the total occupation of the country.[24]

The orders for the seizure of unoccupied France, in clear violation of the armistice agreement, were given by Hitler at 8:30 P.M. on November 10 and carried out the next morning without any other incident than a futile protest by Pétain. The Italians occupied Corsica, and German planes began flying in troops to seize French-held Tunisia before Eisenhower's forces could get there.

There was one further—and typical—piece of Hitlerian deceit. On November 13 the Fuehrer assured Pétain that neither the Germans nor the Italians would occupy the naval base at Toulon, where the French fleet had been tied up since the armistice. On November 25 the OKW Diary recorded that Hitler had decided to carry out "Lila" as soon as possible.* This was the code word for the occupation of Toulon and the

---

* It is only fair to point out that Hitler strongly suspected, not without reason, that the French fleet might try to sail for Algeria and join the Allies. Despite his treacherous dealings with the Germans and his violent hatred of the British, Admiral

capture of the French fleet. On the morning of the twenty-seventh German troops attacked the naval port, but French sailors held them up long enough to allow the crews, on the orders of Admiral de Laborde, to scuttle the ships. The French fleet was thus lost to the Axis, which badly needed its warships in the Mediterranean, but it was denied also to the Allies, to whom it would have been a most valuable addition.

Hitler won the race against Eisenhower to seize Tunisia, but it was a doubtful victory. At his insistence nearly a quarter of a million German and Italian troops were poured in to hold this bridgehead. If the Fuehrer had sent one fifth as many troops and tanks to Rommel a few months before, the Desert Fox most probably would have been beyond the Nile by now, the Anglo–American landing in Northwest Africa could not have taken place and the Mediterranean would have been irretrievably lost to the Allies, thus securing the soft undercover of the Axis belly. As it was, every soldier and tank and gun rushed by Hitler to Tunisia that winter as well as the remnants of the Afrika Korps would be lost by the end of the spring and more German troops would be marched into prisoner-of-war cages than at Stalingrad, to which we must now return.*

DISASTER AT STALINGRAD

Hitler and the principal generals of OKW were lingering on in the pleasant Alpine surroundings of Berchtesgaden when the first news of the Russian counteroffensive on the Don reached them a few hours after it had been launched in a blizzard at dawn on November 19. Though a Soviet attack in this region had been expected it was not believed at OKW that it would amount to enough to warrant Hitler and his chief military advisers, Keitel and Jodl, hurrying back to headquarters in East Prussia after the Fuehrer's ringing beerhouse speech to the old party comrades in Munich on the evening of November 8. So they had puttered about on the Obersalzberg taking in the mountain air.

Their peace and quiet was abruptly broken by an urgent telephone call from General Zeitzler, the new Chief of the Army General Staff, who had remained behind at Rastenburg. He had what the OKW Diary recorded

---

Darlan, who happened to be visiting an ailing son at Algiers, had been pressed into service by Eisenhower as French commander in North Africa not only because he seemed to be the only officer who could get the French Army and Navy to cease resisting the Anglo–American landings but also in the hope that he could get the admiral commanding in Tunisia to oppose the German landings there and also induce the French fleet in Toulon to make a dash for North Africa. The hopes proved vain, although Darlan tried. To his message ordering Admiral de Laborde to bring the fleet over from Toulon he received an answer in one expressive—if indelicate—word: "*Merde.*" (See the *Procès du M. Pétain.*)

* Some 125,000 Germans, according to General Eisenhower, out of a total of 240,000 Axis troops, the rest being Italian. This number includes only those who surrendered during the last week of the campaign—May 5 to 12, 1943. (*Crusade in Europe,* p. 156.)

as "alarming news." In the very first hours of the attack an overwhelming Russian armored force had broken clean through the Rumanian Third Army between Serafimovich and Kletskaya on the Don just northwest of Stalingrad. South of the besieged city other powerful Soviet forces were attacking strongly against the German Fourth Panzer Army and the Rumanian Fourth Army and threatening to pierce their fronts.

The Russian objective was obvious to anyone who looked at a map and especially obvious to Zeitzler who, from Army intelligence, knew that the enemy had massed thirteen armies, with thousands of tanks, in the south to achieve it. The Russians were clearly driving in great strength from the north and the south to cut off Stalingrad and to force the German Sixth Army there to either beat a hasty retreat to the west or see itself surrounded. Zeitzler later contended that as soon as he saw what was happening he urged Hitler to permit the Sixth Army to withdraw from Stalingrad to the Don bend, where the broken front could be restored. The mere suggestion threw the Fuehrer into a tantrum.

"I won't leave the Volga! I won't go back from the Volga!" he shouted, and that was that. This decision, taken in such a fit of frenzy, led promptly to disaster. The Fuehrer personally ordered the Sixth Army to stand fast around Stalingrad.[25]

Hitler and his staff returned to headquarters on November 22. By this time, the fourth day of the attack, the news was catastrophic. The two Soviet forces from the north and south had met at Kalach, forty miles west of Stalingrad on the Don bend. In the evening a wireless message arrived from General Paulus, commander of the Sixth Army, confirming that his troops were now surrounded. Hitler promptly radioed back, telling Paulus to move his headquarters into the city and form a hedgehog defense. The Sixth Army would be supplied by air until it could be relieved.

But this was futile talk. There were now twenty German and two Rumanian divisions cut off at Stalingrad. Paulus radioed that they would need a minimum of 750 tons of supplies a day flown in. This was far beyond the capacity of the Luftwaffe, which lacked the required number of transport planes. Even if they had been available, not all of them could have got through in the blizzardy weather and over an area where the Russians had now established fighter superiority. Nevertheless, Goering assured Hitler that the Air Force could do the job. It never began to.

The relief of the Sixth Army was a more practical and encouraging possibility. On November 25 Hitler had recalled Field Marshal von Manstein, the most gifted of his field commanders, from the Leningrad front and put him in charge of a newly created formation, Army Group Don. His assignment was to push through from the southwest and relieve the Sixth Army at Stalingrad.

But now the Fuehrer imposed impossible conditions on his new commander. Manstein tried to explain to him that the only chance of success lay in the Sixth Army's breaking out of Stalingrad to the west while his own forces, led by the Fourth Panzer Army, pressed northeast against the Russian armies which lay between the two German forces. But once again Hitler refused to draw back from the Volga. The Sixth Army must remain in Stalingrad and Manstein must fight his way to it there.

This, as Manstein tried to argue with the Supreme warlord, could not be done. The Russians were too strong. Nevertheless, with a heavy heart, Manstein launched his attack on December 12. It was called, appropriately, "Operation Winter Gale," for the full fury of the Russian winter had now hit the southern steppes, piling up the snow in drifts and dropping the temperature below zero. At first the offensive made good progress, the Fourth Panzer Army, under General Hoth, driving northeast up both sides of the railroad from Kotelnikovski toward Stalingrad, some seventy-five miles away. By December 19 it had advanced to within some forty miles of the southern perimeter of the city; by the twenty-first it was within thirty miles, and across the snowy steppes the besieged troops of the Sixth Army could see at night the signal flares of their rescuers.

At this moment, according to the later testimony of the German generals, a breakout from Stalingrad of the Sixth Army toward the advancing lines of the Fourth Panzer Army would almost certainly have succeeded. But once again Hitler forbade it. On December 21, Zeitzler had wrung permission from the Leader for the troops of Paulus to break out *provided* they also held on to Stalingrad. This piece of foolishness, the General Staff Chief says, nearly drove him insane.

"On the following evening," Zeitzler related later, "I begged Hitler to authorize the breakout. I pointed out that this was absolutely our last chance to save the two hundred thousand men of Paulus' army."

Hitler would not give way. In vain I described to him conditions inside the so-called fortress: the despair of the starving soldiers, their loss of confidence in the Supreme Command, the wounded expiring for lack of proper attention while thousands froze to death. He remained as impervious to arguments of this sort as to those others which I had advanced.

In the face of increasing Russian resistance in front of him and on his flanks General Hoth lacked the strength to negotiate that last thirty miles to Stalingrad. He believed that if the Sixth Army broke out he could still make a junction with it and then both forces could withdraw to Kotelnikovski. This at least would save a couple of hundred thousand German lives.* Probably for a day or two—between December 21 and 23—this could

---

* In his postwar memoirs, Field Marshal von Manstein says that on December 19, in disobedience to Hitler's orders, he actually directed the Sixth Army to begin to break out of Stalingrad to the southwest and make a junction with the Fourth Panzer Army. He publishes the text of the directive. But it contained certain reservations and Paulus, who still was under orders from Hitler not to break out, must have been greatly confused by it. "This," declares Manstein, "was our one and only chance of saving the Sixth Army." (Manstein, *Lost Victories*, pp. 336–41, 562–63.)

have been done, but by the latter date it had become impossible. For unknown to Hoth the Red Army had struck farther north and was now endangering the left flank of Manstein's whole Army Group Don. On the night of December 22, Manstein telephoned Hoth to prepare himself for drastic new orders. The next day they came. Hoth was to abandon his drive on Stalingrad, dispatch one of his three panzer divisions to the Don front on the north, and defend himself where he was and with what he had left as well as he could.

The attempt to relieve Stalingrad had failed.

Manstein's drastic new orders had come as the result of alarming news that reached him on December 17. On the morning of that day a Soviet army had broken through the Italian Eighth Army farther up the Don at Boguchar and by evening opened a gap twenty-seven miles deep. Within three days the hole was ninety miles wide, the Italians were fleeing in panic and the Rumanian Third Army to the south, which already had been badly pummeled on the opening day of the Russian offensive on November 19, was also disintegrating. No wonder Manstein had had to take part of Hoth's armored forces to help stem the gap. A chain reaction followed.

Not only the Don armies fell back but also Hoth's forces, which had come so close to Stalingrad. These retreats in turn endangered the German Army in the Caucasus, which would be cut off if the Russians reached Rostov on the Sea of Azov. A day or two after Christmas Zeitzler pointed out to Hitler, "Unless you order a withdrawal from the Caucasus now, we shall soon have a second Stalingrad on our hands." Reluctantly the Supreme Commander issued the necessary instructions on December 29 to Kleist's Army Group A, which comprised the First Panzer and Seventeenth armies, and which had failed in its mission to grab the rich oil fields of Grozny. It too began a long retreat after having been within sight of its goal.

The reverses of the Germans in Russia and of the Italo–German armies in North Africa stirred Mussolini to thought. Hitler had invited him to come to Salzburg for a talk around the middle of December and the ailing Duce, now on a strict diet for stomach disorders, had accepted, though, as he told Ciano, he would go on one condition only: that he take his meals alone "because he does not want a lot of ravenous Germans to notice that he is compelled to live on rice and milk."

The time had come, Mussolini decided, to tell Hitler to cut his losses in the East, make some sort of deal with Stalin and concentrate Axis strength on defending the rest of North Africa, the Balkans and Western Europe. "Nineteen forty-three will be the year of the Anglo–American effort," he told Ciano. Hitler was unable to leave his Eastern headquarters in order to meet Mussolini, so Ciano made the long journey to Rastenburg on December 18 on his behalf, repeating to the Nazi leader the Duce's proposals. Hitler scorned them and assured the Italian Foreign Minister that without at all weakening the Russian front he could send additional forces to North Africa, which must, he said, be held. Ciano found German spirits at a low ebb at headquarters, despite Hitler's confident assurances.

The atmosphere is heavy. To the bad news there should perhaps be added the sadness of that humid forest and the boredom of collective living in the barracks . . . No one tries to conceal from me the unhappiness over the news of the breakthrough on the Russian front. There were open attempts to put the blame on us.

At that very moment the survivors of the Italian Eighth Army on the Don were scurrying for their lives, and when one member of Ciano's party asked an OKW officer whether the Italians had suffered heavy losses he was told, "No losses at all: they are running."[26]

The German troops in the Caucasus and on the Don, if not running, were getting out as quickly as they could to avoid being cut off. Each day, as the year 1943 began, they withdrew a little farther from Stalingrad. The time had now come for the Russians to finish off the Germans there. But first they gave the doomed soldiers of the Sixth Army an opportunity to save their lives.

On the morning of January 8, 1943, three young Red Army officers, bearing a white flag, entered the German lines on the northern perimeter of Stalingrad and presented General Paulus with an ultimatum from General Rokossovski, commander of the Soviet forces on the Don front. After reminding him that his army was cut off and could not be relieved or kept supplied from the air, the note said:

The situation of your troops is desperate. They are suffering from hunger, sickness and cold. The cruel Russian winter has scarcely yet begun. Hard frosts, cold winds and blizzards still lie ahead. Your soldiers are unprovided with winter clothing and are living in appalling sanitary conditions . . . Your situation is hopeless, and any further resistance senseless.

In view of [this] and in order to avoid unnecessary bloodshed, we propose that you accept the following terms of surrender . . .

They were honorable terms. All prisoners would be given "normal rations." The wounded, sick and frostbitten would receive medical treatment. All prisoners could retain their badges of rank, decorations and personal belongings. Paulus was given twenty-four hours to reply.

He immediately radioed the text of the ultimatum to Hitler and asked for freedom of action. His request was curtly dismissed by the Supreme warlord. Twenty-four hours after the expiration of the time limit on the demand for surrender, on the morning of January 10, the Russians opened the last phase of the Battle of Stalingrad with an artillery bombardment from five thousand guns.

The fighting was bitter and bloody. Both sides fought with incredible bravery and recklessness over the frozen wasteland of the city's rubble—but not for long. Within six days the German pocket had been reduced by half, to an area fifteen miles long and nine miles deep at its widest. By January 24 it had been split in two and the last small emergency airstrip lost. The planes which had brought in some supplies, especially medicines for the sick and wounded, and which had flown out 29,000 hospital cases, could no longer land.

Once more the Russians gave their courageous enemy a chance to surrender. Soviet emissaries arrived at the German lines on January 24 with a new offer. Again Paulus, torn between his duty to obey the mad Fuehrer and his obligation to save his own surviving troops from annihilation, appealed to Hitler.

Troops without ammunition [he radioed on the twenty-fourth] or food . . . Effective command no longer possible . . . 18,000 wounded without any supplies or dressings or drugs . . . Further defense senseless. Collapse inevitable. Army requests immediate permission to surrender in order to save lives of remaining troops.

Hitler's answer has been preserved.

Surrender is forbidden. Sixth Army will hold their positions to the last man and the last round and by their heroic endurance will make an unforgettable contribution toward the establishment of a defensive front and the salvation of the Western world.

The Western world! It was a bitter pill for the men of the Sixth Army who had fought against that world in France and Flanders but a short time ago.

Further resistance was not only senseless and futile but impossible, and as the month of January 1943 approached its end the epic battle wore itself out, expiring like the flame of an expended candle which sputters and dies. By January 28 what was left of a once great army was split into three small pockets, in the southern one of which General Paulus had his headquarters in the cellar of the ruins of the once thriving Univermag department store. According to one eyewitness the commander in chief sat on his camp bed in a darkened corner in a state of near collapse.

He was scarcely in the mood, nor were his soldiers, to appreciate the flood of congratulatory radiograms that now began to pour in. Goering, who had whiled away a good part of the winter in sunny Italy, strutting about in his great fur coat and fingering his jewels, sent a radio message on January 28.

The fight put up by the Sixth Army will go down in history, and future generations will speak proudly of a Langemarck of daredeviltry, an Alcázar of tenacity, a Narvik of courage and a Stalingrad of self-sacrifice.

Nor were they cheered when on the last evening, January 30, 1943, the tenth anniversary of the Nazis' coming to power, they listened to the fat Reich Marshal's bombastic broadcast.

A thousand years hence Germans will speak of this battle [of Stalingrad] with reverence and awe, and will remember that in spite of everything Germany's ultimate victory was decided there . . . In years to come it will be said of the heroic battle on the Volga: When you come to Germany, say that you have seen us lying at Stalingrad, as our honor and our leaders ordained that we should, for the greater glory of Germany.

The glory and the horrible agony of the Sixth Army had now come to an end. On January 30, Paulus radioed Hitler: "Final collapse cannot be delayed more than twenty-four hours."

This signal prompted the Supreme Commander to shower a series of promotions on the doomed officers in Stalingrad, apparently in the hope that such honors would strengthen their resolve to die gloriously at their bloody posts. "There is no record in military history of a German Field Marshal being taken prisoner," Hitler remarked to Jodl, and thereupon conferred on Paulus, by radio, the coveted marshal's baton. Some 117 other officers were jumped up a grade. It was a macabre gesture.

The end itself was anticlimactic. Late on the last day of January Paulus got off his final message to headquarters.

The Sixth Army, true to their oath and conscious of the lofty importance of their mission, have held their position to the last man and the last round for Fuehrer and Fatherland unto the end.

At 7:45 P.M. the radio operator at Sixth Army headquarters sent a last message on his own: "The Russians are at the door of our bunker. We are destroying our equipment." He added the letters "CL"—the international wireless code signifying "This station will no longer transmit."

There was no last-minute fighting at headquarters. Paulus and his staff did not hold out to the last man. A squad of Russians led by a junior officer peered into the commander in chief's darkened hole in the cellar. The Russians demanded surrender and the Sixth Army's chief of staff, General Schmidt, accepted. Paulus sat dejected on his camp bed. When Schmidt addressed him—"May I ask the Field Marshal if there is anything more to be said?"—Paulus was too weary to answer.

Farther north a small German pocket, containing all that was left of two panzer and four infantry divisions, still held out in the ruins of a tractor factory. On the night of February 1 it received a message from Hitler's headquarters.

The German people expect you to do your duty exactly as did the troops holding the southern fortress. Every day and every hour that you continue to fight facilitates the building of a new front.

Just before noon on February 2, this group surrendered after a last message to the Supreme Commander: ". . . Have fought to the last man against vastly superior forces. Long live Germany!"

Silence at last settled on the snow-covered, blood-spattered shambles of the battlefield. At 2:46 P.M. on February 2 a German reconnaissance plane flew high over the city and radioed back: "No sign of any fighting at Stalingrad."

By that time 91,000 German soldiers, including twenty-four generals, half-starved, frostbitten, many of them wounded, all of them dazed and broken, were hobbling over the ice and snow, clutching their blood-caked blankets over their heads against the 24-degrees-below-zero cold toward the dreary, frozen prisoner-of-war camps of Siberia. Except for some 20,000 Rumanians and the 29,000 wounded who had been evacuated by air they were all that was left of a conquering army that had numbered 285,000 men two months before. The rest had been slaughtered. And of those 91,000 Germans who began the weary march into captivity that winter day, only 5,000 were destined ever to see the Fatherland again.*

Meanwhile back in the well-heated headquarters in East Prussia the Nazi warlord, whose stubbornness and stupidity were responsible for this disaster, berated his generals at Stalingrad for not knowing how and when to die. The records of a conference held by Hitler at OKW with his generals on February 1 survive and shed enlightenment on the nature of the German dictator at this trying period in his life and that of his Army and country.

They have surrendered there—formally and absolutely. Otherwise they would have closed ranks, formed a hedgehog, and shot themselves with their last bullet . . . The man [Paulus] should have shot himself just as the old commanders who threw themselves on their swords when they saw that the cause was lost . . . Even Varus gave his slave the order: "Now kill me!"

Hitler's venom toward Paulus for deciding to live became more poisonous as he ranted on.

You have to imagine: he'll be brought to Moscow—and imagine that rat-trap there. There he will sign anything. He'll make confessions, make proclamations—you'll see. They will now walk down the slope of spiritual bankruptcy to its lowest depths . . . You'll see—it won't be a week before Seydlitz and Schmidt and even Paulus are talking over the radio† . . . They are

---

* According to the figure given by the Bonn government in 1958. Many of the prisoners died during an epidemic of typhus in the following spring.

† Hitler was correct in his forecast, except for the timing. By July of the following summer Paulus and Seydlitz, who became the leaders of the so-called National Committee of Free Germany, did take to the air over the Moscow radio to urge the Army to eliminate Hitler.

going to be put into the Liublanka, and there the rats will eat them. How can one be so cowardly? I don't understand it . . .

What is life? Life is the Nation. The individual must die anyway. Beyond the life of the individual is the Nation. But how can anyone be afraid of this moment of death, with which he can free himself from this misery, if his duty doesn't chain him to this Vale of Tears. Na!

. . . So many people have to die, and then a man like that besmirches the heroism of so many others at the last minute. He could have freed himself from all sorrow and ascended into eternity and national immortality, but he prefers to go to Moscow! . . .

What hurts me most, personally, is that I still promoted him to field marshal. I wanted to give him this final satisfaction. That's the last field marshal I shall appoint in this war. You mustn't count your chickens before they're hatched.[27]

There followed a brief exchange between Hitler and General Zeitzler on how to break the news of the surrender to the German people. On February 3, three days after the act, OKW issued a special communiqué:

The battle of Stalingrad has ended. True to their oath to fight to the last breath, the Sixth Army under the exemplary leadership of Field Marshal Paulus has been overcome by the superiority of the enemy and by the unfavorable circumstances confronting our forces.

The reading of the communiqué over the German radio was preceded by the roll of muffled drums and followed by the playing of the second movement of Beethoven's Fifth Symphony. Hitler proclaimed four days of national mourning. All theaters, movies and variety halls were closed until it was over.

Stalingrad, wrote Walter Goerlitz, the German historian, in his work on the General Staff, "was a second Jena and was certainly the greatest defeat that a German army had ever undergone."[28]

But it was more than that. Coupled with El Alamein and the British–American landings in North Africa it marked the great turning point in World War II. The high tide of Nazi conquest which had rolled over most of Europe to the frontier of Asia on the Volga and in Africa almost to the Nile had now begun to ebb and it would never flow back again. The time of the great Nazi blitz offensives, with thousands of tanks and planes spreading terror in the ranks of the enemy armies and cutting them to pieces, had come to an end. There would be, to be sure, desperate local thrusts—at Kharkov in the spring of 1943, in the Ardennes at Christmas time in 1944—but they formed part of a defensive struggle which the Germans were to carry out with great tenacity and valor during the next two—and last—years of the war. The initiative had passed from Hitler's hands, never to return. It was his enemies who seized it now, and held it.

And not only on land but in the air. Already on the night of May 30, 1942, the British had carried out their first one-thousand-plane bombing of Cologne, and more followed on other cities during the eventful summer. For the first time the civilian German people, like the German soldiers at Stalingrad and El Alamein, were to experience the horrors which their armed forces had inflicted on others up to now.

And finally, in the snows of Stalingrad and in the burning sands of the North African desert, a great and terrible Nazi dream was destroyed. Not only was the Third Reich doomed by the disasters to Paulus and Rommel but also the gruesome and grotesque so-called New Order which Hitler and his S.S. thugs had been busy setting up in the conquered lands. Before we turn to the final chapter, the fall of the Third Reich, it might be well to pause and see what this New Order was like—in theory and in barbarous practice—and what this ancient and civilized continent of Europe barely escaped after a brief nightmare of experiencing its first horrors. It must necessarily be for this book, as it was for the good Europeans who lived through it, or were massacred before it ended, the darkest chapter of all in the history of the Third Reich.

Book Five

✝ ✝ ✝

BEGINNING OF THE END

27

THE NEW ORDER

N O COMPREHENSIVE BLUEPRINT for the New Order was ever drawn up, but it is clear from the captured documents and from what took place that Hitler knew very well what he wanted it to be: a Nazi-ruled Europe whose resources would be exploited for the profit of Germany, whose people would be made the slaves of the German master race and whose "undesirable elements"—above all, the Jews, but also many Slavs in the East, especially the intelligentsia among them—would be exterminated.

The Jews and the Slavic peoples were the *Untermenschen*—subhumans. To Hitler they had no right to live, except as some of them, among the Slavs, might be needed to toil in the fields and the mines as slaves of their German masters. Not only were the great cities of the East, Moscow, Leningrad and Warsaw, to be permanently erased* but the culture of the Russians and Poles and other Slavs was to be stamped out and formal education denied them. Their thriving industries were to be dismantled and shipped to Germany and the people themselves confined to the pursuits of agriculture so that they could grow food for Germans, being allowed to keep for themselves just enough to subsist on. Europe itself, as the Nazi leaders put it, must be made "Jew-free."

"What happens to a Russian, to a Czech, does not interest me in the slightest," declared Heinrich Himmler on October 4, 1943, in a confidential address to his S.S. officers at Posen. By this time Himmler, as chief of the S.S. and the entire police apparatus of the Third Reich, was next to Hitler in importance, holding the power of life and death not only over eighty million Germans but over twice that many conquered people.

What the nations [Himmler continued] can offer in the way of good blood of our type, we will take, if necessary by kidnaping their children and raising

---

* As early as September 18, 1941, Hitler had specifically ordered that Leningrad was to be "wiped off the face of the earth." After being surrounded it was to be "razed to the ground" by bombardment and bombing and its population (three millions) was to be destroyed with it. See above, pp. 853–54.

them here with us. Whether nations live in prosperity or starve to death like cattle interests me only in so far as we need them as slaves to our *Kultur;* otherwise it is of no interest to me.

Whether 10,000 Russian females fall down from exhaustion while digging an antitank ditch interests me only in so far as the antitank ditch for Germany is finished . . .[1]

Long before Himmler's Posen speech in 1943 (to which we shall return, for it covers other aspects of the New Order) the Nazi chiefs had laid down their thoughts and plans for enslaving the people of the East.

By October 15, 1940, Hitler had decided on the future of the Czechs, the first Slavic people he had conquered. One half of them were to be "assimilated," mostly by shipping them as slave labor to Germany. The other half, "particularly" the intellectuals, were simply to be, in the words of a secret report on the subject, "eliminated."[2]

A fortnight before, on October 2, the Fuehrer had clarified his thoughts about the fate of the Poles, the second of the Slavic peoples to be conquered. His faithful secretary, Martin Bormann, has left a long memorandum on the Nazi plans, which Hitler outlined to Hans Frank, the Governor General of rump Poland, and to other officials.[3]

The Poles [Hitler "emphasized"] are especially born for low labor . . . There can be no question of improvement for them. It is necessary to keep the standard of life low in Poland and it must not be permitted to rise . . . The Poles are lazy and it is necessary to use compulsion to make them work . . . The Government General [of Poland] should be used by us merely as a source of unskilled labor . . . Every year the laborers needed by the Reich could be procured from there.

As for the Polish priests,

they will preach what we want them to preach. If any priest acts differently, we shall make short work of him. The task of the priest is to keep the Poles quiet, stupid and dull-witted.

There were two other classes of Poles to be dealt with and the Nazi dictator did not neglect mention of them.

It is indispensable to bear in mind that the Polish gentry must cease to exist; however cruel this may sound, they must be exterminated wherever they are . . .

There should be one master only for the Poles, the German. Two masters, side by side, cannot and must not exist. Therefore, all representatives of the Polish intelligentsia are to be exterminated. This sounds cruel, but such is the law of life.

This obsession of the Germans with the idea that they were the master race and that the Slavic peoples must be their slaves was especially virulent in regard to Russia. Erich Koch, the roughneck Reich Commissar for the Ukraine, expressed it in a speech at Kiev on March 5, 1943.

We are the Master Race and must govern hard but just . . . I will draw the very last out of this country. I did not come to spread bliss . . . The population must work, work, and work again . . . We definitely did not come here to give out manna. We have come here to create the basis for victory.

We are a master race, which must remember that the lowliest German worker is racially and biologically a thousand times more valuable than the population here.[4]

Nearly a year before, on July 23, 1942, when the German armies in Russia were nearing the Volga and the oil fields of the Caucasus, Martin Bormann, Hitler's party secretary and, by now, right-hand man, wrote a long letter to Rosenberg reiterating the Fuehrer's views on the subject. The letter was summed up by an official in Rosenberg's ministry:

The Slavs are to work for us. In so far as we don't need them, they may die. Therefore compulsory vaccination and German health services are superfluous. The fertility of the Slavs is undesirable. They may use contraceptives or practice abortion—the more the better. Education is dangerous. It is enough if they can count up to 100. . . . Every educated person is a future enemy. Religion we leave to them as a means of diversion. As for food they won't get any more than is absolutely necessary. We are the masters. We come first.[5]

When the German troops first entered Russia they were in many places hailed as liberators by a population long ground down and terrorized by Stalin's tyranny. There were, in the beginning, wholesale desertions among the Russian soldiers. Especially in the Baltic, which had been under Soviet occupation but a short time, and in the Ukraine, where an incipient independence movement had never been quite stamped out, many were happy to be freed from the Soviet yoke—even by the Germans.

There were a few in Berlin who believed that if Hitler played his cards shrewdly, treating the population with consideration and promising relief from Bolshevik practices (by granting religious and economic freedom and making true co-operatives out of the collectivized farms) and eventual self-government, the Russian people could be won over. They might then not only co-operate with the Germans in the occupied regions but in the unoccupied ones strive for liberation from Stalin's harsh rule. If this were done, it was argued, the Bolshevik regime itself might collapse and the Red Army disintegrate, as the Czarist armies had done in 1917.

But the savagery of the Nazi occupation and the obvious aims of the German conquerors, often publicly proclaimed, to plunder the Russian lands, enslave their peoples and colonize the East with Germans soon destroyed any possibility of such a development.

No one summed up this disastrous policy and all the opportunities it destroyed better than a German himself, Dr. Otto Bräutigam, a career diplomat and the deputy leader of the Political Department of Rosenberg's newly created Ministry for the Occupied Eastern Territories. In a bitter confidential report to his superiors on October 25, 1942, Bräutigam dared to pinpoint the Nazi mistakes in Russia.

In the Soviet Union we found on our arrival a population weary of Bolshevism, which waited longingly for new slogans holding out the prospect of a better future for them. It was Germany's duty to find such slogans, but they remained unuttered. The population greeted us with joy as liberators and placed themselves at our disposal.

Actually, there was a slogan but the Russian people soon saw through it.

With the inherent instinct of the Eastern peoples [Bräutigam continued], the primitive man soon found out that for Germany the slogan "Liberation from Bolshevism" was only a pretext to enslave the Eastern peoples according to her own methods . . . The worker and peasant soon perceived that Germany did not regard them as partners of equal rights but considered them only as the objective of her political and economic aims . . . With unequaled presumption, we put aside all political knowledge and . . . treat the peoples of the occupied Eastern territories as "Second-Class Whites" to whom Providence has merely assigned the task of serving as slaves for Germany . . .

There were two other developments, Bräutigam declared, which had turned the Russians against the Germans: the barbaric treatment of Soviet prisoners of war and the shanghaiing of Russian men and women for slave labor.

It is no longer a secret from friend or foe that hundreds of thousands of Russian prisoners of war have died of hunger or cold in our camps . . . We now experience the grotesque picture of having to recruit millions of laborers from the occupied Eastern territories after prisoners of war have died of hunger like flies . . .

In the prevailing limitless abuse of the Slavic humanity, "recruiting" methods were used which probably have their origin only in the blackest periods of the slave traffic. A regular man hunt was inaugurated. Without consideration of health or age the people were shipped to Germany . . .*

---

* Neither the extermination of masses of Soviet prisoners of war nor the exploitation of Russian slave labor was a secret to the Kremlin. As early as November 1941, Molotov had made a formal diplomatic protest against the "extermination" of Russian POWs, and in April of the following year he made another protest against the German slave labor program.

German policy and practice in Russia had "brought about the enormous resistance of the Eastern peoples," this official concluded.

Our policy has forced both Bolshevists and Russian nationalists into a common front against us. The Russian fights today with exceptional bravery and self-sacrifice for nothing more or less than recognition of his human dignity.

Closing his thirteen-page memorandum on a positive note Dr. Bräutigam asked for a complete change of policy. "The Russian people," he argued, "must be told something concrete about their future."[6]

But this was a voice in the Nazi wilderness. Hitler, as we have seen, already had laid down, before the attack began, his directives on what would be done with Russia and the Russians* and he was not a man who could be persuaded by any living German to change them by one iota.

On July 16, 1941, less than a month after the commencement of the Russian campaign but when it was already evident from the initial German successes that a large slice of the Soviet Union would soon be within grasp, Hitler convoked Goering, Keitel, Rosenberg, Bormann and Lammers (the last, head of the Reich Chancellery) to his headquarters in East Prussia to remind them of his aims in the newly conquered land. At last his goal so clearly stated in *Mein Kampf* of securing a vast German *Lebensraum* in Russia was in sight and it is clear from the confidential memorandum of the meeting drawn up by Bormann (which showed up at Nuremberg)[7] that he wanted his chief lieutenants to understand well what he intended to do with it. His intentions, he admonished, must however not be "publicized."

There is no need for that [Hitler said] but the main thing is that we ourselves know what we want . . . Nobody must be able to recognize that it initiates a final settlement. This need not prevent our taking all necessary measures—shooting, resettling, etc.—and we shall take them.

In principle, Hitler continued,

we now have to face the task of cutting up the cake according to our needs in order to be able:

> first, to dominate it;
> second, to administer it;
> third, to exploit it.

He did not mind, he said, that the Russians had ordered partisan warfare behind the German lines; "it enables us to eradicate everyone who opposes us."

In general, Hitler explained, Germany would dominate the Russian

---

* See above, pp. 830–34.

territory up to the Urals. None but Germans would be permitted to carry weapons in that vast space. Then Hitler went over specifically what would be done with various slices of the Russian cake.

The entire Baltic country will have to be incorporated into Germany . . . The Crimea has to be evacuated by all foreigners and settled by Germans only, [becoming] Reich territory . . . The Kola Peninsula will be taken by Germany because of the large nickel mines there. The annexation of Finland as a federated state should be prepared with caution . . . The Fuehrer will raze Leningrad to the ground and then hand it over to the Finns.

The Baku oil fields, Hitler ordered, would become a "German concession" and the German colonies on the Volga would be annexed outright. When it came to a discussion as to which Nazi leaders would administer the new territory a violent quarrel broke out.

Rosenberg states he intends to use Captain von Petersdorff, owing to his special merits; general consternation; general rejections. The Fuehrer and the Reich Marshal [Goering] both emphasize there was no doubt that Von Petersdorff was insane.

There was also an argument on the best methods of policing the conquered Russian people. Hitler suggested the German police be equipped with armored cars. Goering doubted that they would be necessary. His planes could "drop bombs in case of riots," he said.

Naturally [Goering added] this giant area would have to be pacified as quickly as possible. The best solution would be to shoot anybody who looked sideways.*

Goering, as head of the Four-Year Plan, was also put in charge of the economic exploitation of Russia.† "Plunder" would be a better word, as Goering made clear in a speech to the Nazi commissioners for the occupied territories on August 6, 1942. "It used to be called plundering," he said. "But today things have become more humane. In spite of that, I intend to plunder and to do it thoroughly."[8] On this, at least, he was as good as his word, not only in Russia but throughout Nazi-conquered Europe. It was all part of the New Order.

---

* A year before, it will be remembered, Goering had told Ciano that "this year between twenty and thirty million persons will die of hunger in Russia" and that "perhaps it is well that it should be so." Already, he said, Russian prisoners of war had begun "to eat each other." See above, p. 854n.
† In a directive of Goering's Economic Staff, East, on May 23, 1941, the destruction of the Russian industrial areas was ordered. The workers and their families in these regions were to be left to starve. "Any attempt to save the population there," the directive stated, "from death by starvation by importing [food] surpluses from the black-soil zone [of Russia]" was prohibited. See above, p. 833.

THE NAZI PLUNDER OF EUROPE

The total amount of loot will never be known; it has proved beyond man's capacity to accurately compute. But some figures are available, many of them from the Germans themselves. They show with what Germanic thoroughness the instructions which Goering once gave to his subordinates were carried out.

Whenever you come across anything that may be needed by the German people, you must be after it like a bloodhound. It must be taken out . . . and brought to Germany.[9]

A great deal was taken out, not only in goods and services but in banknotes and gold. Whenever Hitler occupied a country, his financial agents seized the gold and foreign holdings of its national bank. That was a mere beginning. Staggering "occupation costs" were immediately assessed. By the end of February 1944, Count Schwerin von Krosigk, the Nazi Minister of Finance, put the total take from such payments at some 48 billion marks (roughly $12,000,000,000), of which France, which was milked heavier than any other conquered country, furnished more than half. By the end of the war, receipts from occupation assessments amounted to an estimated 60 billion marks ($15,000,000,000).

France was forced to pay 31.5 billions of this total, its annual contributions of more than 7 billions coming to over four times the yearly sums which Germany had paid in reparations under the Dawes and Young plans after the first war—a tribute which had seemed such a heinous crime to Hitler. In addition the Bank of France was forced to grant "credits" to Germany totaling 4.5 billion marks and the French government to pay a further half billion in "fines." At Nuremberg it was estimated that the Germans extracted in occupation costs and "credits" two thirds of Belgium's national income and a similar percentage from the Netherlands. Altogether, according to a study by the U.S. Strategic Bombing Survey, Germany extracted in tribute from the conquered nations a total of 104 billion marks ($26,000,000,000).*

But the goods seized and transported to the Reich without even the formality of payment can never possibly be estimated. Figures kept pouring in at Nuremberg until they overwhelmed one; but no expert, so far as I know, was ever able to straighten them out and compute totals. In France, for example, it was estimated that the Germans carted off (as "levies in kind") 9 million tons of cereals, 75 per cent of the total production of oats, 80 per cent of oil, 74 per cent of steel, and so on, for a grand total of 184.5 billion francs.

Russia, devastated by warfare and German savagery, proved harder to

---

* At the official rate of exchange (2.5 Reichsmarks to the dollar) this would amount to 40 billion dollars. But I have used the unofficial rate of four Reichsmarks to the dollar. In terms of purchasing power it is more accurate.

milk. Nazi documents are full of reports of Soviet "deliveries." In 1943, for example, 9 million tons of cereals, 2 million tons of fodder, 3 million tons of potatoes, 662,000 tons of meat were listed by the Germans among the "deliveries," to which the Soviet Committee of Investigation added— for the duration of the occupation—9 million cattle, 12 million pigs, 13 million sheep, to mention a few items. But Russian "deliveries" proved much less than expected; the Germans calculated them as worth a net of only some 4 billion marks ($1,000,000,000).*

Everything possible was squeezed out of Poland by the greedy Nazi conquerors. "I shall endeavor," said Dr. Frank, the Governor General, "to squeeze out of this province everything that is still possible to squeeze out." This was at the end of 1942, and in the three years since the occupation he had already squeezed out, as he continually boasted, a great deal, especially in foodstuffs for hungry Germans in the Reich. He warned, however, that "if the new food scheme is carried out in 1943 a half-million people in Warsaw and its suburbs alone will be deprived of food."[10]

The nature of the New Order in Poland had been laid down as soon as the country was conquered. On October 3, 1939, Frank informed the Army of Hitler's orders.

Poland can only be administered by utilizing the country through means of ruthless exploitation, deportation of all supplies, raw materials, machines, factory installations, etc., which are important for the German war economy, availability of all workers for work within Germany, reduction of the entire Polish economy to absolute minimum necessary for bare existence of the population, closing of all educational institutions, especially technical schools and colleges in order to prevent the growth of the new Polish intelligentsia. Poland shall be treated as a colony. The Poles shall be the slaves of the Greater German Reich.[11]

Rudolf Hess, the Nazi deputy Fuehrer, added that Hitler had decided that "Warsaw shall not be rebuilt, nor is it the intention of the Fuehrer to rebuild or reconstruct any industry in the Government General."[12]

By decree of Dr. Frank, all property in Poland belonging not only to Jews but to Poles was subject to confiscation without compensation. Hundreds of thousands of Polish-owned farms were simply grabbed and handed over to German settlers. By May 31, 1943, in the four Polish districts annexed to Germany (West Prussia, Posen, Zichenau, Silesia) some 700,000 estates comprising 15 million acres were "seized" and 9,500 estates totaling 6.5 million acres "confiscated." The difference between "seizure" and "confiscation" is not explained in the elaborate table prepared by the German "Central Estate Office,"[13] and to the dispossessed Poles it must not have mattered.

---

* According to Alexander Dallin in his exhaustive study of German rule in Russia, Germany could have obtained more from Russia in normal trade. (See Dallin, *German Rule in Russia.*)

Even the art treasures in the occupied lands were looted, and, as the captured Nazi documents later revealed, on the express orders of Hitler and Goering, who thereby greatly augmented their "private" collections. The corpulent Reich Marshal, according to his own estimate, brought his own collection up to a value of 50 million Reichsmarks. Indeed, Goering was the driving force in this particular field of looting. Immediately upon the conquest of Poland he issued orders for the seizure of art treasures there and within six months the special commissioner appointed to carry out his command could report that he had taken over "almost the entire art treasury of the country."[14]

But it was in France where the bulk of the great art treasures of Europe lay, and no sooner was this country added to the Nazi conquests than Hitler and Goering decreed their seizure. To carry out this particular plunder Hitler appointed Rosenberg, who set up an organization called Einsatzstab Rosenberg, and who was assisted not only by Goering but by General Keitel. Indeed one order by Keitel to the Army in France stated that Rosenberg "is entitled to transport to Germany cultural goods which appear valuable to him and to safeguard them there. The Fuehrer has reserved for himself the decision as to their use."[15]

An idea of Hitler's decision "as to their use" is revealed in a secret order issued by Goering on November 5, 1940, specifying the distribution of art objects being collected at the Louvre in Paris. They were "to be disposed of in the following way":

1. Those art objects about which the Fuehrer has reserved for himself the decision as to their use.

2. Those . . . which serve the completion of the Reich Marshal's [i.e., Goering's] collection . . .

4. Those . . . that are suited to be sent to German museums . . .[16]

The French government protested the looting of the country's art treasures, declaring that it was a violation of the Hague convention, and when one German art expert on Rosenberg's staff, a Herr Bunjes, dared to call this to the attention of Goering, the fat one replied:

"My dear Bunjes, let me worry about that. I am the highest jurist in the state. It is my orders which are decisive and you will act accordingly."

And so according to a report of Bunjes—it is his only appearance in the history of the Third Reich, so far as the documents show—

those art objects collected at the Jeu de Paume which are to go into the Fuehrer's possession and those which the Reich Marshal claims for himself will be loaded into two railroad cars which will be attached to the Reich Marshal's special train . . . to Berlin.[17]

Many more carloads followed. According to a secret official German report some 137 freight cars loaded with 4,174 cases of art works comprising 21,903 objects, including 10,890 paintings, made the journey from the West to Germany up to July 1944.[18] They included works of, among others, Rembrandt, Rubens, Hals, Vermeer, Velázquez, Murillo, Goya, Vecchio, Watteau, Fragonard, Reynolds and Gainsborough. As early as January 1941, Rosenberg estimated the art loot from France alone as worth a billion marks.[19]

The plunder of raw materials, manufactured goods and food, though it reduced the occupied peoples to impoverishment, hunger and sometimes starvation and violated the Hague Convention on the conduct of war, might have been excused, if not justified, by the Germans as necessitated by the harsh exigencies of total war. But the stealing of art treasures did not help Hitler's war machine. It was a case merely of avarice, of the personal greed of Hitler and Goering.

All this plunder and spoliation the conquered populations could have endured—wars and enemy occupation had always brought privation in their wake. But this was only a part of the New Order—the mildest part. It was in the plunder not of material goods but of human lives that the mercifully short-lived New Order will be longest remembered. Here Nazi degradation sank to a level seldom experienced by man in all his time on earth. Millions of decent, innocent men and women were driven into forced labor, millions more tortured and tormented in the concentration camps and millions more still, of whom there were four and a half million Jews alone, were massacred in cold blood or deliberately starved to death and their remains—in order to remove the traces—burned.

This incredible story of horror would be unbelievable were it not fully documented and testified to by the perpetrators themselves. What follows here—a mere summary, which must because of limitations of space leave out a thousand shocking details—is based on that incontrovertible evidence, with occasional corroboration from the eyewitness accounts of the few survivors.

SLAVE LABOR IN THE NEW ORDER

By the end of September 1944, some seven and a half million civilian foreigners were toiling for the Third Reich. Nearly all of them had been rounded up by force, deported to Germany in boxcars, usually without food or water or any sanitary facilities, and there put to work in the factories, fields and mines. They were not only put to work but degraded, beaten and starved and often left to die for lack of food, clothing and shelter.

In addition, two million prisoners of war were added to the foreign labor force, at least a half a million of whom were made to work in the armaments and munitions industries in flagrant violation of the Hague and Geneva conventions, which stipulated that no war prisoners could be employed in such tasks.* This figure did not include the hundreds of thousands of other POWs who were impressed into the building of fortifications and in carrying ammunition to the front lines and even in manning antiaircraft guns in further disregard of the international conventions which Germany had signed.†

In the massive deportations of slave labor to the Reich, wives were torn away from their husbands, and children from their parents, and assigned to widely separated parts of Germany. The young, if they were old enough to work at all, were not spared. Even top generals of the Army co-operated in the kidnaping of children, who were carted off to the homeland to perform slave labor. A memorandum from Rosenberg's files of June 12, 1944, reveals this practice in occupied Russia.

Army Group Center intends to apprehend forty to fifty thousand youths from the age of 10 to 14 . . . and transport them to the Reich. The measure was originally proposed by the Ninth Army . . . It is intended to allot these juveniles primarily to the German trades as apprentices. . . . This action is being greatly welcomed by the German trade since it represents a decisive measure for the alleviation of the shortage of apprentices.

This action is not only aimed at preventing a direct reinforcement of the enemy's strength but also as a reduction of his biological potentialities.

The kidnaping operation had a code name: "Hay Action." It was also being carried out, the memorandum added, by Field Marshal Model's Army Group Ukraine-North.[22]

Increasing terrorization was used to round up the victims. At first, comparatively mild methods were used. Persons coming out of church or the movies were nabbed. In the West especially, S.S. units merely blocked off a section of a town and seized all able-bodied men and women. Villages were surrounded and searched for the same purposes. In the East, when there was resistance to the forced-labor order, villages were simply burned down and their inhabitants carted off. Rosenberg's captured files are replete with *German* reports of such happenings. In Poland, at least one German official thought things were going a little too far.

The wild and ruthless man hunt [he wrote to Governor Frank], as exercised everywhere in towns and country, in streets, squares, stations, even in churches, at night in homes, has badly shaken the feeling of security of the inhabitants. Everybody is exposed to the danger of being seized anywhere and at any time

---

* Albert Speer, Minister for Armament and War Production, admitted at Nuremberg that 40 per cent of all prisoners of war were employed in 1944 in the production of weapons and munitions and in subsidiary industries.[20]

† A captured record shows Field Marshal Milch of the Air Force in 1943 demanding 50,000 more Russian war prisoners to be added to the 30,000 already manning antiaircraft artillery. "It is amusing," Milch laughed, "that Russians must work the guns."[21]

by the police, suddenly and unexpectedly, and of being sent to an assembly camp. None of his relatives knows what has happened to him.[23]

But rounding up the slave workers was only the first step.* The condition of their transport to Germany left something to be desired. A certain Dr. Gutkelch described one instance in a report to Rosenberg's ministry on September 30, 1942. Recounting how a train packed with returning worked-out Eastern laborers met a train at a siding near Brest Litovsk full of "newly recruited" Russian workers bound for Germany, he wrote:

Because of the corpses in the trainload of returning laborers a catastrophe might have occurred . . . In this train women gave birth to babies who were thrown out of the windows during the journey. Persons having tuberculosis and venereal diseases rode in the same car. Dying people lay in freight cars without straw, and one of the dead was thrown on the railway embankment. The same must have occurred in other returning transports.[25]

This was not a very promising introduction to the Third Reich for the *Ostarbeiter,* but at least it prepared them somewhat for the ordeal that lay ahead. Hunger lay ahead and beatings and disease and exposure to the cold, in unheated quarters and in their thin rags. Long hours of labor lay ahead that were limited only by their ability to stand on their feet.

The great Krupp works, makers of Germany's guns and tanks and ammunition, was a typical place of employment. Krupp employed a large number of slave laborers, including Russian prisoners of war. At one point during the war, six hundred Jewish women from the Buchenwald concentration camp were brought in to work at Krupp's, being "housed" in a bombed-out work camp from which the previous inmates, Italian POWs, had been removed. Dr. Wilhelm Jaeger, the "senior doctor" for Krupp's slaves, described in an affidavit at Nuremberg what he found there when he took over.

Upon my first visit I found these females suffering from open festering wounds and other diseases. I was the first doctor they had seen for at least a fortnight . . . There were no medical supplies . . . They had no shoes

---

* The entire slave labor program was put in charge of Fritz Sauckel, who was given the title of Plenipotentiary General for the Allocation of Labor. A second-string Nazi, he had been Gauleiter and Governor of Thuringia. A pig-eyed little man, rude and tough, he was, as Goebbels mentioned in his diary, "one of the dullest of the dull." In the dock at Nuremberg, he struck this writer as being a complete nonentity, the sort of German who in other times might have been a butcher in a small-town meat market. One of his first directives laid it down that the foreign workers were "to be treated in such a way as to exploit them to the highest possible extent at the lowest conceivable degree of expenditure."[24] He admitted at Nuremberg that of all the millions of foreign workers "not even 200,000 came voluntarily." However at the trial he denied all responsibility for their ill-treatment. He was found guilty, sentenced to death, and hanged in the Nuremberg jail on the night of October 15–16, 1946.

and went about in their bare feet. The sole clothing of each consisted of a sack with holes for their arms and head. Their hair was shorn. The camp was surrounded by barbed wire and closely guarded by S.S. guards.

The amount of food in the camp was extremely meager and of very poor quality. One could not enter the barracks without being attacked by fleas . . . I got large boils on my arms and the rest of my body from them . . .

Dr. Jaeger reported the situation to the directors of Krupp and even to the personal physician of Gustav Krupp von Bohlen und Halbach, the owner—but in vain. Nor did his reports on other Krupp slave labor camps bring any alleviation. He recalled in his affidavit some of these reports of conditions in eight camps inhabited by Russian and Polish workers: overcrowding that bred disease, lack of enough food to keep a man alive, lack of water, lack of toilets.

The clothing of the Eastern workers was likewise completely inadequate. They worked and slept in the same clothing in which they had arrived from the East. Virtually all of them had no overcoats and were compelled to use their blankets as coats in cold and rainy weather. In view of the shortage of shoes many workers were forced to go to work in their bare feet, even in winter . . .

Sanitary conditions were atrocious. At Kramerplatz only ten children's toilets were available for 1,200 inhabitants . . . Excretion contaminated the entire floors of these lavatories . . . The Tartars and Kirghiz suffered most; they collapsed like flies [from] bad housing, the poor quality and insufficient quantity of food, overwork and insufficient rest.

These workers were likewise afflicted with spotted fever. Lice, the carrier of the disease, together with countless fleas, bugs and other vermin tortured the inhabitants of these camps . . . At times the water supply at the camps was shut off for periods of from eight to fourteen days . . .

On the whole, Western slave workers fared better than those from the East—the latter being considered by the Germans as mere scum. But the difference was only relative, as Dr. Jaeger found at one of Krupp's work camps occupied by French prisoners of war in Nogerratstrasse at Essen.

Its inhabitants were kept for nearly half a year in dog kennels, urinals and in old baking houses. The dog kennels were three feet high, nine feet long, six feet wide. Five men slept in each of them. The prisoners had to crawl into these kennels on all fours . . . There was no water in the camp.*[26]

---

* Besides obtaining thousands of slave laborers, both civilians and prisoners of war for its factories in Germany, the Krupp firm also built a large fuse factory at the extermination camp at Auschwitz, where Jews were worked to exhaustion and then gassed to death.

Baron Gustav Krupp von Bohlen und Halbach, the chairman of the board, was

Some two and a half million slave laborers—mostly Slavs and Italians—
were assigned to farm work in Germany and though their life from the very
force of circumstances was better than that of those in the city factories it
was far from ideal—or even humane. A captured directive on the "Treatment of Foreign Farm Workers of Polish Nationality" gives an inkling of
their treatment. And though applied to Poles—it is dated March 6, 1941,
before Russians became available—it was later used as guidance for those
of other nationalities.

Farm workers of Polish nationality no longer have the right to complain,
and thus no complaints will be accepted by any official agency . . . The visit
of churches is strictly prohibited . . . Visits to theaters, motion pictures or
other cultural entertainment are strictly prohibited . . .
Sexual intercourse with women and girls is strictly prohibited.

If it was with German females, it was, according to an edict of Himmler
in 1942, punishable by death.*
The use of "railroads, buses or other public conveyances" was prohibited for slave farm workers. This apparently was ordained so that they
would not escape from the farms to which they were bound.

Arbitrary change of employment [the directive stated] is strictly prohibited.
The farm workers have to labor as long as is demanded by the employer.
There are no time limits to the working time.

---

indicted as a major war criminal at Nuremberg (along with Goering, *et al.*) but
because of his "physical and mental condition" (he had had a stroke and had faded
into senility), he was not tried. He died on January 16, 1950. An effort was made
by the prosecution to try in his stead his son, Alfried, who had acquired sole owner-
ship of the company in 1943, but the tribunal denied this.

Alfried Krupp von Bohlen und Halbach was subsequently tried before a Nuremberg military tribunal (a purely American court) along with nine directors of the
firm in the *United States v. Alfried Krupp et al.* case. On July 31, 1948, he was
sentenced to twelve years imprisonment and confiscation of all his property. He was
released from Landsberg prison (where Hitler had served his sentence in 1924) on
February 4, 1951, in a general amnesty issued by John J. McCloy, the U.S. High
Commissioner. Not only was the confiscation of his corporate property annulled
but his personal fortune of some $10,000,000 was returned to him. The Allied
governments had ordered the breakup of the vast Krupp empire but Alfried Krupp,
who took over the active management of the firm after his release from prison,
evaded the order and at the time of writing (1959) announced, with the approval of
the Bonn government, that not only would the company not be broken up but that
it was acquiring new industries.
* Himmler's directive of February 20, 1942, was directed especially against Russian
slave workers. It ordered "special treatment" also for "severe violations against
discipline, including work refusal or loafing at work." In such cases

special treatment is requested. Special treatment is hanging. It should not take
place in the immediate vicinity of the camp. A certain number [however] should
attend the special treatment.[27]

The term "special treatment" was a common one in Himmler's files and in Nazi
parlance during the war. It meant just what Himmler in this directive said it meant.

Every employer has the right to give corporal punishment to his farm workers . . . They should, if possible, be removed from the community of the home and they can be quartered in stables, etc. No remorse whatever should restrict such action.[28]

Even the Slav women seized and shipped to Germany for domestic service were treated as slaves. As early as 1942 Hitler had commanded Sauckel to procure a half million of them "in order to relieve the German housewife." The slave labor commissar laid down the conditions of work in the German households.

There is no claim to free time. Female domestic workers from the East may leave the household only to take care of domestic tasks . . . It is prohibited for them to enter restaurants, movies, theaters and similar establishments. Attending church is also prohibited . . .[29]

Women, it is obvious, were almost as necessary as men in the Nazi slave labor program. Of some three million Russian civilians pressed into service by the Germans, more than one half were women. Most of them were assigned to do heavy farm work and to labor in the factories.

The enslavement of millions of men and women of the conquered lands as lowly toilers for the Third Reich was not just a wartime measure. From the statements of Hitler, Goering, Himmler and the others already cited—and they are only a tiny sampling—it is clear that if Nazi Germany had endured, the New Order would have meant the rule of the German master race over a vast slave empire stretching from the Atlantic to the Ural mountains. To be sure, the Slavs in the East would have fared the worst.

As Hitler emphasized in July 1941, scarcely a month after he had attacked the Soviet Union, his plans for its occupation constituted "a final settlement." A year later, at the high tide of his Russian conquests, he admonished his aides:

As for the ridiculous hundred million Slavs, we will mold the best of them to the shape that suits us, and we will isolate the rest of them in their own pigsties; and anyone who talks about cherishing the local inhabitant and civilizing him, goes straight off to a concentration camp![30]

THE PRISONERS OF WAR

Though it was a flagrant violation of the Hague and Geneva conventions to use prisoners of war in armament factories or in any labor connected with the fighting at the front such employment, massive as it was, constituted the least of worries for the millions of soldiers captured by the Third Reich.

Their overwhelming concern was to survive the war. If they were Russian the odds were greatly against them. There were more Soviet war prisoners than all others put together—some five and three-quarter million of them. Of these barely one million were found alive when Allied troops liberated the inmates of the POW camps in 1945. About a million had either been released during the war or allowed to serve in the collaborator units set up by the German Army. Two million Russian prisoners of war died in German captivity—from starvation, exposure and disease. The remaining million have never been accounted for and at Nuremberg a good case was made that most of them either had died from the above causes or had been exterminated by the S.D. (S.S. Security Service). According to the German records 67,000 were executed, but this is most certainly a partial figure.[31]

The bulk of the Russian war prisoners—some 3,800,000 of them— were taken by the Germans in the first phase of the Russian campaign, in the great battles of encirclement which were fought from June 21 to December 6, 1941. Admittedly it was difficult for an army in the midst of combat and rapid advance to care adequately for such a large number of captives. But the Germans made no effort to. Indeed the Nazi records show, as we have seen, that the Soviet prisoners were deliberately starved and left out in the open without shelter to die in the terrible subzero snowbound winter of 1941–42.

"The more of these prisoners who die, the better it is for us," was the attitude of many Nazi officials according to no less an authority than Rosenberg.

The clumsy Minister for the Occupied Eastern Territories was not a humane Nazi, particularly in regard to the Russians, with whom, as we have seen, he had grown up. But even he was moved to protest the treatment of Russian prisoners in a long letter to General Keitel, the Chief of OKW, dated February 28, 1942. This was the moment when the Soviet counteroffensive which had hurled the Germans back before Moscow and Rostov had reached its farthest penetrations that winter and when the Germans had realized at last that their gamble of destroying Russia in one short campaign—or perhaps ever—had failed and that just possibly, now that the U.S.A. had been added to Russia and Britain as their enemies, they might not win the war, in which case they would be held accountable for their war crimes.

> The fate of the Soviet prisoners of war in Germany [Rosenberg wrote Keitel] is a tragedy of the greatest extent. Of the 3,600,000 of them, only several hundred thousand are still able to work fully. A large part of them have starved, or died because of the hazards of the weather.

This could have been avoided, Rosenberg continued. There was food enough in Russia to provide them.

> However, in the majority of cases the camp commanders have forbidden food to be put at the disposal of the prisoners; they have rather let them

starve to death. Even on the march to the camps, the civilian population was not allowed to give the prisoners food. In many cases when the prisoners could no longer keep up on the march because of hunger and exhaustion, they were shot before the eyes of the horrified civilian population and the corpses were left. In numerous camps no shelter for the prisoners was provided at all. They lay under the open sky during rain or snow . . .

Finally, the shooting of prisoners of war must be mentioned. These . . . ignore all political understanding. For instance, in various camps all the "Asiatics" were shot . . .[32]

Not only Asiatics. Shortly after the beginning of the Russian campaign an agreement was reached between OKW and the S.S. Security Service for the lat'er to "screen" Russian prisoners. The objective was disclosed in an affidavit by Otto Ohlendorf, one of the S.D.s great killers and like so many of the men around Himmler a displaced intellectual, for he had university degrees both in the law and in economics and had been a professor at the Institute for Applied Economic Science.

All Jews and Communist functionaries [Ohlendorf testified] were to be removed from the prisoner-of-war camps and were to be executed. To my knowledge this action was carried out throughout the entire Russian campaign.[33]

But not without difficulties. Sometimes the Russian captives were so exhausted that they could not even walk to their execution. This brought a protest from Heinrich Mueller, the chief of the Gestapo, a dapper-looking fellow but also a cold, dispassionate killer.*

The commanders of the concentration camps are complaining that 5 to 10 per cent of the Soviet Russians destined for execution are arriving in the camps dead or half dead . . . It was particularly noted that when marching, for example, from the railroad station to the camp, a rather large number of prisoners collapsed on the way from exhaustion, either dead or half dead, and had to be picked up by a truck following the convoy. It cannot be prevented that the German people take notice of these occurrences.

The Gestapo didn't care a rap about the Russian captives falling dead from starvation and exhaustion, except that it robbed the executioners of their prey. But they didn't want the German people to see the spectacle. "Gestapo Mueller," as he was known in Germany, therefore ordered that

effective from today [November 9, 1941] Soviet Russians obviously marked by death and who therefore are not able to withstand the exertions of even

---

* Mueller was never apprehended after the war. He was last seen in Hitler's bunker in Berlin on April 29, 1945. Some of his surviving colleagues believe he is now in the service of the Soviet secret police, of which he was a great admirer.

a short march shall in the future be excluded from the transport into the concentration camps for execution.[34]

Dead prisoners or even starved and exhausted ones could not perform work and in 1942, when it became obvious to the Germans that the war was going to last considerably longer than they had expected and that the captive Soviet soldiers constituted a badly needed labor reservoir, the Nazis abandoned their policy of exterminating them in favor of working them. Himmler explained the change in his speech to the S.S. at Posen in 1943.

At that time [1941] we did not value the mass of humanity as we value it today, as raw material, as labor. What after all, thinking in terms of generations, is not to be regretted but is now deplorable by reason of the loss of labor, is that the prisoners died in tens and hundreds of thousands of exhaustion and hunger.[35]

They were now to be fed enough to enable them to work. By December 1944, three quarters of a million of them, including many officers, were toiling in the armament factories, the mines (where 200,000 were assigned) and on the farms. Their treatment was harsh, but at least they were allowed to live. Even the branding of the Russian war captives, which General Keitel had proposed, was abandoned.*

The treatment of Western prisoners of war, especially of the British and Americans, was comparatively milder than that meted out by the Germans to the Russians. There were occasional instances of the murder and massacre of them but this was due usually to the excessive sadism and cruelty of individual commanders. Such a case was the slaughter in cold blood of seventy-one American prisoners of war in a field near Malmédy, Belgium, on December 17, 1944, during the Battle of the Bulge.

There were other occasions when Hitler himself ordered the murder of Western prisoners, as he did in the case of fifty British flyers who were caught in the spring of 1944, after escaping from a camp at Sagan. At Nuremberg Goering said he "considered it the most serious incident of the whole war" and General Jodl called it "sheer murder."

Actually it seemed to be part of a deliberate German policy, adopted after Anglo–American bombing of Germany became so extensive from 1943 on, to encourage the killing of Allied airmen who had bailed out over Germany. Civilians were encouraged to lynch the flyers as soon as they had parachuted to the ground and a number of these Germans were tried after the war for having done so. In 1944 when the Anglo–American

---

* On July 20, 1942, Keitel had drafted the order.

    1. Soviet prisoners of war are to be branded with a special and durable mark.

    2. The brand is to consist of an acute angle of about 45 degrees with a one-centimetre length of side, pointing downward on the left buttock, at about a hand's width from the rectum.[36]

bombings were reaching their peak Ribbentrop urged that airmen shot down be summarily executed but Hitler took a somewhat milder view. On May 21, 1944, in agreement with Goering, he merely ordered that captured flyers who had machine-gunned passenger trains or civilians or German planes which had made emergency landings be shot without court-martial.

Sometimes captured flyers were simply turned over to the S.D. for "special treatment." Thus some forty-seven American, British and Dutch flyers, all officers, were brutally murdered at Mauthausen concentration camp in September 1944. An eyewitness, Maurice Lampe, a French inmate at the camp, described at Nuremberg how it was done.

The forty-seven officers were led barefooted to the quarry . . . At the bottom of the steps the guards loaded stones on the backs of these poor men and they had to carry them to the top. The first journey was made with stones weighing about sixty pounds and accompanied by blows . . . The second journey the stones were still heavier, and whenever the poor wretches sank under their burden they were kicked and hit with a bludgeon . . . in the evening twenty-one bodies were strewn along the road. The twenty-six others died the following morning.[37]

This was a familiar form of "execution" at Mauthausen and was used on, among others, a good many Russian prisoners of war.

From 1942 on—that is, when the tide of war began to surge against him—Hitler ordered the extermination of captured Allied commandos, especially in the West. (Captured Soviet partisans were summarily shot as a matter of course.) The Fuehrer's "Top-Secret Commando Order" of October 18, 1942, is among the Nazi documents.

From now on all enemies on so-called commando missions in Europe or Africa challenged by German troops, even if they are in uniform, whether armed or unarmed, in battle or in flight, are to be slaughtered to the last man.[38]

In a supplementary directive issued the same day Hitler explained to his commanders the reason for his order. Because of the success of the Allied commandos, he said,

I have been compelled to issue strict orders for the destruction of enemy sabotage troops and to declare noncompliance with these orders severely punishable . . . It must be made clear to the enemy that all sabotage troops will be exterminated, without exception, to the last man.

This means that their chance of escaping with their lives is nil . . . Under no circumstances can [they] expect to be treated according to the rules of the Geneva Convention . . . If it should become necessary for reasons of interrogation to initially spare one man or two, then they are to be shot immediately after interrogation.[39]

This particular crime was to be kept strictly secret. General Jodl appended instructions to Hitler's directive, underlining his words: *"This order is intended for commanders only and must not under any circumstances fall into enemy hands."* They were directed to destroy all copies of it after they had duly taken note.

It must have remained imprinted on their minds, for they proceeded to carry it out. A couple of instances, of many, may be given.

On the night of March 22, 1944, two officers and thirteen men of the 267th Special Reconnaissance Battalion of the U.S. Army landed from a naval craft far behind the German lines in Italy to demolish a railroad tunnel between La Spezia and Genoa. They were all in uniform and carried no civilian clothes. Captured two days later they were executed by a firing squad on March 26, without trial, on the direct orders of General Anton Dostler, commander of the LXXVth German Army Corps. Tried by a U.S. military tribunal shortly after the war, General Dostler justified his action by contending that he was merely obeying Hitler's Commando Order. He argued that he himself would have been court-martialed by the Fuehrer if he had not obeyed.*

Some fifteen members of an Anglo–American military mission—including a war correspondent of the Associated Press, and all in uniform—which had parachuted into Slovakia in January 1945 were executed at Mauthausen concentration camp on the orders of Dr. Ernst Kaltenbrunner, the successor of Heydrich as head of the S.D. and one of the defendants at Nuremberg.† Had it not been for the testimony of a camp adjutant who witnessed their execution, their murder might have remained unknown, for most of the files of the mass executions at this camp were destroyed.[40]

NAZI TERROR IN THE CONQUERED LANDS

On October 22, 1941, a French newspaper *Le Phare* published the following notice:

Cowardly criminals in the pay of England and Moscow killed the Feldkommandant of Nantes on the morning of October 20. Up to now the assassins have not been arrested.

As expiation for this crime I have ordered that 50 hostages be shot, to begin with . . . Fifty more hostages will be shot in case the guilty should not be arrested between now and October 23 by midnight.

This became a familiar notice in the pages of the newspapers or on red posters edged with black in France, Belgium, Holland, Norway, Poland

---

* General Dostler was condemned to death by the U.S. military tribunal in Rome on October 12, 1945.
† Kaltenbrunner was hanged at Nuremberg jail on the night of October 15–16, 1946.

and Russia. The proportion, publicly proclaimed by the Germans, was invariably 100 to 1—a hundred hostages shot for every German killed.

Though the taking of hostages was an ancient custom, much indulged in for instance by the Romans, it had not been generally practiced in modern times except by the Germans in the First World War and by the British in India and in South Africa during the Boer War. Under Hitler, however, the German Army carried it out on a large scale during the second war. Dozens of secret orders signed by General Keitel and lesser commanders were produced at Nuremberg ordering the taking—and shooting—of hostages. "It is important," Keitel decreed on October 1, 1941, "that these should include well-known leading personalities or members of their families"; and General von Stuelpnagel, the German commander in France, a year later stressed that "the better known the hostages to be shot the greater will be the deterrent effect on the perpetrators."

In all, 29,660 French hostages were executed by the Germans during the war and this figure did not include the 40,000 who "died" in French prisons. The figure for Poland was 8,000 and for Holland some 2,000. In Denmark what became known as a system of "clearing murders" was substituted for the publicly proclaimed shooting of hostages. On Hitler's express orders reprisals for the killing of Germans in Denmark were to be carried out in secret "on the proportion of five to one."[41] Thus the great Danish pastor-poet-playwright, Kaj Munk, one of the most beloved men in Scandinavia, was brutally murdered by the Germans, his body left on the road with a sign pinned to it: "Swine, you worked for Germany just the same."

Of all the war crimes which he claimed he had to commit on the orders of Hitler "the worst of all," General Keitel said on the stand at Nuremberg, stemmed from the *Nacht und Nebel Erlass*—"Night and Fog Decree." This grotesque order, reserved for the unfortunate inhabitants of the conquered territories in the West, was issued by Hitler himself on December 7, 1941. Its purpose, as the weird title indicates, was to seize persons "endangering German security" who were not to be immediately executed and make them vanish without a trace into the night and fog of the unknown in Germany. No information was to be given their families as to their fate even when, as invariably occurred, it was merely a question of the place of burial in the Reich.

On December 12, 1941, Keitel issued a directive explaining the Fuehrer's orders. "In principle," he said, "the punishment for offenses committed against the German state is the death penalty." But

if these offenses are punished with imprisonment, even with hard labor for life, this will be looked upon as a sign of weakness. Efficient intimidation can only be achieved either by capital punishment or by measures by which the relatives of the criminal and the population do not know his fate.[42]

The following February Keitel enlarged on the Night and Fog Decree. In cases where the death penalty was not meted out within eight days of a person's arrest,

the prisoners are to be transported to Germany secretly . . . these measures will have a deterrent effect because

(a) the prisoners will vanish without leaving a trace,
(b) no information may be given as to their whereabouts or their fate.[43]

The S.D. was given charge of this macabre task and its captured files are full of various orders pertaining to "NN" (for *Nacht und Nebel*), especially in regard to keeping the burial places of the victims strictly secret. How many Western Europeans disappeared into "Night and Fog" was never established at Nuremberg but it appeared that few emerged from it alive.

Some enlightening figures, however, were obtainable from the S.D. records concerning the number of victims of another terror operation in conquered territory which was applied to Russia. This particular exercise was carried out by what was known in Germany as the Einsatzgruppen— Special Action Groups, or what might better be termed, in view of their performance, Extermination Squads. The first round figure of their achievement came out, as if by accident, at Nuremberg.

One day some time before the trial began a young American naval officer, Lieutenant Commander Whitney R. Harris, of the American prosecution staff, was interrogating Otto Ohlendorf on his wartime activities. It was known that this attractive-looking German intellectual of youthful appearance—he was 38—had been head of Amt III of Himmler's Central Security Office (R.S.H.A.) but during the last years of the war had spent most of his time as a foreign trade expert in the Ministry of Economics. He told his interrogator that apart from one year he had spent the war period on official duty in Berlin. Asked what he had done during the year away, he replied, "I was chief of Einsatzgruppe D."

Harris, a lawyer by training and by this time something of an intelligence authority on German affairs, knew quite a bit about the *Einsatz* groups. So he asked promptly:

"During the year you were chief of Einsatzgruppe D, how many men, women and children did your group kill?"

Ohlendorf, Harris later remembered, shrugged his shoulders and with only the slightest hesitation answered:

"Ninety thousand!"[44]

The *Einsatz* groups had first been organized by Himmler and Heydrich to follow the German armies into Poland in 1939 and there round up the Jews and place them in ghettos. It was not until the beginning of the Russian campaign nearly two years later that, in agreement with the German Army, they were ordered to follow the combat troops and to carry out one phase of the "final solution." Four Einsatzgruppen were formed for this purpose, Groups A, B, C, D. It was the last one which Ohlendorf commanded between June 1941 and June 1942, and it was assigned the southernmost sector in the Ukraine and attached to the Eleventh Army. Asked on the stand by Colonel John Harlan Amen what instructions it received, Ohlendorf answered:

"The instructions were that the Jews and the Soviet political commissars were to be liquidated."

"And when you say 'liquidated,' do you mean 'killed'?" Amen asked.

"Yes, I mean killed," Ohlendorf answered, explaining that this took in the women and children as well as the men.

"For what reason were the children massacred?" the Russian judge, General I. T. Nikitchenko, broke in to ask.

OHLENDORF: The order was that the Jewish population should be totally exterminated.

THE JUDGE: Including the children?

OHLENDORF: Yes.

THE JUDGE: Were all the Jewish children murdered?

OHLENDORF: Yes.

In response to further questioning by Amen and in his affidavit, Ohlendorf described how a typical killing took place.

The *Einsatz* unit would enter a village or town and order the prominent Jewish citizens to call together all Jews for the purpose of "resettlement."* They were requested to hand over their valuables and shortly before execution to surrender their outer clothing. They were transported to the place of executions, usually an antitank ditch, in trucks—always only as many as could be executed immediately. In this way it was attempted to keep the span of time from the moment in which the victims knew what was about to happen to them until the time of their actual execution as short as possible.

Then they were shot, kneeling or standing, by firing squads in a military manner and the corpses thrown into the ditch. I never permitted the shooting by individuals, but ordered that several of the men should shoot at the same time in order to avoid direct personal responsibility. Other group leaders demanded that the victims lie down flat on the ground to be shot through the nape of the neck. I did not approve of these methods.

"Why?" asked Amen.

"Because," replied Ohlendorf, "both for the victims and for those who carried out the executions, it was, psychologically, an immense burden to bear."

In the spring of 1942, Ohlendorf then recounted, an order came from

---

* I.e., they were told they were being resettled elsewhere.

Himmler to change the method of execution of the women and children.*
Henceforth they were to be dispatched in "gas vans" specially constructed
for the purpose by two Berlin firms. The S.D. officer described to the
tribunal how these remarkable vehicles worked.

The actual purpose of these vans could not be seen from the outside. They
looked like closed trucks and were so constructed that at the start of the motor
the gas [exhaust] was conducted into the van causing death in ten to fifteen
minutes.

"How were the victims induced to enter the vans?" Colonel Amen
wanted to know.

"They were told they were to be transported to another locality," Ohlendorf replied.†

The burial of the victims of the gas vans, he went on to complain, was a
"great ordeal" for the members of the Einsatzgruppen. This was confirmed by a certain Dr. Becker, whom Ohlendorf identified as the con-
structor of the vans, in a document produced at Nuremberg. In a letter to
headquarters Dr. Becker objected to German S.D. men having to unload
the corpses of the gassed women and children, calling attention to

the immense psychological injuries and damage to their health which that work
can have for these men. They complained to me about headaches which
appeared after each unloading.

Dr. Becker also pointed out to his superiors that

the application of gas usually is not undertaken correctly. In order to come to
an end as fast as possible, the driver presses the accelerator to the fullest extent.
The persons to be executed suffer death from suffocation and not death by
dozing off, as was planned.

Dr. Becker was quite a humanitarian—in his own mind—and ordered
a change in technique.

My directions now have proved that by correct adjustment of the levers
death comes faster and the prisoners fall asleep peacefully. Distorted faces
and excretions, such as could be seen before, are no longer noticed.[45]

But the gas vans, as Ohlendorf testified, could dispatch only from fifteen to twenty-five persons at a time, and this was entirely inadequate for

---

* There was a special reason for this. See below, p. 962n.
† Ohlendorf was tried at Nuremberg by a U.S. military tribunal along with twenty-
one others in the "Einsatzgruppen Case." Fourteen of them were condemned to
death. Only four, Ohlendorf and three other group commanders, were executed—on
June 8, 1951, at Landsberg prison, some three and a half years after being sentenced.
The death penalties for the others were commuted.

the massacres on the scale which Hitler and Himmler had ordered. Inadequate, for example, for the job that was done at Kiev, the capital of the Ukraine, in just two days, September 29 and 30, 1941, when according to an official *Einsatz* report 33,771 persons, mostly Jews, were "executed."[46]

An eyewitness report by a German of how a comparatively minor mass execution was carried out in the Ukraine brought a hush of horror over the Nuremberg courtroom when it was read by the chief British prosecutor, Sir Hartley Shawcross. It was a sworn affidavit by Hermann Graebe, the manager and engineer of a branch office in the Ukraine of a German construction firm. On October 5, 1942, he witnessed the *Einsatz* commandos, supported by Ukrainian militia, in action at the execution pits at Dubno in the Ukraine. It was a matter, he reported, of liquidating the town's 5,000 Jews.

. . . My foreman and I went directly to the pits. I heard rifle shots in quick succession from behind one of the earth mounds. The people who had got off the trucks—men, women and children of all ages—had to undress upon the order of an S.S. man, who carried a riding or dog whip. They had to put down their clothes in fixed places, sorted according to shoes, top clothing and underclothing. I saw a heap of shoes of about 800 to 1,000 pairs, great piles of under-linen and clothing.

Without screaming or weeping these people undressed, stood around in family groups, kissed each other, said farewells and waited for a sign from another S.S. man, who stood near the pit, also with a whip in his hand. During the fifteen minutes that I stood near the pit I heard no complaint or plea for mercy . . .

An old woman with snow-white hair was holding a one-year-old child in her arms and singing to it and tickling it. The child was cooing with delight. The parents were looking on with tears in their eyes. The father was holding the hand of a boy about 10 years old and speaking to him softly; the boy was fighting his tears. The father pointed to the sky, stroked his head and seemed to explain something to him.

At that moment the S.S. man at the pit shouted something to his comrade. The latter counted off about twenty persons and instructed them to go behind the earth mound . . . I well remember a girl, slim and with black hair, who, as she passed close to me, pointed to herself and said: "twenty-three years old."

I walked around the mound and found myself confronted by a tremendous grave. People were closely wedged together and lying on top of each other so that only their heads were visible. Nearly all had blood running over their shoulders from their heads. Some of the people were still moving. Some were lifting their arms and turning their heads to show that they were still alive. The pit was already two-thirds full. I estimated that it contained about a thousand people. I looked for the man who did the shooting. He was an S.S. man, who sat at the edge of the narrow end of the pit, his feet dangling into the pit. He had a tommy gun on his knees and was smoking a cigarette.

The people, completely naked, went down some steps and clambered over the heads of the people lying there to the place to which the S.S. man directed them. They lay down in front of the dead or wounded people; some caressed those who were still alive and spoke to them in a low voice. Then I heard a series of shots. I looked into the pit and saw that the bodies were twitching or the heads lying already motionless on top of the bodies that lay beneath them. Blood was running from their necks.

The next batch was approaching already. They went down into the pit, lined themselves up against the previous victims and were shot.

And so it went, batch after batch. The next morning the German engineer returned to the site.

I saw about thirty naked people lying near the pit. Some of them were still alive . . . Later the Jews still alive were ordered to throw the corpses into the pit. Then they themselves had to lie down in this to be shot in the neck . . . I swear before God that this is the absolute truth.[47]

How many Jews and Russian Communist party functionaries (the former vastly outnumbered the latter) were massacred by the Einsatzgruppen in Russia before the Red Army drove the Germans out? The exact total could never be computed at Nuremberg but Himmler's records, uncoordinated as they were, give a rough idea.

Ohlendorf's Einsatzgruppen D, with its 90,000 victims, did not do as well as some of the other groups. Group A, for instance, in the north reported on January 31, 1942, that it had "executed" 229,052 Jews in the Baltic region and in White Russia. Its commander, Franz Stahlecker, reported to Himmler that he was having difficulty in the latter province because of a late start "after the heavy frost set in, which made mass executions much more difficult. Nevertheless," he reported, "41,000 Jews [in White Russia] have been shot up to now." Stahlecker, who was disposed of later in the year by Soviet partisans, enclosed with his report a handsome map showing the number of those done to death—symbolized by coffins—in each area under his command. In Lithuania, alone, the map showed, 136,421 Jews had been slain; some 34,000 had been spared for the time being "as they were needed for labor." Estonia, which had relatively few Jews, was declared in this report to be "Jew-free."[48]

The Einsatzgruppen firing squads, after a letup during the severe winter, banged away all through the summer of 1942. Some 55,000 more Jews were exterminated in White Russia by July 1, and in October the remaining 16,200 inhabitants of the Minsk ghetto were dispatched in one day. By November Himmler could report to Hitler that 363,211 Jews had been killed in Russia from August through October, though the figure was probably somewhat exaggerated to please the bloodthirsty Fuehrer.[49]*

---

* On August 31, Himmler had ordered an *Einsatz* detachment to execute a hundred inmates of the Minsk prison, so that he could see how it was done. According to Bach-Zalewski, a high officer in the S.S. who was present, Himmler almost swooned

All in all, according to Karl Eichmann, the head of the Jewish Office of the Gestapo, two million persons, almost all Jews, were liquidated by the Einsatzgruppen in the East. But this is almost certainly an exaggeration; it is strange but true that the S.S. bigwigs were so proud of their extermination that they often reported swollen figures to please Himmler and Hitler. Himmler's own statistician, Dr. Richard Korherr, reported to his chief on March 23, 1943, that a total of 633,300 Jews in Russia had been "resettled"—a euphemism for massacre by the Einsatzgruppen.[51] Surprisingly enough this figure tallies fairly well with exhaustive studies later made by a number of experts. Add another hundred thousand slain in the last two years of the war and the figure is probably as accurate as we will ever have.*

High as it is, it is small compared to the number of Jews who were done to death in Himmler's extermination camps when the "final solution" came to be carried out.

THE "FINAL SOLUTION"

One fine June day of 1946 at Nuremberg three members of the American prosecution staff were interrogating S.S. Obergruppenfuehrer Oswald Pohl, who, among other things, had been in charge of work projects for the inmates of the Nazi concentration camps. Pohl, a naval officer before he joined the S.S., had gone into hiding after the German collapse and had not been apprehended until a year later—in May 1946—when he was discovered working on a farm disguised as a farmhand.†

In answer to one question Pohl used a term with which the Nuremberg prosecution, busy for months in poring over millions of words from the captured documents, had begun to become familiar. A certain colleague by the name of Hoess had, Pohl said, been employed by Himmler "in the final solution of the Jewish question."

"And what was that?" Pohl was asked.

"The extermination of Jewry," he answered.

The expression crept with increasing frequency into the vocabulary and

---

when he saw the effect of the first volley from the firing squad. A few minutes later, when the shots failed to kill two Jewish women outright, the S.S. Fuehrer became hysterical. One result of this experience was an order from Himmler that henceforth the women and children should not be shot but dispatched in the gas vans.[50] (See above, p. 960.)

* The number of Soviet Communist party functionaries slain by the Einsatzgruppen has never even been estimated, as far as I know. Most S.D. reports lumped them together with the Jews. In one report of Group A, dated October 15, 1941, some 3,387 "Communists" are listed among the 121,817 executed, the rest being Jews. But the same report often lists the two together.

† Pohl was condemned to death in the so-called "Concentration Camp Case" by a U.S. military tribunal on November 3, 1947, and hanged in Landsberg prison on June 8, 1951, along with Ohlendorf and others.

the files of the leading Nazis as the war progressed, its seeming innocence apparently sparing these men the pain of reminding one another what it meant and perhaps too, they may have thought, furnishing a certain cover for their guilt should the incriminating papers ever come to light. Indeed at the Nuremberg trials most of the Nazi chiefs denied that they knew what it signified, and Goering contended he had never used the term, but this pretense was soon exploded. In the case against the fat Reich Marshal a directive was produced which he had sent Heydrich, the chief of the S.D., on July 31, 1941, when the Einsatzgruppen were already falling with gusto to their extermination tasks in Russia.

I herewith commission you [Goering instructed Heydrich] to carry out all preparations with regard to . . . a *total solution* of the Jewish question in those territories of Europe which are under German influence . . .

I furthermore charge you to submit to me as soon as possible a draft showing the . . . measures already taken for the execution of the intended *final solution* of the Jewish question.*[52]

Heydrich knew very well what Goering meant by the term for he had used it himself nearly a year before at a secret meeting after the fall of Poland, in which he had outlined "the first step in the final solution," which consisted of concentrating all the Jews in the ghettos of the large cities, where it would be easy to dispatch them to their final fate.†

As it worked out, the "final solution" was what Adolf Hitler had long had in mind and what he had publicly proclaimed even before the war started. In his speech to the Reichstag on January 30, 1939, he had said:

If the international Jewish financiers . . . should again succeed in plunging the nations into a world war the result will be . . . the annihilation of the Jewish race throughout Europe.

This was a prophecy, he said, and he repeated it five times, verbatim, in subsequent public utterances. It made no difference that not the "international Jewish financiers" but he himself plunged the world into armed conflict. What mattered to Hitler was that there was now a world war and that it afforded him, after he had conquered vast regions in the East where most of Europe's Jews lived, the opportunity to carry out their "annihilation." By the time the invasion of Russia began, he had given the necessary orders.

What became known in high Nazi circles as the "Fuehrer Order on the Final Solution" apparently was never committed to paper—at least no

---

* The emphasis is this writer's. A faulty translation of the last line, rendering the German word *Endloesung* as "desired solution" instead of "*final* solution" in the English copy of the document, led Justice Jackson, who did not know German, to allow Goering under cross-examination to get away with his contention that he never used the sinister term. (See n. 54.) "The first time I learned of these terrible exterminations," Goering exclaimed at one point, "was right here in Nuremberg."
† See above, p. 661.

copy of it has yet been unearthed in the captured Nazi documents. All the evidence shows that it was most probably given verbally to Goering, Himmler and Heydrich, who passed it down during the summer and fall of 1941. A number of witnesses testified at Nuremberg that they had "heard" of it but none admitted ever seeing it. Thus Hans Lammers, the bullheaded chief of the Reich Chancellery, when pressed on the witness stand replied:

> I knew that a Fuehrer order was transmitted by Goering to Heydrich . . . This order was called "Final Solution of the Jewish Problem."[53]

But Lammers claimed, as did so many others on the stand, that he did not really know what it was all about until Allied counsel revealed it at Nuremberg.*

By the beginning of 1942 the time had come, as Heydrich said, "to clear up the fundamental problems" of the "final solution" so that it could at last be carried out and concluded. For this purpose Heydrich convened a meeting of representatives of the various ministries and agencies of the S.S.-S.D. at the pleasant Berlin suburb of Wannsee on January 20, 1942, the minutes of which played an important part in some of the later Nuremberg trials.[54] Despite the current setback of the Wehrmacht in Russia the Nazi officials believed that the war was almost won and that Germany would shortly be ruling all of Europe, including England and Ireland. Therefore, Heydrich told the assembly of some fifteen high officials, "in the course of this Final Solution of the European Jewish problem, approximately eleven million Jews are involved." He then rattled off the figures for each country. There were only 131,800 Jews left in the original Reich territory (out of a quarter of a million in 1939), but in the U.S.S.R., he said, there were five million, in the Ukraine three million, in the General Government of Poland two and a quarter million, in France three quarters of a million and in England a third of a million. The clear implication was that all eleven million must be exterminated. He then explained how this considerable task was to be carried out.

> The Jews should now in the course of the Final Solution be brought to the East . . . for use as labor. In big labor gangs, with separation of sexes, the

---

* Lammers was sentenced in April 1949 to twenty years' imprisonment by a U.S. military tribunal at Nuremberg, chiefly because of his responsibility in the anti-Jewish decrees. But as in the case of most of the other convicted Nazis whose sentences were greatly reduced by the American authorities, his term was commuted in 1951 to ten years and he was released from Landsberg prison at the end of that year, after serving a total of six years from the date of his first imprisonment. It might be noted here that most Germans, at least so far as their sentiment was represented in the West German parliament, did not approve of even the relatively mild sentences meted out to Hitler's accomplices. A number of them handed over by the Allies to German custody were not even prosecuted—even when they were accused of mass murder—and some of them quickly found employment in the Bonn government.

966 THE RISE AND FALL OF THE THIRD REICH

Jews capable of work are brought to these areas and employed in road building, in which task undoubtedly a great part will fall through natural diminution.

The remnant that finally is able to survive all this—since this is undoubtedly the part with the strongest resistance—must be treated accordingly, since these people, representing a natural selection, are to be regarded as the germ cell of a new Jewish development.

In other words, the Jews of Europe were first to be transported to the conquered East, then worked to death, and the few tough ones who survived simply put to death. And the Jews—the millions of them—who resided in the East and were already on hand? State Secretary Dr. Josef Buehler, representing the Governor General of Poland, had a ready suggestion for them. There were nearly two and a half million Jews in Poland, he said, who "constituted a great danger." They were, he explained, "bearers of disease, black-market operators and furthermore unfit for work." There was no transportation problem with these two and a half million souls. They were already there.

I have only one request [Dr. Buehler concluded], that the Jewish problem in my territory be solved as quickly as possible.

The good State Secretary betrayed an impatience which was shared in high Nazi circles right up to Hitler. None of them understood at this time—not, in fact, until toward the end of 1942, when it was too late—how valuable the millions of Jews might be to the Reich as slave labor. At this point they only understood that working millions of Jews to death on the roads of Russia might take some time. Consequently long before these unfortunate people could be worked to death—in most cases the attempt was not even begun—Hitler and Himmler decided to dispatch them by quicker means.

There were two—principally. One of them, as we have seen, had begun shortly after the invasion of Russia in the summer of 1941. This was the method of mass slaughter of the Polish and Russian Jews by the flying firing squads of the Einsatzgruppen, which accounted for some three quarters of a million.

It was this method of achieving the "final solution" that Himmler had in mind when he addressed the S.S. generals at Posen on October 4, 1943.

. . . I also want to talk to you quite frankly on a very grave matter. Among ourselves it should be mentioned quite frankly, and yet we will never speak of it publicly . . .

I mean . . . the extermination of the Jewish race . . . Most of *you* must know what it means when 100 corpses are lying side by side, or 500, or 1,000. To have stuck it out and at the same time—apart from exceptions caused by human weakness—to have remained decent fellows, that is what has made us hard. This is a page of glory in our history which has never been written and is never to be written . . .[55]

No doubt the bespectacled S.S. Fuehrer, who had almost fainted at the sight of a hundred Eastern Jews, including women, being executed for his own delectation, would have seen in the efficient working by S.S. officers of the gas chambers in the extermination camps an even more glorious page in German history. For it was in these death camps that the "final solution" achieved its most ghastly success.

THE EXTERMINATION CAMPS

All the thirty odd principal Nazi concentration camps were death camps and millions of tortured, starved inmates perished in them.[*] Though the authorities kept records—each camp had its official *Totenbuch* (death book)—they were incomplete and in many cases were destroyed as the victorious Allies closed in. Part of one *Totenbuch* that survived at Mauthausen listed 35,318 deaths from January 1939 to April 1945.[†] At the end of 1942 when the need of slave labor began to be acute, Himmler ordered that the death rate in the concentration camps "must be reduced." Because of the labor shortage he had been displeased at a report received in his office that of the 136,700 commitments to concentration camps between June and November 1942, some 70,610 had died and that in addition 9,267 had been executed and 27,846 "transferred."[57] To the gas chamber, that is. This did not leave very many for labor duties.

But it was in the extermination camps, the *Vernichtungslager,* where most progress was made toward the "final solution." The greatest and most renowned of these was Auschwitz, whose four huge gas chambers and adjoining crematoria gave it a capacity for death and burial far beyond that of the others—Treblinka, Belsec, Sibibor and Chelmno, all in Poland. There were other minor extermination camps near Riga, Vilna, Minsk, Kaunas and Lwów, but they were distinguished from the main ones in that they killed by shooting rather than by gas.

For a time there was quite a bit of rivalry among the S.S. leaders as to which was the most efficient gas to speed the Jews to their death. Speed was an important factor, especially at Auschwitz, where toward the end the camp was setting new records by gassing 6,000 victims a day. One of the camp's commanders for a period was Rudolf Hoess, an ex-convict once found guilty of murder, who deposed at Nuremberg on the superiority of the gas he employed.[‡]

---

[*] Kogon estimates the number at 7,125,000 out of a total of 7,820,000 inmates, but the figure undoubtedly is too high. (Kogon, *The Theory and Practice of Hell,* p. 227.)

[†] The camp commander, Franz Ziereis, put the total number at 65,000.[56]

[‡] Born in 1900, the son of a small shopkeeper in Baden-Baden, Hoess was pressured by his pious Catholic father to become a priest. Instead he joined the Nazi Party in 1922. The next year he was implicated in the murder of a school teacher who allegedly had denounced Leo Schlageter, a German saboteur in the Ruhr who

The "Final Solution" of the Jewish question meant the complete extermination of all Jews in Europe. I was ordered to establish extermination facilities at Auschwitz in June 1941. At that time there were already in the General Government of Poland three other extermination camps: Belzec, Treblinka and Wolzek . . .

I visited Treblinka to find out how they carried out their extermination. The camp commandant at Treblinka told me that he had liquidated 80,000 in the course of half a year. He was principally concerned with liquidating all the Jews from the Warsaw ghetto.*

He used monoxide gas and I did not think that his methods were very efficient. So when I set up the extermination building at Auschwitz, I used Zyklon B, which was a crystallized prussic acid which we dropped into the death chamber from a small opening. It took from three to fifteen minutes to kill the people in the death chamber, depending upon climatic conditions.

We knew when the people were dead because their screaming stopped. We usually waited about a half hour before we opened the doors and removed the bodies. After the bodies were removed our special commandos took off the rings and extracted the gold from the teeth of the corpses.

Another improvement we made over Treblinka was that we built our gas chambers to accommodate 2,000 people at one time, whereas at Treblinka their ten gas chambers only accommodated 200 people each.

Hoess then explained how the victims were "selected" for the gas chambers, since not all the incoming prisoners were done away with—at least not at once, because some of them were needed to labor in the I. G. Farben chemical works and Krupp's factory until they became exhausted and were ready for the "final solution."

We had two S.S. doctors on duty at Auschwitz to examine the incoming transports of prisoners. These would be marched by one of the doctors, who would make spot decisions as they walked by. Those who were fit to work were sent into the camp. Others were sent immediately to the extermination plants. Children of tender years were invariably exterminated since by reason of their youth they were unable to work.

---

was executed by the French and became a Nazi martyr. Hoess received a life sentence.

He was released in a general amnesty in 1928, joined the S.S. two years later and in 1934 became a member of the Death's Head group of the S.S., whose principal job was the guarding of the concentration camps. His first job in this unit was at Dachau. Thus he spent almost his entire adult life first as a prisoner and then as a jailer. He freely—and even exaggeratedly—testified to his killings both on the stand at Nuremberg and in affidavits for the prosecution. Turned over later to the Poles, he was sentenced to death and in March 1947 hanged at Auschwitz, the scene of his greatest crimes.

* A task which because of the large numbers involved and because of, at the end, armed resistance, could not be completed (as we shall see) until 1943.

Always Herr Hoess kept making improvements in the art of mass killing.

Still another improvement we made over Treblinka was that at Treblinka the victims almost always knew that they were to be exterminated, while at Auschwitz we endeavored to fool the victims into thinking that they were to go through a delousing process. Of course, frequently they realized our true intentions and we sometimes had riots and difficulties. Very frequently women would hide their children under the clothes but of course when we found them we would send the children in to be exterminated.

We were required to carry out these exterminations in secrecy, but of course the foul and nauseating stench from the continuous burning of bodies permeated the entire area and all of the people living in the surrounding communities knew that exterminations were going on at Auschwitz.

Sometimes, Hoess explained, a few "special prisoners"—apparently Russian prisoners of war—were simply killed by injections of benzine. "Our doctors," he added, "had orders to write ordinary death certificates and could put down any reason at all for the cause of death.*[58]

To Hoess's blunt description may be added a brief composite picture of death and disposal at Auschwitz as testified to by surviving inmates and jailers. The "selection," which decided which Jews were to be worked and which ones immediately gassed, took place at the railroad siding as soon as the victims had been unloaded from the freight cars in which they had been locked without food or water for as much as a week—for many came from such distant parts as France, Holland and Greece. Though there were heart-rending scenes as wives were torn away from husbands and children from parents, none of the captives, as Hoess testified and survivors agree, realized just what was in store for them. In fact some of them were given pretty picture postcards marked "Waldsee" to be signed and sent back home to their relatives with a printed inscription saying:

We are doing very well here. We have work and we are well treated. We await your arrival.

The gas chambers themselves and the adjoining crematoria, viewed from a short distance, were not sinister-looking places at all; it was impossible to make them out for what they were. Over them were well-kept lawns with flower borders; the signs at the entrances merely said BATHS. The unsuspecting Jews thought they were simply being taken to the baths for the delousing which was customary at all camps. And taken to the accompaniment of sweet music!

---

* Usually "heart disease" was written down. Kogon, himself in Buchenwald for eight years, gives samples: ". . . Patient died after prolonged suffering on ＿＿＿ at ＿＿＿ o'clock. Cause of death: cardiac weakness complicated by pneumonia." (Kogon, *The Theory and Practice of Hell*, p. 218.) Such formalities were dispensed with at Auschwitz when the massive gassings began. Often the day's dead were not even counted.

For there was light music. An orchestra of "young and pretty girls all dressed in white blouses and navy-blue skirts," as one survivor remembered, had been formed from among the inmates. While the selection was being made for the gas chambers this unique musical ensemble played gay tunes from *The Merry Widow* and *Tales of Hoffmann*. Nothing solemn and somber from Beethoven. The death marches at Auschwitz were sprightly and merry tunes, straight out of Viennese and Parisian operetta.

To such music, recalling as it did happier and more frivolous times, the men, women and children were led into the "bath houses," where they were told to undress preparatory to taking a "shower." Sometimes they were even given towels. Once they were inside the "shower-room"—and perhaps this was the first moment that they may have suspected something was amiss, for as many as two thousand of them were packed into the chamber like sardines, making it difficult to take a bath—the massive door was slid shut, locked and hermetically sealed. Up above where the well-groomed lawn and flower beds almost concealed the mushroom-shaped lids of vents that ran up from the hall of death, orderlies stood ready to drop into them the amethyst-blue crystals of hydrogen cyanide, or Zyklon B, which originally had been commercially manufactured as a strong disinfectant and for which, as we have seen, Herr Hoess had with so much pride found a new use.

Surviving prisoners watching from blocks nearby remembered how for a time the signal for the orderlies to pour the crystals down the vents was given by a Sergeant Moll. "*Na, gib ihnen schon zu fressen*" ("All right, give 'em something to chew on"), he would laugh and the crystals would be poured through the openings, which were then sealed.

Through heavy-glass portholes the executioners could watch what happened. The naked prisoners below would be looking up at the showers from which no water spouted or perhaps at the floor wondering why there were no drains. It took some moments for the gas to have much effect. But soon the inmates became aware that it was issuing from the perforations in the vents. It was then that they usually panicked, crowding away from the pipes and finally stampeding toward the huge metal door where, as Reitlinger puts it, "they piled up in one blue clammy blood-spattered pyramid, clawing and mauling each other even in death."

Twenty or thirty minutes later when the huge mass of naked flesh had ceased to writhe, pumps drew out the poisonous air, the large door was opened and the men of the *Sonderkommando* took over. These were Jewish male inmates who were promised their lives and adequate food in return for performing the most ghastly job of all.* Protected with gas masks and rubber boots and wielding hoses they went to work. Reitlinger has described it.

---

* They were inevitably and regularly dispatched in the gas chambers and replaced by new teams who continued to meet the same fate. The S.S. wanted no survivors to tell tales.

Their first task was to remove the blood and defecations before dragging the clawing dead apart with nooses and hooks, the prelude to the ghastly search for gold and the removal of teeth and hair which were regarded by the Germans as strategic materials. Then the journey by lift or rail-wagon to the furnaces, the mill that ground the clinker to fine ash, and the truck that scattered the ashes in the stream of the Sola.*

There had been, the records show, some lively competition among German businessmen to procure orders for building these death and disposal contraptions and for furnishing the lethal blue crystals. The firm of I. A. Topf and Sons of Erfurt, manufacturers of heating equipment, won out in its bid for the crematoria at Auschwitz. The story of its business enterprise was revealed in a voluminous correspondence found in the records of the camp. A letter from the firm dated February 12, 1943, gives the tenor.

To the Central Construction Office of the S.S. and Police, Auschwitz:

Subject: Crematoria 2 and 3 for the camp.

We acknowledge receipt of your order for five triple furnaces, including two electric elevators for raising the corpses and one emergency elevator. A practical installation for stoking coal was also ordered and one for transporting ashes.[60]

The correspondence of two other firms engaged in the crematorium business popped up at the Nuremberg trials. The disposal of the corpses at a number of Nazi camps had attracted commercial competition. One of the oldest German companies in the field offered its drawings for crematoria to be built at a large S.S. camp in Belgrade.

For putting the bodies into the furnace, we suggest simply a metal fork moving on cylinders.

Each furnace will have an oven measuring only 24 by 18 inches, as coffins will not be used. For transporting the corpses from the storage points to the furnaces we suggest using light carts on wheels, and we enclose diagrams of these drawn to scale.[61]

Another firm, C. H. Kori, also sought the Belgrade business, emphasizing its great experience in this field since it had already constructed four furnaces for Dachau and five for Lublin, which, it said, had given "full satisfaction in practice."

---

* There was testimony at the Nuremberg trials that the ashes were sometimes sold as fertilizer. One Danzig firm, according to a document offered by the Russian prosecution, constructed an electrically heated tank for making soap out of human fat. Its "recipe" called for "12 pounds of human fat, 10 quarts of water, and 8 ounces to a pound of caustic soda . . . all boiled for two or three hours and then cooled."[59]

Following our verbal discussion regarding the delivery of equipment of simple construction for the burning of bodies, we are submitting plans for our perfected cremation ovens which operate with coal and which have hitherto given full satisfaction.

We suggest two crematoria furnaces for the building planned, but we advise you to make further inquiries to make sure that two ovens will be sufficient for your requirements.

We guarantee the effectiveness of the cremation ovens as well as their durability, the use of the best material and our faultless workmanship.

Awaiting your further word, we will be at your service.

Heil Hitler!

C. H. KORI, G.M.B.H.[62]

In the end even the strenuous efforts of German free enterprise, using the best material and providing faultless workmanship, proved inadequate for burning the corpses. The well-constructed crematoria fell far behind at a number of camps but especially at Auschwitz in 1944 when as many as 6,000 bodies (Hoess put it at as many as 16,000) had to be burned daily. For instance, in forty-six days during the summer of 1944 between 250,000 and 300,000 Hungarian Jews alone were done to death at this camp. Even the gas chambers fell behind and resort was made to mass shootings in the *Einsatzkommando* style. The bodies were simply thrown into ditches and burned, many of them only partly, and then earth was bulldozed over them. The camp commanders complained toward the end that the crematoria had proved not only inadequate but "uneconomical."

The Zyklon-B crystals that killed the victims in the first place were furnished by two German firms which had acquired the patent from I. G. Farben. These were Tesch and Stabenow of Hamburg, and Degesch of Dessau, the former supplying two tons of the cyanide crystals a month and the latter three quarters of a ton. The bills of lading for the deliveries showed up at Nuremberg.

The directors of both concerns contended that they had sold their product merely for fumigation purposes and were unaware that lethal use had been made of it, but this defense did not hold up. Letters were found from Tesch and Stabenow offering not only to supply the gas crystals but also the ventilating and heating equipment for extermination chambers. Besides, the inimitable Hoess, who once he started to confess went the limit, testified that the directors of the Tesch company could not have helped knowing how their product was being used since they furnished enough to exterminate a couple of million people. A British military court was convinced of this at the trial of the two partners, Bruno Tesch and Karl Weinbacher, who were sentenced to death in 1946 and hanged. The director of the second firm, Dr. Gerhard Peters of Degesch of Dessau, got off more lightly. A German court sentenced him to five years' imprisonment.[63]

Before the postwar trials in Germany it had been generally believed that

the mass killings were exclusively the work of a relatively few fanatical
S.S. leaders. But the records of the courts leave no doubt of the complicity
of a number of German businessmen, not only the Krupps and the directors
of the I. G. Farben chemical trust but smaller entrepreneurs who outwardly
must have seemed to be the most prosaic and decent of men, pillars—like
good businessmen everywhere—of their communities.

How many hapless innocent people—mostly Jews but including a fairly
large number of others, especially Russian prisoners of war—were
slaughtered at the one camp of Auschwitz? The exact number will never
be known. Hoess himself in his affidavit gave an estimate of "2,500,000
victims executed and exterminated by gassing and burning, and at least
another half million who succumbed to starvation and disease, making a
total of about 3,000,000." Later at his own trial in Warsaw he reduced
the figure to 1,135,000. The Soviet government, which investigated the
camp after it was overrun by the Red Army in January 1945, put the figure
at four million. Reitlinger, on the basis of his own exhaustive study,
doubts that the number gassed at Auschwitz was "even as high as three
quarters of a million." He estimates that about 600,000 died in the gas
chambers, to which he adds "the unknown proportion" of some 300,000 or
more "missing," who were shot or who died of starvation and disease. By
any estimate the figure is considerable.[64]

The bodies were burned, but the gold fillings in the teeth remained and
these were retrieved from the ashes if they had not already been yanked
out by special squads working over the clammy piles of corpses.* The gold
was melted down and shipped along with other valuables snatched from
the condemned Jews to the Reichsbank, where under a secret agreement
between Himmler and the bank's president, Dr. Walther Funk, it was
deposited to the credit of the S.S. in an account given the cover name of
"Max Heiliger." This prize booty from the extermination camps included,
besides gold from dentures, gold watches, earrings, bracelets, rings, neck-
laces and even spectacles frames—for the Jews had been encouraged to
bring all their valuables with them for the promised "resettlement." There
were also great stocks of jewelry, especially diamonds and much silver-
ware. And there were great wads of banknotes.

The Reichsbank, in fact, was overwhelmed by the "Max Heiliger"
deposits. With its vaults filled to overflowing as early as 1942, the bank's
profit-minded directors sought to turn the holdings into cold cash by disposing of them through the municipal pawnshops. One letter from the
Reichsbank to the Berlin municipal pawnshop dated September 15 speaks

---

* Sometimes they were pulled out before the victims were slain. A secret report of
the German warden of the prison at Minsk disclosed that after he had commandeered
the services of a Jewish dentist all the Jews "had their gold bridgework, crowns and
fillings pulled or broken out. This happens always one to two hours before the
special action." The warden noted that of 516 German and Russian Jews executed
at his prison during a six-week period in the spring of 1943, some 336 had the gold
yanked from their teeth.[65]

of a "second shipment" and begins, "We submit to you the following valuables with the request for the best possible utilization." The list is long and itemized and includes 154 gold watches, 1,601 gold earrings, 132 diamond rings, 784 silver pocket watches and "160 diverse dentures, partly of gold." By the beginning of 1944 the Berlin pawnshop itself was overwhelmed by the flow of these stolen goods and informed the Reichsbank it could accept no more. When the Allies overran Germany they discovered in some abandoned salt mines, where the Nazis had hidden part of their records and booty, enough left over from the "Max Heiliger" account to fill three huge vaults in the Frankfurt branch of the Reichsbank.[66]

Did the bankers know the sources of these unique "deposits"? The manager of the Precious Metals Department of the Reichsbank deposed at Nuremberg that he and his associates began to notice that many shipments came from Lublin and Auschwitz.

We all knew that these places were the sites of concentration camps. It was in the tenth delivery in November, 1943, that dental gold appeared. The quantity of dental gold became unusually great.[67]

At Nuremberg the notorious Oswald Pohl, chief of the Economic Office of the S.S., who handled the transactions for his organization, emphasized that Dr. Funk and the officials and directors of the Reichsbank knew very well the origins of the goods they were trying to pawn. He explained in some detail "the business deal between Funk and the S.S. concerning the delivery of valuables of dead Jews to the Reichsbank." He remembered a conversation with the bank's vice-president, Dr. Emil Pohl.

In this conversation no doubt remained that the objects to be delivered [came from] Jews who had been killed in concentration camps. The objects in question were rings, watches, eyeglasses, gold bars, wedding rings, brooches, pins, gold fillings and other valuables.

Once, Pohl related, after an inspection tour through the vaults of the Reichsbank where the valuables "from the dead Jews" were inspected, Dr. Funk tendered the party a pleasant dinner in which the conversation turned around the unique origins of the booty.[68]*

"THE WARSAW GHETTO IS NO MORE"

More than one eyewitness has commented on the spirit of resignation with which so many Jews met their deaths in the Nazi gas chambers or in the great execution pits of the *Einsatz* squads. Not all Jews submitted to extermination so gently. In the spring days of 1943 some 60,000 Jews

---

* Dr. Funk was sentenced to life imprisonment at Nuremberg.

walled up in the Warsaw ghetto—all that remained of 400,000 who had been herded into this place like cattle in 1940—turned on their Nazi tormentors and fought.

Perhaps no one has left a more grisly—and authoritative—account of the Warsaw ghetto rebellion than the proud S.S. officer who put it down.* This German individual was Juergen Stroop, S.S. Brigadefuehrer and Major General of Police. His eloquent official report, bound in leather, profusely illustrated and typed on seventy-five pages of elegant heavy bond paper has survived.† It is entitled *The Warsaw Ghetto Is No More.*[69]

By the late autumn of 1940, a year after the Nazi conquest of Poland, the S.S. had rounded up some 400,000 Jews and sealed them off within a high wall from the rest of Warsaw in an area approximately two and a half miles long and a mile wide around the old medieval ghetto. The district normally housed 160,000 persons, so there was overcrowding, but this was the least of the hardships. Governor Frank refused to allot enough food to keep even half of the 400,000 barely alive. Forbidden to leave the enclosure on the pain of being shot on sight, the Jews had no employment except for a few armament factories within the wall run by the Wehrmacht or by rapacious German businessmen who knew how to realize large profits from the use of slave labor. At least 100,000 Jews tried to survive on a bowl of soup a day, often boiled from straw, provided by the charity of the others. It was a losing struggle for life.

But the ghetto population did not die fast enough from starvation and disease to suit Himmler, who in the summer of 1942 ordered the Jews in the Warsaw ghetto to be removed altogether "for security reasons." On July 22 a great "resettlement" action was instituted. Between then and October 3 a total of 310,322 Jews, according to Stroop, were "resettled." That is, they were transported to the extermination camps, most of them to Treblinka, where they were gassed.

Still Himmler was not satisfied. When he paid a surprise visit to Warsaw in January 1943 and discovered that 60,000 Jews were still alive in the ghetto he ordered that the "resettlement" be completed by February 15. This proved to be a difficult task. The severe winter and the demands of the Army, whose disaster at Stalingrad and whose consequent retreats in southern Russia gave it first claim to transportation facilities, made it difficult for the S.S. to obtain the necessary trains to carry out the final "resettlement." Also, Stroop reported, the Jews were resisting their final liquidation "in every possible way." It was not until spring that Himmler's order could be carried out. It was decided to clear out the ghetto in a "special action" lasting three days. As it turned out, it took four weeks.

---

* John Hersey's novel *The Wall,* based on the Jewish records, is an epic story of the uprising.

† But not Stroop. He was caught after the war, sentenced to death by an American court at Dachau on March 22, 1947, for the shooting of hostages in Greece, and then extradited to Poland, where he was tried for the slaughter of the Jews in the Warsaw ghetto. He was again sentenced to death and hanged at the scene of the crime on September 8, 1951.

The deportation of more than 300,000 Jews had enabled the Germans to reduce the size of the walled-in ghetto and as S.S. General Stroop turned his tanks, artillery, flame throwers and dynamite squads on it on the morning of April 19, 1943, it comprised an area measuring only 1,000 by 300 yards. It was honeycombed, though, with sewers, vaults and cellars which the desperate Jews had converted into fortified points. Their arms were few: some pistols and rifles, a dozen or two machine guns that had been smuggled in, and homemade grenades. But they were now on that April morning determined to use them—the first time and the last in the history of the Third Reich that the Jews resisted their Nazi oppressors with arms.

Stroop had 2,090 men, about half of them Regular Army or Waffen-S.S. troops, and the rest S.S. police reinforced by 335 Lithuanian militia and some Polish police and firemen. They ran into unexpected resistance the first day.

Hardly had operation begun [Stroop reported in the first of his many teletyped daily reports], than we ran into strong concerted fire by the Jews and bandits. The tank and two armored cars pelted with Molotov cocktails . . . Owing to this enemy counterattack we had to withdraw.

The German attack was renewed but found heavy going.

About 1730 hours we encountered very strong resistance from one block of buildings, including machine-gun fire. A special raiding party defeated the enemy but could not catch the resisters. The Jews and criminals resisted from base to base and escaped at the last moment . . . Our losses in first attack: 12 men.

And so it went for the first few days, the poorly armed defenders giving ground before the attacks of tanks, flame throwers and artillery but keeping up their resistance. General Stroop could not understand why "this trash and subhumanity," as he referred to the besieged Jews, did not give up and submit to being liquidated.

Within a few days [he reported] it became apparent that the Jews no longer had any intention to resettle voluntarily, but were determined to resist evacuation . . . Whereas it had been possible during the first days to catch considerable numbers of Jews, who are cowards by nature, it became more and more difficult during the second half of the operation to capture the bandits and Jews. Over and over again new battle groups consisting of 20 to 30 Jewish men, accompanied by a corresponding number of women, kindled new resistance.

The women belonged to the Chalutzim, Stroop noted, and had the habit, he said, of "firing pistols with both hands" and also of unlimbering hand grenades which they concealed in their bloomers.

On the fifth day of the battle, an impatient and furious Himmler ordered Stroop to "comb out" the ghetto "with the greatest severity and relentless tenacity."

I therefore decided [Stroop related in his final report] to destroy the entire Jewish area by setting every block on fire.

He then described what followed.

The Jews stayed in the burning buildings until because of the fear of being burned alive they jumped down from the upper stories . . . With their bones broken, they still tried to crawl across the street into buildings which had not yet been set on fire . . . Despite the danger of being burned alive the Jews and bandits often preferred to return into the flames rather than risk being caught by us.

It was simply incomprehensible to a man of Stroop's stripe that men and women preferred to die in the flames fighting rather than to die peacefully in the gas chambers. For he was shipping off the captured whom he did not slaughter to Treblinka. On April 25 he sent a teletype to S.S. headquarters reporting that 27,464 Jews had been captured.

I am going to try to obtain a train for T2 [Treblinka] tomorrow. Otherwise liquidation will be carried out here tomorrow.

Often it was, on the spot. The next day Stroop informed his superiors: "1,330 Jews pulled out of dugouts and immediately destroyed; 362 Jews killed in battle." Only thirty prisoners were "evacuated."

Toward the end of the rebellion the defenders took to the sewers. Stroop tried to flush them out by flooding the mains but the Jews managed to stop the flow of water. One day the Germans dropped smoke bombs into the sewers through 183 manholes but Stroop ruefully reported that they failed to "have the desired results."

The final outcome could never be in doubt. For a whole month the cornered Jews fought with reckless courage though Stroop, in one daily report, put it differently, complaining about the "cunning fighting methods and tricks used by the Jews and bandits." By April 26 he reported that many of the defenders were "going insane from the heat, the smoke and the explosions."

During the day several more blocks of buildings were burned down. This is the only and final method which forces this trash and subhumanity to the surface.

The last day was May 16. That night Stroop got off his last daily battle report.

One hundred eighty Jews, bandits and subhumans were destroyed. The former Jewish quarter of Warsaw is no longer in existence. The large-scale action was terminated at 2015 hours by blowing up the Warsaw synagogue . . .

Total number of Jews dealt with: 56,065, including both Jews caught and Jews whose extermination can be proved.

A week later he was asked to explain that figure, and he replied:

Of the total of 56,065 caught, about 7,000 were destroyed in the former ghetto during large-scale operation. 6,929 Jews were destroyed by transporting them to Treblinka; the sum total of Jews destroyed is therefore 13,929. Beyond that, from five to six thousand Jews were destroyed by being blown up or by perishing in the flames.

General Stroop's arithmetic is not very clear since this report leaves some 36,000 Jews unaccounted for. But there can be little doubt that he was telling the truth when he wrote in his handsomely bound final report that he had caught "a total of 56,065 Jews whose extermination can be proved." The gas chambers no doubt accounted for the 36,000.

German losses, according to Stroop, were sixteen killed and ninety wounded. Probably the true figures were much higher, given the nature of the savage house-to-house fighting which the general himself described in such lurid detail, but were kept low so as not to disturb Himmler's fine sensibilities. The German troops and police, Stroop concluded, "fulfilled their duty indefatigably in faithful comradeship and stood together as exemplary models of soldiers."

The "final solution" went on to the very end of the war. How many Jews did it massacre? The figure has been debated. According to two S.S. witnesses at Nuremberg the total was put at between five and six millions by one of the great Nazi experts on the subject, Karl Eichmann, chief of the Jewish Office of the Gestapo, who carried out the "final solution" under the prodding hand of its originator, Heydrich.* The figure given in the Nuremberg indictment was 5,700,000 and it tallied with the calculations of the World Jewish Congress. Reitlinger in his prodigious study of the Final Solution concluded that the figure was somewhat less— between 4,194,200 and 4,581,200.[71]

There were some ten million Jews living in 1939 in the territories occupied by Hitler's forces. By any estimate it is certain that nearly half of them were exterminated by the Germans. This was the final consequence

---

* Eichmann, according to one of his henchmen, said just before the German collapse that "he would leap laughing into the grave because the feeling that he had five million people on his conscience would be for him a source of extraordinary satisfaction."[70] Probably he never leaped into the grave, laughing or otherwise. He escaped from an American internment camp in 1945. (NOTE: As this book went on press, the government of Israel announced that it had apprehended Eichmann.)

and the shattering cost of the aberration which came over the Nazi dictator in his youthful gutter days in Vienna and which he imparted to—or shared with—so many of his German followers.

THE MEDICAL EXPERIMENTS

There were some practices of the Germans during the short-lived New Order that resulted from sheer sadism rather than a lust for mass murder. Perhaps to a psychiatrist there is a difference between the two lusts though the end result of the first differed from the second only in the scale of deaths.

The Nazi medical experiments are an example of this sadism, for in the use of concentration camp inmates and prisoners of war as human guinea pigs very little, if any, benefit to science was achieved. It is a tale of horror of which the German medical profession cannot be proud. Although the "experiments" were conducted by fewer than two hundred murderous quacks—albeit some of them held eminent posts in the medical world—their criminal work was known to thousands of leading physicians of the Reich, not a single one of whom, so far as the record shows, ever uttered the slightest public protest.*

In the murders in this field the Jews were not the only victims. The Nazi doctors also used Russian prisoners of war, Polish concentration camp inmates, women as well as men, and even Germans. The "experiments" were quite varied. Prisoners were placed in pressure chambers and subjected to high-altitude tests until they ceased breathing. They were injected with lethal doses of typhus and jaundice. They were subjected to "freezing" experiments in icy water or exposed naked in the snow outdoors until they froze to death. Poison bullets were tried out on them as was mustard gas. At the Ravensbrueck concentration camp for women hundreds of Polish inmates—the "rabbit girls" they were called—were given gas gangrene wounds while others were subjected to "experiments" in bone grafting. At Dachau and Buchenwald gypsies were selected to see how long, and in what manner, they could live on salt water. Sterilization experiments were carried out on a large scale at several camps by a variety of means on both men and women; for, as an S.S. physician, Dr. Adolf Pokorny, wrote Himmler on one occasion, "the enemy must be not only conquered but exterminated." If he could not be slaughtered—and the need for slave labor toward the end of the war made that practice question-

---

* Not even Germany's most famous surgeon, Dr. Ferdinand Sauerbruch, though he eventually became an anti-Nazi and conspired with the resistance. Sauerbruch sat through a lecture at the Berlin Military Medical Academy in May of 1943 given by two of the most notorious of the doctor-killers, Karl Gebhardt and Fritz Fischer, on the subject of gas gangrene experiments on prisoners. Sauerbruch's only argument on this occasion was that surgery was better than sulfanilamide! Professor Gebhardt was sentenced to death at the so-called "Doctors' Trial" and hanged on June 2, 1948. Dr. Fischer was given life imprisonment.

able, as we have seen—then he could be prevented from propagating. In fact Dr. Pokorny told Himmler he thought he had found just the right means, the plant *Caladium seguinum,* which, he said, induced lasting sterility.

The thought alone [the good doctor wrote the S.S. Fuehrer] that the three million Bolsheviks now in German captivity could be sterilized, so that they would be available for work but precluded from propagation, opens up the most far-reaching perspectives.[72]

Another German doctor who had "far-reaching perspectives" was Professor August Hirt, head of the Anatomical Institute of the University of Strasbourg. His special field was somewhat different from those of the others and he explained it in a letter at Christmas time of 1941 to S.S. Lieutenant General Rudolf Brandt, Himmler's adjutant.

We have large collections of skulls of almost all races and peoples at our disposal. Of the Jewish race, however, only very few specimens of skulls are available . . . The war in the East now presents us with the opportunity to overcome this deficiency. By procuring the skulls of the Jewish-Bolshevik commissars, who represent the prototype of the repulsive, but characteristic, subhuman, we have the chance now to obtain scientific material.

Professor Hirt did not want the skulls of "Jewish-Bolshevik commissars" already dead. He proposed that the heads of these persons first be measured while they were alive. Then—

Following the subsequently induced death of the Jew, whose head should not be damaged, the physician will sever the head from the body and will forward it . . . in a hermetically sealed tin can.

Whereupon Dr. Hirt would go to work, he promised, on further scientific measurements.[73] Himmler was delighted. He directed that Professor Hirt "be supplied with everything needed for his research work."

He was well supplied. The actual supplier was an interesting Nazi individual by the name of Wolfram Sievers, who spent considerable time on the witness stand at the main Nuremberg trial and at the subsequent "Doctors' Trial," in the latter of which he was a defendant.* Sievers, a former bookseller, had risen to be a colonel of the S.S. and executive secretary of the Ahnenerbe, the Institute for Research into Heredity, one of the ridiculous "cultural" organizations established by Himmler to pursue one of his many lunacies. It had, according to Sievers, fifty "research branches," of which one was called the "Institute for Military Scientific Research," which Sievers also headed. He was a shifty-eyed, Mephistophelean-looking fellow with a thick, ink-black beard and at

---

* And in which he was condemned to death, and hanged.

Nuremberg he was dubbed the "Nazi Bluebeard," after the famous French killer. Like so many other characters in this history, he kept a meticulous diary, and this and his correspondence, both of which survived, contributed to his gallows end.

By June 1943 Sievers had collected at Auschwitz the men and women who were to furnish the skeletons for the "scientific measurements" of Professor Dr. Hirt at the University of Strasbourg. "A total of 115 persons, including 79 Jews, 30 Jewesses, 4 'Asiatics' and 2 Poles were processed," Sievers reported, requesting the S.S. main office in Berlin for transportation for them from Auschwitz to the Natzweiler concentration camp near Strasbourg. The British cross-examiner at Nuremberg inquired as to the meaning of "processing."

"Anthropological measurements," Sievers replied.

"Before they were murdered they were anthropologically measured? That was all there was to it, was it?"

"And casts were taken," Sievers added.

What followed was narrated by S.S. Captain Josef Kramer, himself a veteran exterminator from Auschwitz, Mauthausen, Dachau and other camps and who achieved fleeting fame as the "Beast of Belsen" and was condemned to death by a British court at Lueneburg.

Professor Hirt of the Strasbourg Anatomical Institute told me of the prisoner convoy en route from Auschwitz. He said these persons were to be killed by poison gas in the gas chamber of the Natzweiler camp, their bodies then to be taken to the Anatomical Institute for his disposal. He gave me a bottle containing about half a pint of salts—I think they were cyanide salts—and told me the approximate dosage I would have to use to poison the arriving inmates from Auschwitz.

Early in August 1943, I received eighty inmates who were to be killed with the gas Hirt had given me. One night I went to the gas chamber in a small car with about fifteen women this first time. I told the women they had to go into the chamber to be disinfected. I did not tell them, however, that they were to be gassed.

By this time the Nazis had perfected the technique.

With the help of a few S.S. men [Kramer continued] I stripped the women completely and shoved them into the gas chamber when they were stark naked.

When the door closed they began to scream. I introduced a certain amount of salt through a tube . . . and observed through a peephole what happened inside the room. The women breathed for about half a minute before they fell to the floor. After I had turned on the ventilation I opened the door. I found the women lying lifeless on the floor and they were covered with excrements.

Captain Kramer testified that he repeated the performance until all eighty inmates had been killed and turned the bodies over to Professor

Hirt, "as requested." He was asked by his interrogator what his feelings were at the time, and he gave a memorable answer that gives insight into a phenomenon in the Third Reich that has seemed so elusive of human understanding.

I had no feelings in carrying out these things because I had received an order to kill the eighty inmates in the way I already told you.
That, by the way, was the way I was trained.[74]

Another witness testified as to what happened next. He was Henry Herypierre, a Frenchman who worked in the Anatomical Institute at Strasbourg as Professor Hirt's laboratory assistant until the Allies arrived.

The first shipment we received was of the bodies of thirty women . . . These thirty female bodies arrived still warm. The eyes were wide open and shining. They were red and bloodshot and were popping from their sockets. There were also traces of blood about the nose and mouth. No *rigor mortis* was evident.

Herypierre suspected that they had been done to death and secretly copied down their prison numbers which were tattooed on their left arms. Two more shipments of fifty-six men arrived, he said, in exactly the same condition. They were pickled in alcohol under the expert direction of Dr. Hirt. But the professor was a little nervous about the whole thing. "Peter," he said to Herypierre, "if you can't keep your trap shut, you'll be one of them."

Professor Dr. Hirt went about his work nonetheless. According to the correspondence of Sievers, the professor severed the heads and, as he wrote, "assembled the skeleton collection which was previously non-existent." But there were difficulties and after hearing them described by Dr. Hirt—Sievers himself had no expert medical or anatomical knowledge—the chief of the Ahnenerbe reported them to Himmler on September 5, 1944.

In view of the vast amount of scientific research involved, the job of reducing the corpses has not yet been completed. This requires some time for 80 corpses.

And time was running out. Advancing American and French troops were nearing Strasbourg. Hirt requested "directives as to what should be done with the collection."

The corpses can be stripped of the flesh and thereby rendered unidentifiable [Sievers reported to headquarters on behalf of Dr. Hirt]. This would mean, however, that at least part of the whole work had been done for nothing and that this unique collection would be lost to science, since it would be impossible to make plaster casts afterwards.

The skeleton collection as such is inconspicuous. The flesh parts could be declared as having been left by the French at the time we took over the Anatomical Institute* and would be turned over for cremating. Please advise me which of the following three proposals is to be carried out: 1. The collection as a whole to be preserved; 2. The collection to be dissolved in part; 3. The collection to be completely dissolved.

"Why were you wanting to deflesh the bodies, witness?" the British prosecutor asked in the stillness of the Nuremberg courtroom. "Why were you suggesting that the blame should be passed on to the French?"

"As a layman I could have no opinion in this matter," the "Nazi Bluebeard" replied. "I merely transmitted an inquiry from Professor Hirt. I had nothing to do with the murdering of these people. I simply carried through the function of a mailman."

"You were the post office," the prosecutor rejoined, "another of these distinguished Nazi post offices, were you?"

It was a leaky defense offered by many a Nazi at the trials and on this occasion, as on others, the prosecution nailed it.[75]

The captured S.S. files reveal that on October 26, 1944, Sievers reported that "the collection in Strasbourg has been completely dissolved in accordance with the directive. This arrangement is for the best in view of the whole situation."[76]

Herypierre later described the attempt—not altogether successful—to hide the traces.

In September, 1944, the Allies made an advance on Belfort, and Professor Hirt ordered Bong and Herr Maier to cut up these bodies and have them burned in the crematory . . . I asked Herr Maier the next day whether he had cut up all the bodies, but Herr Bong replied: "We couldn't cut up all the bodies, it was too much work. We left a few bodies in the storeroom."

They were discovered there by an Allied team when units of the U.S. Seventh Army, with the French 2nd Armored Division in the lead, entered Strasbourg a month later.†[77]

Not only skeletons but human skins were collected by the masters of the New Order though in the latter case the pretense could not be made that the cause of scientific research was being served. The skins of concentration camp prisoners, especially executed for this ghoulish purpose, had merely decorative value. They made, it was found, excellent lamp shades, several of which were expressly fitted up for Frau Ilse Koch, the wife of the commandant of Buchenwald and nicknamed by the inmates

---

* Germany had annexed Alsace after the fall of France in 1940 and the Germans had taken over the University of Strasbourg.
† Professor Dr. Hirt disappeared. As he left Strasbourg he was heard boasting that no one would ever take him alive. Apparently no one has—alive or dead.

the "Bitch of Buchenwald."* Tattooed skins appear to have been the most sought after. A German inmate, Andreas Pfaffenberger, deposed at Nuremberg on this.

. . . All prisoners with tattooing on them were ordered to report to the dispensary . . . After the prisoners had been examined the ones with the best and most artistic specimens were killed by injections. The corpses were then turned over to the pathological department where the desired pieces of tattooed skin were detached from the bodies and treated further. The finished products were turned over to Koch's wife, who had them fashioned into lamp shades, and other ornamental household articles.[78]

One piece of skin which apparently struck Frau Koch's fancy had the words "Haensel and Gretel" tattooed on it.

At another camp, Dachau, the demand for such skins often outran the supply. A Czech physician prisoner, Dr. Frank Bláha, testified at Nuremberg as to that.

Sometimes we would not have enough bodies with good skin and Dr. Rascher would say, "All right, you will get the bodies." The next day we would receive twenty or thirty bodies of young people. They would have been shot in the neck or struck on the head, so that the skin would be uninjured . . . The skin had to be from healthy prisoners and free from defects.[79]

It was this Dr. Sigmund Rascher who seems to have been responsible for the more sadistic of the medical experiments in the first place. This horrible quack had attracted the attention of Himmler, among whose obsessions was the breeding of more and more superior Nordic offspring, through reports in S.S. circles that Frau Rascher had given birth to three children after passing the age of forty-eight, although in truth the Raschers had simply kidnaped them at suitable intervals from an orphanage.

In the spring of 1941, Dr. Rascher, who was attending a special medical course at Munich given by the Luftwaffe, had a brain storm. On May 15, 1941, he wrote Himmler about it. He had found to his horror that research on the effect of high altitudes on flyers was at a standstill because "no tests with human material had yet been possible as such experiments are very dangerous and nobody volunteers for them."

---

* Frau Koch, whose power of life and death over the inmates of Buchenwald was complete, and whose very whim could bring terrible punishment to a prisoner, was sentenced to life imprisonment at the "Buchenwald Trial," but her sentence was commuted to four years, and she was soon released. On January 15, 1951, a German court sentenced her to life imprisonment for murder. Her husband was sentenced to death by an S.S. court during the war for "excesses" but was given the option of serving on the Russian front. Before he could do this, however, Prince Waldeck, the leader of the S.S. in the district, had him executed. Princess Mafalda, daughter of the King and Queen of Italy and wife of Prince Philip of Hesse, was among those who died at Buchenwald.

Can you make available two or three professional criminals for these experiments . . . The experiments, by which the subjects can of course die, would take place with my co-operation.[80]

The S.S. Fuehrer replied within a week that "prisoners will, of course, be made available gladly for the high-flight research."

They were, and Dr. Rascher went to work. The results may be seen from his own reports and from those of others, which showed up at Nuremberg and at the subsequent trial of the S.S. doctors.

Dr. Rascher's own findings are a model of scientific jargon. For the high-altitude tests he moved the Air Force's decompression chamber at Munich to the nearby Dachau concentration camp where human guinea pigs were readily available. Air was pumped out of the contraption so that the oxygen and air pressure at high altitudes could be simulated. Dr. Rascher then made his observations, of which the following one is typical.

The third test was without oxygen at the equivalent of 29,400 feet altitude conducted on a 37-year-old Jew in good general condition. Respiration continued for 30 minutes. After four minutes the TP [test person] began to perspire and roll his head.

After five minutes spasms appeared; between the sixth and tenth minute respiration increased in frequency, the TP losing consciousness. From the eleventh to the thirtieth minute respiration slowed down to three inhalations per minute, only to cease entirely at the end of that period . . . About half an hour after breathing had ceased, an autopsy was begun.[81]

An Austrian inmate, Anton Pacholegg, who worked in Dr. Rascher's office, has described the "experiments" less scientifically.

I have personally seen through the observation window of the decompression chamber when a prisoner inside would stand a vacuum until his lungs ruptured . . . They would go mad and pull out their hair in an effort to relieve the pressure. They would tear their heads and face with their fingers and nails in an attempt to maim themselves in their madness. They would beat the walls with their hands and head and scream in an effort to relieve pressure on their eardrums. These cases usually ended in the death of the subject.[82]

Some two hundred prisoners were subjected to this experiment before Dr. Rascher was finished with it. Of these, according to the testimony at the "Doctors' Trial," about eighty were killed outright and the remainder executed somewhat later so that no tales would be told.

This particular research project was finished in May 1942, at which time Field Marshal Erhard Milch of the Luftwaffe conveyed Goering's "thanks" to Himmler for Dr. Rascher's pioneer experiments. A little later, on October 10, 1942, Lieutenant General Dr. Hippke, Medical Inspector of the Air Force, tendered to Himmler "in the name of German aviation medicine and research" his "obedient gratitude" for "the Dachau experiments." However, he thought, there was one omission in them. They had not taken into account the extreme cold which an aviator faces at high altitudes. To rectify this omission the Luftwaffe, he informed Himmler, was building a decompression chamber "equipped with full refrigeration and with a nominal altitude of 100,000 feet. Freezing experiments," he added, "along different lines are still under way at Dachau."[83]

Indeed they were. And again Dr. Rascher was in the vanguard. But some of his doctor colleagues were having qualms. Was it Christian to do what Dr. Rascher was doing? Apparently a few German Luftwaffe medics were beginning to have their doubts. When Himmler heard of this he was infuriated and promptly wrote Field Marshal Milch protesting about the difficulties caused by "Christian medical circles" in the Air Force. He begged the Luftwaffe Chief of Staff to release Rascher from the Air Force medical corps so that he could be transferred to the S.S. He suggested that they find a "non-Christian physician, who should be honorable as a scientist," to pass on Dr. Rascher's valuable works. In the meantime Himmler emphasized that he

personally assumed the responsibility for supplying asocial individuals and criminals who deserve only to die from concentration camps for these experiments.

Dr. Rascher's "freezing experiments" were of two kinds: first, to see how much cold a human being could endure before he died; and second, to find the best means of rewarming a person who still lived after being exposed to extreme cold. Two methods were selected to freeze a man: dumping him into a tank of ice water or leaving him out in the snow, completely naked, overnight during winter. Rascher's reports to Himmler on his "freezing" and "warming" experiments are voluminous; an example or two will give the tenor. One of the earliest ones was made on September 10, 1942.

The TPs were immersed in water in full flying uniform . . . with hood. A life jacket prevented sinking. The experiments were conducted at water temperatures between 36.5 and 53.5 degrees Fahrenheit. In the first test series the back of the head and the brain stem were above water. In another series the back of the neck and cerebellum were submerged. Temperatures as low as 79.5 in the stomach and 79.7 in the rectum were recorded electrically. Fatalities occurred only when the medulla and the cerebellum were chilled.

In autopsies of such fatalities large quantities of free blood, up to a pint, were always found inside the cranial cavity. The heart regularly showed extreme distention of the right chamber. The TPs in such tests inevitably died when body temperature had declined to 82.5, despite all rescue attempts.

These autopsy findings plainly prove the importance of a heated head and neck protector for the foam suit now in the process of development.[84]

A table which Dr. Rascher appended covers six "Fatal Cases" and shows the water temperatures, body temperature on removal from water, body temperature at death, the length of stay in the water and the time it took the patient to die. The toughest man endured in the ice water for one hundred minutes, the weakest for fifty-three minutes.

Walter Neff, a camp inmate who served as Dr. Rascher's medical orderly, furnished the "Doctors' Trial" with a layman's description of one water-freezing test.

It was the worst experiment ever made. Two Russian officers were brought from the prison barracks. Rascher had them stripped and they had to go into the vat naked. Hour after hour went by, and whereas usually unconsciousness from the cold set in after sixty minutes at the latest, the two men in this case still responded fully after two and a half hours. All appeals to Rascher to put them to sleep by injection were fruitless. About the third hour one of the Russians said to the other, 'Comrade, please tell the officer to shoot us.' The other replied that he expected no mercy from this Fascist dog. The two shook hands with a 'Farewell, Comrade' . . . These words were translated to Rascher by a young Pole, though in a somewhat different form. Rascher went to his office. The young Pole at once tried to chloroform the two victims, but Rascher came back at once, threatening us with his gun . . . The test lasted at least five hours before death supervened.[85]

The nominal "chief" of the initial cold-water experiments was a certain Dr. Holzloehner, Professor of Medicine at the University of Kiel, assisted by a Dr. Finke, and after working with Rascher for a couple of months they believed that they had exhausted the experimental possibilities. The three physicians thereupon drew up a thirty-two-page top-secret report to the Air Force entitled "Freezing Experiments with Human Beings" and called a meeting of German scientists at Nuremberg for October 26–27, 1942, to hear and discuss their findings. The subject of the meeting was "Medical Questions in Marine and Winter Emergencies." According to the testimony at the "Doctors' Trial," ninety-five German scientists, including some of the most eminent men in the field, participated, and though the three doctors left no doubt that a good many human beings had been done to death in the experiments there were no questions put as to this and no protests therefore made.

Professor Holzloehner* and Dr. Finke bowed out of the experiments at this time but the persevering Dr. Rascher carried on alone from October 1942 until May of the following year. He wanted, among other things, to

---

* Professor Holzloehner may have had a guilty conscience. Picked up by the British he committed suicide after his first interrogation.

pursue experiments in what he called "dry freezing." Auschwitz, he wrote to Himmler,

is much better suited for such tests than Dachau because it is colder there and because the size of the grounds causes less of a stir in the camp. (The test persons yell when they freeze.)

For some reason the change of locality could not be arranged, so Dr. Rascher went ahead with his studies at Dachau, praying for some real winter weather.

Thank God, we have had another intense cold snap at Dachau [he wrote Himmler in the early spring of 1943]. Some people remained out in the open for 14 hours at 21 degrees, attaining an interior temperature of 77 degrees, with peripheral frostbite . . .[86]

At the "Doctors' Trial" the witness Neff again provided a layman's description of the "dry-freezing" experiments of his chief.

A prisoner was placed naked on a stretcher outside the barracks in the evening. He was covered with a sheet, and every hour a bucket of cold water was poured over him. The test person lay out in the open like this into the morning. Their temperatures were taken.

Later Dr. Rascher said it was a mistake to cover the subject with a sheet and to drench him with water . . . In the future the test persons must not be covered. The next experiment was a test on ten prisoners who were exposed in turn, likewise naked.

As the prisoners slowly froze, Dr. Rascher or his assistant would record temperatures, heart action, respiration and so on. The cries of the suffering often rent the night.

Initially [Neff explained to the court] Rascher forbade these tests to be made in a state of anesthesia. But the test persons made such a racket that it was impossible for Rascher to continue these tests without anesthetic.[87]

The TPs (test persons) were left to die, as Himmler said they deserved to, in the ice-water tanks or lying naked on the ground outside the barracks at Dachau on a winter evening. If they survived they were shortly exterminated. But the brave German flyers and sailors, for whose benefit the experiments were ostensibly carried out, and who might find themselves ditched in the icy waters of the Arctic Ocean or marooned in some frozen waste above the Arctic Circle in Norway, Finland or northern Russia, had to be saved if possible. The inimitable Dr. Rascher therefore took to performing on his human guinea pigs at Dachau what he termed "warming experiments." What was the best method, he wanted to know, for warming a frozen man and thus possibly saving his life?

Heinrich Himmler, never backward in offering "practical" solutions to his corps of busy scientists, suggested to Rascher that warming by "animal heat" be tried, but at first the doctor did not think much of the idea. "Warming by animal heat—the bodies of animals or women—is much too slow," he wrote the S.S. chief. But Himmler kept after him.

I am very curious [he wrote Rascher] about the experiments with animal heat. Personally I believe these experiments may bring the best and the most sustained results.

Though skeptical, Dr. Rascher was not the man to ignore a suggestion from the leader of the S.S. He promptly embarked on a series of the most grotesque "experiments" of all, recording them for posterity in every morbid detail. Four inmates from the women's concentration camps at Ravensbrueck were sent to him at Dachau. However there was something about one of them—they were classified as prostitutes—that disturbed the doctor and he so reported to his superiors.

One of the women assigned showed impeccably Nordic racial characteristics . . . I asked the girl why she had volunteered for brothel service and she replied, "To get out of the concentration camp." When I objected that it was shameful to volunteer as a brothel girl, I was advised, "Better half a year in a brothel than half a year in the concentration camp . . ."

My racial conscience is outraged by the prospect of exposing to racially inferior concentration camp elements a girl who is outwardly pure Nordic . . . For this reason I decline to use this girl for my experimental purposes.[88]

But he used others, whose hair was less fair and the eyes less blue. His findings were duly reported to Himmler in a report marked "Secret" on February 12, 1942.[89]

The test persons were chilled in the familiar way—dressed or undressed—in cold water at various temperatures . . . Removal from the water took place at a rectal temperature of 86 degrees.

In eight cases the test persons were placed between two naked women on a wide bed. The women were instructed to snuggle up to the chilled person as closely as possible. The three persons were then covered with blankets . . .

Once the test persons regained consciousness, they never lost it again, quickly grasping their situation and nestling close to the naked bodies of the women. The rise of body temperature then proceeded at approximately the same speed as with test persons warmed by being swathed in blankets . . . An exception was formed by four test persons who practiced sexual intercourse between 86 and 89.5 degrees. In these persons, after coitus, a very swift temperature rise ensued, comparable to that achieved by means of a hot-water bath.

Dr. Rascher found, somewhat to his surprise, that one woman warmed a frozen man faster than two women.

I attribute this to the fact that in warming by means of one woman personal inhibitions are avoided and the woman clings more closely to the chilled person. Here too, return of full consciousness was notably rapid. In the case of only one person did consciousness fail to return and only a slight degree of warming was recorded. This test person died with symptoms of a brain hemorrhage, later confirmed by autopsy.

Summing up, this murderous hack concluded that warming up a "chilled" man with women "proceeds very slowly" and that hot baths were more efficacious.

Only test persons [he concluded] whose physical state permitted sexual intercourse warmed up surprisingly fast and also showed a surprisingly rapid return of full bodily well-being.

According to the testimony at the "Doctors' Trial" some four hundred "freezing" experiments were performed on three hundred persons of whom between eighty and ninety died directly as a result thereof, and the rest, except for a few, were bumped off subsequently, some of them having been driven insane. Dr. Rascher himself, incidentally, was not around to testify at this trial. He continued his bloody labors on various new projects, too numerous to mention, until May 1944, when he and his wife were arrested by the S.S.—not for his murderous "experiments," it seems, but on the charge that he and his wife had practiced deceit about how their children came into the world. Such treachery Himmler, with his worship of German mothers, could not brook—he had sincerely believed that Frau Rascher had begun to bear her three children at the age of forty-eight and he was outraged when he learned that she had kidnaped them. So Dr. Rascher was incarcerated in the political bunker at his familiar Dachau camp and his wife was carted off to Ravensbrueck, from which the doctor had procured his prostitutes for the "warming" tests. Neither survived, and it is believed that Himmler himself, in one of the last acts of his life, ordered their execution. They might have made awkward witnesses.

A number of such awkward witnesses did survive to stand trial. Seven of them were condemned to death and hanged, defending their lethal experiments to the last as patriotic acts which served the Fatherland. Dr. Herta Oberheuser, the only woman defendant at the "Doctors' Trial," was given twenty years. She had admitted giving lethal injections to "five or six" Polish women among the hundreds who suffered the tortures of the damned in a variety of "experiments" at Ravensbrueck. A number of doctors, such as the notorious Pokorny, who had wanted to sterilize millions of the enemy, were acquitted. A few were contrite. At a second trial of medical underlings Dr. Edwin Katzenellenbogen, a former member of the faculty of the Harvard Medical School, asked the court for the death sentence. "You have placed the mark of Cain on my forehead," he exclaimed. "Any physician who committed the crimes I am charged with deserves to be killed." He was given life imprisonment.[90]

THE DEATH OF HEYDRICH AND THE END OF LIDICE

Midway through the war there was one act of retribution against the gangster masters of the New Order for their slaughtering of the conquered people. Reinhard Heydrich, chief of the Security Police and the S.D., deputy chief of the Gestapo, this long-nosed, icy-eyed thirty-eight-year-old policeman of diabolical cast, the genius of the "final solution," Hangman Heydrich, as he became known in the occupied lands, met a violent end.

Restless for further power and secretly intriguing to oust his chief, Himmler, he had got himself appointed, in addition to his other offices, Acting Protector of Bohemia and Moravia. Poor old Neurath, the Protector, was packed off on indefinite sick leave by Hitler in September 1941, and Heydrich replaced him in the ancient seat of the Bohemian kings at Hradschin Castle in Prague. But not for long.

On the morning of May 29, 1942, as he was driving in his open Mercedes sports car from his country villa to the Castle in Prague a bomb of British make was tossed at him, blowing the car to pieces and shattering his spine. It had been hurled by two Czechs, Jan Kubis and Josef Gabeik, of the free Czechoslovak army in England, who had been parachuted from an R.A.F. plane. Well equipped for their assignment, they got away under a smoke screen and were given refuge by the priests of the Karl Borromaeus Church in Prague.

Heydrich expired of his wounds on June 4 and a veritable hecatomb followed as the Germans took savage revenge, after the manner of the old Teutonic rites, for the death of their hero. According to one Gestapo report, 1,331 Czechs, including 201 women, were immediately executed.[91] The actual assassins, along with 120 members of the Czech resistance who were hiding in the Karl Borromaeus Church, were besieged there by the S.S. and killed to the last man.* It was the Jews, however, who suffered the most for this act of defiance against the master race. Three thousand of them were removed from the "privileged" ghetto of Theresienstadt and shipped to the East for extermination. On the day of the bombing Goebbels had 500 of the few remaining Jews at large in Berlin arrested and on the day of Heydrich's death 152 of them were executed as a "reprisal."

But of all the consequences of Heydrich's death the fate of the little village of Lidice near the mining town of Kladno not far from Prague will

---

* According to Schellenberg, who was there, the Gestapo never learned that the actual assassins were among the dead in the church. (Schellenberg, *The Labyrinth*, p. 292.)

perhaps be longest remembered by the civilized world. For no other reason except to serve as an example to a conquered people who dared to take the life of one of their inquisitors a terrible savagery was carried out in this peaceful little rural place.

On the morning of June 9, 1942, ten truckloads of German Security Police under the command of Captain Max Rostock* arrived at Lidice and surrounded the village. No one was allowed to leave though anyone who lived there and happened to be away could return. A boy of twelve, panicking, tried to steal away. He was shot down and killed. A peasant woman ran toward the outlying fields. She was shot in the back and killed. The entire male population of the village was locked up in the barns, stables and cellar of a farmer named Horak, who was also the mayor.

The next day, from dawn until 4 P.M., they were taken into the garden behind the barn, in batches of ten, and shot by firing squads of the Security Police. A total of 172 men and boys, over sixteen, were executed there. An additional nineteen male residents, who were working in the Kladno mines during the massacre, were later picked up and dispatched in Prague.

Seven women who were rounded up at Lidice were taken to Prague and shot. All the rest of the women of the village, who numbered 195, were transported to the Ravensbrueck concentration camp in Germany, where seven were gassed, three "disappeared" and forty-two died of ill treatment. Four of the Lidice women who were about to give birth were first taken to a maternity hospital in Prague where their newly born infants were murdered and they themselves then shipped to Ravensbrueck.

There remained for the Germans the disposal of the children of Lidice, whose fathers were now dead, whose mothers were imprisoned. It must be said that the Germans did not shoot them too, not even the male children. They were carted off to a concentration camp at Gneisenau. There were ninety in all and from these seven, who were less than a year old, were selected by the Nazis, after a suitable examination by Himmler's "racial experts," to be sent to Germany to be brought up as Germans under German names. Later, the others were similarly disposed of.

"Every trace of them has been lost," the Czechoslovak government, which filed an official report on Lidice for the Nuremberg tribunal, concluded.

Happily, some of them, at least, were later found. I remember in the autumn of 1945 reading the pitiful appeals in the then Allied-controlled German newspapers from the surviving mothers of Lidice asking the German people to help them locate their children and send them "home."†

Actually Lidice itself had been wiped off the face of the earth. As soon as the men had been massacred and the women and children carted off,

---

* Hanged in Prague in August 1951.
† UNRRA reported on April 2, 1947, that seventeen of them had been found in Bavaria and sent back to their mothers in Czechoslovakia.

the Security Police had burned down the village, dynamited the ruins and leveled it off.

Lidice, though it became the most widely known example of Nazi savagery of this kind, was not the only village in the German-occupied lands to suffer such a barbaric end. There was one other in Czechoslovakia, Lezhaky, and several more in Poland, Russia, Greece and Yugoslavia. Even in the West, where the New Order was relatively less murderous, the example of Lidice was repeated by the Germans though in most cases, such as that of Televaag in Norway, the men, women and children were merely deported to separate concentration camps after every building in the village had been razed to the ground.

But on June 10, 1944, two years to a day after the massacre of Lidice, a terrible toll of life was taken at the French village of Oradour-sur-Glane, near Limoges. A detachment of the S.S. division Das Reich, which had already earned a reputation for terror—if not for fighting—in Russia, surrounded the French town and ordered the inhabitants to gather in the central square. There the people were told by the commandant that explosives were reported to have been hidden in the village and that a search and the checking of identity cards would be made. Whereupon the entire population of 652 persons was locked up. The men were herded into barns, the women and children into the church. The entire village was then set on fire. The German soldiers next set upon the inhabitants. The men in the barns who were not burned to death were machine-gunned and killed. The women and children in the church were also peppered with machine-gun fire and those who were not killed were burned to death when the German soldiers set fire to the church. Three days later the Bishop of Limoges found the charred bodies of fifteen children in a heap behind the burned-out altar.

Nine years later, in 1953, a French military court established that 642 inhabitants—245 women, 207 children and 190 men—had perished in the massacre at Oradour. Ten survived. Though badly burned they had simulated death and thus escaped it.*

Oradour, like Lidice, was never rebuilt. Its ruins remain a monument to Hitler's New Order in Europe. The gutted church stands out against the peaceful countryside as a reminder of the beautiful June day, just before the harvest, when the village and its inhabitants suddenly ceased to exist. Where once a window stood is a little sign: "Madame Rouffance, the only survivor from the church, escaped through this window." In front there is a small figure of Christ affixed to a rusty iron cross.

---

* Twenty members of the S.S. detachment were sentenced to death by this court but only two were executed, the remaining eighteen having their sentences commuted to prison terms of from five to twelve years. The commander of the Das Reich Division, S.S. Lieutenant General Heinz Lammerding was condemned to death *in absentia*. So far as I know he was never found. The actual commander of the detachment at Oradour, Major Otto Dickmann, was killed in action in Normandy a few days later.

Such, as has been sketched in this chapter, were the beginnings of Hitler's New Order; such was the debut of the Nazi Gangster Empire in Europe. Fortunately for mankind it was destroyed in its infancy—not by any revolt of the German people against such a reversion to barbarism but by the defeat of German arms and the consequent fall of the Third Reich, the story of which now remains to be told.

28

THE FALL OF MUSSOLINI

FOR THREE SUCCESSIVE WAR YEARS when summer came, it had been the Germans who had launched the great offensives on the continent of Europe. Now in 1943 the tables turned.

With the capture in early May of that year of the Axis forces in Tunisia, all that remained of a once mighty army in North Africa, it was obvious that General Eisenhower's Anglo–American armies would next turn on Italy itself. This was the kind of nightmare which had haunted Mussolini in September of 1939 and which had made him delay Italy's entry into the war until neighboring France had been conquered by the Germans and the British Expeditionary Force driven across the Channel. The nightmare now returned, but this time it was rapidly turning into reality.

Mussolini himself was ill and disillusioned; and he was frightened. Defeatism was rife among his people and in the armed forces. There had been mass strikes in the industrial cities of Milan and Turin, where the hungry workers had demonstrated for "bread, peace and freedom." The discredited and corrupt Fascist regime itself was fast crumbling, and when Count Ciano at the beginning of the year was relieved as Foreign Minister and sent to the Vatican as ambassador the Germans suspected that he had gone there to try to negotiate a separate peace with the Allies, as Antonescu, the Rumanian dictator, was already urging.

For several months Mussolini had been bombarding Hitler with appeals to make peace with Stalin, so that his armies could be withdrawn to the West to make a common defense with the Italians against the growing threat of the Anglo–American forces in the Mediterranean and of those which he believed were assembling in England for a cross-Channel invasion. The time had come again, Hitler realized, for a meeting with Mussolini in order to buck up his sagging partner and to put him straight. This was arranged for April 7, 1943, at Salzburg, and though the Duce arrived determined to have his way—or at least his say—at last, he once more succumbed to the Fuehrer's torrents of words. Hitler later described his success to Goebbels, who jotted it down in his diary.

By putting every ounce of energy into the effort, he succeeded in pushing Mussolini back on the rails . . . The Duce underwent a complete change . . . When he got out of the train on his arrival, the Fuehrer thought, he looked like a broken old man; when he left [after four days] he was in high fettle, ready for any deed.[1]

But in point of fact Mussolini was not ready for the events which now followed in quick succession. The Allied conquest of Tunisia in May was followed by the successful Anglo–American landings in Sicily on July 10. The Italians had little stomach for battle in their own homeland. Reports soon reached Hitler that the Italian Army was "in a state of collapse," as he put it to his advisers at OKW.

Only barbaric measures [Hitler told a war council on July 17] like those applied by Stalin in 1941 or by the French in 1917 can help to save the nation. A sort of tribunal or court-martial should be set up in Italy to remove undesirable elements.[2]

Once again he summoned Mussolini to discuss the matter, the meeting taking place on July 19 at Feltre in northern Italy. This, incidentally, was the thirteenth conference of the two dictators and it followed the pattern of the most recent ones. Hitler did all the talking, Mussolini all the listening—for three hours before lunch and for two hours after it. Without much success the fanatical German leader tried to rekindle the sunken spirits of his ailing friend and ally. They must continue the fight on all fronts. Their tasks could not be left "to another generation." The "voice of history" was still beckoning them. Sicily and Italy proper could be held if the Italians fought. There would be more German reinforcements to help them. A new U-boat would soon be in operation and would deal the British a "Stalingrad."

Despite Hitler's promises and boasts the atmosphere, Dr. Schmidt found, was most depressing. Mussolini was so overwrought that he could no longer follow his friend's tirades and at the end asked Schmidt to furnish him with his notes. The Duce's despair worsened when during the meeting reports came in of the first heavy daylight Allied air attack on Rome.[3]

Benito Mussolini, tired and senile though he was only going on sixty, he who had strutted so arrogantly across Europe's stage for two decades, was at the end of his rope. When he returned to Rome he found much worse than the aftermath of the first heavy bombing. He faced revolt from some of his closest henchmen in the Fascist Party hierarchy, even from his son-in-law, Ciano. And behind it there was a plot among a wider circle that reached to the King to overthrow him.

The rebellious Fascist leaders, led by Dino Grandi, Giuseppe Bottai and Ciano, demanded the convocation of the Fascist Grand Council, which had not met since December 1939 and which had always been a rubber-stamp body completely dominated by the Duce. It convened on the night of July 24–25, 1943, and Mussolini for the first time in his career as dictator found himself the target of violent criticism for the disaster into which he had led the country. By a vote of 19 to 8, a resolution was carried demanding the restoration of a constitutional monarchy with a democratic Parliament. It also called for the full command of the armed forces to be restored to the King.

The Fascist rebels, with the possible exception of Grandi, do not appear to have had any idea of going further than this. But there was a second and wider plot of certain generals and the King, which was now sprung. Mussolini himself apparently felt that he had weathered the storm—after all, decisions in Italy were not made by a majority vote in the Grand Council but by the Duce—and he was taken completely by surprise when on the evening of July 25 he was summoned to the royal palace by the King, summarily dismissed from office and carted off under arrest in an ambulance to a police station.*

So fell, ignominiously, the modern Roman Caesar, a bellicose-sounding man of the twentieth century who had known how to profit from its confusions and despair, but who underneath the gaudy façade was made largely of sawdust. As a person he was not unintelligent. He had read widely in history and thought he understood its lessons. But as dictator he had made the fatal mistake of seeking to make a martial, imperial Great Power of a country which lacked the industrial resources to become one and whose people, unlike the Germans, were too civilized, too sophisticated, too down to earth to be attracted by such false ambitions. The Italian people, at heart, had never, like the Germans, embraced fascism. They had merely suffered it, knowing that it was a passing phase, and Mussolini toward the end seems to have realized this. But like all dictators he was carried away by power, which, as it inevitably must, corrupted him, corroding his mind and poisoning his judgment. This led him to his second fatal mistake of tying his fortunes and those of Italy to the Third Reich. When the bell began to toll for Hitler's Germany it began to toll for Mussolini's Italy, and as the summer of 1943 came the Italian leader heard it. But there was nothing he could do to escape his fate. By now he was a prisoner of Hitler.

Not a gun was fired—not even by the Fascist militia—to save him. Not a voice was raised in his defense. No one seemed to mind the humiliating nature of his departure—being hauled away from the King's presence to jail in an ambulance. On the contrary, there was general rejoicing at his

---

* "I was completely free of any forebodings," Mussolini wrote later in describing his state of mind as he set out for the palace. King Victor Emmanuel lost no time in bringing him down to earth.

"My dear Duce," Mussolini quotes him as saying at the outset, "it's no longer any good. Italy has gone to bits . . . The soldiers don't want to fight any more . . . At this moment you are the most hated man in Italy . . ."

"You are making an extremely grave decision," Mussolini says he replied. But even by his own account he made little attempt to induce the monarch to change his mind. He ended by "wishing luck" to his successor. (Mussolini, *Memoirs, 1942–1943,* pp. 80–81.)

fall. Fascism itself collapsed as easily as its founder. Marshal Pietro Badoglio formed a nonparty government of generals and civil servants, the Fascist Party was dissolved, Fascists were removed from key posts and anti-Fascists released from prison.

The reaction at Hitler's headquarters to the news of Mussolini's fall may be imagined, though it need not be—for voluminous secret records abound as to what it was.[4] It was one of deep shock. Certain parallels were immediately evident even to the Nazi mind, and the danger that a terrible precedent might have been set in Rome greatly troubled Dr. Goebbels, who was summoned posthaste to Rastenburg headquarters on July 26. The Propaganda Minister's first thought, we learn from his diary, was how to explain the overthrow of Mussolini to the German people. "What are we to tell them, anyway?" he asked himself, and he decided that for the moment they were to be told only that the Duce had resigned "for reasons of health."

Knowledge of these events [he wrote in his diary] might conceivably encourage some subversive elements in Germany to think they could put over the same thing here that Badoglio and his henchmen accomplished in Rome. The Fuehrer ordered Himmler to see to it that most severe police measures be applied in case such a danger seemed imminent here.

Hitler, however, Goebbels added, did not think the danger was very imminent in Germany. The Propaganda Minister finally assured himself that the German people would not "regard the crisis in Rome as a precedent."

Though the Fuehrer had observed the signs of cracking in Mussolini at their meeting but a fortnight before, he was taken completely by surprise when the news from Rome began to trickle in to headquarters on the afternoon of July 25. The first word was merely that the Fascist Grand Council had met, and Hitler wondered why. "What's the use of councils like that?" he asked. "What do they do except jabber?"

That evening his worst fears were confirmed. "The Duce has resigned," he announced to his astounded military advisers at a conference that began at 9:30 P.M. "Badoglio, our most bitter enemy, has taken over the government."

For one of the last times of the war Hitler reacted to the news with that ice-cold judgment which he had displayed in crises in earlier and more successful days. When General Jodl urged that they wait for more complete reports from Rome, Hitler cut him short.

Certainly [he said], but still we have to plan ahead. Undoubtedly in their treachery they will proclaim that they will remain loyal to us, but that is treachery. Of course they won't remain loyal . . . Although that so-and-so [Badoglio] declared immediately that the war would be continued, that won't make any difference. They have to say that, but it remains treason. We'll play the same game while preparing everything to take over the whole crew with one stroke, to capture all that riffraff.

That was Hitler's first thought: to seize those who had overthrown Mussolini and restore the Duce to power.

Tomorrow [he went on] I'll send a man down there with orders for the commander of the Third Panzergrenadier Division to the effect that he must drive into Rome with a special detail and arrest the whole government, the King and the whole bunch right away. First of all, to arrest the Crown Prince and to take over the whole gang, especially Badoglio and that entire crew. Then watch them cave in, and in two or three days there'll be another coup.

Hitler turned to the OKW Chief of Operations.

HITLER: Jodl, work out the orders . . . telling them to drive into Rome with their assault guns . . . and to arrest the government, the King, and the whole crew. I want the Crown Prince above all.
KEITEL: He is more important than the old man.
BODENSCHATZ [a general of the Luftwaffe]: That has to be organized so that they can be packed into a plane and flown away.
HITLER: Right into a plane and off with them.
BODENSCHATZ: Don't let the Bambino get lost at the airfield.

At a later conference shortly after midnight the question was raised as to what to do with the Vatican. Hitler answered it.

I'll go right into the Vatican. Do you think the Vatican embarrasses me? We'll take that over right away . . . The entire diplomatic corps are in there . . . That rabble . . . We'll get that bunch of swine out of there . . . Later we can make apologies . . .

That night also Hitler gave orders to secure the Alpine passes, both between Italy and Germany and between Italy and France. Some eight German divisions from France and southern Germany were hastily assembled for this purpose and established as Army Group B under the command of the energetic Rommel. Had the Italians, as Goebbels noted in his diary, blown the Alpine tunnels and bridges, the German forces in Italy, some of them already heavily engaged in Sicily by Eisenhower's armies, would have been cut off from their source of supplies. They could not have held out for long.

But the Italians could not suddenly turn on the Germans overnight. Badoglio had first to establish contact with the Allies to see if he could get an armistice and Allied support against the Wehrmacht divisions. Hitler had been correct in assuming that that was exactly what Badoglio would do, but he had no inkling it would take as long as it did. Indeed, this assumption dominated the discussion at a war conference at the Fuehrer's headquarters on July 27 attended by most of the bigwigs in the Nazi government and armed forces, among them Goering, Goebbels, Himmler, Rommel and the new Commander in Chief of the Navy, Admiral Karl Doenitz—who had succeeded Grand Admiral Raeder in January, when the latter had fallen from favor.* Most of the generals, led by Rommel, urged caution, arguing that any contempla ed action in Italy be carefully prepared and well thought out. Hitler wanted to move at once even though it meant withdrawing key panzer divisions from the Eastern fron', where the Russians had just launched (July 15) their first summer offensive of the war. For once the generals seem to have had their way and Hitler was persuaded to withhold action. In the meantime as many German troops as could be rounded up would be rushed over the Alps into Italy. Goebbels took a dim view of the hesitancy of the generals.

They don't take into account [he wrote in his diary after the war powwow] what the enemy is going to do. Undoubtedly the English won't wait a week while we consider and prepare for action.

He and Hitler need not have worried. The Allies waited not a week, but six weeks. By then Hitler had his plans and the forces to carry them out ready.

In his feverish mind he had in fact hastily conceived the plans by the time the war conference on July 27 convened. There were four of them: (1) Operation *Eiche* ("Oak") provided for the rescue of Mussolini either by the Navy, if he were located on an island, or by Luftwaffe parachu.ists, if he were found on the mainland; (2) Operation *Student* called for the sudden occupation of Rome and the restoration of Mussolini's government there; (3) Operation *Schwarz* ("Black") was the code name for the mili ary occupation of all of Italy; (4) Operation *Achse* ("Axis") envisaged the capture or destruction of the Italian fleet. Later the last two operations were combined under the code name of "Axis."

Two events early in September 1943 set the Fuehrer's plans in operation. On September 3 Allied troops landed on the boot of southern Italy, and on September 8 public announcement was made of the armistice

---

* Hitler had become furious with Raeder, who had commanded the German Navy since 1928, for the Navy's failure to destroy Allied convoys to Russia in the Arctic Ocean and for heavy losses suffered there. In a hysterical outburst at headquarters on January 1, the warlord had ordered the immediate decommissioning of the German High Seas Fleet. The vessels were to be broken up for scrap. On January 6 there was a stormy showdown between Hitler and Raeder at the Wolfsschanze headquarters. The Fuehrer accused the Navy of inaction and lack of the will to fight and take risks. Raeder thereupon asked to be relieved of his command, and his resignation was formally and publicly accepted on January 30. Doenitz, the new Commander in Chief, had been commander of U-boats, knew little of the problems of surface vessels and henceforth concentrated on submarine warfare.

(secretly signed on September 3) between Italy and the Western Powers.

Hitler had flown to Zaporozhe in the Ukraine that day to try to restore the sagging German front, but, according to Goebbels, he had been seized "by a queer feeling of unrest" and had returned that evening to Rastenburg headquarters in East Prussia, where the news awaited him that his principal ally had deserted. Though he had expected it and prepared for it, the actual timing took him by surprise and for several hours there was great confusion at headquarters. The Germans had first learned of the Italian armistice from a BBC broadcast from London, and when Jodl put through a call from Rastenburg to Field Marshal Kesselring at Frascati, near Rome, to ask if it were true the commander of the German armies in southern Italy confessed that it was news to him. However, Kesselring, whose headquarters that morning had been destroyed by an Allied bombing and who was preoccupied with rounding up troops to meet a new Allied landing somewhere on the west coast, was able to get out the code word "Axis," which set in motion the plans to disarm the Italian Army and occupy the country.

For a day or two the situation of the German forces in central and south Italy was extremely critical. Five Italian divisions faced two German divisions in the vicinity of Rome. If the powerful Allied invasion fleet which had appeared off Naples on September 8 moved north and landed near the capital and was reinforced by parachutists seizing the nearby airfields, as Kesselring and his staff at first expected, the course of the war in Italy would have taken a different turn than it did and final disaster might have overtaken the Third Reich a year earlier than happened. Kesselring later contended that on the evening of the eighth Hitler and OKW "wrote off" his entire force of eight divisions as irretrievably lost.[5] Two days later Hitler told Goebbels that southern Italy was lost and that a new line would have to be established north of Rome in the Apennines.

But the Allied Command did not take advantage of its complete command of the sea, which permitted it to make landings almost anywhere on both coasts of Italy, nor did it exploit its overwhelming air superiority, as the Germans had feared. Moreover, no effort seems to have been made by Eisenhower's Command to try to utilize the large Italian forces in conjunction with its own, especially the five Italian divisions in the vicinity of Rome. Had Eisenhower done so—at least such was the contention of both Kesselring and his chief of staff, General Siegfried Westphal, later—the predicament of the Germans would have become hopeless. It was simply beyond their powers, they declared, to fight off Montgomery's army advancing up the peninsula from the "boot," throw back General Mark Clark's invasion force, wherever it landed, and deal with the large Italian armed formations in their midst and in their rear.*[6]

---

* According to Captain Harry C. Butcher, Eisenhower's naval aide, both the American and British chiefs of staff, General George C. Marshall and Field Marshal Sir John G. Dill, complained that Eisenhower was not showing sufficient initiative in pressing forward in Italy. Butcher points out, in defense of his chief, that insufficient landing craft limited Eisenhower's plans and that to have launched a seaborne

Both generals breathed a sigh of relief when the American Fifth Army landed not near Rome but south of Naples, at Salerno, and when the Allied parachutists failed to appear over the Rome airfields. Their relief was all the greater when the Italian divisions surrendered almost without firing a shot and were disarmed. It meant that the Germans could easily hold Rome and, for the time being, even Naples. This gave them possession of two thirds of Italy, including the industrial north, whose factories were put to work turning out arms for Germany. Almost miraculously Hitler had received a new lease on life.*

Italy's withdrawal from the war had embittered him. It was, he told Goebbels, who had again been summoned to Rastenburg, "a gigantic example of swinishness." Moreover, the overthrow of Mussolini made him apprehensive of his own position. "The Fuehrer," Goebbels noted in his diary on September 11, "invoked final measures to preclude similar developments with us once and for all."

In his broadcast to the nation on the evening of September 10, which Goebbels had persuaded him to make only after much pleading—"The people are entitled to a word of encouragement and solace from the Fuehrer in this difficult crisis," the Propaganda Minister told him—Hitler spoke somewhat defiantly on the subject:

Hope of finding traitors here rests on complete ignorance of the character of the National Socialist State; a belief that they can bring about a July 25 in Germany rests on a fundamental illusion as to my personal position, as well as to the attitude of my political collaborators and my field marshals, admirals and generals.

Actually, as we shall see, there were a few German generals and a handful of former political collaborators who were beginning once more, as the military setbacks mounted, to harbor treasonable thoughts, which, when the next July rolled around, would be translated into an act more violent but less successful than that carried out against Mussolini.

---

invasion as far north as the vicinity of Rome would have put the operation beyond the range of Allied fighter planes, which had to take off from Sicily. Eisenhower himself points out that after the capture of Sicily he was ordered to return seven divisions, four American and three British, to England in preparation for the Channel invasion, which left him woefully short of troops. Butcher also states that Eisenhower originally planned to drop airborne troops on the Rome airfields to help the Italians defend the capital against the Germans, but that at the last minute Badoglio begged that this operation be "suspended temporarily." General Maxwell D. Taylor, who at great personal risk had secretly gone to Rome to confer with Badoglio, reported that because of Italian defeatism and German strength the dropping of an American airborne division there appeared to be suicidal. (See Eisenhower, *Crusade in Europe*, p. 189, and Butcher, *My Three Years with Eisenhower*, pp. 407–25.)

* The King, Badoglio and the government, much to Hitler's anger, escaped from Rome and a little later established themselves in Allied-liberated southern Italy. Most of the Italian fleet also got away to Malta despite intricate plans of Admiral Doenitz to capture or destroy it.

One of Hitler's measures to quash any incipient treason was to order all German princes discharged from the Wehrmacht. Prince Philip of Hesse, the former messenger boy of the Fuehrer to Mussolini, who had been hanging around headquarters, was arrested and turned over to the tender mercies of the Gestapo. His wife, Princess Mafalda, the daughter of the King of Italy, was also arrested and, with her husband, incarcerated in a concentration camp. The King of Italy, like the kings of Norway and Greece, had escaped the clutches of Hitler, who took what revenge he could by arresting his daughter.*

For several weeks the Fuehrer's daily military conferences had devoted a great deal of time to a problem that burned in Hitler's mind: the rescue of Mussolini. "Operation Oak," it will be remembered, was the code name for this plan, and in the records of the conferences at headquarters Mussolini was always referred to as "the valuable object." Most of the generals and even Goebbels doubted whether the former Duce was any longer a very valuable object, but Hitler still thought so and insisted on his liberation.

He not only wanted to do a favor to his old friend, for whom he still felt a personal affection. He also had it in mind to set up Mussolini as head of a new Fascist government in northern Italy, which would relieve the Germans of having to administer the territory and help safeguard his long lines of supply and communication against an unfriendly populace from whose midst troublesome partisans were now beginning to emerge.

By August 1, Admiral Doenitz was reporting to Hitler that the Navy believed it had spotted Mussolini on the island of Ventotene. By the middle of August Himmler's sleuths were sure the Duce was on another island, Maddalena, near the northern tip of Sardinia. Elaborate plans were made to descend upon the island with destroyers and parachutists, but before they could be carried out Mussolini had again been moved. According to a secret clause of the armistice agreement he was to be turned over to the Allies, but for some reason Badoglio delayed in doing this and early in September the "valuable object" was spirited away to a hotel on top of the Gran Sasso d'Italia, the highest range in the Abruzzi Apennines, which could be reached only by a funicular railway.

The Germans soon learned of his whereabouts, made an aerial reconnaissance of the mountaintop and decided that glider troops could probably make a landing, overcome the *carabinieri* guards and make away with the Duce in a small Fieseler-Storch plane. This daring plan was carried out on September 13 under the leadership of another one of Himmler's resourceful S.S. intellectual roughnecks, an Austrian by the name of Otto Skorzeny,

---

* Hitler had never cared for her personally. "I had to sit next to Mafalda," he told his generals during a military conference at headquarters in May that year. "What do I care about Mafalda? . . . Her intellectual qualities aren't such that she would charm you— to say nothing of her looks." (From the secret records of Hitler's daily military conferences, in Felix Gilbert's *Hitler Directs His War*, p. 37.)

who will appear again toward the very end of this narrative in another daredevil exploit.* Virtually kidnaping an Italian general, whom he packed into his glider, Skorzeny landed his airborne force a hundred yards from the mountaintop hotel, where he espied the Duce looking out hopefully from a second-story window. Most of the *carabinieri,* at the sight of German troops, took to the hills, and the few who didn't were dissuaded by Skorzeny and Mussolini from making use of their arms, the S.S. leader yelling at them not to fire on an Italian general—he pushed his captive officer to the front of his ranks—and the Duce shouting from his window, as one eyewitness remembered, "Don't shoot, anybody! Don't shed any blood!" And not a drop was shed.

Within a few minutes the overjoyed Fascist leader, who had sworn he would kill himself rather than fall into Allied hands and be exhibited, as he later wrote, in Madison Square Garden in New York,† was bundled into a tiny Fieseler-Storch plane and after a perilous take-off from a small rock-strewn meadow below the hotel flown to Rome and from there, the same evening, to Vienna in a Luftwaffe transport aircraft.[7]

Though Mussolini was grateful for his rescue and embraced Hitler warmly when they met a couple of days later at Rastenburg, he was by now a broken man, the old fires within him turned to ashes, and much to Hitler's disappointment he showed little stomach for reviving the Fascist regime in German-occupied Italy. The Fuehrer made no attempt to hide his disillusionment with his old Italian friend in a long talk with Goebbels toward the end of September.

The Duce [Goebbels confided to his diary after the talk] has not drawn the moral conclusions from Italy's catastrophe that the Fuehrer had expected of him . . . The Fuehrer expected that the first thing the Duce would do would be to wreak full vengeance on his betrayers. But he gave no such indication and thereby showed his real limitations. He is not a revolutionary like the Fuehrer or Stalin. He is so bound to his own Italian people that he lacks the broad qualities of a world-wide revolutionary and insurrectionist.

Hitler and Goebbels were also incensed that Mussolini had had a reconciliation with Ciano and seemed to be under the thumb of his daughter, Edda, who was Ciano's wife—both of them had found refuge in Munich.‡

---

* Skorzeny had been summoned to the Fuehrer's headquarters for the first time in his life the day after Mussolini's fall and personally assigned by Hitler to carry out the rescue.

† Just before Mussolini was liberated Captain Harry Butcher reported receiving a cablegram at Eisenhower's headquarters from a theater chain in Cape Town offering to donate ten thousand pounds to charity "if you arrange for Mussolini's personal appearance on the stages of our Cape Town theatres. Three weeks' engagement." (Butcher, *My Three Years with Eisenhower*, p. 423.)

‡ Actually, or at least according to a letter which Ciano later wrote to King Victor Emmanuel, he was tricked into coming to Germany in August by the Germans, who had informed him that his children were in danger and that the German government would be happy to convey him and his family to Spain—via Germany. (*The Ciano Diaries*, p. v.)

They thought he should have had Ciano immediately executed and Edda, as Goebbels put it, whipped.* They objected to Mussolini's putting Ciano—"that poisoned mushroom," Goebbels called him—in the forefront of the new Fascist Republican Party.

For Hitler had insisted that the Duce immediately create such a party, and on September 15, at the Fuehrer's prodding, Mussolini proclaimed the new Italian Social Republic.

It never amounted to anything. Mussolini's heart was not in it. Perhaps he retained enough sense of reality to see that he was now merely a puppet of Hitler, that he and his "Fascist Republican Government" had no power except what the Fuehrer gave them in Germany's interests and that the Italian people would never again accept him and Fascism.

He never returned to Rome. He set himself up at an isolated spot in the extreme north—at Rocca delle Caminate, near Gargnano, on the shores of Lake Garda, where he was closely guarded by a special detachment of the S.S. Leibstandarte. To this beautiful lake resort Sepp Dietrich, the veteran S.S. tough, who was detached from his reeling Ist S.S. Armored Corps in Russia for the purpose—such were the goings on in the Third Reich—escorted Mussolini's notorious mistress, Clara Petacci. With his true love once more in his arms, the fallen dictator seemed to care for little else in life. Goebbels, who had had not one mistress but many, professed to be shocked.

The personal conduct of the Duce with his girl friend [Goebbels noted in his diary on November 9], whom Sepp Dietrich had to bring to him, is cause for much misgiving.

A few days before, Goebbels had noted that Hitler had begun "to write off the Duce politically." But not before, it should be added, the Fuehrer forced him to "cede" Trieste, Istria and the South Tyrol to Germany with the understanding that Venice would be added later on. Now no humiliation was spared this once proud tyrant. Hitler brought pressure on him to arrest his son-in-law, Ciano, in November, and to have him executed in the jail at Verona on January 11, 1944.†

---

* "Edda Mussolini," Goebbels wrote in his diary, "is acting like a wildcat in her Bavarian villa. She smashes china and furniture on the slightest provocation." (*The Goebbels Diaries*, p. 479.)

† Ciano's last diary entry is dated "December 23, 1943, Cell 27, Verona Jail." It is a moving piece. How he smuggled this last note as well as a letter of the same date to the King of Italy out of his death cell I do not know. But he remarks that he had hidden the rest of the diary before the Germans got him. The papers were smuggled out of German-occupied Italy by Edda Ciano, who, disguised as a peasant woman and concealing the papers under her skirt, succeeded in getting over the border into Switzerland.

All the other Fascist leaders who had voted against the Duce in the Grand Council and whom the Duce could get his hands on were tried for treason by a special tribunal and, with one exception, sentenced to death and shot along with Ciano. Among them was one of the Duce's erstwhile staunchest followers, Marshal Emilio de Bono, one of the quadrumvirate who had led the march on Rome which put Mussolini in power.

By the early autumn of 1943, Adolf Hitler could well claim to have mastered the gravest threats to the Third Reich. The fall of Mussolini and the unconditional surrender of the Badoglio government in Italy might easily have led, as Hitler and his generals for a few crucial weeks feared, to exposing the southern borders of Germany to direct Allied attack and opening the way—from northern Italy—into the weakly held Balkans in the very rear of the German armies fighting for their lives in southern Russia. The meek departure of the Duce from the seat of power in Rome was a severe blow to the Fuehrer's prestige both at home and abroad, as was the consequent destruction of the Axis alliance. Yet within a couple of months Hitler, by a daring stroke, had restored Mussolini—at least in the eyes of the world. The Italian areas of occupation in the Balkans, in Greece, Yugoslavia and Albania, were secured against Allied attack, which OKW had expected any day that late summer; the Italian forces there, amounting to several divisions, surrendered meekly and were made prisoners of war. And instead of having to write off Kesselring's forces, as he had first done, and retreating to northern Italy, the Fuehrer had the satisfaction of seeing the Field Marshal's armies digging in south of Rome, where they easily halted the advance of the Anglo–American–French troops up the peninsula. There was no disputing that Hitler's fortunes in the south had been considerably restored by his daring and resourcefulness and by the prowess of his troops.

Elsewhere, though, his fortunes continued to fall.

On July 5, 1943, he had launched what was to prove his last great offensive of the war against the Russians. The flower of the German Army—some 500,000 men with no less than seventeen panzer divisions outfitted with the new heavy Tiger tanks—was hurled against a large Russian salient west of Kursk. This was "Operation Citadel" and Hitler believed it would not only entrap the best of the Russian armies, one million strong—the very forces which had driven the Germans from Stalingrad and the Don the winter before—but enable him to push back to the Don and perhaps even to the Volga and swing up from the southeast to capture Moscow.

It led to a decisive defeat. The Russians were prepared for it. By July 22, the panzers having lost half of their tanks, the Germans were brought to a complete halt and started to fall back. So confident of their strength were the Russians that without waiting for the outcome of the offensive they launched one of their own against the German salient at Orel, north of Kursk, in the middle of July, quickly penetrating the front. This was the first Russian summer offensive of the war and from this moment on the Red armies never lost the initiative. On August 4 they pushed the Germans out of Orel, which had been the southern hinge of the German drive to capture Moscow in December 1941.

Now the Soviet offensive spread along the entire front. Kharkov fell on August 23. A month later, on September 25, three hundred miles to the northwest, the Germans were driven out of Smolensk, from which city they, like the Grande Armée, had set out so confidently in the first months of the Russian campaign on the high road to Moscow. By the end of September Hitler's hard-pressed armies in the south had fallen back to the line of the Dnieper and a defensive line they had established from Zaporozhe at the bend of the river south to the Sea of Azov. The industrial Donets basin had been lost and the German Seventeenth Army in the Crimea was in danger of being cut off.

Hitler was confident that his armies could hold on the Dnieper and on the fortified positions south of Zaporozhe which together formed the so-called "Winter Line." But the Russians did not pause even for regrouping. In the first week of October they crossed the Dnieper north and southeast of Kiev, which fell on November 6. By the end of the fateful year of 1943 the Soviet armies in the south were approaching the Polish and Rumanian frontiers past the battlefields where the soldiers of Hitler had achieved their early victories in the summer of 1941 as they romped toward the interior of the Russian land.

This was not all.

There were two other setbacks to Hitler's fortunes that year which also marked the turning of the tide: the loss of the Battle of the Atlantic and the intensification of the devastating air war day and night over Germany itself.

In 1942, as we have seen, German submarines sank 6,250,000 tons of Allied shipping, most of it bound for Britain or the Mediterranean, a tonnage which far outstripped the capacity of the shipyards in the West to make good. But by the beginning of 1943 the Allies had gained the upper hand over the U-boats, thanks to an improved technique of using long-range aircraft and aircraft carriers and, above all, of equipping their surface vessels with radar which spotted the enemy submarines before the latter could sight them. Doenitz, the new commander of the Navy and the top U-boat man in the service, at first suspected treason when so many of his underwater craft were ambushed and destroyed before they could even approach the Allied convoys. He quickly learned that it was not treason but radar which was causing the disastrous losses. In the three months of February, March and April they had amounted to exactly fifty vessels; in May alone, thirty-seven U-boats were sunk. This was a rate of loss which the German Navy could not long sustain, and before the end of May Doenitz, on his own authority, withdrew all submarines from the North Atlantic.

They returned in September but in the last four months of the year sank only sixty-seven Allied vessels against the loss of sixty-four more submarines—a ratio which spelled the doom of U-boat warfare and definitely settled the Battle of the Atlantic. In 1917 in the First World War, when her armies had become stalled, Germany's submarines had almost brought Britain to her knees. They were threatening to accomplish this in 1942, when Hitler's armies in Russia and North Africa had also been stopped, and when the United States and Great Britain were straining themselves not only to halt the drive of the Japanese in Southeast Asia but to assemble men and arms and supplies for the invasion of Hitler's European empire in the West.

Their failure to seriously disrupt the North Atlantic shipping lanes during 1943 was a bigger disaster than was realized at Hitler's headquarters, depressing though the actual news was.* For it was during the twelve months of that crucial year that the vast stocks of weapons and supplies were ferried almost unmolested across the Atlantic which made the assault of Fortress Europe possible in the following year.

And it was during that period too that the horrors of modern war were brought home to the German people—brought home to them on their own doorsteps. The public knew little of how the U-boats were doing. And though the news from Russia, the Mediterranean and Italy grew increasingly bad, it dealt after all with events that were transpiring hundreds or thousands of miles distant from the homeland. But the bombs from the British planes by night and the American planes by day were now beginning to destroy a German's home, and the office or factory where he worked.

Hitler himself declined ever to visit a bombed-out city; it was a duty which seemed simply too painful for him to endure. Goebbels was much distressed at this, complaining that he was being flooded with letters "asking why the Fuehrer does not visit the distressed air areas and why Goering isn't to be seen anywhere." The Propaganda Minister's diary authoritatively describes the growing damage to German cities and industries from the air.

May 16, 1943. . . . The day raids by American bombers are creating extraordinary difficulties. At Kiel . . . very serious damage to military and technical installations of the Navy . . . If this continues we shall have to face serious consequences which in the long run will prove unbearable . . .

May 25. The night raid of the English on Dortmund was extraordinarily heavy, probably the worst ever directed against a German city . . . Reports from Dortmund are pretty horrible . . . Industrial and munition plants have been hit very hard . . . Some eighty to one hundred thousand inhabitants without shelter . . . The people in the West are gradually beginning to lose courage. Hell like that is hard to bear . . . In the evening I received a [further] report on Dortmund. Destruction is virtually total. Hardly a house is habitable . . .

July 26. During the night a heavy raid on Hamburg . . . with most serious

---

* "There can be no talk of a letup in submarine warfare," Hitler had stormed at Admiral Doenitz when on May 31 the latter informed him that the U-boats had been withdrawn from the North Atlantic. "The Atlantic," he added, "is my first line of defense in the West."

It was easier said than done. On November 12 Doenitz wrote despairingly in his diary: "The enemy holds every trump card, covering all areas with long-range air patrols and using location methods against which we still have no warning . . . The enemy knows all our secrets and we know none of his."[8]

consequences both for the civilian population and for armaments production
. . . It is a real catastrophe . . .

July 29. During the night we had the heaviest raid yet made on Hamburg
. . . with 800 to 1,000 bombers . . . Kaufmann [the local Gauleiter] gave
me a first report . . . He spoke of a catastrophe the extent of which simply
staggers the imagination. A city of a million inhabitants has been destroyed in
a manner unparalleled in history. We are faced with problems that are almost
impossible of solution. Food must be found for this population of a million.
Shelter must be secured. The people must be evacuated as far as possible.
They must be given clothing. In short, we are facing problems there of which
we had no conception even a few weeks ago . . . Kaufmann spoke of some
800,000 homeless people who are wandering up and down the streets not
knowing what to do . . .

Although considerable damage was done to specific German war plants,
especially to those turning out fighter planes, ball bearings, naval ships,
steel, and fuel for the new jets, and to the vital rocket experimental station
at Peenemunde on which Hitler had set such high hopes,* and though rail
and canal transport were continually disrupted, over-all German armament production was not materially reduced during the stepped-up Anglo–
American bombings of 1943. This was partly due to the increased output
of factories in the occupied zones—above all, those in Czechoslovakia,
France, Belgium and northern Italy, which escaped bombing.

The greatest damage inflicted by the Anglo–American air forces, as
Goebbels makes clear in his diary, was to the homes and the morale of
the German people. In the first war years they had been buoyed up, as
this writer remembers, by the lurid reports of what Luftwaffe bombing had
done to the enemy, especially to the British. They were sure it would help
bring the war to an early—and victorious—end. Now, in 1943, they
themselves began to bear the full brunt of air warfare far more devastating
than any the Luftwaffe had dealt to others, even to the populace of London
in 1940–41. The German people endured it as bravely and as stoically as
the British people had done. But after four years of war it was all the more
a severe strain, and it is not surprising that as 1943 approached its end,
with all its blasted hopes in Russia, in North Africa and in Italy, and with
their own cities from one end of the Reich to the other being pulverized

---

* In May 1943, an R.A.F. reconnaissance plane had photographed the Peenemunde
installation following a tip to London from the Polish underground that both a
pilotless jet-propelled aircraft (later known as the V-1, or buzz bomb) and a rocket
(the V-2) were being developed there. In August British bombers attacked Peenemunde, badly damaging the installation and setting back research and tests by
several months. By November the British and American air forces had located
sixty-three launching sites for the V-1 on the Channel and between December and
the following February bombed and destroyed seventy-three of the sites, which by
that time had increased to ninety-six. The terms "V-1" and "V-2" came from the
German word *Vergeltungswaffen,* or weapons of reprisal, of which Dr. Goebbels'
propaganda was to make so much of in the dark year of 1944.

from the air, the German people began to despair and to realize that this was the beginning of the end that could only spell their defeat.

"Toward the end of 1943 at the latest," the now unemployed General Halder would later write, "it had become unmistakably clear that the war was militarily lost."[9]

General Jodl, in a gloomy off-the-record lecture to the Nazi gauleiters in Munich on November 7, 1943—the eve of the anniversary of the Beer Hall Putsch—did not go quite so far. But the picture he painted of the situation at the beginning of the fifth year of the war was dark enough.

What weighs most heavily today on the home front and consequently by reaction on the front line [he said] is the enemy terror raids from the air on our homes and so on our wives and children. In this respect . . . the war has assumed forms solely through the fault of England such as were believed to be no longer possible since the days of the racial and religious wars.

The effect of these terror raids, psychological, moral and material, is such that they must be relieved if they cannot be made to cease completely.

The state of German morale as the result of the defeats and the bombings of 1943 was vividly described by this authoritative source, who on this occasion was speaking for the Fuehrer.

Up and down the country the devil of subversion strides. All the cowards are seeking a way out, or—as they call it—a political solution. They say we must negotiate while there is still something in hand . . .*

It wasn't only the "cowards." Dr. Goebbels himself, the most loyal and faithful—and fanatical—of Hitler's followers, was, as his diary reveals, seeking a way out before this year of 1943 was ended, racking his brains not over whether Germany should negotiate for peace but with whom— with Russia or with the West. He did not talk behind Hitler's back about the necessity of searching for peace, as certain others had begun to do. He was courageous and open enough to pour out his thoughts directly to the Leader. On September 10, 1943, while at the Fuehrer's headquarters at Rastenburg, whither he had been summoned on the news of Italy's capitulation, Goebbels broached the subject of possible peace negotiations for the first time in his diary.

---

* Jodl's lecture, entitled "The Strategic Position in the Beginning of the Fifth Year of the War," is perhaps the most exhaustive firsthand account we have of the German predicament at the end of 1943 as seen by Hitler and his generals. It is more than a mere confidential lecture to the Nazi political leaders. It is studded with dozens of highly secret memoranda and documents stamped "Fuehrer's GHQ" to which Jodl referred in his talk and which, taken together, give a revealing history of the war as it appeared to the Fuehrer, who seems to have supervised the preparation of the lecture. Gloomy though he was as to the present, Jodl was even more discouraging about the future, correctly predicting that the coming Anglo–American invasion in the West "will decide the war" and that "the forces at our disposal will not be adequate" to repel it.[10]

The problem begins to present itself as to which side we ought to turn to first—the Muscovite or the Anglo–American. Somehow we must realize clearly that it will be very difficult to wage war successfully against both sides.

He found Hitler "somewhat worried" over the prospect of an Allied invasion in the West and the "critical" situation on the Russian front.

The depressing thing is that we haven't the faintest idea as to what Stalin has left in the way of reserves. I doubt very much whether under these conditions we shall be able to transfer divisions from the East to the other European theaters of war.

Having put down some of his own ideas—which would have seemed treasonably defeatist to him a few months before—in his confidential diary, Goebbels then approached Hitler.

I asked the Fuehrer whether anything might be done with Stalin sooner or later. He said not for the moment . . . And anyway, the Fuehrer believes it would be easier to make a deal with the English than with the Soviets. At a given moment, the Fuehrer believes, the English would come to their senses . . . I am rather inclined to regard Stalin as more approachable, for Stalin is more of a practical politician than Churchill. Churchill is a romantic adventurer, with whom one can't talk sensibly.

It was at this dark moment in their affairs that Hitler and his lieutenants began to clutch at a straw of hope: that the Allies would fall out, that Britain and America would become frightened of the prospect of the Red armies overrunning Europe and in the end join Germany to protect the old Continent from Bolshevism. Hitler had dealt at some length on this possibility in a conference with Doenitz in August, and now in September he and Goebbels discussed it.

The English [Goebbels added in his diary] don't want a Bolshevik Europe under any circumstances . . . Once they realize that . . . they have a choice only between Bolshevism or relaxing somewhat toward National Socialism they will no doubt show an inclination toward a compromise with us . . . Churchill himself is an old anti-Bolshevik and his collaboration with Moscow today is only a matter of expediency.

Both Hitler and Goebbels seemed to have forgotten who collaborated with Moscow in the first place and who forced Russia into the war. Summing up the discussion of a possible peace with Hitler, Goebbels concluded:

Sooner or later we shall have to face the question of inclining toward one enemy side or the other. Germany has never yet had luck with a two-front war; it won't be able to stand this one in the long run either.

But was it not late in the day to ponder this? Goebbels returned to headquarters on September 23 and in the course of a morning stroll with the Nazi leader found him much more pessimistic than a fortnight before about the possibility of negotiating for peace with one side so that he could enjoy a one-front war.

The Fuehrer does not believe that anything can be achieved at present by negotiation. England is not yet groggy enough . . . In the East, naturally, the present moment is quite unfavorable . . . At present Stalin has the advantage.

That evening Goebbels dined with Hitler alone.

I asked the Fuehrer whether he would be ready to negotiate with Churchill . . . He does not believe that negotiations with Churchill would lead to any result as he is too deeply wedded to his hostile views and, besides, is guided by hatred and not by reason. The Fuehrer would prefer negotiations with Stalin, but he does not believe they would be successful . . .

Whatever may be the situation, I told the Fuehrer that we must come to an arrangement with one side or the other. The Reich has never yet won a two-front war. We must therefore see how we can somehow or other get out of a two-front war.

This was a task far more difficult than they seem to have realized, they who had so lightly plunged Germany into a two-front war. But on that September evening of 1943, at least for a few moments, the Nazi warlord finally shed his pessimism and ruminated on how sweet peace would taste. According to Goebbels, he even said he "yearned" for peace.

He said he would be happy to have contact with artistic circles again, to go to the theater in the evening and to visit the Artists' Club.[11]

Hitler and Goebbels were not the only ones in Germany who, as the war entered its fifth year, speculated on the chances and means of procuring peace. The frustrated, talkative anti-Nazi conspirators, their numbers somewhat larger now but still pitifully small, were again giving the problem some thought, now that they saw the war was lost though Hitler's armies still fought on foreign soil. Most of them, but by no means all, had come reluctantly, and only after overcoming the greatest qualms of conscience, to the conclusion that to get a peace for Germany which would leave the Fatherland with some prospect for decent survival they would have to remove Hitler by killing him and at the same time wipe out National Socialism.

As 1944 came, with the certainty that the Anglo–American armies would launch an invasion across the Channel before the year was very far along and that the Red armies would be approaching the frontiers of the

Reich itself and that the great and ancient cities of Germany would soon be reduced to utter rubble by the Allied bombing,* the plotters in their desperation girded themselves to make one final attempt to murder the Nazi dictator and overthrow his regime before it dragged Germany over the precipice to complete disaster.

They knew there was not much time.

---

* "The work of a thousand years is nothing but rubble," wrote Goerdeler to Field Marshal von Kluge in July 1943, after visiting the bombed-out areas in the west. In his letter Goerdeler beseeched the vacillating general to join the conspirators in putting an end to Hitler and his "madness."

29

THE ALLIED INVASION OF WESTERN

EUROPE AND THE ATTEMPT

TO KILL HITLER

THE CONSPIRATORS had made at least half a dozen attempts to assassinate Hitler during 1943, one of which had miscarried only when a time bomb, planted in the Fuehrer's airplane during a flight behind the Russian front, failed to explode.

A considerable change had taken place that year in the resistance movement, such as it was. The plotters had finally given up on the field marshals. They were simply too cowardly—or thickheaded—to use their position and military power to overthrow their Supreme warlord. At a secret meeting in November 1942 in the forest of Smolensk, Goerdeler, the political spark plug of the resisters, had pleaded personally with Field Marshal von Kluge, the commander of Army Group Center in the East, to take an active part in getting rid of Hitler. The unstable General, who had just accepted a handsome gift from the Fuehrer,* assented, but a few days later got cold feet and wrote to General Beck in Berlin to count him out.

A few weeks later the plotters tried to induce General Paulus, whose Sixth Army was surrounded at Stalingrad and who, they presumed, was bitterly disillusioned with the Leader who had made this possible, to issue an appeal to the Army to overthrow the tyrant who had condemned a quarter of a million German soldiers to such a ghastly end. A personal appeal from General Beck to Paulus to do this was flown into the beleaguered city by an Air Force officer. Paulus, as we have seen, responded by

---

* On his sixtieth birthday, October 30, 1942, Kluge received from the Fuehrer a check for 250,000 marks ($100,000 at the official rate of exchange) and a special permit to spend half of it on the improvement of his estate. Notwithstanding this insult to his honesty and honor as a German officer, the Field Marshal accepted both. (Schlabrendorff, *They Almost Killed Hitler*, p. 40.) Later when Kluge turned against Hitler the Fuehrer told his officers at headquarters, "I personally promoted him twice, gave him the highest decorations, gave him a large estate . . . and a large supplement to his pay as Field Marshal . . ." (Gilbert, *Hitler Directs His War*, pp. 101–02, a stenographic account of Hitler's conference at headquarters on August 31, 1944.)

sending a flood of radio messages of devotion to his Fuehrer, experiencing an awakening only after he got to Moscow in Russian captivity.

For a few days the conspirators, disappointed by Paulus, pinned their hopes on Kluge and Manstein, who after the disaster of Stalingrad were flying to Rastenburg, it was understood, to demand that the Fuehrer turn over command of the Russian front to them. If successful, this *démarche* was to be a signal for a *coup d'état* in Berlin. Once again the plotters were victims of their wishful thinking. The two field marshals did fly to Hitler's headquarters, but only to reaffirm their loyalty to the Supreme Commander.

"We are deserted," Beck complained bitterly.

It was obvious to him and his friends that they could expect no practical aid from the senior commanders at the front. In desperation they turned to the only remaining source of military power, the Ersatzheer, the Home or Replacement Army, which was scarcely an army at all but a collection of recruits in training and various garrison troops of overage men performing guard duty in the homeland. But at least its men were armed, and, with the fit troops and Waffen-S.S. units far away at the front, it might be sufficient to enable the conspirators to occupy Berlin and certain other key cities at the moment of Hitler's assassination.

But on the necessity—or even the desirability—of that lethal act, the opposition was still not entirely agreed.

The Kreisau Circle, for instance, was unalterably opposed to any such act of violence. This was a remarkable, heterogeneous group of young intellectual idealists gathered around the scions of two of Germany's most renowned and aristocratic families: Count Helmuth James von Moltke, a great-great-nephew of the Field Marshal who had led the Prussian Army to victory over France in 1870, and Count Peter Yorck von Wartenburg, a direct descendant of the famous General of the Napoleonic era who, with Clausewitz, had signed the Convention of Tauroggen with Czar Alexander I by which the Prussian Army changed sides and helped bring the downfall of Bonaparte.

Taking its name from the Moltke estate at Kreisau in Silesia, the Kreisau Circle was not a conspiratorial body but a discussion group* whose members represented a cross section of German society as it had been in the pre-Nazi times and as they hoped it would be when the Hitlerite nightmare had passed. It included two Jesuit priests, two Lutheran pastors, conservatives, liberals, socialists, wealthy landowners, former trade-union leaders, professors and diplomats. Despite the differences in their backgrounds and thoughts they were able to find a broad common ground which enabled them to provide the intellectual, spiritual, ethical, philosophical and, to some extent, political ideas of the resistance to Hitler. Judging by the documents which they have left—almost all of these men were hanged before the war's end—which included plans for

---

* "We are to be hanged," Moltke wrote to his wife just before his execution, "for thinking together."

the future government and for the economic, social and spiritual foundations of the new society, what they aimed at was a sort of Christian
socialism in which all men would be brothers and the terrible ills of
modern times—the perversions of the human spirit—would be cured.
Their ideals were noble, high in the white clouds, and to them was added
a touch of German mysticism.

But these high-minded young men were unbelievably patient. They
hated Hitler and all the degradation he had brought on Germany and
Europe. But they were not interested in overthrowing him. They thought
Germany's coming defeat would accomplish that. They turned their
attention exclusively to the thereafter. "To us," Moltke wrote at the
time, ". . . Europe after the war is a question of how the picture of man
can be re-established in the breasts of our fellow citizens."

Dorothy Thompson, the distinguished American journalist, who had
been stationed for many years in Germany and knew it well, appealed to
Moltke, an old and close friend of hers, to come down from the mountaintop. In a series of short-wave broadcasts from New York during the
summer of 1942 addressed to "Hans" she begged him and his friends to
do something to get rid of the demonic dictator. "We are not living in a
world of saints, but of human beings," she tried to remind him.

> The last time we met, Hans, and drank tea together on that beautiful terrace
> before the lake . . . I said that one day you would have to demonstrate by
> deeds, drastic deeds, where you stood . . . and I remember that I asked you
> whether you and your friends would ever have the courage to act . . .[1]

It was a penetrating question, and the answer seems to have turned out
to be that Moltke and his friends had the courage to talk—for which they
were executed—but not to act.

This flaw in their minds rather than in their hearts—for all of them met
their cruel deaths with great bravery—was the main cause of the differences between the Kreisau Circle and the Beck–Goerdeler–Hassell group
of conspirators, though they also were in dispute about the nature and
the make-up of the government which was to take over from the Nazi
regime.

There were several meetings between them following a full-dress conference at the home of Peter Yorck on January 22, 1943, presided over by
General Beck, who, as Hassell reported in his diary, "was rather weak and
reserved."[2] A spirited argument developed between the "youngsters" and
the "oldsters"—Hassell's terms—over future economic and social policy,
with Moltke clashing with Goerdeler. Hassell thought the former mayor
of Leipzig was quite "reactionary" and noted Moltke's "Anglo–Saxon and
pacifist inclinations." The Gestapo also took note of this meeting and at
the subsequent trials of the participants turned up a surprisingly detailed
account of the discussions.

Himmler was already closer on the trail of the conspirators than any of
them realized. But it is one of the ironies of this narrative that at this point,

in 1943, with the prospect of victory lost and of defeat imminent, the mild-mannered, bloodthirsty S.S. Fuehrer, the master policeman of the Third Reich, began to take a personal and not altogether unfavorable interest in the resistance, with which he had more than one friendly contact. And it is indicative of the mentality of the plotters that more than one of them, Popitz especially, began to see in Himmler a possible replacement for Hitler! The S.S. chief, so seemingly fanatically loyal to the Fuehrer, began to see this himself, but until almost the end played a double game, in the course of which he snuffed out the life of many a gallant conspirator.

The resistance was now working in three fields. The Kreisau Circle was holding its endless talks to work out the millennium. The Beck group, more down to earth, was striving in some way to kill Hitler and take over power. And it was making contact with the West in order to apprise the democratic Allies of what was up and to inquire what kind of peace they would negotiate with a new anti-Nazi government.* These contacts were made in Stockholm and in Switzerland.

In the Swedish capital Goerdeler often saw the bankers Marcus and Jakob Wallenberg, with whom he had long been friends and who had intimate business and personal contacts in London. At one meeting in April 1942 with Jakob Wallenberg, Goerdeler urged him to get in touch with Churchill. The conspirators wanted in advance an assurance from the Prime Minister that the Allies would make peace with Germany if they arrested Hitler and overthrew the Nazi regime. Wallenberg replied that from what he knew of the British government no such assurance was possible.

A month later two Lutheran clergymen made direct contact with the British in Stockholm. These were Dr. Hans Schoenfeld, a member of the Foreign Relations Bureau of the German Evangelical Church, and Pastor Dietrich Bonhoeffer, an eminent divine and an active conspirator, who on hearing that Dr. George Bell, the Anglican Bishop of Chichester, was visiting in Stockholm hastened there to see him—Bonhoeffer traveling incognito on forged papers provided him by Colonel Oster of the Abwehr.

Both pastors informed the bishop of the plans of the conspirators and, as had Goerdeler, inquired whether the Western Allies would make a decent peace with a non-Nazi government once Hitler had been overthrown. They asked for an answer—by either a private message or a public announcement. To impress the bishop that the anti-Hitler conspiracy was a serious business, Bonhoeffer furnished him with a list of the

---

* It is said in some of the German memoirs that in 1942 and 1943 the Nazis were in contact with the Russians about a possible peace negotiation and even that Stalin had offered to initiate talks for a separate peace. Ribbentrop on the stand at Nuremberg made a good deal of his own efforts to get in touch with the Russians and said he actually made contact with Soviet agents at Stockholm. Peter Kleist, who acted for Ribbentrop in Stockholm, had told of this in his book.[3] I suspect that when all the secret German papers are sorted, a revealing chapter on this episode may come to light.

names of the leaders—an indiscretion which later was to cost him his life and to help make certain the execution of many of the others.

This was the most authoritative and up-to-date information the Allies had had on the German opposition and its plans, and Bishop Bell promptly turned it over to Anthony Eden, the British Foreign Secretary, when he returned to London in June. But Eden, who had resigned this post in 1938 in protest against Chamberlain's appeasement of Hitler, was skeptical. Similar information had been conveyed to the British government by alleged German plotters since the time of Munich and nothing had come of it. No response was made.[4]

The German underground's contacts with the Allies in Switzerland were mainly through Allen Dulles, who headed the U.S. Office of Strategic Services there from November 1942 until the end of the war. His chief visitor was Hans Gisevius, who journeyed to Berne frequently from Berlin and who also was an active member of the conspiracy, as we have seen. Gisevius worked for the Abwehr and was actually posted to the German consulate general in Zurich as vice-consul. His chief function was to convey messages to Dulles from Beck and Goerdeler and to keep him informed of the progress of the various plots against Hitler. Other German visitors included Dr. Schoenfeld and Trott zu Solz, the latter a member of the Kreisau Circle and also of the conspiracy, who once journeyed to Switzerland to "warn" Dulles, as had so many others, that if the Western democracies refused to consider a decent peace with an anti-Nazi German regime the conspirators would turn to Soviet Russia. Dulles, though he was personally sympathetic, was unable to give any assurances.[5]

One marvels at these German resistance leaders who were so insistent on getting a favorable peace settlement from the West and so hesitant in getting rid of Hitler until they had got it. One would have thought that if they considered Nazism to be such a monstrous evil as they constantly contended—no doubt sincerely—they would have concentrated on trying to overthrow it regardless of how the West might treat their new regime. One gets the impression that a good many of these "good Germans" fell too easily into the trap of blaming the outside world for their own failures, as some of them had done for Germany's misfortunes after the first lost war and even for the advent of Hitler himself.

OPERATION FLASH

In February 1943, Goerdeler told Jakob Wallenberg in Stockholm that "they had plans for a coup in March."

They had.

The preparations for Operation Flash, as it was called, had been worked out during January and February by General Friedrich Olbricht, chief of the General Army Office (Allgemeines Heeresamt) and General von Tresckow, chief of staff of Kluge's Army Group Center in Russia. Olbricht, a deeply religious man, was a recent convert to the conspiracy, but, because of his new post, had rapidly become a key figure in it. As deputy to General Friedrich Fromm, commander of the Replacement Army, he was in a position to rally the garrisons in Berlin and the other large cities of the Reich behind the plotters. Fromm himself, like Kluge, was by now disillusioned with his Fuehrer but was not regarded as sufficiently trustworthy to be let in on the plot.

"We are ready. It is time for the Flash," Olbricht told young Fabian von Schlabrendorff, a junior officer on Tresckow's staff, at the end of February. Early in March the plotters met for a final conference at Smolensk, the headquarters of Army Group Center. Although not participating in the action, Admiral Canaris, the chief of the Abwehr, was aware of it and arranged the meeting, flying Hans von Dohnanyi and General Erwin Lahousen of his staff with him to Smolensk ostensibly for a conference of Wehrmacht intelligence officers. Lahousen, a former intelligence officer of the Austrian Army and the only plotter in the Abwehr to survive the war, brought along some bombs.

Schlabrendorff and Tresckow, after much experimenting, had found that German bombs were no good for their purpose. They worked, as the young officer later explained,[6] with a fuse that made a low hissing noise which gave them away. The British, they discovered, made a better bomb. "Prior to the explosion," Schlabrendorff says, "they made no noise of any kind." The R.A.F. had dropped a number of these weapons over occupied Europe to Allied agents for sabotage purposes—one had been used to assassinate Heydrich—and the Abwehr had collected several of them and turned them over to the conspirators.

The plan worked out at the Smolensk meeting was to lure Hitler to the army group headquarters and there do away with him. This would be the signal for the coup in Berlin.

Enticing the warlord, who was now suspicious of most of his generals, into the trap was not an easy matter. But Tresckow prevailed upon an old friend, General Schmundt (as he now was), adjutant to Hitler, to work on his chief, and after some hesitation and more than one cancellation the Fuehrer agreed definitely to come to Smolensk on March 13, 1943. Schmundt himself knew nothing of the plot.

In the meantime Tresckow had been renewing his efforts to get *his* chief, Kluge, to take the lead in bumping off Hitler. He suggested to the Field Marshal that Lieutenant Colonel Freiherr von Boeselager,* who commanded a cavalry unit at headquarters, be allowed to use it to mow Hitler and his bodyguard down when they arrived. Boeselager was more than willing. All he needed was an order from the Field Marshal. But the vacillating commander could not bring himself to give it. Tresckow and Schlabrendorff therefore decided to take matters into their own hands.

They would simply plant one of their British-made bombs in Hitler's plane on its return flight. "The semblance of an accident," Schlabrendorff

---

* Executed by the Nazis.

later explained, "would avoid the political disadvantages of a murder. For in those days Hitler still had many followers who, after such an event, would have put up a strong resistance to our revolt."

Twice that afternoon and evening of March 13 after Hitler had arrived the two anti-Nazi officers were tempted to change their plan and set the bomb off, first in Kluge's personal quarters, where Hitler conferred with the top generals of the army group, and later in the officers' mess where the gathering supped.* But this would have killed some of the very generals who, once relieved of their personal oaths of allegiance to the Fuehrer, were counted upon to help the conspirators take over power in the Reich.

There still remained the task of smuggling the bomb onto the Fuehrer's plane, which was due to take off immediately after dinner. Schlabrendorff had assembled what he calls "two explosive packets" and made of them one parcel which resembled a couple of brandy bottles. During the repast Tresckow had innocently asked a Colonel Heinz Brandt of the Army General Staff, who was in Hitler's party, whether he would be good enough to take back a present of two bottles of brandy to his old friend General Helmuth Stieff,† who was chief of the Organization Branch of the Army High Command. The unsuspecting Brandt said he would be glad to.

At the airfield Schlabrendorff nervously reached through a small opening in his parcel, started the mechanism of the time bomb and handed it to Brandt as he boarded the Fuehrer's plane. This was a cleverly built weapon. It had no telltale clockwork. When the young officer pressed on a button it broke a small bottle, releasing a corrosive chemical which then ate away a wire that held back a spring. When the wire gave out, the spring pressed forward the striker, which hit a detonator that exploded the bomb.

The crash, Schlabrendorff says, was expected shortly after Hitler's plane passed over Minsk, about thirty minutes' flying time from Smolensk. Feverish with excitement, he rang up Berlin and by code informed the conspirators that Flash had begun. Then he and Tresckow waited with pounding hearts for the great news. They expected the first word would come by radio from one of the fighter planes which was escorting the Fuehrer's plane. They counted off the minutes, twenty, thirty, forty, an hour . . . and still there was no word. It came more than two hours later. A routine message said that Hitler had landed at Rastenburg.

We were stunned, and could not imagine the cause of the failure [Schlabrendorff later recounted]. I immediately rang up Berlin and gave the code word indicating that the attempt had miscarried. Then Tresckow and I consulted

---

* At the first meeting, Schlabrendorff says, he had an opportunity to examine Hitler's oversize cap. He was struck by its weight. On examination it proved to be lined with three and a half pounds of steel plating.
† Executed by the Nazis.

as to what action to take next. We were deeply shaken. It was serious enough that the attempt had not succeeded. But even worse would be the discovery of the bomb, which would unfailingly lead to our detection and the death of a wide circle of close collaborators.

The bomb was never discovered. That night Tresckow rang up Colonel Brandt, inquired casually whether he had had time to deliver his parcel to General Stieff and was told by Brandt that he had not yet got around to it. Tresckow told him to hold it—there had been a mistake in the bottles—and that Schlabrendorff would be arriving the next day on some official business and would bring the really good brandy that he had intended to send.

With incredible courage Schlabrendorff flew to Hitler's headquarters and exchanged a couple of bottles of brandy for the bomb.

I can still recall my horror [he later related] when Brandt handed me the bomb and gave it a jerk that made me fear a belated explosion. Feigning a composure I did not feel I took the bomb, immediately got into a car, and drove to the neighboring railway junction of Korschen.

There he caught the night train to Berlin and in the privacy of his sleeping compartment dismantled the bomb. He quickly discovered what had happened—or rather, why nothing had happened.

The mechanism had worked; the small bottle had broken; the corrosive fluid had consumed the wire; the striker had hit forward; but—the detonator had not fired.

Bitterly disappointed but not discouraged, the conspirators in Berlin decided to make a fresh attempt on Hitler's life. A good occasion soon presented itself. Hitler, accompanied by Goering, Himmler and Keitel, was due to be present at the Heroes' Memorial Day (*Heldengedenktag*) ceremonies on March 21 at the Zeughaus in Berlin. Here was an opportunity to get not only the Fuehrer but his chief associates. As Colonel Freiherr von Gersdorff, chief of intelligence on Kluge's staff, later said, "This was a chance which would never recur." Gersdorff had been selected by Tresckow to handle the bomb, and this time it would have to be a suicidal mission. The plan was for the colonel to conceal in his overcoat pockets two bombs, set the fuses, stay as close to Hitler during the ceremony as possible and blow the Fuehrer and his entourage as well as himself to eternity. With conspicuous bravery Gersdorff readily volunteered to sacrifice his life.

On the evening of March 20 he met with Schlabrendorff in his room at the Eden Hotel in Berlin. Schlabrendorff had brought two bombs with ten-minute fuses. But because of the near-freezing temperature in the glassed-over courtyard of the Zeughaus it might take from fifteen to twenty minutes before the weapons exploded. It was in this courtyard that Hitler, after his speech, was scheduled to spend half an hour examining an exhibition of captured Russian war trophies which Gersdorff's staff had arranged. It was the only place where the colonel could get close enough to the Fuehrer to kill him.

Gersdorff later recounted what happened.[7]

The next day I carried in each of my overcoat pockets a bomb with a ten-minute fuse. I intended to stay as close to Hitler as I could, so that he at least would be blown to pieces by the explosion. When Hitler . . . entered the exhibitional hall, Schmundt came across to me and said that only eight or ten minutes were to be spent on inspecting the exhibits. So the possibility of carrying out the assassination no longer existed, since even if the temperature had been normal the fuse needed at least ten minutes. This last-minute change of schedule, which was typical of Hitler's subtle security methods, had once again saved him his life.*

General von Tresckow, Gersdorff says, was anxiously and expectantly following the broadcast of the ceremonies from Smolensk, "a stop watch in his hand." When the broadcaster announced that Hitler had left the hall only eight minutes after he had entered it, the General knew that still another attempt had failed.

There were at least three further "overcoat" attempts at Hitler's life, as the conspirators called them, and each, as we shall see, was similarly frustrated.

Early in 1943 there was one spontaneous uprising in Germany which, though small in itself, helped to revive the flagging spirits of the resistance, whose every attempt to remove Hitler had been thus far thwarted. It also served as a warning of how ruthless the Nazi authorities could be in putting down the least sign of opposition.

The university students in Germany, as we have seen, had been among the most fanatical of Nazis in the early Thirties. But ten years of Hitler's rule had brought disillusionment, and this was sharpened by the failure of Germany to win the war and particularly, as 1943 came, by the disaster at Stalingrad. The University of Munich, the city that had given birth to Nazism, became the hotbed of student revolt. It was led by a twenty-five-year-old medical student, Hans Scholl, and his twenty-one-year-old sister, Sophie, who was studying biology. Their mentor was Kurt Huber, a professor of philosophy. By means of what became known as the "White

---

* One of the difficulties of piecing together the deeds of the plotters is that the memories of the few survivors are far from perfect, so that their accounts not only often differ but are contradictory. Schlabrendorff, for example, who had brought the bombs to Gersdorff, recounts in his book that because they could not find a short enough time fuse the Zeughaus attempt "had to be given up." He apparently was unaware, or forgot, that Gersdorff actually went to the Zeughaus to try to carry out his assignment, though the colonel says that the night before he told him he was "determined to do it" with the fuses he had.

Rose Letters" they carried out their anti-Nazi propaganda in other universities; they were also in touch with the plotters in Berlin.

One day in February 1943, the Gauleiter of Bavaria, Paul Giesler, to whom the Gestapo had brought a file of the letters, convoked the student body, announced that the physically unfit males—the able-bodied had been drafted into the Army—would be put to some kind of more useful war work, and with a leer suggested that the women students bear a child each year for the good of the Fatherland.

"If some of the girls," he added, "lack sufficient charm to find a mate, I will assign each of them one of my adjutants . . . and I can promise her a thoroughly enjoyable experience."

The Bavarians are noted for their somewhat coarse humor, but this vulgarity was too much for the students. They howled the Gauleiter down and tossed out of the hall the Gestapo and S.S. men who had come to guard him. That afternoon there were anti-Nazi student demonstrations in the streets of Munich, the first that had ever occurred in the Third Reich. Now the students, led by the Scholls, began to distribute pamphlets openly calling on German youth to rise. On February 19 a building superintendent observed Hans and Sophie Scholl hurling their leaflets from the balcony of the university and betrayed them to the Gestapo.

Their end was quick and barbaric. Haled before the dreaded People's Court, which was presided over by its president, Roland Freisler, perhaps the most sinister and bloodthirsty Nazi in the Third Reich after Heydrich (he will appear again in this narrative), they were found guilty of treason and condemned to death. Sophie Scholl was handled so roughly during her interrogation by the Gestapo that she appeared in court with a broken leg. But her spirit was undimmed. To Freisler's savage browbeating she answered calmly, "You know as well as we do that the war is lost. Why are you so cowardly that you won't admit it?"

She hobbled on her crutches to the scaffold and died with sublime courage, as did her brother. Professor Huber and several other students were executed a few days later.[8]

This was a reminder to the conspirators in Berlin of the danger that confronted them at a time when the indiscreetness of some of the leaders was becoming a source of constant worry to the others. Goerdeler himself was much too talkative. The efforts of Popitz to sound out Himmler and other high S.S. officers on joining the conspiracy were risky in the extreme. The inimitable Weizsaecker, who after the war liked to picture himself as such a staunch resister, became so frightened that he broke off all contact with his close friend Hassell, whom he accused (along with Frau von Hassell) of being "unbelievably indiscreet" and whom, he warned, the Gestapo was shadowing.*

---

* Hassell describes the painful scene in his diary. "He asked me to spare him the embarrassment of my presence," Hassell writes. "When I started to remonstrate he interrupted me harshly." (*The Von Hassell Diaries,* pp. 256–57.) Only when Weizsaecker was safely settled down in the Vatican later, as German ambassador

The Gestapo was watching a good many others, especially the breezy, confident Goerdeler, but the blow which it dealt the conspirators immediately after the frustrating month of March 1943 during which their two attempts to kill Hitler had miscarried came, ironically, as the result not so much of expert sleuthing but of the rivalry between the two intelligence services, the Wehrmacht's Abwehr and Himmler's R.S.H.A.—the Central Security Office—which ran the S.S. secret service, and which wanted to depose Admiral Canaris and take over his Abwehr.

In the autumn of 1942, a Munich businessman had been arrested for smuggling foreign currency across the border into Switzerland. He was actually an Abwehr agent, but the money he had long been taking over the frontier had gone to a group of Jewish refugees in Switzerland. This was the height of crime for a German in the Third Reich to commit even if he were an Abwehr agent. When Canaris failed to protect this agent, he began to tell the Gestapo what he knew of the Abwehr. He implicated Hans von Dohnanyi, who, with Colonel Oster, had been in the inner circle of the plotters. He told Himmler's men of the mission of Dr. Josef Mueller to the Vatican in 1940 when contact was made with the British through the Pope. He revealed Pastor Bonhoeffer's visit to the Bishop of Chichester at Stockholm in 1942 on a false passport issued by the Abwehr. He hinted at Oster's various schemes to get rid of Hitler.

After months of investigation the Gestapo acted. Dohnanyi, Mueller and Bonhoeffer were arrested on April 5, 1943, and Oster, who had managed to destroy most of the incriminating papers in the meantime, was forced to resign in December from the Abwehr and placed under house arrest in Leipzig.*

This was a staggering blow to the conspiracy. Oster—"a man such as God meant men to be, lucid and serene in mind, imperturbable in danger," as Schlabrendorff said of him—had been one of the key figures since 1938 in the attempt to get Hitler, and Dohnanyi, a jurist by profession, had been a resourceful assistant. Bonhoeffer, the Protestant, and Mueller, the Catholic, had not only brought a great spiritual force to the resistance but had given an example of individual courage in their various missions abroad—as they were to do in their refusal, even after the torture which followed their arrests, to betray their comrades.

But most serious of all, with the breakup of the Abwehr the plotters lost their "cover" and the principal means of communication with each other, with the hesitant generals and with their friends in the West.

Some further discoveries by Himmler's sleuths put the Abwehr and its chief, Canaris, out of business altogether within a few months.

---

there, did he urge the conspirators to action. "This is easy to do from the Vatican," Hassell commented. Weizsaecker survived to write his somewhat shabby memoirs. Hassell's diary was published after his execution.

* Bonhoeffer, Dohnanyi and Oster were all executed by the S.S. on April 9, 1945, less than a month before Germany's capitulation. Their extinction seems to have been an act of revenge on the part of Himmler. Mueller alone survived.

One sprang out of what came to be known in Nazi circles as "the Frau Solf Tea Party," which took place on September 10, 1943. Frau Anna Solf, the widow of a former Colonial Minister under Wilhelm II who had also served as ambassador to Japan under the Weimar Republic, had long presided over an anti-Nazi *salon* in Berlin. To it came often a number of distinguished guests, who included Countess Hanna von Bredow, the granddaughter of Bismarck, Count Albrecht von Bernstorff, the nephew of the German ambassador to the United States during the First World War, Father Erxleben, a well-known Jesuit priest, Otto Kiep, a high official in the Foreign Office, who once had been dismissed as German consul general in New York for attending a public luncheon in honor of Professor Einstein but who eventually had got himself reinstated in the diplomatic service, and Elisabeth von Thadden, a sparkling and deeply religious woman who ran a famous girls' school at Weiblingen, near Heidelberg.

To the tea party at Frau Solf's on September 10 Fräulein von Thadden brought an attractive young Swiss doctor named Reckse, who practiced at the Charité Hospital in Berlin under Professor Sauerbruch. Like most Swiss Dr. Reckse expressed bitter anti-Nazi sentiments, in which he was joined by the others present, especially by Kiep. Before the tea party was over the good doctor had volunteered to carry any letters which Frau Solf or her guests wished to send to their friends in Switzerland—German anti-Nazi émigrés and British and American diplomatic officials—an offer which was quickly taken up by more than one present.

Unfortunately for them Dr. Reckse was an agent of the Gestapo, to whom he turned over several incriminating letters as well as a report on the tea party.

Count von Moltke learned of this through a friend in the Air Ministry who had tapped a number of telephone conversations between the Swiss doctor and the Gestapo, and he quickly warned his friend Kiep, who tipped off the rest of the Solf circle. But Himmler had his evidence. He waited four months to act on it, perhaps hoping to widen his net. On January 12, everyone who had been at the tea party was arrested, tried and executed, except Frau Solf and her daughter, the Countess Ballestrem.* The Solfs were confined at the Ravensbrueck concentration camp and miraculously escaped death.† Count von Moltke, implicated with his friend Kiep, was

---

* Apparently Himmler *had* widened his net in the intervening four months. According to Reitlinger some seventy-four persons were arrested as the result of Dr. Reckse's spying. (Reitlinger, *The S.S.*, p. 304.)

† First the Japanese ambassador intervened to delay their trial. Then on February 3, 1945, a bomb dropped during a daylight attack by the American Air Force not only killed Roland Freisler, while he was presiding over one of his grisly treason trials, but destroyed the dossier on the Solfs, which was in the files of the People's Court. They were nevertheless scheduled to be tried by this court on April 27, but by that time the Russians were in Berlin. Actually the Solfs were released from Moabit prison on April 23, apparently because of an error. (Wheeler-Bennett, *Nemesis*, p. 595n., and Pechel, *Deutscher Widerstand*, pp. 88–93.)

also arrested at this time. But that was not the only consequence of Kiep's arrest. The repercussions spread as far as Turkey and paved the way for the final liquidation of the Abwehr and the turning over of its functions to Himmler.

Among Kiep's close anti-Nazi friends were Erich Vermehren and his stunningly beautiful wife, the former Countess Elisabeth von Plettenberg, who like other opponents of the regime had joined the Abwehr and who had been posted as its agents in Istanbul. Both were summoned to Berlin by the Gestapo to be interrogated in the Kiep case. Knowing what fate was in store for them, they refused, got in touch with the British secret service at the beginning of February 1944 and were flown to Cairo and thence to England.

It was believed in Berlin—though it turned out not to be true—that the Vermehrens had absconded with all the Abwehr's secret codes and handed them over to the British. This was the last straw for Hitler, coming after the arrests of Dohnanyi and others in the Abwehr and coupled with his growing suspicion of Canaris. On February 18, 1944, he ordered that the Abwehr be dissolved and its functions taken over by R.S.H.A. This was a new feather in the cap of Himmler, whose war against the Army officer corps went back to his faking charges against General von Fritsch in 1938. It deprived the armed forces of any intelligence service of their own. It enhanced Himmler's power over the generals. It was also a further blow to the conspirators, who were now left without any secret service whatsoever through which to work.*

They had not ceased trying to kill Hitler. Between September 1943 and January 1944 another half-dozen attempts were organized. In August Jakob Wallenberg had come to Berlin to see Goerdeler, who assured him that all preparations were now ready for a coup in September and that Schlabrendorff would then arrive in Stockholm to meet a representative of Mr. Churchill to discuss peace.

"I was awaiting the month of September with great suspense," the Swedish banker later told Allen Dulles. "It passed without anything happening."[9]

A month later General Stieff, the sharp-tongued hunchback to whom Tresckow had sent the two bottles of "brandy" and whom Himmler later referred to as "a little poisoned dwarf," arranged to plant a time bomb at Hitler's noon military conference at Rastenburg, but at the last moment got cold feet. A few days later his store of English bombs which he had received from the Abwehr and hidden under a watch tower in the head-quarters enclosure exploded, and it was only because an Abwehr colonel,

---

* Canaris was made chief of the Office for Commercial and Economic Warfare. With the assumption of this empty title the "little Admiral" faded out of German history. He was so shadowy a figure that no two writers agree as to what kind of man he was, or what he believed in, if anything much. A cynic and a fatalist, he had hated the Weimar Republic and worked secretly against it and then turned similarly on the Third Reich. His days, like those of all the other prominent men in the Abwehr save one (General Lahousen), were now numbered, as we shall see.

Werner Schrader, who was in on the conspiracy, was entrusted by Hitler with the investigation that the plotters were not discovered.

In November another "overcoat" attempt was organized. A twenty-four-year-old infantry captain, Axel von dem Bussche, was selected by the conspirators to "model" a new Army overcoat and assault pack which Hitler had ordered designed and now wanted to personally inspect before approving for manufacture. Bussche, in order to avoid Gersdorff's failure, decided to carry in the pockets of his model overcoat two German bombs which would go off a few seconds after the fuse was set. His plan was to grab Hitler as he was inspecting the new overcoat and blow the two of them to pieces.

The day before the demonstration an Allied bomb destroyed the models, and Bussche returned to his company on the Russian front. He was back at Hitler's headquarters in December for a fresh attempt with new models, when the Fuehrer suddenly decided to leave for Berchtesgaden for the Christmas holidays. Shortly afterward Bussche was badly wounded at the front, so another young front-line infantry officer was pressed into service to substitute for him. This was Heinrich von Kleist, son of Ewald von Kleist—the latter one of the oldest conspirators. The demonstration of the new overcoat was set for February 11, 1944, but the Fuehrer for some reason—Dulles says it was because of an air raid—failed to appear.*

By this time the plotters had come to the conclusion that Hitler's technique of constantly changing his schedules called for a drastic overhauling of their own plans.† It was realized that the only occasions on which he could definitely be counted to appear were his twice-daily military conferences with the generals of OKW and OKH. He would have to be killed at one of them. On December 26, 1943, a young officer by the name of Stauffenberg, deputizing for General Olbricht, appeared at the Rastenburg headquarters for the noon conference, at which he was to make a report on

---

* The Kleists, father and son, were later arrested. The father was executed on April 16, 1945; his son survived.
† Hitler often discussed this technique with his old party cronies. There is a stenographic record of a monologue of his at headquarters on May 3, 1942. "I quite understand," he said, "why ninety per cent of the historic assassinations have been successful. The only preventive measure one can take is to live irregularly—to walk, to drive and to travel at irregular times and unexpectedly . . . As far as possible, whenever I go anywhere by car I go off unexpectedly and without warning the police." (*Hitler's Secret Conversations*, p. 366.)

Hitler had always been aware, as we have seen, that he might be assassinated. In his war conference on August 22, 1939, on the eve of the attack on Poland, he had emphasized to his generals that while he personally was indispensable he could "be eliminated at any time by a criminal or an idiot."

In his ramblings on the subject on May 3, 1942, he added, "There can never be absolute security against fanatics and idealists . . . If some fanatic wishes to shoot me or kill me with a bomb, I am no safer sitting down than standing up." He thought, though, that "the number of fanatics who seek my life on idealistic grounds is getting much smaller . . . The only really dangerous elements are either those fanatics who have been goaded to action by dastardly priests or nationalist-minded patriots from one of the countries we have occupied. My many years of experience make things fairly difficult even for such as these." (*Ibid.*, p. 367.)

Army replacements. In his briefcase was a time bomb. The meeting was canceled. Hitler had left to have his Christmas on the Obersalzberg.

This was the first such attempt by the handsome young lieutenant colonel, but not the last. For in Klaus Philip Schenk, Count von Stauffenberg, the anti-Nazi conspirators had at last found their man. Henceforth he would not only take over the job of killing Hitler by his own hand in the only way that now seemed possible but would breathe new life and light and hope and zeal into the conspiracy and become its real, though never nominal, leader.

THE MISSION OF COUNT VON STAUFFENBERG

This was a man of astonishing gifts for a professional Army officer. Born in 1907, he came from an old and distinguished South German family. Through his mother, Countess von Uxkull-Gyllenbrand, he was a great-grandson of Gneisenau, one of the military heroes of the war of liberation against Napoleon and the cofounder, with Scharnhorst, of the Prussian General Staff, and through her also a descendant of Yorck von Wartenburg, another celebrated general of the Bonaparte era. Klaus's father had been Privy Chamberlain to the last King of Wuerttemberg. The family was congenial, devoutly Roman Catholic and highly cultivated.

With this background and in this atmosphere Klaus von Stauffenberg grew up. Possessed of a fine physique and, according to all who knew him, of a striking handsomeness, he developed a brilliant, inquisitive, splendidly balanced mind. He had a passion for horses and sports but also for the arts and literature, in which he read widely, and as a youth came under the influence of Stefan George and that poetic genius's romantic mysticism. For a time the young man thought of taking up music as a profession, and later architecture, but in 1926, at the age of nineteen, he entered the Army as an officer cadet in the 17th Bamberg Cavalry Regiment—the famed *Bamberger Reiter*.

In 1936 he was posted to the War Academy in Berlin, where his all-round brilliance attracted the attention of both his teachers and the High Command. He emerged two years later as a young officer of the General Staff. Though, like most of his class, a monarchist at heart, he was not up to this time an opponent of National Socialism. Apparently it was the anti-Jewish pogroms of 1938 which first cast doubts in his mind about Hitler, and these increased when in the summer of 1939 he saw that the Fuehrer was leading Germany into a war which might be long, frightfully costly in human lives, and, in the end, lost.

Nevertheless, when the war came he threw himself into it with characteristic energy, making a name for himself as a staff officer of General Hoepner's 6th Panzer Division in the campaigns in Poland and France. It was in Russia that Stauffenberg seems to have become completely disillusioned with the Third Reich. He had been transferred to the Army High Command (OKH) early in June 1940, just before the assault on

Dunkirk, and for the first eighteen months of the Russian campaign spent most of his time in Soviet territory, where, among other things, he helped organize the Russian "volunteer" units from among the prisoners of war. By this time, according to his friends, Stauffenberg believed that while the Germans were getting rid of Hitler's tyranny these Russian troops could be used to overthrow Stalin's. Perhaps this was an instance of the influence of Stefan George's wooly ideas.

The brutality of the S.S. in Russia, not to mention Hitler's order to shoot the Bolshevik commissars, opened Stauffenberg's eyes as to the master he was serving. As chance had it, he met in Russia two of the chief conspirators who had decided to make an end to that master: General von Tresckow and Schlabrendorff. The latter says it took only a few subsequent meetings to convince them that Stauffenberg was their man. He became an active conspirator.

But he was still only a junior officer and he soon saw that the field marshals were too confused—if not too cowardly—to do anything to remove Hitler or to stop the grisly slaughter of Jews, Russians and POWs behind the lines. Also the needless disaster at Stalingrad sickened him. As soon as it was over, in February 1943, he asked to be sent to the front and was posted as operations officer of the 10th Panzer Division in Tunisia, joining it in the last days of the battle of the Kasserine Pass in which his unit had thrown the Americans out of the gap.

On April 7 his car drove into a mine field—some say it was also attacked by low-flying Allied aircraft—and Stauffenberg was gravely wounded. He lost his left eye, his right hand and two fingers of the other hand and suffered injuries to his left ear and knee. For several weeks it seemed probable that he would be left totally blind, if he survived. But under the expert supervision at a Munich hospital of Professor Sauerbruch, he was restored to life. Almost any other man, one would think, would have retired from the Army and thus from the conspiracy. But by midsummer he was writing General Olbricht—after much practice in wielding a pen with the three fingers of his bandaged left hand—that he expected to return to active duty within three months. During the long convalescence he had had time to reflect and he had come to the conclusion that, physically handicaped though he was, he had a sacred mission to perform.

"I feel I must do something now to save Germany," he told his wife, the Countess Nina, mother of his four young children, when she visited his bedside one day. "We General Staff officers must all accept our share of the responsibility."[10]

By the end of September 1943, he was back in Berlin as a lieutenant colonel and chief of staff to General Olbricht at the General Army Office. Soon he was practicing with a pair of tongs how to set off one of the English-made Abwehr bombs with the three fingers of his good hand.

He was doing much more. His dynamic personality, the clarity of his mind, the catholicity of his ideas and his marked talents as an organizer infused new life and determination into the conspirators. And also some differences, for Stauffenberg was not satisfied with the kind of stodgy, conservative, colorless regime which the old rusty leaders of the conspiracy, Beck, Goerdeler and Hassell, envisaged as soon as National Socialism was overthrown. More practical than his friends in the Kreisau Circle, he wanted a new dynamic Social Democracy and he insisted that the proposed anti-Nazi cabinet include his new friend Julius Leber, a brilliant Socialist, and Wilhelm Leuschner, a former trade-union official, both deep and active in the conspiracy. There was much argument, but Stauffenberg rapidly achieved dominance over the political leaders of the plot.

He was equally successful with most of the military men. He recognized General Beck as the nominal leader of these and held the former General Staff Chief in great admiration, but on returning to Berlin he saw that Beck, recovering from a major cancer operation, was only a shell of his former self, tired and somewhat dispirited, and that moreover he had no concept of politics, being in this field completely under the spell of Goerdeler. Beck's illustrious name in military circles would be useful, even necessary, in carrying out the putsch. But for active help in supplying and commanding the troops which would be needed, younger officers who were on active duty had to be mobilized. Stauffenberg soon had most of the key men he needed.

These were, besides Olbricht, his chief: General Stieff, head of the Organization Branch of OKH General Eduard Wagner, the First Quartermaster General of the Army; General Erich Fellgiebel, the Chief of Signals at OKW; General Fritz Lindemann, head of the Ordnance Office; General Paul von Hase, chief of the Berlin *Kommandantur* (who could furnish the troops for taking over Berlin); and Colonel Freiherr von Roenne, head of the Foreign Armies Section, with his chief of staff, Captain Count von Matuschka.

There were two or three key generals, chief of whom was Fritz Fromm, the actual commander in chief of the Replacement Army, who like Kluge, blew hot and cold and could not be definitely counted on.

The plotters also did not yet have a field marshal on active duty. Field Marshal von Witzleben, one of the original conspirators, was slated to become Commander in Chief of the Armed Forces but he was on the inactive list and had no troops at his command. Field Marshal von Rundstedt, who now commanded all troops in the West, was approached, but declined to go back on his oath to the Fuehrer—or such, at least, was his explanation. Likewise the brilliant but opportunistic Field Marshal von Manstein.

At this juncture—early in 1944—a very active and popular Field Marshal made himself, at first without the knowledge of Stauffenberg, somewhat available to the conspirators. This was Rommel, and his entrance into the plot against Hitler came as a great surprise to the resistance leaders and was not approved by most of them, who regarded the "Desert Fox" as a Nazi and as an opportunist who had blatantly courted Hitler's favor and was only now deserting him because he knew the war was lost.

In January 1944 Rommel had become commander of Army Group B in the West, the main force with which the expected Anglo–American invasion across the Channel was to be repelled. In France he began to see a good deal of two old friends, General Alexander von Falkenhausen, the military governor of Belgium and northern France, and General Karl Heinrich von Stuelpnagel, military governor of France. Both generals had already joined the anti-Hitler conspiracy and gradually initiated Rommel into it. They were aided by an old civilian friend of Rommel, Dr. Karl Stroelin, the Oberbuergermeister of Stuttgart, who like so many other characters in this narrative had been an enthusiastic Nazi and now, with defeat looming and the cities of Germany, including his own, rapidly becoming rubble from the Allied bombing, was having second thoughts. He, in turn, had been helped along this path by Dr. Goerdeler, who in August 1943 had persuaded him to join in drawing up a memorandum to the Ministry of the Interior—now headed by Himmler—in which they jointly demanded a cessation of the persecution of the Jews and the Christian churches, the restoration of civil rights and the re-establishment of a system of justice divorced from the party and the S.S.-Gestapo. Through Frau Rommel, Stroelin brought the memorandum to the attention of the Field Marshal, on whom it appears to have had a marked effect.

Toward the end of February 1944, the two men met at Rommel's home at Herrlingen, near Ulm, and had a heart-to-heart talk.

I told him [the mayor later recounted] that certain senior officers of the Army in the East proposed to make Hitler a prisoner and to force him to announce over the radio that he had abdicated. Rommel approved of the idea.

I went on to say to him that he was our greatest and most popular general, and more respected abroad than any other. "You are the only one," I said, "who can prevent civil war in Germany. You must lend your name to the movement."[11]

Rommel hesitated and finally made his decision.

"I believe," he said to Stroelin, "it is my duty to come to the rescue of Germany."

At this meeting and at all subsequent ones which Rommel had with the plotters, he opposed assassinating Hitler—not on moral but on practical grounds. To kill the dictator, he argued, would be to make a martyr of him. He insisted that Hitler be arrested by the Army and haled before a German court for crimes against his own people and those of the occupied lands.[12]

At this time fate brought another influence on Rommel in the person of General Hans Speidel, who on April 15, 1944, became the Field Marshal's chief of staff. Speidel, like his fellow conspirator Stauffenberg—though they belonged to quite separate groups—was an unusual Army officer. He was not only a soldier but a philosopher, having received *summa cum laude* a doctorate in philosophy from the University of

Tuebingen in 1925. He lost no time in going to work on his chief. Within a month, on May 15, he arranged a meeting at a country house near Paris between Rommel, Stuelpnagel and their chiefs of staff. The purpose, says Speidel, was to work out "the necessary measures for ending the war in the West and overthrowing the Nazi regime."[13]

This was a large order, and Speidel realized that in preparing it closer contacts with the anti-Nazis in the homeland, especially with the Goerdeler–Beck group, were urgently necessary. For some weeks the mercurial Goerdeler had been pressing for a secret meeting between Rommel and— of all people—Neurath, who, having done his own share of Hitler's dirty work, first as Foreign Minister and then as the Reich Protector of Bohemia, was also experiencing a rude awakening now that terrible disaster was about to overtake the Fatherland. It was decided that it would be too dangerous for Rommel to meet with Neurath and Stroelin, so the Field Marshal sent General Speidel, at whose home in Freudenstadt the conference was held on May 27. The three men present, Speidel, Neurath and Stroelin, were, like Rommel himself, all Swabians and this affinity appears not only to have made the meeting congenial but to have led to ready agreement. This was that Hitler must be quickly overthrown and that Rommel must be prepared to become either the interim head of state or Commander in Chief of the Armed Forces—neither of which posts, it must be said, Rommel at any time ever demanded for himself. A number of details were worked out, including plans for contacting the Western Allies for an armistice, and a code for communication between the conspirators in Germany and Rommel's headquarters.

General Speidel is emphatic in his assertion not only that Rommel frankly informed his immediate superior in the West, Field Marshal von Rundstedt, as to what was up, but that the latter was "in complete agreement." There was a flaw, however, in the character of this senior officer of the Army.

During a discussion on the formulation of joint demands to Hitler [Speidel later wrote] Rundstedt said to Rommel: "You are young. You know and love the people. You do it."[14]

After further conferences that late spring the following plan was drawn up. Speidel, almost alone among the Army conspirators in the West, survived to describe it:

An immediate armistice with the Western Allies but not unconditional surrender. German withdrawal in the West to Germany. Immediate suspension of the Allied bombing of Germany. Arrest of Hitler for trial before a German court. Overthrow of Nazi rule. Temporary assumption of executive power in Germany by the resistance forces of all classes under the leadership of General Beck, Goerdeler, and the trade-union representative, Leuschner. No military dictatorship. Preparation of a "constructive peace" within the framework of a United States of Europe. In the East, continuation of the war. Holding a shortened line between the mouth of the Danube, the Carpathian Mountains, the River Vistula and Memel.[15]

The generals seem to have had no doubts whatsoever that the British and American armies would then join them in the war against Russia to prevent, as they said, Europe from becoming Bolshevik.

In Berlin General Beck agreed, at least to the extent of continuing the war in the East. Early in May he sent through Gisevius a memorandum to Dulles in Switzerland outlining a fantastic plan. The German generals in the West were to withdraw their forces to the German frontier after the Anglo–American invasion. While this was going on, Beck urged that the Western Allies carry out three tactical operations: land three airborne divisions in the Berlin area to help the conspirators hold the capital, carry out large-scale seaborne landings on the German coast near Hamburg and Bremen, and land a sizable force across the Channel in France. Reliable anti-Nazi German troops would in the meantime take over in the Munich area and surround Hitler at his mountain retreat on the Obersalzberg. The war against Russia would go on. Dulles says he lost no time in trying to bring the Berlin conspirators down to earth. They were told there could be no separate peace with the West.[16]

Stauffenberg, his friends in the Kreisau Circle and such members of the conspiracy as Schulenburg, the former ambassador in Moscow, had come to realize this. In fact most of them, including Stauffenberg, were "Easterners"—pro-Russian though anti-Bolshevik. For a time they believed that it might be easier to get a better peace with Russia—which through statements from Stalin himself had emphasized in its radio propaganda that it was fighting not against the German people but against "the Hitlerites"—than with the Western Allies, who harped only of "unconditional surrender."* But they abandoned such wishful thinking in October 1943, when the Soviet government at the Moscow Conference of Allied Foreign Ministers formally adhered to the Casablanca declaration of unconditional surrender.

And now, as the fateful summer of 1944 approached, they realized that with the Red armies nearing the frontier of the Reich, the British and American armies poised for a large-scale invasion across the Channel, and the German resistance to Alexander's Allied forces in Italy crumbling, they must quickly get rid of Hitler and the Nazi regime if any kind of peace at all was to be had that would spare Germany from being overrun and annihilated.

In Berlin, Stauffenberg and his confederates had at last perfected their plans. They were lumped under the code name "Valkyrie"—an appropriate term, since the Valkyrie were the maidens in Norse-German mythology,

---

* At their meeting at Casablanca Churchill and Roosevelt had issued on January 24, 1943, their declaration of unconditional surrender for Germany. Goebbels naturally made a great deal of this in trying to whip the German people into a state of all-out resistance but in the opinion of this author his success has been grossly exaggerated by a surprisingly large number of Western writers.

beautiful but terrifying, who were supposed to have hovered over the ancient battlefields choosing those who would be slain. In this case, Adolf Hitler was to be slain. Ironically enough, Admiral Canaris, before his fall, had sold the Fuehrer the idea of Valkyrie, dressing it up as a plan for the Home Army to take over the security of Berlin and the other large cities in case of a revolt of the millions of foreign laborers toiling in these centers. Such a revolt was highly unlikely—indeed, impossible—since the foreign workers were unarmed and unorganized, but to the suspicious Fuehrer danger lurked everywhere these days, and, with almost all the able-bodied soldiers absent from the homeland either at the front or keeping down the populace in the far-flung occupied areas, he readily fell in with the idea that the Home Army ought to have plans for protecting the internal security of the Reich against the hordes of sullen slave laborers. Thus Valkyrie became a perfect cover for the military conspirators, enabling them to draw up quite openly plans for the Home Army to take over the capital and such cities as Vienna, Munich and Cologne as soon as Hitler had been assassinated.

In Berlin their main difficulty was that they had very few troops at their disposal and that these were outnumbered by the S.S. formations. Also there were considerable numbers of Luftwaffe units in and around the city manning the antiaircraft defenses, and these troops, unless the Army moved swiftly, would remain loyal to Goering and certainly make a fight of it to retain the Nazi regime under their chief even if Hitler were dead. Their flak guns could be used as artillery against the Army detachments. On the other hand, the police force in Berlin had been won over through its chief, Count von Helldorf, who had joined the conspiracy.

In view of the strength of the S.S. and Air Force troops, Stauffenberg laid great stress on the timing of the operation to gain control of the capital. The first two hours would be the most critical. In that short space of time the Army troops must occupy and secure the national broadcasting headquarters and the city's two radio stations, the telegraph and telephone centrals, the Reich Chancellery, the ministries and the headquarters of the S.S.-Gestapo. Goebbels, the only prominent Nazi who rarely left Berlin, must be arrested along with the S.S. officers. In the meantime, the moment Hitler was killed his headquarters at Rastenburg must be isolated from Germany so that neither Goering nor Himmler, nor any of the Nazi generals such as Keitel and Jodl, could take over and attempt to rally the police or the troops behind a continued Nazi regime. General Fellgiebel, Chief of Signals, who was stationed at the Fuehrer's headquarters, had undertaken to see to this.

Only then, after all these things had been accomplished within the first couple of hours of the coup, could the messages, which had been drawn up and filed, be sent out by radio, telephone and telegraph to the commanders of the Home Army in other cities and to the top generals commanding the troops at the front and in the occupied zones, announcing that Hitler was dead and that a new anti-Nazi government had been formed in Berlin. The revolt would have to be over—and achieved—within twenty-four hours and the new government firmly installed. Otherwise the vacillating generals might have second thoughts. Goering and Himmler might be able to rally them, and a civil war would ensue. In that case the fronts would cave in and the very chaos and collapse which the plotters wished to prevent would become inevitable.

All depended for success, after Hitler had been assassinated—and Stauffenberg personally would see to this—on the ability of the plotters to utilize for their purposes, and with the utmost speed and energy, the available Army troops in and around Berlin. This posed a knotty problem.

Only General Fritz Fromm, the commander in chief of the Home or Replacement Army, could normally give the order to carry out Valkyrie. And to the very last he remained a question mark. All through 1943 the conspirators had worked on him. They finally concluded that this wary officer could be definitely counted upon only after he saw that the revolt had succeeded. But since they were sure of its success, they proceeded to draft a series of orders under Fromm's name, though without his knowledge. In case he wavered at the crucial moment, Fromm was to be replaced by General Hoepner, the brilliant tank commander who had been cashiered by Hitler after the battle for Moscow in 1941 and forbidden to wear his uniform.

The problem of another key general in Berlin also plagued the plotters. This was General von Kortzfleisch, an out-and-out Nazi, who commanded Wehrkreis III, which included Berlin and Brandenburg. It was decided to have him arrested and replaced by General Freiherr von Thuengen. General Paul von Hase, the commandant of Berlin, was in on the plot and could be counted upon to lead the local garrison troops in the first, all-important step of taking over the city.

Besides drawing up detailed plans for seizing control of Berlin, Stauffenberg and Tresckow, in collaboration with Goerdeler, Beck, Witzleben and others, drafted papers giving instructions to the district military commanders on how they were to take over executive power in their areas, put down the S.S., arrest the leading Nazis and occupy the concentration camps. Furthermore, several ringing declarations were composed which at the appropriate moment were to be issued to the armed forces, the German people, the press and the radio. Some were signed by Beck, as the new head of state, others by Field Marshal von Witzleben, as Commander in Chief of the Wehrmacht, and by Goerdeler, as the new Chancellor. Copies of the orders and appeals were typed in great secrecy late at night in the Bendlerstrasse by two brave women in the plot, Frau Erika von Tresckow, the wife of the general who had done so much to further the conspiracy, and Margarete von Oven, the daughter of a retired general and for years the faithful secretary of two former commanders in chief of the Army, Generals von Hammerstein and von Fritsch. The papers were then hidden in General Olbricht's safe.

The plans, then, were ready. In fact, they had been perfected by the end of 1943, but for months little had been done to carry them out. Events, however, could not wait on the conspirators. As June 1944 came they realized that time was running out on them. For one thing, the Gestapo was closing in. The arrests of those who were in on the plot, among them Count von Moltke and the members of the Kreisau Circle, were mounting with each week that passed, and there were many executions. Beck, Goerdeler, Hassell, Witzleben and others in the inner circle were being so closely shadowed by Himmler's secret police that they found it increasingly difficult to meet together. Himmler himself had warned the fallen Canaris in the spring that he knew very well that a rebellion was being hatched by the generals and their civilian friends. He mentioned that he was keeping a watch on Beck and Goerdeler. Canaris passed the warning on to Olbricht.[17]

Just as ominous for the conspirators was the military situation. The Russians, it was believed, were about to launch an all-out offensive in the East. Rome was being abandoned to the Allied forces. (It fell on June 4.) In the West the Anglo–American invasion was imminent. Very soon Germany might go down to military defeat—before Nazism could be overthrown. Indeed, there was a growing number of conspirators, perhaps influenced by the thinking of the Kreisau Circle, who began to feel that it might be better to call off their plans and let Hitler and the Nazis take the responsibility for the catastrophe. To overthrow them now might merely perpetrate another "stab-in-the-back" legend, such as that which had fooled so many Germans after the First World War.

THE ANGLO–AMERICAN INVASION, JUNE 6, 1944

Stauffenberg himself did not believe that the Western Allies would attempt to land in France that summer. He persisted in this belief even after Colonel Georg Hansen, a carryover from the Abwehr in Himmler's military-intelligence bureau, had warned him early in May that the invasion might begin on any day in June.

The German Army itself was beset by doubts, at least as to the date and place of the assault. In May there had been eighteen days when the weather, the sea and the tides were just right for a landing, and the Germans noted that General Eisenhower had not taken advantage of them. On May 30 Rundstedt, the Commander in Chief in the West, had reported to Hitler that there was no indication that the invasion was "immediately imminent." On June 4, the Air Force meteorologist in Paris advised that because of the inclement weather no Allied action could be expected for at least a fortnight.

On the strength of this and of what little information he had—the Luftwaffe had been prevented from making aerial reconnaissance of the harbors on England's south coast where Eisenhower's troops at that moment were swarming aboard their ships, and the Navy had withdrawn its reconnaissance craft from the Channel because of the heavy seas—Rommel drew up a situation report on the morning of June 5 reporting to Rundstedt that the invasion was not imminent, and immediately set off by car for his home at Herrlingen to spend the night with his family and then to proceed to Berchtesgaden the next day to confer with Hitler.

June 5, General Speidel, Rommel's chief of staff, later recalled, "was a quiet day." There seemed no reason why Rommel should not make his somewhat leisurely journey back to Germany. There were the usual reports from German agents about the possibility of an Allied landing—this time between June 6 and June 16—but there had been hundreds of these since April and they were not taken seriously. Indeed, on the sixth General Friedrich Dollmann, who commanded the Seventh Army in Normandy, on whose beaches the Allied forces were about to land, ordered a temporary relaxation of the standing alert and convoked his senior officers for a map exercise at Rennes, some 125 miles south of those beaches.

If the Germans were in the dark about the date of the invasion, they were also ignorant of where it would take place. Rundstedt and Rommel were certain it would be in the Pas-de-Calais area, where the Channel was at its narrowest. There they had concentrated their strongest force, the Fifteenth Army, whose strength during the spring was increased from ten to fifteen infantry divisions. But by the end of March Adolf Hitler's uncanny intuition was telling him that the *Schwerpunkt* of the invasion probably would be in Normandy, and during the next few weeks he ordered considerable reinforcements to the region between the Seine and the Loire. "Watch Normandy!" he kept warning his generals.

Still, the overwhelming part of German strength, in both infantry and panzer divisions, was retained north of the Seine, between Le Havre and Dunkirk. Rundstedt and his generals were watching the Pas-de-Calais rather than Normandy and they were encouraged in this by a number of deceptive maneuvers carried out during April and May by the British–American High Command which indicated to them that their calculations were correct.

The day of June 5, then, passed in relative quiet, so far as the Germans were concerned. Severe Anglo–American air attacks continued to disrupt German depots, radar stations, V-1 sites, communications and transport, but these had been going on night and day for weeks and seemed no more intense on this day than on others.

Shortly after dark Rundstedt's headquarters was informed that the BBC in London was broadcasting an unusually large number of coded messages to the French resistance and that the German radar stations between Cherbourg and Le Havre were being jammed. At 10 P.M. the Fifteenth Army intercepted a code message from the BBC to the French resistance which it believed meant that the invasion was about to begin. This army was alerted, but Rundstedt did not think it necessary to alert the Seventh Army, on whose sector of the coast farther west, between Caen and Cherbourg, the Allied forces were now—toward midnight—approaching on a thousand ships.

It was not until eleven minutes past 1 A.M., June 6, that the Seventh Army, its commander not yet returned from his map exercise at Rennes, realized what was happening. Two American and one British airborne divisions had begun landing in its midst. The general alarm was sounded at 1:30 A.M.

Forty-five minutes later Major General Max Pemsel, chief of staff of the Seventh Army, got General Speidel on the telephone at Rommel's headquarters and told him that it looked like "a large-scale operation." Speidel did not believe it but passed on the report to Rundstedt, who was equally skeptical. Both generals believed the dropping of parachutists was merely an Allied feint to cover their main landings around Calais. At 2:40 A.M. Pemsel was advised that Rundstedt "does not consider this to be a major operation."[18] Not even when the news began to reach him shortly after dawn on June 6 that on the Normandy coast between the rivers Vire and Orne a huge Allied fleet was disembarking large bodies of troops, under cover of a murderous fire from the big guns of an armada of warships, did the Commander in Chief West believe that this was to be the main Allied assault. It did not become apparent, Speidel says, until the afternoon of June 6. By that time the Americans had a toehold on two beaches and the British on a third and had penetrated inland for a distance of from two to six miles.

Speidel had telephoned Rommel at 6 A.M. at his home and the Field Marshal had rushed back by car without going on to see Hitler, but he did not arrive at Army Group B headquarters until late that afternoon.* In the meantime Speidel, Rundstedt and the latter's chief of staff, General Blumentritt, had been on the telephone to OKW, which was then at Berchtesgaden. Due to an idiotic order of Hitler's not even the Commander in Chief in the West could employ his panzer divisions without the specific permission of the Fuehrer. When the three generals early on the morning of the sixth begged for permission to rush two tank divisions to Normandy, Jodl replied that Hitler wanted first to see what developed. Whereupon the Fuehrer went to bed and could not be disturbed by the frantic calls of the generals in the West until 3 P.M.

When he woke up, the bad news which had in the meantime arrived finally stirred the Nazi warlord to action. He gave—too late, as it turned out—permission to engage the Panzer Lehr and 12th S.S. Panzer divisions in Normandy. He also issued a famous order which has been preserved for posterity in the log of the Seventh Army:

> 16:55 hours. June 6, 1944
> Chief of Staff Western Command emphasizes the desire of the Supreme Command to have the enemy in the bridgehead annihilated by the evening of June 6 since there exists the danger of additional sea- and airborne landings for support . . . The beachhead must be cleaned up by not later than tonight.

In the eerie mountain air of the Obersalzberg, from which Hitler was now trying to direct the most crucial battle of the war up to this moment—

---

* Because of Allied air superiority in the West, Hitler had forbidden his senior commanders to travel by plane.

he had been saying for months that Germany's destiny would be decided in the West—this fantastic order seems to have been issued in all seriousness, concurred in by Jodl and Keitel. Even Rommel, who passed it on by telephone shortly before 5 o'clock that afternoon, an hour after his return from Germany, seems to have taken it seriously, for he ordered Seventh Army headquarters to launch an attack by the 21st Panzer Division, the only German armored unit in the area, "immediately regardless of whether reinforcements arrive or not."

This the division had already done, without waiting for Rommel's command. General Pemsel, who was on the other end of the line when Rommel called Seventh Army headquarters, gave a blunt reply to Hitler's demand that the Allied beachhead—there were actually now three—"be cleaned up by not later than tonight."

"That," he replied, "would be impossible."

Hitler's much-propagandized Atlantic Wall had been breached within a few hours. The once vaunted Luftwaffe had been driven completely from the air and the German Navy from the sea, and the Army taken by surprise. The battle was far from over, but its outcome was not long in doubt. "From June 9 on," says Speidel, "the initiative lay with the Allies."

Rundstedt and Rommel decided that it was time to say so to Hitler, face to face, and to demand that he accept the consequences. They enticed him to a meeting on June 17 at Margival, north of Soissons, in the elaborate bombproof bunker which had been built to serve as the Fuehrer's headquarters for the invasion of Britain in the summer of 1940, but never used. Now, four summers later, the Nazi warlord appeared there for the first time.

He looked pale and sleepless [Speidel later wrote], playing nervously with his glasses and an array of colored pencils which he held between his fingers. He sat hunched upon a stool, while the field marshals stood. His hypnotic powers seemed to have waned. There was a curt and frosty greeting from him. Then in a loud voice he spoke bitterly of his displeasure at the success of the Allied landings, for which he tried to hold the field commanders responsible.[19]

But the prospect of another stunning defeat was emboldening the generals, or at least Rommel, whom Rundstedt left to do most of the talking when Hitler's diatribe against them had come to a momentary pause. "With merciless frankness," says Speidel, who was present, "Rommel pointed out . . . that the struggle was hopeless against the [Allied] superiority in the air, at sea and on the land."*[20] Well, not quite hopeless,

---

* "If, in spite of the enemy's air superiority, we succeed in getting a large part of our mobile force into action in the threatened coast defense sectors in the first hours, I am convinced that the enemy attack on the coast will collapse completely on its first day," Rommel had written General Jodl on April 23, less than two months before. (*The Rommel Papers,* ed. Liddell Hart, p. 468.) Hitler's strict orders had made it impossible to throw in the armored divisions "in the first hours" or even the first days. When they finally arrived they were thrown in piecemeal and failed.

if Hitler abandoned his absurd determination to hold every foot of ground and then to drive the Allied forces into the sea. Rommel proposed, with Rundstedt's assent, that the Germans withdraw out of range of the enemy's murderous naval guns, take their panzer units out of the line and re-form them for a later thrust which might defeat the Allies in a battle fought "outside the range of the enemy's naval artillery."

But the Supreme warlord would not listen to any proposal for withdrawal. German soldiers must stand and fight. The subject obviously was unpleasant to him and he quickly changed to others. In a display which Speidel calls "a strange mixture of cynicism and false intuition," Hitler assured the generals that the new V-1 weapon, the buzz bomb, which had been launched for the first time the day before against London, "would be decisive against Great Britain . . . and make the British willing to make peace." When the two field marshals drew Hitler's attention to the utter failure of the Luftwaffe in the West, the Fuehrer retorted that "masses of jet fighters"—the Allies had no jets, but the Germans had just put them into production—would soon drive the British and American flyers from the skies. Then, he said, Britain would collapse. At this juncture the approach of Allied planes forced them to adjourn to the Fuehrer's air-raid shelter.

Safe in the underground concrete bunker, they resumed the conversation,* and at this point Rommel insisted on steering it into politics.

He predicted [says Speidel] that the German front in Normandy would collapse and that a breakthrough into Germany by the Allies could not be checked . . . He doubted whether the Russian front could be held. He pointed to Germany's complete political isolation . . . He concluded . . . with an urgent request that the war be brought to an end.

Hitler, who had interrupted Rommel several times, finally cut him short: "Don't you worry about the future course of the war, but rather about your own invasion front."

The two field marshals were getting nowhere, either with their military or political arguments. "Hitler paid no attention whatsoever to their warnings," General Jodl later recalled at Nuremberg. Finally the generals urged the Supreme Commander at least to visit Rommel's Army Group B headquarters to confer with some of the field commanders on what they were up against in Normandy. Hitler reluctantly agreed to the visit for June 19—two days hence.

He never showed up. Shortly after the field marshals had departed from Margival on the afternoon of June 17 an errant V-1 on its way to London turned around and landed on the top of the Fuehrer's bunker.

---

* The talks lasted from 9 A.M. to 4 P.M., with a break for lunch—"a one-dish meal," Speidel recounts, "at which Hitler bolted a heaped plate of rice and vegetables, after it had been previously tasted for him. Pills and liqueur glasses containing various medicines were ranged around his place, and he took them in turn. Two S.S. men stood guard behind his chair."

No one was killed or even hurt, but Hitler was so upset that he set off immediately for safer parts, not stopping until he got to the mountains of Berchtesgaden.

There more bad news shortly arrived. On June 20 the long-awaited Russian offensive on the central front began, developing with such overwhelming power that within a few days the German Army Group Center, in which Hitler had concentrated his strongest forces, was completely smashed, the front torn wide open and the road to Poland opened. On July 4 the Russians crossed the 1939 Polish eastern border and converged on East Prussia. All available reserves of the High Command were quickly rounded up to be rushed—for the first time in World War II—to the defense of the Fatherland itself. This helped to doom the German armies in the West. From now on they could not count on receiving any sizable reinforcements.

Once more, on June 29, Rundstedt and Rommel appealed to Hitler to face realities both in the East and in the West and to try to end the war while considerable parts of the German Army were still in being. This meeting took place on the Obersalzberg, where the Supreme warlord treated the two field marshals frostily, dismissing their appeals curtly and then lapsing into a long monologue on how he would win the war with new "miracle weapons." His discourse, says Speidel, "became lost in fantastic digressions."

Two days later Rundstedt was replaced as Commander in Chief West by Field Marshal von Kluge.* On July 15 Rommel wrote a long letter to Hitler and dispatched it by Army teletype. "The troops," he wrote, "are fighting heroically everywhere, but the unequal struggle is nearing its end." He added a postscript in his own handwriting:

I must beg you to draw the proper conclusions without delay. I feel it my duty as Commander in Chief of the Army Group to state this clearly.[21]

"I have given him his last chance," Rommel told Speidel. "If he does not take it, we will act."[22]

Two days later, on the afternoon of July 17, while driving back to headquarters from the Normandy front, Rommel's staff car was shot up

---

* Rundstedt's dismissal may have come partly as the result of his blunt words to Keitel the night before. The latter had rung him up to inquire about the situation. An all-out German attack on the British lines by four S.S. panzer divisions had just floundered and Rundstedt was in a gloomy mood.

"What shall we do?" cried Keitel.

"Make peace, you fools," Rundstedt retorted. "What else can you do?"

It seems that Keitel, the "telltale toady," as most Army field commanders called him, went straight to Hitler with the remarks. The Fuehrer was at that moment conferring with Kluge, who had been on sick leave for the last few months as the result of injuries sustained in a motor accident. Kluge was immediately named to replace Rundstedt. In such ways were top commands changed by the Nazi warlord. General Blumentritt told of the telephone conversation to both Wilmot (*The Struggle for Europe*, p. 347) and Liddell Hart (*The German Generals Talk*, p. 205).

by low-flying Allied fighter planes and he was so critically wounded that it was first thought he would not survive the day. This was a disaster to the conspirators, for Rommel had now—Speidel swears to it[23]—made up his mind irrevocably to do his part in ridding Germany of Hitler's rule (though still opposing his assassination) within the next few days. As it turned out, his dash and daring were sorely missing among the Army officers who, at long last, as the German armies crumbled in the East and West that July of 1944, made their final bid to bring Hitler and National Socialism down.

The conspirators, says Speidel, "felt themselves painfully deprived of their pillar of strength."*[24]

THE CONSPIRACY AT THE ELEVENTH HOUR

The successful Allied landing in Normandy threw the conspirators in Berlin into great confusion. Stauffenberg, as we have seen, had not believed it would be attempted in 1944, and that, if it were, there was a fifty-fifty chance that it would fail. He seems to have wished that it would, since then the American and British governments, after such a bloody and costly setback, would be more willing to negotiate a peace in the West with his new anti-Nazi government, which in this case could get better terms.

When it became evident that the invasion had succeeded, that Germany had suffered another crucial defeat, and that a new one was threatening in the East, Stauffenberg, Beck and Goerdeler wondered whether there was any point in going ahead with their plans. If they succeeded they would only be blamed for bringing on the final catastrophe. Though they knew it was now inevitable, this was not generally realized by the mass of the German people. Beck finally concluded that though a successful anti-Nazi revolt could not now spare Germany from enemy occupation, it could bring the war to an end and save further loss of blood and destruction of the Fatherland. A peace now would also prevent the Russians from overrunning Germany and Bolshevizing it. It would show the world that there was "another Germany" besides the Nazi one. And—who knew?—perhaps at least the Western Allies, despite their terms of unconditional surrender, might not be too hard on a conquered Germany. Goerdeler agreed and pinned even greater hopes on the Western democracies. He knew, he said, how much Churchill feared the danger of "a total Russian victory."

The younger men, led by Stauffenberg, were not entirely convinced. They sought advice from Tresckow, who was now chief of staff of the

---

* Speidel quotes the writer Ernst Juenger, whose books had once been popular in Nazi Germany but who eventually had turned and had joined the Paris end of the plot: "The blow that felled Rommel on the Livarot Road on July 17 deprived our plan of the only man strong enough to bear the terrible weight of war and civil war simultaneously." (Speidel, *Invasion 1944*, p. 119.)

Second Army on the crumbling Russian front. His reply brought the stumbling plotters back on the track.

> The assassination must be attempted at any cost. Even should it fail, the attempt to seize power in the capital must be undertaken. We must prove to the world and to future generations that the men of the German Resistance Movement dared to take the decisive step and to hazard their lives upon it. Compared with this object, nothing else matters.[25]

This inspired answer settled the matter and revived the spirits and dissolved the doubts of Stauffenberg and his young friends. The threatened collapse of the fronts in Russia, France and Italy impelled the plotters to act at once. Another event helped to speed them on their way.

From the beginning the Beck–Goerdeler–Hassell circle had declined to have anything to do with the Communist underground, and vice versa. To the Communists the plotters were as reactionary as the Nazis and their very success might prevent a Communist Germany from succeeding a National Socialist one. Beck and his friends were well aware of this Communist line, and they knew also that the Communist underground was directed from Moscow and served chiefly as an espionage source for the Russians.* Furthermore, they knew that it had become infiltrated with

---

* This came out in the "Rote Kapelle" affair in 1942, when the Abwehr discovered a large number of strategically placed Germans, many of them from old, prominent families, running an extensive espionage network for the Russians. At one time they were transmitting intelligence to Moscow over some 100 clandestine radio transmitters in Germany and in the occupied countries of the West. The leader of the "Rote Kapelle" (Red Orchestra) was Harold Schulze-Boysen, a grandson of Grand Admiral von Tirpitz, a picturesque leader of the "lost generation" after the First World War and a familiar Bohemian figure in those days in Berlin, where his black sweater, his thick mane of blond hair and his passion for revolutionary poetry and politics attracted attention. At that time he rejected both Nazism and Communism, though he considered himself a man of the Left. Through his mother he got into the Luftwaffe as a lieutenant at the outbreak of the war and wormed himself into Goering's "research" office, the Forschungsamt, which, as we have seen in connection with the Anschluss, specialized in tapping telephones. Soon he was organizing a vast espionage service for Moscow, with trusted associates in every ministry and military office in Berlin. Among these were Arvid Harnack, nephew of a famous theologian, a brilliant young economist in the Ministry of Economics, who was married to an American woman, Mildred Fish, whom he had met at the University of Wisconsin; Franz Scheliha in the Foreign Office; Horst Heilmann in the Propaganda Ministry; and Countess Erika von Brockdorff in the Ministry of Labor.

Two Soviet agents who parachuted into Germany and were later apprehended gave the "Rote Kapelle" away, and a large number of arrests followed.

Of the seventy-five leaders charged with treason, fifty were condemned to death, including Schulze-Boysen and Harnack. Mildred Harnack and Countess von Brockdorff got off with prison sentences but Hitler insisted that they be executed too, and they were. To impress would-be traitors the Fuehrer ordered that the condemned be hanged. But there were no gallows in Berlin, where the traditional form of execution was the ax, and so the victims were simply strangled by a rope around their necks which was attached to a meathook (borrowed from an abattoir) and slowly hoisted. From then on this method of hanging was to be employed, as a special form of cruelty, on those who dared to defy the Fuehrer.

Gestapo agents—"V men," as Heinrich Mueller, the Gestapo chief and himself a student and admirer of the Soviet N.K.V.D., called them.

In June the plotters, against the advice of Goerdeler and the older members, decided to contact the Communists. This was at the suggestion of the Socialist wing and especially of Adolf Reichwein, the Socialist philosopher and celebrated *Wandervogel,* who was now director of the Folklore Museum in Berlin. Reichwein had maintained vague contacts with the Communists. Though Stauffenberg himself was suspicious of them, his Socialist friends Reichwein and Leber convinced him that some contact with them had become necessary in order to see what they were up to and what they would do in case the putsch succeeded, and, if possible, to use them at the last moment to widen the basis of the anti-Nazi resistance. Reluctantly he agreed to Leber and Reichwein meeting with the underground Communist leaders on June 22. But he warned them that the Communists should be told as little as possible.

The meeting took place in East Berlin between Leber and Reichwein, representing the Socialists, and two individuals named Franz Jacob and Anton Saefkow who claimed to be—and perhaps were—the leaders of the Communist underground. They were accompanied by a third comrade whom they introduced as "Rambow." The Communists turned out to know quite a bit about the plot against Hitler and wanted to know more. They asked for a meeting with its military leaders on July 4. Stauffenberg refused, but Reichwein was authorized to represent him at a further meeting on that date. When he arrived at it, he, along with Jacob and Saefkow, were promptly arrested. "Rambow," it turned out, was a Gestapo stool pigeon. The next day Leber, on whom Stauffenberg was counting to become the dominant political force in the new government, was also arrested.*

Stauffenberg was not only deeply upset by the arrest of Leber, with whom he had become a close personal friend and whom he regarded as indispensable to the proposed new government, but he saw at once that the whole conspiracy was in dire peril of being snuffed out now that Himmler's men were so close on its trail. Leber and Reichwein were courageous men and could be counted on, he thought, not to reveal any secrets even under torture. Or could they be? Some of the plotters were not so sure. There might be limits beyond which even the bravest man could not keep silent when his body was being racked by insufferable pain.

The arrest of Leber and Reichwein was a further spur to immediate action.

THE COUP OF JULY 20, 1944

Toward the end of June the plotters received one good stroke of fortune. Stauffenberg was promoted to full colonel and appointed chief of staff to General Fromm, the commander in chief of the Home Army.

---

* All four, Leber, Reichwein, Jacob and Saefkow, were executed.

This post not only enabled him to issue orders to the Home Army under Fromm's name but gave him direct and frequent access to Hitler. Indeed, the Fuehrer began to summon the chief of the Replacement Army, or his deputy, to headquarters two or three times a week to demand fresh replacements for his decimated divisions in Russia. At one of these meetings Stauffenberg intended to plant his bomb.

Stauffenberg had now become the key man in the conspiracy. On his shoulders alone rested its only chance for success. As the one member of the plot who could penetrate the heavily guarded Fuehrer headquarters it was up to him to kill Hitler. As chief of staff of the Replacement Army it would have to be left to him—since Fromm had not been won over completely and could not be definitely counted on—to direct the troops that were to seize Berlin after Hitler was out of the way. And he had to carry out both objectives on the same day and at two spots separated by two or three hundred miles—the Fuehrer's headquarters, whether on the Obersalzberg or at Rastenburg, and Berlin. Between the first and the second acts there must be an interval of two or three hours while his plane was droning back to the capital during which he could do nothing but hope that his plans were being energetically initiated by his confederates in Berlin. That was one trouble, as we shall shortly see.

There were others. One seems to have been an almost unnecessary complication that sprang up in the minds of the now desperate conspirators. They came to the conclusion that it would not suffice to kill Adolf Hitler. They must at the same time kill Goering and Himmler, thus ensuring that the military forces under the command of these two men could not be used against them. They thought too that the top generals at the front who had not yet been won over would join them more quickly if Hitler's two chief lieutenants were also done away with. Since Goering and Himmler usually attended the daily military conferences at the Fuehrer headquarters, it was believed that it would not be too difficult to kill all three men with one bomb. This foolish resolve led Stauffenberg to miss two golden opportunities.

He was summoned to the Obersalzberg on July 11 to report to the Fuehrer on the supply of badly needed replacements. He carried with him on the plane down to Berchtesgaden one of the Abwehr's English-made bombs. It had been decided at a meeting of the plotters in Berlin the night before that this was the moment to kill Hitler—and Goering and Himmler as well. But Himmler was not present at the conference that day and when Stauffenberg, leaving the meeting for a moment, rang up General Olbricht in Berlin to tell him so, stressing that he could still get Hitler and Goering, the General urged him to wait for another day when he could get all three. That night, on his return to Berlin, Stauffenberg met with Beck and Olbricht and insisted that the next time he must attempt to kill Hitler, regardless of whether Goering and Himmler were present or not. The others agreed.

The next time was soon at hand. On July 14 Stauffenberg was ordered to report the next day to the Fuehrer on the replacement situation—every available recruit was needed to help fill the gaps in Russia, where Army Group Center, having lost twenty-seven divisions, had ceased to exist as a fighting force. That day—the fourteenth—Hitler had moved his head-quarters back to Wolfsschanze at Rastenburg to take personal charge of trying to restore the central front, where Red Army troops had now reached a point but sixty miles from East Prussia.

Again, on the morning of July 15, Colonel Stauffenberg set out by plane for the Fuehrer's headquarters* with a bomb in his briefcase. This time the conspirators were so certain of success that it was agreed that the first Valkyrie signal—for the troops to start marching in Berlin and for the tanks from the panzer school at Krampnitz to begin rolling toward the capital—should be given two hours before Hitler's conference, scheduled for 1 P.M., began. There must be no delay in taking over.

At 11 A.M. on Saturday, July 15, General Olbricht issued Valkyrie I for Berlin and before noon troops were moving toward the center of the capital with orders to occupy the Wilhelmstrasse quarter. At 1 P.M. Stauffenberg, briefcase in hand, arrived at the Fuehrer's conference room, made his report on replacements, and then absented himself long enough to telephone Olbricht in Berlin to say—by prearranged code—that Hitler was present and that he intended to return to the meeting and set off his bomb. Olbricht informed him that the troops in Berlin were already on the march. At last success in the great enterprise seemed at hand. But when Stauffenberg returned to the conference room Hitler had left it and did not return. Disconsolate, Stauffenberg hurriedly rang up Olbricht with the news. The General frantically canceled the Valkyrie alarm and the troops were marched back to their barracks as quickly and as incon-spicuously as possible.

The news of still another failure was a heavy blow to the conspirators, who gathered in Berlin on Stauffenberg's return to consider what next to do. Goerdeler was for resorting to the so-called "Western solution." He proposed to Beck that both of them fly to Paris to confer with Field Marshal von Kluge on getting an armistice in the West whereby the Western Allies would agree not to push farther than the Franco–German border, thus releasing the German armies in the West to be shunted to the Eastern

---

* There is disagreement among the historians whether Stauffenberg set out for Rastenburg or the Obersalzberg. The two most authoritative German writers on the subject, Eberhard Zeller and Professor Gerhard Ritter, give contradictory accounts. Zeller thinks Hitler was still at Berchtesgaden, but Ritter is sure this is a mistake and that the Fuehrer had returned to Rastenburg. Unfortunately Hitler's daily calendar book, which has proved an unfailing guide to this writer up to this point, was not captured intact and does not cover this period. But the best evidence, including a report on Stauffenberg's movements drawn up at Fuehrer headquarters on July 22, indicates pretty conclusively that on July 15 Hitler was at Rastenburg and that it was there that Stauffenberg planned to kill him. Though the two places from which Hitler tried to conduct the war—he was rarely in Berlin, which was being unmercifully bombed—were about equidistant from the capital, Berchtesgaden, being more centrally located and near Munich, where the Army garrison was believed to be loyal to Beck, had certain advantages over Rastenburg for the conspirators.

front to save the Reich from the Russians and their Bolshevism. Beck had a clearer head. The idea that they could now get a separate peace with the West, he knew, was a pipe dream. Nevertheless the plot to kill Hitler and overthrow Nazism must be carried out at all costs, Beck argued, if only to save Germany's honor. Stauffenberg agreed. He swore he would not fail the next time. General Olbricht, who had received a dressing down from Keitel for moving his troops in Berlin, declared that he could not risk doing it again, since that would unmask the whole conspiracy. He had barely got by, he said, with an explanation to Keitel and Fromm that this was a practice exercise. This fear of again setting the troops in motion until it was known definitely that Hitler was dead was to have disastrous consequences on the crucial following Thursday.

On Sunday evening, July 16, Stauffenberg invited to his home at Wannsee a small circle of his close friends and relatives: his brother, Berthold, a quiet, introspective, scholarly young man who was an adviser on international law at naval headquarters; Lieutenant Colonel Caesar von Hofacker, a cousin of the Stauffenbergs and their liaison man with the generals in the West; Count Fritz von der Schulenburg, a former Nazi who was still deputy police president of Berlin; and Trott zu Solz. Hofacker had just returned from the West, where he had conferred with a number of generals—Falkenhausen, Stuelpnagel, Speidel, Rommel and Kluge. He reported an imminent German breakdown on the Western front but, more important, that Rommel would back the conspiracy regardless of which way Kluge jumped, though he still opposed killing Hitler. After a long discussion the young conspirators agreed, however, that ending Hitler's life was now the only way out. They had no illusions by this time that their desperate act would save Germany from having to surrender unconditionally. They even agreed that this would have to be done to the Russians as well as to the Western democracies. The important thing, they said, was for Germans—and not their foreign conquerors—to free Germany from Hitler's tyranny.[26]

They were terribly late. The Nazi despotism had endured for eleven years and only the certainty of utter defeat in a war which Germany had launched, and which they had done little to oppose—or, in many cases, not opposed at all—had roused them to action. But better late than never. There remained, however, little time. The generals at the front were advising them that collapse in both the East and the West was probably only a matter of weeks.

For the plotters there seemed to be only a few more days left to them to act. The premature march of the troops in Berlin on July 15 had aroused the suspicions of OKW. On that day came news that General von Falkenhausen, one of the leaders of the plot in the West, had been suddenly dismissed from his post as military governor of Belgium and northern France. Someone, it was feared, must be giving them away. On July 17 they learned that Rommel had been so seriously wounded that he would have to be left out of their plans indefinitely. The next day Goerdeler was tipped off by his friends at police headquarters that Himmler had issued an order for his arrest. At Stauffenberg's insistence Goerdeler went, protesting, into hiding. That same day a personal friend in the Navy, Captain Alfred Kranzfelder, one of the very few naval officers in on the conspiracy, informed Stauffenberg that rumors were spreading in Berlin that the Fuehrer's headquarters were to be blown up in the next few days. Again it seemed that someone in the conspiracy must have been indiscreet. Everything pointed to the Gestapo's closing in on the inner ring of the conspiracy.

On the afternoon of July 19 Stauffenberg was again summoned to Rastenburg, to report to Hitler on the progress being made with the new *Volksgrenadier* divisions which the Replacement Army was hurriedly training to be thrown in on the dissolving Eastern front. He was to make his report at the first daily conference at Fuehrer headquarters the next day, July 20, a 1 P.M.* Field Marshal von Witzleben and General Hoepner, who lived some distance outside Berlin, were notified by Stauffenberg to appear in the city in good time. General Beck made his last-minute preparations for directing the coup until Stauffenberg could return by air from his murderous deed. The key officers in the garrisons in and around Berlin were apprised that July 20 would be *Der Tag.*

Stauffenberg worked at the Bendlerstrasse on his report for Hitler until dusk, leaving his office shortly after 8 o'clock for his home at Wannsee. On his way he stopped off at a Catholic church in Dahlem to pray.† He spent the evening at home quietly with his brother, Berthold, and retired early. Everyone who saw him that afternoon and evening remembered that he was amiable and calm, as if nothing unusual was in the offing.

JULY 20, 1944

Shortly after 6 o'clock on the warm, sunny summer morning of July 20, 1944, Colonel Stauffenberg, accompanied by his adjutant, Lieutenant Werner von Haeften, drove out past the bombed-out buildings of Berlin to the airport at Rangsdorf. In his bulging briefcase were papers concerning the new *Volksgrenadier* divisions on which at 1 P.M. he was to report to Hitler at the "Wolf's Lair" at Rastenburg in East Prussia. In between the papers, wrapped in a shirt, was a time bomb.

---

* General Adolf Heusinger, Chief of Operations of the Army High Command, recounts that on July 19 the news from the Ukrainian front was so bad that he inquired at OKW whether the Replacement Army had any troops in training in Poland which might be thrown into the Eastern front. Keitel suggested that Stauffenberg be summoned the next day to advise them. (Heusinger, *Befehl im Widerstreit*, p. 350.)

† FitzGibbon says (*20 July*, p. 150) "it is believed that he had previously confessed, but of course could not be granted absolution." The author recounts that Stauffenberg had told the Bishop of Berlin, Cardinal Count Preysing, of what he intended to do, and that the bishop had replied that he honored the young man's motives and did not feel justified in attempting to restrain him on theological grounds. (*Ibid.*, p. 152.)

It was identical to the one which Tresckow and Schlabrendorff had planted in the Fuehrer's airplane the year before and which had failed to explode. Of English make, as we have seen, it was set off by breaking a glass capsule, whose acid then ate away a small wire, which released the firing pin against the percussion cap. The thickness of the wire governed the time required to set off the explosion. On this morning the bomb was fitted with the thinnest possible wire. It would dissolve in a bare ten minutes.

At the airport Stauffenberg met General Stieff, who had produced the bomb the night before. There they found a plane waiting, the personal craft of General Eduard Wagner, the First Quartermaster General of the Army and a ringleader in the plot, who had arranged to put it at their disposal for this all-important flight. By 7 o'clock the plane was off, landing at Rastenburg shortly after 10 A.M. Haeften instructed the pilot to be ready to take off for the return trip at any time after twelve noon.

From the airfield a staff car drove the party to the Wolfsschanze headquarters, set in a gloomy, damp, heavily wooded area of East Prussia. It was not an easy place to get into or, as Stauffenberg undoubtedly noted, out of. It was built in three rings, each protected by mine fields, pillboxes and an electrified barbed-wire fence, and was patrolled day and night by fanatical S.S. troops. To get into the heavily guarded inner compound, where Hitler lived and worked, even the highest general had to have a special pass, good for one visit, and pass the personal inspection of S.S. Oberfuehrer Rattenhuber, Himmler's chief of security and commander of the S.S. guard, or of one of his deputies. However, since Hitler himself had ordered Stauffenberg to report, he and Haeften, though they were stopped and their passes examined, had little trouble in getting through the three check points. After breakfast with Captain von Moellendorff, adjutant to the camp commander, Stauffenberg sought out General Fritz Fellgiebel, Chief of Signals at OKW.

Fellgiebel was one of the key men in the plot. Stauffenberg made sure that the General was ready to flash the news of the bombing to the conspirators in Berlin so that action there could begin immediately. Fellgiebel was then to isolate the Fuehrer headquarters by shutting off all telephone, telegraph and radio communications. No one was in such a perfect position to do this as the head of the OKW communications network, and the plotters counted themselves lucky to have won him over. He was indispensable to the success of the entire conspiracy.

After calling on General Buhle, the Army's representative at OKW, to discuss the affairs of the Replacement Army, Stauffenberg walked over to Keitel's quarters, hung up his cap and belt in the anteroom and entered the office of the Chief of OKW. There he learned that he would have to act with more dispatch than he had planned. It was now a little after 12 noon, and Keitel informed him that because Mussolini would be arriving by train at 2:30 P.M. the Fuehrer's first daily conference had been put forward from 1 P.M. to 12:30. The colonel, Keitel advised, must make his report brief. Hitler wanted the meeting over early.

Before the bomb could go off? Stauffenberg must have wondered if once again, and on what was perhaps his last try, fate was robbing him of success. Apparently he had hoped too that this time the conference with Hitler would be held in the Fuehrer's underground bunker, where the blast from the bomb would be several times more effective than in one of the surface buildings. But Keitel told him the meeting would be in the *Lagebaracke*—the conference barracks.* This was far from being the flimsy wooden hut so often described. During the previous winter Hitler had had the original wooden structure reinforced with concrete walls eighteen inches thick to give protection against incendiary and splinter aerial bombs that might fall nearby. These heavy walls would add force to Stauffenberg's bomb.

He must soon set it to working. He had briefed Keitel on what he proposed to report to Hitler and toward the end had noticed the OKW Chief glancing impatiently at his watch. A few minutes before 12:30 Keitel said they must leave for the conference immediately or they would be late. They emerged from his quarters, but before they had taken more than a few steps Stauffenberg remarked that he had left his cap and belt in the anteroom and quickly turned to go back for them before Keitel could suggest that his adjutant, a Lieutenant von John, who was walking alongside, should retrieve them for him.

In the anteroom Stauffenberg swiftly opened his briefcase, seized the tongs with the only three fingers he had, and broke the capsule. In just ten minutes, unless there was another mechanical failure, the bomb would explode.

Keitel, as much a bully with his subordinates as he was a toady with his superiors, was aggravated at the delay and turned back to the building to shout to Stauffenberg to get a move on. They were late, he yelled. Stauffenberg apologized for the delay. Keitel no doubt realized that it took a man as maimed as the colonel a little extra time to put on his belt. As they walked over to Hitler's hut Stauffenberg seemed to be in a genial mood and Keitel's petty annoyance—he had no trace of suspicion as yet—was dissipated.

Nevertheless, as Keitel had feared, they were late. The conference had already begun. As Keitel and Stauffenberg entered the building the latter paused for a moment in the entrance hall to tell the sergeant major in charge of the telephone board that he expected an urgent call from his office in Berlin, that it would contain information he needed to bring his

---

* A number of writers have declared that Hitler's daily military conferences at Rastenburg usually took place in his underground bunker and that because of repairs being made to it and because of the hot, humid day, the meeting on July 20 was shifted to the building aboveground. "This accidental change of place saved Hitler's life," Bullock writes (*Hitler*, p. 681). It is to be doubted if there was any accidental change of place. The *Lagebaracke*, as its name implies, was, so far as I can make out, the place where the daily conferences were usually held. Only in case of threatened air raids were the meetings adjourned to the underground bunker which, at that, would have been cooler on this sweltering day. (See Zeller, *Geist der Freiheit*, p. 360, n.4.)

report up to the minute (this was for Keitel's ear), and that he was to be summoned immediately when the call came. This too, though it must have seemed most unusual—even a field marshal would scarcely dare to leave the Nazi warlord's presence until he had been dismissed or until the conference was over and the Supreme Commander had left *first*—did not arouse Keitel's suspicions.

The two men entered the conference room. About four minutes had ticked by since Stauffenberg reached into his briefcase with his tongs and broke the capsule. Six minutes to go. The room was relatively small, some thirty by fifteen feet, and it had ten windows, all of which were wide open to catch the breezes on this hot, sultry day. So many open windows would certainly reduce the effect of any bomb blast. In the middle of the room was an oblong table, eighteen by five feet, made of thick oak planks. It was a peculiarly constructed table in that it stood not on legs but on two large heavy supports, or socles, placed near the ends and extending to nearly the width of the table. This interesting construction was not without its effect on subsequent history.

When Stauffenberg entered the room, Hitler was seated at the center of the long side of the table, his back to the door. On his immediate right were General Heusinger, Chief of Operations and Deputy Chief of Staff of the Army, General Korten, Air Force Chief of Staff, and Colonel Heinz Brandt, Heusinger's chief of staff. Keitel took his place immediately to the left of the Fuehrer and next to him was General Jodl. There were eighteen other officers of the three services and the S.S. standing around the table, but Goering and Himmler were not among them. Only Hitler, playing with his magnifying glass—which he now needed to read the fine print on the maps spread before him—and two stenographers were seated.

Heusinger was in the midst of a lugubrious report on the latest break-through on the central Russian front and on the perilous position, as a consequence, of the German armies not only there but on the northern and southern fronts as well. Keitel broke in to announce the presence of Colonel von Stauffenberg and its purpose. Hitler glanced up at the one-armed colonel with a patch over one eye, greeted him curtly, and announced that before hearing his report he wanted to have done with Heusinger's.

Stauffenberg thereupon took his place at the table between Korten and Brandt, a few feet to the right of Hitler. He put his briefcase on the floor, shoving it under the table so that it leaned against the *inside* of the stout oaken support. It was about six feet distant from the Fuehrer's legs. The time was now 12:37. Five minutes to go. Heusinger continued to talk, pointing constantly to the situation map spread on the table. Hitler and the officers kept bending over to study it.

No one seems to have noticed Stauffenberg stealing away. Except perhaps Colonel Brandt. This officer became so absorbed in what his General was saying that he leaned over the table the better to see the map, discovered that Stauffenberg's bulging briefcase was in his way, tried to shove it aside with his foot and finally reached down with one hand and lifted it to the *far side* of the heavy table support, which now stood between the bomb and Hitler.* This seemingly insignificant gesture probably saved the Fuehrer's life; it cost Brandt his. There was an inexplicable fate involved here. Colonel Brandt, it will be remembered, was the innocent officer whom Tresckow had induced to carry a couple of "bottles of brandy" back on Hitler's plane from Smolensk to Rastenburg on the evening of March 13, 1943, and he had done so without the faintest suspicion that they were in reality a bomb—the very make of bomb which he had now unostentatiously moved farther away under the table from the warlord. Its chemical had by this time almost completed the eating away of the wire that held back the firing pin.

Keitel, who was responsible for the summoning of Stauffenberg, glanced down the table to where the colonel was supposed to be standing. Heusinger was coming to the end of his gloomy report and the OKW Chief wanted to indicate to Stauffenberg that he should make ready to report next. Perhaps he would need some aid in getting his papers out of his briefcase. But the young colonel, he saw to his extreme annoyance, was not there. Recalling what Stauffenberg had told the telephone operator on coming in, Keitel slipped out of the room to retrieve this curiously behaving young officer.

Stauffenberg was not at the telephone. The sergeant at the board said he had hurriedly left the building. Nonplused, Keitel turned back to the conference room. Heusinger was concluding, at last, his report on the day's catastrophic situation. *"The Russian,"* he was saying, *"is driving with strong forces west of the Duna toward the north. His spearheads are already southwest of Dunaburg. If our army group around Lake Peipus is not immediately withdrawn, a catastrophe . . ."*[27]

It was a sentence that was never finished.

At that precise moment, 12:42 P.M., the bomb went off.

Stauffenberg saw what followed. He was standing with General Fellgiebel before the latter's office in Bunker 88 a couple of hundred yards away, glancing anxiously first at his wrist watch as the seconds ticked off and then at the conference barracks. He saw it go up with a roar in smoke and flame, as if, he said later, it had been hit directly by a 155-mm. shell. Bodies came hurtling out of the windows, debris flew into the air. There was not the slightest doubt in Stauffenberg's excited mind that every single person in the conference room was dead or dying. He bade a hasty farewell to Fellgiebel, who was now to telephone the conspirators in Berlin that the attempt had succeeded and then cut off communications until the plotters in the capital had taken over the city and proclaimed the new government.†

---

* According to the account given Allied interrogators by Admiral Kurt Assmann, who was present, Stauffenberg had whispered to Brandt, "I must go and telephone. Keep an eye on my briefcase. It has secret papers in it."

† A good many writers have contended that at this moment General Fellgiebel was to have blown up the communications center and that his failure to do so was disastrous to the conspiracy. Thus Wheeler-Bennett (*Nemesis*, p. 643) writes that "General Fellgiebel failed lamentably in the execution of his task." Since the various communications centers were housed in several different underground bunkers,

Stauffenberg's next task was to get out of the Rastenburg headquarters camp alive and quickly. The guards at the check points had seen or heard the explosion at the Fuehrer's conference hall and immediately closed all exits. At the first barrier, a few yards from Fellgiebel's bunker, Stauffenberg's car was halted. He leaped out and demanded to speak with the duty officer in the guardroom. In the latter's presence he telephoned someone—whom is not known—spoke briefly, hung up and turned to the officer, saying, "Herr Leutnant, I am allowed to pass."

This was pure bluff, but it worked, and apparently, after the lieutenant had dutifully noted in his log: "*12:44. Col. Stauffenberg passed through,*" word was sent along to the next check point to let the car through. At the third and final barrier, it was more difficult. Here an alarm had already been received, the rail had been lowered and the guard doubled, and no one was to be permitted to enter or leave. Stauffenberg and his aide, Lieutenant Haeften, found their car blocked by a very stubborn sergeant major named Kolbe. Again Stauffenberg demanded the use of the telephone and rang up Captain von Moellendorff, adjutant to the camp commander. He complained that "because of the explosion," the guard would not let him through. "I'm in a hurry. General Fromm is waiting for me at the airfield." This also was bluff. Fromm was in Berlin, as Stauffenberg well knew.

Hanging up, the colonel turned to the sergeant. "You heard, Sergeant, I'm allowed through." But the sergeant was not to be bluffed. He himself rang through to Moellendorff for confirmation. The captain gave it.[28]

The car then raced to the airport while Lieutenant Haeften hurriedly dismantled a second bomb that he had brought along in *his* briefcase, tossing out the parts on the side of the road, where they were later found by the Gestapo. The airfield commandant had not yet received any alarm. The pilot had his engines warming up when the two men drove onto the field. Within a minute or two the plane took off.

It was now shortly after 1 P.M. The next three hours must have seemed the longest in Stauffenberg's life. There was nothing he could do as the slow Heinkel plane headed west over the sandy, flat German plain but to hope that Fellgiebel had been able to get through to Berlin with the all-important signal, that his fellow plotters in the capital had swung immediately into action in taking over the city and sending out the prepared messages to the military commanders in Germany and in the West, and that his plane would not be forced down by alerted Luftwaffe fighters or by prowling Russian craft, which were increasingly active over East Prussia. His own plane had no long-distance radio which might have enabled him to tune in on Berlin and hear the first thrilling broadcasts which he expected the conspirators would be making before he landed. Nor, for

---

heavily guarded by S.S., it is most improbable that Stauffenberg's plans ever called for blowing them up—an impossible task for the General. What Fellgiebel agreed to do was to shut off communication with the outside world for two or three hours after he had sent word to Berlin of the explosion. This, except for an unavoidable lapse or two, he did.

this lack, could he himself communicate with his confederates in the capital and give the signal that General Fellgiebel might not have been able to flash.

His plane droned on through the early summer afternoon. It landed at Rangsdorf at 3:45 P.M. and Stauffenberg, in high spirits, raced to the nearest telephone at the airfield to put through a call to General Olbricht to learn exactly what had been accomplished in the fateful three hours on which all depended. To his utter consternation he found that nothing had been accomplished. Word about the explosion had come through by telephone from Fellgiebel shortly after 1 o'clock but the connection was bad and it was not quite clear to the conspirators whether Hitler had been killed or not. Therefore nothing had been done. The Valkyrie orders had been taken from Olbricht's safe but not sent out. Everyone in the Bendlerstrasse had been standing idly by waiting for Stauffenberg's return. General Beck and Field Marshal von Witzleben, who as the new head of state and Commander in Chief of the Wehrmacht, respectively, were supposed to have started issuing immediately the already-prepared proclamations and commands and to have gone on the air at once to broadcast the dawn of a new day in Germany, had not yet showed up.

Hitler, contrary to Stauffenberg's firm belief, which he imparted to Olbricht on the telephone from Rangsdorf, had not been killed. Colonel Brandt's almost unconscious act of shoving the briefcase to the far side of the stout oaken table support had saved his life. He had been badly shaken but not severely injured. His hair had been singed, his legs burned, his right arm bruised and temporarily paralyzed, his eardrums punctured and his back lacerated by a falling beam. He was, as one eyewitness later recalled, hardly recognizable as he emerged from the wrecked and burning building on the arm of Keitel, his face blackened, his hair smoking and his trousers in shreds. Keitel, miraculously, was uninjured. But most of those who had been at the end of the table where the bomb had exploded were either dead, dying or badly wounded.*

In the first excitement there were several guesses as to the origin of the explosion. Hitler thought at first it might have been caused by a sneak attack of an enemy fighter-bomber. Jodl, nursing a blood-spattered head —the chandelier, among other objects, had fallen on him—was convinced that some of the building laborers had planted a time bomb under the floor of the building. The deep hole which Stauffenberg's bomb had blown in the floor seemed to confirm this. It was some time before the colonel became suspected. Himmler, who came running to the scene on hearing the explosion, was completely puzzled and his first act was to telephone— a minute or two before Fellgiebel shut down communications—Artur

---

* The official stenographer, Berger, was killed, and Colonel Brandt, General Schmundt, Hitler's adjutant, and General Korten died of their wounds. All the others, including Generals Jodl, Bodenschatz (Goering's chief of staff) and Heusinger, were more or less severely injured.

Nebe, the head of the criminal police in Berlin, to dispatch by plane a squad of detectives to carry out the investigation.

In the confusion and shock no one at first remembered that Stauffenberg had slipped out of the conference room shortly before the explosion. It was at first believed that he must have been in the building and was one of those severely hurt who had been rushed to the hospital. Hitler, not yet suspicious of him, asked that the hospital be checked.

Some two hours after the bomb went off the clues began to come in. The sergeant who operated the telephone board at the *Lagebaracke* reported that "the one-eyed colonel," who had informed him he was expecting a long-distance call from Berlin, had come out of the conference room and, without waiting for it, had left the building in a great hurry. Some of the participants at the conference recalled that Stauffenberg had left his brief-case under the table. The guardhouses at the check points revealed that Stauffenberg and his aide had passed through immediately after the explosion.

Hitler's suspicions were now kindled. A call to the airfield at Rastenburg supplied the interesting information that Stauffenberg had taken off from there in great haste shortly after 1 P.M., giving as his destination the airport at Rangsdorf. Himmler immediately ordered that he be arrested on landing there, but his order never got through to Berlin because of Fellgiebel's courageous action in closing down communications. Up to this minute no one at headquarters seems to have suspected that anything untoward might be happening in Berlin. All now believed that Stauffenberg had acted alone. It would not be difficult to apprehend him unless, as some suspected, he had landed behind the Russian lines. Hitler, who, under the circumstances, seems to have behaved calmly enough, had something else on his mind. He had to greet Mussolini, who was due to arrive at 4 P.M., his train having been delayed.

There is something weird and grotesque about this last meeting of the two fascist dictators on the afternoon of July 20, 1944, as they surveyed the ruins of the conference hall and tried to fool themselves into thinking that the Axis which they had forged, and which was to have dominated the continent of Europe, was not also in shambles. The once proud and strutting Duce was now no more than a Gauleiter of Lombardy, rescued from imprisonment by Nazi thugs, and propped up by Hitler and the S.S. Yet the Fuehrer's friendship and esteem for the fallen Italian tyrant had never faltered and he greeted him with as much warmth as his physical condition permitted, showed him through the still smoking debris of the *Lagebaracke* where his life had almost been snuffed out a few hours before, and predicted that their joint cause would soon, despite all the setbacks, triumph.

Dr. Schmidt, who was present as interpreter, has recalled the scene.[29]

Mussolini was absolutely horrified. He could not understand how such a thing could happen at Headquarters. . . .

"I was standing here by this table [Hitler recounted]; the bomb went off just in front of my feet . . . It is obvious that nothing is going to happen to me; undoubtedly it is my fate to continue on my way and bring my task to completion . . . What happened here today is the climax! Having now escaped death . . . I am more than ever convinced that the great cause which I serve will be brought through its present perils and that everything can be brought to a good end."

Mussolini, carried away as so often before by Hitler's words, says Schmidt, agreed.

"Our position is bad [he said], one might almost say desperate, but what has happened here today gives me new courage. After [this] miracle it is inconceivable that our cause should meet with misfortune."

The two dictators, with their entourages, then went to tea, and there now ensued—it was about 5 P.M.—a ludicrous scene that gives a revealing, if not surprising, picture of the shabby, tattered Nazi chiefs at the moment of one of the supreme crises in the Third Reich. By this time the communications system of Rastenburg had been restored by the direct order of Hitler and the first reports from Berlin had begun to come in indicating that a military revolt had broken out there and perhaps one on the Western front. Mutual recriminations, long suppressed, broke out between the Fuehrer's captains, their shouting echoing through the rafters though at first Hitler himself sat silent and brooding while Mussolini blushed with embarrassment.

Admiral Doenitz, who had rushed by air to Rastenburg at the news of the *attentat* and arrived after the tea party had begun, lashed out at the treachery of the Army. Goering, on behalf of the Air Force, supported him. Then Doenitz lit on Goering for the disastrous failures of the Luftwaffe, and the fat Reich Marshal, after defending himself, attacked his pet hate, Ribbentrop, for the bankruptcy of Germany's foreign policy, at one point threatening to smack the arrogant Foreign Minister with his marshal's baton. "You dirty little champagne salesman! Shut your damned mouth!" Goering cried, but this was impossible for Ribbentrop, who demanded a little respect, even from the Reich Marshal. "I am still the Foreign Minister," he shouted, "and my name is *von* Ribbentrop!"*

Then someone brought up the subject of an earlier "revolt" against the Nazi regime, the Roehm "plot" of June 30, 1934. Mention of this aroused Hitler—who had been sitting morosely sucking brightly colored medicinal pills supplied by his quack physician, Dr. Theodor Morell—to a fine fury. Eyewitnesses say he leaped from his chair, foam on his lips, and screamed

---

* Ribbentrop had been a champagne salesman and then had married the daughter of Germany's leading producer of the wine. His "von" had come through adoption by an aunt—Fräulein Gertrud von Ribbentrop—in 1925, when he was thirty-two years old.

and raged. What he had done with Roehm and his treasonable followers was nothing, he shouted, to what he would do to the traitors of this day. He would uproot them all and destroy them. "I'll put their wives and children into concentration camps," he raved, "and show them no mercy!" In this case, as in so many similar ones, he was as good as his word.

Partly because of exhaustion but also because the telephone from Berlin began to bring further details of a military uprising, Hitler broke off his mad monologue, but his temper did not subside. He saw Mussolini off to his train—it was their final parting—and returned to his quarters. When told at about 6 o'clock that the putsch had not yet been squelched, he grabbed the telephone and shrieked orders to the S.S. in Berlin to shoot everyone who was the least suspect. "Where's Himmler? Why is he not there!" he yelled, forgetful that only an hour before, as his party sat down to tea, he had ordered the S.S. chief to fly to Berlin and ruthlessly put down the rebellion, and that his master policeman could not possibly have arrived as yet.[30]

The long and carefully prepared rebellion in Berlin had, as Stauffenberg learned to his dismay when he landed at Rangsdorf at 3:45 P.M., got off to a slow start. Three precious, vital hours, during which the Fuehrer headquarters had been shut off from the outside world, had been lost.

Stauffenberg, for the life of him, could not understand why, nor can a historian trying to reconstitute the events of this fateful day. The weather was hot and sultry, and perhaps this had a certain effect. Though the chief conspirators had known that Stauffenberg had left for Rastenburg that morning "heavily laden," as General Hoepner was informed, to attend the 1 P.M. Fuehrer conference, only a few of them, and these mostly junior officers, began to drift leisurely into the headquarters of the Replacement Army—and of the plot—in the Bendlerstrasse toward noon. On Stauffenberg's last previous attempt to get Hitler, on July 15, it will be recalled, General Olbricht had ordered the troops of the Berlin garrison to start marching two hours before the bomb was timed to go off. But on July 20, perhaps mindful of the risk he had run, he did not issue similar orders. Unit commanders in Berlin and in the training centers in nearby Doeberitz, Jueterbog, Krampnitz and Wuensdorf had been tipped the night before that they would most probably be receiving the Valkyrie orders on the twentieth. But Olbricht decided to wait until definite word had come from Fellgiebel at Rastenburg before again setting his troops in motion. General Hoepner, with the uniform which Hitler had forbade him to wear in his suitcase, arrived at the Bendlerstrasse at thirty minutes past noon—at the very moment Stauffenberg was breaking the capsule of his bomb—and he and Olbricht went out for lunch, where they toasted the success of their enterprise with a half bottle of wine.

They had not been back in Olbricht's office very long when General Fritz Thiele, chief signals officer of OKH, burst in. He had just been on the telephone to Fellgiebel, he said excitedly, and though the line was bad and Fellgiebel was very guarded in what he said, it seemed that the explosion had taken place but that Hitler had not been killed. In that case Thiele concluded that the Valkyrie orders should not be issued. Olbricht and Hoepner agreed.

So between approximately 1:15 P.M. and 3:45, when Stauffenberg set down at Rangsdorf and hurried to the telephone, nothing was done. No troops were assembled, no orders were sent out to the military commands in other cities and, perhaps strangest of all, no one thought of seizing the radio broadcasting headquarters or the telephone and telegraph exchanges. The two chief military leaders, Beck and Witzleben, had not yet appeared.

The arrival of Stauffenberg finally moved the conspirators to action. On the telephone from Rangsdorf he urged General Olbricht not to wait until he had reached the Bendlerstrasse—the trip in from the airfield would take forty-five minutes—but to start Valkyrie going at once. The plotters finally had someone to give orders—without such, a German officer seemed lost, even a rebellious one, even on this crucial day—and they began to act. Colonel Mertz von Quirnheim, Olbricht's chief of staff and a close friend of Stauffenberg, fetched the Valkyrie orders and began to dispatch them by teleprinter and telephone. The first one alerted the troops in and around Berlin, and a second one, signed by Witzleben as "Commander in Chief of the Wehrmacht" and countersigned by Count von Stauffenberg— they had been drawn up months before—announced that the Fuehrer was dead and that Witzleben was "transferring executive power" to the Army district commanders at home and to the commanders in chief of the fighting armies at the front. Field Marshal von Witzleben had not yet arrived at the Bendlerstrasse. He had got as far as Zossen, twenty miles southeast of Berlin, where he was conferring with the First Quartermaster General, Wagner. He was sent for, as was General Beck. The two senior generals in the plot were acting in the most leisurely manner on this fateful day.

With the orders going out, some of them signed by General Fromm, though without his knowledge, Olbricht went to the office of the commander of the Replacement Army, told him that Fellgiebel had reported that Hitler had been assassinated and urged him to take charge of Valkyrie and assure the internal security of the State. Fromm's orders, the conspirators realized, would be obeyed automatically. He was very important to them at this moment. But Fromm, like Kluge, was a genius at straddling; he was not the man to jump until he saw where he was landing. He wanted definite proof that Hitler was dead before deciding what to do.

At this point Olbricht made another one of the disastrous mistakes committed by the plotters that day. He was sure from what Stauffenberg had told him on the telephone from Rangsdorf that the Fuehrer was dead. He also knew that Fellgiebel had succeeded in blocking the telephone lines to Rastenburg all afternoon. Boldly he picked up the telephone and asked for a "blitz" telephone connection with Keitel. To his utter surprise— communications, as we have seen, had now been reopened, but Olbricht did not know this—Keitel was almost instantly on the line.

FROMM: What has happened at General Headquarters? Wild rumors are afloat in Berlin.

KEITEL: What should be the matter? Everything is as usual here.

FROMM: I have just received a report that the Fuehrer has been assassinated.

KEITEL: That's all nonsense. It is true there has been an attempt, but fortunately it has failed. The Fuehrer is alive and only slightly injured. Where, by the way, is your Chief of Staff, Colonel Count Stauffenberg?

FROMM: Stauffenberg has not yet returned to us.[31]

From that moment on Fromm was lost to the conspiracy, with consequences which would soon prove catastrophic. Olbricht, momentarily stunned, slipped out of the office without a word. At this moment General Beck arrived, attired in a dark civilian suit—perhaps this was a gesture toward playing down the military nature of the revolt—to take charge. But the man really in charge, as everyone soon realized, was Colonel von Stauffenberg, who, hatless and out of breath, bounded up the stairs of the old War Ministry at 4:30 P.M. He reported briefly on the explosion, which he emphasized he had seen himself from a couple of hundred yards away. When Olbricht interjected that Keitel himself had just been on the phone and sworn that Hitler was only slightly wounded, Stauffenberg answered that Keitel was playing for time by lying. At the very least, he contended, Hitler must have been severely wounded. In any case, he added, there was only one thing they could now do: use every minute to overthrow the Nazi regime. Beck agreed. It did not make too much difference to him, he said, whether the despot was alive or dead. They must go ahead and destroy his evil rule.

The trouble was that after the fateful delay and in the present confusion they did not, for all their planning, know how to go ahead. Not even when General Thiele brought word that the news of Hitler's survival was shortly to be broadcast over the German national radio network does it seem to have occurred to the conspirators that the first thing they had to do, and at once, was to seize the broadcasting central, block the Nazis from getting their word out, and begin flooding the air with their own proclamations of a new government. If troops were not yet at hand to accomplish this, the Berlin police could have done it. Count von Helldorf, the chief of police and deep in the conspiracy, had been waiting impatiently since midday to swing into action with his sizable and already alerted forces. But no call had come and finally at 4 o'clock he had driven over to the Bendlerstrasse to see what had happened. He was told by Olbricht that his police would be under the orders of the Army. But as yet there was no rebel army— only bewildered officers milling about at headquarters without any soldiers to command.

Instead of seeing to this at once Stauffenberg put in an urgent telephone call to his cousin, Lieutenant Colonel Caesar von Hofacker, at General von Stuelpnagel's headquarters in Paris, urging the conspirators to get busy there. This was of the utmost importance, to be sure, since the plot had been better organized in France and was supported by more important Army officers than in any other place save Berlin. Actually Stuelpnagel was to show more energy than his fellow generals at the center of the revolt. Before dark he had arrested and locked up all 1,200 S.S. and S.D. officers and men in Paris, including their redoubtable commander, S.S. Major General Karl Oberg. Had similar energy and similar direction of energy been shown in Berlin that afternoon, history might have taken a different turn.

Having alerted Paris, Stauffenberg next turned his attention to the stubborn Fromm, whose chief of staff he was, and whose refusal to go along with the rebels after he had learned from Keitel that Hitler was alive was seriously jeopardizing the success of the plot. Beck had no stomach to quarrel with Fromm so early in the game and excused himself from joining Stauffenberg and Olbricht, who went to see him. Olbricht told Fromm that Stauffenberg could confirm Hitler's death.

"That is impossible," Fromm snapped. "Keitel has assured me to the contrary."

"Keitel is lying, as usual," Stauffenberg put in. "I myself saw Hitler's body being carried out."

This word from his chief of staff and an eyewitness gave Fromm food for thought and for a moment he said nothing. But when Olbricht, trying to take advantage of his indecision, remarked that, at any rate, the code word for Valkyrie had already been sent out, Fromm sprang to his feet and shouted, "This is rank insubordination! Who issued the order?" When told that Colonel Mertz von Quirnheim had, he summoned this officer and told him he was under arrest.

Stauffenberg made one last effort to win his chief over. "General," he said, "I myself set off the bomb at Hitler's conference. The explosion was as if a fifteen-millimeter shell had hit. No one in that room can still be alive."

But Fromm was too ingenious a trimmer to be bluffed. "Count Stauffenberg," he answered, "the attempt has failed. You must shoot yourself at once." Stauffenberg coolly declined. In a moment Fromm, a beefy, red-faced man, was proclaiming the arrest of all three of his visitors, Stauffenberg, Olbricht and Mertz.

"You deceive yourself," Olbricht answered. "It is we who are now going to arrest you."

An untimely scuffle among the brother officers ensued in which Fromm, according to one version, struck the one-armed Stauffenberg in the face. The General was quickly subdued and put under arrest in the room of his adjutant, where Major Ludwig von Leonrod was assigned to guard him.* The rebels took the precaution of cutting the telephone wires in the room.

---

* A few weeks before, Leonrod had asked an Army chaplain friend of his, Father Hermann Wehrle, whether the Catholic Church condoned tyrannicide and had been given a negative answer. When this came out in Leonrod's trial before the People's Court, Father Wehrle was arrested for not having told the authorities and, like Leonrod, was executed.

Stauffenberg returned to his office to find that Oberfuehrer Piffraeder, an S.S. ruffian who had distinguished himself recently by superintending the exhuming and destroying of 221,000 bodies of Jews murdered by the Einsatzgruppen in the Baltic regions before the advancing Russians got to them, had come to arrest him. Piffraeder and his two S.D. plain-clothes men were locked up in an adjacent empty office. Then General von Kortzfleisch, who had over-all command of the troops in the Berlin-Brandenburg district (Wehrkreis III), arrived to demand what was up. This strictly Nazi General insisted on seeing Fromm but was taken to Olbricht, with whom he refused to speak. Beck then received him, and when Kortzfleisch proved adamant he too was locked up. General von Thuengen, as planned, was appointed to replace him.

Piffraeder's appearance reminded Stauffenberg that the conspirators had forgotten to place a guard around the building. So a detachment from the Guard Battalion Grossdeutschland, which was supposed to be on guard duty but wasn't, was posted at the entrance. By a little after 5 P.M., then, the rebels were at least in control of their own headquarters, but that was all of Berlin they were in control of. What had happened to the Army troops that were supposed to occupy the capital and secure it for the new anti-Nazi government?

A little after 4 P.M., when the conspirators had finally come to life following Stauffenberg's return, General von Hase, the Berlin commandant, telephoned the commander of the crack Guard Battalion Grossdeutschland at Doeberitz and instructed him to alert his unit and himself to report at once to the *Kommandantur* on the Unter den Linden. The battalion commander, recently appointed, was Major Otto Remer, who was to play a key role this day, though not the one the plotters had counted on. They had investigated him, since his battalion had been allotted an all-important task, and satisfied themselves that he was a nonpolitical officer who would obey the orders of his immediate superiors. Of his bravery there could be no doubt. He had been wounded eight times and had recently received from the hand of Hitler himself the Knight's Cross with Oak Leaves—a rare distinction.

Remer alerted his battalion, as instructed, and sped into the city to receive his specific orders from Hase. The General told him of Hitler's assassination and of an attempted S.S. putsch and instructed him to seal off the ministries in the Wilhelmstrasse and the S.S. Security Main Office in the nearby Anhalt Station quarter. By 5:30 P.M. Remer, acting with dispatch, had done so and reported back to Unter den Linden for further orders.

And now another minor character nudged himself into the drama and helped Remer to become the nemesis of the conspiracy. A Lieutenant Dr. Hans Hagen, a highly excitable and self-important young man, had been posted as National Socialist guidance officer to Remer's guard battalion. He also worked for Dr. Goebbels at the Propaganda Ministry and at the moment was actually stationed at Bayreuth where he had been sent by the Minister to work on a book which Martin Bormann, Hitler's secretary, wanted written—a "History of National Socialist Culture." His presence in Berlin was quite fortuitous. He had come to deliver a memorial address in tribute to an obscure writer who had fallen at the front and he sought to take advantage of his visit by also delivering a lecture that afternoon to his battalion—though it was a hot and sultry day—on "National Socialist Guidance Questions." He had a passion for public speaking.

On his way to Doeberitz the excitable lieutenant was sure he saw Field Marshal von Brauchitsch in a passing Army car attired in full uniform, and it immediately occurred to him that the old generals must be up to something treasonable. Brauchitsch, who had been booted out of his command long before by Hitler, was not in Berlin that day, in uniform or out, but Hagen swore he had seen him. He spoke of his suspicions to Remer, with whom he happened to be talking when the major received his orders to occupy the Wilhelmstrasse. The orders kindled his suspicions and he persuaded Remer to give him a motorcycle and sidecar, in which he promptly raced to the Propaganda Ministry to alert Goebbels.

The Minister had just received his first telephone call from Hitler, who told him of the attempt on his life and instructed him to get on the air as soon as possible and announce that it had failed. This seems to have been the first news the usually alert Propaganda Minister had of what had occurred at Rastenburg. Hagen soon brought him up to date on what was about to happen in Berlin. Goebbels was at first skeptical—he regarded Hagen as somewhat of a nuisance—and, according to one version, was on the point of throwing his visitor out when the lieutenant suggested he go to the window and see for himself. What he saw was more convincing than Hagen's hysterical words. Army troops were taking up posts around the ministry. Goebbels, who though a stupid man was extremely quick-witted, told Hagen to send Remer to him at once. This Hagen did, and thereupon passed out of history.

Thus while the conspirators in the Bendlerstrasse were getting in touch with generals all over Europe and giving no thought to such a junior officer as Remer, indispensable as his job was, Goebbels was getting in touch with the man who, however low in rank, mattered most at this particular moment.

The contact was inevitable, for in the meantime Remer had been ordered to arrest the Propaganda Minister. Thus the major had an order to nab Goebbels and also a message from Goebbels inviting him to see him. Remer entered the Propaganda Ministry with twenty men, whom he instructed to fetch him if he did not return from the Minister's office within a few minutes. With drawn pistols he and his adjutant then went into the office to arrest the most important Nazi official in Berlin on that day.

Among the talents which had enabled Joseph Goebbels to rise to his eminence in the Third Reich was a genius for fast talking in tight situations —and this was the tightest and most precarious of his stormy life. He reminded the young major of his oath of allegiance to the Commander in Chief. Remer retorted crisply that Hitler was dead. Goebbels said that the Fuehrer was very much alive—he had just talked with him on the telephone. He would prove it. Whereupon he picked up the phone and put in an urgent call to the Commander in Chief at Rastenburg. Once more the failure of the conspirators to seize the Berlin telephone exchange or at least cut its wires compounded disaster.* Within the matter of a minute or two Hitler was on the line. Goebbels quickly handed his telephone to Remer. Did the major recognize his voice? asked the warlord. Who in Germany could fail to recognize that husky voice, since it had been heard on the radio hundreds of times? Moreover, Remer had heard it directly a few weeks before when he received his decoration from the Fuehrer. The major, it is said, snapped to attention. Hitler commanded him to crush the uprising and obey only the commands of Goebbels, Himmler, who he said had just been named the commander of the Replacement Army and who was en route by plane to Berlin, and General Reinecke, who happened to be in the capital and had been ordered to take over the command of all troops in the city. The Fuehrer also promoted the major forthwith to colonel.

This was enough for Remer. He had received orders from on high and he proceeded with an energy which was lacking in the Bendlerstrasse to carry them out. He withdrew his battalion from the Wilhelmstrasse, occupied the *Kommandantur* in the Unter den Linden, sent out patrols to halt any other troops that might be marching on the city and himself set out to find where the headquarters of the conspiracy was so that he could arrest the ringleaders.

Why the rebelling generals and colonels entrusted such a key role to Remer in the first place, why they did not replace him at the last moment with an officer who was heart and soul behind the conspiracy, why at least they did not send a dependable officer along with the guard battalion to see that Remer obeyed orders—these are among the many riddles of July 20. But then, why was not Goebbels, the most important and the most dangerous Nazi official present in Berlin, arrested at once? A couple of Count von Helldorf's policemen could have done this in two minutes, for the Propaganda Ministry was completely unguarded. But why then did the plotters not seize the Gestapo headquarters in the Prinz Albrechtstrasse and not only suppress the secret police but liberate a number of their fellow conspirators, including Leber, who were incarcerated there? The Gestapo headquarters were virtually unguarded, as was the central office of the R.S.H.A., the nerve center of the S.D. and S.S., which, one would have thought, would be among the first places to be occupied. It is impossible to answer these questions.

Remer's quick turnabout did not become known in the Bendlerstrasse

---

* "To think that these revolutionaries weren't even smart enough to cut the telephone wires!" Goebbels is said to have exclaimed afterward. "My little daughter would have thought of that." (Curt Riess, *Joseph Goebbels: The Devil's Advocate*, p. 280.)

headquarters for some time. Apparently very little of what was happening in Berlin became known there until too late. And it is difficult even today to find out, for the eyewitness reports are filled with bewildering contradictions. Where were the tanks, where were the troops from the outlying stations?

A brief announcement broadcast shortly after 6:30 P.M. over the Deutschlandsender, a radio station with such a powerful transmitter that it could be heard all over Europe, announcing that there had been an at'empt to kill Hitler but that it had failed, came as a severe blow to the harried men in the Bendlerstrasse, but it was a warning that the detachment of troops which was supposed to have occupied the Rundfunkhaus had failed to do so. Goebbels had been able to telephone the text of the announcement to broadcasting headquarters while he was waiting for Remer. At a quarter to seven Stauffenberg sent out a signal by teleprinter to the Army commanders, saying that the radio announcement was false and that Hitler was dead. But the damage to the putschists was almost irreparable. The commanding generals in Prague and Vienna, who had already proceeded to arrest the S.S. and Nazi Party leaders, began to backtrack. Then at 8:20 P.M. Keitel managed to get out by Army teleprinter to all Army commands a message from Fuehrer headquarters announcing that Himmler had been appointed chief of the Replacement Army and that "only orders from him and myself are to be obeyed." Keitel added, "Any orders issued by Fromm, Witzleben or Hoepner are invalid." The Deutschlandsender's announcement that Hitler was alive and Keitel's crisp order that only his commands and not those of the conspirators were to be obeyed had, as we shall see, a decisive effect upon Field Marshal von Kluge, who off in France was on the point of throwing in his lot with the conspirators.*

Even the tanks, on which the rebel officers had counted so much, failed to arrive. It might have been thought that Hoepner, an outstanding panzer general, would have seen to the tanks, but he did not get around to it. The

---

* There are conflicting stories as to why the Berlin radio was not seized. According to one account, a unit from the infantry school at Doeberitz had been assigned this task, which was to be carried out by the commandant, General Hitzfeld, who was in on the plot. But the conspirators failed to warn Hitzfeld that July 20 was the day, and he was away in Baden attending the funeral of a relative. His second-in-command, a Colonel Mueller, was also away on a military assignment. When Mueller finally returned about 8 P.M. he found that his best battalion had left for a night exercise. By the time he rounded up his troops at midnight, it was too late. According to a different story, a Major Jacob succeeded in surrounding the Rundfunkhaus with troops from the infantry school but could get no clear orders from Olbricht as to what to do. When Goebbels phoned the text of the first announcement Jacob did not interfere with its being broadcast. Later the major contended that if Olbricht had given him the necessary orders the German radio network could easily have been denied the Nazis and put at the service of the conspirators. The first version is given by Zeller (*Geist der Freiheit*, pp. 267–68), the most authoritative German historian on the July 20 plot; the second is given by Wheeler-Bennett (*Nemesis*, pp. 654–55n.) and Rudolf Sammler (*Goebbels: The Man Next to Hitler*, p. 138), both of whom say Major Jacob gave the above testimony.

commandant of the panzer school at Krampnitz, which was to supply the tanks, Colonel Wolfgang Glaesemer, had been ordered by the conspirators to start his vehicles rolling into the city and himself to report to the Bendlerstrasse for further instructions. But the tank colonel wanted no part in any military putsch against the Nazis, and Olbricht, after pleading with him in vain, had to lock him up too in the building. Glaesemer, however, was able to whisper to his adjutant, who was not arrested, instructions to inform the headquarters of the Inspectorate of Panzer Troops in Berlin, which had jurisdiction over the tank formations, of what had happened and to see to it that only the inspectorate's commands were obeyed.

Thus it happened that the badly needed tanks, though some of them reached the heart of the city at the Victory Column in the Tiergarten, were denied the rebels. Colonel Glaesemer escaped from his confinement by a ruse, telling his guards that he had decided to accept Olbricht's orders and would himself take command of the tanks, whereupon he slipped out of the building. The tanks were soon withdrawn from the city.

The panzer colonel was not the only officer to slip away from the haphazard and gentlemanly confinement imposed on those who would not join the conspiracy—a circumstance which contributed to the swift end of the revolt.

Field Marshal von Witzleben, when he finally arrived in full uniform and waving his baton shortly before 8 P.M. to take over his duties as the new Commander in Chief of the Wehrmacht, seems to have realized at once that the putsch had failed. He stormed at Beck and Stauffenberg for having bungled the whole affair. At his trial he told the court that it was obvious to him that the attempt had misfired when he learned that not even the broadcasting headquarters had been occupied. But he himself had done nothing to help at a time when his authority as a field marshal might have rallied more of the troop commanders in Berlin and abroad. Forty-five minutes after he had entered the Bendlerstrasse building he stamped out of it—and out of the conspiracy, now that it seemed certain to fail—drove his Mercedes back to Zossen, where he had whiled away the seven hours that were decisive that day, told Quartermaster General Wagner that the revolt had failed, and drove on to his country estate thirty miles beyond, where he was arrested the next day by a fellow General named Linnertz.

The curtain now went up on the last act.

Shortly after 9 P.M. the frustrated conspirators were struck dumb at hearing the Deutschlandsender announce that the Fuehrer would broadcast to the German people later in the evening. A few minutes afterward it was learned that General von Hase, the Berlin commandant, who had started Major—now Colonel—Remer on his fateful errand, had been arrested and that the Nazi General, Reinecke, backed by the S.S., had taken over command of all troops in Berlin and was preparing to storm the Bendlerstrasse.

The S.S. had at last rallied, thanks mostly to Otto Skorzeny, the tough S.S. leader who had shown his prowess in rescuing Mussolini from captivity. Unaware that anything was up that day Skorzeny had boarded the night express for Vienna at 6 P.M., but had been hauled off the train when it stopped at the suburb of Lichterfelde, at the urging of S.S. General Schellenberg, the Number Two man in the S.D. Skorzeny found the unguarded S.D. headquarters in a most hysterical state, but being the cold-blooded man he was, and a good organizer to boot, he quickly rounded up his armed bands and went to work. It was he who first persuaded the tank school formations to remain loyal to Hitler.

The energetic counteraction at Rastenburg, the quick thinking of Goebbels in winning over Remer and in utilizing the radio, the revival of the S.S. in Berlin and the unbelievable confusion and inaction of the rebels in the Bendlerstrasse caused a good many Army officers who had been on the point of throwing in their lot with the conspirators, or had even done so, to think better of it. One of these was General Otto Herfurth, chief of staff to the arrested Kortzfleisch, who at first had co-operated with the Bendlerstrasse in trying to round up the troops, and then, when he saw how things were going, changed sides, ringing up Hitler's headquarters around 9:30 P.M. to say that he was putting down the military putsch.*

General Fromm, whose refusal to join the revolt had put it in jeopardy from the beginning and who, as a result, had been arrested, now bestirred himself. About 8 P.M., after four hours of confinement in his adjutant's office, he had asked to be allowed to retire to his private quarters on the floor below. He had given his word of honor as an officer that he would make no attempt to escape or to establish contact with the outside. General Hoepner had consented and moreover, since Fromm had complained that he was not only hungry but thirsty, had sent him sandwiches and a bottle of wine. A little earlier three generals of Fromm's staff had arrived, had refused to join the rebellion, and had demanded to be taken to their chief. Inexplicably, they were taken to him in his private quarters, though put under arrest. They had no sooner arrived than Fromm told them of a little-used rear exit through which they could escape. Breaking his word to Hoepner, he ordered the generals to organize help, storm the building, liberate him and put down the revolt. The generals slipped out unnoticed.

But already a group of junior officers on Olbricht's staff, who at first had either gone along with the rebels or stuck around in the Bendlerstrasse to see how the revolt would go, had begun to sense that it was failing. They had begun to realize too, as one of them later said, that they would all be hanged as traitors if the revolt failed and they had not turned against it in time. One of them, Lieutenant Colonel Franz Herber, a former police officer and a convinced Nazi, had fetched some Tommy guns and ammunition from the arsenal of Spandau, and these were secreted on the second floor. About 10:30, these officers called upon Olbricht and demanded to

---

* His treachery did not prevent his being arrested for complicity in the plot and hanged for it.

know exactly what he and his friends were trying to accomplish. The General told them, and without arguing they withdrew.

Twenty minutes later they returned—six or eight of them, led by Herber and Lieutenant Colonel Bodo von der Heyde—brandishing their weapons and demanded further explanations from Olbricht. Stauffenberg looked in to see what all the noise was about and was seized. When he tried to escape, bolting out the door and down the corridor, he was shot in the arm—the only one he had. The counterrebels began shooting wildly, though apparently not hitting anyone except Stauffenberg. They then roved through the wing which had been the headquarters of the plot, rounding up the conspirators. Beck, Hoepner, Olbricht, Stauffenberg, Haeften and Mertz were herded into Fromm's vacated office, where Fromm himself shortly appeared, brandishing a revolver.

"Well, gentlemen," he said, "I am now going to treat you as you treated me." But he didn't.

"Lay down your weapons," he commanded, and informed his former captors that they were under arrest.

"You wouldn't make that demand of me, your old commanding officer," Beck said quietly, reaching for his revolver. "I will draw the consequences from this unhappy situation myself."

"Well, keep it pointed at yourself," Fromm warned.

The curious lack of will to act of this brilliant, civilized former General Staff Chief had finally brought his downfall at the supreme test of his life. It remained with him to the very end.

"At this moment it is the old days that I recall . . ." he began to say, but Fromm cut him short.

"We don't want to hear that stuff now. I ask you to stop talking and do something."

Beck did. He pulled the trigger, but the bullet merely scratched his head. He slumped into his chair, bleeding a little.

"Help the old gentleman," Fromm commanded two young officers, but when they tried to take the weapon Beck objected, asking for another chance. Fromm nodded his consent.

Then he turned to the rest of the plotters. "And you gentlemen, if you have any letters to write I'll give you a few more minutes." Olbricht and Hoepner asked for stationery and sat down to pen brief notes of farewell to their wives. Stauffenberg, Mertz, Haeften and the others stood there silently. Fromm marched out of the room.

He had quickly made up his mind to eliminate these men and not only to cover up the traces—for though he had refused to engage actively in the plot, he had known of it for months, sheltering the assassins and not reporting their plans—but to curry favor with Hitler as the man who put down the revolt. In the world of the Nazi gangsters it was much too late for this, but Fromm did not realize it.

He returned in five minutes to announce that "in the name of the Fuehrer" he had called a session of a "court-martial" (there is no evidence that he had) and that it had pronounced death sentences on four officers: "Colonel of the General Staff Mertz, General Olbricht, this colonel whose name I no longer know [Stauffenberg], and this lieutenant [Haeften]."

The two generals, Olbricht and Hoepner, were still scratching their letters to their wives. General Beck lay sprawled in his chair, his face smeared with blood from the bullet scratch. The four officers "condemned" to death stood like ramrods, silent.

"Well, gentlemen," Fromm said to Olbricht and Hoepner, "are you ready? I must ask you to hurry so as not to make it too difficult for the others."

Hoepner finished his letter and laid it on the table. Olbricht asked for an envelope, put his letter in it and sealed it. Beck, now beginning to come to, asked for another pistol. Stauffenberg, the sleeve of his wounded good arm soaked in blood, and his three "condemned" companions were led out. Fromm told Hoepner to follow him.

In the courtyard below in the dim rays of the blackout-hooded headlights of an Army car the four officers were quickly dispatched by a firing squad. Eyewitnesses say there was much tumult and shouting, mostly by the guards, who were in a hurry because of the danger of a bombing attack—British planes had been over Berlin almost every night that summer. Stauffenberg died crying, "Long live our sacred Germany!"[32]

In the meantime Fromm had given General Hoepner a certain choice. Three weeks later, in the shadow of the gallows, Hoepner told of it to the People's Court.

"Well, Hoepner [Fromm said], this business really hurts me. We used to be good friends and comrades, you know. You've got yourself mixed up in this thing and must take the consequences. Do you want to go the same way as Beck? Otherwise I shall have to arrest you now."

Hoepner answered that he did "not feel so guilty" and that he thought he could "justify" himself.

"I understand that," Fromm answered, shaking his hand. Hoepner was carted off to the military prison at Moabit.

As he was being taken away he heard Beck's tired voice through the door in the next room: "If it doesn't work this time, then please help me." There was the sound of a pistol shot. Beck's second attempt to kill himself failed. Fromm poked his head in the door and once more told an officer, "Help the old gentleman." This unknown officer declined to give the *coup de grâce,* leaving that to a sergeant, who dragged Beck, unconscious from the second wound, outside the room and finished him off with a shot in the neck.[33]

It was now sometime after midnight. The revolt, the only serious one ever made against Hitler in the eleven and a half years of the Third Reich, had been snuffed out in eleven and a half hours. Skorzeny arrived at the Bendlerstrasse with a band of armed S.S. men, forbade any more executions—as a policeman he knew enough not to kill those who could be tortured into giving much valuable evidence of the *extent* of the plot— handcuffed the rest of the plotters, sent them off to the Gestapo prison on the Prinz Albrechtstrasse and put detectives to work collecting incriminating papers which the conspirators had not had time to destroy. Himmler, who had reached Berlin a little earlier and set up temporary headquarters in Goebbels' ministry, now protected by part of Remer's guard battalion, telephoned Hitler and reported that the revolt had been crushed. In East Prussia a radio van was racing from Koenigsberg to Rastenburg so that the Fuehrer could make his long-heralded broadcast which the Deutschlandsender had been promising every few minutes since 9 P.M.

Just before 1 A.M. Adolf Hitler's hoarse voice burst upon the summer night's air.

My German comrades!

If I speak to you today it is first in order that you should hear my voice and should know that I am unhurt and well, and secondly, that you should know of a crime unparalleled in German history.

A very small clique of ambitious, irresponsible and, at the same time, senseless and stupid officers had concocted a plot to eliminate me and, with me, the staff of the High Command of the Wehrmacht.

The bomb planted by Colonel Count Stauffenberg exploded two meters to the right of me. It seriously wounded a number of my true and loyal collaborators, one of whom has died. I myself am entirely unhurt, aside from some very minor scratches, bruises and burns. I regard this as a confirmation of the task imposed upon me by Providence . . .

The circle of these usurpers is very small and has nothing in common with the spirit of the German Wehrmacht and, above all, none with the German people. It is a gang of criminal elements which will be destroyed without mercy.

I therefore give orders now that no military authority . . . is to obey orders from this crew of usurpers. I also order that it is everyone's duty to arrest, or, if they resist, to shoot at sight, anyone issuing or handling such orders . . .

This time we shall settle accounts with them in the manner to which we National Socialists are accustomed.

BLOODY VENGEANCE

This time, too, Hitler kept his word.

The barbarism of the Nazis toward their own fellow Germans reached its zenith. There was a wild wave of arrests followed by gruesome torture, drumhead trials, and death sentences carried out, in many cases, by slow strangling while the victims were suspended by piano wire from meathooks borrowed from butchershops and slaughterhouses. Relatives and friends of the suspects were rounded up by the thousands and sent to concentration camps, where many of them died. The brave few who gave shelter to those who were in hiding were summarily dealt with.

Hitler, seized by a titanic fury and an unquenchable thirst for revenge, whipped Himmler and Kaltenbrunner to ever greater efforts to lay their hands on every last person who had dared to plot against him. He himself laid down the procedure for dispatching them.

"This time," he stormed at one of his first conferences after the explosion at Rastenburg, "the criminals will be given short shrift. No military tribunals. We'll hail them before the People's Court. No long speeches from them. The court will act with lightning speed. And two hours after the sentence it will be carried out. By hanging—without mercy."[34]

These instructions from on high were carried out literally by Ronald Freisler, the president of the People's Court (Volksgerichetshof), a vile, vituperative maniac, who as a prisoner of war in Russia during the first war had become a fanatical Bolshevik and who, even after he became, in 1924, an equally fanatical Nazi, remained a warm admirer of Soviet terror and a keen student of its methods. He had made a special study of Andrei Vishinsky's technique as chief prosecutor in the Moscow trials of the Thirties in which the "Old Bolsheviks" and most of the leading generals had been found guilty of "treason" and liquidated. "Freisler is our Vishinsky," Hitler had exclaimed in the conference mentioned above.

The first trial of the July 20 conspirators before the People's Court took place in Berlin on August 7 and 8, with Field Marshal von Witzleben, Generals Hoepner, Stieff and von Hase, and the junior officers, Hagen, Klausing, Bernardis and Count Peter Yorck von Wartenburg, who had worked closely with their idol Stauffenberg, in the dock. They were already pretty well broken by their treatment in the Gestapo cellars and, since Goebbels had ordered every minute of the trial to be filmed so that the movie could be shown to the troops and to the civilian public as an example—and a warning—everything had been done to make the accused look as shabby as possible. They were outfitted in nondescript clothes, old coats and sweaters, and they entered the courtroom unshaven, collarless, without neckties and deprived of suspenders and belts to keep their trousers hitched up. The once proud Field Marshal, especially, looked like a terribly broken, toothless old man. His false teeth had been taken from him and as he stood in the dock, badgered unmercifully by the venomous chief judge, he kept grasping at his trousers to keep them from falling down.

"You dirty old man," Freisler shouted at him, "why do you keep fiddling with your trousers?"

Yet though the accused knew that their fate was already settled they behaved with dignity and courage despite Freisler's ceaseless efforts to degrade and demean them. Young Peter Yorck, a cousin of Stauffenberg, was perhaps the bravest, answering the most insulting questions quietly and never attempting to hide his contempt for National Socialism.

"Why didn't you join the party?" Freisler asked.

"Because I am not and never could be a Nazi," the count replied.

When Freisler had recovered from this answer and pressed the point, Yorck tried to explain. "Mr. President, I have already stated in my interrogation that the Nazi ideology was such that I—"

The judge interrupted him. "—could not agree . . . You didn't agree with the National Socialist conception of justice, say, in regard to rooting out the Jews?"

"What is important, what brings together all these questions," Yorck replied, "is the totalitarian claim of the State on the individual which forces him to renounce his moral and religious obligations to God."

"Nonsense!" cried Freisler, and he cut off the young man. Such talk might poison Dr. Goebbels' film and enrage the Fuehrer, who had decreed, "No long speeches from them."

The court-appointed defense lawyers were more than ludicrous. Their cowardice, as one reads the transcript of the trial, is almost unbelievable. Witzleben's attorney, for example, a certain Dr. Weissmann, outdid the state prosecutor and almost equaled Freisler, in denouncing his client as a "murderer," as completely guilty and as deserving the worst punishment.

That punishment was meted out as soon as the trial had ended on August 8. "They must all be hanged like cattle," Hitler had ordered, and they were. Out at Ploetzensee prison the eight condemned were herded into a small room in which eight meathooks hung from the ceiling. One by one, after being stripped to the waist, they were strung up, a noose of piano wire being placed around their necks and attached to the meathooks. A movie camera whirled as the men dangled and strangled, their beltless trousers finally dropping off as they struggled, leaving them naked in their death agony.[35] The developed film, as ordered, was rushed to Hitler so that he could view it, as well as the pictures of the trial, the same evening. Goebbels is said to have kept himself from fainting by holding both hands over his eyes.*[36]

All that summer, fall and winter and into the new year of 1945 the grisly People's Court sat in session, racing through its macabre trials and grinding out death sentences, until finally an American bomb fell directly on the courthouse on the morning of February 3, 1945, just as Schlabrendorff was being led into the courtroom, killing Judge Freisler and destroying the records of most of the accused who still survived. Schlabrendorff thus miraculously escaped with his life—one of the very few conspirators on

---

* Though the film of this trial was found by the Allies (and shown at Nuremberg, where the author first saw it) that of the executions was never discovered and presumably was destroyed on the orders of Hitler lest it fall into enemy hands. According to Allen Dulles the two films—originally thirty miles long and cut to eight miles—were put together by Goebbels and shown to certain Army audiences as a lesson and a warning. But the soldiers refused to look at it—at the Cadet School at Lichterfelde they walked out as it began to run—and it was soon withdrawn from circulation. (Dulles, *Germany's Underground*, p. 83.)

whom fortune smiled—being eventually liberated from the Gestapo's clutches by American troops in the Tyrol.

The fate of the others must now be recorded.

Goerdeler, who was to be the Chancellor of the new regime, had gone into hiding three days before July 20, after having been warned that the Gestapo had issued an order for his arrest. He wandered for three weeks between Berlin, Potsdam and East Prussia, rarely spending two nights in the same place but always being taken in by friends or relatives, who risked death by giving him shelter, for Hitler had now put a price of one million marks on his head. On the morning of August 12, exhausted and hungry after several days and nights wandering afoot in East Prussia, he stumped into a small inn in the village of Konradswalde near Marienwerder. While waiting to be served breakfast he noticed a woman in the uniform of a Luftwaffe Wac eying him closely, and without waiting for his food he slipped out and made for the nearby woods. It was too late. The woman was an old acquaintance of the Goerdeler family, a Helene Schwaerzel, who had easily recognized him and who promptly confided in a couple of Air Force men who were sitting with her. Goerdeler was quickly apprehended in the woods.

He was sentenced to death by the People's Court on September 8, 1944, but not executed until February 2 of the following year, along with Popitz.* Apparently Himmler delayed the hangings because he thought the contacts of the two men, especially those of Goerdeler, with the Western Allies through Sweden and Switzerland might prove helpful to him if he took over the sinking ship of state—a prospect which began to grow in his mind at this time.[37]

Count Friedrich Werner von Schulenburg, the former ambassador in Moscow, and Hassell, the former ambassador in Rome, both of whom were to have taken over the direction of foreign policy in the new anti-Nazi regime, were executed on November 10 and September 8, respectively. Count Fritz von der Schulenburg died on the gallows August 10. General Fellgiebel, chief of signals at OKW, whose role at Rastenburg on July 20 we have recounted, was executed on the same day.

The death roll is a long one. According to one source it numbered some 4,980 names.[38] The Gestapo records list 7,000 arrests. Among those resistance leaders mentioned in these pages who were executed were General Fritz Lindemann, Colonel von Boeselager, Pastor Dietrich Bonhoeffer, Colonel Georg Hansen of the Abwehr, Count von Helldorf, Colonel von Hofacker, Dr. Jens Peter Jessen, Otto Kiep, Dr. Carl Langbehn, Julius Leber, Major von Leonrod, Wilhelm Leuschner, Artur Nebe (the chief of the criminal police), Professor Adolf Reichwein, Count Berthold von Stauffenberg, brother of Klaus, General Thiele,

---

* Father Alfred Delp, Jesuit member of the Kreisau Circle, was executed with them. Goerdeler's brother, Fritz, was hanged a few days later. Count von Moltke, the leader of the Kreisau Circle, was executed on January 23, 1945, though he had had no part in the assassination plot. Trott zu Solz, a leading light in the Circle and in the conspiracy, was hanged on August 25, 1944.

Chief of Signals, OKH, and General von Thuengen, who was appointed by Beck to succeed General von Kortzfleisch on the day of the putsch.

One group of twenty condemned, whose lives Himmler had prolonged apparently in the belief that they might prove useful to him if he took over power and had to make peace, were shot out of hand on the night of April 22–23 as the Russians began fighting to the center of the capital. The prisoners were being marched from the Lehrterstrasse prison to the Prinz Albrechtstrasse Gestapo dungeon—a good many prisoners escaped in the blackout on occasions such as these in the final days of the Third Reich—when they met an S.S. detachment, which lined them up against a wall and mowed them down, only two escaping to tell the tale. Among those who perished were Count Albrecht von Bernstorff, Klaus Bonhoeffer, brother of the pastor, and Albrecht Haushofer, a close friend of Hess and son of the famous geopolitician. The father committed suicide shortly afterward.

General Fromm did not escape execution despite his behavior on the fateful evening of July 20. Arrested the next day on orders of Himmler, who had succeeded him as head of the Replacement Army, he was haled before the People's Court in February 1945 on charges of "cowardice" and sentenced to death.* Perhaps as a small recognition for his vital service in helping to save the Nazi regime, he was not strangled from a meathook, as were those whom he had arrested on the night of July 20, but merely dispatched by a firing squad on March 19, 1945.

The mystery which surrounded the life of Admiral Canaris, the deposed head of the Abwehr who had done so much to aid the conspirators but was not directly involved in the events of July 20, enveloped for many years the circumstances of his death. It was known that he was arrested after the attempt on Hitler's life. But Keitel, in one of the few decent gestures of his life at OKW, managed to prevent him from being handed over to the People's Court. The Fuehrer, outraged at the delay, then ordered Canaris to be tried by a summary S.S. court. This process was also delayed, but Canaris, along with Colonel Oster, his former assistant, and four others were finally tried at Flossenburg concentration camp on April 9, 1945, less than a month before the war ended, and sentenced to death. But it was not known for sure whether Canaris had been executed. It took ten years to solve the mystery. In 1955 the Gestapo prosecutor in the case was brought to trial and a large number of witnesses testified that they had seen Canaris hanged on April 9, 1945. One eyewitness, the Danish Colonel Lunding, told of seeing Canaris dragged naked from his cell to the gallows. Oster was dispatched at the same time.

Some who were arrested escaped trial and were eventually liberated from the Gestapo by the advancing Allied troops. Among these were General Halder and Dr. Schacht, who had had no part in the July 20 revolt though on the stand at Nuremberg Schacht claimed to have been

---

* "The sentence affected him deeply," Schlabrendorff, who saw a good deal of Fromm at the Prinz Albrechtstrasse Gestapo prison, later recounted. "He had not expected it." (Schlabrendorff, *They Almost Killed Hitler*, p. 121.)

"initiated" into it. Halder was placed in solitary confinement in a pitch-dark cell for several months. The two men, along with a distinguished group of prisoners, German and foreign, including Schuschnigg, Léon Blum, Schlabrendorff and General von Falkenhausen, were freed by American troops on May 4, 1945, at Niederdorf in the South Tyrol just as their Gestapo guard was on the point of executing the whole lot. Falkenhausen was later tried by the Belgians as a war criminal and sentenced on March 9, 1951, after four years in prison awaiting trial, to twelve years' penal servitude. He was released, however, a fortnight later and returned to Germany.

A good many Army officers implicated in the plot chose suicide rather than let themselves be turned over to the tender mercies of the Volks-gericht. On the morning of July 21, General Henning von Tresckow, who had been the heart and soul of the conspiracy among the officers on the Eastern front, took leave of his friend and aide, Schlabrendorff, who has recalled his last words:

"Everybody will now turn upon us and cover us with abuse. But my conviction remains unshaken—we have done the right thing. Hitler is not only the archenemy of Germany: he is the archenemy of the world. In a few hours I shall stand before God, answering for my actions and for my omissions. I think I shall be able to uphold with a clear conscience all that I have done in the fight against Hitler . . .

"Whoever joined the resistance movement put on the shirt of Nessus. The worth of a man is certain only if he is prepared to sacrifice his life for his convictions."[39]

That morning Tresckow drove off to the 28th Rifle Division, crept out to no man's land and pulled the pin on a hand grenade. It blew his head off.

Five days later the First Quartermaster General of the Army, Wagner, took his own life.

Among the high Army officers in the West, two field marshals and one general committed suicide. In Paris, as we have seen, the uprising had got off to a good start when General Heinrich von Stuelpnagel, the military governor of France, arrested the entire force of the S.S. and S.D.-Gestapo. Now all depended on the behavior of Field Marshal von Kluge, the new Commander in Chief West, on whom Tresckow had worked for two years on the Russian front in an effort to make him an active conspirator. Though Kluge had blown hot and cold, he had finally agreed—or so the conspirators understood—that he would support the revolt once Hitler was dead.

There was a fateful dinner meeting that evening of July 20 at La Roche-Guyon, the headquarters of Army Group B, which Kluge had also taken over after Rommel's accident. Kluge wanted to discuss the conflicting reports as to whether Hitler was dead or alive with his chief advisers, General Guenther Blumentritt, his chief of staff, General Speidel, chief of staff of Army Group B, General Stuelpnagel and Colonel von Hofacker, to whom Stauffenberg had telephoned earlier in the afternoon informing him of the bombing and the coup in Berlin. When the officers assembled for dinner it seemed to some of them at least that the cautious Field Marshal had about made up his mind to throw in his lot with the revolt. Beck had reached him by telephone shortly before dinner and had pleaded for his support—whether Hitler was dead or alive. Then the first general order signed by Field Marshal von Witzleben had arrived. Kluge was impressed.

Still, he wanted more information on the situation and, unfortunately for the rebels, this now came from General Stieff, who had journeyed to Rastenburg with Stauffenberg that morning, wished him well, seen the explosion, ascertained that it had not killed Hitler and was now, by evening, trying to cover up the traces. Blumentritt got him on the line and Stieff told him the truth of what had happened, or rather, not happened.

"It has failed, then," Kluge said to Blumentritt. He seemed to be genuinely disappointed, for he added that had it succeeded he would have lost no time in getting in touch with Eisenhower to request an armistice.

At the dinner—a ghostly affair, Speidel later recalled, "as if they sat in a house visited by death"—Kluge listened to the impassioned arguments of Stuelpnagel and Hofacker that they must go ahead with the revolt even though Hitler might have survived. Blumentritt has described what followed.

When they had finished, Kluge, with obvious disappointment, remarked: "Well, gentlemen, the attempt has failed. Everything is over." Stuelpnagel then exclaimed: "Field Marshal, I thought you were acquainted with the plans. Something must be done."[40]

Kluge denied that he knew of any plans. After ordering Stuelpnagel to release the arrested S.S.-S.D. men in Paris, he advised him, "Look here, the best thing you can do is to change into civilian clothes and go into hiding."

But this was not the way out which a proud general of Stuelpnagel's stripe chose. After a weird all-night champagne party at the Hotel Raphaël in Paris in which the released S.S. and S.D. officers, led by General Oberg, fraternized with the Army leaders who had arrested them —and who most certainly would have had them shot had the revolt succeeded—Stuelpnagel, who had been ordered to report to Berlin, left by car for Germany. At Verdun, where he had commanded a battalion in the First World War, he stopped to have a look at the famous battlefield. But also to carry out a personal decision. His driver and a guard heard a revolver shot. They found him floundering in the waters of a canal. A bullet had shot out one eye and so badly damaged the other that it was removed in the military hospital at Verdun, to which he was taken.

This did not save Stuelpnagel from a horrible end. Blinded and helpless, he was brought to Berlin on Hitler's express orders, haled before the People's Court, where he lay on a cot while Freisler abused him, and strangled to death in Ploetzensee prison on August 30.

Field Marshal von Kluge's decisive act in refusing to join the revolt did not save him any more than Fromm, by similar behavior in Berlin, saved himself. "Fate," as Speidel observed apropos of this vacillating general, "does not spare the man whose convictions are not matched by his readiness to give them effect." There is evidence that Colonel von Hofacker, under terrible torture—he was not executed until December 20—mentioned the complicity of Kluge, Rommel and Speidel in the plot. Blumentritt says that Oberg informed him that Hofacker had "mentioned" Kluge in his first interrogations, and that, after being informed of this by Oberg himself, the Field Marshal "began to look more and more worried."[41]

Reports from the front were not such as to restore his spirits.

On July 26, General Bradley's American forces broke through the German front at St.-Lô. Four days later General Patton's newly formed Third Army, racing through the gap, reached Avranches, opening the way to Brittany and to the Loire to the south. This was the turning point in the Allied invasion, and on July 30 Kluge notified Hitler's headquarters, "The whole Western front has been ripped open . . . The left flank has collapsed." By the middle of August all that was left of the German armies in Normandy was locked in a narrow pocket around Falaise, where Hitler had forbidden any further retreat. The Fuehrer had now had enough of Kluge, whom he blamed for the reverses in the West and whom he suspected of considering the surrender of his forces to Eisenhower.

On August 17 Field Marshal Walther Model arrived to replace Kluge—his sudden appearance was the first notice the latter had of his dismissal. Kluge was told by Hitler to leave word as to his whereabouts in Germany—a warning that he had become suspect in connection with the July 20 revolt. The next day he wrote a long letter to Hitler and then set off by car for home. Near Metz he swallowed poison.

His farewell letter to the Fuehrer was found in the captured German military archives.

When you receive these lines I shall be no more . . . Life has no more meaning for me . . . Both Rommel and I . . . foresaw the present development. We were not listened to . . .

I do not know whether Field Marshal Model, who has been proved in every sphere, will master the situation . . . Should it not be so, however, and your cherished new weapons not succeed, then, my Fuehrer, make up your mind to end the war. The German people have borne such untold suffering that it is time to put an end to this frightfulness . . .

I have always admired your greatness . . . . If fate is stronger than your will and your genius, so is Providence . . . Show yourself now also great enough to put an end to a hopeless struggle when necessary . . .

Hitler read the letter, according to the testimony of Jodl at Nuremberg, in silence and handed it to him without comment. A few days later, at his military conference on August 31, the Supreme warlord observed, "There are strong reasons to suspect that had Kluge not committed suicide he would have been arrested anyway."[42]

The turn of Field Marshal Rommel, the idol of the German masses, came next.

As General von Stuelpnagel lay blinded and unconscious on the operating table in the hospital at Verdun after his not quite successful attempt to kill himself, he had blurted out the name of Rommel. Later under hideous torture in the Gestapo dungeon in the Prinz Albrechtstrasse in Berlin Colonel von Hofacker broke down and told of Rommel's part in the conspiracy. "Tell the people in Berlin they can count on me," Hofacker quoted the Field Marshal as assuring him. It was a phrase that stuck in Hitler's mind when he heard of it and which led him to decide that his favorite general, whom he knew to be the most popular one in Germany, must die.

Rommel, who had suffered bad fractures of his skull, temples and cheekbones and a severe injury to his left eye, and whose head was pitted with shell fragments, was first removed from a field hospital at Bernay to St.-Germain to escape capture by the advancing Allied troops and thence, on August 8, to his home at Herrlingen near Ulm. He received the first warning of what might be in store for him when General Speidel, his former chief of staff, was arrested on September 7, the day after he had visited him at Herrlingen.

"That pathological liar," Rommel had exclaimed to Speidel when the talk turned to Hitler, "has now gone completely mad. He is venting his sadism on the conspirators of July 20, and this won't be the end of it!"[43]

Rommel now noticed that his house was being shadowed by the S.D. When he went out walking in the nearby woods with his fifteen-year-old son, who had been given temporary leave from his antiaircraft battery to tend his father, both carried revolvers. At headquarters in Rastenburg Hitler had now received a copy of Hofacker's testimony incriminating Rommel. He thereupon decreed his death—but in a special way. The Fuehrer realized, as Keitel later explained to an interrogator at Nuremberg, "that it would be a terrible scandal in Germany if this well-known Field Marshal, the most popular general we had, were to be arrested and haled before the People's Court." So Hitler arranged with Keitel that Rommel would be told of the evidence against him and given the choice of killing himself or standing trial for treason before the People's Court. If he chose the first he would be given a state funeral with full military honors and his family would not be molested.

Thus it was that at noon on October 14, 1944, two generals from Hitler's headquarters drove up to the Rommel home, which was now surrounded by S.S. troops reinforced by five armored cars. The generals were Wilhelm Burgdorf, an alcoholic, florid-faced man who rivaled Keitel in his slavishness to Hitler, and his assistant in the Army Personnel Office, Ernst Maisel, of like character. They had sent word ahead to Rommel that they were coming from Hitler to discuss his "next employment."

"At the instigation of the Fuehrer," Keitel later testified, "I sent Burgdorf there with a copy of the testimony against Rommel. If it were true, he was to take the consequences. If it were not true, he would be exonerated by the court."

"And you instructed Burgdorf to take some poison with him, didn't you?" Keitel was asked.

"Yes. I told Burgdorf to take some poison along so that he could put it at Rommel's disposal, if conditions warranted it."

After Burgdorf and Maisel arrived it soon became evident that they had not come to discuss Rommel's next assignment. They asked to talk with the Field Marshal alone and the three men retired to his study.

"A few minutes later," Manfred Rommel later related, "I heard my father come upstairs and go into my mother's room." Then:

We went into my room. "I have just had to tell your mother," he began slowly, "that I shall be dead in a quarter of an hour . . . Hitler is charging me with high treason. In view of my services in Africa I am to have the chance of dying by poison. The two generals have brought it with them. It's fatal in three seconds. If I accept, none of the usual steps will be taken against my family . . . I'm to be given a state funeral. It's all been prepared to the last detail. In a quarter of an hour you will receive a call from the hospital in Ulm to say that I've had a brain seizure on the way to a conference."

And that is what happened.

Rommel, wearing his old Afrika Korps leather jacket and grasping his field marshal's baton, got into the car with the two generals, was driven a mile or two up the road by the side of a forest, where General Maisel and the S.S. driver got out, leaving Rommel and General Burgdorf in the back seat. When the two men returned to the car a minute later, Rommel was slumped over the seat, dead. Burgdorf paced up and down impatiently, as though he feared he would be late for lunch and his midday drinks. Fifteen minutes after she had bidden her husband farewell, Frau Rommel received the expected telephone call from the hospital. The chief doctor reported that two generals had brought in the body of the Field Marshal, who had died of a cerebral embolism, apparently as the result of his previous skull fractures. Actually Burgdorf had gruffly forbidden an autopsy. "Do not touch the corpse," he stormed. "Everything has already been arranged in Berlin."

It had been.

Field Marshal Model issued a ringing order of the day announcing that Rommel had died of "wounds sustained on July 17" and mourning the loss "of one of the greatest commanders of our nation."

Hitler wired Frau Rommel: "Accept my sincerest sympathy for the heavy loss you have suffered with the death of your husband. The name of Field Marshal Rommel will be forever linked with the heroic battles in North Africa." Goering telegraphed "in silent compassion":

The fact that your husband has died a hero's death as the result of his wounds, after we all hoped that he would remain to the German people, has deeply touched me.

Hitler ordered a state funeral, at which the senior officer of the German Army, Field Marshal von Rundstedt, delivered the funeral oration. "His heart," said Rundstedt as he stood over Rommel's swastika-bedecked body, "belonged to the Fuehrer."*

"The old soldier [Rundstedt]," Speidel says, "appeared to those present to be broken and bewildered . . . Here destiny gave him the unique chance to play the role of Mark Antony. He remained in his moral apathy."†[45]

The humiliation of the vaunted officer corps of the German Army was great. It had seen three of its illustrious field marshals, Witzleben, Kluge and Rommel, implicated in a plot to overthrow the Supreme warlord, for which one of them was strangled and two forced to suicide. It had to stand idly by while scores of its highest-ranking generals were hauled off to the prisons of the Gestapo and judicially murdered after farcical trials before the People's Court. In this unprecedented situation, despite all its proud traditions, the corps did not close ranks. Instead it sought to preserve its "honor" by what a foreign observer, at least, can only term dishonoring and degrading itself. Before the wrath of the former Austrian corporal, its frightened leaders fawned and groveled.

---

* It is only fair to add that Rundstedt probably did not know of the circumstances of Rommel's death, apparently learning them only from Keitel's testimony at Nuremberg. "I did not hear these rumors," Rundstedt testified on the stand, "otherwise I would have refused to act as representative of the Fuehrer at the state funeral; that would have been an infamy beyond words."[44] Nevertheless the Rommel family noticed that this gentleman of the old school declined to attend the cremation after the funeral and to come to the Rommel home, as did most of the other generals, to extend condolences to the widow.

† General Speidel himself, though incarcerated in the cellars of the Gestapo prison in the Prinz Albrechtstrasse in Berlin and subjected to incessant questioning, became neither broken nor bewildered. Being a philosopher as well as a soldier perhaps helped. He outwitted his S.D. tormentors, admitting nothing and betraying no one. He had one bad moment when he was confronted with Colonel von Hofacker, who, he believes, had been not only tortured but drugged into talking, but on this occasion Hofacker did not betray him and repudiated what he had previously said.

Though never brought to trial, Speidel was kept in Gestapo custody for seven months. As American troops neared his place of confinement near Lake Constance in southern Germany, he escaped with twenty others by a ruse and took refuge with a Catholic priest, who hid the group until the Americans arrived. Speidel omits this chapter of his life in his book, which is severely objective and written in the third person, but he told the story to Desmond Young who gives it in his *Rommel—The Desert Fox* (pp. 251–52 of the paperback edition).

Capping an unusual career, Speidel held an important command at NATO in the late 1950s.

No wonder that Field Marshal von Rundstedt looked broken and bewildered as he intoned the funeral oration over the body of Rommel. He had fallen to a low state, as had his brother officers, whom Hitler now forced to drink the bitter cup to its dregs. Rundstedt himself accepted the post of presiding officer over the so-called military Court of Honor which Hitler created to expel from the Army all officers suspected of complicity in the plot against him so that they could be denied a court-martial and handed over in disgrace as civilians to the drumhead People's Court. The Court of Honor was not permitted to hear an accused officer in his own defense; it acted merely on the "evidence" furnished it by the Gestapo. Rundstedt did not protest against this restriction, nor did another member of the court, General Guderian—who the day after the bombing had been appointed as the new Chief of the Army General Staff—though the latter, in his memoirs, confesses that it was an "unpleasant task," that the court sessions were "melancholy" and raised "the most difficult problems of conscience." No doubt they did, for Rundstedt, Guderian and their fellow judges—all generals—turned over hundreds of their comrades to certain execution after degrading them by throwing them out of the Army.

Guderian did more. In his capacity of General Staff Chief he issued two ringing orders of the day to assure the Nazi warlord of the undying loyalty of the officer corps. The first, promulgated on July 23, accused the conspirators of being "a few officers, some of them on the retired list, who had lost all courage and, out of cowardice and weakness, preferred the road of disgrace to the only road open to an honest soldier—the road of duty and honor." Whereupon he solemnly pledged to the Fuehrer "the unity of the generals, of the officer corps and of the men of the Army."

In the meantime the discarded Field Marshal von Brauchitsch rushed into print with a burning statement condemning the putsch, pledging renewed allegiance to the Fuehrer and welcoming the appointment of Himmler—who despised the generals, including Brauchitsch—as chief of the Replacement Army. Another discard, Grand Admiral Raeder, fearful that he might be suspected of at least sympathy with the plotters, rushed out of retirement to Rastenburg to personally assure Hitler of his loyalty. On July 24 the Nazi salute was made compulsory in place of the old military salute "as a sign of the Army's unshakable allegiance to the Fuehrer and of the closest unity between Army and Party."

On July 29 Guderian warned all General Staff officers that henceforth they must take the lead in being good Nazis, loyal and true to the Leader.

Every General Staff officer must be a National Socialist officer-leader not only . . . by his model attitude toward political questions but by actively co-operating in the political indoctrination of younger commanders in accordance with the tenets of the Fuehrer . . .

In judging and selecting General Staff officers, superiors should place traits of character and spirit above the mind. A rascal may be ever so cunning but in the hour of need he will nevertheless fail because he is a rascal.

I expect every General Staff officer immediately to declare himself a convert or adherent to my views and to make an announcement to that effect in public. Anyone unable to do so should apply for his removal from the General Staff.*

So far as is known no one applied.

With this, comments a German military historian, "the story of the General Staff as an autonomous entity may be said to have come to an end."[46] This elite group, founded by Scharnhorst and Gneisenau and built up by Moltke to be the pillar of the nation, which had ruled Germany during the First World War, dominated the Weimar Republic and forced even Hitler to destroy the S.A. and murder its leader when they stood in its way, had been reduced in the summer of 1944 to a pathetic body of fawning, frightened men. There was to be no more opposition to Hitler, not even any criticism of him. The once mighty Army, like every other institution in the Third Reich, would go down with him, its leaders too benumbed now, too lacking in the courage which the handful of conspirators alone had shown, to raise their voices—let alone do anything— to stay the hand of the one man who they by now fully realized was leading them and the German people rapidly to the most awful catastrophe in the history of their beloved Fatherland.

This paralysis of the mind and will of grown-up men, raised as Christians, supposedly disciplined in the old virtues, boasting of their code of honor, courageous in the face of death on the battlefield, is astonishing, though perhaps it can be grasped if one remembers the course of German history, outlined in an earlier chapter, which made blind obedience to temporal rulers the highest virtue of Germanic man and put a premium on servility. By now the generals knew the evil of the man before whom they groveled. Guderian later recalled Hitler as he was after July 20.

In his case, what had been hardness became cruelty, while a tendency to bluff became plain dishonesty. He often lied without hesitation and assumed that others lied to him. He believed no one any more. It had already been difficult enough dealing with him: it now became a torture that grew steadily worse from month to month. He frequently lost all self-control and his language grew increasingly violent. In his intimate circle he now found no restraining influence.[47]

Nevertheless, it was this man alone, half mad, rapidly deteriorating in body and mind, who now, as he had done in the snowy winter of 1941 before Moscow, rallied the beaten, retreating armies and put new heart into the battered nation. By an incredible exercise of will power which all the others in Germany—in the Army, in the government and among the people—lacked, he was able almost singlehandedly to prolong the agony of war for well nigh a year.

* In his memoirs, Guderian, who constantly emphasizes how he stood up to Hitler and criticizes him bitterly, makes no mention of these orders of the day.

The revolt of July 20, 1944, had failed not only because of the inexplicable ineptness of some of the ablest men in the Army and in civilian life, because of the fatal weakness of character of Fromm and Kluge and because misfortune plagued the plotters at every turn. It had flickered out because almost all the men who kept this great country running, generals and civilians, and the mass of the German people, in uniform and out, were not ready for a revolution—in fact, despite their misery and the bleak prospect of defeat and foreign occupation, did not want it. National Socialism, notwithstanding the degradation it had brought to Germany and Europe, they still accepted and indeed supported, and in Adolf Hitler they still saw the country's savior.

At that time [Guderian later wrote]—the fact seems beyond dispute—the great proportion of the German people still believed in Adolf Hitler and would have been convinced that with his death the assassin had removed the only man who might still have been able to bring the war to a favorable conclusion.[48]

Even after the end of the war General Blumentritt, who was not in on the conspiracy but would have supported it had his chief, Kluge, been of sterner stuff, found that at least "one half of the civil population was shocked that the German generals had taken part in the attempt to overthrow Hitler, and felt bitterly toward them in consequence—and the same feeling was manifested in the Army itself."[49]

By a hypnotism that defies explanation—at least by a non-German—Hitler held the allegiance and trust of this remarkable people to the last. It was inevitable that they would follow him blindly, like dumb cattle but also with a touching faith and even an enthusiasm that raised them above the animal herd, over the precipice to the destruction of the nation.

Book Six

* * *

THE FALL OF THE THIRD REICH

30

THE CONQUEST OF GERMANY

THE WAR CAME HOME to Germany.

Scarcely had Hitler recovered from the shock of the July 20 bombing when he was faced with the loss of France and Belgium and of the great conquests in the East. Enemy troops in overwhelming numbers were converging on the Reich.

By the middle of August 1944, the Russian summer offensives, beginning June 10 and unrolling one after another, had brought the Red Army to the border of East Prussia, bottled up fifty German divisions in the Baltic region, penetrated to Vyborg in Finland, destroyed Army Group Center and brought an advance on this front of four hundred miles in six weeks to the Vistula opposite Warsaw, while in the south a new attack which began on August 20 resulted in the conquest of Rumania by the end of the month and with it the Ploesti oil fields, the only major source of natural oil for the German armies. On August 26 Bulgaria formally withdrew from the war and the Germans began to hastily clear out of that country. In September Finland gave up and turned on the German troops which refused to evacuate its territory.

In the West, France was liberated quickly. In General Patton, the commander of the newly formed U.S. Third Army, the Americans had found a tank general with the dash and flair of Rommel in Africa. After the capture of Avranches on July 30, he had left Brittany to wither on the vine and begun a great sweep around the German armies in Normandy, moving southeast to Orleans on the Loire and then due east toward the Seine south of Paris. By August 23 the Seine was reached southeast and northwest of the capital, and two days later the great city, the glory of France, was liberated after four years of German occupation when General Jacques Leclerc's French 2nd Armored Division and the U.S. 4th Infantry Division broke into it and found that French resistance units were largely in control. They also found the Seine bridges, many of them works of art, intact.*

---

* On August 23, according to Speidel, Hitler had ordered all the Paris bridges and other important installations destroyed "even if artistic monuments are destroyed thereby." Speidel refused to carry out the order, as did General von Choltitz, the

The remnants of the German armies in France were now in full retreat. Montgomery, the victor over Rommel in North Africa, who on September 1 was made a field marshal, drove his Canadian First Army and British Second Army two hundred miles in four days—from the lower Seine past the storied battle sites of 1914–18 and 1940 into Belgium. Brussels fell to him on September 3 and Antwerp the next day. So swift was the advance that the Germans did not have time to destroy the harbor facilities at Antwerp. This was a great stroke of fortune for the Allies, for this port, as soon as its approaches were cleared, was destined to become the principal supply base of the Anglo–American armies.

Farther south of the British–Canadian forces, the U.S. First Army, under General Courtney H. Hodges, advanced with equal speed into southeastern Belgium, reaching the Meuse River, from which the devastating German breakthrough had begun in May 1940, and capturing the fortresses of Namur and Liége, where the Germans had no time to organize a defense. Farther south still, Patton's Third Army had taken Verdun, surrounded Metz, reached the Moselle River and linked up at the Belfort Gap with the Franco–American Seventh Army, which under the command of General Alexander Patch had landed on the Riviera in southern France on August 15 and pushed rapidly up the Rhone Valley.

By the end of August the German armies in the West had lost 500,000 men, half of them as prisoners, and almost all of their tanks, artillery and trucks. There was very little left to defend the Fatherland. The much-publicized Siegfried Line was virtually unmanned and without guns. Most of the German generals in the West believed that the end had come. "There were no longer any ground forces in existence, to say nothing of air forces," says Speidel.[1] "As far as I was concerned," Rundstedt, who was reinstated on September 4 as Commander in Chief in the West, told Allied interrogators after the war, "the war was ended in September."[2]

But not for Adolf Hitler. On the last day of August he lectured some of his generals at headquarters, attempting to inject new iron into their veins and at the same time hold out hope.

If necessary we'll fight on the Rhine. It doesn't make any difference. Under all circumstances we will continue this battle until, as Frederick the Great said, one of our damned enemies gets too tired to fight any more. We'll fight until we get a peace which secures the life of the German nation for the next fifty or a hundred years and which, above all, does not besmirch our honor a second time, as happened in 1918 . . . I live only for the purpose of leading this fight because I know that if there is not an iron will behind it, this battle cannot be won.

---

new commandant of Greater Paris, who surrendered after a few shots had satisfied his honor. For this Choltitz was tried *in absentia* for treason in April 1945, but officer friends of his managed to delay the proceedings until the end of the war. Speidel also reveals that as soon as Paris was lost Hitler ordered its destruction by heavy artillery and V-1 flying bombs, but this order too he refused to obey. (Speidel, *Invasion 1944*, pp. 143–45.)

After excoriating the General Staff for its lack of iron will, Hitler revealed to his generals some of the reasons for his stubborn hopes.

The time will come when the tension between the Allies will become so great that the break will occur. All the coalitions in history have disintegrated sooner or later. The only thing is to wait for the right moment, no matter how hard it is.[3]

Goebbels was assigned the task of organizing "total mobilization," and Himmler, the new chief of the Replacement Army, went to work to raise twenty-five *Volksgrenadier* divisions for the defense of the West. Despite all the plans and all the talk in Nazi Germany concerning "total war" the resources of the country had been far from "totally" organized. At Hitler's insistence the production of civilian goods had been maintained at a surprisingly large figure throughout the war—ostensibly to keep up morale. And he had balked at carrying out the prewar plans to mobilize women for work in the factories. "The sacrifice of our most cherished ideals is too great a price," he said in March 1943 when Speer wanted to draft women for industry.[4] Nazi ideology had taught that the place of the German woman was in the home and not in the factory—and in the home she stayed. In the first four years of the war, when in Great Britain two and a quarter million women had been placed in war production, only 182,000 women were similarly employed in Germany. The number of peacetime domestic servants in Germany remained unchanged at a million and a half during the war.[5]

Now with the enemy at the gates, the Nazi leaders bestirred themselves. Boys between fifteen and eighteen and men between fifty and sixty were called to the colors. Universities and high schools, offices and factories, were combed for recruits. In September and October 1944 a half-million men were found for the Army. But no provision was made to replace them in the factories and offices by women, and Albert Speer, the Minister for Armament and War Production, protested to Hitler that the drafting of skilled workers was seriously affecting the output of arms.

Not since Napoleonic times had German soldiers been forced to defend the sacred soil of the Fatherland. All the subsequent wars, Prussia's and Germany's, had been fought on—and had devastated—the soil of other peoples. A shower of exhortations fell upon the hard-pressed troops.

SOLDIERS OF THE WESTERN FRONT!

. . . I expect you to defend Germany's sacred soil . . . to the very last! . . .

Heil the Fuehrer!

VON RUNDSTEDT,
Field Marshal

SOLDIERS OF THE ARMY GROUP!

. . . None of us gives up a square foot of German soil while still alive . . . Whoever retreats without giving battle is a traitor to his people . . .

Soldiers! Our homeland, the lives of our wives and children are at stake! Our Fuehrer and our loved ones have confidence in their soldiers! . . . Long live our Germany and our beloved Fuehrer!

MODEL,
Field Marshal

Nevertheless, with the roof caving in, there were an increasing number of desertions and Himmler took drastic action to discourage them. On September 10 he posted an order:

Certain unreliable elements seem to believe that the war will be over for them as soon as they surrender to the enemy. . . .

Every deserter . . . will find his just punishment. Furthermore, his ignominious behavior will entail the most severe consequences for his family . . . They will be summarily shot.

A Colonel Hoffmann-Schonforn of the 18th Grenadier Division proclaimed to his unit:

Traitors from our ranks have deserted to the enemy . . . These bastards have given away important military secrets . . . Deceitful Jewish mudslingers taunt you with their pamphlets and try to entice you into becoming bastards also. Let them spew their poison! . . . As for the contemptible traitors who have forgotten their honor—their families will have to atone for their treason.[6]

In September what the skeptical German generals called a "miracle" occurred. To Speidel it was "a German variation of the 'miracle of the Marne' for the French in 1914. The furious advance of the Allies suddenly subsided."

Why it subsided has been a subject of dispute to this day among the Allied commanders from General Eisenhower on down; to the German generals it was incomprehensible. By the second week in September American units had reached the German border before Aachen and on the Moselle. Germany lay open to the Allied armies. Early in September Montgomery had urged Eisenhower to allot all of his supplies and reserves to the British and Canadian armies and the U.S. Ninth and First armies for a bold offensive in the north under his command that would penetrate quickly into the Ruhr, deprive the Germans of their main arsenal, open the road to Berlin and end the war. Eisenhower rejected the proposal.* He wanted to advance toward the Rhine on a "broad front."

---

* "I am certain," Eisenhower wrote in his memoirs (*Crusade in Europe*, p. 305), "that Field Marshal Montgomery, in the light of later events, would agree that this view was a mistaken one." But this is far from being the case, as those who have read Montgomery's memoirs know.

But his armies had outrun their supplies. Every ton of gasoline and ammunition had to be brought in over the beaches in Normandy or through the single port of Cherbourg and transported by truck three to four hundred miles to the advancing front. By the second week of September, Eisenhower's armies were bogging down for lack of supplies. They were also running into unexpected German resistance. By concentrating his available forces at two critical points Rundstedt was able, by the middle of September, to halt at least temporarily Patton's Third Army on the Moselle and Hodges' First Army in front of Aachen.

Eisenhower, prodded by Montgomery, had then agreed to a bold plan to seize a bridgehead over the Lower Rhine at Arnhem and thus obtain a position from which the Siegfried Line could be outflanked on the north. The objective fell far short of Montgomery's dream of racing into the Ruhr and thence to Berlin, but it promised a strategic base for a later try. The attack, led by a massive drop of two American and one British airborne divisions, flying in from bases in Britain, began on September 17, but due to bad weather, to the circumstance that the airborne troops landed right in the midst of two S.S. panzer divisions they did not know were there, and to the lack of adequate land forces pushing up from the south, it failed, and after ten days of savage fighting the Allies withdrew from Arnhem. The British 1st Airborne Division, which had been dropped near the city, lost all but 2,163 of some 9,000 men. To Eisenhower this setback "was ample evidence that much bitter campaigning was to come."[7]

Yet he hardly expected the Germans to recover sufficiently to launch the stunning surprise that burst on the Western Front as Christmas approached that winter.

HITLER'S LAST DESPERATE GAMBLE

On the evening of December 12, 1944, a host of German generals, the senior field commanders on the Western front, were called to Rundstedt's headquarters, stripped of their side arms and briefcases, packed into a bus, driven about the dark, snowy countryside for half an hour to make them lose their bearings, and finally deposited at the entrance to a deep underground bunker which turned out to be Hitler's headquarters at Ziegenberg near Frankfurt. There they learned for the first time what only a handful of the top staff officers and army commanders had known for more than a month: the Fuehrer was to launch in four days a mighty offensive in the West.

The idea had been simmering in his mind since mid-September, when Eisenhower's armies had been brought to a halt on the German frontier west of the Rhine. Although the U.S. Ninth, First and Third armies tried to resume the offensive in October with the objective of "slugging" their way to the Rhine, as Eisenhower put it, the going had been hard and slow. Aachen, the old imperial capital, the seat of Charlemagne, surrendered to First Army on October 24 after a bitter battle—the first German city to fall into Allied hands—but the Americans had been unable to achieve a breakthrough to the Rhine. Still, all along the front they—and the British and Canadians to the north—were wearing down the weakening defenders in battles of attrition. Hitler realized that by remaining on the defensive he was merely postponing the hour of reckoning. In his feverish mind there emerged a bold and imaginative plan to recapture the initiative, strike a blow that would split the U.S. Third and First armies, penetrate to Antwerp and deprive Eisenhower of his main port of supply, and roll up the British and Canadian armies along the Belgian–Dutch border. Such an offensive, he thought, would not only administer a crushing defeat on the Anglo–American armies and thus free the threat to Germany's western border, but would then enable him to turn against the Russians, who, though still advancing in the Balkans, had been halted on the Vistula in Poland and in East Prussia since October. The offensive would strike swiftly through the Ardennes, where the great breakthrough in 1940 had begun, and which German intelligence knew to be defended only by four weak American infantry divisions.

It was a daring plan. It would, Hitler believed, almost certainly catch the Allies by surprise and overcome them before they had a chance to recover.* But there was one drawback. The German Army was not only weaker than it had been in 1940, especially in the air, but it was up against a much more resourceful and far better armed enemy. The German generals lost no time in bringing this to the Fuehrer's attention.

"When I received this plan early in November," Rundstedt later declared, "I was staggered. Hitler had not troubled to consult me . . . It was obvious to me that the available forces were far too small for such an extremely ambitious plan." Realizing, however, that it was useless to argue with Hitler, Rundstedt and Model decided to propose an alternative plan which might satisfy the warlord's insistence on an offensive but which would be limited to pinching off the American salient around Aachen.[8] The German Commander in Chief in the West, however, had so little hope of changing the Fuehrer's mind that he declined to attend a military conference in Berlin on December 2, sending his chief of staff, Blumentritt, instead. But Blumentritt, Field Marshal Model, General Hasso von Manteuffel and S.S. General Sepp Dietrich (the last two were to command two great panzer armies for the breakthrough), who attended

---

* There was an interesting adornment to the plan called "Operation Greif," which seems to have been Hitler's brain child. Its leadership was entrusted by the Fuehrer to Otto Skorzeny, who, following his rescue of Mussolini and his resolute action in Berlin on the night of July 20, 1944, had further distinguished himself in his special field by kidnaping the Hungarian Regent, Admiral Horthy, in Budapest in October 1944, when the latter tried to surrender Hungary to the advancing Russians. Skorzeny's new assignment was to organize a special brigade of two thousand English-speaking German soldiers, put them in American uniforms, and infiltrate them in captured American tanks and jeeps behind the American lines to cut communication wires, kill dispatch riders, misdirect traffic and generally sow confusion. Small units were also to penetrate to the Meuse bridges and try to hold them intact until the main German panzer troops arrived.

the meeting, were unable to shake Hitler's resolve. All through the late autumn he had been scraping the barrel in Germany for this last desperate gamble. In November he had managed to collect nearly 1,500 new or rebuilt tanks and assault guns, and in December another 1,000. He had assembled some twenty-eight divisions, including nine panzer divisions, for the Ardennes breakthrough, with another six divisions allotted for an attack in Alsace to follow the main offensive. Goering promised 3,000 fighter planes.

This was a considerable force, though far weaker than Rundstedt's army group on the same front in 1940. But raising it had meant denying the German forces in the East the reinforcements their commanders thought absolutely necessary to repel the expected Russian winter attack in January. When Guderian, the Chief of the General Staff, who was responsible for the Eastern front, protested Hitler gave him a stern lecture.

"There's no need for you to try to teach me. I've been commanding the German Army in the field for five years and during that time I've had more practical experience than any gentleman of the General Staff could ever hope to have. I've studied Clausewitz and Moltke and read all the Schlieffen papers. I'm more in the picture than you are!"

When Guderian protested that the Russians were about to attack in overwhelming strength and cited figures of the Soviet build-up, Hitler shouted, "It's the greatest bluff since Gengis Khan! Who's responsible for producing all this rubbish?"[9]

The generals who assembled at the Fuehrer's headquarters at Ziegenberg on the evening of December 12, minus their briefcases and revolvers, found the Nazi warlord, as Manteuffel later recalled, "a stooped figure with a pale and puffy face, hunched in his chair, his hands trembling, his left arm subject to a violent twitching which he did his best to conceal. A sick man . . . When he walked he dragged one leg behind him."[10]

Hitler's spirits, however, were as fiery as ever. The generals had expected to be briefed on the over-all military picture of the offensive, but the warlord treated them instead to a political and historical harangue.

Never in history was there a coalition like that of our enemies, composed of such heterogeneous elements with such divergent aims . . . Ultracapitalist states on the one hand; ultra-Marxist states on the other. On the one hand a dying Empire, Britain; on the other, a colony bent upon inheritance, the United States . . .

Each of the partners went into this coalition with the hope of realizing his political ambitions . . . America tries to become England's heir; Russia tries to gain the Balkans . . . England tries to hold her possessions . . . in the Mediterranean . . . Even now these states are at loggerheads, and he who, like a spider sitting in the middle of his web, can watch developments observes how these antagonisms grow stronger and stronger from hour to hour.

If now we can deliver a few more blows, then at any moment this artificially bolstered common front may suddenly collapse with a gigantic clap of thunder . . . provided always that there is no weakening on the part of Germany.

It is essential to deprive the enemy of his belief that victory is certain . . . Wars are finally decided by one side or the other recognizing that they cannot be won. We must allow no moment to pass without showing the enemy that, whatever he does, he can never reckon on [our] capitulation. Never! Never![11]

With this pep talk resounding in their ears the generals dispersed, none of them—or at least so they said afterward—believing that the Ardennes blow would succeed but determined to carry out their orders to the best of their ability.

This they did. The night of December 15 was dark and frosty and a thick mist hung over the rugged snow-laden hills of the Ardennes Forest as the Germans moved up to their assault positions on a seventy-mile front between Monschau, south of Aachen, and Echternach, northwest of Trier. Their meteorologists had predicted several days of such weather, during which it was calculated that the Allied air forces would be grounded and the German supply columns spared the inferno of Normandy. For five days Hitler's luck with the weather held and the Germans, catching the Allied High Command completely by surprise, scored several break-throughs after their initial penetrations on the morning of December 16.

When a German armored group reached Stavelot on the night of December 17, it was only eight miles from the U.S. First Army headquarters at Spa, which was being hurriedly evacuated. More important, it was only a mile from a huge American supply dump containing three million gallons of gasoline. Had this dump been captured the German armored divisions, which were continually being slowed down because of the delay in bringing up gasoline, of which the Germans were woefully short, might have gone farther and faster than they did. Skorzeny's so-called Panzer Brigade 150, its men outfitted in American uniforms and driving captured American tanks, trucks and jeeps, got farthest. Some forty jeeploads slipped through the crumbling front, a few of them getting as far as the River Meuse.*

---

* On the sixteenth a German officer carrying several copies of Operation Greif was taken prisoner and the Americans thus learned what was up. But this does not seem to have curbed the initial confusion spread by Skorzeny's men, some of whom, posing as M.P.s, took up posts at crossroads and misdirected American military traffic. Nor did it prevent First Army's intelligence office from believing the tall tales of some of the captured Germans in American uniform that more than a few of Skorzeny's desperadoes were on their way to Paris to assassinate Eisenhower. For several days thousands of American soldiers as far back as Paris were stopped by M.P.s and had to prove their nationality by telling who won the World Series and what the capital of their native state was—though some could not remember or did not know. A good many of the Germans caught in American uniforms were summarily shot and others court-martialed and executed. Skorzeny himself was tried by an American tribunal at Dachau in 1947 but acquitted. Thereafter he moved to Spain and South America, where he soon established a prosperous cement business and composed his memoirs.

Yet stubborn makeshift resistance by scattered units of the U.S. First Army after the four weak divisions in the Ardennes had been overrun slowed up the German drive and the firm stand on the northern and southern shoulders of the breakthrough at Monschau and Bastogne, respectively, channeled Hitler's forces through a narrow salient. The American defense of Bastogne sealed their fate.

This road junction was the key to the defense of the Ardennes and of the River Meuse behind. If strongly held it not only would block the main roads along which Manteuffel's Fifth Panzer Army was driving for the Meuse River at Dinant but would tie up considerable German forces earmarked for the push beyond. By the morning of December 18, Manteuffel's armored spearheads were only fifteen miles from the town and the only Americans in it belonged to a corps headquarters staff which was preparing to evacuate. However, on the evening of the seventeenth the 101st Airborne Division, which had been refitting at Reims, was ordered to proceed with all speed to Bastogne a hundred miles away. By driving its trucks with headlights on through the night it reached the town in twenty-four hours, just ahead of the Germans. It was a decisive race and the Germans had lost it. Although they encircled Bastogne, they had difficulty in getting their divisions around it to renew the drive toward the Meuse. And they had to leave strong forces behind to contain the road junction and to try to take it.

On December 22, General Heinrich von Luettwitz, commander of the German XLVIIth Armored Corps, sent a written note to General A. C. McAuliffe, commanding the 101st Airborne, demanding surrender of Bastogne. He received a one-word answer which became famous: "NUTS!"

The definite turning point in Hitler's Ardennes gamble came on the day before Christmas. A reconnaissance battalion of the German 2nd Panzer Division had reached the heights three miles east of the Meuse at Dinant the day before and had waited for gasoline for its tanks and some reinforcements before plunging down the slopes to the river. Neither the gasoline nor the reinforcements ever arrived. The U.S. 2nd Armored Division suddenly struck from the north. Already several divisions of Patton's Third Army were moving up from the south, their main objective being to relieve Bastogne. "On the evening of the twenty-fourth," Manteuffel later wrote, "it was clear that the high-water mark of our operation had been reached. We now knew that we would never reach our objective." The pressure on the northern and southern flanks of the deep and narrow German salient had become too great. And two days before Christmas the weather had finally cleared and the Anglo–American air forces had begun to have a field day with massive attacks on German supply lines and on the troops and tanks moving up the narrow, tortuous mountain roads. The Germans made another desperate attempt to capture Bastogne. All day Christmas, beginning at 3 A.M., they launched a series of attacks, but McAuliffe's defenders held. The next day an armored force of Patton's Third Army broke through from the south and relieved the town. For the

Germans it now became a question of extricating their forces from the narrow corridor before they were cut off and annihilated.

But Hitler would not listen to any withdrawal being made. On the evening of December 28 he held a full-dress military conference. Instead of heeding the advice of Rundstedt and Manteuffel to pull out the German forces in the Bulge in time, he ordered the offensive to be resumed, Bastogne to be stormed and the push to the Meuse renewed. Moreover, he insisted on a new offensive being started immediately to the south in Alsace, where the American line had been thinned out by the sending of several of Patton's divisions north to the Ardennes. To the protests of the generals that they lacked sufficient forces either to continue the offensive in the Ardennes or to attack in Alsace he remained deaf.

Gentlemen, I have been in this business for eleven years, and . . . I have never heard anybody report that everything was completely ready . . . You are never entirely ready. That is plain.

He talked on and on.* It must have been obvious to the generals long before he finished that their Commander in Chief had become blinded to reality and had lost himself in the clouds.

The question is . . . whether Germany has the will to remain in existence or whether it will be destroyed . . . The loss of this war will destroy the German people.

There followed a long dissertation on the history of Rome and of Prussia in the Seven Years' War. Finally he returned to the immediate problems at hand. Although he admitted that the Ardennes offensive had not "resulted in the decisive success which might have been expected," he claimed that it had brought about "a transformation of the entire situation such as nobody would have believed possible a fortnight ago."

The enemy has had to abandon all his plans for attack . . . He has had to throw in units that were fatigued. His operational plans have been completely upset. He is enormously criticized at home. It is a bad psychological moment for him. Already he has had to admit that there is no chance of the war being decided before August, perhaps not before the end of next year . . .

Was this last phrase an admission of ultimate defeat? Hitler quickly tried to correct any such impression.

I hasten to add, gentlemen, that . . . you are not to conclude that even remotely I envisage the loss of this war . . . I have never learned to know the

---

* For several hours, judging by the length of the stenographic record of this conference, which has survived almost intact. It is Fragment 27 of the Fuehrer conferences. Gilbert gives the entire text in *Hitler Directs His War*, pp. 158–74.

word "capitulation" . . . For me the situation today is nothing new. I have been in very much worse situations. I mention this only because I want you to understand why I pursue my aim with such fanaticism and why nothing can wear me down. As much as I may be tormented by worries and even physically shaken by them, nothing will make the slightest change in my decision to fight on till at last the scales tip to our side.

Whereupon he appealed to the generals to support the new attacks "with all your fire."

We shall then . . . smash the Americans completely . . . Then we shall see what happens. I do not believe that in the long run the enemy will be able to resist forty-five German divisions . . . We shall yet master fate!

It was too late. Germany lacked the military force to make good his words.

On New Year's Day Hitler threw eight German divisions into an attack in the Saar and followed it with a thrust from the bridgehead on the Upper Rhine by an army under the command of—to the German generals this was a bad joke—Heinrich Himmler. Neither drive got very far. Nor did an all-out assault on Bastogne beginning on January 3 by no less than two corps of nine divisions which led to the most severe fighting of the Ardennes campaign. By January 5 the Germans abandoned hope of taking this key town. They were now faced with being cut off by a British–American counteroffensive from the north which had begun on January 3. On January 8 Model, whose armies were in danger of being entrapped at Houffalize, northeast of Bastogne, finally received permission to withdraw. By January 16, just a month after the beginning of the offensive on which Hitler had staked his last reserves in men and guns and ammunition, the German forces were back to the line from which they had set out.

They had lost some 120,000 men, killed, wounded and missing, 600 tanks and assault guns, 1,600 planes and 6,000 vehicles. American losses were also severe—8,000 killed, 48,000 wounded, 21,000 captured or missing, and 733 tanks and tank destroyers.* But the Americans could

---

* Among the American dead were several prisoners shot in cold blood by Colonel Jochen Peiper's combat group of the 1st S.S. Panzer Division near Malmédy on December 17. According to the evidence presented at Nuremberg 129 American prisoners were massacred; at the subsequent trial of the S.S. officers involved, the figure was reduced to 71. The trial before an American military tribunal at Dachau in the spring of 1946 had a curious denouement. Forty-three S.S. officers, including Peiper, were condemned to death, twenty-three to life imprisonment and eight to shorter sentences. Sepp Dietrich, commander of the Sixth S.S. Panzer Army, which fought in the northern side of the Bulge, received twenty-five years; Kraemer, commander of the Ist S.S. Armored Corps, ten years, and Hermann Priess, commander of the 1st S.S. Panzer Division, eighteen years.

Then a hue and cry arose in the U.S. Senate, especially from the late Senator McCarthy, that the S.S. officers had been treated brutally in order to extort confessions. In March 1948 thirty-one of the death sentences were commuted; in April

make good their losses; the Germans could not. They had shot their last bolt. This was the last major offensive of the German Army in World War II. Its failure not only made defeat inevitable in the West, it doomed the German armies in the East, where the effect of Hitler's throwing his last reserves into the Ardennes became immediately felt.

In his long lecture to the generals in the West three days after Christmas Hitler had been quite optimistic about the Russian front, where, though the Balkans was being lost, the German armies had held firmly on the Vistula in Poland and in East Prussia since October.

Unfortunately [Hitler said] because of the treachery of our dear allies we are forced to retire gradually . . . Yet despite all this it has been possible on the whole to hold the Eastern front.

But for how long? On Christmas Eve, after the Russians had surrounded Budapest, and again on New Year's morning Guderian had pleaded in vain with Hitler for reinforcements to meet the Russian threat in Hungary and to counter the Soviet offensive in Poland which he expected to begin the middle of January.

I pointed out [Guderian says] that the Ruhr had already been paralyzed by the Western Allies' bombing attacks. . . . on the other hand, I said, the industrial area of Upper Silesia could still work at full pressure, the center of the German armament industry was already in the East, and the loss of Upper Silesia must lead to our defeat in a very few weeks. All this was of no avail. I was rebuffed and I spent a grim and tragic Christmas Eve in those most unchristian surroundings.

Nonetheless Guderian returned to Hitler's headquarters for a third time on January 9. He took with him his Chief of Intelligence in the East, General Gehlen, who with maps and diagrams tried to explain to the Fuehrer the precarious German position on the eve of the expected renewal of the Russian offensive in the north.

Hitler [Guderian says] completely lost his temper . . . declaring the maps and diagrams to be "completely idiotic" and ordering that I have the man who had made them shut up in a lunatic asylum. I then lost my temper and said . . . "If you want General Gehlen sent to a lunatic asylum then you had better have me certified as well."

General Lucius D. Clay reduced the death sentences from twelve to six; and in January 1951, under a general amnesty, John J. McCloy, the American High Commissioner, commuted the remaining death sentences to life imprisonment. At the time of writing all have been released. Almost forgotten in the hubbub over the alleged ill-treatment of the S.S. officers was the indisputable evidence that at least seventy-one unarmed U.S. war prisoners were slain in cold blood on a snowy field near Malmédy on December 17, 1944, on the orders—or incitement—of several S.S. officers.

When Hitler argued that the Eastern front had "never before possessed such a strong reserve as now," Guderian retorted, "The Eastern front is like a house of cards. If the front is broken through at one point all the rest will collapse."[12]

And that is what happened. On January 12, 1945, Konev's Russian army group broke out of its bridgehead at Baranov on the upper Vistula south of Warsaw and headed for Silesia. Farther north Zhukov's armies crossed the Vistula north and south of Warsaw, which fell on January 17. Farther north still, two Russian armies overran half of East Prussia and drove to the Gulf of Danzig.

This was the greatest Russian offensive of the war. Stalin was throwing in 180 divisions, a surprisingly large part of them armored, in Poland and East Prussia alone. There was no stopping them.

"By January 27 [only fifteen days after the Soviet drive began] the Russian tidal wave," says Guderian, "was rapidly assuming for us the proportions of a complete disaster."[13] By that date East and West Prussia were cut off from the Reich. Zhukov that very day crossed the Oder near Lueben after an advance of 220 miles in a fortnight, reaching German soil only 100 miles from Berlin. Most catastrophic of all, the Russians had overrun the Silesian industrial basin.

Albert Speer, in charge of armament production, drew up a memorandum to Hitler on January 30—the twelfth anniversary of Hitler's coming to power—pointing out the significance of the loss of Silesia. "The war is lost," his report began, and he went on in his cool and objective manner to explain why. The Silesian mines, ever since the intensive bombing of the Ruhr, had supplied 60 per cent of Germany's coal. There was only two weeks' supply of coal for the German railways, power plants and factories. Henceforth, now that Silesia was lost, Speer could supply, he said, only one quarter of the coal and one sixth of the steel which Germany had been producing in 1944.[14] This augured disaster for 1945.

The Fuehrer, Guderian later related, glanced at Speer's report, read the first sentence and then ordered it filed away in his safe. He refused to see Speer alone, saying to Guderian:

". . . I refuse to see anyone alone any more . . . [He] always has something unpleasant to say to me. I can't bear that."[15]

On the afternoon of January 27, the day Zhukov's troops crossed the Oder a hundred miles from Berlin, there was an interesting reaction at Hitler's headquarters, which had now been transferred to the Chancellery in Berlin, where it was to remain until the end. On the twenty-fifth the desperate Guderian had called on Ribbentrop and urged him to try to get an immediate armistice in the West so that what was left of the German armies could be concentrated in the East against the Russians. The Foreign Minister had quickly tattled to the Fuehrer, who that evening upbraided his General Staff Chief and accused him of committing "high treason."

But two nights later, under the impact of the disaster in the East, Hitler, Goering and Jodl were in such a state that they thought it would not be necessary to ask the West for an armistice. They were sure the Western Allies would come running to them in their fear of the consequences of the Bolshevik victories. A fragment of the Fuehrer conference of January 27 has preserved part of the scene.

HITLER: Do you think the English are enthusiastic about all the Russian developments?

GOERING: They certainly didn't plan that we hold them off while the Russians conquer all of Germany . . . They had not counted on our . . . holding them off like madmen while the Russians drive deeper and deeper into Germany, and practically have all of Germany now . . .

JODL: They have always regarded the Russians with suspicion.

GOERING: If this goes on we will get a telegram [from the English] in a few days.[16]

On such a slender thread the leaders of the Third Reich began to pin their last hopes. In the end these German architects of the Nazi–Soviet Pact against the West would reach a point where they could not understand why the British and Americans did not join them in repelling the Russian invaders.

THE COLLAPSE OF THE GERMAN ARMIES

The end came quickly for the Third Reich in the spring of 1945.

The death throes began in March. By February, with the Ruhr largely in ruins and Upper Silesia lost, coal production was down to one fifth of what it had been the year before and very little of this could be moved because of the dislocation of rail and water transport by Anglo–American bombing. The Fuehrer conferences became dominated by talk of the coal shortage, Doenitz complaining that many of his ships had to lie idle because of lack of fuel and Speer explaining patiently that the power plants and armament factories were in a similar situation for the same reason. The loss of the Rumanian and Hungarian oil fields and the bombing of the synthetic-oil plants in Germany caused such an acute shortage of gasoline that a good part of the desperately needed fighter planes had to be grounded and were destroyed on the fields by Allied air attacks. Many panzer divisions could not move for lack of fuel for their tanks.

The hopes in the promised "miracle weapons," which had for a time sustained not only the masses of the people and the soldiers but even such hardheaded generals as Guderian, were finally abandoned. The launching sites for the V-1 flying bombs and the V-2 rockets directed against Britain were almost entirely lost when Eisenhower's forces reconquered the French and Belgian coasts, though a few remained in Holland. Nearly eight thousand of the two V bombs were hurled against Antwerp and other military targets after the British–American armies reached the German frontier, but the damage they did was negligible.

Hitler and Goering had counted on the new jet fighters driving the Allied air forces from the skies, and well they might have—for the Germans succeeded in producing more than a thousand of them—had the Anglo–American flyers, who lacked this plane, not taken successful counteraction. The conventional Allied fighter was no match for the German jet in the *air,* but few ever got off the ground. The refineries producing the special fuel for them were bombed and destroyed and the extended runways which had to be constructed for them were easily detected by Allied pilots, who destroyed the jets on the ground.

Grand Admiral Doenitz had promised the Fuehrer that the new electro– U-boats would provide a miracle at sea, once more wreaking havoc on the British–American lifelines in the North Atlantic. But by the middle of February 1945 only two of the 126 new craft commissioned had put to sea.

As for the German atom bomb project, which had given London and Washington much worry, it had made little progress due to Hitler's lack of interest in it and Himmler's practice of arresting the atom scientists for suspected disloyalty or pulling them off to work on some of his pet non-sensical "scientific" experiments which he deemed more important. Before the end of 1944 the American and British governments had learned, to their great relief, that the Germans would not have an atom bomb in this war.*

On February 8 Eisenhower's armies, now eighty-five divisions strong, began to close in on the Rhine. They had expected that the Germans would fight only a delaying action and, conserving their strength, retire behind the formidable water barrier of the wide and swift-flowing river. Rundstedt counseled this. But here, as elsewhere throughout the years of his defeats, Hitler would not listen to a withdrawal. It would merely mean, he told Rundstedt, "moving the catastrophe from one place to another." So the German armies, at Hitler's insistence, stood and fought—but not for long. By the end of the month the British and Americans had reached the Rhine at several places north of Duesseldorf, and a fortnight later they had firm possession of the left bank from the Moselle River northward. The Germans had lost another 350,000 men killed, wounded or captured (the prisoners numbered 293,000) and most of their arms and equipment.

Hitler was in a fine fury. He sacked Rundstedt for the last time on March 10, replacing him with Field Marshal Kesselring, who had held out

---

* How they learned is a fascinating story in itself but too long to be set down here. Professor Samuel Goudsmit has told it well in his book *Alsos.* "Alsos" was the code name of the American scientific mission which he headed and which followed Eisenhower's armies into Western Europe.

so stubbornly and long in Italy. Already in February the Fuehrer, in a fit of rage, had considered denouncing the Geneva Convention in order, he said at a conference on the nineteenth, "to make the enemy realize that we are determined to fight for our existence with all the means at our disposal." He had been urged to take this step by Dr. Goebbels, the bloodthirsty noncombatant, who suggested that all captured airmen be shot summarily in reprisal for their terrible bombing of the German cities. When some of the officers present raised legal objections Hitler retorted angrily:

To hell with that! . . . If I make it clear that I show no consideration for prisoners but that I treat enemy prisoners without any consideration for their rights, regardless of reprisals, then quite a few [Germans] will think twice before they desert.[17]

This was one of the first indications to his followers that Hitler, his mission as world conqueror having failed, was determined to go down, like Wotan at Valhalla, in a holocaust of blood—not only the enemy's but that of his own people. At the close of the discussion he asked Admiral Doenitz "to consider the pros and cons of this step and to report as soon as possible."

Doenitz came back with his answer on the following day and it was typical of the man.

The disadvantages would outweigh the advantages . . . It would be better in any case to keep up outside appearances and carry out the measures believed necessary without announcing them beforehand.[18]

Hitler reluctantly agreed and while, as we have seen,* there was no general massacre of captured flyers or of other prisoners of war (except the Russians) several were done to death and the civil population was incited to lynch Allied air crews who parachuted to the ground. One captive French general, Mesny, was deliberately murdered on the orders of Hitler, and a good many Allied POWs perished when they were forced to make long marches without food or water on roads strafed by British, American and Russian flyers as the Germans herded them toward the interior of the country to prevent them from being liberated by the advancing Allied armies.

Hitler's concern to make German soldiers "think twice before they desert" was not ungrounded. In the West the number of deserters, or at least of those who gave themselves up as quickly as possible in the wake of the British–American advances, became staggering. On February 12 Keitel issued an order "in the name of the Fuehrer" stating that any soldier "who deceitfully obtains leave papers, or who travels with false papers,

---

* In Chapter 27, "The New Order."

will . . . be punished by death." And on March 5 General Blaskowitz, commanding Army Group H in the West, issued this order:

All soldiers . . . encountered away from their units . . . and who announce they are stragglers looking for their units will be summarily tried and shot.

On April 12 Himmler added his bit by decreeing that any commander who failed to hold a town or an important communications center "is punishable by death." The order was already being carried out in the case of the unfortunate commanders at one of the Rhine bridges.

On the early afternoon of March 7, a spearhead of the U.S. 9th Armored Division reached the heights above the town of Remagen, twenty-five miles down the Rhine from Koblenz. To the amazement of the American tank crews they saw that the Ludendorff railroad bridge across the river was still intact. They raced down the slopes to the water front. Engineers frantically cut every demolition wire they could find. A platoon of infantry raced across the bridge. As they were approaching the east bank a charge went off and then another. The bridge shook but held. Feeble German forces on the far shore were quickly driven back. Tanks sped over the span. By dusk the Americans had a strong bridgehead on the east bank of the Rhine. The last great natural barrier in Western Germany had been crossed.*

A few days later, on the night of March 22, Patton's Third Army, after overrunning the Saar-Palatinate triangle in a brilliant operation carried out in conjunction with the U.S. Seventh and French First armies, made another crossing of the Rhine at Oppenheim, south of Mainz. By March 25 the Anglo–American armies were in possession of the entire west bank of the river and across it in two places with strong bridgeheads. In six weeks Hitler had lost more than one third of his forces in the West and most of the arms for half a million men.

At 2:30 A.M. on March 24, he called a war conference at his headquarters in Berlin to consider what to do.

HITLER: I consider the second bridgehead at Oppenheim as the greatest danger.

HEWEL [Foreign Office representative]: The Rhine isn't so very wide there.

HITLER: A good two hundred fifty meters. On a river barrier only one man has to be asleep and a terrible misfortune can happen.

The Supreme Commander wanted to know if there was "no brigade or something like that which could be sent there." An adjutant answered:

---

* Hitler had eight German officers who commanded the weak forces at the Remagen bridge executed. They were tried by a "Flying Special Tribunal, West," set up by the Fuehrer and presided over by a fanatical Nazi general by the name of Huebner.

At the present time no unit is available to be sent to Oppenheim. There are only five tank destroyers in the camp at Senne, which will be ready today or tomorrow. They could be put into the battle in the next few days . . .[19]

In the next few days! At that very moment Patton had a bridgehead at Oppenheim seven miles wide and six miles deep and his tanks were heading eastward toward Frankfurt. It is a measure of the plight of the once mighty German Army whose vaunted panzer corps had raced through Europe in the earlier years that at this moment of crisis the Supreme Commander should be concerned with scraping up five broken-down tank destroyers which could only be "put into battle in the next few days" to stem the advance of a powerful enemy armored army.*

With the Americans across the Rhine by the third week of March and a mighty Allied army of British, Canadians and Americans under Montgomery poised to cross the Lower Rhine and head both into the North German plain and into the Ruhr—which they did, beginning on the night of March 23—Hitler's vengeance turned from the advancing enemy to his own people. They had sustained him through the greatest victories in German history. Now in the winter of defeat he thought them no longer worthy of his greatness.

"If the German people were to be defeated in the struggle," Hitler had told the gauleiters in a speech in August 1944, "it must have been too weak: it had failed to prove its mettle before history and was destined only to destruction."[20]

He was fast becoming a physical wreck and this helped to poison his view. The strain of conducting the war, the shock of defeats, the unhealthy life without fresh air and exercise in the underground headquarters bunkers which he rarely left, his giving way to ever more frequent temper tantrums and, not the least, the poisonous drugs he took daily on the advice of his quack physician, Dr. Morell, had undermined his health even before the July 20, 1944, bombing. The explosion on that day had broken the tympanic membranes of both ears, which contributed to his spells of dizziness. After the bombing his doctors advised an extended vacation,

---

* The transcript of this March 23 Fuehrer conference is the last one which was saved, fairly intact, from the flames. It gives a good picture of the frantic mind of the Fuehrer and his obsession with trivial details at the moment when the walls are caving in. For the best part of an hour he discusses Goebbels' proposal to use the broad avenue through the Tiergarten in Berlin as an airstrip. He lectures on the weakness of German concrete in the face of bombing. Much of the conference is given over to scraping up troops. One general raises the question of the Indian Legion.

HITLER: The Indian Legion is a joke. There are Indians who can't kill a louse, who'd rather let themselves be eaten up. They won't kill an Englishman either. I consider it nonsense to put them opposite the English . . . If we used Indians to turn prayer mills, or something like that, they would be the most indefatigable soldiers in the world . . .

And so on far into the night. The meeting broke up at 3:43 A.M.

but he refused. "If I leave East Prussia," he told Keitel, "it will fall. As long as I am here, it will hold."

In September 1944 he suffered a breakdown and had to take to bed, but he recovered in November when he returned to Berlin. But he never recovered control of his terrible temper. More and more, as the news from the fronts in 1945 grew worse, he gave way to hysterical rage. It was invariably accompanied by a trembling of his hands and feet which he could not control. General Guderian has given several descriptions of him at these moments. At the end of January, when the Russians had reached the Oder only a hundred miles from Berlin and the General Staff Chief started to demand the evacuation by sea of several German divisions cut off in the Baltic area, Hitler turned on him.

He stood in front of me shaking his fists, so that my good Chief of Staff, Thomale, felt constrained to seize me by the skirt of my jacket and pull me backward lest I be the victim of a physical assault.

A few days later, on February 13, 1945, the two men got into another row over the Russian situation that lasted, Guderian says, for two hours.

His fists raised, his cheeks flushed with rage, his whole body trembling, the man stood there in front of me, beside himself with fury and having lost all self-control. After each outburst Hitler would stride up and down the carpet edge, then suddenly stop immediately before me and hurl his next accusation in my face. He was almost screaming, his eyes seemed to pop out of his head and the veins stood out in his temples.[21]

It was in this state of mind and health that the German Fuehrer made one of the last momentous decisions of his life. On March 19 he issued a general order that all military, industrial, transportation and communication installations as well as all stores in Germany must be destroyed in order to prevent them from falling intact in'o the hands of the enemy. The measures were to be carried out by the military with the help of the Nazi gauleiters and "commissars for defense." "All directives opposing this," the order concluded, "are invalid."[22]

Germany was to be made one vast wasteland. Nothing was to be left with which the German people might somehow survive their defeat.

Albert Speer, the outspoken Minister for Armament and War Production, had anticipated the barbarous directive from previous meetings with Hitler and on March 15 had drawn up a memorandum in which he strenuously opposed such a criminal step and reiterated his contention that the war was already lost. He presented it to the Fuehrer personally on the evening of March 18.

In four to eight weeks [Speer wrote] the final collapse of the German economy must be expected with certainty . . . After that collapse the war cannot be continued even militarily . . . We must do everything to maintain, even if only in a most primitive manner, a basis for the existence of the nation to the last . . . We have no right at this stage of the war to carry out demolitions which might affect the life of the people. If our enemies wish to destroy this nation, which has fought with unique bravery, then this historical shame shall rest exclusively upon them. We have the duty of leaving to the nation every possibility of insuring its reconstruction in the distant future . . .[23]

But Hitler, his own personal fate sealed, was not interested in the continued existence of the German people, for whom he had always professed such boundless love. He told Speer:

If the war is lost, the nation will also perish. This fate is inevitable. There is no necessity to take into consideration the basis which the people will need to continue a most primitive existence. On the contrary, it will be better to destroy these things ourselves because this nation will have proved to be the weaker one and the future will belong solely to the stronger eastern nation [Russia]. Besides, those who will remain after the battle are only the inferior ones, for the good ones have been killed.

Whereupon the Supreme Warlord promulgated his infamous "scorched earth" directive the next day. It was followed on March 23 by an equally monstrous order by Martin Bormann, the Fuehrer's secretary, a molelike man who had now gained a position at court second to none among the Nazi satraps. Speer described it on the stand at Nuremberg.

The Bormann decree aimed at bringing the population to the center of the Reich from both East and West, and the foreign workers and prisoners of war were to be included. These millions of people were to be sent upon their trek on foot. No provisions for their existence had been made, nor could it be carried out in view of the situation. It would have resulted in an unimaginable hunger catastrophe.

And had all the other orders of Hitler and Bormann—there were a number of supplementary directives—been carried out, millions of Germans who had escaped with their lives up to then might well have died. Speer tried to summarize for the Nuremberg court the various "scorched earth" orders. To be destroyed, he said, were

all industrial plants, all important electrical facilities, water works, gas works, food stores and clothing stores; all bridges, all railway and communication installations, all waterways, all ships, all freight cars and all locomotives.

That the German people were spared this final catastrophe was due to—aside from the rapid advances of the Allied troops, which made the carrying out of such a gigantic demolition impossible—the superhuman efforts of Speer and a number of Army officers who, in direct disobedience (finally!) of Hitler's orders, raced about the country to make sure that vital communications, plants and stores were not blown up by zealously obedient Army officers and party hacks.

The end now approached for the German Army.

While Field Marshal Montgomery's British–Canadian armies, after their crossing of the Lower Rhine the last week of March, pushed northeast for Bremen, Hamburg and the Baltic at Luebeck, General Simpson's U.S. Ninth Army and General Hodges' U.S. First Army advanced rapidly past the Ruhr, the Ninth Army on its northern perimeter, the First Army to the south. On April 1 they linked up at Lippstadt. Field Marshal Model's Army Group B, consisting of the Fifteenth and the Fifth Panzer armies—some twenty-one divisions—was trapped in the ruins of Germany's greatest industrial area. It held out for eighteen days, surrendering on April 18. Another 325,000 Germans, including thirty generals, were captured, but Model was not among them. Rather than become a prisoner he shot himself.

The encirclement of Model's armies in the Ruhr had torn the German front in the West wide open, leaving a gap two hundred miles wide through which the divisions of the U.S. Ninth and First armies not needed to contain the Ruhr now burst toward the Elbe River in the heart of Germany. The road to Berlin lay open, for between these two American armies and the German capital there were only a few scattered, disorganized German divisions. On the evening of April 11, after advancing some sixty miles since daybreak, a spearhead of the U.S. Ninth Army reached the Elbe River near Magdeburg, and on the next day threw a bridgehead over it. The Americans were only sixty miles from Berlin.

Eisenhower's purpose now was to split Germany in two by joining up with the Russians on the Elbe between Magdeburg and Dresden. Though bitterly criticized by Churchill and the British military chiefs for not beating the Russians to Berlin, as he easily could have done, Eisenhower and his staff at SHAEF were obsessed at this moment with the urgency of heading southeast after the junction with the Russians in order to capture the so-called National Redoubt, where it was believed Hitler was gathering his remaining forces to make a last stand in the almost impenetrable Alpine mountains of southern Bavaria and western Austria.

The "National Redoubt" was a phantom. It never existed except in the propaganda blasts of Dr. Goebbels and in the cautious minds at Eisenhower's headquarters which had fallen for them. As early as March 11, SHAEF intelligence had warned Eisenhower that the Nazis were planning to make an impregnable fortress in the mountains and that Hitler himself would command its defenses from his retreat at Berchtesgaden. The icy mountain crags were "practically impenetrable," it said.

Here [it continued], defended by nature and by the most efficient secret weapons yet invented, the powers that have hitherto guided Germany will survive to reorganize her resurrection; here armaments will be manufactured in bombproof factories, food and equipment will be stored in vast underground caverns and a specially selected corps of young men will be trained in guerrilla warfare, so that a whole underground army can be fitted and directed to liberate Germany from the occupying forces.[24]

It would almost seem as though the Allied Supreme Commander's intelligence staff had been infiltrated by British and American mystery writers. At any rate, this fantastic appreciation was taken seriously at SHAEF, where Eisenhower's chief of staff, General Bedell Smith, mulled over the dread possibility "of a prolonged campaign in the Alpine area" which would take a heavy toll of American lives and prolong the war indefinitely.*

This was the last time that the resourceful Dr. Goebbels succeeded in influencing the strategic course of the war by propaganda bluff. For though Adolf Hitler at first considered retiring to the Austro–Bavarian mountains near which he was born and in which he had spent most of the private hours of his life, and which he loved and where he had the only home he could call his own—on the Obersalzberg above Berchtesgaden—and there make a last stand, he had hesitated until it was too late.

On April 16, the day American troops reached Nuremberg, the city of the great Nazi Party rallies, Zhukov's Russian armies broke loose from their bridgeheads over the Oder, and on the afternoon of April 21 they reached the outskirts of Berlin. Vienna had already fallen on April 13. At 4:40 on the afternoon of April 25, patrols of the U.S. 69th Infantry Division met forward elements of the Russian 58th Guards Division at Torgau on the Elbe, some seventy-five miles south of Berlin. North and South Germany were severed. Adolf Hitler was cut off in Berlin. The last days of the Third Reich had come.

---

* "Not until after the campaign ended," General Omar Bradley later wrote, "were we to learn that this Redoubt existed largely in the imaginations of a few fanatic Nazis. It grew into so exaggerated a scheme that I am astonished we could have believed it as innocently as we did. But while it persisted, this legend of the Redoubt was too ominous a threat to ignore and in consequence it shaped our tactical thinking during the closing weeks of the war." (Bradley, *A Soldier's Story*, p. 536.)

"A great deal has been written about the Alpine Fortress," Field Marshal Kesselring commented wryly after the war, "mostly nonsense." (Kesselring, *A Soldier's Record*, p. 276.)

31

GOETTERDAEMMERUNG: THE LAST DAYS

OF THE THIRD REICH

HITLER HAD PLANNED to leave Berlin on April 20, his fifty-sixth birthday, for Obersalzberg and there direct the last stand of the Third Reich in the legendary mountain fastness of Barbarossa. Most of the ministerial offices had already moved south with their trucks full of state papers and of frantic officials desperate to get out of doomed Berlin. The Fuehrer himself had sent most of the members of his household staff to Berchtesgaden ten days before to prepare his mountain villa, the Berghof, for his coming.

He was destined, however, never to see his beloved Alpine retreat again. The end was approaching faster than he had thought possible. The Americans and Russians were driving swiftly to a junction on the Elbe. The British were at the gates of Hamburg and Bremen and threatening to cut off Germany from occupied Denmark. In Italy Bologna had fallen and Alexander's Allied forces were plunging into the valley of the Po. The Russians, having captured Vienna on April 13, were heading up the Danube, and the U.S. Third Army was sweeping down that river to meet them in Hitler's home town of Linz in Austria. Nuremberg, where work had been going on throughout the war on the great auditorium and stadiums which were to mark the ancient town as the capital of the Nazi Party, was besieged and part of the U.S. Seventh Army was sweeping past it toward Munich, the birthplace of the Nazi movement. In Berlin the thunder of Russian heavy artillery could be heard.

"All through the week," Count Schwerin von Krosigk, the puerile Minister of Finance and former Rhodes scholar, who had scooted out of Berlin for the north at the first word of the approaching Bolsheviki, noted in his diary on April 23, "there was nothing but a succession of Job's messengers. Our people seem to be faced with the darkest fate."[1]

Hitler had left his headquarters in Rastenburg in East Prussia for the last time on the previous November 20, as the Russians approached, and had remained in Berlin, which he had scarcely seen since the beginning of the war in the East, until December 10, when he had gone to his Western headquarters at Ziegenberg near Bad Nauheim to direct the great gamble in the Ardennes. After its failure he had returned on January 16 to Berlin, where he was to remain until the end, directing his crumbling armies from the underground bunker fifty feet below the Chancellery, whose great marble halls were now in ruins from Allied bombing.

Physically he was fast deteriorating. A young Army captain who saw him for the first time in February later recalled his appearance.

His head was slightly wobbling. His left arm hung slackly and his hand trembled a good deal. There was an indescribable flickering glow in his eyes, creating a fearsome and wholly unnatural effect. His face and the parts around his eyes gave the impression of total exhaustion. All his movements were those of a senile man.[2]

Since the July 20 attempt on his life he had grown distrustful of everyone, even of his old party stalwarts. "I am lied to on all sides," he fumed to one of his women secretaries in March.

I can rely on no one. They all betray me. The whole business makes me sick . . . If anything happens to me, Germany will be left without a leader. I have no successor. Hess is mad, Goering has lost the sympathy of the people, and Himmler would be rejected by the Party—besides, he [Himmler] is so completely inartistic . . . Rack your brains and tell me who my successor is to be . . .[3]

One would have thought that at this stage of history the question of succession was academic, but it was not—not in this Nazi cuckoo land. Not only the Fuehrer was obsessed by it but the leading candidates to succeed him, as we shall shortly see.

Physical wreck though Hitler now was, with a disastrous end staring him in the face as the Russians approached Berlin and the Western Allies overran the Reich, he and a few of his most fanatical followers, Goebbels above all, clung stubbornly to their hopes of being saved at the last minute by a miracle.

One fine evening early in April Goebbels had sat up reading to Hitler from one of the Fuehrer's favorite books, Carlyle's *History of Frederick the Great*. The chapter he was reading told of the darkest days of the Seven Years' War, when the great King felt himself at the end of his rope and told his ministers that if by February 15 no change for the better in his fortunes occurred he would give up and take poison. This portion of history certainly had its appropriateness and no doubt Goebbels read it in his most dramatic fashion.

"Brave King! [Goebbels read on] Wait yet a little while, and the days of your suffering will be over. Already the sun of your good fortune stands behind the clouds and soon will rise upon you." On February 12 the Czarina died, the Miracle of the House of Brandenburg had come to pass.

The Fuehrer's eyes, Goebbels told Krosigk, to whose diary we owe this touching scene, "were filled with tears."[4]

With such encouragement—and from a British source—they sent for two horoscopes, which were kept in the files of one of Himmler's multitudinous "research" offices. One was the horoscope of the Fuehrer drawn up on January 30, 1933, the day he took office; the other was the horoscope of the Weimar Republic, composed by some unknown astrologer on November 9, 1918, the day of the Republic's birth. Goebbels communicated the results of the re-examination of these two remarkable documents to Krosigk.

An amazing fact has become evident, both horoscopes predicting the outbreak of the war in 1939, the victories until 1941, and the subsequent series of reversals, with the hardest blows during the first months of 1945, particularly during the first half of April. In the second half of April we were to experience a temporary success. Then there would be stagnation until August and peace that same month. For the following three years Germany would have a hard time, but starting in 1948 she would rise again.[5]

Fortified by Carlyle and the "amazing" predictions of the stars, Goebbels on April 6 issued a ringing appeal to the retreating troops:

The Fuehrer has declared that even in this very year a change of fortune shall come . . . The true quality of genius is its consciousness and its sure knowledge of coming change. The Fuehrer knows the exact hour of its arrival. Destiny has sent us this man so that we, in this time of great external and internal stress, shall testify to the miracle . . .[6]

Scarcely a week later, on the night of April 12, Goebbels convinced himself that "the exact hour" of the miracle had come. It had been a day of further bad news. The Americans had appeared on the Dessau–Berlin autobahn and the High Command had hastily ordered the destruction of its last two remaining powder factories, which were in the vicinity. Henceforth the German soldiers would have to get along with the ammunition at hand. Goebbels had spent the day at the headquarters of General Busse on the Oder front at Kuestrin. The General had assured him that a Russian breakthrough was impossible, that (as Goebbels the next day told Krosigk) he was "holding out until the British kick us in the ass."

In the evening [Goebbels recounted] they had sat together at headquarters and he had developed his thesis that according to historical logic and justice things were bound to change, just as in the Seven Years' War there had been the miracle of the House of Brandenburg.

"What Czarina will die this time?" an officer asked.

Goebbels did not know. But fate, he replied, "holds all sorts of possibilities."

When the Propaganda Minister got back to Berlin late that night the center of the capital was in flames from another R.A.F. bombing. The remains of the Chancellery and the Adlon Hotel up the Wilhelmstrasse were burning. At the steps of the Propaganda Ministry, a secretary greeted Goebbels with a piece of urgent news. "Roosevelt," he said, "is dead!"

The Minister's face lit up, visible to all in the light of the flames from the Chancellery across the Wilhelmsplatz.

"Bring out our best champagne!" Goebbels cried. "And get me the Fuehrer on the telephone!"

Hitler was in his deep bunker across the way sitting out the bombing. He picked up the telephone.

"My Fuehrer," Goebbels said. "I congratulate you! Roosevelt is dead! It is written in the stars that the second half of April will be the turning point for us. This is Friday, April the thirteenth. [It was already after midnight.] It is the turning point!"

Hitler's reaction to the news was not recorded, though it may be imagined in view of the encouragement he had been receiving from Carlyle and the stars. But that of Goebbels was. "He was," says his secretary, "in ecstasy."[7]

The fatuous Count Schwerin von Krosigk too. When Goebbels' State Secretary phoned him that Roosevelt was dead he exclaimed—at least in his faithful diary:

This was the Angel of History! We felt its wings flutter through the room. Was that not the turn of fortune we awaited so anxiously?

The next morning Krosigk telephoned Goebbels with *his* "congratulations"—he affirms it proudly in his diary—and, as if this were not enough, followed it with a letter in which he hailed Roosevelt's death, he says, as "a divine judgment . . . a gift from God."

In this atmosphere of a lunatic asylum, with cabinet ministers long in power and educated in Europe's ancient universities, as Krosigk and Goebbels were, grasping at the readings of the stars and rejoicing amidst the flames of the burning capital in the death of the American President as a sure sign that the Almighty would now rescue the Third Reich at the eleventh hour from impending catastrophe, the last act in Berlin was played out to its final curtain.

Eva Braun had arrived in Berlin to join Hitler on April 15. Very few Germans knew of her existence and even fewer of her relationship to

Adolf Hitler. For more than twelve years she had been his mistress. Now in April she had come, as Trevor-Roper says, for her wedding and her ceremonial death.

She is interesting for her role in the last chapter of this narrative but not interesting in herself; she was not a Pompadour or a Lola Montez.* Hitler, although he was undoubtedly extremely fond of her and found relaxation in her unobtrusive company, had always kept her out of sight, refusing to allow her to come to his various headquarters, where he spent almost all of his time during the war years, and rarely permitting her even to come to Berlin. She remained immured at the Berghof on the Obersalzberg, passing her time in swimming and skiing, in reading cheap novels and seeing trashy films, in dancing (which Hitler disapproved of) and endlessly grooming herself, pining away for her absent loved one.

"She was," says Erich Kempka, the Fuehrer's chauffeur, "the unhappiest woman in Germany. She spent most of her life waiting for Hitler."[8]

Field Marshal Keitel described her appearance during an interrogation at Nuremberg.

She was very slender, elegant appearance, quite nice legs—one could see that—reticent and retiring and a very, very nice person, dark blond. She stood very much in the background and one saw her very rarely.[9]

The daughter of lower-middle-class Bavarian parents, who at first strenuously opposed her illicit relation with Hitler, even though he was the dictator, she had been employed in the Munich photograph shop of Heinrich Hoffmann, who introduced her to the Fuehrer. This was a year or two after the suicide of Geli Raubal, the niece of Hitler, for whom, as we have seen, he had the one great passionate love of his life. Eva Braun too, it seems, was often driven to despair by her lover, though not for the same reasons as Geli Raubal. Eva, though installed in a suite in Hitler's Alpine villa, couldn't endure the long separations when he was away and twice tried to kill herself in the early years of their friendship. But gradually she accepted her frustrating and ambiguous role—acknowledged neither as wife nor as mistress—content to be sole woman companion of the great man and making the most of their rare moments together.

She was now determined to share his end. Like Dr. and Frau Goebbels, she had no desire to live in a Germany without Adolf Hitler. "It would not be fit to live in for a true German," she told Hanna Reitsch, the famed German woman test pilot, in the shelter just before the end.[10] Though Eva Braun had a birdlike mind and made no intellectual impression on Hitler at all—perhaps this is one reason he preferred her company to that of intelligent women—it is obvious that his influence on her, as on so many others, was total.

---

* "For all writers of history," Speer told Trevor-Roper, "Eva Braun is going to be a disappointment," to which the historian adds: "—and for readers of history too." (Trevor-Roper, *The Last Days of Hitler*, p. 92.)

HITLER'S LAST GREAT DECISION

Hitler's birthday on April 20 passed quietly enough, although, as General Karl Koller, the Air Force Chief of Staff, who was present at the celebration in the bunker, noted in his diary, it was a day of further catastrophes on the rapidly disintegrating fronts. All the Old Guard Nazis, Goering, Goebbels, Himmler, Ribbentrop and Bormann, were there, as well as the surviving military leaders, Doenitz, Keitel, Jodl and Krebs—the last-named the new, and last, Chief of the Army General Staff. They offered the Fuehrer birthday congratulations.

The warlord was not unusually cast down, despite the situation. He was still confident, as he had told his generals three days before, that "the Russians were going to suffer their bloodiest defeat of all before Berlin." The generals knew better, and at the regular military conference after the birthday party they urged Hitler to leave Berlin for the south. In a day or two, they explained, the Russians would cut off the last escape corridor in that direction. Hitler hesitated; he would not say yes or no. Apparently he could not quite face the appalling fact that the capital of the Third Reich was now about to be captured by the Russians, whose armies, he had announced years before, were as good as destroyed. As a concession to the generals he consented to setting up two separate commands in case the Americans and Russians made their junction on the Elbe. Admiral Doenitz would head that in the north and perhaps Kesselring the one in the south—he was not quite sure about the latter appointment.

That night there was a general getaway from Berlin. Two of the Fuehrer's most trusted and veteran aides got out: Himmler and Goering, the latter in a motor caravan whose trucks were filled with booty from his fabulous estate, Karinhall. Each of these Old Guard Nazis left convinced that his beloved Leader would soon be dead and that he would succeed him.

They never saw him again. Nor did Ribbentrop, who also scurried for safer parts late that night.

But Hitler had not yet given up. On the day after his birthday he ordered an all-out counterattack on the Russians in the southern suburbs of Berlin by S.S. General Felix Steiner. Every available soldier in the Berlin area was to be thrown into the attack, including the Luftwaffe ground troops.

"Any commander who holds back his forces," Hitler shouted to General Koller, who had remained behind to represent the Air Force, "will forfeit his life in five hours. You yourself will guarantee with your head that the last man is thrown in."[11]

All through the day and far into the next Hitler waited impatiently for the news of Steiner's counterattack. It was a further example of his loss of contact with reality. There was no Steiner attack. It was never attempted. It existed only in the feverish mind of the desperate dictator. When he was finally forced to recognize this the storm broke.

April 22 brought the last turning point in Hitler's road to ruin. From early morning until 3 P.M. he had been on the telephone, as he had been the day before, trying to find out from the various command posts how the Steiner counterattack was going. No one knew. General Koller's planes could not locate it, nor could the ground commanders, though it was supposed to be rolling only two or three miles south of the capital. Not even Steiner, though he existed, could be found, let alone his army.

The blowup came at the daily military conference in the bunker at 3 P.M. Hitler angrily demanded news of Steiner. Neither Keitel nor Jodl nor anyone else had any. But the generals had other news. The withdrawal of troops from the north of Berlin to support Steiner had so weakened the front there that the Russians had broken through and their tanks were now within the city limits.

This was too much for the Supreme Warlord. All the surviving witnesses testify that he completely lost control of himself. He flew into the greatest rage of his life. This was the end, he shrieked. Everyone had deserted him. There was nothing but treason, lies, corruption and cowardice. All was over. Very well, he would stay on in Berlin. He would personally take over the defense of the capital of the Third Reich. The others could leave, if they wished. In this place he would meet his end.

The others protested. There was still hope, they said, if the Fuehrer retired to the south, where Field Marshal Ferdinand Schoerner's army group in Czechoslovakia and considerable forces of Kesselring were still intact. Doenitz, who had left for the northwest to take over command of the troops there, and Himmler, who, as we shall see, was up to his own game, telephoned to urge the Leader not to remain in Berlin. Even Ribbentrop called up to say he was about to spring a "diplomatic coup" which would save everything. But Hitler had no more faith in them, not even in his "second Bismarck," as he once, in a moment of folly, had called his Foreign Minister. He had made his decision, he said to all. And to show them that it was irrevocable, he called for a secretary and in their presence dictated an announcement that was to be read immediately over the radio. The Fuehrer, it said, would stay in Berlin and defend it to the end.

Hitler then sent for Goebbels and invited him, his wife and their six young children to move into the *Fuehrerbunker* from their badly bombed house in the Wilhelmstrasse garden. He knew that at least this fanatical and faithful follower, and his family, would stick by him to the end. Next Hitler turned to his papers, sorted out those he wished to be destroyed, and turned them over to one of his adjutants, Julius Schaub, who took them up to the garden and burned them.

Finally that evening he called in Keitel and Jodl and ordered them to proceed south to take over direct command of the remaining armed forces. Both generals, who had been at Hitler's side throughout the war, have left vivid accounts of their final parting with the Supreme Warlord.[12]

When Keitel protested that he would not leave without the Fuehrer, Hitler answered, "You will follow my orders." Keitel, who had never

disobeyed an order from the Leader in his life, not even those commanding him to commit the vilest war crimes, said nothing further, but Jodl, less
a lackey, did. To this soldier, who, despite his fanatical devotion to the
Fuehrer whom he had served so well, still retained some sense of military
tradition, the Supreme Warlord was deserting the command of his troops
and shirking his responsibility for them at a moment of disaster.

"You can't direct anything from here," Jodl said. "If you don't have
your Leadership Staff with you how can you lead anything?"

"Well, then," Hitler retorted, "Goering can take over the leadership
down there."

When one of them pointed out that no soldier would fight for the Reich
Marshal, Hitler cut in. "What do you mean, fight? There's precious little
more fighting to be done!" Even for the mad conqueror the scales at last
were falling from the eyes. Or, at least, the gods were giving him moments
of lucidity in these last nightmarish days of his life.

There were several repercussions to Hitler's outbursts on April 22 and
to his final decision to remain in Berlin. When Himmler, who was at
Hohenlychen, northwest of Berlin, received a firsthand account on the
telephone from Hermann Fegelein, his S.S. liaison officer at headquarters,
he exclaimed to his entourage, "Everyone is mad in Berlin! What am I to
do?"

"You go straight to Berlin," replied one of Himmler's principal aides,
Obergruppenfuehrer Gottlob Berger, the chief of the S.S. head office.
Berger was one of those simple Germans who sincerely believed in National
Socialism. He had no idea that his revered chief, Himmler, under the prod-
ding of S.S. General Walter Schellenberg, was already in touch with Count
Folke Bernadotte of Sweden about surrendering the German armies in the
West. "I am going to Berlin," Berger said to Himmler, "and it is your duty
to go too."

Berger, but not Himmler, went to Berlin that night and his visit is of
interest because of his firsthand description of Hitler on the night of his
great decision. Russian shells were already bursting near the Chancellery
when Berger arrived. To his shock he found the Fuehrer "a broken man—
finished." When he ventured to express his appreciation of Hitler's resolve
to remain in Berlin—"one couldn't desert the people after they had held
out so loyally and long," he says he declared—the very words touched off
the Leader again.

All this time [Berger later recounted] the Fuehrer had never uttered a word;
then suddenly he shrieked: "Everyone has deceived me! No one has told me
the truth! The Armed Forces have lied to me!" . . . He went on and on in
a loud voice. Then his face went bluish purple. I thought he was going to
have a stroke any minute . . .

Berger was also the head of Himmler's Prisoner-of-War Administration,
and after the Fuehrer had calmed down they discussed the fate of a group
of prominent British, French and American prisoners as well as of such

Germans as Halder and Schacht and the former Austrian Chancellor, Schuschnigg, who were being moved southeast to keep them out of the hands of the Americans advancing through Germany. Berger was flying to Bavaria that night to take charge of them. The two men also talked of reports that there had been outbreaks of separatism in Austria and Bavaria. The idea that revolt could break out in his native Austria and in his adopted Bavaria once more convulsed Hitler.

His hand was shaking, his leg was shaking and his head was shaking; and all that he kept saying [Berger reported] was: "Shoot them all! Shoot them all!"[13]

Whether this was an order to shoot all the separatists or all the distinguished prisoners, or both, was not clear to Berger, but apparently to this simple man it meant the whole lot.

GOERING AND HIMMLER TRY TO TAKE OVER

General Koller had stayed away from the Fuehrer's military conference on April 22. He had the Luftwaffe to look after, and "besides," he says in his diary, "I should never have been able to tolerate being insulted all day long."

General Eckard Christian, his liaison officer at the bunker, had rung him up at 6:15 P.M. and in a breathless voice had said, "Historical events, the most decisive of the war, are taking place here!" A couple of hours later Christian arrived at Air Force headquarters at Wildpark-Werder on the outskirts of Berlin to report to Koller in person. "The Fuehrer has broken down!" Christian, an ardent Nazi who had married one of Hitler's secretaries, gasped, but beyond saying that the Leader had decided to meet his end in Berlin and was burning his papers, he was so incoherent that the Luftwaffe Chief of Staff set out, despite a heavy British bombing that had just begun, to find General Jodl and ascertain just what had happened that day in the bunker.

At Krampnitz, between Berlin and Potsdam, where the now Fuehrerless OKW had set up temporary headquarters, he found him, and Jodl told his Air Force friend the whole sad story. He also revealed something which no one else had yet mentioned to Koller and which was to lead to a certain denouement during the next few frantic days.

"When it comes to negotiating [for peace]," Hitler had told Keitel and Jodl, "Goering can do better than I. Goering is much better at those things. He can deal much better with the other side." Jodl now repeated this to Koller.[14]

The Air Force General felt that it was his duty to immediately fly to Goering. It would be difficult and also dangerous, in view of the enemy's monitoring, to try to explain this new development in a radio message. If Goering, who had been officially named by Hitler years before as his successor-designate, were to take over peace negotiations, as the Fuehrer had suggested, there was no time to lose. Jodl agreed. At 3:30 on the morning of April 23 Koller took off in a fighter plane and sped toward Munich.

At noon he arrived on the Obersalzberg and delivered his news to the Reich Marshal. Goering, who had been looking forward, to put it mildly, to the day when he might succeed Hitler, was more circumspect than might have been expected. He did not want to lay himself open, he said, to the machinations of his "deadly enemy," Bormann, a precaution which, as it turned out, was well founded. He perspired under his dilemma. "If I act now," he told his advisers, "I may be stamped as a traitor; if I don't act, I'll be accused of having failed to do something in the hour of disaster."

Goering sent for Hans Lammers, the State Secretary of the Reich Chancellery, who was in Berchtesgaden, for legal advice and also fetched from his safe a copy of the Fuehrer's decree of June 29, 1941. The decree was quite clear. It stipulated that if Hitler died Goering was to be his successor and that if the Fuehrer were incapacitated Goering was to act as his deputy. All agreed that by remaining in Berlin to die, cut off in his last hours from both the military commands and the government offices, Hitler was incapacitated from governing and that it was Goering's clear duty under the decree to take over.

Nevertheless the Reich Marshal drafted his telegram to Hitler with great care. He wanted to make sure of the delegation of authority.

My Fuehrer!

In view of your decision to remain in the fortress of Berlin, do you agree that I take over at once the total leadership of the Reich, with full freedom of action at home and abroad as your deputy, in accordance with your decree of June 29, 1941? If no reply is received by 10 o'clock tonight, I shall take it for granted that you have lost your freedom of action, and shall consider the conditions of your decree as fulfilled, and shall act for the best interests of our country and our people. You know what I feel for you in this gravest hour of my life. Words fail me to express myself. May God protect you, and speed you quickly here in spite of all.

Your loyal
Hermann Goering

That very evening several hundred miles away Heinrich Himmler was meeting with Count Bernadotte in the Swedish consulate at Luebeck on the Baltic. *Der treue Heinrich*—the loyal Heinrich, as Hitler had often fondly referred to him—was not asking for the powers of succession; he was already assuming them.

"The Fuehrer's great life," he told the Swedish count, "is drawing to a close." In a day or two, he said, Hitler would be dead. Whereupon Himmler urged Bernadotte to communicate to General Eisenhower immediately Germany's willingness to surrender to the West. In the East, Himmler added, the war would be continued until the Western Powers themselves had taken over the front against the Russians—such was the naïveté, or stupidity, or both, of this S.S. chieftain who now claimed for himself the dictatorship of the Third Reich. When Bernadotte asked that Himmler put in writing his offer to surrender, a letter was hastily drafted by candlelight—for an R.A.F. bombing that night had shut off the electricity in Luebeck and driven the conferees to the cellar. Himmler signed it.[15]

Both Goering and Himmler had acted prematurely, as they quickly found out. Although Hitler was cut off from all but a scanty radio communication with his armies and his ministries—for the Russians had nearly completed their encirclement of the capital by the evening of the twenty-third—he was now to demonstrate that he could rule Germany by the power of his personality and prestige alone and quell "treason," even by the most eminent of his followers, by a mere word over his creaky wireless transmitter suspended from a balloon above the bunker.

Albert Speer and a remarkable lady witness whose dramatic appearance in the last act of the drama in Berlin will shortly be noted have described Hitler's reaction to Goering's telegram. Speer had flown into the besieged capital on the night of April 23, landing in a cub plane on the eastern end of the East–West Axis—the broad avenue which led through the Tiergarten—at the Brandenburg Gate, a block from the Chancellery. Having learned that Hitler had decided to remain in Berlin to the end, which could not be far off, Speer had come to say his farewell to the Leader and to confess to him that his "conflict between personal loyalty and public duty," as he puts it, had forced him to sabotage the Fuehrer's scorched-earth policy. He fully expected to be arrested for "treason" and probably shot, and no doubt he would have been had the dictator known of Speer's effort two months before to kill him and all the others who had escaped Stauffenberg's bomb.

The brilliant architect and Armament Minister, though he had always prided himself on being apolitical, had had, like some other Germans, a late—a too late—awakening. When he had finally realized that his beloved Fuehrer was determined through his scorched-earth decrees to destroy the German people he had decided to murder him. His plan was to introduce poison gas into the ventilation system in the bunker in Berlin during a full-dress military conference. Since not only the generals but invariably Goering, Himmler and Goebbels now attended these, Speer hoped to wipe out the entire Nazi leadership of the Third Reich as well as the High Command. He procured his gas, inspected the air-conditioning system and then discovered, he says, that the air-intake pipe in the garden was protected by a twelve-foot-high chimney, recently installed on Hitler's personal orders to discourage sabotage, and that it would be impossible to inject his gas into it without being interrupted by the S.S. guards in the garden. So he abandoned his project and Hitler once again escaped assassination.

Now on the evening of April 23 Speer made a full confession of his insubordination in refusing to carry out the wanton destruction of Germany's remaining installations. To his surprise Hitler showed no resentment or anger. Perhaps the Fuehrer was touched by the candor and courage of his young friend—Speer had just turned forty—for whom he had long had a deep affection and whom he regarded as a "fellow artist." Hitler, as Keitel also noted, seemed strangely serene that evening, as though having made up his mind to die in this place within a few days had brought a peace of mind and spirit. But it was the calm not only after the storm—of the previous day—but before the storm.

For Goering's telegram had meanwhile arrived in the Chancellery and after being held up by Bormann, who saw his opportunity at last, was presented to the Fuehrer by this master of intrigue as an "ultimatum" and as a treasonous attempt to "usurp" the Leader's power.

"Hitler was highly enraged," says Speer, "and expressed himself very strongly about Goering. He said he had known for some time that Goering had failed, that he was corrupt and a drug addict"—a statement which "extremely shook" the young architect, since he wondered why Hitler had employed such a man in so high a post so long. Speer was also puzzled when Hitler calmed down and added, "Well, let Goering negotiate the capitulation all the same. It doesn't matter anyway who does it."[16] But this mood lasted only a few moments.

Before the discussion was finished, Hitler, prompted by Bormann, dictated a telegram informing Goering that he had committed "high treason," for which the penalty was death, but that because of his long service to the Nazi Party and State his life would be spared if he immediately resigned all his offices. He was ordered to answer with one word: Yes or No. This did not satisfy the wormlike Bormann. On his own hook he got off a radiogram to the S.S. headquarters in Berchtesgaden ordering the immediate arrest of Goering, his staff and Lammers for "high treason." Before dawn the next day the Number Two man of the Third Reich, the most arrogant—and opulent—of the Nazi princes, the only Reich Marshal in German history and the Commander in Chief of the Air Force, found himself a prisoner of the S.S.

Three days later, on the evening of April 26, Hitler expressed himself even more strongly on the subject of Goering than he had in the presence of Speer.

THE LAST TWO VISITORS TO THE BUNKER

Two more interesting visitors had meanwhile arrived in the madhouse of the Fuehrer's bunker: Hanna Reitsch, the crack woman test pilot who, among other qualities, had a capacity for monumental hatred, especially of Goering, and General Ritter von Greim, who on April 24 had been summoned from Munich to appear personally before the Supreme Warlord and had done so, though the plane in which he and Reitsch flew the last lap on the evening of the twenty-sixth had been torn over the Tiergarten by Russian antiaircraft shells and Greim's foot had been shattered.

Hitler came into the surgery, where a physician was dressing the general's wound.

HITLER: Do you know why I have called you?

GREIM: No, my Fuehrer.

HITLER: Because Hermann Goering has betrayed and deserted both me and his Fatherland. Behind my back he has established contact with the enemy. His action was a mark of cowardice. Against my orders he has gone to save himself at Berchtesgaden. From there he sent me a disrespectful telegram. It was . . .

At this point, says Hanna Reitsch, who was present, the Fuehrer's face began to twitch and his breath came in explosive puffs.

HITLER: . . . an ultimatum! A crass ultimatum! Now nothing remains. Nothing is spared me. No allegiances are kept, no honor lived up to, no disappointments that I have not had, no betrayals that I have not experienced, and now this above all else! Nothing remains. Every wrong has already been done me.

I immediately had Goering arrested as a traitor to the Reich, took from him all his offices, and removed him from all organizations. That is why I have called you.[17]

Then and there he named the startled General lying wounded on his cot the new Commander in Chief of the Luftwaffe—a promotion he could have made by radio, which would have spared Greim a crippled foot and left him at headquarters, the only place from which what was left of the Air Force could be directed. Three days later Hitler ordered Greim, who by now, like Fräulein Reitsch, expected and indeed desired to die in the bunker at the side of the Leader, to depart in order to deal with a new case of "treachery." For "treason," as we have seen, was not confined among the leaders of the Third Reich to Hermann Goering.

During those three days Hanna Reitsch had ample opportunity to observe the lunatic life in the underground madhouse—indeed, she participated in it. Since she was as emotionally unstable as her distinguished host, the account she has left of it is lurid and melodramatic, and yet it is probably largely true and even fairly accurate, for it has been checked against other eyewitness reports, and is thus of importance for the closing chapter of this history.

Late on the night of her arrival with General von Greim—it was April 26—Russian shells began falling on the Chancellery and the thud of the explosions and the sound of crashing walls above increased the tension in the bunker. Hitler took the aviatrix aside.

"My Fuehrer, why do you stay?" she said. "Why do you deprive Germany of your life? . . . The Fuehrer must live so that Germany can live. The people demand it."

"No, Hanna," she says the Fuehrer replied. "If I die it is for the honor of our country, it is because as a soldier I must obey my own command that I would defend Berlin to the last."

My dear girl [he continued], I did not intend it so. I believed firmly that Berlin would be saved on the banks of the Oder . . . When our best efforts failed I was the most horror-struck of all. Then when the encirclement of the city began . . . I believed that by staying all the troops of the land would take example from my act and come to the rescue of the city . . . But, my Hanna, I still have hope. The army of General Wenck is moving up from the south. He must and will drive the Russians back long enough to save our people. Then we will fall back to hold again.[18]

That was one mood of Hitler that evening; he still had hope in General Wenck's relieving Berlin. But a few moments later, as the Russian bombardment of the Chancellery reached great intensity, he was in despair again. He handed Reitsch a vial of poison for herself and one for Greim. "Hanna," he said, "you belong to those who will die with me . . . I do not wish that one of us falls to the Russians alive, nor do I wish our bodies to be found by them . . . Eva and I will have our bodies burned. You will devise your own method."

Hanna took the vial of poison to Greim and they decided that "should the end really come" they would swallow the poison and then, to make sure, pull a pin from a heavy grenade and hold it tightly to their bodies.

A day and a half later, on the twenty-eighth, Hitler's hopes seem to have risen again—or at least his delusions. He radioed Keitel:

"I expect the relief of Berlin. What is Heinrici's army doing? Where is Wenck? What is happening to the Ninth Army? When will Wenck and Ninth Army join?"[19]

Reitsch describes the Supreme Warlord that day, striding

about the shelter, waving a road map that was fast disintegrating from the sweat of his hands and planning Wenck's campaign with anyone who happened to be listening.

But Wenck's "campaign," like the Steiner "attack" of a week before, existed only in the Fuehrer's imagination. Wenck's army had already been liquidated, as had the Ninth Army. Heinrici's army, to the north of Berlin, was beating a hasty retreat westward so that it might be captured by the Western Allies instead of by the Russians.

All through April 28 the desperate men in the bunker waited for news of the counterattacks of these three armies, especially that of Wenck. Russian spearheads were now but a few blocks from the Chancellery and advancing slowly toward it up several streets from the east and north and through the nearby Tiergarten from the west. When no news of the relieving forces came, Hitler, prompted by Bormann, began to expect new treacheries. At 8 P.M. Bormann got out a radiogram to Doenitz.

Instead of urging the troops forward to our rescue, the men in authority are silent. Treachery seems to have replaced loyalty! We remain here. The Chancellery is already in ruins.

Later that night Bormann sent another message to Doenitz.

Schoerner, Wenck and others must prove their loyalty to the Fuehrer by coming to the Fuehrer's aid as soon as possible.[20]

Bormann was now speaking for himself. Hitler had made up his mind to die in a day or two, but Bormann wanted to live. He might not succeed the Fuehrer but he wanted to continue to pull the strings behind the scenes for whoever did.

Finally, that night Admiral Voss got out a message to Doenitz saying that all radio connection with the Army had broken down and urgently requesting the Navy to send over the naval wave length some news of what was happening in the outside world. Very shortly some news came, not from the Navy but from the listening post in the Propaganda Ministry, and it was shattering for Adolf Hitler.

Besides Bormann there was another Nazi official in the bunker who wanted to live. This was Hermann Fegelein, Himmler's representative at court and typical of the type of German who rose to prominence under Hitler's rule. A former groom and then a jockey and quite illiterate, he was a protégé of the notorious Christian Weber, one of Hitler's oldest party cronies and himself a horse fancier, who by fraudulence had amassed a fortune and a great racing stable after 1933. Fegelein, with Weber's help, had climbed quite high in the Third Reich. He was a general in the Waffen S.S. and in 1944, shortly after being appointed Himmler's liaison officer at Fuehrer headquarters, he had further advanced his position at court by marrying Eva Braun's sister, Gretl. All the surviving S.S. chiefs agree that, in alliance with Bormann, Fegelein lost no time in betraying his own S.S. chief, Himmler, to Hitler. But disreputable, illiterate and ignorant though he was, Fegelein seems to have been possessed of a simon-pure instinct for survival. He knew a sinking ship when he saw one.

On April 26 he quietly left the bunker. By the next afternoon Hitler had noticed his disappearance. The Fuehrer's easily aroused suspicions were kindled and he sent out an armed S.S. search party to try to find the man. He was found, in civilian clothes, resting in his home in the Charlottenburg district, which the Russians were about to overrun. Brought back to the Chancellery, he was stripped of his S.S. rank of Obergruppenfuehrer and placed under arrest. Fegelein's attempt at desertion made Hitler immediately suspicious of Himmler. What was the S.S. chief up to, now that he had deliberately absented himself from Berlin? There had been no news since his liaison officer, Fegelein, had quit his post. It now came.

April 28, as we have seen, had been a trying day in the bunker. The Russians were getting close. The expected news of Wenck's counterattack, or of any counterattack, had not come through. Desperately the besieged had asked, through the Navy's radio, for news of developments outside the encircled city.

The radio listening post of the Propaganda Ministry had picked up from a broadcast of the BBC in London one piece of news of what was happening outside Berlin. It was a Reuter dispatch from Stockholm and it was so sensational, so incredible, that one of Goebbels' assistants, Heinz Lorenz, had scampered across the shell-torn square late on the evening of April 28 to the bunker with copies of it for his Minister and for the Fuehrer.

The dispatch, says Reitsch, struck "a deathblow to the entire assembly. Men and women alike screamed with rage, fear and desperation, all mixed into one emotional spasm." Hitler's spasm was the worst. "He raged," says the aviatrix, "like a madman."

Heinrich Himmler—*der treue Heinrich*—had also deserted the sinking ship of state. The Reuter dispatch told of his secret negotiations with Count Bernadotte and his offer to surrender the German armies in the West to Eisenhower.

To Hitler, who had never doubted Himmler's absolute loyalty, this was the heaviest blow of all. "His color," says Reitsch, "rose to a heated red and his face was virtually unrecognizable . . . After the lengthy outburst Hitler sank into a stupor and for a time the entire bunker was silent." Goering at least had asked the Leader's permission to take over. But the "*treue*" S.S. chief and Reichsfuehrer had not bothered to ask; he had treasonably contacted the enemy without saying a word. This, Hitler told his followers when he had somewhat recovered, was the worst act of treachery he had ever known.

This blow—coupled with the news received a few minutes later that the Russians were nearing the Potsdamerplatz, but a block away, and would probably storm the Chancellery on the morning of April 30, thirty hours hence—was the signal for the end. It forced Hitler to make immediately the last decisions of his life. By dawn he had married Eva Braun, drawn up his last will and testament, dispatched Greim and Hanna Reitsch to rally the Luftwaffe for an all-out bombing of the Russian forces approaching the Chancellery, and ordered them also to arrest Himmler as a traitor.

"A traitor must never succeed me as Fuehrer!" Hanna says he told them. "You must get out to insure that he will not."

Hitler could not wait to begin his revenge against Himmler. He had the S.S. chief's liaison man, Fegelein, in his hands. The former jockey and present S.S. General was now brought out of the guardhouse, closely questioned as to Himmler's "betrayal," accused of having been an accomplice in it, and on the Fuehrer's orders taken up to the Chancellery garden and shot. The fact that Fegelein was married to Eva Braun's sister did not help him. Eva made no effort to save her brother-in-law's life.

"Poor, poor Adolf," she whimpered to Hanna Reitsch, "deserted by everyone, betrayed by all. Better that ten thousand others die than that he be lost to Germany."

He was lost to Germany but in those final hours he was won by Eva Braun. Sometime between 1 A.M. and 3 A.M. on April 29, as a crowning award for her loyalty to the end, he accorded his mistress's wish and formally married her. He had always said that marriage would interfere with his complete dedication to leading first his party to power and then his nation to the heights. Now that there was no more leading to do and his life was at an end, he could safely enter into a marriage which could last only a few hours.

Goebbels rounded up a municipal councilor, one Walter Wagner, who was fighting in a unit of the Volkssturm not many blocks away, and this surprised official performed the ceremony in the small conference room of the bunker. The marriage document survives and gives part of the picture of what one of the Fuehrer's secretaries described as the "death marriage." Hitler asked that "in view of war developments the publication of the banns be done orally and all other delays be avoided." The bride- and groom-to-be swore they were "of complete Aryan descent" and had "no hereditary disease to exclude their marriage." On the eve of death the dictator insisted on sticking to form. Only in the spaces given to the name of his father (born Schicklgruber) and his mother and the date of their marriage did Hitler leave a blank. His bride started to sign her name "Eva Braun," but stopped, crossed out the "B" and wrote "Eva Hitler, born Braun." Goebbels and Bormann signed as witnesses.

After the brief ceremony there was a macabre wedding breakfast in the Fuehrer's private apartment. Champagne was brought out and even Fräulein Manzialy, Hitler's vegetarian cook, was invited, along with his secretaries, the remaining generals, Krebs and Burgdorf, Bormann and Dr. and Frau Goebbels, to share in the wedding celebration. For a time the talk gravitated to the good old times and the party comrades of better days. Hitler spoke fondly of the occasion on which he had been best man at the Goebbels wedding. As was his custom, even to the very last, the bridegroom talked on and on, reviewing the high points in his dramatic life. Now it was ended, he said, and so was National Socialism. It would be a release for him to die, since he had been betrayed by his oldest friends and supporters. The wedding party was plunged into gloom and some of the guests stole away in tears. Hitler finally slipped away himself. In an adjoining room he summoned one of his secretaries, Frau Gertrude Junge, and began to dictate his last will and testament.

HITLER'S LAST WILL AND TESTAMENT

These two documents survive, as Hitler meant them to, and like others of his papers they are significant to this narrative. They confirm that the man who had ruled over Germany with an iron hand for more than twelve years, and over most of Europe for four, had learned nothing from his experience; not even his reverses and shattering final failure had taught him anything. Indeed, in the last hours of his life he reverted to the young man he had been in the gutter days in Vienna and in the early rowdy beer hall period in Munich, cursing the Jews for all the ills of the world, spinning his half-baked theories about the universe, and whining that fate once more had cheated Germany of victory and conquest. In this valedictory to the German nation and to the world which was also meant to be a last, conclusive appeal to history, Adolf Hitler dredged up all the empty claptrap of *Mein Kampf* and added his final falsehoods. It was a fitting epitaph of a power-drunk tyrant whom absolute power had corrupted absolutely and destroyed.

The "Political Testament," as he called it, was divided into two parts, the first consisting of his appeal to posterity, the second of his specific directions for the future.

More than thirty years have passed since I made my modest contribution as a volunteer in the First World War, which was forced upon the Reich.

In these three decades, love and loyalty to my people alone have guided me in all my thoughts, actions and life. They gave me power to make the most difficult decisions which have ever confronted mortal man . . .

It is untrue that I or anybody else in Germany wanted war in 1939. It was wanted and provoked exclusively by those international statesmen who either were of Jewish origin or worked for Jewish interests.

I have made too many offers for the limitation and control of armaments, which posterity will not for all time be able to disregard, for responsibility for the outbreak of this war to be placed on me. Further, I have never wished that after the appalling First World War there should be a second one against either England or America. Centuries will go by, but from the ruins of our towns and monuments the hatred of those ultimately responsible will always grow anew. They are the people whom we have to thank for all this: international Jewry and its helpers.

Hitler then repeated the lie that three days before the attack on Poland he had proposed to the British government a reasonable solution of the Polish–German problem.

It was rejected only because the ruling clique in England wanted war, partly for commercial reasons, partly because it was influenced by propaganda put out by the international Jewry.

Next he placed "sole responsibility" not only for the millions of deaths suffered on the battlefields and in the bombed cities but for his own massacre of the Jews—on the Jews. Then he turned to the reasons for his decision to remain in Berlin to the last.

After six years of war, which in spite of all setbacks will one day go down in history as the most glorious and heroic manifestation of the struggle for existence of a nation, I cannot forsake the city that is the capital of this state . . . I wish to share my fate with that which millions of others have also taken upon themselves by staying in this town. Further, I shall not fall in the hands of the enemy, who requires a new spectacle, presented by the Jews, to divert their hysterical masses.

I have therefore decided to remain in Berlin and there to choose death voluntarily at that moment when I believe that the position of the Fuehrer and the Chancellery itself can no longer be maintained. I die with a joyful heart in my knowledge of the immeasurable deeds and achievements of our peasants and workers and of a contribution unique in history of our youth which bears my name.

There followed an exhortation to all Germans "not to give up the struggle." He had finally forced himself to recognize, though, that National Socialism was finished for the moment, but he assured his fellow Germans that from the sacrifices of the soldiers and of himself

the seed has been sown that will grow one day . . . to the glorious rebirth of the National Socialist movement of a truly united nation.

Hitler could not die without first hurling one last insult at the Army and especially at its officer corps, whom he held chiefly responsible for the disaster. Though he confessed that Nazism was dead, at least for the moment, he nevertheless adjured the commanders of the three armed services

to strengthen with every possible means the spirit of resistance of our soldiers in the National Socialist belief, with special emphasis on the fact that I myself, as the founder and creator of this movement, prefer death to cowardly resignation or even to capitulation.

Then the jibe at the Army officer caste:

May it be in the future a point of honor with the German Army officers, as it already is in our Navy, that the surrender of a district or town is out of the question and that, above everything else, the commanders must set a shining example of faithful devotion to duty unto death.

It was Hitler's insistence that "a district or town" must be held "unto death," as at Stalingrad, which had helped bring about military disaster. But in this, as in other things, he had learned nothing.

The second part of the Political Testament dealt with the question of succession. Though the Third Reich was going up in flames and explosions, Hitler could not bear to die without naming his successor and dictating the exact composition of the government which that successor must appoint. First he had to eliminate his would-be successors.

Before my death, I expel former Reich Marshal Hermann Goering from the party and withdraw from him all the rights that were conferred on him by the decree of June 20, 1941 . . . In his place I appoint Admiral Doenitz as President of the Reich and Supreme Commander of the Armed Forces.

Before my death, I expel the former Reichsfuehrer of the S.S. and the Minister of Interior Heinrich Himmler from the party and from all his state offices.

The leaders of the Army, the Air Force and the S.S., he believed, had betrayed him, had cheated him of victory. So his only possible choice of successor had to be the leader of the Navy, which had been too small to play a major role in Hitler's war of conquest. This was a final jibe at the Army, which had done most of the fighting and lost most of the men killed in the war. There was also a last parting denunciation of the two men who had been, with Goebbels, his most intimate collaborators since the early days of the party.

Apart altogether from their disloyalty to me, Goering and Himmler have brought irreparable shame on the whole nation by secretly negotiating with the enemy without my knowledge and against my will, and also by illegally attempting to seize control of the State.

Having expelled the traitors and named his successor, Hitler then proceeded to tell Doenitz whom he must have in his new government. They were all "honorable men," he said, "who will fulfill the task of continuing the war with all means." Goebbels was to be the Chancellor and Bormann the "Party Minister"—a new post. Seyss-Inquart, the Austrian quisling and, most recently, the butcher governor of Holland, was to be Foreign Minister. Speer, like Ribbentrop, was dropped. But Count Schwerin von Krosigk, who had been Minister of Finance continuously since his appointment by Papen in 1932, was to retain that post. This man was a fool, but it must be admitted that he had a genius for survival.

Hitler not only named his successor's government. He imparted one last typical directive to it.

Above all, I enjoin the government and the people to uphold the racial laws to the limit and to resist mercilessly the poisoner of all nations, international Jewry.[21]

With that the Supreme German Warlord was finished. The time was now 4 A.M. on Sunday, April 29. Hitler called in Goebbels, Bormann and Generals Krebs and Burgdorf to witness his signing of the document, and to affix their own signatures. He then quickly dictated his personal will. In this the Man of Destiny reverted to his lower-middle-class origins in Austria, explaining why he had married and why he and his bride were killing themselves, and disposing of his property, which he hoped would be enough to support his surviving relatives in a modest way. At least

Hitler had not used his power to amass a vast private fortune, as had Goering.

Although during the years of struggle I believed that I could not undertake the responsibility of marriage, now, before the end of my life, I have decided to take as my wife the woman who, after many years of true friendship, came to this city, already almost besieged, of her own free will in order to share my fate.

She will go to her death with me at her own wish as my wife. This will compensate us both for what we lost through my work in the service of my people.

My possessions, insofar as they are worth anything, belong to the party, or, if this no longer exists, to the State. If the State too is destroyed, there is no need for any further instructions on my part. The paintings in the collections bought by me during the years were never assembled for private purposes but solely for the establishment of a picture gallery in my home town of Linz on the Danube.

Bormann, as executor, was asked

to hand over to my relatives everything that is of value as a personal memento or is necessary for maintaining a petty-bourgeois [*kleinen buergerlichen*] standard of living . . .*

My wife and I choose to die in order to escape the shame of overthrow or capitulation. It is our wish that our bodies be burned immediately in the place where I have performed the greater part of my daily work during the twelve years of service to my people.

Exhausted by the dictation of his farewell messages, Hitler went to bed as dawn was breaking over Berlin on this last Sabbath of his life. A pall of smoke hung over the city. Buildings crashed in flames as the Russians fired their artillery at point-blank range. They were now not far from the Wilhelmstrasse and the Chancellery.

While Hitler slept, Goebbels and Bormann made haste. In his Political Testament, which they had signed as witnesses, the Fuehrer had specifically ordered them to leave the capital and join the new government. Bormann was more than willing to obey. For all his devotion to the Leader, he did not intend to share his death, if he could avoid it. The only thing in life he wanted was power behind the scenes, and Doenitz might still offer him this. That is, if Goering, on learning of the Fuehrer's death, did not try to usurp the throne. To make sure that he did not, Bormann now got out a radio message to the S.S. headquarters at Berchtesgaden.

---

* Who these relatives were Hitler did not say, but from what he told his secretaries he had in mind his sister, Paula, and his mother-in-law.

. . . If Berlin and we should fall, the traitors of April 23 must be exterminated. Men, do your duty! Your life and honor depend on it![22]

This was an order to murder Goering and his Air Force staff, whom Bormann had already placed under S.S. arrest.

Dr. Goebbels, like Eva Braun but unlike Bormann, had no desire to live in a Germany from which his revered Fuehrer had departed. He had hitched his star to Hitler, to whom alone he owed his sensational rise in life. He had been the chief prophet and propagandist of the Nazi movement. It was he who, next to Hitler, had created its myths. To perpetuate those myths not only the Leader but his most loyal follower, the only one of the Old Guard who had not betrayed him, must die a sacrificial death. He too must give an example that would be remembered down the ages and help one day to rekindle the fires of National Socialism.

Such seem to have been his thoughts when, after Hitler retired, Goebbels repaired to his little room in the bunker to write his own valedictory to present and future generations. He entitled it "Appendix to the Fuehrer's Political Testament."

The Fuehrer has ordered me to leave Berlin . . . and take part as a leading member in the government appointed by him.

For the first time in my life I must categorically refuse to obey an order of the Fuehrer. My wife and children join me in this refusal. Apart from the fact that feelings of humanity and personal loyalty forbid us to abandon the Fuehrer in his hour of greatest need, I would otherwise appear for the rest of my life as a dishonorable traitor and a common scoundrel and would lose my self-respect as well as the respect of my fellow citizens . . .

In the nightmare of treason which surrounds the Fuehrer in these most critical days of the war, there must be someone at least who will stay with him unconditionally until death . . .

I believe I am thereby doing the best service to the future of the German people. In the hard times to come, examples will be more important than men . . .

For this reason, together with my wife, and on behalf of my children, who are too young to be able to speak for themselves and who, if they were old enough, would unreservedly agree with this decision, I express my unalterable resolution not to leave the Reich capital, even if it falls, but rather, at the side of the Fuehrer, to end a life that for me personally will have no further value if I cannot spend it at the service of the Fuehrer and at his side.[23]

Dr. Goebbels finished writing his piece at half past five on the morning of April 29. Daylight was breaking over Berlin, but the sun was obscured by the smoke of battle. In the electric light of the bunker much remained to be done. The first consideration was how to get the Fuehrer's last will and testament out through the nearby Russian lines so that it could be delivered to Doenitz and others and preserved for posterity.

Three messengers were chosen to take copies of the precious documents out: Major Willi Johannmeier, Hitler's military adjutant; Wilhelm Zander, an S.S. officer and adviser to Bormann; and Heinz Lorenz, the Propaganda Ministry official who had brought the shattering news of Himmler's treachery the night before. Johannmeier, a much decorated officer, was to lead the party through the Red Army's lines. He himself was then to deliver his copy of the papers to Field Marshal Ferdinand Schoerner, whose army group still held out intact in the Bohemian mountains and whom Hitler had named as the new Commander in Chief of the Army. General Burgdorf enclosed a covering letter informing Schoerner that Hitler had written his Testament "today under the shattering news of Himmler's treachery. It is his unalterable decision." Zander and Lorenz were to take their copies to Doenitz. Zander was given a covering note from Bormann.

DEAR GRAND ADMIRAL:
Since all divisions have failed to arrive and our position seems hopeless, the Fuehrer dictated last night the attached political Testament. Heil Hitler.

The three messengers set out on their dangerous mission at noon, edging their way westward through the Tiergarten and Charlottenburg to Pichelsdorf at the head of the Havel lake, where a Hitler Youth battalion held the bridge in anticipation of the arrival of Wenck's ghost army. To get that far they had successfully slipped through three Russian rings; at the Victory Column in the middle of the Tiergarten, at the Zoo Station just beyond the park, and on the approaches to Pichelsdorf. They still had many other lines to penetrate, and much adventure lay ahead of them,* and though they eventually got through it was much too late for their messages to be of any use to Doenitz and Schoerner, who never saw them.

The three messengers were not the only persons to depart from the bunker that day. At noon on April 29, Hitler, who had now been restored to a period of calm, held his customary war conference to discuss the military situation, just as he had daily at this hour for nearly six years—and just as if the end of the road had not been reached. General Krebs reported that the Russians had advanced farther toward the Chancellery during the night and early morning. The supply of ammunition of the city's defenders, such as they were, was getting low. There was still no news from Wenck's rescue army. Three military adjutants, who now

---

* Trevor-Roper, in *The Last Days of Hitler*, has given a graphic account of their adventures. But for an indiscretion of Heinz Lorenz, the farewell messages of Hitler and Goebbels might never have become known. Major Johannmeier eventually buried his copy of the documents in the garden of his home at Iserlohn in Westphalia. Zander hid his copy in a trunk which he left in the Bavarian village of Tegernsee. Changing his name and assuming a disguise, he attempted to begin a new life under the name of Wilhelm Paustin. But Lorenz, a journalist by profession, was too garrulous to keep his secret very well and a chance indiscretion led to the discovery of his copy and to the exposure of the other two messengers.

found little to do and who did not want to join the Leader in self-inflicted death, asked if they could leave the bunker in order to try to find out what had happened to Wenck. Hitler granted them permission and instructed them to urge General Wenck to get a move on. During the afternoon the three officers left.

They were soon joined by a fourth, Colonel Nicolaus von Below, Hitler's Luftwaffe adjutant, who had been a junior member of the inner circle since the beginning of the war. Below too did not believe in suicide and felt that there was no longer any useful employment in the Chancellery shelter. He asked the permission of the Fuehrer to leave and it was granted. Hitler was being most reasonable this day. It also occurred to him that he could utilize the Air Force colonel to carry out one last message. This was to be to General Keitel, whom Bormann already suspected of treason, and it would contain the warlord's final blast at the Army, which, he felt, had let him down.

No doubt the news at the evening situation conference at 10 P.M. increased the Fuehrer's already monumental bitterness at the Army. General Weidling, who commanded the courageous but ragged overage Volkssturm and underage Hitler Youth troops being sacrificed in encircled Berlin to prolong Hitler's life a few days, reported that the Russians had pushed ahead along the Saarlandstrasse and the Wilhelmstrasse almost to the Air Ministry, which was only a stone's throw from the Chancellery. The enemy would reach the Chancellery, he said, by May 1 at the latest—in a day or two, that is.

This was the end. Even Hitler, who up until now had been directing nonexistent armies supposed to be coming to the relief of the capital, saw that—at last. He dictated his final message and asked Below to deliver it to Keitel. He informed his Chief of OKW that the defense of Berlin was now at an end, that he was killing himself rather than surrender, that Goering and Himmler had betrayed him, and that he had named Admiral Doenitz as his successor.

He had one last word to say about the armed forces which, despite his leadership, had brought Germany to defeat. The Navy, he said, had performed superbly. The Luftwaffe had fought bravely and only Goering was responsible for its losing its initial supremacy in the war. As for the Army, the common soldiers had fought well and courageously, but the generals had failed them—and him.

The people and the armed forces [he continued] have given their all in this long and hard struggle. The sacrifice has been enormous. But my trust has been misused by many people. Disloyalty and betrayal have undermined resistance throughout the war.

It was therefore not granted to me to lead the people to victory. The Army General Staff cannot be compared with the General Staff in the First World War. Its achievements were far behind those of the fighting front.

At least the Supreme Nazi Warlord was remaining true to character to the very end. The great victories had been due to him. The defeats and final failure had been due to others—to their "disloyalty and betrayal."

And then the parting valediction—the last recorded written words of this mad genius's life.

The efforts and sacrifices of the German people in this war have been so great that I cannot believe that they have been in vain. The aim must still be to win territory in the East for the German people.*

The last sentence was straight out of *Mein Kampf.* Hitler had begun his political life with the obsession that "territory in the East" must be won for the favored German people, and he was ending his life with it. All the millions of German dead, all the millions of German homes crushed under the bombs, even the destruction of the German nation had not convinced him that the robbing of the lands of the Slavic peoples to the East was— morals aside—a futile Teutonic dream.

THE DEATH OF HITLER AND HIS BRIDE

During the afternoon of April 29 one of the last pieces of news to reach the bunker from the outside world came in. Mussolini, Hitler's fellow fascist dictator and partner in aggression, had met his end and it had been shared by his mistress, Clara Petacci.

They had been caught by Italian partisans on April 27 while trying to escape from Como into Switzerland, and executed two days later. On the Saturday night of April 28 the bodies were brought to Milan in a truck and dumped on the piazza. The next day they were strung up by the heels from lampposts and later cut down so that throughout the rest of the Sabbath day they lay in the gutter, where vengeful Italians reviled them. On May Day Benito Mussolini was buried beside his mistress in the paupers' plot in the Cimitero Maggiore in Milan. In such a macabre climax of degradation Il Duce and Fascism passed into history.

It is not known how many of the details of the Duce's shabby end were communicated to the Fuehrer. One can only speculate that if he heard many of them he was only strengthened in his resolve not to allow himself or his bride to be made a "spectacle, presented by the Jews, to divert their hysterical masses,"—as he had just written in his Testament—not their live selves or their bodies.

Shortly after receiving the news of Mussolini's death Hitler began to make the final preparations for his. He had his favorite Alsatian dog, Blondi, poisoned and two other dogs in the household shot. Then he

---

* Colonel Below destroyed the message when he learned of Hitler's death while he was still making his way toward the Allied Western armies. He has reconstructed it from memory. See Trevor-Roper, *op. cit.,* pp. 194–95.

called in his two remaining women secretaries and handed them capsules of poison to use if they wished to when the barbarian Russians broke in. He was sorry, he said, not to be able to give them a better farewell gift, and he expressed his appreciation for their long and loyal service.

Evening had now come, the last of Adolf Hitler's life. He instructed Frau Junge, one of his secretaries, to destroy the remaining papers in his files and he sent out word that no one in the bunker was to go to bed until further orders. This was interpreted by all as meaning that he judged the time had come to make his farewells. But it was not until long after midnight, at about 2:30 A.M. of April 30, as several witnesses recall, that the Fuehrer emerged from his private quarters and appeared in the general dining passage, where some twenty persons, mostly the women members of his entourage, were assembled. He walked down the line shaking hands with each and mumbling a few words that were inaudible. There was a heavy film of moisture on his eyes and, as Frau Junge remembered, "they seemed to be looking far away, beyond the walls of the bunker."

After he retired, a curious thing happened. The tension which had been building up to an almost unendurable point in the bunker broke, and several persons went to the canteen—to dance. The weird party soon became so noisy that word was sent from the Fuehrer's quarters requesting more quiet. The Russians might come in a few hours and kill them all— though most of them were already thinking of how they could escape— but in the meantime for a brief spell, now that the Fuehrer's strict control of their lives was over, they would seek pleasure where and how they could find it. The sense of relief among these people seems to have been enormous and they danced on through the night.

Not Bormann. This murky man still had work to do. His own prospects for survival seemed to be diminishing. There might not be a long enough interval between the Fuehrer's death and the arrival of the Russians in which he could escape to Doenitz. If not, while the Fuehrer still lived and thus clothed his orders with authority, Bormann could at least exact further revenge on the "traitors." He dispatched during this last night a further message to Doenitz.

DOENITZ!

Our impression grows daily stronger that the divisions in the Berlin theater have been standing idle for several days. All the reports we receive are controlled, suppressed, or distorted by Keitel . . . The Fuehrer orders you to proceed at once, and mercilessly, against all traitors.

And then, though he knew that Hitler's death was only hours away, he added a postscript, "The Fuehrer is alive, and is conducting the defense of Berlin."

But Berlin was no longer defensible. The Russians already had occupied almost all of the city. It was now merely a question of the defense of the Chancellery. It too was doomed, as Hitler and Bormann learned at the situation conference at noon on April 30, the last that was ever to take place. The Russians had reached the eastern end of the Tiergarten and broken into the Potsdamerplatz. They were just a block away. The hour for Adolf Hitler to carry out his resolve had come.

His bride apparently had no appetite for lunch that day and Hitler took his repast with his two secretaries and with his vegetarian cook, who perhaps did not realize that she had prepared his last meal. While they were finishing their lunch at about 2:30 P.M., Erich Kempka, the Fuehrer's chauffeur, who was in charge of the Chancellery garage, received an order to deliver immediately 200 liters of gasoline in jerricans to the Chancellery garden. Kempka had some difficulty in rounding up so much fuel but he managed to collect some 180 liters and with the help of three men carried it to the emergency exit of the bunker.[24]

While the oil to provide the fire for the Viking funeral was being collected, Hitler, having done with his last meal, fetched Eva Braun for another and final farewell to his most intimate collaborators: Dr. Goebbels, Generals Krebs and Burgdorf, the secretaries and Fräulein Manzialy, the cook. Frau Goebbels did not appear. This formidable and beautiful blond woman had, like Eva Braun, found it easy to make the decision to die with her husband, but the prospect of killing her six young children, who had been playing merrily in the underground shelter these last days without an inkling of what was in store for them, unnerved her.

"My dear Hanna," she had said to Fräulein Reitsch two or three evenings before, "when the end comes you must help me if I become weak about the children . . . They belong to the Third Reich and to the Fuehrer, and if these two cease to exist there can be no further place for them. My greatest fear is that at the last moment I will be too weak." Alone in her little room she was now striving to overcome her greatest fear.*

Hitler and Eva Braun had no such problem. They had only their own lives to take. They finished their farewells and retired to their rooms. Outside in the passageway, Dr. Goebbels, Bormann and a few others waited. In a few moments a revolver shot was heard. They waited for a second one, but there was only silence. After a decent interval they quietly entered the Fuehrer's quarters. They found the body of Adolf Hitler sprawled on the sofa dripping blood. He had shot himself in the mouth. At his side lay Eva Braun. Two revolvers had tumbled to the floor, but the bride had not used hers. She had swallowed poison.

It was 3:30 P.M. on Monday, April 30, 1945, ten days after Adolf Hitler's fifty-sixth birthday, and twelve years and three months to a day since he had become Chancellor of Germany and had instituted the Third Reich. It would survive him but a week.

The Viking funeral followed. There were no words spoken; the only sound was the roar of Russian shells exploding in the garden of the Chan-

---

* The children and their ages were: Hela, 12; Hilda, 11; Helmut, 9; Holde, 7; Hedda, 5; Heide, 3.

cellery and on the shattered walls around it. Hitler's valet, S.S. Sturm-
bannfuehrer Heinz Linge, and an orderly carried out the Fuehrer's body,
wrapped in an Army field-gray blanket, which concealed the shattered
face. Kempka identified it in his own mind by the black trousers and
shoes which protruded from the blanket and which the warlord always
wore with his field-gray jacket. Eva Braun's death had been cleaner, there
was no blood, and Bormann carried out her body just as it was to the
passage, where he turned it over to Kempka.

Frau Hitler [the chauffeur later recounted] wore a dark dress . . . I could
not recognize any injuries to the body.

The corpses were carried up to the garden and during a lull in the
bombardment placed in a shell hole and ignited with gasoline. The
mourners, headed by Goebbels and Bormann, withdrew to the shelter
of the emergency exit and as the flames mounted stood at attention and
raised their right hands in a farewell Nazi salute. It was a brief ceremony,
for Red Army shells began to spatter the garden again and the survivors
retired to the safety of the bunker, leaving the gasoline-fed flames to complete the work of eradicating the last earthly remains of Adolf Hitler and
his wife.* For Bormann and Goebbels, there were still tasks to perform
in the Third Reich, now bereft of its founder and dictator, though they
were not the same tasks.

There had not yet been time for the messengers to reach Doenitz with
the Fuehrer's testament appointing him as his successor. The admiral
would now have to be informed by radio. But even at this point, with
power slipped from his hands, Bormann hesitated. It was difficult to one
who had savored it to give it up so abruptly. Finally he got off a message.

GRAND ADMIRAL DOENITZ:
In place of the former Reich Marshal Goering the Fuehrer appoints you as
his successor. Written authority is on its way. You will immediately take all
such measures as the situation requires.

There was not a word that Hitler was dead.
The Admiral, who was in command of all German forces in the north
and had moved his headquarters to Ploen in Schleswig, was flabbergasted
at the news. Unlike the party leaders, he had no desire to succeed Hitler;
the thought had never entered his sailor's head. Two days before, believing that Himmler would inherit the succession, he had gone to the S.S.

---

* The bones were never found, and this gave rise to rumors after the war that Hitler
had survived. But the separate interrogation of several eyewitnesses by British and
American intelligence officers leaves no doubt about the matter. Kempka has given
a plausible explanation as to why the charred bones were never found. "The traces
were wiped out," he told his interrogators, "by the uninterrupted Russian artillery
fire."

chief and offered him his support. But since it would never have occurred to him to disobey an order of the Fuehrer, he sent the following reply, in the belief that Adolf Hitler was still alive.

My FUEHRER!

My loyalty to you will be unconditional. I shall do everything possible to relieve you in Berlin. If fate nevertheless compels me to rule the Reich as your appointed successor, I shall continue this war to an end worthy of the unique, heroic struggle of the German people.

GRAND ADMIRAL DOENITZ

That night Bormann and Goebbels had a fresh idea. They decided to try to negotiate with the Russians. General Krebs, the Chief of the Army General Staff, who had remained in the bunker, had once been the assistant military attaché in Moscow, spoke Russian, and on one famous occasion had even been embraced by Stalin at the Moscow railway station. Perhaps he could get something out of the Bolsheviks; specifically, what Goebbels and Bormann wanted was a safe-conduct for themselves so that they could take their appointed places in the new Doenitz government. In return for this they were prepared to surrender Berlin.

General Krebs set out shortly after midnight of April 30–May 1 to see General Chuikov,* the Soviet commander of the troops fighting in Berlin. One of the German officers accompanying him has recorded the opening of their conversation.

KREBS: Today is the First of May, a great holiday for our two nations.†

CHUIKOV: We have a great holiday today. How things are with you over there it is hard to say.[25]

The Russian General demanded the unconditional surrender of everyone in the Fuehrer's bunker as well as of the remaining German troops in Berlin.

It took Krebs some time to carry out his mission, and when he had not returned by 11 A.M. on May 1 the impatient Bormann dispatched another radio message to Doenitz.

The Testament is in force. I will join you as soon as possible. Till then, I recommend that publication be held up.

This was still ambiguous. Bormann simply could not be straightforward enough to say that the Fuehrer was dead. He wanted to get out to be the first to inform Doenitz of the momentous news and thereby help to insure

---

* Not Marshal Zhukov, as most accounts have had it.
† May 1 was the traditional Labor Day in Europe.

his favor with the new Commander in Chief. But Goebbels, who with his wife and children was about to die, had no such reason for not telling the Admiral the simple truth. At 3:15 P.M. he got off his own message to Doenitz—the last radio communication ever to leave the beleaguered bunker in Berlin.

GRAND ADMIRAL DOENITZ

MOST SECRET

The Fuehrer died yesterday at 1530 hours [3:30 P.M.]. Testament of April 29 appoints you as Reich President . . . [There follow the names of the principal cabinet appointments.]

By order of the Fuehrer the Testament has been sent out of Berlin to you . . . Bormann intends to go to you today and to inform you of the situation. Time and form of announcement to the press and to the troops is left to you. Confirm receipt.

GOEBBELS

Goebbels did not think it necessary to inform the new Leader of his own intentions. Early in the evening of May 1, he carried them out. The first act was to poison the six children. Their playing was halted and they were given lethal injections, apparently by the same physician who the day before had poisoned the Fuehrer's dogs. Then Goebbels called his adjutant, S.S. Hauptsturmfuehrer Guenther Schwaegermann, and instructed him to fetch some gasoline.

"Schwaegermann," he told him, "this is the worst treachery of all. The generals have betrayed the Fuehrer. Everything is lost. I shall die, together with my wife and family." He did not mention, even to his adjutant, that he had just had his children murdered. "You will burn our bodies. Can you do that?"

Schwaegermann assured him he could and sent two orderlies to procure the gasoline. A few minutes later, at about 8:30 P.M., just as it was getting dark outside, Dr. and Frau Goebbels walked through the bunker, bade goodbye to those who happened to be in the corridor, and mounted the stairs to the garden. There, at their request, an S.S. orderly dispatched them with two shots in the back of the head. Four cans of gasoline were poured over their bodies and set on fire, but the cremation was not well done.[26] The survivors in the bunker were anxious to join the mass escape which was just getting under way and there was no time to waste on burning those already dead. The Russians found the charred bodies of the Propaganda Minister and his wife the next day and immediately identified them.

By 9 o'clock on the evening of May 1, the *Fuehrerbunker* had been set on fire and some five or six hundred survivors of the Fuehrer's entourage, mostly S.S. men, were milling about in the shelter of the New Chancellery —like chickens with their heads off, as one of them, the Fuehrer's tailor, later recalled—preparatory to the great breakout. The plan was to go by foot along the subway tracks from the station below the Wilhelmsplatz, opposite the Chancellery, to the Friedrichstrasse Bahnhof and there cross the River Spree and sift through the Russian lines immediately to the north of it. A good many got through; some did not, among them Martin Bormann.

When General Krebs had finally returned to the bunker that afternoon with General Chuikov's demand for unconditional surrender Hitler's party secretary had decided that his only chance for survival lay in joining the mass exodus. His group attempted to follow a German tank, but according to Kempka, who was with him, it received a direct hit from a Russian shell and Bormann was almost certainly killed. Artur Axmann, the Hitler Youth leader, who had deserted his battalion of boys at the Pichelsdorf Bridge to save his neck, was also present and later deposed that he had seen Bormann's body lying under the bridge where the Invalidenstrasse crosses the railroad tracks. There was moonlight on his face and Axmann could see no sign of wounds. His presumption was that Bormann had swallowed his capsule of poison when he saw that his chances of getting through the Russian lines were nil.

Generals Krebs and Burgdorf did not join in the mass attempt to escape. It is believed that they shot themselves in the cellar of the New Chancellery.

THE END OF THE THIRD REICH

The Third Reich survived the death of its founder by seven days.

A little after 10 o'clock on the evening of the first of May, while the bodies of Dr. and Frau Goebbels were burning in the Chancellery garden and the inhabitants of the bunker were herding together for their escape through a subway tunnel in Berlin, the Hamburg radio interrupted the playing of a recording of Bruckner's solemn Seventh Symphony. There was a roll of military drums and then an announcer spoke.

Our Fuehrer, Adolf Hitler, fighting to the last breath against Bolshevism, fell for Germany this afternoon in his operational headquarters in the Reich Chancellery. On April 30 the Fuehrer appointed Grand Admiral Doenitz his successor. The Grand Admiral and successor of the Fuehrer now speaks to the German people.

The Third Reich was expiring, as it had begun, with a shabby lie. Aside from the fact that Hitler had not died that afternoon but the previous one, which was not important, he had not fallen fighting "to the last breath," but the broadcasting of this falsehood was necessary if the inheritors of his mantle were to perpetuate a legend and also if they were to hold control of the troops who were still offering resistance and who would surely have felt betrayed if they had known the truth.

Doenitz himself repeated the lie when he went on the air at 10:20 P.M. and spoke of the "hero's death" of the Fuehrer. Actually at that moment he did not know how Hitler had met his end. Goebbels had radioed only that he had "died" on the previous afternoon. But this did not inhibit the Admiral either on this point or on others, for he did his best to muddy the confused minds of the German people in the hour of their disaster.

It is my first task [he said] to save Germany from destruction by the advancing Bolshevik enemy. For this aim alone the military struggle continues. As far and as long as the achievement of this aim is impeded by the British and Americans, we shall be forced to carry on our defensive fight against them as well. Under such conditions, however, the Anglo–Americans will continue the war not for their own peoples but solely for the spreading of Bolshevism in Europe.

After this silly distortion, the Admiral, who is not recorded as having protested Hitler's decision to make the Bolshevik nation Germany's ally in 1939 so that a war could be fought against England and later America, assured the German people in concluding his broadcast that "God will not forsake us after so much suffering and sacrifice."

These were empty words. Doenitz knew that German resistance was at an end. On April 29, the day before Hitler took his life, the German armies in Italy had surrendered unconditionally, an event whose news, because of the breakdown in communications, was spared the Fuehrer, which must have made his last hours more bearable than they otherwise would have been. On May 4 the German High Command surrendered to Montgomery all German forces in northwest Germany, Denmark and Holland. The next day Kesselring's Army Group G, comprising the German First and Nineteenth armies north of the Alps, capitulated.

On that day, May 5, Admiral Hans von Friedeburg, the new Commander in Chief of the German Navy, arrived at General Eisenhower's headquarters at Reims to negotiate a surrender. The German aim, as the last papers of OKW make clear,[27] was to stall for a few days in order to have time to move as many German troops and refugees as possible from the path of the Russians so that they could surrender to the Western Allies. General Jodl arrived at Reims the next day to help his Navy colleague draw out the proceedings. But it was in vain. Eisenhower saw through the game.

I told General Smith [he later recounted] to inform Jodl that unless they instantly ceased all pretense and delay I would close the entire Allied front and would, by force, prevent any more German refugees from entering our lines. I would brook no further delay.[28]

At 1:30 A.M. on May 7 Doenitz, after being informed by Jodl of Eisenhower's demands, radioed the German General from his new headquarters at Flensburg on the Danish frontier full powers to sign the document of unconditional surrender. The game was up.

In a little red schoolhouse at Reims, where Eisenhower had made his headquarters, Germany surrendered unconditionally at 2:41 on the morning of May 7, 1945. The capitulation was signed for the Allies by General Walter Bedell Smith, with General Ivan Susloparov affixing his signature as witness for Russia and General François Sevez for France. Admiral Friedeburg and General Jodl signed for Germany.

Jodl asked permission to say a word and it was granted.

With this signature the German people and the German Armed Forces are, for better or worse, delivered into the hands of the victors . . . In this hour I can only express the hope that the victor will treat them with generosity.

There was no response from the Allied side. But perhaps Jodl recalled another occasion when the roles were reversed just five years before. Then a French general, in signing France's unconditional surrender at Compiègne, had made a similar plea—in vain, as it turned out.

The guns in Europe ceased firing and the bombs ceased dropping at midnight on May 8–9, 1945, and a strange but welcome silence settled over the Continent for the first time since September 1, 1939. In the intervening five years, eight months and seven days millions of men and women had been slaughtered on a hundred battlefields and in a thousand bombed towns, and millions more done to death in the Nazi gas chambers or on the edge of the S.S. Einsatzgruppen pits in Russia and Poland—as the result of Adolf Hitler's lust for German conquest. A greater part of most of Europe's ancient cities lay in ruins, and from their rubble, as the weather warmed, there was the stench of the countless unburied dead.

No more would the streets of Germany echo to the jack boot of the goose-stepping storm troopers or the lusty yells of the brown-shirted masses or the shouts of the Fuehrer blaring from the loudspeakers.

After twelve years, four months and eight days, an Age of Darkness to all but a multitude of Germans and now ending in a bleak night for them too, the Thousand-Year Reich had come to an end. It had raised, as we have seen, this great nation and this resourceful but so easily misled people to heights of power and conquest they had never before experienced and now it had dissolved with a suddenness and a completeness that had few, if any, parallels in history.

In 1918, after the last defeat, the Kaiser had fled, the monarchy had tumbled, but the other traditional institutions supporting the State had remained, a government chosen by the people had continued to function, as did the nucleus of a German Army and a General Staff. But in the spring of 1945 the Third Reich simply ceased to exist. There was no longer any German authority on any level. The millions of soldiers, airmen and sailors were prisoners of war in their own land. The millions of civilians were governed, down to the villages, by the conquering enemy troops, on whom they depended not only for law and order but throughout that summer and bitter winter of 1945 for food and fuel to keep them alive. Such was the state to which the follies of Adolf Hitler—and their own folly in following him so blindly and with so much enthusiasm—had brought them, though I found little bitterness toward him when I returned to Germany that fall.

The people were there, and the land—the first dazed and bleeding and hungry, and, when winter came, shivering in their rags in the hovels which the bombings had made of their homes; the second a vast wasteland of rubble. The German people had not been destroyed, as Hitler, who had tried to destroy so many other peoples and, in the end, when the war was lost, themselves, had wished.

But the Third Reich had passed into history.

A BRIEF EPILOGUE

I WENT BACK that autumn to the once proud land, where I had spent most of the brief years of the Third Reich. It was difficult to recognize. I have described that return in another place.[29] It remains here merely to record the fate of the remaining characters who have figured prominently in these pages.

Doenitz's rump government, which had been set up at Flensburg on the Danish border, was dissolved by the Allies on May 23, 1945, and all its members were arrested. Heinrich Himmler had been dismissed from the government on May 6, on the eve of the surrender at Reims, in a move which the Admiral calculated might win him favor with the Allies. The former S.S. chief, who had held so long the power of life and death over Europe's millions, and who had often exercised it, wandered about in the vicinity of Flensburg until May 21, when he set out with eleven S.S. officers to try to pass through the British and American lines to his native Bavaria. Himmler—it must have galled him—had shaved off his mustache, tied a black patch over his left eye and donned an Army private's uniform. The party was stopped the first day at a British control point between Hamburg and Bremerhaven. After questioning, Himmler confessed his identity to a British Army captain, who hauled him away to Second Army headquarters at Lueneburg. There he was stripped and searched and made to change into a British Army uniform to avert any possibility that he might be concealing poison in his clothes. But the search was not thorough. Himmler kept his vial of potassium cyanide concealed in a cavity of his gums. When a second British intelligence officer arrived from Montgomery's headquarters on May 23 and instructed a medical officer to examine the prisoner's mouth, Himmler bit on his vial and was dead in twelve minutes, despite frantic efforts to keep him alive by pumping his stomach and administering emetics.

The remaining intimate collaborators of Hitler lived a bit longer. I went down to Nuremberg to see them. I had often watched them in their hour of glory and power at the annual party rallies in this town. In the

dock before the International Military Tribunal they looked different.
There had been quite a metamorphosis. Attired in rather shabby clothes,
slumped in their seats fidgeting nervously, they no longer resembled the
arrogant leaders of old. They seemed to be a drab assortment of medioc-
rities. It seemed difficult to grasp that such men, when last you had seen
them, had wielded such monstrous power, that such as they could conquer
a great nation and most of Europe.

There were twenty-one of them* in the dock: Goering, eighty pounds
lighter than when last I had seen him, in a faded Luftwaffe uniform without
insignia and obviously pleased that he had been given the Number One
place in the dock—a sort of belated recognition of his place in the Nazi
hierarchy now that Hitler was dead; Rudolf Hess, who had been the
Number Three man before his flight to England, his face now emaciated,
his deep-set eyes staring vacantly into space, feigning amnesia but leaving
no doubt that he was a broken man; Ribbentrop, at last shorn of his
arrogance and his pompousness, looking pale, bent and beaten; Keitel, who
had lost his jauntiness; Rosenberg, the muddled party "philosopher,"
whom the events which had brought him to this place appeared to have
awakened to reality at last.

Julius Streicher, the Jew-baiter of Nuremberg, was there. This sadist
and pornographer, whom I had once seen striding through the streets of
the old town brandishing a whip, seemed to have wilted. A bald, decrepit-
looking old man, he sat perspiring profusely, glaring at the judges and
convincing himself—so a guard later told me—that they were all Jews.
There was Fritz Sauckel, the boss of slave labor in the Third Reich, his
narrow little slit eyes giving him a porcine appearance. He seemed
nervous, swaying to and fro. Next to him was Baldur von Schirach, the
first Hitler Youth Leader and later Gauleiter of Vienna, more American
by blood than German and looking like a contrite college boy who has
been kicked out of school for some folly. There was Walther Funk, the
shifty-eyed nonentity who had succeeded Schacht. And there was Dr.
Schacht himself, who had spent the last months of the Third Reich as a
prisoner of his once revered Fuehrer in a concentration camp, fearing
execution any day, and who now bristled with indignation that the Allies
should try *him* as a war criminal. Franz von Papen, more responsible
than any other individual in Germany for Hitler's coming to power, had
been rounded up and made a defendant. He seemed much aged, but the
look of the old fox, who had escaped from so many tight fixes, was still
imprinted on his wizened face.

Neurath, Hitler's first Foreign Minister, a German of the old school,
with few convictions and little integrity, seemed utterly broken. Not
Speer, who made the most straightforward impression of all and who during the long trial spoke honestly and with no attempt to shirk his respon-

---

* Dr. Robert Ley, head of the Arbeitsfront, who was to have been a defendant, had
hanged himself in his cell before the trial began. He had made a noose from rags
torn from a towel, which he had tied to a toilet pipe.

sibility and his guilt. Seyss-Inquart, the Austrian quisling, was in the dock, as were Jodl and the two Grand Admirals, Raeder and Doenitz—the latter, the successor to the Fuehrer, looking in his store suit for all the world like a shoe clerk. There was Kaltenbrunner, the bloody successor of "Hangman Heydrich," who on the stand would deny all his crimes; and Hans Frank, the Nazi Inquisitor in Poland, who would admit some of his, having become in the end contrite and, as he said, having rediscovered God, whose forgiveness he begged; and Frick, as colorless on the brink of death as he had been in life. And finally Hans Fritzsche, who had made a career as a radio commentator because his voice resembled that of Goebbels, who had made him an official in the Propaganda Ministry. No one in the courtroom, including Fritzsche, seemed to know why he was there—he was too small a fry—unless it were as a ghost for Goebbels, and he was acquitted.

So were Schacht and Papen. All three later drew stiff prison sentences from German denazification courts though, in the end, they served very little time.

Seven defendants at Nuremberg drew prison sentences: Hess, Raeder and Funk for life, Speer and Schirach for twenty years, Neurath for fifteen, Doenitz for ten. The others were sentenced to death.

At eleven minutes past 1 A.M. on October 16, 1946, Ribbentrop mounted the gallows in the execution chamber of the Nuremberg prison, and he was followed at short intervals by Keitel, Kaltenbrunner, Rosenberg, Frank, Frick, Streicher, Seyss-Inquart, Sauckel and Jodl.

But not by Hermann Goering. He cheated the hangman. Two hours before his turn would have come he swallowed a vial of poison that had been smuggled into his cell. Like his Fuehrer, Adolf Hitler, and his rival for the succession, Heinrich Himmler, he had succeeded at the last hour in choosing the way in which he would depart this earth, on which he, like the other two, had made such a murderous impact.

AFTERWORD

This book had a surprising reception.

No one—not my publisher, my editor, my agent, my friends—believed that the public would buy a book so long, so full of footnotes, so expensive, and on such a subject. My lecture agent had told me there was no more interest in Hitler and the Third Reich and that I would have to talk about something else. My publisher printed only 12,500 copies in advance.

The fact that the book started at once to attract considerable readership was therefore a pleasant surprise to us all. I never kept track of the sales myself—either of the hardcover edition brought out by Simon and Schuster or the mass-market paperback edition brought out by Fawcett. I was surprised to hear two or three years ago that the Book-of-the-Month Club had sold more copies of *The Rise and Fall of the Third Reich* than of any other book in its history. But how many copies, I have no idea. The book also did well abroad—in Britain, France, and Italy, though less well in Germany.

The reviews of the book, except in Germany, were much more perceptive than I had expected. And though the academic historians, on the whole, were cool to the book and to me (as if I were a usurper with no right to invade their field—to *write* good history, they said, you had to *teach* it), there were notable exceptions.

H. R. Trevor-Roper, for instance. I felt some trepidation when I first heard that the Sunday *New York Times Book Review* had given him the book to review. He was a prestigious historian at Oxford whom I much admired—I had found his book *The Last Days of Hitler* very valuable. But British book reviewers at that time had been rather hard on American authors, and besides, as an eminent academic, Trevor-Roper might share, I thought, the disdain of his American colleagues for journalists who try to write history. So I concluded I would probably be clobbered in the publication that was most important for American writers and their books.

1145

But Trevor-Roper too surprised. The headline above his page-one review gave a hint as to what he would have to say:

LIGHT ON OUR CENTURY'S DARKEST NIGHT
The Awful Story of Hitler's Germany
Is Movingly Told in Masterly Study

"In ordinary circumstances," Trevor-Roper began, "it would be impossible, only half a generation after its end . . . to write its history. But with the Third Reich, nothing was ordinary, not even its end. In that total annihilation all the secrets of [Hitler's] rule were broken open, all the archives captured. . . .

"Now, as never before, the living witnesses can converge with the historical truth. All they need is a historian. In William L. Shirer they have found one. . . ."

This was heady stuff, and at the very beginning of the review. It almost took my breath away. The concluding lines were almost as breathtaking. "This is a splendid work of scholarship, objective in method, sound in judgment, inescapable in its conclusions."

I was brought down to earth by the front-page review in the rival *New York Herald-Tribune Book Review*. Its author, Gordon A. Craig, then a historian at Princeton, did not agree at all with his Oxford colleague that the Third Reich had found its historian in me. By no means! He thought the book was too long and "out of balance." He regretted that I had not read the book of an obscure German historian. The fact that the book was based not on what other historians had written but on original sources—captured secret German documents—did not impress him, if he noticed it.

In Germany, to put it mildly, the book did not fare very well with the reviewers. The Germans simply could not face up to their past. Led by the chancellor of West Germany, Konrad Adenauer, the book was furiously attacked and the author maligned. "A German-hater!" Adenauer called me. Since the book dealt objectively with Nazi Germany and the crimes the Germans committed against the human spirit and against their neighbors and against the Jews of Europe, and since I allowed the documented facts to speak for themselves, I was somewhat taken back by the vehemence of the German reaction, but not entirely surprised.

And now, as the thirtieth-anniversary edition of *The Rise and Fall* goes to press, the world is suddenly confronted with a new reunification of Germany. Soon, united, Germany will be strong again economically and, if it wishes, militarily, as it was in the time of Wilhelm II and Adolf Hitler. And Europe will be faced again with the German problem. If the past is any guide, the outlook is not very promising for Germany's neighbors, who twice in my lifetime have been invaded by the Teutonic armies. The last time, under Hitler, as the readers of this book are reminded, the German behavior was a horror in its barbarism.

People ask now: Have the Germans changed? Many in the West appear to believe so. I myself am not so sure, my view no doubt clouded by the personal experience of having lived and worked in Germany in the Nazi time. The truth is that no one really knows the answer to that crucial question. And quite understandably the nations that were former victims of German conquest do not want to take any chances again.

Is there a solution to the German problem? Perhaps. It lies in enmeshing reunited Germany in a European security system out of which it could never break loose to pursue its past policies of aggression.

In one fundamental sense, the situation has changed since the fall of the Third Reich. The development of the hydrogen bomb, as I mentioned at the end of my Foreword, written in 1959, has rendered an old-fashioned conqueror like Adolf Hitler obsolete. If ever a new adventurer such as Hitler tried to lead the Germans to new conquests, he would be repelled by a nuclear response. That would put a quick end to German aggression. But, unfortunately, it would put an end to the world too.

So maybe the H-bomb and the rockets and planes and submarines designed to deliver it, horrible threat though they are to the survival of the planet, will, ironically, help, at least, to solve the German problem. No more bloody conquests by the Germans, or by anyone else.

Perhaps it will help too if the erring governments and the wondering people of this world will remember the dark night of Nazi terror and genocide that almost engulfed our world and that is the subject of this book. Remembrance of the past helps us to understand the present.

William L. Shirer
May 1990

NOTES

Abbreviations used in these notes:

DBrFP—Documents on British Foreign Policy. Files of the British Foreign Office.

DDI—I Documenti diplomatica italiani. Files of the Italian government.

DGFP—Documents on German Foreign Policy. Files of the German Foreign Office.

FCNA—Fuehrer Conferences on Naval Affairs. Summary records of Hitler's conferences with the Commander in Chief of the German Navy.

NCA—Nazi Conspiracy and Aggression. Part of the Nuremberg documents.

N.D.—Nuremberg document.

NSR—Nazi–Soviet Relations. From the files of the German Foreign Office.

TMWC—Trial of the Major War Criminals. Nuremberg documents and testimony.

TWC—Trials of War Criminals before the Nuremberg Military Tribunals.

CHAPTER 1

1. The Hammerstein memorandum, cited by Wheeler-Bennett in his *The Nemesis of Power*, p. 285. The memorandum was written for Wheeler-Bennett by Dr. Kunrath von Hammerstein, son of the General, and was based on his father's notes and diaries. It is entitled "Schleicher, Hammerstein and the Seizure of Power."
2. Joseph Goebbels, *Vom Kaiserhof zur Reichskanzlei*, p. 251.
3. Hammerstein memorandum, cited by Wheeler-Bennett, *op. cit.*, p. 280.
4. Goebbels, *op. cit.*, p. 250.
5. *Ibid.*, p. 252.
6. *Ibid.*, p. 252.
7. André François-Poncet, *The Fateful Years*, p. 48. He was French ambassador in Berlin 1930–38.
8. Goebbels, Kaiserhof, pp. 251–54.
9. Proclamation of Sept. 5, 1934, at Nuremberg.
10. Friedrich Meinecke, *The German Catastrophe*, p. 96.
11. Adolf Hitler, *Mein Kampf*, American edition (Boston, 1943), p. 3. In a good number of quotations from this book I have altered the English translation somewhat to bring it closer to the original text in German.
12. Konrad Heiden, *Der Fuehrer*, p. 36. All who write on the Third Reich are indebted to Heiden for material on the early life of Hitler.
13. *Ibid.*, p. 41.
14. *Ibid.*, p. 43.
15. *Ibid.*, p. 43.
16. *Mein Kampf*, p. 6.
17. *Ibid.*, p. 8.
18. *Ibid.*, pp. 8–10.
19. *Ibid.*, p. 10.
20. *Hitler's Secret Conversations, 1941–44*, p. 287.
21. *Ibid.*, p. 346.
22. *Ibid.*, p. 547.
23. *Ibid.*, pp. 566–67.
24. August Kubizek, *The Young Hitler I Knew*, p. 50.
25. *Ibid.*, p. 49.
26. *Mein Kampf*, pp. 14–15.
27. Kubizek, *op. cit.*, p. 52, and *Hitler's Secret Conversations*, p. 567.
28. Kubizek, *op. cit.*, p. 44.
29. *Mein Kampf*, p. 18.
30. *Ibid.*, p. 21.
31. Kubizek, *op. cit.*, p. 59.
32. *Ibid.*, p. 76.
33. *Ibid.*, pp. 54–55.
34. Konrad Heiden, *Der Fuehrer*, p. 52.
35. *Mein Kampf*, p. 20.
36. *Ibid.*, p. 18.
37. *Ibid.*, p. 18.
38. *Ibid.*, p. 21.
39. *Ibid.*, pp. 21–22.
40. *Ibid.*, p. 34.
41. Heiden, *Der Fuehrer*, p. 54.
42. *Ibid.*, p. 68.
43. *Mein Kampf*, p. 34.
44. *Ibid.*, p. 22.
45. *Ibid.*, pp. 35–37.

46. *Ibid.*, pp. 22, 125.
47. *Ibid.*, pp. 38–39.
48. *Ibid.*, p. 41.
49. *Ibid.*, pp. 43–44.
50. *Ibid.*, pp. 116–17.
51. *Ibid.*, p. 118.
52. *Ibid.*, pp. 55, 69, 122.
53. Stefan Zweig, *The World of Yesterday*, p. 63.
54. *Mein Kampf*, p. 100.
55. *Ibid.*, p. 107.
56. *Ibid.*, p. 52.
57. Kubizek, *op. cit.*, p. 79.
58. *Mein Kampf*, p. 52.
59. *Ibid.*, p. 56.
60. *Ibid.*, pp. 56–57.
61. *Ibid.*, p. 59.
62. *Ibid.*, pp. 63–64.
63. *Ibid.*, pp. 123–24.
64. *Ibid.*, pp. 161, 163.

CHAPTER 2

1. *Mein Kampf*, pp. 204–5.
2. *Ibid.*, p. 202.
3. Heiden, *Der Fuehrer*, p. 84.
4. Rudolf Olden, *Hitler, the Pawn*, p. 70.
5. *Mein Kampf*, p. 193.
6. *Ibid.*, pp. 205–6.
7. *Ibid.*, p. 207.
8. *Ibid.*, pp. 215–16.
9. *Ibid.*, pp. 210, 213.
10. *Ibid.*, pp. 218–19.
11. *Ibid.*, p. 220.
12. *Ibid.*, pp. 221–22.
13. *Ibid.*, p. 224.
14. *Ibid.*, p. 687*n.*
15. *Ibid.*, p. 687.
16. *Ibid.*, p. 354.
17. *Ibid.*, p. 355.
18. *Ibid.*, pp. 369–70.
19. Konrad Heiden, *A History of National Socialism*, p. 36.
20. *Mein Kampf*, pp. 496–97. The italics are Hitler's.
21. Heiden, *A History of National Socialism*, pp. 51–52.
22. Heiden, *Der Fuehrer*, pp. 98–99.
23. Heiden, *A History of National Socialism*, p. 52.
24. Heiden, *Hitler*, pp. 90–91.

CHAPTER 3

1. Wheeler-Bennett, *Wooden Titan: Hindenburg*, pp. 207–8.
2. *Ibid.*, p. 131.
3. Wheeler-Bennett's *Nemesis*, p. 58.

4. Franz L. Neumann, *Behemoth*, p. 23.
5. Heiden, *Der Fuehrer*, pp. 131–33.
6. *Ibid.*, p. 164.
7. Lt. Gen. Friedrich von Rabenau, *Seeckt, aus seinem Leben*, II, p. 342.
8. *Ibid.*, p. 371.
9. Karl Alexander von Mueller, quoted by Heiden in *Der Fuehrer*, p. 190.
10. The record of the court proceedings is contained in *Der Hitler Prozess.*

CHAPTER 4

1. The figures are from a study of Eher Verlag's royalty statements made by Prof. Oron James Hale and published in *The American Historical Review*, July 1955, under the title "Adolf Hitler: Taxpayer."
2. The quotations are from *Mein Kampf*, pp. 619, 672, 674.
3. *Ibid.*, pp. 138–39.
4. *Ibid.*, p. 140.
5. *Ibid.*, pp. 643, 646, 652.
6. *Ibid.*, p. 649.
7. *Ibid.*, p. 675.
8. *Ibid.*, p. 654.
9. *Ibid.*, pp. 150–53.
10. *Adolf Hitlers Reden*, p. 32. Quoted by Bullock, *op. cit.*, p. 68.
11. *Mein Kampf*, pp. 247–53.
12. *Ibid.*, pp. 134–35, 285, 289.
13. *Ibid.*, p. 290.
14. *Ibid.*, pp. 295–96.
15. *Ibid.*, p. 296, for this and the two quotations above it.
16. *Ibid.*, p. 646.
17. *Ibid.*, pp. 383–84.
18. *Ibid.*, p. 394.
19. *Ibid.*, pp. 402–4.
20. *Ibid.*, p. 396.
21. *Ibid.*, pp. 449–50.
22. A. J. P. Taylor, *The Course of German History*, p. 24.
23. Wilhelm Roepke, *The Solution of the German Problem*, p. 153.
24. *Mein Kampf*, pp. 154, 225–26.
25. *Hitler's Secret Conversations*, p. 198.
26. See his study of Chamberlain in *The Third Reich*, ed. by Baumont, Fried and Vermeil.
27. The foregoing, from Chamberlain back to Fichte and Hegel, is based

on the works of the authors and on quotations and interpretations in such books as *German Philosophy and Politics,* by John Dewey; *The German Catastrophe,* by Friedrich Meinecke; *The Solution of the German Problem,* by Wilhelm Roepke; *A History of Western Philosophy,* by Bertrand Russell; *Thus Speaks Germany,* ed. by W. W. Coole and M. F. Potter; *The Third Reich,* ed. by Baumont, Fried and Vermeil; *German Nationalism: The Tragedy of a People,* by Louis L. Snyder; *German History: Some New German Views,* ed. by Hans Kohn; *The Rise and Fall of Nazi Germany,* by T. L. Jarman; *Der Fuehrer,* by Konrad Heiden; *The Course of German History,* by A. J. P. Taylor; *L'Allemagne Contemporaine,* by Edmond Vermeil; *History of Germany,* by Hermann Pinnow.

E. Eyck's *Bismarck and the German Empire* is an invaluable study.

The limitations of space in a work of this kind prohibited discussion of the considerable influence on the Third Reich of a number of other German intellectuals whose writings were popular and significant in Germany: Schlegel, J. Goerres, Novalis, Arndt, Jahn, Lagarde, List, Droysen, Ranke, Mommsen, Constantin Frantz, Stoecker, Bernhardi, Klaus Wagner, Langbehn, Lange, Spengler.

28. *Mein Kampf,* p. 381.
29. *Ibid.,* p. 293.
30. *Ibid.,* pp. 212–13.
31. Hegel, *Lectures on the Philosophy of History,* pp. 31–32. Quoted by Bullock, *op. cit.,* p. 351.
32. Quoted in *The Third Reich,* ed. by Baumont *et al.,* pp. 204–5, from two works of Nietzsche: *Zur Genealogie der Moral* and *Der Wille zur Macht.*

CHAPTER 5

1. Kurt Ludecke, *I Knew Hitler,* pp. 217–18.
2. Baynes (ed.), *The Speeches of Adolf Hitler,* I, pp. 155–56.
3. Curt Riess, *Joseph Goebbels,* p. 8.
4. This and the other quoted Hitler reminiscences of January 16–17,

1942, about Obersalzberg are from *Hitler's Secret Conversations.*
5. Such authorities as Heiden and Bullock tell of the Raubals coming to Haus Wachenfeld in 1925, when Geli Raubal was seventeen. But Hitler makes it clear that he did not acquire the villa until 1928, at which time he says, "I immediately rang up my sister in Vienna with the news, and begged her to be so good as to take over the part of mistress of the house." See *Hitler's Secret Conversations,* p. 177.
6. Heiden, *Der Fuehrer,* pp. 384–86.
7. See the fascinating analysis of Hitler's income tax returns made by Prof. Oron James Hale in *The American Historical Review,* July 1955.
8. *Ibid.*
9. *Ibid.*
10. Heiden, *Der Fuehrer,* p. 419.
11. The speech does not appear in Baynes or in Roussy de Sales's collection of Hitler's speeches (Hitler, *My New Order*). It was published verbatim in the *Voelkischer Beobachter* (special Reichswehr edition) on March 26, 1929, and is quoted at length in "Blueprint of the Nazi Underground," *Research Studies of the State College of Washington,* June 1945.
12. The quotations are from the *Frankfurter Zeitung,* September 26, 1930.
13. *Nazi Conspiracy and Aggression* [hereafter referred to as *NCA*], Supplement A, p. 1194 (Nuremberg Document [hereafter, N.D.] EC–440).
14. Otto Dietrich, *Mit Hitler in die Macht.*
15. Funk's testimony, *NCA,* Suppl. A, pp. 1194–1204 (N.D. EC–440), and *NCA,* V., pp. 478–95 (N.D. 2328–PS). Thyssen's declarations are from his book *I Paid Hitler,* pp. 79–108.
16. *NCA,* VII, pp. 512–13 (N.D. EC–456).

CHAPTER 6

1. According to Heiden, *Der Fuehrer,* p. 433.
2. Heiden, *History of National Socialism,* p. 166.

3. Goebbels, *Kaiserhof*, pp. 19–20.
4. *Ibid.*, pp. 80–81.
5. Wheeler-Bennett, *Nemesis*, p. 243.
6. The above quotes are from Goebbels, *Kaiserhof*, pp. 81–104.
7. François-Poncet, *op. cit.*, p. 23.
8. Franz von Papen, *Memoirs*, p. 162.
9. *NCA*, Suppl. A, p. 508 (N.D. 3309–PS).
10. Hermann Rauschning, *The Voice of Destruction*.
11. Goebbels was not caught napping this time, as he had been on August 13. He immediately gave the press the exchange of correspondence and it was published in the morning papers of Nov. 25. It is available in the *Jahrbuch des Oeffenlichen Rechts*, Vol. 21, 1933–40.
12. Papen, *op. cit.*, pp. 216–17.
13. *Ibid.*, p. 220.
14. *Ibid.*, p. 222.
15. François-Poncet, *op. cit.*, p. 43. He says erroneously, "seventy days."
16. *NCA*, II, pp. 922–24.
17. Kurt von Schuschnigg, *Farewell, Austria*, pp. 165–66.
18. Meissner affidavit, *NCA*, Suppl. A, p. 511.
19. The Hammerstein memorandum, Wheeler-Bennett's *Nemesis*, p. 280.
20. *Hitler's Secret Conversations*, p. 404.
21. Papen, *op. cit.*, pp. 243–44.

CHAPTER 7

1. *NCA*, III, pp. 272–75 (N.D. 351–PS).
2. Goebbels, *Kaiserhof*, p. 256.
3. See affidavit of Georg von Schnitzler, *NCA*, VII, p. 501 (N.D. EC–439); speeches of Goering and Hitler, *NCA*, VI, p. 1080 (N.D. D–203); Schacht's interrogation, *NCA*, VI, p. 465 (N.D. 3725–PS); Funk's interrogation, *NCA*, V, p. 495 (N.D. 2828–PS).
4. Goebbels, *Kaiserhof*, pp. 269–70.
5. Papen, *op. cit.*, p. 268.
6. Rudolf Diels, *Lucifer ante Portas*, p. 194.
7. For sources on the responsibility for the Reichstag fire see: Halder's affidavit, *NCA*, VI, p. 635 (N.D. 3740–PS); transcript of Gisevius' cross-examination on April 25, 1946, *Trial of the Major War Criminals* [hereafter cited as *TMWC*], XII, pp. 252–53; Diehl's affidavit, Goering's denial, *TMWC*, IX, pp. 432–36, and *NCA*, VI, pp. 298–99 (N.D. 3593–PS); Willy Frischauer, *The Rise and Fall of Hermann Goering*, pp. 88–95; Douglas Reed, *The Burning of the Reichstag;* John Gunther, *Inside Europe* (Gunther attended the trial at Leipzig). There are many alleged testaments and confessions by those claiming to have participated in the Nazi firing of the Reichstag or to have positive knowledge of it, but none, so far as I know, has ever been substantiated. Of these, memoranda by Ernst Oberfohren, a Nationalist deputy, and Karl Ernst, the Berlin S.A. leader, have been given some credence. Both men were slain by the Nazis within a few months of the fire.
8. *NCA*, III, pp. 968–70 (N.D. 1390–PS).
9. *NCA*, IV, p. 496 (N.D. 1856–PS).
10. *NCA*, V, p. 669 (N.D. 2962–PS).
11. *Dokumente der deutschen Politik*, I, 1935, pp. 20–24.
12. François-Poncet, *op. cit.*, p. 61.
13. Text of law, *NCA*, IV, pp. 638–39 (N.D. 2001–PS).
14. Laws of March 31 and April 7, 1933, and January 30, 1934, all in *NCA*, IV, pp. 640–43.
15. *NCA*, III, p. 962 (N.D. 1388–PS).
16. Goebbels, *Kaiserhof*, p. 307.
17. *NCA*, III, pp. 380–85 (N.D. 392–PS).
18. Law of May 19, 1933, *NCA*, III, p. 387 (N.D. 405–PS).
19. Goebbels, *op. cit.*, p. 300.
20. N. S. *Monatshefte*, No. 39 (June 1933).
21. The July 1 and 6 quotations in Baynes, I, p. 287 and pp. 865–66.
22. From a study entitled *My Relations with Adolf Hitler and the Party*, which Admiral Raeder wrote in Moscow after his capture by the Russians and which was made available at Nuremberg. *NCA*, VIII, p. 707.
23. Baynes, I, p. 289.
24. Spengler, *Jahre der Entscheidung*, p. viii.
25. Blomberg's directive, *TMWC*, XXXIV, pp. 487–91 (N.D. C–140).

26. Quoted by Telford Taylor in *Sword and Swastika*, p. 41. The Seeckt papers are now at the National Archives in Washington.

27. The source for the "Pact of the *Deutschland*" is *Weissbuch ueber die Erschiessung des 30 Juni, 1934* (Paris, 1935), pp. 52–53. Herbert Rosinski in his *The German Army*, pp. 222–23, confirms the terms of the pact. Bullock and Wheeler-Bennett accept it in their books on this period. The source for the May 16 meeting of the generals is Jacques Bénoist-Méchin's *Histoire de l'Armée Allemande depuis l'Armistice*, II, pp. 553–54.

28. *Rede des Vizekanzlers von Papen vor dem Universitaetsbund, Marburg, am 17 Juni, 1934* (Berlin: Germania-Verlag).

29. Papen, *op. cit.*, p. 310.

30. *NCA*, V, pp. 654–55 (N.D. 2950–PS).

31. Papen, *op. cit.*, pp. 330–33.

CHAPTER 8

1. Leo Stein, *I Was in Hell with Niemoeller*, p. 80.

2. Neumann, *Behemoth*, p. 109. He states that the quotations are from the research project "Antisemitism" of the Institute of Social Research, published in *Studies in Philosophy and Social Science*, 1940.

3. Rauschning, *The Voice of Destruction*, p. 54.

4. Stewart W. Herman, Jr., *It's Your Souls We Want*, pp. 157–58. Herman was pastor of the American Church in Berlin from 1936 to 1941.

5. The text is given in Herman, *op. cit.*, pp. 297–300; also in the New York *Times* of Jan. 3, 1942.

6. Affidavit of Nov. 19, 1945, *NCA*, V, pp. 735–36 (N.D. 3016–PS).

7. Most foreign correspondents in Berlin kept a collection of such gems. My own has been lost. The quotations are from Philipp Lenard, *Deutsche Physik*, preface; Wallace Deuel, *People under Hitler*; William Ebenstein, *The Nazi State*.

8. Wilhelm Roepke, *The Solution of the German Problem*, p. 61.

9. Quoted in Frederic Lilge's *The Abuse of Learning: The Failure of the German University*, p. 170.

10. Schirach's American ancestry is given by Douglas M. Kelley, the American psychiatrist at the Nuremberg jail during the trial of the major war criminals, in his book, *22 Cells in Nuremberg*, pp. 86–87.

11. *Reichsgesetzblatt*, 1936, Part 1, p. 933. Quoted in *NCA*, III, pp. 972–73 (N.D. 1392–PS).

12. From his book, *Basic Facts for a History of German War and Armament Economy*. Quoted in *NCA*, I, p. 350 (N.D. 2353–PS).

13. The ministry's report of September 30, 1934, *NCA*, VII, pp. 306–9 (N.D. EC–128); Schacht's report of May 3, 1935, *NCA*, III, pp. 827–30 (N.D. 1168–PS); text of the secret Reich Defense Law, *NCA*, IV, pp. 934–36 (N.D. 2261–PS).

14. *NCA*, VII, p. 474 (N.D. EC–419).

15. Thyssen, *I Paid Hitler*, pp. xv, 157.

16. Quoted by Neumann in *Behemoth*, p. 432.

17. Ebenstein, *op. cit.*, p. 84.

18. *NCA*, III, pp. 568–72 (N.D. 787, 788–PS).

19. *The Third Reich*, ed. by Baumont *et al.*, p. 630.

20. Eugen Kogon's phrase. See his *Der SS Staat—das System der deutschen Konzentrationslager*. A somewhat abridged version appeared in English, *The Theory and Practice of Hell*. It is the best study of Nazi concentration camps yet written. Kogon spent seven years in them.

21. Quoted in *NCA*, II, p. 258 (N.D. 1852–PS).

22. *NCA*, VIII, pp. 243–44 (N.D. R–142).

23. *Voelkischer Beobachter*, May 20, 1936.

CHAPTER 9

1. Friedelind Wagner, *Heritage of Fire*, p. 109.

2. Papen, *op. cit.*, p. 338.

3. *Daily Mail*, Aug. 6, 1934.

4. *Le Matin*, Nov. 18, 1934.

5. Wolfgang Foerster, *Ein General kaempft gegen den Krieg*, p. 22. This book is based on Beck's papers.

6. *NCA*, VII, p. 333 (N.D. EC–177).
7. *NCA*, I, p. 431 (N.D. C–189).
8. *NCA*, VI, p. 1018 (N.D. C–190).
9. *Ibid.*
10. *TMWC*, XX, p. 603.
11. *My New Order*, ed. by Roussy de Sales, pp. 309–33. The text of the speech is also in Baynes, II, pp. 1218–47.
12. *My New Order*, pp. 333–34.
13. Pertinax, *The Grave Diggers of France*, p. 381.
14. The author's *Berlin Diary*, p. 43.
15. François-Poncet, *op. cit.*, pp. 188–89.
16. *NCA*, VI, pp. 951–52 (N.D. C–139), the text of the order. See also *TMWC*, XV, pp. 445–48.
17. *NCA*, VII, pp. 454–55 (N.D. EC–405), minutes of the meeting.
18. *NCA*, VI, pp. 974–76 (N.D. C–159).
19. *TMWC*, XV, p. 252, for Jodl's evidence; *Hitler's Secret Conversations*, pp. 211–12, for Hitler's figure.
20. François-Poncet, *op. cit.*, p. 193.
21. *Berlin Diary*, pp. 51–54.
22. François-Poncet, *op. cit.*, p. 190.
23. *Ibid.*, pp. 194–95.
24. *TMWC*, XV, p. 352.
25. *Hitler's Secret Conversations*, pp. 211–12. Remarks of January 27, 1942.
26. Paul Schmidt, *Hitler's Interpreter*, p. 41.
27. *TMWC*, XV, p. 352.
28. *TMWC*, XXI, p. 22.
29. *Hitler's Secret Conversations*, p. 211.
30. Quoted by François-Poncet, *op. cit.*, p. 196.
31. *NCA*, VII, p. 890 (N.D. L–150).
32. Kurt von Schuschnigg, *Austrian Requiem*, p. 5.
33. *NCA*, I, p. 466 (N.D. 2248–PS).
34. *Documents on German Foreign Policy* [hereafter referred to as *DGFP*], Series D, I, pp. 278–81 (No. 152).
35. Papen, *op. cit.*, p. 370.
36. *DGFP*, III, pp. 1–2.
37. *Ibid.*, pp. 892–94.
38. *DGFP*, I, p. 37.
39. *Ibid.*, III, p. 172.
40. *Ciano's Diplomatic Papers*, ed. by Malcolm Muggeridge, pp. 43–48.
41. Milton Shulman, *Defeat in the West*, p. 76. His source is given as a British War Office Intelligence

Review, December 1945. It would seem to be from an interrogation of Goering.
42. Text of the secret protocol, *DGFP*, I, p. 734.
43. *TWC*, XII, pp. 460–65 (N.D. NI–051).
44. *TMWC*, IX, p. 281.
45. *DGFP*, I, p. 40.
46. *Ibid.*, pp. 55–67.
47. *NCA*, VI, pp. 1001–11 (N.D. C–175).
48. The Hossbach minutes, dated Nov. 10, 1937. The German text is given in *TMWC*, XXV, pp. 402–13, and the best English translation is in *DGFP*, I, pp. 29–39. A hasty English version was done at Nuremberg and printed in *NCA*, III, pp. 295–305 (N.D. 386–PS). Hossbach also gives an account of the meeting in his book *Zwischen Wehrmacht und Hitler*, pp. 186–94. The brief testimony of Goering, Raeder and Neurath on the conference is printed in *TMWC*.

CHAPTER 10

1. Affidavit of Baroness von Ritter, a relative of Neurath, *TMWC*, XVI, p. 640.
2. *TMWC*, XVI, p. 640.
3. *Ibid.*, p. 641.
4. Schacht, *Account Settled*, p. 90.
5. Jodl's diary, *TMWC*, XXVIII, p. 357.
6. *Ibid.*, p. 356.
7. *Ibid.*, pp. 360–62.
8. *Ibid.*, p. 357.
9. Telford Taylor, *Sword and Swastika*, pp. 149–50. The manuscript of Blomberg's unpublished memoirs is in the Library of Congress.
10. Bullock, *op. cit.*, p. 381, and Wheeler-Bennett, *Nemesis*, p. 369.
11. Wolfgang Foerster, *Ein General kaempft gegen den Krieg, op. cit.*, pp. 70–73.
12. *TMWC*, IX, p. 290.
13. *The Von Hassell Diaries, 1938–1944*, p. 23.

CHAPTER 11

1. Dispatch to Hitler, Dec. 21, 1937, *DGFP*, I, p. 486.
2. Papen, *op. cit.*, p. 404.
3. *Ibid.*, p. 406.
4. Schuschnigg, *Austrian Requiem*,

pp. 12–19; *NCA*, V, pp. 709–12 (N.D. 2995–PS).

5. Draft of protocol submitted to Schuschnigg, *DGFP*, I, pp. 513–15.

6. *NCA*, V, p. 711 (N.D. 2995–PS).

7. Schuschnigg, *Austrian Requiem*, p. 23.

8. N.D. 2995–PS, *op. cit.*

9. Schuschnigg gave slightly different versions of Hitler's threats in his book, p. 24, and in his Nuremberg affidavit, 2995–PS (*NCA*, V, p. 712). I have used both in abbreviated form.

10. *Austrian Requiem*, p. 24.

11. *Ibid.*

12. *Ibid.*, p. 25, and Schuschnigg's affidavit, N.D. 2995–PS, *op. cit.*

13. *Austrian Requiem*, p. 25.

14. *NCA*, IV, p. 357 (N.D. 1775–PS).

15. *NCA*, IV, p. 361 (N.D. 1780–PS).

16. From my own notes taken during the broadcast.

17. Dispatch to the German Foreign Office on Feb. 25, 1938, marked "Very Secret," *DGFP*, I, p. 546.

18. For Miklas' testimony, see *NCA*, Suppl. A, p. 523. Papen's suggestion is in his *Memoirs*, p. 425.

19. *Austrian Requiem*, pp. 35–36.

20. *NCA*, IV, p. 362 (N.D. 1780–PS).

21. *NCA*, VI, pp. 911–12 (N.D. C–102).

22. *Ibid.*, VI, p. 913 (N.D. C–103).

23. *DGFP*, I, pp. 573–76.

24. *NCA*, V, pp. 629–54 (N.D. 2949–PS).

25. *Austrian Requiem*, p. 47.

26. Testimony of Wilhelm Miklas on January 30, 1946, during anti-Nazi court proceedings against Dr. Rudolf Neumayer. Though the former President is a bit hazy about exact times and the exact sequence of events on the fateful day, his testimony is of great value and interest. *NCA*, Suppl. A, pp. 518–34 (N.D. 3697–PS).

27. *Austrian Requiem*, p. 51.

28. See *NCA*, Suppl. A, pp. 525–34 (N.D. 3697–PS). Also, *NCA*, V, p. 209 (N.D. 2465–PS, 2466–PS).

29. *NCA*, VI, p. 1017 (N.D. C–182).

30. *DGFP*, I, pp. 584–86.

31. *Ibid.*, pp. 553–55.

32. *TMWC*, XVI, p. 153.

33. *DGFP*, I, p. 263.

34. *Ibid.*, pp. 273–75.

35. *Ibid.*, p. 578.

36. *NCA*, I, pp. 501–2 (N.D. 3287–PS).

37. Text of circular cipher telegram, *DGFP*, I, pp. 586–87.

38. *TMWC*, XX, p. 605.

39. *TMWC*, XV, p. 632.

40. Memorandum of Seyss-Inquart at Nuremberg, Sept. 9, 1945, *NCA*, V, pp. 961–92 (N.D. 3254–PS).

41. *TMWC*, XIV, p. 429.

42. Text of Schacht's address, *NCA*, VII, pp. 394–402 (N.D. EC–297–A).

43. *NCA*, IV, p. 585 (N.D. 1947–PS).

CHAPTER 12

1. The file for Case Green was kept at Hitler's headquarters and was captured intact by American troops in a cellar at Obersalzbreg. The summary of the Apr. 21 Hitler–Keitel discussion is the second paper in the collection. The entire file was introduced in evidence at Nuremberg as N.D. 388–PS. An English translation is in *NCA*, III, pp. 306–709; a better English version of the Apr. 21 talks is in *DGFP*, II, pp. 239–40.

2. Secret memorandum of the German Foreign Office, Aug. 19, 1938, *NCA*, VI, p. 855 (N.D. 3059–PS).

3. *DGFP*, II, pp. 197–98.

4. *Ibid.*, p. 255.

5. Weizsaecker memorandum, May 12, 1938, *DGFP*, II, pp. 273–74.

6. Text of four telegrams exchanged, *NCA*, III, pp. 308–9 (N.D. 388–PS).

7. *Ibid.*, pp. 309–10.

8. Text of Keitel's letter and of the directive, *DGFP*, II, pp. 299–303.

9. *Ibid.*, pp. 307–8.

10. Dispatch of the German minister and military attaché in Prague, May 21, 1938, *ibid.*, pp. 309–10.

11. Dispatch of Ambassador von Dirksen, May 22, 1938, *ibid.*, pp. 322–23.

12. Speech to the Reichstag, Jan. 30, 1939, in *My New Order*, ed. by Roussy de Sales, p. 563.

13. According to Fritz Wiedermann, one of the Fuehrer's adjutants, who was present and who later swore that he "was considerably shaken by this statement." *NCA*, V, pp. 743–44 (N.D. 3037–PS).

14. Undated Jodl diary entry, *TMWC*, XXVIII, p. 372 (N.D. 1780-PS).
15. Item 11 of Case Green, *NCA*, III, pp. 315-20 (N.D. 388-PS); also *DGFP*, II, pp. 357-62.
16. *TMWC*, XXVIII, p. 373. The *TMWC* volume gives the German text. An English translation of excerpts of Jodl's diary is in *NCA*, IV, pp. 360-70.
17. The texts of the memoranda are given by Wolfgang Foerster in *Ein General kaempft gegen den Krieg*, pp. 81-119.
18. Jodl's diary, *TMWC*, XXVIII, p. 374. English translation, *NCA*, IV, p. 364 (N.D. 1780-PS).
19. *Ibid.*
20. *TMWC*, XX, p. 606.
21. *The Von Hassell Diaries*, p. 6.
22. *Ibid.*, p. 347.
23. Foerster, *op. cit.*, p. 122.
24. Dispatches of June 8 and 9, 1938, *DGFP*, II, pp. 395, 399-401.
25. Dispatch of June 22, *ibid.*, p. 426.
26. *Ibid.*, pp. 529-31.
27. *Ibid.*, p. 611.
28. Item 17 of the "Green" file, *NCA*, III, pp. 332-33 (N.D. 388-PS).
29. *TMWC*, XXVIII, p. 375.
30. Minutes of the Sept. 3, 1938, meeting, *NCA*, III, pp. 334-35 (N.D. 388-PS).
31. Schmundt's minutes of the Sept. 9 meeting, *ibid.*, pp. 335-38. It is Item 19 in the "Green" file.
32. Jodl's diary note for Sept. 13, *TMWC*, XXVIII, pp. 378-79 (N.D. 1780-PS).
33. *DGFP*, II, p. 536.
34. Reports of Kleist's visit are in *Documents on British Foreign Policy* [hereafter referred to as *DBrFP*], Third Series, II.
35. Most of the text of Churchill's letter is in *DGFP*, II, p. 706.
36. *DBrFP*, Third Series, II, pp. 686-87.
37. Nevile Henderson, *Failure of a Mission*, pp. 147, 150.
38. *DBrFP*, Third Series, I.
39. Erich Kordt gives his brother's account of this meeting in his book *Nicht aus den Akten*, pp. 279-81.
40. *DGFP*, II, p. 754.
41. *Ibid.*, p. 754.
42. L. B. Namier, *Diplomatic Prelude*, p. 35.
43. There is a considerable amount of material about the conference.

The text of the official report drawn up by Paul Schmidt, who acted as interpreter and was the only other person present, is in *DGFP*, II, pp. 786-98. Schmidt has given an eyewitness account of the meeting in his book *Hitler's Interpreter*, pp. 90-95. Chamberlain's notes are in *DBrFP*, Third Series, pp. 338-41; his letter to his sister on the meeting is in Keith Feiling's *Life of Neville Chamberlain*, pp. 366-68. See also Nevile Henderson's *Failure of a Mission*, pp. 152-54.

44. *DGFP*, II, p. 801.
45. *Ibid.*, p. 810.
46. Feiling, *op. cit.*, p. 367.
47. *NCA*, VI, p. 799 (N.D. C-2).
48. *DGFP*, II, pp. 863-64.
49. British White Paper, Cmd. 5847, No. 2. Text also in *DGFP*, II, pp. 831-32.
50. See *Berlin Diary*, p. 137.
51. The chief sources for the Godesberg conference are: Schmidt's notes on the two Godesberg meetings, *DGFP*, II, pp. 870-79, 898-908; Schmidt's description of the talks, *Hitler's Interpreter*, pp. 95-102; texts of correspondence exchanged between Hitler and Chamberlain on September 23, *DGFP*, II, pp. 887-92; notes by Kirkpatrick on the meeting, *DBrFP*, Third Series, II, pp. 463-73, 499-508; Henderson's description in *Failure of a Mission*, pp. 156-62.
52. *NCA*, IV, p. 367 (N.D. 1780-PS).
53. Jodl's diary, Sept. 26, 1938, *ibid.*
54. Text of the Godesberg memorandum, *DGFP*, II, pp. 908-10.
55. The *Times*, London, Sept. 24, 1938.
56. Text of the Czech reply, British White Paper, Cmd. 5847, No. 7.
57. Text of Chamberlain's letter to Hitler of Sept. 26, 1938, *DGFP*, II, pp. 994-95.
58. Though Dr. Schmidt's notes on this meeting are missing from the German Foreign Office papers, his own account of it appears in his book, *op. cit.*, pp. 102-3. Kirkpatrick's notes are in *DBrFP*, Third Series, II, No. 1, p. 118. Henderson's version in his book, *op. cit.*, p. 163.
59. Items 31-33 of "Green" file, *NCA*, III, pp. 350-52 (N.D. 388-PS).

60. Dispatch from Paris, *DGFP*, II, p. 977.

61. The text of Roosevelt's two appeals and Hitler's answer to the first one are in *DGFP*, II.

62. Dispatch from Prague, *DGFP*, II, p. 976.

63. Text of Hitler's letter of Sept. 27, 1938, *DGFP*, II, pp. 966–68.

64. Chamberlain's plan, *DGFP*, II, pp. 987–88. The Prime Minister's messages are quoted by Wheeler-Bennett in *Munich*, pp. 151–52, 155, from the Czech Archives.

65. *Ibid.*, p. 158.

66. Text in British White Paper, Cmd. 5848, No. 1. The letter was handed to Hitler by Henderson at noon the next day.

67. Henderson, *op. cit.*, p. 144. *DBrFP*, Third Series, II, p. 614.

68. Jodl's diary, Sept. 28, 1938, *NCA*, IV, p. 368 (N.D. 1780–PS).

69. Sources: Halder's interrogation at Nuremberg by Capt. Sam Harris, a New York attorney, *NCA*, Suppl. B, pp. 1547–71; also Halder's memorandum, which was given to the press at Nuremberg but is not included in either the *NCA* or *TMWC* volumes. Gisevius, *To the Bitter End*, pp. 283–328; his testimony at Nuremberg, *TMWC*, XII, pp. 210–19. Schacht, *Account Settled*, pp. 114–25.

70. Gisevius, *To the Bitter End*, p. 325. Also his testimony on the stand at Nuremberg, *TMWC*, XII, p. 219.

71. Erich Kordt's memorandum, made available to the writer. Allen Dulles, *Germany's Underground*, p. 46, also gives an account of the call.

72. Accounts of the meetings in the Chancellery on the forenoon of Sept. 28 are given by some of the participants: Schmidt, *op. cit.*, pp. 105–8; François-Poncet, *op. cit.*, pp. 265–68; Henderson, *op. cit.*, pp. 166–71.

73. Schmidt, *op. cit.*, p. 107.

74. *Ibid.*, p. 107.

75. Henderson, *op. cit.*, pp. 168–69. Schmidt, *op. cit.*, p. 108.

76. Masaryk later described this scene to the writer, as he did to many other friends. But my notes on it were lost, and I have used Wheeler-Bennett's moving account in *Munich*, pp. 170–71.

77. From Halder's interrogation, Feb. 25, 1946, *NCA*, Suppl. B, pp. 1553–58.

78. Schacht, *op. cit.*, p. 125.

79. Gisevius, *op. cit.*, p. 326.

80. *Ciano's Hidden Diary, 1937–1938*, p. 166. In a telegram dated June 26, 1940, Mussolini reminded Hitler that at Munich he had promised to take part in the attack on Britain. The text of the telegram is in *DGFP*, X, p. 27.

81. Text of the Chamberlain and Beneš notes, *DBrFP*, Third Series, II, pp. 599, 604.

82. The minutes of the two Munich meetings, *DGFP*, II, pp. 1003–8, 1011–14.

83. Henderson, *op. cit.*, p. 171. François-Poncet, *op. cit.*, p. 271.

84. Schmidt, *op. cit.*, p. 110.

85. Text of the Munich Agreement. *DGFP*, II, pp. 1014–16.

86. From the official report of Dr. Masarik to the Czech Foreign Office. The sources for this section on the Munich Conference are: *DGFP*, II, as cited above in note 83; text of the Munich Agreement, *ibid.*, pp. 1014–16; *DBrFP*, Third Series, II, No. 1, p. 227; and Ciano, Schmidt, Henderson, François-Poncet and Weizsaecker, *op. cit.*

87. *Berlin Diary*, p. 145.

88. The sources for this Chamberlain–Hitler meeting are: *DGFP*, II, p. 1017, for text of declaration; *DGFP*, IV, pp. 287–93, for Schmidt's official memorandum on the meeting; Schmidt's book, *op. cit.*, pp. 112–13. *DBrFP*, Third Series, II, No. 1228, gives a slightly different version of the conversation.

89. *DGFP*, IV, pp. 4–5.

90. Jodl's diary, *NCA*, IV, p. 368 (N.D. 1780–PS).

91. Keitel's testimony, April 4, 1946, *TMWC*, X, p. 509.

92. Manstein's testimony, Aug. 9, 1946, *TMWC*, XX, p. 606.

93. Jodl's testimony, June 4, 1946, *TMWC*, XV, p. 361.

94. Gamelin, *Servir*, pp. 344–46. A disappointing book! Pertinax, *The Grave Diggers of France*, p. 3, confirms the General here. These are also the sources of Gamelin's advice on Sept. 26 and 28.

95. Churchill, *The Gathering Storm*, p. 339.
96. *DGFP*, IV, pp. 602–4.
97. Schacht on the stand at Nuremberg, *TMWC*, XII, p. 531.
98. Speech to the commanders in chief, Nov. 23, 1939, *NCA*, III, p. 573 (N.D. 789–PS).

CHAPTER 13

1. "Green" file, Item 48, *NCA*, III, pp. 372–74 (N.D. 388–PS).
2. *Ibid.*
3. Hitler's directive, Oct. 21, 1938, *NCA*, VI, pp. 947–48 (N.D. C–136).
4. *DGFP*, IV, p. 46.
5. Heydrich's orders to the police for organizing the pogrom, *NCA*, V, pp. 797–801 (N.D. 3051–PS); Heydrich's report to Goering on the damage and the number of killed and wounded, *NCA*, V. p. 854 (N.D. 3058–PS). Report of Walter Buch, chief party judge, on the pogrom, *NCA*, V, pp. 868–76 (N.D. 3063–PS); Major Buch gives lurid details of numerous murders of Jews and blames Goebbels for the excesses. Stenographic report of the meeting of Goering with cabinet members and government officials and a representative of the insurance companies on Nov. 12, *NCA*, IV, pp. 425–57 (N.D. 1816–PS). Though the complete report is missing, the part which was found runs to 10,000 words.
6. *TMWC*, IX, p. 538.
7. *DGFP*, IV, pp. 639–49.
8. *DBrFP*, Third Series, IV, No. 5.
9. *Ciano's Hidden Diary*, entry for Oct. 28, 1938, p. 185; *Ciano's Diplomatic Papers*, pp. 242–46.
10. *DGFP*, IV, pp. 515–20.
11. Schmidt, *op. cit.*, p. 118; his notes on the meeting, *DGFP*, IV, pp. 471–77.
12. *DGFP*, IV, pp. 69–72.
13. *Ibid.*, pp. 82–83.
14. *Ibid.*, pp. 185–86; also in *NCA*, VI, pp. 950–51 (N.D. C–138).
15. Dispatch of the chargé, *DGFP*, IV, pp. 188–89.
16. *DGFP*, IV, p. 215.
17. Memoranda of Chvalkovsky's two talks, with Hitler and Ribbentrop,

on Jan. 21, 1939, *DGFP*, IV, pp. 190–202. Chvalkovsky's own report to the Czechoslovak cabinet on Jan. 23, Czech Archives, quoted by Wheeler-Bennett in *Munich*, pp. 316–17. Also see *French Yellow Book*, pp. 55–56.
18. Text, *DGFP*, IV, pp. 207–8.
19. Text, *ibid.*, pp. 218–20.
20. Memorandum of meeting, *ibid.*, pp. 209–13.
21. Text, *ibid.*, pp. 234–35.
22. Based on an account later given by the British minister in Prague, *NCA*, VII, pp. 88–90 (N.D. D–571).
23. Secret minutes of Tiso–Hitler talk, *DGFP*, IV, pp. 243–45.
24. See *DGFP*, IV, p. 250.
25. *Ibid.*, pp. 249, 255, 260. For Ambassador Coulondre's dispatch, see *French Yellow Book*, p. 96 (No. 77).
26. Dispatch from Prague, March 13, 1939, *DGFP*, IV, p. 246.
27. *TMWC*, IX, pp. 303–4.
28. The sources for the foregoing section, "The Ordeal of Dr. Hácha," are: Secret minutes of the meeting of Hitler and Hácha, *DGFP*, IV, pp. 263–69; it is also in the Nuremberg documents, *NCA*, V, pp. 433–40 (N.D. 2798–PS). Text of the declaration of the German and Czechoslovak governments, March 15, 1939, *DGFP*, IV, pp. 270–71; the first part was issued as a communiqué; it was actually drafted in the Foreign Office on March 14. Proclamation of the Fuehrer to the German People, March 15, *NCA*, VIII, pp. 402–3 (N.D. TC–50). Coulondre's dispatch, *French Yellow Book*, p. 96 (No. 77). Schmidt's description of meeting, his book, *op. cit.*, pp. 123–26. Henderson on, his book, *op. cit.*, Ch. 9. Scene with secretaries, A. Zoller, ed., *Hitler Privat*, p. 84.
29. *TMWC*, XVI, pp. 654–55.
30. Text, *DGFP*, VI, pp. 42–45.
31. Text, *DGFP*, IV, p. 241.
32. *Berlin Diary*, p. 156.
33. *The Ciano Diaries, 1939–1943*, pp. 9–12.
34. Text, *DGFP*, IV, pp. 274–75.
35. *Ibid.*, pp. 273–74.
36. *DGFP*, VI, pp. 20–21.
37. *Ibid.*, pp. 16–17, 40.

38. Reports of Dirksen, March 18, 1939, *ibid.*, pp. 24–25, 36–39.
39. *Ibid.*, p. 39.

CHAPTER 14

1. German memo of meeting, *DGFP*, VI, pp. 104–7. Lipski's report to Beck, *Polish White Book*, No. 44; given in *NCA*, VIII, p. 483 (N.D. TC–73, No. 44).
2. Hitler's assurance to Lipski, Nov. 15, 1937, *DGFP*, VI, pp. 26–27; assurance to Beck, Jan. 14, 1938, *ibid.*, p. 39.
3. Beck's instructions to Lipski, Oct. 31, 1938, *Polish White Book*, No. 45; *NCA*, VII, pp. 484–86. Ribbentrop's memo on meeting with Lipski, Nov. 19, *DGFP*, V, pp. 127–29.
4. German memo of meeting by Dr. Schmidt, *DGFP*, V, pp. 152–58. Polish minutes on, *Polish White Book*, No. 48; *NCA*, VIII, pp. 486–88 (N.D. TC–73).
5. Ribbentrop's memo of the meeting, *DGFP*, V, pp. 159–61. Polish minutes on, *Polish White Book*, No. 49; *NCA*, VIII, p. 488 (N.D. TC–73).
6. Ribbentrop's memo of his meeting with Beck in Warsaw, Jan. 26, 1939, *DGFP*, V, pp. 167–68; Beck's version is given in the *Polish White Book*, No. 52.
7. Dispatch of Moltke, Feb. 26, 1939, *DGFP*, VI, p. 172.
8. Lipski's dispatch to Warsaw on the meeting, *Polish White Book*, No. 61; also in *NCA*, VIII, pp. 489–92 (N.D. TC–73, No. 61). Ribbentrop's memo of the meeting, *DGFP*, VI, pp. 70–72.
9. Foreign Office memo of the meeting, *DGFP*, V, pp. 524–26.
10. *Ibid.*, pp. 502–4.
11. Source for this paragraph: *DGFP*, V, pp. 528–30.
12. *DGFP*, VI, p. 97.
13. *Ibid.*, pp. 110–11.
14. *NCA*, VII, pp. 83–86 (N.D. R–100).
15. Text in *DGFP*, VI, pp. 122–24. Ribbentrop's report on March 26 meeting with Lipski, *ibid.*, pp. 121–22; Polish version, *White Book*, No. 63.
16. Dr. Schmidt's memo of the meeting, *DGFP*, VI, pp. 135–36.

17. Moltke's dispatch, *ibid.*, pp. 147–48; Polish version, *White Book*, No. 64.
18. *DBrFP*, IV, No. 538.
19. See *DBrFP*, IV, Nos. 485, 518, 538 (text of Anglo–French proposal), 561, 563, 566, 571, 573.
20. *Ibid.*, No. 498.
21. *DBrFP*, V, No. 12.
22. Quoted by Gisevius, *op. cit.*, p. 363.
23. The text of Case White, *NCA*, VI, pp. 916–28; a partial translation is in *DGFP*, VI, pp. 186–87, 223–28 (N.D. C–120). The text of the original German is in *TMWC*, XXXIV, pp. 380–422.
24. Confidential German memos on the Goering–Mussolini talks are in *DGFP*, VI, pp. 248–53, 258–63. See also *The Ciano Diaries*, pp. 66–67.
25. The circular telegram of April 17, 1939, *DGFP*, VI, pp. 264–65; Foreign Office memo of the answers, *ibid.*, pp. 309–10; Weizsaecker's call to German minister in Riga, April 18, *ibid.*, pp. 283–84.
26. *Ibid.*, pp. 355, 399.
27. *DGFP*, IV, pp. 602–7.
28. *Ibid.*, pp. 607–8 (dispatch of Oct. 26, 1938).
29. *Ibid.*, pp. 608–9.
30. *Ibid.*, p. 631.
31. *DGFP*, VI, pp. 1–3.
32. Davies, *Mission to Moscow*, pp. 437–39. Ambassador Sieds's dispatch, *DBrFP*, IV, No. 419.
33. Boothby, *I Fight to Live*, p. 189. Halifax statement to Maisky, *DBrFP*, IV, No. 433.
34. *DGFP*, VI, pp. 88–89.
35. *Ibid.*, p. 139.
36. German memo of Goering–Mussolini talk, April 16, 1939, *ibid.*, pp. 259–60.
37. *Ibid.*, pp. 266–67.
38. *Ibid.*, pp. 419–20.
39. *Ibid.*, p. 429.
40. *Ibid.*, pp. 535–36.
41. *Nazi–Soviet Relations, 1939–41* [hereafter referred to as *NSR*], pp. 5–7, 8–9.
42. *French Yellow Book*, Dispatches Nos. 123, 125. I have used the French-language edition (*Le Livre Jaune Français*), but I believe the English edition carries the same numbers for dispatches.
43. *DGFP*, VI, pp. 1, 111. Appendix I

of this volume contains a number of memoranda on the staff talks taken from the German naval archives.

44. *The Ciano Diaries*, pp. 67–68.
45. German memo on the Milan meeting, *DGFP*, VI, pp. 450–52. Ciano's minutes, *Ciano's Diplomatic Papers*, pp. 282–87.
46. Text of the treaty of alliance, *DGFP*, VI, pp. 561–64. A secret protocol contained nothing of significance.
47. Schmundt's minutes, May 23, 1939, *NCA*, VII, pp. 847–54 (N.D. L–79). There is also an English translation in *DGFP*, VI, pp. 574–80. The German text is in *TMWC*, XXXVII, pp. 546–56.
48. For details of the plan, see N.D. NOKW–2584. This is in the *TWC* volumes [*Trials of War Criminals before the Nuremberg Military Tribunals*].
49. *NCA*, VI, pp. 926–27 (N.D. C–120).
50. *TMWC*, XXXIV, pp. 428–42 (N.D. C–126). The English translation of this document in *NCA*, VI, pp. 937–38, is so abbreviated that it has little value.
51. *NCA*, VI, p. 827 (N.D. C–23).
52. Text of the Anglo–French draft, *DBrFP*, V, No. 624; the British ambassador's account of Molotov's reaction is in the same volume, Nos. 648 and 657.
53. "Urgent" dispatch of May 31, *DGFP*, VI, pp. 616–17.
54. Dispatch of June 1, *ibid.*, pp. 624–26.
55. *Ibid.*, p. 547.
56. *Ibid.*, pp. 589–93.
57. *Ibid.*, p. 593.
58. Letter, Weizsaecker to Schulenburg, May 27, with postscript of May 30, *ibid.*, pp. 597–98.
59. *Ibid.*, pp. 608–9.
60. *Ibid.*, pp. 618–20.
61. *Ibid.*, pp. 790–91.
62. *Ibid.*, pp. 805–7.
63. *Ibid.*, p. 810.
64. *Ibid.*, p. 813.
65. *DBrFP*, V, Nos. 5 and 38.
66. *Pravda*, June 29, 1939.
67. Dispatch of June 29, *DGFP*, VI, pp. 808–9.
68. *TMWC*, XXXIV, pp. 493–500 (N.D. C–142). It is given much

more briefly in English translation in *NCA*, VI, p. 956.
69. *NCA*, IV, pp. 1035–36 (N.D. 2327–PS).
70. *NCA*, VI, p. 934 (N.D. C–126).
71. The secret minutes of the meeting of the Reich Defense Council, June 23, 1939, *NCA*, VI, pp. 718–31 (N.D. 3787–PS).
72. *DGFP*, VI, pp. 750, 920–21.
73. *Ibid.*, pp. 864–65.
74. Text of notes, *DGFP*, VII, pp. 4–5, 9–10.
75. Report of Burckhardt to the League of Nations, March 19, 1940. Text in *Documents on International Affairs, 1939–1946*, I, pp. 346–47.
76. *DGFP*, VI, pp. 936–38.
77. *Ibid.*, pp. 955–56.
78. Schnurre's memo, *ibid.*, pp. 1106–9.
79. *Ibid.*, pp. 1015–16.
80. *Ibid.*, pp. 1022–23.
81. *Ibid.*, pp. 1010–11.
82. *Ibid.*, p. 1021.
83. *DBrFP*, IV, No. 183.
84. See *DBrFP*, VI, Nos. 329, 338, 346, 357, 358, 376, 399.
85. *Ibid.*, Nos. 376 and 473.
86. Two dispatches of Aug. 1, *DGFP*, VI, pp. 1033–34.
87. *DBrFP*, Appendix V, p. 763.
88. Burnett's letter in *DBrFP*, VII, Appendix II, p. 600; Seeds's telegram, *ibid.*, VI, No. 416.
89. *DGFP*, VI, p. 1047.
90. *Ibid.*, pp. 1048–49.
91. *Ibid.*, pp. 1049–50.
92. *Ibid.*, pp. 1051–52.
93. *Ibid.*, pp. 1059–62.
94. *French Yellow Book*, Fr. ed., pp. 250–51.
95. Text of two letters, *DGFP*, VI, pp. 973–74.
96. Attolico's dispatch on his July 6 meeting with Ribbentrop is printed in *I Documenti diplomatica italiani* [hereafter cited as *DDI*], Seventh Series, XII, No. 503. I have used the quotation and paraphrasing from *The Eve of the War*, ed. by Arnold and Veronica M. Toynbee.
97. Memo of Weizsaecker, *DGFP*, VI, pp. 971–72.
98. *The Ciano Diaries*, pp. 113–14.
99. *Ibid.*, pp. 116–18.
100. *The Ciano Diaries*, pp. 118–19, 582–83. Ciano's minutes of the meeting with Ribbentrop are in

Ciano's Diplomatic Papers, pp. 297–98; also in DDI, Eighth Series, XIII, No. 1. No German record of this meeting has been found.

101. The captured German minutes of the meetings on Aug. 12 and 13 were presented at Nuremberg as documents 1871–PS and TC–77. The latter is the more complete and is published in English translation in NCA, VIII, pp. 516–29. I have used the version signed by Dr. Schmidt, in DGFP, VII, pp. 39–49, 53–56. Ciano's record of his two talks with Hitler are in Ciano's Diplomatic Papers, pp. 303–4, and in DDI, XIII, Nos. 4 and 21. Also the entries for Aug. 12 and 13, 1939, and Dec. 23, 1943, in his Diaries, pp. 119–20, 582–83.

102. This extract from Halder's diary is published in DGFP, VII, p. 556.

103. See DDI, Seventh Series, XIII, No. 28, and DBrFP, VI, No. 662.

CHAPTER 15

1. Schnurre's memo of the meeting, taken from his dispatch to the embassy in Moscow, Aug. 14, 1939, DGFP, VII, pp. 58–59.

2. Text of Schulenburg's letter, ibid., pp. 67–68.

3. Text of Ribbentrop's telegram, ibid., pp. 62–64.

4. The memo of the British businessmen was found in a file of Goering's office and is published in DGFP, VI, pp. 1088–93. There are numerous jottings on the document in Goering's handwriting. "Oho!" he scribbled several times opposite statements that obviously he could not believe. The whole fantastic and somewhat ludicrous story of Dahlerus' peace mission which brought him briefly to the center of the stage at a momentous moment is told in his own book, The Last Attempt. Also in his testimony at Nuremberg, TMWC, IX, pp. 457–91, and in Sir Lewis Namier's Diplomatic Prelude, pp. 417–33; the chapter is entitled "An Interloper in Diplomacy."

5. Interrogation of Halder, Feb. 26, 1946, NCA, Suppl. B, p. 1562.

6. Hassell, op. cit., pp. 53, 63–64.

7. Thomas, "Gedanken und Ereignisse," Schweizerische Monatshefte, December 1945.

8. Memo of Canaris on conversation with Keitel, Aug. 17, 1939, NCA, III, p. 580 (N.D. 795–PS).

9. Naujocks affidavit, NCA, VI, pp. 390–92 (N.D. 2751–PS).

10. Dispatch of Schulenburg, 2:48 A.M., Aug. 16, DGFP, VII, pp. 76–77. The ambassador gave a fuller account in a memo dispatched by courier, and he added details in a letter to Weizsaecker, ibid., pp. 87–90, 99–100.

11. DBrFP, Third Series, VII, pp. 41–42. For Ambassador Steinhardt's reports see U.S. Diplomatic Papers, 1939, I, pp. 296–99, 334.

12. Dispatch of Ribbentrop to Schulenburg, Aug. 16, DGFP, VII, pp. 84–85.

13. Ibid., p. 100.

14. Ibid., p. 102.

15. Dispatch by Schulenburg, 5:58 A.M., Aug. 18, ibid., pp. 114–16.

16. Dispatch of Ribbentrop, 10:48 P.M., Aug. 18, ibid., pp. 121–23.

17. Memo of Schnurre, Aug. 19, ibid., pp. 132–33.

18. Dispatch of Schulenburg, 6:22 P.M., Aug. 19, ibid., p. 134.

19. Dispatch of Schulenburg, 12:08 A.M., Aug. 20, ibid., pp. 149–50.

20. Churchill, The Gathering Storm, p. 392. He does not give his source.

21. Ibid., p. 391.

22. Hitler's telegram to Stalin, Aug. 20, DGFP, VII, pp. 156–57.

23. Dispatch of Schulenburg, 1:19 A.M., Aug. 21, ibid., pp. 161–62.

24. Dispatch of Ribbentrop, Aug. 21, ibid., p. 162.

25. Dispatch of Schulenburg, 1:43 P.M., Aug. 21, ibid., p. 164.

26. Stalin's letter to Hitler, Aug. 21, ibid., p. 168.

27. NCA, Suppl. B, pp. 1103–5.

28. DBrFP, VI, No. 376.

29. See DBrFP, Third Series, VII, Appendix II, pp. 558–614. The appendix contains a detailed day-to-day record of the military conversations in Moscow and constitutes the most comprehensive source I have seen of the Allied version of the talks. It includes reports to London, during the negotiations, by Air Marshal Burnett and Gen. Heywood, and

the final report of the British mission by Adm. Drax. Also, a verbatim account of the dramatic meeting of Gen. Doumenc with Marshal Voroshilov on the evening of Aug. 22, when the chief of the French military mission tried desperately to save the situation despite the public announcement that Ribbentrop was arriving in Moscow the next day. Also, the record of the final, painful meeting of the Allied missions with Voroshilov on Aug. 26. Volume VII also includes many dispatches between the British Foreign Office and the embassy in Moscow which throw fresh light on this episode.

This section of the chapter is based largely on these confidential British papers. Unfortunately the Russians, so far as I know, have never published their documents on the meeting, though a Soviet account is given in Nikonov's *Origins of World War II*, in which much use of the British Foreign Office documents is made. The Soviet version is also given in *Histoire de la Diplomatie*, ed. by V. Potemkin.

30. Paul Reynaud, *In the Thick of the Fight*, p. 212. Reynaud, pp. 210–33, gives the French version of the Allied negotiations in Moscow in August 1939. He gives his sources on p. 211. Bonnet gives his version in his book *Fin d'une Europe*.

31. The documents are in *DBrFP*, VII (see note 29 above). It is interesting that not a line on the Anglo–French diplomatic efforts in Warsaw to get the Poles to accept Russian help nor on the course of the military talks in Moscow was published in either the *British Blue Book* or the *French Yellow Book*.

32. Dispatch of Ribbentrop, 9:05 P.M., Aug. 23, from Moscow, *DGFP*, VII, p. 220.

33. Secret German memoranda, Aug. 24, *ibid.*, pp. 225–29.

34. Text of the Soviet draft, *DGFP*, VII, pp. 150–51.

35. Gaus affidavit at Nuremberg, *TMWC*, X, p. 312.

36. Text of the German–Soviet non-aggression pact and of secret additional protocol, signed in Moscow Aug. 23, 1939, *DGFP*, VII, pp. 245–47.

37. Churchill, *The Gathering Storm*, p. 394.

CHAPTER 16

1. *British Blue Book*, pp. 96–98.

2. Henderson's dispatch, Aug. 23, 1939, *ibid.*, pp. 98–100. German Foreign Office memo of meeting, *DGFP*, VII, pp. 210–15. Henderson reported on the second meeting on Aug. 24 (*British Blue Book*, pp. 100–2).

3. Text of Hitler's letter of Aug. 23 to Chamberlain, *ibid.*, pp. 102–4. It is also printed in *DGFP*, VII, pp. 216–19.

4. Text of Hitler's letter to Mussolini, Aug. 25, *DGFP*, VII, pp. 281–83.

5. Text of verbal declaration of Hitler to Henderson, Aug. 25, drawn up by Ribbentrop and Dr. Schmidt, *DGFP*, VII, pp. 279–84; also in *British Blue Book*, pp. 120–22. Henderson's dispatch of Aug. 25 describing interview, *British Blue Book*, pp. 122–23. See also Henderson's *Failure of a Mission*, p. 270.

6. Coulondre's dispatch, Aug. 25, *French Yellow Book*, Fr. ed., pp. 312–14.

7. *NCA*, VI, pp. 977–98. From a file on Russo–German relations found in the files of the Navy High Command.

8. Schmidt, *op. cit.*, p. 144.

9. *Ibid.*, pp. 143–44.

10. *Ciano Diaries*, pp. 120–29.

11. Weizsaecker memorandum, Aug. 20, *DGFP*, VII, p. 160.

12. Mackensen letter to Weizsaecker, Aug. 23, *ibid.*, pp. 240–43.

13. Dispatch of Mackensen, Aug. 25, *ibid.*, pp. 291–93.

14. See *DGFP*, VII, note on p. 285.

15. Mussolini's letter to Hitler, Aug. 25, *ibid.*, pp. 285–86.

16. *NCA*, VI, pp. 977–78 (N.D. C–170).

17. Ribbentrop's interrogation, Aug. 29, 1945, *NCA*, VII, pp. 535–36; Goering's interrogation, Aug. 29, 1945, *ibid.*, pp. 534–35; Keitel's testimony on the stand at Nuremberg under direct examination, Apr. 4, 1946, *TMWC*, X, pp. 514–15.

18. *NCA*, Suppl. B, pp. 1561–63.
19. Gisevius, *op. cit.*, pp. 358–59.
20. Hassell, *op. cit.*, p. 59.
21. Thomas, "Gedanken und Ereignisse," *loc. cit.*
22. Testimony of Dr. Schacht, May 2, 1946, at Nuremberg, *TMWC*, XII, pp. 545–46.
23. Testimony of Gisevius, Apr. 25, 1946, at Nuremberg, *ibid.*, pp. 224–25.
24. The texts of all these appeals are in the *British Blue Book*, pp. 122–42.
25. Hitler to Mussolini, Aug. 25, 7:40 P.M., *DGFP*, VII, p. 289.
26. *Ciano Diaries*, p. 129.
27. Mussolini to Hitler, Aug. 26, 12:10 P.M., *DGFP*, VII, pp. 309–10.
28. *Ciano Diaries*, p. 129. Mackensen's report, *DGFP*, VII, p. 325.
29. Hitler to Mussolini, Aug. 26, 3:08 P.M., *DGFP*, VII, pp. 313–14.
30. Mussolini to Hitler, 6:42 P.M., Aug. 26, *ibid.*, p. 323.
31. Hitler to Mussolini, 12:10 A.M., Aug. 27, *ibid.*, pp. 346–47.
32. Mussolini to Hitler, 4:30 P.M., Aug. 27, *ibid.*, pp. 353–54.
33. Dispatch of Mackensen, Aug. 27, *ibid.*, pp. 351–53.
34. Daladier to Hitler, Aug. 26, *ibid.*, pp. 330–31. Also in the *French Yellow Book*, Fr. ed., pp. 321–22.
35. Halder's diary, entry of Aug. 28, recapitulating "sequence of events" of previous five days. This portion is in *DGFP*, VII, pp. 564–66.
36. Goering's interrogation, Aug. 29, 1945, at Nuremberg, *NCA*, VIII, p. 534 (N.D. TC–90).
37. *TMWC*, IX, p. 498.
38. The account of the doings of Dahlerus is based on his book, *op. cit.*, and on his testimony at Nuremberg, where he learned how naïve he had been about his German friends. See above, note 4 for Chapter 15. It is substantiated by a great deal of material from the British Foreign Office published in *DBrFP*, Third Series, Vol. VII.
39. *DBrFP*, VII, p. 287.
40. Testimony of Dahlerus at Nuremberg, *TMWC*, IX, p. 465.
41. *DBrFP*, VII, p. 319n.
42. *TMWC*, IX, p. 466.
43. *DBrFP*, VII, pp. 321–22.
44. *British Blue Book*, p. 125, and *DBrFP*, VII, p. 318.

45. Text of British note to Germany, Aug. 28, *British Blue Book*, pp. 126–28.
46. Dispatch of Henderson to Halifax, 2:35 A.M., Aug. 29, *ibid.*, pp. 128–31.
47. Dispatch of Henderson to Halifax, Aug. 29, *ibid.*, p. 131.
48. Dispatch of Henderson, Aug. 29, *DBrFP*, VII, p. 360.
49. *Ibid.*, p. 361.
50. Text of German reply, Aug. 29, *British Blue Book*, pp. 135–37.
51. *DBrFP*, Third Series, VII, p. 393.
52. Henderson, *Failure of a Mission*, p. 281.
53. *British Blue Book*, p. 139.
54. Text of Chamberlain's note to Hitler, Aug. 30, *DGFP*, VII, p. 441.
55. *British Blue Book*, pp. 139–40.
56. *Ibid.*, p. 140.
57. *Ibid.*, p. 142.
58. Schmidt, *op. cit.*, pp. 150–55. Also Schmidt's testimony at Nuremberg, *TMWC*, X, pp. 196–222.
59. *TMWC*, X, p. 275.
60. Schmidt, *op. cit.*, p. 152.
61. *DGFP*, VII, pp. 447–50.
62. Henderson's *Final Report*, Cmd. 6115, p. 17. Also his book, *op. cit.*, p. 287.
63. *DBrFP*, VII, No. 575, p. 433.
64. *TMWC*, IX, p. 493.
65. Henderson's wire to Halifax, 12:30 P.M., Aug. 31, *DBrFP*, VII, p. 440; letter to Halifax, *ibid.*, pp. 465–67; wire, 12:30 A.M., Sept. 1, *ibid.*, pp. 468–69. Kennard's wire to Halifax, Aug. 31, *ibid.*, No. 618.
66. *DBrFP*, VII, pp. 441–43.
67. *British Blue Book*, p. 144.
68. *Ibid.*, p. 147.
69. *Ibid.*, p. 147.
70. Text of Polish written reply to Britain, Aug. 31, *ibid.*, pp. 148–49; Kennard's dispatch, Aug. 31 (it was not received in London until 7:15 P.M.), *ibid.*, p. 148.
71. For Lipski's Final Report, see *Polish White Book*. Extracts are published in *NCA*, VIII, pp. 499–512.
72. *DGFP*, VII, p. 462.
73. Lipski's version in his Final Report, *loc. cit.* Dr. Schmidt's German account of the interview is in *DGFP*, VII, p. 463.
74. The German text of Hitler's directive is in *TMWC*, XXXIV, pp.

456–59 (N.D. C–126). English translations are given in *NCA*, VI, pp. 935–39, and *DGFP*, VII, pp. 477–79.

75. Hassell, *op. cit.*, pp. 68–73.
76. Dahlerus' testimony at Nuremberg, *TMWC*, IX, pp. 470–71; Forbes's answer to questionnaire submitted by Goering's lawyer at Nuremberg is quoted in Namier, *Diplomatic Prelude*, pp. 376–77. Henderson's account is in his *Final Report*, p. 19.
77. *DBrFP*, VII, p. 483. Henderson's later account of the dispatch is given in his *Final Report*, p. 20, and in his book, *op. cit.*, pp. 291–92.
78. *TMWC*, II, p. 451.
79. Naujocks affidavit, *loc. cit.*
80. *DGFP*, VII, p. 472.
81. Gisevius, *op. cit.*, pp. 374–75.

CHAPTER 17

1. *DGFP*, VII, p. 491.
2. From Dahlerus' book, *op. cit.*, pp. 119–20; and from his testimony on the stand at Nuremberg, *TMWC*, IX, p. 471.
3. *DBrFP*, VII, pp. 466–67.
4. *Ibid.*
5. *TMWC*, IX, p. 436. Dahlerus' testimony, as printed here, contains a typographical error which makes him say the Poles "had *been* attacked," and is therefore totally misleading.
6. *DBrFP*, VII, pp. 474–75.
7. *Ibid.*, Nos. 651, 652, pp. 479–80.
8. The text is in *DGFP*, VII, p. 492, and in the *British Blue Book*, p. 168. Dr. Schmidt's notes on Ribbentrop's comments to Henderson and Coulondre are in *DGFP*, VII, pp. 493 and 495, respectively.
9. Schmidt's version of the argument in *DGFP*, VII, p. 493; Henderson gave his account briefly in his dispatch on the evening of Sept. 1, 1939 (*British Blue Book*, p. 169).
10. *DBrFP*, VII, No. 621, p. 459.
11. *Ciano Diaries*, p. 135.
12. *DGFP*, VII, p. 483.
13. *Ibid.*, pp. 485–86.
14. Bonnet to François-Poncet, 11:45 A.M., Sept. 1, *French Yellow Book*, Fr. ed., pp. 377–78. Mussolini's proposal for a conference on September 5 was outlined in a dis-

patch from François-Poncet to Bonnet Aug. 31, *ibid.*, pp. 360–61.

15. *DBrFP*, VII, pp. 530–31.
16. Henderson's *Final Report*, p. 22.
17. Text in *DGFP*, VII, pp. 509–10.
18. From Schmidt's memo, on which this scene is based, *ibid.*, pp. 512–13.
19. Schmidt, *op. cit.*, p. 156.
20. *Ciano Diaries*, pp. 136–37.
21. *DGFP*, VII, pp. 524–25.
22. *Ciano Diaries*, p. 137. De Monzie, a defeatist French senator, confirms the story in his book *Ci-Devant*, pp. 146–47.
23. Corbin's dispatch, *French Yellow Book*, Fr. ed., p. 395.
24. This section is based on *DBrFP*, VII, covering Sept. 2–3. There is an excellent summary, based on the confidential British Foreign Office papers and on the scant French sources available, in *The Eve of the War, 1939*, ed. by Arnold and Veronica M. Toynbee. Namier, *Diplomatic Prelude*, also is useful. I have purposely omitted the references to scores of documents in *DBrFP* in order to avoid cluttering the pages with numerals.
25. Halifax wires to Henderson: 11:50 P.M., Sept. 2, *DBrFP*, VII, No. 746, p. 528; 12:25 A.M., Sept. 3, *ibid.*, p. 533.
26. The text is in the *British Blue Book*, p. 175, and in *DGFP*, VII, p. 529.
27. *DBrFP*, VII, No. 758, p. 535.
28. Schmidt's account is in his book, *op. cit.*, p. 157; see also his testimony on the stand at Nuremberg, *TMWC*, X, p. 200.
29. Schmidt, *op. cit.*, pp. 157–58; also his testimony at Nuremberg, *TMWC*, X, pp. 200–1.
30. *Ibid.*
31. *DBrFP*, VII, No. 762, p. 537, *n.* 1.
32. *Ibid.*
33. *TMWC*, IX, p. 473.
34. Bonnet recounts this himself, *op. cit.*, pp. 365–68.
35. Weizsaecker's memo of the meeting, *DGFP*, VII, p. 532.
36. The text is in *DGFP*, VII, pp. 548–49.
37. The text is given in *DGFP*, VII, pp. 538–39.
38. This is revealed in the German Foreign Office papers, *ibid.*, p. 480.

39. Text of telegram, *ibid.*, pp. 540–41.
40. *Fuehrer Conferences on Naval Affairs* [hereafter referred to as *FCNA*], 1939, pp. 13–14.

CHAPTER 18

1. Text of Russian reply, *DGFP*, VIII, p. 4. A number of these Nazi–Soviet exchanges are printed in *NSR*, but *DGFP* gives a fuller account.
2. *Ibid.*, pp. 33–34.
3. Molotov's congratulations, *ibid.*, p. 34. His promise of military action, p. 35.
4. Schulenburg dispatch, Sept. 10, *ibid.*, pp. 44–45.
5. *Ibid.*, pp. 60–61.
6. *Ibid.*, pp. 68–70.
7. *Ibid.*, pp. 76–77.
8. *Ibid.*, pp. 79–80.
9. Schulenburg dispatch, *ibid.*, p. 92.
10. *Ibid.*, p. 103.
11. *Ibid.*, p. 105.
12. *Ibid.*, pp. 123–24.
13. *Ibid.*, p. 130.
14. The two telegrams, *ibid.*, pp. 147–48.
15. *Ibid.*, p. 162.
16. *Ibid.*, Appendix 1.
17. Text of the treaty, including the secret protocols, a public declaration, and exchanges of two letters between Molotov and Ribbentrop, *ibid.*, pp. 164–68.

CHAPTER 19

1. Maj.-Gen. J. F. C. Fuller, *The Second World War*, p. 55. Quoted from *The First Quarter*, p. 343.
2. Text of Directive No. 3, *DGFP*, VIII, p. 41.
3. Namier, *op. cit.*, pp. 459–60. He quotes the French text of the convention.
4. Testimony of Halder for defendants in the "Ministries Case" trial, on Sept. 8–9, 1948, at Nuremberg, *TWC*, XII, p. 1086.
5. Testimony of Jodl in his own defense on June 4, 1946, at Nuremberg, *TMWC*, XV, p. 350.
6. Testimony of Keitel in his own defense on April 4, 1946, at Nuremberg, *ibid.*, X, p. 519.
7. Churchill, *The Gathering Storm*, p. 478.
8. *FCNA*, 1939, pp. 16–17.

9. Weizsaecker's memorandum of his talk with Kirk, *DGFP*, VIII, pp. 3–4. His testimony at Nuremberg on his talk with Raeder, *TMWC*, XIV, p. 278.
10. *Ibid.*, XXXV, pp. 527–29 (N.D. 804–D). The document gives both Raeder's memorandum of his conversation and the text of the American naval attaché's cable to Washington.
11. Sworn statement of Doenitz at Nuremberg, *NCA*, VII, pp. 114–15 (N.D. 638–D).
12. *Ibid.*, pp. 156–58.
13. Nuremberg testimony of Raeder, *TMWC*, XIV, p. 78; of Weizsaecker, *ibid.*, pp. 277, 279, 293; of Hans Fritzsche, a high official in the Propaganda Ministry and an acquitted defendant in the trial, *ibid.*, XVII, pp. 191, 234–35. The *Voelkischer Beobachter* article is in *NCA*, V, p. 1008 (N.D. 3260–PS). For Goebbels' broadcast, see *Berlin Diary*, p. 238.
14. Schmidt memorandum of the talk, *DGFP*, VIII, pp. 140–45.
15. Brauchitsch's testimony at Nuremberg, *TMWC*, XX, p. 573. A note in the OKW War Diary confirms the quotation.
16. *Ciano Diaries*, pp. 154–55. *Ciano's Diplomatic Papers*, pp. 309–16.
17. *DGFP*, VIII, p. 24.
18. *Ibid.*, pp. 197–98.
19. *DGFP*, VII, p. 414.
20. Hitler's memorandum, *NCA*, VII, pp. 800–14 (N.D. L–52); Directive No. 6, *NCA*, VI, pp. 880–81 (N.D. C–62).
21. The text is in *TWC*, X, pp. 864–72 (N.D. NOKW–3433).
22. Both Schlabrendorff, *op. cit.*, p. 25, and Gisevius, *op. cit.*, p. 431, tell of this plot.
23. Wheeler-Bennett in *Nemesis*, p. 491*n.*, gives the German sources. See also Hassell, *op. cit.*, and Thomas, "Gedanken und Ereignisse," *loc. cit.*
24. Halder's interrogation at Nuremberg, Feb. 26, 1946, *NCA*; Suppl. B, pp. 1564–75.
25. Rothfels, *The German Opposition to Hitler*.
26. They are given in *NCA*, VI, pp. 893–905 (N.D. C–72).
27. Buelow-Schwante testified in the

"Ministries Case" before the Nuremberg Military Tribunal about Goerdeler's message and his own private audience with King Leopold. See transcript, English edition, pp. 9807–11. It is also mentioned in *DGFP*, VIII, p. 384*n*. His telegram of warning to Berlin is printed in *DGFP*, VIII, p. 386.

28. For the varied accounts of the Venlo kidnaping, see S. Payne Best, *The Venlo Incident;* Schellenberg, *The Labyrinth;* Wheeler-Bennett, *Nemesis.*

An official Dutch account is given in the protest of the Netherlands government to Germany, *DGFP*, VIII, pp. 395–96. Additional material was given at the "Ministries Case" trial at Nuremberg. See *TWC*, XII.

29. *TWC*, XII, pp. 1206–8, and *DGFP*, VIII, pp. 395–96.

30. For various accounts of the bomb attempt, see Best, *op. cit.;* Schellenberg, *op. cit.;* Wheeler-Bennett, *Nemesis;* Reitlinger, *The S.S.; Berlin Diary;* Gisevius, *op. cit.* There was also some material at Nuremberg from which I made notes and which I have used here, though I cannot find it in the *NCA* and *TMWC* volumes.

31. The textual notes are given in *NCA*, III, pp. 572–80, and also in *DGFP*, VIII, pp. 439–46 (N.D. 789–PS).

32. Halder's diary for Nov. 23 and his footnote added later. Brauchitsch's testimony at Nuremberg, *TMWC*, XX, p. 575.

33. Halder's interrogation at Nuremberg, *NCA*, Suppl. B, pp. 1569–70. Also see Thomas, "Gedanken und Ereignisse," *loc. cit.*

34. Hassell, *op. cit.*, pp. 93–94, 172.

35. *Ibid.*, pp. 79, 94.

36. From the diary of Admiral Canaris, *NCA*, V, p. 769 (N.D. 3047–PS).

37. *NCA*, VI, pp. 97–101 (N.D. 3363–PS).

38. *TMWC*, I, p. 297.

39. *Ibid.*, VII, pp. 468–69.

40. *Ibid.*, XXIX, pp. 447–48.

41. *NCA*, IV, p. 891 (N.D. 2233–C–PS).

42. *Ibid.*, pp. 891–92.

43. *Ibid.*, pp. 553–54.

44. *DGFP*, VIII, p. 683*n*.

45. The text, *ibid.*, 604–9.

46. *Ibid.*, p. 394.

47. *Ibid.*, p. 213.

48. *Ibid.*, p. 490.

49. *NCA*, IV, p. 1082.

50. *Ibid.*, p. 1082 (N.D. 2353–PS).

51. *DGFP*, VIII, p. 537.

52. *Ibid.*, pp. 591, 753, respectively.

53. Text of trade treaty of Feb. 11, 1940, and figures on deliveries, *ibid.*, pp. 762–64.

54. *NCA*, IV, pp. 1081–82 (N.D. 2353–PS).

55. *DGFP*, VIII, pp. 814–17 (Schnurre memorandum, Feb. 26, 1940).

56. *NCA*, III, p. 620 (N.D. 864–PS).

57. Langsdorff's moving letter is given in *FCNA*, 1939, p. 62. Other German material on the battle and its aftermath, pp. 59–62.

58. I have used some of the original German sources for this account of the forced landing: reports of the German ambassador and the air attaché in Brussels to Berlin, *DGFP*, VIII, and Jodl's diary. The text of the German plan of attack in the West, as salvaged by the Belgians, is given in *NCA*, VIII, pp. 423–28 (N.D. TC–58–A). Karl Bartz has given an account of the incident in *Als der Himmel brannte.* Churchill's comments are in *The Gathering Storm*, pp. 556–57. He gives a wrong date for the forced landing.

CHAPTER 20

1. *NCA*, IV, p. 104 (N.D. 1546–PS); VI, pp. 891–92 (N.D. C–66).

2. *Ibid.*, VI, pp. 928 (N.D. C–122), p. 978 (N.D. C–170).

3. *Ibid.*, p. 892 (N.D. C–166); *FCNA*, 1939, p. 27.

4. Churchill, *The Gathering Storm*, pp. 531–37.

5. *FCNA*, 1939, p. 51.

6. Rosenberg's memorandum, *NCA*, VI, pp. 885–87 (N.D. C–64). It is also given in *FCNA*, 1939, pp. 53–55.

7. *FCNA*, 1939, pp. 55–57.

8. *Ibid.*, pp. 57–58.

9. *DGFP*, VIII, pp. 515, 546–47.

10. Jodl's diary, Dec. 12, 13—obvi-

ously misdated. Halder diary for Dec. 14.

11. Rosenberg memorandum, *NCA,* III, pp. 22–25 (N.D. 004–PS).

12. *DGFP,* VIII, pp. 663–66.

13. Text of the directive, *NCA,* VI, p. 883 (N.D. C–63).

14. Interrogation of Falkenhorst at Nuremberg, *NCA,* Suppl. B, pp. 1534–47.

15. Text of the directive, *NCA,* VI, pp. 1003–5; also in *DGFP,* VIII, pp. 831–33.

16. Jodl's diary, March 10–14, 1940.

17. *DGFP,* VIII, pp. 910–13.

18. *Ibid.,* pp. 179–81, 470–71.

19. *Ibid.,* pp. 89–91.

20. Text of Hitler's directive, *ibid.,* pp. 817–19.

21. Dr. Schmidt's minutes of the meetings of Sumner Welles with Hitler, Goering and Ribbentrop are in *DGFP,* VIII; also Weizsaecker's two memoranda on his talk with Welles. The American envoy also saw Dr. Schacht after the banker, now fallen from grace, had been summoned by Hitler and told what line to take. See Hassell, *op. cit.,* p. 121. Welles has given his own account of his talks in Berlin in *The Time for Decision.*

22. *DGFP,* VIII, pp. 865–66.

23. *DGFP,* VIII, pp. 652–56, 683–84.

24. Text of Hitler's letter to Mussolini, March 8, 1940, *ibid.,* pp. 871–80.

25. Schmidt's minutes of the meetings, *ibid.,* pp. 882–93, 898–909; Ciano's version is in *Ciano's Diplomatic Papers,* pp. 339–59. Also see Schmidt, *op. cit.,* pp. 170–71, and *The Ciano Diaries,* for their personal comments on the meetings. Ribbentrop's two telegrams to Hitler reporting on his interviews are in *DGFP,* VIII.

26. Welles, *op. cit.,* p. 138.

27. *Ciano Diaries,* p. 220.

28. Dr. Schmidt's transcribed shorthand notes of the meeting, *DGFP,* IX, pp. 1–16.

29. Hassell, *op. cit.,* pp. 116–18, on which this account is largely based.

30. Allen Dulles, *Germany's Underground,* p. 59.

31. Shirer, *The Challenge of Scandinavia,* pp. 223–25.

32. Churchill, *The Gathering Storm,* p. 579. The British plans for R–4 are given in Derry, *The Campaign in Norway,* the official British account of the Norwegian campaign.

33. Text of the directive, *DGFP,* IX, pp. 66–68.

34. Text, *ibid.,* pp. 68–73.

35. Text of, *NCA,* VI, pp. 914–15 (N.D. C–115).

36. *TMWC,* XIV, pp. 99, 194.

37. Text of, *NCA,* VIII, pp. 410–14 (N.D. TC–55). Also in *DGFP,* IX, pp. 88–93.

38. Renthe-Fink's dispatch from Copenhagen, *DGFP,* IX, pp. 102–3; Bräuer's dispatch from Oslo, *ibid.,* p. 102.

39. The Danish version of the German occupation is based on the author's *The Challenge of Scandinavia,* and on *Denmark during the Occupation,* ed. by Børge Outze. Lt. Col. Th. Thaulow's contribution is especially valuable. A Guards officer, he was with the King at the time.

40. From the secret German Army Archives. Quoted in *NCA,* VI, pp. 299–308 (N.D. 3596–PS).

41. From the Norwegian State Archives; quoted in the author's *The Challenge of Scandinavia,* p. 38.

42. *DGFP,* IX, p. 124.

43. *Ibid.,* p. 129.

44. *Ibid.,* p. 186.

45. Churchill, *The Gathering Storm,* p. 601.

CHAPTER 21

1. *Belgium—The Official Account of What Happened, 1939–1940,* pp. 27–29.

2. *NCA,* IV, p. 1037 (N.D. 2329–PS).

3. *Ibid.,* VI, p. 880 (N.D. C–62).

4. Allen Dulles, *op. cit.,* pp. 58–61. Dulles says Col. Sas personally confirmed this account to him after the war.

5. There is a vast amount of material on the development of the German plans for the attack in the West. I have drawn on the following: the diaries of Halder and Jodl; Halder's booklet, *Hitler als Feldherr,* Munich, 1949 (an English translation, *Hitler as War Lord,* was published in London in 1950); extracts from the OKW War Diary published in the *NCA* and *TMWC*

volumes of the Nuremberg documents; the various directives of Hitler and OKW, published in the Nuremberg volumes and in *DGFP*, VIII and IX; Manstein, *Verlorene Siege;* Goerlitz, *History of the German General Staff* and *Der Zweite Weltkrieg;* Jacobsen, *Dokumente zur Vorgeschichte des Westfeldzuges, 1939–40;* Guderian, *Panzer Leader;* Blumentritt, *Von Rundstedt;* Liddell Hart, *The German Generals Talk;* considerable German material in the Nuremberg documents of the NOKW series which were produced at the secondary trials. For the British plans, see Churchill's first two volumes of his memoirs; Ellis, *The War in France and Flanders,* which is the official British account; J. F. C. Fuller, *The Second World War;* Draper, *The Six Weeks' War.* The best over-all account, based on all the German material available, is in Telford Taylor's *The March of Conquest.*

6. Churchill, *Their Finest Hour,* pp. 42–43.

7. *DGFP,* IX, pp. 343–44.

8. Both Goering and Kesselring were questioned on the stand at Nuremberg in regard to the bombing of Rotterdam. See *TMWC,* IX, pp. 175–77, 213–18, 338–40.

9. *TMWC,* XXXVI, p. 656.

10. Churchill, *Their Finest Hour,* p. 40.

11. For more detailed accounts, see Walther Melzer, *Albert Kanal und Eben-Emael;* Rudolf Witzig, "Die Einnahme von Eben-Emael," *Wehrkunde,* May 1954 (Lt. Witzig commanded the operation, but because of a mishap to his glider did not arrive until his men, under Sgt. Wenzel, had nearly accomplished their mission); Gen. van Overstraeten, *Albert I–Leopold III; Belgium—The Official Account of What Happened.* Telford Taylor, *The March of Conquest,* pp. 210–14, gives an excellent summary.

12. Churchill, *Their Finest Hour,* pp. 46–47.

13. Hitler to Mussolini, May 18, 1940, *DGFP,* IX, pp. 374–75.

14. From the King's own account of the meeting and that of Premier Pierlot. Published in the official

Belgian Rapport, Annexes, pp. 69–75, and quoted by Paul Reynaud, who was French Premier at the time, in his *In the Thick of the Fight,* pp. 420–26.

15. Lord Gort's dispatches, Supplement to the London *Gazette,* London, 1941.

16. Weygand, *Rappelé au service,* pp. 125–26.

17. Churchill, *Their Finest Hour,* p. 76.

18. Liddell Hart, *The German Generals Talk,* pp. 114–15 (soft-cover edition).

19. *Ciano Diaries,* pp. 265–66.

20. Telford Taylor, *The March of Conquest,* p. 297.

21. Text, Wilhelm II's telegram and draft of Hitler's reply, *DGFP,* IX, p. 598.

22. Texts of the exchange of letters between Hitler and Mussolini in May–June 1940 are in *DGFP,* IX.

23. *Ciano Diaries,* p. 267.

24. *DGFP,* IX, pp. 608–11.

25. *Ciano Diaries,* p. 266.

26. *Ibid.,* p. 266.

27. Though copies of the minutes found in the German Archives are unsigned, Dr. Schmidt has testified that he himself drew them up. Since he acted as interpreter, he was in the best position of anyone to do this. They are printed in *DGFP,* IX, as follows: negotiations of June 21, pp. 643–52; record of the telephone conversations between Gen. Huntziger and Gen. Weygand (at Bordeaux) on the evening of June 21, as drawn up by Schmidt, who had been directed to listen in, pp. 652–54; record of the telephone conversation between Gen. Huntziger and Col. Bourget, Gen. Weygand's adjutant (at Bordeaux), at 10 A.M. on June 22, pp. 664–71; text of the Franco-German Armistice Agreement, pp. 671–76; memorandum of questions raised by the French and answered by the Germans during the negotiations at Compiègne, pp. 676–79. Hitler gave instructions that this document, though not a part of the agreement, was "binding on the German side."

The Germans had placed hidden microphones in the *wagon-lit* and recorded every word spoken. I myself listened to part of the proceedings as they were being recorded in the German communications van. So far as I know, they were never published and perhaps neither the recording nor the transcript was ever found. My own notes are very fragmentary, except for the closing dramatic session.

28. Churchill, *Their Finest Hour*, p. 177.
29. *DGFP*, X, pp. 49–50.
30. *Ibid.*, IX, pp. 550–51.
31. *Ibid.*, IX, pp. 558–59, 585.
32. *Ibid.*, X, pp. 125–26.
33. *Ibid.*, pp. 39–40.
34. *Ibid.*, p. 298.
35. *Ibid.*, pp. 424, 435.
36. Churchill, *Their Finest Hour*, pp. 259–60.
37. *Ibid.*, pp. 261–62.
38. *DGFP*, X, p. 82.
39. OKW directive, signed by Keitel, *FCNA*, 1940, pp. 61–62.
40. *Ciano Diaries*, p. 274.
41. *FCNA*, 1940, pp. 62–66.
42. Letter of Hitler to Mussolini, July 13, 1940, *DGFP*, X, pp. 209–11.
43. Text of Directive No. 16, *NCA*, III, pp. 399–403 (N.D. 442–PS). It is also published in *DGFP*, X, pp. 226–29.
44. *The Ciano Diaries*, pp. 277–78 (for July 19, 22).
45. Churchill, *Their Finest Hour*, p. 261.
46. *DGFP*, X, pp. 79–80.
47. *Ibid.*, p. 148.

CHAPTER 22

1. Naval Staff War Diary, June 18, 1940. Quoted in Ronald Wheatley, *Operation Sea Lion*, p. 16. The author, a member of the British team compiling an official history of the war, had unrestricted access to the captured German military, naval, air and diplomatic archives, a privilege not accorded up to the time of writing to any unofficial American authors by either the British or the American authorities, who hold joint custody of the documents. Wheatley, as a guide to restricted German sources on Sea Lion, is therefore very helpful.
2. OKM (Navy High Command) records. Wheatley, p. 26.
3. Naval Staff War Diary, Nov. 15, 1939. Wheatley, pp. 4–7.
4. Wheatley, pp. 7–13.
5. *FCNA*, p. 51 (May 21, 1940); Naval Staff War Diary, same date, Wheatley, p. 15.
6. Text, *TMWC*, XXVIII, pp. 301–3 (N.D. 1776–PS). A not very good English translation is published in *NCA*, Suppl. A, pp. 404–6.
7. British War Office Intelligence Review, November 1945. Cited by Shulman, *op. cit.*, pp. 49–50.
8. Liddell Hart, *The German Generals Talk*, p. 129.
9. From OKH papers, cited by Wheatley, pp. 40, 152–55, 158. The plan was continually being altered throughout the next six weeks.
10. Naval Staff War Diary, Raeder–Brauchitsch discussion, July 17. Wheatley, p. 40*n*.
11. Halder diary, July 22; *FCNA*, pp. 71–73 (July 21).
12. Naval Staff War Diary, July 30, and memorandum, July 29. Wheatley, pp. 45–46.
13. *FCNA*, Aug. 1, 1940. This is Raeder's confidential report on the meeting. Halder gave his in a long diary entry of July 31.
14. *DGFP*, X, pp. 390–91. It is also given in N.D. 443–PS, which was not published in the *NCA* or *TMWC* volumes.
15. *FCNA*, pp. 81–82 (Aug. 1, 1940).
16. *Ibid.*, pp. 73–75.
17. From the Jodl and OKW papers. Wheatley, p. 68.
18. *FCNA*, pp. 82–83 (Aug. 13).
19. The two directives, *ibid.*, pp. 81–82 (Aug. 16).
20. *Ibid.*, pp. 85–86. Wheatley, pp. 161–62, gives details of Autumn Journey from the German military records.
21. Text of Brauchitsch's instructions, from the OKH files. Wheatley, pp. 174–82.
22. *FCNA*, 1940, p. 88.
23. *Ibid.*, pp. 91–97.
24. Halder's diary of the same date; Assmann, *Deutsche Schicksalsjahre*, pp. 189–90; OKW War Diary, cited by Wheatley, p. 82.
25. Raeder's report, *FCNA*, 1940, pp. 98–101. Halder's diary, Sept. 14.
26. *FCNA*, 1940, pp. 100–1.

27. Naval Staff War Diary, Sept. 17. Wheatley, p. 88.
28. *Ibid.*, Sept. 18. Cited by Wheatley.
29. *FCNA*, 1940, p. 101.
30. *Ciano Diaries*, p. 298.
31. *FCNA*, 1940, p. 103.
32. *Vorstudien zur Luftkriegsgeschichte, Heft 11, Der Luftkrieg gegen England, 1940–1*, by Lt. Col. von Hesler, cited by Wheatley, p. 59. The two to four weeks' estimate was given Halder, who noted it in his diary on July 11.
33. Adolf Galland, *The First and the Last*, p. 26. Also from Galland's interrogation, quoted by Wilmot in *The Struggle for Europe*, p. 44.
34. Luftwaffe General Staff record of directives given by Goering at this conference. Wheatley, p. 73.
35. *Ciano Diaries*, p. 290.
36. See T. H. O'Brien, *Civil Defence*. This is a volume in the official British history of the Second World War, edited by Prof. J. R. M. Butler and published by H. M. Stationery Office.
37. Notes on Goering's conference with air chiefs, Sept. 16. Cited by Wheatley, p. 87.
38. Churchill, *Their Finest Hour*, p. 279.
39. Peter Fleming, *Operation Sea Lion*, p. 293. An excellent book, but Fleming was denied access to restricted documents, though he says he was permitted to glance through—for an hour or two—Wheatley's study shortly before it was published.
40. *DGFP*, X.
41. Schellenberg, *The Labyrinth*, Ch. 2.
42. New York *Times*, Aug. 1, 1957.

CHAPTER 23

1. *DGFP*, IX, p. 108.
2. *Ibid.*, pp. 294, 316.
3. *Ibid.*, pp. 599–600.
4. *Ibid.*, X, pp. 3–4.
5. Churchill, *Their Finest Hour*, pp. 135–36 (the text of his letter to Stalin).
6. *DGFP*, X, pp. 207–8.
7. *Mein Kampf*, p. 654.
8. Speech of Jodl, Nov. 7, 1943, *NCA*, I, p. 795 (N.D. L–172).
9. Sworn testimony of Warlimont, Nov. 21, 1945, *NCA*, V, p. 741;

interrogation of Warlimont, Oct. 12, 1945, *ibid.*, Suppl. B, pp. 1635–37.
10. Halder's diary, July 22, 1940. He records what Brauchitsch told him of the conference with Hitler in Berlin on the previous day.
11. Halder's diary, July 3, 1940.
12. *NCA*, IV, p. 1083 (N.D. 2353–PS).
13. War Diary, OKW Operations Staff, Aug. 26, 1940. Quoted in *DGFP*, X, pp. 549–50.
14. See Warlimont's two affidavits, *NCA*, V, pp. 740–41 (N.D. 3031, 2–PS), and his interrogation, *ibid.*, Suppl. B, p. 1536. Jodl's directive of Sept. 6, 1940, is given in *NCA*, III, pp. 849–50 (N.D. 1229–PS).
15. The directive of Nov. 12, 1940, *NCA*, III, pp. 403–7. The portion dealing with Russia is on p. 406.
16. OKW War Diary, Aug. 28. Quoted in *DGFP*, X, pp. 566–67n.
17. *The Ciano Diaries*, p. 289.
18. *NCA*, VI, p. 873 (N.D. C–53).
19. *NSR*, pp. 178–81.
20. The German memorandum, *ibid.*, pp. 181–83; the Soviet memorandum of Sept. 21 in reply, *ibid.*, pp. 190–94.
21. *Ibid.*, pp. 188–89.
22. *Ibid.*, pp. 195–96.
23. *Ibid.*, pp. 197–99.
24. *Ibid.*, pp. 201–3.
25. *Ibid.*, pp. 206–7.
26. Ribbentrop's letter to Stalin, Oct. 13, 1940, *ibid.*, pp. 207–13.
27. Text of Ribbentrop's indignant telegram, *ibid.*, p. 214.
28. Text of Stalin's reply, *ibid.*, p. 216.
29. *Ibid.*, p. 217.
30. Memoranda of the meetings of Molotov with Ribbentrop and Hitler on Nov. 12–13, 1940, *ibid.*, pp. 217–54.
31. Schmidt, *op. cit.*, p. 212.
32. *Ibid.*, p. 214.
33. Dispatch of Schulenburg, Nov. 26, 1940, *NSR*, pp. 258–59.
34. *FCNA*, 1941, p. 13; Halder's diary, Jan. 16, 1941.
35. Halder diary, Dec. 5, 1940; *NCA*, IV, pp. 374–75 (N.D. 1799–PS). The latter is a translation of part of the War Diary of the OKW Operations Staff, headed by Jodl.
36. Complete German text, *TMWC*, XXVI, pp. 47–52; short English

version, *NCA*, III, pp. 407–9 (N.D. 446–PS).

37. Halder, *Hitler als Feldherr*, p. 22.
38. *FCNA*, 1940, pp. 135–36 (conference of Dec. 27, 1940).
39. *Ibid.*, pp. 91–97, 104–8 (conferences of Sept. 6 and 26, 1940). Raeder signed both reports.
40. *DGFP*, IX, pp. 620–21.
41. Schmidt, *op. cit.*, p. 196. The interpreter gives a fairly complete account of the conversations. The German minutes in the U.S. State Department's *The Spanish Government and the Axis* are fragmentary. Erich Kordt, who was also present, gives a more detailed account in his unpublished memorandum, previously referred to.
42. *Ciano's Diplomatic Papers*, p. 402.
43. Schmidt, *op. cit.*, p. 197.
44. The text of the Montoire Agreement is among the captured German Foreign Office papers but was not released by the State Department at the time of writing. However, William L. Langer, *Our Vichy Gamble* (pp. 94–95), cites it from the German papers made available to him by the Department.
45. *The Ciano Diaries*, p. 300.
46. Ribbentrop on the stand at Nuremberg, and Schmidt in his book, p. 200, recalled the words.
47. Schmidt, *op. cit.*, p. 200.
48. Halder's diary, Nov. 4, 1940; report of Jodl to Adm. Schniewind, Nov. 4, *FCNA*, 1940, pp. 112–17; Directive No. 18, Nov. 12, 1940, *NCA*, III, pp. 403–7 (N.D. 444–PS).
49. *FCNA*, 1940, p. 125.
50. *Ibid.*, p. 124.
51. *The Spanish Government and the Axis*, pp. 28–33.
52. Raeder's report is in *FCNA*, 1941, pp. 8–13; Halder did not record the two-day conference in his diary until Jan. 16, 1941.
53. Text of Directive No. 20, *NCA*, IV, pp. 101–3 (N.D. 1541–PS).
54. Text of Directive No. 22 and supplementary order giving code names, *NCA*, III, pp. 413–15 (N.D. 448–PS).
55. *NCA*, VI, pp. 939–46 (N.D. C–134).
56. Halder, *Hitler als Feldherr*, pp. 22–24.

57. *NCA*, III, pp. 626–33 (N.D. 872–PS).
58. German figures given by Foreign Office, as of Feb. 21, 1941, *NSR*, p. 275.
59. German minutes of conference, *NCA*, IV, pp. 272–75 (N.D. 1746–PS).
60. *NCA*, I, p. 783 (N.D. 1450–PS).
61. A partial text of Directive No. 25, *NCA*, VI, pp. 938–39 (N.D. C–127).
62. OKW minutes of the meeting, *NCA*, IV, pp. 275–78 (N.D. 1746–PS, Part II).
63. Jodl's testimony, *TMWC*, XV, p. 387. His "tentative" plan of operations, *NCA*, IV, pp. 278–79 (N.D. 1746–PS, Part V).
64. Text, letter of Hitler to Mussolini, March 28, 1941, *NCA*, IV, pp. 475–77 (N.D. 1835–PS).
65. For details see text of directive, *NCA*, III, pp. 838–39 (N.D. 1195–PS).
66. Churchill, *The Grand Alliance*, pp. 235–36.
67. From the Russian file of the High Command of the German Navy; entries for May 30 and June 6, *NCA*, VI, pp. 998–1000 (N.D. C–170).
68. *FCNA*, 1941, pp. 50–52.
69. *TMWC*, VII, pp. 255–56.
70. *NCA*, VI, p. 996 (N.D. C–170).
71. Cited by Shulman, *op. cit.*, p. 65.
72. Top-secret directive, April 30, 1941, *NCA*, III, pp. 633–34 (N.D. 873–PS).
73. Halder affidavit, Nov. 22, 1945, at Nuremberg, *NCA*, VIII, pp. 645–46.
74. *TMWC*, XX, p. 609.
75. Testimony of Brauchitsch at Nuremberg, *TMWC*, XX, pp. 581–82, 593.
76. Text of Keitel's order, July 23, 1941, *NCA*, VI, p. 876 (N.D. C–52); July 27 order, *ibid.*, pp. 875–76 (N.D. C–51).
77. Text of the court-martial directive, *NCA*, III, pp. 637–39 (N.D. 886–PS). A slightly different version found in the records of Army Group South and dated a day later, May 14, is given in *NCA*, VI, pp. 872–75 (N.D. C–50).
78. Text of directive, also dated May 13, 1941, *NCA*, III, pp. 409–13 (N.D. 447–PS).

79. Text of Rosenberg's instructions, *NCA*, III, pp. 690–93 (N.D. 1029, 1030–PS).

80. Text, *NCA*, III, pp. 716–17 (N.D. 1058–PS).

81. Text of directive, *NCA*, VII, p. 300 (N.D. EC–126).

82. Memorandum of meeting, *NCA*, V, p. 378 (N.D. 2718–PS).

83. Schmidt, *op. cit.*, p. 233.

84. Keitel interrogation, *NCA*, Suppl. B, pp. 1271–73.

85. The Duke of Hamilton's personal report, *NCA*, VIII, pp. 38–40 (N.D. M–116).

86. Kirkpatrick's reports on his interviews with Hess on May 13, 14, 15, *ibid.*, pp. 40–46 (N.D.s M–117, 118, 119).

87. Churchill, *The Grand Alliance*, p. 54.

88. *TMWC*, X, p. 7.

89. *Ibid.*, p. 74.

90. Douglas M. Kelley, *22 Cells in Nuremberg*, pp. 23–24.

91. *NSR*, p. 324.

92. *Ibid.*, p. 326.

93. *Ibid.*, p. 325.

94. *Ibid.*, p. 318.

95. *Ibid.*, pp. 340–41.

96. *Ibid.*, pp. 316–18.

97. *Ibid.*, p. 328.

98. *Ibid.*, p. 338.

99. Schulenburg's dispatches, May 7, 12, *ibid.*, pp. 335–39.

100. *Ibid.*, p. 334.

101. *Ibid.*, pp. 334–35.

102. Sumner Welles, *The Time for Decision*, pp. 170–71.

103. Churchill, *The Grand Alliance*, pp. 356–61.

104. *NSR*, p. 330.

105. *NCA*, VI, p. 997 (N.D. C–170).

106. *NSR*, p. 344.

107. *Ibid.*, pp. 345–46.

108. *Ibid.*, p. 346.

109. Text of, *NCA*, VI, pp. 852–67 (N.D. C–39).

110. The minutes of this meeting never turned up, so far as I know, but Halder's diary for June 14, 1941, describes it, and Keitel told about it on the stand at Nuremberg (*TMWC*, X, pp. 531–32). The Naval War Diary also mentions it briefly.

111. *NSR*, pp. 355–56.

112. *Ibid.*, pp. 347–49.

113. Schmidt's formal memorandum of the meeting, *ibid.*, pp. 356–57. Also his book, pp. 234–35.

114. Hitler to Mussolini, June 21, 1941, *NSR*, pp. 349–53.

115. *The Ciano Diaries*, pp. 369, 372.

116. *Ibid.*, p. 372.

CHAPTER 24

1. *NCA*, VI, pp. 905–6 (N.D. C–74). The complete text in German, *TMWC*, XXXIV, pp. 298–302.

2. Halder Report (mimeographed, Nuremberg).

3. *NCA*, VI, p. 929 (N.D. C–123).

4. *Ibid.*, p. 931 (N.D. C–124).

5. Article by Gen. Blumentritt in *The Fatal Decisions*, ed. by Seymour Freidin and William Richardson, p. 57.

6. Liddell Hart, *The German Generals Talk*, p. 147.

7. *Ibid.*, p. 145.

8. Halder Report,

9. Heinz Guderian, *Panzer Leader*, pp. 159–62. The page references in this and subsequent chapters are to the Ballentine soft-cover edition.

10. Blumentritt article, *loc. cit.*, p. 66.

11. Interrogation of Rundstedt, 1945. Quoted by Shulman, *op. cit.*, pp. 68–69.

12. Guderian, *op. cit.*, pp. 189–90.

13. *Ibid.*, p. 192.

14. *Ibid.*, p. 194.

15. *Ibid.*, p. 191.

16. *Ibid.*, p. 199.

17. Goerlitz, *History of the German General Staff*, p. 403.

18. *The Goebbels Diaries*, pp. 135–36.

19. *Hitler's Secret Conversations*, p. 153.

20. Halder, *Hitler als Feldherr*, p. 45.

21. *NCA*, IV, p. 600 (N.D. 1961–PS).

22. Blumentritt article, *loc. cit.*, pp. 78–79.

23. Liddell Hart, *The German Generals Talk*, p. 158.

CHAPTER 25

1. *DGFP*, VIII, pp. 905–6.

2. *NCA*, IV, pp. 469–75 (N.D. 1834–PS).

3. The text, *NCA*, VI, pp. 906–8 (N.D. C–75).

4. Raeder's report on the meeting, *FCNA*, 1941, p. 37. Also in *NCA*, VI, pp. 966–67 (N.D. C–152).

5. They are published, along with those of the subsequent talks, including two with Hitler, in *NSR*, pp. 281–316.
6. Schmidt, *op. cit.*, p. 224.
7. *FCNA*, 1941, pp. 47–48.
8. N.D. NG–3437, Document Book VIII–B, *Weizsaecker Case*. Cited by H. L. Trefousse, *Germany and American Neutrality, 1939–1941*, p. 124 and *n*.
9. Text of telegram, *NCA*, VI, pp. 564–65 (N.D. 2896–PS).
10. *Ibid.*, p. 566 (N.D. 2897–PS).
11. *FCNA*, 1941, p. 104.
12. *NCA*, VI, pp. 545–46 (N.D. 3733–PS).
13. Falkenstein memorandum of Oct. 29, 1940, *NCA*, III, p. 289 (N.D. 376–PS).
14. *FCNA*, 1941, p. 57.
15. *Ibid.*, p. 94.
16. *Ibid.*, Annex I (Raeder's report to the Fuehrer, Feb. 4, 1941).
17. *Ibid.*, p. 32 (March 18, 1941).
18. *Ibid.*, p. 47 (April 20, 1941).
19. *Ibid.*, May 22, 1941.
20. *Ibid.*, pp. 88–90 (June 21, 1941).
21. *NCA*, V, p. 565 (N.D. 2896–PS).
22. German Naval War Diary, *TMWC*, XXXIV, p. 364 (N.D. C–118). The partial English translation in *NCA*, VI, p. 916, is quite misleading.
23. *FCNA*, Sept. 17, 1941, pp. 108–10.
24. *Ibid.*, Nov. 13, 1941.
25. *NCA*, Suppl. B, p. 1200 (interrogation of Ribbentrop at Nuremberg, Sept. 10, 1945).
26. N.D. NG–4422E, Document Book IX, "Weizsaecker Case," cited by Trefousse, p. 102.
27. *Ibid.* Numerous telegrams between Ribbentrop and Ott in May 1941, and Ott's testimony in the "Far Eastern Trial" in Tokyo, cited by Trefousse, p. 103.
28. Vice-Minister Amau on Aug. 29 and Foreign Minister Adm. Toyoda on Aug. 30. Japanese minutes of the two meetings are in *NCA*, VI, pp. 546–51 (N.D. 3733–PS).
29. Hull, *Memoirs*, p. 1034. The texts of Toyoda's telegrams to Nomura on Oct. 16, 1941, are given in *Pearl Harbor Attack, Hearings before the Joint Committee on the Investigation of the Pearl Harbor Attack*, XII, pp. 71–72.
30. Hull, *op. cit.*, pp. 1062–63.
31. Documents 4070 and 4070B, *Far Eastern Trial*, cited by Trefousse, pp. 140–41.
32. Hull, *op. cit.*, pp. 1056, 1074.
33. Intercepted message of Oshima to Tokyo, Nov. 29, 1941, *NCA*, VII, pp. 160–63 (N.D. D–656).
34. *Pearl Harbor Attack*, XII, p. 204. The intercepted Tokyo telegram is also given in *NCA*, VI, pp. 308–10 (N.D. 3598–PS).
35. *NCA*, V, pp. 556–57 (N.D. 2898–PS).
36. *NCA*, VI, p. 309 (N.D. 3598–PS).
37. Text of telegram, *ibid.*, pp. 312–13 (N.D. 3600–PS).
38. Schmidt, *op. cit.*, pp. 236–37.
39. *TMWC*, X, p. 297.
40. Intercepted message of Oshima to Tokyo, Dec. 8, 1941, *NCA*, VII, p. 163 (N.D. D–167).
41. N.D. NG–4424, Dec. 9, 1941, Document Book IX, *Weizsaecker Case*.
42. I have combined here Ribbentrop's testimony in direct examination on the stand at Nuremberg—*TMWC*, X, pp. 297–98—and his statements during his pretrial interrogation which are contained in *NCA*, Suppl. B, pp. 1199–1200.
43. *Hitler's Secret Conversations*, p. 396.
44. *NCA*, V, p. 603 (N.D. 2932–PS).
45. Schmidt, *op. cit.*, p. 237.
46. A partial translation of Hitler's speech is published in Gordon W. Prange (ed.), *Hitler's Words*, pp. 97, 367–77.
47. English translation in *NCA*, VIII, pp. 432–33 (N.D. TC–62).
48. *FCNA*, 1941, pp. 128–30 (December 12).

CHAPTER 26

1. *TMWC*, XX, p. 625.
2. Hassell, *op. cit.*, p. 208.
3. *Ibid.*, p. 209.
4. Schlabrendorff, *op. cit.*, p. 36.
5. Hassell, *op. cit.*, p. 243.
6. The text of the first draft drawn up in January–February 1940, Hassell, *op. cit.*, pp. 368–72; text of the second draft, composed at the end of 1941, Wheeler-Bennett, *Nemesis*, Appendix A, pp. 705–15.
7. Hassell, *op. cit.*, pp. 247–48.
8. *Ibid.*, p. 247.

9. *The German Campaign in Russia —Planning and Operations,* 1940– 42 (Washington: Department of the Army, 1955), p. 120. This study is based largely on captured German Army records and monographs prepared by German generals for the Historical Division of the U.S. Army which, at the time of writing, were not generally available to civilian historians. However, I must point out that in the preparation of this and subsequent chapters the Office of the Chief of Military History, Department of the Army, was most helpful in giving access to German documentary material.

10. *TMWC,* VII, p. 260 (Paulus' testimony at Nuremberg). Hitler's remark was made on June 1, 1942, nearly a month before the offensive began.

11. *The Ciano Diaries, op. cit.,* pp. 442–43.

12. *Ibid.,* pp. 478–79.

13. *Ibid.,* pp. 403–4.

14. *FCNA,* 1942, p. 47 (conference at the Berghof, June 15). Also p. 42.

15. Halder, *Hitler als Feldherr,* pp. 50–51.

16. *FCNA,* 1942, p. 53 (conference of Aug. 16 at Hitler's headquarters).

17. Halder, *op. cit.,* p. 50.

18. *Ibid.,* p. 52.

19. The quotations from Hitler and Halder are from the latter's diary and book, and from Heinz Schroeter, *Stalingrad,* p. 53.

20. Quoted by Gen. Bayerlein from Rommel's papers, *The Fatal Decisions,* ed. by Freidin and Richardson, p. 110.

21. Bayerlein quotes the order. *Ibid.,* p. 120.

22. The source for this and for much else in this chapter about Hitler's OKW conferences is the so-called OKW Diary, which was kept until the spring of 1943 by Dr. Helmuth Greiner, and thereafter until the end of the war by Dr. Percy Ernst Schramm. The original diary was destroyed at the beginning of May 1945 on the order of General Winter, deputy to Jodl. After the war Greiner reconstructed the part he had kept from his original notes and drafts and eventually turned it over to the Military History Branch of the Department of the Army in Washington. Part of the material is published in Greiner's book, *Die Oberste Wehrmachtfuehrung, 1939–1943.*

23. *Procès du M. Pétain* (Paris, 1945), p. 202—Laval's testimony.

24. *The Ciano Diaries,* pp. 541–42.

25. Gen. Zeitzler's essay on Stalingrad in Freidin (ed.), *The Fatal Decisions,* from which I have drawn for this section. Other sources: OKW War Diary (see note 22 above), Halder's book, and Heinz Schroeter, *Stalingrad.* Schroeter, a German war correspondent with the Sixth Army, had access to OKW records, radio and teleprinter messages of the various army commands, operational orders, marked maps and the private papers of many who were at Stalingrad. He got out before the surrender and was assigned to write the official story of the Sixth Army at Stalingrad, based on the documents then in the possession of OKW. Dr. Goebbels forbade its publication. After the war Schroeter rescued his manuscript and continued his studies of the battle before rewriting his book.

26. *The Ciano Diaries,* p. 556. Mussolini's proposals are given on pp. 555–56 and confirmed from the German side in the OKW War Diary of December 19.

27. Felix Gilbert, *Hitler Directs His War,* pp. 17–22. This is a compilation of the stenographic record of Hitler's military conferences at OKW. Unfortunately only a fragment of the records were recovered.

28. Goerlitz, *History of the German General Staff,* p. 431.

CHAPTER 27

1. *NCA,* IV, p. 559 (N.D. 1919–PS).

2. *Ibid.,* III, pp. 618–19 (N.D. 862–PS), report of Gen. Gotthard Heinrici, Deputy General of the Wehrmacht in the Protectorate.

3. Bormann's memorandum. Quoted in *TMWC,* VII, pp. 224–26 (N.D. USSR 172).

4. *NCA,* III, pp. 798–99 (N.D. 1130–PS).

5. *Ibid.,* VIII, p. 53 (N.D. R–36).

6. Dr. Bräutigam's memorandum of Oct. 25, 1942. Text in *NCA*, III, pp. 242–51; German original in *TMWC*, XXV, pp. 331–42 (N.D. 294–PS).

7. *NCA*, VII, pp. 1086–93 (N.D. L–221).

8. *TMWC*, IX, p. 633.

9. *Ibid.*, p. 634.

10. *TMWC*, VIII, p. 9.

11. *NCA*, VII, pp. 420–21 (N.D.s EC–344–16 and –17).

12. *Ibid.*, p. 469 (N.D. EC–411).

13. *Ibid.*, VIII, pp. 66–67 (N.D. R–92).

14. *Ibid.*, III, p. 850 (N.D. 1233–PS).

15. *Ibid.*, p. 186 (N.D. 138–PS).

16. *Ibid.*, pp. 188–89 (N.D. 141–PS).

17. *Ibid.*, V, pp. 258–62 (N.D. 2523–PS).

18. *Ibid.*, III, pp. 666–70 (N.D. 1015–B–PS).

19. *Ibid.*, I, p. 1105 (N.D. 090–PS).

20. *NCA*, VI, p. 456 (N.D. 1720–PS).

21. *Ibid.*, VIII, p. 186 (N.D. R–124).

22. *Ibid.*, III, pp. 71–73 (N.D. 031–PS).

23. *Ibid.*, IV, p. 80 (N.D. 1526–PS).

24. *Ibid.*, III, p. 57 (N.D. 016–PS).

25. *Ibid.*, III, p. 144 (N.D. 084–PS).

26. *Ibid.*, VII, pp. 2–7 (N.D. D–288).

27. *Ibid.*, V, pp. 744–54 (N.D. 3040–PS).

28. *Ibid.*, VII, pp. 260–64 (N.D. EC–68).

29. *Ibid.*, V, p. 765 (N.D. 3044–B–PS).

30. *Hitler's Secret Conversations*, p. 501.

31. Based on an exhaustive study from the German records made by Alexander Dallin, *German Rule in Russia*, pp. 426–27. He used figures compiled by OKW–AWA in *Nachweisungen des Verbleibs der sowjetischen Kr. Gef. nach den Stand vom 1.5.1944.* AWA are the initials for the General Armed Forces Department of OKW (*Allgemeines Wehrmachtsamt*).

32. *NCA*, III, pp. 126–30 (N.D. 081–PS).

33. *Ibid.*, V, p. 343 (N.D. 2622–PS).

34. *Ibid.*, III, p. 823 (N.D. 1165–PS).

35. *Ibid.*, IV, p. 558 (N.D. 1919–PS).

36. *TMWC*, XXXIX, pp. 48–49.

37. *Ibid.*, VI, pp. 185–86.

38. *NCA*, III, pp. 416–17 (N.D. 498–PS).

39. *Ibid.*, pp. 426–30 (N.D. 503–PS).

40. *NCA*, VII, pp. 798–99 (N.D. L–51).

41. *TMWC*, VII, p. 47.

42. *NCA*, VII, pp. 873–74 (N.D. L–90).

43. *Ibid.*, pp. 871–72 (N.D. L–90).

44. Harris, *Tyranny on Trial*, pp. 349–50.

45. Ohlendorf's testimony on the stand at Nuremberg, *TMWC*, IV, pp. 311–23; his affidavit, based on Harris' interrogation, *NCA*, V, pp. 341–42 (N.D. 2620–PS). Dr. Becker's letter, *ibid.*, III, pp. 418–19 (N.D. 501–PS).

46. *NCA*, VIII, p. 103 (N.D. R–102).

47. *Ibid.*, V, pp. 696–99 (N.D. 2992–PS).

48. *Ibid.*, IV, pp. 944–49 (N.D. 2273–PS).

49. Case IX of the *Trials of War Criminals* [*TWC*] (N.D. NO–511). This was the so-called "Einsatzgruppen Case," entitled "*United States v. Otto Ohlendorf, et al.*"

50. *Ibid.* (N.D. NO–2653).

51. Cited by Reitlinger in *The Final Solution*, pp. 499–500. Reitlinger's studies in this book and in his *The S.S.* are the most exhaustive on the subject that I have seen.

52. *NCA*, III, pp. 525–26 (N.D. 710–PS). The English translation here of the last line misses the whole point. The German word *Endloesung* ("final solution") is rendered as "desirable solution." See the German transcript.

53. *TMWC*, XI, p. 141.

54. *TWC*, XIII, pp. 210–19 (N.D. NG–2586–G).

55. *NCA*, IV, p. 563 (N.D. 1919–PS).

56. *Ibid.*, VI, p. 791 (N.D. 3870–PS).

57. *Ibid.*, IV, pp. 812, 832–35 (N.D. 2171–PS).

58. Hoess affidavit, *NCA*, VI, pp. 787–90 (N.D. 3868–PS).

59. N.D. USSR–8, p. 197. Transcript.

60. *TMWC*, VII, p. 584.

61. *Ibid.*, p. 585.

62. *Ibid.*, p. 585 (N.D. USSR 225). Transcript.

63. *Law Reports of Trials of War Criminals*, I, p. 28. London, 1946. This is a summary of the twelve secondary Nuremberg trials, covered in the *TWC* volumes.

64. The above section on Auschwitz is based on, aside from the sources

quoted, the testimony at Nuremberg of Mme. Vaillant-Couturier,
a Frenchwoman who was confined
there, *TMWC*, VI, pp. 203–40;
Case IV, the so-called "Concentration Camp Case," entitled *United
States v. Pohl*, et al.," in the *TWC*
volumes; *The Belsen Trial*, London, 1949; G. M. Gilbert, *Nuremberg Diary, op. cit.;* Filip Friedman, *This Was Oswiecim* [Ausch-
witz]; and the brilliant survey of
Reitlinger in *The Final Solution*
and *The SS*.

65. *NCA*, VIII, p. 208 (N.D. R–135).
66. *NCA*, Suppl. A, pp. 675–82
(N.D.s 3945–PS, 3948–PS, 3951–
PS).
67. *Ibid.*, p. 682 (N.D. 3951–PS).
68. *Ibid.*, pp. 805–7 (N.D. 4045–PS).
69. The text, *ibid.*, III, pp. 719–75
(N.D. 1061–PS).
70. *TMWC*, IV, p. 371.
71. Reitlinger, *The Final Solution*, pp.
489–501. The author analyzes the
Jewish exterminations country by
country.
72. *TMWC*, XX, p. 548.
73. *Ibid.*, p. 519.
74. Examination of Josef Kramer,
Case I of the *Trials of the War
Criminals*—the so-called "Doctors'
Trial," entitled *"United States v.
Brandt*, et al."
75. Sievers' testimony, *TMWC*, XX,
pp. 521–25.
76. *Ibid.*, p. 526.
77. The testimony of Henry Herypierre is in the transcript of the
"Doctors' Trial."
78. *NCA*, VI, pp. 122–23 (N.D. 3249–
PS).
79. *Ibid.*, V, p. 952 (N.D. 3249–PS).
80. *Ibid.*, IV, p. 132 (N.D. 1602–PS).
81. Report of Dr. Rascher to Himmler, April 5, 1942, in the transcript of the "Doctors' Trial,"
Case I, *"United States v. Brandt,
et al."* Dr. Karl Brandt was Hitler's personal physician and Reich
Commissioner for Health. He was
found guilty at the trial, sentenced
to death and hanged.
82. *NCA*, Suppl. A, pp. 416–17
(N.D. 2428–PS).
83. Letter of Prof. Dr. Hippke to
Himmler, Oct. 10, 1942, in transcript, Case I.
84. *NCA*, IV, pp. 135–36 (N.D. 1618–
PS).

85. Testimony of Walter Neff, transcript, Case I.
86. Letter of Dr. Rascher to Himmler,
April 4, 1943, transcript, Case I.
87. Testimony of Walter Neff, *ibid.*
88. Himmler's letter and Rascher's
protest, *ibid.*
89. 1616–PS, in transcript of Case I.
The document is not printed in
TMWC, and the English translation in *NCA* is too brief to be of
any help.
90. Alexander Mitscherlich, M.D., and
Fred Mielke, *Doctors of Infamy*,
pp. 146–70. This is an excellent
summary of the "Doctors' Trial"
by two Germans. Dr. Mitscherlich
was head of the German Medical
Commission at the trial.
91. *Wiener Library Bulletin*, 1951, V,
pp. 1–2. Quoted by Reitlinger in
The S.S., p. 216.

CHAPTER 28

1. *The Goebbels Diaries*, p. 352.
2. *FCNA*, 1943, p. 61.
3. The Italian minutes of the Feltre
meeting are in *Hitler e Mussolini*,
pp. 165–90; also in Department of
State Bulletin, Oct. 6, 1946, pp.
607–14, 639; Dr. Schmidt's description of the meeting is in his
book, *op. cit.*, p. 263.
4. The chief sources are the stenographic records of Hitler's conferences with his aides at his headquarters in East Prussia on July 25
and 26, published in Felix Gilbert,
Hitler Directs His War, pp. 39–71;
also *The Goebbels Diaries*, entries
for July 1943, pp. 403–21; and the
*Fuehrer Conferences on Naval Af-
fairs* [*FCNA*], entries for July and
August 1943, made by Adm. Doenitz, the new commander of the
German Navy.
5. *The Memoirs of Field Marshal
Kesselring* (London, 1953), pp.
177, 184. I have used this British
edition of Kesselring's memoirs;
they have been published in America under the title *A Soldier's Record*.
6. See Kesselring, *op. cit.*, and Gen.
Siegfried Westphal, *The German
Army in the West*, pp. 149–52.
7. Firsthand accounts of Mussolini's
rescue are given in Otto Skorzeny,
Skorzeny's Secret Missions, by the

Duce himself in his *Memoirs, 1942–43,* and by the Italian manager and manageress of the Hotel Campo Imperatore in a special article included in the British edition of the *Memoirs.*

8. Hitler quotation from *FCNA,* 1943, p. 46; the item from Doenitz' diary is quoted by Wilmot, *op. cit.,* p. 152.

9. Halder, *Hitler als Feldherr,* p. 57.

10. I have quoted the lecture at length in *End of a Berlin Diary,* pp. 270–86. The text (in English) is in *NCA,* VII, pp. 920–75.

11. The above excerpts from Goebbels' diary are from *The Goebbels Diaries,* pp. 428–42, 468, 477–78. Hitler's talk with Doenitz in August 1943 was noted by the Admiral in *FCNA,* 1943, pp. 85–86.

CHAPTER 29

1. Dorothy Thompson, *Listen, Hans,* pp. 137–38, 283.

2. Hassell, *op. cit.,* p. 283.

3. *Zwischen Hitler und Stalin.* Ribbentrop's testimony, *TMWC,* X, p. 299.

4. George Bell, *The Church and Humanity,* pp. 165–76. Also Wheeler-Bennett, *Nemesis,* pp. 553–57.

5. Allen Dulles, *op. cit.,* pp. 125–46. Dulles gives the text of a memorandum written for him by Jakob Wallenberg on his meetings with Goerdeler.

6. The account of this whole episode is based largely on the report of Schlabrendorff, *op. cit.,* pp. 51–61.

7. To Rudolf Pechel, who quotes him at length in his book, *Deutscher Widerstand.*

8. There are a number of accounts, some of them firsthand, of the students' revolt: Inge Scholl, *Die weisse Rose* (Frankfurt, 1952); Karl Vossler, *Gedenkrede fuer die Opfer an der Universitaet Muenchen* (Munich, 1947); Ricarda Huch, "Die Aktion der Muenchner Studenten gegen Hitler," *Neue Schweizer Rundschau,* Zurich, September–October 1948; "Der 18 Februar: Umriss einer deutschen Widerstandsbewegung," *Die Gegenwart,* October 30, 1940; Pechel, *op. cit.,* pp. 96–104; Wheeler-Bennett, *Nemesis,* pp. 539–41; Dulles, *op. cit.,* pp. 120–22.

9. Dulles, *op. cit.,* pp. 144–45.

10. Quoted by Constantine FitzGibbon in *20 July,* p. 39.

11. Desmond Young, *Rommel,* pp. 223–24. Stroelin gave Young a personal account of the meeting. See also Stroelin's Nuremberg testimony, *TMWC,* X, p. 56, and his book, *Stuttgart in Endstadium des Krieges.*

12. Speidel emphasizes the point in his book *Invasion 1944,* pp. 68, 73.

13. *Ibid.,* p. 65.

14. *Ibid.,* p. 71.

15. *Ibid.,* pp. 72–74.

16. Dulles, *op. cit.,* p. 139.

17. Schlabrendorff, *op. cit.,* p. 97.

18. The telephone log of the Seventh Army headquarters. This revealing document was captured intact in August 1944 and provides an invaluable source for the German version of what happened to Hitler's armies on D Day and during the subsequent Battle of Normandy.

19. Speidel, *op. cit.,* p. 93.

20. *Ibid.,* pp. 93–94, on which this account is largely based. Gen. Blumentritt, Rundstedt's chief of staff, has also left an account, and there is additional material in *The Rommel Papers,* ed. by Liddell Hart, p. 479.

21. The text of the letter is given in Speidel, *op. cit.,* pp. 115–17. A slightly different version is in *The Rommel Papers,* pp. 486–87.

22. Speidel, *op. cit.,* p. 117.

23. *Ibid.,* pp. 104–17.

24. *Ibid.,* p. 119.

25. Schlabrendorff, *op. cit.,* p. 103. He was still attached to Tresckow's staff.

26. The sources for these meetings of the conspirators on July 16 are the stenographic account of the trial of Witzleben, Hoepner *et al.;* Kaltenbrunner's reports on the July 20 uprising; Eberhard Zeller, *Geist der Freiheit,* pp. 213–14; Gerhard Ritter, *Carl Goerdeler und die deutsche Widerstandsbewegung,* pp. 401–3.

27. Heusinger, *Befehl im Widerstreit,* p. 352, tells of his last words that day.

28. Zeller, *op. cit.,* p. 221.

29. Schmidt, *op. cit.*, pp. 275–77.
30. A number of guests at the tea party, Italian and German, have given eyewitness accounts of it. Eugen Dollmann, an S.S. liaison officer with Mussolini, has rendered the fullest description both in his book, *Roma Nazista*, pp. 393–400, and in his interrogation by Allied investigators, which is summed up by Dulles, *op. cit.*, pp. 9–11. Zeller, *op. cit.*, p. 367, *n*.69, and Wheeler-Bennett, *Nemesis,* pp. 644–46, have written graphic accounts, based mostly on Dollmann.
31. The transcript of this telephone conversation was put in evidence before the People's Court. Schlabrendorff, *op. cit.*, quotes it on p. 113.
32. Zeller, *op. cit.*, p. 363*n*., cites two eyewitnesses to the executions, an Army chauffeur who observed them from a nearby window, and a woman secretary of Fromm.
33. This account of what went on in the Bendlerstrasse that evening is taken largely from General Hoepner's frank testimony before the People's Court during his trial and that of Witzleben and six other officers on Aug. 6–7, 1944. The records of the People's Court were destroyed in an American bombing on Feb. 3, 1945, but one of the stenographers at this trial—at the risk of his life, he says—purloined the shorthand records before the bombing and after the war turned them over to the Nuremberg tribunal. They are published verbatim in German in *TMWC*, XXXIII, pp. 299–530.

There is a great deal of material on the July 20 plot, much of it conflicting and some quite confusing. The best reconstruction of it is by Zeller, *op. cit.*, who gives a lengthy list of his sources on pp. 381–88. Gerhard Ritter's book on Goerdeler, *op. cit.*, is an invaluable contribution, though it naturally concentrates on its subject. Wheeler-Bennett's *Nemesis* gives the best account available in English and uses, as does Zeller, Otto John's unpublished memorandum. John, who after the war got into difficulties with the Bonn government and

was imprisoned by it, was present at the Bendlerstrasse that day and recorded a great deal of what he saw and what Stauffenberg told him. Constantine FitzGibbon, *op. cit.*, gives a lively account, based mostly on German sources, especially Zeller.

Also invaluable, though they must be read with caution, are the daily reports on the investigation of the plot carried out by the S.D.–Gestapo, which date from July 21 to Dec. 15, 1944. They were signed by Kaltenbrunner and sent to Hitler, being drawn up in extra-large type so that the Fuehrer could read them without his spectacles. They represent the labors of the "Special Commission for July 20, 1944," which numbered some 400 S.D.–Gestapo officials divided into eleven investigation groups. The Kaltenbrunner reports are among the captured documents. Microfilm copies are available at the National Archives in Washington—No. T–84, Serial No. 39, Rolls 19–21. See also Serial No. 40, Roll 22.
34. Zeller, *op. cit.*, p. 372, *n*.10, quotes an officer who was present.
35. The account of the executions was later related by the prison warder, Hans Hoffmann, a second warden and the photographer, and is given in Wheeler-Bennett, *Nemesis,* pp. 683–84, among others.
36. Wilfred von Oven, *Mit Goebbels bis zum Ende*, II, p. 118.
37. Ritter, *op. cit.*, pp. 419–29, gives the details of this interesting sidelight.
38. This figure is given in a commentary in the records of the Fuehrer's conferences on naval affairs (*FCNA*, 1944, p. 46) and is accepted by Zeller, *op. cit.*, p. 283. Pechel, *op. cit.*, who found the official "Execution Register," says, p. 327, there were 3,427 executions recorded in 1944, though a few of these probably were not connected with the July 20 plot.
39. Schlabrendorff, *op. cit.*, pp. 119–20. I have altered the English text here given to make it conform more to the original German.
40. Gen. Blumentritt gave this account

to Liddell Hart (*The German Generals Talk*, pp. 217–23).

41. *Ibid.*, p. 222. There is considerable source material on the Paris end of the plot, including the account given by Speidel in his book and numerous articles in German magazines by eyewitnesses. The best over-all account has been rendered by Wilhelm von Schramm, an Army archivist stationed in the West: *Der 20 Juli in Paris*.

42. Felix Gilbert, *op. cit.*, p. 101.

43. Speidel, *op. cit.*, p. 152. My account of the death of Rommel is based on, besides Speidel, who questioned Frau Rommel and other witnesses, the following sources: two reports written by the Field Marshal's son, Manfred, the first for British intelligence, quoted by Shulman, *op. cit.*, pp. 138–39, the second for *The Rommel Papers*, ed. by Liddell Hart, pp. 495–505; and Gen. Keitel's interrogation by Col. John H. Amen on Sept. 28, 1945, at Nuremberg (*NCA*, Suppl. B, pp. 1256–71). Desmond Young, *op. cit.*, has also given a full account, based on talks with the Rommel family and friends and on Gen. Maisel's denazification trial after the war.

44. *TMWC*, XXI, p. 47.

45. Speidel, *op. cit.*, pp. 155, 172.

46. Goerlitz, *History of the German General Staff*, p. 477.

47. Guderian, *op. cit.*, p. 273.

48. *Ibid.*, p. 276.

49. Liddell Hart, *The German Generals Talk*, pp. 222–23.

CHAPTER 30

1. Speidel, *op. cit.*, p. 147.

2. British War Office interrogation, cited by Shulman, *op. cit.*, p. 206.

3. Fuehrer conference, Aug. 31, 1944. Felix Gilbert, *op. cit.*, p. 106.

4. Fuehrer conference, March 13, 1943.

5. United States Strategic Bombing Survey, *Economic Report*, Appendix, Table 15.

6. From U.S. First Army G-2 reports, quoted by Shulman, *op. cit.*, pp. 215–19.

7. Eisenhower, *Crusade in Europe*, p. 312.

8. Rundstedt to Liddell Hart, *The German Generals Talk*, p. 229.

9. Guderian, *op. cit.*, pp. 305–6, 310.

10. Manteuffel, in Freidin and Richardson (eds.), *op. cit.*, p. 266.

11. Fuehrer conference, Dec. 12, 1944.

12. Guderian, *op. cit.*, p. 315.

13. *Ibid.*, p. 334.

14. Albert Speer to Hitler, Jan. 30, 1945, *TMWC*, XLI.

15. Guderian, *op. cit.*, p. 336.

16. Fuehrer conference, Jan. 27, 1945. This is included in Felix Gilbert, *op. cit.*, pp. 111–32. I have slightly altered the sequence of the text.

17. Fuehrer conference, undated, but probably on Feb. 19, 1945, since Adm. Doenitz notes the discussion in his record of that date. See *FCNA*, 1945, p. 49. Gilbert, *op. cit.*, gives the Hitler quotation, p. 179.

18. *FCNA*, 1945, pp. 50–51.

19. Fuehrer conference, March 23, 1945. This is the last transcript preserved. Gilbert, *op. cit.*, gives it in full, pp. 141–74.

20. Testimony of Albert Speer at Nuremberg, *TMWC*, XVI, p. 492.

21. Guderian, *op. cit.*, pp. 341, 43.

22. Text of Hitler's order, *FCNA*, 1945, p. 90.

23. Speer, *TMWC*, XVI, pp. 497–98. This section, including the quotations from Hitler and Speer, is taken from the latter's testimony on the stand at Nuremberg on June 20, 1946, the text of which is given in *TMWC*, XVI; and from the documents which he presented in his defense, which are given in Vol. XLI.

24. SHAEF intelligence summary, March 11, 1945. Quoted by Wilmot, *op. cit.*, p. 690.

CHAPTER 31

1. Count Lutz Schwerin von Krosigk's unpublished diary. I have given the essential extracts in *End of a Berlin Diary*, pp. 190–205.

Trevor-Roper, in *The Last Days of Hitler*, also quotes from it. Trevor-Roper, the historian, who was a British intelligence officer during the war, was assigned the task of investigating the circumstances of Hitler's end. The results are given in his brilliant book, to which all who attempt to write this final chapter of the Third Reich are indebted. I have availed myself of a number of other sources, especially the firsthand accounts of eyewitnesses such as Speer, Keitel, Jodl, Gen. Karl Koller, Doenitz, Krosigk, Hanna Reitsch, Capt. Gerhardt Boldt and Capt. Joachim Schultz, as well as one of Hitler's women secretaries and his chauffeur.

2. Gerhardt Boldt, *In the Shelter with Hitler*, Ch. 1. Capt. Boldt was A.D.C. to Guderian and then to Gen. Krebs, the last Chief of the Army General Staff, and spent the final days in the bunker.

3. Albert Zoller, *Hitler Privat*, pp. 203–5. According to the French edition (*Douze Ans auprès d'Hitler*) Zoller was a captain in the French Army attached as interrogation officer to the U.S. Seventh Army and in this capacity questioned one of Hitler's four women secretaries; later, in 1947, he collaborated with her in the writing of this book of recollections of the Fuehrer. She is probably Christa Schroeder, who served Hitler as stenographer from 1933 to a week before his end.

4. Krosigk's diary.

5. *Ibid.*

6. Quoted by Wilmot, *op. cit.*, p. 699.

7. Trevor-Roper, *op. cit.*, p. 100. The account was given by one of Goebbels' secretaries, Frau Inge Haberzettel.

8. Michael A. Musmanno, *Ten Days to Die*, p. 92. Judge Musmanno, a U.S. Navy intelligence officer during the war, personally interrogated the survivors who had been with Hitler during his last days.

9. Keitel interrogation, *NCA*, Suppl. B, p. 1294.

10. *NCA*, VI, p. 561 (N.D. 3734–PS). This is a lengthy summary of a U.S. Army interrogation of Hanna Reitsch on the last days of Hitler in the bunker. She later repudiated parts of her statement, but Army authorities have confirmed its substantial accuracy as containing what she said during the interrogation on Oct. 8, 1945. Though Frl. Reitsch is a highly hysterical person, or was during the months that followed her harrowing experience in the bunker, her account, when checked against the evidence of the others, is a valuable record of Hitler's very last days.

11. Gen. Karl Koller, *Der letzte Monat*, p. 23. This is Koller's diary covering the period from April 14 to May 27, 1945, and is an invaluable source for the last days of the Third Reich.

12. Keitel in his interrogation at Nuremberg, *NCA*, Suppl. B, pp. 1275–79. Jodl's account was given to Gen. Koller the same night and recorded in the latter's diary of April 22–23. See Koller, *op. cit.*, pp. 30–32.

13. Trevor-Roper, *op. cit.*, pp. 124, 126–27. The author gives Berger's account, he says, "with some reservations."

14. Keitel recalled the remark in his interrogation, *loc. cit.*, p. 1277. Jodl's version is in Koller's diary, *op. cit.*, p. 31.

15. Bernadotte, *The Curtain Falls*, p. 114; Schellenberg, *op. cit.*, pp. 399–400. They agree substantially in their versions of the meeting.

16. Speer on the stand at Nuremberg, *TMWC*, XVI, pp. 554–55.

17. Hanna Reitsch interrogation, *loc. cit.*, pp. 554–55.

18. *Ibid.*, p. 556. All the subsequent quotations and the events described by Hanna Reitsch are taken from this interrogation and are found in *NCA*, VI, pp. 551–71 (N.D. 3734–PS). They will not therefore be cited in each case.

19. Keitel, in his interrogation, *loc. cit.*, pp. 1281–82, quoted the message from memory. The German naval records give a similarly worded radio message from Hitler to Jodl dated 7:52 P.M., April 29 (*FCNA*, 1945, p. 120), and Schultz's OKW Diary (p. 51), which gives the same text, records it as received by Jodl at 11 P.M. on April 29. This is probably an error, since by that hour of that evening Hitler, judging by his actions, no longer cared where any army was.

20. Trevor-Roper, *op. cit.*, p. 163,

gives the first message. The second I have found in the Navy's records, *FCNA*, 1945, p. 120. The further message from the naval liaison officer in the bunker, Adm. Voss, is also given in *FCNA*, p. 120.

21. The text of Hitler's Political Testament and personal will is given in N.D. 3569–PS. A copy of his marriage certificate was also presented at Nuremberg. I have given the texts of all three in *End of a Berlin Diary*, pp. 177–83, *n.* A rather hastily written English translation of the will and testament is published in *NCA*, VI, pp. 259–63. The original German is in *TMWC*, XLI, under the Speer documents.

22. Gen. Koller, *op. cit.*, p. 79, gives the text of Bormann's radiogram.

23. The text of Goebbels' appendix was presented at the Nuremberg trial. I have given it in *End of a Berlin Diary*, p. 183*n*.

24. Kempka's account of the death of Hitler and his bride is given in two sworn statements published in *NCA*, VI, pp. 571–86 (N.D. 3735–PS).

25. Juergen Thorwald, *Das Ende an der Elbe*, p. 224.

26. This account of the death of the Goebbels family is given by Trevor-Roper, *op. cit.*, pp. 212–14, and is based largely on the later testimony of Schwaegermann, Axmann and Kempka.

27. Joachim Schultz, *Die letzten 30 Tage*, pp. 81–85. These notes are based on the OKW diaries for the last month of the war and I have used them to bolster a good many pages of this chapter. The book is one of several published under the direction of Thorwald under the general title *Dokumente zur Zeitgeschichte*.

28. Eisenhower, *op. cit.*, p. 426.

29. *End of a Berlin Diary*.

ACKNOWLEDGMENTS

Though for this book, as for all others that I have written, I have done my own research and planning, I owe a great deal to a number of persons and institutions for their generous help during the five years that this work was in the making.

The late Jack Goodman, of Simon and Schuster, and Joseph Barnes, my editor at this publishing house, got me started and Barnes, an old friend from our days as correspondents in Europe, stuck it out over many ups and downs, offering helpful criticism at every turn. Dr. Fritz T. Epstein, of the Library of Congress, a fine scholar and an authority on the captured German documents, guided me through the mountains of German papers. A good many others also came to my aid in this. Among them were Telford Taylor, chief counsel for the prosecution at the Nuremberg war crimes trials, who already has published two volumes of a military history of the Third Reich. He loaned me documents and books from his private collection and proferred much good advice.

Professor Oron J. Hale, of the University of Virginia, chairman of the American Committee for the Study of War Documents, American Historical Association, led me to much useful material, including the results of some of his own research, and one hot summer day in 1956 did me a signal service by yanking me out of the manuscript room of the Library of Congress and sternly advising me to get back to the writing of this book lest I spend the rest of my life peering into the German papers, which one easily could do. Dr. G. Bernard Noble, chief of the Historical Division of the State Department, and Paul R. Sweet, a Foreign Service officer in the Department, who was one of the American editors of the *Documents on German Foreign Policy,* also helped me through the maze of Nazi papers. At the Hoover Library at Stanford University, Mrs. Hildegard R. Boeninger, by mail, and Mrs. Agnes F. Peterson, in person, were generous of their aid. At the Department of the Army, Colonel W. Hoover, acting Chief of Military History, and Detmar Finke, of his staff, put me on the track of German military records, of which this office has a unique collection.

Hamilton Fish Armstrong, editor of *Foreign Affairs,* took a personal interest in seeing me through this book, as did Walter H. Mallory, then executive director of the Council on Foreign Relations. To the Council, to Frank Altschul and to the Overbrook Foundation I am grateful for a generous grant which enabled me to devote all of my time to this book during its final year of preparation. I must also thank the staff of the Council's excellent library, on whose members I made many wearisome demands. The staff of the New York Society Library also experienced this and, despite it, proved most patient and understanding.

Lewis Galantière and Herbert Kriedman were good enough to read most of the manuscript and to offer much valuable criticism. Colonel Truman Smith, who was a U.S. military attaché in Berlin when Adolf Hitler first began his political career in the early Twenties and later after he came to power, put at my disposal some of his notebooks and reports, which shed light on the beginnings of National Socialism and on certain aspects of it later. Sam Harris, a member of the U.S. prosecution staff at Nuremberg and now an attorney in New York, made available the *TMWC* Nuremberg volumes and much additional unpublished material. General Franz Halder, Chief of the German Army General Staff during the first three years of the war, was most generous in answering my inquiries and in pointing the way to German sources. I have mentioned elsewhere the value to me of his unpublished diary, a copy of which I kept at my side during the writing of a large part of this book. George Kennan, who was serving in the U.S. Embassy in Berlin at the beginning of the war, has refreshed my memory on certain points of historical interest. Several old friends and colleagues from my days in Europe, John Gunther, M. W. Fodor, Kay Boyle, Sigrid Schultz, Dorothy Thompson, Whit Burnett and Newell Rogers, discussed various aspects of this work with me—to my profit. And Paul R. Reynolds, my literary agent, provided encouragement when it was most needed.

Finally I owe a great debt to my wife, whose knowledge of foreign languages, background in Europe and experience in Germany and Austria were of great help in my research, writing and checking. Our two daughters, Inga and Linda, on vacation from college, aided in a dozen necessary chores.

To all these and to others who have helped in one way or another, I express my gratitude. The responsibility for the book's shortcomings and errors is, of course, exclusively my own.

BIBLIOGRAPHY

This book is based principally on the captured German documents, the interrogations and testimony of German military officers and civilian officials, the diaries and memoirs which some of them have left, and on my own experience in the Third Reich.

Millions of words from the German archives have been published in various series of volumes, and millions more have been collected or microfilmed and deposited in libraries—in this country chiefly the Library of Congress and the Hoover Library at Stanford University—and in the National Archives at Washington. In addition, the Office of the Chief of Military History, Department of the Army, at Washington is in possession of a vast collection of German military records.

Of the published volumes of documents the most useful for my purposes have been three series. The first is *Documents on German Foreign Policy*, Series D, comprising a large selection in English translation of the papers of the German Foreign Office from 1937 to the summer of 1940. Through the courtesy of the State Department I have been given access to a number of additional German Foreign Office papers, not yet translated or published, which deal primarily with Germany's declaration of war on the United States.

Two series of published documents dealing with the main Nuremberg trial have been invaluable in taking one behind the scenes in the Third Reich. The first is the forty-two-volume *Trial of the Major War Criminals*, of which the first twenty-three volumes contain the text of the testimony at the trial and the remainder the text of the documents accepted in evidence, which are published in their original language, mostly German. Additional documents, interrogations and affidavits collected for that trial and translated rather hurriedly into English are published in the ten-volume series *Nazi Conspiracy and Aggression*. Unfortunately, the extremely valuable testimony given before the commissioners of the International Military Tribunal is mostly omitted from the latter series and is available only in mimeographed form on deposit with a few leading libraries.

There were twelve subsequent trials at Nuremberg, conducted by United States military tribunals, but the fifteen bulky published volumes of testimony and documents presented at these trials, titled *Trials of War Criminals before the Nuremberg Military Tribunals*, contain less than one tenth of the material. However, the rest may be found in mimeograph or photostats in some libraries. Summaries of other trials which shed much light on the Third Reich may be found in *Law Reports of Trials of War Criminals*, published by His Majesty's Stationery Office in London, 1947–49.

Of the unpublished German documents other than the rich collections in the Hoover Library, the Library of Congress and the National Archives—which contain, among other things, the Himmler files and a number of Hitler's private papers—one of the most valuable finds has been that of the so-called "Alexandria Papers," a good proportion of which have now been microfilmed and deposited at the National Archives. Information about a number of other captured papers will be found in the notes. Among the unpublished German material, incidentally, is General Halder's diary—seven volumes of typescript with annotations added by the General after the war to clarify certain passages—which I found to be one of the most valuable records of the Third Reich.

Some of the books which have been helpful to me are listed below. They are of three types: first, the memoirs and diaries of some of the leading figures in this narrative; second, books based on the new documentary material, such as those of John W. Wheeler-Bennett, Alan Bullock, H. R. Trevor-Roper and Gerald Reitlinger in England, of Telford Taylor in America, and of Eberhard Zeller, Gerhard Ritter, Rudolf Pechel and Walter Goerlitz in Germany; and third, books which provide background.

A comprehensive bibliography of works on the Third Reich has been published in Munich as a special number of the *Vierteljahrshefte fuer Zeitgeschichte* under the auspices of the Institut fuer Zeitgeschichte. The catalogues of the Wiener Library in London also contain excellent bibliographies.

PUBLISHED DOCUMENTARY MATERIAL

Der Hitler Prozess. Munich: Deutscher Volksverlag, 1924. (The record of the court proceedings of Hitler's trial in Munich.)

Documents and Materials relating to the Eve of the Second World War, 1937–39. 2 vols. Moscow: Foreign Language Publishing House, 1948.

Documents concerning German–Polish Relations and the Outbreak of Hostilities between Great Britain and Germany. London: His Majesty's Stationery Office, 1939. (The *British Blue Book.*)

Documents on British Foreign Policy, 1919–39. London: H. M. Stationery Office, 1947– . (Referred to in the notes as *DBrFP.*)

Documents on German Foreign Policy, 1918–45. Series D, 1937–45. 10 vols. (as of 1957). Washington: U.S. Department of State. (Referred to as *DGFP.*)

Dokumente der deutschen Politik, 1933–40. Berlin, 1935–43.

Fuehrer Conferences on Naval Affairs (mimeographed). London: British Admiralty, 1947. (Referred to as *FCNA.*)

Hitler e Mussolini—Lettere e documenti. Milan: Rizzoli, 1946.

I Documenti diplomatica italiani. Ottavo series, 1935–39. Rome: Libreria della Stato, 1952–53. (Referred to as *DDI.*)

Le Livre Jaune Français. Documents diplomatiques, 1938–39. Paris: Ministère des Affaires Étrangères. (The *French Yellow Book.*)

Nazi Conspiracy and Aggression. 10 vols. Washington: U.S. Government Printing Office, 1946. (Referred to as *NCA.*)

Nazi–Soviet Relations, 1939–41. Documents from the Archives of the German Foreign Office. Washington: U.S. Department of State, 1948. (Referred to as *NSR.*)

Official Documents concerning Polish–German and Polish–Soviet Relations, 1933–39. London, 1939. (The *Polish White Book.*)

Pearl Harbor Attack. Hearings before the Joint Committee on the Investigation of the Pearl Harbor Attack. 39 vols. Washington: U.S. Government Printing Office, 1946.

Soviet Documents on Foreign Policy. 3 vols. London: Royal Institute of International Affairs, 1951–53.

Spanish Government and the Axis, The. Washington: U.S. State Department, 1946. (From the German Foreign Office papers.)

Trial of the Major War Criminals before the International Military Tribunal. 42 vols. Published at Nuremberg. (Referred to as *TMWC.*)

Trials of War Criminals before the Nuremberg Military Tribunals. 15 vols. Washington: U.S. Government Printing Office, 1951–52. (Referred to as *TWC.*)

HITLER'S SPEECHES

Adolf Hitlers Reden. Munich, 1934.

BAYNES, NORMAN H., ed.: *The Speeches of Adolf Hitler, April 1922–August 1939.* 2 vols. New York, 1942.

PRANGE, GORDON W., ed.: *Hitler's Words.* Washington, 1944.

ROUSSY DE SALES, COUNT RAOUL DE, ed.: *My New Order.* New York, 1941. (The speeches of Hitler, 1922–41.)

GENERAL WORKS

ABSHAGEN, K. H.: *Canaris.* Stuttgart, 1949.

AMBRUSTER, HOWARD WATSON: *Treason's Peace.* New York, 1947.

ANDERS, WLADYSLAW: *Hitler's Defeat in Russia.* Chicago, 1953.

ANONYMOUS: *De Weimar au Chaos—Journal politique d'un Général de la Reichswehr.* Paris, 1934.

ARMSTRONG, HAMILTON FISH: *Hitler's Reich.* New York, 1933.

ASSMANN, KURT: *Deutsche Schicksalsjahre.* Wiesbaden, 1950.

BADOGLIO, MARSHAL PIETRO: *Italy in the Second World War.* London, 1948.

BARRACLOUGH, S.: *The Origins of Modern Germany.* Oxford, 1946.

BARTZ, KARL: *Als der Himmel brannte.* Hanover, 1955.

BAUMONT, FRIED AND VERMEIL, eds.: *The Third Reich.* New York, 1955.

BAYLE, FRANÇOIS: *Croix gammée ou caducée.* Freiburg, 1950. (A documented account of the Nazi medical experiments.)

BELGIAN MINISTRY OF FOREIGN AFFAIRS: *Belgium: The Official Account of What Happened, 1939–1940.* New York, 1941.

BENEŠ, EDUARD: *Memoirs of Dr. Eduard Beneš. From Munich to New War and New Victory.* London, 1954.

BÉNOIST-MÉCHIN, JACQUES: *Histoire de l'Armée allemande depuis l'Armistice.* Paris, 1936–38.

BERNADOTTE, FOLKE: *The Curtain Falls.* New York, 1945.

BEST, CAPTAIN S. PAYNE: *The Venlo Incident.* London, 1950.

Bewegung, Staat und Volk in ihren Organisationen. Berlin, 1934,

BLUMENTRITT, GUENTHER: *Von Rundstedt.* London, 1952.

BOLDT, GERHARD: *In the Shelter with Hitler.* London, 1948.

BONNET, GEORGES: *Fin d'une Europe.* Geneva, 1948.

BOOTHBY, ROBERT: *I Fight to Live.* London, 1947.

BORMANN, MARTIN: *The Bormann Letters: the Private Correspondence between Martin Bormann and his Wife, from Jan. 1943 to April 1945.* London, 1954.

BRADLEY, GENERAL OMAR N.: *A Soldier's Story.* New York, 1951.

BRADY, ROBERT K.: *The Spirit and Structure of German Fascism.* London, 1937.

BRYANS, J. LONSDALE: *Blind Victory.* London, 1951.

BRYANT, SIR ARTHUR: *The Turn of the Tide—A History of the War Years Based on the Diaries of Field Marshal Lord Alanbrooke, Chief of the Imperial General Staff.* New York, 1957.

BULLOCK, ALAN: *Hitler—A Study in Tyranny.* New York, 1952.

BUTCHER, HARRY C.: *My Three Years with Eisenhower.* New York, 1946.

CARR, EDWARD HALLETT: *German–Soviet Relations between the Two World Wars, 1919–1939.* Baltimore, 1951.

———, *The Soviet Impact on the Western World.* New York, 1947.

CHURCHILL, SIR WINSTON S.: *The Second World War.* 6 vols. New York, 1948–1953.

CIANO, COUNT GALEAZZO: *Ciano's Diplomatic Papers,* edited by Malcolm Muggeridge. London, 1948.

———, *Ciano's Hidden Diary, 1937–1938.* New York, 1953.

———, *The Ciano Diaries, 1939–1943,* edited by Hugh Wilson. New York, 1946.

CLAUSEWITZ, KARL VON: *On War.* New York, 1943.

COOLE, W. W., AND POTTER, M. F.: *Thus Speaks Germany.* New York, 1941.

CRAIG, GORDON A.: *The Politics of the Prussian Army, 1940–1945.* New York, 1955.

CROCE, BENEDETTO: *Germany and Europe.* New York, 1944.

Czechoslovakia Fights Back. Washington: American Council on Public Affairs, 1943.

DAHLERUS, BIRGER: *The Last Attempt.* London, 1947.

DALLIN, ALEXANDER: *German Rule in Russia, 1941–1944.* New York, 1957.

DALUCES, JEAN: *Le Troisième Reich.* Paris, 1950.

DAVIES, JOSEPH E.: *Mission to Moscow.* New York, 1941.

DERRY, T. K.: *The Campaign in Norway.* London, 1952.

DEUEL, WALLACE: *People under Hitler.* New York, 1943.

DEWEY, JOHN: *German Philosophy and Politics.* New York, 1952.

DIELS, RUDOLF: *Lucifer ante Portas.* Stuttgart, 1950.

DIETRICH, OTTO: *Mit Hitler in die Macht.* Munich, 1934.

DOLLMANN, EUGEN: *Roma Nazista.* Milan, 1951.

DRAPER, THEODORE: *The Six Weeks' War.* New York, 1944.

DUBOIS, JOSIAH E., JR.: *The Devil's Chemists.* Boston, 1952.

DULLES, ALLEN: *Germany's Underground.* New York, 1947.

Bibliography 1189

EBENSTEIN, WILLIAM: *The Nazi State.* New York, 1943.
EISENHOWER, DWIGHT D.: *Crusade in Europe.* New York, 1948.
ELLIS, MAJOR L. F.: *The War in France and Flanders, 1939–1950.* London, 1953.
EYCK, E.: *Bismarck and the German Empire.* London, 1950.

FEILING, KEITH: *The Life of Neville Chamberlain.* London, 1946.
FEUCHTER, GEORG W.: *Geschichte des Luftkriegs.* Bonn, 1954.
FISHER, H. A. L.: *A History of Europe.* London, 1936.
FISHMAN, JACK: *The Seven Men of Spandau.* New York, 1954.
FITZGIBBON, CONSTANTINE: *20 July.* New York, 1956.
FLEMING, PETER: *Operation Sea Lion.* New York, 1957.
FLENLEY, RALPH: *Modern German History.* New York, 1953.
FOERSTER, WOLFGANG: *Ein General kaempft gegen den Krieg.* Munich, 1949. (The papers of General Beck.)
FRANÇOIS-PONCET, ANDRÉ: *The Fateful Years.* New York, 1949.
FREIDIN, SEYMOUR, AND RICHARDSON, WILLIAM, eds.: *The Fatal Decisions.* New York, 1956.
FRIEDMAN, FILIP: *This Was Oswiecim* [Auschwitz]. London, 1946.
FRISCHAUER, WILLY: *The Rise and Fall of Hermann Goering.* Boston, 1951.
FULLER, MAJOR-GENERAL J. F. C.: *The Second World War.* New York, 1949.

GALLAND, ADOLF: *The First and the Last. The Rise and Fall of the Luftwaffe Fighter Forces, 1938–45.* New York, 1954.
GAMELIN, GENERAL MAURICE GUSTAVE: *Servir.* 3 vols. Paris, 1949.
GAY, JEAN: *Carnets Secrets de Jean Gay.* Paris, 1940.
Germany: A Self-Portrait. Harland R. Crippen, ed. New York, 1944.
GILBERT, FELIX: *Hitler Directs His War.* New York, 1950. (The partial text of Hitler's daily military conferences.)
GILBERT, G. M.: *Nuremberg Diary.* New York, 1947.
GISEVIUS, BERND: *To the Bitter End.* Boston, 1947.
Glaubenskrise im Dritten Reich. Stuttgart, 1953.
GOEBBELS, JOSEPH: *Vom Kaiserhof zur Reichskanzlei.* Munich, 1936.
———, *The Goebbels Diaries, 1942–1943,* edited by Louis P. Lochner. New York, 1948.
GOERLITZ, WALTER: *History of the German General Staff, 1657–1945.* New York, 1953.
———, *Der zweite Weltkrieg, 1939–45.* 2 vols. Stuttgart, 1951.
GOUDIMA, CONSTANTIN: *L'Armée Rouge dans la Paix et la Guerre.* Paris, 1947.
GREINER, HELMUTH: *Die Oberste Wehrmachtfuehrung, 1939–1945.* Wiesbaden, 1951.
GREINER, JOSEF: *Das Ende des Hitler-Mythos.* Vienna, 1947.
GUDERIAN, GENERAL HEINZ: *Panzer Leader.* New York, 1952.
GUILLAUME, GENERAL A.: *La Guerre Germano-Soviétique, 1941.* Paris, 1949.

HABATSCH, WALTHER: *Die deutsche Besetzung von Daenemark und Norwegen, 1940,* 2nd ed. Goettingen, 1952.

HALDER, FRANZ: *Hitler als Feldherr*. Munich, 1949.

HALIFAX, LORD: *Fullness of Days*. New York, 1957.

HALLGARTEN, GEORGE W. F.: *Hitler, Reichswehr und Industrie*. Frankfurt, 1955.

HANFSTAENGL, ERNST: *Unheard Witness*. New York, 1957.

HARRIS, WHITNEY R.: *Tyranny on Trial—The Evidence at Nuremberg*. Dallas, 1954. (A selection of the German documents at Nuremberg from the *TMWC* and *NCA* volumes.)

HASSELL, ULRICH VON: *The Von Hassell Diaries, 1938–1944*. New York, 1947.

HEGEL: *Lectures on the Philosophy of History*. London, 1902.

HEIDEN, KONRAD: *A History of National Socialism*. New York, 1935.

————, *Hitler—A Biography*. New York, 1936.

————, *Der Fuehrer*. Boston, 1944.

HENDERSON, NEVILE: *The Failure of a Mission*. New York, 1940.

HERMAN, STEWART W., JR.: *It's Your Souls We Want*. New York, 1943.

HEUSINGER, GENERAL ADOLF: *Befehl im Widerstreit—Schicksalsstunden der deutschen Armee, 1923–1925*. Stuttgart, 1950.

HINDENBURG, FIELD MARSHAL PAUL VON BENECKENDORF UND VON: *Aus meinem Leben*. Leipzig, 1934.

HITLER, ADOLF: *Mein Kampf*. Boston, 1943. This is the unexpurgated edition in English translation published by Houghton Mifflin. (The German original: Munich, 1925, 1927. The first volume, *Eine Albrechnung*, was published in 1925; the second, *Die Nationalsozialistische Bewegung*, in 1927. Thereafter the two were published in one volume.)

Hitler's Secret Conversations, 1941–44. New York, 1953.

Les Lettres Sécrètes Échangées par Hitler et Mussolini. Paris, 1946.

HOETTL, WILHELM (WALTER HAGEN): *The Secret Front: The Story of Nazi Political Espionage*. New York, 1954.

HOFER, WALTHER: *War Premeditated, 1939*. London, 1955. (English translation from *Die Entfesselung des zweiten Weltkrieges*.)

HOSSBACH, GENERAL FRIEDRICH: *Zwischen Wehrmacht und Hitler*. Hanover, 1949.

HULL, CORDELL: *The Memoirs of Cordell Hull*. 2 vols. New York, 1948.

JACOBSEN, HANS-ADOLF: *Dokumente zur Vorgeschichte des Westfeldzuges, 1939–40*. Goettingen, 1956.

JARMAN, T. L.: *The Rise and Fall of Nazi Germany*. London, 1955.

JASPER, KARL: *The Question of German Guilt*. New York, 1947.

KELLEY, DOUGLAS M.: *22 Cells in Nuremberg*. New York, 1947.

KESSELRING, ALBERT: *A Soldier's Record*. New York, 1954.

KIELMANNSEGG, GRAF: *Der Fritsch Prozess*. Hamburg, 1949.

KLEE, CAPTAIN KARL: *Das Unternehmen Seeloewe*. Goettingen, 1949.

KLEIN, BURTON: *Germany's Economic Preparations for War*. Cambridge, 1959.

KLEIST, PETER: *Zwischen Hitler und Stalin*. Bonn, 1950.

KNELLER, GEORGE FREDERICK: *The Educational Philosophy of National Socialism*. New Haven, 1941.

KOGON, EUGEN: *The Theory and Practice of Hell.* New York, 1951. (The German original: *Der SS Staat und das System der deutschen Konzentrationslager.* Munich, 1946.)

KOHN, HANS, ed.: *German History: Some New German Views.* Boston, 1954.

KOLLER, GENERAL KARL: *Der letzte Monat.* Mannheim, 1949. (The diary of the last Chief of the Luftwaffe General Staff.)

KORDT, ERICH: *Nicht aus den Akten.* (*Die Wilhelmstrasse in Frieden und Krieg, 1928–1945.*) Stuttgart, 1950.

————, *Wahn und Wirklichkeit.* Stuttgart, 1947.

KREIS, ERNST, AND SPEIER, HANS: *German Radio Propaganda.* New York, 1946.

KROSIGK, COUNT LUTZ SCHWERIN VON: *Es geschah in Deutschland.* Tuebingen, 1951.

KUBIZEK, AUGUST: *The Young Hitler I Knew.* Boston, 1955.

LANGER, WILLIAM L.: *Our Vichy Gamble.* New York, 1947.

LANGER AND GLEASON: *The Undeclared War, 1940–1941.* New York, 1953.

LAVAL, PIERRE: *The Diary of Pierre Laval.* New York, 1948.

LENARD, PHILIPP: *Deutsche Physik,* 2nd ed. Munich–Berlin, 1938.

LICHTENBERGER, HENRI: *L'Allemagne Nouvelle.* Paris, 1936.

LIDDELL HART, B. H.: *The German Generals Talk.* New York, 1948.

————(ed.): *The Rommel Papers.* New York, 1953.

LILGE, FREDERIC: *The Abuse of Learning: The Failure of the German University.* New York, 1948.

LITVINOV, MAXIM: *Notes for a Journal.* New York, 1955.

LORIMER, E. O.: *What Hitler Wants.* London, 1939.

LOSSBERG, GENERAL BERNHARD VON: *Im Wehrmacht Fuehrungsstab.* Hamburg, 1950.

LUDECKE, KURT: *I Knew Hitler.* London, 1938.

LUDENDORFF, GENERAL ERIC: *Auf dem Weg zur Feldherrnhalle.* Munich, 1937.

LUDENDORFF, MARGARITTE: *Als ich Ludendorffs Frau war.* Munich, 1929.

LUEDDE-NEURATH, WALTER: *Die letzten Tage des Dritten Reiches.* Goettingen, 1951.

MANSTEIN, FIELD MARSHAL ERIC VON: *Verlorene Siege.* Bonn, 1955. (English translation: *Lost Victories.* Chicago, 1958.)

MARTIENSEN, ANTHONY K.: *Hitler and His Admirals.* New York, 1949.

MEINECKE, FRIEDRICH: *The German Catastrophe.* Cambridge, 1950.

MEISSNER, OTTO: *Staatssekretaer unter Ebert–Hindenburg–Hitler.* Hamburg, 1950.

MELZER, WALTHER: *Albert Kanal und Eben-Emael.* Heidelberg, 1957.

MITSCHERLICH, ALEXANDER, M.D., and MIELKE, FRED: *Doctors of Infamy.* New York, 1949.

MONZIE, ANATOLE DE: *Ci-Devant.* Paris, 1942.

MORISON, SAMUEL ELIOT: *History of the United States Naval Operations in World War II.* Vol. I, *The Battle of the Atlantic, September 1939–May 1943.* Boston, 1948.

MOURIN, MAXIME: *Les Complots contre Hitler.* Paris, 1948.

MUSMANNO, MICHAEL A.: *Ten Days to Die.* New York, 1950.
MUSSOLINI, BENITO: *Memoirs 1942–1943.* London, 1949.

NAMIER, SIR LEWIS B.: *In the Nazi Era.* London, 1952.
————, *Diplomatic Prelude, 1938–1939.* London, 1948.
NATHAN, OTTO: *The Nazi Economic System: Germany's Mobilization for War.* Durham, N.C., 1944.
NEUMANN, FRANZ L.: *Behemoth.* New York, 1942.

O'BRIEN, T. H.: *Civil Defence.* London, 1955. (A volume in the official British history of the Second World War, edited by J. R. M. Butler.)
OLDEN, RUDOLF: *Hitler, the Pawn.* London, 1936.
OUTZE, BØRGE, ed.: *Denmark during the Occupation.* Copenhagen, 1946.
OVEN, WILFRED VON: *Mit Goebbels bis zum Ende.* Buenos Aires, 1949.
OVERSTRAETEN, GENERAL VAN: *Albert I–Leopold III.* Brussels, 1946.

PAPEN, FRANZ VON: *Memoirs.* New York, 1953.
PECHEL, RUDOLF: *Deutscher Widerstand.* Zurich, 1947.
PERTINAX: *The Grave Diggers of France.* New York, 1944.
PINNOW, HERMANN: *History of Germany.* London, 1936.
POLIAKOV, LEON, AND WULF, JOSEF: *Das Dritte Reich und die Juden.* Berlin, 1955.
POTEMKIN, V. V., ed.: *Histoire de la Diplomatie.* Paris, 1946–47. (A French edition of a Soviet Russian work.)

RABENAU, LIEUTENANT GENERAL FRIEDRICH VON: *Seeckt, aus seinem Leben.* Leipzig, 1940.
RAUSCHNING, HERMANN: *Time of Delirium.* New York, 1946.
————, *The Revolution of Nihilism.* New York, 1939.
————, *The Conservative Revolution.* New York, 1941.
————, *The Voice of Destruction.* New York, 1940.
REED, DOUGLAS: *The Burning of the Reichstag.* New York, 1934.
REITLINGER, GERALD: *The Final Solution—The Attempt to Exterminate the Jews of Europe, 1939–1945.* New York, 1953.
————, *The SS—Alibi of a Nation.* New York, 1957.
REYNAUD, PAUL: *In the Thick of the Fight.* New York, 1955.
RIBBENTROP, JOACHIM VON: *Zwischen London und Moskau. Erinnerungen und letzte Aufzeichnungen.* Leone am Starnberger See, 1953.
RIESS, CURT: *Joseph Goebbels: The Devil's Advocate.* New York, 1948.
RITTER, GERHARD: *Carl Goerdeler und die deutsche Widerstandsbewegung.* Stuttgart, 1955.
ROEPKE, WILHELM: *The Solution of the German Problem.* New York, 1946.
ROSINSKI, HERBERT: *The German Army.* Washington, 1944.
ROTHFELS, HANS: *The German Opposition to Hitler.* Hinsdale, Ill., 1948.
ROUSSET, DAVID: *The Other Kingdom.* New York, 1947.
RUSSELL, BERTRAND: *A History of Western Philosophy.* New York, 1945.

SAMMLER, RUDOLF: *Goebbels: The Man Next to Hitler.* London, 1947.
SASULY, RICHARD: *I. G. Farben.* New York, 1947.

SCHACHT, HJALMAR: *Account Settled*. London, 1949.

SCHAUMBURG-LIPPE, PRINZ FRIEDRICH CHRISTIAN ZU: *Zwischen Krone und Kerker*. Wiesbaden, 1952.

SCHELLENBERG, WALTER: *The Labyrinth*. New York, 1956.

SCHLABRENDORFF, FABIAN VON: *They Almost Killed Hitler*. New York, 1947.

SCHMIDT, PAUL: *Hitler's Interpreter*. New York, 1951. (This English translation omits about one half of the original, *Statist auf diplomatischer Buehne, 1923–45*, Bonn, 1949, which covered the pre-Hitlerian period.)

SCHOLL, INGE: *Die weisse Rose*. Frankfurt, 1952.

SCHRAMM, WILHELM VON: *Der 20. Juli in Paris*. Bad Woerishorn, 1953.

SCHROETER, HEINZ: *Stalingrad*. New York, 1958.

SCHUETZ, WILLIAM WOLFGANG: *Pens under the Swastika, a Study in Recent German Writing*. London, 1946.

SCHULTZ, JOACHIM: *Die letzten 30 Tage—aus dem Kriegstagebuch des O.K.W.* Stuttgart, 1951.

SCHULTZ, SIGRID: *Germany Will Try It Again*. New York, 1944.

SCHUMANN, FREDERICK L.: *The Nazi Dictatorship*. New York, 1939.

———, *Europe on the Eve*. New York, 1939.

———, *Night Over Europe*. New York, 1941.

SCHUSCHNIGG, KURT VON: *Austrian Requiem*. New York, 1946. (This is an English translation of the original: *Ein Requiem in Rot-Weiss-Rot*. Zurich, 1946.)

———, *Farewell, Austria*. London, 1938.

SCOLEZY, MAXINE S.: *The Structure of the Nazi Economy*. Cambridge, 1941.

SEABURY, PAUL: *The Wilhelmstrasse: A Study of German Diplomats under the Nazi Regime*. Berkeley, 1954.

SHERWOOD, ROBERT E.: *Roosevelt and Hopkins*. New York, 1948.

SHIRER, WILLIAM L.: *Berlin Diary*. New York, 1941.

———, *End of a Berlin Diary*. New York, 1947.

———, *The Challenge of Scandinavia*. Boston, 1955.

SHULMAN, MILTON: *Defeat in the West*. New York, 1948.

SKORZENY, OTTO: *Skorzeny's Secret Memoirs*. New York, 1950.

SNYDER, LOUIS L.: *The Tragedy of a People*. Harrisburg, 1952.

SPEIDEL, GENERAL HANS: *Invasion 1944*. Chicago, 1950.

SPENGLER, OSWALD: *Jahre der Entscheidung*. Munich, 1935.

STEED, HENRY WICKHAM: *The Hapsburg Monarchy*. London, 1919.

STEIN, LEO: *I Was in Hell with Niemoeller*. New York, 1942.

STIPP, JOHN L.: *Devil's Diary*. Yellow Springs, Ohio, 1955. (A selection of German documents from the *NCA* volumes.)

STROELIN, KARL: *Stuttgart im Endstadium des Krieges*. Stuttgart, 1950.

SUAREZ, GEORGES, AND LABORDE, GUY: *Agonie de la Paix*. Paris, 1942.

TANSILL, CHARLES C.: *Back Door to War*. New York, 1952.

TAYLOR, A. J. P.: *The Course of German History*. New York, 1946.

TAYLOR, TELFORD: *Sword and Swastika*. New York, 1952.

———, *The March of Conquest*. New York, 1958.

THOMAS, GENERAL GEORG: *Basic Facts for a History of German War and Armament Economy* (mimeographed). Nuremberg, 1945.

THOMPSON, DOROTHY: *Listen, Hans*. Boston, 1942.

THORWALD, JUERGEN: *Das Ende an der Elbe*. Stuttgart, 1950.
————, *Flight in Winter: Russia, January to May 1945*. New York, 1951.
THYSSEN, FRITZ: *I Paid Hitler*. New York, 1941.
TOLISCHUS, OTTO D.: *They Wanted War*. New York, 1940.
TOYNBEE, ARNOLD, ed.: *Hitler's Europe*. London, 1954.
TOYNBEE, ARNOLD AND VERONICA M., eds.: *The Eve of the War*. London, 1958.
TREFOUSSE, H. L.: *Germany and American Neutrality, 1939–1941*. New York, 1951.
TREVOR-ROPER, H. R.: *The Last Days of Hitler*. New York, 1947.

VERMEIL, EDMOND: *L'Allemagne Contemporaine, Sociale, Politique et Culturale, 1890–1950*. 2 vols. Paris, 1952–53.
VOSSLER, KARL: *Gedenkrede fuer die Opfer an der Universitaet Muenchen*. Munich, 1947.
VOWINCKEL, KURT: *Die Wehrmacht im Kampf*, Vols. 1, 3, 4, 7, 8, 9, 10, 11. Heidelberg, 1954.

WAGNER, FRIEDELIND: *Heritage of Fire*. New York, 1945.
WEISENBORN, GUENTHER: *Der lautlose Aufstand*. Hamburg, 1953.
WEIZSAECKER, ERNST VON: *The Memoirs of Ernst von Weizsaecker*. London, 1951.
WELLES, SUMNER: *The Time for Decision*. New York, 1944.
WESTPHAL, GENERAL SIEGFRIED: *The German Army in the West*. London, 1951.
WEYGAND, GENERAL MAXIME: *Rappelé au Service*. Paris, 1947.
WHEATLEY, RONALD: *Operation Sea Lion*. London, 1958.
WHEELER-BENNETT, JOHN W.: *Wooden Titan: Hindenburg*. New York, 1936.
————, *Munich: Prologue to Tragedy*. New York, 1948.
————, *The Nemesis of Power: The German Army in Politics, 1918–1945*. New York, 1953.
WICHERT, ERWIN: *Dramatische Tage in Hitlers Reich*. Stuttgart, 1952.
WILMOT, CHESTER: *The Struggle for Europe*. New York, 1952.
WRENCH, JOHN EVELYN: *Geoffrey Dawson and Our Times*. London, 1955.

YOUNG, DESMOND: *Rommel—The Desert Fox*. New York, 1950.

ZELLER, EBERHARD: *Geist der Freiheit*. Munich, 1954.
ZIEMER, GREGOR: *Education for Death*. New York, 1941.
ZOLLER, A., ed.: *Hitler Privat*. Duesseldorf, 1949. (French edition: *Douze Ans auprès d'Hitler*. Paris, 1949.)
ZWEIG, STEFAN: *The World of Yesterday*. New York, 1943.

PERIODICALS

HALE, PROFESSOR ORON JAMES: "Adolf Hitler: Taxpayer." *The American Historical Review*, LX, No. 4 (July 1955).
HUCH, RICARDA: "Die Aktion der Muenchner Studenten gegen Hitler." *Neue Schweizer Rundschau*, Zurich, September–October 1948.

Huch, Ricarda: "Der 18. Februar: Umriss einer deutschen Widerstands-bewegung." *Die Gegenwart,* October 30, 1946.

Kempner, Robert M. W.: "Blueprint of the Nazi Underground." *Research Studies of the State College of Washington,* June 1945.

Thomas, General Georg: "Gedanken und Ereignisse." *Schweizerische Monatshefte,* December 1945.

Witzig, Rudolf: "Die Einnahme von Eben-Emael." *Wehrkunde,* May 1945.

INDEX

INDEX

ABOUT THE AUTHOR

William L. Shirer had a distinguished career as a foreign correspondent, news commentator, and historian of the contemporary world. He reported from Berlin for the Universal News Service and for CBS on the rise of the Nazis and he covered their fall as a war correspondent. Out of these reports grew his best-sellers *Berlin Diary* and *The Rise and Fall of the Third Reich*.

Shirer authored many other best-selling books, including *The Collapse of the Third Republic, Love and Hatred: The Stormy Marriage of Leo and Sonya Tolstoy,* and an autobiography, *20th Century Journey: A Memoir of a Life and the Times,* composed of three volumes—*The Start: 1904–1930, The Nightmare Years: 1930–1940,* and *A Native's Return: 1945–1988.* Shirer died in 1993 in Boston, Massachusetts.